*f*P

THE NEW

Bill James Historical Baseball Abstract

BILL JAMES

THE FREE PRESS

New York   London   Toronto   Sydney   Singapore

All photographs and illustrations courtesy of *The Sporting News*.

THE FREE PRESS
A division of Simon & Schuster, Inc.
1230 Avenue of the Americas
New York, NY 10020

THE FREE PRESS and colophon are trademarks of Simon & Schuster, Inc.

For information about special discounts for bulk purchases,
please contact Simon & Schuster Special Sales:
1-800-456-6798 or business@simonandschuster.com

Designed by Helene Berinsky

Manufactured in the United States of America

10   9   8   7   6   5   4   3   2   1

Library of Congress Cataloging-in-Publication Data

James, Bill, 1949–
        The new Bill James historical baseball abstract / Bill James.
            p.   cm.
        Rev. ed. of: The Bill James historical baseball abstract. Rev. ed. 1988.
        Includes bibliographical references.
        1. Baseball—United States—History.   2. Baseball—Records—United States.   I. James,
    Bill, 1949– Bill James historical baseball abstract.   II. Title.

GV863.A1 J36   2001
796.357′0973—dc21

                                                                                2001040062

ISBN 0-684-80697-5

This book is for Isaac James
whose love of life renews me every morning.

ACKNOWLEDGMENTS

This volume is a major revision of a book which was originally published fifteen years ago. Many people contributed to that book in its first form, including;

Jim Baker, who worked with me while I was writing the first edition of this book, and provided invaluable assistance in helping to develop the library necessary to research it, helping to research it, helping to write it, writing some parts of it, and taking care of other duties.

Pete Palmer, David Frank, Gordon Herman, Randy Lakeman, and Chuck Waseleski, who also provided information and data.

Jim Carothers, who contributed time and intelligence to his own project within these pages.

Tom Heitz, Jeff Kernin, and Donna Cornell of the Hall of Fame Library in Cooperstown (at that time), who were invaluable in certain parts of the research.

Peter Gethers, who edited the original book.

Liz Darhansoff, who represented my interests in the publishing business fifteen years ago, and still does.

In the revision:

Rob Neyer contributed very heavily, doing most of the work on the pitch selection files in Part 3, and many other things.

John Sickels worked with me for several years, remains a good friend, and also made important contributions to the book.

Mike Webber has the job now.

Bill Rosen edited this version of the book, and has been extraordinarily patient with me while I struggled to re-write it. This book was supposed to come out years ago, sometime in the last millennium.

Andrea Au works with Bill, and with me when I work with Bill, and has been, at times, the major engine driving the project.

My good friend Mike Kopf has worked with me at various times over the last 15 years, and some articles that he wrote have gotten dragged into this book in edited versions. Mike also proofed and copy edited this manuscript before it was sent to the publisher.

Steve Getschier and James R. Meier, the archivist and librarian of *The Sporting News*, assisted me in doing other research by use of the *The Sporting News* morgue.

Lloyd Johnson also provided me with some research materials.

Jill Rosen is running the public relations effort for the book.

Numerous other people provided ideas, made suggestions, helped me to solve problems, or wrote articles that were used as background research. As the book has been revised, this list has no doubt grown. I have tried to acknowledge these throughout the book, as appropriate, and not to appear to take credit for the work that other people have done. To anyone that I have failed to credit for their research, I send my apologies, and I would ask that if you feel that I borrowed your research and didn't properly credit it, you might contact me and let me know.

The people who form that maligned franchise known as "the media" have been kind to me, most of the time on purpose, but failing that by accident. Thanks to all.

Behind every great man there is a great woman, and some of us ordinary Joes get lucky, too. Susan McCarthy would do credit to a man of far greater accomplishments than mine. She also wrote some bits of the book, articles about baseball uniforms and how they have changed over time. She has her own work to do (she is an artist), but this has never stopped her from carrying a good bit of my load, too, particularly as book deadlines draw near. When the first edition of this book was produced in the mid-1980s she pitched in as a typist, secretary, statistician, office manager, bookkeeper, proofreader, schedule-maker, and editor. Since we now have three children her role in producing the book is different, but she remains patient of husbands who work until 4 o'clock in the morning, neglect their share of the household duties, grow irritable when their work does not go well, and make unreasonable demands on those around them. Without her help, this book would not be what it is.

To write a book is awfully hard on your family; this one, in particular, has been a killer. My children are Rachel, now 15, Isaac, 12, and Reuben, 8. When I undertook to revise this book they were Rachel, 10, Isaac, 7, and Reuben, 3. They have given up an awful lot of me to let me re-write this book, and while that might be a welcome sacrifice to many people, they seem to miss me. I miss them, and I appreciate what they haven't given. I love you guys.

Thanks to all.

Bill James

CONTENTS

INTRODUCTION

Hi. My name is Bill James. Through most of the 1980s I wrote an annual book called *The Baseball Abstract*. It was a kind of a technical book, at times, and there were essays in it that were not real easy to understand. I was very happy to spend eight pages discussing how many camels could rest in the on-deck circle of a theoretical ballpark. Some people liked it, some people didn't. I was once described by a now defunct publication as "the guru of baseball statistics," and by Sparky Anderson as "a little fat guy with a beard who knows nothing about nothing." Actually, I'm seven inches taller than Sparky is, but what the heck, three out of four ain't bad, and it sure beats being described as the guru of baseball statistics.

Anyway, the editor of *The Baseball Abstract* was Peter Gethers, a man of many talents. Peter wondered whether I could adapt the premises of the annual book to cover the history of baseball, since this would create a book that had a shelf life longer than a package of Oreos. I said I could, and I did, and the *Historical Baseball Abstract* was first published in 1985.

That book did well, and it has an odd quality about it, which is that it can never really be finished, as long they're still playing baseball. I always had it in mind to write periodic updates. Time is getting away from me. I sat down a couple of years ago to revise the *Historical Baseball Abstract* and discovered a funny thing: I didn't like a lot of it. It's odd, really; people come up to me all the time and tell me how much they love that book, and I figured when I got into it, I wouldn't have too much to do. But when I started re-editing it, I spent six months saying, "Why the hell did I do that?" Times and people change, and I'm not saying that I'm a better writer now than I was then, but I'm different.

So this book, depending on how you want to look at it, is either:

(a) a revision of the original *Historical Baseball Abstract,* or

(b) a new book that uses some of the old material.

Certain premises of the book remain the same; it is an effort to create a picture of the game of baseball as that game has evolved over the years, but focuses on the fact that baseball exists to be enjoyed, that we enjoy it by wrestling with it, trying to get a handle on it. I would explain how this is different now than in the first edition, except that, in some respects, I'm not really sure what I was trying to do fifteen years ago.

The book has three sections. Strategy in baseball never comes to rest; it is in constant search of an equilibrium that, the Lord willing, I will never find. The first section of this book, called "The Game" is, in a sense, about that search for equilibrium, about how the game of each decade was different from the game of the years before. But if each decade is different in some ways, in many more ways it is the same, and the first section of the book is also about that, about the repeating patterns and habits that come as fresh revelations to each generation of baseball fans.

The second section of the book, called "The Players," could be described as the Who-Was-Better-Than-Whom section, and consists in the main of information and arguments about the relative merits of the hundred best players at each position in the history of the game. I'm an argumentative cuss by nature, and how much you enjoy that section of the book is likely to depend to an extent on how much you like to argue about baseball players.

The third section of the book, now called "Reference," is an effort to put on record a couple of types of information which escape the Encyclopedias.

This book is not intended to studied; it is intended to be enjoyed. It is intended that you pick it up, leaf through, find something that looks interesting, read it, react to it, decide that I'm right, decide that I'm wrong, put it down, pick it up some other time. To those of you who enjoyed the first version, I hope that you'll feel we have met the standard. To those of you who didn't see the first one, I thank you for joining in, and I hope you'll feel some connection to it. Thanks for reading.

Bill James

PART 1

THE GAME

The first section of this book looks at the history of baseball as it has unfolded, decade by decade, since 1870. There are fourteen sub-sections, one for each decade since the 1870s, plus one for the Negro Leagues.

As I had originally envisioned the *Historical Baseball Abstract*, this was to have been a small, almost perfunctory look at the history of the game to set to the table for Section II, a detailed look at the players. But as I began to do research on the history of baseball (in order to discuss the players more intelligently) I began to feel that there was a history of baseball that had not been written at that time, a history of good and ordinary players, a history of being a fan, a history of games that meant something at the time but mean nothing now.

In American society, our ways of teaching about baseball are better than our ways of teaching about anything else. No matter how it is that your mind works, baseball reaches out to you. If you're an emotional person, baseball asks for your heart. If you are a thinking man or a thinking woman, baseball wants your opinion. Whether you are left-brain or right-brain, Type A or Type Z, whether your mind is

bent toward mathematics or toward history or psychology or geometry, whether you are young or old, baseball has its way of asking for you. If you are a reader, there is always something new to read about baseball, and always something old. If you are a sedentary person, a TV watcher, baseball is on TV; if you always have to be going somewhere, baseball is somewhere you can go. If you are a collector, baseball offers you a hundred things that you can collect. If you have children, baseball is something you can do with children; if you have parents and cannot talk to them, baseball is something you can still talk to them about.

It is this fact, spun through into dollars and cents, that explains the paradox of which the disaffected so often complain, that baseball players make a hundred times as much money as cancer researchers. If cancer researchers had box scores and statistics (which, of course, could easily be created), if those box scores were in the paper in the morning, if they had baseball cards, if those cards were for sale in convenience stores, if cancer research programs were on six channels every evening, if there were annual books about cancer research and daily newspaper personality profiles, if there were cancer researchers encyclopedias to sustain the memory of old, dead cancer researchers, if there was an oral tradition, if cancer research had a vocabulary that made sense to us, if you could go and watch them do their job, if there were someone there to explain to you what was happening and to sell you a beer ... well, then, cancer researchers would be on their way toward multimillion dollar salaries. Instead, cancer researchers—most of them, anyway—swat down our interest with self-righteousness and jargon, with demands that we dedicate ourselves to the field before we can really understand anything about it.

School teachers and academics, in ways they seem constitutionally incapable of understanding, tell us to go away and leave them alone whenever we show any interest in what they are doing. The very essence of baseball is that it does not. The essential definition of baseball is that baseball is a thing which welcomes and sustains our interest. Whoever we are, however we think, however old we are, wherever we live, whatever we like to do, baseball wants us—and this is what makes baseball what it is.

It is, then, peculiarly unsatisfying to read a railroad track history of baseball—this happened, and then this happened, and then this happened. Baseball doesn't preach at us; baseball surrounds us. It was the goal of this book to create a history of baseball that would surround you, that would reach out to you and take your hand. This is done, of course, with details: hundreds and hundreds of tiny little details. What was it like to be a baseball fan in 1923? Who were the heroes, who were the rogues, who were the comedians? What was in the paper in the mornings?

A linear history of baseball drops the details once those details no longer mean anything—

once they no longer serve to move the narrative of baseball forward. Thus, in an odd way, it drops the things that make baseball what it is. An academic, writing a history of baseball, often sounds very much like an academic writing about cancer research. He leaves out the details that make it fun.

Well, I don't meant to criticize anyone, but if baseball exists only to be enjoyed, and you leave out the details that make it fun, then aren't you leaving out what makes it what it is? We cover each decade in a box with a series of questions. These questions are a way of reaching into baseball history for the details. Who was the handsomest player; who was the ugliest? Who was the best hitter; who was the worst? Who was different from everybody else? What was right with the game; what was wrong with it? Who disgraced the game, and who ennobled it? Who threw the best curve ball; who threw the best heat? Who was the best bunter? Little, tiny details that don't mean anything anymore, except for the fact that it is those details that enable baseball to embrace us. Baseball is and was a billion details. Perhaps I have saved a couple of thousand from the crush of time.

My goal isn't to tell you what happened in baseball in 1913. My goal is to give you a sense of what it was like to be a baseball fan in 1913, as best I can in this forum. The citations for the best-looking and ugliest players were made by a qualified expert: my wife. In her twenties, Susie spent many hours poring over every photograph in my library, and emerged with a list of the handsomest and homeliest from each period. These selections are exactly as good as anybody else's; it's just opinion. For the new version of the book she handed off that assignment to our children.

I was interested in uniforms, since the types of uniforms worn by players in 1913 are essential to the sense of being at a game in that season. If you've ever seen me on a weekday you know that I don't know anything about clothes, so I also assigned that duty to my wife. Her comments on baseball uniforms over time accompany each Decade in a Box, plus she wrote an introduction of her own, which appears next.

Susie felt the need to emphasize that she is not an expert on the history of uniforms or cloth or clothes in general. I've never claimed to be an expert, either; my view is that when you write something it is either true or false, and being an expert or not being an expert really has nothing to do with it. She worked hard to double-check the things she wrote and see that they were true, and while she might have bobbled a ground ball or two, I'm sure that for the most part she got it right.

ABOUT THE
"APPEARANCE" AWARDS

Just before my study was complete, I stumbled across an article entitled "Baseball's Ten Handsomest Men" in the September 1957 issue of *Sport* magazine. The author talked about how women (giggly girls) swooned when the strikingly tall, dark and handsome Ted Williams walked to the plate. He was "all man," you know; she wrote about how women just love a strong, dominant man, and she went on (and on) about a particular "boy" being the one you would have wanted to carry your books, while another was the one you would have wanted to ask you to the prom, or the boy you would have wanted to marry. Some other classic lines: of Jerry Coleman, "Brown eyes that sparkle and dark brown curly hair make women's eyes roll like ball bearings." Of Vinegar Bend Mizell, "He

flips female hearts with his masculinity." Of Eddie Mathews, "but with those beautiful muscles, he can make a girl believe anything."

Just for the record, I wanted to say that this study was not conducted to do any of the things that the *Sport* article seems to be about. I have yet to see a baseball card that made me want to marry anybody, and it would take me months to get the mothball smell out of my prom dress. Come to think of it, I don't have a prom dress.

The study was done, basically, just for the fun of it. We can't claim that there is any reason you should accept our findings. We could claim that we had to do it because nobody else would. Handsome players and ugly players are a part of every decade, just like minor leaguers and major leaguers, fast runners and slow runners and tobacco chewers. I got to pick them because I seemed to be the appropriate sex for the task. For another thing, I come to the history of baseball with a clean slate, being largely unfamiliar with the players, their numbers or faces, and this ignorance should prevent me from making the "I know he's ugly but he sure could play second base" type of calls. On the other hand, no doubt I glanced quickly over some faces that I should have paid more attention to. Bill gave me only one hint about who he thought I ought to pick: Donald Mossi. I did have to scout around for a picture of him, but he was worth it.

Fifteen years have passed since I wrote these paragraphs. Bill and I have three kids. Since I am now over 40 and old enough to be the mother of a major league player (yikes) I thought it prudent to let the kids make the new selections. This doesn't mean I didn't put forward a few of my own candidates, though.

—Susan McCarthy

THE 1870s

HOW THE GAME WAS PLAYED

The national sport in the last century, having distinguished itself from rounders by an accretion of changes in the period 1830–70, has since fractured into any number of related games—baseball, softball, slow-pitch softball, tee-ball for small ones, stickball for the streets, work-up for the sandlot, and that weird and wonderful game that they play in Chicago where they swing a stick at something about the size of your head. Of those games, baseball in 1870 resembled fast-pitch softball more than any other, including modern baseball. The pitch was delivered underhand from a distance of 45 feet. The rules required a stiff arm so as to limit velocity, but the rules were not tightly enforced, and pitchers could move the ball in there pretty good with a flick of the wrist. The ball was not wound as tight as it would be later; it was a handmade ball of yarn with a cover on it, not terribly standard in size or shape, and to hit the thing 400 feet would probably have been impossible.

Basic play in other respects was largely then as now, much of which is common to the family of games. Bases were 90 feet apart and touched in the same sequence as now. The rule specifying a putout by hitting the runner with a thrown ball had disappeared during the 1850s. The rule allowing an out for a ball caught on one bounce was on the way out after 1863. The batters batted in order, as they do now, although the order did not have to be announced ahead of time, allowing managers to react to events in the game the first time through the order.

In other small respects, the game was different, but many features of the modern game were present despite somewhat different rules. "Anyone who searches through old records" wrote Harold Seymour in his classic history of the development of baseball (*Baseball: The Early Years*), "is bound to be impressed with how much was already known about the fundamentals of the game, playing the various positions, and 'inside baseball'." Seymour insists that Charles Comiskey in the 1880s was not the first man to play off the bag at first, as others have written, and that "this method of play was familiar and commonly used back in the 1860s." (Another historian, David Voight, credits Joe Start with originating this play.)

Seymour also ticks off the following list of developments prior to 1870:

- First basemen held the runner on first if needed, and played off the bag when the base was empty.
- Left-handed first basemen were regarded as having an advantage.
- The expression "long ball" was used, though, since few parks had outfield walls within reach, it rarely referred to the automatic home run that we know now.
- Pitchers changed speeds.
- The controversy about whether or not a pitcher could make a ball curve was already going.
- Teams in 1870 would put their most agile infielder at shortstop, and the infielder with the best arm at third base.
- Speed and throwing arms were valued in the outfield, and the fastest man on the team was often the center fielder.
- The system of relaying throws in from the outfield already existed.
- Outfielders shifted their positions to play the hitters.
- Sliding was becoming more common.
- Baserunners would tag up and advance after a play.
- Dickey Pearce, a shortstop, had invented bunting.

But in a lot of ways, the baseball of 1876 was, in fact, extremely primitive. A ball was fair if it bounced in fair territory, which effectively required the fielders to cover a larger area. (Ross Barnes hit .404 or .429 in the first season of the National League, 1876, by perfecting the "fair-foul bunt"—that is, landing the ball in fair territory so that it would roll foul. At the time, a batter who walked was charged with an at bat, thus creating a discrepancy between his batting average as it was then and as

it is now.) The batter called for a high pitch or a low pitch, to his liking, which in some respects is like a football team calling for a run or a pass, but in another sense can be seen as a reflection of one of baseball's unique features: It is the only sport in which the team that has the ball is on defense.

Nine innings and three strikes antedate professionalism in baseball, but it took nine balls to walk somebody, so nobody got too many. Not many walks, not many homers, but lots of singles and lots of errors. That's the one largest difference between the offensive constructions of 1870 and those of 1920—all those errors. The Boston Red Stockings hit .295 as a team in 1871 and did not hit a huge number of home runs. But they scored more than twelve runs a game because of the great number of errors. Fielding gloves were not introduced until 1875, were not universally adopted for more than a decade after that, and had no padding even then, so a fielder's hands would swell up something fierce. It wasn't at all unusual for a team to make three, four, maybe more errors in an inning—and that made the innings long enough to get out of hand. Though stolen base records for the period do not exist, base stealing does not seem to have been as common in the early days of the professionals as it had been in the amateur baseball of the 1860s or as it would be later. George Wright confirmed that in his day they had never realized the potential value of base stealing.

Teams at the beginning of the 1870s played only about thirty "league" or "association" games a year and used but one pitcher; as the decade progressed the schedules grew longer almost every year, and by 1879 all teams carried a spare pitcher to give their number one—who might start seventy or eighty games, for example—an occasional day off. Another point with regard to the schedule is that the teams often played non-league teams. In 1871, when the Association teams only played about thirty games each, they might well have played another fifty or sixty games or even more against teams from other leagues—non-professional leagues, city all-star teams, anything. The season stretched until November 15.

When the National League teams became distinctly superior to any other teams is very much an open question. Sportswriters often insisted, until the mid-eighties, that the National League teams were no better than other teams. It would be a worthy study to go back and find a city that had good sports coverage in the era, like Louisville or Syracuse, and see how many games the city's team played against nonleague competition in this period, and what their record was. I'm sure that the Boston teams under Harry Wright regularly demolished their opponents, but I think it likely that some of the weaker teams in the National League in 1880 were really no stronger than a hundred other teams around the country.

When you arrived at a game in 1878, a player might take your ticket; this was still true as late as 1890. George Wright, who lived to be ninety, recalled the era in an interview with the *New York Sun* in 1915: "Youngsters who are accustomed to see 1 to 0 and 2 to 1 games may well wonder," he said, "how it was that the early Base Ball nines were able to score so many runs. The fact is that the pitchers in those days were not the skilled artists of the present and depended mainly on an underhand ball, which was easy to hit; and then again, the fielders did not gobble up the grounders so skillfully or try to stop with their bare hands the wicked liners that are 'speared' nowadays." Wright also said that "Batting was not done as scientifically in those days as now. The sacrifice hit was unthought of and the catcher was not required to have as good a throwing arm because no one had discovered the value of the stolen base. Long drives were more common than at present." The long drives would shortly return.

But it was baseball; you wouldn't have any trouble recognizing it. The games were a little long and the scores were a little high, but it was baseball. The skills in demand were the same, the personalities were the same, the arguments were the same. Baseball was baseball before it was professional baseball.

And with that blithe assurance, I'm going to have to warn you that the picture presented here of baseball in the nineteenth century is, of necessity, rather incomplete. Just to answer fully one of the questions that make up the boxes on these first three decades could easily use up a book. Team vs. team in the 1890s? There are volumes on that subject. Player vs. team (salary battles, player/management battles) of the 1880s? There could be books written on that subject. Overlooked stars of the nineteenth century? They're almost all overlooked—all your average fan knows about baseball in the nineteenth century is Willie Keeler and the Baltimore Orioles. How the game was changing from decade to decade? New strategies in use? New terms in use? You got a million words there. It is far beyond the scope this book to repair the common ignorance of baseball in the nineteenth century. If you are really interested in the subject, read Harold Seymour's book, mentioned earlier, or David Voight's *American Baseball: From Gentleman's Sport to the Commissioner System,* or join the Society for American Baseball Research and start collecting their stuff. I am neither competent nor at leisure to write the volumes that would be required to do this century justice.

WHERE THE GAME WAS PLAYED

We're talking about two leagues here. The first avowedly professional league, the National Association of Professional Baseball Players (the Association), which dominated from 1871 to 1875 and lasted past that, allowed whoever wanted to join in, provided that they pay the entry fee and abide by the other rules of the league. The entry fee was initially $10, equivalent to maybe $200 today. The teams drew up their own schedules, agreeing only to play at least five games against each of the other teams. Initially, the league had teams from Boston, Chicago, Cleveland, Fort Wayne, New York, Philadelphia, Rockford, Troy (New York), and Washington, D.C. Some teams would drop out and others join in; before being pushed aside the Association would include Baltimore, Brooklyn, Middletown (Connecticut), Elizabeth, Hartford, St. Louis, New Haven, and Keokuk. The Association started out with a Midwestern flavor, based around Chicago, and gradually moved east, anchoring around New York.

The National Association is to the National League precisely as the American States under the Articles of Confederation are to the United States under the Constitution: Agreements but no provisions for enforcing them, no strong central authority. Teams would not schedule the games that they were required to or schedule them and then not play them. There was no uniformity in umpiring, ticket pricing, or field conditions. Teams haggled over how the gate was to be shared between visiting and home teams; some stronger teams demanded and got inequitable relationships with the weaker teams. The association was plagued with "revolvers," players who jumped from one team to another. Eventually the stronger teams got tired of putting up with the tentative and ineffectual management of the Keokuks and Middletowns of the Association, and broke off to form the National League.

The National League—officially the National *League* of Professional Baseball *Clubs*—transferred power from the players to the financial backers, the "owners" as we would call them today. They created a structure for the league—a league president, secretary/treasurer, board of directors—and assessed each club $100 a year

for the costs of doing business. The league covenant implied that the central organization had authority and would use it, and it did. The man who had organized this palace revolt, and would wield the power in the league until his death in 1881, was William Hulbert.

In 1876 the league started with teams in Boston, Chicago, Cincinnati, Hartford, Louisville, New York, Philadelphia, and St. Louis—a good selection of the biggest and best baseball cities in the nation as it was then. But at the end of the 1876 season, New York and Philadelphia refused to make their final, western road trip, figuring they had lost enough money on the year. For this, New York and Philadelphia were kicked out of the league. It was, to extend the parallel, the National League's Whiskey Rebellion, and authority was effectively asserted.

The wisdom of this action has been debated regularly over the course of the last 125 years. On the one hand, it was necessary to establish respect for the rules of the league; on the other, it deprived the young league of the nation's two largest cities, eventually forcing the league back into cities like Syracuse and Troy, and endangering its position as the nation's strongest league.

Anyway, to resume the list of cities which hosted major league baseball . . . Buffalo, Indianapolis, Milwaukee, Providence, Syracuse, and Troy.

WHO THE GAME WAS PLAYED BY

Entrepreneurs, immigrants, and people from Brooklyn, Philadelphia, and Baltimore. The entrepreneurs were few in number but large in impact, for this was the era in which a young player with brains, ambition, and self-discipline could wind up owning his own team, as Albert Spalding did, and Alfred Reach, and John Montgomery Ward, and as a few more players from the next decade would (Comiskey, Griffith,

Connie Mack). Many players, up until 1920, would become the owners of minor league teams. Of course, players who combined brains, ambition, and self-discipline were in a distinct minority, and the entrepreneurial ambitions of many of the players involved fixing an appropriate price at which to sell the game to the gamblers. Harry Wright had trouble with alcoholism and poor training habits of the very first professional champions, and baseball players as a group would acquire an unsavory reputation within ten years of the beginning of professionalism.

In *American Baseball,* Voight commented on the large number of Irish names on the rosters of teams as early as 1871, and certainly there were many. The list of names in the National Association also included intriguing entries like "Cherokee Fisher" and "Count Sensenderfer." There were several Jewish players, and a good many immigrants. Without tracing the ancestry of all the names, it doesn't seem to me that the Irish influence in 1870 was as strong as it was in 1890 or 1895.

The Philadelphia influence . . . well, that's another story. Going through the birthplaces of men who played in the National Association, it would seem that at least half must have been born in Brooklyn, Philadelphia, or Baltimore. This is not nearly as true of the best players as it is of the ordinary ones, suggesting that the teams of this period still retained some of the flavor of small local organizations, in which a man brought his brother along and recommended a neighbor who could play the outfield. The Middletown, Connecticut, team had several members who were actually from Middletown. But the best players were likely to come from anywhere. Spalding was from Byron, Illinois. Ross Barnes was from Mt. Morris, New York. Cap Anson was from Marshalltown, Iowa. Candy Cummings was from Ware, Massachusetts. Harry Wright was born in Sheffield, England.

CHECKING IN:

1870— Jesse Burkett, Wheeling, West Virginia

1871— Buck Freeman, Catasauqua, Pennsylvania
Orville Wright, Dayton, Ohio

1872— Willie Keeler, Brooklyn

1873— John McGraw, Truxton, New York
Harry Davis, Philadelphia
Jimmy Collins, Niagara Falls

1874— Honus Wagner, Carnegie, Pennsylvania
Fielder Jones, Shinglehouse, Pennsylvania
Bill Klem, Rochester, New York
Robert Frost, San Francisco

1875— Nap Lajoie, Woonsocket, Rhode Island

1876— Mordecai Brown, Nyesville, Indiana
Ginger Beaumont, Rochester, Wisconsin
Rube Waddell, Bradford, Pennsylvania

1877— Frank Chance, Fresno, California

1878— Mike Donlin, Erie, Pennsylvania

1879— Miller Huggins, Cincinnati
Josef Stalin, Tiflis, Georgia, Russia

CHECKING OUT:

1870— Robert E. Lee, 63

1872— Al Thake, 22

1875— Andrew Johnson, 67

1876— Bub McAtee, 31

1879— Jimmy Hallinan, inflammation of the bowels, 30

THE 1870s IN A BOX

Attendance Data:

Highest:	St. Louis, 1875	78,500
	Chicago, (1871–1879)	500,304
Lowest:	Keokuk, 1875	4,000

According to new research by Robert L. Tiemann and Pete Palmer, total attendance for the National Association/National League was between 205,000 and 269,000 throughout the decade except for 1875, and was flat throughout the decade. The one exception is the last year of the Association, 1875, when league attendance was about 387,000.

Most Home Runs:

Charley Jones, 1879	9
Charley Jones	18

All leaders of categories here are based on the totals for the National League only, 1876–79, unless otherwise noted.

Best Won/Lost Record by Team:

Chicago,	1876	52-14	.788
Boston		176-98	.642

Worst Won/Lost Record by Team:

Cincinnati,	1876	9-56	.138
Cincinnati		104-158	.397

The Philadelphia team, expelled after only one season, had a winning percentage for that one season of .237.

Index of Competitive Balance: 21%

Percentage of Regulars Hitting .300: 24%

Home-Field Winning Percentage: .563

Heaviest Player: Though Cap Anson's listed weight of 227 pounds was probably not attained until later, he was probably the biggest man in the league almost from the day play began.

Lightest Player: Candy Cummings, who weighed only 120.

Most Strikeouts by Pitcher:

Monte Ward,	1879	239
Tommie Bond		595

Highest Batting Average:

Ross Barnes,	1876	.404
Cap Anson		.352

As mentioned, Ross Barnes' 1876 batting average was .429 if walks are not counted as at bats. Barnes' batting average for the five years of the American Association was also .379, making him the true batting champion of the era.

Lowest Batting Average:
Redleg Snyder,   1876   .151
Joe Quest   .206

Best Major League Players (By Years):
1876— Ross Barnes
1877— Deacon White
1878— Paul Hines
1879— Paul Hines

Best Major League Pitchers (By Years):
1876— Albert Spalding
1877— Jim Devlin
1878— Tommy Bond
1879— Pud Galvin

Hardest-Throwing Pitcher: George Zettelein was reputed to be a very hard thrower at the start of the decade, though his record suggests that he had lost most of his speed by the time league play began. Al Spalding threw very hard, and Tommy Bond threw hard.

Best Curve: Tommy Bond

Best Switch Hitter: Bob Ferguson

Iron Man: Tommy Bond

Best Baseball Books: Henry Chadwick's *Beadle's Dime Baseball Player*, the first guide, began publication in 1860 and lasted through 1881. (The dime referred to the cost of the book; the ballplayer was much more.) The *Spalding Guide* began publication in 1877, edited by Lewis Meacham; Chadwick later came over and ran it, instead.

Five Largest Changes in Baseball During the Decade:

1. Organization of the first professional leagues

2. Transfer of power from the players to the financial backers

3. Expansion of league schedules from a few games to about 80 at end of decade

4. Standardization/codification of the rules

5. Refinement of defensive play

Best Outfield Arm: Jim Hatfield, a member of the famous Cincinnati team that is often described as the first professional team, threw a baseball 400 feet, 7½ inches on October 15, 1872, a record that was not matched for many years.

Most Runs Batted In:
Jim O'Rourke,   1879   62
Charley Jones, 1879   62
Deacon White   190
for the four years (1876–1879)

Most Aggressive Baserunner: King Kelly

Fastest Player: Lip Pike

On August 27, 1873, Pike, a sprinter, beat a racehorse (a trotter) in a 100-yard dash to win a bet. The trotter was allowed to start 25 yards behind the line, and Pike took off when the horse reached him. They held even for most of the race, and when Pike began to pull ahead late in the race the horse broke into a run. But Pike still beat it by four yards (item based on note by Al Kermisch in 1979 *Baseball Research Journal*).

Slowest Player: Pop Snyder

Best Control Pitcher: No one stands out. With nine balls to work with, most pitchers could avoid walks. Besides, as George Wright said in the 1915 interview, "This method of reaching base [the walk] was unusual because it was an unwritten law that the hitter should do his utmost to connect with the ball and he was not handicapped by any rule as to where he should step in order to hit it."

Most Stolen Bases: Unknown

Best-Looking Players: King Kelly, Smiling Mickey Welch

Ugliest Player: Charlie Gould

O.J. Simpson Award: Pacer Smith

Best Offense: 1879 Providence Grays

Retrobermanisms:
Joe (Quest For) Fire
Davy (Magnum) Force
Hick (If I Were a) Carpenter
Joe (When Do We) Start

First of His Kind: Everybody

One of a Kind: Jim Devlin in 1877 was the only pitcher to pitch 100% of his team's innings in a season.

Best Infield: 1879 Cincinnati Red Stockings (1B—Cal McVey, 2B—Joe Gerhardt, 3B—King Kelly, SS—Ross Barnes)

Best Outfield: 1879 Providence Grays (Tom York, Paul Hines, Jim O'Rourke)

A Better Man than a Ballplayer: Tim Murnane

Mr. Dickens, I'd Like You to Meet: Trick McSorley

Best Defensive Team: 1879 Red Stockings

Clint Hartung Award: Steve King

Outstanding Sportswriter: Henry Chadwick

Most Admirable Superstar: Deacon White

Least Admirable Superstar: George Hall

Gold Glove Team:
C— Pop Snyder
1B— Joe Start
2B— Jack Burdock
3B— Bill Hague

SS— George Wright
OF— Charley Jones
Paul Hines
Jack Remsen

Franchise Shifts: A "franchise" as we know it now—a collection of contracts with players, stadiums, and fans—did not exist. Teams dropped out of the league or were dismissed and new ones came in, but there was no concept of doing business somewhere else.

New Stadiums: Primitive Parks

Best Pennant Race: 1871 National League

In 1871, the Chicago White Stockings were in the middle of an exciting three-team race with the Philadelphia Athletics and the Boston Red Stockings when their park was destroyed by the Great Chicago Fire. Despite losing their uniforms, and equipment, despite being without funds, the players saw the season through on the generosity of their competitors. They eventually lost the "pennant" to the Athletics in Philadelphia in the last game of the season.

Best World Series: No World Series

Best-Hitting Pitcher: Albert Spalding

Worst-Hitting Pitcher: Candy Cummings

Best Minor League Team: 1878 Buffalo Bisons

Best Minor League Player: Pud Galvin

Odd Couple: Albert Spalding and William Hulbert

Drinking Men: Jim Devlin, Charlie Jones, Asa Brainard, The Only Nolan, Jack Burdock, Bill Craver

New Strategies:
Catchers moving closer to the plate
Fielders backing up one another

New Equipment:
1875—Catcher's mask
1875—First fielding gloves introduced
1876—Turnstiles

The National Association had no standard baseball. Some teams used red baseballs.

Player vs. Team:
Davy Force vs. the White Stockings

Team vs. Team:
Chicago (Hulbert) against Philadelphia
Chicago (Hulbert) against New York
Chicago (Hulbert) against Cincinnati

From Hulbert against Philadelphia (see comments on Force Case, if you haven't), it degenerated to Hulbert against the National League, and seemed to be headed for Hulbert against the World. New York and Philadelphia were kicked out of the new league in 1877 for not making a road trip. Louisville fell apart in 1878 during a gambling scandal. Cincinnati was expelled in 1881 for playing ball on Sunday and selling beer at the games. Not to be too harsh, but the death of Hulbert in 1882 was probably the best thing that could have happened to the league at that point. He was a strong man and a strong leader, but he had the league under too tight a rein.

Uniform Changes: See Susie's comments on pages 20 and 21.

New Terms or Expressions: During a tour of England in 1874, Henry Chadwick drew up a lexicon of the game for the benefit of the British writers. It included such terms as assists, passed balls, balks, fungoes, grounders, pop-ups, double plays, overthrows, and white-washed. Other terms are not now in use, such as muffed balls, daisy cutters, and line balls (which became line drives).

Most Wins by Pitcher:
Al Spalding,	1876	47
Monte Ward,	1879	47
Tommy Bond		154

Spalding was the best pitcher in the years of the National Association, winning as many as 57 games in a season (he was 57–5 in 1875) and leading the Association in wins every year. He won 207 in the Association, 48 in the league for a total of 255.

Highest Winning Percentage:
Al Spalding,	1876	47-12	.797
Tommy Bond		154-68	.694

Lowest Winning Percentage:
Dory Dean,	876	4-26	.133
Bobby Mathews		36-52	.409

Nicknames: See page 18

Best Manager: Harry Wright

Ozzie Guillen Award: Shortstop Tom Carey batted 274 times in 1877, 253 times in 1878, without drawing a single walk either season.

Minor Leagues Were:
100 percent free
0 percent slaves to the majors

Best Double Play Combination: Chuck Fulmer and Davy Force, 1879 Buffalo Bisons

Worst Double Play Combination: Billy Craver and Jimmy Hallinan, 1876 New York Mutuals

Craver was banned from baseball after the 1877 season. He had been accused for years of throwing games, and (according to one report) several times was beaten up by his teammates, who believed that he was crooked. A converted catcher, in 1876 he turned only 7 double plays and committed 41 errors in 42 games at second base.

Hallinan, an Irish immigrant, was a fine hitter but no shortstop; he had 7 double plays and 67 errors in 50 games, after which he never played another game at shortstop. He died of gastritis in October, 1879, at the age of 30. (And thanks to Bill Deane, who found Hallinan's obituary in the *New York Clipper.*)

Best Unrecognized Player: Levi Meyerle or Charley Jones

Highest-Paid Player: Probably Harry Wright at $2,500 (Modern Equivalent, about $45,000)

New Statistics: Statistics made available by the National League in 1879 were games played, at bats, hits, runs, batting average, average runs per game, times reached first base (which apparently included reaching by an error or forceout), on-base percentage, putouts, assists, errors, total chances, fielding average, passed balls for catchers, batters facing pitcher, runs allowed, average runs allowed (per game), hits allowed, opposition batting average, walks, average walks per game, and wild pitches. Some of this material, such as passed balls and batters facing pitcher,

fell out of use—and will be noted when it returns. In many cases I have changed to modern terminology—that is "batting average" rather than "percentage of base hits per times at bat."

A Very Good Movie Could Be Made About: The 1872 Chicago White Stockings, fighting for a pennant and for survival at the same time.

Five Biggest Things Wrong with Baseball:

1. Crooked players

2. Segregation

3. Lack of an organized, predictable schedule

4. Drunkenness of the players (some of whom were visibly drunk on the field)

5. Primitive rules/frequent rule changes

I Don't Know What This Has to Do with Baseball, But I Thought I'd Mention It Anyway: Pitcher Joseph Borden played baseball under the name "Nedrob" (Borden spelled backwards) because his parents objected to his playing professionally.

BEST MINOR LEAGUE TEAM OF THE 1870S

Joseph M. Overfield, writing in the 1977 *Baseball Research Journal*, makes a case for the prowess of the 1878 Buffalo Bisons of the International Association. They were a team with such established stars as Dave Eggler and Davy Force and players with great futures in the majors, like Pud Galvin and Joe Hornung. They won the International Association championship and a good many exhibition games, including a 10–7 record against National League opponents. In 1879 the Bisons moved into the

National League, with essentially the same team, and finished third.

In 1877 the *Louisville Commercial* printed a standing of the best clubs in America at the end of the season, sort of like a modern college football poll. The list made no distinction between the National League teams and teams in other leagues, which may show the position that the league held in public opinion at that time. It was a good league, but it was just another league; it later became the major league.

—Jim Baker

NICKNAMES OF THE 1870s

There were no rules for nicknames, to begin with, and a sportswriter—who might be the only one in town—could call a player whatever he wanted. Charlie Pabor was called "The Old Woman in the Red Cap," probably the only seven-word nickname ever; a similarly outstanding handle was "Death to Flying Things," assigned to the overbearing defensive wizard Bob Ferguson. Will White was called "Whoop-La," a forerunner of "Ee-Yah Jennings" and "The Say-Hey Kid." Hardy Richardson was called "Old True Blue," Billy Reilly "Pigtail Billy," George Bradley was called "Grin" and Jim O'Rourke "Orator Jim." Bob Addy was called "The Magnet," and Joe Gerhardt was called "Move Up Joe" because of something he always yelled to his teammates as a young man.

But as there was no rule as to what a nickname might be, there was also not such a strong feeling that a player had to have one. The game, remember, was still on a much more human level then; it is not unrealistic to think that a hard-core fanatic—a breed that existed from the very first day—might have personally known the players for whom he rooted. Players did talk to the fans; attempts were made to prohibit this, but those attempts were still being made thirty years later, which suggests that they were not initially very successful. The cities were much smaller; the National League had a rule that a team must represent a city of at least 75,000 people, but several cities did not meet the standard. A fan probably knew where a player lived and who his wife or girlfriend was. Or both.

There was not the need, then, to give the player a human face by assigning him a name; nicknames probably were used more for opposition players than for the members of the home team. Nicknames didn't really get rolling until the late eighties, when the scale of the operation changed and the distance between the players and fans increased.

THE LOUISVILLE SCANDAL

In 1877, the Louisville Grays had built a large lead over Boston. With a quarter of the season to go (fifteen games), the Grays needed to win only half of their remaining games to clinch the flag. Louisville was sparked by outfielder George Hall, sort of an early-day Hal Chase, who had developed a reputation for dishonesty while in the National Association. They also had star pitcher Jim Devlin, who boasted a pretty mean "drop" pitch.

With the pennant seemingly assured, the Grays began dropping games due to a variety of "bonehead" plays; strikeouts, pick-offs, and costly errors abounded. Louisville consequently blew its lead and finished second to Boston. Certainly this would have qualified as the pennant race of the decade, except for the stench in the air.

At the conclusion of the season a Louisville paper, the *Courier-Journal,* made accusations that the team had gone in the tank. The primary culprit was alleged to be Jim Devlin, who was now, according to some reports, sporting a variety of fancy jewelry. After the season he pitched well in exhibitions after doing quite poorly in the stretch run. A league investigation followed and resulted in the lifetime expulsion of Devlin, Hall, shortstop Bill Craver, and Al Nichols. Nichols was only a substitute, but it was said that he had key connections to New York gamblers.

For years after, Devlin literally begged for reinstatement. He was often seen hanging around the National League offices, pleading and dressed in rags. Devlin died in Philadelphia at the age of 33, reportedly working at the time as a police officer.

—Jim Baker

NATIONAL LEAGUE ALL-STAR TEAM 1876–1879

Records in seasonal notation, based on 75 games played. Pitchers based on 60 starts.

Pos.	Player	Years	Hits	HR	RBI	Avg.	Other
C	Deacon White	3.52	113	1	54	.343	61 Runs
1B	Joe Start	3.24	113	1	33	.320	
2B	Ross Barnes	2.20	114	1	43	.329	
3B	Cap Anson	3.14	119	0	53	.352	20 Doubles
SS	Johnny Peters	3.52	104	1	40	.302	20 Doubles
LF	Charley Jones	3.54	99	5	50	.307	9 Triples
CF	Paul Hines	3.62	114	2	51	.334	
RF	Jim O'Rourke	3.62	109	1	39	.331	

Pitcher	Years	Won-Lost	SO	ERA	Other
Tommy Bond	3.77	41–18	158	1.97	535 Innings
Monte Ward	1.78	37–17	199	1.92	516 Innings

INDEX FINGERED

The "Index of Competitive Balance," which is a new measurement introduced here, is composed of two elements. Those two elements are:

1. The standard deviation of winning percentage for teams in each single season during the decade, averaged.

2. The standard deviation of winning percentages among franchises for the decade as a whole.

The first of these measures the extent to which the best teams in any season are able to dominate the weakest teams. The second measures the extent to which the same teams win season after season throughout the decade.

If baseball was perfectly competitive—that is, if every team was exactly as good as every other team, and the only differences between them were in luck—then the first measure above would be .039, and the second would be .014.

The actual figures for the 1870s were .170 and .081; I'd have to spend about three more paragraphs to fully explain the parameters used to derive these numbers, and I'm going to skip that, because it's boring. These two figures (in each decade) are then added together, and the sum is divided by .053, which is what the sum would be in a perfectly competitive environment. This figure is then divided into 100 to produce the index of competitive balance. In other words, if the sum of these two standard deviations was .106, that would be 2.00 times what it would be in a perfectly competitive environment, which would produce an index of 50%. A perfectly competitive index is therefore 100%.

You may not have understood all of that, and you don't need to. The essential point is that the greater the difference is between the best teams and the worst, the lower the index of competitive balance. The 1870s are the *least* competitive decade in baseball history, with an index of 21%.

INTRODUCTION TO THE UNIFORM COMMENTS

What men wore to play baseball in the early days now seems quaint and a little odd, but their dress reminds us of the great luxury of beginnings, the freedom from tradition. Not that baseball was the first organization of its kind to need a uniform. Baseball men undoubtedly looked to other sports, such as cricket and horseback riding, as a guide to appropriate dress. They were also influenced by military uniforms of the day. Once the form was established and accepted, though (as it was by about 1910), change came slowly through a series of gradual refinements—with a few exceptions.

This study is intended to be a general overview of changes in the baseball uniform. It is not meant to date precisely where something began or to include every change in uniforms, only to give a sense of what the uniforms of the time looked like. The study is based mostly on observations from photographs in guides, magazines, and books, plus occasional references to uniforms in texts. A SABR publication, *The National Pastime: A Special Pictorial Issue—The Nineteenth Century*, was very useful for examining the first thirty years, plus being a delight in itself, with photographs dating back to the 1850s. The text, by John Thorn and Mark Rucker, illustrates the photographs, not the other way around.

When we did this fifteen years ago, not many reference materials were available. Since the original edition of the *Historical Baseball Abstract* was published in 1985, a fine book by Marc Okkonen, *Baseball Uniforms of the 20th Century*, came out in 1991. It has been an excellent resource as I've attempted to re-evaluate my earlier comments and add new material. Half of Okkonen's book consists of year-by-year illustrations of home and road uniforms for each team from 1901 to 1991, which were extremely useful in making comparisons.

Let's get started. Small town teams or college teams of the 1850s dressed simply and practically in long dark pants, with long-sleeved light-colored shirts. The club teams of the period seemed intent on designing a suit of clothes that designated the members as ballplayers, but was still stylish in the fashion of the day. With this in mind, they disregarded completely the fact that

(continued)

NEW STRATEGIES OF THE 1870s

According to David Voight, Deacon White in 1875 introduced the practice of the catcher standing right behind the batter to take the throw. This practice did not become standard for nearly another thirty years, but there is some doubt about when it started. The *New York Times* article on Nat Hicks at the time of his death (1907) states that Hicks was the first catcher to do this, at a date unspecified apparently in the sixties, and further that after he did so the other catchers followed suit. So this practice had a vogue before 1875.

Harry Wright during the decade developed the practice of one fielding backing up another one. The first season tickets were sold by Cleveland in 1871.

a close-fitting collar with a bow tie and a shirt with long sleeves and cuffs was just not very comfortable for playing ball.

A few examples: The Lowells of Boston wore what looked like leftover military trousers from the Civil War: a white, long-sleeved, bibbed shirt with a small bow or ribbon tie, high leather-top shoes and a cloth cap. A large oval area on the shirt front—the bib—extended from the collar down to the midsection and was detachable, with button closures all round. The 1864 Mutuals of New York looked smashing indeed in all-white dress—long pants, long-sleeved and collared shirts, with a dark belt at midsection spelling out "Mutuals."

In contrast, the 1867 Niagaras of Buffalo were not a very homogeneous group; it looks like they borrowed from each other's closets. A few wore ties, some wore long-sleeved shirts with bib closures, while others wore button-up shirts with no collar. Long trousers were common to all, but some were checked, while others have checked tops. The editors of *The National Pastime* noted that the first major league team to wear checked uniforms was the Brooklyn Robins.

Shown on the first baseball card in 1868, the Brooklyn Athletics were dressed in dark military-style pants with a white stripe up the side and pant clips around the ankles. In 1869 photographs we find the first appearance of true sports clothes, in the form of knickerbockers, which became widely accepted by ball teams in the seventies and become fashionable in public dress in the eighties. Knickers, a variation of the European breeches popular at the time of the French Revolution and before, were worn by hunters in the 1860s, and later adopted by golfers and cyclists. Members of the Red Stockings Base Ball Club of Cincinnati—the club whose success sparked the formation of the National Association—were photographed in knickers and long stockings, with the initial of their town embroidered on the bib of their shirts.

A historic note—the first uniform was officially adopted by the Knickerbockers of New York in 1849. It consisted of long blue trousers, white shirts, and straw hats. The term "knickerbocker" originally referred to descendants of Dutch settlers in New York, and by extension meant any New Yorker.

—Susan McCarthy

STATE OF THE UNION

What does it mean to be a "major" league? In baseball encyclopedias dating back to 1922, including those with my name on them, the Union Association has always been treated as a major league. Searching through old records for an exception to this rule, I found none, although I did discover an instructive error.

The 1951 edition of *Daguerreotypes* (from *The Sporting News*) contains only one player who played in the Union Association, Tommy McCarthy. McCarthy's record, as it appears in *Daguerreotypes,* considers the Union Association to be not one major league, but two major leagues. To make McCarthy's record add up to his "major league" totals, you not only have to include the Union Association, you have to count it twice. Apparently the statistician wasn't sure whether to include the Union Association in the major league totals or not, decided to include them, then went to get a second opinion on the subject. When the source said to include the Union Association, he apparently forgot that he had already included them, and added them back in again.

In any case, all baseball encyclopedias—*The Baseball Cyclopedia* by Ernest Lanigan (1922), *The Official Encyclopedia of Baseball,* by Hy Turkin and S. C. Thompson (1951), Macmillan's *Baseball Encyclopedia* (1969), *Total Baseball* (1989), and the *All-Time Handbook* and *All-Time Sourcebook* from STATS Inc. (1998)—treat the Union Association as a major league, although *Total Baseball* sometimes applies a statistical discount to the league's records. The sundry record books published by *The Sporting News,* which date back to about 1940, have always treated the Union Association as a major league, except *Daguerreotypes,* which treats it as one major league or two, depending on the edition.

Laying aside eighty years of tradition, however, suppose that we face this issue on its own terms: Was the Union Association actually a major league?

When I sat down to take a hard look at that issue, I was astonished to discover how weak the Union Association's argument to be considered a major league actually is. On every conceivable ground, the Union Association's argument to be considered a major league is vastly weaker than that of, for example, the Pacific Coast League in the 1920s or 1930s, the Negro National League in the 1930s or early 1940s, the American League in 1900, or the California Winter League in the early 1920s.

Founded by a St. Louis millionaire, Henry V. Lucas, the Union Association existed for only one summer, 1884. According to the article "The Development of Baseball" in *The Baseball Encyclopedia* (Macmillan, 1969), the Union Association started the season with twelve franchises, but "of the twelve franchises that started the season, only five finished." This is not exactly correct; actually, thirteen teams participated in the Union Association at some point, three of which dropped out in mid-season, and five of which apparently joined in the fun after the season was underway. This is

merely an interpretation; there is one team which is either a resumption of an earlier franchise or a new effort, depending on the source.

In any case, only five teams in the league played something resembling a full schedule—that is, somewhere between 105 and 113 games. The league had no pennant race. Lucas' St. Louis team won 94 games and lost 19, finishing miles ahead of anyone else, the second-place finisher being somewhat hard to determine, as some teams had good percentages, but played as few as eight games.

Now, we don't know what the standards of a "major" league are, so let me ask you: Is this what you think of as a major league? A league that exists for only one season, a "league" in which several teams drop out in mid-season and others appear for the stretch run, a league in which the best team hardly ever loses . . . is this, in your experience, what is meant by the term, a "major" league?

Much of what is implied by a "major" league in the modern vernacular is that it is *not* a minor league, that it rests atop a pyramid of organized competition. This definition is difficult to apply to 1884, because the structure was just getting organized then. The International Association was organized in 1877, The Western League in 1879, the Eastern Championship Association in 1881 . . . by 1884 there were actually eight minor leagues, a good many of which probably could have kicked the Union Association's butt and stolen their lunch money, but I'm getting ahead of the story.

Sorry

In 1877, the *Utica Herald* published a report of a game played there that had this appended to the summary: "Apologies by pitchers for hitting batsmen, Morgan 4, Neale 3."

UNIFORMS OF THE 1870s

By 1875, the style was just about set for the rest of the century. Teams wore baggy knickers, long stockings, lace up high-top leather shoes, long sleeves with cuffs. Shirts had stiff-looking collars, which gradually relaxed and were often turned up to sort of fan the face. A tie was worn in the early years, but when incidents of players choking to death while trying to make plays increased, the custom soon faded. The bib was still around, but by the late seventies shirts began to appear with a different closure. The opening from the waist to the neckline, where buttons would be now, was secured by lacing one side to the other. The team's city was usually spelled out across the chest. A wide, dark belt with rather fancy clasps was worn around the middle, and sometimes bore the team name.

The Ithacas, an independent team from New York, followed this general style, but their stockings were striped and their caps were more like bowlers than baseball caps. Several club teams from this period looked remarkably modern in uniform, with round necks on shirts made of what looks like a stretch knit material. An early Harvard team even wore short sleeves, and their knickers were much more form-fitting. While wool and flannel (and even silk) were the fabrics commonly used, some of these tighter fitting pants would almost have to have been made out of some sort of jersey or other knit material.

Albert Spalding in 1876 put different-colored hats on his players to designate positions, making the team look, according to the *Chicago Tribune,* like a "Dutch bed of tulips." Unfortunately, Spalding's foray into gardening lasted only one season. The first instances I found of teams using a descriptive symbol on their uniforms, rather than the initial or name of the city, were the Skull and Bones team from Massachusetts and the Maple Leafs of Guelph, Ontario, both in 1876. The two teams later joined to form the Cemetery League.

–Susan McCarthy

Editor's Note: Susie is just joking about the players choking to death with those neckties. Didn't happen.

The Union Association did do one thing that helps to identify them as a major league: they moved into major league cities. Like Altoona. No, they did have a team in Altoona and a team in Wilmington, but the Union Association cities were, in the main, major league cities: Baltimore, Boston, Chicago, Cincinnati, Kansas City, Milwaukee, Pittsburgh, Philadelphia, St. Louis, St. Paul, and Washington.

On the other hand . . . well, I've been to Los Angeles a dozen times, and that doesn't make me a movie star. The Union Association didn't *stick* in any of those towns; they didn't stick anywhere.

The key question, of course, is whether or not they had major league talent. They may have played a phony schedule with a jumble of teams and somebody could have finished 89–2, but if they did it with major league talent, we'll accept them as a major league. So who *were* the players who made up this league?

I made a study of that issue. There were 272 players who played in the Union Association. Of those 272 players, how many were established major league players? How many were major league fringe players? How many were major league virgins, guys who never played a game in the majors in any other league?

Of the 272 players in the league, 107 never played at all in any other major league–before the Union Association, after the Union Association, anytime. 107, or 39%, had *no* major league identification, other than the Union Association.

Many of these players were regulars in the Union Association, (although, since the number of games played by Union Association teams is so variable, it is impossible to establish meaningful standards by which to define the regulars). Harry Moore led the UA in Games Played (111), was third in the league in hits (155), and third in batting average (.336). Moore never played another inning in anything recognized as a major league. While Moore was the best of the Union Association regulars who never played at all in other leagues, about one-fourth of the league's regulars have no history in any other league.

I did a parallel study of the players who played in the International League in 1960. There were 236 players who played in that league. Of those 236 players, all but 45 played in the American League or the National League at some point in their careers. The percentage of International League players who never played in the majors was 19%. The parallel percentage for the Union Association was more than twice as high.

Of the other 165 Union players, who played in the UA but also played in the established major leagues, another 72 played only very briefly. These players all:

- Had fewer than 300 at bats in the other leagues.
- Had fewer than 50 hits in the real major leagues.

Actually, some other Union Association players don't meet either of these standards, but they were excluded from this group of 72 because they were pitchers who enjoyed some little bit of success somewhere.

Anyway, these 72 players had an average of 14 hits in some other major league. Most of the 14 hits were in 1884. When the Union Association tried to establish itself in competition with the existing leagues, the American Association expanded from eight teams to twelve, rather than concede territory to the new league. The result was a huge demand for new ballplayers. Any number of ballplayers had a kind of tryout with one of the American Association teams, failed that, and then went to play in the Union Association, or the other way around.

Fairly typical of these 72 players would be John Tilley; with 112 at bats in other leagues he ranks in the top one-third of this group. Tilley had played 15 games for Cleveland in August and September, 1882, going 5-for-56 as a hitter, and making six errors in the outfield. He was out of the majors in 1883, but in 1884 the American Association placed a new team in Toledo, and Tilley got another 56 at bats there before Toledo decided they could live without him; he had hit .179 and, rather amazingly, fielded .632 in the outfield–7 errors in 19 fielding chances. Despite these misadventures, when St. Paul organized a Union Association team that fall, they needed ballplayers, and Tilley got a third chance. That was his entire major league career.

This is a group of 72 players who, like Tilley, got very brief trials in the real major leagues, but sank like a stone. The group includes Redleg Snyder, who had played in the National League in 1876, hitting .151 (31-for-205), after which he had disappeared from the major league scene for eight seasons. In 1884 he re-appeared, with Wilmington in the Union Association.

MOST-ADMIRABLE SUPERSTAR, 1870s

Deacon White was catcher and third baseman for several teams from 1876 to 1890. Henry Chadwick admired him because he was never known to complain, and wrote about him that "there is one thing in which White stands pre-eminent, and that is the integrity of his character." The *Cincinnati Enquirer* wrote that "Mr. White has few peers as a ballplayer and he has always been a gentleman in his professional and private life." He picked up his nickname from the strange habit of going to church.

White also got off the quote of the decade in 1889, when battling against the reserve rule. An excellent article about White was written by Joseph Overfield, and appeared in the 1975 *Baseball Research Journal;* most of these facts are taken from that article. In 1888 the Detroit franchise in the National League went out of business, and sold its players around the league. Deacon White and Jack Rowe were sold to Pittsburgh, but instead of reporting to their new team, that December the two of them purchased a team in Buffalo, New York, in the International League, intending to play for themselves. They weren't too happy about the fact that they had been sold for $7,000 and were being asked to report to Pittsburgh for a fraction of that. Things didn't go well in Buffalo, and eventually they capitulated and reported to Pittsburgh, but were paid $1,250 each plus good salaries, $500 a month.

White told a Buffalo reporter, "We are satisfied with the money, but we ain't worth it. Rowe's arm is gone. I'm over 40 and my fielding ain't so good, though I can still hit some. But I will say this. No man is going to sell my carcass unless I get half."

Near the top of this group is Dick Burns, who had been released by Detroit in midsummer, 1883, after hitting .186 in 37 games for that team. He was one of the best players in the Union Association, which earned him another look in the NL the next season, where he lasted 14 games. His career total of 38 hits in the "real" major leagues is the seventh-highest in this group.

The *highest* hit total in the group? Well, that would be Scrappy Carroll, who parlayed his nine-game trial with St. Paul in 1884 into a 13-game trial with Buffalo (National League) in 1885, where he went 3-for-40. He survived that experience to play 57 games for Cleveland in the American Association in 1887, hitting .199 with 16 outfield errors. This gave him 46 hits in the real major leagues, highest total in this group of 72.

Tilley, Burns, and Carroll were among the best of this group of 72 players. Ten of the 72 played in the real majors but never had a hit, and 37 of them played in the majors but did not get their hit total out of single digits. These players, then, were *clearly* not major league caliber. Adding them to the 107 discussed before, that makes 179 of the 272 Union Association players who obviously could not play in the real majors.

But what about the other 93?

Lee Allen, in *The Development of Baseball,* says that Henry V. Lucas "was able to lure many players from the other leagues." The assumption that this is true appears to underlie the identification of the Union Association as a major league.

But in fact, this statement is flatly wrong: Lucas was not able to lure "many players" from the established leagues. Of the 272 players who played in the Union Association, at most about a dozen were established players, lured away from the National League or the American Association. None were stars of real significance.

Continuing to sort through the players, the other 93 who represent the Union Association's creme-de-la-creme... Did any of you see spring training games in 1995, when the major leaguers were on strike? The remaining 93 players were predominantly composed of players whose credentials were very similar to those of the replacement players—teenagers, washed up veterans, and sub-regulars who were looking for a chance to break through.

This group includes, for example:

- **Buster Hoover.** The 21-year-old Hoover was one of the best players in the Union, hitting .364 as a regular for Philadelphia. The Philadelphia franchise folded in August, and Hoover signed with or was sold to the National League franchise in the same city, where he hit .190 in 10 games. He went back to the minors then, but got a chance to play in the American Association in 1886, hitting .217 in 40 games for Baltimore. After that he disappeared for six seasons, re-appearing with Cincinnati (the Reds) in 1892. He lasted 14 games, hitting .176.
- **Jumbo Schoeneck.** Schoeneck, a 22-year-old 223-pounder, was also among the best hitters in the league, hitting .308 in 106 games, and leading the league's first basemen in games, putouts, and fielding percentage. After the Union Association

folded he disappeared for four seasons, re-surfacing with Indianapolis in late 1888. He hit .237 in 1888, .242 early in 1889, and then was gone forever.
- **Frank Olin.** Played well in the American Association in 1884, also played briefly in the Union, but played only one major league game other than the 1884 season.
- **Sleeper Sullivan.** A bench warmer in the National League in 1881, the American Association in 1882–1883, had been released by an American Association team early in 1883. Played briefly in the Union, and then never played again.
- **Peek-A-Boo Veach.** A pitcher/outfielder in the Union Association, he pitched one game in the American Association in 1887 (which he lost), and played the outfield for a National League team in 1890, when the *real* National League players revolted and formed their own league. That's his entire career.
- **George Strief.** A regular outfielder for Cleveland (NL) in 1879, he hit just .174, and disappeared until 1882, when he re-emerged with the American Association. He hit .195 and .225 in two seasons in the American Association, then played for four teams in the summer of 1884—two teams in the Union Association, one in the National League, one in the American Association. Career ended in mid-season, 1885.
- **Tim Murnane.** More famous as a sportswriter than a player. He had played in the National Association (1872–1875) and the National League (1876–1878), but had been out of the major leagues for six years before returning with the Union Association in Boston, a team of which he was also a part-owner.
- **Will Foley.** A 38-year-old veteran who, like Murnane, had played in the National Association and the National League, but

had dropped out of the majors since 1879, except for a five-game look with Detroit in 1881. The Union Association gave him one more "major league" experience.

Of the 93 players not already discussed, about 53 are of this type, which could be sub-divided into these four types:

1. Young players who played well in the Union, earned trials by the real major leagues, but failed those trials.

2. Guys whose "other major league" career was just the 1884 season.

3. National League and American Association fringe players.

4. Washed up veterans who had been out of the majors for years.

OK, that leaves about 40 players to be dealt with, depending on where you sort the hard cases. About 40 players (a) were good or at least fairly decent major league players, and (b) did play in the Union Association.

About two-thirds of these players were men who got their first taste of "major league" play in the Union Association, and who then went on to be major league players.

Does the presence of these players certify the Union Association as a "major" league? Obviously it does not. If producing two dozen players who went on to have decent major league careers certified the Union as a major league, then the International League could be certified as a major league in any season from 1890 to 1990. Let's pick a season at random—say, 1941. Players who played in the International League in 1941 included Fred Hutchinson, Jimmy Ripple, Pat Mullin, Sid Gordon, Erv Dusak, Hank Majeski, Tommy Holmes, Johnny Lindell, Herman Franks, Goodie Rosen, Whitey Kurowski, Tony Cuccinello, Tommy Byrne, Snuffy Stirnweiss, Ray Mueller, Lennie Merullo, Hal White, Hank Borowy, Clem Dreisewerd, Max Surkont, Virgil Trucks, Ed Head, and Stan Musial.

The young players who came out of the Union Association weren't nearly that good, weren't nearly as good as the young players produced by the International League in 1941, or the International League in 1951, or the Pacific Coast League in 1926, or the Eastern League in 1968. If the presence of 25 to 30 future major league players makes a league a major league, baseball encyclopedias will need to be the size of pianos.

Still, if two dozen young men playing in the Union Association went on to star in the National League or the American Association in the next few years, that certainly would show that the level of competition in the UA was pretty good, just as the large number of players who vaulted from the Negro Leagues to major league stardom pretty much proves that the competition in the Negro Leagues was of high quality. But the Union Association fails this test, for three reasons:

1. The young players who came out of the UA weren't all that good. There's no Willie Mays here, no Henry Aaron, no Jackie Robinson.

2. To get to 25 players, you have to count a bunch of guys who played less than ten games in the Union.

3. Many of the young players who used the UA as a springboard to major league careers actually didn't emerge as legitimate major leaguers until years later.

I'll give you a list of all the young players who could be included in this group, so you can form your own summary of their accomplishments if you want to take the time. I have a list of 26 players: Kid Baldwin, Lady Baldwin, Charlie Bastian, Henry Boyle, Oyster Burns, Jack Clements, Con Daily, Jumbo Davis, Jim Donnelly, Frank Foreman, Joe Gunson, Bill Hutchison, Bill Johnson, Al Maul, Tommy McCarthy, Chippy McGarr, Mox McQuery, Bert Myers, Billy O'Brien, Joe Quinn, Yank Robinson, Emmett Seery, Germany Smith, Phenomenal Smith, Perry Werden, and Joe Werrick.

Exactly one-half of those players played twelve games or fewer in the Union Association. Oyster Burns, for example, was certainly a quality major league player, and he did play in the Union Association. Two games. He was 19 years old. How much does the presence of the 19-year-old Oyster Burns in two games actually do to certify the Union Association as a major league? Realistically, nothing.

Bill Hutchison was certainly an exceptional major league pitcher—in the 1890s. He also played two games in the Union. After that, his major league career doesn't start until 1889.

Tommy McCarthy, while his selection to the Hall of Fame is generally conceded to have been unfortunate, was certainly a good major league player, and he did play in the Union. He was twenty years old. It would be four years

PARKS OF THE 1870s

To state the matter without hyperbole, the finest ballpark in the United States in 1879 would today be considered substandard for the Florida State League. The first enclosed ballpark was the Union and Capitoline Grounds, commonly known as the Union Grounds, in Brooklyn, built in 1864 by William Cammeyer. It seated about 1,500 people on long benches.

The "stadiums" where baseball was played in the 1870s would seem to be not too different from the accommodations at which I witnessed rodeos in small towns in Kansas in the late 1950s and early 1960s—actually, the rodeo places might be closer to the parks of the late 1880s than the late 1970s. The owners bought some wood and threw up fences and primitive bleachers and maybe a clubhouse or a dugout; the players often assisted in the construction. In a couple of years the thing fell down or burned down or rotted out, or they just got tired of it and built another one. The average occupancy of a park before 1890 wasn't more than a couple of years. These teams, remember, were not the only teams in town; the gentlemen's clubs that had dominated baseball in the 1850s and 1860s were still around, frequently competed against the professionals,

and almost always shared parks with them. By 1880 most teams probably owned their own parks, but it was not unusual for a team to switch accommodations in mid-season, entering into or departing an arrangement with one of these clubs or with someone who rented a ballpark out as a business.

Under those circumstances, if a team drew 4,000 people, it looked like an enormous number; people would be spilling off the bleachers and standing along the foul lines to watch the game. The crowd was not necessarily confined to the seats well into the twentieth century. For large crowds as late as 1935, there might be ropes put up in the outfield and fans standing behind the ropes.

In the first edition of this book, I commented that to make a full accounting of all the parks that teams played in during this period would be a massive undertaking. That undertaking was undertaken by Philip Lowry, who produced the book *Green Cathedrals,* published by the Society of American Baseball Research in 1986. Lowry attempted to document and describe every park used in the major leagues from day one to the present, as well as some minor league parks and other miscellaneous information. It is a wonderful reference book.

until he was ready to play regularly in the American Association, in 1888.

Joe Gunson is on the list above. He has the same problem as Hutchison and McCarthy (his career doesn't *really* begin until years later), plus another problem: Joe Gunson was the Tim Spehr of the 1890s. Does the presence of the 21-year-old Joe Gunson in this league suggest that the UA was a major league, or that it wasn't? I don't know; where was Tim Spehr when he was 21?

How many guys were there who *really* played in the Union, not ten games but who really played there, and who *really* went on to become major league players, not years later but right away? About five, none of them stars.

Joe Quinn, a 19-year-old Australian, played regularly in the Union, and stayed with his team (St. Louis) when that team moved to the National League the next season. He struggled, hitting .213 in 1885 and .232 in 1886, but he kept his job, and he went on to have a good major league career.

Jack Clements, a 19-year-old catcher for Philadelphia, was purchased by the Philadelphia National League team when the Union team folded. He, too, struggled for two seasons, hitting .191 in 1885 and .205 in 1886, but he survived, played in the National League until 1900, and became one of the best catchers in nineteenth-century baseball (and the best left-handed catcher in baseball history).

Germany Smith, a 21-year-old shortstop for Altoona, hit .315 before the Altoona franchise folded in May, and leveraged that to a successful major league career, although he was a .240 hitter, not a .315 hitter. He was a glove man.

Emmett Seery, a 23-year-old outfielder who hit .313 in the Union and led the league's outfielders in assists and putouts, also moved to the National League in 1885. He hit .162, but survived to have a modestly successful major league career.

Yank Robinson, an infielder, led the Union in walks with 37, and later led the American Association in walks twice, with 116 and 118.

Henry Boyle, a young pitcher who went 15-3 for St. Louis, pitched in the National League from 1885 through 1889, although he had a losing record every season.

That's it.

OK, we come, then, to the last group of players who might somehow legitimize the Union Association as a "major" league, the twelve to fifteen players who could reasonably be described as established major league players, who did play in the Union Association.

Two points. First, none of these players was a legitimate star at that time (although Jack Glasscock and Fred Dunlap later became minor stars).

Second, the performance of these players, the good players who did come over from the established major leagues, is so extraordinary that, rather than suggesting that the Union Association *was* a major league, it provides definitive proof of the opposite proposition.

I've got a working list of fourteen "legitimate" major league players, although there are all kinds of questions about whether he should be included on such a list. That list, alphabetically, is: Jersey Bakely, Tommy Bond, George Bradley, One Arm Dailey, Buttercup Dickerson, Fred Dunlap, Charlie Ganzel, Jack Glasscock, Jack Gleason, Jim McCormick, Dave Rowe, Orator Shaffer, Charlie Sweeney, and Billy Taylor.

This collection of run-of-the-mill and journeymen ballplayers, transported to the new major league, became superstars. Fred Dunlap, a career .277 hitter in ten years in the National League (before and after 1884) hit .412 in the Union, leading the league in hits (185), home runs (13), runs scored (160), total bases, batting average, on-base percentage, slugging percentage ... basically everything. Returning to the National League the next season, he hit .270.

Would this suggest to you that Dunlap in 1884 was hitting against major league competition? If it does, look at the other players who came over. Pebbly Jack Glasscock, a career .287 hitter in a 17-year National League career, hit .249 that summer in the National League, but played 38 games in the Union, and hit .419.

Orator Shaffer, a career .271 hitter in the National League and the American Association, also played in the Union Association, as a regular. He hit .360.

Buttercup Dickerson, a career .273 hitter in the NL and AA, played 46 games in the Union. He hit .365.

Jack Gleason, a career .248 hitter in the real major leagues, played 92 games in the Union. He hit .324.

Bollicky Billy Taylor was an American Association fringe player, a utility man who also pitched on occasion. His career average in the real major leagues was .261, his won-lost record 25-32. In the Union, he hit .366 and went 25-4.

Jim McCormick, a good National League pitcher, spent part of that summer with Cleveland (NL) and part with Cincinnati (UA). He went 19-22 in the National League, 21-3 in the Union.

Are there any counter-examples, any real major league players who came to the Union and didn't perform as if this was a Mickey Mouse league where they could do whatever they wanted to? Well, not really. One Arm Daily, whose career record was 45-59 in the real major leagues, did go "just" 28-28 in the Union Association, although he had gone 23-19 the previous season in the National League. But Daily, whose career high in strikeouts would otherwise be 171, struck out 483 Union Association batters. Dave Rowe, a fringe player in other leagues, led the UA in at bats (485) and hit "only" .293; he had hit .313 the

previous season in the American Association, in limited playing time.

Jersey Bakely, who had pitched well in the American Association in 1883, did not pitch well in the UA in 1884. But Bakely was a twenty-year-old who had behind him only eight games in the AA (as a teenager), making it a stretch to describe him as an established player. Tommy Bond was just 13-9 in the UA, but Bond was washed up, a player who had been essentially out of baseball for three years before the 1884 season brought him back into circulation.

One of the most famous Union Association stars, whose story is frequently cited in telling the league's history, was Charlie Sweeney. On June 7, 1884, Sweeney struck out 19 men in a National League game, winning 2-1; incidentally, Sweeney also batted cleanup in that game. A few weeks later, Sweeney showed up for a game drunk, took the mound, and refused to come out of the game when his manager relieved him, thus forcing his release, and thus enabling him to sign with the Union Association.

Sweeney, because of the attention which followed his 19 strikeout effort, may have been the closest thing the Union had to a real star—Sweeney, or Dunlap. He is not, in general, an exception to the pattern of the league. He left the majors shortly after his 24th birthday in 1887, leaving a career won-lost mark of 24-7 in the Union Association—but 40-45 in the real major leagues.

Summarizing, this is the way the 272 players break down (and I have been as generous as I could possibly be in classifying players):

1. No other major league connection   107
2. Had brief trials but failed   72
3. Major league fringe players   53
4. Overaged and inexperienced players   26
5. Legitimate major league players   14
6. Major league stars   0

Doesn't it seem pretty obvious what the level of competition in this league was? It was a league that made .270 hitters into .400 hitters, and .450 pitchers into Sandy Koufax. In modern baseball, Al Martin is a career .280 hitter. Let me ask you: if there was a new league now, and if Al Martin hit .400 in that league and Donovan Osborne went 23–4, would you accept that as a major league?

There is one other thing to point out here. The St. Louis "powerhouse"—the St. Louis team that went 94–19 in this tacky little league—survived the league's collapse, augmented their roster with the best players available from the collapse of the rest of the league, and went into the National League in 1885; they eventually became the St. Louis Cardinals. And they finished last. Retaining their best players from the team that went 94–19 in 1884 (Dunlap, Shaffer, Rowe, Sweeney, and Taylor), but moving to a real major league, they dropped from 94–19 to 36–72.

So how bad *was* this league? If a 94–19 team goes 36–72 in a real league, where is the center of the league?

Is there any standard by which the Union Association would rate ahead of, let us say, the Pacific Coast League of the 1920s? I can't find any. Let's quickly tick off the various things that *might* be considered indicators of major league status:

1. *Stability.* The Union Association had three teams fold in less than a season. The Pacific Coast League, in ten seasons, had two franchises move, but none fold. Every team completed its schedule every season.

2. *Competitiveness.* The Union Association had no pennant race. In fact, according to the 1885 *Spalding Guide,* they didn't even have a pennant winner, as Spalding reported that "No official records were kept, and no club legally won the pennant." The Pacific

Coast League, on the other hand, had reasonably good, competitive pennant races every year.

3. *Quality players.* Let's see, the UA had Charlie Sweeney, Joe Quinn, Jack Glasscock, and Fred Dunlap. The PCL in the 1920s had Lefty Gomez, Earl Averill, Dave Bancroft, Mickey Cochrane, Ernie Lombardi, Lloyd Waner, Paul Waner, Lefty O'Doul, Tony Lazzeri, Babe Herman, and dozens of other players who had substantial major league careers.

4. *Size of cities.* The UA had St. Louis, Kansas City, Baltimore, and Altoona. The PCL, on the other hand, had Los Angeles, San Francisco, Seattle, Oakland, and Portland.

5. *Ballparks.* I didn't research it, but a safe guess would be that the PCL had a big advantage.

6. *Attendance.* Again, we are short of data, but you won't lose money betting that the PCL crowds in the 1920s were much larger.

7. *Major league media coverage.* Big advantage for the PCL, which had coverage by multiple newspapers in almost every city.

8. *A structure to attract talent.* No Union Association team had any minor league supporting it, and many or most of the UA teams signed players from walk-in tryouts. The PCL teams in the late 1920s, on the other hand, had organized scouting, and had their own farm teams feeding them talent.

One could argue, I suppose, the "source" theory. If you trace back a great river, you will eventually find a small stream which has been proclaimed by local boosters to be the river's source—and hence, a part of the river. Maybe you could tie the Union Association to the modern majors by the source theory. I can't see how.

But you know what is most astonishing here? After researching this thing for about a week, and realizing finally that there is just absolutely no way in hell to categorize the UA as a major league, I started trying to figure out where the idea that this *was* a major league originally came from.

As I mentioned, Ernest Lanigan classified the UA as a major league when he put together the first baseball encyclopedia in the early 1920s. I assumed that Lanigan had done this based on the *Reach* and *Spalding Guides* from 1885, which are basic sources of historical information.

But when I located those guides, guess what? It is very clear in the 1885 *Guides,* both of them, that the editors of those publications *didn't* regard the Union Association as a major league, at all. The distinction between a "major" league and a "minor" league is just beginning to emerge at that time; there are references to "minor" associations, but that is just an informal description, as opposed to an actual classification.

But the 1885 *Reach Guide,* after recapping briefly the fortunes of the American Association, the National League, the Eastern League and the Northwestern League, has a passage entitled "Other Failures," which leads into the Union Association. "Though they spent money unstintingly and used it to tempt professional players to revolt against the Reserve Rule," reported *Reach, "they did not succeed except in a very limited manner."*

Later, recapping the pennant races, the *Reach Guide* again discusses the American Association and the National League, the Eastern League, the Western League, and the Southern League before getting to the Union. About the Union pennant race, it says that "the St. Louis member had a walk over from the start, owing to the relative weakness of the other teams. Besides there was so much apparent hippodroming done in this body and so many games which were uncertain in their championship nature, that it becomes of no interest what was

the further result of the season's contest in the Union Association." This is part of a paragraph, which the Union Association shares with the Iron and Oil League and the Ohio State League.

In its statistical section this *Reach Guide,* after investing 51 pages in the 1884 records of the American Association and the National League and devoting six pages in the Eastern League, gives a page and a half to the Union statistics, with the comment that "weak pitching had much to do with putting the record so high."

The *Spalding Guide* for 1885 gives even more cursory treatment to the Union Association. After many pages of analysis of the American Association and the National League season, the *Spalding Guide* then covers the Eastern League, the Northwestern League, and the Union Association in a little less than one page apiece, the Union Association third. They gave the Union Association one-eighth as much space as they gave the "Inter-Collegiate Association," which is what we would now call the Ivy League, and one-third as much space as they gave the "Northwestern College Association," which was a forerunner of the Big Ten.

So where, then, does the idea come from that this is a major league, since (a) it clearly wasn't, and (b) the leading experts of the day clearly knew that it wasn't.

How did the Union Association magically become a major league, years after the fact?

It is as simple, I think, as this: Ernest Lanigan made a mistake, and the rest of us haven't done our jobs. If it *isn't* as simple as that, then the question I would ask is, what were the sources that Lanigan relied on, to support his judgment that this should be considered a major league?

Very little baseball history, after all, had been *written* before then. Lanigan, like all of us, is remembered not for what he did *best,* but

THE DAVY FORCE CASE

The National Association was a player-dominated outfit that had no reserve clause and no real protection against one team stealing players from another. The players who went from team to team were called "revolvers." The most famous of them was Davy Force, a 5-foot-4-inch shortstop.

Force was described by Francis Richter as the greatest shortstop of his day, except for George Wright. Force hit extremely well in the National Association (.412 in 1872), although he never hit much after the National League was formed in 1876. He seems to have been hurt by a rule change that allowed a pitcher to throw sidearm, as a small player might. He was built funny; "his legs," said Richter, "were muscular, but short and bowed, he being in these respects a miniature Honus Wagner . . . he had, like Wagner, a sort of awkward grace."

Force's contract problems were one of the keys to the alliance of powers that made the National League possible. During the winter of 1874–75, Davy negotiated with both Chicago, for whom he had played the previous year, and Philadelphia. This created no particular problem, there being no reserve rule, until he signed contracts with both teams, which a good many players in that time did. The prior contract was signed with Chicago, and on that basis the Association's Judiciary Committee awarded him to the White Stockings. However, there was another meeting of the Association later in the spring in Philadelphia, at which Mr. Spering, of Philadelphia, was elected president of the Association—and appointed a new Judiciary Committee. The new Judiciary Committee reversed the old one, and awarded Force to Philadelphia.

This reversal made William Hulbert, Chicago's financial backer, livid. Hulbert's anger resulted in the dissolution of the National Association and the formation of the National League. Hulbert generalized his own ailments, and concluded that the Association was not being run properly—too lax, too player-oriented, not enough protection for the "owners"—and so began drawing up a new set of by-laws, and organizing the league's other financial backers. Further, Harry Wright, though not directly involved, felt that the Association had handled the matter badly by allowing Force to play for Philly. Wright was the most influential figure in baseball at this time, with the possible exception of Henry Chadwick, and his view of the issue may have led him to side with Hulbert in the ensuing battle.

for what he did *first*. The most significant baseball history written between the failure of the Union Association and Lanigan's *Baseball Cyclopedia* is Albert G. Spalding's *America's National Game* (1911). That work dismisses the Union Association in two paragraphs, stating that "the season was a humiliating failure." Lanigan, who was eleven years old in 1884, apparently based his decision that this should be considered a major league upon his own childhood memory.

There are a very small group of us who have engineered the baseball encyclopedias—Lanigan, Hy Turkin, S. C. Thompson, John Tattersall, Lee Allen, Pete Palmer, John Thorn, Don Zminda, John Dewan, Neil Munro, myself . . . you could put all of us in a small room, if you had a good ventilation system. Lanigan made a mistake; the rest of us, out of sloppiness and laziness, have failed to correct it. That's about all there is to it.

At the end of World War II, moneyed interests in Mexico attempted to promote the Mexican League into a major league by luring major leaguers away from their contracts with big dollars. They attracted a few players—Mickey Owen, Sal Maglie, Danny Gardella—but ultimately failed, first because they could not attract the players they wanted, and second because they could not generate enough income to sustain their largesse.

The story of the Union Association is almost precisely the same—the same in terms of the effort which was being made, the same in terms of the approach that was used, essentially the same in terms of the number of quality players who took the bait, essentially the same in terms of the outcome of the experiment.

It would be farcical to list the 1946 Mexican League as a major league—and it is a farce to allow the Union Association to continue to masquerade in the records as a major league. We are polluting major league record books by including statistics from a league that wouldn't properly be included in an encyclopedia of the good minors. Maybe it's premature to say that we ought to take them out, but we sure ought to talk about it.

THE 1880s

HOW THE GAME WAS PLAYED

The 1880s were a time of extensive experimenting with the rules of the game, as the entrepreneurs of professional baseball, now in charge of the game, began to adapt baseball to their commercial needs. The committee on playing rules accepted suggestions all summer, and every winter issued new rules. The number of balls required for a walk, which was nine before, was changed to eight in 1880, to seven in 1882, to six in 1884, back to seven in 1886, to five in 1887, and to four in 1889. This was done in an effort to speed up the game, and to require the pitcher to get the ball in there where it could be hit. The pitcher's box was moved back from 45 feet to 50, and the dimensions of the box were changed twice (a pitcher at this time was allowed to take a short run before delivering the ball). The rules were changed several times on how high a pitcher could raise his arm, but by the end of the decade he was allowed to throw overhand and raise his arm to the moon if he could get it up there. Flat bats were legal for a few years. These experiments were conducted in an attempt to find the right balance between offense and defense. In 1887, the rule allowing the batter to call for a high pitch or a low pitch was eliminated, and a standard strike zone was defined. For one year a strikeout required four strikes. Batters were given first base if hit by a pitch.

With truly independent minor leagues and two major leagues (three if you count the Union Association), rule changes were not always adopted in unison. This resulted in some confusion. The scoring rules were fiddled around with continuously—what to count as a hit, what not to count as a hit, what to charge as an at bat, what not to charge as an at bat, when to charge an error and to whom—all that was in constant flux.

The number of runs jumped up and down, but wound up the decade around six per team per game in both leagues. Fielding gloves were adopted during the decade, and errors consequently diminished. The stolen base was in its heyday, in part because catchers, with pitchers throwing overhand and from 50 feet away, were unable to deal with pitches as they do today. (Stolen bases were counted beginning in 1887, but, since players could be credited with a stolen base when they took an extra base on the basepaths, it is difficult to know how many stolen bases there were in the modern meaning of the term. It is clear, though, that there were many.)

The game began to get rough. In the 1850s and sixties, baseball's ethics were set by gentlemen's clubs. As they developed more interest in won and lost records, the gentlemen's clubs took in the better athletes. The first generation of professional players came from that background, from the experience of being hired soldiers of the gentlemen's clubs. Respect for the umpires was the accepted norm, and prominent citizens often served as volunteer umpires.

With the coming of professionalism, and professional umpires, this went out the window, and the game turned rough. The center of rowdyism in the 1880s was the St. Louis team in the American Association, led by Arlie Latham (The Freshest Man on Earth) and manager Charles Comiskey. This great team—and many think them the greatest team of the nineteenth century—attempted to drive opponents off their game with constant verbal abuse. Since they won, others imitated them. Players acting as coaches ran up and down the baselines hurling insults and obscenities at the pitcher; this led to the coach's box being established in 1887. Latham was known for his talents and enthusiasm as an antagonist, leading to constant fights. The Association would fine them and Chris Von der Ahe, the owner, would pay the fines, believing such tactics to encourage attendance.

The fans got involved. Visiting players had no dugouts to hide in, only a bench, exposed to hostile fans sitting close enough to be heard, close enough to hurl, close enough to reach out and touch. And the way they treated the umpires! Well, we'll deal with that later, but many people felt that you just couldn't win in St. Louis; if the fans didn't get to you, they'd get to

the umpire. The Browns from 1883 through 1889 won more than three-fourths of their home games.

King Kelly was noted for his innovative circumvention of the rulebook; someone said that half of the National League's rules were written to keep King Kelly from stealing ballgames. When the rules were changed to allow in-game substitutions, all a player had to do was call himself into the game. This was the practice until one day when the third out of the ninth inning was popped up over the head of King Kelly, seated on the Chicago bench. Kelly stood up, called himself into the game, and caught the ball (or so, at least, the story goes). Whether that story is true or not, he certainly cut across the infield while running the bases when he could get by with it, and pioneered such tactics as limping to first base in great pain, then suddenly recovering to steal second, and dropping

King Kelly

his catcher's mask where the baserunner would trip over it.

One could make too much of this. The rowdy behavior was far worse in the American Association, which charged a twenty-five cent admission and sold beer, than in the National League, which preferred the fifty-cent admission and did not. But the average man in the 1880s, while rougher than today, was not a thug, nor was the average ballplayer helpless to defend himself. Many games were marked by the best of sportsmanship on all sides. The surprise at the time was to see so many games which were not, and so that's what people wrote about.

Throughout the decade, the "official" schedule lengthened steadily, as "league" games became more profitable than exhibitions. As teams began to play 90, 100, 120, 130 (league) games a year, and as pitchers began to throw overhand, the one-man pitching staffs died out; by 1889 most teams were using three pitchers, not exactly in a modern rotation, but alternating.

WHERE THE GAME WAS PLAYED

We're talking basically about two leagues here—the National League, which was already in place in 1880, and the American Association, which came along in 1882. There was also the Union Association (see page **000**), which occupied some major league cities for a few weeks with minor league talent, but the teams represented in the two majors were:

National	American
Boston	Baltimore
Buffalo	Brooklyn
Chicago	Cincinnati
Cincinnati	Cleveland
Cleveland	Columbus
Detroit	Indianapolis
Indianapolis	Kansas City
Kansas City	Louisville
New York	New York
Philadelphia	Philadelphia
Pittsburgh	Pittsburgh
Providence	Richmond
St. Louis	St. Louis
Troy	Toledo
Washington	Washington
Worcester	

There were efforts to place major league ball as far west as Kansas City and as far south as Richmond, but these efforts failed, in part because of the transportation difficulties, and in part because the press in those towns was not robust enough to nurture and sustain the public's interest. Baseball remained concentrated in the northeast corner of the nation, where the population densities were highest.

At the beginning of the decade, the National League had been forced into smaller cities by William Hulbert's wars with other teams. Hulbert made a remark, often quoted, that he would rather be a lamppost in Chicago than a millionaire in any other city. Combined with his record of antipathy toward the teams in New York and Philadelphia, this suggests a personal bias against the big cities of the east. This enabled the American Association, opening shop in 1882, to move unchallenged into the nation's largest cities. Denny McKnight, first president of the Association, estimated that the Association drew from a population base of 2,370,000 fans, whereas the National League served only 1,156,000. But following the death of Hulbert, the National League marched into the big cities of the east, and balanced the scales.

WHO THE GAME WAS PLAYED BY

One thing about the players of the nineteenth century that should be noted is their size. Few were over six feet tall.

The players were still mostly eastern, mostly Irish, and a little rough. The stories about their having been unwelcome in the best hotels are true, if over-stated.

This man played more than 1,000 major league games, and is mentioned only once in passing in this book. And none of you has any idea who he is.

CHECKING IN:

1880– Christy Mathewson, Factoryville, Pennsylvania
    Sam Crawford, Wahoo, Nebraska
    Joe Tinker, Muscotah, Kansas
1881– Branch Rickey, Lucasville, Ohio
    Ed Walsh, Plains, Pennsylvania
    Johnny Evers, Troy, New York
1883– Hal Chase, Los Gatos, California
1884– Chief Bender, Brainerd, Minnesota
    Eddie Cicotte, Detroit
1885– George S. Patton, San Gabriel, California
1886– Ty Cobb, Narrows, Georgia
    Home Run Baker, Trappe, Maryland
1887– Eddie Collins, Millerton, New York
    Walter Johnson, Humboldt, Kansas
    Grover Alexander, St. Paul, Nebraska
    Joe McCarthy, Philadelphia
1888– Tris Speaker, Hubbard City, Texas
    Joe Jackson, Brandon Mills, South Carolina
    Eugene O'Neill, New York City
1889– Smokey Joe Wood, Kansas City, Missouri

CHECKING OUT:

1881– James Garfield, gunshot, 50
1882– William Hulbert, heart attack, 49
1884– Jim Devlin, 33
1885– Ulysses S. Grant, 63
1888– Asa Brainard, 47

THE 1880s IN A BOX

Attendance Data:

Highest: Brooklyn (AA), 1889   353,690

        St. Louis (AA)   1,509,000

Lowest: Worcester (Mass), 1882   11,000

        (National League team)

According to the research of Robert L. Tiemann and Pete Palmer, total attendance for major league baseball began 1880 at 256,428 and peaked in 1887 at 4,115,769. Attendance for the decade was about 23,276,002 fans, split among 146 franchise/seasons, making about 159,400 fans per team per season.

The average American in this era probably attended a major league baseball game about once every 27 years.

Most Home Runs:

Ned Williamson, Chicago,   1884   27

Harry Stovey,   91

Williamson's twenty-seven home runs were a fluke, the result of a short fence at Lakefront Park, which created inflated home run totals for the entire team. In all other seasons, balls hit over that fence were considered doubles.

Best Won/Lost Record by Team:

1885 Chicago White Sox   87-25   .777

St. Louis Browns (A.A.)   618-323   .656

Worst Won/Lost Record by Team:

1883 Philadelphia (N.L.)   17-81   .173

Washington (NL)   163-337   .326

Index of Competitive Balance: 24%

Home-Field Winning Percentage: .583

Percentage of Regulars Hitting .300: 17%

Largest Home-Field Advantage: Louisville (AA)

Louisville during the decade was 261-195 at home (.572) but 171-315 on the road (.352), a 220-point home-field advantage.

Having Their Best Decade: The Chicago Cubs (then known by other names, including "White Sox" and "Colts"), had their best decade ever. The team now known as the San Francisco Giants was launched in 1883, and also had a better winning percentage than in any other decade.

Heaviest Player: Roger Connor or Cap Anson (220-plus)

Lightest Player: Davy Force (130)

Most Strikeouts by Pitcher:

Matt Kilroy,   1886   513

Tim Keefe   2,195

Highest Batting Average:

Tip O'Neill,   1887   .435

Dan Brouthers   .348

The only .400 hitters of the decade were O'Neill and Pete Browning, both in the American Association in 1887, in a season in which four strikes were required for a strikeout. At the time, the American Association counted walks as hits in batting average, and reported a batting average for O'Neill of .492.

Lowest Batting Average:

Jack Burdock,	1888	.142
Tom McLaughlin		.189

Best Major League Players (by Years):

1880— George Gore
1881— Cap Anson
1882— Dan Brouthers
1883— Dan Brouthers
1884— Paul Hines
1885— Roger Connor
1886— King Kelly
1887— Tip O'Neill
1888— Jimmy Ryan
1889— Tommy Tucker

Best Major League Pitchers (by Years):

1880— Jim McCormick
1881— Grasshopper Jim Whitney
1882— Old Hoss Radbourn
1883— Old Hoss Radbourn
1884— Old Hoss Radbourn
1885— John Clarkson
1886— Dave Foutz
1887— Bob Caruthers
1888— Silver King
1889— John Clarkson

Hardest-Throwing Pitcher: Charlie Sweeney

The 1924 *Spalding Guide* said that "Modern Base Ball enthusiasts would find it hard to realize the amount of speed that Sweeney could put into his work. Walter Johnson is called the 'speed king', but he never pitched with more speed than Sweeney, and perhaps not as much." See note about Sweeney under "Negotiating Tactic."

Best Curve: Mickey Welch

Best Power/Speed Combination: Harry Stovey

Best Switch Hitter: Tommy Tucker

Iron Man: Old Hoss Radbourn

Best Bunter: Joe Start

Best Baseball Books:

The Sporting News began publication in 1886. The *Reach Guide* and *The Sporting Life*, both eventually edited by the incomparable Francis Richter, started in 1883 (Richter founded *The Sporting Life* and assumed the position as *Reach* editor later on). "Casey at the Bat" first appeared in the *San Francisco Examiner* in 1888. Among the popular books of the period were Mike Kelly's *Play Ball: Stories of the Ball Field*, in 1888, and Fred Pfeffer's *Scientific Ball*, in 1889.

Five Largest Changes in Baseball During the Decade:

1. Wholesale revisions of the rules/elimination of primitive elements

2. Establishment of the two-league format

3. Extension of schedules to something like modern length

4. Growth/development of stadiums

5. Consolidation of the authority of professionals over the amateurs who had previously controlled the game

Best Outfield Arm: George Gore

Most Runs Batted In:

Sam Thompson,	1887	166
Cap Anson		967

Early rules did not require the batting order to be announced prior to game time. Before this was changed in the early eighties, Anson would sometimes wait and see if the first two men got on. If they did, he would bat; if not, he would wait and hit in the next inning.

Most Aggressive Baserunners:
King Kelly
Arlie Latham
Harry Stovey

Fastest Player: Billy Sunday

When he got old, Cap Anson said that Billy Sunday had been a greater player than Ty Cobb. The 1919 *Reach Guide,* conceding Sunday's greatness as a baserunner, found it necessary to rebut this at some length . . . see also note about Arlie Latham, page 570.

Slowest Player: Dick Buckley

Best Control Pitcher: Jim Whitney

Most Stolen Bases:

Hugh Nicol,	1887	138
Arlie Latham		367

Best-Looking Player: Billy Sunday

Ugliest Player: Grasshopper Jim Whitney

A reporter once wrote that Whitney had "a head about the size of a wart with the forehead slanting at an angle of 45 degrees."

O.J. Simpson Award: Terry Larkin (see page 51)

Cap Anson Award: Cap Anson

Three Finger Brown Award: One Arm Daily

Ozzie Guillen Trophy: Hick Carpenter

Bound for Glory:
Billy Sunday (Evangelist)
John K. Tener (Future Governor of Pennsylvania)
Robert M. Keating (Inventor)
Frank Olin (Industrialist)

Best Pitching Staff: 1887 St. Louis Browns (Bob Caruthers, Dave Foutz, Silver King)

Best Offense: 1885 Chicago White Stockings

Retrobermanisms:
Jimmy (Power to the) Peoples
(See a doctor immediately if your) Dick Burns
George (It's all a matter of whose Ox is) Gore

First of His Kind: Tommy Tucker (first switch hitter to win a batting title)

Last of His Kind: Jack Clements (the last left-handed catcher)

The notion that a left-handed person *could not* be a major league catcher is absurd. The practical disadvantage of having to "throw through" the hitters 65% of the time on a steal of second (as opposed to 35%) is not prohibitive. If you think about it, a left-handed catcher would in general have an *advantage* in scrambling after a ball tapped in front of the plate. If the ball is tapped along the first base line, the play is in front of the catcher, and it makes little difference whether the catcher is right-handed or left. But on a ball tapped along the third base line, a left-handed catcher would have an advantage, since the right-hander has to reach across his body to grab the ball, thus has to "run past" the play in order to avoid screening himself.

The biggest reason there are no left-handed catchers is natural selection. Catchers need good throwing arms. If you have a kid on your baseball team who is left-handed and has a strong arm, what are you going to do with him?

One of a Kind: Old Hoss Radbourn (only man to win 59 games in a season)

Best Infield: 1885 Chicago White Sox (Cap Anson, Fred Pfeffer, Ned Williamson, Tom Burns)

Best Outfield: 1889 New York Giants (Jim O'Rourke, Mike Tiernan, George Gore)

A Better Man Than a Ballplayer: Pop Snyder was a brilliant defensive catcher, possibly better than Charlie Bennett, although I picked Bennett as the Gold Glove catcher of the decade. Anyway, in 1882 Snyder made $11,000, and played well, hitting .291 and earning almost twice as many Win Shares for his fielding as any other catcher in the league. That winter the Reds sent him a contract calling for $18,000 in 1883. Snyder returned it, explaining that it was too much. He asked that the Reds take a thousand dollars off of his offer, and give it to a teammate who he felt was underpaid. The Reds agreed, and Snyder played for $17,000.

Mr. Dickens, I'd Like You to Meet:
Eddie Fusselback (St. Louis, 1882, Baltimore, 1884) Cannonball Titcomb (Philadelphia, 1886–87, Giants, 1888–89)

Platoon Combinations I Would Like to See:
Chicken Wolf and Harry Koons

Best Defensive Teams: Charles Comiskey's St. Louis Browns were by far the best defensive team of the 1880s.

Charles Comiskey has been credited with inventing the practice of having the pitcher cover first base on a ground ball to the right side, thus enabling the first baseman to come off the bag and cover the hole. This is based on news reports and memories…really, not much more than gossip. Cap Anson, who liked to take credit for inventing all defensive teamwork, once claimed, in a 1918 interview, that his pitchers were doing this before Comiskey's.

It occurred to me that, with modern baseball encyclopedias, it would be simple to check and see how many putouts actually were recorded by pitchers, and whether the totals for St. Louis (or Chicago) were larger than those for other teams, as they would certainly have to be if the claim for Comiskey was valid. Here's what I found:

1. Putout rates for pitchers in 1876 were not really very different than they are now. In 1876 there were 520 major league games played, and pitchers recorded 346 putouts—.66 per game. In 1996 there were 4,534 major league games, and pitchers recorded 2,630 putouts—.58 per game.

2. In the first ten years of the majors, however, putout rates for pitchers *declined* substantially, from .66 per game in 1876 to .40 in 1885. I believe that this happened because the practice developed of pitchers not catching pop ups. There aren't very many PO1s, you know. The pitcher only catches a pop out if no one else can. This practice almost certainly developed shortly after 1876.

3. In the first four years of the St. Louis Browns, 1882–1885, their pitchers recorded no more putouts than any other team. They were in the middle of the league in pitcher putouts. (Comiskey took over management of the team late in the 1883 season.)

4. In 1886, however, putouts by St. Louis pitchers suddenly vaulted far ahead of anyone else in the league. In 1886 St. Louis pitchers recorded 106 putouts, whereas the record for a team in a season before 1886 was 81. They led the majors again in 1887, with 108 (Brooklyn was second in the league with 76), and in 1888, with 89.

Conclusion? Charles Comiskey did in fact invent the practice of pitchers covering first base on a grounder to the right side.

Clint Hartung Award: *Ebenezer Beatin

Outstanding Sportswriter: Oliver Perry Caylor

Most Admirable Superstar: Bid McPhee

Least Admirable Superstar: Cap Anson

Gold Glove Team:
C— Charlie Bennett
1B— Charlie Comiskey
2B— Bid McPhee
3B— Ed Williamson
SS— Germany Smith
OF— Curt Welch
     Jim Fogarty
     Pop Corkhill

New Stadiums:
1882— Exposition Park, Pittsburgh
1883— Lakefront Park, Chicago (remodeled)
        Washington Park, Brooklyn
        Recreation Park, Philadelphia
1884— Redland Park, Cincinnati
1886— Capitol Park, Washington
1887— Huntington Grounds, Philadelphia

Best Pennant Race: 1889 National League

The Giants won and Boston lost on the last day of the season to give the Giants a one-game victory.

Best World Series: 1886 Series, won by St. Louis over Chicago, 0-6, 12-0, 4-11, 8-5, 10-3, and 4-3.

Best-Hitting Pitchers: Guy Hecker, Dave Foutz, and Bob Caruthers

Worst-Hitting Pitcher: Cannonball Titcomb

Best Minor League Team: Dallas Hams, 1888

Best Minor League Player: Bill Krieg

Odd Couple: Cap Anson and King Kelly

Drinking Men:
Charlie Sweeney
King Kelly
Jim McCormick
Gid Gardner
Lee Viau
Mickey Welch
Pete Browning
Jack Farrell

New Equipment:
Flat-sided bats legal, 1885–1893
Sliding pads introduced by Sam Morton
First made-to-order bats, by Hillerich
Umpires indicators invented
Chest protectors for catchers (1888 or 1889, experiments earlier)
Catchers mitts
First night baseball game played at Hull, Massachusetts, September 2, 1880
Prior to 1887, home plate was made of stone, iron, or wood. Numerous players were injured by the plate. A major league player/inventor, Robert M. Keating, invented the two-part rubber home plate, white with a black border, which has been used ever since.

Player vs. Team: The owner's reserve clause, developed in 1879, was submitted to a number of court tests during this era, and lost them all. In the first big test, the case of Charlie Bennett, the court ruled that the clause Bennett had signed was merely an agreement to execute a contract at a later date, and not a contract in and of itself. This implied that Bennett had a right to reject the later offer. This was merely the first of many courtroom defeats for baseball's reserve arrangement, which survived nonetheless for eighty-five more years.

Team vs. Team: A Detroit owner named Frederick Kimball Stearns spent $25,000 between 1885 and 1887 to turn Detroit into a powerhouse team. The Detroit area at this time was not able to support his expenditures, and Stearns needed to get some of the money back from the road gate. The other National League owners, reacting to Stearns' strategy, reduced the road gate to a limit of $125 a game, thus preventing Stearns from recovering his investment, and forcing him to sell off his stars.

Uniform Changes: Position-coded uniforms

New Terms or Expressions: Fans at this time were called "cranks" or "kranks." Thomas Lawson wrote a little book, *The Krank: His Language and What it Means* (1888) which listed such terms as "willow" or "ash" for bat, "circus catches" for circus catches, "robber" or "tenth man" for umpire, as well as "butter fingers" and "back up" fielders.

Most Wins by Pitcher:
Old Hoss Radbourn, 1884   59
Tim Keefe   291

Highest Winning Percentage:
Fred Goldsmith,   1880   21-3   .875
Bob Caruthers   175-64   .732

Lowest Winning Percentage:
Sam Moffett,   1884   3-19   .136
Egyptian Healy   44-98   .310

Nicknames: See page 48

All Offense/No Defense: 1885 Philadelphia Athletics

All Defense/No Offense: 1885 New York Metropolitans

Homer: Ned Williamson hit 64 home runs in his career—57 of them at home (Chicago), only 7 on the road. His teammate Fred Pfeffer also hit 81 of his 94 home runs at home, while Hick Carpenter of Cincinnati, who hit 18 career home runs, hit all but one in his home park.

Yellowstone Park Award: Henry Larkin

This probably comes under the heading of "You Learn Something Useless Every Day," but unlike modern baseball, in which almost exactly 50% of home runs are hit by the home team, in the 1880s a very high percentage of home runs were hit by the home team. All prominent players of the 1880s with any power hit more career home runs at home than they did on the road except Henry Larkin, an American Association first baseman who hit 35 of his 53 home runs on the road.

Minor Leagues Were: 100% percent free

Best Double Play Combination: Bid McPhee and Frank Fennelly, Cincinnati, 1885–1888.

Fennelly and McPhee were about 20 double plays a year better than the National League average.

Worst Double Play Combination: Joe Farrell and Sadie Houck, 1886 Baltimore Orioles.

Paul Krichell Talent Scout Award: Cap Anson

In early 1890, Cap Anson journeyed to Canton, Ohio, to see Cy Young pitch. He reported that Young was "just another farmer."

Best Unrecognized Player: Tony Mullane

Highest-Paid Player: Varying reports. Management in the late eighties was trying to enforce a salary limit. Players, of course, tried to avoid the limit, and there were side deals by which players received cash payments outside the contract.

New Statistics:
1883— Total bases
          Wild pitches
1884— Runs earned by opponents (earned runs) and earned run average temporarily adopted by National League
1886— Stolen bases
1888— Pitcher's walks
1889— Pitcher's strikeouts and hit by pitch

Wild pitches and walks were originally part of a pitcher's fielding record, later switched to the pitching ledger. The *Chicago Tribune* introduced RBI in 1880, but the concept didn't catch on until twenty years later. Existing RBI records for the period were figured later.

A Very Good Movie Could Be Made About: Baseball in St. Louis, 1883–86. It's got everything—great teams, unbelievable characters like Lucas, Von der Ahe, Comiskey, Sweeney, and Latham, pennant races, World Series.

Five Biggest Things Wrong with Baseball:

1. Segregation
2. On-field violence
3. Constant bickering between players and owners
4. Excessive movement of players
5. Player drunkenness

I Don't Know What This Has to Do with Baseball, But I Thought I'd Mention It Anyway: The original "Louisville Slugger" was Pete Browning, the Louisville slugger who discovered the batmaking talents of Bud Hillerich. Browning, like Ted Williams, absolutely loved his bats, and did a lot to change bats from crude nineteenth-century table legs into modern tools of the trade. Browning had over 200 bats, each of which had a name. He used names from the Bible if he didn't have anything else in mind.

Browning was released from an insane asylum in Louisville in 1905, and died in a city hospital later in the year.

1882:
THE SECRET SCORER

When Albert Spalding was president of the Chicago National League team from 1882 to 1891 (the team now known as the Cubs) he felt that the official scorer should be independent, not subject to criticism or pressure. According to an article by Alex Haas, Spalding successfully kept secret the identity of his official scorer—for ten years. Cap Anson, the manager, did not know who it was. The league president, who received the accounts, did not know who was sending them. The press had no idea who the official scorer was. The man who mailed them to the league office did not know what he was mailing; he was just dropping something off for his mother.

His mother was Elisa Green Williams, and she was the official scorer. She attended every game and sat between the wives of two of the team's stars, Cap Anson and Abner Dalrymple. She scored every play without ever tipping them off that hers was the official account.

1885: THE GOOD PEOPLE
OF THE EARTH VERSUS
PETE SOMMERS

On May 28, 1885, Joseph Andrews Sommers, later a major league catcher, was arrested in Cleveland and charged with playing ball on Sunday with the Cleveland team in a minor league. A jury trial was held. The team wished to admit evidence showing that baseball had been played on Sunday in Cleveland for several years without interference, and that other entertainments were permitted under the law. The judge would admit no evidence relating to those issues, but instructed the jury to consider only the question of whether Sommers had, indeed, played ball on Sunday. Sommers acknowledged that he had.

The Cleveland club appealed, claiming that the law was unconstitutional in that it made no provisions for someone who might wish to keep a different holy day. They also argued that the law did not apply to Sommers, who was not "playing" the game, but merely following his avocation, as permitted under the law, and that the judge had erred in restricting the scope of the issues before the jury.

MAJOR LEAGUE ALL-STAR TEAM 1880–1889

Records in seasonal notation, based on 130 games. Pitchers based on 60 starts.

Pos.	Player	Years	Hits	HR	RBI	Avg.	Other
C	Buck Ewing	5.92	157	7	72	.295	19 Triples
1B	Dan Brouthers	7.24	186	11	91	.348	37 Doubles
2B	H. Richardson	7.49	171	7	71	.307	114 Runs
3B	Pete Browning	8.14	185	6	74	.344	66 Steals
SS	Jack Glasscock	8.10	156	2	56	.296	
LF	Harry Stovey	8.22	170	11	73	.313	135 Runs
CF	George Gore	7.32	164	5	65	.308	
RF	Sam Thompson	3.82	173	14	118	.319	
U	King Kelly	7.92	170	7	85	.314	78 Steals

Pitcher	Years	Won-Lost	SO	ERA	Other
RH Tim Keefe	8.15	36-22	270	2.71	472 Innings
RH John Clarkson	5.46	40-18	276	2.54	523 Innings

@ATHLETICS.DIS

In 1883 a Philadelphia zookeeper named Jim Murray introduced a system of relaying scores almost instantly all over the city of Brotherly Love, by means of carrier pigeons. Homing pigeons would be released at the park with the up-to-date scores after each half-inning, and the workers at the zoo would "know how the inning went before the men are out in the field for the next one." A few fans from other parts of the city heard about this and wanted in on it, so provisions were made for them, too. On some days as many as a half-dozen birds would be released at the end of each frame. (Item based on a note in the delightful book, *The Scrapbook History of Baseball*.)

RECRUITING POSTER

In 1886 the owners of the two leagues agreed to hold salaries to a maximum of $2,000. More creatively, the owners decided to charge players for the use of their uniforms, and also to charge them 50 cents a day for expenses while on road trips.

John Montgomery Ward, a star player and a graduate of Columbia Law School, decided to form a union.

OUT

The only known case of a dishonest umpire in professional baseball was that of Dick Higham, fired by the National League in June, 1882, after confessing to collusion with gamblers.

Higham was also the first umpire to wear a face mask.

BEST WORLD SERIES OF THE 1880s

The American Association began play as a major league in 1882. For two years the National League tried to run them out of town, but the leagues made peace in 1883. This made it possible, in theory, to arrange a championship series between the two leagues.

The problem was that nobody really knew how to arrange such a series. Since they didn't know how to do it, they tried a lot of things that didn't work. They played varying numbers of games—seven, nine, ten, fifteen games. They tried putting it on the road, as a traveling show. These things didn't work, and substandard umpiring caused one championship series (1885) to degenerate into a walkout, with both teams claiming victory. When the championship series did not degenerate into anger and confusion, they tended to meander off into exhibition contests.

The one successful championship series of the 1880s was the 1886 series, which pitted St. Louis of the American Association, led by Charles Comiskey, against Chicago of the National League, led by Cap Anson. The series featured many of the great players of the era, including Arlie Latham, Tip O'Neill, Bob Caruthers, and Dave Foutz of St. Louis, and Fred Pfeffer, Jimmy Ryan, Ned Williamson, King Kelly, and John Clarkson of the White Sox. Both managers, Comiskey and Anson, were playing managers, both first basemen, both men known for being tough, aggressive, intelligent and creative.

And a great deal was at stake. The American Association was trying to prove that they belonged, that their teams could play with the big boys. The two teams had hard feelings, left over from the series of the year before, which they had failed to complete. American Association fans claimed that the St. Louis Browns

were the finest team the world had ever seen. National League fans said the same about the White Sox.

That said, the series still had the odor of an exhibition lingering about it. The first three games were blowouts. John Clarkson pitched a shutout for Chicago in Game One, 6–0. Parisian Bob Caruthers returned the compliment in the second game, 12–0; Tip O'Neill hit two home runs. Clarkson came back in Game Three, with one day's rest, while Caruthers skipped the rest and started for St. Louis. Chicago won, 11–4, in an eight-inning game, and Chicago was up 2–1 as the series moved to St. Louis.

Moving to St. Louis, in 1886, meant saying hello to the most notorious fans in the sporting world. Clarkson, pitching for the third time in four days, was rocked, 8–5, in a game stopped by the umpire after seven innings. Outfielder Jimmy Ryan started the fifth game (you tell me why), and was pounded, 10–3, in a game discontinued by darkness and disinterest after seven innings. St. Louis led, 3 games to 2.

Game Six saved the series. Interest in the games had mounted as the series ran, despite the scores. The White Sox led in the seventh inning, 3–0; a light rain was falling, and there was talk of calling the game. The fans would have none of that. The Browns erased a 3–0 lead in the bottom of the eighth, and went on to win with one out in the tenth on a legendary steal of home by Curt Welch. This was the most famous play in nineteenth-century baseball, the $15,000 slide, so-called because the Browns grabbed all the receipts on the strength of the victory. Bob Caruthers was the winning pitcher for St. Louis—and the American Association could claim its only undisputed championship of the baseball world.

NICKNAMES IN THE 1880s

Nicknames of the 1880s reflect a variety of primitive forms, some of which caught on, and some of which didn't. Nicknames with allusions to literature or the heroic past were used, but never caught on; Tony Mullane was "The Apollo of the Box," Charles Comiskey "The Old Roman," Milt Scott "Mikado Milt," and Pete Browning "The Gladiator." But Jim Galvin became the first of dozens of hard-throwing pitchers to be likened to a train, when he was called "The Steam Engine," and Ed Morris served a like function in being called "Cannonball." Long nicknames disappeared quickly; Arlie Latham's five-word handle was one of the last of those. But Mickey Welch, being called "Smiling Mickey," set a pattern for hundreds of players, and for the first time animals came to be used (though infrequently) to suggest images. Pete Hotaling was called "Monkey," Jim Whitney was "Grasshopper Jim," and Willard Mains just plain "Grasshopper." Those particular animals, however, are no longer used to conjure player images.

Two forms of nicknames that were popular were those that suggested places or movement, such as "Parisian Bob" Caruthers and "The Little Globetrotter" (Billy Earle). A few nicknames alluded to a player's voice, and a player named George Miller, who must have had one of the greatest voices ever, had three of them: "Doggie," "Foghorn," and "Calliope" (if that kid grew up today they'd send him to a speech therapist). Tim O'Rourke was called "Voiceless Tim," and Mike Tiernan, a quiet man, was "Silent Mike."

Elton Chamberlain was called "Icebox" Chamberlain because he was cool and collected on the mound. George Tebeau was called "White Wings." Jim Baker noticed in going through some 1890's newspapers that garbage workers of the time were called "White Wings," and I speculated in the first edition of this book that Tebeau may have been a garbage worker in the off season. Somebody who seemed to know what he was talking about wrote me a letter, saying that he thought it was very improbable that Tebeau would have been a garbage worker in the off season, so I backed off that when the book was reprinted in paperback. But then later, I found a fairly prominent player from the 1930s, and I'm sorry but I forgot to note who it was, who was called "The Junk Man" because he was, in fact, a garbage worker in the off season. So I don't know where that's going, but anyway, Tebeau was called "White Wings," and garbage workers in that time were called "White Wings." The decade of the 1880s had as many great one-of-a-kind nicknames as any period of baseball history, of which I present a few:

Sureshot (Fred Dunlap)

Bloody Jake (Jake Evans)

Scissors (Dave Foutz)

Pebbly Jack (Jack Glasscock)

Prune (George Moolic)

Dandelion (Fred Pfeffer)

Peach Pie (Jack O'Connor)

Bolicky Billy Taylor Razzle Dazzle (Con Murphy)

Skyrocket Smith (Samuel J. Smith)

All deaf and dumb players were called "Dummy."

BALLPARKS OF THE 1880s

Some parks were built in the 1880s which, if not successful as long-term domiciles for major league teams, at least had pretensions in that direction. With the great increases in attendance early in the decade, there was (1) a recognized need for larger parks, and (2) a new belief in the stability of the institution. One must remember that a National League owner in 1876 had no reason to believe that the National League would last thirty or fifty years, and thus no incentive to build a permanent ballpark, and no way to finance it.

The palace of baseball in the 1880s was Lakefront Stadium in Chicago. Lakefront, built in 1887, benefited from constant renovations by Albert Spalding, and after a major facelift in 1883 seated 10,000 fans, making it the largest baseball park in the country. Spalding's private box was equipped with a gong to call his lackeys, and (believe it or not) a private telephone line, so that he could conduct business during the game. The park featured eighteen private boxes with armchairs and curtains to keep the sun out and the vandal hordes at bay; it also had a pagoda built to accommodate a small brass band, which entertained before and after the games and between innings, but which never, as far as we know, played anything like "Ring of Fire" when Tommy Burns came to bat, religious hymns for Billy Sunday, or imitated the sound of popcorn popping for Fred Pfeffer.

The new ballparks of the decade . . . Washington Park in Brooklyn (1883) was a little 2,000-seater, built for a minor league team. That burned down in 1889. When Alfred Reach bought the Worcester, Massachusetts, team and moved it to Philadelphia in 1883, he built a small park called Recreation Park. The Phillies quickly outgrew this, so he built the Huntington Grounds in 1887. This was perhaps the finest new park of the decade, a big double-decker seating 20,000 people, and no doubt Reach intended it to last a few years. It burned in 1894, not completely, was rebuilt and collapsed in 1903, killing twelve people. The park survived this, too, and eventually became the Baker Bowl. The American Association team in Cincinnati in 1884 threw up a jerry-built park in the month before the 1884 season opened. A section of the seats collapsed on opening day, killing one spectator and injuring many others.

Henry Lucas, the enthusiastic millionaire who backed the Union Association, laid out a small but pretentious ballpark on his private estate in St. Louis, while crosstown rival Chris Von der Ahe spent $6,500 to convert old Sportsman's Park (built 1876) to the task of simultaneously accommodating baseball games, horse races, beer sales, and fireworks shows. The Hewitt brothers built Capitol Park in Washington in 1886; it seated 6,000. The Giants from 1883 onward were playing at the first Polo Grounds, which would receive large crowds, if not necessarily seat them; they left in a Tammany Hall wrangle in 1890. I doubt that any team except the White Sox spent the entire decade in one park. But with crowds of 30,000 by the end of the decade, the day when that would change was drawing into view.

UNIFORMS OF THE 1880s

Remember Spalding's "tulip bed" of the 1870s? The Detroit Wolverines tried it again in 1882. From the *National Pastime:* "Each player's jersey, belt and cap were designated by position—1B, red and white stripes; CF— red and black; SS—brown; P, sky blue; and so on, with team colors reflected only in the stockings. The heavy silk "clown" shirts were not only humiliating to the players, but uncomfortable in the heat; the experiment was mercifully ended in June." (Can't you just see how this ended. About June, the manager looked out there and said, "You know, I think you can tell what position the man is playing just by looking at where he is on the field.") The Wolverines continued to wear striped stockings of black and yellow— like a Tiger. They came to be called the De- troit Tigers. Later on we'll look at the evolution of the Detroit "D," which is an in- teresting study in itself.

A few other notes . . . with no identifica- tion numbers on the uniforms, did you ever wonder how players kept track of their own stuff? A photograph of Wee Willie Keeler's shirt provides an answer. "W. Keeler" was embroidered on the front shirt tail, the part that would be tucked in. A close-up view of the shirt belonging to a member of the Bara- boo Base Ball Club shows the detachable bib I've mentioned before, but also has the long sleeves with buttons just above the elbow, enabling the player to detach part of the sleeve.

More and more uniforms were going all dark about this time, probably following the famous black uniforms of the New York Giants. The Chicago uniform, for instance, was changed to dark pants and top, con- trasting white caps, stockings, lace-up clo- sure, belt, and lettering. One more little tidbit from the *National Pastime;* Will White was the only prominent player of the nineteenth century to wear glasses.

—Susan McCarthy

NEGOTIATING TACTIC

Charlie Sweeney was a young pitcher in the first glow of his fame. On July 21, 1884, he arrived at the park indisposed, and announced that he had been out drinking all night. His manager sent him to the mound anyway, but Sweeney was hit- ting the sauce between innings, with predictable effects. Since a substitution could not be made without the consent of the opposition, in the fifth inning Sweeney was told to go to right field, where a standby pitcher was stowed away for such an occasion. Sweeney, however, refused to go to right field, and continued to pitch.

According to an article by Frederick Ivor- Campbell, the manager after a couple of in- nings became insistent, at which point Sweeney walked off the field, forcing his team to play a man short. Sweeney was released that evening.

Which didn't turn out badly. The emanci- pated Sweeney signed with St. Louis of the Union Association, earning a nice raise. It is suspected that the incident may have been planned to force his release.

TERRY LARKIN

This is not a pretty story, and you may not wish to read it. Terry Larkin was a pitcher with Hartford and Chicago from 1877 through 1879, winning eighty-nine games. One day in 1883 his wife, Catherine, got on him for coming home drunk. He pulled a pistol from his hip pocket and shot her, afterwards (a) threatening to kill anyone who came near him, and (b) cutting his own throat with a razor. He was arrested and held in a hospital where, under the impression that his wife would die, he again attempted suicide, this time by banging his head against a steam register, causing an ugly gash. Restrained, he begged a policeman to "For God's sake hit me in the head and put an end to my suffering."

His wife recovered, but Larkin's suffering did not end yet. Larkin returned briefly to the majors in 1884, and permanently to crime in 1886. Fired from a job as a saloon keeper in Brooklyn, Larkin showed up at the bar with two loaded pistols, and demanded that the saloon owner fight a duel. The owner was unwilling, but Larkin insisted, and forced him at the point of one gun to take the other. When they were marching off their ten paces, the owner marched out the door and locked Larkin in, returning with a policeman who arrested the old ballplayer. "Larkin's examination," reported a local paper, "was adjourned for a week, so that he could get the liquor out of him."

According to Richard Malatzsky "Larkin appeared in *The Sporting Life* periodically after his baseball career with regard to slashing police officers and other relatives." Mr. Malatzsky searched for ten years for the time and place of Larkin's death, finally learning that Larkin's unhappy life had ended in Brooklyn on September 16, 1894.

THE ALLENTOWN WONDER

In 1887 a twenty-year-old pitcher by the name of Ebenezer Beatin shamelessly signed contracts with several professional teams, including Detroit, Cincinnati, and Indianapolis of the National League. He was called "The Allentown Wonder" due to his pitching prowess in that city. The matter of his contractual polygamy was put before the league, and decided in favor of the Detroit Wolverines, who used him in two games en route to the 1887 National League pennant. He put in a mediocre year there in 1888, then moved on to Cleveland, where he was 20–15 in 1889 (of course, winning twenty games was not a standard of excellence at that time, as the league leader would normally win more than forty). This was to be the highlight of his career. The next year Eb was Beatin thirty-one times, and the fans were more impressed with an Ohio youngster named Denton Young. Eb departed in 1891 with an 0–3 record. The pitcher that everybody had wanted four years earlier had a final record of 48–57, making everybody wonder what was so wonderful back there in Allentown. He signed five contracts, but was only allowed to dishonor one with his pitching.

—Jim Baker

THE 1890s

HOW THE GAME WAS PLAYED

Dirty. Very, very dirty. The tactics of the eight-ies were aggressive; the tactics of the nineties were violent. The game of the eighties was crude; the game of the nineties was criminal. The baseball of the eighties had ugly elements; the game of the nineties was just ugly.

Players spiked one another. A first baseman would grab the belt of the baserunner to hold him back a half-second after the ball was hit. Players tripped one another as they rounded the bases. Fights broke out more days than not. Players shoved umpires, spat on them, and punched them. Fans hurled insults and beer bottles at the players of opposing teams.

The great team of the time, and the team responsible for promoting this style of play, was the Baltimore Orioles, the team of John McGraw, Hughie Jennings and Willie Keeler. Writing about them in *The Ultimate Baseball Book,* Robert Creamer said that John McGraw "had a genius for making enemies. He had been knocked down in spring training by a rival manager after blocking a player on the

basepaths. He did grab base runners' belts to slow them down as they passed, stood in their way deliberately to make them run around him, stepped on their feet as he took throws at the bag." McGraw himself recalled a game in which "the other team had a runner on first who started to steal second, but . . . spiked our first baseman on the foot. Our man retaliated by trying to trip him. He got away, but at sec-ond Heinie Reitz tried to block him off while Hughie . . . covered the bag to take the throw and tag him. The runner evaded Reitz and jumped feet first at Jennings to drive him away from the bag. Jennings dodged the fly-ing spikes and threw himself bodily at the runner, knocking him flat. In the meantime the batter hit our catcher over the hands with his bat so he couldn't throw, and our catcher trod on the umpire's feet with his spikes and shoved his big mitt in his face so he couldn't see the play."

Great fun, huh? The Cleveland team, under Patsy Tebeau, developed a set play where, on a pre-arranged signal, the first baseman would shove the baserunner off base just as the pitcher threw the ball to first. They tried that against Honus Wagner. Honus slapped the first baseman with the back of his hand and knocked him flat. *The Sporting News* said that the Orioles were "playing the dirtiest ball ever seen in the country," and that they would maim an opponent if need be. One of my heroes, one of the finest and sharpest men ever associated with major league baseball, was John Heydler, later National League president but at that time an umpire. Heydler said of the old Orioles that "they were mean, vicious, ready at any time to maim a rival player or an umpire, if it helped their cause. The things they would say to an umpire were unbelievably vile, and they broke the spirits of some fine men. I've seen umpires bathe their feet by the hour after McGraw and others spiked them through their shoes . . . the worst of it was that they got by with much of their brow beating and hooliganism. Other clubs patterned after them, and I feel the lot of the umpires was never worse." David Voight said that "umpires were cursed, bombarded with beer bottles and rotten eggs, and subjected to beatings."

It was hell to be an umpire in the 1890s; it's a wonder anyone would do it. One of the best was Bob Ferguson, old "Death to Flying Things." But as nearly as I can figure out, the fans never actually killed an umpire. They tried. Umpires required police protection countless times, and there was an incident in Minnesota in 1906 in which a crowd got hold of an umpire with apparent intent to do bodily harm, but was dissuaded by a local athlete. A good many umpires have been killed in on-field accidents, some of them in the minors. But if they didn't kill one (deliberately) in the 1890s, then it just wasn't destined to happen, because they sure tried.

The mess was preserved by a persistent myth that the fans liked this kind of thing. Many owners believed this, what we might call the Von der Ahe myth, after the St. Louis owner

of the 1880s who deliberately encouraged rowdyism, and was largely responsible for giving it a toehold in professional baseball. Some fans, of course, did like it. In 1918 Christy Mathewson (of all people) said that baseball had gotten too tame, and that what it needed was "a real old-fashioned feud." Horrified, Francis Richter responded with an article entitled "The Cost of Rowdy Ball." A witness to the entire period, Richter wrote that "in the 80s there developed a spirit of rivalry which led to much abuse of umpires by players and of players by each other." He cited Anson and Comiskey, from the eighties, as being the worst offenders, but "the situation developed nothing more serious than an occasional riot." But then "the steady growth of rowdyism reached its apogee in the decade of the 90s, during the sole reign of the 12 club National League. Obscene and indecent language between players and to the umpires reached such a pitch that . . . some of the magnates could not stand the raw work of the players, and protested continually against it. But the larger number of the magnates condoned and excused every act of rowdyism, no matter how flagrant."

As to offensive styles, it has been written that the baseball of the 1890s was the first "modern" baseball, a statement that I think reflects a fundamental misunderstanding about the game—namely, that the way in which the game is played is defined largely by the rules. It isn't; the way in which the game is played is defined mostly by the conditions under which the game is played, with the parks as the paramount condition. It is defined no more by the rules than by the players, the ethics, the strategies, the equipment, or the expectation of the public. These people played seven-run-a-game baseball, and we could play seven-run-a-game baseball today or two-run-a-game baseball with the same basic rule structure; it all depends on how and when we fine-tune the game. But it is true that the rules attained essentially their modern form after 1893, when the pitching distance was moved back to 60 feet, 6 inches.

In the early nineties the pitchers were in control. Batting averages in 1891–92 were in the range of .250, though teams still scored in excess of five runs per game because an average team still committed over three errors a game. Still, five runs a game were regarded at that time as too few, and in 1893 the pitching mound was moved to 60 and 6. After that the hitters took over; league batting averages went up near .300 (.309 in 1894) and runs per team per game were around seven. Base stealing declined throughout the decade, as catchers developed protective equipment which enabled them to move up close to the batter, where they are now.

WHERE THE GAME WAS PLAYED

The major league cities were Baltimore, Boston, Brooklyn, Buffalo, Chicago, Cincinnati, Cleveland, Columbus, Louisville, Milwaukee, New York, Philadelphia, Pittsburgh, Rochester, St. Louis, Syracuse, Toledo, and Washington.

By 1890 the National League had occupied the big cities of the east, but the American Association was doing alright for itself in the midwest, in cities like St. Louis, Louisville, Columbus, and Toledo. A reserve arrangement was in place. The Players League opened (and closed) in 1890, going head to head with the National League in the big eastern cities, in several cases in ballparks separated by just blocks. By 1892 two of the three leagues had folded, with the stronger American Association teams joining the National League.

This created a twelve-team National League monopoly, and one that should have provided good ammunition for Joe Cronin in 1968 when he was arguing for adoption of the division setup. His argument then was "You can't sell a twelfth-place team." They sure couldn't. With the weakest teams in the leagues finishing forty-five, fifty, fifty-five, sixty games behind every year, the bottom of the league began to atrophy. Every year three teams opened the gates on opening day and died. Only the fans of Boston, Baltimore, and Brooklyn were entitled to dream of a pennant. Eventually, this led to the second abomination of baseball in the 1890s, syndicate ownership.

Baseball in the 1890s allowed a man to own stock in two different teams, or for that matter in several different teams. By a series of trades, sales, and gambling debts, there arose a system in which the same men owned stock in different teams all over the National League. When the weak teams in the league, losing by fifty games a year, grew weak enough, the strong teams simply bought them. It was as if George Steinbrenner could, for example, purchase the Montreal Expos, and transfer all their best players to the Yankees. Montreal comes up with a Vladimir Guerrero; the Yankees get him. Montreal would continue to function in the National League, with a manager doing the best he could under the circumstances, but every time he succeeds in coming up with a winner . . . well, there he goes again.

Several of these diseased arrangements infected the National League. As the decade wore on, it reached the point of absurdity, or obscenity, or both. The Robison brothers owned both the Cleveland and St. Louis entries. A cabal of the same men owned both Baltimore and Brooklyn. Barney Dreyfuss and company owned both Louisville and Pittsburgh. If one team had a chance to win, it got all the players—and it needed them to compete against the other superteams. They had formed, in effect, a hybrid major/minor league, with teams competing against their own farm teams.

While the top teams each year won almost 70% of their games, the worst teams lost 75%. In 1894, '95 and '96 Louisville finished more than 50 games out of first place. In 1897 and '98 St. Louis finished more than 60 games out of first place. In 1899 Cleveland finished more than 80 games out of first place.

Given the inequality between teams and the high-scoring game, there must have been an endless series of 12–1 and 16–3 games. Can you imagine trying to convince the Cleveland fans to support the 1899 Cleveland Spiders? Well, neither could anybody else. No one went to their home games, and eventually they stopped playing them, and wound up traveling from road game to road game, serving as virtually an automatic victory for their opponents—and, by acclamation, the worst major league team ever.

And baseball's greatest disgrace. The 1919 White Sox sold out the big series. The Cleveland owners sold out the whole season.

WHO THE GAME WAS PLAYED BY

The Irish. Baseball in the 1890s was dominated by Irish players to such an extent that many people, in the same way that people today believe that blacks are born athletes, thought that the Irish were born baseball players.

Of course, people also associated the roughness and unruliness of the players with their ethnic background. The Irish have, indeed, long been credited with that, but there is evidence that a good many of the players were thoroughly disgusted with the way the game was being run. By the middle of the decade an educated element was filtering into the game. By 1900, a good many college players had joined the majors. When the Western League/American League went for major league status as a "clean" league, many found this attractive and

CHECKING IN:

1890– Casey Stengel, Kansas City
Larry MacPhail, Cass City, Michigan
Sam Rice, Morocco, Indiana
Dwight D. Eisenhower, Denison, Texas
1891– Dazzy Vance, Iowa
1893– George Sisler, Manchester, Ohio
1894– Harry Heilmann, San Francisco
Ford Frick, Wawaka, Indiana
Norman Rockwell, New York City
1895– Babe Ruth, Baltimore
1896– Rogers Hornsby, Winters, Texas
1898– Frankie Frisch, Queens, New York
1899– Pie Traynor, Framingham, Massachusettes

CHECKING OUT:

1891– Larry Corcoran, 32
Jim Whitney, 34
P. T. Barnum, 81
1892– Alexander Cartwright, 72
Darby O'Brien (pitcher), consumption, 25
1893– Darby O'Brien (outfielder), 29
1894– Bob Ferguson, 49
King Kelly, typhoid fever or pneumonia, 36
Ned Williamson, liver and heart problems, 36
E.J. McNabb, murder/suicide, 28
1895– Harry Wright, Pneumonia, 60
Pacer Smith, hanged, 42
1896– Cannonball Crane, accidental overdose of chloral, 34
1897– Old Hoss Radbourn, paresis, 42
1899– Minnie McGraw (wife of John) died following appendix operation, 23

helped the league to acquire quality players and establish credibility.

It was in this period also that the ballplayers developed an exaggerated reputation as unsavory characters. Many of the players realized that they were losing respect, as men, because of the way the game was played on the field. They couldn't have been very happy about that, but as with any arms race, the first to disdain the tactic allows his opponent an advantage . . . so no one does.

MAJOR LEAGUE ALL-STAR TEAM 1890–1899
Records in seasonal notation, based on 154 games. Pitchers based on 50 starts.

Pos.	Player	Years	Hits	HR	RBI	Avg.	Other
C	Chief Zimmer	5.67	157	4	86	.278	
1B	Roger Conner	5.95	182	12	106	.310	
2B	Cupid Childs	8.21	187	2	88	.316	109 Walks
3B	John McGraw	5.51	193	2	72	.336	116 BB, 153 Runs
SS	H. Jennings	6.49	191	2	107	.323	
LF	Ed Delahanty	8.25	226	10	131	.354	130 RBI
CF	Billy Hamilton	7.67	220	4	74	.357	176 Runs, 94 SB
RF	Willie Keeler	5.37	256	3	85	.387	

	Pitcher	Years	Won-Lost	SO	ERA	Other
RH	Kid Nichols	9.41	32-16	158	2.96	427 Innings
RH	Amos Rusie	8.34	28-18	220	2.74	447 Innings
RH	Cy Young	9.92	27-15	96	3.05	375 Innings

THE 1890s IN A BOX

Attendance Data:

In 1890 it was reported that the Player's League drew 981,000 fans, the National League 814,000. There were eight teams in each league. That was with two teams going head to head in most markets, dividing the crowds, and was considered poor attendance.

My best estimate is that total major league attendance for the decade was about 24,800,000. The Philadelphia Phillies have the highest reported attendance for the decade, with a high of 474,971 in 1895, and 2,981,541 for the decade. The Cleveland Spiders of 1899 probably had the lowest single-season attendance, and the Washington Senators probably had the lowest attendance for the decade as a whole.

The average American in this era probably attended a major league baseball game about once every 30 years.

Most Home Runs:

Buck Freeman,	1899	25
Hugh Duffy		80

Best Won/Lost Record by Team:

Boston, 1897	93-39	.705
Boston (NL)	869-508	.631

It is interesting to note that while the Orioles are thought of as the great team of their generation, the Beaneaters won more championships (4–3), had the best one-year record of the decade, and had the best overall record. The Boston team was the true offensive innovator of the period, and was noted for playing clean ball, at least by contrast. Boston was the only team in the decade to lead the National League in both runs scored and fewest runs allowed, which they did in both 1891 and 1897. Boston in the American Association also did this in 1891.

Worst Won/Lost Record by Team:

Cleveland, 1899	20-134	.130
St. Louis	400-707	.361

A lesser-known sidelight on the disastrous 1899 season of the Cleveland Spiders: Their owners decided to skip spring training. While the other teams spent a month or more in Hot Springs or New Orleans, the Cleveland team worked out in a gymnasium in Terre Haute, Indiana.

Index of Competitive Balance: 27%

Home-Field Winning Percentage: .603

Percentage of Regulars Hitting .300: 35%

Largest Home-Field Advantage: Cleveland and Washington (NL)

As you know, things got so bad for the 1899 Cleveland Spiders that they canceled their home games, and turned the last two months of the season into a long road trip. No one was going to their home games, so short-term economics favored playing road games and taking their cut of the gate. The team finished with 134 losses, including 101 losses on the road (now *there* is a record that will be tough to beat) and a 1-34 record after September first.

Three things about this, however, are not well known.

1. It wasn't just Cleveland that canceled home games; the practice spread around the

league. Louisville, Washington, and St. Louis also sacrificed home games to play on the road.

2. The practice did not begin in 1899. It began in 1892 in Washington. The Spiders were a good team until 1897; the Washington Senators and the St. Louis Cardinals, the league's doormats in the mid-nineties, had been moving games for years.

3. The Spiders home-field winning percentage in the 1890s was .625; on the road it was .385. Washington also had a 240-point home/road disparity in the 1890s (.494 vs. .255). These are the largest home/road differentials in baseball history. Home teams won 60.3% of their games in the 1890s, easily the highest percentage of any decade.

Of course, the practice of abandoning home games for road games made the home/road disparity larger, because it meant that bad teams played more road games than good teams, which drove the winning percentage of road teams down, and the winning percentage of home teams up.

Having Their Best Decade Ever: Boston Braves and Philadelphia Phillies

Having Their Worst Decade: St. Louis Cardinals

Heaviest Player: Wilbert Robinson, 5'8½" and listed at 215 pounds, but often described as weighing even more. Another candidate who should be mentioned, if only for his name, was Carlton Molesworth, who pitched briefly for the Washington Nationals in 1895. He stood just 5 feet 6 inches, but weighed 200. Carlton Molesworth is such a great name for a factotum. Can't you see this portly man in a butler's garb, waddling to the beck and call of an even more portly industrialist?

RICH FOP: Molesworth, draw my bath.
MOLESWORTH: As you wish, sir. Will there be anything else, sir?
RICH FOP: No, Molesworth, you are free to go after that task is complete. However, I do not wish you to "raid" the larder on your way out, as has been your custom of late.
MOLESWORTH: Very good, sir. Good night.

—Jim Baker

Lightest Player: Willie Keeler, 140

Most Strikeouts by Pitcher:
Amos Rusie,	1890	345
Amos Rusie	1891	

Highest Batting Average:
Hugh Duffy,	1894	.438
Willie Keeler		.387

Lowest Batting Average:
Jim Canavan,	1892	.166
Yank Robinson		.196

Best Major League Players (by Years):
1890— Cupid Childs
1891— Billy Hamilton
1892— Dan Brouthers
1893— Ed Delahanty
1894— Hugh Duffy
1895— Jesse Burkett
1896— Hughie Jennings
1897— Willie Keeler
1898— Ed Delahanty
1899— Ed Delahanty

Best Major League Pitchers (by Years):
1890— Bill Hutchison
1891— Bill Hutchison
1892— Jack Stivetts
1893— Frank Killen
1894— Amos Rusie
1895— Pink Hawley
1896— Cy Young
1897— Kid Nichols
1898— Kid Nichols½
1899— Vic Willis

Hardest-Throwing Pitcher: Amos Rusie

Best Curve: Vic Willis

Best Power/Speed Combination: Ed Delahanty

Best Switch Hitter: George Davis

Iron Man: Kid Nichols

Best Bunter: Willie Keeler

Best Baseball Books: The first Frank Merriwell story was published in the *Tip Top Weekly* on April 18, 1896. Eventually 986 Merriwell stories were collected into 245 books, some written by Gilbert Patten under the pseudonym Burt L. Standish, some written by other people under Patten's supervision. Frank could make a curve break twice, regularly got the game-winning hit for Yale, and was the best and finest baseball player who ever lived.

—Jim Carothers

Largest Change in Baseball During the Decade:

1. Standardization of Rules to Present Form

Everything else is negative and temporary. The American Association died, but the effects of that are temporary, as it was replaced in the next decade by the American League. This decade exposed the evils of interlocking ownership, which is a principle that still holds—even today, you can't own parts of two major league teams. But really, baseball went almost entirely backward during this decade. Nothing good was accomplished, and nothing much was contributed to the future of the game.

Best Outfield Arm: George Van Haltren

Worst Outfield Arm: Sliding Billy Hamilton

Most Runs Batted In:
Sam Thompson,	1895	165
Hugh Duffy		1,088

Most Aggressive Baserunner: John McGraw

Fastest Player: Billy Hamilton

Slowest Player: Malachi Kittridge

On June 24, 1899, Cleveland pitcher Charlie Knepper hit a double. The *Cleveland Plain Dealer* reported the next day that "a hay wagon drawn by lame horses could have reached third, but Knepper is no hay wagon and had no lame horses to assist him."

On May 31, 1899, the *Boston Globe* described Chief Zimmer as "jogging around the path like a six-day walker with first money in sight." (Both quotes are taken from *Misfits: The Cleveland Spiders of 1899*.)

Best Control Pitcher: Cy Young

Most Stolen Bases:
Billy Hamilton,	1891	115
Billy Hamilton		730

Best-Looking Players:
John Clarkson
Billy Nash

Ugliest Player: Fred Tenney

O.J. Simpson Award: Marty Bergen

Three Finger Brown Award: Dummy Hoy

Ozzie Guillen Trophy: Frank Bowerman

Bound for Glory:
Robert Gibson (Federal Judge)
Fred Brown (Governor and U.S. Senator from New Hampshire)
Alfred W. Lawson (Aviation Pioneer)
Edward Morgan Lewis (Educator)

Best Pitching Staff: Boston Beaneaters, 1892
Kid Nichols, Jack Stivetts, Harry Staley, and John Clarkson.

Boston's pitching staffs were the best in baseball almost every year through the 1890s.

Best Offense: Philadelphia Phillies, 1899

Retrobermanisms:
George (Double) Decker
Bill (You're Lookin' Great) Dahlen
Charlie (Dear) Abbey
Gus (Pre-Fight) Weyhing

First of His Kind: Frank Selee

(First manager to use the hit and run)

Last of His Kind: Jeremiah Denny

Denny was the last barehanded defensive player. Hick Carpenter, the only player to have a career as a left-handed third baseman, played one game in the 1890s, although his career basically ends in 1889.

One of a Kind: John Montgomery Ward

Best Infield: 1894 Baltimore Orioles

Dan Brouthers, Heinie Reitz, Hughie Jennings, and John McGraw

Best Outfield: The Philadelphia Phillies had the best outfields in baseball throughout the decade. From 1891 through 1895 their out-field was Ed Delahanty, Billy Hamilton, and Sam Thompson, all Hall of Famers, and often cited as the best outfield of all time. The Win Shares system ranks the Phillies 1899 outfield of Delahanty, Roy Thomas, and Elmer Flick as even greater than the earlier outfield, which was undeniably brilliant.

A Better Man Than a Ballplayer: Mike Tiernan

A Better Ballplayer Than a Human Being: Patsy Tebeau

Tebeau, though not fast, was Cleveland's John McGraw, a tough, aggressive player with no excess of manners. The 1919 *Reach Guide* says that "early in life [he] was given the name 'Pat' by his neighbors because of his fondness for shoveling sand and also carry-ing a dinner pail." Guess you had to be there . . . anyway, Tebeau managed in the ma-jors for ten years and had a good record, though he kept finishing second. In 1894 he was involved in a confusing scandal in which he was drunk, beaten, robbed, and paid $250

blackmail to avoid a lawsuit. After his retire-ment in 1899 he ran a saloon in St. Louis until he shot himself, committing suicide, in 1918, aged fifty-four.

Mr. Dickens, I'd Like You to Meet:
Pop Swett
George Hogriever
Malachi Jeddidah Kittridge
Henry Carl Gastright

Platoon Combinations I Would Like to See:
Jake Virtue and Bill Goodenough

Best Defensive Team: 1898 Cincinnati Reds

Clint Hartung Award: Lou Sockalexis

Outstanding Sportswriter: Tim Murnane

Most Admirable Superstar: Dummy Hoy

Gold Glove Team:
C—   Chief Zimmer
1B— Fred Tenney
2B— Bid McPhee
3B— Lave Cross
SS— Hughie Jennings
OF— Bill Lange
       Hugh Duffy
       Jimmy McAleer

Least Admirable Superstar: Ed Delahanty

Franchise Shifts: In fall, 1891, two American Association teams, Louisville and Columbus, folded. The National League then persuaded Chris Von der Ahe, the power in the AA and owner of the St. Louis team, to come over to the National League. Von der Ahe brought Washington, Baltimore, and a refinanced Louisville team with him. The four American Association teams finished ninth, tenth, eleventh, and twelfth in the National League in 1892, but after that the league was stable for the rest of the decade. In 1900, the Na-tional League contracted to eight teams by getting rid of three of the old American Association teams (Washington, Louisville, and Baltimore), plus Cleveland.

New Stadiums:
1890— Manhattan Field, New York (became new Polo Grounds in 1891, seated 16,000)

1891— League Park, Cleveland (wooden structure)

1892— National Park, Washington (seated 6,500)

1895— Union Park, Baltimore (concrete and steel, but seated only 6,500)

1899— Robison Field, St. Louis

The exciting new park of the decade was the Polo Grounds. A renovation of Redlands Park in Cincinnati also apparently made that into quite an attractive, modern stadium with some concrete and steel. Several parks, as usual, burned down during the decade, and at one point three parks burned in a few weeks, causing concern that there was a "baseball arsonist" loose.

Best Pennant Race: *1897 National League

Best World Series: None

The "World Series" of the 1890s were the Temple Cup games, a post-season series pitting the first-place against the second-place team. It never worked. The winning team was supposed to get 65% of the gate, but there were persistent rumors that the players had agreed to split the take, and were just going through the motions. Having the first-place team play the second-place team was anticlimatic at best, and undercut the pennant race.

Best-Hitting Pitcher: Jack Stivetts

Worst-Hitting Pitcher: Tully Sparks

Best Minor League Player: Perry Werden

Drinking Men:
Marty Bergen
Harry Decker
Jack McCarthy
Willie McGill
Jerry Nops
Lou Sockalexis
Patsy Tebeau

New Strategies:

The practice of catchers signaling for the pitch became common in the 1890s, although this had been done before.

The split season was tried for the first time.

The practice of chopping down on the ball—The Baltimore Chop—was developed.

Brooklyn in the mid-nineties invented the cut-off play.

Philadelphia became the first team to use an illegal electric sign-stealing system.

Hit and run developed by Boston Beaneaters.

New Equipment:
Pitching machines
Cincinnati painted center field fence black to help hitters

Player vs. Team: Amos Rusie of the New York Giants was the dominant strikeout pitcher of the 1890s, leading the league in Ks in 1890, '91, '93, '94 and '95. He was a consistent winner, going 36-13 in 1894, and 22-21 with a bad team in 1895. The Giants owner at this time was Andrew Freedman, who could be described as George Steinbrenner on Quaaludes, with a touch of Al Capone. Mean sum'bitch. Amos Rusie had several run-ins with this madman, but when he drew his last paycheck in 1895, he found that Freedman had withheld $200. The most you could make in a season at the time was $2,500; $200 was a substantial reduction, arbitrarily imposed by Freedman for unspecified violations of training and indifferent pitching late in the season.

That was the last straw. Rusie knew that Freeman was simply lowering his salary without going to the trouble of negotiating the change. He refused to report to the Giants in 1896 until the money was refunded. Freedman refused to give it back. Rusie held out. All year. The press supported him. The fans organized a boycott. Freedman would not relent.

With John Montgomery Ward representing him, Rusie appealed to the league. He lost. He sued. The other owners, realizing that a loss in court was nearly inevitable and would undermine their position, pleaded with Freedman to be reasonable. He refused.

Finally, the other owners got together and paid Rusie a reported $3,000 for the season he had missed (1896). Rusie rejoined the Giants.

Team vs. Team: Nothing dies without a lawsuit. When the American Association fell apart in 1891, the owners of two of the teams cut out of the settlement threatened to sue, as well they should have, having just been deprived of their property. The case would have been a precedent for the case filed by the Baltimore Terrapins twenty-five years later, which resulted in the Supreme Court ruling that baseball was immune to anti-trust action. The suit was settled out of court for a payment to the two teams of $131,000.

*Uniform Changes: How women dressed for baseball—see page 67.

New Terms or Expressions:
Fan
Texas Leaguer
Baltimore Chop
Big League

Most Wins By Pitcher:

Bill Hutchinson,	1890	42
Bill Hutchinson,	1891	42
Kid Nichols		297

Highest Winning Percentage:

Jim Hughes,	1899	28-6	.824
Kid Nichols		297-148	.667

Lowest Winning Percentage:

Les German,	1896	1-19	.050
Jim Hughey		24-76	.240

Nicknames: Pink Hawley, who won 167 games between 1892 and 1901, had an identical twin brother, Blue Hawley, who died in 1891, when they were 18. The two played together as the pitcher and catcher on a semi-pro team in Wisconsin until Blue died, thus forming the "Pink and Blue Battery."

Their parents had pink and blue ribbon on hand before the twins were born, to be ready for either a boy or a girl. When they got twin boys they tied pink ribbon to one and blue to the other to keep them straight, and then got in the habit of calling them "Pink" and "Blue."

Flameout: Tuck Turner

At the age of 21, Tuck Turner hit .416 and scored 91 runs in 80 games, he also drove in 82 runs. His career degenerated quickly after that. I can't remember that I have ever read anything about him, and I have no idea what the story was.

All Offense/No Defense: 1894–95 Philadelphia Phillies

All Defense/No Offense: 1896 Cincinnati Reds

Homer: Bobby Lowe

Yellowstone Park Award: Cupid Childs

Cupid Childs and Bobby Lowe were both second basemen of the 1890s, both good ballplayers. Lowe was the first player to hit four home runs in a game (May 30, 1894), while Childs never hit more than four home runs in a season, and only once hit four (1895).

But the power difference between them is totally a park illusion; Childs actually hit more home runs in road games than Bobby Lowe. Childs hit twenty career home runs—four at home, but 16 on the road. In a career of about the same length, Lowe hit 71 home runs—but only 14 in road games.

Tough-Luck Season: Ed Doheny, 1898

Could I Try This Career Over? George Treadway

Minor Leagues Were:
98 percent free
2 percent slaves to the majors

Best Double Play Combination: The Boston Beaneaters of 1891–1892, with the double play combination of Joe Quinn and Herman Long, were +18 and +31 in double plays versus expected double plays. From 1893 through 1895, with Bobby Lowe and Herman Long, they were +28, +21, and +17.

Two other teams in the 1890s had outstanding double play combinations. The Baltimore Orioles of 1894 through 1897, the Beaneaters rivals for National League dominance, had the combination of Heinie Reitz and Hughie Jennings, who were also quite outstanding.

Cap Anson's Chicago Colts shuffled second basemen throughout the decade. In mid-1897, Anson's last season, they acquired minor league veteran Jim Connor, who was well past 30. Connor was too weak a hitter to stay in the major leagues, but apparently outstanding on the double play. In 1897 the Chicago Orphans, with the double play combination of Connor and Bill Dahlen, turned 40 double plays more than expected, the highest figure of the decade, and one of the highest of all time.

Worst Double Play Combination: Tommy Dowd and Monte Cross, 1896 St. Louis Browns.

Paul Krichell Talent Scout Award: As an 18-year-old, Roger Bresnahan appeared in six games as a pitcher for the Washington Senators, going 4-0 and also hitting .375. But when Bresnahan demanded a raise the next spring, Washington manager Gus Schmelz thought he was a cheeky kid (which he was, of course) and let him go back to the minor leagues.

Best Unrecognized Player: Herman Long

Highest-Paid Player: Unknown, but surely someone in the first two years of the decade, before the National League monopoly. It was reported that salaries increased 100% in 1890–1891, because of the Player's League. If true, this would have made salaries of $6,000 or more common. After 1892 a system of salary limits was in place and was effective (unlike that of the late eighties, which was widely circumvented). Although some teams no doubt paid bonuses in excess of the $2,500 salary ceiling, that probably was done only for exceptional players, and the system kept salaries low. Stagnant attendance through the decade also helped to contain salaries.

New Statistics: 1893—Sacrifice Hits
(see page 65)

A Very Good Movie Could Be Made About: A great movie could be made about the 1897 pennant race, capped by the series which will be described later. It's good versus evil, clean baseball versus Muggsy and assorted thugs—and good triumphs. It would be easy to root for Kid Nichols and Jimmy Collins and Herman Long and Hugh Duffy against McGraw and Jennings and Reitz.

Five Biggest Things Wrong with Baseball:
1. On-field violence
2. Segregation
3. Syndicate ownership resulting in sold-out, non-competitive teams
4. Lack of a clear championship
5. Player/management bickering (early in decade)

I Don't Know What This Has to Do with Baseball, But I Thought I'd Mention It Anyway: The Designated Hitter rule was first proposed in the 1890s. The first serious discussion of it was about 1930. In both cases, the advantages proposed for the DH had little to do with increasing offense.

I Don't Know What This Has to Do with Baseball, Either, But I Thought I'd Mention It, Too: A woman by the name of Elizabeth Stround, playing under the name of Lizzie Arlington, played briefly in the Atlantic League in 1898.

And While I'm Just Mentioning Stuff: Billy Earle, who played for five teams between 1889 and 1894, was a hypnotist, or, as they said at the time, "the only ball player endowed with hypnotic powers." The 1893 *Reach Guide* reported that "in belief he is a spiritualist, and practices hypnotism, magnetism, and spiritual healing."

Some memory of this survived at least until 1949, when Bill Stern published *Bill Stern's Favorite Baseball Stories.* Stern claims that "strange things began to happen from the moment Billy Earle joined the club. He had a pair of piercing eyes that seemed to blaze with a strange light. When he looked at a teammate, that player would get a creepy, helpless feeling ... from 1886 to 1895, in less than nine baseball seasons, Billy Earle, although the best catcher of his time, was ... forced out of baseball, because of nothing more than superstition, the belief that he was a hypnotist with the power of 'the evil eye.'"

BASEBALL STATISTICS IN THE 1890s

The New England League, a good minor league, began counting batter's strikeouts in 1890, twenty years before the majors did.

In 1898 one of the Washington owners, to quote Harold Seymour, "admitted getting the official scorer to add 40 base hits to infielder Gene DeMontreville's record, to bring his batting average above .300 so he could sell him to Baltimore for a higher price." He thought this a legitimate tactic.

The Washington owner was probably stretching the story. If that were true, DeMontreville's average would probably have dropped 70 points on joining Baltimore. It did drop 20, but not 70. I believe that he may have told the official scorer to give DeMontreville a break on any hit/error decision to make him look a little better in the stats, but I doubt that the effect of this was anything like 40 hits.

THANK YOU, SIR, MAYBE I WILL TAKE MY VACATION THERE

Honus Wagner was once asked about his greatest thrill in baseball. "Well, the greatest thrill I ever got was one time a Giant batter hit a home run. As he ran past me I said, 'Nice hit,' and he said 'Go to hell.'"

Pause.

Alright, Honus, why was that your greatest thrill?

"I'd been in the league for three years," said Honus. "And he was the first player to speak to me."

BASEBALL STRATEGY IN THE 1890s

By 1890 the sacrifice bunt was an established, if controversial, strategic weapon. If you read sports pages from the early nineties, it sometimes seems that the bunt is all that anybody wants to talk about . . . it should be made illegal, it shouldn't be made illegal, the batter should be given credit for it, he shouldn't be given credit for it, he should be charged with an at bat, he shouldn't, it should be legal but it's a bad play, no, it's a good play . . . on and on. They changed the rules on how to score it a couple of times and talked about changing the rules the rest of the time. A lot of this was still going on in the late 1890s.

Exactly when the hit and run developed is a matter of some confusion. During this decade the teams developed the practice of passing signals among players, offensively and defensively. The Boston team, especially Tommy McCarthy, gets a lot of the credit for developing runner-to-batter signals. John Montgomery Ward said that "I have never, in my twelve years' experience on the diamond, seen such skillful playing. The Boston players use more head-work and private signals than any other team in the country, and that alone is the reason why they can win the championship with apparent ease. McCarthy is the chief schemer. He is the man who has introduced this new style of play into the team and he has been ably assisted by Nash, Duffy, Long, Lowe, and Carroll . . . 'Team-work in the field' used to be a prime factor in a pennant-winning team, but now 'team-work at the bat' is the latest wrinkle, and the Bostons have it down fine."

These quotes are from the 1895 *Spalding Guide*, but were offered in 1893. Ward also added a surprising description of the sacrifice bunt. "Say, for instance, that they have a man on first and nobody out. *Under the old style of play a sacrifice bunt would be the proper thing.* (Italics mine.) . . . The Bostons, however, work this scheme: The man on first makes a bluff attempt to steal second, but runs back to first. By this it becomes known whether the second baseman or the short stop is going to cover second for the throw from the catcher. Then the batsman gets a signal from the man on first that (he) is going to steal on a certain pitched ball. The moment he starts for second the batsman just pushes the ball for the place occupied only a moment before by the infielder who has gone to cover second base."

What Ward has described, of course, is essentially the hit and run play, with a twist. The play has an extra element of deceit. The fact that this trick might work sometimes suggests that the play is new; later on, the play would be worked without the false start.

So it was clear, at this point, that Tommy McCarthy and the Boston Beaneaters had developed a new play, the hit and run. Two things happened after the fact to confuse the issue. Number one, John McGraw spent thirty years as the darling of the New York press corps, during which time he was able to effectively shift credit for these innovations from Boston, which really developed them, to the Orioles. And number two, Harold Seymour wrote a classic history of baseball, in which he suggested that the hit and run play was used in the eighties. His evidence? Cap Anson said, in a post-career interview, that the White Stockings were using it then.

Well, Cap Anson was a blowhard, and the older he got, the harder he blew. The fact that Cap Anson said, twenty or thirty years after the fact, that his team was using the hit and run play first—that really just doesn't mean anything.

Monte Ward was the smartest, most alert player of his time. It is clear from his comments that he had never seen this play before.

The best evidence is that Tommy McCarthy invented the hit and run play. Monte Ward picked up on it and taught it to Willie Keeler, and Keeler brought it to Baltimore. The term "hit and run" probably was used earlier–but it was used for the play that we now call the run and hit.

PENNANT RACES OF THE 1890s

Among its many shortcomings, the twelve-team league produced few good pennant races. The league stumbled to an inauspicious start in 1892 with the idea of a split season, which was reviled by everyone. The "big league" never produced a three-team race. Third-place teams never got closer than eight games off the mark, and there were only a few decent two-team races.

The 1895 race, though decided by only three games, suffered from poor scheduling since, in the last ten days of the season, first-place Baltimore played seven games but second-place Cleveland played only two. Baltimore went 6–1 while Cleveland split, so that the half-game lead of September 21 edged up by the day, with Cleveland powerless to do anything about it.

In 1897, however, there was a great two-team race. The Boston Beaneaters started poorly, but went 21–2 in June to roar back into the race. On August 21, the defending champion Baltimore Orioles trailed Boston by three games. By August 28, Boston had pulled ahead by percentage points, but were still a half-game behind because they had played fewer games:

	Won	Lost	Pct	GB
Baltimore	69	32	.683	.5
Boston	72	34	.679	—

And then, for twenty-eight days, the margin between the two teams never grew larger than one full game. Baltimore won eleven in a row from September 4 through September 16. Boston answered with eight out of nine. By

September 23, nothing much had changed except that time was running out:

	Won	Lost	Pct	GB
Baltimore	87	36	.707	.5
Boston	89	37	.706	—

Another problem with the twelve-team league, familiar to fans of a hundred years later, was the dilution of the schedule. The two teams warring for the top spot rarely met. But on this date, September 24, Boston began a three-game set in Baltimore; they would have one series left when this series was over.

A crowd of 12,900 turned out to see Boston move into first place with a 6–4 victory. The crowd included 135 "Rooters" down from Boston under the leadership of John Fitzgerald, wearing Red Badges and armed with tin horns. The Orioles had the tying runs on base when Willie Keeler ripped a liner, speared by Herman Long, Boston shortstop, who doubled a runner off second base.

On Saturday, September 25, 18,750 people saw the Orioles come back, 6–3, to reclaim first place. The Orioles took a quick 3–0 lead, but the Beaneaters in the seventh had the tying run on third (Billy Hamilton) and another man on first (Bobby Lowe). When Lowe got caught in a rundown between first and second, Hamilton headed home. Dirty Jack Doyle spun and threw home. The heavy-set Wilbert Robinson landed hard on the smaller Hamilton, according to a newspaper report, "almost crushing him with his two hundred and fifty pounds of solid flesh." The game was described as a "nerve destroyer," and it was said that the series so far had comprised two of the most exciting games in the history of baseball.

No Sunday ball. Game Three was played on Monday, September 27, and was attended by 25,375 cranks, bringing the three-day total to a remarkable 57,000. It was a wide-open slugfest, a nineties type of ballgame. Baltimore scored

UNIFORMS IN THE 1890s

There was a time in the nineteenth century when women's teams were in vogue as a small-time entertainment. And what did women wear to play baseball? A photograph of one such team, the "Young Ladies Base Ball Club No. 1" of 1890–91, has the team posed like any male team. The women are wearing regular striped baseball caps, knee-length dark-and-light striped dresses, gathered at the waist and held with a wide clasp belt. The sleeves are long and the neckline is tightly fastened with a big polka dot bow. They wear long, dark, heavy-looking stockings and pointed, ankle-high leather shoes with a small heel. (Smart to put those dress heels in the closet, ladies.) The team members look relaxed, several are holding bats and a ball is in the foreground. Women who played baseball around this time were called "fair base ballists."

For the men, a photo taken at spring training in 1896 shows the New York Giants in their heavy woolen gear. Quilted knickers are worn along with hip-length wool sweaters, heavy stockings, and baseball caps. One would think that wool uniforms in general would be more than warm enough, but quilted knickers can be seen at times other than just in spring training. The quilting was probably justified for the extra sliding protection it offered. Later on actual sliding pads were affixed to the inside of the knickers.

One interesting feature about uniforms in the 1890s was the importance of the stockings. Teams such as the White and Red Stockings, the Browns and the Tigers derived their names from the color of their stockings. In fact, with no identifying name on the jersey front, the stockings and caps actually proclaimed the team's identity.

—Susan McCarthy

(Baseball men in this era were big on the medicinal value of sweating.)

five early off the great Kid Nichols, but Boston exploded for nine runs in the seventh, and won it 19–10. Baltimore's three top pitchers all worked in the effort, but Boston had climbed back into first place with three to play.

The Baltimore crowd seemed to enjoy the barrage. The papers reported them laughing good-naturedly at the onslaught. Billy Hamilton was cheered lustily when, "after being trampled upon and severely stunned by Jennings at second, he made a grand run for home on Lowe's single, collided with Baltimore's fleshy backstop and, falling heavily, pluckily crawled toward the base, almost fainting as he touched it." On-the-scene reports paint a pleasant picture, different from the one we usually see of the period. When the game was over "ten thousand people congratulated the visitors with handshakes and cheers and told them what good fellows and fine players they were." Then again, the size of the crowd suggests that these were not the regular fans of the era, so much as people who got caught up in the excitement of the race.

In what was probably the greatest series in nineteenth-century baseball, Germany Long had nine hits, three of them doubles, and scored four runs. Willie Keeler and Hughie Jennings had seven hits apiece for Baltimore, Wilbert Robinson six. There were twenty-two doubles in the three games, four by Jennings.

Boston won two of its last three, and took the pennant by two games.

1897: THE GOOD OF THE EARTH VERSUS JOHN POWELL

John Joseph (Jack) Powell, pitcher for the Cleveland Spiders, was brought to trial in June, 1897, on a charge of playing ball on Sunday. He was fined $5 and court costs, which came to a healthy $153. Stanley Robison, owner of the Spiders, announced his intention to appeal the issue, but Sunday ball in Cleveland was discontinued for the rest of the century.

1894: THE LAST REAL MAN RETIRES

The last position player who did not wear a glove in the field was Jerry Denny, an ambidextrous third baseman who retired from the Louisville team following the 1894 season. Though a right-handed batter and thrower, Denny could catch the ball with either hand, and, if the pressures of time required, fire it to first with whichever hand it happened to be in.

Pitcher Gus Weyhing, who lasted until 1901, also did not wear a glove.

1890: WANTED: ONE SEXY SHORTSTOP

On August 26, 1890, a New York gentleman named W. S. Franklin announced his intention to form a Women's Professional Base Ball League. His help-wanted advertisement said that applicants "must be young, not over 20, good looking and good figure." Applicants out of the city were requested to send photographs.

1899: GOD'S DOUBLE AGENT

On July 10, 1899, the Reverend Sherman Powell bought a ticket to a baseball game in Fort Wayne, Indiana, and began copying down the names of players, spectators, and ticket takers, apparently intending to use this evidence to convict the pagans of playing baseball on Sunday. When he was discovered, a nasty crowd encircled him, took away his pen and his notebook, and made him fear for his safety. The police were called, and they escorted the indignant reverend from the ballpark.

Reverend Powell issued a statement saying that the Good Citizen's League would continue its fight against violations of the Sabbath in Fort Wayne.

BUMPUS

Bumpus Jones started the 1892 season with Joliet in the Two-I League. You might say he started out well: He won his first fifteen starts, allowing only fifteen runs. He lost a few after that, but finished the season 24–5 with ten shutouts. The Two-I League folded, and Jones was sold to Atlanta (Southern Association) where he went 3–4, and was purchased by the Cincinnati Reds in early October.

On the last day of the 1892 season (October 15, 1892), Bumpus made his major league debut. He pitched a no-hitter, winning the game 7 to 1.

He would win only one more major league game, being released in mid-season, 1893, with a career record of two wins, four losses, and a 7.99 ERA.

BASEBALL LANGUAGE IN THE 1890s

The term "fan" for what was earlier called "crank" is supposed to have been coined by Ted Sullivan, who preceded Charles Comiskey as manager of the Browns. It existed in the 1880s but was rarely used.

It has been often written that the term "Texas Leaguer" comes from the major league debut of Ollie Pickering, who got four hits in his first game after being called up from the Texas League. Each hit just blooped over the infield. The next day a reporter who missed a play saw Pickering on first base and asked what happened. "Oh, he just made another one of those Texas League hits," said another reporter. However, Robert McConnell looked up the game stories for Ollie Pickering's 1896 debut, and reports that the record does not support this story.

The term "Baltimore chop," of course, owes its origin to Willie Keeler.

The term "big league" apparently referred originally to the size of the one major league, which had twelve teams. But the "big league" came to stand for the "major league," and "big leagues" became a synonym for "majors."

SHOVE IT, LOUIS C. KRAUTHOFF

The National League in 1898 established a "court" or "board" to "try and to punish all cases of indecent conduct or obscene language of ballplayers." A wealthy attorney named Louis C. Krauthoff was to head the court. The players hated the idea and the press ridiculed it. The court was dissolved in 1899, having heard not a single case.

EDGAR McNABB

Edgar McNabb was a pitcher for the Baltimore Orioles in 1893. He posted an 8–7 record with a 4.12 ERA. Not asked to return to the team in 1894, he had signed on with Grand Rapids.

Aside from pitching, McNabb was involved in other sport, namely an illicit affair with actress Louise Kellogg, a.k.a. Mrs. Louis Rockwell. She was a good-looking and "shapely" blond who was married to R.E. Rockwell, a Seattle ice merchant. In his spare time he was president of the Pacific and Northwest League.

McNabb and Mrs. Rockwell had been carrying on their affair for "at least a year" when the wages of sin caught up with the couple at the Hotel Eiffel, in Pittsburgh on February 28, 1894. Despite witness testimony that their manner that night was "gay" and "jolly," McNabb was apparently not in the best of spirits. They were registered at the Eiffel as "E.J. McNabb and wife." At approximately eight in the evening they went up to their room to prepare for a trip to the theatre. Pistol shots were heard, as well as scuffling and screaming. The door was broken in by one L. Gilliland, himself a former minor league baseball player, and a friend of McNabb's.

Gilliland found Mrs. Rockwell on the floor in a pool of blood, shot twice through the neck. McNabb was down for the count and going fast, having shot himself in the mouth. Mrs. Rockwell survived for a time, paralyzed from the waist down by a bullet that had lodged in her spinal column.

The newspapers speculated that the couple was penniless and McNabb saw this route as an end to their problems.

—Jim Baker

QUOTES FROM THE 1892 *SPALDING GUIDE*

The rowdy habit of "slugging" which prevailed to such an extent in the foot ball arena in 1891, showed very plainly what folly it would have been to allow the base-ball professionals to become foot-ball players at the close of the base-ball championship campaign. The professionals encounter risks of dangerous injuries in their own game frequently enough to make them exciting; but in comparison with the risks of foot ball, base ball is harmless. With a record of twenty-one lives lost on the English foot ball ground during the season of '90 and '91, with over a hundred dangerous injuries, base-ball players may congratulate themselves that they are not in the foot-ball arena.

The evil of drunkenness in the ranks of the professional players in 1890 and '91 was carried to an excess almost equaling that of the demoralized period of the decade of the seventies . . . Season after season have clubs become bankrupt solely through the failure of their teams to accomplish successful field work owing to the presence of two or three drunkards in their team.

Three years ago the swift pitching, which had then about reached the highest point of speed, proved to be so costly in its wear and tear upon the catchers, that clubs had to engage a corps of reserve catchers in order to go through a season's campaign with any degree of success. Afterward, however, the introduction of the catcher's breast pad and protective gloves led to some relief being afforded the catchers who had been called upon to face the swift pitching of the "cyclone" pitchers of the period.

This last remark is interesting for two reasons. First, it implies that the pitchers of the 1890 era threw much harder than the pitchers of fifteen years earlier. Later writers would claim that Sweeney, Zettlein, Devlin, and others threw as hard as Walter Johnson. This more contemporary comment unmistakably suggests that they didn't.

Second, some historians have dated the use of chest protectors by catchers as early as 1875. This comment, which seems fairly unambiguous, places their introduction to the majors in the late 1880s.

PERSPECTIVE

Baseball historians dwell considerably on the "days of violence." These days make exciting reading, but it should be considered in proper perspective, that during these same times there was violence everywhere; it was an age of violence. There was violence in the Wild West when it was being settled. There was violence in the upbuilding of the country. Political campaigns had their riots. Three Presidents were assassinated. Labor had its uprisings. Early baseball was characteristic of its times.

—Connie Mack

THE 1900s

HOW THE GAME WAS PLAYED

Clean baseball arrived in 1901 with the emergence of the American League. Byron Bancroft "Ban" Johnson became president, in 1893, of an established minor league known as the Western League. Through an aggressive investment strategy, good public relations, and a policy of acquiring the best players available and moving into the largest and most progressive cities, Johnson placed this league on the path toward becoming a second major league. This was announced in 1901, under the name of the American League, and accomplished by 1903.

Johnson realized that the bad manners and frequent fistfights the National League permitted were restraining the public's enthusiasm for the game. In combating these things, Johnson was high-handed, arbitrary, imperious, and highly effective—all the things that Judge Landis would later be, in controlling scandals of integrity. As the American League quickly became not only a major league, but clearly the better of the two leagues in the eyes of the public, the National League was forced to follow suit, and clean up its innings.

When the blood stopped flowing and the game resumed, stolen bases per team per season ranged between 150 to 200, while home runs per team per season lay in the range of 15 to 30. At the time, this decline in baserunning was regarded as calamitous. In the 1906 *Spalding Guide,* Henry Chadwick was certain that baseball owners would take some action to restore baserunning once they saw in print just how few stolen bases there were. "By way of further illustration of the remarkable falling off in base running due to the foul strike rule, we give below the percentages of stolen bases made by all of the players of the National League clubs in 1905, who had a credit of not less than 20 stolen bases. The table in question will astonish the magnates of the leading clubs when they see by the figures what a comparatively poor record their crack players made in base running last season to that of four years ago." The "percentages" referred to show stolen bases as a percentage of games played, not as a percentage of stolen base attempts. Caught stealing were not recorded.

The rule change referred to, the foul strike rule, was probably the major defining force of

Ty Cobb spiked Frank Baker on this play in September, 1909, provoking Connie Mack to denounce Cobb as "an undesirable person who will stop at nothing to gain his ends." This became the most famous spiking incident of Cobb's career, and he received several death threats at the time.

What I also like about this photo is that peg, sticking four to five inches above the ground, to which third base has been attached. Less intrusive ways of fastening the bags were developed within a few years.

the decade. Prior to 1901, a foul ball was not a strike. This change, instituted in 1901 in the National League and 1903 in the American League, shifted the balance of power dramatically toward the pitcher. Batting averages dropped from near .280 down to the .240–.250 zone for the rest of the decade. Strikeouts went up by more than 50 percent. Base stealing, as Chadwick notes, was reduced. Even power hitting, which then meant doubles and triples more than home runs, was curtailed, as hitters became defensive with two strikes on them.

Errors continued to drop sharply, as gloves grew in size and padding. All of these things tended to reduce the number of runs scored. With runs becoming dear and outs comparatively

cheap, one-run strategies dominated. With a runner on first and nobody out, a bunt was so automatic that many managers didn't even have a sign for it. The hit and run, popularized in the 1890s as an aggressive, big-inning tactic, now became a defensive, get-one-base-if-nothing-else maneuver. By 1915, traditionalists were complaining that the hit and run had ruined baseball.

WHERE THE GAME WAS PLAYED

After some experiments early in the decade, the major leagues settled by 1903 into the eleven cities that were to be privileged to have it for the next half-century. Major league cities during the decade included Baltimore (until 1902), Boston, Brooklyn, Chicago, Cincinnati, Cleveland, Detroit, Milwaukee (in 1901), New York, Philadelphia, Pittsburgh, St. Louis, and Washington.

WHO THE GAME WAS PLAYED BY

No other epoch of baseball history has featured such a diverse, wide-ranging, non-homogeneous cast of characters as the baseball of the first twenty years of this century. The Irish dominance of the previous two decades was broken by the emergence of the American League, which had been a Midwestern league staffed largely by Midwestern players. The National League gradually began to shed its Irish flavor, though some of that was retained until about 1915.

This may be one of the keys to the booming attendance of the decade, for whereas baseball in the nineteenth century was in danger of becoming a game of the Irish, by the Irish, and for the Irish, it now appealed to a broader cross-section of the public. In a nation of immigrants, ethnic identity was important; when you knew a man, you knew where his family came from and when they got off the boat. Many of the game's biggest stars were the heavily accented sons of immigrants, and in particular German and French immigrants (though at that, I'd say at a guess that the immigrant population in baseball was smaller than in the society at large); immigration to the U.S. totaled 13.6 million between 1899 and 1914. There were several Native American players, some of them stars, and a few Jewish players.

The college sports programs about 1905 adopted a quasiprofessional outlook, and began fighting for the right to educate the young men who could run the fastest and throw the hardest. When these players became professional, baseball teams emerged as combinations of college-educated alcoholics and marginally literate or outright illiterate, but still self-disciplined, young men from the backwoods; dapper dandies from state universities formed double-play combinations with street-tough muscle men who carried razors and shoeless southern farm boys who carried handguns or Bibles or both. Players sometimes went directly from the coal mines into the majors, and went straight back to the coal mines. Davy Jones commented directly on this in *The Glory of Their Times*. "The players were more colorful," he said, "drawn from every walk of life. We had stupid guys, smart guys, tough guys, mild guys, crazy guys, college men, slickers from the city and hicks from the country." No decade was ever richer in odd couples. Sam Crawford, an educated man of great dignity, spent over ten years in the outfield with a cagey ruffian from the backwoods of Georgia who packed a pistol. They never did learn to get along. Tinker and Evers hated each other but played together like Tracy and Hepburn, and one cannot but wonder what kind of chill traced the spine of Christy Mathewson when he first learned that the salty John McGraw was to be his new manager. Sometimes they made it work, and sometimes the teams simply disintegrated, splitting into warring tribes. It was wonderful when it worked.

Baseball in the years 1905 to 1919 was soaked in strategy as never before, never since. It is possible to see a connection between that and the diverse nature of the rosters. Strategies in baseball are *team* actions; they require two or more people to know about them in advance, and cooperate in their execution. It could be argued that managers, sensing the danger that a team could disintegrate into factions, demanded of their players more cooperation—and thus more strategy—than was really necessary. Or rather, that the strategy was necessitated not by the game situations, but by the roster.

CHECKING IN:

1900— Lefty Grove, Lonaconing, Maryland
      Louis Armstrong, New Orleans
1902— Charles Lindbergh, Detroit
1903— Charlie Gehringer, Fowlerville,
      Michigan
      Lou Gehrig, New York City
      Tom Yawkey, Detroit
      Carl Hubbell, Carthage, Missouri
      Mickey Cochrane, Bridgewater,
      Massachusetts
      Chuck Klein, Indianapolis
1905— Leo Durocher, West Springfield,
      Massachusetts
      Howard Hughes, Houston
1906— Joe Cronin, San Francisco
      Satchel Paige, Mobile, Alabama
1907— Jimmie Foxx, Sudlersville,
      Maryland
1909— Mel Ott, Gretna, Louisiana

Carl Hubbell was born on the same day as John Dillinger—June 22, 1903.

CHECKING OUT:

1900— Jack Taylor, Bright's disease, 28
      Marty Bergen, murder/suicide, 28
1901— William McKinley, gunshot, 58
1902— Pud Galvin, catarrh of the
      stomach, 36
      Fred Dunlap, 43
1903— Win Mercer, suicide by gas, 28
      Ed Delahanty, drowned, 35
      Twelve people killed in collapse of
      bleachers at Phillies game, August 6
1905— Pete Browning, complications from
      mastoiditis, 44
1906— Susan B. Anthony, 86
      Buck Ewing, 47

1907— Chick Stahl, suicide by swallowing
      acid, 34
      Cozy Dolan, typhoid fever, 34
      Stahl and Dolan, regular outfielders
      for the two Boston teams, died
      within a few hours of one another.
1909— Geronimo, 75
      Frank Selee, tuberculosis, 49
      John Clarkson, pneumonia, 47
      Foghorn Miller, kidney disease, 42
      Henry Clay Pulliam, suicide by
      gunshot, 40
      Herman Long, tuberculosis, 38
      Jimmy Sebring, convulsions, 27

Henry Chadwick, called the Father of Baseball, had a head cold but insisted on attending the Dodgers home opener in wet, cold weather. He developed pneumonia and died April 20, 1908, at the age of eighty-three.

YANNIGAN

The term "yannigan" was used as the name for any rookie, replacement, or second-line player. It has a quirky, vaguely negative connotation to it, like the 1980s term "scrubeenie"; it just *sounds* derogatory. The term occasionally achieved a kind of official recognition. After the San Francisco earthquake in 1906, Brooklyn played a benefit game for the relief effort, and split the squad into "Regulars" and "Yannigans." Since rosters were smaller then, several pitchers started for the Yannigans, as well as manager Patsy Donovan and Sammy Strang, a yannigan from the rival New York Giants. The Yannigans won, 3-2; 5,000 were on hand, and $12,000 was raised for the people of San Francisco.

—Jim Baker

THE 1900s IN A BOX

Attendance Data:

Total: 50 million (49,880,718, 1901–1909)

Highest: New York Giants, 1908   estimated 910,000

New York Giants   4,977,481

Lowest: Philadelphia (NL), 1902   112,066

Boston Braves   1,492,753

Attendance boomed during this period. Attendance in 1901 was 3.6 million, or about 230,000 per team. This increased every year except for a small decline in 1906, and by the end of the decade had more than doubled. The primary causes were the effective control of vulgar and unseemly behavior on the field, a series of outstanding pennant races, the organization of the nation's media through formation of the Associated Press and other organizations, huge popular interest in the World Series, and—both cause and effect—the construction of grand, permanent stadiums.

The average American in this era attended a major league baseball game about once every twenty years.

Most Home Runs:

Sam Crawford,   1901   16

Socks Seybold,   1902   16

Harry Davis   67

Best Won/Lost Record by Team:

Chicago (NL),   1906   116-36   .763

Pittsburgh Pirates   938-538   .636

Worst Won/Lost Record by Team:

Washington Senators,   1904 38-113 .252

Washington Senators   490-833 .366

Index of Competitive Balance: 30%

The standard deviation of winning percentage in 1909 was .131, the highest of the twentieth century. The Pirates won 110 games. Four major league teams finished 55 games or more out of first place.

The second-highest standard deviation of winning percentage of the twentieth century was in 1906, the third-highest in 1904. This is perhaps misleading, as the figures were even higher in the 1890s, and even higher than that in the 1880s. Baseball was still getting organized. The weakest teams were slowly pulling up toward the level of the strongest.

Home-Field Winning Percentage: .552

Percentage of Regulars Hitting .300: 18%

Largest Home-Field Advantage: Philadelphia Athletics

The White Elephants were 432-216 in Philadelphia, .667, but 302-352 on the road. The home-field advantage in this decade was twice as large in the American League as in the National League.

Having Their Best Decade Ever: Pittsburgh Pirates, Chicago White Sox

The Philadelphia Athletics had a better winning percentage in this decade (.564) than that organization has had in any other decade, although this was probably not the A's best decade. This was the only decade in which the A's were *uniformly* good, as opposed to great for half the decade.

Having Their Worst Decade: Boston Braves, Brooklyn Dodgers, Washington Senators

Heaviest Player: The heaviest weight listed is for Ed Walker, a 6-foot-5-inch, 242-pound pitcher who appeared in only four games. Harry Lumley, though his weight is unlisted, appears to have run up some pretty good tabs in the hotel coffee shops. Lumley led the league in triples and home runs as a rookie in 1904, and in 1906 was among the best players in the National League, hitting .324 with 35 stolen bases, also leading the league in slugging percentage. A picture of him taken in 1908 is suggestive of Roger Ebert, and during that season he hit just .216 with four stolen bases in 127 games.

Lightest Player: Probably Sammy Strang or Jimmy Dygert. Johnnie Evers is the smallest player for whom a weight is listed, weighing but 125.

When the first modern baseball encyclopedia was published in 1969, many players from this era had unlisted weights, since no one at that time was systematically collecting data on players' weights. Most of these weights have since been filled in, apparently, with numbers that are invented. I do not object to estimating weights when they are missing, but many of those now listed are wildly inaccurate. Jimmy Dygert is listed at 5'10," 185 pounds—a huge man, by the standards of that era. Alfred H. Spink's *The National Game* (1910) gives this description of him:

J. Dygert is the toy pitcher of the Athletics of the American League. He only weighs 115 pounds, but this is made up mostly of nerve and muscle. Clubs who have opposed the Athletics say the little fellow has bluffed his way through the American League ever since Connie Mack discovered him at New Orleans in 1904.

George Winter, another American League pitcher, is listed at 155 pounds. He actually weighed 131 to 133. Sammy Strang has been listed at weighing 160 pounds—ten pounds lighter than Henry Aaron. I doubt that Strang weighed 120. Many other listed weights in this era are just absolutely nuts.

Most Strikeouts by Pitcher:
Rube Waddell,   1904 about 349
Rube Waddell   2,251
(1904 figure is disputed)

Highest Batting Average:
Nap Lajoie,   1901   .426
Honus Wagner   .352

Lowest Batting Average:
Bill Bergen,   1909   .139
Bill Bergen   .175

Best Major League Players (by Years):
1900— Honus Wagner
1901— Nap Lajoie
1902— Honus Wagner
1903— Honus Wagner
1904— Honus Wagner
1905— Honus Wagner
1906— Honus Wagner
1907— Honus Wagner
1908— Honus Wagner
1909— Ty Cobb

Best Major League Pitchers (by Years):
1900— Joe McGinnity
1901— Cy Young
1902— Cy Young
1903— Joe McGinnity
1904— Jack Chesbro
1905— Christy Mathewson
1906— Three Finger Brown
1907— Ed Walsh
1908— Ed Walsh
1909— Three Finger Brown

Hardest-Throwing Pitcher: Walter Johnson

Best Curve: Three Finger Brown

Best Power/Speed Combination: Honus Wagner

Best Switch Hitter: John Anderson

Iron Man: Joe McGinnity

Best Bunter: Roy Thomas

Best Baseball Books:
1900— *A Ballplayer's Career* by Cap Anson
      The first baseball autobiography
1907— *History of Colored Baseball* by Sol
      White
1908— *Baseball Magazine* begins publication

Seven Largest Changes in Baseball During the Decade:

1. Arrival of the American League
2. Great leap forward in newspaper coverage
3. Beginning of the World Series
4. First modern stadiums
5. Tremendous reduction of on-field violence
6. Explosion of attendance
7. Sharp reduction in runs scored due to foul
   strike rule

Best Outfield Arm: Mike Mitchell

Worst Outfield Arm: Topsy Hartsel

Most Runs Batted In:
Honus Wagner,   1901   126
Honus Wagner   956

Most Aggressive Baserunner: Ty Cobb or Kid Elberfeld

Fastest Player: Harry Bay

Slowest Player: Piano Legs Hickman

Best Control Pitcher: Cy Young

Most Stolen Bases:
Ty Cobb,   1909   76
Honus Wagner   488

Best-Looking Players: Christy Mathewson, Sam Crawford

Ugliest Players: Ray Collins, Phil Geier

O.J. Simpson Award: Tacks Latimer was a catcher who played for five major league teams, but only 27 games, which may be some sort of record. Anyway, in 1924 he was working as a police officer, but got involved in an off-duty dispute with his lieutenant, and shot the man three times in the back.

Latimer was given a life sentence. In 1926 the prisoners rioted, and during this riot Latimer courageously came to the defense of the warden's young daughter. For this, he was granted a pardon by the Governor of Ohio in 1930.

Cap Anson Award: Ty Cobb

Three Finger Brown Award: Three Finger Brown

Best Pitching Staff: Chicago Cubs, 1906

Best Offense: Pittsburgh Pirates, 1902

Football Players: Christy Mathewson, Eddie Collins

Retrobermanisms:
Socks (If I May Be) Seybold
Jim (Citizen) Kane

First of His Kind: Dode Criss (first player to be used regularly as a pinch hitter)

Last of His Kind: Luther Taylor (last mute player)

One of a Kind: Rube Waddell

Best Infield: Chicago Cubs, 1903–1910

Best Outfield: Detroit Tigers, 1905–1910
(Matty McIntyre, Ty Cobb, Sam Crawford)

A Better Man Than a Ballplayer: Sam Leever

A Better Ballplayer Than a Human Being: Mike Donlin

Mr. Dickens, I'd Like You to Meet: Homer Smoot (Cardinals, 1902–1906)

Platoon Combinations I Would Like to See: Elmer Flick and Max Flack

Best Defensive Team: 1908 Chicago Cubs

Clint Hartung Award: Johnny Lush

Outstanding Sportswriter: Frances Richter, editor of the *Sporting Life* and the *Reach Guide*

Most Admirable Superstar: Christy Mathewson

Least Admirable Superstar: Hal Chase

Gold Glove Team:
C—   Ossee Schreckengost
1B— Frank Isbell
2B— Johnny Evers
3B— Jimmy Collins
SS— Joe Tinker
OF— Fielder Jones
     Jimmy Sheckard
     Joe Birmingham

Ozzie Guillen Trophy: Whitey Alperman in 1909 batted 442 times, drawing only two walks. This was the lowest single-season walk rate in the twentieth century, among players with 300 or more plate appearances.

Franchise Shifts:

Milwaukee to St. Louis (American League), 1902

Baltimore to New York (American League), 1903

New Stadiums:
1901— Huntington Avenue Grounds, Boston (for Red Sox)
        South Side Park, Chicago (for White Sox)
        Bennett Park, Detroit
        Columbia Park, Philadelphia
        American League Park, Washington

1903— Hilltop Stadium, New York (Highlanders)
1909— Shibe Park, Philadelphia
        Forbes Field, Pittsburgh
        League Park, Cleveland (concrete version)
        Sportsman's Park, St. Louis (renovated)

Best Pennant Race: National League, 1908

Best World Series: 1903

The first real World Series; respect for the new league was at stake. Boston, with Cy Young and Bill Dineen, rallied from a three games to one deficit to beat Pittsburgh in eight games.

Red Sox fans taunted Honus Wagner by singing an amended version of "Tessie" ("Honus, why do you hit so badly?" instead of "Tessie, you know I love you madly.")

Best-Hitting Pitcher: Al Orth

Worst-Hitting Pitcher: Red Ames or Howie Camnitz

Ames inability to hit was a running joke in the New York newspapers. A sporting goods company once advertised that they had a bat that even Leon Ames could get a hit with. Red hit .123 for the decade; Camnitz hit .092.

Best Minor League Team: 1900 Chicago White Sox

Best Minor League Player: Emil Frisk, the "Wagner of the minors," had 272 hits in the PCL in 1904, and had over 2,000 hits in his minor league career, despite spending several years as a pitcher.

Odd Couple: John McGraw and Christy Mathewson

Drinking Men:
Howie Camnitz
Rube Waddell
Bugs Raymond
Slim Sallee
Wild Bill Donovan
Ed Reulbach

Christy Mathewson in *Pitching in a Pinch* discussed the drinking habits of several contemporaries. "Like great artists in other fields of endeavor," he wrote, "many Big League pitchers are temperamental. 'Bugs' Raymond, 'Rube' Waddell, 'Slim' Sallee and 'Wild Bill' Donovan are ready examples of the temperamental type. The first three are the sort of men of whom the manager is never sure. He does not know, when they come into the ball park, whether or not they are in condition to work. They always carry with them a delightful atmosphere of uncertainty."

By 1920, it would have been impossible to write that without risking a lawsuit.

New Equipment:
Shin Guards (1907)
Tarpaulin (1908)

The first tarpaulin to protect the field from rain was devised by the Pittsburgh Waterproof Company, and was purchased by the Pittsburgh Pirates on April 28, 1908.

Player vs. Team: On April 11, 1909, Johnny Evers stated that he desired to lay off for a season, and had completed correspondence with the Chicago club to that end. He said he wanted to take a complete rest for the 1909 season.

On May 11, 1909, Evers signed a two-year contract, and rejoined the Cubs.

Team vs. Team: Philadelphia vs. Philadelphia, Nap Lajoie in the middle

Uniforms:
High collars
Blousy shirts
Special undershirts for pitchers
Handmade shoes
Long stockings
Team sweaters
Sunglasses

New Terms or Expressions: Yannigan

Most Wins by Pitcher:
Jack Chesbro, 1904   41
Christy Mathewson   236

Highest Winning Percentages:
Wild Bill Donovan, 1907   25-4   .862
Ed Reulbach   97-39   .713
Sam Leever   167-82   .699

Lowest Winning Percentage:
Joe Harris, 1906   2-21   .087
Jack Townsend   34-82   .293

Nicknames: Animals and hometowns were the dominant themes of a decade blessed with classic nicknames; see page 83.

Flameout: Harry Lumley

All Offense/No Defense: 1901 St. Louis Cardinals

All Defense/No Offense: 1901 Boston Braves

Tough-Luck Season: Ned Garvin was the tough-luck pitcher of the decade, if not the hard-luck pitcher of all time. In 1900 he posted a 2.41 ERA for the Cubs; the league ERA was 3.69, but Garvin finished 10-18. In 1901, for Milwaukee in the American League, he again bested the league ERA (3.46 to 3.66), but finished 7-20. In 1902 he cut his ERA to 2.09, but finished 11-11. In 1903 his ERA was again better-than-league (3.08 vs. 3.26), but he finished 15-18 for Brooklyn, and in 1904, capping it off, he posted a 1.72 ERA (league ERA, 2.72), but finished 5-16. He was pretty much the tough-luck pitcher of the year every year.

Could I Try This Career Over? Otto Hess

Minor Leagues Were:
90 percent free
10 percent slaves to the majors

Best Double Play Combination: Nap Lajoie and Terry Turner, 1906–1907 Cleveland Naps.

The famous Tinker to Evers to Chance combination was together from 1903 through

1910. Their first season the Cubs turned two fewer double plays than expected, 78 to 80. From then on they were always positive: +6 in 1904, +13 in 1905, +20 in 1906, +15 in 1907, +3 in 1908, +9 in 1909, and +5 in 1910. Although Chance was injured in 1911, Tinker and Evers stayed together most of two more years, scoring at +5 and +12.

Tinker to Evers to Chance surely was not the greatest double play combination of all time, and probably was not the best in baseball at that time. They were good—but they were B/B+ good, not A/A+ material.

Worst Double Play Combination: Jack Doyle and Bones Ely, 1902 Washington Senators.

Paul Krichell Talent Scout Award: Con Strouthers

Strouthers managed the Augusta team in the Sally League in 1904. He signed Ty Cobb to play center field while his regular center fielder was suspended by the league. When his center fielder was reinstated, he released Cobb.

Ira Thomas Talent Scout Award: Mike Lynch

Tacoma manager, Northwestern League, 1906. Released Walter Johnson, and was kind enough to suggest to Walter that he ought to forget about pitching, and maybe try his luck as an outfielder.

Cy Slapnicka Talent Scout Award: Horace Fogel

Christy Mathewson won 20 games (20-17) for an awful New York Giants team in 1902. The next spring, Fogel toyed with the idea of converting him to a third baseman.

Johnny Lucadello Talent Scout Award: John McGraw

After Tris Speaker played seven games with the Boston Red Sox in 1907, the Sox were so unimpressed that they forgot to send him a contract that winter. The Giants went to spring training in Marlin, Texas, near Speaker's home. Speaker went to their camp twice, and begged McGraw to work him out. McGraw said he already had more players in camp than he knew what to do with.

Best Unrecognized Player: The best player from this era who is not in the Hall of Fame is Jimmy Sheckard or Bill Dahlen.

Highest-Paid Player: Probably Nap Lajoie

New Statistics: The basic pitching record took form during this decade. Innings Pitched first appeared in a *Guide* in this decade. It may seem curious that innings pitched were not reported sooner, but one should remember that:

1. Until 1890, virtually all games were complete games, hence all one needed to know was how many games the pitcher had worked, not how many innings.

2. Even today, official statistics do not give defensive innings at other positions.

A Very Good Movie Could Be Made About: The final days of the 1908 season.

Five Biggest Things Wrong with Baseball:
1. Segregation
2. Substandard umpiring
3. Labor/management bickering
4. Fan violence
5. Rumors of player dishonesty

I Don't Know What This Has to Do with Baseball, But I Thought I'd Mention It Anyway: The first congressional baseball game was played in Washington in 1909. The center of attention was Republican Representative John Tener of Pennsylvania, who had pitched for Cap Anson's Colts. Despite Tener's presence, the Democrats squeaked out a 26-16 victory.

Tener later became Governor of Pennsylvania and President of the National League. At the same time, no less.

BEAR CUBS

The Chicago Cubs in 1906 won 116 games. This remains the record for wins in one season. The Cubs also won 223 games in two years (1906–1907), which is the record for wins in a two-season span, and 322 games over three years (1906–1908), which is the record for wins over a three-season span. They won 426 games over a four-season span (1906–1909), which is the record for wins over a four-year span, and they won 530 games over a five-season span (1906–1910), which is the record for wins over a period of five years.

The Cubs won 622 games over a six-year period (1905–1910), which is a record, by far. The only other team to win 600 games in a six-year span was the Cardinals of the 1940s, although many teams have *lost* 600 games in six years, proving that it is easier to stay in last place than it is to stay in first.

The Cubs won 715 games in seven years (1904–1910); this also is a record. They won 807 games in an eight-year period (1904–1911), which, again, is a record; the Yankees won 799 between 1936 and 1943. They won 898 games between 1904 and 1912, which is a record for wins over a nine-year period, and they won 986 between 1904 and 1913, which is a record for wins over a ten-year period.

It has become common to bash the selection of Tinker, Evers, and Chance to the Hall of Fame, saying that Franklin P. Adams' famous poem put them in. It is easy to quote their batting statistics, which are but marginally impressive, to show that the trio does not belong—and, indeed, they may not. But at the same time, this is perilously near an absurd argument, to wit: Tinker, Evers, and Chance were not really great ballplayers, they merely happened to win a huge number of games. The definition of a great ballplayer is a ballplayer who helps his team to win a lot of games.

I go back and forth on this issue; sometimes I think they were great players, sometimes I think not. But if you're going to say that these guys *don't* belong in the Hall of Fame, it seems to me, you have to deal somehow with the phenomenal success of their team. This team won more games, over any period of years, than the Yankees with Ruth and Gehrig, more games than the Dodgers with Robinson, Reese, Snider, and Campy, more games than the Reds with Bench, Morgan, Rose, and Concepcion—more games than anybody. When you start explaining their wins, as Ricky Ricardo would say, you've got a lot of 'splaining to do.

Is the rest of the team so great that no weight need be carried by these three players?

It is not. The catcher, Johnny Kling, was good, but probably not as good as any of the three. Third baseman Harry Steinfeldt was in the same range. No outfielder on the team was Ty Cobb or Babe Ruth or Mickey Mantle; none was even Tris Speaker or Al Simmons or Duke Snider.

When you look carefully at the Cubs of those years, it is impossible to avoid the conclusion that this team won more games with infield defense than any other team in the history of baseball. First of all, they won more *games* than any other team in the history of baseball. And they didn't do it with .350 hitters, and they didn't do it with 40 homer men.

Their pitching was good. Three Finger Brown was great; the rest of the staff was good. But it is also apparent that the Cubs' defense was so good that anybody they put on the mound was effective. Nineteen pitchers pitched 150 or more innings for the Cubs in their ten best years, 1904–1913. Seventeen of those 19 pitchers posted ERAs below 3.00, including guys like Chick Fraser, Buttons Briggs, and Orval Overall who had never had comparable success with other teams. Even Three Finger Brown had been acquired by the Cubs after posting a 9-13 record for the Cardinals as a rookie in 1903.

The essential question is this: If Tinker, Evers, and Chance were not great players, how do you explain the success of this team? The Yankees of 1936–1945 had DiMaggio, Dickey, Gehrig for a couple of years, Red Ruffing, Lefty Gomez, Lazzeri, and Joe Gordon at second, Red Rolfe, Tommy Henrich, Johnny Murphy, George Selkirk, Frankie Crosetti, and numerous other stars. The Yankees had enough success to justify the brilliant reputations those men still enjoy—but they couldn't match the win totals of the Cubs.

SUGAR, PLEASE

Danny Shay was, so to speak, the Roger Metzger of his time. Shay was a light-hitting shortstop who had a finger amputated in 1905, but tried to come back and play. He wasn't very successful at the major league level, but went back to the minor leagues and continued his career.

Ten years later, while employed as the Milwaukee manager, Shay shot and killed a "colored" waiter in an Indianapolis hotel. The papers don't say what color the waiter was, but I'd say dark brown was a good guess. The shooting followed an argument over the amount of sugar in the sugar bowl at Shay's table. The manager was arrested and charged with murder, and a grand jury indicted him. Shay pleaded self defense, claiming that the man had called him a bad name and attempted to assault him.

He was acquitted.

MAJOR LEAGUE ALL-STAR TEAM 1900–1909

Records in seasonal notation, based on 154 games. Pitchers based on 45 starts.

Pos.	Player	Years	Hits	HR	RBI	Avg.	Other
C	Roger Bresnahan	6.34	147	3	60	.285	79 Walks
1B	Frank Chance	6.72	158	3	75	.299	53 Steals
2B	Nap Lajoie	7.95	210	6	100	.347	45 Doubles
3B	Jimmy Collins	7.14	175	4	76	.288	
SS	Honus Wagner	9.05	204	6	106	.351	
LF	Mike Donlin	5.22	200	7	107	.338	
CF	Ty Cobb	3.86	198	5	101	.338	49 Steals
RF	Sam Crawford	9.16	183	6	88	.307	18 Triples

Pitcher		Years	Won-Lost	SO	ERA	Other
RH	Christy Mathewson	8.23	29-14	218	1.97	361 Innings
RH	Cy Young	8.64	27-15	182	2.12	46 Walks
RH	Three Finger Brown	5.01	29-13	159	1.63	

NICKNAMES OF THE 1900s

Animals, always a staple of player nicknames, were in vogue in the first decade of this century, usually modified or described in some way. Mike Donlin was "Turkey Mike," Clark Griffith was "The Old Fox," Frank Isbell was "The Bald Eagle," and Jake Beckley was "Eagle Eye." Davy Jones was called "Kangaroo," Lou Ritter was "Old Dog," Bill Shipke was "Muskrat Bill," Jimmy Slagle was called "The Human Mosquito" (a nickname that in subsequent generations would have been shortened to "Skeeter"). Sammy Strang was "The Dixie Thrush," and Jesse Burkett and Johnny Evers were both called "The Crab."

We also see in this decade the emergence of the "hometown" nicknames. There were a few before this time (Amos Rusie was "The Hoosier Thunderbolt") but very few, because, for one thing, most of the nineteenth century players came from just a few towns. A few of these (from the turn of the century) include "The Duke of Tralee" (Roger Bresnahan), "Wahoo Sam" (Sam Crawford), "The Goshen Schoolmaster" (Sam Leever), and "Wabash George" (George Mullin). Albert Schweitzer, who certainly did not need a nickname, was called "Cheese." A few others, from the time when people believed in good nicknames:

The Peerless Leader (Frank Chance)
The Tabasco Kid (Kid Elberfeld)
Wagon Tongue (Bill Keister)
Little All Right (Claude Ritchey)
The Flying Dutchman (Honus Wagner)
Miner (Three Finger Brown)
Frosty Bill (Bill Duggleby)
Crossfire (Earl Moore)
Yip (Frank Owen)
The Knight of the Wallop (Mike Donlin)
The Piano Mover (Frank Smith)
All Indian players were called "Chief."
All players who could run were called "Deerfoot."

THE OPEN ROAD OUT

Harry Clay Pulliam was one of many executives in baseball's early years who came into the game through the newspapers. Pulliam was born in a small town in Kentucky in 1869. After receiving a law degree from the University of Virginia he worked for a newspaper in Louisville. He became secretary to the president of the American Association, made enough of a name for himself in Louisville to serve a two-year term in the Kentucky Assembly, and became acquainted with Barney Dreyfuss, owner of the Louisville and Pittsburgh franchises in the National League. From 1900 to 1903 he was secretary/ treasurer of the Pirates. Late in this period the National League abolished the office of the presidency, an unsuccessful experiment that ended in less than a year. When the office was restored in 1903, Pulliam, at the age of thirty-four, became president of the National League.

Pulliam seems to have been generally an able executive, at least in his first years. He was sharp, a good administrator, and a man of considerable charm. He assisted in organizing the peace with the American League, and adopted Ban Johnson's policies toward rowdiness on the field, successfully completing the clean-up of the game. His first re-election in 1904 was unanimous. Somehow he made an enemy of John T. Brush, owner of the Giants, which it wasn't at all difficult to do. His second re-election was by a vote of 7–1. Brush converted to his side Garry Herrmann, the owner of the Reds, and these Machiavellian cohorts, both of whom seem to have gotten into the game mostly because they liked the power plays, would annually vote against him, so that he was re-elected several times by a 6–2 vote.

Pulliam had, of course, other disagreements on specific issues. On June 6, 1905, Pulliam gave a speech in which he publicly attacked Brush, charging that Brush had attempted "by common law" to subvert a National League rule of which he (Brush) was the author, that rule having to do with disciplining players. He took his battles with Herrmann and Brush rather hard. He became, said Francis Richter, "obsessed with the idea that the success of the league rested entirely on his shoulders." Pulliam was what you might call a wimp. Though a nice-looking man, he was frail and of a nervous temperament. "He was an idealist," quoting Richter again, "a dreamer, a lover of solitude and nature, of books, of poetry, of music and flowers." The nervous temperament grew steadily worse. His disagreements with owners grew more and more to occupy his mind, and his policies became more rigid and more arbitrary.

In late September, 1908, Harry Pulliam was called upon to make an immensely controversial decision about a critical game in the National League pennant race, as a result of Merkle's boner. He ruled against the New York team. He got stacks of hate mail. His nervous intensity worsened. At the February, 1909, meeting of the National League, Pulliam apparently fell apart. Though his specific behavior is not recorded, it was reported that "Mr. Pulliam suffered such a complete physical and nervous breakdown that a long rest in seclusion had to be forced upon him."

John Heydler acted as president for a few months while Pulliam recovered, on full salary. He returned to work in June, looking well, though a certain buoyancy in spirit for which he had been noted had passed with the nervousness. On the evening of June 28, 1909, in his room at the New York Athletic Club, the president of the National League fired a shot through his temple, leaving him sightless and in great pain for a few hours, before he died the next morning. He was forty.

In his wake, Brush's enemies in the New York press twisted Pulliam's death into a martyrdom. Richter thought he should have

married, and wrote that "heart-hunger had much to do with Harry Pulliam's death." No doubt it did. Pulliam was president of the National League at a time when half the owners wanted the man who held that office to be an autocrat, and half wanted him to be an office boy. The twisted remains of this struggle are buried in a grave in Louisville.

There were, or seemed to be, many more suicides in the game then than there are now; certainly the necrologies of the game contain many, many more violent deaths. In our time, if a Donnie Moore or a Bruce Gardner does himself in, that becomes a big story. I drew up a partial list of baseball-related suicides from 1900 through 1925, but my library is incomplete, and I'm sure I didn't get all of them. Was this true of the country as a whole—were suicide rates higher then? I would guess that they were. I'm not sure that anyone knows. America was at the end of a time when men were allowed to have dreams larger than life, getting late in the generation of Ford and Edison and Firestone and Rockefeller and Spalding. I suspect that in 1910 the great majority of American men owned guns, and a good many carried them. When one's dreams collapse, when one finds oneself suffocating in a small reality and powerless to escape it on this earth, what could be easier than to take leave of it?

I'VE HAD THOSE SEATS

The Baseball Writers Association of America was formed at the World Series in 1908, after out-of-town writers in Chicago were placed in the back row of the grandstand, while at Detroit they were asked to climb a ladder to the roof of the first base pavilion, and try to write their stories in the rain and snow.

UNIFORMS OF THE 1900s

As we come into the twentieth century, high collars were still the rule of the day. Blousy shirts were often worn with a long T-shirt underneath, shirt-sleeves being shortened to half or three-quarters length. Upper and lower garments were even more sacklike and shapeless than before. A wide belt hitched the two together and was often fastened on the side, since there was a belt loop right in front where we fasten our belts today.

Pitchers, when the weather recommended it, wore a special wool, fleece-lined T-shirt with a roll collar (turtleneck). Uniforms in the early 1900s were made either of wool or a wool and cotton mix.

Handmade shoes were still in use, looking a little like short hiking boots, but they were always black in color. The leather was calfskin or kangaroo hide, and steel plates with spikes "were riveted to heel and sole." Long stockings of a heavy wool were worn with knickers, either light or dark in color and occasionally striped. An ad in the 1908 *Sporting News* shows a diagram of a baseball stocking extending up over the knees to the thigh, but no clue is given as to how it was fastened and there are no advertisements for garters. According to Marc Okkonen, author of *Baseball Uniforms of the 20th Century,* the stirrup stocking, as separate from the foot covering part, first came into use in 1905. The stirrup added new fashion possibilities, particularly as a way to jazz up the uniform with a little more color.

In the early 1900s the Tigers uniform featured the city name in full across the jersey front. By 1903 a simple "D" stood for Detroit but must have been deemed rather boring because by 1904, it was changed to the fancy Old English style "D" which is still

used. Once again according to Marc Okkonen, this fancy style "D" is the oldest team symbol still in use today. A simpler version of the "D" appeared briefly in 1916 and 1919, but otherwise the form has held. The Old English or "Black Letter" "W" was also used by Washington on their 1906 road uniforms, while the Cleveland Indians about the same time used an elegant script "C." The first instance of a team's nickname gracing the front of the jersey was the Washington Nationals in 1905. And as long as we're talking about firsts . . . in 1909, the Cubs were the first team to spell out their city name in a vertical fashion down the lapel of their shirts.

A double-breasted suit jacket was part of a team's standard wardrobe, as was a vest sweater or hip length "ribbed coat." Players wore their team sweaters (an early form of warm-up jackets) during batting practice and for team photos. Speaking of team photos, those from the nineteenth and early twentieth centuries make today's obligatory team shot look staid and formal. We get a closer and more personal view of team members, partly because the teams were smaller and the pictures not so crowded, but also because the approach seems more relaxed. Players are pictured with, God forbid, an arm draped around a teammate's neck or a hand resting on another's shoulder. In today's team photos, the photographer rules. Everybody is uniformly lined up, seated players' hands are on their own knees, standing players keep their arms behind their backs. Now if we could just get that guy in the back row to remove his nose ring.

A few other notes . . . caps were of several basic forms and varied from team to

(continued)

(Continued)

team, but all had a shorter bill than in today's model. Some used contrasting dark/light colors for the bill and head-fitting part, while others used stripes radiating from the button at the apex. Some had the city initial in front, as all do now. Caps with horizontal stripes looked rather boxy and were known as the Chicago Style, although we would identify this style more recently as the Pittsburgh Pirates style of the 1980s. The home/road distinction in uniforms was clearly established by the early 1900s, with white being for the home team and gray for the visitors. Sunglasses were in use, as evidenced by a 1908 photo of Bill Hinchman.

A brief note about umpires. Formal dress, replete with suit jacket, slacks, and bow tie, typified the uniforms for umpiring officials during this period. Crowning touch—a cap which looked a little like a golf cap. For the home plate umpires standard protective gear developed for catchers (masks and chest protectors) was added to umpire's uniforms by the 1890s.

—Susan McCarthy

QUICK HITS

Three players just after the turn of the century had really interesting short careers. Those three are:

1. Jim Nealon, who led the National League in RBI in 1906, at the age of 21. Nealon contracted tuberculosis in mid-season, 1907, and died in 1910, at the age of 25.

2. Henry Schmidt, who won 21 games for Brooklyn in 1903 (21-13), but never pitched in the majors before or after that season. Schmidt was a Texan who hated living in the East, and refused to report to Brooklyn for the 1904 season.

Schmidt resurfaced in the news in 1905, when he was released by the Oakland Club of the Pacific Coast League, which alleged that he had thrown a game. Schmidt demanded an investigation by the league president. I don't know how it came out.

3. Erwin (Zaza) Harvey, who played for the White Sox and the (now) Indians in 1901 and 1902. In 1901, at the age of 23, Harvey pitched in 16 games for the White Sox, not too badly; he was 3-6 with a 3.62 ERA. The White Sox sold him to the Indians, and the Indians converted him to the outfield.

As an outfielder, he was sensational. Playing 45 games for the Indians in 1901, he hit .353, drove in 24 runs and stole 15 bases. Then he played 12 games in 1902, and hit .348 (16/46). Then his career ended. I know nothing about him; I can't recall that I have ever seen any reference to him, other than his entry in the encyclopedias. There has to be a story here, but does anyone know what it is?

1905: VE KNOW VERR TO FIND CHEW, BROOKLYN PLAYERS

For several Sunday games in 1904 and 1905, the Brooklyn Dodgers evaded local Blue Laws by not charging admission to the games. (Laws which regulated what business could be done on Sunday were called Blue Laws.) Instead, they sold scorecards, which usually cost a nickel, for four different prices: a dollar, seventy-five cents, fifty cents, and a quarter. Describing the game of April 23, 1905, the *New York Times* reported that several dozen policemen were on hand, and the names of all players and scorecard sellers were taken down, but neither the police nor the Sabbath Observance Association attempted to stop the game. A crowd of 11,642 heathens was in attendance.

SUICIDES IN BASEBALL
1900–1925
(A PARTIAL LISTING)

January 19, 1900. Worcester, Massachusetts. Marty Bergen, National League catcher, killed his wife and two children with an ax and then slit his own throat.

January 12, 1903. San Francisco. Win Mercer, Detroit pitcher, inhaled poisonous gas at the age of twenty-eight. He had apparently gambled and lost not only his own money, but also some money that didn't belong to him, that he was "holding" for his teammates. He left a suicide note warning of the evils of women and gambling.

January 10, 1904. Utica, New York. Clinton Bradley, a former Eastern League pitcher, committed suicide due to business failure.

February 1, 1904. Springfield, Massachusetts. Daniel Mahoney, 39, a major league catcher in the mid-1890s, committed suicide by drinking carbolic acid.

November 28, 1904. New Haven, Connecticut. Steve Ashe, a pitcher for the New Haven team, committed suicide at a New Haven hospital during a fit of insanity.

June 7, 1905. Cleveland. Lottie Bruce, the sister of Lave Cross, was shot and wounded by her husband, who then committed suicide.

July 11, 1905. Kansas City. Mrs. Frank Bonner, wife of the second baseman of the Kansas City team (American Association) committed suicide. Her husband Frank, who had played in the majors for six years, died on December 31 of the same year of blood poisoning.

July 15, 1905. San Francisco. Eugene F. Bert, president of the Pacific Coast League, shot himself in a suicide attempt. Subsequently recovered.

March 28, 1907. West Baden, Indiana. Chick Stahl, player-manager of the Red Sox, drank carbolic acid, aged thirty-four.

January 2, 1909. Chandler, South Carolina. Edward Strickland, a pitcher with Greenville, shot his girlfriend and himself, aged twenty-six.

January 15, 1909. Factoryville, Pennsylvania. Nicholas Mathewson, younger brother of Christy Mathewson, shot himself, aged twenty-two.

July 29, 1909. New York City. Harry Pulliam.

March 14, 1910. Albion, New York. Charles Nelson Brown, twenty-seven, a minor league player, hanged himself.

September 28, 1910. Cleveland. James Payne, former trainer of the team that is now the Indians, committed suicide in the presence of his wife and mother, aged thirty-five.

December 13, 1910. Louisville. Dan McGann, longtime major league first baseman (1895–1908), shot himself, aged thirty-three.

February 6, 1911. Chester, Pennsylvania. Thomas Senior, minor league umpire, shot himself at the age of thirty-two.

November 29, 1911. Johnstown, Pennsylvania. Randolph Blanch, Johnstown sports editor, suicide at the age of thirty.

January 14, 1914. Dallas. Walt Goldsby, major league player, 1884–1888, later a minor league umpire and manager, died by his own hand.

October 11, 1916. Canton, Ohio. Carl Britton, minor league pitcher, committed suicide at the age of forty.

April 23, 1918. Chicago. A man named James McDonough, attempting a reconciliation with his wife, shot both her and himself when this failed. The papers at the time reported that McDonough had played for the Chicago Federal League team, but I can find no record of his having done so, or of anyone with a similar name, nor did I find any James McDonough in the high minors at the time. I don't know who he was.

May 6, 1918.   Chicago. E. F. Egan, manager of the Waterloo team in the Central Association, committed suicide in grief over the death of his wife.

August 18, 1920.   St. Louis. Otto Stifel, at one time a major stockholder in the St. Louis Browns, shot himself following a series of business reversals.

May 21, 1921.   Frankfort, Kentucky. Clay Dailey, a young pitcher, committed suicide in his depression over being cut by the Louisville team in spring training.

July 16, 1921.   Arthur Irwin, a major league player from 1880 to 1894, briefly a manager of the Giants, the man credited with inventing modern (padded) fielder's gloves, disappeared while en route from New York to Boston on a steamer. Irwin, who also invented other things such as a football scoreboard, and who spent several years as the secretary of the Yankees, was in poor health, despondent, and had stated before the trip that he was "going home to die." When the ship arrived in Boston he was not on board. His body was never found, and nothing more was ever learned of the circumstances of his death.

October 11, 1921.   Paris, Missouri. Noel Bruce, longtime minor league pitcher of the 1880s and 1890s, shot himself at the age of fifty-six.

December 25, 1923.   Orlando, Florida. Mrs. Joe Tinker, wife of the Hall of Fame shortstop, shot herself, aged 41.

December 11, 1924.   Memphis. John Wakefield, a young player who was the property of the St. Louis Cardinals, shot and killed himself after an argument with a girlfriend.

See also Johnny Mostil, CF#99 (page 779). If you'll look, you'll see that ballplayers almost never commit suicide in the summer. January is a big month for it, and December and March. June, July, August, and September are almost suicide-free for baseball players.

TEAM VERSUS TEAM

The acceptance of the American League as a major loop was not accomplished without a shot being fired. There is some disagreement among the experts as to how serious the National League was about the battle. David Voight, certainly one of the game's most qualified historians, opines that all the National League owners did was to "go through the motions of a war," but his is a minority opinion, and the facts upon which it is based are not apparent. "'Face' had to be saved," Voight says, and he goes on to detail the following list of face-saving gestures: snubs, court battles, ticket price-wars, counter salary offers to defectors, and encouraging other major league pretenders to move in on the Americans. The list is not exhaustive.

The major court battle was the Lajoie case. Napoleon Lajoie was the star second baseman of the Philadelphia team in the National League. The team would not initially meet Lajoie's 1901 salary request, and a bitter dispute ensued, after which Lajoie refused to sign with the Phillies at any price, and agreed instead to play for their new cross-town rivals under Connie Mack. The National League team sued, and attempted to force Lajoie to play for them. On May 17, 1901, a Philadelphia court turned them down, saying that the Phillies had made a one-way contract with Lajoie for 1901, and Lajoie was not bound by it. But on April 22, 1902, the supreme court of Pennsylvania ruled on appeal "that the provisions of the contract are reasonable and the consideration is fully adequate," meaning that Lajoie was bound by the National League contract after all.

American League President Ban Johnson got around that by transferring Lajoie (and other affected players) out of the state of Pennsylvania. Lajoie, playing for Cleveland, did not play in or travel through Pennsylvania, where he could have been arrested (a technique still used today by players being chased by paternity suits or other legal nuisances). The matter was put to rest when the two leagues made peace later in the 1902 season.

Voight feels that a settlement was reached so quickly because the National League teams quietly recognized the virtues of the old two-league system, under which baseball had thrived in the 1880s. It seems equally likely that this baseball war was short because the American League won it quickly and decisively. While there may have been something of a fudge factor involved, reported attendance in the American League in 1902 exceeded that of the established league by a whopping 32 percent. The American League team in Philadelphia was outdrawing the National League team almost 4 to 1. The National League accepted the American League as an equal not because they liked the idea, but because they had no choice.

THE 1908 PENNANT RACES

To give a modern fan the sense of it, the National League pennant race in 1908 was like the American League race in 1967, only with one of the teams being in New York and the other in Los Angeles, and with Kerry Wood or Livan Hernandez being called up by another team in September so he could make four starts against one of the teams that was trying to win the thing, and with one of the key games suddenly erupting into a major controversy which would necessitate the New York team making a special trip to Los Angeles for their 162nd game, which Roger Clemens is to pitch against Pedro Martinez, with a few odd death threats, riots, attempts to fix the game, fights between players and fans, and some loose talk about a strike thrown in for good measure. The world has never seen the like of it.

The American League race was equally phenomenal. On September first, four teams were separated by two and a half games. Three of those teams would stay hot in September, with the fourth dropping gradually out of the race.

The Cleveland Naps had opened a two-and-a-half game lead by September 24. When they staged a dramatic come-from-behind rally on September 26, the Cleveland crowd and three bands marched around the field in celebration.

They thought they had it won, but the Tigers had just commenced a ten-game winning streak that would put them a half-game in front by the end of September. On October 2, the Indians and the third team still in it, the White Sox, hooked up in perhaps the greatest pitcher's duel in the history of the game: Addie Joss threw a perfect game, while Ed Walsh struck out 15 in eight innings, losing 1–0. The Tigers kept their streak alive that day, but lost the next despite Ed Killian's one-hitter.

The last day of the season opened with three teams within half a game of one another. The Tigers had a previous rain-out which, under the rules of the time, did not have to be made up. On that basis, when the Tigers won that day they had won the race. No race has ever been closer.

The National League race of 1908 is now remembered as the greatest of all pennant races. But up until 1930, when people *actually* remembered the season, the two pennant races were remembered together, the greatest pennant races there ever were. The 1908 National League race has been the subject of classic sports journalism. A chapter on the final game of the National League campaign in *Pitching in a Pinch* is as fine a 5,000-word piece about baseball as has ever been written. The Merkle incident and the Harry Coveleski story are center-stage items in the incomparable *The Glory of Their Times*, and G. H. Fleming did a clippings book about the race, *The Unforgettable Season*, which is the standard of its field. There is another recent book about the season, *More Than Merkle;* I haven't had time to review it thoroughly yet.

1909: A MONKEY
ON THE LOOSE

The New Orleans team in the Southern League in 1909 kept some kind of a monkey as a mascot—a rather large creature, perhaps a chimp, known for his surly disposition. His name was Henry. On July 18, 1909, Henry escaped from his cage behind home plate and got into the stands, terrorizing the patrons and starting a stampede. The game was held up for several minutes as patrons headed for the exits and threw pop bottles at the rampaging ape. They finally succeeded in driving him back to the field where he could be captured and returned to his cage.

1909: THE MODERN
BALLPARK ARRIVES

When the American League went big time in 1901, it found itself several short in the ballpark department, and so it did what teams had been doing for forty years: they threw up a bunch of them. Three American League teams moved into or remained in existing facilities, while the other five ordered some wood to be purchased and pointed down the line that way and the other way and said, "Put up a ballpark here."

They were not, you see, "ballparks" in the modern sense of the word. The concept of the huge, permanent, sturdy, fireproof, grand, spacious, elegant thing that we now call a ballpark sprang into existence in 1907 or 1908. The first concrete-and-steel ballpark was Shibe Park, built in Philadelphia by one of the game's great innovators, Benjamin Shibe, in 1909. The second was built in 1909, the third in 1909, the fourth in 1909, and by 1916 there was hardly anything else in baseball.

The dramatic increase in the popularity of the sport had rendered the old ballparks archaic in two ways. The larger crowds demanded more seating, and the fattened wallets of the owners could now undertake larger investments. Shibe

Park opened on April 12, 1909. On opening day, 30,162 paying customers and several thousand invited guests attended, and were filled with an appropriate sense of history: nothing like this had ever existed before. It had three decks. It would be hard to overstate the excitement that the occasion generated. It was the first time that anyone had experienced something that is special to each of us now, that experience of looking around a grand ballpark for the first time and saying helplessly, "This place is really something, isn't it?" Thirty thousand people were experiencing that together. The park "has inaugurated a new era in base ball," said *The Sporting Life*.

Forbes Field in Pittsburgh opened on June 30 of the same year. Slightly smaller than Shibe (it seated 23,000), Forbes was regarded for years somewhat the way Camden Yards is regarded today, as the crown jewel in the diamond tiara. It was never the biggest, but it seemed the best—the sight lines were the best, it contained and expressed the enthusiasm of the crowd the best; it was just the best place to watch a baseball game. It was the first park to have the open walkway under the top deck. "Under the main seating area of the grand stand is a broad promenade, nearly as long as three city blocks and wider than most streets," reported the *Reach Guide*. The sense of grace and comfort that this imparted to the park was part of its charm, and so the promenade found its way into modern stadium design.

League Park in Cleveland and Sportsman's Park in St. Louis, existing parks, were reborn in concrete and steel by the time the year was up. While they didn't have the same stature or impact, those parks (with renovations) would serve major league teams for many years, and become a part of the affectionate memories of millions of people. The early years of the next decade would see more of the same. The throw-'em-up and let-'em-burn-down era of ballparks was over.

THE 1900 WHITE SOX

The American League was not built in a day into a major league. When the National League contracted in 1900, shrinking from a twelve-team to an eight-team league, the American League took in many of the dispossessed players. The American League was a minor league at that time; taking in these players was a strong step toward major league status.

The championship team in the American League in 1900, as it would be in 1901, was the Chicago White Sox. They were a minor league team in name only; almost all of the White Sox players had played in the major leagues before and would play in the majors again, and were near their prime. Their regular lineup was this:

1B–Frank Isbell
2B–Dick Padden
3B–Fred Hartman
SS–Frank Shugart
LF–Herm McFarland
CF–Dummy Hoy
RF–Steve Brodie
C– Joe Sugden
P– John Katoll
P– Roger Dezner
P– Chauncey Fisher
P– Roy Patterson

The team finished 82-53. An excellent article about them appears in the 1978 *Baseball Research Journal*.

1909: ALL QUIET ON THE EASTERN LEAGUE FRONT

On Sunday, April 18, 1909, the New York Highlanders (now the Yankees) played an exhibition game against the Jersey City team in the Eastern League, at Jersey City. The team, having had several run-ins with the law over playing ball on Sunday, distributed cards asking the patrons to avoid all cheering and rooting, so as to keep the noise down. The request was almost universally obeyed, and the Highlanders won, 6 to 3, in what was probably the quietest baseball game ever played before an audience of more than a thousand people.

A FEW WORDS ABOUT THE OLD MINORS

The minor leagues did not start out as what they are. By a long series of actions and agreements, inducements and rewards, the minor leagues were reduced in tiny degrees from entirely independent sovereignties into vassal states, existing only to serve the needs of major league baseball.

It is not my purpose to trace that march into bondage, who was where at what moment, what agreements had been signed, and who had signed them. That's another book. All I am trying to do is say a few things about minor league baseball, and have them understood by modern readers. I cannot do that if, when I say "minor leagues" you think of the minor leagues as they exist today. We are talking about a completely different animal.

The minor leagues as they existed a hundred years ago were something more like today's Mexican League, or perhaps a Japanese baseball league, except that rather than operating in another country in a foreign language, they operated in the hinterlands of the United States. They were *independent*. My experience has been that it is difficult to get people to internalize this concept to the point that they can stop coloring their understanding of what happened then with modern notions about "minor league" baseball. My experience has been that if you tell somebody about the brilliant minor league career of Ox Eckhardt, who had a career average of .367, they will say, "Wow, why didn't he ever get a chance?" No, no—it's not like that. He's not a player who *might* have done things if he'd had the chance. He's a player who *did* things. He played baseball. He made a good living playing baseball. His picture was on baseball cards; he was a local celebrity. The fact that he did these things in a league that was not the American or the National is important in its own way, but it doesn't make the things he did unreal or meaningless, as it would today; he *did* them. If he hit .370 one year, the reason he wanted to hit .380 the next was not so he would get "called up," but so he would get a better contract, just as if he were a major leaguer, or so his team might win the pennant, just as if that were a major league pennant.

Or Lefty Grove. Lefty Grove pitched for Baltimore in the International League for five years, going 12-2, 25-10, 18-8, 27-10, and 27-6. You tell people that and they say, "Why didn't he get called up sooner?" So you explain that his was an independent business; the Orioles were not inside of any structure for him to get "called up" through. It was up to the Baltimore owner to keep him, trade him, or sell him. So the next comment is usually, "Oh, I see. They were keeping him to run up his value to the major leagues." No, no, no; the major leagues didn't have anything to do with it. They were keeping him to win ball games. They were keeping him to draw crowds. He was *just playing baseball.*

When the major leagues were evolving, arbitrary decisions were made about where to put teams. St. Louis wound up with two teams and Milwaukee with none. Transportation placed geographic boundaries on the major leagues. San Francisco and Los Angeles grew into great cities without being drawn into the web, and these cities, along with others (like Atlanta, Kansas City, Louisville, Montreal, Seattle . . .) were condemned for fifty years to wear the label "bush league." They formed their own leagues, and they played their own baseball. It was not baseball at the "highest level"; the International League, though a good league, did not have as many good players as the American League or the National League. But the difference between the majors and the minors was a difference in *degree,* a difference in *calibre*—not an inequality of status. The Baltimore team was just as important to the Baltimore fans then as it is today.

While the major leagues were, as a whole, the best baseball going, there was not a one-to-one relationship between a ballplayer's abilities and major league status. A conservative assessment is that some of the players who made their living in the minor leagues were

JOHNNY LUSH

An eighteen-year-old first baseman/pitcher for the Phillies in 1904, Johnny Lush was the youngest regular player of this century. He hit a respectable .276 as a rookie (the league average was .249), though he lost all six of his starts as a pitcher. Despite this, Lush was converted to a more-or-less fulltime pitcher in 1906, winning eighteen games with a decent ERA. He faded after that, winding up with a career batting average of .249 (Clint Hartung's was .238) and a won-lost record of 66-86.

just as good as some of those who played for years in the majors. We know that this is true in several ways. For one thing, almost every player autobiography written between 1900 and 1960 says so. Unless the man writing the autobiography was a superstar, he would almost always say that there was a lot of luck involved in who made the majors and who didn't—that "several of the guys I played with back there were just as good as I was, but they didn't get the breaks." Many minor league players did get to play in the majors after long minor league careers, and often they were successful when that opportunity finally came. Minor league players sometimes earned more money than major league players. That is, not every minor league player was paid less than every major league player, as is the case today.

A more adventurous assessment would be that some of the best players in the game were in the minor leagues. Buzz Arlett may have been one of the best players in baseball between 1918 and 1937, at any level. Tony Freitas may have been one of the best pitchers of the 1930s. That statement would find many defenders among knowledgeable people and among people who played baseball in the 1920s and '30s. Many others would disagree.

A man tells his grandson now that he played twenty years in the minor leagues, and the grandson envisions him locked in a kind of perpetual adolescence, waiting twenty years for a chance to play some real baseball. Maybe they were not great players. Maybe they were not even as good as I think they were. But they were professional players, and they played it to the best of their abilities. That fact, at least, deserves to be remembered.

THE 1910s

HOW THE GAME WAS PLAYED

A cork-center baseball was invented by Ben Shibe in 1909 and marketed by the Reach company, which supplied baseballs for the American League, in 1911. Spalding followed, developing a cork-center ball for the National League. This caused batting levels to jump in 1911 and 1912. Runs scored per game in the American League in 1911 went from 3.6 to 4.6. Ty Cobb hit .420 in 1911 and .410 in 1912, and Joe Jackson hit .408 in 1911. Those are the only .400 seasons between 1901 and 1920.

In 1913 the pitchers regained control, largely due to the spreading use of the emery ball. While Ben Shibe was working on the new cork center ball, a modestly talented minor league pitcher named Russ Ford accidentally scuffed a baseball against a concrete wall, and noticed that it dived on the next pitch. Experimenting, Ford realized out that if you put just a little scratch on a baseball, you could make the thing dive like a falcon. He reached the majors in 1910, and went 26-6 his first year.

Ford had just put a little scratch on the ball, about the size of a dime, and had kept his pitch a secret by faking a spitball, which was a legal pitch. But after Ford lost his effectiveness, his secret spread around the American League, then the National; by 1913 everybody in baseball knew that you could make the ball dive by scratching it. And, as Roger Peckinpaugh recalled in *Baseball Between the Wars,* "now they weren't satisfied with a little spot the size of a dime, they wanted a bigger spot. They wound up scuffing about half the ball." Policy was that baseballs were used as long as they could be seen. If a ball was scratched, accidentally or on purpose, it remained in the game. By the middle part of the decade, all new baseballs were immediately defaced, dropped in the dirt, scratched on a button, or rubbed with sandpaper—and all games were played entirely with those kind of baseballs. By 1914 runs per game in the American League were back down to 3.7, 3.8 in the National League.

Baseball for the rest of the decade was a resumption of the dead-ball game of the years

1902–1910. Batting averages were low (around .250), home runs were rare (the normal league-leading figure was about twelve), and much of the basis of an offense was baserunning and strategy. Control pitchers again dominated the decade.

WHERE THE GAME WAS PLAYED

Major league cities during the decade, considering the Federal League to be a major league, included Baltimore, Boston, Brooklyn, Buffalo, Chicago, Cincinnati, Cleveland, Detroit, Indianapolis, Kansas City, Newark, New York, Philadelphia, Pittsburgh, St. Louis, and Washington. St. Louis in 1914 and 1915 had three major league teams.

WHO THE GAME WAS PLAYED BY

Shysters, con men, drunks, and outright thieves; I'm sure they were only a tiny portion of the baseball populace, but they are the ones who gave the decade its character, and the ones who are remembered.

The Irish tone of the game continued to wash out, and the game became to a considerable extent the property of midwestern farm boys who came out of cow pasture Sunday leagues. My father used to go to those games, and played in the leagues when he was older, and he talked about them some. Most of the dominant pitchers of the era were from my part of the country. Grover Cleveland Alexander was from Elba, Nebraska, about three hours drive from where I grew up. Jesse Barnes, who led the National League in wins in 1919 (25-9) was born in Oklahoma but grew up in the same county in Kansas that I did; his brother Virgil was also a pretty good pitcher.

I repeated that last paragraph as it appeared in the first edition of this book in 1985. What I did not know then, fifteen years ago, was that Jesse Barnes' mother was a James. My father was very proud of Jesse and Virgil Barnes, just because they were local boys who made good— but he never knew that they were his cousins. His father (my grandfather) had fallen out with his family after my great-grandfather divorced and re-married in the early 1880s. The Barneses were married in 1890, moved to Oklahoma (where Jesse was born in 1892), and then moved back to Kansas a year or two later. We all knew some of the Barneses; I played sports myself against members of the same family when I was growing up. But we had no idea, until recently, that they were relatives.

Anyway, resuming what I wrote fifteen years ago . . . Claude Hendrix, who led the National League in winning percentage while pitching for the Pirates in 1912 (24-9) and in 1917 while pitching for the Cubs (19-7), and who also won 29 games in the Federal League in 1914, was from Olathe, Kansas. The fabled 1912 matchup between Walter Johnson and Smokey Joe Wood was a matchup of two Kansans. Babe Adams, hero of the 1909 World Series and a 20-game winner in 1911 and 1913, began his career pitching for Parsons, Kansas, and was often referred to as a Kansan, although he was born in Indiana and grew up with relatives in Missouri.

Jeff Tesreau, who led the N.L. in ERA in 1912 and followed up with seasons of 22-13 and 26-10, was from Ironton, Missouri. Black Sox star Lefty Williams (23-11 in 1919, 22-14 in 1920) was from Aurora, Missouri, which was also the home town of even more famous crooks: Ma Barker and her boys and Alvin "Creepy" Karpis. Many fine position players also came from this area, including Sam Crawford, Ivy Olsen, Joe Tinker, Casey Stengel, and Fred Clarke, but for some reason the pitchers were most numerous.

The 1924 World Series featured the Senators, with Walter Johnson, against the Giants, with Virgil Barnes. This prompted Bill Corum to write that "Virgil prove(s) that while all the great pitchers may come from his state, they do not all come to Washington." To my regret, the Sunday leagues did not regain their momentum after World War I, and mostly died at the outset of the Depression. This region has produced relatively few good ballplayers since that time.

CHECKING IN:

1910— Wally Moses, Uvalda, Georgia
      Dixie Walker, Villa Rica, Georgia
1911— Walt Alston, Venice, Ohio
      Hank Greenberg, New York City
      Dizzy Dean, Lucas, Arkansas
      Joe Medwick, Carteret, New Jersey
1913— Richard Nixon, Yorba Linda, California
      Johnny Mize, Demorest, Georgia
1914— Joe DiMaggio, Martinez, California
      Jonas Salk, New York City
1915— Orson Welles, Kenosha, Wisconsin
      Kirby Higbe, Columbia, South Carolina
      Allie Reynolds, Bethany, Oklahoma
1916— Enos Slaughter, Roxboro, North Carolina
1917— Frank Sinatra, Hoboken
1918— Lou Boudreau, Illinois
      Bob Feller, Van Meter, Iowa
      Ted Williams, San Diego
      Pee Wee Reese, Ekron, Kentucky
1919— Jackie Robinson, Cairo, Georgia
      Ralph Houk, Lawrence, Kansas

CHECKING OUT:

1910— Mark Twain, 74
1911— Jack Rowe, 66
      Joseph Pulitzer, 64
      Will White, drowned, 62
      Bob Caruthers, 47 (1912 *Reach Guide* says he died of a nervous breakdown)
      Addie Joss, tubercular meningitis, 31
1912— Cupid Childs, 44
1914— Rube Waddell, tuberculosis, 37
      Harry Steinfeldt, paralysis, 38
1915— Albert Spalding, 65
      Booker T. Washington, 59
      Dave Orr, 55
      Ross Barnes, stomach illness, 54
1916— Rasputin, numerous causes, 45
1917— Wee Willie Sudhoff, 41
1918— Jim McCormick, 62
      Patsy Tebeau, suicide by gunshot, 54
      Jake Beckley, heart disease, 54
      Silent Mike Tiernan, tuberculosis, 51
      Eddie Grant, killed in the Argonne Forest, 35
1919— Jim O'Rourke, 66
      Teddy Roosevelt, 60

THE 1910s IN A BOX

Attendance Data:

Total: 56 million (55,681,347)

Highest: New York Giants, 1919   708,857
          Chicago White Sox   5,577,496

Lowest: Brooklyn Dodgers, 1918   83,831
          Boston Braves   2,088,310

Attendance, which exploded from 1900 to 1910, stagnated early in the decade and declined as the decade progressed, due to the distractions of the war, national and international chaos, and corruption in baseball. Attendance for the decade as a whole was up slightly from the previous decade, but was 22 percent less than it would have been had attendance per game simply stayed where it was in 1908–1909.

The average American in this era attended a major league baseball game about once every eighteen years.

Most Home Runs:

Babe Ruth,   1919   29

Gavy Cravath   116

Best Won/Lost Record by Team:

Boston Red Sox,   1912   105-47   .691

New York Giants   889-587   .602

In a decade dominated by the superteams of the A's, Red Sox, White Sox, and Giants, a much-maligned team missed by .005 of having the best won-lost record of the decade. That was the Cincinnati Reds of 1919, whose .686 winning percentage was the second-best of the ten-year period.

Worst Won/Lost Record by Team:

Philadelphia Athletics,   1916   36-117   .235

St. Louis Browns   599-892   .402

Index of Competitive Balance: 36%

The teens were the most competitive decade in baseball history up until the 1960s; each decade since the 1960s has been more competitive.

Most of this competition occurred in the National League. The National League was

highly competitive simply because no team in the league was actually very good.

At the end of the previous decade, 1906–1910, the National League was dominated by two great teams, the Cubs and the Pirates, with the Giants being the only other team which had any realistic chance to make a run. In 1911 the Giants slipped past the other two teams to become the dominant team, which is a historically normal type of rotation. Teams tend to take turns winning a few pennants, with rotations normally lasting about three to five years and gradual transitions between them.

After the Giants rotation, however (after their pennants in 1911 through 1913), the pennant was stolen by the Boston Braves, a down-and-out franchise having a miracle season. The legend of the Miracle Braves was one of baseball's most often-told stories for fifty years thereafter, until they were effectively ousted from their niche in baseball lore by the 1969 Mets.

In 1915 the National League pennant was won by the Philadelphia Phillies, who were essentially a similar team—a team which had finished sixth the previous season, and a team which had been in the National League since 1883 without winning anything. In 1916 it happened again; the Dodgers, who had been flat on their backs from 1904 through 1914, rose up and won the league. The Giants won in 1917, and the Cubs were in first place when the war terminated the 1918 season, but in 1919 there was yet another upset, as the Cincinnati Reds, who had been in the league since 1890, finally won the thing.

So this was one of the most competitive leagues in baseball history, with six different champions in six years. The problem was that most of these teams weren't really very good. The American League was nowhere near as competitive—because the American League had great teams.

The consequence of this was that the American League won the World Series in 1910, in 1911, in 1912, in 1913, in 1915, in 1916, in 1917, and in 1918. This is why the White Sox were prohibitive favorites in the 1919 World Series, a fact which has been misinterpreted by baseball historians. Any number of people have written that the 1919 White Sox were one of the greatest teams of all time. The 1919 Chicago White Sox were not a great team, at all, not by any standard.

The White Sox were heavy favorites not because the White Sox were a great team, but because they were the American League team, and the American League had been winning the World Series since 1910, with one exception. You know how people are; anything happens twice, a lot of people are going to figure it is destined to happen a third time. After the American League had won the World Series eight times in nine years, the American League team was a prohibitive favorite in the tenth.

Home-Field Winning Percentage: .540

Percentage of Regulars Hitting .300: 18%

Largest Home-Field Advantage: Brooklyn Dodgers, .105

The Dodgers were 383-350 in their home parks (.523), but 313-437 (.417) on the road. Ebbets Field opened in 1913; the gap is even wider if you exclude the years 1910–1912.

Having Their Best Decade Ever: New York Giants, Boston Red Sox

Having Their Worst Decade: New York Yankees

Heaviest Player: *Larry McLean

Lightest Player: A player named Larry McClure, who batted only once in the major leagues, is listed at 130 pounds. The smallest player of note was The Mighty Mite, Miller Huggins, who was 5′6½″ and weighed 140 pounds. Huggins used his size to good advantage, leading the National League in walks four times.

Listed at 5′6½″, 165 pounds, Pittsburgh infielder Buster Caton was probably even smaller than that. The 1919 *Reach Guide* refers to him as "the Pittsburgh Lilliputian," and there are many other references to his small size.

Most Strikeouts by Pitcher:

Walter Johnson,	1910	313
Walter Johnson		2,219

Highest Batting Average:

Ty Cobb,	1911	.420
Ty Cobb,		.387
	(1,951 for 5,037)	

Lowest Batting Average:

Tony Smith,	1910	.181
Sam Agnew		.204

Best Major League Players (By Years):
1910— Nap Lajoie
1911— Ty Cobb
1912— Tris Speaker

1913— Eddie Collins
1914— Tris Speaker
1915— Ty Cobb
1916— Tris Speaker
1917— Ty Cobb
1918— Babe Ruth
1919— Babe Ruth

Best Major League Pitchers (By Years):
1910— Jack Coombs
1911— Pete Alexander
1912— Walter Johnson
1913— Walter Johnson
1914— Walter Johnson
1915— Pete Alexander
1916— Pete Alexander
1917— Pete Alexander
1918— Walter Johnson
1919— Eddie Cicotte

Hardest-Throwing Pitcher: Walter Johnson

Best Curve: Jack Coombs

Best Power/Speed Combination: Home Run Baker

Best Switch Hitter: Max Carey

Iron Man: Everett Scott

Best Bunter: Ray Chapman

Best Baseball Books:
1912— *Pitching in a Pinch* (Christy Mathewson)
1915— *Alibi Ike* (Ring Lardner)
1916— *You Know Me, Al* (Ring Lardner)

Five Largest Changes in Baseball During the Decade:

1. Appearance of modern stadiums (actually begins 1909)
2. Strong move toward more players, see note below
3. Organization/structure of minor leagues
4. Hiring of coaches
5. Movements toward the commissioner system

Managers in this era (1910–1919) began to use a lot more players to play a game. From the beginning of professional baseball until the year 2000, managers have constantly expanded the number of players they used. This current was moving more rapidly about 1915 than at any other time.

Platooning, really began in 1914, although there had been experiments before, and by 1919 was as pervasive as it ever has ever been. The first true relief pitchers can be dated to 1915 (Sad Sam Jones) and 1917 (Dave Danforth). The record for relief appearances in a season in 1905 was 18. By 1919 the record was 41, and 20 was a commonplace figure.

John McGraw from 1910 to 1919 used several players as full-time pinch runners. Pinch hitting became much more common in this era. In 1904 several American League players tied for the league lead in pinch hits, with two apiece. That was no fluke; a common league-leading figure in that era was three or four. By 1914 Ham Hyatt had 58 at bats as a pinch hitter, and totals of 45 or more appearances were quite common by the end of the decade.

A relevant question is, "When was the roster fixed at 25 players?" I don't know the answer, but I believe that it was about 1917, and that this was done for two reasons. First, as managers began finding ways to use more players in a game—pinch hitters, pinch runners, relief pitchers, platoon players—the team's owners found a need to put a limit on it to control the expense. Second, as the minor leagues were organized, they wanted to limit the number of players who could be controlled by each franchise.

Best Outfield Arm: Tris Speaker

Worst Outfield Arm: George Burns

Most Runs Batted In:
Home Run Baker,   1912   130
Ty Cobb   828

Most Aggressive Baserunner: Ty Cobb

Fastest Player: Jim Thorpe or Hans Lobert

Slowest Player: Steve O'Neill

Best Control Pitcher: Babe Adams

Most Stolen Bases:
Ty Cobb, 1915	96
Ty Cobb	577

Best-Looking Player: Smokey Joe Wood

Ugliest Player: Rabbit Maranville

O.J. Simpson Award: Danny Shay or Sam Crane

Cap Anson Award: Ty Cobb

Ozzie Guillen Trophy: Art Fletcher

Bound for Glory: Harry Harper, a good left-handed pitcher with the Senators in 1916, went into the trucking and road construction businesses after he was out of baseball, and became a multimillionaire. He also ran (unsuccessfully) for the U.S. Senate from New Jersey.

Best Pitching Staff: 1913 New York Giants

Best Offense: 1913 Philadelphia Athletics

Football Players: Greasy Neale, Art Griggs, George Halas, Jim Thorpe, Ralph Capron, Shorty DesJardien, Al Elliott, Norm Glockson, Bruno Haas

Retrobermanisms:
Jack (Hi!) Nabors
Ray (Electric) Schalk

First of His Kind: Dolf Luque (first Latin American star)

Last of His Kind: Stan Baumgartner (Last player to become a prominent sportswriter after his playing career.)

One of a Kind: Ty Cobb

Best Infield: Philadelphia A's, 1911–1914
The famous $100,000 infield—Stuffy McInnis, Eddie Collins, Jack Barry, and Home Run Baker

Best Outfield: Detroit Tigers, 1915–1919 (Cobb, Bobby Veach, and Sam Crawford/Harry Heilmann)

A Better Man Than a Ballplayer: Sam Crawford

A Better Ballplayer Than a Human Being: Hal Chase

Mr. Dickens, I'd Like You to Meet: Eugene Hamlet Krapp (Also known as "Rubber Arm." Led American League in walks in 1911, but finished 14-9.)

Platoon Combinations I Would Like to See: Rebel Oakes and Slippery Ellam

Best Defensive Team: 1915 Boston Red Sox

*Clint Hartung Award: Walter Barbare

Outstanding Sportswriter: Heywoud Broun

Most Admirable Superstar: Christy Mathewson

Least Admirable Superstar: Ty Cobb

Gold Glove Team:
C—	Ray Schalk
1B—	Ed Konetchy
2B—	Eddie Collins
3B—	Heinie Groh
SS—	Rabbit Maranville
OF—	Hi Myers
	Tris Speaker
	Max Carey

Franchise Shifts: None (except the Federal League). However, in 1915 the Washington Senators were rumored to be moving to Toronto.

*New Stadiums:

1910— Comiskey Park, Chicago
Concrete Polo Grounds, New York
National Park, Washington
Destroyed by fire and rebuilt (became
Griffith Stadium)

1912— Fenway Park, Boston

1913— Ebbets Field, Brooklyn
Navin Park, Detroit

1914— Terrapin Park, Baltimore
Weegham Park, Chicago (became
Wrigley Field in 1916)

1915— Braves Field, Boston

Best Pennant Race: 1915 Federal League

*Best World Series: 1912, Boston (A) defeated New York (N) in eight games, series remembered for Snodgrass' Muff

Best-Hitting Pitcher: I'd guess maybe Babe Ruth

Worst-Hitting Pitcher: Rip Hagerman or Ernie Koob

Best Minor League Team: Minneapolis Millers, 1910–11

The Millers picked up players who bounced out of the major leagues, paid them good salaries, and gave them a chance to play their way back to the show. The team in 1910 and/or 1911 included Gavy Cravath, Rube Waddell, Sam Leever, Claude Rossman, Jimmy Williams, Hobe Ferris, Dave Altizer, Otis Clymer, Nick Altrock, and Long Tom Hughes.

Best Minor League Player: Joe Riggert

Odd Couple: Two men more different than Christy Mathewson and John McGraw would be difficult to find; they were the Billy Martin and the Greg Maddux of their time. They got along great. McGraw wanted to win more than he wanted anything else, and Mathewson could win games for him. Matty wanted to

be respected more than he wanted anything else, and McGraw treated him with respect. When McGraw was suspended for a time during 1914, a board of three men ran the team. Larry Doyle ran the team on the field and made pinch-hitting decisions, Mathewson ran the pitching staff, and Mike Donlin took care of the umpires.

Drinking Men:

Slim Sallee
Pete Alexander
Josh Devore
Mike Donlin
Larry McLean
Ray Caldwell
Billy Southworth
Oscar Stanage
Stan Baumgartner

New Equipment:

Resin bags (about 1910)

Player vs. Team: Ty Cobb regularly battled the Tigers for more money. He usually was asking to be paid more than Tris Speaker. The Tigers doggedly refused to match Speaker's salary. When the Federal League started in 1914, Cobb held out and threatened to jump. The Tigers responded by threatening to trade him for Speaker. At one point, a Cobb-for-Speaker swap reportedly was near to completion, but the Tigers eventually agreed to make Cobb the highest paid player in the game. Until the Federal League folded.

Team vs. Team: See article, "The Feds"

Uniform Changes:

Stirrups
Smaller collars
Team nicknames on uniforms

New Terms or Expressions: For a few years, from about 1910 to 1916, baseball fans were commonly known as "bugs." Then the older term "fans" came back into use.

The term "rookie" was apparently first used about this time, although it was not common for another twenty years. The term "bush leagues," although in existence earlier, became common in this era. The term "pinch hitter" developed in its modern sense during this period. The term "pinch" was used at the turn of the century the way the word "clutch" is used today; a "clutch" situation was referred to as "in a pinch," and a player who hit well in those situation was "a good pinch hitter." Since a substitute batter was most often used in such a situation, the term pinch hitter came to mean a substitute hitter, and the original usage of the term died out.

Most Wins by Pitcher:
Walter Johnson,　1913　　　36
Walter Johnson　　　　　265

Highest Winning Percentage:
Smokey Joe Wood,　1912　34-5　　.872
Smokey Joe Wood　　　　104-49　.680
(Pete Alexander had almost the same winning percentage as Wood, .675, with more than twice as many decisions.)

Lowest Winning Percentage:
Jack Nabors,　1916　　　1-20　　.048
Pete Schneider　　　　58-86　　.403
(See Article, Pete Schneider)

Flameout: Josh Devore

All Offense/No Defense: 1915 New York Giants. The 1914 Brooklyn Dodgers had four of the top five hitters in the National League, but nonetheless finished fifth. Their offense wasn't really very good—they just had a bunch of guys who hit singles.

All Defense/No Offense: 1919 Chicago Cubs

Homer: Gavy Cravath led the National League in home runs in 1913, 1914, 1915, 1917, 1918, and 1919, although he had only 219 at bats in 1919. A lot of people think that Cravath was the first great power hitter, or the Babe Ruth of his era or something.

But Cravath played in a park, the Baker Bowl, which was by far the easiest place in baseball to hit a home run. In 1914, when Cravath led the National League with 19 home runs, he never homered in any other park; all 19 were hit in the Baker Bowl. In 1918, same thing; Cravath led the National League in home runs with 8, but all of them were at home.

Cravath in his career actually hit fewer home runs in road games (26) than Nellie Fox (30).

Yellowstone Park Award: Ty Cobb

Cravath and Cobb, who were about the same age, hit almost the same number of career home runs (119 for Cravath, 117 for Cobb). But Cobb hit only 35 home runs in his home park. In road games, he hit more than three times as many as Cravath (82 to 26).

Tough-Luck Season: Ed Walsh, 1910

Could I Try This Career Over? George Whiteman [See page 117]

Minor Leagues Were:
85 percent free
15 percent slaves to the majors

Best Double Play Combination: Dots Miller and Honus Wagner, 1911 Pittsburgh Pirates.

Worst Double Play Combination: Donie Bush was the shortstop for the Detroit Tigers from 1909 until mid-season, 1921. He was a good offensive player, and the Win Shares system rates him as deserving of the American League's gold glove at shortstop in 1909 and 1911, but he was apparently terrible at turning the double play. During the first half of the Bush era, the Tigers changed their regular second baseman every year—Germany Schaefer in 1909, Jim Delahanty in 1910, Charlie O'Leary in 1911, Baldy Louden in 1912, Ossie Vitt in 1913, Marty Kavanaugh in 1914. In spite of this effort, or because of it, the Tigers had the poorest double play results in the league every single season, −18 in 1909, −28 in 1910, −25 in 1911, −33 in 1912, −20 in 1913, and −20 in 1914.

In 1915 the Tigers settled on Ralph Young as their second baseman; he held the position for the rest of the Donie Bush era. They did better with Young, but not much. They were −5 in 1915, −18 in 1916, −25 in 1917, −23 in 1918, and −19 in 1919, avoiding finishing last in the league in all of those seasons except 1918. In 1920–21, however, they dropped back to −38 and −33, finishing last in the league once again. For the thirteen seasons that Bush was their regular shortstop, the Tigers were almost 300 double plays below expectation.

In 1914, under player/manager Red Dooin, the Philadelphia Phillies missed their expected double plays by a whopping 36, and finished sixth in the National League with a record of 74-80. Pat Moran took over the team in 1915, and, while the rest of the Phillies' lineup remained largely intact, changed the double play combination. The second baseman, Bobby Byrne, was sent to third base, and the starting shortstop, Jack Martin, was released; they were replaced by Bert Niehoff, acquired in exchange for Red Dooin, and Dave Bancroft, a rookie. The 1915 Phillies slightly exceeded their double play expectation, and vaulted to the pennant.

Paul Krichell Talent Scout Award: Tom Meany wrote a book in 1949, *Baseball's Greatest Teams*, in which he wrote that "the key man on the 1917 White Sox was Arnold (Chick) Gandil, who two years later was to be the key man of the scandal . . . Be that as it may, it was Gandil who made the 1917 Sox." That is a terrific book, and I respect the fact that Meany was closer to the team than I am, writing about it thirty years later, as opposed to eighty years later.

But the White Sox decision to dump Jack Fournier at first base and replace him with Chick Gandil has got to rank among the worst talent decisions in the history of baseball. I will grant you that

(a) Gandil was a better defensive first baseman, and

(b) Defense at first base may have been dramatically more important at that time than it is now.

But Fournier was an adequate first baseman, and one of the outstanding hitters of his generation. He hit .311 in 1914, .322 in 1915—with a lot of walks, and with power. That was battling the dead baseballs. When the lively ball era arrived, and Fournier re-established himself in the majors, then he posted some real numbers. But he was just as good a hitter in Chicago as he would be in Brooklyn; it's just that the numbers don't look as good because in Chicago he was playing in a pitcher's park in a league with a 2.73 ERA. Fournier's 1914 season in Chicago, in context, was a tremendous season—28 Win Shares, by my math. A good many people have won MVP Awards with less.

Fournier had a slow start in 1916, and Clarence Rowland replaced him with a player who

(a) contributed absolutely nothing with the bat, even if he hit .280, and

(b) engineered the fixing of the World Series.

I don't know if honesty can be considered a talent, but that is one lousy exchange.

Best Unrecognized Player: The three best players of this era who are not in the Hall of Fame are Sherry Magee, Larry Doyle, and Ed Konetchy.

Highest-Paid Player: Tris Speaker (about $18,000)

New Statistics:
Earned Run Averages
Batters Facing Pitcher
Sacrifice Hits Allowed
Strikeouts and walks (for batters)

The strikeout and walk totals for early batters which exist now were figured in the late 1960s by Information Concepts, Incorporated in the process of making the first Macmillan Encyclopedia. The early players who walked a lot, like Topsy Hartsel, Roy Thomas, and Miller Huggins, did not know at the time how many walks they had drawn.

Batter's strikeouts and walks as official statistics were introduced in 1910, by John A. Heydler, then Secretary of the National League. Acknowledging them in the 1911 *Reach Guide*, Francis Richter wrote that "The figures are of no special value or importance—first, because the number of strikeouts affords no real line on the player's batting ability, especially under the foul-strike rule; and second,

because bases on balls are solely charged to the pitcher, beyond the control of the batsman, and therefore not properly to be considered in connection with his individual work, except as they may indicate in a vague way his ability to 'wait out' or 'work' the pitcher."

A Very Good Movie Could Be Made About: The Miracle Braves

Five Biggest Things Wrong with Baseball:

1. Crooked players
2. Segregation
3. Constant lawsuits
4. Dirty, scratched-up baseballs/poor fields
5. Lack of central authority/inability to fix problems

I Don't Know What This Has to Do with Baseball, But I Thought I'd Mention It Anyway: In the fall of 1914, pitcher Jim Scott was taking a tour of the Illinois State Reformatory at Pontiac, Illinois. The inmates were playing a Sunday afternoon baseball game and Scott sat down to watch. In the third inning one of the pitchers faded. The convicts asked Scott to join in. Scott went to the mound, and pitched six-plus innings of one-hit, shutout baseball, for which he was given a standing ovation by the prisoners. He was, said the 1915 *Reach Guide*, the first player to pitch in prison without being detained after the game.

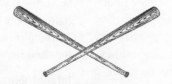

THE FEDS

The existence of the Federal League is the central fact of baseball in the 1910–19 era.

In 1914 some rich guys got together and decided to start a new major league, which they called the Federal League. This is abbreviating the story to the point of distortion; the Federal League actually played in 1913, although not as a major league, and not everybody involved in the effort was rich. Anyway, the league built eight new parks, one of which is now known as Wrigley Field. The league attempted to attract major league stars away from the American and National Leagues, and had fair success. Among those who played in the league were Joe Tinker, Chief Bender, Claude Hendrix, Three Finger Brown, Ed Konetchy, Hal Chase, Ed Reulbach, Russ Ford, Doc Crandall, Howie Camnitz, and many others with unmistakable major league pedigrees. The Federal League copied the economic form that the other leagues had refined through years of trial and error. It was an eight-team league playing a 154-game schedule—exactly the form arrived at by the National and American Leagues. Bidding wars erupted after the Feds lured away a couple of stars, and salaries went through the roof. The Federals didn't attract enough customers to pay their bills, and so, at the end of the 1915 season, most of the Federal League owners sold out their assets to the existing leagues, forcing the league to fold.

The Federal League was a well-organized, well-financed, well-thought-out effort to construct a new league. I am inclined to believe that, had the Federal League been born at another time, it might have well have become established. It happened to come at a remarkable moment in American history, a time of strife and dissension, a period of high expectations and revolutionary fervor:

The year 1914 will ever be a black one in human history, owing to world-wide dissensions and upheavals which culminated in the World War . . . External causes of decline [in baseball include] the political unrest and revolution in the nation; the constant harassment and depression of the country's big and little business; [and the] incessant distracting and disquieting exploitation of social, individual and financial theories, which had become a local as well as a national mania. —1915 *Reach Baseball Guide*

This coincided with a fierce recession in the baseball business, a recession which broke not just the Federal League, but more than twenty other leagues as well—the original Appalachian League, the Atlantic League, the Bi-State league, the Border League, the Buckeye League, the California State League, the Canadian League, etc. It was just the wrong time to be starting a new baseball league, and the Federal League couldn't overcome that.

But while the Federal League did not survive, it changed everything. The Federal League sent salaries sky-rocketing. The salary rocket forced the breakup of the best team in baseball, the Philadelphia Athletics, whose players were sold off. The salaries forced Jack Dunn, owner/manager of the minor league Baltimore Orioles, to put his 19-year-old star pitcher, Babe Ruth, up for sale (otherwise Ruth would have spent several years, perhaps even a decade, in Baltimore.) The two teams that were able to buy talent, the Boston Red Sox and the Chicago White Sox, replaced the Athletics as the best teams in baseball.

When the Federal League folded, salaries tumbled. Players in their prime were forced to sign new contracts for a third of what they had gotten when the Federal League was standing. Some players were bitter about that. Some of those bitter players are the key figures in the big story of the decade: the Black Sox scandal.

When the rest of the Federal League owners folded, the owner of the Baltimore Terrapins had his own agenda: he wanted a major league team in Baltimore. He filed suit against major league baseball, charging Organized Baseball with violations of the Sherman Antitrust Act—that is, acting as a monopoly. This suit eventually reached the Supreme Court, and resulted in baseball being declared outside the reach of antitrust law. This ruling, while it has long since been acknowledged to be peculiar, allowed Organized Baseball to operate as a legal monopoly for many years.

The ruling in *Federal Baseball Club of Baltimore, Inc. v. National League of Prof'l Baseball Clubs, Inc.,* 259 U.S. 200 (1922), which was written by Oliver Wendell Holmes, has been routinely characterized as ruling that "Baseball is a sport, not a business." If you read the decision, you will realize that this is a grotesque misrepresentation. It is true that the defendants in this case—Organized Baseball—did make a legal argument which could accurately be summarized as "Baseball is a sport, not a business." It is true that the people making that argument won. But the federal appeals court which ruled in favor of Organized Baseball, and the Supreme Court in the Oliver Wendell Holmes opinion, clearly stated that the sale of baseball games was a business, and emphasized this point by drawing parallels between baseball and other businesses.

The ruling in *Federal Baseball* was, appropriately, a federalist decision. Baseball was beyond the reach of antitrust law, the Supreme Court ruled, because it was not, at its core, an *interstate* business. A baseball team, the Supreme Court said, is in the business of selling baseball games to the people in its own state. It is not selling anything that comes from out of state, therefore it is not interstate commerce, therefore it cannot be regulated by the federal government.

But while the ruling absolutely does not say anything that can be represented as "Baseball is a sport, not a business," it is, nonetheless, an odd and puzzling decision. People who write about this decision often seem to miss a very obvious reason why the case was decided in an odd way.

In *Total Baseball,* Gary D. Hailey and Douglas R. Pappas report that "the court of appeals (which wrote the decision later affirmed by the Supreme Court) heard oral arguments on October 15, 1920, only three days after the final game of the World Series was played between the Cleveland Indians and the Brooklyn Dodgers." What is not mentioned, but what is a thousand times more important, is that the case was heard only three weeks after the Black Sox scandal broke. Revelations about baseball being sold out were appearing in the newspapers daily *while the appeal was being heard.*

And when you think about it, what does a crooked baseball player believe? *He believes that baseball is a business, not a sport.* Isn't that a precise statement of the thought process of the athlete who sells out? What does the crook who sets it up say to his teammates? He says, "We're in this for the money, aren't we? We're not doing this for our health; we're not doing this for fun. We're *professionals.* We're doing it for the money."

So the appeals court which ruled in favor of Organized Baseball heard the case with a monster looking over their shoulders: the monster of professionalism run amok. The court was asked, in essence, "Must the issues of money govern the sport?" But the court was asked that question in a highly unusual context, in which the worst consequences of putting money ahead of the sporting interest had just been dramatically demonstrated. This unusual circumstance is reflected in an odd decision.

MAJOR LEAGUE ALL-STAR TEAM 1910–1919

Records in seasonal notation, based on 154 games. Pitchers based on 45 starts.

Pos.	Player	Years	Hits	HR	RBI	Avg.	Other
C	Chief Meyers	5.86	131	2	57	.293	
1B	Ed Konetchy	9.29	159	5	74	.282	
2B	Eddie Collins	9.36	180	2	73	.326	89 BB, 52 SB
3B	Home Run Baker	8.15	185	9	97	.310	
SS	Honus Wagner	6.77	166	5	77	.296	
LF	Joe Jackson	7.62	203	6	86	.354	19 Triples
CF	Tris Speaker	9.34	195	4	78	.344	45 Doubles
RF	Ty Cobb	8.66	225	5	96	.387	67 Steals

Pitcher	Years	Won-Lost	SO	ERA	Other
RH Walter Johnson	9.25	29–15	240	1.59	371 Innings
RH Pete Alexander	7.55	28–13	204	2.07	
RH Christy Mathewson	5.13	27–15	139	2.39	Only 39 Walks
LH Hippo Vaughn	6.90	22–16	182	2.32	

1916: OLD BALLPLAYERS NEVER DIE

"Base ball today is not what it should be. The players do not try to learn all the fine points of the game as in the days of old, but simply try to get by. They content themselves if they get a couple of hits every day or play an errorless game. The first thing they do each morning is to get the papers and look at the hit and error columns. If they don't see them, some sportswriter gets a terrific panning, of which he never hears.

"When I was playing ball, there was not a move made on the field that did not cause every one of the opposing team to mention something about it. All were trying to figure why it had been done and to watch and see what the result would be. That same move could never be pulled again without every one on our bench knowing just what was going to happen.

"I feel sure that the same conditions do not prevail today. The boys go out to the plate, take a slam at the ball, pray that they'll get a hit, and let it go at that. They are not fighting as in the days of old. Who ever heard of a gang of ball players after losing going into the clubhouse singing at the top of their voices? That's what happens every day after the games at the present time.

"In my days, the players went into the clubhouse after a losing game with murder in their hearts. They would have thrown out any guy on his neck if they had even suspected him of intentions of singing. In my days the man who was responsible for having lost a game was told in a man's way by a lot of men what a rotten ball player he really was. It makes me weep to think of the men of the old days who played the game and the boys of today. It's positively a shame, and they are getting big money for it, too."

—Bill Joyce

As quoted in the 1916 *Spalding Base Ball Guide*. Joyce was a third baseman and manager in the 1890s.

PETE SCHNEIDER

Pete Schneider pitched for the Cincinnati Reds from 1914 to 1918, also pitched briefly for the Yankees in 1919. He won 20 games in 1917 (20-19), but had a losing record the other years, and had the worst winning percentage of any pitcher with 100 decisions in the decade (58-86), although actually that's not all that bad.

Schneider moved to the outfield after he had an arm injury in 1919. On May 11, 1923, Schneider was playing right field for Vernon of the Pacific Coast League, at Salt Lake City. In his first at bat, in the first inning, he hit a two-run home run. Vernon scored four in the first, three more in the second, bringing Schneider back to the plate in the second inning. He hit into a forceout, making him one for two.

In the third inning Vernon batted around again, scoring four runs and re-loading the bases before Schneider came back to the plate. Schneider hit a grand slam home run, making it 15 to 2; Schneider had two homers, six RBI.

Up again in the fourth inning, Schneider added a three-run homer; it was 20-2, and Schneider had nine RBI. He didn't bat in the fifth, but in the sixth he drilled the ball off the very top of the centerfield wall for a double. (You may remember that Joe Adcock, in his four-homer game against the Dodgers in 1954, also hit a line drive double off the very top of the centerfield fence.) Vernon scored four in that inning, making it 24-4.

Seventh inning, 24-5; Schneider batted with the bases loaded. Home Run. His second Grand Slam of the game; he had four homers, a double, and 13 RBI. The inning went on, and on, and on; by the time Schneider came back to the plate the bases were empty, but the score was 34-5. Schneider homered again, his second of the inning, fifth of the game; he had 14 RBI.

He batted again in the ninth inning, and hit a screeching liner to center field, caught by the center fielder. The game ended 35-11.

Schneider's five homers in a game are not a record. Jay Clarke, you may remember, hit eight home runs in a game for Corsicana in July, 1902. But that was in a 51-3 game in a borrowed park in a league so low on the ladder that the players still had one foot in the primordial swamp. This was in a good minor league, against two pretty good pitchers—Walt Kinney, who would be back in the majors before the season was out, and Fritz Coumbe, who had been a major league pitcher for several years.

Schneider never made it back to The Show. He was third in the PCL in batting average that year, .360, with 43 doubles, 23 triples, 19 home runs, and he was only 27 years old. But in 434 major league at bats (in his years as a pitcher), Schneider had struck out 100 times, and drawn only 5 walks. He would never get the chance to improve on his .221 lifetime major league average.

BASEBALL WRITING IN THE TEENS

1912—Christy Mathewson's *Pitching In a Pinch* (ghosted by John Wheeler) is one of the first "inside" views of the game.

1912—The beginning of Lester Chadwick's (one of the many pseudonyms of Edward Stratemeyer, who also used the name Franklin Dixon to write the Hardy Boys books, and Carolyn Keane for Nancy Drew) "Baseball Joe" novels. Joe, a combination of Frank Merriwell and Christy Mathewson, was a model to his young readers, including Mark Harris.

1915—Ring Lardner's "Alibi Ike," the classic story of the rookie who middle name, X., stood for "excuse me."

1916—Ring Lardner's *You Know Me, Al,* the first baseball novel for grown-ups, and still one of the best.

—Jim Carothers

NICKNAMES

Quite a few "modified proper names" emerged as nicknames in the teens, often enriched by alliteration. Larry Doyle was "Laughing Larry," Solly Hofman was "Circus Solly," Bill Raridon was "Bedford Bill," Joe Jackson was "Shoeless Joe," Hal Janvrin "Childe Harold," and Hal Chase the first baseball "Prince Hal." Otherwise, one-word nicknames were the rule of the day. Walter Barbare was "Dinty," Lena Blackburne was called "Slats," Eddie Collins was called "Cocky," Fritz Maisel was "Flash," Fritz Moll-witz was "Zip," Everett Scott was "Deacon," Ray Schalk was "Cracker," George Stovall was "Firebrand," and Dick Rudolph was "Baldy." These nicknames were useful, because they carried an image of the player, of something he could do or the way he looked. On occasion they could place a nickname among the classics, such as for Benny Meyer, who was called "Earache," or Jim Shaw, who was called "Grunting Jim."

The three-word form of nickname, beginning with "The ..." emerged in the teens. The only four players from this decade for whom I noted that form of nicknames were Ty Cobb (The Georgia Peach), Walter Johnson (The Big Train), Tris Speaker (The Grey Eagle), and Miller Huggins (The Mighty Mite). This was a popular form for more than fifty years. Mickey Mantle was "The Commerce Comet," Ted Williams was "The Splendid Splinter," Joe DiMaggio was "The Yankee Clipper," Frankie Frisch was called "The Fordham Flash," Stan Musial was "The Donora Greyhound," and Carl Hubbell was known as "The Meal Ticket." Dozens of medium level stars had nicknames in that form, like Carl Furillo (The Reading Rifle) and Dom DiMaggio (The Little Professor), but very few poor or mediocre players. The use of the definite article "The" implies a uniqueness on the part of the player named. The adjective (the second word) serves to enhance that uniqueness. If more than three words are involved the name tends to acquire a comic tone (The Freshest Man on Earth, The Wild Horse of the Osage).

WELL TONED

Fred Toney is remembered for pitching a ten-inning no-hitter in the same game that another big horse, Hippo Vaughn, threw nine innings of no-hit ball. Toney was famous for his great strength. He is listed at 195 pounds in the encyclopedias, but the 1918 *Reach Guide* described him as "well over 200 pounds in perfect physical condition." When he came to the big leagues he used to amaze his teammates by performing feats of strength. It was said that he could lift more weight than any two of his teammates combined.

In the minors in 1909, Toney threw a seventeen-inning no-hitter. He was pitching for Winchester, Kentucky, in the Blue Grass League.

It was May 10th, and Winchester had only one loss; they were facing the only team which had beaten them, Lexington. The 1910 *Reach Guide* reported that "throughout the city business was almost suspended, the bulletin boards being the only thing people thought of. When the victory was announced all the whistles in the town sounded and crowds went wild." They were just excited about the win; remember, the term and concept of the "no-hitter" did not exist at that time. In the seventeen innings Toney struck out nineteen and walked only one; his pitching opponent also went the distance, allowing six hits. The 17-inning game was completed in two hours, forty-five minutes.

UNIFORMS OF THE TEENS

Uniform developments in this decade were mostly in the form of refinements. The collars became smaller. Many more uniforms featured a short, stand-up collar, similar to that of a Nehru jacket. A contrasting band around the neck and sleeve was common, as well as a bit of trim work up the sides of the pants and around the neckline. An ad in one guide proudly offers a uniform with "Gusset Ventilated Sleeves" which allow the player greater movement and better ventilation. The belt loops on the left and right sides of some uniforms were elongated and called tunnel loops; the loops of today are much the same. Belts became narrower. Most teams were still using the traditional dark solid stockings, as the popularity of stripes and garish colors ran its course, for the time. The double breasted suit jacket which was probably intended as a warm up jacket (but perhaps was only worn for formal occasions) faded from use by 1910. Big, bulky sweaters took over, sometimes in spectacular knitted forms. The cover of a *Baseball Magazine* in 1914 features Walter Johnson wearing a beautiful knitted sweater/jacket uniform in colors of red, gold and blue.

The basic style of the uniform was by now traditional, and much the same from team to team. The next area for experimentation was the team name. Philadelphia, the two Chicago teams, the Red Sox and Pirates used their team nicknames (which ten years earlier had been informal, and subject to change at the whim of a sportswriter) on their uniforms. On one, "Chicago Cubs" is spelled out in full; on a second is a large C with a little cubbie inside, and on a third, a rectangular C encloses the letters UBS. Chicago seems to have been a hotbed for

this kind of innovation, because the other team in town showed similar diversity. A big S on the left side of the shirt enclosed an O in the top loop and an X in the bottom. The big S is variously decorated with little balls or bats or socks. Flags on the sleeve denote either post-war patriotism or league loyalty. The Washington team also displayed an American flag on the left breast pocket, with a weak-looking W on the sleeve. The Philadelphia White Elephants attached a little elephant to the left breast pocket, and the Denver Bears used a bear symbol in the same place.

In 1911 the Yankees and the Athletics were given permission by the league to use for their home uniform a white flannel cloth with "fine stripes." But there were earlier instances of pinstripes. The Detroit Wolverines in 1888 wore white shirts with thin stripes, dark pants; pinstripes show up in Chicago in 1907 and in St. Louis in 1910. In the *Ultimate Baseball Book* a photo of Larry Lajoie shows him in a Cleveland pinstriped uniform; no date is given but a blurrier version of the same photo, much smaller, appears in the 1910 *Spalding Guide,* meaning that it was taken no later than 1909. The Boston Braves introduced a checkered look, which would make a used car salesman proud, in the 1907 road uniform.

As noted in *Baseball Uniforms of the 20th Century,* numbers on uniforms first appear in Cleveland in 1916. The numbers were attached to the sleeves. The practice did not catch on immediately, and we will wait until the early thirties for the large numbers to establish themselves on the backs of uniforms where they're supposed to be.

1910: GLAD YOU NOTICED

For the first thirty-plus years of major league baseball, a no-hitter had no particular significance. When Lee Richmond and John Montgomery Ward threw perfect games just a few days apart in 1880, the press took no particular note of it. When Henry Porter of Kansas City threw a no-hitter at Baltimore in June of 1888, a Kansas City paper reported the game the next day without commenting on the uniqueness of the event. A week later, they observed that when Porter had pitched the game without giving up a hit in Baltimore, this was "believed to be the first time all season" that it had been done. They were wrong. Adonis Terry of Brooklyn had hurled a no-hitter ten days earlier.

As late as 1907, the no-hitter still meant little. When Frank Pfeffer of Boston threw a no-hitter on May 8, the summary of the game in the *New York Times* read: "Pfeffer shut out Cincinnati without a hit or a run today and Boston won easily, 6 to 0. Runs came through bunching hits in four innings." That, and the box score, was all there was; it was the briefest account given to any game played that day.

Within a few years this would change; when Miles Main threw a no-hitter in the Federal League in 1915, the Kansas City paper reported that he had knocked on the door of the

Hall of Fame and been admitted, presenting the no-hitter as his credential.

Why, how, and yet more precisely when the recognition of no-hitters began is an interesting question. A game in there somewhere may have grabbed the public's imagination, although I doubt it. The *Reach Guides* in 1911 inaugurated a special feature on low-hit games—a feature so successful that it is still a part of the modern guides. My guess is that that was the lens which focused attention on outstanding performances in general, of which the no-hitter was of course the king.

From our vantage, the question seems to be not how it developed, but how it could have taken so long to develop. It's such a perfect diversion for the early innings of a game. Although I have been to hundreds of games and have never seen a no-hitter, I still think about it almost every time I'm at the park. I think about it when the first batter gets out or when he gets a hit, I think about it when either side goes in order in the first, and I think about it whenever I look up at the scoreboard and see that 0 0 0. Each day the pitcher plays Russian Roulette with sudden immortality, and each day he loses, and after the fourth inning it is all forgotten.

WALTER BARBARE

The 1915 *Reach Guide,* published after Barbare had played only fifteen major league games, said that several observers, who are named in the article, "claim that Walter Barbare . . . is the best young infielder they have seen in years. [He] is a freak in build and endowed with nature's ball-playing weapons. He has abnormally long arms and wide hands, and possesses wonderful natural knowledge of batsmen. He never rests his hands upon his

knees . . . but stands in a crouched position with his long arms swinging and his hands almost touching the ground. He reminds one of a gorilla and is remarkably fast in starting from this peculiar, but natural, position. He is a fast man on the bases and looks like a hard and natural hitter." Barbare hit .191 in 77 games that year, and played but 500 games in the major leagues, hitting .260 with only one home run.

LARRY McLEAN

Although three pitchers who didn't pitch fifty innings among them are listed at 230, the biggest player of the time was a lean, mean, fightin' machine named (would I make this up?) Larry McLean. His legal name was John Bannerman McLean, and he was born in Cambridge, Massachusetts, and grew to be 6'5", 228 pounds. He played thirteen years in the major leagues, hitting .262, and hit .500 in the 1913 World Series (6 for 12).

According to the 1922 *Reach Guide,* "McLean was a man of great size, a convivial disposition and a bad temper when under the influence of liquor, which led him into many more or less serious rows during his baseball career ... (after the) 1913 World Series, his habits were such that Manager McGraw was forced to release him." After that he was reportedly connected with the movie business for several years.

On March 24, 1921, McLean was shot and killed by a bartender in Boston's South End. His friend Jack McCarthy, who also played in the National League for several years, was injured in the fracas. The bartender was given a light sentence, it being shown that McLean and McCarthy were the aggressors in the incident.

1914: THE OLD FOG SCAM

The Memphis Park in the Southern League, like many parks of the era, minor and major league, had several signs painted on the outfield walls. Hit This Sign and Win a Suit ... Knock it Here and Win a Quart of Red Eye ... Bump This Fence and get a dozen Never-Wear-Out socks, etc. Mickey Finn, who managed the Memphis team in 1914, claimed that one time a fog moved in so thick you couldn't see the outfield fence. One of his outfielders hit a drive out there somewhere and collected a suit, two bottles of booze, the sox, a hat and a pound of coffee.

Many hitters of the time claimed that these outfield signs were distracting, and interfered with their hitting. This poem, unattributed, appeared in the 1915 *Reach Guide:*

> The fence signs at the ballpark are yellow, green and red,
> Their fierce glare queers the hitting; the batting eye goes dead,
> It seems to hurt the Giants even more than other nines,
> But Cobb and old Sam Crawford—they just don't believe in signs!

(When I first wrote this item fifteen years ago, signs on outfield fences were almost extinct. Since then they have come back in fashion, but protecting the center field area as a hitter's background.)

1917: HOLY FUNGOES, BATMAN, THAT MAN IS FIRING REAL BULLETS

On April 16, 1917, five persons were injured when a gun battle erupted at the ballpark in Vernon (Los Angeles) California. The game in progress was between two semipro teams, one black and one white, and the gun battle was between two men who had bet on the game.

The Vernon park had a reputation as a tough spot. In 1919 Vernon won the Pacific Coast League, and then beat St. Paul (American Association) in the first minor league World Series. However, the St. Paul manager charged the Vernon team with unsportsmanlike play, and swore that the American Association would never again meet the PCL champion, if Vernon was going to represent the PCL.

This became a moot point. After 1919, the Pacific Coast League adopted a long schedule, which made it impossible for them to participate in the Junior World Series anyway. After that, the Junior World Series was between the champions of the American Association and the International League.

1917: ESCAPE FROM ST. LOUIS

On September 5, 1917, owner Phil Ball of the St. Louis Browns charged that the Browns' players were deliberately playing badly in an attempt to escape the Browns and their manager, Fielder Jones. "Every $1,000 I lose on the Browns this season will cost the ballplayers $100," he was quoted as saying. "Salaries will be cut next season. These fellows are all wrong when they think they will get away from the Browns by laying down on the job. Because they dislike their manager is no reason the Browns should not put forth their best efforts."

Three days later, Ball's double-play combination filed suit against him. Shortstop Doc Lavan (who, by the way, really was a doctor) and Del Pratt (who really was a ballplayer) filed separate suits, each asking $50,000, charging that Ball had slandered them by alleging "that the plaintiffs were unfaithful and dishonest in their profession of base ball."

Among the hundreds of lawsuits filed in baseball in that decade, this was surely the most justified. The other suits were all about money; Lavan and Pratt sued to defend their integrity. But it had a side benefit. Both players were traded that winter.

1917: ANOTHER BASTION OF CLEAN LIVING FALLS TO SIN

On August 21, 1917, Judge R. E. Blake of the circuit court in Tennessee refused a request by the state attorney general to issue an injunction against Sunday ball in Nashville. The court declined to overturn the decision of a lower court, whose magistrate had attended a Sunday ball game and concluded that the game was not a public nuisance, as the attorney general had asserted.

REMIND ME NOT TO SAY THAT

When Babe Ruth hit 29 home runs in 1919, the record was thought to be one that would stand for a long time. The 1920 *Spalding Guide* opined that "Perhaps, and most likely, Ruth will not be so successful in 1920. The pitchers will eye him with more than ordinary caution and they will twist their fingers into knots to get more curve and still more curve on the ball. They will give one another private little tips."

The editor, John Foster, also penned this verse:

> King of the Realm of Swat,
>   Omnipotent in the Land of Slug;
> You surely set a mark
>   At which others will plug—and plug.
> To beat that "29"
>   Will take some breadth of shoulder,
> And when they put a "30" up;
>   Well—we'll most likely be some older.

NEW STADIUMS OF THE TEENS

The building of new and impressive stadiums continued apace as the decade opened. Comiskey Park opened in 1910, and was promptly declared "the finest Ball Park in the United States, which means the finest in the world" by the *Reach Guide*. It seated 48,600 people, including 12,600 in the bleachers, and was constructed at a cost of $750,000.

The new Polo Grounds (the old ones having been consumed by fire) were rebuilt into the largest baseball stadium in the country in 1911, though at its opening it did not receive, or deserve, the barrels of praise that were carried to the other new parks. The Yankees moved in with the Giants in 1913.

Boston had a park war. Fenway Park opened in 1912. It was small when it was built (about 27,000 seats) and would quickly become tiny.

In 1914, when the Braves won the pennant, the Red Sox invited them to play the World Series in Fenway, which could accommodate larger crowds than the South End Grounds, where the Braves played. The Braves accepted, but began building the huge, bland, Braves Field, which opened in 1915. (Legend has it that a dozen horses and mules were buried alive in a cave-in during construction, and lay beneath the third-base line as long as ball was played there.) The Red Sox won the pennant in 1915, and the Braves invited them to play the World Series at Braves Field, which seated 40,000 and would hold more . . . The Red Sox accepted.

National Park in Washington was destroyed by fire in 1911 and rebuilt in only eighteen days; with a number of remodelings, it stayed on the scene until the sixties. Crosley Field in Cincinnati was also destroyed by fire in 1911, and was rebuilt and rededicated May 18, 1912. As attendance declined, the parks became less ambitious. Ebbets Field, small but gorgeous, opened in 1913, as did Navin Field (now Tiger Stadium). When it opened it was a single-decked stadium seating 23,000. When the Federal League started in 1914 they had several new parks, the most important of which were Weegham Park in Chicago (later Wrigley Field), and Terrapin Park in Baltimore, where the Baltimore Orioles, the greatest of minor league teams, played until the 1940s.

And that was it. Baseball surveyed what it had done, and saw that it was good. By 1916 every major league team except the Phillies was playing in a concrete-and-steel park less than ten years old. The teams were tied down then, with investments too expensive to walk away from. The parks not only stood but improved with age, and with a few exceptions no new parks would be built for forty years. Those parks defined baseball in that era. The Pirates played the way that they could play the best in spacious Forbes Field; the Dodgers and Giants built for power to accommodate the Polo Grounds and Ebbets Field. By the time the teams began to think about new parks no open space was left in the cities, and the investment involved in constructing a park had become massive. Baseball had been living in apartments since the birth of the National League; now each team had a house. It would be many years before anyone was ready to move again.

A DECADE WRAPPED IN GREED

There are three essential news stories of Ty Cobb's decade, in each of which are buried many dollar signs. The first of these is the founding of the Player's Fraternity in the closing days of the 1912 season. This organization started well. President David Fultz, a religious man, gained respect from all sides for the professionalism with which he conducted his business, and in reviewing the 1914 season was able to report that the organization "has made remarkable progress, both in increased membership and in concessions gained for its members . . . a large majority of the sporting writers have given us very flattering notices." Players who were veterans of ten seasons or more gained the right to have an outright release when their teams were through with them, and could not be optioned to the minors without consent.

In the winter of 1913–14, Fultz declared an embargo on contract signing to gain leverage in one negotiation, and received the needed compliance. This, too, was unfortunate, for it gave the impression that the Fraternity had more muscle than it ever really did. Holding out is easy in the winter, and it would soon become obvious that the Fraternity was carrying an unloaded weapon. The organization concentrated much of its work on trying to secure gains for players who were released, sold, traded, or optioned between teams, and thus had its largest impact at the minor league level. This was a deliberate strategy on the part of Fultz, who recognized that the structure of the game was a pyramid, with the largest numbers buried at the bottom. It was not an unwise strategy, but it was to prove an unfortunate one, for in the coming wars minor leagues dropped like tulips in a hailstorm, sending frightened minor leaguers scurrying peaceably into the arms of their employers.

The second news story was not related to the first, but the two quickly became friends. In 1914 the Federal League set up shop as a third major. For two years salaries boomed and the National Commission—the forerunner of the Commissioner's Office—looked left and right and, with that unerring instinct for the physics of power plays that major league owners had from 1875 to 1969, decided that the threat from the left was the one they could live with: they issued recognition to the Fraternity and began to schedule meetings with them.

The Federal League folded after two years, the National Commission stopped meeting with the Fraternity, and major league players realized suddenly that they were as powerless as before. In the end, the Federal League killed the Player's Fraternity, for as a player's salary went from $4,000 to $12,000 and back to $4,000, the infant Fraternity stood by, helpless to stop it, and was crushed by the scattering anger.

In the muck of this were innumerable lawsuits. I should make an accounting of them, but I haven't the heart for it. On opening day, 1915, the Kansas City *Star* expressed relief that "the umpires have taken the indicators away from the Judges." There was the Hageman case, the Kraft case, the Terrapins case, the Johnson case (Cincinnati versus Kansas City) . . . players sued players, teams sued teams, leagues sued teams, Curly sued Moe, Moe sued Larry, Larry sued Curly and they all got together and sued the cameraman; Lord, it was an awful time, and then the war started.

World War I came about, I am told, because the expansionist dreams of the imperial powers reached the limits of the earth and began to crush against one another. When no more territory remained to be claimed and conquered, the great powers began to fight over the ones already in tow. It was a greedy time; there's no other way to put it. Remember how the decade started? In 1910 the Chalmers company decided to give a car to the batting champion, and you would have thought it was made of gold, the things they did for it. The Browns' third baseman played ten feet behind third base while Nap Lajoie dropped bunt singles in front of him, trying to cheat Ty Cobb out of an automobile. Ban Johnson, seeking an essential truth in lieu of true facts, made up a couple of extra hits for Cobb and declared him the champion anyway, and Chalmers gave them a car apiece. In discussing the decline of the Detroit team that year, the *Reach Guide* observed that "it is believed that factional troubles also existed, which were apparently augmented by rows growing out of Cobb's personal ambition and his desire to win an automobile offered as a batting prize." Of the ten greatest players in baseball history—you pick 'em—Ty Cobb was the only one so badly marked by greed.

The *Spalding Guides* of the period feature recurring headlines that, stumbled over in isolation, provoke a laugh:

Base Ball in France
Base Ball Booming in Australia
Base Ball in the Philippines
Base Ball Around the World
Base Ball in Yucatan
Base Ball in the Canal Zone
Base Ball in Guatemala

But Albert Spalding was quite in earnest about these headlines, for, having consolidated a virtual monopoly of the sporting goods market in the United States, he was intent upon spreading the game of baseball to every corner of the earth where a man might have two nickels to spend on a bat or a glove.

When attendance collapsed in 1914, these expansionist goals, in baseball, were suddenly focused on a diminishing universe. The 1970s in baseball were a greedy decade, but while baseball in the seventies was booming—the owners were unhappy because the players were consuming *marginal* revenues—baseball in the teens was collapsing, leaving the players and owners fighting over the pieces of a shrinking pie.

It was bound to get ugly, and it did. The third major story of the decade was a product of the unhappy marriage of the first two. The players started selling ball games.

It is not my intention to make apologies for the dishonest ballplayers. But you have to know two things to understand what happened. Number one, there was a generation of players to whom baseball made a lot of promises which it didn't keep. And number two, every baseball headline in the decade has a dollar sign attached to it. The great infield of the time was called the "$100,000 infield." The label was intended as a figure of speech, but Connie Mack took it literally, and the members of this great infield were priced and sold. Marty O'Toole was called "the $22,000 beauty." Stars and superstars—the biggest stars in the game, including Babe Ruth, were auctioned from one set of fans to another for whatever they would bring, and then ordered to report to camp for a fifth or a tenth of that amount.

It is a hard thing to know that another man is making money off of your labor, and has no intention of dealing fairly with you. This is not to say that Joe Jackson or Happy Felsch or Heinie Zimmerman were not guilty of their own crimes, because they were. But the archvillain of this villainous era was Charles Albert Comiskey. He had no reason in the world not to deal fairly with his players. The White Sox drew the largest crowds in baseball in this period—even larger than the Giants—yet the White Sox were one of the lowest-paying teams. Comiskey held all the power in the relationship between owner and players, and he had to rub their noses in it.

Other than the Black Sox, many or most of the dishonest players—at least those who were exposed—were refugees from the Federal League. Heinie Zimmerman had been an officer in the fraternity. It wasn't young, reckless players who fell in with the gamblers, but the sour veterans of the decade's bright beginnings. They all wanted the money, and they all wanted it all.

The game was saved by two men. One was Comiskey's one-time ally, now his bitterest enemy, Ban Johnson. The other was a man Comiskey could never have comprehended, a man with a great lust for everything *except* money. Put Joe Jackson in the Hall of Fame? How about if we kick Comiskey out? Bury them all in a common grave, and put up a marker with an eleven-word epitaph. They all wanted the money, and they all wanted it all.

1916: AN OBVIOUS IMPOSTER

Hughie Jennings got a letter from a small town in Michigan, a letter from a pitcher who claimed he could strike out Ty Cobb anytime on three pitches. The guy said it would only cost $1.80—his train fare to Detroit—for Jennings to find out. Hughie figured well, you never know, and sent the dollar-eighty. The pitcher showed up—great, big, gangly kid, 6-foot-4 and all joints. They let him warm up and called out Cobb.

Cobb hit his first pitch against the right field wall. His second pitch went over the right field wall. The third pitch went over the center field wall. Cobb was thinking they ought to keep this guy around to help him get in a groove.

"Well," said Jennings. "What have you got to say?"

The pitcher stared hard at the batter in the batter's box. "You know," he said, "I don't believe that's Ty Cobb in there."

A CAPSULE HISTORY OF PLATOONING

1871—First professional league opens with Bob Ferguson, the first switch hitter. (Switch hitting implies a recognition of the platoon advantage. Why would you switch hit, if you didn't think there was an advantage to batting left against a right-hander?)

1887—First known platoon arrangement in Indianapolis. (Indianapolis Hoosiers, a team that finished 37-89, platooned a right-handed hitting outfielder, Gid Gardner, with a left-hander, Tom Brown, and also platooned at first base.)

1889—Tommy Tucker, first outstanding switch hitter, wins American Association batting title at .372.

1906—Detroit experiments with platooning their catchers. (The Tigers had a switch-hitting catcher, Boss Schmidt, who couldn't hit a left-hander. The Tigers for several years sat Schmidt down and played Freddie Payne, Oscar Stanage or Ira Thomas against left-handed pitchers.)

1914—First widespread, aggressive platooning helps Boston win World Series title. George Stallings celebrated as "miracle man" for winning a pennant with a down-and-out team.

1915–1925—Heyday of platooning. Widespread platooning on almost every team.

1926–1940—Platooning falls into disfavor because of resistance by players. The players hated platooning because sitting a player down against lefties was a way of saying that he had a weakness, that he couldn't hit these pitchers. Most managers backed off of it because they didn't want to irritate their players.

1940—Leo Durocher becomes first manager to try to keep a lefty in the bullpen to pitch to left-handed batters.

1940—Billy Southworth makes limited but open use of platooning in St. Louis. Cardinals become dominant team of the 1940s.

1940s—Two-platoon football becomes the rule. The term "platooning" is adapted from football. Before that, it was just called "sitting a guy down" or something—hard to sell as a positive strategy.

1949—Casey Stengel hired in New York. Platoons aggressively and talks about it openly. His success brings platooning out of its dormant stage.

1968—Earl Weaver hired by Baltimore, adds batter/pitcher records and evolves personal style in platooning. Weaver and Stengel are the most successful platoon managers.

1986—Tony LaRussa hired in Oakland; begins using *multiple* left-handed relievers. Works for him; backfires everywhere else.

1987–1998—Constant expansion of the bullpens effectively shrinks the rosters, making platooning rare from an offensive standpoint. Managers scramble to find two or three left-handed relievers per team, creating an artificial shortage of pitching, and limiting options on offense. Has incidental benefit of creating long, boring games.

GEORGE WHITEMAN

"I Have Had My Day"

George Whiteman was probably a very good player. He had a trial with the Red Sox in 1907 (actually, the Sox purchased Whiteman and Tris Speaker at the same time), but was let go after just three games. He had an 11-game trial with the Yankees in 1913, hitting .344 with a secondary average of .438, but he didn't stick.

In 1918, with Duffy Lewis in the Army, the Red Sox acquired the 35-year-old Whiteman from Toronto. Whiteman platooned in left field with Babe Ruth; he played left when a lefty was on the mound, or when Ruth pitched. He played OK, nothing sensational, but in the 1918 World Series the Cubs started lefties all six games. Whiteman, a 35-year-old with only 257 major league at bats, batted cleanup for the Sox all six games, reducing Babe Ruth to a pitcher/pinch hitter.

The Red Sox won the series in six games, despite scoring only nine runs in the six games; they won 1-0, 2-1, 3-2, and 2-1, and lost 3-0 and 3-1. Whiteman was acknowledged as the star of the series. His .250 batting average was the best of the Red Sox regulars, but his stardom was in the field:

> After giving due credit to Vaughn, Mays, Scott and Schang, I have come to the conclusion that the real hero of the World's Series was George Whiteman, formerly of the Toronto Maple Leafs. Here is a veteran player whom unkind fate has exiled for years to a minor role in obscure leagues. Here is a player with the proved ability to play on a great team, the real star of the world's champions. And yet he went begging for a big league job through all the best years of his career and found his proper place late in life, too late to realize the just reward of his talents.
>
> I talked with Whiteman immediately after the final game, while the stands were still ringing with applause of his sensational work. As we talked members of the passing crowd continually accosted the now famous athlete. "They all want to talk to me now," said Whiteman, with a trace of wistfulness in his voice. It came late, but I got my chance at last. I was sure I could make good and I guess I have. Not that the experience was so trying to me at that, but somehow or other I never seemed to land in the majors. I was strongly

considered many years ago. In fact, I was traded to Boston, this same club, along with Tris Speaker. But I never got a show. Speaker didn't connect at first either, you may remember. But he got his chance and he sure made good. But I never seemed to get a chance. I was allowed to drift back to the minors, and though I was signed several seasons later on, and played some 14 games with a fine batting average, I drifted back just the same. It seemed to be my luck.

> I think I have been good enough to play in the majors for some years. But I never seemed to get the publicity that some fellows got. If people don't know about you it's a cinch they won't care a great deal to get you on their club. The writers seem to come around to some fellows and write them up. But they seldom came to me. So I went plodding along year after year, hoping that something would break. I had about given up hope when this chance came, and I said to myself, "It's the last chance you will ever get and it is up to you to make good." I worked hard all the time. I did my best. I am not sure I could do as well again, but it will always be a satisfaction to me to know that I was able to do good work.
>
> If it hadn't been for this season, no one would ever have heard of George Whiteman. I suppose. And there you are. I don't know how many other players there have been in the minors that no one ever heard of either, who might have delivered the goods if they had a chance. It's a hard game, professional base ball, and no one can tell me that you don't have to have luck as well as ability to rise very far in it.
>
> But while I think that I should have had a chance a long time ago, I am satisfied. I have had my day, brief as it is. I am certainly better off than hundreds of other fellows who never had their day at all. —Frank Lane, 1919 *Reach Guide* (Edited to one-third of original length)

Whiteman never played again in the major leagues. Scouting in this era was extremely haphazard, and many of the best players either never played in the major leagues, or were recognized very late. Whiteman was a small man, a right-handed batter; major league teams look first for big guys and lefties. He had very good control of the strike zone, but that's an invisible skill. He played good defense, but that doesn't always get you a lot of respect. He had an even balance of skills, as opposed to one or two attention-grabbing abilities, and he was just never lucky.

1911: BENDER AND BROTHER

Chief Bender, the Athletics great pitcher from 1903 to 1914, had a brother who pitched in the minor leagues. The two of them seem to have been something of a good Indian/bad Indian combination out of an old John Wayne western. Chief Bender won 210 major league games, and after taking off a year to work in the shipyards during World War I, came back to go 29-2 in the minors at the age of thirty-six, and 7-3 with an ERA of 1.33 at the age of forty-three. He was employed in baseball until the day he died in 1954, as a scout, minor league manager, and a coach for both John McGraw (1931) and Connie Mack (1947–1950). In 1928 he coached at the U.S. Naval Academy. Although he was suspended for a while in 1911 (along with Rube Oldring) for his creative interpretation of good conditioning, his is a record that, on balance, would suggest a balanced individual.

His brother John C. Bender, on the other hand, seems to have been a little moody. While with the Columbia team in the South Atlantic League in 1908, John had some harsh words with his manager, Win Clark, and eventually pulled a knife on him. And used it. For this he was suspended from baseball for more than two years, being allowed to join the Western Canada League in 1911.

Albert (Chief) Bender is in the Hall of Fame, but his brother achieved an even higher honor. In Edmonton, Alberta, on September 25, 1911, he died on the mound during the course of a game.

LIVE WIRE

Johnny Evers, the 125-pound center of Tinker to Evers to Chance, was known as "The Crab" because of his intensity. A lot of people didn't like him, but he had an unquestioned desire to win. He missed a good part of the 1911 season after a nervous breakdown.

It was said of Evers that he was so full of electricity that he could not wear a watch. It was a common practice at that time to give watches in testimonial dinners. Evers was given several fine watches, but when you put a watch on Johnny Evers' body it would not keep accurate time. He'd always give the nice ones away and buy a cheap one, then throw it away when it stopped running.

THE 1920s

HOW THE GAME WAS PLAYED

The change between the baseball of the teens and the baseball of the twenties was the most sudden and dramatic of the twentieth century. The Black Sox scandal and related embarrassments, coming on the heels of seven seasons of poor attendance, so terrified major league owners that they were willing to accept changes; desperate, indeed, to climb aboard any ship that looked like it might be headed toward a safe port no matter which direction. From a structural standpoint, Judge Landis provided that ship. From an economic standpoint, Babe Ruth was the vessel.

The fans were galvanized by the Ruth phenomenon; his explosion on the New York scene in 1920 was the biggest news story that baseball has ever had. When the Black Sox scandal broke late in the 1920 season, major league magnates were faced with sudden prosperity on the one hand, and doom and disaster on the other. Under those unique circumstances, the owners did not do what they would have done at almost any other time, which would have

been to take some action to prevent Ruth, as they would see it, from making a mockery of the game. Instead they gave Ruth room to operate, allowed him to pull the game wherever it wanted to go. Baseball then moved forcefully in the direction in which it had been trying to move since the coming of parks with permanent seats in the outfield. Home run totals soared beyond anyone's imagination. Batting averages jumped 20 to 50 points over the previous decade. The stolen base, the sacrifice bunt, and every other symbol of tyrannical strategy was sent scurrying for the portholes as baseball men, made suddenly wealthy by the explosive popularity of the new baseball, lined up to draw arms in support of it.

This was in some measure a return to the form of baseball in the early 1870s, but no one except the baseball historians—and there were fewer then than now—knew that. It was all new to the fans. For years, baseball fans believed that a change of baseballs was instituted in 1920 that, a "lively ball" was adopted which made possible the home run explosion by Babe Ruth, who hit the unimaginable total of fifty-four in a season. There was no such switch in baseballs. A better quality of yarn was available after World War I, and this may have increased the resiliency of the balls, but that was incidental, and its effect was not dramatic. The 1922 *Reach Guide* reported that "An attempt was made by many writers, during the greater part of the season, to blame the heavy batting on the ball, assuming that it had been changed so as to make it much more 'lively' than the old cork-center ball. This the manufacturers flatly denied, asserting that the ball was precisely the same as had always been used." Early in the 1921 season, National League president John Heydler launched an investigation to see if the league was being sold some "rabbit balls." He concluded that the balls in use were the same as always, and that the changes were due to the abolition of the spitball and other freak deliveries, plus the example of Babe Ruth, who had shown that it was possible to hit home runs with much greater consistency than was previously thought. Besides, as Pete Palmer and John Thorn have pointed out, Ruth's fifty-four-homer explosion would have happened in 1919 had the circumstances been different. Ruth hit 29 home runs in 1919, but:

1. The American League was playing a shortened schedule (140 games).

2. Ruth was playing in an extremely tough home run park, hitting 20 of 29 home runs on the road.

3. Ruth in 1919 was still pitching 133 innings.

In 1920, moving to the homer-friendly Polo Grounds, playing a full schedule and not pitching, Ruth's home runs on the road increased only from 20 to 25—but his home runs in his home park jumped from 9 to 29.

More than that, the *one-year* increases in offensive totals were not extraordinary. In 1920, runs per game in the American League increased by .65, whereas in 1911 they had increased by

.97. In the National League, the 1920 increase was only .32, whereas in 1911 it was .39. But whereas in other years the increases in offense were resisted by baseball men, and consequently negated by later events, the changes of 1920 were accepted, and sustained by measures taken to consolidate the effect. The gap between the offensive levels of the 1920s and the 1910s is remarkable—but the gap between the levels of 1920 and 1919 is not.

Of the increase in offense in 1920 alone, probably a more important change was the limited ban of the spitball in the winter of 1919–20. One of the motives for action against the spitball was a fear that it might be dangerous. In a symposium on the spitball (Should it be banned?) in the 1909 *Spalding Guide,* most of the writers who responded expressed a dislike of the spitball, and several cited the danger of one getting away and someone being hurt as one reason for their opposition.

In 1920, then, we get one of the real keys to the lively ball era. A pitch, probably not a spitball, did get away from a pitcher, Carl Mays, and killed the batter. Although a good many players had been killed in on-field incidents at the minor league level, the death of Ray Chapman was a shock to the baseball community. Chapman was killed by a dirty gray ball that he probably did not pick up as quickly as he could have. News reporters ferreted out the information that American League president Ban Johnson, some weeks earlier, had issued a directive to the league's umpires to conserve baseballs, throwing them out of play only when they were "dangerous." Carl Mays claimed that the umpire (Tommy Connolly) had permitted a ball to remain in play that was dangerous, a ball with a rough spot on it that caused it to sail. This provoked two other American League umpires, Billy Evans and Bill Dineen, to issue a statement that "No pitcher in the American League has resorted to more trickery than Carl Mays in attempting to get a break on the ball which would make it more difficult to hit."

Priorities changed overnight, in any case, and from then on much more effort was made to keep a clean, fresh ball in play. In *The Glory of Their Times,* Fred Snodgrass reflected that "We hardly ever saw a new baseball, a clean one. If the ball went into the stands and the ushers couldn't get it back from the spectators, only then would the umpire throw out a new one." The infielders would chew tobacco and licorice and spit into their gloves, to help make the ball as dark as possible.

This ended in 1921, when the spitball and the "emery ball" were banned, and clean balls kept in play. The pitchers complained that the new baseballs were difficult to grip. The 1922 *Reach Guide* reported that "the pitchers claimed that they were unable to curve the new balls, because they were not able to get a proper grip on them by reason of the excessive gloss upon them, and asked for permission to rub the gloss off with a small amount of resin. They also complained loudly of the number of new balls thrown constantly into the games by the umpires." In response to the complaints about the gloss, the practice of having the umpires "rub down" the game balls, a practice that continues to this day, was begun in 1921. The clean, new balls were incidentally much more "lively" than the old, soiled, batted and spit upon baseballs of the previous decade.

When the owners discovered that the fans *liked* to see home runs, and when the foundations of the game were simultaneously imperiled by disgrace, then there was no turning back. In 1925 a new "cushioned cork center" ball was introduced, perhaps more lively than those before it, and offense was allowed to dominate the remainder of the decade.

WHO THE GAME WAS PLAYED BY

Country boys. With the exploding popularity of baseball after the turn of the century, baseball began to draw more of its personnel from the minor league teams, and less from the colleges. College-educated players, of whom there were scores in the first fifteen years of this century, now became rare. Second-generation immigrants and fourth-generation farm boys played Sunday baseball in the pastures and parks of small cities, formed semipro alliances and caught the eye of the local press or the local manager, and found their way into the lowest levels of an increasingly structured talent system. The earlier an athlete entered that system, the more time he had to make it to the top. It did not behoove a young player to waste precious years in college.

Wild Bill Donovan, Tiger star of twenty years earlier, was killed in a train wreck on December 9, 1923. National League president John Heydler and Hall of Fame executive George Weiss were also passengers on the train. The three men had been sitting in the smoking car trading stories until about midnight, when that car was closed down. Donovan and Weiss, who were sharing a cabin, invited Heydler to come back with them and continue the evening. Heydler started to go, but decided at the last minute to call it a day.

It was a foggy night with a light rain falling. A car stalled on the tracks. The train slammed into the vehicle, and the car in which Donovan and Weiss were sleeping crumpled. Weiss was thrown through the roof, landed on a heap of rubbish, and was not badly hurt, Heydler was unhurt, but Donovan was killed.

CHECKING IN:

1920– Stan Musial, Donora, Pennsylvania
      Bob Lemon, San Bernardino, California
      Early Wynn, Hartford, Alabama
1921– Warren Spahn, Buffalo, New York
      Roy Campanella, Philadelphia
1922– Ralph Kiner, Santa Rita, New Mexico
      Minnie Minoso, Havana, Cuba
1923– Bobby Thompson, Glasgow, Scotland
      Larry Doby, Camden, South Carolina
      Norman Mailer, Long Branch, New Jersey
      Hoyt Wilhelm, Huntersville, North Carolina
1925– Yogi Berra, St. Louis
      Malcolm X, Omaha, Nebraska
1926– Don Newcombe, Madison, New Jersey
      Duke Snider, Los Angeles
      Marilyn Monroe, Los Angeles
      Robin Roberts, Springfield, Illinois
1927– Nellie Fox, St. Thomas, Pennsylvania
1928– Billy Martin, Berkeley, California
      Whitey Ford, New York City

CHECKING OUT:

1921– Socks Seybold, car wreck, 51
      Larry McLean, gunshot, 39
1922– Ben Shibe, 83
      Alexander Graham Bell, 75
      Cap Anson, 69
      Sam Thompson, heart attack, 62
      Austin McHenry, brain tumor, 26
1923– Jimmy Ryan, 60
      Pancho Villa, 45
1924– Candy Cummings, 75
      Frank Chance, pulmonary trouble, 47
      Jake Daubert, complications following surgery, 40
      Tony Boeckel, car wreck, 29
1925– Monte Ward, 65
      William Jennings Bryan, 65
      Christy Mathewson, tuberculosis, 47
1926– Cal McVey, 75
      Eddie Plank, 49
1927– Lave Cross, 60
      Hughie Jennings, 58
      Ross Youngs, Bright's desease, 29
1928– Al Reach, 87
1929– Miller Huggins, 50

SWING

Frank Gibson in 1924 hit .359 when playing the field (71-for-198)—but went 0 for 31 as a pinch hitter.

WHERE THE GAME WAS PLAYED

Major league cities during the decade were Boston, Brooklyn, Chicago, Cincinnati, Cleveland, Detroit, New York, Philadelphia, Pittsburgh, St. Louis, and Washington.

THE 1920s IN A BOX

Attendance Data:
Total: 93 million (92,652,885)
Highest: Chicago Cubs, 1929   1,485,166
          New York Yankees   10,527,508
Lowest: Boston Braves, 1924   117,478
          Boston Braves   2,499,518

Attendance boomed. After a record-shattering nine million plus in 1920 (five million plus in the American League), attendance took a half-step backward following the revelation of the fixing of the 1919 World Series. The damage was contained, however, and new attendance peaks were set in 1924 (9.45 million), 1925 (9.54 million), 1926 (9.8 million) and 1927 (9.9 million). The Yankees drew over a million almost every year, and the Tigers (1924) and Cubs (1927–1929) also made it over the million mark.

The average American in this era attended a major league baseball game about once every twelve years.

Most Home Runs:
Babe Ruth,   1927   60
Babe Ruth   467

Best Won/Lost Record by Team:
New York Yankees,   1927   110-44   .714
New York Yankees   933-602   .608

Worst Won/Lost Record by Team:
Philadelphia Phillies,   1928   43-109   .283
Philadelphia Phillies   566-962 .370

Ranking the sixteen major league teams in winning percentage for the decade as a whole, the two Boston teams rank fourteenth and fifteenth. The Braves were 603-928, .394, and the Red Sox 595-938, .388.

Index of Competitive Balance: 34%

The early part of the decade was much more competitive than the latter part. When the lively ball came in, some teams adapted to it readily, while other teams continued to try to play the game the way it had been played before.

At the start of the decade the two New York teams won every year, but the races, with one exception, were close. As the decade progressed the teams changed, but the races opened up; by 1929 the Yankees and Athletics were just miles ahead of the rest of the American League.

The first game of the 1929 World Series was set up by the fact that the pennant races that year were over by mid-August. By September first the A's knew not only that they would win but who they would play—one of the few times in baseball history that both races were basically over before Labor Day. This enabled Mack to send Howard Ehmke out to spend two weeks scouting the Cubs. Ehmke, rested, thoroughly briefed on the Cub hitters, and knowing that he was pitching perhaps the last game of a long career, struck out 13 batters, enabling the A's to seize a leg up in the series. Anyway, in 1920 baseball had very good competitive balance—but by 1929, it was pretty much gone.

Home-Field Winning Percentage: .543

Percentage of Regulars Hitting .300: 46%

Largest Home-Field Advantage: Cincinnati Reds

Reds were .576 at home, .465 on the road.

The New York Yankees in the 1920s had a better winning percentage on the road (.574) than any other American League team did at home.

Having Their Best Decade Ever: St. Louis Browns

Having Their Worst Decade: Philadelphia Phillies, Boston Red Sox

Changing Direction: Cardinals, White Sox, Red Sox, Yankees

The St. Louis Cardinals, a hapless organization for almost 40 years, began the decade as one of baseball's worst teams, and ended the decade as one of the best. The 1920s were the first of five straight decades in which the Cardinals would be one of baseball's better teams.

The Chicago White Sox, a quality organization from 1901 to 1920, collapsed in 1921 after the core of their team was banned from baseball. They would not become respectable again until the 1950s.

The Red Sox, a powerhouse from 1900 to 1919, collapsed after the sale of Babe Ruth, and would not recover until the late 1930s. The Yankees, a weak organization until the late teens, emerged as the class of the league.

The Phillies, a strong team in the mid-teens, went to hell in a handbasket after they sold Grover Cleveland Alexander. Beginning in the early 1920s they would lose almost 100 games a season for 25 years—an unmatched record for long-term futility.

Heaviest Player: Garland Buckeye, known as Gob Buckeye, was a left-handed pitcher in the American League, stood six feet tall and weighed a reported 260 pounds. Another player who collected a few hits in the meat and potatoes league was Fats Fothergill, who was 5 feet 10 and a half and weighed 230 pounds, but hit .326 in a twelve-year career.

Lightest Player: Doc Gautreau, a 5'4", 129-pound second baseman who played for the Braves, 1925–1928.

Most Strikeouts by Pitcher:
Dazzy Vance, 1924   262
Dazzy Vance   1,464

Vance was the only major league pitcher to strike out 200 batters in the 1920s. He did it three times, and reached 197 a fourth season.

Highest Batting Average:
Rogers Hornsby,   1924   .424
Rogers Hornsby   .382

Lowest Batting Average:
Heinie Sand,   1928   .211
Harvey McClellan   .220

Best Major League Players (by Years):
1920— Babe Ruth
1921— Babe Ruth
1922— Rogers Hornsby
1923— Babe Ruth
1924— Babe Ruth
1925— Rogers Hornsby
1926— Babe Ruth
1927— Babe Ruth
1928— Babe Ruth
1929— Rogers Hornsby

Best Major League Pitchers (by Years):
1920— Pete Alexander
1921— Red Faber
1922— Red Faber

1923— Dolf Luque
1924— Dazzy Vance
1925— Pete Donohue
1926— George Uhle
1927— Ted Lyons
1928— Dazzy Vance
1929— Lefty Grove

Hardest-Throwing Pitcher: Lefty Grove

Charlie Gehringer said that Grove threw "much harder" than Bob Feller. Joe Cronin said that no one threw harder than Grove.

Best Curve: Sad Sam Jones

Top Power/Speed Combination: Kenny Williams

Best Switch Hitter: Frankie Frisch

Iron Man: Lou Gehrig

Best Bunter: Eddie Collins

Collins may have been the best bunter of all time.

Resident Intellectual: Johnny Rawlings

Rawlings, who played twelve years in the majors and was a regular second baseman for six years, had a law degree from Stanford.

Best Baseball Books: *Babe Ruth's Own Book of Baseball* (1928)

Five Largest Changes in Baseball During the Decade:

1. Beginning of the Lively Ball Era
2. Transfer of player acquisition/development responsibility from managers to front offices
3. Effective capture of the minor leagues as major league servants
4. Arrival of the Commissioner System
5. Elimination of gambling/corruption

Best Outfield Arm: Bob Meusel

Worst Outfield Arm: Earle Combs

Most Runs Batted In:
Lou Gehrig,   1927   175
Babe Ruth   1,328

Most Aggressive Baserunner: Frankie Frisch

In years in which caught stealing were counted, National League outfielder Ray Powell was 21-for-77 as a base stealer.

Fastest Player: Maurice Archdeacon

Before a minor league game in 1921, Archdeacon circled the bases in 13.4 seconds, which broke the previous record held by Hans Lobert. Archdeacon was born ten years too late. He hit .333 in 127 major league games, but he had no power, and his speed, which would have made him a valuable player ten years earlier, didn't mean as much in the Babe Ruth era.

Slowest Player: Johnny Bassler

Best Control Pitcher: Grover Cleveland Alexander

Most Stolen Bases:
Sam Rice,   1920   63
Max Carey   346

Best-Looking Players: George Pipgras, Bill Walker

Ugliest Player: Joe Martina

Cap Anson Award: Kenesaw Mountain Landis

Three Finger Brown Award: Lefty Stewart

Walter Stewart was a right-handed pitcher, but lost one finger on his right hand in an accident as a young man. He switched to pitching left-handed, won 20 games for the St. Louis Browns in 1930, and won 100 games in the major leagues.

Ozzie Guillen Trophy: Joe Dugan

Best Pitching Staff: 1926 Philadelphia A's

Lefty Grove, Howard Ehmke, Rube Walberg, Sam Gray, Eddie Rommel, Jack Quinn and Joe Pate. The team posted a 3.00 ERA in a hitter's park in a league with a 4.02 ERA.

Best Offense: 1927–28 New York Yankees

Football Players: Red Badgro, Gene Bedford, Howard Berry, Hinkey Haines, Jack Perrin, Riggs Stephenson, Bruce Caldwell, Chuck Corgan, Waddy MacPhee, Dick Reichle, Johnny Mohardt, Ossie Orwoll, Pid Purdy, Red Smith, Evar Swanson, Luke Urban, Ernie Vick, Russ Young

Retrobermanisms:
Joe (Here Come De) Judge
Frank (I'd Follow You to) Shellenback
Pitcher Carmen Hill was actually called Bunker Hill

Basketball Guys: Bucky Harris played pro basketball, back in the days when basketball games were played inside wire mesh cages, thus making the players "cagers." Others include Rusty Saunders, Harry Riconda, Carl Husta, Ted Kearns, Ralph Miller

First of His Kind: Firpo Marberry (the first true relief ace)

Last of His Kind: Carl Mays was the last power pitcher who threw underhanded. There have been thirty to fifty underhand pitchers since then, but mostly they were guys who didn't throw hard enough to pitch overhand.

One of a Kind: Dazzy Vance was the only player who had a Hall of Fame career entirely after age 30.

Best Infield: 1927 New York Giants

Bill Terry, Rogers Hornsby, Fred Lindstrom, Travis Jackson

Best Outfield: New York Yankees, 1925–29

Bob Meusel, Earle Combs, Babe Ruth

A Better Man Than a Ballplayer: Jimmy Wilson

A Better Ballplayer Than a Human Being: Carl Mays

Mr. Dickens, I'd Like You to Meet:
Yats Wuestling (Detroit, 1929–1930)
Nemo Gaines (Washington, 1920)

Platoon Combinations I Would Like to See:
Aaron Ward and Harley Boss

Best Defensive Teams:

1. 1924 Pittsburgh Pirates
2. 1924 Washington Senators

Clint Hartung Award: Moe Solomon

Outstanding Sportswriter: Ring Lardner

Most Admirable Superstar: Lou Gehrig

Least Admirable Superstar: Rogers Hornsby

Gold Glove Team:
C—   Muddy Ruel
1B— George Kelly
2B— Frankie Frisch
3B— Willie Kamm
SS— Everett Scott
OF— Johnny Mostil
     Al Simmons
     Max Carey

Franchise Shifts: None

New Stadiums: Yankee Stadium (1923)

Best Pennant Race: American League, 1920

Best World Series: Impossible to pick; there are too many good ones. The 1921 series was won by the Giants over their roommates, [Note: Stadium-mates? Park-mates?] the

Yankees, and featured every kind of game and every kind of play. The 1923 series, won by the Yankees 4-2, is remembered for Casey Stengel's two game-winning home runs, after the second of which he thumbed his nose at the pitcher as he rounded third base, for which he was reprimanded by Commissioner Landis. The 1924 series featured four one-run games, was won by the Senators, and was regarded by some observers as the greatest World Series ever played. The 1925 series, won by Pittsburgh over Washington, featured a disputed diving-into-the-seats catch by Sam Rice, and is one of the few times that a team has come back from a 3-1 deficit to win the series. The 1926 series, won by St. Louis over the Yankees, was highlighted by the infinitely rehashed story of Grover Cleveland Alexander, thirty-nine going on seventy, coming in to strike out Lazzeri in the seventh game. Any of those can be called the best series of the time.

Best-Hitting Pitcher: George Uhle

Uhle's lifetime batting average, .288, is the highest of any pitcher with 500 or more at bats.

Worst-Hitting Pitcher: Win Ballou

Best Minor League Team: 1920–25 Baltimore Orioles

Best Minor League Player: Buzz Arlett

Odd Couple: Babe Ruth and Lou Gehrig

Drinking Men:
Pete Alexander
Flint Rhem
Paul Waner
Phil Douglas

Player vs. Team: After leading the St. Louis Cardinals to the World Championship in 1926 as a player/manager, Rogers Hornsby broke into a feud with Cardinals owner Sam Breadon. Hornsby accused Breadon of being too concerned with the dollar signs and not enough with the players, and said that he had, among other things, scheduled too many exhibition games on off days. Hornsby was traded to the Giants for Frankie Frisch and a pitcher.

Team vs. Team: The New York Giants, apparently jealous of the success of the Yankees, threw them out of the Polo Grounds in 1922.

Uniform Changes: Sanitary factories!

New Terms or Expressions: The term "General Manager" was first applied to Billy Evans, a former American League umpire who became General Manager of the Cleveland Indians in 1927. The term "Commissioner" is, if you stop to think about it, an odd thing to call an all-powerful ruler of the baseball world. The Commissioner was called Commissioner rather than Admiral, Czar, General, Commander, Sultan, President, Boss, Ruler, Potentate, King, or Prime Minister because baseball, before the Commissioner was hired, was ruled by the National Commission, a three-man group which had final authority to rule on baseball-related disputes. The Commissioner, for all practical purposes, subsumed the role of his commission.

Most Wins by Pitcher:

Jim Bagby,	1920	31
Burleigh Grimes		190

Highest Winning Percentage:

Emil Yde,	1924	16– 3	.842
Ray Kremer		107–55	.660

Lowest Winning Percentage:

Roy Smith,	1921		
and Roy Wilkinson,	1921	4–20	.167
Red Ruffing		39–93	.295

Nicknames:
Union Man (Walter Holke)
Poosh 'Em Up (Tony Lazzeri)
Spinach (Oscar Melillo)
The Sultan of Swat (Babe Ruth)
The Crown Prince of Swat (Lou Gehrig)
The Rajah of Swat (Rogers Hornsby)
The Rabbi of Swat (Moe Solomon)
Bucketfoot Al (Al Simmons)
Big Poison (Paul Waner)
Little Poison (Lloyd Waner)
The Mississipi Mudcat (Guy Bush)
Shufflin' Phil (Phil Douglas)
Camera Eye (Max Bishop)
Turkeyfoot (Frank Brower)
Trolley Line (Johnny Butler)
Governor (Frank Ellerbee)
Slug (Harry Heilmann)
Ol' Stubblebeard (Burleigh Grimes)

Flameout: Carson Bigbee

All Offense/No Defense: 1928 New York Yankees

All Defense/No Offense: 1926 Philadelphia Athletics

Homer: Ken Williams hit 196 career home runs, 142 at home and 54 on the road. Another Williams, Cy, was almost as imbalanced—161 home runs at home, 90 on the road.

Yellowstone Park Award: Goose Goslin in 1926 hit 17 home runs—all 17 on the road. Griffith Stadium was by far the toughest home run park in the major leagues from 1920 until the early 1950s. Goslin also hit 11 of 12 on the road in 1924, 8 of 9 on the road (1923 and again in 1935), 15 of 18 on the road (1929), and 13 of 17 on the road (1928). His "explosion" to 37 home runs in 1930 was caused just by getting into a fair home run park. Had he played in St. Louis or Detroit or Cleveland, he would have hit 30+ every year.

Tough-Luck Season: Dolf Luque, 1922

Could I Try This Career Over? Frank Shellenback

Minor Leagues Were:
50 percent free
50 percent slaves to the majors

Best Double Play Combination: Hughie Critz and Hod Ford, 1928 Cincinnati Reds.

Worst Double Play Combination: The double play combination of the 1926 Brooklyn Dodgers, Johnny Butler and Chick Fewster, was probably the worst of all time. The National League average in 1926 was 148 double plays per team. The Dodgers were essentially average in terms of opposition baserunners and ground balls, yet they turned only 95 double plays on the season—52 less than their expectation. This is the worst figure of all time in that category.

Johnny Butler, a 33-year-old rookie shortstop in 1926, had a decent year with the bat, but ended the season playing third base. Fewster, three years younger than Butler but playing his tenth major league season, was a bench player promoted to semi-regular status by an injury to second baseman Milt Stock.

The statement that they were the worst double-play combination of all time comes with a caveat, which is that it was a time of rapidly increasing expectations in this area. In the dead ball era stolen base attempts and sacrifice bunts were so common as to be pervasive. When a runner was on first with less than two out, it was more or less *assumed* that the manager would do something to move the runners; the only real question was "What?" Will they bunt, will they sacrifice, will they hit and run? In that environment, 6-4-3 and 4-6-3 Double Plays were so rare that the skill was not central to the position.

The coming of Babe Ruth changed baseball offense to greater reliance on a station-to-station strategy, which increased the number of double play opportunities. This, in turn, increased the defensive expectations for a second baseman, particularly in regard to his ability to make a pivot. This change was so significant that it created the only clear alteration in the defensive spectrum to have occurred in the twentieth century, and can be described as a fundamental re-definition of a second baseman's job. Prior to 1925, second base was a *hitter's* position. By 1940, it had become a fielder's position.

The 1926 Dodgers, who were managed by an old dead-ball manager and had old dead-ball players at second base and shortstop, were simply behind the curve. Butler and Fewster were the worst of all time not because they were any worse at turning the double play than some combinations of earlier years, but because they were playing a game in which more was expected of them.

Paul Krichell Talent Scout Award: The Detroit Tigers owned the rights to Carl Hubbell from late 1925 through 1927, but never allowed him to throw a pitch in the major leagues. Hubbell was with the Tigers in spring training, 1926 and 1927, but their managers (Ty Cobb in 1926, George Moriarty in 1927) thought he was wasting his time with the screwball, and wanted him to throw fastballs and curves. Hubbell failed to impress anybody with his curve or fastball, and was released to the Texas League after the 1927 season.

Best Unrecognized Player: Milt Stock

Highest-Paid Player: Babe Ruth, of course

Ruth's $80,000 would be roughly equivalent to $750,000 in today's money.

New Statistics:
1920— Caught Stealing
1923— Double Plays
1920 NL, 1925 AL— Passed Balls
1920–25— American League counted stolen bases against pitchers

Best Baseball Movies:
1924— *Battling Orioles*
1925— *Life's Greatest Game*
1927— *Casey At the Bat*
1927— *Slide, Kelly, Slide*

A Very Good Movie Could Be Made About: Babe Ruth, maybe

Five Biggest Things Wrong with Baseball:

1. Segregation
2. Domination of the game by New York teams
3. Rapid decay of the minor leagues
4. Management squabbling
5. Fan drinking and rowdyism

I Don't Know What This Has to Do with Baseball, But I Thought I'd Mention It Anyway: One time in 1922, Pirate first baseman Charlie Grimm fielded a hard hit ground ball by a slow runner, no one on base. Instead of going over to touch first, he fired the ball to second baseman Cotton Tierney, singing out loud enough to be heard in the bleachers, "Have we got him, Mr. Tierney?" Tierney sang back, "Absolutely, Mr. Grimm"—an echo of a famous vaudeville routine by Gallagher and Shean. The runner was out at first, 3-6-3.

THE GREATEST TEAM WHAT EVER WAS
Part I

What is the greatest team in baseball history?

I have been asked several times if I would be interested in writing a book on that subject, and have actually written several chapters of such a book; I was going to call it *The Greatest Team What Ever Was*. I am never going to publish that stuff, and never going to get the book written, because:

(a) You can't write a book saying that the 1927 Yankees were the greatest team ever, because it's already been said too many times, and

(b) You can't write a book saying that the 1927 Yankees *weren't* the greatest team ever, because they were.

What I was going to do with the book . . . I can give this away because I'm not going to get it done . . . was to pick the sixteen greatest teams ever, eight American League teams and eight National, make up a 154-game schedule for those sixteen teams, and then "play" them through an imaginary season. When the 1961 Yankees played the 1911 Philadelphia A's, for example, they would have to travel not only to Philadelphia, but also to 1911. They would have to play the game, in other words, the way that it was played in 1911, when Frank Baker led the American League in home runs with eleven. They would have to find a way to win the game *without* hitting home runs; they have to run and claw and move baserunners the way that teams did at that time. Conversely, when the 1911 A's traveled to 1961 to play the '61 Yankees, they'd have to get used to the fact that the games were longer and slower and everybody in the lineup could hit a home run, so their starting pitchers couldn't coast along waiting for the tight spots, so they couldn't get a hundred complete games. If you tried to make your starting pitchers finish out their wins in 1961, you'd just get annihilated in the late innings.

It would be a lot of fun, except for the rather serious fact that it doesn't go anywhere. At the end of the book the '27 Yankees win anyway, and everybody says, "Well, what was that all about? Like we didn't *know* about the 1927 Yankees."

Now, the 1998 Yankees, in all honesty, do tend to reinvigorate the debate, since the '98 Yankees may well have been better than the '27 Yankees. But the 1998 Yankees present a similar dilemma, which is: What assumption do you make about the quality of play over time?

If you assume that the quality of play has improved over time, then obviously, the 1998 Yankees have to be the greatest team ever. In fact, I do believe that the quality of play has generally improved over the years, and thus I could argue that the 1998 Yankees are the greatest team the game has ever seen.

But the problem with taking that approach is that:

(a) Whatever assumption you make about the quality of play over time is absolutely going to determine who you decide was the greatest team ever, and

(b) You can't convince anybody.

In my experience, if you are talking to somebody who believes that the greatest baseball ever played was in the years 1957 to 1961, you can talk to him until you're blue in the face and say anything you want to, and you are not going to change his opinion, except maybe to include 1962. If I were to write a book arguing that the 1998 Yankees were the greatest team ever because the quality of play has gotten constantly better over the years, the people who believed that at the start of the book would still believe it at the end of the book, and the people who didn't believe it at the start of the book still wouldn't believe it at the end of the book.

So that's a waste of time. What I fall back to is, in that book it's not the destination that counts, it's the scenery—and that's just not me. I've got to have a point to make, or I don't know what to say. Two of my friends, Eddie Epstein and Rob Neyer, wrote a book on the subject which came out just before this one went to the publisher. They had a different approach and a different solution to the problem, plus they are both outstanding researchers with original approaches, so that's a terrific book, I will leave it to them.

BREAK ON THROUGH

When the National League began in 1876, the top pitchers were worth about three times as much as the best position players. The top pitchers in the National League in 1876 were Albert Spalding (57 Win Shares), George Bradley (57), and Jim Devlin (53). The top position players were Ross Barnes (20), Jim O'Rourke (17), Lip Pike (17), and George Wright (17).

The relative values of the two groups began to even out immediately, however, so that by 1900 the best player in the game (Honus Wagner) was more than equal in value to the best pitcher (Joe McGinnity). This happened for two reasons. One is just innings pitched. In 1876, since teams preferred to use only one pitcher, the top pitchers worked almost 100% of their team's innings. By 1890 teams were using three or four pitchers, and by 1900 they were using five to eight (not counting the guys who just pitched in one or two games).

Second, in 1876 the best pitchers hit about as well as the position players. Of the four top pitchers of 1876 (Devlin, Bradley, Spalding, and Bond) three were above-average hitters (in terms of runs created per out) and the fourth (Bradley) was nearly average. Spalding hit .312 with 14 doubles, driving in 44 runs and scoring 54. Devlin hit .315, also with 14 doubles, and scored 38 runs. Bond hit .275 with 21 RBI.

Thus, in comparing the value of a pitcher to a position player in that era, the pitcher might have 70% of the OFFENSIVE value of the position player—plus five or ten times the defensive value. On balance, he was contributing a lot more.

By 1890 pitchers hit much less than players at the other positions, and by 1900 they had deteriorated still further—while a top pitcher's playing time had also declined from nearly 100% of the team's innings to 25%. In 1876 a pitcher might have had 70% of the offensive value of a position player. By 1900, few pitchers would have had 7%. Still, as late as 1915 to 1920, it probably was true that, on most teams, the top pitcher was worth more than the top position player.

After 1920 this was no longer true; after 1920 the top pitchers were *sometimes* more valuable than the best position players, but more often not. It is interesting to note that, right when this shift occurred—1915 to 1920—a whole group of young players who had entered baseball as pitchers moved to the field. Babe Ruth is, of course, the most famous, but a dozen or more players born within a few years of Ruth made similar, if less spectacular, transitions. These include:

George Sisler. Two years older than Babe Ruth, Sisler reached the American League as a left-handed pitcher a year after Ruth did (1915)—and he was quite good, posting a career ERA of 2.35. Nonetheless, his managers felt that he would be more valuable as an everyday player.

Rube Bressler. Three months older than Babe Ruth, Bressler was the 19-year-old left-handed sensation of the American League in 1914, finishing 10–4 with a 1.77 ERA. He lost his effectiveness when Connie Mack sold off the defense behind him, and he began to have arm trouble shortly after that. He pitched well with Cincinnati in 1918 (8-5, 2.46), but moved to the outfield in 1921, and played in the National League until 1932, retiring with a lifetime average of .301.

Reb Russell. Another hard-throwing young left-hander in the American League at the same time as Ruth, Sisler, and Bressler. A 22-game winner in 1913, he was 18-11 in 1916, 15-5 in 1917, and 7-5 in 1918, before injuries forced him to the minor leagues. Converting to the outfield in 1920/21, he made it back to the majors in 1922, driving in 75 runs in 60 games that year—the highest RBI/game ratio in twentieth century baseball. He left baseball a year later, probably because he could make more money running his vaudeville/wild west traveling show than he could make as a ballplayer.

Smokey Joe Wood. Five years older than Ruth, he was a teammate of Ruth's when Ruth came to the majors; made the transition to the outfield in 1918, hit .366 as a part-time player in 1921, drove in 92 runs in 1922.

Buzz Arlett, the Babe Ruth of the minor leagues. Four years younger than Ruth, he began his career as a pitcher, and won 22, 29, 19, and 25 games in the Pacific Coast League between 1919 and 1922, the highlight being a 29-17 season in 1920. Switching to the outfield in 1922/23, he became perhaps the greatest slugger in the history of minor league baseball, hitting .341 in a twenty-year career with 432 minor league home runs. His one season in the majors, 1931, he hit .313 with a .538 slugging percentage. The following year, with Baltimore in the International League, he hit 54 homers, and twice hit four in a game.

Lefty O'Doul. Two years younger than Babe Ruth, he also began his career as a left-handed pitcher, and vaulted to the majors after going 25-9 with San Francisco (PCL) in 1921. Failing as a major league pitcher, he switched to the outfield in 1924, and went on to win two National League batting titles.

Pete Schneider. Major league pitcher; won 20 games in 1917. Converted to the outfield in 1920/21, and had a big year in the PCL in 1922, although he never made it back to the majors.

Sam Rice. Five years older than Ruth, he began his career in the same year as Ruth (1914), and made the majors in 1915 after going 9-2 in the Virginia League in 1914. Though he posted a 2.52 ERA as a major league pitcher, he switched to the outfield nonetheless, and went on to a Hall of Fame career as a major league outfielder.

Charlie Jamieson. Two years older than Ruth, he began his career as a left-handed pitcher in 1912, in the International League. When he made the majors in 1915 he was an outfielder/pitcher, and he pitched in 13 major league games early in his career, but emerged as a full-time outfielder, a lifetime .303 hitter.

Jack Graney. Nine years older than Babe Ruth, he began his career as a left-handed pitcher, and reached the majors as a left-handed pitcher in 1908. Pitching poorly in two games, he returned to the minors, and re-emerged as a major league outfielder two years later. He played 1400 major league games, and was the first ex-player to become a broadcaster.

Bill Barrett. Five years younger than Ruth; began his career as a pitcher, and reached the majors as a pitcher/outfielder in 1921. Switched full-time to the outfield in 1922 and 1923, and hit .288 in a nine-year major league career.

Harry Wolter. Ten years older than Ruth, he began his major league career as a pitcher in 1907. Having limited success on the mound, he moved to the outfield in 1910, and was a regular for four seasons.

Wilbur Good. Nine years older than Ruth; began his major league career as a pitcher in 1905. Switched to the outfield in 1908, and was able to stay in the majors until 1918.

Clarence Mitchell. Four years older than Ruth, he was a decent left-handed pitcher who won 125 major league games between 1911 and 1932. Beginning in 1916, he also filled in occasionally at first base, and in 1922, when he was battling a sore arm, tried to convert full-time to first base. He hit .290 that year with 3 homers, 28 RBI in 155 at bats, but went back to the mound when his arm recovered.

Jack Bentley. One month younger than Babe Ruth, Bentley was a sensational minor league combination player, a left-handed pitcher and first baseman. With Baltimore (International League) from 1920 through 1922 Bentley went 16-3, 12-1 and 13-2 on the mound (total 41-6), and also hit .371, .412 and .351 as a first baseman, driving in 161, 120 and 128 runs in the three seasons. After the 1922 season Bentley was the object of a bidding war by major league teams. Most of the teams that sought to purchase him intended to use him as a first baseman, but the Giants wound up with him, and John McGraw, who was a contrarian, determined to use him primarily as a pitcher. He had a modestly successful major

league career, going 13-8 in 1923 (but hitting .427) and then going 16-5 in 1924, hitting .265.

Johnny Cooney. Six years younger than Babe Ruth, Cooney was a major league pitcher from 1921 through 1926, with modest success. Moving to the outfield, Cooney battled for almost ten years to get back to the major leagues, finally breaking through in 1936, after he had hit .371 at Indianapolis, collecting 224 hits. He was 35 years old when he got back to the majors, but despite the late start he was a regular major league outfielder for six years, and is the only major league player ever to have his best season at the age of 40 (1941).

Not to mislead anyone . . . at any given period a certain number of players make or attempt to make these transitions, and there are always other factors in the switch, other than the relative value of a good pitcher as opposed to a good hitter. It seems clear to me that *more* of these transitions occurred around 1915–1925 than at any other time, and I think it is likely that one reason is that, at about this time, a good hitter became more valuable than a good pitcher.

1921: THE ROWDY ELEMENT

About the time of World War I the throwing of pop bottles and beer bottles at players became a serious problem. John Heydler helped to bring it under control by devising a plan wherein the concessionaires who sold the bottles were asked to instruct vendors to keep an eye out for offenders. The league would prosecute, and vendors would serve as witnesses. It must have worked, because references to the problem declined rapidly after that.

PITCHER PLUS

Using the Win Shares system (see intro to Part 2), I established a method to identify the greatest pitcher/hitter combinations of all time. It's a simple method: Take the Win Shares earned by each player as a pitcher and those earned by the player as a hitter, and find the harmonic mean. It's the same method used to make power/speed numbers. Babe Ruth earned 609.21 Win Shares as a hitter, 101.84 as a pitcher; put them together you get 174.51. The top ten, according to this method, are:

1. **Babe Ruth.**

2. **Monte Ward.** Nineteenth-century Hall of Famer who has career batting numbers similar to Maury Wills, pitching numbers similar to Addie Joss.

3. **Bob Caruthers.** Hit .357 in 1887, scored 102 runs, also went 29-9 on the mound. Caruthers twice won 40 games (1885, 1889), and won 218 games in his career, also hit .282 lifetime.

4. **Dave Foutz.** Caruthers teammate in St. Louis and Brooklyn; also hit .357 in 1887 and went 25-12, also won 41 games in 1886. When Foutz would pitch, Caruthers played the outfield, and vice versa. Silver King, the third pitcher on the staff in St. Louis, also was a good hitter.

5. **Elmer Smith.** Led the NL in ERA in 1887, switched to the outfield after an arm injury and had a career average of .310.

6. **Kid Gleason.** Won 138 games between 1888 and 1895, switched to second base after his arm went. Wasn't as good a hitter as Caruthers, Foutz, or Smith, but played longer than any of them because of his defensive ability.

7. **Guy Hecker.** Won 52 games in 1884, hit .283 lifetime and .341 in 1886.

8. **Cy Seymour.** Led the NL in strikeouts in 1898, won 25 games, but always had control trouble. He jumped to Baltimore when the American League started in 1901, and John McGraw moved him to the outfield, where he had an outstanding career. Led the National League in batting, RBI, hits, doubles and triples in a fluke season in 1905, but had many other decent seasons.

9. **Nixey Callahan.** Won 99 games from 1894 to 1903, moved to the outfield and hung around another ten years as a fourth outfielder.

10. **Grasshopper Jim Whitney.** One of the best pitchers of the early 1880s, also played some at first base and in the outfield, and was a lifetime .261 hitter.

Eleven through twenty-five are, in order, Tony Mullane, Smokey Joe Wood, George Van Haltren, Adonis Terry, George Mullin, Walter Johnson, Old Hoss Radbourn, Red Ruffing, Johnny Cooney, Bobby Wallace, Charlie Ferguson, Charlie Buffinton, Ed Daily, and Win Mercer.

Those are all pre-World War II players (Red Ruffing is the most recent), so I drew up a list of the top twelve post-war players, a few of whom are crossover players, but most of whom are just pitchers who could also hit:

1. Bob Lemon
2. Don Newcombe
3. Early Wynn
4. Hal Jeffcoat
5. Johnny Lindell
6. Fred Hutchinson
7. Earl Wilson
8. Tommy Byrne
9. Bob Forsch
10. Rick Rhoden
11. Warren Spahn
12. Ed Lopat

TWENTY-TWO MEN OUT

Historians and journalists wrestle with impossibly complex realities to sort out patterns of light and shadow, which are reduced by the popular memory into black and white. But few simplifications of memory are as bizarre as the notion that the Black Sox scandal hit baseball out of the blue, that this one blight sullied an otherwise faultless record of integrity. In fact, of course, the Black Sox scandal was merely the largest wart of a disease that had infested baseball at least a dozen years earlier and had grown, unchecked, to ravage the features of a generation.

One thing that I have always wanted to see is a complete list of the men who were banned from baseball in the various scandals of the 1917–1927 period. I don't think many people realize how many of them there are.

By my count, thirty-eight major league players were involved in the scandals of the era. "Involved" means either that they were banned, or serious charges were made against them. Eighteen active major league players were either banned outright, or clearly unwelcome to continue in the profession, because of issues related to the integrity of the game. Two more were banned but re-instated. Four retired players were seriously implicated in the scandals. One active player was banned for life and three others banned for two years or more in matters less directly related to the integrity of the game. The other ten players were either cleared of the charges made against them, or allowed to stay in the game for lack of hard evidence. By no means do these counts include players who were approached about the possibility of throwing a game, or players who had incidental knowledge of a fix, or players who were alleged to have advance knowledge of a fix; that list would be enormous. I'm not sure I've got them all, but the ones I can find are given next alphabetically:

Rube Benton. Banned by National League, 1922, on a variety of charges including guilty knowledge of 1919 series fix, failing to report offer of $800 from Hal Chase and Heinie Zimmerman to help fix Giants games in 1919, and counter-allegation ensuing from charge that Buck Herzog had attempted to bribe him to lose games in 1920. His story was one of the keys to breaking the scandals. Reinstated by Landis.

Bill Burns. Though out of major league baseball for seven years before the scandal, Burns, a major league pitcher from 1908 to 1912, brought together the White Sox and the gamblers who fixed the series. Burns was discovered hiding in Mexico by Ban Johnson; Arnold Rothstein testified in court that all he knew of the fix was that Burns and Abe Attell had approached him about fixing the series.

Paul Carter. National League pitcher, allegedly involved in attempt to fix Cub games, 1920. Persona non grata after 1920.

Hal Chase. Involved in an endless series of gambling escapades. Prominently mentioned as one of the those constructing 1919 series fix. Accused by his manager, George Stallings, of trying to throw a game in 1910. Formally charged by Christy Mathewson, his manager in 1917, with throwing games that year. Charged by Lee Magee with bribing him to lose games in 1918. Suspended by Giants for allegedly throwing games during 1919. Alleged by Rube Benton to have won $40,000 betting on 1919 series. Banned from Pacific Coast League parks in 1920 for trying to bribe an umpire. Presumably holds the all-time record for games fixed.

Eddie Cicotte. World Series conspirator. His confession breached the fence of silence. Banned for life.

Ty Cobb. Alleged by Dutch Leonard to have conspired with Tris Speaker to fix the final game of the 1919 season. Acknowledged writing of seemingly incriminating letter. Acquitted.

Cozy Dolan. Giants coach; alleged by Jimmy O'Connell to have been behind attempt to fix game in 1924. Gave evasive answers on examination by Landis. Banned for life.

Phil Douglas. Wrote a letter to Les Mann in 1922 (he was drunk at the time) opaquely offering to desert the Giants, if rewarded, so that he wouldn't have to help McGraw win the pennant (he was mad at McGraw for chewing him out). Banned for life.

Jean Dubuc. National League pitcher. Involved with Chase and Zimmerman, 1919. Had advance knowledge of the series fix. Listed as banned for life in 1921, but played organized baseball in Canada a year or two later, either because he was re-instated or because he somehow slid under Judge Landis' radar screen.

Happy Felsch. World Series conspirator. Banned for life.

Ray Fisher. National League pitcher, banned from baseball, 1921, for alleged contract jumping. A respected gentleman and longtime baseball coach at the University of Michigan, Fisher got involved in a contract battle with August Herrmann, Cincinnati owner, at a time when Judge Landis needed Herrmann's support.

Frankie Frisch. Alleged by Jimmy O'Connell to have known about attempt to fix game in 1924. Denied everything; acquitted.

Chick Gandil. World Series conspirator; some have portrayed him as the heavy, the man who wrote the script. Banned for life.

Joe Gedeon. St. Louis second baseman. Friend of Swede Risberg. Served on the Ad Hoc Committee to Throw The World Series. Banned for life.

Joe Harris. American League first baseman/outfielder. Disqualified for two seasons (1920/21) for playing in outlaw league.

Claude Hendrix. Apparently had agreed to throw a game that he was scheduled to start, August 31, 1920. Never officially banned, but persona non grata in baseball after 1920.

Buck Herzog. Alleged by Rube Benton to have joined with Hal Chase in offering Benton $800 to lose a game in 1919. Allegedly involved in attempt to fix Cub game, August 31, 1920. No action taken; played in minors after 1920.

Joe Jackson. World Series conspirator. Banned for life.

Bill James. American League pitcher, 1911–1919. Name was brought up in two incidents. Charged with being a go-between in the 1917 business alleged by Swede Risberg, and with having knowledge of the 1919 Speaker/Cobb incident. Admitted to having collected $850 from Risberg and dividing it among Detroit players, but claimed it was for bearing down harder to help beat Boston in an earlier series. Acquitted. No relation.

Benny Kauff. Name was mentioned several times in connection with the investigation of the fixed series. Allegedly refused $500 offer from Chase and Zimmerman to help throw games in 1919. Later banned from baseball after being charged in New York with auto theft and receiving stolen property. Sued Landis seeking reinstatement following his acquittal, but lost.

George Kelly. Alleged by Jimmy O'Connell to have known about attempt to fix game in 1924. Denied everything; acquitted.

Dickie Kerr. One of the "clean Sox"; suspended 1923–1925 for pitching against outlaw team (including a couple of the Black Sox) during contract dispute.

Dutch Leonard. Incriminated self in the process of bringing charges against Cobb and Speaker, 1927. Never officially banned; persona non grata after career was over.

Fred McMullin. Expressed an interest in helping to throw the 1919 World Series if they would let him play. Banned for life.

Lee Magee. National League outfielder/infielder. Confessed in 1919 to having helped Chase and Zimmerman fix games in 1918. Stated at the time that if barred he would take some famous people with him "for tricks turned ever since 1906." Banned for life.

Billy Maharg. Boxer; one major league game in 1912 and one in 1916. Possibly same person as Peaches Graham, major league catcher, 1902–1912. Enlisted by Bill Burns to act as a go-between in negotiations toward fixing of 1919 World Series. Never officially banned. Persona non grata.

Fred Merkle. Of the famed boner in 1908. Rumored to be involved in fixing of Cubs game, August 31, 1920. Retired following season, never banned or suspended.

Jimmy O'Connell. Told Philadelphia infielder Heinie Sand before a game in 1924 that "it will be worth $500 to you if you don't bear down too hard against us today." On whose behalf he did this has never been ascertained. Banned for life.

Jimmy Ring. Allegedly paid $25 by Chase after losing a game in 1918. No action taken.

Pants Rowland. Chicago manager in 1917. Swede Risberg charged in 1926 that Rowland had participated in the fixing of four games between Detroit and Chicago in 1917, after the pennant race was decided. Acquitted.

Gene Paulette. National League first baseman. Accepted gifts from St. Louis gamblers, 1919. (One of the gamblers was Carl Zork, who was tried with the Black Sox.) Banned for life.

Swede Risberg. World Series conspirator; banned for life.

Tris Speaker. Alleged by Dutch Leonard to have conspired with Ty Cobb to fix the final game of 1919 season. There was and is no evidence against him of any kind (beyond the allegation), and he was acquitted.

Buck Weaver. Participated in meetings where the fixing of the World Series was discussed. Banned for life for guilty knowledge.

Lefty Williams. 0–3 with a 6.61 ERA during the 1919 World Series. Banned for life.

Smokey Joe Wood. Alleged by Dutch Leonard to have been the man who placed bets for Speaker and Cobb. Acquitted.

Ross Youngs. Alleged by Jimmy O'Connell to have known about attempt to fix game in 1924. Denied everything. Acquitted.

Heinie Zimmerman. Outstanding National League third baseman, 1907–1919; batting and home run champion, 1912. In 1919, Zimmerman and Hal Chase allegedly tried to bribe Benny Kauff, Lee Magee, Fred Toney, Rube Benton, Jean Dubuc, and others to help them fix games. Banned for life.

The ten banned players, in addition to the Black Sox eight, were Paul Carter, Chase, Phil Douglas, Joe Gedeon, Claude Hendrix, Benny Kauff, Lee Magee, Jimmy O'Connell, Gene Paulette, and Heinie Zimmerman. The four retired players who were not invited to any old-timers games were Burns, Dolan, Maharg, and Leonard.

UNIFORMS IN THE 1920s

To lead off the twenties, a quote from an ad in the 1923 *Spalding Guide:* "All Spalding base ball uniforms are made by us in our own sanitary factories. They are so built and so maintained. Our employees receive the benefits that an abundance of light and air in the workrooms brings to them. When you put on your Spalding uniform, you have our assurance that it was made under clean and healthful conditions." Just thought you might like to be reminded of what kind of stuff was considered important enough to include in an advertisement back then. A recent e-mail chain letter describes an exchange between a guy trying to order personalized shoes from Nike—seems they offer this feature for an additional $50 or so on some of their stuff—and finding their policy prohibited the particular word he requested: "Sweatshop." He finally acquiesced, asking only that they send a picture of the 12-year old Vietnamese girl who sewed his sneakers.

The ad goes on to describe various styles of uniforms, from the "World Series" down to the "Amateur Special." Two styles of shirts are offered—one with a V-neck and the other with a "military" collar (what I've been referring to as a Nehru jacket collar). For length of sleeves, there was a choice between full, half, three-quarter, or detachable. The big selection on baseball pants is between elastic or tape bottoms. There was a choice of block or fancy lettering. Colors offered were mostly neutrals (white, pearl, gray, brown) but a variety of stripe colors were available for the asking. The cost of the top-of-the-line uniform consisting of cap, shirt, pants, belt, and stockings was $25, if ordered for an entire team, or $30 for one individual outfit.

Baseball caps featured in another ad range from the solid color "Philadelphia Style" to the "Boston Style," which had a solid color visor but a pinstriped crown. The Chicago style or pillbox style was available along with the New York and Brooklyn styles, which appear to be deeper and rounder in the back. All styles were fully equipped and ready to wear with "ventilated crowns, no lining . . . stitched visor and perspiration proof sweatband."

More movement on team name representation. In 1921 the Cleveland Indians chose to identify themselves not by city or symbol but with "World Champions" ablaze across their shirts. The two Cardinals seesawing on a bat was in place by the same time. (Incidentally, the original nickname for the St. Louis team was not derived from the bird. It referred to the cardinal red trimming on the uniform first used in the nineteenth century. They were called the "Cardinals" as earlier St. Louis teams had been called "Browns" and "Maroons.") Through 1920, the Boston Braves used a circular symbol on the left breast pocket featuring a red Indian head in profile on a blue background. Philadelphia came out with a new look in 1921, with pinstripes and a simple red "P" enclosed in a circle. In 1923 the circle disappears, the big P stays on the front pocket and an additional P appears on the cap.

—Susan McCarthy

THE BALTIMORE ORIOLES

Year	Won	Lost	Pct	Position
1919	100	49	.671	1st (+8)
1920	110	43	.719	1st (+1½)
1921	119	47	.717	1st (+20)
1922	115	52	.689	1st (+10)
1923	113	54	.677	1st
1924	117	48	.709	1st (+19)
1925	105	61	.633	1st

The greatest minor league team of all time was the Baltimore Orioles of the International League from 1919 to 1925. The Orioles owner was Jack Dunn, an ex-major leaguer who was not a wealthy man; he was running the Orioles as a small business. From the time he first owned the team, Dunn scouted the bushes to find the best young players he could find, and he kept them as long as he could. He was aided by a strong baseball tradition in Baltimore, which produced several hometown players, and supported the team in the manner they deserved.

When the Federal League brought major league baseball to Baltimore in 1914, Dunn complained loudly that he had a better team than the Federal League Baltimore Terrapins, but that the "minor league" label was killing his attempts to sell the team to the public. But since he couldn't sell the team he was hard up for cash, and had to sell his most promising players, including the nineteen-year-old Babe Ruth, to the Boston Red Sox. He always regretted that, and from then on swore that he would never sell a star player unless he could replace him. Dunn survived the Federal League challenge, and in time purchased their park.

In the critical years 1915 to 1925 the minor leagues were reduced, by a series of agreements, more and more to a subservient relationship to the majors. Dunn always refused to

go along. His concept of the minor leagues was that they were simply in smaller cities than the major leagues, but not in any other sense unequal, and he was not about to sign any agreement that might have required him, for example, to sell his best players to the major leagues at a set price, or to recognize territorial rights of the major league teams that they did not recognize for him. He felt that for the minor league teams to sell their best players to the majors would lead ultimately to the destruction of the minors. Though the wisdom of this view is now self-evident, it was not a popular opinion at the time. The 1922 *Reach Guide* scoffed at the minor leagues' need for independence, and in discussing the refusal of the top minor leagues to agree to a draft agreement with the majors, argued that "to off-set this rather shadowy advantage, they cannot secure new blood from lesser leagues, and will be forced to purchase such players as they need." The editor also argued that "The Baltimore Club's idea that a AA League Club should not sell a star player at any price is all wrong, as the sale of real stars not only helps to equalize teams, but the money derived from sales to the major leagues amply compensates for possible lessened gate receipts."

Jack Dunn never accepted that nonsense, and by 1920 there was no doubt his team was as good as many of the major league teams. The same *Reach Guide* observed a few pages later that the "Baltimore team was universally regarded as of real major league caliber." Unfortunately, all the other minor league teams eventually did accept it, and thus the minor leagues were suckered into a relationship of complete dependence on their major league partners, who were determined to cripple them.

The Orioles star pitcher was Robert Moses Groves (Lefty Grove), who was only perhaps the greatest pitcher who ever lived. Lefty's records with Baltimore were 12-2, 25-10, 18-8, 27-10, and 27-6. He led the league in strikeouts from 1921 through 1924, with totals ranging from 205 to 330. Eventually, Dunn would relent and sell him to Philadelphia for $106,000, surpassing the amount New York paid for Babe Ruth in 1920 . . . the highest figure ever spent for a ballplayer at any level up to that time.

The 1922 Orioles probably had a better pitching staff than the 1927 Yankees. While Grove was 109-36 during those five years, a pitcher named Johnny Ogden was 118-45. Ogden was 27-9 in 1920, 31-8 in 1921, and generally accepted as the best pitcher in the minors at that time. John McGraw wanted him for the Giants, Connie Mack wanted him for the A's, and Pat Moran wanted him for the Reds, but Baltimore had him, and Baltimore kept him.

Between Ogden and Grove came an eccentric named Rube Parnham. Parnham pitched briefly for the Philadelphia Athletics in 1916, perhaps the worst major league team of this century, and won two of three starts. Parnham pitched eleven innings with Philadelphia in 1917 before being acquired by the Orioles, for whom he was 16-9 in 1917, 22-10 in 1918, and 28-12 in 1919. In 1920 he jumped the team after starting out 5-0. Returning in 1922, he went 33-7 in 1923 (making Grove the number two pitcher on the staff at 27-10), and ended the season with twenty straight wins. He had won 18 straight games with a week to play when he jumped the team again. He showed up at the park on the final day of the season, and won both ends of a double-header to make it twenty straight. He left baseball again in 1924.

When those three weren't pitching, Jake Bentley, the regular first baseman would take occasional turns on the mound (see article, "Break On Through"). Other pitchers who passed through included George Earnshaw, Tommy Thomas, and Clifford Jackson, the former two

successful pitchers in the major leagues later on. A pitcher named Harry Frank went 25-12 in 1920. In 1925, the first year without Grove, Tommy Thomas won 32 games, George Earnshaw 29, and Johnny Ogden 28.

The end of the Oriole dynasty was visible in the east by that time. The rest of the league was tired of getting beaten. Under the leadership of Dunn, the International League had been the last minor league to hold out against the major league draft arrangement, refusing to have their best players taken from them for $5,000. But with the Orioles able to keep their best players, they were able to dominate the league, and so the rest of the league began to tire of supporting this policy. In 1924 the major leagues agreed to modifications of the draft agreement, and the International League capitulated.

In fairness to the other owners, there was a conflict between what was good for the minor leagues in the long run, and what was good for each team in the short run. It was not healthy for the International League to be dominated by Baltimore, and while it is no doubt true that they would have been better off in the long run to have emulated Dunn and developed their own stars, it is also true that many of them had neither the resources nor the know-how to do this. Anyway, faced with the prospect of losing his star players for $5,000 apiece, Dunn was forced to sell them to the major leagues, and the Oriole dynasty crumbled. By 1927 the ashes of the great Oriole team were spread around the American League, and Baltimore was without its champions.

1920: A CLIMATE OF FEAR

In order to combat gambling on the games, Tris Speaker did not name his starting pitchers until game time during the 1920 World Series.

THE 1920 AMERICAN LEAGUE PENNANT RACE

The American League pennant chase in 1920 was a three-team race among Indians (98-56), White Sox (96-58), and Yankees (95-59). Enormous excitement was generated around the league by Ruth's great season, which evolved into a pennant race worthy of its own book when (a) Ray Chapman of Cleveland was killed by a pitch (the Indians replaced him with a Hall of Famer, Joe Sewell) and (b) the story of the Black Sox broke in the last week of the season. Ranks with the 1908 National League race, 1978 American League East race and one or two others as the greatest of pennant races, combining great baseball with powerful drama.

1924: OLD BALLPLAYERS NEVER DIE

The 1924 *Spalding Guide* reported that Joe McGinnity, the Iron Man of twenty years earlier (and still an active pitcher with Dubuque of the Missouri Valley League, where he was 15-12 in 1923) was of the opinion that "the pitchers of the present time are not as good as they were in other days . . . McGinnity calls attention to the faults of the present-day pitchers and is depressed by the fact that so few of them possess a good curve or try to acquire one. He thinks this is due to the fact that so many pitchers 'got by' in the past with a straight delivery because they pretended to have a spitball, or some other method of pitching that was out of the ordinary."

MAJOR LEAGUE ALL-STAR TEAM 1920–1929

Records in seasonal notation, based on 154 games. Pitchers based on 40 starts.

Pos.	Player	Years	Hits	HR	RBI	Avg.	Other
C	Gabby Hartnett	4.60	137	18	79	.287	
1B	Lou Gehrig	4.98	185	29	127	.335	127 Runs
2B	Rogers Hornsby	9.29	225	27	124	.382	44 Doubles
3B	Pie Traynor	7.70	194	5	104	.322	
SS	Joe Sewell	9.12	186	3	90	.322	11 Strikeouts
LF	Harry Heilmann	9.21	209	15	123	.364	43 Doubles
CF	Al Simmons	5.32	220	22	105	.356	.570 Slugging
RF	Babe Ruth	9.08	191	51	146	.355	136 Walks

Pitcher		Years	Won-Lost	SO	ERA	Other
RH	Dazzy Vance	6.41	23-14	228	3.10	
RH	Pete Alexander	7.77	21-14	84	3.04	45 Walks
RH	Burleigh Grimes	8.96	21-15	114	3.52	
LH	Herb Pennock	8.15	20-14	90	3.46	

MOSES SOLOMON

In the fall of 1923, John McGraw paid $4,500 to acquire a player who had just established a new minor league record for home runs in a season. Four and a half thousand wasn't a lot of money for a prospect even then—the A's would shell out $106,000 for another Moses a year later—but Moses H. Solomon came with special credentials, and became the immediate darling of the Big City press. He was christened the Rabbi of Swat, and he was supposed to hit home runs, and he was supposed to have a special appeal to the New York audience. He had hit 49 home runs at Hutchinson in the Southwestern League, and no one but the Babe had ever hit that many. Anywhere.

Moe Solomon's lifetime major league batting average was .375—three for eight. Seems like he had a lot of trouble with the glove, and a certain amount of trouble with batting practice curve balls. The Giants had a couple of other rookies in 1924 that they preferred to go with, Bill Terry and Hack Wilson. Moses was out of baseball in a few years. His 49 home runs in 1923 were over half of his career total in professional baseball. He had a successful post-playing career, investing in real estate. The pressure that was put upon him to become New York's Jewish superstar is something that no one, to this point, has been able to live up to. (More details on the story of Moses Solomon can be found in an article by Howard Lavelle in the 1976 *Baseball Research Journal*. See also comment about Wally Moses, RF #73.)

1923: 325 HITS

The minor league record for hits in a season was set in 1923, by Paul Strand, with Salt Lake City in the Pacific Coast League. Strand's complete record for the season appears below:

Year	G	AB	R	H	2B	3B	HR	RBI	SB	Avg
1923	194	825	180	325	66	13	43	187	22	.394

Strand led the Pacific Coast League in 1923 in runs, hits, home runs, RBI, and batting average. Salt Lake city finished with a record if 94 wins, 105 losses.

In one documented incident, veteran pitcher Harry Krause intentionally walked Strand with the bases loaded—and was cheered by the fans for so doing.

1924: 100 DOUBLES

In the Western League in 1924, an outfielder named Lyman Lamb hit 100 doubles, one of the more remarkable minor league records. No other player in organized ball ever hit more than 75 doubles in a season, even in the long seasons of the Pacific Coast League. Lamb's record appears below:

Year	G	AB	R	H	2B	3B	HR	RBI	SB	Avg
1924	168	699	149	261	100	4	19	—	15	.373

The Western League did not count RBI at this time. Lamb led the league in hits, 261, but was third on the Tulsa team in batting, behind someone named Lelivet, presumably Jack, and somebody named Washburn, presumably not Ray. Washburn hit .375 with 53 doubles, 48 homers and 458 total bases. Tulsa finished third, with a record of 98–69.

1929: 553 TOTAL BASES

In the Pacific Coast League in 1929, Ike Boone had 553 total bases, a minor league record. (Paul Strand in 1923 had 546, the second-highest total.) Boone's batting record:

Year	G	AB	R	H	2B	3B	HR	RBI	SB	Avg
1929	198	754	195	323	49	8	55	218	9	.407

Boone had a lifetime minor league batting average of .370, and also hit .319 in 355 games in the major leagues.

THE 1930s

HOW THE GAME WAS PLAYED

Following the 1930 season, when runs scored rose to historic levels and any number of batting records were established, the National League acted to deaden the baseball a little bit. The baseball of the 1930s was, from that point on, fundamentally a resumption of the baseball of the twenties. Batting averages and home run totals stayed high—actually, batting averages dropped off a little and home runs continued to increase, as more and more players came into the game who had mastered the uppercut. Stolen bases and sacrifice hits continued to decline throughout the decade.

A gap developed between the offensive levels of the two leagues; the American League offenses continued to rip, but the National League became more of a pitcher's league. The American League scored more runs than the National every year from 1931 through 1942, and in much of that period the differences were large. In 1933 American League teams scored almost five runs per game (4.96), while National League teams less than four per game. This is the widest and most persistent gap between the two leagues in the history of baseball.

The game was rich in characters, but not particularly rich in strategy. Night baseball began to arrive late in the decade, but there probably is no other decade in the history of the sport in which the game changed as little as it did between 1929 and 1939.

WHERE THE GAME WAS PLAYED

Major league cities during the thirties were Boston, Brooklyn, Chicago, Cincinnati, Cleveland, Detroit, New York, Philadelphia, Pittsburgh, St. Louis, and Washington. By 1939 the location of the major league teams was out of whack with the nation's population distribution. The transportation system was still at a point where a truly national schedule would have been difficult to sustain.

WHO THE GAME WAS PLAYED BY

By 1930 the generation of players that Kirby Higbe called the Babe Ruth generation was strongly entrenched. The ethnic identity of the players was still observable; many of these players were still second-generation or third-generation immigrants. The Italian population in baseball at this time has been much commented upon, in part perhaps because many Italian stars have easily recognizable names (DiMaggio, Dolph Camilli, Ernie Lombardi), but in truth baseball probably always had more players of German descent than Italian. For the first time, the state of California became prominent as the garden of young baseball stars, with Joe DiMaggio (1936) and Ted Williams (1939) the most conspicuous California products. In terms of numbers, the South was the most productive region, and in particular the hill country of Arkansas, Tennessee, and Oklahoma. The number of educated players was probably at an all-time low.

Branch Rickey, mastermind of the St. Louis Cardinals, said, "I offered mill hands, plowboys, high school kids a better way of life. They rose on sandlots to big city diamonds. They earned more in a month than they could have earned in a year." Heywood Broun wrote of John McGraw that "he would take kids out of the coal mines and out of the wheat fields and make them walk and talk and chatter and play ball with the look of eagles." Dizzy Dean was perhaps the quintessential player of the era. Dean would drop by Rickey's office, prop his feet up on the desk and "talk country."

"If there was one more like him," Rickey said, "I'd get out of the game." Rickey muttered to his family that he wondered what a lawyer and educated man like himself was doing dealing with the likes of Dizzy Dean for a living. Yet, although Rickey was a kind of a snob who didn't drink, swear, or attend baseball games on Sunday, his teams both in St. Louis and Brooklyn were always the hardest-drinking, loudest-swearing, most raucous in the league. And in that as in everything else, all baseball men followed the leadership of Branch Rickey.

CHECKING IN:

1930– Earl Weaver, St. Louis
1931– Willie Mays, Westfield, Alabama
    Ernie Banks, Dallas
    Mickey Mantle, Spavinaw, Oklahoma
    Eddie Mathews, Texarkana, Texas
1932– Maury Wills, Washington, D.C.
    Ray Charles, Albany, Georgia
1933– Rocky Colavito, New York City
1934– Hank Aaron, Mobile, Alabama
    Roger Maris, Fargo, North Dakota
    Roberto Clemente, Carolina, Puerto Rico
    Al Kaline, Baltimore
1935– Frank Robinson, Beaumont, Texas
    Bob Gibson, Omaha, Nebraska
    Sandy Koufax, Brooklyn
    Harmon Killebrew, Fayette, Idaho
1937– Brooks Robinson, Little Rock, Arkansas
    Juan Marichal, Laguna Verde, Dominican Republic
1938– Willie McCovey, Mobile, Alabama
1939– Lou Brock, El Dorado, Arkansas
    Carl Yastrzemski, Southampton, New York

As many players who would hit 500 home runs were born in 1931 (four) as in all of history before then.

No United States presidents were born in the 1930s.

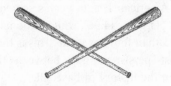

CHECKING OUT:

1930— William Howard Taft, 73
1931— Thomas Edison, 84
    Charles Comiskey, 72
1932— Dan Brouthers, 74
1933— Bill Veeck, Sr., influenza, 55
    Ring Lardner, 48
1934— Wilbert Robinson, 70
    John McGraw, uremia, 60
1935— Paul Hines, 80
    Hank O'Day, bronchial
    pneumonia, 74
    Billy Sunday, 72
    Len Koenecke, fire extinguisher, 29

1936— Deacon McGurie, 72
    Charles Stoneham, Bright's
    disease, 59
1937— John D. Rockefeller, 98
    George Wright, 90
    Rube Benton, car wreck, 49
1938— Silver King, 70
    Bob Fothergill, 38
    Col. Tillinghast Huston, 71
1939— Deacon White, 92
    Abner Dalrymple, 81
    Col. Jacob Ruppert, phlebitis, 71
    Al Munro Elias, 67

MAJOR LEAGUE ALL-STAR TEAM 1930–1939

Records in seasonal notation, based on 154 games. Pitchers based on 40 starts.

Pos.	Player	Years	Hits	HR	RBI	Avg.	Other
1C	Bill Dickey	7.88	182	21	119	.320	
1B	Lou Gehrig	9.07	199	38	150	.343	.638 Slugging
2B	C. Gehringer	9.31	200	16	108	.331	127 Runs
3B	Stan Hack	6.09	170	5	61	.300	99 Runs
SS	Arky Vaughn	7.46	189	10	85	.329	
LF	Paul Waner	9.50	206	8	79	.333	39 Doubles
CF	Joe DiMaggio	3.60	220	38	155	.341	92 X-Base hits
RF	Mel Ott	9.58	175	32	119	.313	

Pitcher		Years	Won-Lost	SO	ERA	Other
RH	Dizzy Dean	6.77	22-12	168	2.97	
RH	Red Ruffing	8.88	20-11	142	3.59	Hit .285
LH	Carl Hubbell	8.77	21-12	146	2.70	
LH	Lefty Grove	7.94	25-10	165	2.91	

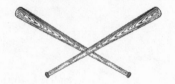

THE 1930s IN A BOX

Attendance Data:

Total:	81 million (81,013,329)	
Highest:	Chicago Cubs, 1930	1,463,624
	New York Yankees	9,089,953
Lowest:	St. Louis Browns, 1935	80,922
	St. Louis Browns	1,184,076

You sometimes hear it said that entertainment industries thrive during a recession. Any idea that baseball thrived during the Great Depression of the 1930s is erroneous. After a good start, attendance during the years 1932–1935 rolled back to the levels of twenty-five years earlier. Crowds recovered somewhat after that, but never returned to the peaks of the mid- and late-twenties. Few industries in this country had a good decade, and baseball certainly did not.

The average American in this era attended a major league baseball game about once every sixteen years.

Most Home Runs:

Jimmie Foxx,	1932	58
Hank Greenberg,	1938	58
Jimmie Foxx		415

Best Won/Lost Record by Team:

Philadelphia A's,	1931	107-45	.704
New York Yankees		970-554	.636

Worst Won/Lost Record by Team:

Boston Braves,	1935	38-115	.248
St. Louis Browns		578-951	.378

Index of Competitive Balance: 31%

The 1930s were the *least* competitive decade in baseball since 1910.

Home-Field Winning Percentage: .553

Percentage of Regulars Hitting .300: 41%

Largest Home-Field Advantage: Philadelphia Phillies

The Phillies were 336-414 (.448) in Philadelphia, just 245-529 (.317) on the road.

Having Their Best Decade Ever: Washington Senators

The Yankees had their best winning percentage ever in this decade, although they didn't win as many championships as they would in the 1950s.

Having Their Worst Decade: Chicago White Sox, St. Louis Browns

The Cincinnati Reds had their worst winning percentage ever in this decade, but saved the decade with a pennant in 1939.

Changing Direction: Although the Washington Senators are often thought of as a perpetually down-and-out organization, the Senators actually had winning records for the decades of the teens, the twenties, and the thirties, and won pennants in the twenties and thirties. The team fell into a 25-year malaise after they sold Joe Cronin in 1934.

Heaviest Player: Jumbo Brown, a pitcher with the Yankees and Giants, was 6′4″, and dented the scales at 295. As far as I know, this is the greatest weight ever acknowledged by a major league player.

Lightest Player: Pat Ankenman, who played one game for the Browns in 1936, was 5′4″ and weighed 125. The smallest player of note was Charlie Dressen, who stood 5′6″ and weighed a little under 150.

Most Strikeouts by Pitcher:
Bob Feller,   1939   246
Lefty Gomez   1,337

Highest Batting Average:
Bill Terry,   1930   .401
Bill Terry   .352

Lowest Batting Average:
Jim Levey,   1933   .195
Merv Shea   .208

Best Major League Players (by Years):
1930— Lou Gehrig
1931— Babe Ruth
1932— Jimmie Foxx
1933— Jimmie Foxx
1934— Lou Gehrig
1935— Arky Vaughan
1936— Lou Gehrig
1937— Joe Medwick
1938— Mel Ott
1939— Joe DiMaggio

Best Major League Pitchers (by Years):
1930— Lefty Grove
1931— Lefty Grove
1932— Lefty Grove
1933— Carl Hubbell
1934— Dizzy Dean
1935— Wes Ferrell
1936— Carl Hubbell
1937— Lefty Gomez
1938— Bill Lee
1939— Bucky Walters

Hardest-Throwing Pitcher: Bob Feller

Best Curve: Tommy Bridges

Best Power/Speed Combination: Ben Chapman

Best Switch Hitter: Ripper Collins

Iron Man: Lou Gehrig, of course

Best Bunter: Dick Bartell

Resident Intellectual: Moe Berg, and also Charlie Devens. Devens was a Harvard graduate, a member of an upper-class Boston family. His father had been Attorney General of Massachusetts; his grandfather, a classmate and friend of Oliver Wendell Holmes.

Best Baseball Books:
1930— *Buck's Winning Hit,* by Elmer Dawson
1935— *Standing the Gaff,* by Steamboat Johnson (reminiscences of a minor league umpire)

Five Largest Changes in Baseball During the Decade:

1. Beginning of night baseball
2. Growth of awards
3. Explosion of interest in baseball history (see note)
4. Acceptance of Sunday baseball/stabilization of pitching staffs
5. Segregating of pitchers into starters and relievers

In the late 1930s there was a sudden awareness that the early history of the game was slipping away. In 1930 professional baseball had been around for about 60 years, meaning that old men still remembered the first generation of professional players. Fan interest in baseball had exploded just after the turn of the century. In 1930 that generation of fans was in mid-life.

By 1940 the first generation of players was mostly dead, the first generation of sportswriters was mostly gone, and the generation of fans spawned at the turn of the century had turned gray. Anxiety about baseball's fading past crystalized around the creation of the Hall of Fame in Cooperstown. Baseball in 1940 had an awareness of its past, which provoked publication of the first wave of books about baseball history in the early 1940s.

Best Outfield Arms:
Mel Ott
Chick Hafey

Worst Outfield Arm: Riggs Stephenson

Most Runs Batted In:
Hack Wilson, 1930   191
Jimmie Foxx   1403

Most Aggressive Baserunner: Pepper Martin

Fastest Player: Evar Swanson

Slowest Player: Shanty Hogan

Best Control Pitcher: Red Lucas or Carl Hubbell

Most Stolen Bases:
Ben Chapman, 1931   61
Ben Chapman   269

Best-Looking Player: Hank Greenberg

Ugliest Players:
Ernie Lombardi
Suitcase Seeds

Cap Anson Award: Jake Powell

Three Finger Brown Award: Tom Sunkel, National League pitcher from 1937 to 1944, had lost the sight in his left eye due to a childhood accident with a pop gun.

Ozzie Guillen Trophy: Lloyd Waner

Bound for Glory: Johnny Berardino

Best Pitching Staff: 1931 Philadelphia A's

Best Offense: 1931 New York Yankees

Best Defense: 1939 Cincinnati Reds

Football Players: Ray Berry, Spud Chandler, Ace Parker, Larry Bettencourt, Howard Maple, Ox Eckhardt, Wally Gilbert, Bump Hadley, Jim Levey, Ab Wright

Retrobermanisms:
Smead ('Tis the Season to be) Jolley

Basketball Guys: Lou Boudreau, Red Rolfe

First of His Kind: Harlond Clift, the first modern power-hitting third baseman.

Last of His Kind: Wes Ferrell in 1933 tried to play the outfield between starts. People said he would hurt his arm, and sure enough he did, which made him the last significant player to attempt this double duty.

Also Last of His Kind: Burleigh Grimes, the last legal spitball pitcher

One of a Kind: Willard Hershberger (only player to commit suicide during the season)

Best Infield: 1934-35 Detroit Tigers (Hank Greenberg, Charlie Gehringer, Marv Owen, and Billy Rogell)

Best Outfield: 1931-33 New York Yankees (Babe Ruth, Earle Combs, and Ben Chapman)

A Better Man Than a Ballplayer: Larry French

A Better Ballplayer Than a Human Being: Hack Wilson

Mr. Dickens, I'd Like You to Meet:
Heinie Meine
Emil (Hill Billy) Bildilli

Platoon Combinations I Would Like to See: Boze Berger and Lonnie Frey

Best Defensive Teams: The Detroit Tigers were the best defensive team in the American League through most of the decade; the Chicago Cubs were the best in the National. The Cincinnati Reds, an absolutely awful defensive team through most of the decade, improved dramatically in 1938-39 when Bill McKechnie was hired, and changed the focus of the organization. By 1939 McKechnie had put a great defensive team on the field.

Clint Hartung Award: Don Padgett

Outstanding Sportswriter: Grantland Rice [Note: I dunno. Can you read him any more without getting purple ink all over your fingers?]

Most Admirable Superstar: Frank Graham

Least Admirable Superstar: Joe Medwick

Gold Glove Team:
C—   Gabby Hartnett
1B— Bill Terry
2B— Burgess Whitehead
3B— Billy Werber
SS— Leo Durocher
OF— Mike Kreevich
       Joe DiMaggio
       Lloyd Waner

Franchise Shifts: None

New Stadiums: 1931—Memorial Stadium in Cleveland (baseball, 1932. Indians played there only on weekends until 1948)

Best Pennant Race: 1930 National League

The Cardinals in 1930 were 13½ behind on August 8, in fourth place and only one game over .500 (53-52). They went 39-10 the rest of the way, taking a three-game series against Brooklyn in late September (remembered for the alleged kidnapping of Flint Rhem) to move into first place.

The National League had good pennant races almost every year, while the American League had poor pennant races almost every year.

Best World Series: 1931 (Pepper Martin vs. Mickey Cochrane)

Best-Hitting Pitcher: Wes Ferrell

Worst-Hitting Pitcher: Johnny Broaca

Best Minor League Teams:
1937 Newark Bears
1934 Los Angeles Angels

Best Minor League Player: Nick Cullop

Odd Couple: Joe DiMaggio and Lefty Gomez

Joe McCarthy assigned Gomez to room with DiMaggio when DiMag first arrived in 1936. The two men were personality opposites, DiMaggio shy and taciturn, Gomez gregarious and hyperactive. That's probably why McCarthy put them together, feeling that Gomez' good humor would help keep DiMaggio relaxed. The men became the best of friends.

Another odd couple was Moe Berg, the super-intellectual catcher of the Washington Senators, and his longtime roommate Dave Harris, a slow-moving Southerner who was called "Sheriff" because he had been briefly deputized to help track down a man who stole a mule. Once, when Harris was feeling a little off, Berg studied his tongue and informed Harris solemly that he was just suffering from a little bout of intestinal fortitude.

Harris, the next day, duly informed reporters that he had shaken off that little bit of intestinal fortitude. "Moe," Harris once told him, "I can drive in more runs in a month than you smart guys can think across the plate all season."

Drinking Men:
Jimmie Foxx
Hack Wilson
Len Koenecke
Bobo Newsome
Earl Whitehill
Paul Waner
Van Lingle Mungo

New Equipment: After the 1933 season, the National League made a widely and deliberately publicized effort to add more life to the baseball they were using. National League runs per game did increase by 22 percent in 1934, but offense in the NL remained well below the levels of the American League.

Player vs. Team: Joe DiMaggio vs. the Yankees

Team vs. Team: The essential battles of the 1920s and thirties were between major league and minor league teams, as the majors gradually consolidated their domination of the lower leagues. When Bob Feller was signed in 1936, his first professional activity was at the major league level, with Cleveland, and he was a seventeen-year-old sensation of the highest order. The Des Moines club in the Western League, which had been trying to sign Feller, protested that its rights had been violated as, under the major-minor agreement of 1921, the major leagues had agreed not to sign players (other than college players) who were not already in organized ball. In a controversial and much-publicized case, Judge Landis allowed Feller to stay with Cleveland but awarded Des Moines $7,500 in damages. The protections for the minors in the major/minor agreement of 1921 soon became a dead letter, and the majors just basically did whatever the hell they wanted to.

Uniform Changes: Glass buttons: gone forever

New Terms or Expressions: Base ball became one word

In 1930 the term "rookie" was rarely used, was normally placed in quotation marks when it was used, and was usually spelled "rooky." By 1939 it was in common usage.

Most Wins by Pitcher:
Lefty Grove,	1931	31
Lefty Grove		199

Highest Winning Percentage:
Johnny Allen,	1938	15-1	.938
Lefty Grove		199-76	.724

Lowest Winning Percentage:
Ben Cantwell,	1935	4-25	.138
Milt Gaston		36-81	.308

Nicknames: A mean streak emerges

Worst Award Selection: 1938, Ernie Lombardi over Mel Ott as National League MVP

Best Player Who Never Won the MVP Award: Mel Ott

Flameout: Bill DeLancey (illness)

All Offense/No Defense: 1930 New York Yankees

All Defense/No Offense: 1933 Boston Braves

Homer: Mel Ott hit 323 career home runs at home, 188 on the road—by far the largest home park home run advantage in baseball history. Ott gained about 135 home runs by playing in a good home run park; no one else is more than +90.

Chuck Klein (190/110) and Hank Greenberg (205/126) also gained a lot of home runs by playing in home run parks.

Yellowstone Park Award: Joe DiMaggio probably lost more home runs to playing in a poor home run park (for a right-handed hitter) than anyone else in history. DiMaggio hit 213 career home runs on the road, 148 at home— thus, he lost about 65 home runs to Yankee Stadium.

Tough-Luck Season: Paul Derringer, 1933

Could I Try This Career Over? Hal Trosky

Minor Leagues Were:
30 percent free
70 percent slaves to the majors

Best Double Play Combination: Billy Herman and Billy Jurges teamed as the double play combination of the Chicago Cubs from September, 1931, through 1938. The Cubs led the league in Double Plays in 1933 and 1935, with 163 each season. They led the league in Double Plays minus expected DP in 1933 (+20), 1935 (+35), and 1936 (+25), and were above expectation in the other seasons. The Cubs won three pennants with Jurges and Herman manning the middle of the infield.

Worst Double Play Combination: In 1939, with Johnny Berardino playing second base and Don Heffner playing shortstop, the 1939 St. Louis Browns turned only 144 Double Plays, 42 less than expected in view of their baserunners allowed and ground balls. They lost 111 games. In 1940 the Browns returned Berardino and Heffner, but flip-flopped them, sending Heffner to second base and Berardino to short. The team's double play performance improved sharply, and their won-lost record improved by 24 games.

Paul Krichell Talent Scout Award: Phil Rizzuto grew up as a Brooklyn Dodger fan, dreaming of playing for the Dodgers. In 1936 Rizzuto's high school baseball coach arranged for him to have a tryout at Ebbets Field, under the supervision of Casey Stengel. But the Dodgers didn't really look at him; they just asked him to run a little bit, told him he was too small to play baseball, and sent him home.

Highest-Paid Player: Babe Ruth (about $80,000)

New Statistics:
1933— Hit into double play (NL)
1939— Grounded into double play (both leagues)

A Very Good Movie Could Be Made About: The Kansas City Monarchs

Five Biggest Things Wrong with Baseball:

1. Segregation
2. Domination of the game by New York teams
3. Declining attendance
4. Misalignment of the teams with the nation's population (no teams in California, by now a populace state, none in Texas or the south)
5. Prevalence of hero worship journalism/ complete lack of good books about the game

I Don't Know What This Has to Do with Baseball, But I Thought I'd Mention It Anyway: Ted Lyons went to Baylor on a trombone scholarship; I'm guessing that he was maybe the only major league baseball player ever to attend college on a trombone scholarship. But at a football game against Texas A&M a fight broke out, and Lyons put down his trombone to participate in the fight. His trombone was crushed in the melee, and Lyons lost his scholarship.

THE DEATH OF COMMON
SENSE IN BASEBALL

Between 1937 and 1943 an instructive series of small controversies occurred over batting championships and other league leaders—not that I'm teaching a class here, but the way these things were handled tells us something about how people thought about "rules" at that time.

When major league baseball began, batting statistics were official, but batting championships were not. The National League rules in 1876—and for almost 75 years thereafter—contained no standards of qualification for a batting championship, slugging championship, ERA championship, or any similar championship.

Over the years, however, a set of rules developed, the cornerstones of which were that a batting champion had to play in 100 games and a pitching champion had to pitch ten complete games. This wasn't a quick development; as late as 1918, when Billy Southworth hit .341 in 64 games, he was recognized by some publications as the National League batting champion. That apparently was a watershed event, however, because in the following season, when Gavy Cravath also hit .341 in about the same number of games and at bats (again the highest average in the league), the same publications declined to list him as the batting champ.

In 1932 Jimmie Foxx hit .364 with 58 homers, 169 RBI—for all practical purposes, winning the American League's triple crown. Dale Alexander, however, had played 124 games, batting 392 times, and had hit .367. The 1933 *Reach Guide* dutifully reported that "Dale Alexander, Boston first baseman, won the batting championship of the American League with .367." But while Alexander was recognized by the league, a lot of people felt that Foxx had been jobbed, losing by

three points to a player with less than 400 at bats.

In 1938, however, Taffy Wright went Dale Alexander one step better. Wright, a rookie, was a part-time outfielder. By pinch-hitting him every day in the closing week, the White Sox were able to get him up to 100 games on the nose. And he did, in fact, have the highest batting average in the league. He hit .350, while Jimmie Foxx (who had almost as many RBI as Wright had at bats) hit a mere .349.

Now this obviously wasn't Wright; Jimmie Foxx clearly had a better claim to the title than Taffy. If Foxx had been swindled in 1932, he was now being robbed at gunpoint. The American League, acting sensibly in my view, announced that, regardless of what the rules might say, Jimmie Foxx would be recognized as the American League's batting champion. To cover themselves a little, they said that a hundred games meant 100 games in the field, not counting pinch hitting appearances. Wright had played only sixty games in the field, a good many of those being partial games.

Two years later, a similar thing happened in the battle for the American League's ERA title. The rules at the time required that a pitcher pitch ten complete games in order to qualify for the league ERA title. Bob Feller, clearly the league's best pitcher, went 27-11 with a 2.61 ERA. But another rookie, Tiny Bonham, was called up in early August, made twelve starts between August 5 and the end of the season—and completed ten of them, with a 1.90 ERA.

Bonham, like Wright, was technically qualified for the league title, but the American League did the same thing they had done before: they ignored the rule, and did what common sense told them was right. They recognized Bob Feller as the league ERA leader, incidentally the only time Feller would ever lead the league in ERA.

If this happened now, of course, the league would say, "Well, it may not seem right, but that's the rule, we have to do what the rule says." In fact, in 1981, a similar thing did happen. Sammy Stewart had the best ERA in the American League (2.32); Steve McCatty was second at 2.33. But the rule at the time called for partial innings to be rounded off to integers before ERA was figured, and when you did that, Fatty McCatty dropped to 2.32 and Stewart went up to 2.33, making McCatty the leader. The league officials said, "Well, a rule is a rule, it may be wrong but that's what the rules say, so we have to live with it."

This change is reflective of a change in our culture, a change which has been called the death of common sense. Up until about 1930, if a criminal fled out of state, it was common for the sheriff to simply go get him. When a criminal who was wanted in Colorado was captured in Oklahoma, the sheriff in Oklahoma might just call up the sheriff in Colorado and say, "Hey, I've got your man over here," and the Colorado sheriff would go get him—no warrant, no *habeus corpus*, no request for extradition, no bookkeeping.

The law may have technically required extradition, but if the lawmen decided to skip a few steps, that wasn't the end of the world. Until about 1930, this did not make those cases reversible. The attitude of the lawmen toward the law can be summarized as:

1. The purpose of the law is to deliver justice.

2. The law must accommodate the effort to deliver justice.

3. If you miss a step of the dance, that's not important so long as the system delivers justice.

This is a perfectly sensible way to think about the issue, although it is now out of fashion. It is not hard to codify this as law; the Supreme Court could perfectly well state that judges may set aside issues of law which interfere with the legitimate pursuit of justice—indeed, there is an argument that the court eventually *will* be forced to adopt such a doctrine, because absent such latitude, technicalities demanding enforcement will multiply until they paralyze the system. But until we reach that point, the prevailing opinion is that the laws must be written so as to produce justice, but that the laws, once adopted, must be followed whether they lead to justice or to outrage.

In baseball, the parallel shift has been from this:

1. The purpose of the rules is to recognize the best players.

2. The recognition should go to the best players.

3. Recognize the best players, whether this accommodates the rules or not.

To this:

1. The rules must be written to identify the best players, but

2. You have to follow the rules, regardless of whether they work or whether they don't.

The difficulty with this approach is that it in essence requires that you step on every land mine in the process of mapping the minefield. One can illustrate this by looking at the National League batting races of 1940 and 1942. In 1940 the National League batting leader was Debs Garms, whose playing time was somewhere between Taffy Wright and Dale Alexander—more than Wright, but less than Alexander. National League President Ford Frick winced, but accepted Garms as the batting champion (again splitting the recognition, since *The Sporting News,* among others, did not). Many people felt that this was unfair to Ernie Lombardi, and more than forty years later Jimmy Gleeson told Jack Etkin that the "leading hitter, Ernie Lombardi, hit .319, but that was the year they gave the batting championship to Debs Garms. I think he only played in about 80 games and was more of a fill-in guy and pinch hitter at Pittsburgh." (*Innings Ago,* Walsworth Publishing, 1987. Garms had actually played 103 games, but only 84 in the field.)

Anyway, Frick tried to "cure" the problem by announcing that, in the future, the National League would also observe the Taffy Wright rule—100 games would mean 100 games in the field.

But two years later, guess what? This doesn't work either. In 1942 Ernie Lombardi again had the highest average in the National League, .342—but this time he was on the wrong side of the Taffy Wright line. So now, Lombardi is being screwed twice—in 1940, he loses the batting championship because the Taffy Wright rule *isn't* enforced, and in 1942 he's going to lose it because it is enforced.

So Ford Frick threw up his hands and said the hell with it; I'm going to recognize Lombardi anyway, because he deserves it. And that, eventually, is the policy that the American legal system may be forced to accept. Write the rule as carefully as you can, respect the rule, obey the rule—but remember that in the final analysis you are not a slave to the rule. The law is a servant of justice; the pursuit of justice is not a servant of the law.

UNIFORMS OF THE 1930s

The thirties might be called the decade of the patch. Patches had been used by the 1907 White Sox to commemorate the 1906 World Championship, and by most teams to signal patriotism during World War I, but the use of patches proliferated during the thirties. According to Marc Okkonen, there was a tercentenary patch for the Braves and Red Sox in 1930, a new St. Louis Browns crest, a World's Fair patch for the New York teams in 1938, and a patch worn by all major league teams in 1939 commemorating the centennial of baseball's imaginary invention.

Another interesting note, again from *Baseball Uniforms of the 20th Century,* concerns the first All Star Game in 1933. The Nationals chose to shell out the bucks for matching uniforms for all players. The American League had players wear the home uniforms of their regular teams, but then the money that would have been spent for matching uniforms paid for a big pizza party after the game.

A few miscellaneous notes: All teams were identified by city and nickname now. About half used the nicknames on their uniforms, and half didn't. A note under "Base Ball Condensed Data" in the back of a *Spalding Guide* notes 1931 as the year glass buttons and polished metal on uniforms were forbidden...I knew you would be anxious to hear when that happened. Knickers were stretching out to about mid-calf. The Tigers started another trend in name lettering by spelling out "Detroit" in script. Oh, and a big innovation in Chicago: a jersey that zips up. Sure, it saves time, but watch out for those chest hairs, guys.

—Susan McCarthy

NICKNAMES

Nicknames in the thirties got nasty. There have always been a few less-than-complimentary nicknames around, sometimes more than a few. In the thirties, under the pressure of economic catastrophe on the one hand and hero-worship journalism on the other, nicknames emerged as a way of accenting limitations. Harry Davis was called "Stinky." Frankie Hayes was called "Blimp," Red Lucas was "The Nashville Narcissus," Ernie Lombardi "Schnozz," and Eric Mc-Nair "Boob." Hugh Mulcahy, who lost seventy-six games in four years, was therefore called "Losing Pitcher Mulcahy" (from the box scores: Losing Pitcher—Mulcahy), and Lynn Nelson was called "Line Drive Nelson" because everything he threw up there came rocketing back at him. Walter Beck, a pitcher with a career record of 38-69, was called "Boom Boom." George Grantham, who led National League second basemen in errors whenever they let him play second base, was called "Boots"; that actually began in the twenties.

You didn't want to be fat in this climate, or it became part of your name. Freddie Fitzsimmons, a fine pitcher, was called "Fat Freddie." Babe Phelps was also called "Blimp," Walter Brown was called "Jumbo," and Alfred Dean was called "Chubby" Dean although he actually wasn't chubby at all. Bob Fothergill was called "Fatty," and a couple of players were called "Porky." Johnny Riddle was called "Mutt," and Bob Seeds was called "Suitcase" either because of his huge shoes or because he changed teams so often. Nicknames tended to call attention not to the player's strengths, but to his weaknesses. Leo Durocher was not "The Peerless Leader" or "The Little General" but "The Lip." Nick Cullop, whose face was beet red, was called "Old Tomato Face." Harvey Hendrick was called "Gink." Sammy Byrd, a

defensive replacement for the Bambino, was called "Babe Ruth's Legs," Dom Dallessandro was called "Dim Dom," and Bill Zuber was called "Goober Zuber."

In this context, even nicknames that were intended to be complimentary, or at least innocent, start to sound suspicious. Morris Arnovich was "Snooker." Harry Danning was "Harry the Horse." Marv Breuer was "Baby Face." Odell Hale was "Bad News." Dick Bartell was "Rowdy Richard"; actually, at the time he was called "Rowdy Dick," but that's been dropped from the encyclopedias for reasons of taste. George Selkirk was called "Twinkletoes"; try hanging that one on a major league player today. Merrill May was called "Pinky," according to his son, because "he had the red ass." I'm sure no harm was intended, but would you want the nicknames assigned to Vernon Gomez (Goofy), Dick Porter (Twitchy), Lloyd Brown (Gimpy), Atley Donald (Swampy), Link Blakely (Blinky), or Mel Harder (Wimpy)? It sounds like the Seven Dwarfs against Popeye the Sailor Man. Roy Mahaffey, by the way, was called "Popeye." Bill Dietrich, who wore glasses and was slightly pop-eyed, was called "Bullfrog Bill." Alan Strange was called "Inky," but got even by tagging his teammate Harlond Clift with the nickname "Darkie." Hazen Shirley Cuyler, who stuttered as a youth, was called "Kiki" because that was what he would say when attempting to pronounce his last name; at any odds, I'm sure he preferred that to being called Hazen Shirley. Another player, Johnny Tyler, was called "Ty Ty," but I don't know why.

Great players were more fortunate, but not immune. How would a major league star react today if you called him "Bobo," like Buck Newsome (who incidentally usually referred to himself in the third person, saying "Bobo did this" or "Bobo will do that"). Jerome Dean was "Dizzy." Johnny Murphy, an outstanding relief pitcher, was called "Grandma" and "Rocking Chair Johnny." Al Simmons was called "Bucketfoot Al"—again, calling attention to his supposed weakness. Joe Medwick's name has been politely shortened to "Ducky" by subsequent generations, because people are loathe to believe that a Hall of Fame player was actually called "Ducky Wucky." Let's make up an All-Star team to finish this off:

Left-Handed Pitcher	Gimpy
Right-Handed Pitcher	Wimpy
Catcher	Blimp
First Base	Stinky
Second Base	Inky
Third Base	Pinkie
Shortstop	Rowdy Richard
Left Field	Twitchy
Center Field	Snooker
Right Field	Ducky Wucky

ALDORA APPLETON

Pete Jablonowski was a graduate of the University of Michigan, 1927. He was a major league pitcher on and off for the next several seasons, but changed his name in 1934 to Pete Appleton. He did better as Pete Appleton, winning 23 games for Toronto in 1935, then having his best major league season with the Senators in 1936. He was able to stay in the majors until 1942, when he left to join the Navy.

In Bill Stern's version of the Jablonowski/Appleton story, Jablonowski changed his name to change his luck, and sure enough, his luck did change as soon as he changed his name. But you know what? On November 9, 1933, Jablonowski got married. His wife's maiden name—I am not making this up—was Aldora Leszcynski. He changed his name to Appleton a few months later—and don't you just know what the real reason was? After all those years of being Aldora Leszcynski, the woman just couldn't stomach the prospect of going through the rest of her life as Aldora Lescynski Jablonowski.

1937: OLD BALLPLAYERS NEVER DIE

Hooks Wiltse, pitching star of Honus Wagner's era, was interviewed by *The Sporting News* in 1937. He lamented "the paucity of real major league talent" in baseball, and listed five reasons for it:

1. Softball was cutting into the game.
2. Colleges weren't developing as much good talent as they once had.
3. The attention of college athletes was being diverted by spring football practice, lacrosse and track.
4. Too many younger boys were caddying, and then getting interested in golf.
5. There weren't as many sandlot diamonds as there used to be.

"Some of the young players today are as good as in the old days," said Hooks. "But there aren't enough of 'em. The boys don't take the game as seriously as we used to. I remember in my day we ate, slept and lived baseball. Swing music and the automobile have changed the temperament of youth."

BEST MINOR LEAGUE TEAMS OF THE 1930s

The two most celebrated minor league teams of the thirties were the 1937 Newark Bears, a farm team of the Yankees, and the 1934 Los Angeles Angels, who were the personal property of William Wrigley, who also owned the Cubs. The two teams make for an interesting contrast on several levels. The Bears, benefiting from close contact with New York City, are much the more ballyhooed, and are often cited as the greatest minor league team of all time, which they clearly were not. Philip Roth wrote a fine essay about them, and they were the subject of an informative and detailed book by Ron Mayer. But the Angels, playing two thousand miles from New York, were a much better team.

The '37 Bears were impressive. They won their league by 25½ games, going 109-43, then cemented the title by winning two rounds of playoffs, 4-0 and 4-0. They met the Columbus Red Birds, led by Enos Slaughter, in the Little World Series. The Bears' Charlie Keller was the Minor League Player of the Year, although that award should have gone to Slaughter, who had hit .382 with 245 hits including 42 doubles, 26 homers, and 122 RBI. Keller had a fine year, but wasn't close to any of Slaughter's standards. Anyway, the Bears lost three straight close games at home, then rallied to win the World Series by taking four straight in Columbus—surely one of the few times in history that the home team has lost all seven games of a championship series.

The Newark team, besides King Kong Keller, had several future major league players, led by first baseman George McQuinn and second baseman Joe Gordon. Other major leaguers included Babe Dahlgren (who played third for Newark), Willard Hershberger, Buddy Rosar, and Bob Seeds. Seeds had a historic explosion the following year in which he had nine hits,

seven of them home runs, and drove in seventeen runs in two consecutive games. In 1937 Dahlgren and McQuinn hit .340 and .330 with doubles, triples and home runs aplenty. Gordon's stats at Newark were the same as they would be in a typical major league season for him, and both catchers (Rosar and Hershberger) hit over .300, as both would do in the majors in their best seasons.

The pitching staff listed a number of so-so major league pitchers, good enough to win with the Yankees, but never rotation anchors; these included Atley Donald, Steve Sundra, Joe Beggs, Marius Russo, Kemp Wicker, and Vito Tamulis. Beggs, later the relief ace of the Cincinnati Reds, was a starter that season and was 21-4, while Swampy Donald was 19-2.

To understand why I say that they were not the equal of the 1934 Los Angeles Angels, you have to go back and take a look at the crossroads occupied by the minor leagues at that moment. The major league owners and general managers, under the leadership of Branch Rickey, were converting the minor leagues into servants of the major leagues. Commissioner Landis was fighting a losing battle to keep them independent, existing for their own purposes.

In a well-known incident in 1937, Landis freed ninety-one St. Louis Cardinal farmhands, ruling that the relationships between the Cardinals and the minor league teams were illegal. When this confrontation is discussed today, the idea usually comes across that the Cardinals had been guilty of some sort of covert shenanigans in signing and controlling minor league players. This is an unfortunate misunderstanding, because what Landis in fact ruled was that the arrangements between the Cardinals and their minor league affiliates—arrangements that were, in Landis' words, "Big as a house. Big as the Universe"—were in and of themselves prohibited. Those same relationships, within ten years of Landis' death, became standard practice throughout baseball—and, indeed, were soon surpassed by new and even more restrictive arrangements that would have horrified the old judge even more.

Landis ruled that the Cardinal contracts had trapped the minor league teams in a relationship in which they were prohibited from taking actions that they might need to take to win a league championship—and thus, in effect, that they constituted a breach of faith with those team's fans, the same as surrendering the attempt to win the pennant in any other way. Once this breach of faith was complete, once the minor leagues teams no longer were able to pursue victory for themselves only, they could no longer survive without subsidies. Let me quote from the exchanges between Rickey and Landis at that time, as released by the commissioner's office:

LANDIS: You have this arrangement which obligates Springfield to take optional players only from the owner of the Danville club, it's competitor . . . suppose Springfield and Danville are in first and second positions, making a fight, and that Springfield can get an optional player who will strengthen Springfield. Have you a right under this agreement to say to Springfield, "You shall not take that player?"

RICKEY: I think we have.

LANDIS: Is that good?

RICKEY: It is not good for Springfield.

LANDIS: Is it good for the league? Is it good for the whole institution?

RICKEY: Many a club makes an agreement that is bad for itself. It is entirely a question of can a man make a deal for himself.

LANDIS: I am not dealing with the question of the selfish interest of Springfield in the deal. I am dealing with this question: *Here is a pennant race in the Three-I League that is, as far as the principle is concerned, just as important as if it were a pennant race in the National or American Leagues.* They are fighting your club. You have the power to say to them: "This avenue of strength to your club is shut off." It is pretty plain that would be bad for the league, wouldn't it?

RICKEY: I get your point: Danville and Springfield are contending for the pennant in the same league. All right. Suppose . . . we withhold the benevolent hand and say, "You can't have any optional player from us, and other sources of supply are stopped; there, that will leave you in second place and Danville will win." . . . Yes, that is in it; you are right.

LANDIS: That is in this (the agreement with Springfield); isn't it?

RICKEY: Yes, that is in there.

LANDIS: Big as a house, isn't it?

RICKEY: It is not big as a house.

LANDIS: I think it is as big as the universe. *This is just as important in the Three-I League as it would be in the National or American Leagues.*

Regrettably, journalists interpreted this action on a personal level, as Landis against Rickey. The minor leagues decayed because the point was lost that Landis was trying to make: that minor league teams cannot survive if their fans are asked to support units which are, in reality, extensions of a foreign power.

The minor leagues before Branch Rickey were a small war. After Rickey, they were merely boot camp.

In the 1930s, the minor league teams were poised between what they had been and what they were to become. The Newark Bears were a vassal team. They may have been the strongest vassal team ever, a reflection of a time when the strength of the teams was imbalanced, but they were a vassal team in a vassal league—and, to my mind, could not possibly have been as strong as the strongest of the free minor league teams. The 1934 Angels, while not entirely free as the Orioles had been a decade earlier, were more free than the Bears—and the league in which they competed was, from 1930 until 1955, the most independent of the minor leagues. The Pacific Coast League teams had their own stars, whom they kept for years.

Yet, ironically, this tends to work against the Angels in their evaluation by fans fifty or seventy years later. A modern fan, looking at the players involved, tries to figure out how good the team was by looking at what their players did when they got to the majors. But the Pacific Coast League was a good league, and the things that were done there did not need to be validated by major league performance in order to become real.

The Pacific Coast League had used a split schedule (first half, second half)—for several years before 1931. They stopped in 1932. The Los Angeles Angels of 1934 were such an awesome team that they had to split the schedule again, or the Angels were going to win it by thirty-five games. Their first-half record was 66-18, winning by nineteen and a half games (or rather, the Angels were nineteen and a half ahead when the rest of the league decided that they wanted to call it off and start over). It didn't help. In the second half the Angels were 71-32, winning by twelve games. Their combined record was 137-50, a .733 percentage. The second-best combined record in the league was 101-85. To make a playoff, they chose an all-star team from the rest of the league. The Angels beat the all-star team in six games.

Who were those guys? The star of the team was Frank Demaree, who started the All-Star

game for the National League in 1936 and 1937. Demaree had quite a season, hitting .383 with 45 homers, 173 RBI, 51 doubles, and 41 stolen bases, one of three 40/40 seasons in minor league history. The top pitcher was Fay Thomas, who had the misfortune of being drafted after the season by the St. Louis Browns, but who was a good pitcher for many years in the minors.

That's what many of the Angels were—minor league stars. Jigger Statz was a durable singles hitter who had nine straight .300 seasons in the Pacific Coast League; he was probably fairly comparable to the American League's Doc Cramer, as a player. Third Baseman Gene Lillard was an outstanding offensive and defensive player, who I think could have been a major league star with better luck. The double play combination was Jimmy Reese (who had been Babe Ruth's roommate) and Carl Dittmar, another longtime minor league star. First baseman Jim Oglesby was laid up by blood poisoning in 1936, during the time that he was trying to establish himself in the major leagues (bad timing, Jim).

A book about the Angels by Richard E. Beverage was published by Deacon Press in Placentia, California in 1981. The Angels were probably not as good as the Baltimore Orioles of a decade earlier, and quite possibly not even as good as the San Francisco Seals of 1922–25 or the Minneapolis Millers of 1911. By 1934 most of the structures were already in place to take all of the best players out of the minors and concentrate them in the majors. But I think the Angels were the best minor league team of the 1930s.

FRANK SHELLENBACK

Frank Shellenback may have been the best pitcher in the history of the minor leagues. His major league career was respectable but not distinguished. In 1918 he was 10-12 with a 2.66 ERA, that figure ranking 27th among 55 American League starters. He got his chance that year when Red Faber went into the Army and Claude Williams left the team early in the season. The White Sox had an off year, finishing sixth after winning the pennant in 1917. When Faber and Williams returned in 1919, and Shellenback started slowly, he was released to Minneapolis. He was twenty-seven years old.

Shellenback was a spitball pitcher, and he had the misfortune of being in the minor leagues at the moment that the spitball was banned. Each team was allowed to protect a couple of spitball pitchers, so that those who relied on the pitch would not be put out of the game. Shellenback, being in the minors, was not put on a major league protected list. He did make the Pacific Coast League protected list a year later, however, and so he continued to pitch for almost twenty years thereafter—in the Pacific Coast League.

Shellenback would win 315 games in the minor leagues. This is not one of the top ten totals in minor league history, but there are several reasons for citing Shellenback as perhaps the best minor league pitcher of all time. His won-lost record, 315-192, is 123 games over .500 with a .621 percentage, both figures the best among minor league 300-game winners. His record was all compiled in the top minors; he was 9-6 in the International League, 11-8 in the American Association, and 295-178 in the Pacific Coast League. And, while he did pitch for some good teams, he also pitched for a lot of not-very-good teams. He was 18-10 in 1921 for a Vernon team that was under .500 when he wasn't pitching. In 1923 he was 19-19 for a terrible team. In the following four seasons (1924–1927) he was 14-7, 14-17, 16-12 and 19-12 with PCL teams that were nowhere near .500 with other pitchers. When his teams were decent his records got better: 23-11 in 1928, 26-12 in 1929, 19-7 in 1930, 27-7 in 1931, 26-10 in 1932, and 21-12 in 1933. The Hollywood Stars, for whom Shellenback was 27-7 in 1931, were only one game over .500 when Shellenback wasn't pitching. After 1934 he went back to pitching for bad teams.

Shellenback is best remembered today as Leo Durocher's pitching coach.

FETTERED COMPETITION

They went to bed 21-5, and woke up 0-26. Unfortunately, due to the obvious timidity of team owner Joe Cambria, they were not called the "Steaks." They were called the Indians. They were called the Indians because they had once been an Indians farm team, although by 1937 they were affiliated with the Senators. At the start of the 1937 season, the Salisbury Indians, of Salisbury, Maryland, were title favorites. With a hard-throwing right-hander from Atlantic City, a Cuban kid, a smooth second baseman named Jerry Lynn, and some fence-busting outfielders, Salisbury seemed as good a bet as any to win the Eastern Shore League in the summer of 1937.

They won a few games, and then they lost one, and then they won several more, and they lost one, and then they won several more, and then suddenly one morning—it was June 20th, after a meeting at the league president's office on the 19th—they were 0 and 26. The problem was that the Eastern Shore League, a Class D League at the bottom of baseball's food chain, had a rule that each team was permitted to sign no more than four "experienced" players. The Indians had signed four experienced players, but had not listed their first baseman, Robert Brady, as an "experienced" player. Other teams protested that Brady had signed a contract three years earlier with another team.

Yes, said Joe Cambria, but he never played. He signed a pro contract three years ago, but he never put on a uniform.

To a modern fan, this whole approach—limiting the number of "experienced" players who may play for each team—probably seems a bit odd. You can liken it to the NCAA. In the NCAA, teams are sometimes forced to forfeit games because the team has scheduled too many practices, or because one of the team's fans has allowed a player to borrow his sports car for a weekend, or some other damned thing. That's where minor league baseball was at that time—it was trying to create a structure for vigorous competition within carefully specified limits.

The league president, one J. Thomas Kibler, ruled that Brady should have been considered an experienced player—and, in what can only be considered a draconian sanction, forfeited all of Salisbury's games. This ruling was more than draconian: it was stupid, and it was unjust. Harris *had* no professional experience, and Salisbury had not intentionally violated the rules. Harris had not even appeared in almost

half of the Salisbury games, and had hit only .246 with no homers, 7 RBI. To take away 21 wins because of an error which was both inadvertent and inconsequential was unfair to the team's fans, unfair to the players, and a breach of the fundamental principle that sports events are supposed to be decided on the field, and not in a back room.

Joe Cambria appealed the decision to Judge William G. Bramham, president of the National Association. The minor league Landis. "Before the season opened," Cambria explained, "the Salisbury club submitted a list of players to the league president. Kibler okayed the list. Kibler had as much knowledge about Brady as Salisbury did." Bramham upheld the ruling. "We're floored," Cambria said, "but we'll never quit. I've instructed the manager and the team to carry on the fight on and off the ball field."

The Indians picked themselves up, dusted themselves off, and soldiered on. Oh and 26. Their manager, Jake Flowers, did not protest Kibler's action, for an odd reason: personal loyalty. Kibler had been his college baseball coach. "We ask no quarter and we offer none," said Flowers. "We'll be back in the first division before Labor Day." Labor Day was when the season ended. It was a nearly impossible goal, at 0 and 26. Not only were their wins in the bank converted to losses, but also losses by the opposition had been converted into wins, pushing Easton's record up from 18-12 to 20-10. Salisbury was 20 games behind with 72 to play. If they won two-thirds of the remaining games, that wouldn't get them back to .500.

They won their first game, 10 to 0, and then their second. Two and 26, three and 27, five and 28. In a month they were 20 and 31. They moved out of the cellar on July 28, with five weeks left in the season. They reached .500 on August 9. They had three weeks left to make a run for the top.

What they had going for them was two pitchers who never lost. Although the Kibler elf had taken away 21 wins, he had left the individual statistics, including won-lost records, as they were. George Comellas, a 19-year-old Cuban right-hander, was 20 and 0, and had struck out 21 men in one nine-inning victory. He was the number two pitcher on the staff. The number one pitcher, Atlantic City product Joe Kohlman, pitched a four-hitter in his first start, but took a loss. After that he didn't lose . . . five in a row, ten, fifteen, twenty. At one time, the Salisbury Indians of 1937 had two pitchers working on winning streaks of twenty games or more. The Indians also had the league's two leading hitters, second baseman Jerry Lynn and shortstop Frank Trechock, and a power-hitting catcher, Mike Guerra.

In the end, Salisbury's spectacular battle back from a near-death sanction was a bonanza for the league. Although attendance totals were never posted, Salisbury drew an estimated 1,500 fans a game, and Salisbury fans began following the team around the state, creating overflow attendance wherever they played. (Seven of the eight teams in the Eastern Shore League played in Maryland, the other being warehoused in Dover, Delaware.)

By August 19 the Salisbury Indians had pulled to within one game of the first-place Easton Yankees. On August 20, however, Comellas took his first loss of the season, dropping them two back. They won on the 21st, but so did Easton; they weren't scheduled to play on the 22nd, and then they were rained out on the 23rd and the 24th. On August 25th, with the end of the race ten days away, they were still in second place.

Joe Kohlman's 22nd consecutive win was a five-hitter in which he struck out 12, lowering his earned run average to 1.25. They won again the next day, edging into first place, but then lost a game and dropped back to second.

On August 30 the Indians played an odd double-header, making up for a rainout by playing Centreville that afternoon, and Crisfield that night. Kohlman won the afternoon contest for his 23rd consecutive victory. Comellas won the evening game, moving to 22-1. They were back in first.

Five members of the Salisbury team (Comellas, Kohlman, Lynn, Trechock, and Guerra) were sold to the Washington Senators, for delivery at season's end. Clark Griffith himself came out to see them play on September 1. A crowd of 3,000 wedged into Salisbury to see Griffith, and to see the players receive jeweled watches and cars and candy in tribute to their comeback. They won, of course, 10 to 2, but Easton was coming to town on September 2.

Joe Kohlman was ready for them. He really did it. He pitched a no-hitter, striking out nine and walking two. Salisbury didn't even have to make up a couple of rainouts; they had the pennant won, at 59-37. After the 0-26 start, they were 59-11.

The Indians cruised in the first round of the playoffs, but lost two straight to open the second round. They rallied to tie it, and sent Joe Kohlman out for the final game. No problem. No hits, no runs, no problem. His second no-hitter in just over two weeks, the first one clinching the pennant, and the second one deciding the playoffs. He finished 25-1 for a team that played only 96 games. He struck out 257 batters in 227 innings, and had a string of 27 straight victories including the playoffs. His ERA was not carried in the official stats, but was unofficially reported at 1.18.

None of the five players who vaulted to the majors became stars. The Senators exploited the local publicity by letting them play one game apiece that September. Joe Kohlman pitched a complete-game victory for the Senators, and finished his major league career with a 1-0 record, although he pitched in a few other games. Jerry Lynn played only one major league game, but had two hits to retire with a career average of .667, a slugging percentage of 1.000, and seven clean plays at second base. Frank Trechock also played only one game, the same game; he also had two hits, and finished with a major league batting average of .500.

Mike Guerra played that game, too, and then went back to the minors for seven seasons. The war got him back to the majors, and he had an eight-year career as a backup catcher, all of that after his thirtieth birthday.

Jake Flowers, the manager, was named the Minor League Manager of the Year by *The Sporting News.* He was the only man ever to win that award for managing a Class D ballclub—and the only manager to win a pennant after starting the season 0 and 26.

(My thanks to Lloyd Johnson for his help with this article.)

THANK GOD I'M A COUNTRY BOY

Kirby Higbe says in his autobiography that he developed his strong arm by throwing rocks at the Negroes. Satchel Paige says in his that he developed his arm by throwing rocks at the white boys.

THE NEGRO LEAGUES

When we speak of the Negro Leagues, we often mean something more than the leagues themselves. Segregation in baseball dates back at least to 1867; Cap Anson's famous refusal to play against black players, which came twenty years later, is more properly described as a time when efforts to break the color line were turned back, rather than the time when the color line was established. From 1867 forward, when African Americans wanted to play baseball, they had to play it, in the main, within the walls of segregation.

In the fifty years following those walls contained countless black baseball teams, some leagues of black teams, dozens of black superstars, and many memorable contests. The economic form that the game favored was the exhibition series or championship series, a model somewhat analogous to modern boxing, albeit without the TV money. As the twentieth century progressed, and transportation became easier, this evolved into the exhibition tour. By 1920 there were prominent black teams in many or most northern cities, teams which

dominated local competition and sometimes traveled to play against one another or to meet other opposition. Rube Foster, a great player himself, considered the 1910 Chicago American Giants, a team with no league, to be the greatest baseball team ever assembled, black or white. The Kansas City Giants, a forerunner of the Monarchs, won 54 straight games in 1909.

The Chicago Giants remained a formidable team throughout the teens, but by their end Foster realized that the teams needed the stability and structure of a league organization, in part to combat the influence of Nat Strong, who controlled the booking of stadiums and the promotion of games on the East Coast. In 1920, on the initiative of Foster, the men who operated eight of these teams met in Kansas City to form the Negro National League (NNL). It was a Midwestern league, not a league of new teams, but an agreement of existing operations to play in a league format.

But the new league did not entirely supplant the existing operations of its member teams. The teams, which had toured for years, continued to schedule 50 or 100 or 150 exhibition games a year, mixed in with league contests. The teams continued to control their own scheduling. Thus, in the first year of the Negro National League, the Kansas City Monarchs played 81 league games, while the Chicago Giants played only 42, and this continued to be the pattern; the Negro League teams never played 100 or more league games, and never had a balanced schedule.

After a couple of seasons, as the Negro National League began to enjoy some success, the better east coast teams decided to organize a league of their own. This was the Eastern Colored League (ECL), which began play in 1923.

Rube Foster was good with money. The story told about him, which was passed along for sixty years before it was written down, and which therefore appears in different guises, is that when he was in his late teens (about 1899) he pitched a game in a small city in Texas, a game attended by several hundred fans. Rube was doing the math in his head; several hundred fans, a quarter or fifty cents a head, a dime for the kids; that's $300 or more. But when his team got their cut, it was a pittance, a few dollars.

Rube went to the team's manager and demanded to know what had happened. The manager, a veteran player, said that he had made the best deal he could. Well, said Rube, if you don't want to deal with these guys, let me do it. The veteran said fine, you do it. He did— and for the rest of his life, Rube Foster's team never took less than 50% of the gate.

Rube Foster grew to be a great baseball player, and also the visionary businessman of black baseball—a promoter of games, an organizer of teams, and ultimately, the organizer of the league. He was also the backbone of the league—the financier, the negotiator, the innovator, the authority, the booking agent, and the league's *de facto* commissioner.

The white National League was organized in 1876 by a strong-willed Chicago businessman, William Hulbert, who died six years later. But whereas the premature death of William Hulbert was beneficial to that National League—Hulbert had made his contribution, and his strong personality was obstructing the league's growth—the premature death of Rube Foster ripped the heart out of the Negro National. Foster lost his mind in 1926 (probably due to organic causes) and died in 1930. Foster, like Hulbert, was so strong-willed as to be regarded by many as a tyrant, but he brought to the league indispensable skills.

Foster had big plans for the National League. He was, for one thing, reportedly planning to put a few white players in the league. His death came at a particularly bad time, with attendance down throughout the league, and Foster's estate entangled with the finances of almost all the teams. The league stumbled and fell, failing to play out the 1928 season. It staggered to its feet, played through the 1929 and 1930 seasons, but then collapsed again. Meanwhile, the Eastern Colored League also collapsed in 1928, also staggered through the 1929 season, and then expired.

While the Negro Leagues were inert, the teams that had comprised the league soldiered on. They went back to fulltime exhibition tours—barnstorming, as it came to be called (after the pilots of the era, who used barns as hangars). The Kansas City Monarchs, with no league affiliation from 1931 to 1936, still played between 80 and 250 games every year.

In 1933 Gus Greenlee, king of the numbers racket in Pittsburgh, decided to re-launch the National League. The guys that he knew who had both the money and the interest to back other teams were (you guessed it) the guys who ran the numbers rackets in some other eastern cities. Thus, the Negro National League was restarted in 1933 with management that was . . . well, not quite gangsters, but men who made their living by running a gambling enterprise that happened to be illegal.

Now, there is little evidence that these were really bad guys. They were men who owned nightclubs, restaurants, hotels, and theaters in the black communities (Greenlee's team was called the Pittsburgh Crawfords, after his Crawford Bar and Grille). They paid their bills, they met their obligations; games were not fixed, and players were not dropped in the river when they went into a slump. Still, the marginal nature of the league's financing had significant consequences . . . The league was careless in issuing franchises, and some teams entered the league with no money behind them and no real commitment to the enterprise. No one in the league much respected player contracts, and there was no central authority to speak of.

The Negro National League of the 1930s, although it picked up the name of the NNL, was more the successor of the Eastern Colored League than of the original NNL, which was a Midwestern league. In 1937 the Midwestern teams got back together to form the Negro American League (the NAL). People thus began to refer to teams as "Eastern" and "Western," rather than by league names. As a consequence, when we speak of the Negro major leagues we are really describing four leagues—

The Negro National League I (1920–1930)

The Eastern Colored League (1923–1929)

The Negro National League II (1933–1947)

The Negro American League (1937–1950)

These years are not too precise. Leagues sometimes started and played games, but decided the hell with it in mid-season, and failed to post won-lost records. The NAL stumbled along after 1950, its final demise being located somewhere between 1955 and the first Reagan

administration, but after 1950 it had lost all pretense of being a major league. And the leagues themselves were never the whole of elite Negro League baseball, as the Majors were in the white world. The Leagues were more the yolk of the egg, the nucleus of a world that extended from the Dominican Republic to Alberta, from the ice up north to the equator and below and included dozens of other leagues, organized at various times.

Jackie Robinson signed with the Dodgers in late 1945, and played in the major leagues in 1947. The end of the color line brought the inevitable end of the Negro Leagues. Negro League historians are wont to rant that the white club owners did not respect the "contracts" of the Negro League teams in the period of the league's disintegration. They miss, it seems to me, an obvious point: these teams didn't respect one another's contracts, either. They operated on letters of agreement, which players and teams felt free to discard as soon as they became inconvenient. Why would we expect the white club owners to respect "contracts" that the Negro Leagues themselves didn't respect?

From 1920 on, the Negro National League tried to imitate certain aspects of major league baseball, and ultimately they failed, as an economic enterprise. One can fault the leagues for failing to issue, insist upon and honor standard player contracts. One can fault the leagues for tolerating selfish behavior by the teams, such as refusing to commit to a regular schedule and forgetting to file score sheets and statistics with the league office.

But before we make that judgment, there is something else to remember, which I have never seen pointed out in any book about the Leagues. The entire black population of the United States in 1920 was about 10.5 million people. By 1945, it was 13.5 million. In 1920,

Buck Leonard homers at Giffith Stadium, 1945

MOST of those ten million were living in the south, most of those on farms, and most of those in conditions not very far removed from slavery. The situation that Buck O'Neil recalls from his childhood—working from dawn to dark as a box boy on a celery farm, having his father thrown in jail because the county needed road workers—was fairly representative of America at that time.

The Negro League teams were northern, urban operations, with their appeal based largely on the black population (except for barnstorming, which was destructive of stability). That audience was drawn from an entire population, in 1920, of about 2 million people, most of them poor, and spread around 15 to 20 cities. Two of the glamour teams of the Negro Leagues, the Homestead Grays and the Pittsburgh Crawfords, were based in Pittsburgh—at a time when the black population of Pittsburgh, according to Donn Rogosin in *Invisible Men,* was less than 80,000. It is just not realistic to think that the Negro League organizations, even had Foster lived, could have reached the scale and stability that we associate with major league baseball.

Beyond that, Negro League management was cut off from capital. Most banks wouldn't talk to black businessmen in that era, wouldn't even talk to them. To survive, a Negro League team needed a financial wizard juggling the money, or risked collapse the first time attendance slackened. There were about five of those guys involved in the league who were really good at handling money—Rube Foster, J. L. Wilkinson, Cum Posey, Gus Greenlee, and Abe Manley. The rest of them were just getting by day to day.

Now, I have known a good many men who run major league baseball teams, and I can tell you, very few of them are financial wizards. A certain number of them are just dumb as a post. If you cut them off from access to capital and forced them to live on the money they could generate in on-going operations, 80% of them would be bankrupt within two years. That was the situation that the Negro Leagues faced: inevitable failure met anybody who was just a sporting promoter, just a baseball man, and just ordinary at handling money.

Understanding this, it is rather remarkable that they were able to accomplish what they did. They developed outstanding players; they set up a league which was immensely successful at identifying the best black athletes in the country. They organized All-Star games that drew large crowds, and were major league operations in every sense of the word. They sustained themselves economically by traveling from Puerto Rico to Canada, promoting relentlessly an endless series of games in an endless series of small towns. They set the stage for Jackie Robinson. By the time integration arrived, baseball was more ready for it than almost any other segment of American society.

HOW THE GAME WAS PLAYED

In some respects, Negro League baseball in the years 1920–1950 mirrored white baseball of the years 1870–1900. Negro League teams in the 1920s played league schedules of 50 to 80 games, with exhibition loads of perhaps a

hundred games more—exactly as National Association and National league teams had in the 1870s. Negro League teams in the 1920s sometimes refused to make scheduled road trips on which the owners thought they would lose money, just as National Association teams had done. The stronger teams in the Negro Leagues sometimes extorted 70% of the gate receipts from the weaker teams, just as had happened in the National Association.

Negro League players did not have strong contracts, and players jumped from team to team when more money was offered, just as had happened in the Association. In the 1890s several National League teams bought into others, creating a situation in which teams were essentially competing with their farm clubs. Similar things happened in the Negro Leagues, where the shortage of capital forced competing businesses into an unhealthy embrace.

In other respects, the organization of the Negro Leagues was up to or ahead of the white leagues. The Negro League teams used lights and played night baseball years before the major leagues did. Negro League players invented and refined many strategies. Most significantly, the networking system by which the Negro Leagues identified and developed talent was certainly far more sophisticated than nineteenth century baseball, and appears to have been probably more effective than the methods used by the white teams—different, but certainly no less effective (see "Who The Game Was Played By").

Negro League teams carried fourteen to sixteen men, which forced players to be more versatile than in the white leagues. From the standpoint of the fan, I would regard this as a large advantage for the Negro League game. I have always believed that the 25-man roster is too large. It enables managers to hide weaknesses; players who can't hit left-handers don't have to hit left-handers, players who can't throw don't have to throw. Specialization in sports reduces the dimensions of the player that can be exposed in the contest, and thus dehumanizes the players, making the game, in my opinion, less interesting. A fourteen-man roster is small, but a sixteen-man roster is a lot closer to where it ought to be than 25.

When you read the oral histories of the Negro Leagues, you could get the impression that the game was like dead ball era baseball. The spitball, banned in white baseball since 1920, remained legal in the Negro Leagues. With a big-hitting team coming to town, white teams would occasionally (surreptitiously) "freeze" baseballs, sharply reducing the resiliency of the balls. Black teams did this openly without repercussions. One of the most famous games in Negro League history is the "Battle of the Butchered Balls," a 1930 pitcher's duel played under the lights at Muehlebach Field in Kansas City. The 12-inning game ended 1-0, with Smokey Joe Williams striking out 27 men (and winning), and Chet Brewer striking out 19 (and losing). Both pitchers threw emery balls, spit balls, and "goo balls" to which a small amount of tar had been applied. Combined with the dim lights of the Kansas City park, Brewer and Williams had the hitters praying to see tomorrow.

Such stories create the image of a dead ball game, dominated by strategy and baserunning. Donn Rogosin wrote that "Negro Leaguers realized that they possessed a distinctive style of Baseball. The central difference stemmed from the Negro League's emphasis on speed and its rejection of the Babe Ruth-inspired long-ball game." Phil Dixon gives a different impression in *The Negro Baseball Leagues,* reporting what happened after Bill Robinson (Bojangles) offered to pay members of the Los Angeles White Sox $5 per home run. The White Sox hit so many home runs that "Robinson reduced the offer to $1 per

home run. He finally stopped giving money altogether when Norman (Turkey) Stearns hit four home runs in one game. Robinson stated 'It's time for me to stop handing out money; you fellows are breaking me.'"

While I am not knowledgeable enough to interpose myself in a dispute among experts here, the statistical record—such as it is—suggests that Rogosin's argument that the Negro Leagues rejected the Babe Ruth revolution is incorrect. The statistics printed in the *Macmillan Encyclopedia* (1993) show Oscar Charleston hitting 15 homers in 60 games in 1921, 16 homers in 66 games in 1922, 14 homers in 56 games in 1924, 20 homers in 68 games in 1925, 11 homers in 49 games in 1927, and 10 homers in 40 games in 1933—home run rates comparable to Rogers Hornsby or Hack Wilson. John Beckwith, barely mentioned among discussions of the league's stars, is reported to have homered 46 times in 141 games between 1929 and '31. Cool Papa Bell, much more famous for speed than power, is reported to have homered 15 times in 85 games in 1926. The immortal Josh Gibson homered about as often, per game, as Babe Ruth. Chino Smith homered 20 times in 60 games in 1929. Turkey Stearns hit 17, 18, 20, 20, 24, and 19 homers in various seasons, never playing more than 88 games. Mule Suttles has almost the same career data as Stearns. Willard Brown, Rap Dixon, Buck Leonard, Dobie Moore, Willie Wells, and others had impressive home run rates.

The St. Louis Stars of the late 1920s, playing in Sportsman's Park (which was a hitters' paradise) compiled phenomenal hitting stats from the top of the lineup to the bottom. Cool Papa Bell is reported to have batted 370 times in 85 games in 1926, and more than four times per game every year between 1925 and 1930. It is impossible to bat that many times unless your team scores a lot of runs.

On the other hand, these teams probably played an honest offense: nobody was up there looking for a walk. Terris McDuffie walked only five men in 108 innings in 1937. Many pitchers posted extremely low walk totals.

Bruce Petway, a star catcher in the days before the league was organized, hit a reported .253, .208, and .200 from 1916 to 1918, with a .171 average in exhibitions against major leaguers. In trips to Cuba from 1908 to 1916 he compiled an average of .210. But in the Negro National from 1921 to 1924 he hit .313, .268, .337, and .341—and he was 38 when that stretch started. This and other examples suggest that the lively ball era may have come to Negro baseball about the same time it came to white baseball.

My best guess, based on what I know, is that Negro League baseball featured wide-open baserunning and a good number of pitchers duels, but high batting averages, lots of home runs, a good number of errors, with runs scored held somewhat in check by a shortage of walks.

WHERE THE GAME WAS PLAYED

Black baseball was played everywhere in North America. Negro *League* baseball was played at the highest level in 27 cities: Atlanta, Atlantic City, Baltimore, Birmingham, Brooklyn, Chicago, Cincinnati, Cleveland, Columbus, Dayton, Detroit, Harrisburg, Houston, Indianapolis, Jacksonville, Kansas City, Louisville, Memphis, Milwaukee, Nashville, New York, Newark, Philadelphia, Pittsburgh, St. Louis, Toledo, and Washington.

These 27 cities were represented by a total of 55 franchises, although it is sometimes impossible to say for sure what is a new franchise and what is a continuation of an existing franchise. The Newark Stars, a 1926 effort in the Eastern Colored League, melted into the ocean of history after winning only one game in 11 efforts. Ten other franchises won ten league games or fewer, and 33 of the 55 franchises won 75 league games or fewer in their entire existence.

The ten strongest teams of the Negro Leagues, in order, were:

1. The Kansas City Monarchs
2. The Chicago American Giants
3. The St. Louis Stars
4. The Homestead Grays
5. The Detroit Stars
6. The Newark Eagles
7. Hilldale (Philadelphia)
8. The Baltimore Elite Giants
9. The Birmingham Black Barons
10. The Pittsburgh Crawfords

There are countless other teams which could be mentioned, but I'm trying to keep this a little bit simple.

A fascinating feature of Negro League baseball, which has little parallel in white baseball, is the phenomenon of great teams that existed for only a year, only a few months, or only a few weeks, and had no connection to the strongest leagues. The most famous of these teams was the Trujillo team, which was formed in Santo Domingo in 1937, but other great teams were formed in Cuba, in Mexico, and in Bismarck, North Dakota, among many other places.

This happened because Negro League players were not bound by strong, enforceable contracts. A man who had money, if he dreamed of putting together a powerhouse baseball team, had little chance of attracting Lou Gehrig, Joe DiMaggio, Carl Hubbell, and Charlie Gehringer—but he could attract African-American players of the same quality.

WHO THE GAME WAS PLAYED BY

Almost all of the stars of the Negro Leagues were born in the South, and became a part of the urban northward migration. Only a handful of players were born in the north.

The Negro League teams almost from the beginning had networks of city teams and semi-pro teams which fed them talent, and at least one team (the Monarchs) did have an organized farm team. Negro League teams had an immense advantage over white teams in finding and developing talent: they traveled. Boy, did they travel. Negro League teams barnstormed coast to coast for several months every year, playing against local competition. League teams would play a league series in Pittsburgh on Saturday afternoon, then race to Altoona to play a local team on Saturday night. That gave their managers and players the opportunity to see literally thousands of young players every year. It gave local athletes a chance to reach out to the teams and say "Here I am. I can play."

When the players did go home (December through February) everybody on the team essentially became a scout, trolling their acquaintances for players who might be able to help their teams. It was different from the major league system, but it was highly effective.

Apart from skin color and the fact that there were even more southerners, the sociological mix of the Negro Leagues was probably not very different from that of the major leagues in the same era. There were some college men in the mix, some tough guys, some rubes and some slickers. The best Negro League teams, the Monarchs and Giants, set a high standard of behavior for their players, and were quite effective in enforcing that standard.

CHECKING IN:

1856— Fleetwood Walker
1865— Frank Grant
1874— J. L. Wilkinson
1879— Charlie Grant
1879— Rube Foster
1881— Branch Rickey
1884— John Henry Lloyd
1885— Smokey Joe Williams
1886— Spotswood Poles
1890— Louis Santop
1896— Oscar Charleston
1898— Bullet Joe Rogan
1903— Cool Papa Bell
1906— Satchel Paige
1907— Buck Leonard
1911— Buck O'Neil
1911— Josh Gibson
1919— Jackie Robinson

CHECKING OUT:

1924— Fleetwood Walker
1930— Rube Foster
1932— Charlie Grant
1937— Frank Grant
1942— Louis Santop
1946— Smokey Joe Williams
1947— Josh Gibson
1954— Oscar Charleston
1962— Spotswood Poles
1962— Bullet Joe Rogan
1964— J. L. Wilkinson
1964— John Henry Lloyd
1965— Branch Rickey
1972— Jackie Robinson
1982— Satchel Paige
1991— Cool Papa Bell

THE NEGRO LEAGUES IN A BOX

Attendance Data:

Systematic attendance data about the Negro Leagues does not exist. The first Negro League World Series in 1924 drew crowds ranging from a low of 584 fans to a high of 8,661. Opening day was a big crowd, and big games sometimes drew crowds over 10,000. It would be my guess that Negro League games in the 1920s were typically attended by 500 to 5,000 fans, with somewhat larger crowds in the earlier part of the decade, dropping after 1925.

The restart of the Negro National in 1933 brought in crowds even smaller than that at first, but the numbers probably built steadily. Attendance for the East-West All-Star game in Chicago, the Negro Leagues biggest spectacle, started at about 20,000 in 1933, and increased to about 45,000–50,000 from 1941 through 1948. By the early 1940s, Negro League games were probably drawing crowds of 3,000 to 10,000 as a regular thing, and more when some publicity could be generated.

In 1942 it was reported that a Washington Senators game drew less than 5,000. That same night, 29,000 came to the park to see Satchel Paige pitch against the Homestead Grays. The Grays, playing in Washington at that time, were regularly drawing 15,000 and more. Buck Leonard said in *Voices from the Great Black Baseball Leagues* that "In 1945 we drew more than the Senators, and we weren't playing as many games." In October and November, 1946, Satchel and Bob Feller put together a tour, traveling through the West and in particular California. They played 32 games in 26 days, reporting attendance of more than 400,000.

On October 4, 1933, a game between the Kansas City Monarchs and a team billed as the St. Louis Cardinals drew six thousand fans at Oxford, Nebraska. In quieter times, thousands of games were played in front of a few hundred fans, a hundred, a few dozen.

Most Home Runs:

Mule Suttles,	1926	27
Willie Wells,	1929	27
Mule Suttles		190

The leaders here are based on the Negro League data given in the 1993 *Macmillan* *Encyclopedia*. Josh Gibson was generally regarded as the greatest power hitter in Negro baseball.

Best Won/Lost Record by Team:

Kansas City Monarchs,	1929	62-17	.785
Kansas City Monarchs		680-363	.652

Worst Won/Lost Record by Team:

Memphis Red Sox,   1945   17-61   .218
New York Black Yankees   71-217   .247

Heaviest Player: Heavy Johnson, 250 pounds

Tubby Barnes' (also known as Fat Barnes) weight is unknown, but surely went over 250 on a bad doughnut day.

Lightest Player: Paul Jake Stevens (115 to 155)

Stevens roomed at the 1935 All Star Game with Boojum Wilson, who was hardly any taller than Stevens, but outweighed him about two to one. Stevens got drunk after the game, really drunk, and picked a fight with Wilson. Wilson, according to Stevens, picked him up with one hand and dangled him by his throat out the fourth-floor window. (In more recent versions of this story, Stevens has been dangled out a sixteenth-story window by his ankle. I'm giving you the older, more conservative version.)

Most Strikeouts by Pitcher:

Satchel Paige,   1929   184
Satchel Paige,   1927–1950   1084

The most strikeouts by a pitcher in a season was probably by John Donaldson, 1915.

In a career, surely the most was by Satchel Paige, who probably struck out several thousand hitters more than Nolan Ryan in his long career.

Highest Batting Average:

Josh Gibson,   1943   .517
Chino Smith,   1925–1930   .428

The 44-year-old John Henry (Pop) Lloyd hit a reported .564 in 37 games with the Lincoln Giants in 1928. I was using a 50-game standard here; Josh hit .517 in 57 games.

Best Negro League Players (by Years):

1900 to 1903— Charlie Grant
1904 to 1906— Bill Monroe
1907 to 1909— John Henry Lloyd
1910 to 1913— Louis Santop
1914 to 1916— Spotswood Poles
1917 to 1919— Oscar Charleston or Cristobal Torriente
1920— Jimmy Lyons
1921— Oscar Charleston
1922— Oscar Charleston
1923— Cristobal Torriente
1924— Dobie Moore
1925— Oscar Charleston
1926— Mule Suttles or Cool Papa Bell
1927— Fats Jenkins
1928— John Henry Lloyd
1929— Willie (Devil) Wells or Chino Smith
1930— John Beckwith
1931— Mule Suttles
1932— Cool Papa Bell
1933— Oscar Charleston
1934— Josh Gibson
1935— Turkey Stearns
1936— Josh Gibson
1937— Willard Brown
1938— Josh Gibson
1939— Buck Leonard
1940— Buck Leonard
1941— Mule Suttles
1942— Josh Gibson
1943— Josh Gibson
1944— Eugene Benson
1945— Sam Jethroe
1946— Willard Brown
1947— Buck Leonard
1948— Buck Leonard
1949— Bob Boyd

Best Negro League Pitchers (by Years):

1900 to 1903— Danny McClellan
1904 to 1906— Rube Foster

1907 to 1909— Walter Ball
1910 to 1913— Harry Buckner
1914 to 1916— Smokey Joe Williams or John
                Donaldson
1917 to 1919— Dick Redding
1920— Jose Mendez
1921— Plunk Drake
1922— Bullet Rogan
1923— Andy Cooper
1924— Bullet Rogan or Nip Winters
1925— Reuben Curry or Joe Rogan
1926— Nip Winters
1927— Bill Foster
1928— Ted Trent
1929— Connie Rector
1930— Ted Trent
1931— Bill Foster
1932— Bill Foster
1933— Chet Brewer
1934— Slim Jones
1935— Leroy Matlack
1936— Satchel Paige
1937— Leon Day
1938— Terris McDuffie
1939— Hilton Smith
1940— Ray Brown
1941— Hilton Smith
1942— Hilton Smith
1943— Eugene Bemer
1944— Bill Byrd
1945— Eugene Bemer
1946— Max Manning or Leon Day
1947— Luis Tiant Sr.
1948— Bill Byrd
1949— Bill Byrd

Hardest-Throwing Pitcher: Smokey Joe
Williams

Best Curve: John Donaldson in the teens, Bullet Rogan in the twenties, Chet Brewer in the
thirties. Big Florida Trent also had an outstanding curve, according to some sources the

best in the league. Rogan threw a hard curve
that broke almost straight down. Donaldson's
curve was a pitch more like a slider, a breaking
pitch thrown as hard as a fastball.

Best Power/Speed Combination: Oscar
Charleston

Best Switch Hitter: Cool Papa Bell

Iron Man: Larry Brown

Best Bunter: Bingo DeMoss

Flameout: Slim Jones

Slim was a skyscraper, 6'6", and thin as a
rail...they list him at 185, but he looks more
like 170, and at 6'6," that's thin. A hard-
throwing lefty, he was probably the best
pitcher in the league at age 21, when he went
22-3 for the Philadelphia Stars (1934). He died
just four years later. He had a terrible drinking
problem, and froze to death on a Baltimore
street at the age of 25.

Best Baseball Books:
20 Years Too Soon—Quincy Trouppe
The Negro Baseball Leagues (A Photographic
History)—Phil Dixon
*The Biographical Encyclopedia of the Negro
Baseball Leagues*—James A. Riley
Blackball Stars—John Holway
Invisible Men—Donn Rogosin
History of Colored Base Ball—Sol White
I Was Right on Time—Buck O'Neil
Black Diamonds—John Holway
The Kansas City Monarchs—Janet Bruce
Voices From the Great Black Baseball Leagues—
John Holway

These are all fine books, as are some biographies and other collections. James Riley's
Biographical Encyclopedia is the most indispensable research collection. Holway's books
are the most indispensable original research. If

you're just looking for something fun to read, you absolutely can't beat Buck O'Neil's *I Was Right On Time* (Buck O'Neil with Steve Wulf and David Conrads).

Best Outfield Arm: Jelly Gardner or Martin Dihigo. Possibly Christobal Torriente.

Worst Outfield Arm: Chaney White

Most Runs Batted In: No Stats. Probably Torriente in a season, Mule Suttles in a career.

Most Aggressive Baserunner: Perhaps Clint Thomas. Cool Papa, Oscar Charleston, Bullet Rogan, Chaney White, and Turkey Stearns were aggressive baserunners

Fastest Player: Cool Papa Bell

Slowest Players: Eldridge (Head) Mayweather, Gene Benson

Jesse Williams said that "Buck O'Neil was the greatest you ever saw stealing third base. And couldn't run fast enough to get out of a shower of rain. But he could take third base."

Best Control Pitcher: Satchel Paige

Best-Looking Players: Terris McDuffie, Dink Mothell, Tom Wilson

Effa Manley, owner of the Newark Eagles, once ordered the manager to pitch McDuffie out of turn so she could show him off for some of her girl friends.

McDuffie described himself as "the second best-dressed man in New York" behind Ray Robinson. He used to wear a jacket that said "The Great Terris McDuffie" on the back.

Ugliest Player: Otto (Jay Bird) Ray

Strangest Batting Stances: Jim Binder, Turkey Stearns, Gene Benson

O.J. Simpson Award: Dave Brown

Three Finger Brown Award: Hilton Smith, who was a truly outstanding pitcher, had an arm that was short and bent.

Bound For Glory: Charlie Pride

Best Pitching Staff: The Kansas City Monarchs of the mid- to late-thirties had one of the greatest pitching staffs ever assembled, with Satchel Paige, Hilton Smith, Lefty Bryant, and Chet Brewer.

Best Offense: St. Louis Stars, 1926–1930

Football Players: Jackie Robinson, Jesse Williams

Retrobermanisms: Pitcher Andy Porter was actually called Pullman Porter, a Bermanesque nickname fifty years before the style was popularized by the Boomer.

Basketball Guys: Dick Seay, although he was tiny, was an outstanding basketball player. Ted Strong, Sweetwater Clifton, Piper Davis, Winfield Welch, Fats Jenkins, Bill Yancey, Garnet Blair, Wilmer Fields. Goose Tatum (star of the Harlem Globetrotters) was an outfielder/first baseman for the Indianapolis Clowns.

First of His Kind: Jackie Robinson

Last of His Kind: Fleetwood Walker

One of a Kind: Buck O'Neil

Best Infield: Newark Eagles of the late thirties (1B–Mule Suttles, 2B–Dick Seay, 3B–Ray Dandridge, SS–Devil Wells)

Best Outfield: St. Louis Stars, late twenties (Frog Redus, Cool Papa Bell, Johnny Russell)

A Better Man Than a Ballplayer: Buck O'Neil or Dave Malarcher

A Better Ballplayer Than a Human Being: Plunk Drake or John Beckwith

Mr. Dickens, I'd Like You to Meet: Patricio Scantlebury

Platoon Combinations I Would Like to See: Heavy Johnson and Tank Carr

Best Defensive Team: 1910 Chicago American Giants

Outstanding Sportswriter: Ric Roberts, *Pittsburgh Courier*

Most Admirable Superstar: Rube Foster. Buck Leonard was a respected, quiet, intellectual man.

Gold Glove Team:
C— Biz Mackey
1B— Buck O'Neil
2B— Newt Allen
3B— Dave Malarcher
SS— Dick Lundy
OF— Christobal Torriente
     Oscar Charleston
     Jelly Gardner

New Stadiums: The only park I know of built specifically for the Negro Leaguers was White Sox Park in Los Angeles, built by Joe Pirrone, who was the man behind the California Winter Leagues.

Best World Series: 1924

Best-Hitting Pitcher: Bullet Rogan

Odd Couple: Satchel Paige and Buck O'Neil

Drinking Men:
Tank Carr
Ollie Marcelle
Bill Riggins
Slim Jones
John Beckwith
Sam Bankhead

Charles Blackwell
Christobal Torriente

New Equipment: Negro League aficionados are prone to claiming that Negro Leaguers invented almost everything new in baseball since the pitching mound. Many or most of these claims are spurious. Often people think that because something was used in the Negro Leagues before it was generally adopted in the white leagues, it was invented by the Negro Leaguers—overlooking the fact that there may have been earlier or simultaneous experiments by white players.

An easy example is batting helmets. Willie Wells in 1942 was hit in the head by a pitch, perhaps (in one version of the story) when he was distracted by Effa Manley's legs. The next time he faced the same pitcher, Wells borrowed a construction helmet, and thus became the "first" player to use a batting helmet.

Except that players had been experimenting with batting helmets for at least thirty years. Roger Bresnahan tested a batting helmet in a major league game after being beaned in 1909. Branch Rickey had tried to require his players to use batting helmets in spring training, 1921 (after the death of Ray Chapman) although most of the players rejected them after a quick trial, and it is unclear whether any were actually used in regular-season games. Minor leaguers had certainly used batting helmets, at times, in the 1920s.

In fact, according to *Only the Ball was White*, this wasn't even the first time batting helmets had been used in the Negro Leagues. According to Robert Peterson (page 146), when Satchel Paige pitched in the *Denver Post* tournament in 1936, his fastball so terrified opponents that a team from Borger, Texas, showed up to face him with specially made batting helmets. There are a hundred people who claim to have invented batting helmets.

Most Wins by Pitcher:

Ray Brown, 1940	24
Bill Foster	137

Highest Winning Percentage:

Leroy Matlack, 1935	18-0	1.000
Ray Brown, 1932–1945	101-30	.771

(Some sources list Matlack, 1935, at 20–0 or 21-0.)

Nicknames:

Boojum Wilson
Duro Davis
Bingo DeMoss
Ankleball Moss
Crush Holloway
Colt (Newt Allen, also called the Black Diamond)
Doctor Cyclops (Max Manning)
Packinghouse Adams
Rainey Bibbs
Streak Milton
Cool Papa Bell
Biz Mackey (also called the Silver Eagle)
Chick Pullman
Candy Jim Taylor
Frog Redus
Tully McAdoo
Gold Tooth (Lenny Pearson)
Bullet Joe (Wilber Rogan)
Sparkplug Reese (also known as Speed Boy Reese)
Jelly Gardner
Subby (Dick Byas)
Two Sides (Charles Wesley)
Boogie-Woogie Pardue
High Pockets (Robert Hudspeth)
Rats Henderson
Fats Jenkins

Tank Carr
Heavy Johnson
Jumbo Kimbro
Tubby Scales
Chino (Charlie Smith)
Turkey (Norman Stearnes)
Mule (George Suttles)
Showboat Thomas
Devil Wells
Satan Taylor
Shifty (Jim West)
Double Duty (Ted Radcliffe)
Steel Arm Davis
Jewbaby Floyd (trainer)
Jet (Sam Jethroe)
Sug (Willie Cornelius. Sug was short for "Sugar")
Tacky (Andrew Payne)
Winky James
Goose (Reuben) Curry
Big Florida (Ted Trent)
Dink (Carroll Mothell)

Chet Brewer was called "Dooflackem" after a term he would yell while shooting dice.

Head Mayweather was called "Head" because he had a huge head.

Olan Taylor was originally called "Satan" because he could knock the devil out of the ball. His nickname was changed to "Jelly" after his mother refused to attend games at which her son was called Satan.

Ankleball Moss, as you might guess, threw a hard sinker. He died at the age of (about) 28, after he was accidentally shot during a dice game, and a white doctor refused to treat him.

Quote from Buck O'Neil, *I Was Right on Time:*
"Boy, did we have names. We had Sea Boy and Gunboat, Steel Arm and Copperknee, Dark Knight and Skin Down, Mosquito and

Jitterbug, Popsickle and Popeye, Suitcase and, of course, Satchel."

Among the nicknames applied to Satchel Paige by the white press was "The Chocolate Whizbang."

Willie Powell was sometimes called "Hoggy Baby."

James Brown was called "Bad Blood," according to Phil Dixon, because of "his habit of physically abusing umpires."

Could I try this career over? Everybody

Best Double Play Combination: Newt Allen and Dobie Moore, Kansas City Monarchs, 1922–1926

Best Unrecognized Player: Dobie Moore

Highest-Paid Player: Satchel Paige

I Don't Know What This Has to Do with Baseball, But I Thought I'd Mention It Anyway: There were dozens of black teams called the "Giants" or the "Cuban Giants" or the "American Giants." At one time the two best teams in Chicago were the Giants and the American Giants. The term "Giants" was a code that meant a Negro team. There were other barnstorming teams at that time. Newspapers would print ads for barnstorming teams, but most papers refused to run pictures of black players. When teams put up fliers or posted advertisements promoting a ballgame, the name "Giants" was a way of letting people know that this was a black team.

RATINGS OF THE TOP NEGRO LEAGUE PLAYERS BY POSITION

CATCHER

1. **Josh Gibson.** Probably the greatest catcher in baseball history, and probably the greatest right-handed power hitter. Bill Veeck said that Gibson was the greatest hitter he ever saw. So did countless other Negro League participants and observers.

Gibson was strong in all the parts of his body—short, powerful arms, huge wrists, massive, round shoulders. He was a disciplined hitter with enormous self-confidence. He could pick up a curve the moment it left the pitcher's hand, could hit it 500 feet if he could reach it or let it go by if he couldn't. His defensive skills were good; he was quick, had soft hands, and could throw. His career was not exceptionally long, but I believe that he would have hit over 500 home runs had he played in the majors—150 more than any other catcher.

2. **Louis Santop.** A huge left-handed power hitter who was a superstar in the Walter Johnson era. A genial, easy-going man with a gruff voice, immensely popular with the fans. Good defensive skills; limited mobility, particularly as he aged, but a good arm and, at 240 pounds, a world beater at blocking the plate. Was destroyed by criticism following a critical error in the 1924 World Series.

3. **Biz Mackey.** A dangerous switch hitter, and regarded as the finest defensive catcher in the Negro Leagues. Six-foot even and 200 pounds, he was quick behind the plate and snapped throws to the bases without breaking his squat. Hit a reported .423 with 20 homers for Hilldale (Eastern Colored League) in 1923, also hit .400 in 1930.

4. **Double Duty Radcliffe.** Given the nickname by Damon Runyon after he caught the first game of a double header and pitched the second. He was both a fine pitcher and a fine catcher. Well liked and

intelligent, he played for more than twenty years and managed on after that.

5. **Bruce Petway.** Most famous as a defensive catcher in the Ty Cobb era. Once threw out Ty Cobb three times in one game. A pretty decent right-handed hitter, and could rank higher.

6. **Roy Campanella.** Played in the Negro Leagues almost ten years before the color line was broken. He wasn't as dominant a player in Black baseball as he was in the National League, but he could do a lot of things.

7. **Quincy Trouppe.** Called "El Roro" (the Baby) because of his baby face, he was the author of a book which is a good source of frank and reliable information on the era in which he played. Trouppe surfaced in the majors (1952) at the tag end of a twenty-two year career. Switch hitter; a perpetual .300 hitter who walked a lot, made the All-Star team in 23 leagues over his long career.

8. **Joe Greene.** A top player for a short period of time before World War II. He was a right-handed power hitter, had a strong arm, and solid defensive skills. No speed, and except for a few years probably struck out too much to be considered a great hitter, but had real power. As a soldier in World War II, he reportedly was assigned to the detail that cut down the bodies of Benito Mussolini and his mistress.

9. **Larry Brown.** Defensive catcher, not a great hitter and probably not top-notch as a handler of pitchers, but soft hands, quick as a cat, and a powerful arm. Benito Santiago/Tony Pena/Jim Sundberg type receiver. Switch hitter.

10. **Frank Duncan.** A great competitor, wonderful sense of balance, quick, and blessed with a strong arm. An excellent handler of pitchers, caught for the Kansas City

Monarchs throughout the 1920s, and later managed them.

FIRST BASE

1. **Buck Leonard.** Short and weighing only 185 pounds, Leonard had a compact left-handed stroke that generated enormous power with a quick, easy motion—a little bit, perhaps, like a left-handed Henry Aaron. A strong person, a respected gentleman, he was 40 years old before the color line was broken, but lived to see himself inducted into the Hall of Fame.

(Mule Suttles, if ranked as a first baseman, would rival Leonard as the top man at the spot. I'd bet that Mule played more games at first base than at any other position, but he is listed by everybody as an outfielder, so I'll go along with it.)

2. **Luke Easter.** I know that I have him ranked higher than almost anyone else would rank him, but I'll say this. I know that he didn't "do" all that much either in the Negro Leagues or the white majors—but if you could clone him and bring him back, you'd have the greatest power hitter in baseball today, if not ever. He was immense (6'4½", 240) with shoulders that crossed three lanes of traffic.

Easter was an amiable, fun-loving man who gambled, wasn't 100% honest, and had a temper. He didn't get into baseball until he was past 30, yet he performed sensationally everywhere he went. With the Homestead Grays in 1948, he hit .363 in 58 games, with most of his hits going for extra bases. Signed by the Indians and assigned to San Diego in the Pacific Coast League, he was a genuine phenomenon on the West Coast in 1949, drawing immense crowds everywhere along the coast. He again hit .363 in the PCL, hitting 25 homers and driving in 92 runs in 80 games.

As a 35-year-old rookie for the Indians in 1950 he drove in 107 runs, 103 more his second season. Battling injuries in 1952, he still hammered 31 homers and drove in 97 runs in 127 games.

When an ankle injury left him unable to move faster than a good walk, he returned to the minors, and continued to bat home runs at a Ruthian pace. In 1955, aged 40, he led the International League in home runs (35) and RBI (106); he was playing for Buffalo. In 1956 he upped the ante to 40 and 128, and defended his titles. In 1958, now 43, he hit .307 for Buffalo with 38 homers, 109 RBI. More injuries reduced his playing time, but he continued to hit home runs and drive in runs for years thereafter. In 1960, aged 45, he hit .302 with 14 homers, 57 RBI in 275 at bats for Rochester. Two years later he hit 15 homers, drove in 60 runs in 249 at bats.

Easter was killed in a payroll robbery in 1979. He was carrying the payroll for a construction company that he worked for, was jumped and murdered.

3. Ben Taylor. Left-handed line drive hitter of the Ty Cobb era, hit about .334 lifetime. Exceptional fielder and also a fine pitcher, going 30-1 against all competition in 1911.

4. Buck O'Neil. The Great Soul of Negro League baseball, a warm, wonderful man and an immensely talented story teller. A Mark Grace/Mickey Vernon type player (except right-handed), a line drive hitter and Gold Glove first baseman, very graceful, good baserunner, excellent arm. Won the Negro American League batting title in 1946.

5. Tank Carr. Heavy-set switch hitter but could run, led the Eastern Colored League in stolen bases and triples in 1925. Good hitter with power, but career was shortened by his fondness for the bottle.

6. George Giles. Sometimes called the Black Bill Terry. Similar player to Buck O'Neil except left-handed, a hustling, aggressive, first baseman who played way off the line and raced hitters to the bag. Grandfather of Brian Giles, who played for the Mets, Brewers, and White Sox in the eighties.

7. Highpockets Hudspeth. Six-foot-six, 235-pound, left-handed power hitter. A Willie McCovey type player, had bad feet and trouble handling low throws. Could hit and hit for power, but wasn't greatly respected in the Negro Leagues, where there was more emphasis on defense at first base than in white baseball (post-1920). Died of tuberculosis in 1933, age unknown but probably less than 40.

8. Ed Rile. Big switch-hitter for the Detroit Stars in the late twenties, hit around .350 with power in a short career.

9. Bob Boyd. The Rope. Starred in the last days of the league.

10. Showboat Thomas. The fanciest fielding first baseman in the Negro Leagues, lots of razzle-dazzle. Inconsistent hitter.

xx. Edgar Wesley. Left-handed power hitter from the twenties, rated high by some observers. Batted fourth behind Turkey Stearnes for several years.

SECOND BASE

1. Bingo DeMoss. "When Bingo DeMoss made the double play he hardly ever looked directly toward first base. He could make the play by a half glance," (Sam Bennett, quoted by Quincy Trouppe in *20 Years Too Soon*) . . . the best bunter in Negro League baseball, also extremely good at handling the bat, could hold off to the last second and slap the ball behind the runner. Fast. Played 1910 to 1930.

2. **Newt Allen.** Played baseball almost every day for 25 years beginning in 1920. A graceful, slick-fielding, second baseman in the mold of Tony Taylor, Manny Trillo, Julian Javier, Cookie Rojas, and Frank White, but had more good years than any of them. Had a shortstop's arm, and was extremely quick.

3. **George Scales.** Listed by Quincy Trouppe as the best second baseman he ever saw. A right-handed hitter with power, he was both fast and quick, but tended to put on weight (he was called "Tubby"). Outstanding hitter, perhaps comparable to Bill Madlock. Got into a terrible fight with Ted Page, who was his roommate, in 1937. Page knocked out his two front teeth, and the two men slept facing each other that night, both clutching weapons.

4. **Sammy T. Hughes.** A complete player, a Ryne Sandberg-type second baseman. Comparable to Barry Larkin, perhaps; taller and perhaps more athletic than Sandberg. A smart player who did everything well; James Riley in *The Biographical Encyclopedia of the Negro Baseball Leagues* says that he was "considered the premier second baseman of the Negro National League."

5. **Bill Monroe.** Could rank higher. Turn-of-the-century player, batted cleanup for Rube Foster's Chicago American Giants in 1911. He stayed with that team after they added John Henry Lloyd to become, in the opinion of some, the greatest team of all time. Died suddenly of unknown causes at the end of a 19-year career.

6. **Frank Grant.** Nineteenth century player, played in the minors for several years before the color line was clearly fixed, hitting .337 with power. Actual name was Ulysses F. Grant ... was called the "Black Dunlap."

7. **Charlie Grant** (Chief Tokahoma). Signed by John McGraw in 1901; McGraw was going to pretend he was an Indian, and end run the color line. Probably had great talent, but career was short, and stats are unavailable.

8. **Frank Warfield** (The Weasel). A complete defensive wizard, very fast, excellent reactions, tremendous range, good arm, made few mistakes. Used to snap the throw underhanded to first base. Slap hitter. Quiet but tough, carried a knife. Sarcastic, not universally liked; his harsh criticism of Louis Santop after the 1924 World Series contributed to Santop's demise as a player. Fought with umpires, to the point of alienating both umpires and teammates. See also Ollie Marcelle.

9. **Dick Seay.** A tiny jitterbug-type player. One of the few Negro League stars who was raised in the North, he was a resource for his teammates on the social mores and customs of the northern cities, how to go along and get along. When the teams traveled South the roles were reversed, and the Southerners had to explain to Seay how to play the game without getting in trouble.

10. **Dink Mothel.** Kind of a sixth man star, played everywhere on the field. He was most outstanding at second base, but was a teammate of Newt Allen for years, and Allen never came out of the lineup.

xx. **Bonnie Serrell.** Also called Bunny and Barney, and ranked much higher by some people. Was nicknamed "The Vacuum Cleaner" thirty years before they called Brooks Robinson "Hoover," but for the same reason. A left-handed hitter, also hit .376 to lead the Negro American League in 1942, then hit .556 to lead the Monarchs to a

World Series sweep over the Homestead Grays.

Many or most of the Negro Leaguers played in Mexico during the winters. Serrell liked Mexico, and seethed at the racism in the United States. Finally he settled in Mexico, eventually married a Mexican woman. When he didn't come north in 1945 the Monarchs signed Jackie Robinson, who was three years older than Serrell and not considered to be as good a player. When Robinson signed with the Dodgers Serrell looked for some way to break into Organized Ball, but never could. Played periodically north of the border into the early fifties, but played mostly in Mexico, and still lives in Mexico as far as anybody knows.

THIRD BASE

1. **Ray Dandridge.** Really a shortstop in terms of ability, but played third base in some of his best years because he was a teammate of Devil Wells. He was bowlegged; the line that appears everywhere about him is that a train could go between his legs but a ground ball couldn't. Fast, an amazing third baseman, and a .350–.370 hitter, he was signed by the Giants when he was 35 years old (nearly 36), and was the best player in the American Association the second half of 1949 (hitting .363) and all of 1950 (when he won the league's MVP Award), but the Giants (who needed a third baseman) wouldn't bring him up. Durable, consistent; did everything exceptionally well except that he wasn't a power hitter. Is in the Hall of Fame, and deserves to be.

2. **Judy Johnson.** Odd player, comparable to Dandridge except smaller and not quite as fast. Not truly comparable to anybody in white baseball except maybe Pie Traynor and George Kell. A right-handed hitter, clean, smooth third baseman, powerful arm—but small, thin, a high-average hitter with little power. As a hitter he was probably along the lines of Carney Lansford—a right-handed line drive hitter, but he was a much better fielder than Lansford. If you can imagine Charlie Hayes with another 60 points on his batting average, then you could compare him to Hayes.

3. **Ollie Marcelle.** Frankie Frisch type player—fast, smart, aggressive on the bases, a better fielder at third base than Frisch. Perhaps not as good a hitter as Dandridge or Johnson, but equal to them or more in the field. Could charge a bunt like nobody else. Picked by the *Pittsburgh Courier* as the top third baseman in the history of the leagues; also picked number one by John Henry Lloyd.

Marcelle was handsome, vain, and prone to reckless behavior off the field. His teammates called him "The Ghost" because he would disappear after games; they never saw him at the hotel. He was with Dave Brown the night that Brown killed a man in a fight (1924), and, years later (1930), got into a fight with Frank Warfield over a dice game, during which Warfield bit off the end of his nose. There was no plastic surgery at that time, and Marcelle had to go around for the rest of his life with a piece of tape on the end of his nose. Fans taunted him about the disfigurement, which hastened the end of his career.

4. **Jud (Boojum) Wilson.** A left-handed hitter, and a great one. Wilson was built like Hack Wilson or Kirby Puckett—short, but powerful. Huge, huge shoulders, arms like a gorilla, big, bear-trap hands, but a small waist, short but powerful lower body.

Wilson had a temper, like John Beckwith, although not as bad; he was easygoing most of the time, as opposed to Beckwith, who was never very far from breaking into outright assault. John Holway says that "both Jud and Beck could punch an umpire as quickly as they could swat a pitch. They both got into a memorable fight with an ump that (1925) summer. Wilson was arrested; Beckwith left town for a few days." Holway's book, *Blackball Stars,* tells many stories about fights that Wilson got into and people he assaulted. If an umpire ruled against him he'd swat the umpire; if a baserunner kicked the ball out of his glove he was as likely to chase the baserunner as he was to chase the baseball. But he was kind and generous most of the time; he just couldn't or wouldn't control his temper. As a third baseman he was awkward but adequate, played everything off his chest.

5. **Dave Malarcher.** A quiet, classy, dignified man, much respected; he was known as "Gentleman Dave" and "Preacher." A small switch-hitter; most of his value was in his glove, his head, and his legs, but he could hit OK. Managed the Chicago Giants for several years after the death of Rube Foster. Attended Dillard University in New Orleans; also attended a couple of SABR conventions in his later years.

6. **John Beckwith.** Most of the Negro League third basemen were like major league third basemen pre-1930—that is, they were defensive players first, closer to shortstops than to modern third basemen, who tend to be slow power hitters. Negro League third basemen were small and fast, chosen first of all for their ability to field a bunt.

Beckwith and Boojum Wilson were the exceptions to this rule. Beckwith was a real boomer. He hit .480 in 1930, with 19 homers in 50 games; also hit 16 homers in 51 games in 1931, which still led the league. Built about like Bobby Bonilla, he was by far the biggest third baseman, and one of the biggest and strongest men in the league.

Beckwith was a right-handed hitter who pulled everything, so other teams would stack their defense against him, putting a third infielder on the left side of the infield. Babe Ruth, who played against him, said that "not only can Beckwith hit harder than any Negro ball player, but any man in the world." James Riley writes that he was "moody, brooding, hot-tempered and quick to fight. Combined with a severe drinking problem, and an often lazy, unconcerned attitude about playing, his character deficiencies often negated his performance value." He was known to show up drunk for games, at times, and to beat the hell out of teammates. He was kind of an underworld character, a bootlegger, possibly a pimp. He was a fantastic hitter, but it was always a close call whether it was worthwhile to have him around.

7. **Newt Joseph.** Played in Kansas City along with Newt Allen—the two Newts. They were roommates and best of friends.

As a young man, Joseph hitch-hiked to Kansas City from his home in Oklahoma, showed up at the ballpark and demanded a uniform. Nobody knew what to say, so they gave him a uniform and a lot of attitude, kind of preparing to make fun of him. Once they worked him out they decided to let him keep the uniform.

Joseph was a left-handed hitter, faster and with more power than Judy Johnson, but not a .300 hitter and not as smooth in the field. A hustling, aggressive player, always chattering at third base, always hopped up. Had a bad temper, and could turn mean. Ran a taxi stand in Kansas City in the off-season and kept it after his career. Died of tuberculosis at age 53.

8. **Alex Radcliffe.** Brother of Ted "Double Duty" Radcliffe. Had a good arm, was a good fielder, ran well, hit close to .300 with some power.

9. **Candy Jim Taylor.** A member of Rube Foster's great team, the Chicago American Giants, about 1910. More famous as a manager than as a player. A quick-thinking third baseman, a pretty good hitter in the years before the League was organized. Had several brothers who also played baseball, including an older brother called Steel Arm Johnny Taylor, who was really outstanding.

10. **Dewey Creasy.** Hit .341 with 23 homers for St. Louis in 1926. A good player for a long time after that, helped St. Louis to several pennants, but not usually a big hitter. Slow, adequate in the field.

SHORTSTOP

1. **John Henry (Pop) Lloyd.** Tall, rangy player, powerful, extremely fast. Often described as The Black Honus Wagner; hit .368 in twelve years of the Negro Leagues, which weren't organized until he was 36 years old, including a .564 average with a league-leading 11 home runs in 37 games in 1928, when he was 44.

Lloyd had an odd face, with a sharp chin that pointed out from the bottom of his jaw almost like a finger. Quincy Trouppe wrote that "We called him El Cuchara, which in Spanish means 'spoon chin.'" Buck O'Neil says that he was called "Cuchara," which means "tablespoon" because he "set the table" by getting on base all the time.

Connie Mack said that you could put Honus Wagner and Pop Lloyd in a bag, pull out whichever one and not go wrong either way. Lloyd grew up fatherless, but became a father figure to players that he played beside, finding ways to share his experience, and to build confidence in younger players.

2. **Willie (Devil) Wells.** A generation later than Lloyd, but a comparable player; did everything outstanding except throw.

Macmillan stats show him hitting .382 with 23 homers in 96 games in 1927, .368 with 27 homers in 1929, .403 with 14 homers in 1930, and .344 as late as 1944, when he was 36. Often hit by pitches, he was one of the first players to wear a batting helmet, picking up a construction worker's helmet and wearing it to the plate. Was given the nickname "El Diablo" in Mexico, where he played winters for thirty years.

3. **Dick Lundy.** A spectacular shortstop and a showman, also a switch hitter who hit .330–.340. Chance Cummings, a Negro League first baseman, said that "Lundy could go behind second base and get a ball and throw you out, go behind third and do the same thing." Satchel Paige said that "it looked like he knowed where you were going to hit the ball," and that he was "just like Lou Boudreau." Probably a better fielder than Lloyd, certainly a better fielder than Wells, and regarded by some as a better all-around player.

4. **Dobie Moore.** Short, barrel-chested man with long arms, hit .453 for Kansas City in 1924, with 139 hits in 79 games, leading Kansas City to a pennant and World Series victory. Lifetime .365 hitter; probably the best 230-pound shortstop in baseball history. Casey Stengel saw him playing ball in the army during World War I, and recommended him to J.L. Wilkinson, who ran the Kansas City Monarchs, and was a friend of Stengel's. Moore's career ended prematurely when he was shot by his girlfriend while jumping out the window of a whorehouse. He had some sort of quarrel with his girlfriend, who apparently ran the brothel; she claimed that he hit her three times in the face, while he said, plausibly enough, that if he had hit her three times she wouldn't have been able to go get her gun. Anyway, his leg was fractured so badly that it ended his career.

5. **Bill Riggins.** Real name was Orville. A good switch hitter and a good shortstop, but a heavy drinker.

6. **Pee Wee Butts.** Born in the same year and the same state as Jackie Robinson (Georgia, 1919), teamed with Junior Gilliam on the Baltimore Elite Giants to form the outstanding double play combination of the latter days of the Negro Leagues. A fine shortstop, very strong for a 145-pound man, he was a decent hitter with some pop, probably as good a player as Gilliam. He was devastated by his failure to get an offer from the major leagues when Junior did, which was attributed to his age, his affection for the night life, and the fact that once, in his younger days, he had been arrested for assaulting an umpire.

7. **Sam Bankhead.** Shortstop on the Pittsburgh Crawfords, later the Homestead Grays. Older brother of Dan Bankhead, who pitched for the Dodgers. The Bankheads were the Delahantys of the Negro Leagues, with five brothers playing in the league; Sam was considered to be the best. .285 hitter, originally an outfielder, moved to shortstop in his thirties and did an excellent job. Jimmy Powers urged the New York Giants to sign him in 1938.

Wilmer Fields said that "The most respected man I met in baseball was Sam Bankhead." He worked as a garbage man in Pittsburgh after his career. Holway says that he was the model for Troy Maxson in the Broadway show "Fences," by August Wilson. Shot to death in a barroom fight, 1976.

8. **Paul Stevens.** Tiny, tiny little man with unlimited energy, listed at 158 pounds in *Macmillan,* but I have seen him listed as small as 120 pounds. He was called "Country Jake." James Riley describes him as "fast, aggressive, argumentative, temperamental, and controversial," and says that "Jake was cat-quick and used this attribute to make acrobatic plays." A light hitter; the Mark Belanger of the Negro Leagues. Sam Bankhead said he "couldn't hit a bull in the ass."

Like Ty Cobb, Stevens promoted his career as a young man by sending fake telegrams to reporters and managers, pretending to be somebody else, and raving about what a great player he was. He was a funny guy, always making jokes, even in the field. "Always when you would meet his team, he would jive you a little," said Buck Leonard. "He'd be beating you, and he'd be joking."

9. **Silvio Garcia.** Originally a pitcher, moved to shortstop after being hit by a line drive in 1940. Tommy Lasorda, who pitched to Garcia when he was in his thirties, said that he was one of the toughest hitters he ever faced. Leo Durocher said that Marty Marion couldn't carry his glove.

10. **Abe Harrison.** Starred with the Cuban X Giants in the 1880s. At that time Negro players were expected to be comedians as well as players, so he had a comedy routine along with his play, but he was regarded as the best shortstop of his time. Played in the minor leagues in the 1890s, hitting .305.

11. **Pelayo Chacon.** Cuban defensive wizard, slap hitter. Father of Elio Chacon. Friendly, well-liked man. Played in Venezuela in 1933, which was hard duty for Negro Leaguers; sent Clint Thomas a card reading "I hope you be well. I be well. Thomas, I have been here 14 month, and I am weary. Regards to all boys. Your friend Chacon."

LEFT FIELD

1. **Turkey Steares.** Left-handed hitter, comparable to Ted Williams or Mel Ott. Turkey loved to hit. He was a lifetime .352

hitter with Willie Stargell power...he loved his bats, and he would talk to them like they were children. He had a 34-inch bat and a 35-inch bat, and had special cases for each of them, like violin cases. Buck O'Neil said he went to Stearnes' room one time and Stearnes was sitting there in his pajamas, talking to his bats. "I used you and only hit the ball up against the fence," he said to the 34-incher. "If I had picked you," he said to the 35-inch model, "I would have hit the ball over the fence."

He was called "Turkey" because of the way he flapped his arms when he ran...Macmillan shows him with 181 career home runs in 903 games, placing him second on the all-time list behind Mule Suttles...listed by Riley's *Biographical Encyclopedia* as a center fielder.

2. **Mule Suttles.** Right-handed hitter, career batting stats a lot like Stearns. Hit .418 in 1926 with 27 homers in 87 games, giving him a slugging percentage over .800. Swung at everything and struck out a lot, but hit prodigious home runs, and connected often enough to compile a .329 lifetime average. Worked as a coal miner as a youth, and started playing ball on the mine teams.

3. **Monte Irvin.** Second half of career in majors.

4. **Pete Hill.** Left-handed line drive hitter, was the captain of Rube Foster's Chicago American Giants from 1911 to 1918, Rube Foster's right-hand man. When Foster spun off a second team (the Detroit Stars) Hill went to manage them. Cum Posey said he was "The most consistent hitter of his time." Often compared to Ty Cobb as a player, but probably more comparable to Sam Crawford, leaving aside the question of quality. He was more of a solid, sane, consistent player than an erratic ball of fire like Cobb,

also not as fast as Cobb. Ran well, but was very bowlegged.

5. **Gene Benson.** Kind of a Tony Gwynn type, a short, squat, left-handed line drive hitter. He had an odd stance and an inside-out swing, never looked like he was ready to hit. Monte Irvin said that the best chance to get him out was after he hit the ball because "when he ran, he'd kind of waddle." Good-natured man (Holway described him as "cherubic"), and a story teller. Bob Feller called him "Cousin," because he couldn't get him out...close friend of Jackie Robinson. Used the basket catch; some have suggested that Mays learned it directly or indirectly from him. Was a good outfielder, and played some in center field.

6. **Vic Harris.** Leadoff man for the Homestead Grays in the mid-thirties, hit about .300 with a little power. Real name was "Elander," but was called, among other things, "Vicious Vic" for his use of his fists and spikes. Excellent defensive left fielder.

7. **Chaney White.** The Don Baylor of the Negro Leagues. He would lean into a pitch to get on base, then steal second. Riley quotes an unidentified opposition player as saying that he was "built like King Kong, but ran like Jesse Owens," and claims that he once circled the bases in 14-flat on a sprained ankle. No arm, and regarded as a dirty player, but a .300 hitter with a lot of other skills.

8. **Heavy Johnson.** Johnson was an army buddy of Bullet Rogan and Dobie Moore; they all joined the Monarchs together, on the recommendation of Casey Stengel. He was immense, a 250-pound right-handed hitter who, according to Jocko Conlan "could hit the ball out of any park." In 1924 he is supposed to have hit more than 60 home runs against all levels of competition, although the Monarchs probably

played 250 games, and the feat is not documented. In 182 league games from 1922 to 1924 he hit almost .400, with 30 triples and 32 home runs. No fielder, and didn't have a long career.

9. **Frog Redus.** Five-foot-five-inch right-handed hitter who played left beside Cool Papa Bell in St. Louis through the late twenties, hitting .357, .393, .330, .357, .345, and .321 from 1924 through 1929, with surprising power, although Sportsman's Park probably accounts for a good percentage of the home runs. One of several Negro League stars who came from Muskogee, Oklahoma.

10. **Hurley McNair.** Reputed to be the best two-strike hitter in the Negro Leagues. George Giles said he "could have taken two strikes on Jesus Christ" and gotten a base hit on the third pitch. Willie Wells told John Holway that McNair taught him to hit the curve ball by tying his front foot to home plate so that he couldn't back out, and then throwing him curve ball after curve ball after curve ball. Worked as an umpire after his playing days; reportedly once pulled a knife on a player who complained about his call.

CENTER FIELD

1. **Oscar Charleston.** Regarded by many knowledgeable people as the greatest baseball player who ever lived. Buck O'Neil said that Willie Mays was the greatest major league player he ever saw, but Charleston was better. According to O'Neil, "Charlie was a tremendous left-handed hitter who could also bunt, steal a hundred bases a year, and cover center field as well as anyone before him or since ... he was like Ty Cobb, Babe Ruth and Tris Speaker rolled into one."

Bernie Borgan, a longtime scout for the St. Louis Cardinals who signed many major league players, said that Charleston was the greatest player he ever saw, including Babe Ruth and Ty Cobb.

Cuban pitcher Juanelo Mirabal said that Charleston "would try to beat you any way he could. Just like Ty Cobb, rip your pants or your legs, just to beat you out of a game. To me, I don't know which one was best. Both of them were great."

Dave Malarcher said he "could play the whole outfield by himself" and Paige said "He used to play right in back of second base. He would outrun the ball. You had to see him to believe him."

Hollis (Sloppy) Thurston barnstormed against him, said that he hit a home run every night.

Jimmy Crutchfield said "If I had to pick the best player I saw in my time, it would be hard to pick between Charleston and Josh Gibson."

John Johnson of the *Kansas City Call* wrote that Charleston was so fast that "he makes Ty Cobb look like a runner with a handicap."

Charleston was a barrel-chested man with thin legs, like Ruth. He was intense, focused, bright, and did everything exceptionally well.

2. **Christobel Torriente.** Cuban superstar, a teammate of Charleston's at one time; played center field, moving Charleston to left, probably because his arm was even stronger than Oscar's. Left-handed hitter with power to all fields; hit vicious line drives. Light-skinned enough to have "passed" and played in the majors, except that he had crinkly hair.

Torriente was born in 1895, the same year as Babe Ruth, one year before Charleston; he, too, had the large upper body and thin legs of Ruth and Charleston. Webster McDonald compared his build to Muhammad

Ali, although he was not nearly as tall as Ali. Easy-going; liked to clown around on the field. Holway quotes him as complaining about U.S. income taxes, in broken English: "The ducks got it. Me going back to Cuba this winter. Don't want the ducks to get my money." Deductions.

3. **Cool Papa Bell.** Lou Brock type player, probably better than Brock. Famous for his speed, but also hit some home runs. Hit .430 in Mexico when he was 43 years old. Would have been a 3,000-hit man in the majors easily, in my opinion.

Quincey Trouppe grew up in St. Louis when Cool Papa was in his prime; Cool Papa scouted him, got him into baseball, and kept him under his wing for several years. According to Trouppe Cool Papa "was always a well-conditioned ballplayer who managed to keep his weight on an even keel. He was a good-looking man, one of the best dressed in baseball."

4. **Spotswood (or Spottsford) Poles.** Ty Cobb contemporary, switch-hitting singles hitter who hit .610 (25 for 41) in documented exhibitions against major league players. Extremely fast. Often called "The Black Ty Cobb," usually by John Holway.

5. **Jimmy Lyons.** Described by James Riley as "one of the fastest men ever to wear a baseball uniform," he was the leadoff hitter for Rube Foster's Giants in the first years of the league, and was probably the best player in the league in 1920, when he hit .406 and stole 22 bases in 56 games. In 1912 a Chicago writer wrote that Lyons "steals bases as easy as he gets on a street car." He was a left-handed hitter without a lot of power, but an expert drag bunter. During World War I he played in the Allied Expeditionary Force League, where he played against Ty Cobb's brother, who reportedly remarked that Lyons was better than Ty. A gentleman; a close friend of Dave Malarcher.

6. **Clint Thomas.** A five-skill player, starred for Hilldale in the early 1920s, later made a habit of turning up on teams just before they folded. .300 hitter with power, some speed, excellent defensive skills.

7. **Jimmy Crutchfield.** Small man, left-handed singles hitter, good defensive center fielder and base runner, often compared to Lloyd Waner. Lived until 1995 and gave countless interviews about the leagues after they became popular in the late seventies, thus is frequently quoted about life and players in the leagues. Probably not a .300 hitter.

8. **Fats Jenkins.** Not fat at all; a member of the Basketball Hall of Fame. Hit .398 in 1927, .335 lifetime in a 20-year career. In the off season he was the captain of the Renaissance basketball team, which won 88 straight games in 1934–35. A smart, hustling player, he slapped the ball and bunted, was like lightning getting to first base. Saved his money, opened a package store in the Bronx after his career, and did very well. Also worked as a boxing referee.

9. **Charles Blackwell.** A star in the first years of the league, hitting .448 in 1921 with 10 homers, 27 stolen bases in 62 games, career average of .324 as best we know. Led the Negro National League (the West) in batting in 1921 and 1922. No one knows for sure how old he was then or how long he had been playing the game, but he played until 1929, albeit often under the influence of alcohol. He died in 1935, once more of undocumented causes, presumably related to the drinking.

10. **Eddie Dwight.** Reportedly almost as fast as Cool Papa Bell, kept his average in the black by bunting, played a spectacular center field although he didn't have much

of an arm. Worked as a chemist for the state of Kansas after his career. His son was the first black American accepted for astronaut training, and later on was the sculptor of the Henry Aaron statue at the ballpark in Atlanta.

RIGHT FIELD

1. **Martin Dihigo.** Fast, graceful, blessed with a powerful arm, he played every position on the field, and played them all well; this claim seems improbable but is well documented. A fine pitcher. Johnny Mize, who played with him one winter in the Dominican Republic, said that Dihigo "was the only guy I ever saw who could play all nine positions, manage, run, and switch-hit. I thought I was having a pretty good year myself down there, and they were walking him to pitch to me."

2. **Willard Brown.** Tremendous right-handed power hitter, maybe comparable to Jose Canseco, Juan Gonzalez, Andre Dawson, or Frank Robinson. Hit hundreds and hundreds of home runs in the Negro Leagues, Puerto Rico (where he still holds many records), and Mexico. Quincey Trouppe said that "Brown is one who challenged the feats of Josh Gibson. He was like Gibson in some respects. He could hit the ball out of the park, but swung at a lot of bad pitches, whereas Gibson did not. Who knows? Brown may have been as great, or greater, than Gibson, if he had been a little more patient and waited for strikes."

Relaxed, casual player, often accused (perhaps unfairly) of not hustling. Buck O'Neil said he hustled; he was just so easy-going he sometimes rubbed people the wrong way. He used to carry a copy of *Reader's Digest* in his hip pocket to give him something to do in the outfield when things

ground to a halt. Was first black player to hit a home run in the American League. See note about Jeff Heath in Section II (LF, #49).

3. **Ted Strong.** Kind of a switch-hitting Dave Winfield, a long, lean fellow with a strong arm and good speed. An original member of the Harlem Globetrotters. Started the All-Star game at three different positions (shortstop, right field, first base). According to Buck O'Neil, "Ted was the type of guy who, if I came down and met him in the hotel lobby and said, 'Come on, Ted, let's go to church,' he'd want to go. But somebody could beat me down there and say, 'Let's go to this dive down the street and drink all night,' and he'd be all for it. That was Ted—he'd blow either way."

4. **Wild Bill Wright.** Six-foot-four-inch, 225-pound switch hitter who was also one of the fastest men in the league. Reportedly circled the bases in 13.2 seconds. Good drag bunter. Lifetime .336 hitter with line drive power . . . also was a big star in Mexico, where he won the Triple Crown in 1943. Retired in Mexico, ran a restaurant down there that was popular with the players.

5. **Alejandro Oms.** Cuban player, same age as Babe Ruth, comparable to Paul Waner, a consistent .330 to .370 hitter in a long career, did other things well enough but not anything special. A natural entertainer; if the game wasn't close he would clown around in the outfield, catching the ball behind his back and doing 720-degree spins before throwing the ball back to the infield. Often pretended not to speak English.

6. **Chino Smith.** Hit .428 with lots of power in a five-year career, died (probably of yellow fever) at the age of 29. Satchel Paige said that he was the best hitter in the Negro Leagues except possibly Josh Gibson. Fast, and a good outfielder. Was called "Chino" because of his eyes.

7. **Cherokee Davis.** Also a pitcher. Dead Red hitter, had trouble with the curve. Had a Babe Ruth-type personality—big, good-natured guy, always playing around; basically just a big kid. He had been raised in a Catholic orphan house; used to run away from home regularly. Played in the Pacific Coast League at the end of his career; was reportedly going to be purchased by the Chicago White Sox, but broke his leg just as the deal was going through. John Holway said that, as an older man, he "looked and sounded exactly like a tanned Walter Matthau."

8. **Jelly Gardner.** Left-handed leadoff man, very fast, had a phenomenal throwing arm. Gardner played for years for Rube Foster. Foster always smoked a big, heavy pipe. One time he signaled for Gardner to bunt, but Gardner hit a triple. When he got back to the dugout, Foster smashed him across the head with the pipe . . .

9. **Rap Dixon.** Got his nickname from the Rappahannock River in Virginia, where he grew up. A good hitter, not the greatest hitter in the league, but a player who did everything well. Hit three home runs in the first Negro League game ever played in Yankee Stadium (1930) . . . On a tour of Japan in 1927 he raced around the bases in 14.5 seconds, then amazed the Japanese by standing at home plate and throwing several balls over the outfield fence, 328 feet away. . .

10. **Nat Rogers.** Good left-handed line drive hitter; adequate fielder, ordinary base runner. Hit in 31 straight games for the Chicago American Giants in the pennant race in 1927. One of nine brothers; built himself up as a child by working on railroad gangs, driving spikes. James Riley says that off the field he was characterized as "evil," but doesn't even hint at why.

MY TWO CENTS

There are many people who know vastly more than I do about the Negro Leagues. If any of those people choose to criticize or differ with my ratings, I would ask you to assume that they are right and I am wrong. I was just trying to organize some information; this is the best I can do based on what I know.

There are three Negro League players that I believe have a good argument to rank at the top of the list at their positions. I have little doubt that Josh Gibson was the greatest catcher in the history of baseball. Gibson, a right-handed hitting catcher with good defensive skills, is essentially comparable to Johnny Bench, Carlton Fisk, Gary Carter, Roy Campanella, and Gabby Hartnett—except that, as a hitter, he was more like Foxx or Ruth than Bench or Carter. His career isn't exceptionally long; his defense probably was not the equal of Campanella or Sundberg. But many people said that Gibson was the greatest hitter they ever saw, and if you just look at photographs of Gibson at bat, it is easy to believe it. There are some guys who just *look* like hitters—and nobody ever looked more like a hitter than Josh Gibson.

Four or five of the greatest players in baseball history are center fielders—Cobb, DiMaggio, Mays, Mantle, and possibly Speaker. The two most nearly perfect players in major league history were DiMaggio and Mays. Well, Wagner . . . anyway, the other three center fielders, while flawed, were equally great. Oscar Charleston probably rates right with them. Some say he was better. It's hard to imagine how anyone could have been better, but Charleston, in a sense, put Mays and Mantle together. He combined the grace, athleticism, and all-around skills of Mays with the upper body strength of Mantle, plus he was a left-handed hitter. His hands were so strong that when he was playing first base, late in his career, pitchers would use him to rub down new baseballs, as he could rub a baseball so hard that he would open up the seams. He played shallow, like Speaker, and ran down everything hit over his head. He was an intense player—more intense than any of these five except Cobb, and his intensity was less destructive than Cobb's. Buck O'Neil said that "Oscar had a stop sign on his chest." Later, as a manager, his players recalled that if he lost a game, he would chew on it all night, unable to sleep. It's impossible to compare him to the other center fielders without head to head numbers; it's impossible to imagine that he was much better than they were. But he was a hell of a package.

Third, Satchel Paige. Yeah, I know that there is a question about whether Satchel was the greatest pitcher in the history of the league. In the literature of the league there are numerous places where people say that Bullet Joe Rogan was better than Satchel, or Hilton Smith was just as good, or Chet Brewer was the ace of the staff. Dave Malarcher said that Bill Foster was "the greatest pitcher of our time, not even barring Satchel." There was a poll of Negro League veterans in 1952 which picked Smokey Joe Williams over Satchel as the greatest pitcher in the history of the league. Rogan and Williams threw as hard as Satchel, and Rogan had a much better curve.

But you know why you read that stuff? Satchel was the frame of reference. A St. Louis newspaper in 1912 said that George Baumgardner threw harder than Walter Johnson. A 1915 *Baseball* magazine article said that Ed Reulbach threw as hard as Walter Johnson; a *Reach Guide* said that George Zettlein threw as hard as Walter Johnson, maybe harder; a *Spalding Guide* said the same about Charlie Sweeney. A Washington newspaper in 1944 said that Junior Ortiz threw as hard as Walter Johnson. Honus Wagner said that Cy Young was faster

than Johnson. Johnson himself said that nobody threw harder than Smokey Joe Wood. Walter was the frame of reference.

Somebody once said, comparing Paige to Rogan, that "all Satchel had is the fastball." Well, that's not *quite* all. Satchel had a Grade A fastball and fantastic control. In addition, as Warren Spahn once said, "Hitting is timing. Pitching is destroying the hitter's timing." Satchel, Warren Spahn, Juan Marichal, and Jim Kaat were probably the greatest ever at destroying a hitter's timing. There is a second line about pitching, that the three most important things in pitching—like real estate—are location, location, and location. Satchel could locate it.

Great pitchers are intelligent; almost all are articulate. The pitcher is the only man on the field who can *plan* what he wants to do, and for this reason, intelligence is more critical in pitching than in any other element of the game.

Satchel was enormously intelligent, and he was driven; life batted him down a thousand times, and he got right up off the floor and started punching a thousand and one times. He had fantastic composure on the mound. Jimmy Crutchfield said it best: he said that the Lord always had an arm around Satchel. So what you have, in Satchel Paige, is a great fastball, great control, a tremendous change, a great understanding of how to pitch, intelligence, determination, absolute composure—and a forty-year career. Bullet Joe Rogan, Joe Williams, Hilton Smith—I'm sure those guys were all great pitchers. I think that Satchel deserves to rank, with Cy Young, Lefty Grove, and Walter Johnson, as the guys that you talk about when you're trying to figure out who was the greatest that ever lived.

If there is a fourth who might deserve to rank at the top of his position, I guess that might be John Henry Lloyd at shortstop. The other guys . . . well, who knows? The fascination of player rankings is that, if you work meticulously through the arguments, you can achieve the illusion of great accuracy. If we were to try to mix Ray Dandridge, Oliver Marcelle, and Newt Joseph in with Clete Boyer, Ron Santo, and George Brett we would not only be unable to sustain the illusion of great accuracy, we would destroy it such as it exists now.

The strongest *position* for the Negro Leaguers vis-a-vis their white counterparts is probably catcher; Gibson, Petway, Mackey, Radcliffe, Greene, and Duncan were probably better players, top to bottom, than the white catchers of their era. The weakest position for the Negro Leaguers in the same comparison is probably left field. It was a league in which players played all over the field; everybody had to play center, almost everybody pitched at least once in a while. The people I have listed in left field mostly played as much in center or right as they did in left.

MAYBE IT'S JUST ME

One of the basic references about the Negro Leagues, which was useful to me in compiling this section, is *Invisible Men,* by Donn Rogosin (Atheneum, 1983). It is quite a good book, although flawed by self-righteousness. Rogosin writes condescendingly, almost contemptuously, about Branch Rickey, because in his opinion Rickey's motives, in destroying the ninety-year-old practice of baseball apartheid, were insufficiently pure and lofty.

But what were Rickey's motives? . . . Rickey's motive in this case was, in all likelihood, to establish an organization that would give him control of, and first crack at, the pool of black talent, should the integration of the major leagues occur.

Almost every reference that Rogosin makes to Rickey implies that Rickey was morally unworthy to associate with modern liberals. I find this kind of crap to be almost nauseating. Yeah, Rogosin; let's see you attack injustice on the scale that Branch Rickey attacked it, and then you can pass judgment on his motives. That's just my opinion.

Anyway, Rogosin tells a story about a player that he identifies as "Johnny Dunlap of the Boston Braves." No one named Johnny Dunlap ever played for the Boston Braves, and I'm not sure who he means, but that's a side issue. His story is that one winter, when he was playing in Cuba, Dunlap became friendly with Willie Wells. One day, when Dunlap and Wells were at the race track, Dunlap spotted Early Wynn, and invited him over for a beer. According to Rogosin:

Wynn took one look at Dunlap's darkcomplexioned companion and said, "I don't drink with niggers." "What'd you say?" quizzed Dunlap. "You heard what I said. I don't drink with niggers," responded Early Wynn. Dunlap swiftly got up and broke Early Wynn's jaw.

Hoo, boy; you can almost hear Rogosin breathing hard in the background, fantasizing about all the racists whose jaws he would have broken, if only he'd been there in time.

But when you think about it, aren't Dunlap's actions a great deal more offensive than Wynn's? Obviously, Wynn's comments are inappropriate, and let's offer no excuses for Wynn because he grew up in Alabama in the twenties and thirties; he was a grown man, and he should have known better.

But Early Wynn used a vulgar and insulting term. Dunlap's response was assault and battery. Who is more wrong?

What do you think, guys? Am I the one who is out of step here, or is Rogosin's story, on reflection, reckless and insensitive? Do we really want to applaud those who respond to ignorance with violence? Does this seem right to you?

You decide.

BOBBY ESTALELLA

How much did the Negro League players walk? In general, we assume that the Negro League players, like Latin players today, tended not to focus on the walk as an offensive weapon, preferring to play straight-up baseball. But, as Bobby Estalella shows, this is not necessarily true.

When I first saw the records of Bobby Estalella in the *Macmillan Encyclopedia*, I was puzzled by why his career didn't take off sooner and last longer. In a 15-game trial with the Senators in September, 1935, Estalella was dynamite, hitting .314 with 2 homers, 10 RBI, and also drawing 17 walks in 15 games; he finished with a .471 slugging percentage, .485 on-base percentage. Despite this rather extraordinary performance, Estalella got only 13 plate appearances in 1936, all of those as a pinch hitter. He had two triples and four walks, which gave him a .667 slugging percentage and a .462 on-base percentage.

Well, the Senators didn't need anybody like that, so Estalella returned to the minor leagues for two and half years, finally latching on to a major league job in 1939. He hit .275 with 8 homers in 82 games, which, since the Senators played in a park where a home run was an occasion for a feast, almost led the team. Buddy Lewis actually led the team with 10 homers, but nobody else had more than 4. Estallela scored 51 runs and drove in 41 as a half-time player for a team that finished 41.5 games out of first place.

So they sent him back to the minors in 1940. He resurfaced briefly with the St. Louis Browns in 1941, then played through the war years, and played well. He hit .298 in 1944, and .299 in 1945; in 1945 he was fourth in the league in batting average, fifth in slugging percentage, third in on-base percentage (.399). But as soon as the war was over, he was gone. He disappeared entirely from the major league

scene until 1949, when he played eight games with the Philadelphia A's, which was the end of his major league experience.

Just knowing that much, I always thought that was a fascinating and puzzling career. To a certain extent, you could explain this by defensive skill or by simple ignorance. Baseball men of that era didn't pay any attention to the "walk" column. The thinking at the time was that walks were something the pitcher did, and the hitter didn't, or shouldn't, have much to do with it. Bill DeWitt, who ran the St. Louis Browns during the war, said that he got rid of Roy Cullenbine after the 1941 season because Cullenbine was a lazy player, always trying to get on base with a walk. The lazy bastard had hit .317 in 1941 with 9 homers, 98 RBI and 121 walks.

This kind of high-octane ignorance no doubt worked against Estalella as well, plus Estalella was not a good defensive player. But I got even more intrigued by Estalella's career a few years later, when I picked up a war-time *Baseball Register,* and got a look at Estalella's minor league numbers. They're eye-popping. Estalella had earned his major league trial in 1935 by hitting .316 at Harrisburg, with a .563 slugging percentage. After "failing" his major league trial in 1935–36 he went to Albany in the International League, where he hit .331, slugging .545.

That earned him a demotion to the Piedmont League, where he hit .349 in 1937, swatting 33 homers and driving in 89 runs in 106 games, slugging percentage of .706. Back in the Piedmont League in 1938 he stepped it up to .378, winning the league's triple crown (38, 123, .378) and also leading the league in runs scored, 134. He also drew 117 walks, was 28-for-32 as a base stealer, and was second in the league in outfield assists, with 19, making only five errors.

That got him one full year with the Senators, where he was a part-time outfielder, albeit perhaps the team's most productive hitter. After that he was sent to Minneapolis (American Association), where he hit .341 with 36 doubles, 32 homers, drove in 121 runs, drew 132 walks, and scored 147 runs in 147 games.

This, then, was clearly a player who got a raw deal from baseball, and I always wondered what the story behind the story was. It turns out, he was actually a black guy—not *very* black, but black enough to retard his career in that era. He was a Cuban star, and his skin tone was such that the Senators, by giving him a chance to play in the major leagues at all, were skating on thin ice. The unwritten rule was that you could play Cubans or other Latin American players, but only if they were light enough to pass for white guys. Estalella was not exactly an Albino; he looked more like Jackie Robinson than Richie Ashburn, and while he had never actually played in the Negro Leagues, he had mixed often with the Negro League players in Cuba.

So here, at least, is one latin/black player whose walk tendencies are documented, and who was *not* reluctant to let the pitcher beat himself. Whether this says anything at all about the style of baseball prevailing in Cuba at that time, I don't know. Estalella's grandson and namesake is now a major league player. His career got off to an oddly similar start: he hit .353 in a brief trial in 1996 (.706 slugging percentage) so they sent him back down to Scranton. In a late trial in 1997 he hit .345, slugging percentage .793, on-base percentage .472, so they sent him back to Scranton again in '98.

Maybe it's the same player, still trying to make a breakthrough by shaving sixty years off his baseball age. No, Bobby Estalella the first was a fine player who could have had an excellent career, but then, that's true of them all, from Eufemio Abreau to Charlie Zomphier. He was a peculiar player, in a peculiar time, with peculiar rules, and somehow he slipped past the bouncer and got a chance to play. But not much of a chance.

THE 1940s

HOW THE GAME WAS PLAYED

In 1941, as you probably know unless you failed a number of history classes, America went to war. During wartime the quality of the baseballs used was inferior, as there was something in regular baseballs that was needed to make explosives or O.D. green paint or something, and the balls manufactured were rather lifeless. The quality of the play wasn't too lively, either. With most of the good players in the service, a collection of old men and children and men with one arm and seven dependents gathered regularly and batted around a dull spheroid, and this was called "major league baseball" for three years.

This baseball was characterized by low batting averages, low home run totals, and an unusual number of bases being stolen by anyone aged thirty-seven or younger. Strategy came to the fore, as it always does when talent is short, plus there were some terrific pennant races and an unlimited supply of fresh human interest stories. On that basis the baseball of the war years was probably, in its own way, as enjoyable as any.

The game that the Williamses, DiMaggios, Fellers, and Musials returned to in 1946 was different from the game they had departed four years earlier. There was night baseball, and for that reason or some other, batting averages were lower. Thirty-five regular players had hit over .350 in the ten years before the war (1932–41); only eight would do so in the ten years after (1946–55). The offensive philosophies of Babe Ruth, as espoused by Ted Williams, dominated the latter part of the decade: Get a pitch you can hit and uppercut. As batters declined to swing at any pitch they couldn't hit into the seats, walks per game reached astonishing levels. One team in 1949 had a starting pitcher who walked 179 men in 196 innings, another who walked 123 in 214 innings, and a third who walked 138 in 275. Their relief ace walked 75 men in 135 innings, and other pitchers on this same team had totals of 57 walks in 95 innings, 48 walks in 49 innings, 29 walks in 58 innings, and 43 walks in 52 innings. That team used fourteen pitchers, of whom only one allowed less than one walk per two innings. That team was the New York Yankees, and they were the World Champions.

And in the next season, 1950, they issued even more walks than that (three of their four starters averaged 138 walks apiece) and they were World Champions again.

The definitive player of the era was Pat Seerey, who in 1948 hit .231 with 102 strike-outs in 105 games, but also drew 90 walks and drove in 70 runs in 105 games. I could recite odd combinations like that for paragraphs, but instead I will recommend that you look up Eddie Joost, Eddie Lake, Eddie Stanky, and Ed Yost in a baseball encyclopedia. Multiply the results by Tom, Dick, and Harry, and you'll get the idea.

Baseball boomed in the late forties, but this kind of baseball would drive a purist nuts—in fact, after a while it would even start to drive me nuts. Run production was high, but they were doing it all wrong. At its best, it was the baseball of the ticking bomb, the danger building up and up until somebody finally put one in the seats. At its worst it was station-to-station baseball with the trains running late, baseball with no action except the few seconds of the long fly.

After 1950, home runs became even more plentiful but the walks became much more scarce. It is hard to say why. The strike zone was redefined in 1950, but the change went the other way. Perhaps what happened is that baseball moved from the Bob Feller generation of pitchers to the Robin Roberts generation—that is, toward a reliance on control pitchers, rather than on pitchers who lived by fire. A manager in 1949 could reasonably have said to himself, "Look, if these guys are going to stand there and wait for my pitcher to get himself in a hole and make a mistake, I'll just go find some pitchers who aren't afraid of the strike zone. If the hitters want to hit 0 and 2, we'll let them." Whatever, the basic trends both of this generation and of the next were in line with those of the entire period beginning in 1920 and not ending until the late sixties—

more home runs, more strikeouts, and lower batting averages.

WHERE THE GAME WAS PLAYED

S. O. C. (Same old cities).

WHO THE GAME WAS PLAYED BY

At a guess, about 40 percent of the major league players of the wartime period were truly of major league quality. Of the sixty-four National League regulars of the 1945 season, only twenty-two played a hundred or more games in the majors the next season (1946) and only eleven played a hundred or more games in the majors four years later (1949). As a control, I checked the same figures for the 1950 season. Of the sixty-four National League regulars of 1950, forty-four played a hundred or more games the next year, and twenty-nine played a hundred or more games four years later.

Baseball may not have been great in the forties, but there have been as many good books written *about* baseball in the forties as about any era. Bill Mead's *Even the Browns,* Kirby Higbe's *The High Hard One,* and Leo Durocher's *Nice Guys Finish Last* all make good reading, as do numerous books about the end of the color line, such as *The Year All Hell Broke Loose* and a couple on the war years. Robert Creamer's *Baseball in '41* may be my favorite Bob Creamer book. These books portray a generation of rough, boozing, poorly educated but thoroughly trained ballplayers, many of them southerners, who helped to fight a war and returned to find a game and society changing on them in ways that many of them found threatening and difficult to deal with. They faced the horrible challenge of the war with great courage, and the bright challenge of the future with great confusion.

CHECKING IN:

1940— Willie Stargell, Earlsboro,
　　　　Oklahoma
　　　　Tony Oliva, Cuba
1941— Pete Rose, Cincinnati
　　　　Bill Freehan, Detroit
　　　　Bob Dylan, Minnesota
1942— Muhammad Ali, Kentucky
　　　　Tony Perez, Cuba
1943— Joe Morgan, Texas
　　　　Fergie Jenkins, Ontario, Canada
1944— Tom Seaver, Fresno, California
　　　　Steve Carlton, Miami
1945— Rod Carew, Panama
1946— Reggie Jackson, Pennsylvania
1947— Nolan Ryan, Texas
　　　　Johnny Bench, Oklahoma
1949— Mike Schmidt, Dayton, Ohio
　　　　Bruce Springsteen, Freehold,
　　　　New Jersey

CHECKING OUT:

1940— Sliding Billy Hamilton, 74
　　　　George Davis, 70
　　　　Willard Hershberger, suicide, 29
1941— Tommy Bond, 84
　　　　Mickey Welch, 82
　　　　Lou Gehrig, amyotrophic lateral
　　　　sclerosis, 37
1942— Amos Rusie, 71
1943— Jimmy Collins, 73
　　　　Joe Kelley, 71
1944— Tony Mullane, 85
　　　　Kenesaw Mountain Landis, 78
　　　　Roger Bresnahan, 64
1945— Adolph Hitler, 56

291,557 American Servicemen were killed
in World War II—about eighteen times as
many men as have ever played major
league baseball, from 1870 to the present.

This accounted for a little less than 2% of
the total combat deaths for all countries
involved in the war.
1946— Gertrude Stein, 72
　　　　Walter Johnson, brain tumor, 59
　　　　Tony Lazzeri, 41
　　　　Nine members of the Spokane
　　　　team, Western International
　　　　League, were killed when their bus
　　　　careered off a mountain road.
1947— Jack Glasscock, 87
　　　　Jimmy Scheckard, 68
　　　　Johnny Evers, 66
　　　　Hal Chase, 64
1948— Henry Ford, 84
　　　　Mordecai Brown, 71
　　　　Joe Tinker, 68
　　　　Babe Ruth, throat cancer, 53
　　　　Hack Wilson, 48
　　　　Five members of the Duluth team,
　　　　Northern League, were killed when
　　　　the team bus collided with a truck.
1949— Buck Freeman, 77
　　　　Wildfire Schulte, 67

JOE DIMAGGIO SQUARED

Joe DiMaggio's batting streak ended on July
17, 1941. That same day, numbers were being
picked out of a fishbowl in New York City to
see who would be drafted into the U.S. Army.
Each number picked, unlike the Vietnam era
draft that you may remember, represented just
one young man. The second number chosen,
number 90, belonged to a twenty-one-year-old
kid named Joe DiMaggio. You can imagine the
resulting publicity; the media just loves that
kind of thing. The kid welcomed the publicity,
but he said he felt awful bad that Joe's streak
had come to an end.

THE 1940s IN A BOX

Attendance Data:

Total:	135 million (134,853,739)	
Highest:	Cleveland, 1948	2,620,627
	New York Yankees	14,391,690
Lowest:	St. Louis Browns, 1941	176,240
	St. Louis Browns	3,330,861

The average American in this era attended a major league baseball game about once every eleven years.

Most Home Runs:

Ralph Kiner, 1949	54	
Ted Williams	234	

Best Won/Lost Record by Team:

Cardinals, 1942	106-48	.688
Cardinals	960-580	.623

Worst Won/Lost Record by Team:

Phillies, 1941	42-109	.278
Phillies	584-951	.380

Index of Competitive Balance: 34%

Home-Field Winning Percentage: .544

Percentage of Regulars Hitting .300: 19%

Largest Home-Field Advantage: Boston Red Sox, by far

The Red Sox in the 1940s had a .646 winning pecentage in Fenway Park (499-274), but just .465 on the road (355-409). Projected to 154 games, that's equivalent to 99–55 at home, but 72–82 on the road.

The Red Sox in the years 1944 to 1953 had the largest year-in, year-out home-field advantage of any team in the twentieth century. They were 17 games better at home than on the road in 1944, 13 games better in 1945, 18 games better in 1946, 13 games better in 1947, 13 and a half better in 1948, 26 games better in 1949 (61-16 at home, 35-42 on the road), 16 games better in 1950, 15 games better in 1951, and 24 games better in 1952 (50-27 at home, 26-51 on the road). For the nine years total they were 470-224 at home (.677), 314-379 on the road (.453).

As to why this happened . . . well, the Red Sox had a veteran team in a unique park. This period ended abruptly in 1953, when Dom DiMaggio, Johnny Pesky, and Vern Stephens all left, the Red Sox two best pitchers were left-handers, and the team played better on the road than in Fenway.

Having Their Best Decade Ever: St. Louis Cardinals

Having Their Worst Decade: New York Giants

Changing Direction: The Brooklyn Dodgers from 1900 to 1939 had losing records in every decade, and up until 1938 were best known as baseball's resident eccentrics. They improved dramatically in 1939, under the guidance of Larry MacPhail and Leo Durocher, and would remain one of baseball's best organizations for the next fifty years.

The Chicago Cubs had seven decades of excellence beginning with the formation of the

National League in 1876. They were outstanding in the 1870s and 1880s, good in the 1890s, great after the turn of the century, good in the teens, good in the twenties, outstanding in the thirties, good in the 1940s up until 1946. They collapsed in 1947 due to their failure to develop a productive farm system.

The Phillies, down and out for thirty years, began to put things together at about the same time, and for the same reason: their farm system had a very productive phase in the late 1940s.

Heaviest Player: Johnny Hutchings, a National League pitcher, stood 6'2" and weighed 250.

Lightest Player: Barney Koch, who played second base for Brooklyn briefly in 1944, weighed but 140.

Most Strikeouts by Pitcher:

Bob Feller,	1946	348
Hal Newhouser		1,579

Highest Batting Average:

Ted Williams,	1941	.406
Ted Williams		.356

Lowest Batting Average:

Eddie Joost,	1943	.185
Al Glossop		.210

Best Major League Players (by Years):
1940— Johnny Mize
1941— Joe DiMaggio
1942— Ted Williams
1943— Luke Appling
1944— Stan Musial
1945— Snuffy Stirnweiss
1946— Ted Williams
1947— Ted Williams
1948— Stan Musial
1949— Stan Musial

Best Major League Pitchers (by Years):
1940— Bob Feller
1941— Thornton Lee
1942— Mort Cooper
1943— Spud Chandler
1944— Dizzy Trout
1945— Hal Newhouser
1946— Hal Newhouser
1947— Warren Spahn
1948— Johnny Sain
1949— Mel Parnell

Hardest-Throwing Pitcher: Bob Feller

Best Curve: Johnny Sain

Best Power/Speed Combination: Joe DiMaggio

Best Switch Hitter: Red Schoendienst

Iron Man: Stan Musial

Best Baseball Books: See comment, Baseball Books of the 1940s

Five Largest Changes in Baseball During the Decade:

1. Breaking of the color line/collapse of the Negro Leagues
2. Switch to night baseball
3. Spread of farm systems
4. Player/managers replaced by professional managers
5. Bonus wars

Let me explain the number three item there. In 1940, about three organizations had well developed farm systems, about eight had some farm systems, and about five had almost nothing. The Cardinals in 1940 had a vast farm system controlling more than 600 players. The Yankees and Indians had smaller but highly professional farm systems.

But on the other end, the Browns, the Senators, the Boston Braves, and the two

Philadelphia teams had virtually no player development operations. They were still trying to compete the way they had competed twenty years earlier—signing exceptional kids out of high school and from college programs, and buying players from minor league operators.

Players continued to come out of the walls until the mid-1920s. The Philadelphia A's in the early twenties got Jimmie Foxx (from high school), Cochrane, Simmons, Grove, and Bishop (from minor league independent operators), George Earnshaw from a college campus, and were the best team in the league in the early 1930s. The Washington Senators, although they did have some working arrangements with minor league teams, won the American League in 1933 with what was, in essence, an overgrown shoestring operation, collecting ballplayers here and there. But by 1935 these streams of talent were drying up, and by 1940 they had all but stopped. The aggressive organizations—the Cardinals, Yankees, Indians, Red Sox, Tigers, and Dodgers—were locking up so much of the talent in their farm systems that the teams without aggressive farm systems were falling off the edge of the earth.

Through the 1940s, the other teams scrambled to build their player development operations, and by 1950 all the teams had farm operations of some sort. This led to the Bonus Baby wars; by 1947 outstanding high school kids were bombarded with offers from a dozen or more major leagues teams, and ended up signing contracts for several times the money paid to major league stars. This, in turn, led to the Bonus Baby Rule, which required players who signed contracts for bonuses of $10,000 or more to spend two years on the major league roster before they could enter the farm system. But the teams that had been slow to develop farm systems—the five mentioned before, plus the Cubs and the Pirates—were so far behind that it would take them years or decades to catch up.

Best Outfield Arm: Indian Bob Johnson or Vince DiMaggio

Worst Outfield Arm: Pete Gray (sorry)

Most Runs Batted In:

Ted Williams,	1949,	159
Vern Stephens,	1949,	159
Bob Elliott		903

Most Aggressive Baserunner: Jackie Robinson

Fastest Player: George Case

Slowest Player: Ernie Lombardi

Best Control Pitcher: Tiny Bonham

Most Stolen Bases:

George Case,	1943	61
George Case		285

Best-Looking Players:
Whitlow Wyatt
Lou Boudreau

Ugliest Players: Ewell Blackwell, Jim Castiglia, Charlie Keller

Strangest Batting Stance: Stan Musial

Cap Anson Award: Ben Chapman

Three Finger Brown Award: Lou Brissie

Ozzie Guillen Trophy: Pete Suder

Bound for Glory: Dom DiMaggio

Best Pitching Staff: St. Louis Cardinals, 1942–46

Best Offense: 1946–1949 Boston Red Sox

Football Players: Alvin Dark, Jim Castiglia, Steve Filipowicz, Snuffy Stirnweiss, Sam Chapman, Charlie Keller

Retrobermanisms:
Hank (Purple Mountained) Majeski
Johnny (Hip) Hopp
George (War) Munger
Eddie (Hold the) Mayo
Bob (Fall of the House of) Usher

Basketball Guys: Howie Schultz, Frankie Baumholtz

First of His Kind: Jackie Robinson

Last of His Kind: Ted Williams (the last .400 hitter)

One of a Kind: Rip Sewell

Best Infield: 1946 St. Louis Cardinals (Musial, Schoendienst, Kurowski, and Marion)

Best Outfield: New York Yankees

The Yankees had Joe DiMaggio, Charlie Keller, and Tommy Henrich on their roster from 1939 through 1949, although the three probably didn't play 600 games together because of injuries, the war, and the fact that there were other good outfielders on the team. They were arguably the greatest outfield of all time. Both Keller and Henrich had better careers than several Hall of Fame outfielders, even with no allowances for time missed in the war. In 1941 all three hit 30+ home runs—the only outfield before the 1980s to have three 30-homer men. They averaged 110 runs scored, 111 RBI among them (in '41). They were all three still good players after the war.

A Better Man Than a Ballplayer: Sam Chapman

A Better Ballplayer Than a Human Being: Jeff Heath

Mr. Dickens, I'd Like You to Meet: Cookie Cuccurullo, Pittsburgh (1943–45)

Platoon Combinations I Would Like to See:
Sibby Sisti and Creepy Crespi
Johnny Dickshot and Rusty Peters

Best Defensive Team: 1940 Cincinnati Reds

Clint Hartung Award: Clint Hartung, a spring training phenom in 1947, was promoted as having superstar ability either as a pitcher or a hitter. He had a modest career, and his name has become synonymous with the over-hyped prospect who fails to live up to his clippings.

Outstanding Sportswriter: Red Smith

Most Admirable Superstar: Stan Musial

Gold Glove Team:
C—   Jim Hegan
1B—   Frank McCormick
2B—   Lonnie Frey
3B—   Ken Keltner
SS—   Marty Marion
OF—   Terry Moore
      Joe DiMaggio
      Dom DiMaggio

Franchise Shifts: None

New Stadiums: None

Best Pennant Race: The Best Decade Ever for pennant races Best World Series: 1947

In the 1947 World Series the Dodgers hit .230 as a team, and their starting pitcher was knocked out early in every game of the series. Brooklyn somehow rallied often enough to stretch it to seven games. Bill Bevens pitched a one-hitter but lost; Gionfriddo robbed DiMaggio of a homer. The Dodgers wound up using Hal Gregg as the starting pitcher in the seventh game. Gregg had finished the season with 4 wins, 5 losses, and a 5.88 ERA—by far the worst pitcher ever to start Game Seven of a World Series.

Best-Hitting Pitcher: Schoolboy Rowe

Worst-Hitting Pitcher: Preacher Roe

Best Minor League Teams:
1941   Columbus (American Association)
1946   San Francisco (PCL)
1948   Montreal (International League)

Best Minor League Players:
Bill Thomas
Frank Kelleher

Odd Couple: Leo Durocher and Larry MacPhail

Drinking Men:
Sig Jackucki
Tex Shirley
Tom Seats
Kirby Higbe
Jim Tabor

Player vs. Team: The most celebrated salary wrangle of the decade involved Hank Greenberg, a threat to retire, a desire to play for the Yankees, a trade, and a racehorse.

Team vs. Team: Yankees/Dodgers feud, spring of 1947

Uniform Changes: Nothing changed much

Most Wins by Pitcher:
Hal Newhouser,   1944   29
Hal Newhouser   170

Highest Winning Percentage:
Freddie Fitzsimmons,   1940   16-2   .889
Spud Chandler   85-34   .719

Lowest Winning Percentage:
George Caster, 1940   4-19   .174
Vern Kennedy   37-68   .352

Worst Award Selection: 1942, Joe Gordon over Ted Williams as American League MVP

Best Player Who Never Won the MVP Award: Johnny Mize

Best Bunter: Harry Walker

Flameout: Dick Wakefield

All Offense/No Defense: 1940 Pittsburgh Pirates

All Defense/No Offense: 1945 St. Louis Cardinals

Homer: Bobby Doerr (145 of 223 career home runs in Fenway Park)

Yellowstone Park Award: Ed Yost.

Through 1953 Ed Yost had hit 55 career home runs—3 in Washington, 52 on the road.

Tough-Luck Season: Eddie Smith, 1942

Smith finished 14–17 in '41, 7–20 in 1942. Warren Brown wrote a poem about him, a small part of which goes:

Under a spreading luckless spell the White Sox Ed Smith works,

The Smith, a loser now by rote, knows all misfortunes quirks;

He's beaten by the best there is, he's beaten by the jerks.

Week in, week out, by day or night, he gives it all he's got,

But loses just the same because some wallop wasn't caught,

Or his own hitters failed in turn when they were on the spot.

Could I Try This Career Over? Isaac (Ike) Pearson had a career record of 13 wins, 50 losses, which is the lowest winning percentage in major league history (.206) for a pitcher with 50 or more decisions. I'm not sure Roger Clemens could have done a whole lot better under the same conditions. Pearson, a star athlete at Ole Miss, was signed to a bonus contract the day he graduated from Mississippi in 1939, and went straight to the major leagues with no training or experience. Once there, he pitched for teams that were among the worst in major league history, because they had no farm system and consequently did lots of things like putting college kids on the major league roster. The Phillies were 45-106, 50-103, 43-111, and 42-109 in the four years he pitched for them. In 1941 Pearson registered a 3.57 ERA, better than the league average of 3.63, but still finished 4-14.

Returning from the war in 1946, Pearson pitched a few innings for a Phillies team that was 69-85. His next opportunity was in 1948, when he got to pitch 53 innings for a White Sox team that lost only 101 games—actually the best team he ever pitched for, other than those few innings in 1946.

Minor Leagues Were:
20 percent free
80 percent slaves to the majors

Best Double Play Combination: The combination of Joe Gordon and Phil Rizzuto, who played for the Yankees in 1941–42 and in 1946, was probably the greatest combination in the history of baseball, based strictly on their ability to turn the double play. Comparing the Yankees double plays to expected double plays, we have the Yankees at +57 in 1942 (the highest figure of all time) and +52 in 1941 (the second-highest figure of all time). They were +20 in 1946.

Both Rizzuto and Gordon were individually outstanding on the double play. Gordon, teamed with other partners, was +36 in 1939, +15 or more five other times. Rizzuto, teamed with other partners, had the Yankees at a comparable level: +37 in 1952, +15 or more six other times. Individually, they were very, very good. Teamed together, they were historic.

The connection between turning the double play and winning was closer in the 1940s and

1950s than in any other era in baseball history. Teams that are good at turning the double play have always had *some* tendency to win, of course. But in the 1940s, 18 of the 20 championship teams were above average at turning the double play, and half of them, 10 of 20, were +20 or more in DP versus expected DP.

Worst Double Play Combination: Al Kozar and Sam Dente, 1949 Washington Senators.

Paul Krichell Talent Scout Award: Larry Woodall

George Digby, the Red Sox scout in Alabama, tried to talk the Red Sox into signing Willie Mays in 1949. The Sox sent Larry Woodall to check him out. Woodall reported that Mays was not the Red Sox' type of player.

Best Unrecognized Player: Tommie Holmes

Highest-Paid Player: Bob Feller

New Statistics: None

Best Baseball Movies:
Pride of the Yankees, 1942
It Happened in Flatbush, 1942
The Stratton Story, 1949
It Happens Every Spring, 1949 .

A Very Good Movie Could Be Made About: The end of the Color line. Actually the movie—*The Jackie Robinson Story,* with Jackie playing himself—was made in 1950. Somebody should try again.

Five Biggest Things Wrong with Baseball:

1. Shortage of talent due to the war
2. Poor alignment of teams in regard to the population
3. Aging stadiums in declining neighborhoods
4. Long-term competitive imbalances (Yankees by 1950 had been winning for thirty years, Phillies had been losing almost 100

games a year for thirty years, White Sox had been bad for twenty-five years, etc.)

5. Substandard equipment (baseballs) due to the war

I Don't Know What This Has to Do with Baseball, But I Thought I'd Mention It Anyway: Rube Melton was called "Rube" because his name was "Reuben." He was, incidentally, a world-class Rube.

When he reported to spring training one year, his manager asked him why his spikes were caked with red clay. "Been huntin' in 'em all winter," replied Rube, as if this would have been obvious to a more intelligent manager. One time, plagued with mosquitoes in his

hotel room, Rube made a pile of rags in the middle of the floor and lighted them afire, intending to smoke the buggers out. He was quite offended when his teammate stomped out the fire before it could smoke good.

My favorite Rube Melton story, however, involves the first time Rube was invited to a major league spring training camp, with the Phillies in 1942. To the surprise of manager Hans Lobert, he showed up with a substantial family in tow. Just as Lobert had opened his mouth to explain that it wasn't the practice to take wives and children to spring training Melton cut him off. "Mistah Lobut," he said genially. "I'd like to make you acquainted with my puppy..."

MAJOR LEAGUE ALL-STAR TEAM 1940–1949

Records in seasonal notation, based on 154 games. Pitchers based on 40 starts, 67 relief appearances, or equivalent combination.

Pos.	Player	Years	AB	R	H	2B	3B	HR	RBI	BB	SO	SB	Avg.
C	Walker Cooper	5.71	536	68	154	27	5	19	96	32	35	2	.287
1B	Johnny Mize	6.16	572	106	174	29	6	35	121	80	42	4	.304
2B	Joe Gordon	7.59	568	90	153	26	5	24	94	75	70	8	.270
3B	Bob Elliott	9.45	567	85	165	31	8	12	96	77	44	6	.292
SS	Lou Boudreau	9.25	569	82	171	37	6	7	75	76	29	5	.299
LF	Stan Musial	6.96	594	117	206	43	16	21	101	81	29	6	.346
CF	Joe DiMaggio	6.02	592	114	192	32	11	30	131	75	30	2	.325
RF	Ted Williams	6.72	544	142	194	40	7	35	133	148	46	2	.356

	Pitcher	Years	G	GS	IP	Won	Lost	Pct	SO	BB	ERA
RH	Bob Feller	6.63	42	37	301	22	13	.629	222	131	2.90
LH	Hal Newhouser	8.71	43	35	282	20	14	.590	181	123	2.84
RH	Mort Cooper	5.79	42	36	277	20	12	.626	133	80	2.92
RH	Spud Chandler	3.99	41	38	304	21	9	.700	136	97	2.67
RA	Joe Page	4.07	59	11	178	13	10	.565	119	94	3.31

THE GREATEST TEAM WHAT EVER WAS
Part II

One of the things you can do to try to figure out how great a team was is to count the positions at which they were above average, and those at which they were below average. A team looked at in this way consists of thirteen "spots"—eight regulars, four starters, a relief ace; I'm not saying the bench doesn't count.

If you look at a team as consisting of thirteen slots, then one-half of all teams will be above average at catcher, one-half will be above average at first base, one-half will be above average at second base, etc. But how many teams will be above average at all thirteen spots?

Statistically, we would expect only one team in each 8,192 to be above average at all thirteen spots. In major league history there have only been about 2,500 teams. Thus we would expect, given a random distribution of talent, that there most likely would not be any team in major league history which is above average at every position.

Just theory, right? But when you look hard at the question of what the greatest team might have been, you realize how profoundly true this is. It is very hard to find that perfect team, that team that you can say *was* the greatest ever—but there are many teams that were just *almost* perfect, teams that just missed perfection by one big "if."

Look at the 1941 Dodgers, for example. The '41 Dodgers were just that close to being a perfect team. They had a quality catcher (Mickey Owen), the MVP at first base (Dolph Camilli), a Hall of Famer at second base (Billy Herman), a Hall of Famer at shortstop (Pee Wee Reese), a quality player at third base (Cookie Lavagetto), a Hall of Famer in left field (Joe Medwick), the MVP runner-up in center field (Pete Reiser),

and a near-Hall of Famer in right field (Dixie Walker).

In the history of baseball, that is probably as close as any team has ever come to putting out a lineup of eight legitimate stars, plus they had a Hall of Fame manager (Leo Durocher), two outstanding starting pitchers (Kirby Higbe and Whitlow Wyatt, who won 22 games apiece), a good relief ace (Hugh Casey), and half a dozen other decent pitchers.

You could say that this is the greatest team ever, and you might be right, except for two problems. First, they lost the World Series. And second, with the same team on the field the next season, they failed to repeat. They won 104 games in '42 (four more than '41), but they didn't win the pennant. So you've got a team with one pennant, no World Championships, and I just don't see how you can pick a team with one pennant and no World Championship as the greatest team ever.

The '54 Indians, of course, have the same problem: greatest pitching staff before the Braves of the late '90s, tremendous lineup except for shortstop, won 111 games, but at the end of the day, they've got one pennant and no World Championship.

The '62 Dodgers . . . man, what a team. The first half of the 1962 season, the Dodgers were unbeatable. This team, again, is close to having star players at every position—catcher John Roseboro, first base Ron Fairly, second base Junior Gilliam, third base Daryl Spencer, shortstop Maury Wills, outfield of Frank Howard, Willie Davis, Tommy Davis. They've got Wally Moon and Duke Snider for extra outfielders. Unbelievable offense; Tommy Davis hit .346 with 153 RBI, Frank Howard missed 30 games and still drove in 119, Maury Wills was the

MVP and stole 104 bases, Willie Davis had power and speed, hit .285 and scored 103 runs, Junior Gilliam hit .270 and drew 93 walks and could still run some... just an unbelievable offense. They scored more runs than the '61 Yankees, despite playing in a park that reduced runs scored by 18%.

For pitchers, they started with Drysdale and Koufax, added in a veteran left-hander (Johnny Podres), a smoke-throwing right-hander (Stan Williams), and backed them up with three outstanding relievers—Ron Perranoski, Ed Roebuck, and Larry Sherry. By early August they were 40 games over .500, 78-38.

And you know what happened: Koufax got hurt, and they lost. The Giants beat 'em. So it would be the greatest team ever, except they didn't win. They won in '63, swept the Yankees in a four-game World Series, but 1962 is the year they should have been at their best.

The 1930 Cubs... if Hornsby had been healthy, that had to be the greatest team ever put together. Rogers Hornsby missed most of the year with an injury, and they still scored 998 runs. The 1929 Cubs... if they hadn't blown an 8-0 lead in a World Series game, if Hartnett hadn't been hurt, if they'd repeated in 1930, that would be maybe the greatest team that ever was. The 1942 or 1946 St. Louis Cardinals... if they hadn't sold Johnny Mize to the Giants after the '41 season, that had to be the greatest team ever.

The Big Red Machine... if they had gotten Tom Seaver in '75, rather than in mid-season 1977, that would be the greatest team ever. Maybe they were the greatest team ever anyway, but if they'd had Seaver, picking the greatest team ever would be a no-brainer. The Kansas City Royals of 1976–1980... phenomenal team. Strong at every position except in October.

Could any of these teams have handled the '27 Yankees? Probably not. The '27 Yankees had poor catching, erratic defense in the middle infield, an aging third baseman, and a big doofus reliever who was just a one-year fluke—but Ruth and Gehrig were so good that they count as two superstars apiece, and Combs was the fourth-best player in the league.

There is a gentleman who has written some articles claiming that the 1929–1931 Philadelphia A's were really the great team of that era. His argument is that of these two great teams (the Yankees and A's) the Yankees were "built first," but that when both teams were complete, the A's had a better team. After all, he will point out, in 1929 the Yankees still had Ruth and Gehrig and Combs and Meusel and Lazzeri, and had *added* Bill Dickey—but the A's beat them by almost twenty games.

The A's beat them by twenty games because, by 1929, the Yankee pitching staff had fallen apart. The 1927 Yankee pitching staff was outstanding, but old. By 1929 Herb Pennock was barely hanging on, Dutch Ruether was retired, Urban Shocker was dead, Waite Hoyt was ineffective, and Wilcy Moore was back in the minors. OK, he didn't go back to the minors until 1930, but you get my point; the 1929–31 A's were a great team, but they were able to beat the Yankees because the Yankees were pitching Hank Johnson and Ed Wells and Roy Sherid. There are many teams which are one "if" away from being clearly the greatest ever. Only the '27 and '98 Yankees, in different ways, failed to trip over an "if."

Left to right, Terry Moore, Mel Allen, Hank Gowdy, Billy Hillenbrand. Gowdy was trying to teach Hillenbrand, an All-American football player at Indiana before being inducted, to play baseball.

MEMORIAL

It is relatively obvious that there must have been at least a dozen men who missed the Hall of Fame due to World War II. If you chart the number of Hall of Famers by decade of birth, you get this:

1890–1899	26 players
1900–1909	32 players
1910–1919	15 players
1920–1929	17 players
1930–1939	22 players so far

The numbers dip about 1910 for various reasons, including the fact that those were the players who went to war in mid-career—the players born 1910 to 1925.

So if we agree that *somebody* missed the Hall of Fame by going to war in mid-career, the question becomes, who? To a certain extent, of course, we can't know. There must have been one or two 18-year-old boys killed or maimed in that war who, had they escaped service, would have gone to be the Joe DiMaggios or Tom Seavers of their generation. We can't know how well players would have played in their missing years. Nonetheless, this is my list of the best candidates for players who lost a Hall of Fame career to World War II:

1. **Cecil Travis.** A shortstop, Travis hit .317 or better (as a regular) seven times between 1934 and 1941, with a career high of .359 in 1941, two points better than DiMaggio. Williams hit .400; Travis led the American League in hits, with 218. He was only 27 years old at that time, turned 28 late in the season, and had about a 37% chance to get 3,000 career hits.

Travis was a soldier during the war, not a ballplayer in uniform but a soldier. There is a story, printed many times, that he suffered frostbite on his feet during the war; I have also seen stories denying this, but in any case Travis played briefly and ineffectively after the war.

2. **Mickey Vernon.** Mickey Vernon had a long career punctuated by several brilliant seasons. There are four things that kept Vernon from making it to Cooperstown:

a. He played for years with back trouble, which finally disappeared after he was operated on for appendicitis. The years in which he had back trouble are obvious in his batting stats.

b. He played most of his career in the worst home run park in baseball, Griffith Stadium. In his career he hit only 55 home runs in his home parks, as opposed to 117 on the road.

c. He played much of his career for poor teams.

d. He missed two prime seasons during the war.

Even with all of these setbacks, Vernon earned 295 Win Shares in his career, which ranks him ahead of five Hall of Fame first basemen, more than a hundred Win Shares ahead of George Kelly (193). He did an awful lot of things well in a long career. But with 20 Win Shares in 1942, 21 in 1943, and 33 in 1946 (his first season back), we have to assume Vernon would

have earned *at least* 40 more in the two missing seasons. That would put him at 331 career Win Shares, which is strong Hall of Fame territory. Thus, despite the presence of the other factors, it may well be that the war, by itself, kept Mickey Vernon out of the Hall of Fame.

3. **Dom DiMaggio.** With 220 career Win Shares, he rates ahead of at least 18 Hall of Famers, not including those elected as managers or for other service. But he missed three full seasons during the war, so he also could well be up around 300 career Win Shares . . . I'll cut the Win Shares comments and put the Win Shares for the rest of these guys in a chart.

4. **Johnny Pesky.** Johnny Pesky was a great player as a rookie in 1942, hitting .331, scoring over 100 runs, and leading the American League in hits with 205. He was a great player when he got back in 1946–47, almost duplicating his rookie stats each year, although with a few more walks. The war cut his great seasons from six to three, which weakened enormously his Hall of Fame credentials.

5. **Dick Wakefield.** Received a reported bonus of $52,000 when he was signed by the Tigers, the largest bonus in history at that time. He hit .345 in the Texas League, then hit .326 in 240 major league games before reporting to the U.S. Army in mid-1944. Big (6'4", 210 pounds), fast, strong, and possessing a smooth left-handed stroke, he was never the same player after the war.

6. **Joe Gordon.** American League MVP in 1942. Like Mickey Vernon, he had a career which was very near to Hall of Fame standards despite missing two full seasons due to the war.

7. **Tommy Henrich.** A tremendous player both before and after the war, missed three prime seasons due to military service.

8. **Alvin Dark.** Career started late, in part because of the war, in which he was an officer. He was 26 by the time of his rookie season, four or five years later than normal for a player of his calibre, but had a near-Hall of Fame career anyway.

9. **Sam Chapman.** A fine defensive center fielder who hit .322 with 106 RBI in 1941, aged 25. His four best seasons, aged 26 through 29, were lost to World War II, although he came back to drive in over 200 runs in 1949–1950.

10. **Buddy Lewis.** A left-handed line drive hitter, Lewis had already piled up 1,112 hits and had just turned 25 by the end of the 1941 season, owning a career average of .304. He missed three and a half seasons due to the war—the seasons when he would have been 25, 26, 27, and 28—and was never the same player afterward.

11. **Hank Sauer.** This is more speculative than the others, but the war was one of the factors which kept Sauer from getting a major league foothold until he was 31.

12. **Sid Gordon.** A longshot, obviously, but there are guys in the Hall of Fame who didn't have careers as good as Gordon's, and Sid missed two full seasons due to the war.

The chart, as promised, follows. I marked players as "No" to the question "Ability Suffered?" if their ability did not deteriorate dramatically during the war. But obviously, missing three years of your development period isn't going to *help* anybody's skill level, except maybe a pitcher, who could be shielded from overusing an immature arm by three years away from the game.

Player	Born	Career Win Shares	Missed Seasons	Ability Suffered?
Cecil Travis	1913	169	Almost Four	Yes
Mickey Vernon	1918	295	Two Full	No
Dom DiMaggio	1917	220	Three Full	No
Johnny Pesky	1919	188	Three Full	No
Dick Wakefield	1921	95	1.50	Dramatically
Joe Gordon	1915	244	Two Full	Perhaps
Tommy Henrich	1913	208	Three Full	No
Alvin Dark	1922	227	Two Full	No
Sam Chapman	1916	144	Almost Four	Some
Buddy Lewis	1916	178	Three and a half	Yes
Hank Sauer	1917	174	1.80	No
Sid Gordon	1917	200	Two	No
Virgil Trucks	1917	197	1.97	No
Hank Bauer	1922	182	Four Full	No
Barney McCosky	1917	146	Three Full	Some
Wally Judnich	1917	102	Three Full	Lots
Ferris Fain	1921	161	Three Full	No
Eddie Robinson	1920	126	Three Full	No

13. **Virgil Trucks.** Missed almost two full seasons due to the war, still won 177 major league games. Would almost certainly have won over 200 games, were it not for the war.

14. **Hank Bauer.** Missed four crucial developmental seasons (1942–1945), and was still a heck of a player.

15. **Barney McCosky.** Hit .316 in 571 games before the war. Missed three full seasons and lost his speed during the war, although he still hit .325 in his first three post-war seasons.

16. **Wally Judnich.** A five-tool player for three years before the war, a left-handed hitting center fielder who hit .299 with a .491 slugging percentage from 1940–1942. Missed three full seasons, and was not the same player afterward.

17. **Ferris Fain.** Had a good career anyway, but career was delayed three years at its outset by the war.

18. **Eddie Robinson.** Like Fain, a first baseman who had a good career anyway, but his career was delayed by three full seasons before it was really underway.

UNIFORMS OF THE 1940s

We have reached the dead-pan era. From 1920 until 1960, there doesn't seem to be much to report in the way of significant changes in uniform style. I mentioned to Bill that I was having trouble finding many things of interest in here, and he said that during this period the game in general doesn't change quickly; it just evolves slowly. Likewise in baseball fashion.

From team to team, uniforms in the forties and fifties look much alike—all white home suits, road uniforms usually gray. The form is still boxy and baggy; shirts have round necks, either button or zip up, with half-length sleeves, and a T-shirt worn underneath. In 1940 the Chicago Cubs wore a sleeveless vest which zipped up the front, a matching blue sweater underneath. Some teams are a little heavy handed with the trim work on the sides, outlining the front button flap of the shirt, running several times around the neck and down the sleeves. Other clubs seem to prefer the stark simplicity of a plain white suit with no decoration save for the team name. The Boston Braves uniforms of the early '40s have no trimwork. The stripes on the stockings are cut out by 1943, and yet the city and team name are still under revision, going from a fancy B to plain capital letters.

As night games increased in popularity during the '40s, some baseball people thought a shiny reflective fabric for the uniforms might add to the enjoyment of the spectators. Only a few teams added the "satins" to their playbill though.

—Susan McCarthy

NICKNAMES

After a decade of use as instruments of torture, nicknames became almost apologetically pleasant again in the forties. Players of ordinary skills were bestowed with such mildly flattering nicknames as "Mercury" if they ran well, "Scrap Iron" if they were tough, or "Old Reliable" or "Steady Eddie" if they showed up every day and put on a good show. Of the few derogatory nicknames of the forties, all were bestowed on players who didn't go to the war. It was hard to say anything rude about a man who had risked his life for you; you just didn't do that kind of thing in the forties. A few nicknames, more or less at random:

Ding-a-Ling (Dain Clay)

Bow Wow (Hank Arft)

The Gay Reliever (Joe Page)

The Little Professor (Dom DiMaggio)

Four Sack Dusack (Erv Dusack)

Slats (Marty Marion)

The Man (Stan Musial)

Foghorn (George Myatt)

Swish (Bill Nicholson)

L'il Abner (Paul Erickson)

The Mad Monk (Russ Meyer)

Country (Enos Slaughter)

The Brat (Eddie Stanky)

Mountain Music (Cliff Melton)
   (Also known as "Rabbit Ears" and "Mickey Mouse")

Abba Dabba (Jim Tobin)

The People's Cherce (Dixie Walker)

The Mad Russian (Lou Novikoff)

The Volga Batman (Mike Chartak)

Sabu (Bill Schuster)

The Arm (Tom Hafey)

Hot Potato (Luke Hamlin)

All Jewish players were called "Moe."

UTILITY MAN

With Houma of the Evangeline League in 1948 (the same team that Bill Thomas had won thirty-five games for two seasons earlier), Roy (Tex) Sanner won the league's triple crown, hitting .386 with 34 homers, 126 RBI. When not playing the outfield, Sanner pitched, winning 21 games and losing only 2, striking out a league-record 251 batters in 199 innings, and posting a 2.58 ERA.

THAT'S WOMEN FOR YOU

In 1941 and 1942 the Brooklyn Dodgers went to Cuba for spring training. Ernest Hemingway used to hang around with the ballplayers some, and he and Hugh Casey became good friends. They used to go to a dove-shooting club every day after practice, seven days a week. Sometimes afterward, and after spending some hours in a casino, Ernest would take a few of the ballplayers to his house up in the hills for a little boxing. Hemingway and Casey would put on the gloves and beat the hell out of each other and the furniture until Hemingway's wife couldn't stand it anymore and would make them leave.

THANK YOU, MA'AM

The Las Vegas team of the Sunset League in 1947 hit .338 for the season, with 271 home runs in 140 games. The statistics for the team's regulars are given next:

The team scored 1,261 runs, nine per game, but allowed 1,235. They finished 73-67.

Pos.	Player	G	AB	R	H	2B	3B	HR	RBI	BB	SO	SB	Avg.	Runs Created
C	Castro	129	539	101	191	34	1	28	121	25	69	2	.354	119
1B	Myers	139	459	118	139	13	2	33	121	136	54	3	.303	118
2B	P. Godfrey	118	509	93	163	26	7	14	103	32	65	5	.320	88
3B	Gregory	102	366	83	120	28	0	17	75	51	50	1	.328	82
SS	Kelly	126	508	153	170	33	2	33	99	93	114	7	.335	134
OF	R. Godfrey	134	571	111	183	28	4	32	123	26	118	5	.320	110
OF	Felix	140	610	173	236	35	8	52	182	76	105	18	.387	201
OF	Zaby	133	531	158	213	47	7	18	132	104	78	22	.401	164

BLOCKING AND TACKLING THE PLATE

The modern method of blocking the plate is, quite simply, illegal. If you read the rule book (Rule 7.06 B), it is clear that the catcher is not allowed to block home plate in any way, shape, or form without having the ball in his hand. Period. The rules say that, and until about 1940 that is exactly what they meant. In the "Knotty Problems of Baseball" in the 1938 *Spalding Guide*, there occurs this exchange:

Q. I would like your opinion on a play where the catcher squats in front of the plate to prevent the runner from touching it. The runner cannot go around the catcher and does not want to slide into him to reach the base for fear of injuring him.

A. The position occupied by the catcher is illegal unless he has the ball in his hand ready to touch the runner.

Note, first of all, the tone of the inquiry. He doesn't ask "What do the rules really say about the catcher blocking the plate?" He doesn't ask "How far can the catcher legally go in blocking home plate?" He discusses a catcher who "squats" in front of home plate, and goes on to explain the unique purpose of this action.

Next, consider the response: He can't do that. Not "The rules really say that he's not supposed to do that, but we all know they do." Not "A technical interpretation of the rules would hold the catcher to be obstructing the baserunner." Just "That's illegal. You can't do it."

And when you consider, finally, that this exchange occurs in the knotty problems of baseball, a typical paragraph of which concerns itself with what happens when a ball in play lodges in the pocket of a passing marsupial, I think we can conclude that this was not, at that time, a common practice.

I went through guides of the twenties and thirties, looking for home-plate collisions. There aren't any that would register by modern standards. There are plenty of photographs of plays at home plate, and sometimes they run into each other, but not like now.

Basepath obstruction was a major problem in the 1880s and nineties, when baseball was in danger of becoming a contact sport. In 1897 the rules on obstruction were tightened up, and the principle of free access to the bases met with general acceptance—at the other three positions. There was always something of a problem with catchers blocking the plate, but there were always limits. In 1922 two games were protested because of the intractability of catchers. National League President John Heydler ruled against the protests, writing that "the unpopular practice of 'blocking off' runners at the plate . . . has always been the cause of dispute, ill-feeling among and serious injury to players, but against which no practical remedy has been found." However, it is, again, quite clear that what was meant by "blocking off" the plate was tame indeed by the standards of the 1990s. Heydler continues, "The decisions to be made by the umpires in this regard are usually the most important of the game, but they are decisions based solely upon the umpire's judgment *as to whether or not the runner beat the ball.*" In other words, the principle that you were not to block the plate until you actually had the ball was still taken seriously at that time. And what did they mean by "blocking off" the plate? "Umpire Moran reports that catcher [Earl] Smith's left knee was in front of the corner of the plate nearest the left foul line, the imprint of his shin guard being plain on the rain soaked ground, but that there remained considerable uncovered plate for Schmandt to touch."

And that is, more or less, the position the catcher occupies in all of the shots of home-plate collisions that you will see from that era. There are no pictures of collisions occuring several feet up the line.

In the modern game, of course, the catcher sets up five feet down the third-base line and wrestles the runner until help arrives. Lance Parrish occupied a position that will allow a runner to ramble all over the ballpark, buy a hotdog and a beer, and touch anything he wants to as long as it doesn't show up on the scoreboard. No modern catcher is expected to leave part of the plate open.

So when did the rule fall into disuse? There isn't any moment at which it began. They didn't wake up one morning and say, "Let's start letting the catchers obstruct the baserunners." I believe that the *de facto* interpretation of this rule drifted to where it now is between 1965, and 1980. Maybe my memory is playing tricks on me, but I don't remember Elston Howard or Earl Battey doing the things catchers do now.

To end with a digression, it is in principle most dangerous to have one set of rules on the books, but another set in use in practice. That is exactly how many of the game's greatest controversies have erupted, including the Pine Tar incident and Merkle's Boner. Giant fans always claimed that what Merkle did (he failed to touch second to ceremonially complete the play) was common practice at that time. If, in fact, it was common practice, then the umpire used poor judgment in deciding to commence enforcement of the rule at that particular moment, when the pennant was on the line. My friend Mike Kopf says that has nothing to do with it; a rule is a rule, and the rule says he is supposed to touch second.

Perhaps, but would you want to lose the pennant on a rule that hadn't been enforced in twenty years? In the army, or in any fascist state, they have laws against almost everything, rules which are never enforced as long as you behave yourself. Then you make somebody mad, or the captain wakes up on the wrong side of the cot, and *whammo*. You just broke fifteen laws. Having laws on the books which are not enforced puts every policeman in the robes of a judge, empowered to decide who the guilty are today. In a free society, since the law cannot be arbitrarily or selectively enforced, a statute that is not enforced is not enforceable. What we have here is another situation from which no good can arise.

(Since I first wrote this article more than 15 years ago, the practice of blocking the plate has conformed somewhat to the rules. Catchers in the early 1980s actually would run several feet up the third base line and wrestle the baserunner while waiting for the throw; this was not exaggeration to make a point. This practice, which was always illegal, has gradually modified over the last twenty years.

Now if we can just get them to do something about the phantom tag at second base . . .)

DUROCHER AND RICKEY

Leo Durocher was the manager and Branch Rickey the General Manager of the Brooklyn Dodgers from 1942 to 1946. Whenever Leo strayed from the reasonably straight and something approaching narrow, Rickey would call him in and narrate the parable of the Prodigal Son, always ostensibly discussing someone else. "Through our many years together," wrote Durocher in *Nice Guys Finish Last*, "Mr. Rickey recited the parable of the Prodigal Son to me many, many times . . . always about some other sinner or wastrel, but always at a time when I knew he looked on me as something less than the leading candidate for secretary of the YMCA." Rickey was a religious man, but he understood that ballplayers had their ways, and he never took it upon himself to reform them or to straighten out Leo. "It would have been impossible for him," said Durocher, "to come right out and say that he disapproved of sleeping with loose women on the Sabbath." Leo's value system was largely structured around loose women. Durocher said he was always afraid to lie to Rickey because he always figured Rickey had the answer before he asked the question.

TOM SEATS

Same subject, Rickey and Durocher. One time when Leo almost pushed it too far was in the matter of Tom Seats. This was 1945, and Seats, a 33-year-old journeyman, had a good year in the low minors in 1944, and suddenly found himself in the major leagues. He was hit hard early in the season. Durocher called him in for a conference before his next start, during which it was decided that the problem was nerves, and that a couple of fingers of brandy before each game was just the thing to settle him down. Seats got settled down and finished the year with a 10-7 record, but when Rickey found out about it he was apoplectic. "You . . . gave . . . a . . . man . . . in . . . uniform . . . whiskey?" inquired the Mahatma.

"Yes, sir," Leo replied.

Rickey thought about it a while and said, "He will never pitch again for Brooklyn," and added that he should fire Leo as well.

Leo responded with a terse, definitive comment that is a perfect summary of the thinking of every good manager. "There is a 'W' column and an 'L' column," he said. "I thought when I signed my contract . . . it was my obligation to put as many as I could under that 'W' column." But Tom Seats never pitched in the major leagues again.

1946: LIFE BEGINS AT HOUMA

Bill Thomas won 383 games in the minor leagues, and never threw a pitch at the major league level. His won-lost records for most of his career aren't very good—a seemingly endless series of 15-18 and 20-17 seasons—but he was one of those guys who had a talent for picking losers. He went 16-17 with Charleroi in the Middle Atlantic League in 1927, but you have to understand that the rest of the pitchers on the Charleroi team were 26-58, so he was almost 200 points better-than-team. It took him several years to reach the good minor leagues (he took the 1930 season off, for some reason) and when he did it was with Indianapolis, a middle-of-the-pack American Association team, and later he pitched for several years with Portland and Hollywood, then the ugly step-sisters of the Pacific Coast League. His records in what would now be called Triple A baseball total up to a little under .500. He was 17-9 for Mobile in the Southern League in 1944, and the team still finished eleven games under .500.

In 1946 he was 41 years old, and he was pitching for Houma, which emerged as the powerhouse of the Evangeline League. Houma played 131 games that year. Thomas won 35 games and lost 7. Now granted, that wasn't much of a league, but 35 wins are a bunch. No other pitcher, anywhere in organized baseball, at any age, has won 35 games in any other season since 1922.

What happened then I but partially understand. The 1947 *Baseball Guide* contains a one-paragraph note, "Five Banned in Gambling Probe," and says that on January 25, 1947, five players were placed on Organized Baseball's Ineligible List after an investigation of allegations involving thrown games and association with known gamblers. Thomas was one of the five. He was suspended for "conduct detrimental to baseball"—something which, apparently, extended beyond winning thirty-five games at the age of 41.

An article by George Hilton in the 1982 *Baseball Research Journal* discusses the Evangeline League scandal, which was the only one of its kind to hit organized baseball since 1919. It began when the owner of the Abbeville franchise, Mr. I.N. Goldberg, alleged that the players of Houma and Alexandria had conspired to fix the outcomes of three playoff games. The allegation against Thomas was that he had been in contact with gamblers who had asked him to throw games; he testified that he had, indeed, been approached by one such gambler, but had categorically refused any such involvement, and had not gone even so far as to learn the man's name. Unfortunately for Thomas, Judge Landis had established the principle of expulsion for guilty knowledge.

As Jim Baker points out, this raises some fascinating questions, such as "Where do you go to place a bet on the Evangeline League?" Do you just walk into a Las Vegas casino one afternoon and say, "I'd like to put down ten grand on Thibodaux to beat New Iberia next Saturday?" Apparently, illegal gambling was then flourishing in Louisiana, and the primary beneficiary of these dark deeds was an Alexandria bookmaker.

Charges extended as far as money being handed into the dugout from the stands during and after games. It is not clear whether any games were successfully thrown. A Houma player, years later, said that all of the games that were supposed to be thrown were won by mistake, as the would-be Rothsteins were carrying insufficient protection, and one player accidentally hit a double while attempting to strike out.

Anyway, for associating with these ne'er-do-wells, Thomas was banned from baseball. It is clear that Bill Thomas had not thrown any games; for one thing, he was 5-0 during the playoffs. He was angry and defiant about his banishment from baseball. Out of baseball, he worked as a roustabout in Texaco's refinery at Houma, and alternately threatened to sue and petitioned for reinstatement, which eventually was granted. Almost three years later. The next time he broke camp, he was forty-five.

In 1950 Thomas went 23-8 for two teams in the Evangeline League. Then he moved on to the Rio Grande Valley League, where he pitched nine more games, pushing his season's record to 26-12. After that season, though, he was to win only twenty-three more games in the minor leagues.

In 6,000 minor league innings, Thomas walked less than two men per nine innings. Thomas must be dead by now; if not, he would be pushing 100, but it is not known where he lives or where he was buried. He was probably not a major league pitcher, or at least not very much of a major league pitcher, but at any level it doesn't seem right to let the memory of such a remarkable career drop entirely from sight. How many games he might have won with good minor league teams, and if he had had the four missing seasons of his career, it is impossible to imagine. It was a great service of Ray Nemec, Robert Hoie, and the other SABR members who compiled the book, *Minor League Baseball Stars*, which traces the statistical outline of Thomas' career, and allows us to envision a memory of him.

PENNANT RACES OF THE 1940s

The decade of the 1940s was rich in pennant races, at least in the American League. Of the twenty pennant races in the decade, there were at least ten outstanding ones:

1. 1940 American League
2. 1944 American League
3. 1948 American League
4. 1946 National League
5. 1949 National League
6. 1949 American League
7. 1942 National League
8. 1941 National League
9. 1945 American League
10. 1945 National League

The 1940 American League race is recounted in Dick Bartell's 1980s autobiography, *Rowdy Richard*. It was a five-team race with three teams hanging in until the last weekend, a race filled with controversies and heroics. The 1944 AL race is immortalized in Bill Mead's classic, *Even The Browns*. The 1948 race is documented in David Kaiser's *Epic Season* (haven't got to it yet), and the 1949 American League race is re-created in David Halberstam's *Summer of '49*. The 1941 race is covered in Robert Creamer's wonderful *Baseball in '41*.

With one exception, all of the close National League races in the decade involved only two teams—Brooklyn and St. Louis.

1948: 254 RBI

Playing for Amarillo in the West Texas-New Mexico League in 1948, Bob Crues drove in 254 runs, thirty more than any other player in the history of baseball. His complete batting record for that season follows:

Year	G	AB	R	H	2B	3B	HR	RBI	BB	Avg.
1948	140	565	185	228	38	3	69	254	90	.404

There were five small-time leagues down there, the West Texas-New Mexico League, the Big State League, the Arizona-Texas League, the Lone Star League, and the Longhorn League. They were all hitter's leagues. Lots of people hit .380, hit 50 home runs. Just that season, someone named S.V. Washington hit .384 with 29 home runs, 124 RBI in 124 games for Texarkana in the Big State League, while Gainesville's Les Goldstein hit 58 doubles. In the Arizona-Texas League, which was Class C, Gene Lillard hit .364 with 20 homers, 92 RBI in 90 games, while Pete Hughes hit .347 with 21 homers and 118 RBI, and also drew 207 walks to give him an on-base percentage of .566. Lillard and Hughes were teammates, and the team finished fifth in a six-team circuit.

In the Lone Star League the batting champion, Joe Kracher, hit .433 to help Kilgore win the pennant. In the West Texas-New Mexico League, in addition to Bob Crues there was Herschel Martin, who won the batting title at .425 with 61 doubles (as well as managing the pennant-winning Albuquerque team), and Ed Carnett, who hit .409 with 59 doubles and 33

homers, and Virgil Richardson of Lubbock, who hit .397 with 196 RBI. By my count, these five regional leagues in 1948 produced seventy-two players who drove in 100 runs, and eleven who drove in 150 runs.

Bob Crues began his career as a pitcher, and went 20-5 in the same league in 1940. Then he hurt his arm and the war came, and he sort of got derailed, wound up as an outfielder. He had some mobility and a good arm. In his big year in 1948, he played 57 games in center field (the West Texas-New Mexico League maintained separate statistics for each outfield position, as every league should do). When he wasn't in center he was in right; he had sixteen baserunner kills. Crues spent most of his career in the West Texas Leagues.

BASEBALL BOOKS OF THE 1940s

Although no individual title had great significance, the Putnam series of team histories were collectively important. Other publishing events of note:

1940   *The Kid from Tompkinsville* introduces Roy Tucker, a worthy successor to Frank Merriwell, and a precursor, of sorts, of Malamud's Roy Hobbs.

1941   "You Could Look It Up," James Thurber's story of the pinch-hitting midget, is published in *The Saturday Evening Post,* ten years before Bill Veeck produces Eddie Gaedel.

1942   *Baseball Digest* begins publication.

1949   *Bill Stern's Favorite Baseball Stories.* A treasure trove of legend, myth, and anecdote. Individual stories in this collection can be trusted about as far as you can throw the average piano.

—Jim Carothers

Bill Stern in the 1940s wrote books of apocryphal baseball stories, which he presented as gospel truth. Today his name is synonymous with the worst in journalism—grand disregard for the truth or even plausibility of his stories, a lack of original research, sweeping interpretations of events based on limited knowledge. This is fair in the sense that Stern was guilty of the offenses alleged, and on one level the truth is always fair. Stern's standards were accepted in sports journalism at the time. Other people wrote the same kind of books, but are not subject to the same ridicule today, not because they were more accurate but because there were less successful. Many, many of Fred Lieb's stories don't check out if you track back on them, but Lieb remains respected, even revered, by many of us. Like Norman Rockwell, Edgar Guest, and J. Edgar Hoover, Bill Stern has given his name to the failings of his generation and his genre.

THE 1950s

HOW THE GAME WAS PLAYED

The baseball of the 1950s was perhaps the most one-dimensional, uniform, predictable version of the game which has ever been offered to the public. By 1950, the stolen base was a rare play, a "surprise" play. In the first seven years of the decade, no team stole a hundred bases in a season. In 1920, or arguably even earlier, powerful trends had gone into motion toward an offense based more and more around the home run, and less and less around anything else. Batting averages, which had jumped early in the lively ball era, began dropping after 1930. In the early 1950s, every team approached the game with the same essential offensive philosophy: get people on base and hit home runs. Every team, whether one of the best or one of the worst, featured players in the class of Gus Zernial, Ralph Kiner, Hank Sauer, Roy Sievers, Jim Lemon, Luke Easter, Eddie Robinson, Bob Nieman, Gus Triandos, Vic Wertz, Bobby Thomson, Sid Gordon, Rocky Colavito, and Ted Kluszewski, muscular men not long in grace nor noted for acceleration, but men who commanded large salaries for occasional home runs.

I wouldn't state it for a fact, but it is possible that the attendance problems of the early fifties were in some measure attributable to this. Since every team's offense was so much the same, a baseball game was not a clash of opposing philosophies or unlike skills, but rather a simple test of quality, a day-to-day worry about which pitcher had his control and which one would slip a pitch into the wheelhouse of the other's behemoth and how many men would be on base. Perhaps this was exciting baseball if your team was the Yankees or the Dodgers or (early in the decade) the Giants, and you figured each day that yours would be the fortunate team; besides, those three teams—the Yankees, Dodgers, and Durocher's Giants—truly did play an exciting, aggressive game of baseball, as did a few other managers.

Another point on which baseball drew heavy criticism from the media in the fifties was the length of time that it took to play the games. The average length of a major league game rose from two hours, twenty-three minutes

Eddie Mathews and friend. Life is good

in 1951 to two hours, thirty-eight minutes in 1960, and the number of games played in less than two hours dropped in those years from 166 to 41. This engendered criticism that baseball had become too slow, and in the early sixties a series of steps was taken to speed up the game. It was at this time that the rule was enacted requiring a manager to remove his pitcher if he went to the mound more than once in an inning. This was done to stop repeated, and time-consuming, visits to the mound.

The game evolved slowly. Strikeouts, on the rise since the early thirties, continued to ascend throughout the decade, with batting averages consequently in decline, and doubles and triples declining with batting averages. The trends in

motion did not break during the decade—they did not break until 1969—but they did bend into a new shape. The stolen base began to make a comeback. A new breed of power pitcher was emerging.

Perhaps even more than the *games,* the stifling effect of this baseball of so few dimensions was felt upon the *pennant races,* and thus upon the imagination of the fans. People tell me that baseball should never change, that it should remain forever locked the way it was the moment that they first discovered how wonderful it was. I cannot understand how people can think that way. Baseball didn't change much between 1920 and 1960; it crept forward like a scout on his knees, but it admitted no revolutions and no upheavals. They kept playing the same game in the same cities as long as they could, and they kept playing by the same unwritten rules and the same strategies, testing and retesting the same already proven theories about the game, and the same teams just kept winning. It sure doesn't seem like much of a way to greet the morning.

The decade ended on an optimistic note for fans who were growing weary of the reruns. In 1959 every team in baseball hit at least a hundred home runs *except* the American League champion White Sox, who hit but ninety-seven, and were considered at the time to have a "running" offense.

WHERE THE GAME WAS PLAYED

In 1953, major league baseball broke from the east coast and headed for the midwest. In 1958, it made it all the way to the west coast. Major league cities included Baltimore, Boston, Brooklyn, Chicago, Cincinnati, Cleveland, Detroit, Kansas City, Los Angeles, Milwaukee, New York, Philadelphia, Pittsburgh, St. Louis, San Francisco, and Washington.

WHO THE GAME WAS PLAYED BY

With the breaking of the color barrier, other ethnic identities ceased to have much meaning. Second-generation immigrants became third-generation immigrants became fourth-generation, and the accents ceased to be of languages and became the accents of regions. While some players still grew up in Little Italy or Fisherman's Wharf or Germantown, Illinois, more grew up in places with names like McAllister and Houston. But the difference between black and white was still deeply felt, and

where the Blacks were, everybody else was just White.

There weren't that many blacks, really—about eight percent. There were probably more Polish players in the fifties than African Americans (Kluszewski, Mazeroski, Kubek, and Musial were among the good ones. The Polish population in baseball was at its all-time high.) A myth has developed that for a time each team could have two blacks, the star and his roommate. No such pattern ever existed, but no blacks and whites roomed together during the fifties. Latins could room with blacks, and Latins could room with whites—but blacks and whites never roomed together. There were quite a few more Latin players as the decade wore on.

It is often written that the National League was integrated more quickly than the American League, which is how the National League caught and surpassed the American League after forty-five years as the weaker league. This is generally true, but integration was team-by-team, rather than league-by-league. Cleveland in the American League was well integrated by 1951, whereas the Cardinals in the National League did not have a black regular until Curt Flood in 1958. (Tom Alston, a regular early in 1954 season, had a nervous breakdown precipitated in part by racist abuse, and Charlie Peete, who would probably have been the Cardinals first black regular in 1957, was killed in a plane crash while returning from playing winter ball.)

As to regions, the South and California still produced a disproportionate share of the talent. Willie and Mickey were southerners; the Duke was from California (I consider Oklahoma southern because they drawl). Educated players began slowly to filter back into the game. The Yankees, in particular, had a number of players among the educated minority, including Moose Skowron, Bobby Brown, Andy Carey, and Bob Cerv.

CHECKING IN:

1951– Dave Winfield, St. Paul, Minnesota

1952– Fred Lynn, Chicago
    Vladimir Putin, Leningrad

1953– Dan Quisenberry, Santa Monica
    George Brett, West Virginia
    Keith Hernandez, San Francisco
    Jim Rice, South Carolina

1954– Gary Carter, California

1955– Robin Yount, Danville, Illinois
    Steve Jobs, San Francisco
    Bill Gates, Seattle

1956– Dale Murphy, Portland
    Eddie Murray, Los Angeles

1958– Rickey Henderson, Chicago
    Jamie Lee Curtis, Los Angeles

1959– Ryne Sandberg, Spokane
    Tim Raines, Florida

CHECKING OUT:

1950– Kiki Cuyler, 50
    Pete Alexander, alcoholism and
    epilepsy, 63

1951– Eddie Collins, 63
    Joe Jackson, 63
    Ludwig Wittgenstein, 62
    Harry Heilmann, 56
    Bill Klem, 77

1952– Arlie Latham, 93
    Arky Vaughan, boating accident, 40

1953– Jesse Burkett, 84
    Josef Stalin, 74
    Jim Tabor, 36

1954– Hugh Duffy, 87
    Chief Bender, 70

1955– Cy Young, 88
    Honus Wagner, 81
    Harry Agganis, pneumonia and
    pulmonary embolism, 25

1956– Connie Mack, 93
    Al Simmons, 56

1957– Sen. Joseph McCarthy, 48
    Tris Speaker, heart attack, 70
    Chuck Klein, 52
    Mel Ott, head-on collision, 52

1959– Frank Lloyd Wright, 89
    Nap Lajoie, 83
    Ed Walsh, 78
    Jim Bottomley, 59

THE BEST BASEBALL BOOKS OF THE 1950s

1951–Hy Turkin and S.C. Thompson, in *The Official Encyclopedia of Baseball,* produce the first modern compendium of individual player season and career statistics. Unique and invaluable B. M. (Before Macmillan).

1952–Bernard Malamud's *The Natural,* a satiric fantasy baseball novel on the theme that nobody ever really learns anything. Malamud's book, which owes much to Eddie Waitkus and T. S. Eliot, bears occasional resemblances to the 1984 Robert Redford vehicle.

1953–With *The Southpaw,* Mark Harris begins the saga of Henry Wiggin, left-handed pitcher and tale-teller extraordinaire.

1954–Douglas Wallop, *The Year the Yankees Lost the Pennant,* reworks Goethe's *Faust* into *Damn Yankees.*

—Jim Carothers

1955–*Fear Strikes Out* is my own addition to the list.

—Bill

THE 1950s IN A BOX

Attendance Data: 165 million (165,067,231)
Highest: Milwaukee Braves,   1957   2,215,404
          New York Yankees   16,133,658
Lowest: St. Louis Browns,   1950   247,131
          Washington Senators   5,598,081

The average American in this era attended a major league baseball game about once every ten years.

Most Home Runs:
Mickey Mantle,   1956   52
Duke Snider   326

Best Won/Lost Record by Team:
Cleveland Indians,   1954   111–43   .721
New York Yankees   955–582   .621

Worst Won/Lost Record by Team:
Pittsburgh Pirates,   1952   42–112   .273
Pittsburgh Pirates   616–923   .400

Index of Competitive Balance: 34%

The 1958 season was the most competitive in baseball history, in terms of having the smallest difference between the best teams and the worst. No team in either league won more than 92 games or lost more than 93 games, and six teams in each league were huddled between 71 and 84 wins. The standard deviation of team winning percentage in 1958 was .050, an all-time record low. The same figure in 1959 was .055, which is the fourth-lowest on record.

This happened because the Yankees of the late 1950s, while they remained good enough to win, were not as strong as either the Yankees of the early 1950s or the Yankees of the early 1960s—indeed, they were certainly no better than the Cleveland Indians of the early 1950s.

In the National League, there really was no championship team between the collapse of the Dodgers in 1957 and the reemergence of the Dodgers and Giants in 1962. The Milwaukee Braves had phenomenal front-line talent, and *should* have dominated that era, but couldn't keep their act together.

But the decade was not at all "competitive" in the sense that anybody had a fair chance to win. The decade was dominated by two teams—the Yankees and the Dodgers.

Home-Field Winning Percentage: .539

Percentage of Regulars Hitting .300: 19%

Largest Home-Field Advantage: Boston Red Sox, .132

Having Their Best Decade Ever: Cleveland Indians, Brooklyn-Los Angeles Dodgers

Having Their Worst Decade: Chicago Cubs, Pittsburgh Pirates, Washington Senators, Philadelphia-Kansas City Athletics.

Changing Direction: The White Sox, wandering in the wilderness for thirty years, found themselves in the active hands of Frank Lane. Lane made a series of brilliant trades. The

White Sox improved their record almost every year from 1948 (51-103) to 1954 (94-60), and remained a good team for fifteen years thereafter.

The Braves, struggling in Boston for a half-century, improved dramatically as soon as they moved to Milwaukee. The St. Louis Browns, whose history was similar, also began to crawl toward respectability soon after they moved to Baltimore, although they would not become competitive until 1960.

Heaviest Player: Ted Kluszewski had the highest listed weight, at 235, with Steve Bilko at 230. Both estimates are conservative. No one in baseball at this time would admit to a weight over 235, although baseball in the fifties probably had more 250-pounders than at any other time until the 1990s.

Lightest Player: Eddie Gaedel, 65 pounds

Lightest Real Player: YoYo Davalillo, 140

Most Strikeouts by Pitcher:

Herb Score, 1956	263
Early Wynn	1,544

Highest Batting Average:

Ted Williams, 1957	.388
Ted Williams	.336

Lowest Batting Average:

Gair Allie, 1954	.199
Ted Kazanski	.217

Best Major League Players (by Years):
1950— Phil Rizzuto
1951— Stan Musial
1952— Stan Musial
1953— Al Rosen
1954— Willie Mays
1955— Mickey Mantle and Willie Mays
1956— Mickey Mantle
1957— Mickey Mantle
1958— Mickey Mantle and Willie Mays
1959— Hank Aaron

Best Major League Pitchers (by Years):
1950— Robin Roberts
1951— Sal Maglie
1952— Bobby Shantz
1953— Robin Roberts
1954— Robin Roberts
1955— Robin Roberts
1956— Early Wynn
1957— Jim Bunning
1958— Warren Spahn
1959— Vern Law

Hardest-Throwing Pitcher: Steve Dalkowski

Hardest-Throwing Major League Pitcher: Herb Score

Best Curve: Camilo Pascual

Best Power/Speed Combination: Willie Mays

Best Switch Hitter: Mickey Mantle

Iron Man: Robin Roberts

Best Baseball Books:
1951— *The Official Encyclopedia of Baseball* by Hy Turkin and S.C. Thompson
1952— *The Natural* by Bernard Malamud
1953— *The Southpaw* by Mark Harris
1954— *The Year the Yankees Lost the Pennant* by Douglass Wallop
1955— *Fear Strikes Out* by Jimmy Piersall and Al Hirschberg

Five Largest Changes in Baseball During the Decade:

1. Franchises shifting rapidly after 50 years of stability.
2. Growth/threat of televised baseball.
3. End of the railroad era/players and media travelling by plane.
4. Collapsing attendance due to televised baseball and urban decay.
5. Onset of the eternal problem of games getting longer.

Best Outfield Arm: Carl Furillo

An outfielder named Glen Gorbous, playing for Omaha at the time, established a record in 1957 when he threw a baseball 445 feet, 10 inches on the fly. Gorbous could throw but not hit. For the Phillies in 1955, he had ten Baserunner Kills in just sixty-two games, but hit only .244.

Worst Outfield Arm: Dick Williams

Most Runs Batted In:

Al Rosen, 1953	145
Duke Snider	1,031

Duke Snider and Gil Hodges were the only major leaguers to hit 300 home runs during the 1950s, and also the only two to drive in 1,000 runs.

Most Aggressive Baserunner: Minnie Minoso

Fastest Player: Mickey Mantle

Pedro Ramos, a pitcher for the Senators, was often used as a pinch runner, and always insisted he was the fastest player in baseball. He repeatedly challenged Mickey Mantle to a footrace in an effort to prove this, but the race never happened.

Slowest Player: Gus Triandos

Best Control Pitcher: Lew Burdette or Robin Roberts

Most Stolen Bases:

Luis Aparicio, 1959	56
Willie Mays	179

Best-Looking Players:
Eddie Mathews
Mickey Mantle

Ugliest Player: Don Mossi

Three Finger Brown Award: Bud Daley, a natural right hander, had polio as a child, and had to learn to use his left hand. He won 16

games twice in a row for the Kansas City A's, which was the most ever won for that franchise.

Ozzie Guillen Trophy: Don Mueller

Bound for Glory, or at least Congress:
Chuck Connors
Larry Jackson
Vinegar Bend Mizell

Best Pitching Staff: 1954 Cleveland Indians

Best Offense: 1953 Brooklyn Dodgers

Football Players: Vic Janowicz, Jackie Jensen, Bob Cerv, Moose Skowron, Ted Kluszewski

Retrobermanisms: Gino (Holy) Cimoli

Basketball Guys: Gene Conley, Joe Adcock, Bill Sharman, Dick Groat, Johnny and Eddie O'Brien

First of His Kind: Don Newcombe (first Cy Young Winner)

Last of His Kind: Connie Mack

One of a Kind: Gene Conley (Only player ever to sustain successful careers in both the NBA and the majors. Also, for many years, the only player to win the Minor League player of the year award more than once. Sandy Alomar finally matched that accomplishment.)

Best Infield: 1950–1952 Brooklyn Dodgers, Gil Hodges, Jackie Robinson, Billy Cox, and Pee Wee Reese. 1950 Red Sox had better stats, but not in context.

Best Outfield: 1959 Cleveland Indians (Minnie Minoso, Tito Francona, Rocky Colavito, and Jimmy Piersall)

A Better Man Than a Ballplayer: Gus Zernial

A Better Ballplayer Than a Human Being:
Johnny Temple

Mr. Dickens, I'd Like You to Meet:
Angelo Dagres (Baltimore, 1955)
Odbert Hamrick (Brooklyn, 1955, Baltimore, 1958)

Platoon Combinations I Would Like to See:
Coot Veal and Cot Deal
Bob Hale and Carroll Hardy

Best Defensive Team: 1959 Chicago White Sox

Clint Hartung Award: Billy Consolo

Outstanding Sportswriter: Arnold Hano

Most Admirable Superstar: Ernie Banks

Gold Glove Team:
C— Roy Campanella
1B— Vic Power
2B— Nellie Fox
3B— Billy Cox
SS— Roy McMillan
OF— Jimmy Piersall
      Willie Mays
      Jim Busby

Franchise Shifts:
Boston (N) to Milwaukee, 1952
St. Louis (A) to Baltimore, 1953
Philadelphia (A) to Kansas City, 1955
Brooklyn to Los Angeles, 1958
New York (N) to San Francisco, 1958

New Stadiums: Two of the cities that attracted teams, Baltimore and Milwaukee, built new stadiums to help them do that. Memorial Stadium in Baltimore was built in 1950, and the upper deck was added in 1953. Milwaukee's County Stadium, also completed in 1953, was the first stadium to be built with public money. The other teams that moved did so initially into existing parks, and no new parks were built for other teams. However, Minneapolis and St. Paul got together in 1957 to construct Midway Park, to which a major league team was attracted in 1961.

Best Pennant Race: 1951 National League

Best World Series: 1952, Yankees over Dodgers in seven

Best-Hitting Pitcher: Don Newcombe

Worst-Hitting Pitcher: Bob Buhl

Best Minor League Team: 1954 Indianapolis Indians

Best Minor League Players:
Ray Perry
Al Pinkston

Odd Couple: Yogi Berra and Dr. Bobby Brown were roommates and best of friends, although at a glance they seemed to have nothing in common.

Resident Intellectual: Jim Brosnan

Drinking Men:
Ryne Duren
Don Newcombe
Ellis Kinder
Don Larsen

New Equipment: Batting helmets were a pet project of Branch Rickey. He had asked the Cardinals to wear them in spring training in the early 1920s, and required all of the Pirates to wear them in 1952, so that these valuable stars who went 42-112 that year wouldn't get hurt and leave him with a bad team. The National League adopted them in 1955, the American League in 1956, with a grandfather clause to exempt players who were already in the league.

Uniform Changes: See page 239.

Most Wins by Pitcher:
Robin Roberts, 1952   28
Warren Spahn   202

Highest Winning Percentage:

| Elroy Face, | 1959 | 18-1 | .947 |
| Whitey Ford | | 121-50 | .708 |

Lowest Winning Percentage:

| Don Larsen, | 1954 | 3-21 | .125 |
| Camilo Pascual | | 45-76 | .372 |

Nicknames: Animal House (see note)

Worst Award Selection: 1952, Hank Sauer selected as National League MVP.

Best Player Who Never Won the MVP Award: Eddie Mathews or Duke Snider

Best Bunters: Phil Rizzuto, Nellie Fox, and Richie Ashburn

Flameout: Johnny Groth

All Offense/No Defense: 1950 Boston Red Sox

All Defense/No Offense: 1959 Baltimore Orioles

Homer: Yogi Berra hit 210 of 358 career home runs in Yankee Stadium.

Yellowstone Park Award: Joe Adcock lost more home runs to playing in poor home run parks (primarily County Stadium in Milwaukee) than anyone except Joe DiMaggio and Goose Goslin. Adcock hit 199 career home runs on the road—more than Tony Perez, Orlando Cepeda, Darrell or Dwight Evans, Johnny Bench, Duke Snider, Rocky Colavito, Dale Murphy, Jim Rice, Graig Nettles, Al Kaline, or Mel Ott. But he hit only 137 in his home parks—far fewer than any of the players listed before.

Tough-Luck Season: Virgil Trucks, 1952

Could I Try This Career Over? Bob Cerv

Minor Leagues Were:
5 percent free
95 percent slaves to the majors

Best Double Play Combination: Phil Rizzuto and Gil McDougald, New York Yankees. I discussed this in my last book, but Casey Stengel's Yankees turned a huge number of double plays regardless of who was playing second and short.

Worst Double Play Combination: Dick Cole and Curt Roberts, 1954 Pittsburgh Pirates.

Paul Krichell Talent Scout Award: Quincy Trouppe, scouting for the St. Louis Cardinals in the spring of 1953, recommended that the Cardinals sign Ernie Banks. The Cardinals sent another scout to check him out. The Cardinal scout reported that "I don't think he is a major league prospect. He can't hit, he can't run, he has a pretty good arm but it's a scatter arm. I don't like him."

Ira Thomas Talent Scout Award: The Detroit Tigers, desperate for a shortstop, had a purchase option on Maury Wills. They worked him out, and returned him to the Dodger organization.

Highest-Paid Player: Ted Williams, 1959 $125,000

New Statistics:
1954— Sacrifice flies
1955— Intentional walks

A Very Good Movie Could Be Made About: A day in the life of Casey Stengel

Five Biggest Things Wrong with Baseball:

1. Franchises jumping around, abandoning loyal fans.
2. Old stadiums in bad neighborhoods with little parking and poor public transportation.
3. Minor leagues dying off.
4. Complete domination by New York teams.
5. Long, boring games/limited offensive variety.

THE GREATEST TEAM WHAT EVER WAS

Part III

What are the standards of a great team? To me, three things define greatness in a team:

1. A great team needs to win more than once. A great team needs to dominate over a period of three to five years, at least.

2. A great team should have great players, in their prime. There is a difference between a player having a great season—Wilcy Moore in 1927, Ripper Collins in 1934, Zoilo Versalles in 1965—and a great player. You cannot be a great player for one year, because that isn't what greatness means.

3. A great team needs to be able to win anywhere, anytime. I'm not saying that the team needs to win on demand, but having a bunch of fast guys, a couple of .300 hitters and some pitchers who throw strikes may be enough to win 100 games if you're playing in a big park—but you've got to go into Yankee Stadium and beat the Yankees, so let's look at your left-handed power.

Of those three factors, one is easily measured. You can make a fairly objective evaluation of what a team has accomplished over a period of years by doing something simple like counting the positives over a five-year period. Let's say we set up a six-point scale for each season, based on:

1. Finishing over .500.
2. Winning 90 games.
3. Winning 100 games.
4. Winning the division.
5. Winning the league.
6. Winning the World Series.

If you meet all of those standards in a season, that's a six-point season. If you were to meet all of those standards every year for five years (which no team has ever come close to doing), that would be thirty success points over the five-year run. I'll talk more of that in a moment.

You could make the second standard (the number of great players on the team) somewhat objective by sorting players into "star" classes, perhaps by using the Win Shares system to make objective determinations about who is a star, who is a superstar, and so on. Then you could scan the rosters and credit the team, perhaps, with ten points for each legitimate superstar, seven points for an all-star, four points for a minor star, and three points for a quality regular.

Why would you want to do that? You would want to do something like that if

(a) you were seriously interested in identifying the greatest team in the history of baseball, and

(b) you bought the theory that a great team must have great players.

The third standard, ability to win under any conditions, would be the most difficult to make purely objective since it must measure the breadth of a team's talents. How many different things did this team do well? Did they have speed *and* left-handed power *and* right-handed power *and* infield defense *and* outfield defense *and* starting pitching *and* relief pitching *and* right-handed pitching *and* left-handed pitching *and* .300 hitters *and* leadoff men? Again, you could make that objective, but imperfectly.

The top five-year runs in baseball history, by the "accomplishment count" system, would be:

New York Yankees	1935–1939	25
New York Yankees	1949–1953	25
Chicago Cubs	1906–1910	24
St. Louis Cardinals	1942–1946	24
New York Yankees	1960–1964	24
Philadelphia Athletics	1910–1914	23
Oakland A's	1971–1975	22
Atlanta Braves	1995–1999	22
Philadelphia Athletics	1928–1932	21
New York Yankees	1954–1958	21
Cincinnati Reds	1972–1976	21
New York Yankees	1976–1980	21
Boston Red Sox	1912–1916	20
Brooklyn Dodgers	1952–1956	20
Baltimore Orioles	1969–1973	20
New York Giants	1921–1925	19
Oakland A's	1988–1992	19
New York Yankees	1995–1999	19
New York Giants	1909–1913	18
New York Yankees	1926–1930	18
Atlanta Braves	1994–1998	18
New York Yankees	1941–1945	18

The teams that won their league before the split into divisions in 1969 were counted as winning the division as well as the league. I will run a list in a separate chart of the top five-year periods for each franchise.

There are six teams in baseball history which have had back-to-back six-point seasons: the Philadelphia A's in 1910–1911, the Yankees in 1927–1928, the A's again in 1929–1930, the Yankees again in 1936–1937, the Cincinnati Reds in 1975–1976, and the Yankees again in 1977–1978. The record for a three-year period is 17 points, by the A's from 1929–1931 (they won 100 games for the third straight year, but lost the World Series), the Yankees from 1936–1938 (or 1937–39), and the St. Louis Cardinals from 1942–1944. All records for team accomplishment in periods longer than four years are held either by Joe McCarthy's Yankees (1936–44) or by the Casey Stengel/Ralph Houk Yankees (1949–1964).

I'm not suggesting that we could use a system like this to make a sole determination of the best team in the history of the game. The method uses arbitrary cutoffs, and a five-year list isn't necessarily any better than a six-year list or a seven-year list. But this system is useful in sorting out the candidates. I mentioned before the 1941 Dodgers and the 1954 Indians, both of which teams are sometimes listed among the greatest ever. They don't make the list. They didn't do enough, over a period of seasons, to be considered among the best teams ever.

Some people have made efforts to evaluate the greatest teams ever by, for example, looking at the norms and standard deviations of runs scored by teams, so that they can say that this team's offense was 2.1 standard deviations above the norm, while their pitching and defense were 1.4 standard deviations below the norm, making the team + 3.5 standard run deviations. Maybe it's just me, but I can't really see that that type of analysis leads anywhere except back to the team's won-lost record.

To state the runs scored in terms of standard deviations from the norm, you're going to have to look at standard deviations over a period of several years, or you're going to be subject to an irrelevant influence based on whether there was or was not another team in the league which could score runs and whether or not there happened to be a real bad team in the league. In the American League in 1974 the standard deviation of runs scored was 24.5. In the National League the number of runs scored was almost the same, but the standard deviation was 72.0. The Red Sox scored 696 runs but were 1.3 standard deviations above the league norm; the Pirates scored 751 runs but were 1.1 standard deviations above their league norm. That doesn't make the Red Sox offense better than the Pirates, does it?

If you use multi-year standard deviations, then you're inevitably going to conclude that the best team was the team that won the most games. While the won-lost record of the team is certainly a good starting point, it is, after all, a starting point; if you keep coming back to that you're walking in circles.

One team often listed among the greatest ever is the 1919 Chicago White Sox (the Black Sox). There is no foundation to consider that team among the all-time greats. The White Sox top score for five-year performance is 12 points, from 1916 to 1920. That's nothing. Their multi-year accomplishments rank them below the Detroit Tigers (1907–1911), the Red Sox (1901–1905), the Tigers of the thirties, the Indians of the fifties, the Baltimore Orioles of 1979–1983, the Kansas City Royals of 1976–1980, the Tigers of 1983–1987, and dozens of other teams that no one suggests we should list among the greatest of all time.

Even if we assume that the 1919 Chicago White Sox could have won the World Series, even if we assume that that team could have won the American League in 1920 had eight players not been expelled in late September, it still isn't enough. The team just didn't win often enough to be considered an all-time great team.

If you look at the personnel of the 1919 White Sox, once again they're not very impressive. Sure, they had some good players; they also had Nemo Leibold, Swede Risberg, and Chick Gandil. As everyday players. Their everyday lineup was two superstars (Eddie Collins

PERIODS OF GREATEST SUCCESS FOR EACH FRANCHISE

	Years	Points
Anaheim Angels	1982–1986	9
Atlanta Braves	1995–1999	22
Baltimore Orioles	1969–1973	20
Boston Braves	(Several)	7
Boston Red Sox	1912–1916	20
Brooklyn Dodgers	1952–1956	20
Chicago Cubs	1906–1910	24
Chicago White Sox	1916–1920	12
Cincinnati Reds	1972–1976	21
Cleveland Indians	1995–1999	17
Detroit Tigers	1907–1911	14
Houston Astros	1995–1999	11
Kansas City A's		0
Kansas City Royals	1976–1980	15
Los Angeles Dodgers	1962–1966	17
New York Yankees	1935–1939	25
New York Yankees	1949–1953	25
Milwaukee Braves	1955–1959	13
Milwaukee Brewers	1978–1982	10
Minnesota Twins	1965–1969	11
and again	1987–1991	11
Montreal Expos	1979–1983	8
New York Giants	1921–1925	19
New York Mets	1984–1988	16
Oakland A's	1971–1975	22
Philadelphia Athletics	1910–1914	23
Philadelphia Phillies	1976–1980	17
Pittsburgh Pirates	1901–1905	16
San Diego Padres	1994–1998	7
San Francisco Giants	1962–1966	12
St. Louis Browns	1941–1945	5
St. Louis Cardinals	1942–1946	24
Texas Rangers	1995–1999	9
Washington Senators I	1923–1927	11
Washington Senators II	(1969)	1

and Joe Jackson), three pretty good players (Buck Weaver, Ray Schalk, and Happy Felsch), and three guys who frankly weren't very good. That's not a great team.

Anything that makes a player or team famous tends to make them over-rated. The White Sox wind up terribly over-rated, ironically, because they threw the World Series.

VALUING RELIEVERS

What is the relationship between the value of a good starting pitcher and the value of a good reliever? A starting pitcher, pitching 200 to 270 innings a season, saves many more runs than a relief ace, who typically pitches less than 100 innings in a season. But the relief ace might still be as valuable or more valuable, because his job is to pitch at critical moments of the game, when a run allowed would be especially damaging. Everyone would expect and everyone would acknowledge, I think, that one run saved by a relief ace has more impact on the won-lost record of the team than one run saved by a starter, but *how much* more impact? 30% more? 50% more? Twice as much? Who knows?

Nobody knows. I designed a study to address that question and related questions. One central issue is that outlined above: What is the value of one run saved by a relief ace, as contrasted with one run saved by a starting pitcher? The other central issue is: Is the modern style of using the ace reliever, which involves using him almost exclusively in "save" situations, the optimal usage pattern? Does the reliever actually have more impact on the won-lost record of his team when he is used in that way than when he is used in some other way?

I needed to know the answers to these questions in order to develop the Win Shares system. If you don't make any adjustment for the "situational importance" of runs saved by a relief ace, then, following the logic of the system, you will reach the conclusion that relief aces are nowhere near as valuable as good starters. Among the relievers who have won Cy Young

or MVP Awards—Konstanty, Sparky Lyle, Rollie Fingers, Guillermo Hernandez, Dennis Eckersley—few were anywhere near the league lead in runs saved for his team. Some adjustment seems to be both logically necessary and consistent with general assessments of player value. But what is that adjustment?

I designed a series of tests to study that. These studies are based on a very simple simulation of a baseball game, in which the smallest event is a half-inning. I set up two identical teams, Teams A and B, playing a 50/50 mix of home games and road games, with the home team having a home-field advantage, and with both teams having an equal ability to recognize a one-run situation and to play for one run.

Having constructed and tested this simple model, I began to modify it by adding a quality pitcher to one of the teams. First, to establish a base line (for the relievers), I added three starting pitchers (one at a time)—a pitcher who pitched complete games only, a high-quality pitcher pitching in a more realistic pattern, and a lesser-quality starting pitcher, also pitching in a realistic fashion.

What I wanted to know is, what is the relationship between runs saved (by a starting pitcher) and extra wins? If a starting pitcher saves his team 100 runs scored, a thousand runs scored, how many extra games does his team win?

I found that, for a starting pitcher, there was a gain of one win for each eight to nine runs saved. Actually, for the three starting pitchers, I got values of one extra win for each 8.01 runs, 8.35 runs, and 8.79 runs, respectively.

Then, having established the value of a run saved by a starting pitcher, I took the starting pitchers out and began substituting relievers.

I put relief pitchers into the study in five different patterns, corresponding roughly to the way that relievers have been used in various periods of baseball history. The relief ace was used in one of five patterns, which were:

1. The Clint Brown pattern.
2. The Elroy Face pattern.
3. The Hoyt Wilhelm pattern.
4. The Bruce Sutter pattern.
5. The Robb Nenn pattern.

The relief pitcher, in every case, was of exactly the same effectiveness; the only thing that changed was *the way in which he was used*. He was always a highly effective pitcher—more effective, per inning, than the starters.

The pitcher used in the Clint Brown pattern would come into the game whenever:

(a) the starting pitcher was knocked out, and

(b) the relief ace wasn't tired.

In other words, his work load was essentially regulated by chance, and by his own fatigue. Occasionally the reliever used in this way would come in the game early and pitch five, six, seven, or more innings, then be out for several days. Most often, he would come in when the starter was knocked out and pitch an inning or two of relief until the game was over or he would be replaced by a pinch hitter. The computer wasn't *reluctant* to use this reliever in a "game" situation, but it didn't put any priority on saving him for that type of situation. Just whenever the starter was knocked out, the relief ace came into the game, if he hadn't been used or used much in the last couple of days, and wasn't tired.

This model was intended to reflect the usage of relief aces from the mid-1930s, the Clint Brown era, up until the early 1950s, the time of Ellis Kinder and Harry Dorish. A reliever used in this way would pitch 58 games, 106 innings in an average season, and would record an average of ten saves. These numbers are very typical of Clint Brown and others of that era including Mace Brown, Clyde Shoun, Hugh Casey, Ace Adams, Ted Wilks, Les Webber, Joe Berry, Tom Ferrick, Dick Coffman, Jack Russell, and Ellis Kinder. The reliever's ERA in all patterns would be a little over 2.50, although it varies a tiny bit because different usage patterns cause the relief ace to be used in more or fewer situations in which the other team would be playing for one run.

The relief ace used in the Elroy Face pattern was used similarly, except that the computer would tend to save him for the late innings of a close game. He wouldn't pitch more than 2 or 3 innings at a time, ordinarily, and he wouldn't often come into the game before the seventh inning, and the computer wouldn't ordinarily put him into the game if it wasn't fairly close. But the computer still

(a) tried to rest the reliever a day or two between appearances, and

(b) was as likely to bring the relief ace in when his team was two runs behind as it was to bring him in when they were two runs ahead.

The computer manager at this stage paid no attention to the "save" situation, in other words. This was intended to model the way that relief aces were used from the mid-1950s until about 1962. Used in this way, the relief ace would pitch 59 games, 96 innings in an average season, and would record 15 saves—numbers that are very typical of Elroy Face (1957–1964), and also consistent with Turk Farrell (1957–1961 and 1967–68), Clem Labine

(1957–59), Turk Lown (1957–1962), and others including Hersh Freeman, Gerry Staley, Don McMahon, Marv Grissom, Bill Henry, Don Elston, and the young Ron Perranoski.

When the relief ace was used in the Hoyt Wilhelm pattern, the emphasis began to switch from bringing the reliever in when the starting pitcher was knocked out, to bringing the reliever in *in preference to* the starter. In this pattern, the relief ace would be brought into the game in the late innings of any close game, unless he had been worked hard in the previous games.

This usage pattern was intended to represent the 1963–1978 era, when relief aces were just worked to death, and new records for relief appearances were set almost every season.

In our study, the reliever pitched an average of 72 games, 128 innings per season, recording an average of 24 saves. Mike Marshall is the defining pitcher of the era, working 92 games in 1973, 106 in 1974, and 90 in 1979, and working almost two innings per game. That was extreme, but Dick Radatz, John Wyatt, Ted Abernathy, Mudcat Grant, Eddie Fisher, Wilbur Wood, Bob Locker, Dave Guisti, John Hiller, Sparky Lyle, Goose Gossage (up to 1978), Kent Tekulve, and Wayne Granger are others who were used this way. Ron Perranoski was used in this pattern, beginning in 1963; so was Hoyt Wilhelm, who had also worked a lot of innings in some seasons in the fifties.

MAJOR LEAGUE ALL-STAR TEAM 1950–1959

Records in seasonal notation, based on 154 games. Pitchers based on 40 starts.

Pos.	Player	Years	Hits	HR	RBI	Avg.	Other
C	Yogi Berra	9.06	165	26	110	.287	Only 29 strikeouts
1B	Stan Musial	9.45	187	28	103	.330	38 Doubles
2B	Jackie Robinson	6.03	161	16	79	.311	
3B	Eddie Mathews	7.62	160	39	103	.281	99 Walks
SS	Ernie Banks	5.99	176	38	110	.295	
LF	Ted Williams	6.46	165	35	113	.336	131 Walks
CF	Willie Mays	6.92	187	36	103	.317	26 Stolen bases
RF	Mickey Mantle	8.09	172	35	104	.311	110 Walks

Pitcher		Years	Won-Lost	SO	ERA	Other
RH	Christy Mathewson	8.23	29-14	218	1.97	361 Innings
RH	Robin Roberts	9.78	20-15	155	3.32	308 Innings
RH	Early Wynn	9.00	21-13	172	3.28	
LH	Warren Spahn	9.34	22-14	157	2.92	
LH	Whitey Ford	5.76	21-9	159	2.66	
RA	Ellis Kinder	5.54	10-7	70	3.12	17 Saves

When the relief ace was used in the Bruce Sutter pattern, the computer manager became reluctant to bring him into the game unless it was a "save" situation. After fifteen years of relief aces being worked more and more, by the late 1970s it was becoming apparent that the load was too heavy, and managers were looking for some way to limit the use of their relief aces, while getting the maximum value from them. When Bruce Sutter crashed in the second half of the 1977 and 1978 seasons, his manager, Herman Franks, decided to hold Sutter back for "save" situations, not to use him when the score was tied or the team was a run behind. Within a year or two, this became the way that all relief aces were used.

A reliever used in the Bruce Sutter pattern (in our study) pitched an average of 61 games, 111 innings per season, registering an average of 38 saves. These numbers are fairly typical of Dave Righetti, Joe Sambito, Rick Camp, Greg Minton, Rollie Fingers, and Goose Gossage (post-1978), Bill Caudill, Ron Davis, the aging Gene Garber, and the young Jeff Reardon, and the young Lee Smith.

This was a transitional step toward the 1990s reliever, the Robb Nen pattern—the era of the one-inning save. Pitchers used in the Robb Nen pattern in our study pitched 77 games, 91 innings in a typical season, registering an average of 41 saves per season.

Essentially, these five usage patterns represent two transitions:

1. From relievers being brought into the game when starters failed, to relief aces brought in when "their" situation—the save situation—arose.

2. From relievers' workloads being regulated by their own fatigue, to workloads being kept very light so that the relief ace would always be available for "his" situation.

That's a simplification. In all five stages of the study, the reliever's recent workload still controls his availability to some extent, and in all five stages of the study, the team would *sometimes* find itself in a situation in which the relief ace just had to come in and pitch an inning or two, no matter how tired he was. Sixteenth inning, no matter how hard he has worked, he has to pitch. In all five patterns, if the pitcher hasn't worked in the last five days, the computer manager knows that it needs to get him in there for an inning or two. If the fatigue level is low and it's the ninth inning of a tie game, the relief ace has to pitch—just as he does in real life. The computer manager is always balancing the team's need for a pitcher against the reliever's fatigue level. But in broad terms, that's the change the computer makes—from bringing in the reliever when the starter is gone, to bringing him in to pitch the ninth inning of a save situation, period.

I tested relief aces used in each of these five patterns over a period of 2,000 or more test seasons. Having done this, we are in a better position to answer the two questions that I began by asking:

1. What is the value of one run saved by a relief ace, as contrasted with one run saved by a starting pitcher?

2. Is the modern style of using the ace reliever, which involves using him almost exclusively in "save" situations, the optimal usage pattern?

My findings on these two issues can be summarized in five statements:

1. A hundred runs saved by a relief ace have substantially more impact than a hundred runs saved by a starting pitcher in all cases, even when the reliever's job is just to come in and pitch when the starter is knocked out.

2. As to how much more impact a run saved by a relief ace has, you can get answers

ranging from 36% more to 97%, depending on exactly what comparison you are making.

3. The best short answer is that 100 runs saved by relief pitchers will have 70% more impact on the team's won-lost record than 100 runs saved by starting pitchers.

4. The modern usage pattern of a relief ace—the Robb Nen pattern, using relievers in one-inning "save" situations—is clearly and absolutely not the optimal usage pattern.

5. The relief aces of the Hoyt Wilhelm era (1963–1978) were about 50% more valuable than modern relief aces, mostly because they pitched more innings, but also because the runs that they saved had more impact, one for one, than those saved by modern relief aces.

Whereas there was a gain of one win for each eight to nine runs saved by starting pitchers, the parallel figures for relief aces were:

1. One win for each 5.88 runs by a reliever used in the Clint Brown pattern.

2. One win for each 5.14 runs by a reliever used in the Elroy Face pattern.

3. One win for each 4.47 runs by a reliever used in the Hoyt Wilhelm pattern.

4. One win for each 4.73 runs by a reliever used in the Bruce Sutter pattern.

5. One win for each 4.64 runs by a reliever used in the Robb Nen pattern.

Why was the value of a run saved higher in the Hoyt Wilhelm era than it is now? Essentially, because

(a) the situation in which a run saved has the greatest impact is when the game is tied (in the late innings), and

(b) because the relief aces of that era were used most often when the game was tied.

There are really two situations in which a run saved has a very high impact—when the game is tied, and when the reliever's team is one run ahead. In those two situations, a run

saved has a huge impact on the team's won-lost record.

I isolated situations (as opposed to usage patterns) by "switching off" all the rest of the computer manager's logic as to when a reliever should be used, and telling the computer to bring in the relief ace for one inning (and one inning only) in each of six situations:

1. Team trailing by two runs after 7.5 or 8 innings.

2. Team trailing by one run after 7.5 or 8 innings.

3. Team tied up after 7.5, 8, or 8.5 innings.

4. Team leading by one run after 8 or 8.5 innings.

5. Team leading by two runs after 8 or 8.5 innings.

6. Team leading by three runs after 8 or 8.5 innings.

When a relief ace was called in to pitch one inning in a tie game, the winning percentage of his team was .574. When he *wasn't* called in to pitch that inning, of course, it was very near to .500. The relief ace could swing the game, used in that way, 7.4% of the time. And there was a gain of one game, in that situation, for each 2.51 runs saved by the reliever. Let me put the results of all six situations in chart form:

Situation	With Relief Ace	Without Relief Ace	Difference	Runs for each Win
−2	.074	.068	.006	25.18
−1	.223	.197	.026	7.13
±0	.574	.500	.074	2.51
+1	.867	.810	.057	3.21
+2	.964	.945	.019	10.29
+3	.990	.982	.008	21.87

Each run saved in a tie game has more than eight times the impact of a run saved with a three-run lead. If you use your relief ace to save a three-run lead in the ninth inning, you'll win that game 99% of the time. If you *don't* use your ace in that situation, you'll win 98% of the time. So is that a smart thing to do, to use a precious asset in that situation?

The conclusion of this study is very clear. There are two situations in which the use of a relief ace is particularly helpful: when the teams are tied, and when the team is ahead by one run. But no other situation is even remotely the same. Using your relief ace when you're two runs ahead has less than one-third the impact of using him when you're one run ahead—and is less effective than using the relief ace for an inning when you're behind by a run.

Pitchers used in the modern way, in the Robb Nen pattern, DO often pitch when the game is tied, even though this is not the core of their job description. They do pitch often in that situation, however, because they pitch 75 times a year, and teams don't have 75 one-inning save situations. Teams have 50 to 60 one-inning save situations. The remaining games that a modern reliever pitches are games when it's tied in the late innings, and he's fresh.

But the earlier relievers pitched more often in tie games, plus the modern relievers are very often used in situations in which their presence in the game may be psychologically comforting to the manager, but has little practical benefit. Modern relievers are used to pitch the ninth inning with a three-run lead. While I don't mean to dismiss the intangible costs of blowing a three-run lead, an average team would win 97% of those games if they brought in Bryan Rekar in that situation. Even bad pitchers don't give up three runs in one inning a very high percentage of the time, and even if the reliever does give up three runs, the team

has a good chance to win the game anyway; it takes at least four to beat you. It is simply not logical to make a special effort to get your best pitcher into the game when you have a three-run lead with one inning to play.

Essentially, using your relief ace to protect a three-run lead is like a business using a top executive to negotiate fire insurance. It's not that fire insurance isn't important. If you have a fire and you're not insured, obviously that's a huge loss. But the reality is that, even if you don't carry any insurance, you're not *likely* to have a fire. And while you may desperately need insurance, that doesn't mean that it is therefore essential to assign your best executive to negotiate it. There are other people who can take care of that kind of work.

One more question before I go. What is the absolutely perfect way to use a relief ace? Suppose that you have one reliever who is clearly better than anyone else on your staff. What is the very best way to use him, so that he will have maximum impact on the won-lost record of his team?

The answer that I am going to offer is a guess, albeit a guess informed by research. The very optimal usage pattern, I believe, would be to use the relief ace:

- two innings a game when the game is tied,
- two innings a game when you have a one-run lead, and
- one inning at a time in other games when the game is close at the end and the relief ace hasn't been used for a day or two.

In other words, bring in your man when you're ahead by one after seven innings, when you're tied after seven innings, or when the game is close and the relief ace isn't tired.

If a reliever pitched two innings two days in a row, he would need to rest the third day. This situation, then, would create a workload of about 69 games, 113 innings per season. Now, that is NOT a workload that is going to destroy anybody. In all honesty, I can't see one iota of evidence that a workload of 70 games, 130 innings is dangerous to a reliever. A hundred and thirty innings isn't very many. Goose Gossage had several seasons working that way, and he threw 95 until he was 40. The relievers of that era who stayed within that range were as healthy and as durable as the relievers of any other era. Look at them—Gossage, Wilhelm, Ted Abernathy, Sparky Lyle, Rollie Fingers, Quisenberry, Tekulve, Ron Perranoski, Bob Locker, Wilbur Wood, Clay Carroll, Gene Garber. Those guys had about 100 good seasons among them. I don't see any reason to believe that a 70-game, 130-inning workload for a reliever is dangerous.

Some relievers in that same era stepped over the line—Mike Marshall, Wayne Granger, Bill Campbell. Bruce Sutter in the first half of the 1978 season was on target to pitch 87 games and 157 innings. He crashed in the second half, and no wonder. It was necessary to limit the relief pitcher's role, to prevent relievers from being destroyed by overwork.

But while it was necessary to limit a relief pitcher's role, many modern relievers now are working 70 to 85 innings a season—*and they're not even working the right 75 innings*. Managers in the late 1970s had one good idea, which was to define and limit the relief pitcher's role so that he wasn't overworked, and one bad idea, which was to use the reliever only in "save" situations. Almost any reliever CAN work more than 90 innings a season without any excessive risk to his career; he can work 120, 130 innings.

My definition of when to use a relief ace targets the reliever toward the innings which have the greatest impact, but also has flexibility built into it, to stabilize the reliever's workload and allow his arm to recover. Twenty-five of his expected 69 or 70 appearances are re-

served for games when he hasn't pitched lately. Used in that way, I just can't believe that a pitcher would have any accelerated risk of arm injury.

Incidentally, I just finished reviewing Whitey Herzog's new book about managing, *You're Missin' a Great Game*. On page 129 of that book, Herzog outlines *his* ideas on the most effective use of a relief ace, which are consistent with mine up to a point:

> First of all, it's better to have your closer go two innings every other day than one inning every day . . . Today a guy will have 65 appearances and go 55 innings . . . You're going to pay a guy $4 million and only get 55 innings? That's a joke . . .

Arbitration forces *everyone* to overvalue the kind of statistics that can be used to generate big bucks come contract time. As a result, the manager has a situation where his start reliever is now *demanding* to be in during a save situation. The ego-driven or salary-driven use of statistics takes precedence over the logical use of statistics only when you allow it to.

I essentially agree with Herzog, except that I would go a little bit further. Herzog is still advocating using his closer *primarily* for "save" situations, but also extending it into other games under certain circumstances. I would argue that when you're defining the most effective use of your closer, you should START with the tie games. That is when the impact of a run saved is the largest, when the game is tied.

A relief ace, used in this way, would not save 50 games—but he could win 20, and he might win 30. A reliever used in this way, having an outstanding season, could win 20 games and also save 20.

I'm not saying that that's the right way to use a reliever for all teams; different teams have different needs. If you had a team with a great offense, it would probably be smart to use him to pitch the top of the ninth in a home game even when you were *behind* by one run. But if the manager wants to win as many games as possible, he can get a lot bigger bang

from his relief ace by pitching him in tie games than he can by pitching him with a three-run lead—eight times bigger.

As percentage baseball goes, 800% is a big percentage.

UNIFORMS OF THE 1950s

As mentioned in the last decade, there isn't much happening with uniforms in the middle of the century, but here are a few miscellaneous notes. To honor 50 years of leadership by Connie Mack the Philadelphia A's adopted gold thread for their trim color; their jerseys also sported a golden anniversary sleeve patch. When the Athletics moved to Kansas City one of my all time favorite symbols, the elephant balancing on a baseball, was added to the left sleeve. The elephant symbol goes back to the 1901–1902 era, when John McGraw disdainfully referred to the Athletics as "white elephants." What a wonderful and unique symbol for a baseball team, to take a derogatory comment and turn it around like that; a lot of spunk there. The elephant was last seen on the A's uniform in 1928 before it was resurrected in KC in 1955.

The Brooklyn Dodgers started a new trend in numbering in the 50s. The player's

number now appeared not only on the back but also on the front, on the lower left side of the jersey, in red. Speaking of red, the Philadelphia Phillies in 1950 switched to solid red caps, stirrups, undershirts, and pinstripes, after decades of blue or blue-and-red mixes. Their success in 1950, their first pennant in 35 years, caused the uniform of that season to stick with them.

The Pirates tried playing baseball with fiberglass caps—not just as batting helmets, mind you, but all game. That didn't last long. From the mid-fifties to the end of the decade, the Cardinals see-saw act is broken up, and one lone bird is banished to the left sleeve, but take heart; the act is booked again in 1960.

The umpires still dress out in full suit regalia, jackets, baseball cap, black shoes, and long ties. The suit jacket was frequently shed during hot weather.

—Susan McCarthy

1951: WHERE IS EARL WEAVER
WHEN YOU NEED HIM?

Bobby Thomson's pennant-winning home run against Ralph Branca, who was called into the game to pitch to him, was his third home run that season off of Branca. Teammate Monte Irvin had hit five home runs off of Branca. Altogether, the Giants that year hit eleven home runs off of Branca, and beat him six times, one less than the record for a single team defeating a single pitcher during a single season.

A year and a half before Thomson's home run, Brooklyn's then-GM Branch Rickey was interviewed by John Lardner for *The Saturday Evening Post* on a more-or-less unrelated subject, but commented on Branca's penchant for gophers. "Branca pitched a hundred and eighty-seven innings last year," Rickey said without looking at notes, "and gave twenty-one home runs. Why, my goodness, that's awful. That's terrible." His 1951 figures were almost the same—yet Dressen chose to bring him in to pitch to a right-handed power hitter with the left field fence just 279 feet away.

THE FIFTIES NOBODY TALKS ABOUT:
BASEBALL IN TROUBLE

Baseball in the early 1950s suffered alarming declines in attendance. It was often written in that era that baseball was in trouble—that television, which was usually blamed for the decline, was threatening the very existence of the game (somehow, this always gets left out of those nostalgic books about how great baseball was in the golden fifties). "TV MUST GO . . . OR BASEBALL WILL" screamed the headline in the November, 1952, issue of *Baseball Magazine,* and then that venerable publication itself bit the dust. (*Sport* magazine wrote much the same story, but survived it.) Before the Kefauver Committee in 1958, Commissioner Ford Frick predicted that major league baseball would be out of existence within ten years if baseball could not get control of indiscriminate broadcasting.

The Negro Leagues died. Minor leagues were dropping like turkeys in November, and major league attendance, after a peak just short of 21 million in 1948, dropped to 17.5 million in 1950, and was fading every year . . . 16.1 million in 1951, 14.7 million in 1952, 14.4 million in 1953. The teams felt helpless. They felt the need for better facilities. Most of the teams at this time were playing in parks built between 1909 and 1915, but the costs involved in constructing a new stadium had become prohibitive.

Finally, in a mood near panic, the teams began to pick up and pursue the fans. The Braves, after drawing just 281,000 fans in Boston in 1952, moved to Milwaukee, where they drew the largest crowds in baseball for the remainder of the decade. This held the 1953 attendance decline, which was 13 percent for the other fifteen teams, to a less ominous two percent. Baseball's other weak sister, the Browns, followed suit in 1953, and met with similar, though less impressive, results, and then the Athletics picked up and went to Kansas City.

Buoyed by the attendance gains of the new cities, baseball refused to sink, and attendance began to grow slowly late in the decade. In 1959, aided by two terrific pennant races, major league attendance was up to 18.3 million. I have deep sympathy for the fans of the Giants and the Dodgers, but the problems faced by those teams in New York were very real. The Dodgers, who drew 1.8 million in 1946, put a great team on the field for ten years after that, and suffered ten years of box office reversals, dropping to 1.03 million by 1957. The Giants, after a peak of 1.6 million in 1947, suffered catastrophic reverses for most of the next ten years, down to 629,000 in 1956, 654,000 in 1957. Think about it: in the biggest city in the nation, a team with an unparalleled wealth of tradition, boasting uncounted millions of loyal fans who would wail and lament thirty years for their lost team, a team featuring one of the greatest and most exciting players who has ever played this game—was drawing 9,000 people a game.

Perhaps I should make this a separate article, called "Sympathy for the Devil," but consider honestly the position of Walter O'Malley in 1957. After purchasing a property in receivership, historically mismanaged and with more failures than successes behind it, after having built that team, by hard work and astute judgment, into the strongest franchise in the league, he continues *for ten years* to produce outstanding baseball teams—yet he watches that position of leadership slip away from him, as the attendance of his team falls to fifth in the league, and less than one-half of that enjoyed by the owners of the Milwaukee franchise, who had the courage to seize new territory. His protests about inadequate parking and facilities are ignored, merely lame complaints of a pampered businessman. What is he then to do?

The cities were dying. The slums were clinging to the walls of the ballparks, eating out the core of the city. The crime rate was rising. Public transportation was dying. People were afraid to go to ball games. Perhaps night baseball, the economic godsend of the forties, was responsible for that. Perhaps night baseball killed the neighborhoods—neighborhoods the teams then discarded. I don't know. They didn't intend to, but (with the exception of Mr. Wrigley) they didn't worry about it.

This does not make it right that the Dodgers in 1958 abandoned a city that loved them, but the true story of baseball in the 1950s is not a story about greedy men who betrayed the trust of loyal rooters and brought the golden age of sport crashing down as they foraged for even greener pastures. It is a story about fear and urban decay, about a panic-stricken industry scrambling for survival. It is a story about old ballparks that had come to symbolize the rotting neighborhoods in which they rested, and were smashed apart so that something new and full of promise could be put in their place. We know now that this was a mistake, and we wish now that they had saved the old ballparks. But we must also hope that history will have compassion in surveying our mistakes, and for that reason we must try not to judge too harshly the mistakes of the generation before us.

THE BEST WORLD SERIES OF THE 1950s

The 1952 World Series is among the least remembered World Series of the fifties—just another in a string of Yankee victories—but nonetheless it was one hell of a duel. The most remembered contests of the decade are the 1955 World Series, which is the one Brooklyn finally won, and the 1956 World Series, in which Larsen reached perfection. The 1954 World Series is remembered for Willie's catch on Wertz, etc. . . .

The 1952 World Series was a seven-game series with six great games. If you're interested, let's wallow in the details for a while:

Game 1: Brooklyn won, 4-2. The game was 1-1 through five, and the Yankees missed chances to open a lead in the fourth and again in the fifth. Rizzuto led off the fourth with a single, and Mantle beat out a bunt to put two on with nobody out. With one out and Rizzuto on third Joe Collins lined to right, but Carl Furillo fired a strike to home plate, and Rizzuto had to hold. The Yankees didn't score. Then in the fifth inning, Gil McDougald led off with a walk and Billy Martin singled, but Andy Pafko threw out McDougald trying for third. Then, with two out, Pafko made a diving catch, and the Yankees again did not score. Brooklyn cashed two in the sixth and held on.

Game 2: Yankees won, 7-1. Sixth-inning explosion after Hodges dropped a double play ball.

Game 3. Dodgers won, 5-3. Yankees loaded the bases in the fourth but didn't score; got two more on in the fifth and didn't score again. Yanks later got two solo home runs, but Dodgers scored two runs in the top of the ninth with the aid of a Reese/Robinson double steal and a passed ball charged to Yogi.

Game 4. Yankees won, 2-0, as Dodgers wasted chances. With one out and one on first, Billy Martin stumbled while fielding a ground ball and then threw it away, putting runners at first and third. Allie Reynolds struck out Robinson and Campanella to get out of it.

In the third inning, Reese singled but was caught stealing.

In the fifth inning of Game Four, Pafko led off with a single, Hodges walked and

Furillo sacrificed, putting two men in scoring position with one out. Furillo was batting eighth, after his worst year, so his sacrifice brought the pitcher, Joe Black, to the plate. On a suicide squeeze, Black missed the bunt and the runner was dead at the plate; the Yankees got out of it.

Game 5. One of the greatest World Series games ever, won by Brooklyn, 6-5. Pafko in the second inning and Furillo in the eleventh made sensational leaping catches of balls at the right field wall—both of them certain home runs if they got past the glove. (Dressen had switched his defense in the outfield after he got a lead, which is how both men happened to be playing right field.) Other plays of note: With Robinson on second in the second inning, Campy faked a bunt. McDougald broke IN to cover the bunt and Robinson stole third, which was momentarily unprotected.

Later in the same inning the bases were loaded. Carl Erskine made a good bunt down the first base line, but Ewell Blackwell (Yankee pitcher) fielded it and flipped it backhand to Yogi for a force at home. But in the fifth inning, Blackwell set up a three-run explosion by attempting to make the play at second on another sac bunt. Cox lined a single off McDougald's glove to start the winning rally in the eleventh.

Game 6. Yankees won, 3-2, despite two home runs by the Duke. Cox led off the first with a double, but Reese popped out trying to bunt, and the Dodgers failed to score except for Snider's shots.

Game 7. Yankees won, 4-2. In the fourth inning, Snider led off with a single, and then two straight Dodgers (Robinson and Campanella) bunted for base hits, both hits rolling slowly down the third base line. Bases loaded, nobody out. Allie Reynolds was brought in in relief, making his fourth series appearance (he pitched a shutout in Game Four, then relieved in Games Six and Seven). Allie got out of it with just one run scoring.

In the seventh inning, the Dodgers loaded the bases again, this time with one out, but Snider and Robinson coming up. Bob Kuzava, the fourth Yankee pitcher of the afternoon, got them out of it.

The series was a Monday morning quarterback's dream, with countless managerial openings on each side. *The Sporting News* review of the series said that it was "packed with strategy which was contrary to the book, but . . . both Stengel and Charley Dressen profited by the moves. Dressen went an unusually long way with his starters, sometimes too long." Dressen's affection for the sacrifice bunt was without limit. He *always* bunted when he had the

opportunity, no matter who was up. The Dodgers lost several runners on the bases, but mostly in games that they won, and they also created some runs by being aggressive on the bases. Gil Mc-Dougald played badly in the series—four errors, a couple of mistakes on the basepaths; he hit .200 and the Dodgers kept dropping bunts in front of him. The Dodgers took many liberties with Gene Woodling's arm. Johnny Mize was the hero of the series. He's not mentioned here because I focused on what could have happened but didn't, rather than on what did.

Stan Baumgartner, reviewing the series for *The Sporting News Guide* the next year, called it one of the most thrill-packed series in history. The description seems accurate; the outcome of the series hung in doubt from beginning to end, with little relief. The Yankees had to win the last two games at Ebbets Field to remain champions of the world, and they did it.

RAYMOND LAWRENCE PERRY

My favorite minor league baseball star of all was a 5-foot-7-inch third baseman named Ray Perry. In the Far West League in 1950, Perry hit .366 with 44 home runs and 170 RBI in 138 games. Despite hitting .366, Perry had more walks than hits, 179-169, giving him an on-base percentage of .547, by dint of which he scored 162 runs. Speed? He stole 23 bases, putting him among the league's top ten. His slugging percentage was .734. As a glove man, Perry led the league's third basemen in fielding percentage and was second in range factor. He filled in at second base in sixteen games, making only one error there. He didn't play shortstop that year. In his spare time, Perry managed the Redding team, which finished 86-54, a game and a half out of first. It was, all things considered, not one of Perry's better seasons.

The Far West League was a Class D League, and Perry at this time was in his prime, at the

age of twenty-nine. Even so, his domination of the league across the board was remarkable. The Far West was not a hitter's paradise, like the Longhorn League or the West Texas-New Mexico League or the Sunset League, where sluggers regularly cranked out 50 or 60 home runs and hit .400. With 44 home runs, Perry led the league by 10, and with 170 RBI he led by 28. In batting average he was second, behind a singles hitter. And Perry was not, like Joe Baumann or many of the other players who compiled these spectacular numbers, a slugging behemoth, a two-dimensional offensive player. Perry led the leagues in which he played in everything—and he did it for several years.

Ray Perry began his minor league career at the age of 19, with Salt Lake City of the Pioneer League. The Pioneer League was not, as it is today, a "rookie" league. I had once assumed that that was what was meant by the name

"Pioneer," that it was for players just starting out. Not true; the Pioneer League has a long history, dating back before the modern farm system. The Pioneer League in 1939 was just a low-level league.

Anyway, Perry hit .295 with 17 homers, 94 RBI, scored 115 runs in 130 games, and led the league with 41 doubles. In 1941 he moved up to Tacoma in the Western International League, where he had pretty much the same season, hitting .313 with 41 doubles, 12 homers and 88 RBI. He did not draw the huge walk numbers then (49 that season), but he led the league's third basemen in fielding percentage and putouts, and finished second in assists in double plays. Late in the season he was purchased by San Francisco in the Pacific Coast League. He had the look of a man who would be in the majors in a year or two.

He had a so-so year his first season in the Pacific Coast League. As a 21-year-old who had proven he could play in the PCL, Perry remained a good prospect.

The first of Ray Perry's misfortunes was that of his entire generation: the War came. At the ages of 22 and 23, when Perry should have been sharpening his skills and earning his first serious looks from the big leagues, he was out of baseball. Had it not been for the war, Perry likely would have been in the majors by the end of 1944.

He returned to baseball, with the Seals, in 1945. He hit .271 with 5 home runs, 58 RBI—decent numbers with the soggy baseballs of wartime. He was becoming a more patient hitter, taking 70 walks in 135 games. Only twenty-five, he was still in position to fight for a role in postwar baseball.

On April 21, 1946, Perry was hitting .346 in the infant season (9 for 26). He fractured his leg on that date, so severely that he was out for the rest of the year. And the next.

That finished him as a prospect. He was 27 years old when he joined Redding of the Far West League in 1948 as a player/manager. Nothing he could do after that would ever restore his chance to play in the majors. He had been able to play baseball only one of the previous five years.

In the Far West League in 1948, Perry hit .411. A loud .411. He hit 36 home runs in 122 games, drove in 163 runs, and scored 138. He drew 139 walks. He led the league in batting average by 63 points, in runs batted in by 48, and hit five more home runs than any other two players combined. His on-base percentage was .549, his slugging percentage .727. He stole 18 bases and played first base, second base, third base, the outfield, and catcher as well as managing.

This was to become a fairly typical Ray Perry season. In 1949 he hit .404 with 45 homers, 155 RBI in 120 games. He drew 169 walks, giving him an on-base percentage of .600. He stole 20 bases, had a slugging percentage of .846, managed, and played second base, third, and short, with the best fielding percentage in the league at third. I described his 1950 season at the outset—.366, 44 homers, 170 RBI, 179 walks. In 1951 he slumped to .349 with 18 homers, 128 RBI, though he still led the league in home runs and RBI, and with 180 walks his on-base percentage remained a respectable .554. He stole 19 bases.

In 1952 Perry went back to the Pacific Coast League—briefly. Conceivably, Perry might still have advanced in his profession if he had gotten hot at the start of the season. But he was past thirty. He didn't get hot. He drifted down to El Dorado in the Cotton States League, arriving there in time to play 84 games and lead the league in home runs, drawing 79 walks and hitting .307. In 1953 he was in the California State League, hitting .337, leading the league in doubles (41), home runs (36), and runs scored (120), plus, of course, walks (142). In 1954 he hit .341 with 37 homers, 128 RBI, marking the seventh consecutive season he had led his league in home runs. That year he drew a career-high 184 walks and served as the first professional manager for Don Drysdale.

He began to fade a little after that. He hit just .268 in the Three-I League in 1955, with 23 homers and 82 RBI in 112 games. He was, for the first time in years, not the dominant player in the league. In the California League the next two seasons, he hit .316 and .350 and drove in over a hundred runs a year. In 1958, aged 37, he retired in mid-season after hitting .293 and driving in just 50 runs in 77 games. He continued to manage in the minor leagues for several seasons after that. I don't know exactly when or why he drifted out of baseball, but he died in 1973 in Fremont, California, at the age of 52.

Was Perry capable of playing major league baseball? If you ask a hundred people you'll get a hundred different answers, but my answer is "of course he was." I know that the leagues that Perry dominated were a long way from the major leagues, and that there is all the difference in the world between playing major

league baseball and having a low minor league roped and tied. But even in the low minors, the man played against any number of future or past major leaguers. He was always better than they were—a lot better. He played against Vince DiMaggio, Don Demeter, Chuck Essegian, Al Gionfriddo, Eddie Lake, Ron Hansen, Albie Pearson, Marty Keough, Gene Green, Wally Westlake, and Johnny Callison. If they all went to the major leagues together, what was going to happen to make them better than he was?

Perry missed four key years in youth, due to wartime and injuries. Who could miss four key years of his youth, and still make the majors? A few guys did; a lot of people didn't. My best guess is that Ray Perry, as a player, was somewhere between Ed Yost and Stan Hack. He probably wasn't a whole lot better hitter than Don Demeter, Wally Westlake, or Vince DiMaggio—but he probably was better. What he would have done, had he had those four key seasons, is something we will just never know.

THE MAN WHO INVENTED WINNING UGLY

I have always kind of identified with Don Mossi. Don Mossi had two careers as a major league pitcher, one as a reliever and one as a starter, and he was pretty darned good both times. No one who saw him play much remembers that, because Mossi's ears looked as if they had been borrowed from a much larger species, and reattached without proper supervision. His nose was crooked, his eyes were in the wrong place, and though he was skinny he had no neck to speak of, just a series of chins that melted into his chest. An Adam's apple poked out of the third chin, and there was always a stubble of beard because you can't shave a face

like that. He looked like Gary Gaetti escaping from Devil's Island.

One of the problems with choosing ugliest and handsomest players is that a player who looks little short of grotesque in one pose or one photograph will look fine in another. Susie showed me a picture of Hoyt Wilhelm in which he looked positively handsome. I assured her it was just a bad shot.

You never have the problem with Don Mossi. Don Mossi was the complete, five-tool ugly player. He could run ugly, hit ugly, throw ugly, field ugly, and ugly for power. He was ugly to all fields. He could ugly behind the runner as well as anybody, and you talk about pressure . . . man, you never saw a player who was uglier in the clutch.

Normally, I might be reluctant to write about this, but Don knows he's ugly. Don was so ugly that the broadcast media's rule of two Negroes applied. A sportscaster will ordinarily never say that two black men look alike, but there is an exception, if you have two players who look *so much* alike that you ruin your credibility if people think you haven't noticed. Ordinarily, sportswriters will seem not to notice a jagged tooth or a creative nostril, but Don was so ugly that people talked openly about it. He was kind of a public service, the ugly man's hero.

BEST WINTER LEAGUE TEAM OF THE 1950s, PRESUMABLY

In the winter of 1953–54, the Santurce team in the Puerto Rican League had an outfield of Bob Thurman, Willie Mays, and Roberto Clemente. Willie led the league in hitting at .395; Clemente, then nineteen years old, was fourth at .344. Toothpick Sam Jones went 14-4 for the team; Ruben Gomez was 13-4.

They won the pennant.

BEST MINOR LEAGUE TEAMS OF THE 1950s

The Indianapolis team of 1954 finished 95-57, winning their league by ten and a half games. They defeated Minneapolis in the first round of the playoffs before losing four of five to Louisville, but I'd still take my chances with them. The team featured three outstanding major league players, Rocky Colavito (.271, 38 homers, 116 RBI), and the pitchers Herb Score (22-5, 330 strikeouts), and Sam Jones (15-8, second in the league in strikeouts with 178). In the following two years Score led the American League in strikeouts (245 and 263) while walking 154 and 129, while Jones led the

National League both years in both strikeouts (198 and 176) and walks (185 and 115); it's safe to say that nobody was digging in on them. There were some other people on the team who could play a little—Suitcase Simpson, Hank Foiles, Billy Harrell, Joe Ginsberg, Joe Caffie, Owen Friend, Hurricane Hazle, and a pitcher named Bob Kelly who had a good year.

The 1952 Milwaukee team, a farm club of the Braves, was also outstanding, particularly the pitching staff, led by Gene Conley (23-9), Dick Donovan, Don Liddle, and Murray Wall. Wall, a so-so major league pitcher, had an outstanding minor league career, and turned up on several of the best minor league teams of the decade. Milwaukee also had some decent everyday players, including Bill Bruton, Gene Mauch, Billy Klaus, and Johnny Logan, and George Crowe for parts of the year. The best minor league eight-man lineup of the decade was the Kansas City Blues of 1953, which included Bill Skowron, Elston Howard, Vic Power, Bob Cerv, and Bill Virdon, among others. That team had no pitching, but finished second in the American Association and won the playoffs anyway. A similar Yankee farm team was Denver in 1956, which had a double-play combination of Kubek and Richardson, accompanied in the infield by Woody Held (.276, 35 homers, 125 RBI) and Marv Throneberry (.315, 42, 145). Their outfield was pretty fair, but they had only one pitcher (Ralph Terry). The consistently strong Montreal teams of 1951–1956 should also be mentioned.

1954: 72 HOME RUNS

The minor league record for home runs in a season is held by Joe Baumann of Roswell in the Longhorn League in 1954, when he hit 72. Baumann's complete record is below:

Year	G	AB	R	H	2B	3B	HR	RBI	BB	Avg.
1954	138	498	188	199	35	3	72	224	150	.400

As I mentioned (see 1947: 254 RBI) the Longhorn League was a hitter's league, but this was a season. Hitting .400 with 150 walks and being hit by pitches nine times, Baumann had an on-base percentage of .545, a slugging percentage of .916, and created about 246 runs for Roswell. Roswell finished second with a record of 87 wins, 51 losses.

Baumann was an enormous man, 6'5" and 235 pounds. He ran a Texaco station in Roswell, pumped gas during the day and hit home runs at night. In his minor league career, which lasted only 1,019 games, he hit .337 with 337 home runs.

OLD BALLPLAYERS NEVER DIE

Wilbur Cooper, star pitcher of the 1920s, told the *Pittsburgh Post-Gazette* in 1953 that there were more top players in his day than in 1950s. "The majors haven't fully recovered from World War II," he explained. "In fact, they're still being hit by war with so many youngsters being called because of the Korean situation."

ANIMAL HOUSE

Animals, for the second time, enjoyed a major vogue as a source of nicknames. Unlike the earlier period, the nicknames are not generally modified or described. One could probably make up an entire all-star team (or an entire zoo) of players whose nickname was simply that of a beast. Harry Brecheen was known as "The Cat," Harvey Haddix as "The Kitten" (because he reminded people of Brecheen), Johnny Mize as "The Big Cat," Leo Kiely as "The Black Cat," and Don Hoak was "Tiger," which about covers the felines. Frank House was called "Pig," Tom Sturdivant was called "Snake," Roy Sievers was called "Squirrel," Don Bessent "The Weasel," and Charlie Peete and Frank Lary were dubbed "Mule." Lary was also called "Yankee Killer," making him, I think, only the third player nicknamed for his ability to defeat one other team (Jack Pfiester and Harry Coveleski were called "Giant Killers"). Jim Owens was called "Bear" and Mike Garcia "The Big Bear"; Johnny Schmitz was "Beartracks" because of his large feet. Dick Farrell was called "Turk," although that may have been a family nickname rather than a baseball nickname, as was true of Moose Skowron, whose nickname actually was short for "Mussolini," a nickname given him as a baby by his grandfather, who thought he bore a resemblance to Il Duce. Somebody is always called "Bull," and in this case it was Brooks Lawrence, as well as "The Baby Bull," Orlando Cepeda, who was called The Baby Bull because his father had been called "The Bull." A few animals were modified. Duke Snider was among several players to be called "The Silver Fox," and Joe Frazier was called "Cobra Joe." Snider was nicknamed "The Duke" by his father due to his evident pride at completing his first day of kindergarten. Other nicknames:

The Nervous Greek (Lou Skizas)

The Chairman of the Board (Whitey Ford)

The Rope (Bob Boyd)

The Say Hey Kid (Willie Mays)

The Horse (Frank Howard)

The Flea (Bob Lillis)

The Toy Bulldog (Clint Courtney)

Scrap Iron (also Courtney)

The Walking Man (Eddie Yost)

The Barber (Sal Maglie)

The Sphinx (Don Mossi)

Owl (Bob Thurman)

Sour Mash (Jack Daniels)

The Little Potato (Camilo Pascual)

Vinegar Bend (Wilmer Mizell)

All very blond players in the fifties were called "Whitey."

I Don't Know What This Has to Do with Baseball, But I Thought I'd Mention It Anyway: Joe McCarthy claimed that he had once had a dream that he had died and gone to heaven. The Old Man called him up and told him to assemble a baseball team. He looked around, and he had Christy Mathewson, Walter Johnson, Babe Ruth, Lou Gehrig . . . all of the greatest players in baseball history.

He was thrilled; he figured it would be the greatest team ever.

Just then the phone rang. It was the devil; he wanted to schedule a game. "You don't have a chance," McCarthy told him.

"I've got all the ballplayers."

"I know," said Satan. "But I've got all the umpires."

THE 1960s

HOW THE GAME WAS PLAYED

As the decade commenced, baseball showed promise of opening up into a new generation of exciting, multi-faceted offense. The use of speed as an offensive weapon, which had atrophied for forty years, began to re-emerge late in the fifties, and by 1962 was a headline story, as Maury Wills stole 104 bases. Batting champions hit in the range of .350, and home run totals were at historic levels. Best of all, the expansion of 1961–62 counteracted the blurring effects of ever-increasing competitive balance, and allowed a few outstanding players to stand out from the crowd in a bolder relief.

On January 26, 1963, the Baseball Rules Committee voted to expand the strike zone. Previously defined as extending from the armpits to the top of the knee, the strike zone was then redefined to include the area from the shoulders to the bottom of the knee. Several things about this should be noted. First, this action was not taken by baseball as a whole. The teams had no direct input and little indirect input into the decision. It was taken by a small, semi-private committee that probably did not intend to dramatically re-shape the way the

game was played. Second, the Rules Committee members apparently thought that they were, in taking this action, returning the strike zone to what it had been prior to 1950; that, at least, is what they announced at the time. If so, they overshot the mark just a little; the definition used prior to 1950 was from the player's *knees* to his shoulders; the new definition said from the *bottom of the knees* to the shoulders.

The effect of this redefinition was dramatic. The action was taken, quietly, because there was a feeling that runs (and in particular home runs) had become too cheap. Roger Maris' breaking Babe Ruth's single-season home run record contributed to that feeling. The thinking was that, by giving the pitchers a few inches at the top and bottom of the strike zone, they could whittle the offense down just a little bit.

The action cut deeper than anticipated. Home run output in 1963 dropped by ten percent, and total runs dropped by 12%, from 4.5 per game to 3.9. Batting averages dropped by twelve points. Baseball's second dead-ball era had begun.

The question which puzzled people at the time was how this apparently minor redefinition of the strike zone could have had such a dramatic impact on the level of offense, when basically the same redefinition of the strike zone thirteen years earlier, in the opposite direction, seemed to have only a small, temporary effect. I would explain it this way. Suppose that, in a period of small but consistent inflation, a man is given an eight percent increase in salary. The effect of this would seem to be small and temporary, as inflation would quickly erode the gains.

Thirteen years later, however, the eight percent raise is taken away from him, and the man is returned to 97% of his original salary, while inflation continues. The impact of this upon his purchasing power would be drastic, and would seem to grow more severe with each passing year.

The hitters were in a period in which the tide was running against them. From 1931 to until the mid-1970s, long-range trends against the hitters were in motion, resulting in constant increases in the number of strikeouts and steady declines in batting average. As batting averages dropped, sequential offense became more difficult to sustain, and it became more and more profitable to attempt to hit home runs. There were several causes of this trend, some of which are still in motion today.

The most important causes of the 1960s game, I believe, were stadium architecture and the lack of an enforcement mechanism regarding the height of the pitcher's mound. The newer parks in that era moved the fans further away, creating more foul territory. Almost every change in ballparks between 1930 and 1968 took hits out of the league. When the Dodgers moved from Ebbets Field into (eventually) Dodger Stadium, that took a huge number of hits out of the National League. When the St. Louis Browns moved to Baltimore, at least a hundred hits a year went out of the American League, because of the change in parks. When the Indians moved from League Park to cold, cavernous Memorial Stadium, that probably took 200 hits a year away from the league.

There is no change in ballparks that I am aware of between 1930 and 1968 that significantly favored batting averages. Some changes favored home run hitters, but none or almost none favored singles hitters.

In addition to this, until 1969 no one was regularly checking the height or the slope of the pitcher's mound. The Cleveland Indians from the 1940s onward were believed to have built their pitching mound higher than the rules allowed. When the Dodgers had Koufax (who was 6-foot-2) and Drysdale (6-5), they built their mound up, and shaved a full run off of Koufax and Drysdale's ERA. (K&D's combined ERAs in Dodger Stadium, 1962–1966, were 1.98, 2.01, 1.46, 1.89, and 2.01. Their ERAs on the road were more than one full run higher every year except 1963.)

Other factors contributing to the pitchers domination were increased night baseball, and a predisposition on the part of the Rules committee to permit those innovations which favored the defense, while prohibiting those which favored the offense. For example, fielder's gloves were allowed to grow larger and larger, but corked bats were prohibited. Colored baseballs for better visibility were prohibited, but advertisements on the center field fence, which interfered with the hitter's sight lines, were permitted until 1969.

Anyway, batting averages dropped in 1963, and would continue to drop. With a large, accommodating strike zone, unregulated pitching mounds, and hitters still swinging for the fences, power pitchers were in complete command of the game. Every team had them, the Bob Veales, the Jim Maloneys, the Dick Radatzes, and the occasional Bob Gibson. With the rules all stacked in their favor, they made sequential offense—four singles in an inning—all but impossible, and thus further encouraged an offense built around the home run. Stolen bases continued to creep back into the game, but the pace of the increase slowed after 1962.

WHERE THE GAME WAS PLAYED

On both coasts and in the middle: Atlanta, Baltimore, Boston, Chicago, Cincinnati, Cleveland, Detroit, Houston, Kansas City, Los Angeles, Milwaukee, Minnesota, Montreal, New York, Oakland, Philadelphia, Pittsburgh, St. Louis, San Diego, San Francisco, Seattle, and Washington. The Southwest and most of the deep South (including Florida) still had no major league ball.

WHO THE GAME WAS PLAYED BY

The game was dominated by power pitchers. The number of black players continued to increase, as did those coming from Latin America. It will probably always be true that star athletes come predominantly from the bottom of the economic spectrum.

CHECKING IN:

1960— Chili Davis, Jamaica
Tony Gwynn, Los Angeles
Cal Ripken, Maryland

1962— Darryl Strawberry, Los Angeles
Don Mattingly, Evansville, Indiana
Roger Clemens, Dayton, Ohio

1963— David Cone, Kansas City

1964— Dwight Gooden, Tampa
Barry Bonds, Riverside, California
Jose Canseco, Havana

1966— Greg Maddux, San Angelo, Texas

1967— Mo Vaughn, Norwalk, Connecticut

1968— Mike Piazza, Norristown, Pennsylvania
Jeff Bagwell, Boston
Frank Thomas, Columbus, Georgia
Sammy Sosa, San Pedro de Macoris, Dominican Republic

1969— Ken Griffey, Jr.
Juan Gonzalez, Arecibo, Puerto Rico
Frank Thomas and Jeff Bagwell, the two 1994 MVPs, were born on the same day, May 27, 1968. They are the only two stars of that magnitude in history who were born on the same day.

CHECKING OUT:

1960— Fred Clarke, 87
Stuffy McInnis, 69

1961— Ty Cobb, cancer, 74
Ernest Hemingway, suicide, 63
Dummy Hoy, 99
Eddie Gaedel, 36
Dazzy Vance, 69

1962— Mickey Cochrane, 59

1963— Rogers Hornsby, heart attack, 66
Home Run Baker, 77
John F. Kennedy, 46

1964— Fred Hutchinson, cancer, 45
Ken Hubbs, plane crash, 22

1965— Winston Churchill, 91
Paul Waner, emphysema, 62
Branch Rickey, heart attack, 83

1966— Charlie Dressen, cancer, 67

1967— Jimmie Foxx, choked on food, 59

1968— Sam Crawford, 88
Babe Adams, 86
Heinie Groh, 78
Vern Stephens, 48

1969— Heinie Zimmerman, 82

THE 1960s IN A BOX

Attendance Data:

Total:	224 million (224,199,594)	
Highest:	Los Angeles Dodgers, 1962	2,755,184
	Los Angeles Dodgers	21,781,262
Lowest:	San Diego Padres, 1969	512,970
	New Washington Senators	5,834,745

The Washington figure covers only nine years, but would still have been the lowest in baseball even if their tenth year had been their best ever.

The average American in this era attended a major league baseball game about once every nine years.

Most Home Runs:

Roger Maris, 1961	61
Harmon Killebrew	393

Best Won/Lost Record by Team:

New York Yankees, 1961	109–53	.673
Baltimore, 1969	109–53	.673
Baltimore	911–698	.566

Worst Won/Lost Record by Team:

New York Mets, 1962	40–120	.250
New York Mets	494–799	.382

Index of Competitive Balance: 40%

Three things happened to make baseball much more competitive by 1970 than it ever had been before. One was the collapse of the Yankee dynasty (1965), which opened the American League up to the kind of competition the National League had periodically enjoyed. The second was the amateur free agent draft—Jim Murray described it as baseball socialism—which began in 1965. The third was expansion, which made the races more competitive simply because a twelve-team league is inherently more difficult to dominate than an eight-team circuit.

Home-Field Winning Percentage: .541

Percentage of Major League Regulars Hitting .300: 12%

Largest Home-Field Advantage: Houston Astros, by far

The Houston Colts/Astros in the sixties were 29 games over .500 in Houston, but 213 games under .500 on the road, a 187-point home-field differential. Per 162 games, the Astros were 85–77 at home, but 54–108 on the road.

Having Their Best Decade Ever: San Francisco Giants, Detroit Tigers, Minnesota Twins

Having Their Worst Decade: New York Mets, Houston Astros

Changing Direction: The Cleveland Indians, a quality organization in the 1920s, 1930s, 1940s, and 1950s, began to fall apart in the mid-1950s, when General Manager Hank Greenberg made a series of poor decisions which cost the Indians Al Lopez and Luis Aparicio, among others. The Indians remained fairly competitive through 1959, coasting on the momentum built up in the early fifties, but their decline actually dates to the winter of 1955–1956. They would be among baseball's have-nots for about 35 years, until restored by John Hart and the Jacobs family.

Heaviest Player: Frank Howard, listed at 6'7" and 275, is the heaviest listed. Dick Radatz, listed at only 235, must have been close to 300 by the end of his playing days.

Lightest Player: Albie Pearson, 140-pound center fielder

Most Strikeouts by Pitcher:

Sandy Koufax, 1965	382
Bob Gibson	2,071

Highest Batting Average:

Norm Cash, 1961	.361
Roberto Clemente	.328

Lowest Batting Average:

George Scott, 1968	.171
Ray Oyler	.176

Best Major League Players (by Years):
1960– Eddie Mathews
1961– Mickey Mantle
1962– Frank Robinson or Willie Mays
1963– Hank Aaron
1964– Dick Allen
1965– Willie Mays
1966– Frank Robinson
1967– Carl Yastrzemski
1968– Carl Yastrzemski
1969– Willie McCovey

Best Major League Pitchers (by Years):
1960– Lindy McDaniel
1961– Warren Spahn
1962– Bob Purkey
1963– Sandy Koufax
1964– Dean Chance
1965– Sandy Koufax
1966– Sandy Koufax
1967– Jim Bunning
1968– Bob Gibson
1969– Tom Seaver

Hardest-Throwing Pitcher: Sudden Sam McDowell

Best Curve: Dave McNally

Best Power/Speed Combination: Willie Mays

Best Switch Hitter: Pete Rose

Iron Man: Brooks Robinson

Best Bunter: Bobby Richardson

Best Baseball Books:
1960– *The Long Season* by Jim Brosnan
1963– *Eight Men Out* by Eliot Asinof
1966– *The Glory of Their Times*
1968– *The Universal Baseball Association, Inc; J. Henry Waugh, Prop.* by Robert Coover
1969– *The Baseball Encyclopedia*, Macmillan

Five Largest Changes in Baseball During the Decade:

1. Expansion (1961 and 1969)

2. Growth of the power of television networks

3. Coming of artificial turf (1965)

4. Reduction in the height of the mound (1969)

5. Free agent amateur draft (1965)

Best Outfield Arm: Roberto Clemente

Worst Outfield Arm: Tito Francona

Most Runs Batted In:

Tommy Davis, 1962	153
Hank Aaron	1,107

Most Aggressive Baserunner: Frank Robinson

Fastest Player: Willie Davis

Slowest Player: Boog Powell

Best Control Pitcher: Juan Marichal

Most Stolen Bases:
Maury Wills, 1962   104
Maury Wills   535

Best-Looking Players:
Bill Mazeroski
Bob Gibson

Ugliest Player:
Bill Skowron
Dick Donovan

O.J. Simpson Award: Denny McLain

Cap Anson Award: Al Dark

Ozzie Guillen Trophy: Bobby Richardson

Bound for Glory: Senator Jim Bunning

Best Pitching Staff: 1966 Los Angeles Dodgers

Best Offense: 1962 Los Angeles Dodgers

Football Players: Bob Allison, Norm Bass, Bernie Allen, Donn Clendenon

Retrobermanisms:
Rocky (I'll Call'a Tony, You) Colavito
Joe (Capital) Gaines
Jose (Who the Hell) Azcue

Basketball Guys: Dave DeBusschere, Costen Shockley, Earl Robinson, Joe Gibbon, Bob Gibson, Frank Howard, Sandy Koufax

First of His Kind: Rick Monday (first player taken in the Amateur Free Agent draft)

Last of His Kind: Denny McLain (the last 30-game winner)

One of a Kind: Ernie Banks

Best Infield: 1963-64 St. Louis Cardinals (Bill White, Julian Javier, Ken Boyer, and Dick Groat)

Best Outfield: 1961 Yankees

A Better Man Than a Ballplayer: Ruben Amaro or George Altman

A Better Ballplayer Than a Human Being: Maury Wills

Mr. Dickens, I'd Like You to Meet: Coco Laboy

Double Play Combinations I Would Like to See:
Bobby Wine and Pete Rose
Frank Bolling and Gene Alley

Infield I Would Like to See: 1B—Norm Cash, 2B—Chuck Schilling, 3B—Don Money, SS—Ernie Banks

Best Defensive Teams: 1960–1964 Yankees and 1963–1967 St. Louis Cardinals

Clint Hartung Award: Mike Epstein

Outstanding Sportswriter: Jim Murray

Most Admirable Superstar: Roberto Clemente

Gold Glove Team:
C—   Elston Howard
1B— Wes Parker
2B— Bill Mazeroski
3B— Brooks Robinson
SS— Dal Maxvill
OF— Willie Mays
       Curt Flood
       Roberto Clemente

Franchise Shifts:
Washington to Minnesota (A.L), 1961
Milwaukee to Atlanta (N.L.), 1966
Kansas City to Oakland (A.L.), 1968

New Stadiums:
1960— Candlestick Park, San Francisco
1962— Dodger Stadium, Los Angeles
1964— Shea Stadium, New York
1965— Astrodome, Houston
        Atlanta-Fulton County Stadium, Atlanta

1966– Anaheim Stadium, Anaheim
Busch Stadium, St. Louis

1967– San Diego Stadium (Major League Baseball, 1969)

Best Pennant Race: 1964 National League and 1967 American League

Best World Series: The Election Years—'60, '64, and '68

Best-Hitting Pitcher: Earl Wilson

Worst-Hitting Pitchers: Ron Herbel and Dean Chance

Best Minor League Team: Birmingham, 1967

Odd Couple: Danny Murtaugh and Roberto Clemente

Drinking Men:
Sam McDowell
Pumpsie Green
Joe Pepitone

New Equipment:
Batting gloves
Weighted doughnuts on bat
Outsized catchers mitts for handling knuckleballs

Player vs. Team:
Marv Throneberry vs. the Mets, 1963
Koufax and Drysdale vs. the Dodgers, 1966

Uniform Changes: Cutesy Logos and Big Guns

Most Wins by Pitcher:

Denny McLain,	1968	31
Juan Marichal		191

Highest Winning Percentage:

Whitey Ford,	1961	25–4	.862
Sandy Koufax		137–60	.695

Lowest Winning Percentage:

Roger Craig,	1963	5–22	.185
Roger Craig		38–67	.355

Worst Award Selection: 1965 National League Rookie of the Year Award, Jim Lefebvre picked over Joe Morgan.

Best Player Who Never Won the MVP Award: Al Kaline

Flameout: Zoilo Versalles

All Offense/No Defense: 1964 Milwaukee Braves

All Defense/No Offense: 1967 Chicago White Sox

Homer: Ron Santo hit 216 career home runs at home, only 126 on the road.

Yellowstone Park Award: Bill Mazeroski hit only 45 career home runs at home, 93 on the road.

Tough-Luck Season: Jim Bunning in 1960 was the best pitcher in the American League—but finished 11-14. Bunning made the Hall of Fame, but he was a tough-luck pitcher much of his career. He had half-a-dozen seasons in which, if a few things had broken different, he could have won the Cy Young Award. In 1964 he was 19-4 with two weeks to go, and had pitched a perfect game. In 1967 He was clearly the best pitcher in the National League, but lost five one-to-nothing games, and was denied the award.

Could I Try This Career Over? Ken Brett

Minor Leagues Were:
2 percent free
98 percent slaves to the majors

Best Double Play Combination: Bill Mazeroski and Gene Alley, 1965–1968 Pittsburgh Pirates.

Worst Double Play Combination: Dick Howser and Jerry Lumpe, 1961–62 Kansas City Athletics. Lumpe and Howser carried good bats, particularly for the middle infielders on a bad team. But they couldn't turn a double play with Stan on first and Ollie running.

Paul Krichell Talent Scout Award: The New York Mets in 1967 had the first pick in the amateur draft. They cut their list to Reggie Jackson and Steve Chilcotte—and drafted Chilcotte.

Ira Thomas Talent Scout Award: When the American League expanded in 1969, Jim Palmer was left off the list of "protected" players for two rounds. Either the Kansas City Royals or the Seattle Pilots could have drafted him—but both teams passed.

(Paul Krichell, if anybody missed the reference, was the key scout who built the New York Yankee dynasty, signing Lou Gehrig, Johnny Allen, Bill Dickey, and Phil Rizzuto, among others. Ira Thomas was Connie Mack's right-hand man in the twenties, signing or recommending Al Simmons, George Earnshaw, and others.)

Best Unrecognized Player: Bill Freehan

Highest-Paid Player: Probably Willie Mays, 1969 (about $145,000)

New Statistics: Saves (unofficial)

A Very Good Movie Could Be Made About: The life and times of Leo Durocher

Five Biggest Things Wrong with Baseball:

1. Lack of offense/action; domination by pitchers

2. Aging stadiums with inadequate access

3. Franchise instability

4. Declining attendance/constant comparisons with exploding popularity of pro football

5. Pervasive media cynicism

I Don't Know What This Has to Do with Baseball, But I Thought I'd Mention It Anyway: 1962, when Joe Pepitone was a rookie, he liked to hang around at the Copacabana with a lot of the rackets guys. He recalled in an autobiography that some of them were pretty upset with Moose Skowron because he was playing ahead of their Italian buddy. "We're gonna help ya out with that little problem ya got with Skowron," one of them said one night. "He's gonna have a little accident," explained another. Pepitone protested, and talked them out of taking any immediate action. But he still insists they were serious.

THE GREATEST TEAM
WHAT EVER WAS
Part IV

There are four things in the world that I am absolutely certain of. If push comes to shove, I will concede that, having thought about these things for forty years, I still do not really know whether Willie Mays or Mickey Mantle was a greater ballplayer, whether Joe DiMaggio was a better defensive center fielder than his brother Vince, whether Rod Carew was a better hitter than Tony Gwynn, whether there will ever be peace in the mideast, whether the Yeti roams the high Himalayas, whether alligators dream of flying, whether Richard Hauptman stole the Lindbergh baby, or whether Judge Crater eloped with Amelia Earhardt. I just don't know. There are, in truth, only four things that I am actually certain of:

1. I am certain that I will never be asked to escort Julia Roberts to the Academy Awards.

2. I am certain that young children should not be allowed to play with vials of anthrax.

3. I am certain that pigs cannot be taught to speak Pig Latin.

4. I am certain that the 1961 New York Yankees were not a great baseball team.

I am not just saying that the 1961 Yankees were not the greatest team ever. I am saying that they were not a great team, period. They were not one of the five greatest teams ever, they were not one of the ten greatest teams ever, they were not one of the twenty greatest teams ever, and they were not one of the thirty greatest teams ever. They probably were one of the fifty best teams ever, which would put them in the top two percent of all major league baseball teams, but perhaps beyond the range of what we usually mean by the term "great."

The strengths of this team have been much discussed: they hit more home runs than any team until the hopped-up 1990s, they won 109 games, and they crushed the Cincinnati Reds in the World Series. Maris and Mantle hit more home runs than any teammates ever, and four other guys hit twenty-plus homers, including Johnny Blanchard, a third catcher/pinch hitter who hit 21 homers in just 243 at bats. Elston Howard hit .348, Whitey Ford went 25-4, Ralph Terry went 16-3, and Luis Arroyo had a spectacular year out of the pen, clocking out at 15-5 with 29 saves and a 2.19 ERA.

All true. What is almost never pointed out about this team is that:

1. Their offense is completely one-dimensional, and not all that impressive,

2. They have no bench, other than Blanchard, and

3. Whitey Ford is really the only quality pitcher on the team.

Let's look at those one at a time:

1. The Offense

In major league history there have been forty teams which led the league both in runs scored and in fewest runs allowed. These are, generally speaking, the greatest teams in the history of the game—the 1927 Yankees, the 1936 Yankees (as well as the 1937, 1938, and 1939 Yankees), the 1953 Brooklyn Dodgers, the Baltimore Orioles of 1970 and '71, the 1984 Detroit Tigers, and the 1998 Yankees.

The 1961 Yankees, on the other hand, did not led the league in *either* runs scored or fewest runs allowed. That's right: the 1961 Yankees, despite their phenomenal home run totals, did not lead the American League in runs scored.

The 1961 Yankees scored 827 runs, 5.1 runs per game. That's a good total. It's not one of the top ten figures of all time; in fact, it's not one of the top twenty, the top thirty, the top fifty, or the top 100 . . . I already used that device, didn't I? It's not one of the top 200. It's probably one of the top 300; I'm not sure.

Even if you focus on a time frame—let's say, 1950 to 1970—the '61 Yankees don't rate among the top offensive teams of that era. They scored fewer runs than the 1962 Giants or the 1962 Dodgers, fewer than the Dodgers of 1950, '51, or '55, fewer than San Francisco in 1970 (who finished third in their division), or the 1950 Detroit Tigers, who finished second. They scored a hundred runs fewer than the 1953 Dodgers, and exactly 200 runs fewer than the 1950 Boston Red Sox, who played only 154 games and finished third. They scored only two runs more than the 1965 Reds, a fourth-place team in the middle of a pitcher's era. 827 runs scored is just not a truly impressive total, in any context.

If you compare their runs scored to the league average, you reach the same conclusion: this was a good offense, but hardly a great one. The American League average in 1961 was 734 runs per team; the Yankees beat that by 93 runs. The 1927 Yankees beat the American League average by 213 runs. The 1936–1939 Yankees beat the league average by at least 143 runs every year. The 1953 Dodgers beat the league average by 216 runs, the '67 Red Sox by 123 runs, the '62 Giants by 150 runs. The 1931 Yankees beat the American League average by 273 runs, and they didn't even win the pennant. Neither did the '63 Cardinals (+ 129 runs) or the '64 Braves (+ 151).

In terms of runs scored, the '61 Yankees are a long, long way from being a great team. Why?

Because they didn't do anything well except hit home runs. You want to see a great offense, look at the '76 Reds. The Reds that year scored 857 runs, 212 more than the National League average.

The 1976 Reds led the National League in home runs, 141. But they also led in hits, doubles, triples, walks drawn, stolen bases, stolen base percentage, batting average, slugging average, on base percentage, and fewest grounded into double plays. They led the league in everything.

The '61 Yankees led the league in home runs—period. Well, home runs, slugging percentage, and intentional walks. They were dead last in the league in doubles (194), tied for fifth in triples (40), next-to-last in walks drawn (543), dead last in stolen bases (which probably doesn't mean anything, because if I had the '61 Yankees, I wouldn't steal bases either), below average in stolen base percentage, and fourth in grounding into (fewest) double plays. They were fourth in batting average. Basically, they were at or below the league average in everything except hitting home runs.

So if you're going to tell me that this is a great offense, what you're telling me is that the only thing that counts is hitting home runs. That's a peculiar way to look at an offense.

One Yankee regular, Clete Boyer, hit .224. Boyer was a better hitter than that, but the real problem with the Yankee lineup was the 1-2 hitters, Richardson and Kubek. They were a couple of .270 hitters who never walked. They used up a huge number of outs—Richardson made more batting outs than any other major league player, and Kubek was among the leaders—and they didn't score very many runs, because they weren't on base. Bobby Richardson, playing every game of the 1961 season and batting leadoff for a team with phenomenal power coming up behind him, scored only 80 runs. Kubek and Richardson together scored only 164 runs.

The Kansas City A's finished ninth that year. Their second baseman and shortstop, Dick Howser and Jerry Lumpe, also batted one-two for that team. They weren't anywhere near Kubek and Richardson in the field, but they scored 189 runs, 25 more than the Milkshake Twins, and they missed more playing time than Kubek and Richardson did.

Of course, this didn't really matter, in the 1961 American League. The Yankees were good enough that they were going to win anyway. But if you envision another level of competition—the 1961 Yankees competing against the greatest teams in the history of the game—then it becomes a real weakness. If you take the home run away from the Yankees, because of the park or because of the pitcher or because they're playing a different type of baseball, then the fact that their leadoff men aren't on base to start the offense . . . well, that matters a whole lot.

2. The Bench

Casey Stengel had a great bench, led by Gil McDougald, who was the best fifth infielder in the history of baseball. He had Elston Howard backing up Yogi Berra, he platooned in the outfield to give him one or two extra outfielders, and he always used more infielders than he really needed.

But in the 1961 expansion, McDougald was chosen by the Los Angeles Angels, as was Bob Cerv. McDougald refused to report and was traded back to the Yankees, but decided to retire instead. Dale Long, the Yankees other left-handed pinch hitter in 1960, was chosen by the other expansion team and became their first baseman, and Elston Howard became a regular at catcher.

How good was the bench of the '61 Yankees? Among all the championship teams of the last fifty years, I would doubt that any other had a bench as thin as the '61 Yankees. There was Johnny Blanchard, who could pinch hit, catch if you weren't planning on seeing any base stealers, and play the outfield in an emergency. There was a good right-handed pinch hitter, in Bob Cerv, who the Yankees re-acquired in a trade with the Angels.

Ten players played for the 1961 Yankees, other than the regulars, the pitchers, Blanchard and Cerv. But of those ten, seven had four hits or fewer. Those seven (Jack Reed, Earl Torgeson, Jesse Gonder, Deron Johnson, Bob Hale, Tom Tresh, and Lee Thomas) were a combined 15-for-85 (.176) and drove in 8 runs. That leaves three players:

1. **Hector Lopez.** He played left field against left-handed pitchers and pinch hit. He hit .222 with 3 homers in 243 at bats, plus he was as bad a defensive player as you would ever want to see.

2. **Billy Gardner.** He played third base an inning or two when Houk pinch hit for Boyer, and he would have played second if Richardson had gotten hurt. He hit .212 with 2 RBI in 99 at bats.

3. **Joe DeMaestri.** Backed up Kubek at shortstop. He hit .146 in 30 games, 41 at bats.

That's it—two good pinch hitters, two real bad infielders, and Hector Lopez. That's all there is. DeMaestri and Gardner between them went 27-for-140 and drove in four runs; add in the magnificent seven guys with less than 20 at bats and you've got 42-for-225 (.187). Add Lopez, and you're up to 468 at bats with a .205 average, 5 homers, and 33 RBI. Every other American League team, including the expansion teams, had a stronger bench than the 1961 Yankees.

3. The Pitching Staff

The pitching staff for the 1961 Yankees consisted essentially of eleven pitchers, of whom nine were on the roster at any moment. The eleven pitchers, alphabetically, were Luis Arroyo, Tex Clevenger, Jim Coates, Bud Daley, Art Ditmar, Whitey Ford, Hal Reniff, Rollie Sheldon, Bill Stafford, Ralph Terry, and Bob Turley.

Of those eleven pitchers, eight either:

(a) had been in the minors for part or all of the 1960 season, or

(b) were veterans hanging on by their fingernails, or

(c) both.

Those eight pitchers, alphabetically except for Arroyo, were:

1. Tex Clevenger. Never more than a major league fringe pitcher, was acquired by the '61 Yankees in mid-season and pitched 32 innings for them, with a 5.68 ERA. Career ended early in the 1962 season.

2. Bud Daley. Daley went 12-17 in 1961—4-8 for Kansas City and 8-9 for the Yankees after a mid-season trade. Pitched OK in relief in '62, but then his career was all but over.

3. Art Ditmar. A fine pitcher in '59 and '60, he was traded to Kansas City (for Daley) after starting out 2-3. He never won a major league game after the trade, and was out of the majors within a year.

4. Hal Reniff. In the minor leagues since 1956, made his major league debut when he was called up in June. Was injured in '62, but recovered to have a modestly successful career.

5. Rollie Sheldon. His entire professional career, before 1961, consisted of 18 games in the New York-Pennsylvania League.

6. Bill Stafford. Came to the majors in August, 1960. Was basically a rookie in 1961, although not technically.

7. Bob Turley. Cy Young Award winner in 1958, he hadn't won more than nine games since, and by 1961 was just hanging on. He walked 51 men in 72 innings, recording a 5.75 ERA and a 3-5 record. Didn't improve much in '62, and was sold to the Angels after the '62 season.

8. Luis Arroyo. Arroyo is immensely famous because he pitched so well in '61, but he is *both* a guy who had been in the minors until mid-1960, and an old guy just hanging on. He was a little fat guy who threw a screwball. After pitching for the Cardinals in '55, he went back to the minors in early '56, and stayed there for most of the '56 season, all of 1957, all of 1958, all of 1959, and the first half of 1960.

Arroyo was sharp in late 1960, fooling hitters with a pitch that almost nobody else threw at that time. The Yankees lost Bobby Shantz, their top left-handed reliever, in the expansion draft. They slid Arroyo into his spot. Ryne Duren, the top right-handed reliever, was ineffective; Arroyo took over his job, too. He ranks as probably the best pitcher in the American League in 1961, Arroyo or Ford.

The Yankees talked him out of playing ball that winter, to save his arm. His arm wasn't in shape the next spring, and he never got back in stride. In the rest of his career, post-1961, he pitched less than 40 innings in the major leagues, with an ERA over 6.00.

Who does that leave? The three pitchers for the 1961 Yankees who were not either raw kids or old guys just hanging on were Whitey Ford, Ralph Terry, and Jim Coates. And one of those three, Jim Coates, was just a long reliever/swing man who had impressive won-lost records because he always entered the game with his team behind, hence in no position to be charged with a loss.

OK, Whitey Ford is an all-time great; I'm not taking anything away from Whitey. I know that a lot of these guys pitched pretty well in 1961—Sheldon did, Stafford did, Arroyo did, and Ralph Terry. But what I am saying is, *there is a vast difference between a good pitcher and a guy who pitched well that year.*

Do you know how many of the pitchers for the '61 Yankees had winning records in the rest of their careers? Three—Ford, Coates (whose won-lost record is a fluke), and Turley (who was completely washed up by 1961). Every other pitcher on that staff, including Ralph Terry, had a losing record in the rest of his career.

They not only had losing records, they had losing records in short careers. Six of the eleven pitchers had 35 wins or fewer in the rest of their careers. The exceptions, other than Whitey Ford, are Bud Daley (52-55), Art Ditmar (70-74), Ralph Terry (91-96), and Bob Turley (98-80).

Compare the front four of the '61 Yankees to the front four of the 1954 Indians, or the 1966 Dodgers, or the 1971 Orioles. The chart at the right on top of the page compares the "focus season" and "rest of career" records for the pitchers on these four teams.

You think I'm picking on the Yankees, comparing their front four to the greatest pitching staffs of that era? OK, compare them to the '57 Braves, with Spahn, Burdette, Buhl, and Conley. Compare them to the '59 Dodgers, with Drysdale, Koufax, Johnny Podres, and Roger Craig. Compare them to the '59 White Sox, with Early Wynn, Billy Pierce, Dick Donovan, and Bob Shaw. Compare them to the '62 Giants, with Marichal, Pierce, Jack Sanford, and Billy O'Dell. Compare them to the '63 Dodgers; compare them to the '64 Cardinals, with Bob Gibson, Curt Simmons, Ray Sadecki, and Roger Craig. Compare them to the '65 Twins, with Jim Kaat, Jim Perry, Mudcat Grant, and Camilo Pascual. Compare them to any championship team you want. You'll have a heck of a time finding

	Season	Rest of Career
1954 Indians		
Bob Lemon	23–7	184–121
Early Wynn	23–11	277–233
Mike Garcia	19–8	123–89
Art Houtteman	15–7	72–84
1961 Yankees		
Whitey Ford	25–4	211–102
Ralph Terry	16–3	91–96
Bill Stafford	14–9	29–31
Rollie Sheldon	11–5	27–31
1966 Dodgers		
Sandy Koufax	27–9	138–78
Don Drysdale	13–16	196–150
Claude Osteen	17–14	179–181
Don Sutton	12–12	312–244
1971 Orioles		
Mike Cuellar	20–9	165–121
Dave McNally	21–5	163–114
Jim Palmer	20–9	248–143
Pat Dobson	20–8	102–121

another championship team that only had one real quality starting pitcher.

Look, Stafford and Sheldon and Reniff and even Terry weren't *really* good major league pitchers. What they were is young guys with good arms. Under the circumstances—pitcher's park, great defense behind them, good offense to help them out—Ralph Houk could say to these guys "Just don't beat us. Just don't walk everybody; don't work behind the hitters. You've got a good arm. Throw fast balls early in the count. If they hit the ball, you've got a great infield behind you. If they hit the ball hard, it's a long, long way to the left field fence. If you give up three or four runs, we'll get them back. Just relax and throw strikes; we're going to win." That works fine, under the circumstances—but it doesn't make anybody a pitcher.

Why does it matter? Well, suppose that there was a higher league, a league in which the Yankees were matched against the '70 Orioles and the '75 Reds and the '77 Dodgers. That stuff is just not going to work, in that higher league. You're going to have more good hitters, more smart hitters, more veteran hitters. If you match Whitey Ford against Mike Cuellar in Game One, you're going to have Rollie Sheldon against Jim Palmer in Game Two, and Bill Stafford against Dave McNally in Game Three. And you're going to get killed.

Not to over-state my argument, there are two things about the '61 Yankees which argue in their favor. One is their defense, and in particular their infield defense. Their infield was Bill Skowron (a good defensive first baseman), Bobby Richardson (a Gold Glove second baseman), Tony Kubek (who deserved the 1961 Gold Glove at shortstop, although he didn't win it), and Cletis Boyer (who was one of the best glove men ever at third base). The catcher, Elston Howard, was also outstanding. That's phenomenal infield defense, and that infield defense deserves a lot of the credit for what the Yankees were able to accomplish.

Second, the Yankees accomplishments over a three-year or five-year period are quite outstanding—among the very best in baseball history. That's an important criteria of greatness in a team, and the '61 Yankees present an impressive credential in that area.

But that doesn't change the fact that, if you put the '61 Yankees in a league against the '75 Reds, the '79 Pirates, the '67 Cardinals, and the 1915 Red Sox, they're going to lose. Could this team play on artificial turf?

Absolutely not. Apart from the other weaknesses of the team, they've got below-average team speed, and their offense would not work in those big 1970s parks, where you could lead the league in homers with 140. And that's not

the big problem. The big problem is their outfield defense. Roger Maris was a good right fielder in Yankee Stadium, a B+ right fielder. But he wasn't quick enough or fast enough to be considered a good right fielder in Three Rivers or Riverfront or Royals' Stadium in 1975. Mickey Mantle was a pretty good center fielder in 1961, but he had bad knees. Bad knees and artificial turf just don't go together.

And in left field, what do the Yankees have? A 36-year-old catcher. Yeah, I know it's Yogi Berra; he's a 36-year-old catcher. You want to try that in Riverfront Stadium, against the '75 Reds? Good luck.

There are some great teams that the '61 Yankees could match up against. The '36 Yankees, the '27 Yankees, the '73 Oakland A's . . . apart from being short on quality pitching, the Yankees would be alright against those teams. But what if they had to play, let's say, the 1911 Philadelphia A's?

In 1911, Frank Baker led the American League in home runs with 11. *If you're going to beat that team, you're going to have to win a lot of games without home runs.* Could the '61 Yankees win, without home runs?

No way in hell. First of all, the '61 Yankee offense did not do anything well, except hit home runs. Second, look at their record against the Washington Senators. The 1961 Washington Senators were an expansion team, losing 100 games—but they played in the toughest home run park in baseball at that time. In Yankee Stadium, the Yankees beat them 7 out of 9. But in Washington, where the park took their power away, guess what? The Senators won 5 out of 9.

Yeah, the '61 Yankees won 109 games—in an expansion year. So did the '69 Orioles. Sure, the '61 Yankees dominated the World Series—in a home run park, against one of the weakest championship teams in the history of the National League, and incidentally against a team (the Reds) that did not have even one player on their roster who had ever appeared in a World Series game before 1961.

I know I'm not going to convince very many of you. The '61 Yankees have been listed among the greatest teams of all time since June of 1961. I'm not going to be able to take them off the list. Pigs don't speak Latin, anthrax is not a toy, I ain't dating Julia, and the '61 Yankees were not a great team. It's my book; that's my opinion.

YOU'D HAVE A HECK OF A TIME PROVING HE WAS WRONG

In 1960 Jackie Robinson went to visit both of the presidential candidates, Richard Nixon and John F. Kennedy. He endorsed Nixon. In 1964 Robinson worked for Barry Goldwater. He felt that Lyndon Johnson, by politicizing the race issue, would ultimately undermine support for civil rights—as, of course, he did. Robinson realized that civil rights gains could not continue without the support of both political parties. "It would make everything I worked for meaningless," Robinson told Roger Kahn, "if baseball is integrated but political parties were segregated."

Ty Cobb with unidentified fan, 1960

UNIFORMS OF THE 1960s

Was there something in the atmosphere of the giddy, half-crazed sixties that gave birth to cutesy logos? Probably not, but the logos began to sizzle, from the sweet-faced Cubbie on the left sleeve of the Chicago uniform to the smiling Oriole bird to the fiercely grinning feathered Indian used by Cleveland and the laughing Indian on the Braves' sleeve. Pity the team whose nickname didn't lend itself to a descriptive character. Silly logos didn't add much distinction to the player or the sport, and so they quieted down for a decade or so, only to reappear in the 1980s as theatrical mascots.

Charlie Finley stirred up many things as the owner of the Kansas City and Oakland Athletics, not the least of which were the uniforms. He ordered that three colors—gold, white, and kelly green—be used in various combinations for the A's uniform. The road uniform for 1963 featured gold pants and gold vests with a green undershirt, green stirrups, and green caps; the rules committee gave them special permission to wear colored uniforms at home, rather than the traditional white. And, of course, one couldn't wear black shoes with vibrant green and gold, so Finley completed the look with white shoes made of—I am not making this up—Kangaroo hide leather. Finley's A's, moving to Oakland, stayed with the color combination.

The expansion Royals reacted to the eccentricities of the departed Finley, who was loathed in Kansas City, by choosing conservative, traditional uniforms, white for home, gray for the road, with Royal blue trim. For the new team in Houston (1962), the Colts chose (ouch) a hand gun for their team symbol. The pistol is shown in side view with a smoky "C" curling out of the barrel. The rest of "COLTS" is spelled out in block letters, and, in case you missed the connection, the front of the caps feature not a symbol or city initial, but ".45s." I'm not sure that would sell anymore, even in Texas. The team renamed itself after a lawsuit or two, exchanging the gun for a shooting star.

Minnesota's new uniform looks classy enough, but what's that on the left sleeve? The logo signifies the twin cities of Minneapolis and St. Paul with cartoon musclemen shaking hands in front of a huge baseball. Cute, but there's too much detail. From a distance of thirty feet it looks like the paw print of an unknown rodent. Montreal uses three colors to create a big puffy "M" for their logo, and repeats the three color pattern in the design of the hat and trim work.

Shirt sleeves, which started out full length and had been getting progressively shorter, finally disappeared from certain uniform styles of the late fifties. The Pirates, Reds, A's, and Indians adopted sleeveless button or zip-up tunics, similar to the Cubs' vest of the forties. With a T-shirt or sweatshirt underneath, the new style apparently allowed more freedom of movement, something further facilitated about 1970 by a change in fabric. For those uniforms which still had regular sleeves, player numbers were affixed there in addition to the jersey back.

By this time, most teams made at least minor changes in design from year to year—a change in lettering, or some additional trimwork. As color began to dominate in the next decade, the changes became more dramatic. Historically, though, a few teams have resisted the impulse to alter, and have kept the same basic design from year to year and decade to decade. The Dodgers, Yankees, Reds, and later the Royals are among those who do little to tamper with the traditional style.

—Susan McCarthy

NICKNAMES

Nicknames in the sixties started to get nasty again. Although not as common nor as harsh as those of the thirties, less than flattering nicknames of the decade included a number of sarcastic handles given to journeyman players who had brief hot streaks. Marv Throneberry was called "Marvellous Marv," Jose Azcue was called "The Immortal Azcue" after he played like an MVP for two months early in 1963, and Willie Smith was called "Wonderful Willie" when the minor league pitcher had a sudden breakthrough as a major league pinch hitter/outfielder. There were also out-and-out uncomplimentary monickers, such as "Dr. Strangeglove" (Dick Stuart), "Motormouth" (Paul Blair), and "Iron Hands" (Chuck Hiller). Yankee pitcher Hal Reniff was probably the last player nicknamed "Porky."

The best nickname, for my money, belonged to Sam McDowell: Sudden Sam. The nickname was original, alliterative, worked in print or on the air, and described both the abilities and the career of the player, whose fame and fastball both arrived suddenly.

Many players before Willie McCovey had been called "Stretch," but Willie made the name his own, as Ruth had done with "Babe." Other nicknames of note:

Moonman (Mike Shannon)
No Neck (Walter Williams)
Superjew (Mike Epstein)
Hoover (Brooks Robinson)
Hondo (Frank Howard)
Honey (John Romano)
The Creeper (Ed Stroud)
Daddy Wags (Leon Wagner)
The Toy Cannon (Jimmie Wynn)
Mudcat (Jim Grant)
Roadblock (Sherman Jones)
The Monster (Dick Radatz)
The Vulture (Phil Regan)

REMIND ME AGAIN NOT TO SAY THAT

The twenty-second of September, 1969, is a day to remember. For on that day a player performed a feat that only one other player in the history of baseball has accomplished, and it very likely will never happen again. Willie Mays hit the 600th home run of his career. Only Babe Ruth (who else?) had done that before him.

Eldon and Harlan Mills,
Player Win Averages

(*Player Win Averages* was published in the spring of 1970. Henry Aaron would hit his 600th career home run in 1971.)

GRAFITTI SEEN IN A BALTIMORE BATHROOM

First Handwriting: JESUS IS THE ANSWER
Second Handwriting: What is the question?
Third Handwriting: Who was Matty and Felipe's brother?

REMIND ME AGAIN NOT TO SAY THAT

Writing about Ty Cobb in *The Greatest in Baseball*, Mac Davis stated that "his career record of 892 stolen bases is not likely to be broken." Lou Brock was then in his rookie season.

MAJOR LEAGUE ALL-STAR TEAM 1960–1969

Records in seasonal notation, based on 162 games. Pitchers based on 40 starts.

Pos.	Player	Years	Hits	HR	RBI	Avg.	Other
C	Bill Freehan	5.97	145	18	70	.262	
1B	Willie McCovey	8.16	146	37	101	.279	
2B	Pete Rose	6.57	202	11	66	.309	103 Runs
3B	Ron Santo	9.48	168	27	99	.281	
SS	Maury Wills	9.30	187	2	40	.286	58 Stolen bases
LF	Frank Robinson	9.06	177	35	112	.304	
CF	Willie Mays	9.25	177	38	114	.300	114 Runs
RF	Hank Aaron	9.51	191	39	116	.308	
OF	R. Clemente	9.04	208	20	95	.328	Nine Gold Gloves

Pitcher	Years	Won-Lost	SO	ERA	Other
RH Juan Marichal	8.12	24–11	227	2.57	314 Innings
RH Bob Gibson	8.06	20–13	257	2.74	
LH Sandy Koufax	6.27	22–10	305	2.36	
LH Whitey Ford	6.10	19–9	171	2.83	
RA Hoyt Wilhelm	8.51	9–8	103	2.16	18 Saves

KIRBY HIGBE

After his playing days, Kirby Higbe had trouble making a living, and eventually he wrote some bad checks and was sentenced to sixty days in the Richland County Jail in South Carolina. He made the acquaintance and won the trust of the warden, and wound up working as a guard there. From there he moved to working as a guard at the state pen.

Higbe started smuggling sleeping pills—at least he says they were sleeping pills—into the penitentiary. Appropriately, he got the pills in there by concealing them inside a baseball, and hurling the baseball over the walls, into the recreation yard. The judge who heard his case said that Kirby had been one of his heroes, and Higbe was sentenced to three years probation. While on probation he collaborated on an honest autobiography, *The High Hard One,* published by Viking in 1967. He does not emerge from his own book as a very likeable man, or as a man of much intelligence or fiber, yet somehow the book is likeable, intelligent, and painfully honest. Higbe had a seventh-grade education and a hell of a fastball, and he did the best he could with each one.

BEST MINOR LEAGUE TEAMS, 1960s

By the 1960s the free minor leagues were long gone. The major leagues had taken their liberty, television had taken their audience, and expansion had taken their territory. The form remained alive, but no life remained in the form.

By 1965 the minor leagues were tightly structured; there was no possibility of a rebel league deciding to get better facilities, upgrade itself and rise in stature, as the Pacific Coast League had tried to do in the fifties. Everything was fixed; each player was an A player, a AA player, or a AAA player (or, early in the decade, a B player, a C player, or a D player).

And yet, ironically, the strongest teams of the decade were not AAA teams, but teams from the lower classifications. Triple A teams had become holding companies for players whose careers had stalled a step away from the majors. When a player took a step forward or showed promise early in the season, up he went. AAA rosters sheltered largely indistinguishable veterans who had failed at the major league level, but whom the team wanted to keep at hand in event of an emergency. Even in the heat of a pennant race, the major league teams would now relieve their minor league affiliates of their best players, even when those players filled but the most minor role on the major league team. Under these circumstances, it was rare for a AAA team to play even .600 baseball, and the best AAA winning percentage of the decade (.642) was by a veteran Tulsa team which had no players of real major league quality.

In the lower minors, however, organizations usually had four to six AA and A teams, and they often played favorites, loading up the roster of one team with all of the organization's hot prospects, so that they would get acquainted, learn to play together, and establish a winning atmosphere. Some of these teams were pretty good, including:

Reno, 1961: Dodger team, finished 97-43. No major league stars on the team, but two ace pitchers. The aces were Bruce Gardner, who was 20-4 that summer, leading the league in ERA; he later committed suicide on the mound at USC. The other was Joe Moeller, who was a big man with a sweeping curve that over-matched players in the low minors. At Reno he was 12-3 with 162 strikeouts in 119 innings, 1.82 ERA. He was equally sensational in other minor league venues, but didn't do much in the majors.

The best position player on the team was Don Williams, the shortstop, who hit .363 and scored 132 runs, driving in 97. He never played in the majors, and there must be a story behind that, but I don't know what it is. First baseman Dick Nen, father of the relief ace Robb Nen, had a monster season, hitting .351 with 32 homers, 144 RBI, and 25 stolen bases; he was a marginal player in the majors. Third baseman Ken McMullen hit 21 homers and drove in 117 for Reno, and had the best major league career of anyone on the team.

Tacoma, 1962: San Francisco Giant farm team, perhaps the best AAA team of the 1960s. Two major league catchers (Tom Haller and John Orsino), a second baseman (Chuck Hiller), a good outfielder (Manny Mota), and a deep pitching staff headed by Gaylord Perry, and including Eddie Fisher, Ron Herbel, and Jim Duffalo. Won the league by ten games.

Birmingham, 1967: Charles O. Finley was a Birmingham boy, so he decided to pool his talent and put on a show for the homies. The show included Reggie Jackson, Joe Rudi, Dave Duncan, Rollie Fingers, and other members of the future three-time World Champions. But the star of the show that summer was George Lauzerique, a 19-year-old Cuban right-hander who went 13-4 with a league-leading 2.30 ERA. Lauzerique kept flirting with no-hitters. On May 11 he pitched no-hit ball for seven innings, but was lifted because the A's had a rule in their farm system against young pitchers throwing more than a hundred pitches. On June 8, facing the major league A's in an exhibition, Lauzerique allowed only one hit in seven innings before coming out, for the same reason. Finally, on July 6, Lauzerique pitched a seven-inning perfect game, throwing only eighty-five pitches. Birmingham finished 84-55, and won their league easily.

THE GOOD OLE DAYS

Don Drysdale was paid a reported $35,000 in 1962, when he went 25-9 and pitched 314 innings. In court proceedings resulting from an appeal on the tax evaluation of Dodger Stadium, the Dodgers reported a profit for the season of $4,347,177.

In 1965 Drysdale went 23-12, and doubled as one of the team's top pinch hitters, hitting .300 with seven home runs. His teammate Sandy Koufax went 26-8, striking out 382 batters, forming one of the greatest pitching one-two punches in baseball history.

The next spring the two men engaged in a joint holdout which became the most celebrated salary battle of the 1960s. The pitchers were asking for a three-year, $1.05 million contract to be divided between the two of them, making $175,000 per pitcher per season. Koufax eventually settled for $125,000, Drysdale for $110,000.

THE BEST BASEBALL BOOKS OF THE 1960s

1960: In *The Long Season,* Jim Brosnan provides the only baseball diary to be written by the ballplayer whose name appears on the title page.

1963: Eliot Asinof's *Eight Men Out.* A careful study of the 1919 Black Sox scandal.

1966: In *The Glory of Their Times,* Lawrence S. Ritter pioneered and perfected the technique of oral history as applied to baseball. Often imitated, never excelled.

1968: *The Universal Baseball Association, Inc.: J. Henry Waugh, Prop.*, by Robert Coover.

1969: *The Baseball Encyclopedia,* published by Macmillan and Information Concepts, Inc. Individual season and career statistics for each season, and much more. *The Baseball Encyclopedia* marked the beginning of advanced statistical analysis of the game.

                                    —Jim Carothers

REALITY THERAPY

After his legendary season in 1962, in which he hit .238 with 49 RBI and led the league in errors, Marv Throneberry held out for more money in the spring of 1963. The Mets responded by sending Marv to Buffalo.

1962: A WARM CUP OF COFFEE

Of all of the thousands of players who have been called up late in the season and given a chance to show what they can do, perhaps the most impressive showing was turned in by a giant named Walter Franklin Bond in September of 1962. Bond got into twelve games with the Cleveland Indians that year, and swatted out nineteen hits good for forty total bases. He hit .380 with 6 homers, 17 RBI. It's arbitrary, but my list of the biggest late-season smashes by young players is shown at the bottom of the page. I used a 20-game limit.

Shane Spencer, 1998, was better than any of these guys, but was called up too early and played too much to qualify. Others who deserve to be mentioned include Charlie Reilly (1889), Jack Crooks (1889), Monte Cross (1894), Piano Legs Hickman (1899), Otto Krueger (1900), Bunk Congalton (1905), Lou Gehrig (1923), George Puccinelli (1930), Merv Connors (1938), Eddie Robinson (1946), Bob Nieman (1951), Tommy Helms (1965), Ted Cox (1977), Randy Ready (1983), and Scott Cooper (1991).

Walt Bond was not destined to be an outstanding player, and in his case, destiny was fairly forceful. Bond was 6'7", ran well for a big guy but was awkward and slow to accelerate. His natural position was first base, but the Indians had him playing in the outfield. He had hit .320 at Salt Lake City, fourth in the Pacific Coast League, with only 11 homers there but 12 triples. The Indians had finished under .500 in '61 and '62, and you might think that a kid with these credentials, including 6 homers in 12 games in the majors, would make an impression on them, but the Indians in those days had no intention of being intimidated by the obvious. Joe Adcock was, like Walt Bond, a big guy who could hit home runs and play first base, and he had the advantage of being thirty-five years old, whereas Bond was only twenty-five. The Indians traded two young outfielders and a pitcher to acquire Adcock, and sent Bond back to Jacksonville to work on his grammar, personal etiquette, and media skills. Or something.

Well, to make a long story short, Walt Bond would be dead of leukemia in five years. He got a chance to play regularly, with Houston in 1964, in the worst hitter's park in baseball, and

Player, Year	G	AB	R	H	2B	3B	HR	RBI	BB	Avg.	SIPct.
Walt Bond, 1962	12	50	10	19	3	0	6	17	4	.380	.800
J. D. Drew, 1998	14	36	9	15	3	1	5	13	4	.417	.972
Joe Jackson, 1910	20	75	15	29	2	5	1	11	8	.387	.587
Gil Goan, 1947	11	42	5	21	3	2	0	3	5	.500	.667
Jim Greengrass, 1952	18	68	10	21	2	1	5	24	7	.309	.588
Rudy Pemberton, 1995	13	41	11	21	8	0	1	10	3	.512	.780
Fred Lynn, 1974	15	43	5	18	2	2	2	10	6	.419	.698
Babe Ganzel, 1927	13	48	7	21	4	2	1	13	7	.438	.667
Gary Ward, 1980	13	41	11	19	6	2	1	10	3	.463	.780
Stan Musial, 1941	12	47	8	20	4	0	1	7	2	.426	.574
Elmer Valo, 1941	15	50	13	21	0	1	2	6	4	.420	.580
TOTAL	156	541	104	225	37	16	25	124	53	.416	.682

when he seemed to be in danger of succeeding anyway, they built a ballpark that was even tougher. In 1964 he hit .254 with 20 homers, 85 RBI—not outstanding numbers, but you might notice that his teammates Rusty Staub, Jimmie Wynn, Pete Runnels, and Joe Morgan hit a combined .215. The Astros were as bad an organization as the Indians in those days. They played in an impossible home run park, and then they looked at their home run totals and figured they needed more power. In early '65 they traded for Jim Gentile, and moved Bond to the outfield. On Astroturf. He struggled, went back to the minors, and died in Detroit on September 14, 1967.

MIRACLES

There were three Miracle teams during the 1960s—the 1969 Mets (the most famous miracle team of all time), the 1967 Red Sox, and the 1961 Cincinnati Reds. This chart compares the performance of the teams in the previous seasons:

	Reds	Red Sox	Mets
Wins	67	72	73
Losses	87	90	89
Percentage	.435	.444	.451
Games behind	28	26	24
Years since last pennant	21	21	—

The Reds improved by 26 games (to 93-61), the Red Sox by 20 games (to 92-70), and the Mets by 27 games (to 100-62). What happened to these teams, to cause them to vault over the league in one giant leap? When a team improves that much, there are basically four things that can explain it:

1. The team can make some good trades.
2. They can come up with some young players.

1960–1961 REDS

Win Shares for the two teams:

Cincinnati, 1960		Cincinnati, 1961	
Frank Robinson	23	Frank Robinson	34
Vada Pinson	20	Vada Pinson	32
Bob Purkey	15	Jim O'Toole	22
Ed Bailey	14	Joey Jay	19
Jim Brosnan	14	Gordy Coleman	19
Eddie Kasko	14	Gene Freese	17
Jim O'Toole	10	Bob Purkey	16
Gus Bell	9	Jim Brosnan	13
Roy McMillan	9	Wally Post	13
Wally Post	8	Eddie Kasko	11
Bill Henry	8	Jerry Lynch	10
Jay Hook	7	Bill Henry	10
Billy Martin	5	Leo Cardenas	9
Willie Jones	5	Ken Hunt	8
Marshall Bridges	5	Ken Johnson	8
Gordy Coleman	5	Don Blasingame	6
Jerry Lynch	5	Jim Maloney	6
Cal McLish	4	Elia Chacon	5
Joe Nuxhall	3	Gus Bell	4
Lee Walls	3	Jerry Zimmerman	3
Leo Cardenas	2	Howie Nunn	3
Dutch Dotterer	2	Deron Johnson	2
Don Newcombe	2	Johnny Edwards	2
Elio Chacon	1	Dick Gernert	2
Bob Grim	1	Ed Bailey	2
Jim Maloney	1	Sherman Jones	2
Cliff Cook	1	Bob Schmidt	1
Tony Gonzalez	1		
Orlando Pena	1		
Harry Anderson	1		
Claude Osteen	1		
Jose Azcue	1		
TOTAL	201	TOTAL	279

3. The young players they have can come through big.

4. They can have guys having career years.

There is a fifth factor now, of course, which is free agency, but there was no free agency at that time.

Since I have the Win Shares system now, I thought it might be instructive to do a Win Shares comparison of these teams before and after the miracle. (See right column, p. 270.)

The Reds improved by 26 games, which is 78 win shares. The point of the Win Shares analysis is that it simplifies the accomplishments of the players, so as to enable us to see patterns more easily. What happened, in simple terms, is three things:

1. *Three key players had better seasons.* Frank Robinson and Vada Pinson were the Reds two best players in 1960—but they were *much* more valuable in 1961:

	HR	RBI	Avg.	Win Shares
Frank Robinson, 1960	31	83	.297	23
Frank Robinson, 1961	37	124	.323	34
Vada Pinson, 1960	20	61	.287	20
Vada Pinson, 1961	16	87	.343	32

In addition, Jim O'Toole, a 24-year-old pitcher, came on strong:

	Won-Lost	ERA	Win Shares
Jim O'Toole	12-12	3.80	10
Jim O'Toole	19-9	3.10	22

These three players improved by a total of 32 Win Shares—about 40% of the team's overall improvement.

2. *Three young players acquired in trade stepped into key roles, and performed better than the older players that they replaced.* The three young players were Gene Freese, Joey Jay, and Gordy Coleman. To get them in the lineup

required some creative adjustments by the Cincinnati front office. The Reds

1. Traded their shortstop, Roy McMillan, to Milwaukee for Joey Jay and Juan Pizzaro,

2. Traded Pizzaro and a pitcher (Cal McLish) to the White Sox for Gene Freese,

3. Put Freese at third base,

4. Moved their third baseman, Kasko, to short,

5. Moved their first baseman, Frank Robinson, back to right field, and

6. Put Gordy Coleman, acquired in an earlier trade, at first base.

Thus, in summary, Gene Freese replaced Roy McMillan, Gordy Coleman replaced Gus Bell, and Joey Jay replaced Cal McLish. This was a net improvement of 34 Win Shares, from a total of 22 to a total of 55:

1960		1961	
McLish	4	Jay	19
Bell	9	Coleman	19
McMillan	9	Freese	17

3. Two veteran outfielder/pinch hitters, Wally Post and Jerry Lynch, also had better years:

	HR	RBI	Avg.	Win Shares
Jerry Lynch, 1960	6	27	.289	5
Jerry Lynch, 1961	13	50	.315	10
Wally Post, 1960	17	38	.281	8
Wally Post, 1961	20	57	.294	13

Adding another 10 Win Shares to the team total. The rest of the team was essentially unchanged:

	1960	1961
Bob Purkey	15	16
Jim Brosnan	14	13
Eddie Kasko	14	11
Bill Henry	8	10
Other players	62	63

1966–1967 RED SOX

This chart compares the 1966 and 1967 Red Sox:

Boston, 1966		Boston, 1967	
Joe Foy	22	Carl Yastrzemski	42
Carl Yastrzemski	21	George Scott	23

Boston, 1966		Boston, 1967	
Tony Conigliaro	20	Rico Petrocelli	23
George Scott	16	Jim Lonborg	19
Rico Petrocelli	14	Reggie Smith	19
Darrell Brandon	10	Mike Andrews	17
Jose Santiago	9	Tony Conigliaro	16
Jim Lonborg	9	John Wyatt	14
Lee Stange	9	Joe Foy	13
Don McMahon	9	Lee Stange	13
George Smith	8	Gary Bell	11
Don Demeter	8	Jose Santiago	10
John Wyatt	7	Jerry Adair	8
Earl Wilson	7	Dan Osinksi	6
Dalton Jones	5	Sparky Lyle	5
Mike Ryan	5	Dalton Jones	5
Dennis Bennett	5	Darrell Brandon	4
Bob Tillman	4	Mike Ryan	4
Dan Osinski	4	Dennis Bennett	3
George Thomas	4	Jerry Stephenson	2
Jim Gosger	4	Gary Waslewski	2
Jose Tartabull	4	Russ Gibson	2
Ken Sanders	3	Elston Howard	2
Hank Fischer	3	Dave Morehead	2
Eddie Kasko	2	Don Demeter	2
Lenny Green	1	Hank Fischer	1
Rollie Sheldon	1	Jose Tartabull	1
Dick Stigman	1	Galen Cisco	1
Dave Morehead	1	Don McMahon	1
Bob Tillman	1		
Ken Harrelson	1		
Tony Horton	1		
George Thomas	1		
Norm Siebern	1		
TOTAL	216	TOTAL	276

The Red Sox improved by 20 games, which is 60 win shares.

With some effort, the things that happened to this team can be wedged into the same groups we had for the Reds:

1. *Four key players had better seasons.* Carl Yastrzemski, Rico Petrocelli, and George Scott were among the Red Sox best players in 1966—but they were quite a bit better in 1967:

	HR	RBI	Avg.	Win Shares
Carl Yastrzesmki, 1966	16	80	.278	21
Carl Yastrzemski, 1967	44	121	.326	42
Rico Petrocelli, 1966	18	59	.238	14
Rico Petrocelli, 1967	17	66	.259	23
George Scott, 1966	27	90	.245	16
George Scott, 1967	19	82	.303	23

In addition, Jim Lonborg, a 25-year-old pitcher, came on strong:

	Won-Lost	ERA	Win Shares
Jim Lonborg, 1966	10-10	3.86	9
Jim Lonborg, 1967	22-9	3.16	19

These four players, then, improved by a total of 47 Win Shares—almost 80% of the team's overall improvement. Of course, Yastrzemski's phenomenal 1967 season is a much larger factor in the surge than Robinson's MVP year in 1961, but we can at least see some sort of a parallel.

2. *Two young players from the farm system stepped into the lineup and played better than the veterans that they replaced.* The two rookies were Reggie Smith and Mike Andrews, who replaced George Smith at second base and Don Demeter, Lenny Green and Jim Gosger in center field:

1966		1967	
G. Smith	8	Andrews	17
Demeter	8	R. Smith	19
Gosger	4		
L. Green	1		

A total improvement of 15 Win Shares, from 21 to 36.

3. *The Red Sox also got more out of pitchers Jose Santiago, John Wyatt, Lee Stange, and Gary Bell in 1967 than they had gotten out of Santiago, Wyatt, Stange, and Darrell Brandon in 1966:*

	Won-Lost	ERA	Saves	Win Shares
Jose Santiago, 1966	12-13	3.66		9
Jose Santiago, 1967	12-4	3.60		10
John Wyatt, 1966	3-4	8	3.12	7
John Wyatt, 1967	10-7	20	2.61	14
Lee Stange, 1966	7-9		3.35	9
Lee Stange, 1967	8-10		2.77	13
Darrell Brandon, 1966	8-8		3.30	10
Gary Bell, 1967	12-8		3.16	11

Adding another 13 Win Shares to the team total.

4. *The Red Sox would have improved even more than they did had it not been for the injury to Conigliaro and the relatively poor season by Joe Foy.* Foy and Conigliaro were both young men at that time. Foy was 24, Conigliaro 22. But Conigliaro got hurt and Foy went backward, rather than forward:

	HR	RBI	Avg.	Win Shares
Joe Foy, 1966	15	63	.262	22
Joe Foy, 1967	16	49	.251	13
Tony Conigliaro, 1966	28	93	.265	20
Tony Conigliaro, 1967	20	67	.287	16

The rest of the team was essentially un-changed—poor catching both years, and not really a lot of help from the rest of the pitchers:

	1966	1967
Yastrzemski, Scott, et al.	60	107
Second Basemen and Shortstops	21	36
Four Pitchers	35	48
Foy and Conigliaro	42	29
Rest of Team	58	56

1968–1969 NEW YORK METS

This chart compares the 1968 and 1969 New York Mets:

New York Mets, 1968		New York Mets, 1969	
Tom Seaver	24	Tom Seaver	33
Jerry Koosman	23	Cleon Jones	30
Cleon Jones	20	Tommie Agee	28
Jerry Grote	16	Jerry Koosman	24
Ed Charles	14	Art Shamsky	17
Ron Swoboda	14	Bud Harrelson	14
Cal Koonce	11	Tug McGraw	14
Dick Selma	10	Gary Gentry	14
Art Shamsky	9	Jerry Grote	14
Ron Taylor	8	Ken Boswell	13
Ken Boswell	7	Ron Taylor	13
Bud Harrelson	7	Don Cardwell	10
Don Cardwell	7	Ron Swoboda	10
J. C. Martin	6	Ed Kranepool	8
Larry Stahl	6	Jim McAndrew	8
Jim McAndrew	6	Wayne Garrett	7
Nolan Ryan	6	Donn Clendenon	7
Tommy Agee	5	Nolan Ryan	6
Ed Kranepool	4	Jack DiLauro	6
Al Weis	3	Rod Gaspar	6
Al Jackson	3	Al Weis	4
Phil Linz	2	J. C. Martin	3
Jerry Buchek	2	Ed Charles	3
Don Shaw	2	Duffy Dyer	3
Kevin Collins	1	Bobby Pfeil	2
Don Bosch	1	Cal Koonce	2
Greg Goossen	1	Amos Otis	1
Danny Frisella	1		
TOTAL	219	TOTAL	300

The Mets improved by 27 games, which is 81 win shares. The largest single factor in this improvement is that Tommie Agee, who was nearly useless in 1968, was an outstanding player in 1969. But returning to the form used before:

1. *Three key players had dramatically better seasons.* In addition to Agee, the Mets got MVP-type seasons from a young outfielder, Cleon Jones, and a 24-year-old pitcher, Tom Seaver:

	HR	RBI	Avg.	Win Shares
Tommie Agee, 1968	5	17	.217	5
Tommie Agee, 1969	26	76	.271	28

Agee in 1968 had driven in 17 runs in 132 games.

	HR	RBI	Avg.	Win Shares
Cleon Jones, 1968	14	55	.297	20
Cleon Jones, 1969	12	75	.340	30

	Won-Lost	ERA	Win Shares
Tom Seaver, 1968	16-13	2.20	24
Tom Seaver, 1969	25-7	2.21	33

These three players improved by a total of 42 Win Shares—more than half of the team's overall improvement.

2. *Two young pitchers from the farm system stepped up and pitched better than the veterans that they replaced.* Essentially, Gary Gentry took over the work of Dick Selma, and Tug McGraw replaced Cal Koonce:

1968		1969	
G. Smith	8	Andrews	17
Koonce	11	McGraw	14
Selma	10	Gentry	14

A total improvement of 7 Win Shares, from 21 to 28.

3. *Beyond that, the situation is a little bit different. Beyond that, there is just a general improvement all up and down the lineup.* Nine players just had somewhat better seasons in 1969 than they had had in 1968:

	1968	1969	Gain
Art Shamsky	9	17	+8
Bud Harrelson	7	14	+7
Ken Boswell	7	13	+6
Ron Taylor	8	13	+5
Ed Kranepool	4	8	+4
Don Cardwell	7	10	+3
Jim McAndrew	6	8	+2
Jerry Koosman	23	24	+1
Al Weis	3	4	+1

These players improved the Mets by a total of 37 Win Shares. The rest of the team was essentially unchanged:

	1968	1969
Jerry Grote	16	14
Ron Swoboda	14	10
J. C. Martin	6	3
Nolan Ryan	6	6
Seaver and Mobile Boys	49	91
Gentry group	21	28
Nine Above	74	111
All others	33	37

So what's the key to Miracle seasons? Two things:

1. You replace a couple of unproductive veterans with young players who can play a little bit, and

2. You get three young players on your team to take a step forward.

Most of the improvement in all three cases came from three established young players, which in all of these cases included a 24- or

25-year-old pitcher and a 26- or 27-year-old outfielder. You've got a star stepping up to the superstar level, a couple of good young players stepping up to the all-star level, and a few people being pulled along by the energy and excitement. The rest of the team is treading water. That, at least in this decade, was the formula for a miracle season.

HARRY'S PARKING

When you went to a Kansas City A's baseball game 1965 into the early seventies, you could pretty much expect your glove compartment to be rifled as a part of the package. My memory may have overdrawn this a little. There wasn't any "official" parking, owned by the city or the team, and the parking on side streets would be gone two hours before game time, even with a small crowd. A guy named Harry had purchased vacant lots in the neighborhood, and turned them into gravel lots, Harry's Parking; actually, his name wasn't Harry, but my publisher has expressed a preference that I not invite unnecessary lawsuits. You could park at one of Harry's lots near the stadium for $2, as I recall; those further away were $1.50 or $1.

The quality of the security offered by Harry's Parking was a little bit inconsistent. Sometimes, if you left something like a pair of sunglasses in your car, they might miss it. I am sure that Harry himself was honest. But Harry had an understanding with the guys who collected the money: I get the gate fee; anything you find in the cars is yours. Experienced fans knew better than to lock the car, because that was just inviting them to break a window. When you got back to Harry's Parking after the game, nobody would be around, except sometimes you would find that you had a flat tire, and there would be a nice man there offering to fix it for $10. It was quite a bit like parking in Manhattan in the early nineties...I don't know if Giuliani has cleaned that up, but it was the same sort of racket.

If you exclude the teams that got new parks, attendance at major league baseball games from 1950 to 1970 was in a sustained nosedive. Was this a common condition, at baseball parks all over the country? I was thinking about this, and I realized that I have never read anything about it. I would bet that it was. Anyway, in trying to explain the attendance figures, or just on its own merits, I thought this was something that could be mentioned.

THE 1970s

HOW THE GAME WAS PLAYED

Changes started deep down in baseball in the 1950s, and by the 1970s those changes had reached maturity. From naturalists we learn that there are three basic defensive reactions in nature: to freeze, to fight, and to run like hell. Baseball, when confronted by any threat, is split among groups who want to freeze, those who want to fight, and those who want to run.

Baseball from 1920 through 1950 was dominated by men who wanted to freeze. In the 1950s, the balance of power shifted to those who wanted to run. When the Dodgers and Giants ran for the coast in the 1950s, they set into motion a chain of events that resulted, eventually, in the baseball of the 1970s. Stadium architecture and game equipment are the two largest dynamics of change in baseball. If you put the players of today in the parks of 1950 with the equipment of 1950, with all of the other differences—the racial composition of the players, inter-league play, the expansion, the strike zone, steroids—with all of those, in three months they would be playing baseball pretty much the way it was played in the 1950s.

Baseball had been played in the same parks, and maybe they were wonderful parks, from 1922 to 1952. The fences had been moved around some, but it was the same parks. When baseball teams moved into new cities they moved into new parks, and that changed the game. The teams mostly moved into pitcher's parks, and that made baseball, in the 1960s, a pitcher's game.

After 1968, when the American League batting champion hit .301, there were a series of steps taken to restore balance between hitters and pitchers. The height of the mound was reduced, and enforcement policies were developed to insure that teams did not build up their mounds higher than the rules allowed. League policy required, for the first time, that efforts be made to protect the visual background for the hitter. Baseball men had known since 1895 (at least) that it interfered with the hitter's ability to pick up the ball if there were fans or advertisements in dead center field, where they would be behind the pitcher in the batter's line of sight. But while this had been known for many years, until 1969 some teams continued to provide the hitters with poor hitting backgrounds.

Several teams moved their fences in, or moved home plate out toward the fences. The strike zone was shrunk. The Designated Hitter Rule was adopted. And, once the cities absorbed the reality that teams could and would move, there was a new round of stadium building. The new stadiums defined a new brand of baseball.

And a great brand of baseball it was. Don't get me wrong: I have nothing good to say about artificial turf. But the baseball of the 1970s, which was derived in part from the artificial turf that was then so popular, was a wonderful brand of baseball. On the field at one time you might have a player who was capable of hitting .350 or better, a baserunner who was capable of stealing 80 or more bases, a hitter who was capable of hitting 35 or 40 homers, and a 20-game winner who could strike out 250 or 300 batters.

The balance between hitting and pitching, which lurched in one direction in the 1960s and in the opposite direction in the 1990s, was at a good point in the 1970s. The obsessive changing of pitchers, which has choked the life out of baseball in the 1990s, was just getting started. It was a fast game, on the turf; artificial turf required quickness and rewarded speed. It was a game that put the full athletic ability of the players on display in a way that was very satisfying, very exciting. Attendance boomed.

WHERE THE GAME WAS PLAYED

Baseball by the late 1970s had gotten significantly behind the population once again. The South and Southwest had grown great metropolises that had no baseball. The additions of baseball to Seattle and Toronto served the North a little better, and baseball (better late than never) arrived in Dallas in 1972. A full list of cities: Anaheim, Atlanta, Baltimore, Boston, Chicago, Cincinnati, Cleveland, Detroit, Dallas,

Houston, Kansas City, Los Angeles, Milwaukee, Minnesota, Montreal, New York, Oakland, Philadelphia, Pittsburgh, St. Louis, San Diego, San Francisco, Seattle, Toronto, and (briefly) Washington.

WHO THE GAME WAS PLAYED BY

By 1970, the suburban generation of players was in place. Playing in organized leagues from the time they could walk, the players of the seventies possessed highly developed skills but a casual attitude toward the game that was difficult for some of the aging stars to accept. The impact of black athletes on the game reached its peak in the mid-seventies, and has declined slowly from 1975 to the present. Latin American and American Latins continued to produce a growing share of the players.

PERFECT TIMING

The absolute, theoretical minimum number of batters that a pitcher can face and be credited with pitching a complete game is thirteen. That can happen if a pitcher pitches four innings, gets twelve guys out, but surrenders a home run to the other hitter, while his team is being shutout, in a game that is stopped by rain at that exact point. And it has happened. In Baltimore on July 30, 1971, Dick Drago of the Royals faced thirteen batters, and got them all out except Frank Robinson, who homered. Jim Palmer stopped the Royals on two hits through five innings, the game was stopped by rain, and the Orioles won, 1-0.

CHECKING IN:

1970— Bernie Williams, Alameda, California

1971— Pedro Martinez, Manoguayabo, Dominican Republic

1972— Chipper Jones, Deland, Florida

1973— Nomar Garciaparra, Whittier, California

Tory Spelling, Los Angeles

Gwyneth Paltrow, Los Angeles

1974— Derek Jeter, Pequannock, New Jersey

1975— Alex Rodriguez, New York, New York

1977— Andruw Jones, Wellemstad, Curacao

CHECKING OUT:

1970— Ray Schalk, 77

1971— Igor Stravinsky, 89

Carl Mays, 79

Goose Goslin, 70

Heinie Manush, 69

Spike Eckert, heart attack, 62

1972— Pie Traynor, 72

Jackie Robinson, 53

Gil Hodges, heart attack, 47

Roberto Clemente, plane crash, 38

1973— Frankie Frisch, automobile accident, 74

Lyndon Johnson, 64

1974— Sam Rice, 84

Dizzy Dean, heart attack, 63

1975— Casey Stengel, 86

Swede Risberg, 81

Lefty Grove, 75

Nellie Fox, 47

Don Wilson, carbon monoxide poisoning, 29

1976— Firpo Marberry, 77

Bob Moose, auto accident, 29

Danny Thompson, leukemia, 29

1977— Ernie Lombardi, 69

1978— Joe McCarthy, 90

Lyman Bostock, murdered, 27

1979— Walter O'Malley, 75

Stan Hack, 70

Luke Easter, shot during holdup, 63

Thurman Munson, plane crash, 32

ATTENDANCE IN THE 1970s

Attendance per game played in the seventies averaged about 16,600, up from 14,500 during the sixties. The improvement from 1969 to 1979 is more striking, from 14,005 per game in 1969 to 20,679 in 1979, an improvement of 48 percent.

The largest reason for the upsurge was probably the quality of baseball played. Other contributing factors might include, as I would gauge their importance:

1. The improved accessibility of the new stadiums.

2. The maturing of the baby boom generation, which reached an age at which interest in baseball often returns.

3. A series of good pennant races.

4. Publication of the *Macmillan Encyclopedia* in 1969, which facilitated and thus encouraged baseball mania.

5. The 1975 World Series, which showed millions how good baseball had become, and annihilated the feeling that the game was pass.

6. The collapse of the Yankee dynasty in 1964, which opened up American League races.

7. The split into divisions in 1969, which increased the number of teams that had a chance to win.

THE 1970s IN A BOX

Attendance Data:

Total:	330 million (329,778,984)		
Highest:	Dodgers,	1978	3,347,845
	Dodgers		24,480,796
Lowest:	Oakland,	1979	306,763
	Oakland		7,646,599

The average American in this era attended a major league baseball game about once every six years.

Most Home Runs:

George Foster,	1977	52
Willie Stargell		296

Best Won/Lost Record by Team:

Cincinnati,	1975	108-54	.667
Baltimore,	1970	108-54	.667
Cincinnati		953-657	.592
Baltimore		944-656	.590

Worst Won/Lost Record by Team:

Toronto,	1979	53-109	.327
Toronto		166-318	.343
San Diego		667-942	.415

Index of Competitive Balance: 45%

Home-Field Winning Percentage: .538

Percentage of Regulars Hitting .300: 15%

Largest Home-Field Advantage: Boston Red Sox, 127 points

Per 162 games, the Boston Red Sox were 100-62 at home, but 80-82 on the road.

Having Their Best Decade Ever: Cincinnati Reds, Baltimore Orioles

Having Their Worst Decade: San Diego Padres, Toronto, and Seattle

Heaviest Player: By the end of his playing days in 1977, Boog Powell's weight was probably around 275.

Lightest Player: Freddie Patek, about 147 pounds. Joe Morgan, two-time National League MVP, weighed but a few pounds more.

Most Strikeouts by Pitcher:

Nolan Ryan,	1973	383
Nolan Ryan		2,678

Highest Batting Average:

Rod Carew,	1977	.388
Rod Carew		.343

Lowest Batting Average:

Dave Roberts,	1974	.157
Bill Plummer		.189

Best Major League Players (by Years):

1970— Carl Yastrzemski
1971— Joe Torre
1972— Dick Allen
1973— Joe Morgan
1974— Joe Morgan
1975— Joe Morgan
1976— Joe Morgan
1977— Rod Carew
1978— Dave Parker
1979— Fred Lynn

Best Major League Pitchers (by Years):

1970— Sam McDowell
1971— Ferguson Jenkins
1972— Steve Carlton
1973— John Hiller

1974— Gaylord Perry
1975— Jim Palmer
1976— Mark Fidrych
1977— Jim Palmer
1978— Ron Guidry
1979— Jim Kern

Hardest-Throwing Pitcher: Nolan Ryan

Best Curve: Bert Blyleven

Best Power/Speed Combination: Bobby Bonds

Best Switch Hitter: Reggie Smith

Iron Man: Pete Rose

Best Bunter: Steve Garvey

Best Baseball Books:
1970— *Ball Four*, by Jim Bouton and Leonard Schecter
1971— *The Boys of Summer*, Roger Kahn
1972— *The Summer Game*, Roger Angell
1973— *The Great American Novel*, Philip Roth
1974— *Babe*, Robert Creamer
1975— *Nice Guys Finish Last*, Leo Durocher with Ed Linn

Five Largest Changes in Baseball During the Decade:

1. Free agency.
2. Arrival of cookie cutter stadiums/prevalence of artificial turf.
3. Designated hitter rule.
4. Continued explosion of the running game.
5. Players hired agents.

Best Outfield Arm: Ellis Valentine

Most Runs Batted In:
George Foster,   1977   149
Johnny Bench   1,013

Most Aggressive Baserunner: Hal McRae

Fastest Player: Herb Washington

Fastest Real Player: Willie Wilson

Slowest Player: Elrod Hendricks

Best Control Pitcher: Ferguson Jenkins

Most Stolen Bases:
Lou Brock,   1974   118
Lou Brock   551

Best-Looking Players:
Carlton Fisk
Ken Singleton

Ugliest Player: George Foster

O.J. Simpson Award: Cesar Cedeno

Cap Anson Award: Paul Kerr

Ozzie Guillen Trophy: Manny Sanguillen

Best Pitching Staff: 1971 Baltimore Orioles

Best Offense: 1976 Cincinnati Reds

Football Players: Dave Parker, Reggie Jackson, Jamie Quirk

Retrobermanisms:
Matt (Tax Deferred) Keough
Morris (Pedal to the) Nettles

Basketball Guys: Danny Ainge, Dave Winfield, Davey Lopes

First of His Kind: Catfish Hunter (the first millionaire free agent)

Last of His Kind: Calvin Griffith (the last owner/operator at the major league level)

One of a Kind: Mark Fidrych

Best Infields:
Cincinnati Reds, 1973–1976
Baltimore Orioles, 1970–1976
Los Angeles Dodgers, 1973–1979

The Dodger infield was intact far longer than any other infield in baseball history, and consisted of four very good ballplayers

(Garvey, Lopes, Cey, and Russell). The Orioles infield was defensively impenetrable and offensively solid (Boog Powell, Dave Johnson, Brooks Robinson, and Mark Belanger; Grich replaced Johnson in 1973 and Lee May replaced Boog in 1975). But the infield of the '75-'76 Reds featured four players of Hall of Fame quality (Tony Perez, Joe Morgan, Pete Rose, and Dave Concepcion), and was clearly the best infield of the decade.

Best Outfield: Boston Red Sox, 1975–1980

LF— Jim Rice
CF— Fred Lynn
RF— Dwight Evans

The best one-year outfield was the 1972 Astros (Cedeno, Jimmie Wynn, and Bob Watson).

A Better Man Than a Ballplayer: Andy Thornton

A Better Ballplayer Than a Human Being: Cleon Jones

Mr. Dickens, I'd Like You to Meet: Alan Mitchell Edward George Patrick Henry Gallagher

Platoon Combinations I Would Like to See: Steve Swisher and Chico Walker

Best Defensive Team: 1973 Baltimore Orioles

Clint Hartung Award: David Clyde

Outstanding Sportswriter: Peter Gammons

Most Admirable Superstar: Willie Stargell

Least Admirable Superstar: Reggie Jackson

Gold Glove Team:

C— Johnny Bench	SS— Mark Belanger
1B— Steve Garvey	OF— Paul Blair
2B— Bobby Grich	Garry Maddox
3B— Graig Nettles	Amos Otis

There are at least five third basemen in the 1970s who would be more deserving of the "Decade Gold Glove" than any third baseman of the 1930s, the 1950s, or the 1990s. Brooks Robinson, the great defensive third baseman of the 1960s, was still at the top of his game as the 1970s began, as was Clete Boyer. Aurelio Rodriguez was an outstanding defensive third baseman, as was Doug Rader. Buddy Bell came up in mid-decade; he was super, too. Mike Schmidt was outstanding; Ron Cey and George Brett were very under-rated defensive players. Sal Bando, Darrell Evans, and Ken Reitz were excellent defensive third basemen.

Ultimately, I decided to go with Graig Nettles, who I think was just an inch below Brooksie, although he never received comparable acclaim. But you can't help but notice that there wasn't anyone in the 1990s who would compare to the top five of the 1970s—Nettles, Robinson, Rodriguez, Schmidt, and Bell.

Franchise Shifts:
1970— Seattle to Milwaukee
1972— Washington to Dallas

New Stadiums:
1970— Three Rivers Stadium, Pittsburgh
1970— Riverfront Stadium, Cincinnati
1971— Veterans Stadium, Philadelphia
1973— Royals Stadium, Kansas City
1976— Renovated Yankee Stadium
1977— Olympic Stadium, Montreal
1977— Kingdome, Seattle

Best Pennant Race: 1978, American League East

Best World Series: 1975, Cincinnati over Boston, 0–6, 3–2, 6–5, 4–5, 6–2, 6–7, 4–3

Best-Hitting Pitcher: Ken Brett

Worst-Hitting Pitcher: Dan Spillner

Odd Couple: Earl Weaver and Jim Palmer

Drinking Men:
Bob Welch
Darrell Porter
Roger Moret

New Equipment:
Neck guard for catchers (invented by Steve Yeager)
Sliding gloves
Dimple on end of bat (brought back from Japan by Jose Cardenal)

Player vs. Team: On December 28, 1975, arbitrator Peter Seitz ruled that the standard player contract allowed a player to become a free agent after one "team option" season.

Uniform Changes:
Synthetic fabrics
Bright colors
Stretch waistbands
Many experiments

New Terms or Expressions:
Rotator cuff injury
Designated hitter

Most Wins by Pitcher:

Steve Carlton,	1972	27
Jim Palmer		186

Highest Winning Percentage:

Ron Guidry,	1978	25-3	.893
Don Gullett		109–50	.686

Lowest Winning Percentage:

Matt Keough,	1979	2–17	105
Bill Greif		31–67	.316

Nicknames:
Sugar Bear (Larvelle Blanks)
Downtown Ollie Brown
Pudge (Carlton Fisk)
Dirty Al (Alan M.E.G.P.H. Gallagher)
Rojo (Doug Rader)
The Rooster (Rick Burleson)
Chicken (Fred) Stanley
The Bird (Mark Fidrych)
Bigfoot (Bob Stanley)

Worst Award Selection: 1979, Willie Stargell as National League co-MVP. Willie Stargell wasn't one of the thirty best players in the National League in 1979. He provided leadership and had four or five game-breaking hits late in the season, and some reporters started a bandwagon for him.

Best Player Who Never Won the MVP Award: Dave Winfield

Flameouts: Bobby Tolan, Mitchell Page

All Offense/No Defense: San Francisco Giants, 1970

All Defense/No Offense: New York Mets, 1973

Believe it or not, the 1972 Baltimore Orioles allowed only 430 runs all season.

Homer: Greg Luzinski

Yellowstone Park Award: Bob Watson hit the same number of career home runs on the road as Ted Kluszewski (117), but nowhere near half as many in his home park (67 for Watson, 162 for Klu). Watson hit more home runs in road games than Vern Stephens, Chuck Klein, Vada Pinson, or Cy Williams.

Tough-Luck Season: Dave Roberts, 1971 (14–17, 2.10 ERA)

Could I Try This Career Over? Cliff Johnson

If somebody had had the sense to make Cliff Johnson a DH/first baseman in a hitter's park when he was 23 years old, he would have hit 500 homers. Instead, the Astros wasted the first half of his career trying to make a catcher out of him.

Wally Moon Eyebrows Award: Gary Gentry

Minor Leagues Were:
0 percent free
100 percent slaves to the majors

Best Double Play Combination: Mark Belanger and Bobby Grich, 1973–1976 Baltimore Orioles.

Worst Double Play Combination: The double play combination of the 1974 San Diego Padres, Derrel Thomas and Enzo Hernandez, was one of the worst of all time.

Paul Krichell Talent Scout Award: The Chicago White Sox made Danny Goodwin the number one player in the amateur draft in 1971. When he didn't sign and went to college instead, the California Angels in 1975 drafted him first again—the only player twice selected as the number one pick.

Best Unrecognized Player: Bobby Grich

Highest-Paid Player: Dave Parker in 1979 became the first player to earn a million dollars a year. The Pirates didn't want to acknowledge openly that they were paying him a million dollars a year, so they hid a lot of the money in bonus clauses and delayed payments that were written in such a way that you almost had to have been there when the contract was negotiated to know that it was a million a year, but it was. Nolan Ryan the next year (1980) became the first player to have a contract that just flat-out called for a million a year.

New Statistics: None

A Very Good Movie Could Be Made About: Dick Williams and the Masters of Chaos, the Oakland A's of 1971 to 1973.

Five Biggest Things Wrong with Baseball:

1. Labor/management battles; 1972 strike.
2. Innumerable lawsuits.
3. Sterile suburban parks with artificial turf.
4. Fan drinking and violence.
5. Pervasive media cynicism.

I Don't Know What This Has to Do with Baseball, But I Thought I'd Mention It Anyway: Reggie Jackson has written two autobiographies, one done with Bill Libby for Playboy Press (1975) and the other with Mike Lupica for Villard (1984). Both books are named *Reggie,* and the jacket of each is entirely covered by a facial picture of Reggie, sans glasses, against a blue-gray background.

MESSERSMITH

One of the pivotal moments in the history of baseball occurred on December 23, 1975, when arbitrator Peter Seitz ruled in favor of the players in grievances filed by Dick Moss on behalf of Dodger pitcher Andy Messersmith and retired Expo Dave McNally.

Let us note a couple of things first. Mr. Seitz did not find that the reserve arrangement was illegal. It is perfectly legal for management and unions to negotiate reserve arrangements if they want to. Also, since the Supreme Court had just ruled three years earlier that the reserve arrangement was legal, it would have been quite remarkable for an arbitrator in a civil matter to overrule the Supreme Court and decide that it was illegal.

Mr. Seitz did not find that the reserve clause was invalid. The clause under dispute is still a part of the basic agreement, and is still in effect.

Mr. Seitz's ruling had nothing whatsoever to do with baseball's position as a legally protected monopoly.

It was assumed throughout the entire proceeding that the clause under dispute was legal and valid. What they were arguing about is what it meant. The clause in question reads:

> If prior to March 1, the Player and the Club have not agreed upon the terms of the contract, then on or before 10 days after said March 1, the Club shall have the right by written notice to the Player to renew this contract for the period of one year.

The clubs argued that this meant one year, and then the next year, and then the next year—in other words, that the contract could be renewed in perpetuity. The players argued that one year meant one year. The arbitrator ruled simply that the players' interpretation would prevail.

During the period of the hearing, the public largely assumed that the players could not win.

The argument made by the owners, relayed to the public by the sportswriters, was that organized baseball could not survive without the reserve clause. That argument was irrelevant to the issues of the case, and insulted the intelligence of the arbitrator. If General Motors designs a defective automobile and finds itself facing lawsuits as a result, can they defend themselves by arguing that if they lose they will be driven out of business? Can tobacco companies protect themselves from liability by arguing that, if they lose, they will be driven out of business? Of course not. The consequences of losing the suit were not the issue.

The arguments made by the owners in front of the arbitrator were not quite the same as the arguments made before the microphones, but they weren't a lot better. They filed a suit to prevent the issue from going before an arbitrator. The judge told them to arbitrate. They argued that to allow free agency would destroy competitive balance, another irrelevant issue. They argued that they had to have the right to reserve players in order to defray the costs of operating a farm system.

"I am not unmindful," wrote Seitz in his decision, "of the testimony of the Commissioner of Baseball and the Presidents of the National and American Leagues . . . that any decision of the arbitration panel sustaining the Messersmith and McNally grievances would have dire results, wreak great harm to the reserve system and do serious damage to the sport of baseball."

You have to understand that an arbitrator is a professional skeptic. He hears self-serving arguments every day. Every day he faces people who are trying to get him to focus on something other than the issues of the case. Very often someone tells the arbitrator that terrible consequences will follow if you rule against me, and sometimes this is quite true. After a while an arbitrator is not a trusting soul. He recognizes a self-serving argument. He carefully distinguishes between relevant and irrelevant issues. The owners served the arbitrator a rich plateful of the same stuff they had been feeding the media for a hundred years. The arbitrator passed.

For several years afterward, I wondered if perhaps the owners hadn't lost a case that might have been won by a better argument. Sam Reich eventually convinced me otherwise. Sam Reich is Tom Reich's brother, a sharp attorney from Pittsburgh. We used to work arbitration cases together, and often, during a lull in the research, we would drift into arguing about stuff like whether Granny Hamner was a better shortstop than Johnny Logan, whether Earl Williams could have made it as a catcher if he had tried harder, and how the Messersmith case should have been presented. Sam recalled that when Tom (Reich) first told him that the Players Association wanted to try this approach, he scoffed at the idea. Tom got Sam a copy of the basic agreement, and Sam read it over a couple of times. "I took it back to Tom," Sam recalls, "and said 'Where is it?' I thought I just couldn't find it. I had heard so much all my life about this reserve clause that I assumed they *had* a reserve clause—you know, some good strong language spelling out what their rights were. I couldn't believe that the owners' entire case hung on this one sentence about renewing the contract for the next year."

But, I argued at first, regardless of the vagueness of the words, hadn't it always been assumed that this meant that the player was bound in perpetuity? Couldn't the owners easily have proven, I argued, that this clause had been around forever, and that both management and labor had always assumed that it meant that the player was bound from year to year? You could demonstrate in many ways that that was what it had always been assumed to mean—for example,

that assumption seems to underly the arguments in the Flood case. Couldn't they have argued that the clause had to be found to mean what both sides had assumed that it meant when they entered into the contract?

"Well," said Sam, "you can try that. But it is a very important principle of contract law that when the language is not specific, the contract will be interpreted against the party that drew up the contract, or against the party that drafted the disputed language. Obviously, it wasn't the players who put this clause in the contract. This was the owner's clause. If the owners had intended to retain the player in perpetuity, they had a responsibility to spell that out. You can't expect an arbitrator to read more into the contract than is there. When Tom finally convinced me that there wasn't anything more than this in the contract, I knew that the owners were in serious trouble."

The reason the owners used the arguments they did, then, is probably not because anyone believed that these were good arguments. The owners used the arguments they did because they were desperate. They had to try to get the arbitrator to put aside his logic and training and the facts of the case, and decide the issue as a baseball fan. "You can't rule against us," they argued, "because we're baseball."

Seitz had no alternative but to find for the players.

THAT EXPLAINS IT

A generation of baseball fans now is too young to remember Mark "the Bird" Fidrych, which is a real shame. Fidrych lasted for only one year, but he was more fun than a barrel of butterflies and a bucket of mud.

Fidrych was a skinny, hyper-active kid with wild hair and nervous eyes who strode around the pitcher's mound as if he were on a mission of earth-shaking importance. As soon as he got the ball back from the catcher he would begin to talk to it, perching the ball on his fingertips like Yoric's skull, explaining to the baseball what its assignment was. It's hard to describe, but he was hypnotic. That was just one of his mannerisms. There was an intensity about him which gave the impression that, when you cared this much about winning baseball games, *of course* you would talk to the baseball. Huge, huge crowds turned out every time he pitched. The Tigers, who had drawn barely over a million fans all season in 1975, drew 605,677 just to Fidrych's "home" starts in 1976 (another 300,000 on the road).

On June 28, 1976, Fidrych was facing the Yankees on national TV. When Fidrych began talking to the baseball, Graig Nettles stepped out of the box and began a conversation with his bat. "Now don't you listen to that ball," said Nettles to the bat. "When it comes in here you hit it right up in that upper deck up there," and Nettles pointed to the upper deck.

Nettles popped out. "Goddamn," he said. "I just realized I was using a Japanese bat. Doesn't understand English."

MAJOR LEAGUE ALL-STAR TEAM 1970–1979

Records in seasonal notation, based on 162 games. Pitchers based on 40 starts.

Pos.	Player	Years	Hits	HR	RBI	Avg.	Other
C	Johnny Bench	8.86	158	33	114	.267	
1B	Rod Carew	8.38	213	7	75	.343	30 SB, 100 Runs
2B	Joe Morgan	9.00	161	19	80	.282	119 Walks, 54 SB
3B	Mike Schmidt	6.69	142	35	100	.255	103 Walks
SS	Dave Concepcion	8.33	152	8	64	.270	
LF	Bobby Bonds	9.13	272	31	94	.274	112 Runs, 2 SB
CF	Bobby Murcer	9.26	167	21	91	.282	
RF	Reggie Jackson	8.89	159	33	104	.275	
U	Pete Rose	9.90	207	8	59	.314	40 Doubles

	Pitcher	Years	Won-Lost	SO	ERA	Other
RH	Jim Palmer	8.85	21-12	176	2.58	
RH	Tom Seaver	8.67	21-12	266	2.65	
RH	Garylord Perry	8.41	20-14	208	2.91	
LH	Steve Carlson	9.18	19-14	228	3.18	
RA	Rollie Fingers	9.89	8-9	98	2.89	21 Saves

GO IMPRESS SOMEBODY ELSE

Did you ever notice that no knuckleball pitcher has ever won the Cy Young Award? The one sort-of exception is Early Wynn, 1959; Wynn threw four pitches, including a knuckleball, but wasn't a true knuckleball pitcher.

When I was developing the Win Shares system, I was interested to see who would be listed as the top pitcher in the American League in 1971. Vida Blue won the MVP Award (24-8, 1.82 ERA) and the Cy Young as well, but the Cy Young was a close and disputed vote, as Mickey Lolich pitched 376 innings that year and won 25 games. I remember having an argument with a friend about who ought to win that award. I said Blue.

According to the Win Shares system, the best pitcher in the American League in 1971, and by a pretty decent margin, was Wilbur Wood. Wood also had a great year—334 innings, 22-13 won-lost record, 1.91 ERA—and he did draw one vote in the Cy Young balloting, but only one. Why wasn't he a larger part of the discussion?

It is the direct and indirect effect of throwing the knuckleball. Looking more carefully at the data, I found that six knuckleball pitchers show up as deserving of the Cy Young Award (actually, three pitchers including Phil Niekro four times)—but none of them won it. The direct effect could be illustrated by looking at the 1962 Award, which was won by Don Drysdale. Both Drysdale and Bob Purkey had fine seasons. Drysdale was 25-9 with a 2.83 ERA. But Bob Purkey, who threw the knuckleball about 20–40% of the time, had a won-lost record just as good (23-5) and almost the same ERA (2.81), although Purkey pitched for a team that wasn't quite as good, and pitched in a park (Crosley Field) that was much tougher for a pitcher than Dodger Stadium. Thus, as the Win Shares

system sees it, Purkey clearly deserves the Award, by a margin of about two full Win Shares.

Why didn't he win it? Well, you've got a big, strong, handsome pitcher with a knockout fastball, pitching in Los Angeles, against an average-sized, average-looking slop pitcher pitching in Cincinnati. Purkey got one vote, the same as Wilbur Wood got in '71. Reporters respect fastballs—just like baseball men.

The pitcher nominated by the Win Shares system as deserving of the Cy Young Award will win that award almost exactly 50% of the time. Through 2000 there have been 79 Cy Young Award winners, 41 of whom are shown by the Win Shares system as deserving of the Award. But many Cy Young decisions are razor thin, according to the Win Shares method. In 1985, for example, Bret Saberhagen won the American League Cy Young although the Win Shares system says that Dave Stieb was better—by a margin of 24.43 to 24.42. The difference is 1% of one Win Share, which is equivalent to about one-thirtieth of one run, which is a silly distinction; for all practical purposes, they're even. In 1993 Greg Maddux won the Cy Young Award, although the Win Shares system thinks that Jose Rijo was better, by a margin of 25.44 to 25.38. You wouldn't expect a statistical method to agree with a panel of voters consistently on distinctions that fine.

However, when one pitcher ranks as clearly better than anybody else in the league, which happens a little more than half the time, then that pitcher will win the Cy Young Award about two-thirds of the time.

The *indirect* effects of the knuckleball on Cy Young voting are greater than the direct effects. The indirect effect can be illustrated best by looking at Phil Niekro, 1978. Phil Niekro in 1978 went 19-18 for a last-place team, the

Atlanta Braves; he pitched 334 innings, which led the National League by 59 innings, struck out 248 men, which was second in the league, and posted a 2.88 ERA despite pitching in what was, at that time, by far the best hitter's park in the National League, the Launching Pad. By the Win Shares method he ranks as the best pitcher in the National League by a huge margin, 8.63 Win Shares (about 25 runs). Every other pitcher since the award began who had led by that kind of a margin, anything even close to that, has won the Cy Young Award. Niekro drew no first-place votes, and was seventh in the Cy Young voting.

But I do *not* attribute this to prejudice against a knuckleball pitcher. After all, the Cy Young winner that year was Gaylord Perry, who was older than Niekro and living on the spitball. If the voters had wanted a fireballer, they could have given the award to J. R. Richard. They didn't give the award to Niekro not because he floated pitches to home plate on moth wings, but because he was 19-18. Yeah, he was 19-18 with a last-place team, but still, he was 19-18. Starting pitchers who finish 19-18 don't win the Cy Young Award.

And that's the larger reason that no knuckleball pitcher has ever won the Cy Young Award: because the Cy Young Award usually goes to the pitcher with the best won-lost record, and most knuckleball pitchers pitch for bad teams.

Almost all baseball men, if they had their druthers, would rather have a hard thrower than a knuckleball pitcher. Managers on good teams have more options: they can get the pitchers they want. Bad teams have limited options, so they have to take chances. Thus bad teams are, on the whole, much more likely than good teams to put a knuckleball pitcher on the mound. But since bad teams are always short on pitching, if the knuckleball pitcher turns out to be effective, he may lead the league in in-

nings pitched. Thus, we get Wilbur Wood leading the American League in innings pitched in 1972 and 1973, Phil Niekro leading the National League in innings pitched in 1974, 1977, 1978, and 1979, Charlie Hough leading the American League in innings pitched in 1987, and Tim Wakefield pitching enough to allow 151 runs to score in 1996 and to lead the league in losses in 1997—mostly for bad teams, and always for teams which were short on pitching.

The other years that Niekro could and perhaps should have won the Cy Young Award are 1974, 1976, and 1979; he also ranks among the top five pitchers in the league in 1967, 1969, 1971, and 1972. Niekro is not the only pitcher who came up empty in the Cy Young voting although the Win Shares system says that he should have won more than once. Dave Stieb also shows as deserving of three Cy Young Awards (1982, 1984, and 1985) and as the runner-up in 1983 and among the leaders in 1981. He never finished higher than fifth in the voting. Jim Bunning, who was anything but a knuckleball pitcher, also shows up as deserving of Cy Young Awards in 1957 and 1967, and as the best pitcher in the American League in 1960, although there was only one Cy Young Award then, and he ranks behind several National League pitchers.

Even the one sort-of knuckleballer who did win the Award, Early Wynn, is offset by the fact that, in the Win Shares system, he ranks below a true knuckleballer: Hoyt Wilhelm. That was the year Wilhelm was a starting pitcher, and led the American League in ERA. He doesn't rank as deserving of the Cy Young Award by the Win Shares method. The Win Shares system thinks the Award should have gone to Vern Law, who won it the next year, and ranks several pitchers as more or less even. But within that group, Hoyt Wilhelm ranks just a hair ahead of Early Wynn.

One of the most underrated pitchers in baseball history is Dutch Leonard, a knuckleball pitcher of the 1930s and 1940s. Leonard had a lifetime record of 191-181, a 3.25 ERA in a hitter's period, never led the league in ERA or wins, but led the league twice in losses.

But what you don't see right away is that Leonard pitched his whole career for terrible teams—in fact, in terms of the teams that he pitched for, I believe that Leonard was the unluckiest pitcher of all time. He went 14-11 in 1934—but that was for a Brooklyn Dodger team that finished sixth. He went 20-8 in 1939 and 18-13 in 1941—but those records were for Washington Senators teams that finished sixth and seventh. He went 14-14 in 1944—with a last-place team. He went 17-12 with a 2.68 ERA in 1947—but that was for a Philadelphia Phillies team that tied for last. Even near the end of his career, 1950 and 1951, he went 5-1 and 10-6—but those records were for Chicago Cub teams that finished seventh and eighth. The only "contending" team that he ever pitched for was the Washington Senators in 1945, and he went 17-7. Leonard wound up his career with 191 wins—but 232 Win Shares.

BIRD THOU NEVER WERT

Play along with me here. Take out your pen, and write down the names of ten pitchers who won 200 or more games in the major leagues. You pick 'em—players from the forties, fifties, sixties, seventies, eighties, lefties, right-handers, American Leaguers, National Leaguers, Hall of Famers or guys who just hung around a long time. Your list.

What do all of those men have in common? I'll tell you: they were all above the league strikeout average early in their careers. Probably seven of your ten led the league in strikeouts at least once.

I got a letter a couple of years ago from somebody who had projected out Mark Fidrych's career, assuming that Fidrych hadn't torn the cartilage in his knee in spring training, 1977. He showed Fidrych winning . . . I don't remember, 320 games or something. In fact, it was always very unlikely that Mark Fidrych would have a career of more than a few seasons. There is simply no such thing as a starting pitcher who has a long career with a low strikeout rate.

I am always amazed that people fail to see this on their own. The career expectation for a strikeout pitcher is so much greater than the career expectation for a non-strikeout pitcher of the same age and ability that the difference is very obvious if you study the issue. Of course, not that many people actually *study* baseball issues, but it is not like this is a trivial matter. Trying to figure out what a pitcher's potential might be is basic to being a baseball fan.

If a pitcher's strikeout rate is less than 4.5 per nine innings, you can pretty much write him off as somebody who is going to have a real career. I first noticed this twenty-some years ago, when Dallas Adams and I were developing a team in a table-game league. In this league you picked rookies and held them through their careers, so you wanted to pick pitchers who would last and develop. This led to a question: is there any way to spot a rookie pitcher who will last and develop?

I drew up a list of the 100 best pitchers since World War II, and then studied the characteristics of those pitchers *as rookies*. As rookies, how many had winning records? As rookies, how many had better-than-league control? As rookies, how many were 22 years old,

23, how many were 24, etc.? How many were good hitters? How many were tall? How many were right-handed, how many were left-handed, how many had outstanding minor league records, how many didn't, etc.

Most of the results were predictable. As rookies, about 55 of the 100 pitchers had winning records, but most of those "winning" records were 9-7 or 4-3 or something; few of the pitchers were actually highly successful as rookies. Their control rates were worse than the league average, their ERAs not significantly better. Their age pattern was not any different than a "control group" consisting of 100 rookie pitchers who had pitched well as rookies, but gone on to less distinguished careers. A few of them had been great in the minor leagues, but their overall minor-league won-lost record was not much over .500.

But then I looked at the question, "How many of these pitchers, as rookies, had strike-out rates better than the league average?" The answer, shockingly, was "All of them." Well, actually it wasn't all of them; it wasn't 100 out of 100, it was like 77 out of a 100. But the rest of the great pitchers, the ones who were below the league strikeout rate as rookies, were all flukes or hard cases. They were the guys who finished 4-11 as rookies with strikeout rates 10% below the league average, but who then dramatically increased their strikeout rates in the next two or three years, or they were the guys who had struck out 200 men in the minors, but had rookie "seasons" of 52 innings with only 21 strikeouts. For all practical purpose, *all* of the best starting pitchers since World War II had been above the league strike-out rate as young pitchers.

From then until now, I've been looking for a starting pitcher who could pitch consistently well with a low strikeout rate. I still haven't found one. Many young pitchers have come up since then who were quite effective with few strikeouts. Mark Fidrych was a superstar for

one season with 97 strikeouts in 250 innings. Dave Rozema was 15-7 in 1977 with 92 strikeouts in 218 innings. Lary Sorensen was 18-12 in 1978 with only 78 strikeouts in 281 innings. Allan Anderson was 16-9 in 1988, led the American League in ERA; he struck out only 83 in 202 innings. Jeff Ballard in 1989 was 18-8 with 62 strikeouts in 215 innings; Andy Hawkins in 1985 was 18-8 with 69 strikeouts in 229 innings. John Farrell was effective at the tag end of the '87 season, then was 14-10 in 1988 with only 92 strikeouts in 210 innings. Greg Hibbard was 14-9 in 1990 with only 92 strikeouts in 211 innings, and Randy Tomlin in 1992 was 14-9 with 90 strikeouts in 209 innings. But all of these pitchers—and all others like them—disappeared quickly after one or two good seasons.

Many of you now have electronic encyclopedias that enable you to assemble data quickly, so let me outline a couple of simple ways to study this issue if you want to. One way is to isolate all the pitchers in major league history who won a certain number of games at a certain age—let's say, all the 25-year-old pitchers in baseball history who won 16 games, or all the 28-year-olds who won 18 games, or something like that. You'll have a small group, ten to thirty pitchers. Sort them by their strikeout rates, relative to the league, and then take the top five pitchers and the bottom five. Then look up how many games the two groups of pitchers win in the rest of their careers.

You will find that the high-strikeout pitchers won more games in the rest of their careers than the low-strikeout pitchers. Even though that is a quick and dirty study, even though five pitchers are ordinarily too small a group to predict what in the hell you might find, you will find this difference. The bias is so large that even when you work with very small groups of pitchers, you still find it.

Second way to study the issue ... pick a year of birth. Let's say all pitchers born in 1955, or 1961 ... you pick. Add 26 years to that year, and look up the records for those pitchers through that season (that is, all pitchers born in 1955, career records through 1981). These are the "BEFORE" records. Then split them into two groups, according to their career strikeouts per nine innings.

Then look up their won-lost records in the rest of their careers, the "AFTER" records. In the "Before" group, some of the best pitchers will be guys with low strikeout rates. But in the "After" group, almost every time, all of the best pitchers will be in the high-strikeout group.

Combining these two almost absolute facts:

1. That all good young pitchers with strikeout rates below 4.00 per game disappear quickly.

2. That all pitchers who have long careers start out with strikeout rates in excess of the league average.

One would think it would be obvious that power pitchers last much longer than finesse pitchers, and one would think that everyone would know this. In fact, very few people seem to know this, large numbers of people persist in believing that the opposite is true, and, when I point this out to people, they almost always want to argue with me.

There are two things that people say to explain why I must be wrong about this. These can be summarized as, "I've seen a lot of pitchers like Tommy John have good long careers without striking batters out, and I've seen a lot of power pitchers like Sandy Koufax burn out early." As to having seen a lot of pitchers have good careers without striking batters out, that's bullshit; you haven't seen any, because there aren't any. Even Tommy John, who is for some reason regarded as the paragon of this type of pitcher, was near the league average in strikeouts for most of his career. In 1965, his first good year, he struck out 126 men in 184 innings, 6.16 per nine innings. The American League average was 5.97. In 1968 he struck out 5.95 batters per nine innings (the league

average was 5.96), and in 1972 he struck out 5.63 (league average: 5.65). In 1978, when the 35-year-old John pitched his last year for the Dodgers, his strikeout rate was 5.24 per nine innings—higher than the National League average, 5.14.

As to the other side of that—power pitchers like Sandy Koufax who burn out early—well, sure. I haven't suggested that *all* power pitchers last a long time. There are lots of power pitchers who burn out before 200 wins—J. R. Richard, Herb Score, Tom Griffin, Mario Soto, Edwin Correa, Gary Nolan, Erik Hanson, Al Downing.

The influence of strikeouts on a pitcher's future can be compared to the effect of height on a man's chances of playing in the NBA. It's not that ALL men who are seven foot tall can play in the NBA—indeed, surveying the whole country, I would suppose that no more than 20% of the men who are 7 foot tall can play in the NBA. But if 20% of seven footers play in the NBA, what is the percentage for men who are 6-foot-10? Probably about one-eighth of that, or about 2.5%. Of people 6-foot-8, if might be one-eighth of that, or three-tenths of one percent, and so on down . . . by the time you get to 5-foot-8, you're down to about one in eighty million.

It's not that ALL seven-footers can play in the NBA, and it isn't true that height is everything. There are other factors. But if you studied the American male population, you could very easily establish that the percentage of men who play in the NBA increases substantially with each one inch of increase in height. The same is true here: there are other factors in having a long career, but if you study the issue, you can easily establish that pitchers who strike out four men per nine innings last longer than pitchers who strike out three men per nine innings, that pitchers who strike out five men per game last longer than those who strike out four, that those who strike out six last longer than those who strike out five, and so on without end; pitchers who strike out nine per game will outlast those who strike out "only" eight. If you *really* study the issue, you can establish that pitchers who strike out 4.1 men per nine innings will last longer than those who strike out 4.0.

Which pitchers have had the longest careers in the last forty years? Nolan Ryan and Steve Carlton. For a baseball fan to fail to see that strikeout rates are closely tied to career length, I would argue, is very much like a basketball fan failing to notice that basketball players tend to be tall. Three more questions, and I'll knock this off:

1. Are there any exceptions to the rule?
2. Could there be an exception to the rule?
3. If this is true, why is it true?

First question . . . are there exceptions? I would argue that there are no clear-cut exceptions to the rule that starting pitchers with low strikeout rates always have short careers. There are some hard cases. Let me review a few of the toughest cases, the best arguments you could make if you're skeptical:

Relievers. I said that there are no *starting* pitchers who have long careers with low strikeout rates. There might be some relievers, like Kent Tekulve.

Jimmy Key. Jimmy Key in his first year as a starter (1985) went 14-6, but struck out only 85 men in 213 innings. Nonetheless, he went on to win 186 major league games.

However, Jimmy Key was *over* the American League strikeout rate in his rookie season, 1984, when he was in the bullpen, and his strikeout rate shot up again in 1986, returning to essentially the league average. Key struck out 173 men as recently as 1993, when he was far over the league average, and his career average was 5.34 strikeouts per nine innings.

Key is not an *exception* to the rule that low-strikeout pitchers never last; rather,

Key defines the limits of the rule. Key was a lefty, he was very smart, he got a lot of ground balls, and he had wonderful control—like Tommy John and Tom Glavine. These type of pitchers define exactly how many strikeouts you absolutely have to have to win consistently in the major leagues, if you're left-handed and you do everything well. If you're left-handed and you do everything well, you can win consistently even if your strikeout rate is a little bit below the league norm.

Scott Erickson. Scott Erickson won 20 games in 1991, striking out only 108 batters. This is a ratio of 5.40 strikeouts for each win. Very few pitchers can sustain a ratio less than ten to one. Erickson's career ratio (through 1998) is 8.74 to 1, which is unusually low for a 1990s pitcher.

Erickson is unusual. Most pitchers with low K rates have modest fastballs, and survive by changing speeds and moving the ball around. Erickson as a rookie had a good fastball, but not a "hopping" fastball like power pitchers; he threw a heavy fastball that burrowed into the ground when the batter made contact.

But since 1991, Erickson's career has drifted toward normalcy. He fell on hard times in 1993–94, as if he was going to have the short career which is normal for a pitcher with few strikeouts. He emerged from that period by learning to use his breaking pitch as a strikeout pitch. Although he continues to get more ground balls than any other American League pitcher, in 1998 he also struck out 186 batters, fourth in the American League. He has eight straight seasons of 100-plus strikeouts.

Lew Burdette. Burdette, again, was a very unusual pitcher, in his case unusual because his control was so exceptional. Burdette averaged only 3.15 strikeouts per nine innings

UNIFORMS OF THE 1970s

In the early seventies, most teams adopted synthetic fabrics. With this, dress became even more informal, and style and comfort became the aims of uniform selection. Doubleknit fabric is well suited to form fitting garments that produce a streamlined look, which is fine in some cases but knits tell all; no more hiding excess flab under loose, baggy suits. Bright colors marched back into the game on the backs of synthetic knits, and teams scrambled to find appropriate color schemes.

Styles swung widely within some organizations, while those with traditionalist sympathies simply adapted the new fabrics to their old style. The Tigers, Yankees, and Dodgers stuck with the old reliable basic white uniform—no flashy colors, no fancy stretch waistbands. The White Sox in the late 70s tried a modernized throwback to the early days, with dark pants just below the knees and a pullover shirt, straight cut, not tucked in and with an open collar. This uniform looked sloppy and disappeared after a few years, but not before a Bermuda shorts version appeared in 1976.

There were new looks around most of baseball—wide stripes here, thin stripes there, here a button-up, there a zip-up, everywhere a V-neck. Horizontal scales of bright yellow and orange blared out "Astros," and both the Pirates and Padres tried combinations of black and gold. There were styles that looked just alike except for slight variations in color and border stripes. The stretch waistband closures became popular and with the new fabrics, piping was replaced by wide fabric stripes.

Batting helmets in the 70s began to track the color schemes of the home cap. The Pirates during the 1976 season brought back one of the old style caps and then kept the style until the late 80s. The Pirates also initiated the practice of mixing up home and road uniforms. The striped top could be worn with gold or black pants; the gold top could be worn with gold pants or black pants. You get the idea—let's see how many possible combinations we can get out of four basic sets; throw in varying colors of stirrups, hats, and undershirts and you could be up half the night just trying to decide what to wear the next day.

—Susan McCarthy

in his career, the lowest strikeout rate of any highly successful post-war pitcher. He was able to win because

    (a) there was an outstanding team behind him, and

    (b) he never walked anybody.

Even though he struck out few batters, his strikeout/walk ratio was still outstanding for the era in which he pitched.

Burdette is arguably the last clear example of a pitcher who could win consistently with few strikeouts. If you were able to name a pitcher who won 200 games with a low strikeout rate (back in the first paragraph of this article), Burdette was probably the pitcher. However, two points:

1. Strikeout rates at that time were much lower than now. Burdette was below the average, but not all that far below average.

2. If you have to go back forty years to find an exception to the rule, that is truly the exception that proves the rule.

Ted Lyons. Lyons won 260 major league games and is in the Hall of Fame, although his strikeout rate is even lower than Burdette's. That was sixty-seventy years ago, and a lot of things were different.

Could there be an exception to the rule?

Sure. Spud Webb and Muggsy Bogues can play in the NBA at 5-6 or whatever. There isn't any major league pitcher now who can sustain a ratio of eight strikeouts per win, but there could be, if there were a pitcher who was exceptional enough in some other respect.

If there were an exception to the rule, it would probably be a Kent Tekulve-type pitcher who threw underhanded or low-sidearm and never walked anybody.

Why is this true?

There are really two ways to explain it. One is that the batting average against a pitcher is inversely related to his strikeout rate. If a pitcher's strikeouts are low, the batting average against him will be high.

Up to a certain point, a pitcher can contend with a high batting average against him by doing other things well—but only up to a point. Beyond that point, no matter how well he does other things, he's going to lose. That point, in modern baseball, is about 4.5 strikeouts per nine innings.

Well, all pitchers, once they establish a level of success, begin to decline in terms of strikeouts per nine innings. Some pitchers decline from the moment they reach the majors; others go up for two or even three years before they begin to decline. Some decline very, very slowly, others decline rapidly, but (almost) every pitcher's strikeout rate goes down over time.

If the strikeout rate starts out at 5.0, the pitcher will hit the bottom when he loses 0.5 strikeouts per game. If he starts out at 6.0, he can pitch until he loses 1.5 strikeouts/game. If he starts out at 7.0, he can pitch until he loses 2.5.

Thus, the higher a pitcher starts out in terms of strikeouts/nine innings, the longer he can pitch before he crashes onto the floor. There are other variables—each pitcher's rate of decline is different, depending on his conditioning, his motion, and other variables, and each pitcher's "floor" is different, depending on how many other things he does well. But the length of the dive depends on the height of the diving board, more than it depends on any other factor.

Second explanation . . . you have heard it said many times, I am sure, that baseball is a game of adjustments. Well, the strikeout rate is one index of a pitcher's room to maneuver in making those adjustments.

The pitcher who doesn't get strikeouts may be very successful for a short period of time, but he is walking a fine line. He lives on the ground ball to short. What happens if the batter makes a small adjustment, and that becomes a ground ball into center field? What does he do then?

Mark Fidrych was walking a tightrope. It was inevitable that he was going to fall off before very long.

1978: OLD BALLPLAYERS NEVER DIE

Observing the 1978 World Series, Joe Sewell offered the opinion that only two members of the '78 Yankees would have been able to make the Yankee team in 1932. And he thought those two, Thurman Munson and Ron Guidry, would both have been in the bullpen.

MY TWO CENTS, 246 WORDS

I have been asked by a reader whether I can explain, in 200 words or less, why I am convinced that the modern practice of constantly switching to left-handed relievers is foolish and counter-productive. OK, let's give it a shot:

The left-handed short reliever gives his team one advantage, but has five problems. The advantage is that he increases the number of times that the pitcher's team will have the platoon advantage. But:

1. He doesn't increase it very much. Every left-handed pitcher in the majors will face more right-handed batters than lefties. At best, a manager might conceivably increase the number of times that he has the platoon advantage by 100.

2. The advantage is just not that large. Gaining the platoon advantage for 100 hitters isn't worth five runs a year.

3. To do this, the manager is taking innings away from his sixth, seventh, and eighth-best pitchers, and giving them to his tenth-, eleventh-, and twelfth-best pitchers. On almost all teams, this creates a demand for more pitchers than are available.

4. To keep two extra pitchers, you have to cut a pinch hitter and a defensive player. Either player, if he is worth a crap, is worth more than five runs. If you pinch hit an outfielder for an infielder, you can get the platoon advantage, but you can also bring up a better hitter. If you work it the other way, you gain *only* the platoon advantage.

5. It is inherently more difficult to control the platoon advantage on defense than it is on offense. Platooning at one position gives a team the platoon advantage on offense an extra 200 times in a season.

246 words. Best I can do.

BEST BASEBALL BOOKS OF THE 1970s

1970—*Ball Four,* called "detrimental to baseball" by Bowie Kuhn, but praised as being "just like junior high" by a Kansas City teenager. Leonard Schecter edited Jim Bouton's tape-recorded musings.
Overrated.

1971—*The Boys of Summer.* Roger Kahn's bittersweet encounters with the Brooklyn Dodgers of 1952–53.
Overrated.

1972—Roger Angell's *The Summer Game,* a gathering of his elegant *New Yorker* pieces, set a new standard for baseball journalism.

1973—Philip Roth, *The Great American Novel.*

1974—Robert W. Creamer, *Babe,* the best of baseball biographies.

—Jim Carothers

Nice Guys Finish Last is my own addition to the list. Done with Ed Linn, Leo Durocher's version of his side of fifty years' worth of controversies is the best book in its genre, at least until Whitey Herzog's 1999 *You're Missin' a Great Game.*

Sometimes what Durocher writes about is still interesting; sometimes the subject has curled up and died sometime in the last half-century. But from page one to page 364, the use of the language is astonishingly good, the pace is right, and all the details are in place. There are no gaps; the book follows a complex, tumultuous life year by year and day by day, giving both a sense of the time and a sense of the event.

That's Jim Carothers' assessment of *Ball Four* and *The Boys of Summer*; I like both books.

—Bill James

THE 1980s

HOW THE GAME WAS PLAYED

Baseball brought into the 1980s a mixture of styles as rich as the game had had in more than half a century. In just the first season of the decade, 1980, three players hit over .340, including one who hit .390, ten players stole 50 or more bases, including three who stole 96 or more, three players hit 40 to 48 home runs, two pitchers won 24 or more games, and one struck out 286 batters. One player hit 49 doubles, four players drew more than a hundred walks, a pitcher completed 28 games, and three pitchers saved 30 or more games. There have been few ten-year periods in history that could boast of players succeeding dramatically in so many different ways.

This could not last forever, but it did last through most of the 1980s. Baseball is normally dominated by relatively few strategies or approaches to the game; only in transition periods do we have highly successful players of many different types. Over time power drives out speed, power pitching controls power hitting, strong bullpens take out strong starting staffs, or vice versa.

In the mid-1980s baseball began to be plagued by the incredible shrinking strike zone. Between 1980 and 1990 unintentional walks increased by 6%, strikeouts by 18%. By the mid-1980s, baseball fans heard the first rumblings of the home run eruption of the 1990s. Home runs per game, which in 1976 had dropped to 1.15 per game (.58 per team per game), were by 1986 up to 1.81 per game, their highest level in twenty years. In 1987 they vaulted to 2.12 per game, a record at the time.

Stolen bases remained at historically high levels throughout the 1980s. Complete games declined from 20% of all starts in 1980 to 10% in 1990.

WHERE THE GAME WAS PLAYED

Same as the 1970s. There were no expansion teams and no franchise shifts during the 1980s. The 1980s were the only decade since the 1940s in which baseball's geography did not change.

WHO THE GAME WAS PLAYED BY

The immense growth of baseball salaries gave ballplayers the opportunity to see themselves as professional men, and did, no doubt, increase professionalism. As late as the early 1970s baseball players—even stars—needed to work off-season jobs to make ends meet. The million-dollar salaries of the 1980s *enabled* players to spend the off-season in conditioning programs. This raised the bar, so that survival in a highly competitive business soon *required* that players spend the off-season in conditioning programs.

As players became more professional, they became more savvy in handling the media, distancing themselves from reporters, showing less of themselves to the public. Reporters at the same time also embraced this peculiar notion of professionalism, and began to distance themselves from the athletes. To older fans, the players no doubt began to look all alike, breaking from the pack only when caught with their pants down or arrested with drugs or prostitutes or underage cheerleaders or some combination thereof. The media, denied access to the players as people, began to portray athletes as villains, as arrogant, over-paid drug abusers. In a decade in which attendance increased at a phenomenal rate, a dozen or more books were written moaning about how dreadful the world of professional sports had become. Drug use did become "rampant" among ballplayers in the early 1980s, although no one really knows whether this rampage involved 5% of the players, or 60%. I'd be inclined to guess that it was closer to five, but you catch the irony: ballplayers cut themselves off from the media to hide their faults, and so the public attributed to all athletes the worst actions of a few, this being the only insight that was left to them.

CHECKING IN:

1980— McCauley Culkin
1986— Rachel James
1988— Isaac James

CHECKING OUT:

1980— Elston Howard, 51
1982— Ken Boyer, 51
       Jackie Jensen, 55
       Dixie Walker, 71
       Indian Bob Johnson, 75
1983— Earl Averill, 81
1984— Joe Cronin, 77
       Waite Hoyt, 84
       Stan Coveleski, 94
1985— Roger Maris, 51
       Burleigh Grimes, 92
1986— Norm Cash, 51
       Red Ruffing, 81
1987— Dick Howser, 51
       Babe Herman, 84
1988— Ted Kluszewski, 63
       Harvey Kuenn, 57
       Carl Hubbell, 85
1989— Donnie Moore, Suicide, 35
       Ted Bundy, executed, 42
       Carl Furillo, 66
       Lefty Gomez, 80
       Bill Terry, 90

THE 1980s IN A BOX

Attendance Data: 459 million (458,858,705)
Highest: Los Angeles Dodgers, 1982   3,608,881
         Los Angeles Dodgers   30,894,722
Lowest: Minnesota Twins,   1981   469,090
        Seattle Mariners   9,841,630

The lowest attendance by a team in a season, not counting the 1981 strike season, was 655,181, by the Cleveland Indians in 1985.

The average American during the 1980s attended a major league baseball game about once every five years.

Most Home Runs:
Mark McGwire,   1987   49
Andre Dawson,   1987   49
Mike Schmidt   313

Best Won/Lost Record by Team:
1986 New York Mets   108-54   .667
New York Yankees   854-708   .547

Worst Won/Lost Record by Team:
1988 Baltimore Orioles   54-107   .335
Seattle Mariners   673-893   .430

Index of Competitive Balance: 56%

Home-Field Winning Percentage: .541

Percentage of Regulars Hitting .300: 15%

Largest Home-Field Advantage: Minnesota Twins, .150

Per 162 games, the Twins in the eighties were 88-74 at home, but 64-98 on the road.

Having Their Best Decade Ever: California Angels, Kansas City Royals, Houston Astros, Milwaukee Brewers, Montreal Expos, Toronto Blue Jays, New York Mets. Basically, most of the expansion teams.

Having Their Worst Decade: Atlanta Braves, Cleveland Indians

Changing Direction: The Cincinnati Reds, a powerhouse from 1961 through 1981, lost 101 games in 1982, and have been up and down ever since.

Heaviest Player: Joey Meyer, listed 260.

Meyer was a talented hitter, big, strong guy, but just fat as a bear in August. Huge, fat thighs, fat arms, immense rump. He was kind of gross, actually.

Lightest Player: Jerry Browne, 140

Most Strikeouts by Pitcher:
Mike Scott,   1986   306
Nolan Ryan   2,399

Highest Batting Average:
George Brett,   1980   .390
Wade Boggs   .352

Lowest Batting Average:
Steve Jeltz, 1988   .187
Darren Daulton   .206

Best Major League Players (by Years):
1980— Mike Schmidt
1981— Mike Schmidt
1982— Robin Yount
1983— Cal Ripken
1984— Ryne Sandberg

1985— George Brett
1986— Wade Boggs
1987— Alan Trammell
1988— Jose Canseco
1989— Will Clark

Best Major League Pitchers (by Years):
1980— Steve Carlton
1981— Steve McCatty
1982— Steve Carlton
1983— Dan Quisenberry
1984— Dave Stieb
1985— Dwight Gooden
1986— Roger Clemens
1987— Roger Clemens
1988— Orel Hershiser
1989— Bret Saberhagen

Hardest-Throwing Pitcher: Nolan Ryan

Best Curve: Mike Boddicker

Best Power/Speed Combination: Rickey Henderson

Best Switch Hitter: Eddie Murray

Iron Man: Cal Ripken

Best Bunter: Brett Butler

Best Baseball Books:
1981— *The Ultimate Baseball Book*—Dan Okrent and Harris Lewine
1984— *Stengel,* Bob Creamer
1989— *The Pitch That Killed,* Mike Sowell

Five Largest Changes in Baseball During the Decade:

1. Development/maturation of the free agent system.
2. Development of the regional television market.
3. Mushrooming of rotisserie/fantasy baseball.
4. Explosion of statistical information about the game.
5. Development of arbitration.

Best Outfield Arm: Jesse Barfield, by far

Worst Outfield Arm: Rudy Law

Most Runs Batted In:
Don Mattingly,   1985   145
Eddie Murray   996

Most Aggressive Baserunner: Alfredo Griffin

One thing I have always wanted to do was to document Alfredo's baserunning exploits. He really was phenomenal. I personally saw him score from second on a ground ball to second, scoring the lead run in the top of the ninth. I have heard about Alfredo doing things like going first-to-third on infield outs, moving second-to-third on a pop up to short, scoring on a pop out to the catcher, and taking second after grounding into a forceout. Alfredo figured that if you left the base ahead of him unguarded, it was his. Somebody ought to make a documented list of those basepath heroics, with dates and specifics, before it gets away from us.

Fastest Player: Willie Wilson or Tim Raines

Slowest Player: Willie Aikens

Most Stolen Bases:
Rickey Henderson,   1982   130
Rickey Henderson   838

Best-Looking Players: Ryne Sandberg, Mark Gubicza, Willie Upshaw

Ugliest Players: Steve Balboni, Pete Vuckovich

Cap Anson Award: Al Campanis

Three Finger Brown Award: Jim Eisenreich

Ozzie Guillen Trophy: Alfredo Griffin and/or Damaso Garcia.

Griffin batted 441 times in 1984, drawing only four walks.

Best Pitching Staff: 1985 Kansas City Royals

Best Offense: 1982 Milwaukee Brewers

Football Players: Kirk Gibson, Bo Jackson, Rick Leach, Phil Bradley

Basketball Guys: Tony Gwynn was an outstanding basketball player at San Diego State.

First of His Kind: Steve Bedrosian in 1985 became the first starting pitcher to pitch 200 innings without pitching a complete game. This is now common.

Last of His Kind: Brian Kingman (the last 20-game loser)

One of a Kind: Rob Deer

Best Infield: Both teams in the 1982 World Series had outstanding infields. The Brewers from 1980 to 1983 had Cecil Cooper, Jim Gantner, Paul Molitor, and Robin Yount, although Molitor was originally the second baseman, with Gantner at third, and Molitor moved to third only after a stint in the outfield. The Cardinal infield was Keith Hernandez, Tommie Herr, Ken Oberkfell, and Ozzie Smith, providing not quite as much punch, but tremendous defense.

Best Outfield: Oakland A's, 1980

Best Control Pitcher: Dan Quisenberry

A Better Man than a Ballplayer: Kevin Bass

A Better Ballplayer Than a Human Being: Dave Parker

Mr. Dickens, I'd Like You to Meet: Drungo LaRue Hazewood (Baltimore Orioles, 1980)
Mickey Klutts (1976–1983)

Platoon Combinations I Would Like to See: Roy Smalley and Bryan Little

Best Defensive Team: 1982 St. Louis Cardinals

Clint Hartung Award: Shawn Abner or Brad Komminsk

Outstanding Sportswriter: Thomas Boswell

Most Admirable Superstar: Dale Murphy

Least Admirable Superstar: Steve Carlton

Gold Glove Team:
C— Jim Sundberg
1B— Keith Hernandez
2B— Frank White
3B— Tim Wallach
SS— Ozzie Smith
OF— Willie Wilson
      Andre Dawson
      Kirby Puckett

Franchise Shifts: None

New Ballparks:
Hubert H. Humphrey Metrodome, Minnesota, 1982
Skydome in Toronto, 1989

Best Pennant Race: 1980 National League West

Best World Series: 1986, New York (N) over Boston

Best-Hitting Pitcher: Don Robinson

Worst-Hitting Pitcher: Don Carman

Best Minor League Team: 1980 Denver Bears

Led by Tim Raines and Tim Wallach, the Bears finished 92–44. Raines was the Minor League Player of the Year, hitting .354 with 77 stolen bases in 108 games, Wallach hit 36 homers and drove in 124 runs, and Randy Bass, who never broke through in the majors, hit .333 with 37 and 143.

Odd Couple: Steve Garvey and Jay Johnstone

Drinking Men:
David Green
Rod Scurry

New Equipment:
Batting helmets with cheek guards
Foot guards for hitters

Uniform Changes: Back to basics

New Terms or Expressions: Rotisserie baseball

Most Wins by Pitcher:

Steve Stone,	1980	25
Jack Morris		162

Highest Winning Percentage:

David Cone,	1988	20-3	.870
Dwight Gooden		100-39	.719

Lowest Winning Percentage:

Jose DeLeon,	1985	2-19	.095
Jim Beattie		43-72	.374

Nicknames: Old Penitentiary Face (Jeffrey Leonard)

Worst Award Selection: Pete Vuckovich won the American League Cy Young Award in 1982. He is probably the worst pitcher ever to win the award.

Best Player Who Never Won the MVP Award: Eddie Murray

Flameouts:
Oddibe McDowell
Juan Samuel

All Offense/No Defense: Harvey's Wallbangers (1982 Brewers)

All Defense/No Offense: 1985 Kansas City Royals

Homer: Bob Horner hit 142 of 218 career home runs in his home park.

Yellowstone Park Award: Jose Cruz Sr. hit 30 home runs more than Bob Horner in road games (106 to 76)—but 83 fewer in his home park (142 to 59).

Tough-Luck Season: Nolan Ryan, 1987

Could I Try This Career Over? Ozzie Canseco

Minor Leagues Were: 100 percent slaves to the majors

Best Double Play Combination: Ozzie Smith and Tommie Herr, 1982–1987 St. Louis Cardinals.

Worst Double Play Combination: 1983 San Francisco Giants, Johnnie LeMaster at shortstop, Brad Wellman and Joel Youngblood at second.

Paul Krichell Talent Scout Award: The New York Yankees in 1982 signed Dave Collins as a free agent—and cut Willie McGee from their 40-man roster to make room.

Best Unrecognized Player: Mickey Tettleton

Highest-Paid Player: Mark Davis ($13 million for four years)

New Statistics: Nothing new officially except Game-Winning RBI, which were dropped after a few years. There was an explosion of new unofficial statistics in the wake of the personal computer revolution, 1981–1983. Among the best of the new unofficial stats was Holds, from STATS, 1987.

Five Biggest Things Wrong with Baseball:

1. Labor/management war and strikes; constant fighting about money.
2. Drug scandals.
3. Fan drinking and violence.
4. Horrible parks.
5. Long, boring games.

DOWN IN FRONT

Between 1977 and 1983, I never went to a major league game at which I was not seated near to a loud, obnoxious drunk. I went to very, very few games in that era at which there was not a fight that broke out somewhere in the vicinity of my seat. I must have gone to 30, 40 games a year during that period, mostly Kansas City Royals games—and there were loud drunks near my seat at every single game.

There were frequent incidents of fans throwing things at players, pouring beer on players. Drunken fans would run onto the field. Sometimes there would be a group of rowdy patrons—four or five guys together, maybe eight, maybe twenty, all drinking and screaming obscenities at the players or trying to pick fights with other fans. The fights would often develop when drunken fans would taunt those who were rooting for the other team. I can remember several times the fans around us would be so loathsome that we would move to other seats to try to get away from them—only to find that there were drunks in that section who were just as offensive. One time, on opening day, a fan fell out of the upper deck at Royals Stadium and was killed. I was there that day, but a friend of mine who was sitting near the place where the fan fell always claimed that he was pushed out, murdered. My friend never went back to the ballpark. Many times we would talk about it on the radio . . . what can be done about this? Is there any way to prevent this stuff from happening?

And then suddenly one spring, the problem was gone. I think it was the spring of 1984, about the third or fourth game that I had gone to. A guy down below me was a little too loud, maybe had had a few drinks, and I suddenly realized that at the other games I had gone to, I hadn't been seated near any of these guys. The problem disappeared so quickly and so cleanly that its absence was hardly noticed. To this day, I have never read a single news story about the successful solution to this problem, Something that doesn't happen isn't news. Dozens of stories had been written decrying the problem—but none even noted its passing.

What happened? Major league baseball teams developed a subtle and diverse program to control alcohol abuse and disruptive behavior. Before the game starts, an announcement is read asking the fans to be courteous to those around them, and to show respect for those who wish to root for the home team or the opposition. By itself, of course, such an announcement would do nothing to prevent bad behavior, but it's part of a plan. Beer sales are terminated after the seventh inning. The number of beer vendors was reduced relative to vendors of other products, and the beer vendors won't sell you more than two beers at a time. Beer vendors are taught to recognize people who have had too much to drink, and to refuse to sell them more beer.

Fans were always prohibited from bringing bottles into the park, but that prohibition is enforced now by security guards who search every bag brought into the park to make sure it doesn't contain a bottle. It's a nuisance, and sometimes I wish they'd cut it out, but it's nothing compared to putting up with the drunks. Drinking in the parking lot before the game is discouraged.

If these things fail, there is a security office where fans can go to report problems. If a fan is loud and abusive, a couple of guys in uniform will sit down on either side of him, and explain to him that his conduct is interfering with other people's enjoyment of the game. If he wants to stay at the game, he needs to behave himself.

They'll throw him out of the park if they have to, but they hardly ever have to. Around the park, a couple of dozen guys with walkie-talkies walk around looking for problems, keeping an eye out for unpleasant situations as they develop. If there's a group of people causing a problem, they can get together a little larger group of men in uniform.

Part of what happened to change the climate regarding fan violence, I think, was the Cesar Cedeno incident in Houston. I should check the details, but there was an incident about 1980 in which Cesar Cedeno went into the stands and attacked a fan. But in the aftermath of the battle, it turned out that the fan had been sitting there in the good seats for

MAJOR LEAGUE ALL-STAR TEAM 1980–1989

Records in seasonal notation, based on 162 games. Pitchers based on 36 starts.

Pos.	Player	Years	Hits	HR	RBI	Avg.	Other
C	Gary Carter	8.10	156	26	99	.264	
1B	Eddie Murray	9.26	177	30	108	.293	
2B	Ryne Sandberg	7.62	183	18	72	.285	33 Stolen bases
3B	Mike Schmidt	8.15	158	38	114	.277	100 Walks
SS	Cal Ripken	8.12	173	25	92	.277	
LF	R Henderson	8.54	177	16	63	.291	98 SB, 131 Runs
CF	Robin Yount	8.93	194	19	92	.305	38 Doubles
RF	Dale Murphy	9.49	164	32	98	.273	

Pitcher	Years	Won-Lost	SO	ERA	Other
RH Dave Stieb	9.33	15-12	148	3.32	
RH Jack Morris	9.22	18-13	177	3.66	
RH Bert Blyleven	8.95	15-13	184	3.64	
LH F Valenzuela	8.16	16-13	202	3.19	
RH Roger Clemens	4.85	20-9	251	3.06	
RA D Quisenberry	9.10	6-5	42	2.67	27 Saves

UNIFORMS OF THE 1980s

At the start of the 1980s, uniforms carry forward a strong flavor of the doubleknit seventies. But as the decade moves forward, a back to basics movement grabs hold, a move toward a plainer, cleaner look. The color schemes are toned down, there is less trim work, home uniforms go back to white, road uniforms back to gray. The mesh waist bands are replaced with belts. The pullover shirt begins to give way to buttons.

The White Sox in 1980 and 1981 continue trying to get more teams to join their pajama party, wearing casual V-necked shirts, not tucked in. In 1982 they give up and go with a real doubleknit look of horizontal blue and red stripes with "sox" spelled out in white. The White Sox also pick up a novelty from the Astros uniforms of 1975–79, and add the player's numbers to the left front pants-pocket area. That doesn't catch on either, and by the later 80s, they're on board the traditionalist train.

Milwaukee's home white uniform had pinstripes and blue trim; the road uniform was of the same style, only in a light blue with gold added to the trim. They revamped their road uniform in the mid-80s, changing their traveling colors to gray and replacing "Brewers" with "Milwaukee." The Brewers stuck with the doubleknit through the end of the eighties, though, resuming their traditionalist refinements in 1990.

The Cleveland Indians uniforms of 1986 revert to a more traditional style. Even Chief Wahoo finds his way back onto the uniform, this time on the cap fronts and the left sleeve. Atlanta in 1987 joins the trend with a uniform featuring button-up jersey, separate belts, and a re-issue of the tomahawk, last seen in 1963. Umpires in the late 1980s look more comfortable, too, in dark gray slacks, short sleeve light blue shirts, dark shoes, and belt. Suit jackets are replaced with sweaters for chilly days. Haven't you always wondered if some umpires sneak packs of gum or mints into their ball bags?

—Susan McCarthy

several days, screaming at Cedeno. "MURDERER!" he would yell, and, what is worse in our society, "NIG---! MURDERER!" Nobody did anything about it, until Cedeno had had as much as he was going to take. Then it occurred to somebody to ask, "Why in the hell didn't the Astros do something about that loudmouth fan *before* then?" I think that incident was a key in changing how baseball thought about fan misbehavior, being pro-active and heading off incidents before they developed into violence.

After a couple of years, people no longer *expected* to be able to go to ballgames to get drunk and scream at people. A whole generation of fans has grown up now to whom the idea of going to a baseball game to drink until you vomit would seem as foreign as the idea of going to Alaska to test out your new fly swatter. No problem, no story; nobody says anything about it—but many times, over the years, I have taken heart when I reflected on this change. We only talk about the things that are wrong with the game, not the things that are right. That's just human nature. Many times problems seem like they are impossible to solve, that things are just going to get worse and worse—but problems do get solved sometimes. If we have a plan, if we devote a few resources to the plan, we can solve problems. We can reduce the crime rate; we can fix our schools, we can get mentally ill people off the streets and into decent housing, we can even make the criminal justice system work if we can get the lawyers out of the room long enough to figure out the problem. We can eliminate the problems that plague baseball at the start of the 21st century. We just need to agree on what to do.

I Don't Know What This Has to Do with Baseball, But I Thought I'd Mention It Anyway: In a 1980 dress rehearsal for the 1981 strike, the players voted 967–1 to authorize a strike. The lone player to vote against the strike was Jerry Terrell—the union representative of the Kansas City Royals.

THE 1990s

HOW THE GAME WAS PLAYED

The outstanding features of baseball in the 1990s were record numbers of strikeouts, home runs, relief pitchers, and new stadiums. The game was essentially defined by batters using bats with very thin handles, and whipping them through the strike zone as fast as possible, producing either extra base hits or strikeouts.

In 1967 there were 11.98 strikeouts for each major league game (5.99 per team). Several things were done to change that. Strikeouts drifted downward until 1981, when there were slightly less than 9.5 strikeouts per game. Since then there has been a resumption of the historical trend toward more strikeouts, which dates to the 1920s. Strikeout rates passed the 1967 high-water mark in 1994 and pushed on to levels about 10 percent higher by decade's end.

But whereas the strikeouts of the 1960s were caused by the dominance of power pitchers, the strikeouts of the 1990s were caused more by the predominance of power hitters. Babe Ruth, in his time, regularly led the league in strikeouts; so did Jimmie Foxx, Mickey Mantle, Reggie Jackson, Mike Schmidt, and many other power hitters. Mark McGwire, Ken Griffey Jr., and

Albert Belle don't strike out any more than Mantle, Jackson, or Schmidt, but there are simply *more* players now who are swinging for the fences—and thus, more strikeouts.

So the 1990s presented the paradox of historically high strikeout rates, simultaneous with historically high batting averages. Major league batting averages have hovered between .265 and .270 since 1994, the highest they have been in fifty years.

The question of why home-run hitting exploded in the 1990s is much debated. There are two popular theories that I will comment on in passing:

1. That the ball is livelier.
2. That there is a shortage of good pitching.

I put little stock in either of these explanations. The resiliency of baseballs is tested regularly, has been for many years; it's probably up some. It might be better if the resiliency of the balls was reduced, but it hasn't increased dramatically.

In all sports, whenever one person succeeds another must fail. When the hitters rule the game, this can always be explained as poor pitching, and vice versa. In addition, there is always a perceived shortage of *good* pitching, because each team needs a dozen or more pitchers. If a team has a shortstop they're not looking around for another, so they're not going to complain about the shortage of good shortstops. But even if a team has eight good pitchers they still need more, so some people are always going to complain about the lack of good pitching. I don't put any stock in this as an explanation for why baseball in the 1990s is the way it is.

Expansion? Expansion favors neither the hitter nor the pitcher, on balance; it does as much to create a shortage of good hitters as it does to create a shortage of good pitchers.

In the early 1990s the strike zone was a real problem, or the umpires if you prefer. From the mid-1980s into the early 1990s many umpires just would not call a strike, particularly strike three, no matter how perfect the pitch. That was maddening, and people still complain about it, but it is really not true anymore; the leagues have addressed the issue, and almost all of the umpires now will call a strike a strike. It hasn't made much difference.

In my opinion, the hitting conditions of the 1990s are created by six factors: the new ballparks, which have tended to be hitter's ballparks, and the culmination of five historical trends, which are:

1. The acceptance of strength training.

2. The abbreviating of pitcher's motions.

3. The use of aluminum bats in amateur ball.

4. The policy of fining and suspending players automatically when there is a fight.

5. The evolution of bat design.

The battle for the acceptance of strength training in baseball took at least seventy years to run its course. Honus Wagner believed in strength training, and used dumbbells as a part of his off-season workouts—but there was, at that time, an entrenched prejudice against weight-lifting by baseball players (and most other athletes). Strength training, it was believed, would make players muscle-bound and result in injuries. In the early 1980s, when Lance Parrish reported to spring training one year sporting ten pounds of extra muscle, Sparky Anderson complained that Parrish needed to decide whether he wanted to be a catcher or a member of the Russian Olympic weight-lifting team. There are still people today who believe this, but they are now badly outvoted.

A second factor is pitcher's motions. Rent a tape of a World Series from the 1950s, even the early 1960s, and you will be struck by the pitchers' mechanics. Pitchers in that era used very high leg kicks, some of them, and pumped their arms vigorously up and down in the process of delivering the pitch. They vaulted forward in completing the pitch, although they would shorten the delivery somewhat with runners on base.

But that was problematic, because many pitchers lost effectiveness with runners on base, and even the shortened "stretch" motions were, in retrospect, not all that short. From the time of Maury Wills (1962) until the mid-1980s, pitching coaches constantly encouraged young pitchers to shorten their deliveries. The pitching motions that are common today are totally different from those of the 1920–1965 era—and it is very likely that, as a consequence of this, the pitchers don't throw as hard. I don't want to generalize, but there may not be as many pitchers now who throw 90-plus miles per hour as there were in the 1950s, primarily because the pitchers use such conservative motions that they don't get much out of their legs.

Third, the aluminum bats. In the 1980s, when the college programs switched to aluminum bats, it was commonly said that this was going to ruin the hitters. With the aluminum bat, even if you don't hit the ball well, it will still carry. If you get jammed with an aluminum bat but happen to meet the ball squarely, you've got a base hit, whereas if the same thing happens with a wooden bat you've got a bat handle. If you swing late at an outside pitch with an aluminum bat, you can drive the ball hard to the opposite field.

In the 1980s, it was widely believed that the use of aluminum bats would ruin young hitters, and might cause another pitcher's era. This proves again that it is impossible to anticipate history. The effect that this has had on major league baseball is exactly the opposite of what was expected.

It has always been considered a sucker's game for a hitter to try to drive an outside pitch. Up until 1990, young hitters were always taught either to lay off the outside pitch or to go with it and guide it into the opposite field. If you try to "drive" that ball, they were told, you're going to wind up with a ground ball to second base (if you're right-handed) or shortstop (if you're a lefty). The aluminum bats were supposed to ruin hitters because they were going to let young hitters get by with this destructive habit of trying to drive the outside pitch.

But in fact, what the hitters learned from using the aluminum bats was not that they *couldn't* hit the outside pitch hard, but that they *could*. The aluminum bat revolution is, in a way, very similar to the Babe Ruth revolution. Before Babe Ruth, hitters had been taught for fifty years that it was a sucker's game to try to hit long flies. Up until 1920, any young hitter who experimented with an uppercut was told to cut it out and swing level, because everybody "knew" that if you uppercut you would hit a few home runs, but you'd hit twenty times as many fly outs and pop ups. Babe Ruth was "allowed" to uppercut, and wasn't coached out of it, because

(1) he was a pitcher, and

(2) it wasn't Ruth's nature to do what he was told.

Well, what's happened here is really the same thing: everybody "knew" that you couldn't make a living by crowding the plate

and driving the outside pitch to the fence, but it turned out that everybody was wrong.

We first noticed this, some STATS guys and I, after a comment that Greg Maddux made. Maddux said that the biggest change in baseball since he came into the league was in the number of hitters who stand right on top of the plate and hit the outside pitch. He said that when he came in the league (1986) he saw maybe a half-dozen opposite-field home runs all season. Now you see them all the time.

We checked that out, since we have mountains of data including things like where home runs are hit, and we found it to be absolutely true. The number of opposite-field home runs has, in fact, nearly tripled since 1987. Meanwhile, the number of hit batsmen has more than doubled, from 32 per 100 games in 1984 (31 in 1980) to 65 per 100 games in 1999. The batters have learned that they can stand right on top of the plate and blast away at the outside pitch.

The people who have picked up bad habits from the aluminum bats haven't been the hitters, but the pitchers. Young pitchers used to be taught to work inside, to jam the hitters. You can't teach that in amateur ball now, because it doesn't work with aluminum bats.

This trend was given a booster rocket in the early 1990s, when the leagues developed policies of automatically expelling players who charge the mound after a brushback, automatically suspending players who leave the dugout during a fight, and automatically expelling a pitcher who throws close to a hitter after a warning.

This, again, is a battle that goes back many, many years; I can show you baseball guides from the twenties, thirties and fifties talking about how fights develop after inside pitches and suggesting what ought to be done to prevent this from happening. The effective policy of the 1990s—and it has been a very effective policy, in terms of limiting fights—is no tolerance for brushback pitches, no tolerance for charging the mound.

In addition, hitters now use batting helmets with ear flaps, which reduce the batter's fear of an inside pitch, at least a bit. For all intents and purposes, the league policy now is that the hitter can stand right on top of home plate, and the pitcher can't do much about it. A few pitchers can still get by with knocking the hitter back off the plate, but not very many; that's pretty much a lost art. The batters own the inside corner.

Finally, there is a hundred-year trend in bat design. Nineteenth-century bats had barrels almost as thick as the hitting area. Bats from 1920 had thinner handles, from 1950, still thinner, from 1980, still thinner, from 1999, thinner yet. More and more of the bat's weight has been concentrated into the sweet spot, the contact area; even the end of the bat has been hollowed out to increase a little bit more the ratio between the bat's weight and its surface area.

The effect of this is to increase bat speed. The hitters of the Nellie Fox/Richie Ashburn type, who choked up on the bat and tried to punch the ball into the outfield, are just about gone. Almost everybody now holds the bat right down on the knob, and tries to hit the ball hard.

Batters used to "bone" their bats, rubbing them hard with a bone or something similar to compact the surface wood just a little, making the bat harder. In the mid-1990s batters learned that they could accomplish the same thing by "double dipping" the bat, putting an extra layer of lacquer on the bat. This also has contributed to the home run explosion.

Finally, the new parks, and in particular the addition of Coors Field to the mix, have contributed somewhat to the increases in home runs and scoring. Although this factor is not as large as I once believed it to be, Coors Field is the best hitter's park in the history of baseball (excepting temporary and transitional

stadiums), and colors the statistics of the entire league. Even apart from Coors, the new parks of the last ten years have tended to improve playing conditions for hitters, as opposed to pitchers.

So putting those things together, we have the baseball of the 1990s—lots of doubles, lots of homers, lots of strikeouts. Sit-on-your-ass baseball, as Whitey Herzog has termed it. Triples have declined from 56 per 100 games in 1977 to 32 per 100 games in 2000, primarily due to the gradual disappearance of artificial turf. Intentional walks have declined from 69 per 100 games in 1989 to 40 in 2000, because everyone is a power hitter now, so it is no longer possible to pitch around the power hitters. Stolen base rates have been declining since 1983, although they remain high by historical standards. Errors are down, double plays up—again, consistent with long-term historical trends.

There is, finally, the revolting development of constant pitching changes. Again, this is the culmination of a hundred-year trend. Teams in 1876 used one pitcher. In 1890 they used three or four, in 1920, using 25-man rosters, seven or eight. When I was young (in the 1960s) teams carried eight or nine pitchers; in the 1970s, nine or ten; in the 1980s, ten to twelve, and in the 1990s, eleven to thirteen.

Well, if you have that many pitchers, or that many people who pretend to be pitchers, of course you have to get them into the game. Thus it is that the latter innings of modern baseball games are constantly delayed by pitching changes which have one-half the entertainment value of a good screen saver, and which incidentally deliver their managers an advantage too small to be detected with the naked microscope. The number of pitchers used per game has been increasing for a hundred years—but increased more rapidly between 1983 and 1995 than ever before. In 1983 major league managers used 1.60 relievers per game; in 1995 they used 2.45, a 53%

increase in 12 years. Projecting that rate of increase for another two generations, by the year 2020 major league managers would be using six relievers per game.

Some of you may believe that every year in the 1990s we saw new and higher levels of home runs and runs scored. This is untrue; in fact, we reached a plateau in 1994. There has been little change since then.

WHERE THE GAME WAS PLAYED

You all know that.

WHO THE GAME WAS PLAYED BY

The largest changes in the player population in the last twenty years have come from the continuation of two trends dating to about 1940: more college players, and more Latin Americans. The domination of the game by black players continues to wane.

CHECKING IN:

1990— JonBenet Ramsey, Atlanta
1993— Reuben James, Lawrence, Kansas
        Elian Gonzalez, Cuba

CHECKING OUT:

1990— Tony Conigliaro, 45
        Larry Jackson, 59
        Joe Sewell, 91
1991— Smoky Burgess, 64
        Luke Appling, 83
1992— Steady Eddie Lopat, 73
        Billy Herman, 83
1993— Tim Crews, 31, Boating Accident
        Steve Olin, 27, Boating Accident
        Don Drysdale, 56
        Roy Campanella, 71
        Charlie Gehringer, 89
1995— Mickey Mantle, 64
1998— Richie Ashburn, 71
1999— Joe DiMaggio, 84

MAJOR LEAGUE ALL-STAR TEAM 1990–1999

Records in seasonal notation, based on 162 games. Pitchers based on 36 starts.

Pos.	Player	Years	Hits	HR	RBI	Avg.	Other
C	Mike Piazza	6.06	198	40	127	.328	.575 Slugging
1B	Frank Thomas	8.46	185	36	123	.320	127 Walks
2B	Craig Biggio	9.35	185	15	69	.297	39 Doubles
3B	Robin Ventura	8.64	164	24	99	.278	
SS	Barry Larkin	7.98	181	17	80	.303	
LF	Barry Bonds	8.85	167	41	122	.302	39 SB, 129 Walks
CF	Ken Griffey	8.69	187	44	126	.302	
RF	Albert Belle	8.25	184	43	133	.299	42 Doubles

Pitcher		Years	Won-Lost	SO	ERA	Other
RH	Roger Clemens	8.47	18-11	263	3.02	
RH	Greg Maddux	9.19	19-10	192	2.54	Only 48 Walks
RH	Kevin Brown	8.75	16-11	181	3.25	
LH	Randy Johnson	8.17	18-9		315	3.14
LH	Tom Glavine	9.08	18-10	161	3.21	
RA	John Wetteland	7.36	5-4	89	2.66	40 Saves

THE 1990s IN A BOX

Attendance Data: 601 million (601,233,401)

Highest:	Colorado Rockies, 1993	4,483,350
	Baltimore Orioles	32,192,618
Lowest:	Montreal Expos, 1999	773,277
	Montreal Expos	13,008,431

Attendance in the early 1990s rolled to record levels. By 1993, 70,257,938 fans attended major league baseball games, a staggering number—up more than 50% from the average per-season figure of the 1980s, which was a record-setting decade. At the time of the 1994 strike we were headed toward an even larger number in 1994.

The 1994/95 strike cooled the ardor of the nation's baseball fans, rolling attendance back to the levels of the late eighties.

Since then attendance has gradually increased. By the end of the decade it had not quite reached the pre-strike levels.

For the 1990s as a whole, attendance was far higher than in any other decade, up 31% from the 1980s. The expansion teams account for an increase of 7%; the other 24% is just bigger crowds. The average American during the 1990s attended a major league baseball game about once every four and a half years.

Most Home Runs:

Mark McGwire, 1998	70
Mark McGwire	405

Best Won/Lost Record by Team:

New York Yankees, 1998	114-48	.704
Atlanta Braves	925-629	.595

Worst Won/Lost Record by Team:

Detroit Tigers, 1996	53-109	.327
Florida Marlins	472-596	.442

(Tampa Bay was 132-192, .407, in their first two seasons.)

Index of Competitive Balance: 57%

The onset of the free agent era in the mid-1970s was accompanied by frequent lamentations that this would destroy competitive balance, as the rich would grow richer and the poor would grow livestock for the rich. This didn't happen, proving once more that it is impossible to anticipate history. The 1980s, the first full decade of free agency, were by far the most competitive years in baseball history up to that point, and also the decade in which the small-city markets enjoyed their most success ever, as Kansas City reached the World Series twice, St. Louis three times, Minnesota twice, Milwaukee once, and Oakland twice. In no other decade in baseball history was the game *less* dominated by New York City teams.

In the early 1990s this continued to be true; baseball was highly competitive, and not at all dominated by Big Market teams. But as the decade has moved on, competitive balance has begun to fray. The standard deviation of winning percentage, which was .054 in 1990 (one of the lowest figures in baseball history) jumped to .081 in 1998, the highest figure since 1977.

When I was in high school we knew this kid who drank like a sponge and drove like a maniac; we all used to say he would kill himself in a car wreck by the time he was 30. Boy, were we wrong; he didn't kill himself in a car wreck until he was almost 40.

It would be a mistake to conclude that, because the destruction of competitive balance by free agency didn't happen when we *expected* it to occur, it therefore isn't going to happen. Many things suggest that free agency now *is* destroying competitive balance, although it took twenty years for this to happen. But it is impossible to anticipate history, and the method I have established to measure competitive balance does show that overall competitive balance was greater in the 1990s than in any other period of baseball history.

Home-Field Winning Percentage: .537

Percentage of Regulars Hitting .300: 20%

Largest Home-Field Advantage: Colorado Rockies

The Rockies were 88-74 per 162 games at home (.545), 67-95 on the road (.412).

Having Their Best Decade Ever: Atlanta Braves, San Diego Padres, Seattle Mariners, Texas Rangers.

The Padres and Mariners were below .500 for the decade, but still better than in any previous decade. The Rangers, after two dismal decades, were 60 games over .500 in the 1990s.

Having Their Worst Decade: Detroit Tigers, Kansas City Royals, Los Angeles Dodgers, Oakland A's.

Changing Directions: The Cleveland Indians, most notably.

Heaviest Player: Probably Cecil Fielder

Fielder acknowledges a weight of 261, leaving unanswered the question of what he might weigh if he put his other foot on the scale. Calvin Pickering is listed at 283 pounds.

Lightest Player: Craig Grebeck, 148 pounds

Most Strikeouts by Pitcher:
Randy Johnson,	1999	364
Randy Johnson		2,538

Highest Batting Average:
Tony Gwynn,	1994	.394
Tony Gwynn		.344

Lowest Batting Average:
Rob Deer,	1991	.179
Rob Deer		.209

Best Major League Players (by Years):
1990— Rickey Henderson
1991— Barry Bonds
1992— Barry Bonds
1993— Barry Bonds
1994— Jeff Bagwell
1995— Barry Bonds
1996— Jeff Bagwell
1997— Frank Thomas
1998— Mark McGwire
1999— Derek Jeter

Best Major League Pitchers (by Years):
1990— Roger Clemens
1991— Roger Clemens
1992— Greg Maddux
1993— Kevin Appier
1994— Greg Maddux
1995— Greg Maddux
1996— John Smoltz
1997— Roger Clemens
1998— Greg Maddux
1999— Pedro Martinez

Hardest-Throwing Pitcher: Randy Johnson

Best Curve: Tom Gordon

Best Power/Speed Combination: Barry Bonds

Best Switch Hitter: Chili Davis

Iron Man: Cal Ripken

Best Bunter: Kenny Lofton

Best Baseball Books:
1990— *Men At Work*, George F. Will
1992— *The Negro Baseball Leagues (A Photo-graphic History)*, Phil Dixon
1992— *Baseball Nicknames*, James J. Skipper
1995— *Walter Johnson*, Henry W. Thomas
1999— *You're Missin' a Great Game*, Whitey Herzog and Jonathon Pitts

Five Largest Changes in Baseball During the Decade:

1. Eruption of new parks.
2. Wild cards in the playoffs.
3. Inter-league play.
4. Hitting explosion.
5. Expansion.

It is possible that ten years from now, we will look back and say that, in retrospect, the biggest thing that happened in baseball in the 1990s was the emergence of the split between the big city teams and the small city teams.

Best Outfield Arm: Vladimir Guerrero

Most Runs Batted In:
Manny Ramirez, 1999   165
Barry Bonds   1,076

Most Aggressive Baserunner: Delino DeShields

Fastest Player: Kenny Lofton

Slowest Player: Cecil Fielder

Best Control Pitcher: Greg Maddux

Most Stolen Bases:
Marquis Grissom, 1992   78
Otis Nixon   478

Best-Looking Players:
Ken Griffey Jr.
John Wetteland
Mark Grudzielanek

Ugliest Players: Randy Johnson, Charlie O'Brien

Cap Anson Award: John Rocker

Three Finger Brown Award: Jim Abbott

Ozzie Guillen Trophy: Ozzie Guillen

Best Pitching Staff: Atlanta Braves, 1993–1999
The Braves pitching staff is probably the best in the history of baseball.

Best Offense: 1998 New York Yankees

Football Players: Deion Sanders, Brian Jordan

First of His Kind: Hideo Nomo

Last of His Kind: Cal Ripken

One of a Kind: Jeff Montgomery (only four-pitch relief ace in major league history)

Best Infield: 1996 Baltimore Orioles (Palmeiro, Alomar, Surhoff, and Ripken)

Best Outfield: 1990-91 Pittsburgh Pirates (Bonds, Bonilla, and Van Slyke)

A Better Man Than a Ballplayer: Doug Drabek

A Better Ballplayer Than a Human Being: Wilfredo Cordero

Mr. Dickens, I'd Like You to Meet:
Heathcliff Slocumb
Archi Cianfrocco
Josias Manzanillo

Platoon Combinations I Would Like to See:
Rob Deer and Brian Hunter
David Justice and Vance Law

Best Defensive Team: 1991 Minnesota Twins

Clint Hartung Award: Brien Taylor

Outstanding Sportswriter: Peter Gammons

Most Admirable Superstar: Kirby Puckett

Least Admirable Superstar: Albert Belle

Gold Glove Team:
C— Ivan Rodriguez
1B— Mark Grace
2B— Mark Lemke
3B— Terry Pendleton
SS— Omar Vizquel
OF— Marquis Grissom
     Devon White
     Kenny Lofton

Franchise Shifts: None

New Ballparks:
1991— New Comiskey in Chicago
1992— Camden Yards in Baltimore
1993— Joe Robbie Stadium, Florida
1994— Jacobs Field in Cleveland
1994— The Ballpark in Arlington
1995— Coors Field
1997— Edison Internation/Remodeled Big A in Anaheim
1997— Turner Field, Atlanta
1998— Bank One Ballpark, Arizona
1998— Tropicana Field, Tampa Bay
1999— Safeco Field, Seattle

More new parks were built in the 1990s than in any other period in baseball history.

Best Pennant Races:
1993— National League West (Atlanta vs. San Francisco)
1995— American League West (Seattle, California, and Texas)

Best World Series: 1991, Jack Morris of the Twins pitched a ten-inning shutout in the seventh game to hold off the Braves. Five of the seven games were decided by one run.

Best-Hitting Pitcher: Tom Glavine

Worst-Hitting Pitcher: Mark Clark

Odd Couple: Sammy Sosa and Mark McGwire

New Equipment:
Small, inside-the-shirt chest protectors for umpires
Sliding pads
Catching helmets

Player vs. Team: See article, The Tenth War

Team vs. Team: See article, The Tenth War

Uniform Changes: See note

Most Wins by Pitcher:
Bob Welch, 1990   27
Greg Maddux   176

Highest Winning Percentage:
Greg Maddux, 1995   19-2   .905
Pedro Martinez   107-50   .682

Lowest Winning Percentage:
Paul Wagner, 1995   5-16   .238
Willie Blair, 1998   5-16   .238
Mark Gubicza   48-69   .410

Nicknames:
El Gato (Tony Pena)
Big Hurt (Frank Thomas)
The Crime Dog (Fred McGriff)
The Hit Dog (Mo Vaughn)
One Dog (Lance Johnson)
Wonder Dog (Rex Hudler)
The Oakland Out Man (Dennis Eckersley)
Rocket (Roger Clemens)

Worst Award Selection: American League Cy Young, 1990 (Bob Welch)

Best Player Who Never Won the MVP Award: Tony Gwynn

Flameout: Phil Plantier

All Offense/No Defense: 1991 Texas Rangers

All Defense/No Offense: 1990 Cincinnati Reds

Homer: Dante Bichette

Yellowstone Park Award: Steve Finley

Finley has hit more home runs on the road than Bichette—but less than 40% as many at home.

Tough-Luck Season: Anthony Young, 1992

Could I Try This Career Over? Rob Ducey

Minor Leagues Were:
0.5 percent free
99.5 percent slaves to the majors

Best Double Play Combination: Robby Thompson and Royce Clayton, 1992–1995 San Francisco Giants.

Worst Double Play Combination: Mark Lewis and Andujar Cedeno, 1996 Detroit Tigers.

Paul Krichell Talent Scout Award: The Boston Red Sox traded Jeff Bagwell to the Astros for a 37-year-old relief pitcher.

Best Unrecognized Player: Craig Biggio

Highest-Paid Player: Albert Belle

New Statistics: Zone Ratings

A Very Good Movie Could Be Made About: El Duque

Seven Biggest Things Wrong with Baseball:

1. Lack of central authority/inability to solve problems.
2. Teams with no real chance to win/declining competitive balance.
3. Constant fighting about money.
4. Excessive player movement between teams.
5. Long, boring games with too much inaction.
6. Excessive domination by hitters.
7. Sub-standard umpiring.

I Don't Know What This Has to Do with Baseball, But I Thought I'd Mention It Anyway: Perhaps the most phenomenal fact of life in baseball today is that major league teams continue to use first-round draft picks for high school pitchers. You could call it the Brien Taylor/Todd Van Poppel phenomenon. If you study the issue, it is just stunningly obvious that the frequency with which these draft picks pay off is something like one-third to one-quarter of the payoff rate for other first-round picks. It has been obvious for twenty years that this is a stupid, stupid gamble, to use a first-round pick for a high school pitcher—yet every year, four to seven first-round picks are invested in these turkeys.

BASEBALL 2015

History shows nothing more clearly than that one cannot anticipate history. This is true, I think, because many of the things that we all know turn out, when put to the test, to be untrue, or to be true only up to a point.

Having said that, four things about the future of baseball seem so obvious to me that I am willing to put them on record in a hardcover book, so that the next generation of sportswriters can make fun of me twenty years from now. Those four things are:

1. That baseball will eventually solve or contain the problem of economics corroding competitive balance.

2. That baseball will eventually gain control of the problem of the ever-lengthening games.

3. That the hundred-year trend of using more and more pitchers will end, and complete games (for the first time ever) will soon become more common, rather than less.

4. That the trend toward more strikeouts and more homers from the top of the order to the bottom will also end soon.

As to why these will happen . . . Baseball will eventually solve or contain the problem of free agency destroying competitive balance because:

　　a. The historical trend in all sports and across many decades is toward ever greater competitive balance.

　　b. There are obvious solutions to the problem.

　　c. If the obvious solutions are not adopted sooner, the problem will become so acute that they will have to be adopted later.

Broad, powerful forces in sports and society tend to level competition within any fixed group. The details of negotiated contracts can obstruct that process for a period of time, but not forever.

Baseball will eventually gain control of the problem of ever-lengthening games because sooner or later, it will occur to the men who market professional baseball to the public that

　　a. We are selling entertainment.

　　b. Long, slow baseball games are boring.

　　c. There are very obvious ways to drain the inaction out of the game.

I'll write about what those ways are in another essay, but what I'm saying is, it's just a blind spot. All groups of people develop blind spots; in politics right now we have a blind spot about privacy. We'll get beyond it.

The hundred-year trend toward more and more pitchers in a game will eventually run its course. In fact, it may already have run its course, because it doesn't make any sense. In order to gain a small, almost miniscule, platoon advantage, managers are using so many pitchers that they are creating an artificial shortage of pitching. Eventually it will occur to them that this doesn't work.

The trend toward more and more homers and more and more strikeouts will also end soon because

　　a. Those trends are cyclical.

　　b. Again, it doesn't really make sense.

A hitter who swings slowly and punches the ball through the infield or over the infield can hit .320, .330—always could, and still can. Nobody in baseball has less bat speed than Tony Gwynn, and look at the result: you've got this man nearing 40, fat, can't run, and he still hits .350.

With all of the crazy hitting records of the 1990s, nobody has made any real run at Hack Wilson's RBI record. No American Leaguer has made a run at Lou Gehrig's American League RBI record. Why? Individually, power hitters have had seasons which are as good as any in history—but they don't drive in as many runs, and their teams do not score as many runs as the great hitting teams of the 1930s. Why?

Because nobody is setting the table. We've got offenses now that are wall-to-wall power hitters. The only people who aren't power hitters are the guys who don't hit anything; there aren't really any good hitters, other than Tony Gwynn and maybe Jose Offerman, who are singles hitters.

We all know why that is: it's because everybody has got the idea that, to make money, you have to hit homers. That won't stand. The winds of history will blow it flat, because there's no real foundation to it. All it takes is one dramatic counter-example to change the way people think about the issue. Sooner or later, we're going to get some little guy with limited athletic ability who just draws walks and punches singles, somebody will put him in the lineup in front of Albert Belle or Ken Griffey or Nomar or Juan Gonzalez, and the big guy will drive in 175 runs, and everybody else will go scrambling around looking for little guys who can get on base.

THE PERFECT MACHINE

An idea has taken root among baseball fans in the last thirty to forty years that baseball is a kind of perfect machine, which maintains its form and proportion through its own internal system of checks and balances. This belief is expressed on the one hand in the quasi-philosophical delight that we take in noting that, after 150 years, shortstops are still throwing batters out at first base by a half-step, and on the other hand, by the sustained petulance of baseball fans who, a quarter-century later, are still angry about the Designated Hitter rule. Anger at the Designated Hitter rule is founded on the premise that baseball, on the field, is a perfect game—that it has its own internal weights and measures, it's own scales and it's own justice, and that no one has the right to monkey with that. No matter how screwed up baseball is off the field, we may think, no matter how irrational its schedule, no matter how insane its salary structure, and no matter how bloody its labor relations, it remains, on the field, the same game it has always been and, Lord willing, always will be.

It is my argument that this prejudice against deliberate change, this belief in baseball's intrinsic purity and perfectness on the field, has become a burden to the game of baseball, and has become the enemy of needed reforms.

I am, like almost everyone who lives in Lawrence, Kansas, a fanatical fan of college basketball in general and the Kansas Jayhawks in particular. The experience of walking into Allen Fieldhouse at the start of a basketball game is virtually indescribable. There is an excitement in the building which is not merely palpable, but visceral. One cannot help but be carried away by it, swept away in a river of anticipation and enthusiasm.

College basketball is a wonderful game, but baseball is a wonderful game, too, and I can remember times, although those memories are growing dim, when we were all swept away in the sheer joy of being at a baseball park. College basketball remains a wonderful sport in large part because those people who control the game are determined not to allow it to be trivialized by the selfish strategies of those who play and coach.

In all sports, in all shared activities, the interests of one party are often at odds with the interests of the game itself. If the rules allowed it, some basketball coaches would instruct their players to just dribble around all game, never shooting except free throws. If the other team is better than you are, your best chance to win is with a game of very few possessions. Basketball has developed many ways to prevent coaches from turning basketball games into long exhibitions of dribbling and free throw shooting. There is the shot clock, the half-court line, the closely guarded rule, and the rule that says that we don't shoot the first few fouls in each half, unless the team with the ball is fouled in the act of shooting.

If you go back 50 years in college basketball, you might be amazed at how many rule changes have been added—not rules added to *improve* the game or to dictate the strategy, but rule changes added to *preserve* the game, and to control the extremes of strategic indulgence. Basketball has added the 3-point shot and the 3-seconds in the lane rule to control the degree to which sheer size can dominate over athletic ability. Basketball has amended its goal-tending rule numerous times, limited the number of timeouts allowed and regulated when time can be called, changed the free throws for fouls, changed when fouls are called, changed the rules on when players can step into the lane (after free throws), eliminated shooting from behind the backboard, amended many of the rules governing in-bounds plays, eliminated 99% of the jump balls, adjusted the rules regarding traveling and physical contact during defensive play, instituted an intentional foul rule for the closing minutes of the half, changed the rules on when the clock stops . . . basketball has amended its rules, in the last 50 years, in literally hundreds of ways. The general effect of these rules is not to make the game something new and different, but simply to stop people from using tricks and gimmicks, and force them to play basketball. Most basketball rules changes, like the new rule designed to prevent a player from calling timeout as he is falling out of bounds, are simply a way of saying to the coaches and players, "Stop messing around and play basketball."

In baseball, we don't send that message. We don't send that message, essentially, for two reasons. One is that baseball has wandered into an egalitarian swamp, in which, even when we can see the changes we need, no one has the power to enforce change. Forty years ago, almost all power in baseball was concentrated in the hands of a small group of club owners, and much of that power was loaned, by the club owners, to the Commissioner. In today's baseball we have 30 owners rather than 16. Many of those owners are corporations rather than identifiable individuals, and much of the power which was held by the club owners as a group is now gone. Some of it has gone to the television networks. Some of it has gone to the agents. Some of it has gone to the Player's Union, and to the judges and lawyers who are in effect agents of the union, given the state of American labor law, which does little to protect the weak and powerless but a great deal to protect the organized wealthy. Even if we all agreed on what needed to be done, given the diffusion of power in modern baseball, getting it done would still be very difficult.

But there is another reason why we don't, in baseball, fix the things that obviously need to be fixed. Many of us refuse to see the things, even the obvious things, that need to be corrected. The presumption that baseball is a perfect, self-correcting machine is so strong, in the minds of many, that it creates a gigantic blind spot. There are some rule changes that need to be made in baseball—obvious rules, really, but changes not designed to make baseball into something new and different, but to restore baseball to what it is supposed to be, and to what it was for a hundred years.

More than ten years ago, in the *Baseball Abstract,* I wrote an article about the Kansas City Royals' wonderful announcer, Denny

UNIFORMS OF THE 1990s

The uniforms of the early 90s are typified by the traditionalist trend which began in the mid to late 80s, and coincides with the building boom in new stadiums. It wouldn't look right to go to all the trouble of building modern parks which look like old parks, if the players were decked out in trendy uniforms, would it?

By 1991 only a few teams, namely Cincinnati and St. Louis, retain their double knit pullover style jerseys. Everyone else has button- up jerseys, separate belts, color coded to match the trim, as are the shoes. The jersey fronts are clean and uncluttered with classic styling; most teams have a small sleeve patch. All caps have the team initial or a small symbol at the front. The vast majority of teams use white for the home uniform, with light gray or blue for the road. Eight of the 26 teams have pinstriped uniforms. Gold chains have apparently become a mandatory part of the uniform.

Later in the decade the conservative look still holds, but we can see a few ripples of change. All teams have a dark colored jersey which is paired with light gray or white pants for an extra ensemble at home or on the road. In addition, there seems to be an extra set of jerseys which are worn only during warm-ups and batting practice. These pullover jerseys use a mesh type knit fabric.

One of the new expansion teams, the Florida Marlins, chose a teal color the likes of which have never been seen before in baseball uniforms. It is a good move for a new team. The Colorado Rockies, the only team named after a land formation, went with basic black and white, but also added a new color in their trimwork, purple.

Almost everyone in the 90s wears their pants down to the ankle, showing only a tiny part of the stirrups. A few players of the nineties wear high socks ... George Brett, Darryl Strawberry, Jim Thome, Chipper Jones. Bill says that Norberto Martin gets the award for the highest socks in baseball.

OK, that's about it from your fashion reporter. I wonder how uniforms will have changed if Bill revises this book again in 15–20 years, and I get to continue my conversation with you. Things will change a little around the edges, and there will no doubt be some innovations in equipment, but the basics will remain the same; I think that's what we've learned.

—Susan McCarthy

Mathews. I felt then, and still feel, that Mr. Mathews is one of the most talented men ever to sit down in front of a microphone, and attempt to describe a baseball game. I did, however, find fault with him on one issue. I criticized him, at that time, for complaining about the length of the games.

Mathews sees more major league games than I do, and I have to say, a few years later, that he wasn't wrong. He was just getting there ahead of me. The problem with long baseball games isn't the time they take. The problem is that the wasted time inside baseball games dissipates tension, and thus makes the games less interesting, less exciting, and less fun to watch.

Baseball's poetic and lyrical celebrants are fond of pointing out that baseball is the only major team sport without a clock. What these people don't understand is that, until about 1945, baseball *did* have a clock. It was called the sun. Baseball games, until the advent of night ball, *had* to be crisply played because they often didn't start until late afternoon, and they had to be finished by sundown, and sundown then was an hour sooner than it is now. Umpires, until World War II, were very much in the habit of enforcing a certain degree of attention to time. Umpires who failed to do this effectively were subject to criticism from the press, and were sometimes fined by the league, simply for failing to "move the games along." Even after the coming of night baseball, the *habit* of moving the games along was well established in the population of baseball umpires—in the umpires who pre-dated Night Baseball, many of whom lasted into the 1960s. Their influence, somewhat attenuated, affected the generation of umpires they trained.

Generations of umpires have come and gone since then, and that idea—that the umpire could or should keep the game moving—has largely been lost. Baseball games in the late 1990s consist of an inordinate amount of just messing around. I have six rules changes that I would like to advocate here. Four of those have to do with that problem, the problem of wasted time.

First, baseball needs to adopt a rule limiting the number of times a pitcher can throw to a base. This, like the strategy of letting the air out of the ball in basketball, is a clear situation in which the interests of the game itself are at odds with the interests of one participant. A major league pitcher has a selfish interest in preventing stolen bases against him. Throwing to first base, even throwing to first base repeatedly, is one way to accomplish this.

Incidentally, if you're curious about this, it does work. STATS Inc. keeps records, including

records of every time a pitcher throws to first base. A few years ago, they did a study comparing the stolen base percentages when pitchers threw to first, and the stolen base percentages when they didn't. The conclusion was clear: throwing to first base does reduce the number and the success rate of stolen bases. Throwing repeatedly is more effective than throwing over just once.

The problem is that while throwing to first base may be good strategy, it is lousy entertainment. If the people who wrote baseball's rule book, most of which was basically drawn into its current form in the 1880s and 1890s—if those people had ever thought that some bastard was going to stand on the mound and throw repeatedly to first base, there is absolutely no question but that they would have immediately prohibited it. After all, they *did* limit the number of times that a pitcher can throw home without getting something accomplished. What kind of sense would it make to say that if you can't get the *batter* out within four throws you have to concede, but if you want to make 35 pointless throws to first base, I guess that's OK. The battle between pitcher and batter, after all, was supposed to be the main object.

But the people who wrote the rule book didn't prohibit this, because it simply never occurred to them that it was going to become a problem. It never was a problem, until about 1970. By that time, the stewards of baseball, having inherited a game that they regarded as near perfect, had forgotten that it was, after all, simply *men* who had written the rules. The idea of baseball as a perfect machine, never in need of a little fine tuning, is objectively ridiculous—yet it blinds baseball men to the fact that those long, tedious interludes when pitchers flip the ball repeatedly to first base can be very easily eliminated by a rule that would fit into the game so seamlessly that few people would ever realize that such a rule existed, if it did exist.

That rule would say, very simply, that a team is allowed two unsuccessful throws to the bases in each inning. Two; that's all. If they make a third unsuccessful throw to the bases in any inning, it is counted as a ball. That is all that it would take—just a tiny, lightweight penalty for wasting time. In reality, the rule would hardly ever be applied, because pitchers would virtually never throw three times in any inning.

This rule would have at least three predictable effects. First, throws to the bases would be greatly reduced. Second, the average major league game would be about four minutes shorter. And third, there would be a little bit more base stealing. That's fine. Stolen base attempts are exciting. The rule would give a tiny advantage to a young player who can run, as opposed to an old fat guy who can hit home runs. That's fine, too; baseball is supposed to be played by young guys who can run, rather than old fat guys who can hit home runs. But basically, you'd never know the rule was there, because it would never come into play.

The second rule that I would like to see implemented doesn't actually need a rules change; it just requires a policy directive to the umpires. The policy should be that once the batter gets into the box to hit, time will not be called.

As I suppose most of you know, but most casual fans do not, baseball players cannot call time. Only the umpire can call time. The problem is, the player can *ask* for time, and the umpire will almost always grant the request.

Well, can you imagine the effect it would have on basketball if teams were allowed to call some indefinite number of timeouts? How about allowing one team to call time out while the other team is running a fast break? Would that work? But that is exactly what we do in

baseball—we allow the batter to call time out for the deliberate purpose of disrupting the pitcher's effort.

It is almost always in the interests of the hitter to throw the pitcher off his game; hitting, the cliché has it, is timing, while pitching is disrupting timing...but it works the other way around, too. Inevitably, some players were going to discover this, and begin to exploit it. It is not in either team's interest, in principle, to allow the hitter to disrupt the pitcher by stepping out on him repeatedly while the pitcher is trying to do his work. Allowing this to happen doesn't work to the advantage of the Yankees, as opposed to the Rangers, or to the advantage of the Rangers, as opposed to the Indians, since all the teams do it. It certainly doesn't work to the advantage of the fans. But it does work to the advantage of the hitter, whoever the hitter happens to be at the moment. This is the classic situation calling out for regulation: the situation in which the selfish interest of the player is at odds with the interest of the game itself.

Again, this policy would be virtually invisible if it did exist, because batters would not step out of the box if they were told in advance that the umpire was *not* going to call time. The only thing you would notice is that the games were a lot more exciting than they used to be, because the energy and excitement natural to baseball would not be dissipated by constant interruptions. I don't mean that the umpire couldn't *ever* call time. If a player loses a contact lens, is stung by a bee or chased by a rabid possum, if Morganna runs onto the field or a paper cup blows into the batter's box, we can make an exception. It should be an exception; it shouldn't be the rule.

The third change I advocate also has to do with the time element, and this one is sure to generate comments about my naivete, or something. I would like to see baseball, which now requires two minutes between innings, cut that to 90 seconds.

The criticism that this is naive would be based upon the assumption that, since baseball advertisers sell the time between innings, a reduction of the amount of time available to be sold would mean a reduction in money. The value of anything, including advertising time, depends upon its scarcity. Baseball revenues now are depressed because baseball has more advertising time to sell than advertisers want to buy. Suppose that we met our goals here, that by making the games more urgent, we would increase interest in the broadcast. The result might be 10% less advertising time, over the course of a season, but 10% more people watching the games, which might mean a 30% increase in the number of interested buyers. The result might be a dramatic improvement in the ratio of the supply of advertising time to the demand for that time—improved, in the view of those who are selling the time. It is not self-evident that this would cost baseball money—indeed, it might be considered self-evident, by some people, that whatever makes baseball a better game will, in the long run, result in making more money for those who own the enterprise.

The fourth rules change is a little more subtle. This story starts in the month my wife was born, which was September 1954. Through mid-September 1954, a wire-thin Chicago rookie shortstop named Ernie Banks, playing every game, had hit 12 home runs. With the Cubs season grinding toward the finish, Banks decided to experiment with a very thin-handled bat. Whipping the thin bat through the strike zone, Banks hit 7 home runs in two weeks. He continued using the bat the next season, and hit 44 home runs, a record for a middle infielder.

Sportswriters naturally asked the slightly built Banks about his unexpected power, and Banks naturally explained about the bat. Players had certainly used thin bats before then; bat handles had been getting thinner, before Banks, for sixty years. But this event was, in a sense, the beginning of the modern era in baseball history, the era of the whip-handled bat. Stan Musial had used a thin-handled bat, but Musial used the light bat because it gave him better bat control; sometimes he was able to flick the head of the bat at the ball and pop it into a corner. The power hitters of earlier eras, from Babe Ruth through Hank Sauer, generally figured the heavier the bat, the better. Joe DiMaggio early in some seasons used a 46-ounce bat. Banks approach was different: get a light bat with all the weight in the head, and whip it through the strike zone as hard as you can.

This, of course, is now an almost universal approach: get as light a bat as possible, and swing it as hard as you can swing it with any reasonable chance of making contact. Bats have gotten lighter and lighter, and handles have gotten thinner and thinner. In 1954 all bats were at least 1.2 inches in circumference at the thinnest point. Now, some bats are as thin as .7 inches around. That's the reason they crack so easily and so often. It isn't the wood; it's the fact that the bat handles are so thin.

But while I do not wish to give any player a career crisis, I wonder if that type of offense, based around everybody swinging for the fences, is really the optimal form of the game, as a spectator sport. I would like to propose a rule to turn this around, very gradually. Baseball bats have a maximum length, a maximum weight (which is a joke, because nobody is within eight ounces of the maximum), and a maximum circumference. I think that they also need a minimum weight, and a minimum circumference. The minimum circumference, I would suggest, should start out at .8 inches next year, and should increase by .05 inches every other year, until it reaches 1.3 inches—in other words, until bat handles are back to the shape they had twenty or thirty years ago.

This change, implemented gradually over twenty years, shouldn't throw anyone into a career panic. Its immediate effect would be negligible. But its long-term effect would be offenses based less around bat speed, and more around bat control; less around power, and more around contact. Baseball would still have power hitters, of course, as it always has. But we'd have fewer strikeouts, fewer walks, fewer homers, more hits, more doubles, and more contests between fielders and baserunners. I think that makes a better game. That's the way the game was played for a hundred years, and there's no reason that can't be the way the game is played in the future.

A side benefit of this rule would be that it would become much more feasible to use wooden bats at lower levels of competition. Lower baseball leagues switched from wooden to aluminum bats because of the soaring cost of wooden bats—a problem that was made far worse because the thin-handled bats break so easily. If the handles were thicker the bats wouldn't break, and the cost would be a lot less.

The fifth change also relates to a change in the game brought about by the aluminum bats—more batters crowding the plate, fewer pitchers who can move them off the plate, resulting in an explosion in the rates of hit batsmen.

I would like to see the batter's box moved back from home plate, eventually, by about four inches. Again, this could be phased in over a period of years to insure that no one's career would be thrown into a tailspin; you could move the batter's box back one inch every four years until it is back four inches.

Again, this would be an invisible change to the fan, even to the hitter; you'd have to be Ted Williams to notice that the batter's box had moved an inch. Most hitters don't stand in the front four inches of the box, and even hitters who do like to crowd the plate sometimes step back a few inches. The effect on any one hitter would be almost inconsequential.

But if you back the hitter off a few inches, you make it a lot harder to hit the outside pitch into the seats. You make it a little bit harder to pull the fastball in the middle of the plate. The result would be fewer home runs, a great many fewer hit batsmen, and thus we would, once again, be encouraging hitters to make contact and run, rather than swing for the seats and walk. We would also reduce injuries, since broken hands and fingers sometimes result from being hit with the pitch.

Finally, I would like to see a rule limiting mid-inning pitching changes. Baseball men have known at least since the late 1870s that right-handed hitters hit better against left-handed pitchers, and vice versa. Leo Durocher in the 1940s was the first manager to feel that it was important to keep a left-hander in the bullpen to get out left-handed hitters.

But what started out as a strategy has evolved into something more like an obsession. The number of relievers used per game has increased by more than 50% since the mid-1980s. Since pinch hitting is *not* increasing (it is decreasing), it seems obvious that almost all of those additional pitching changes are now made inside the inning, between hitters. Almost all of the increase has also occurred in the late innings of close games, at the time when baseball is supposed to be most exciting. This constant shifting of relief pitchers, unheard of a generation ago, has profoundly changed the experience of watching a closely contested baseball game.

Now, as an aside, this not only is not optimal entertainment; it's also not optimal strategy. I think that this hundred-year trend may well reverse itself in the next twenty years, simply because what the managers are doing now, shuttling relievers in and out at the drop of a resin bag, doesn't make any sense. Managers are pursuing a percentage that they cannot possibly catch.

But what is more important it's irritating to watch. It *isn't* entertaining. I am sure that a few of the purists will argue that I want to sacrifice strategy for action, but I doubt that this is true. Limiting a manager's options does not reduce strategy. If chess adopted a rule that pawns could move backward as well as forward, would this increase strategy in chess? Of course not. Increasing options does not, in itself, increase strategy, and decreasing options does not decrease strategy. I simply want to say to the managers, as I want to say to the hitters and to the pitchers, Stop Messing Around and Play Baseball.

My proposed rule would say that each team is allowed to change pitchers in mid-inning:

    a. Once a game.
    b. After the pitcher on the mound has given up at least one run in the inning.

In other words, a manager cannot repeatedly stop the action to shuffle a new pitcher into the game. He's got one free move a game, and he can remove a pitcher who is getting hit. But making two, three, even four pitching changes in the last two innings of the game to get the matchups he wants—no. It's rude to the fans to make them sit through this.

What I am really arguing for, of course, is taking control of baseball, to the extent that we can. I am talking about making baseball back into what it was, by taking positive action to control the game's aimless drifting. If all of these rules were adopted this winter, but were not announced to the public, you would notice immediately that the games were quicker, more focused, and more exciting, but you would have the devil's own time figuring out what had actually changed. All of the rule changes advocated here would be almost completely invisible.

Baseball was *not* designed by the Gods; it was designed by men who wanted to create a marketable sports entertainment. We have paid a high price for forgetting that.

Part of the price is that baseball men have the sense that something is amiss, but propose the crudest and most heavy-handed remedies for what are, in reality, simple problems. The Designated Hitter Rule is a good example. Proposals to put a clock on the pitcher and time him between pitches, ham-fisted efforts to tinker with the balk rules, and incessant arguing about the shape of the strike zone are, to me, symbols of how poorly understood baseball's maladies really are. The people who make these kind of proposals believe fundamentally that baseball is a boring game which needs to be jazzed up for the next century. We don't *need* to take dramatic, flashy actions to change baseball into something new and different. We need to take quiet, gauze-thin actions designed to tell the participants to stop messing around and play baseball. This is understood by the men who run the NFL; it is understood by the men who run college basketball. It is not understood by the men who run baseball. If we'll just do that much, or that little, we can show younger fans how exciting baseball is supposed to be.

LET'S NOT GO THERE

The home run era has been fun. I think a consensus has developed among baseball people that it is beginning to grow tiresome, and that something will soon need to be done to make baseball look more like baseball. Among the suggestions most often made are to restore the balance between hitting and pitching by:

    a. Expanding the strike zone.
    b. Raising the mound.

I think that these suggestions are poorly considered, and would not improve the game as spectator sport.

Why? Because what these remedies would create is more strikeouts. Expand the strike zone, raise the mound, legalize the spitball, and you've got more strikeouts. Strikeouts are already at an all-time high; we don't need any more of them. We take these kind of steps, Randy Johnson is going to strike out 400, maybe 450 batters.

Look, baseball *now* is a game of .300 hitters who hit 50 homers, and .260 hitters who hit 40 homers. If you raise the mound, what you're going to have is a game of .260 hitters who hit 40 homers and .220 hitters who hit 30 homers. In other words, you're going to trade the .300 hitters who hit 50 homers for .220 hitters who hit 30 homers. That is not what we need.

We need gentle adjustments. More strikeouts is a harsh adjustment. We need to make it easier to put together a series of singles and doubles. And to do that, we need fewer strikeouts, not more.

I would be in favor of deadening the baseball a little bit. The people who buy the baseballs insist that they test the resiliency of the baseballs all the time, but what I don't understand is, if you test the baseballs all the time and the resiliency of the baseballs is a problem, then why don't you fix it? Are you just testing them so that you can keep insisting that it isn't a problem?

I didn't list that in the "Rules" article, because the resiliency of the balls isn't specified in the rules. But if we decided to tame the hitters a little bit, it would be a lot easier and lot less dangerous just to deaden the baseballs a tiny bit than it would be to start messing around with the height of the mound (which requires that pitchers and hitters re-learn their job) or with the strike zone (which would require that we re-educate the umpires).

THE TENTH WAR

In a baseball history there have been two kinds of wars—wars between owners and players, and wars between rival leagues or groups of teams. These two occur in intermingled time periods—that is, times of labor/management tension tend also to be times of battles between teams and leagues, and vice versa. When a new league starts up, that pushes salaries up, which causes player/management tension. Or, if it starts with labor action, higher salaries tend to put pressure on teams, which causes splits among teams ... anyway, I thought maybe it would help clarify the discussion if we designated these periods of strife as "wars," and laid out a chronology of them in the simplest possible terms:

1. The Founding Revolution
   Year: 1876
   Combatants: Owners vs. Players
   Won By: Owners
   Resulting In: National League Replacing National Association

2. The First Association Skirmish
   Years: 1882–83
   Combatants: National League vs. American Association
   Won By: American Association
   Resulting In: Two-League System

3. The Union Association Incident
   Year: 1884
   Combatants: Union Association vs. Existing Two Leagues
   Won By: Existing Leagues
   Resulting In: Continuation of the Two-League System

4. The Players Association War (Baseball's World War I)
   Year: 1890
   Combatants: Existing Leagues vs. the Player's Association
   Won By: Existing Leagues
   Resulting In: Collapse of the Player's Association

5. The Second Association Skirmish
   Year: 1891
   Combatants: National League vs. American Association
   Won By: National League
   Resulting In: Death of the American Association
   (Basically a Coup d'etat. National League persuaded some of the American Association owners to stab the rest of them in the back, resulting in the sudden collapse of the Association.)

6. The American League War
   Years: 1901–1903
   Combatants: National League vs. American League
   Won By: American League
   Resulting In: Restoration of the Two-League System

7. The Federal League Insurgency
   Years: 1914–1915
   Combatants: Federal League and Players Brotherhood vs. Existing Two Leagues
   Won By: Existing Two Leagues
   Resulting In: Continuation of the Two-League System, Death of the Brotherhood and the Federal League, Baseball's exemption from anti-trust law

8. The '72 Affair (The First New Union Battle)
   Year: 1972
   Combatants: Players vs. Management
   Won By: Players
   Resulting In: Acceptance of the Players' Association

9. The Free Agency War
   Year: 1981
   Combatants: Players vs. Management
   Won By: Players
   Resulting In: Acceptance of Arbitration and Free Agency Rights

10. The TV Money War (Baseball's Second World War)

Years: 1994–95
Combatants: Players vs. Management and Small Cities vs. Large Cities
Won By: Players and Large Cities
Resulting In: Leagues Dividing into Rich Teams and Poor Teams

I've left out a whole lot of things, like the Owner's Collusion (1987), the Messersmith Case (1975), the battles that surrounded the coming of the Commissioner System (1921–22), and the battles to seize the minor leagues (1910–1925). You are thus entitled to ask what constitutes a "War," since I left out so many battles. The answer is, it's a War if it changes the schedule. If it's guys fighting over money or power, that's business as usual. If games are cancelled or teams die, that's a War.

Anyway, the point I wanted to make . . . The 1994–95 strike got as ugly as it did, in part, because it was not a clean two-sided confrontation, as the previous two wars had been. Baseball Wars alternate between player/management battles, and team vs. team battles. For years, the structure of the contests has been management on one side, players on the other. We've been fighting that way for thirty years, so going into the Tenth War, team owners concentrated on building solidarity among the teams.

But this strategy was doomed to fail, and doomed to fail at a high cost, because *the natural opponents here were not teams and players*. It was a three-sided war: players, small city teams, and large city teams. A strategy based upon keeping two of the natural antagonists together was not going to work.

The 1994–95 strike may be seen, in retrospect, as a turning point. It may have marked the end of the player/management battles which pre-occupied baseball for thirty years— and the beginning of the battles between big city teams and small city teams.

THE BATTLE TO GET TO THE OBVIOUS

The two biggest problems in baseball today are:

1. The fact that nobody is driving the vehicle.

2. The extreme inequality of income between teams.

I try very hard not to rip baseball, but certainly anyone can see that serious things are wrong with the game today, as a commercial entertainment. This business of selling everything you can find to the highest bidder, selling the name of your stadium, selling every camera angle, selling the moment in the broadcast after a player hits a home run . . . maybe it's just me, but I think that's just repeatedly slapping the paying customer in the face with a shoestring.

I could list twenty more flaws in the game, but the basic problem is that many of these specific problems have obvious solutions—but there is no central authority, and thus there is no way to implement the obvious solution.

And I honestly don't have any idea what to do about that. Power is spread all over the map; how do you unify power, in a democracy, without a crisis? I don't think you can. Eventually, major league baseball will face a true crisis, a crisis being defined as something which threatens the continued existence of the enterprise. When that happens, everything will change; people will give up their power to stay alive. But until that happens, I think that baseball will continue to wander all over the road, sideswiping bad ideas, because the controls are broken, and nobody's driving the car.

The solution to the second problem, income equality, on the other hand, is mind-numbingly obvious. The natural rule governing television rights would be that when the New York Yankees and the Minnesota Twins play a baseball game, and the rights to that baseball game are sold to television, both teams should share in the profits of the sale. That's just common sense, isn't it? This isn't a hard concept that I'm explaining here, I don't think.

The essence of the economic problem in baseball is that we have accidentally constructed a situation in which this is not true. Now, I want to stress this: I am not talking about revenue sharing. Revenue Sharing is a peculiar proposal under which the New York Yankees should take some of their money, which they have earned, and give it to the other teams. That has nothing to do with what I am suggesting. I am talking about legal ownership of the television rights.

The leagues have been operating on a set of explicit or implied agreements which were constructed many years ago, and the full implications of which were not thought through. These agreements were constructed on the assumption that *those* revenues—"local" broadcast revenues—would be only a tiny fraction of each team's income. But what happens if that revenue stream swells so that it becomes larger than the team's "central" or basic revenue? The people who set up the policies under which the leagues operate never anticipated that, and constructed an arrangement which doesn't work under those conditions.

Well, that's not unusual; those sorts of things happen all the time in business. What you do is, if you can't live with the arrangement, you renegotiate. You don't assume, if you want to survive, that you are bound in perpetuity by an agreement that was made 60 years ago.

What is needed here just couldn't possibly be any more obvious. We need to apply the natural rule. The natural rule says that when the New York Yankees and the Minnesota Twins play a baseball game and the broadcast rights to that game are sold to television, both teams share equally in those proceeds. It's that's simple: you sell the rights, each team gets half the money.

The team's half of the money, they keep for themselves; the other team's half, they put into a pool which is shared equally by all of the teams in the league. If the New York Yankees sign a cable television deal for $500 million, they put $250 million in the bank, and the other $250 million goes to the league.

This would not wipe out the disparity in TV income. The Twins or the Kansas City Royals would get one share of the league pot, plus half of maybe ten million dollars. The Yankees would get one share of the league pot, plus half of $500 million. But this would mean that the disparity in cable TV income would be about 3 to 1, rather than 50 to 1. The Yankees are still going to have an advantage—but not such a large advantage that the Minnesota Twins can't compete, if they're smart.

I've had people tell me that this is a pipe dream, because the New York Yankees will never agree to re-structure the deal. But what those people are not thinking about is what happens if the Minnesota Twins simply refuse to play the Yankees? What happens if the Minnesota Twins, the Kansas City Royals, the Oakland A's, the Detroit Tigers, and the Tampa Bay Septuagenarians all get together and say,

"Look, we're not coming. You've got a $500 million cable TV deal; good luck to you. I hope you can find somebody to play, but if we don't get half the money for our games, there ain't no New York Yankees on our schedule."

The small-city teams have acted for fifteen years as the powerless victims of baseball economics. But in reality, the small city teams *have* power; they simply lack the courage to use it. Eventually, desperation will make them brave.

The 1994–95 strike was a missed opportunity to address this problem. The opportunity was missed because the focus of the major league owners was:

    a. Keeping *unity* in the management ranks.

    b. Winning one from those damned players.

But that was a mistake, because there was no place, within that structure, to address the real issue, which was the income disparity between the rich and poor teams.

Baseball teams are acting like they have a huge, impossible problem with the TV money. In reality, at least as I see reality, it's obvious what the solution is, and it's obvious how you get there. And that's how it will work itself out, because eventually, nature discovers the obvious solution.

PART 2

PLAYER RATINGS AND COMMENTS

INTRODUCTION TO THE PLAYER RATINGS

There are three things that I need to discuss before I can explain how I arrived at the player ratings which appear throughout this section. Those three things are:

1. Runs Created.
2. Win Shares.
3. The Meaning of Statistics.

Those three things will be the next three articles, after which we will get to:

4. The Ratings System Used Here.
5. Clutch Performance.
6. Win-Based Analysis of Fielding.

RUNS CREATED

A hitter's job is not to compile a high batting average. A hitter's job is not to maintain a high on-base percentage, not to create a high slugging percentage, not to get 200 hits. A hitter's job is not to hit home runs. *Some* hitters might hit home runs as the primary part of their job, but only some hitters, and even those only some of the time; with a runner on second and two out, no manager wants any hitter up there looking for a home run.

Hitting home runs is *part* of a hitter's job, hitting doubles is part of the job, getting on base is part of the job, driving in runs is part of the job, hitting singles is part of the job, stealing bases is part of the job—but what IS the job itself?

The job itself is to create runs. That is what all hitters are trying to do in every plate appearance: they are trying to create runs. The essential measure of a hitter's success is how many runs he has created.

Well then, how do we know how many runs a player has created?

There is a very simple formula which will answer that question quite well 90% of the time. The formula is:

Hits Plus Walks

Times Total Bases

Divided by (At Bats Plus Walks)

If you run this formula for any team since 1920, it will almost always give you a total within 5% of the team's actual runs scored. In 1999 every major league team scored within 5% of the number of runs projected by this formula (although this is unusual; normally three or four teams will wander off for one reason or another). Anyway, you can make a pretty good estimate of how many runs a hitter has created by simply adding together his hits and walks, multiplying by his total bases, and dividing by his (at bats plus walks).

However, if "pretty good" isn't good enough, there are four things you can do to make the estimate more accurate. Those are:

1. Sweat the small stuff.

2. Place the estimate in a team context.

3. Adjust for situational data where it exists.

4. Reconcile the estimates to the runs actually scored by the team.

1. *Sweating the small stuff.* The basic runs created formula doesn't include stolen bases, caught stealing, hit by pitch, grounding into double plays, sacrifice hits, sacrifice flies, or strikeouts. You can make the formula more accurate by building in adjustments for these events.

2. *Placing the estimates in a team context.* One problem with the basic runs created formula as applied to an individual is that it implicitly assumes that the elements of the hitter's offensive contribution are interacting with one another. Suppose that you have two pairs of two hitters. Each pair consists of two players who have 400 (at bats plus walks) apiece, but in the first pair, each player has 150 total bases and 150 (hits plus walks). In the second pair, one player has 100 total bases and 100 (hits plus walks), while the other has 200 of each.

Figured as teams, these two pairs are the same. Figured as individuals, they're different; the first pair creates 112.5 runs (56.25 + 56.25), and the second pair 125 (25 + 100). This is illogical. Or another example ... suppose you have two players who steal ten bases apiece, but one of them is a good hitter, the other is a poor hitter. The individual runs created formula will show that the good hitter is creating more runs by his ten stolen bases than the poor hitter, because the good hitter's stolen bases will have a larger multiplier in the hitter's batting stats. This is illogical.

We fixed this by, in essence, creating a "typical" team, figuring how many runs that team would create WITH this hitter, figuring how many runs they would create WITHOUT this hitter, and subtracting one from the other. This eliminates the problem of the hitter's run elements inter-acting with one another.

3. *Adjusting for situational data where it exists.* A company I work with, STATS Inc., has scored every major league game since 1984, creating a substantial data base of batting averages with runners in scoring position and other "situational" stats. Two items from the situational data base can be easily shown to influence the number of runs a team will score: their batting average with runners in scoring position, and their home runs with men on

base (as opposed to the bases empty). For this reason, we adjust our runs created estimates for this data, where it does exist.

4. *Correcting estimates on the team level.* We figure runs created for all the individuals on each team, and total those up. If the total is too high or too low, we adjust it. If a team scores 760 runs but the individuals on the team have 800 estimated runs created, then we reduce everybody's runs created by 5%, so that the runs created by individuals on the team are the same as the team runs scored total.

Runs Created for every individual season in baseball history are presented in the *All-Time Handbook,* from STATS, Inc., if you're interested. *Total Baseball* in the past has printed my runs created estimates as well . . . I don't know if they're going to embrace the new formulas or not. They're welcome to, anyway; it's up to them.

Not everybody has reacted well to the recent amendments to the Runs Created formula, and I fault myself for this; I'm sure I haven't done a good job of explaining why the changes were made. The purpose of a runs created formula is to estimate as accurately as possible how many runs a player has created. When better data becomes available, we use it. If the runs created estimates for a team total up to 700 and the team has actually scored only 680 runs, then our estimates are wrong, and we should fix them as best we can.

But isn't it possible, someone wonders, that on this team that has 700 runs created and only 680 scored, some players have actually created MORE runs than our estimates show? Of course it's possible; in fact, it's inevitable. We're not making the estimates *perfect;* we're only making them *better.* If a team scores 680 runs but has 700 runs created, we know that the average player on this team is 2.9% less productive than our best estimate shows. If we reduce all

of the estimates by 2.9%, we will be making some of them more accurate and some of them less accurate. What we can be absolutely certain of is that those we are making better outnumber those that we are making worse.

Searching for better runs created methods is an evolving process, and I'm not saying this is the last step. This is just where we are right now.

THE WIN SHARES SYSTEM

For many years, I have wanted to have a system which summarizes each player's value each season into a simple integer. Willie Mays' value in 1954 is $40, in 1955, $40, in 1956, $27, while Mickey Mantle in the same three years is $36, $41, $49. If we had an analytical system *in which we had confidence,* and which delivered results in that simple a form, it would open the door to researching thousands of questions which are virtually inaccessible without such a method. It would reduce enormously the time and effort required to research other questions, which can be accessed by other methods, but only with great difficulty.

This book was two years late getting to the publisher, because I finally figured out how to make that work. Three years ago—November, 1997—I had a conceptual breakthrough on this problem, which I realized would enable me to make those simple integer values for all players. But this created a problem, to wit: this section of the book.

From mid-1993 through summer of 1996, I had drawn up lists of the 100 best players at each position. It was a lot of fun; I messed around with it an hour or two in the evenings for three years. I enjoyed doing it, and I intended to make those lists the basis of Part 2 of this book, the Player Ratings Section. But realizing that I was on the verge of having a Values System that actually worked, this created a problem with what I would be telling you, my reader. On the one hand, I would be telling you in this book how I rated the top 100 players in baseball history and the top 100 at each position—and one year later I would be coming out with another book *(Win Shares)* which presented a statistical method to do the same thing. In other words, I would be saying to you, in July of 2001, "Forget what I said last year; this is how the players really rate. I've figured it out now." I couldn't do that; I had to unify the two. And that meant that I had to hold off on the new *Historical Abstract* until the research for the other book, *Win Shares,* was essentially done.

The conceptual breakthrough was this. Suppose that there were a league in which the average team scored and allowed 662 runs in a 154-game season, and in which the runs scored and allowed by each team were as follows:

Team	R	OR
St. Louis	772	490
Pittsburgh	744	662
Cincinnati	573	537
Chicago	702	669
New York	682	773
Boston	593	674
Brooklyn	690	832
Philadelphia	539	658

What would be the won-lost record of each team?

We know how to answer that, right? The won-lost record of each team will be about the same as the ratio between the square of their runs scored, and the square of their runs allowed. This calculation would produce won-lost records as follows:

Team	R	OR	Won-Lost
St. Louis	772	490	110–44
Pittsburgh	744	662	86–68
Cincinnati	573	537	82–72
Chicago	702	669	81–73
New York	682	773	67–87
Boston	593	674	67–87
Brooklyn	690	832	63–91
Philadelphia	539	658	62–92

And, in fact, that is pretty much how the league worked out. This is the data for the National League in 1944, the actual won-lost records for which were:

Team	R	OR	Won-Lost
St. Louis	772	490	105–49
Pittsburgh	744	662	90–63
Cincinnati	573	537	89–65
Chicago	702	669	75–79
New York	682	773	67–87
Boston	593	674	65–89
Brooklyn	690	832	63–91
Philadelphia	539	658	61–92

What I realized, in November of 1997, is that there is a second way to project won-lost records, based on the runs scored and allowed, which is of almost the same accuracy as the Pythagorean projection.

The second method is to focus on the marginal runs scored by each team. A marginal run is defined as any run scored by the team in excess of one-half the league average, or any run prevented (not allowed) by the team below the level of 1.5 times the league average. Since the National League average in 1944 was 662 runs, the marginal runs *scored* by these teams were all runs scored above 331:

Team	MR
St. Louis	441
Pittsburgh	413
Cincinnati	242
Chicago	371
New York	351
Boston	262
Brooklyn	359
Philadelphia	208

The marginal runs saved are calculated, for this league, by subtracting runs allowed from 993:

Team	MR	MRS
St. Louis	441	503
Pittsburgh	413	331
Cincinnati	242	456
Chicago	371	324
New York	351	220
Boston	262	319
Brooklyn	359	161
Philadelphia	208	335

Adding together the Marginal Runs Scored and the Marginal Runs Saved, we have Total Marginal Runs:

Team	MR	MRS	Total
St. Louis	441	503	944
Pittsburgh	413	331	744
Cincinnati	242	456	698
Chicago	371	324	695
New York	351	220	571
Boston	262	319	581
Brooklyn	359	161	520
Philadelphia	208	335	543

You can project each team's winning percentage by dividing the total by twice the league average of runs scored—1324 in this case. This produces expected winning percentages, for this league, as follows:

Team	MR	MRS	Total	Pct
St. Louis	441	503	944	.713
Pittsburgh	413	331	744	.562
Cincinnati	242	456	698	.527
Chicago	371	324	695	.525
New York	351	220	571	.431
Boston	262	319	581	.439
Brooklyn	359	161	520	.393
Philadelphia	208	335	543	.410

Which creates expected won-lost records as follows:

Team	Won–Lost	Pct
St. Louis	110–44	.713
Pittsburgh	87–67	.562
Cincinnati	81–73	.527
Chicago	81–73	.525
New York	66–88	.431
Boston	68–86	.439
Brooklyn	60–94	.393
Philadelphia	63–91	.410

Compared to the actual won-lost records, as follows:

Team	Projected Won–Lost	Actual Won–Lost
St. Louis	110–44	105–49
Pittsburgh	87–67	90–63
Cincinnati	81–73	89–65
Chicago	81–73	75–79
New York	66–88	67–87
Boston	68–86	65–89
Brooklyn	60–94	63–91
Philadelphia	63–91	61–92

I haven't put in park effects here, and I'll trust you to figure those out. This alternative system of projecting won-lost records, even with park adjustments, is not *quite* as accurate as the Pythagorean system; it has very near the same accuracy, but not quite. But this way of projecting team won-lost records has two tremendous advantages on the Pythagorean method, one of which is so obvious that I suspect that many of you have already spotted it.

The first advantage of projecting won-lost records from marginal runs is that *we can easily figure the marginal runs contributed by each player.* In other words, since we can figure how many runs have been created by each player, since we can easily remove the "sub-marginal" runs, and since we know what the ratio of marginal runs to wins is for each team, we can put these together so as to see how many games have been "won" by each individual hitter. Since the runs saved by each pitcher can be figured by the same method as the runs saved by a team, wins can be easily attributed to individual pitchers. This enables us to take Runs Created one step further, and to figure, in essence, Wins Created.

The second advantage is that *the ratio of marginal runs to team wins is the same on a good team as it is on a bad team.* The best team in this league, the Cardinals, has 944 marginal runs, 105 wins, a ratio of nine to one. The worst team in the league, the Phillies, has 543 marginal runs, 61 wins—again, a nine to one ratio. This is normally true; the ratio of team wins to marginal runs does not vary with the quality of the team (except in unusually extreme cases). If it did, the won-lost projections would be off. And that means that a player contributing 30 marginal runs to a bad team will rate just the same as a player contributing 30 marginal runs to a good team. A player hitting .300 with 15 homers on a bad team will rate just the same,

other things being equal, as a player hitting .300 with 15 homers on a good team—an essential element of a fair rating system.

This realization is the basis of the Win Shares method. A Win Share is simply one-third of a win, equivalent to approximately three marginal runs at normal levels of offense. For such a system to be useful, for it to be adopted by baseball researchers, it must pass at least eight tests of fairness:

1. It must deal fairly with pitchers and position players.

2. It must be fair to hitters, and to glove men.

3. It must be fair to starters, and to relievers.

4. It must be fair to players who play in big-hitting eras, like 1894, 1930, and the 1990s, and to players who play in pitching eras like 1906 and 1968. It must be fair, specifically, to PITCHERS in big-hitting eras, and to hitters in pitching-dominated eras.

5. It must be fair to players who play on good teams, and players who play on bad teams.

6. It must be fair to infielders and outfielders, to catchers and to shortstops and to designated hitters.

7. It must be fair to part-time players who play well, but it must also be fair to ordinary players who play well enough to keep their jobs.

8. For careers, it must be fair to players who have 4,000-at bat careers, and it must be fair to players who have 10,000-at bat careers.

There are probably many others like that. The system has to be fair to power hitters and .300 hitters, it has to be fair to fast guys and slow guys, etc. Those aren't too problematic, because we've been studying offenses for many years, and there is a solid consensus about how to evaluate hitters, with some issues still in dispute.

	1950	51	52	53	54	55	56	57	58	59	60	61	62	63	64	65	Total
Chicago	5	22	22	21	25	25	19	31	22	30	20	11	16	12	13	1	295
Philadelphia	5	8	8	4	3												28

If the system fails any of these eight tests, that limits its use. The Linear Weights method, largely successful on points 1-6 above, is limited because it fails the seventh and eighth tests, which relate to differences in playing time.

Anyway, evaluating hitters is something we've worked on for a long time, and evaluating pitchers is relatively easy. What's hard is three things:

1. Fielding.
2. Relief pitching.
3. Being fair to players on bad teams, and players on good teams.

This system eliminated the third problem. To get from the revelation to the point at which I had actual Win Shares for each player in major league history in each season was more than a year's work. There were a million small problems to be solved, and two big problems, which were how to handle fielding, and how to assess the value of a relief pitcher. A full explanation of the Win Shares system, as well as Win Shares for every player in every season, can be found in a book published (essentially) simultaneously with this one, *Win Shares,* from STATS, Inc.

There are many things that you can do with *Win Shares,* other than compare players. You can evaluate trades. On October 19, 1949, the Philadelphia Athletics traded Nellie Fox to the Chicago White Sox for Joe Tipton. The trade can be "scored" by counting all career Win Shares after the trade for Nellie Fox to the credit of the White Sox, and all those for Tipton to the credit of Philadelphia. This produces the results shown in the table at the top of this page.

Chicago won the trade, 295 to 28—obvious, but recognizing the obvious is the first test that

a method must pass. As an aside, the Win Shares system does see Fox as being the Most Valuable Player in the American League in 1959, when Fox won the MVP Award, whereas the Linear Weights system does not see him as being among the five best players in the league in that season. But both systems agree that 1959 was not his best season; he was even better in 1957, although in 1957 he was nowhere near the level of the 1957 MVP, Mickey Mantle.

A 30-Win Share season is, in general, an MVP candidate-type season. People have won MVP Awards with less; people have failed to win MVP awards with 40 Win Shares. But when a player gets to 30 in an ordinary season, he's probably going to be visible in the MVP voting.

Anyway, if we can evaluate a trade, then we can evaluate trading *strategies.* When teams trade an outfielder for a pitcher of the same age, who usually wins? Making good trades is less important now than it was thirty years ago, but the same type of analysis can be done with the amateur free agent draft. In 1990 the first round of the draft went like this:

1.	Atlanta	Chipper Jones
2.	Detroit	Tony Clark
3.	Philadelphia	Mike Lieberthal
4.	White Sox	Alex Fernandez
5.	Pittsburgh	Kurt Miller
6.	Seattle	Mark Newfield
7.	Cincinnati	Dan Wilson
8.	Cleveland	Tim Costo
9.	Los Angeles	Ron Walden
10.	Yankees	Carl Everett
11.	Montreal	Shane Andrews
12.	Minnesota	Todd Ritchie

13. St. Louis   Donovan Osborne
14. Oakland   Todd Van Poppel
15. San Francisco   Adam Hyzdu
16. Texas   Dan Smith
17. Mets   Jeromy Burnitz
18. St. Louis   Aaron Holbert
19. Giants   Eric Christopherson
20. Baltimore   Mike Mussina
21. Houston   Tom Nevers
22. Toronto   Steve Karsay
23. Cubs   Lance Dickson
24. Montreal   Rondell White
25. San Diego   Robbie Beckett
26. Oakland   Don Peters

This is one of the best first rounds in the history of the draft. Chipper Jones played in the major leagues in 1993, but didn't earn a Win Share until 1995, but since then has earned almost a hundred major league Win Shares:

Rank	Team	Player	1990	91	92	93	94	95	96	97	98	99	2000	Total
1.	Atlanta	Chipper Jones	—	—	—	0	—	20	26	22	29	34	25	156

He ranks ahead of Tony Clark, but Clark has also become a good major league player:

Rank	Team	Player	1990	91	92	93	94	95	96	97	98	99	2000	Total
1.	Atlanta	Chipper Jones	—	—	—	0	—	20	26	22	29	34	25	156
2.	Detroit	Tony Clark	—	—	—	—	—	2	8	24	15	19	5	73

The fourth pick in the draft, Alex Fernandez, paid off quicker but got hurt, and Jones will eventually be worth far more:

Rank	Team	Player	1990	91	92	93	94	95	96	97	98	99	2000	Total
1.	Atlanta	Chipper Jones	—	—	—	0	—	20	26	22	29	34	25	156
2.	Detroit	Tony Clark	—	—	—	—	—	2	8	24	15	19	5	73
4.	White Sox	Alex Fernandez	5	7	6	20	11	12	19	16	—	10	4	110

You may note that Fernandez' Win Shares pretty much track his actual Wins, as credited by the official stats:

		1990	91	92	93	94	95	96	97	98	99	2000	Total
Alex Fernandez	Win shares	5	7	6	20	11	12	19	16	—	10	4	110
Alex Fernandez	Actual wins	5	9	8	18	11	12	16	17	—	7	7	100

Rarely is the relationship this close, but most pitchers in most seasons, and in their careers, will have about the same number of Win Shares as they do Wins. There are many exceptions to this, but in general, a season of 20 Win Shares may be seen as comparable in value to a 20-win season. More on that later.

Anyway, in this way, we could "score" the entire draft. Through 2000, the first round of the 1990 draft would score like this:

			Value
1.	Atlanta	Chipper Jones	156
2.	Detroit	Tony Clark	73
3.	Philadelphia	Mike Lieberthal	61
4.	White Sox	Alex Fernandez	110
5.	Pittsburgh	Kurt Miller	1
6.	Seattle	Mark Newfield	16
7.	Cincinnati	Dan Wilson	77
8.	Cleveland	Tim Costo	1
9.	Los Angeles	Ron Walden	0
10.	Yankees	Carl Everett	88
11.	Montreal	Shane Andrews	39
12.	Minnesota	Todd Ritchie	25
13.	St. Louis	Donovan Osborne	42
14.	Oakland	Todd Van Poppel	17
15.	San Francisco	Adam Hyzdu	0
16.	Texas	Dan Smith	2
17.	Mets	Jeromy Burnitz	90
18.	St. Louis	Aaron Holbert	0
19.	Giants	Eric Christopherson	0
20.	Baltimore	Mike Mussina	161
21.	Houston	Tom Nevers	0
22.	Toronto	Steve Karsay	29
23.	Cubs	Lance Dickson	0
24.	Montreal	Rondell White	94
25.	San Diego	Robbie Beckett	0
26.	Oakland	Don Peters	0

If you can "score" a draft accurately, then you're in a position to evaluate drafting *strategies*. What is the payoff rate for players drafted out of high school, as opposed to those drafted out of college? How long does it take a high-school draft pick to pay off, as opposed to a college pick? What is the payoff rate for a draft pick invested in a pitcher, as opposed to a position player? Is there a difference between an infielder and an outfielder? Is there a difference between the payoff rates of players drafted from the south, and those drafted from other parts of the country?

What is the inherent value of a given draft pick? How much more valuable is a #1 draft pick, as compared to a #2 draft pick?

This is just one of many areas which could be studied, using this method. One could use it to analyze the salary structure, pegging the appropriate salary for each player. We could use it to evaluate agents. Compare two players who have the same or essentially the same value pattern. Who got more money? The one with the better agent.

One could use such a system to measure *consistency,* which is a hard thing to measure without a value clamp. One could use such a system to evaluate the role of racial prejudice in award voting, if there is such an impact.

One could use such a system to analyze aging, in hundreds of ways. If you have a 28-year-old slugging outfielder and a 28-year-old defense-first infielder of the same value, which is likely to be of more value in three years? Is there a difference in the value pattern of a right-handed pitcher versus a left-handed pitcher? A starter versus a reliever? A power pitcher versus a control pitcher?

One could use such a system to determine whether players today age differently than players of 20, 30, or 70 years ago. Forming groups of hundreds of players, one can assess aging patterns within the group by simply adding together the values. One could help evaluate the future of any player, a free agent at the current time, by forming a group of players with the same characteristics, and adding up the season values.

One could use such a system to try to understand the role of the farm system in producing pennant winners in modern baseball, where the players produced are normally retained by the system for only a few years. Evaluating farm system production over a period of years becomes not a matter of opinion, but a subject capable of objective analysis.

In the past I have advocated a method, called the Value Approximation Method, which could be used to analyze the same type of questions. But the Value Approximation Method was ultimately undermined by the lack of logic behind it. The system consisted of arbitrary cutoffs. If a player hit 20 homers, that was a point; if he didn't, that was no point. I argued at the time that the utility of the output was such that we should accept the approximate nature of the value-numbers themselves, because we weren't interested in the value-numbers themselves, but in the conclusions which could be reached by forming groups of seasons. One player's approximation might be a little low, another's a little high, but when you are dealing with *groups* of seasons, that doesn't matter. We're not interested in whether Orlando Cepeda in 1960 should be at 17 or 21; we're interested in all of the groups to which Cepeda contributed— San Francisco Giants, 23-year-old superstars, players from Puerto Rico, first basemen, right-handed sluggers, etc.

The Value Approximation Method fell by the wayside for two reasons. One problem was that, whether or not people *should* be willing to accept the approximate nature of the season-value estimates, some people weren't. Some people, long in the habit of focusing on season ratings as end products in and of themselves, were unwilling to make use of a system which delivered only *approximate* numbers on that level, for the purpose of moving beyond that level. And, of course, when you're figuring salaries, you really can't have approximations; you need an accurate measure.

The other problem was that while the Value Approximation Method was conceptually simple, the Book of Values didn't actually exist. I always wanted to have a volume which contained the approximate values for every major league player every year, but I never actually did. Since the values didn't exist, then in order to study anything involving hundreds of seasons, one had to start by figuring the approximate values for hundreds of seasons. The sheer work involved in using it limited its value.

But among the uses of the Win Shares system, one of the most obvious is its help in rating players—indeed, a player's Career Win Shares could be seen as a "rating" in and of itself. But I don't think that's a completely appropriate use of the Win Shares system, and let me explain why.

THE MEANING OF STATISTICS

Baseball statistics are simplifications of much more complex realities. It may be unnecessary to say this because, of course, all human understanding is based on simplifications of more complex realities. Economic theories are simplified images of how an economy works, replacing billions of complicated facts with a few broad generalizations. The same is true of psychological and sociological theories, it is true in medicine and astronomy. The search for understanding, wherever it roams, is a search for better simplifications—simplifications which explain more and distort less. Even the understanding gained from experience is, of course, a simplification of experience into the generalizations which are distilled from many experiences.

The difference between a good statistical analyst and a poor statistical analyst is that a good statistical analyst, like Pete Palmer or

Craig Wright, understands this, and a bad one implicitly denies it.

A good statistical analyst, in studying the statistical record of a baseball season, asks three or four essential questions:

1. What is missing from this picture?

2. What is distorted here, and what is accurately portrayed?

3. How can we include what has been left out?

4. How can we correct what has been distorted?

We all know many things and many different types of things which are not reflected in the statistical record. Acknowledging this, a good statistical analyst is sometimes able to reach out and draw areas of the game which were previously undocumented inside the tent, inside the focus of the statistical record. Sabermetrics is sometimes able to invent a way to correct for one or another distortion of the statistical picture.

The bad statistical analyst, on the other hand, will *assume* that what the statistical record tells him must be true and complete—and by making that assumption, will forfeit his ability to add anything significant to the record.

Baseball statistics are interesting not because they answer questions for us, but because they may be used to study issues. The value of baseball statistics in identifying the greatest players is not that they answer all of the questions involved, but that they provide definitive answers to *some* of the questions involved, which enables us to focus on the others.

THE RATINGS SYSTEM

The limitation of raw Win Shares as a player rating system can be seen by comparing the

career totals of Joe DiMaggio (385) and Rusty Staub (356). DiMaggio leads, but the margin is uncomfortably thin. We could get near 100% agreement, I suspect, that the margin between DiMaggio and Staub should be larger than that.

This is an extreme case, but what is left out of this comparison? Let's compare them year by year:

Win Shares—Career Totals

	DiMaggio		Staub	
Age 19			1963	12
Age 20			1964	5
Age 21	1936	25	1965	13
Age 22	1937	38	1966	18
Age 23	1938	30	1967	28
Age 24	1939	34	1968	28
Age 25	1940	31	1969	27
Age 26	1941	41	1970	29
Age 27	1942	32	1971	31
Age 28			1972	13
Age 29			1973	23
Age 30			1974	17
Age 31	1946	24	1975	25
Age 32	1947	29	1976	25
Age 33	1948	34	1977	12
Age 34	1949	21	1978	16
Age 35	1950	29	1979	8
Age 36	1951	17	1980	10
Age 37			1981	6
Age 38			1982	3
Age 39			1983	4
Age 40			1984	1
Age 41			1985	2
Total		385		356

I don't believe that any individual season of either DiMaggio or Staub has been inaccurately evaluated. At any age at which they can be directly compared, DiMaggio has more value than Staub, with the exception of 1946, when DiMaggio had torn cartilage in his knee. But what is left out of the comparison is opportunity. Staub has career Win Shares comparable to DiMaggio's because:

- He was a major league regular at age 19.
- DiMaggio missed three prime seasons due to World War II.
- Staub hung around for seven years after he was no longer a regular, picking up five Win Shares a year, whereas DiMaggio retired the moment he began to slip.
- Staub's team's played 162 games a year, whereas DiMaggio's teams played 154, giving Staub another 5% advantage.

Sandy Koufax won 165 major league games; Mark Langston won 179. This does not prove that Mark Langston was a better pitcher than Sandy Koufax; there are other factors. Same with career Win Shares; we have to consider the other factors.

The player ratings below—the top 100 players of all time (page 358) and also the top 100 at each position—are based on Win Shares, but not simply based on the player's career Win Share total. There are six factors which go into the rating, or seven if you include the statistical override. Those six are:

1. The player's career Win Share total.

2. The player's average Win Shares in his three best seasons.

3. The player's average Win Shares in his five best consecutive seasons.

4. The player's career Win Shares per 162 games.

5. An "era adjustment" based on the player's year of birth.

6. A subjective component, intended to enable us to deal with factors not accurately reflected in the statistics.

Let me deal with those one at a time.

1. The Player's Career Win Share Total

Babe Ruth had more Win Shares in his career than anyone else in baseball history, 758. The top ten are:

1.	Babe Ruth	758
2.	Ty Cobb	726
3.	Honus Wagner	655
4.	Henry Aaron	641
5.	Willie Mays	641
6.	Cy Young	635
7.	Tris Speaker	633
8.	Stan Musial	604
9.	Eddie Collins	572
10.	Mickey Mantle	565

I jumped through a few statistical hoops to convert this number into a figure which could be combined with seasonal averages without dwarfing them . . . well, I suppose I should explain, even though I know that 97% of you could care less. I divided the figure above by 10, and then found the harmonic mean between that number and 25. This lists the players in the same order, but with different numbers:

1.	Babe Ruth	37.60
2.	Ty Cobb	37.19
3.	Honus Wagner	36.19
4.	Henry Aaron	35.97
5.	Willie Mays	35.97
6.	Cy Young	35.88
7.	Tris Speaker	35.84
8.	Stan Musial	35.36
9.	Eddie Collins	34.79
10.	Mickey Mantle	34.66

2. The Player's Win Shares in His Three Best Seasons

Babe Ruth earned 51 Win Shares in 1920, 53 Win Shares in 1921, and 55 Win Shares in 1923, an average of 53 for the three best years. This also is the highest average of all time. The top ten are:

					Average
1.	Babe Ruth	55 (1923)	53 (1921)	51 (1920)	53.00
2.	Honus Wagner	59 (1908)	46 (1905)	45 (1906)	50.00
3.	Mickey Mantle	51 (1957)	49 (1956)	48 (1961)	49.33
4.	Walter Johnson	54 (1913)	47 (1912)	42 (1915)	47.67
5.	Ty Cobb	49 (1915)	48 (1911)	46 (Twice)	47.67
6.	Ted Williams	50 (1946)	46 (1942)	44 (1947)	46.67
7.	Tris Speaker	52 (1912)	45 (1914)	41 (1916)	46.00
8.	Stan Musial	47 (1948)	44 (1946)	40 (1949)	43.67
9.	Rogers Hornsby	47 (1922)	42 (1929)	41 (1921)	43.33
10.	Nap Lajoie	47 (1910)	42 (1901)	41 (1904)	43.33

I need to explain one other thing here. The highest Win Share totals of all time were by pitchers in the 1876–1892 era, when pitchers stood 50 feet from the batter and pitched huge numbers of innings. Old Hoss Radbourne in 1884 pitched 679 innings, winning 59 or 60 games, depending on your source, and losing only 12. Obviously, this had an immense impact on the won-lost record of his team, and Radbourne is credited with 89 Win Shares, the highest total of all time.

If Radbourne stood alone, we would be happy to recognize him as an exceptional performer, and to list him among the greatest players ever. But pitchers in that era frequently pitched more than 500 innings in a season, and frequently earned more than 60 Win Shares per season. If we made no adjustment, the list above would be entirely composed of pitchers who pitched before 1893; no one else would even appear on the list, except maybe Babe Ruth, toward the bottom of the top ten. Obviously this is an undesirable conclusion; we are willing to consider pitchers from that era *among* the greatest players in history, but it is probably better to say that that was a different game, and to make some room for the other 96% of the players.

To convert the Win Shares into ratings, then, I divided the Win Shares for pitcher *seasons* before 1893 by two. This still provides healthy totals for those players. Old Hoss Radbourne's 1884 season, even divided by two, still rates as better than any season of Willie Mays, Cy Young, Lou Gehrig, or Henry Aaron. Silver King's season as a twenty-year-old in 1888 (45-21 in 586 innings), even divided by two, still rates as high as any individual season by Robin Roberts, Roberto Clemente, Bob Feller, Sandy Koufax, or Roger Clemens.

Dividing these season totals by two doesn't deprive these players of recognition; it just keeps them from dominating the list. We use their career Win Shares, un-adjusted, in figuring the career rating factors, which are elements I and IV of this system.

3. Five Best Consecutive Seasons

Our third rating standard is the player's five best consecutive seasons. Honus Wagner's Win Shares, beginning in 1904, were 43, 46, 45, 44, and 59. This rates, because of Babe Ruth's suspension for the first part of the 1922 season, as the best five-year run in baseball history:

1.	Honus Wagner	1904–1908	47.40
2.	Babe Ruth	1920–1924	46.60
*3.	Ted Williams	1941–1948	44.20
4.	Walter Johnson	1912–1916	43.40
5.	Mickey Mantle	1954–1958	43.20
6.	Ty Cobb	1907–1911	43.00
7.	Tris Speaker	1912–1916	42.20
8.	Willie Mays	1962–1966	39.40
9.	Joe Morgan	1972–1976	39.20
10.	Eddie Collins	1911–1915	38.80
10.	Stan Musial	1944–1949	38.80

Twelve through 20, if you're curious, are the peak periods of Lou Gehrig, Rogers Hornsby, Kid Nichols, Barry Bonds, Hank Aaron, Cy Young, Pete Alexander, Ed Walsh, and Mel Ott.

I decided, for obvious reasons, to count Ted Williams' 1942 and 1946 seasons as consecutive seasons. I did this for all of the war time stars, including Greenberg and Feller, who had partial seasons in 1945 and (in one case) 1941. It seems to me more fair to do this than not.

You may be surprised to note that, for example, Willie Mays' best seasons are 1962–1966,

rather than 1954–1958, and Ty Cobb's best five-year run does not include 1912, when he hit .410. Willie Mays' numbers in the 1960s may be a little bit less impressive than his numbers in the 1950s because (a) Mays in the 1960s was playing in Candlestick Park, and (b) baseball had entered a pitcher's era. I think that, in context, Mays' performance in the 1960s is a hair better than his performance in the 1950s.

Ty Cobb in 1912, same thing. In 1907 the average American League team scored 564 runs; in 1912 the average team scored 687 runs. Cobb won the batting title both seasons, hitting .350 in 1907, .410 in 1912, but factoring in defense and other elements, we have Cobb at 41 Win Shares in 1907, 40 in 1912, which makes 1907–1911 Cobb's best five-year stretch, rather than 1908–1912. Not that Cobb looks weak if you evaluate him by his worst five-year stretch.

On a broader question, why do we use several different measurements of the player's greatness, rather than one? Because no one measurement is the right one. There is nothing magic about the player's best three years, his best four years, his best seven years, his best nine consecutive years . . . none of those is absolutely the right way to look at the issue. By combining several different measurements, we hope to avoid being thrown off-track by a player who happens to fit the category perfectly, or badly. On an analogous question, one could ask "what is the largest elephant in the zoo?" and we could measure each elephant in many different ways. We could measure the height of the elephant, the weight, the width, the length, the girth, the height at the shoulder, etc. If you answer the question "what is the largest elephant?" with respect to any one measurement, you have an absolute answer, but it may be the wrong one. By combining the measurements, you can make a better approach to the essence of the question.

4. Career Win Shares per Season

Our fourth measurement is the player's career Win Shares per 162 games, or per 43 starts as a pitcher, with a relief appearance counted as one-half of a start.

If we ranked players on their Win Shares per career game, obviously all of the good pitchers would rank ahead of anybody else, even Babe Ruth. We use 43 starts for pitchers rather than 40 or 41 (86 relief appearances rather than 80 or 82) because, frankly, the rating numbers for pitchers are low, and this is a way of bringing them a little bit closer to where we would expect them to be.

Since Babe Ruth is both a pitcher and a hitter, we based his rating on career Win Shares per 147 games—actually, 146.53. The 147 game figure is derived from the fact that 13% of Ruth's career Win Shares were earned as a pitcher . . . you can probably deduce the math from there if you care. It doesn't matter to Babe Ruth, since Ruth is obviously going to rank as the number one player no matter what we do. The top ten players in career win shares per season are:

1.	Babe Ruth	44.33
2.	Ted Williams	39.43
3.	Ty Cobb	38.76
4.	Mickey Mantle	38.12
5.	Honus Wagner	38.00
6.	Tris Speaker	36.76
7.	Lou Gehrig	36.60
8.	Rogers Hornsby	36.00
9.	Joe DiMaggio	35.92
10.	Barry Bonds	35.47

Spots 11 through 20 on this list are occupied by Joe Jackson, Bob Caruthers, Kid Nichols, Willie Mays, Dan Brouthers, Mike Piazza, Billy Hamilton, Joe Medwick, Walter Johnson, and Frank Thomas.

5. The Time Line Adjustment

It is my belief that the quality of play in major league baseball has improved steadily over time, being higher in almost every generation than it was in the previous generation. I recognize that many of you have settled opinions on this issue, that many of you disagree with me, and further, that there is little chance I can change your mind. Nonetheless, let me take a moment to explain the simple facts upon which I base my position.

The major leagues as they existed in 1876 had no organized system of funneling the best players into a few leagues—indeed, I think all knowledgeable people would agree that many of the best players in the country in 1876 did not play in the National League. The process of identifying the best young players, training them, and eventually bringing all of the best players into two leagues was not fully organized until 1925, at the very earliest—50 years into the history of the majors—and even then was far from what it is now. As late as 1900–1905, there were at least two amateur players who showed up at the park, bought a ticket, and wound up playing in that day's game. This is not "major league baseball" as we understand the term today.

Second, while old-timers talk about expansion diluting the quality of play, and have been talking about this for 40 years, a careful consideration of the population base issue tends to favor the more recent years. In 1930 there were 16 major league teams, representing a population of 123 million citizens. Blacks were excluded from the talent pool at that time; that would reduce the talent pool to 112 million citizens—7 million citizens for each team.

By 1990 that ratio was more than 9 million citizens for each team. In addition to that, in 1930 there were only a couple of Latin American players in the majors (Cubans). Now, major league teams scout and draw much of their talent from Latin America—substantially increasing the talent pool from which each team is drawn.

Third, old timers like to claim that players used to spend longer learning the game in the minor leagues than they do now, but this is flatly untrue; the average number of minor league games played by a major league player is almost exactly the same as it has been since 1930, the only changes being that World War II caused a temporary jump in the average number of minor league games played by a major leaguer (as career minor leaguers got to play in the majors), and expansions have caused similar, very temporary jumps in that average. (It is possible that the number of minor league innings pitched have decreased. The number of games played by non-pitchers has not.)

Fourth, standards of performance in most other athletic events have increased steadily over the years, as have standards of health and longevity. It seems unlikely that baseball skills have degenerated while skills in other sports have leaped forward.

Fifth, earlier players dominated their game to a greater extent than more recent players—indeed, the extent to which the best players have dominated their competition has probably decreased in every generation. The reason for this is simple: as the game gets better, it gets harder to dominate. My view of the quality of play over time was essentially summed up by Casey Stengel in his 1962 biography, *Casey At the Bat:*

> But even with the better equipment and the better grounds, you have to have more ability to be an infielder or an outfielder today . . . so in some ways baseball is better now. But as far as the players are concerned—if a man was a good hitter with the dead ball, why couldn't he hit the lively ball? And if he was a good fielder with the little glove, why couldn't he be a good fielder

with a trap glove? And the pitchers who were good then—why couldn't they adjust to the livelier ball and the harder hitting of today?

It is my belief that if Honus Wagner were playing today, he would be a great player today—perhaps the best player in baseball. He wouldn't dominate the game today the way he dominated the game then, because there are *more* good players now, and in some ways the game is harder now. The extent to which the best players dominate the game has steadily decreased because the quality of the average player has moved upward.

If you don't make any time-line adjustments, then, using the Win Shares system or almost any other method, you will wind up with a top 100 list which is dominated by players who played before 1950. Even *making* a time line adjustment, 52 of my top 100 players played in the major leagues or in the Negro Leagues (played at least one game) prior to 1950. Another 14 came up in the 1950s. Only 34 have come to the majors since 1960—that is, in the last 40 years. If I didn't introduce a small time-line adjustment, I'd have 75 or 85 players from the first half of the century in the top 100. I just don't believe that's right or logical.

The time line element is figured as "Year of Birth, minus 1800, divided by ten." This gives Ken Griffey Jr. (the youngest player in my top 100) a seven-point advantage over Babe Ruth, and a ten-point advantage over Cy Young, who was the first born player in the top 100.

6. The Subjective Element

The subjective element in the rating system is a number between one and fifty, chosen to help us adjust for:

1. Statistically undocumented portions of a player's career.

2. Inequalities in the caliber of competition.

3. World Series performance.

4. Positive or negative leadership.

5. Clutch performance.

6. Special contributions of the player undefined by the statistics.

7. Defensive value beyond that accounted for in the win shares system.

Let me deal with those things one at a time:

1. Adjustment for Undocumented Parts of a Player's Career

Joe DiMaggio was in the United States Army in 1943, 1944, and 1945. It is my belief that, in rating players, it is appropriate to make an adjustment for this.

I don't make adjustments for players who are injured; I don't make adjustments for players who are suspended or who voluntarily retire, no matter what the conditions. I make adjustments for any player *who is clearly a major league player, but who is prevented from playing in the major leagues by forces beyond his control.*

One might imagine that it was obvious that we should make an adjustment for this; how in the hell can you evaluate Joe DiMaggio *without* making an adjustment for that? But if it is obvious to me, it is not obvious to everyone:

> Bill James decried the years [Lefty] Grove spent languishing in Baltimore while Jack Dunn held him back from the major leagues, but Grove was no great shakes pitching for a strong second-place club in 1925 when he finally did get a chance, and anyway the "what if" game is silly in this context, and endless. What if Alexander had never touched alcohol? What if Feller hadn't gone to war? What if Satchel Paige had been white? What if Earl Averill hadn't broken Dizzy Dean's toe?—Henry W. Thomas, *Walter Johnson: Baseball's Big Train*

Lefty Grove was injured in 1925, but that's a side issue. I had argued in the first version of this book that Lefty Grove should rank ahead of Walter Johnson, in part because of his very large number of great seasons, some of which were in the minor leagues.

Thomas, who is Johnson's grandson, naturally wants to see Grandpa ranked as the greatest pitcher who ever lived, and I have decided, given the evidence of the Win Shares method, to go along with him. But, it seems to me, he is lumping together arguments which can be easily distinguished, and therefore limited. I am not arguing that Lefty Grove *would have been* a great pitcher in 1923 or 1924. I am arguing that Grove *was* a great pitcher in 1923 and 1924.

Let's start with Satchel Paige. Is it silly to say that Satchel Paige was a great pitcher in 1933? Hell, it's silly to suggest that he *wasn't*. Does he have any statistics to prove this? Not really. But in rating players, why is it silly to give Satchel Paige credit for being what he was?

The same with DiMaggio during the war. I am not arguing that Joe DiMaggio *would have been* a great player in 1945. I am arguing that Joe DiMaggio *was a* great player in 1945. He was prevented from playing in the major leagues by circumstances beyond his control, but that does not mean that he was not a great player. Exactly the same is true of Lefty Grove in 1923 and 1924: He was a great pitcher who was prevented from playing in the major leagues by circumstances beyond his control.

Now, the idea that Dizzy Dean would have been a great pitcher for many years had he not broken his toe—that's a different argument. That's a "what if" argument, arguing that Dean "would have been" great. I don't know that I'd describe it as silly, but it's certainly a dangerous line of analysis, because there's no exact limit to it . . . if Dizzy Dean, why not Herb Score, if Herb Score why not Jim Maloney?

You never give players credit for what they *might have been*—but you always give them credit for what they *were*. In rating players, I give compensatory credit for five types of gaps in playing careers:

1. Wartime service.

2. Seasons missed because of racial segregation.

3. Seasons in which a major league star was trapped in the minor leagues by factors beyond his control.

4. Seasons missed by players born before 1856 who may have been in mid-career before the National League was organized.

5. Players who were blocked from playing by league wars impacting their contracts.

2. Inequalities in the Caliber of the Competition

Hal Newhouser in 1944 was 29-9 with a 2.22 ERA; in 1945 he was 25-9 with a 1.81 ERA. If you ignore the fact that he was pitching against war-time competition, those seasons are the equal of Dizzy Dean's performance in the 1930s, or Sandy Koufax' performance in the 1960s. The Win Shares analysis assumes that a Win is a Win is a Win. We have to build in a subjective adjustment for that which we know to be true, but which our analysis does not reflect.

Jim Gentile was great—in 1961, when there were twenty minor league pitchers in the American League. I don't put very much stock in the "expansion year" argument; the expansion effect is small, and lasts only for two or three years. Still, I think it would be difficult to argue that the quality of American League competition in 1961 was exactly the same as it was in 1960.

Benny Kauff was great—in the Federal League, which had a couple dozen real major league players. Fred Dunlap was dominant in 1884—in a league that is roughly comparable to the Midwest League. Nap Lajoie in 1901—that, again, is an expansion year; the American League in 1901 is a marginal major league.

3. World Series Performance

The Win Shares system gives no credit for World Series performance. This is, perhaps, a necessary and inevitable decision, since World Series stardom is not equally accessible to all players, and it probably isn't appropriate to rate Ernie Banks lower because he played for an organization whose best pitchers were Glen Hobbie and Bob Rush, or Phil Rizzuto higher because he played for the Yankees.

Nonetheless, the unintended consequence of this decision is that, if a pitcher pitches a 2-hit shutout on the last day of the season for a team that finishes 81-81, he'll earn about two Win Shares for the effort. If a pitcher pitches a 2-hit shutout in the first game of the World Series (Vic Raschi, 1950), that's a non-event. This doesn't really make sense.

One of Ted Williams' critics once wrote that, in the eight biggest games of his life, Ted Williams went 6-for-29 with one RBI. He had in mind the 1946 World Series, in which Williams did nothing much, and the 1948 championship playoff game, in which Williams singled and walked. That's completely unfair, and it is absurd; you don't evaluate a man who played in the majors for twenty years by what he did in a handful of games.

But while these games should not count for everything, it does seem to me that they should count for something. A large part of what made Reggie Jackson who he is was a few games in October. Part of what makes Eddie Collins who he was is that he was the greatest World Series performer of the first half of the century, if not the greatest ever. I don't want to throw that out the window.

4. Leadership or Disruptive Behavior

Leadership is only obliquely measured by the Win Shares system, but real and sometimes significant nonetheless. Players who are on-field and clubhouse leaders of outstanding teams, like DiMaggio, Ken Boyer, Bob Gibson, Carlton Fisk, George Brett, Hal McRae, Gil Hodges, Pee Wee Reese, Pete Rose, Joe Morgan—those players should be given credit for that, in evaluating their overall contribution to the team. If a player is cantankerous or unreliable or just a plain old air-head, that's a part of the picture of who he is; there's no rule that says you have to forget about it when you're rating him, even if you don't have statistics on how many times he missed the team bus.

5. Clutch Performance

I'll deal with that in a separate essay.

6. Special Contributions of the Player Utterly Beyond the Reach of the Statistics.

Jackie Robinson. Hal Chase. Eddie Grant. You see where I'm going with this . . .

7. Defensive Value Beyond (or Below) That Estimated by the System.

I put many months of hard work into developing the fielding elements of the Win Shares system, and I am proud of the system. The system rates good defensive players as good defensive players and poor defensive players as poor defensive players, consistently, at every position including catcher and first base.

However, it is one thing to say that the system is good, and another to say that it is perfect. The Win Shares system sees Joe DiMaggio as being among the best defensive outfielders of all time, along with Willie Mays, Tris Speaker, Curt Flood, and a few others. It sees Rusty Staub as being a pretty decent outfielder in his better years, and as having almost no defensive value in his last ten seasons. We believe that DiMaggio played about 15,095 innings in the outfield in his career, and we credit him with 60.49 Win Shares as an outfielder. We believe that Staub played about 14,604 innings in the outfield, earning 29.05 Win Shares, and that he played about 3,468 innings at first base, earning another 6.25 Win Shares. I believe this is a reasonable and accurate comparison of their relative defensive value.

However, to say that this is a *perfect* defensive evaluation—that would be a leap. Is 25 Win Shares enough to reflect the defensive superiority of Joe DiMaggio to Rusty Staub, or should it be 50? Is a 2-1 ratio enough, or should it be 3-1? I don't think I can tell you that I have the absolutely correct answer to that. There are some players who are given subjective ratings higher or lower than the mid-point (25) because I'm not convinced that the Win Shares system makes an adequate evaluation of their defensive contribution.

There are a couple of other things probably worth mentioning. We need to keep in mind the schedule length . . . modern players play 162 games a year, whereas earlier players played 154, and *really* early players played half that. Catchers are at a tremendous rating disadvantage because they play a position that destroys their athletic ability and shortens their careers; some compensation for that is probably appropriate.

The subjective factor is not an excuse to override the logic of the system and rate players however I want to rate them. The subjective adjustment is an acknowledgement that there are factors of the player's contribution which are not documented in the Win Shares analysis.

Here's a hard case, perhaps the hardest case I had to deal with: Mickey Mantle and Ty Cobb. Almost everybody who has ever rated the 100 best players of all time has rated Ty Cobb ahead of Mickey Mantle—maybe everybody, I don't know. Everybody except Bob Costas. But here are the ratings in my system:

	Ty Cobb	Mickey Mantle
Career value	37.19	34.66
Three best years	47.67	49.33
Five best consecutive seasons	43.00	43.20
Career per game	38.76	38.12
Time line adjusted	8.60	13.10
Total	175.22	178.42

Mantle rates three points ahead.

Now, I'll tell you this: If I was starting a major league team today, and I could choose either Ty Cobb or Mickey Mantle to build my team around, I would choose Mickey Mantle in a New York minute. I mean the whole package of both men—the drinking, the racism, the competitiveness, the bad knee, the intelligence, the generosity, the quirky sense of humor, the morbid fixations. I would draft Mantle, I would have no hesitation, I would have no second thoughts, and I am confident that I would never regret it.

Nonetheless, there is a serious problem with the rating, which can be seen in the "career per game" number. Ty Cobb earned not only more career Win Shares than Mickey Mantle, but more Win Shares per game played—in a career that was substantially longer.

Why, then, does Mantle rank higher? Mantle ranks higher because his peak years are so good, and because he came along 45 years later, when (in my opinion) the quality of the competition was tougher. Mantle, at his best, was better than Cobb—and against tougher competition.

But is this a logically compelling argument that Mantle was a better player, or is this a quirk of the ratings system? In the end, I have

to acknowledge that it is a quirk of the ratings system. Mantle rates higher because I rated players on their three best seasons—ignoring the fact that Cobb's fourth-best, fifth-best, sixth-best, and seventh-best seasons are far better than Mantle's; Cobb had eight seasons of 40 or more Win Shares, Mantle had four.

Mantle rates ahead of Cobb on the basis of his five best seasons—but had I chosen to rate players on their *six* best consecutive seasons, Cobb would have rated ahead. Had I rated them on their four best consecutive seasons, Cobb would have rated nearly even. This, again, is a quirk of the rating system.

So I gave Cobb a higher subjective factor than I gave Mantle, and allowed him to edge back ahead. My heart is not in it, but as I see it, the world believes that Cobb was a better player than Mantle, and I would be unable to sustain a logical argument to the contrary under rigorous attack. I have to give Cobb the edge.

Finally, of course, I put in an emergency override for the Negro League players, who cannot be evaluated by the same methods that can be used to evaluate their white contemporaries. I'll outline my feelings about clutch performance and my fielding analysis, and then list the top 100 players in baseball history.

CLUTCH PERFORMANCE

The prominence of clutch performance as an element in player ratings can be attributed to three factors:

1. Hero worship journalism.

2. Self-aggrandizement by athletes, particularly retired athletes serving as TV announcers.

3. The fact that we all need, at times, to escape the implications of our logic.

Retired athletes are immensely fond of "character" and "clutch ability" as explanations for their success. Joe Morgan and Ray Knight are notable in this regard, but Reggie Jackson is (or was) the worst; a baseball game as broadcast by Reggie is essentially a test of "character," "determination," and "fortitude," these traits being revealed in how players play at critical moments of the game.

We are supposed to believe that athletes are athletes not merely because they are fast, strong, quick, and well conditioned, but because there is something special inside them, this "character" that comes to the fore in the crucible of athletic competition. They are athletes, in other words, because they are better people than the rest of us.

My attitude toward this can probably be inferred from my tone. I do not believe that athletes are better people than the rest of us, I do not believe that athletic contests are tests of character, and I do not believe that there is any such thing as an *ability* to perform in clutch situations. It's just a lot of poppycock.

Baseball men often like to attribute the success or failure of a team to clutch performances. Those of us who study baseball systematically know that this is largely untrue, that the number of runs a team scores is a predictable outcome of their hits, their walks, their home runs, and their other offensive accomplishments—and further, that the number of games the team wins is largely a predictable outcome of their runs scored and runs allowed. Clutch performance *can* increase or decrease a team's wins, but clutch successes and failures generally even out over the course of a season, leaving most teams with about the won-lost record they deserve.

But, since this elusive "clutch ability" has no particular statistical dimension, it has become popular within the discussion as a bullshit dump. All discussions have bullshit dumps; we need them. Our logic, whatever it is that we are talking about, can never be completely worked out; all subjects worthy of discussion are too complicated to be fully encased in logic. Thus, in all discussions, the least precise areas become bullshit dumps, elements of the discussion which are used to reconcile our formal logic to our intuitive sense of right or wrong, justice or injustice, accuracy or inaccuracy, reason or madness, moderation or extremity. "Psychology" is a common bullshit dump. I am not saying that psychology is not real or that psychologists do not know what they are talking about. What I am saying is that since human psychology affects almost everything within our sight in undocumented ways which are never fully understood, psychology inevitably becomes a bullshit dump which can be used to justify or explain what is otherwise unjustified or inexplicable.

"Karma" is a popular bullshit dump. In politics, "sensitivity" is a bullshit dump; so is the "influence of the media." Witchcraft used to be a major bullshit dump, but has lost its audience.

If a player rates 53rd at third base in terms of runs scored, RBI, and batting average, but you just *know* that he was one of the greatest players of all time, how do you close that gap? Crediting him with being a great clutch player is an easy way to bridge the gap between your knowledge and your conviction. It's easy to assert; it's impossible to disprove. If Gene Tenace rates as a better player than Garry Maddox, you can easily downgrade him by asserting that he wasn't a "clutch" player; after all, look at his RBI. Whatever you want to prove, clutch performance will get you there—if you don't need logic to get back home again.

Still, the fact that 90% or 99% of what is said about clutch performers in sports is nonsense does not mean that there is nothing here which should have any impact on our ratings. Let me give you a couple of examples of players whose evaluation, I believe, *should* be altered by their clutch performances: Bob Gibson and Don Drysdale. National League right-handed power pitchers of the 1960s, both Hall of Famers, both had historic performances in 1968.

This is an absolute fact that doesn't change depending on how you feel about it: Don Drysdale started 13 games in his career in the heat of the pennant race against the team the Dodgers were trying to beat—and never won. Not even once. He never pitched particularly well without winning; 0 for 13.

I don't believe that this reflects a character failing on Drysdale's part. I think it's just something that happened. Sometimes he had been overworked; sometimes maybe a pitch or two got away from him. Sometimes you make good pitches and get beat. If there was a big game next week, I'd as soon have Drysdale pitching for me as anybody else.

Nonetheless, it did happen; he did, in general, pitch poorly in pennant races (with some exceptions), and he did repeatedly fail to beat the Dodgers' key opponent in the heat of the pennant race. In rating Drysdale's career, is this something that should be ignored, or something that should be considered?

On the other hand, Bob Gibson. In 1964 Gibson had 12 wins on September 1—but won 7 games after September first, driving the Cardinals, eight and a half behind on September first, through the pack. The Cardinals won easily in '67 and '68 (1964 was the only time they won a close race), but in nine World Series starts Gibson pitched 81 innings, striking out 92 hitters, going 7-2 with a 1.89 ERA, 55 hits allowed, and incidentally hitting two home runs, winning two World Series MVP Awards.

There are about twenty players who, in my opinion, should be rated up or rated down a little bit because of their clutch performances. Yogi Berra. Joe Carter. George Brett. Steve Garvey. Reggie Jackson. It's a dangerous area to get into, because when you reach into the bullshit dump, you're not going to come out with a handful of diamonds. But if a player really does come through in big games or fail in big games, I don't think we can afford to ignore that.

WIN-BASED FIELDING ANALYSIS

The Win Shares analysis of fielding performance, which has occupied most of my life for the last year, has been immensely complicated—and, in my humble opinion, largely successful.

The Win Shares system is essentially a method of attributing team wins to individual players—to individual hitters, to individual pitchers, and to individual fielders. There is an absolute 3-to-1 ratio of team wins to Win Shares by individuals on the team; nothing, not even a rounding discrepancy, is allowed to shake that ratio. If a team wins 100 games, their players will be credited with 300 Win Shares, absolutely and without exception.

Wins, then, are the sum of the Win Shares system. The system starts with the team's won-lost Record, and assigns Win Shares to individuals in six stages:

1. Wins are divided between offense and defense.

2. Wins credited to the offense are assigned to individual hitters.

3. Wins credited to the defense are divided between pitching and fielding.

4. Wins credited to pitching are assigned to individual pitchers.

5. Wins credited to fielding are assigned to fielding positions.

6. Wins credited to fielding positions are assigned to individual fielders.

Schematically, it looks like this:

Of these six stages, three are straightforward—the three which don't involve fielding. The three which do involve fielding will require a book-length explanation, but the essential mechanism of the system is "Claim Points." Runs Created by hitters (in excess of the margin) are Claim Points against hitter's wins. Runs Saved by pitchers (below the margin) are Claim Points against pitching wins; pitcher's Wins, Losses, and Saves also count, but Runs Saved are the basis of the system.

The things that would cause a player to rate as a good fielder in any other fielding system will cause him, in the Win Shares system, to have a good number of claim points. There are exceptions to that and limitations, but in general, a good fielding rating in *Total Baseball* or any other fielding analysis will mean a good Claim Percentage in our system, and thus a good number of Claim Points. But how many Win Shares follow from that also depends on the defensive performance of the team as a whole.

Please understand that I am not claiming that the Win Shares analysis of fielding is better than any previous analysis of fielding performance. I am claiming that the Win Shares analysis of fielding is **vastly** better than any previous analysis, light years better. Ultimately, you will have to be the judge of this, but I feel, having worked on this for a year or more, that I have broken the code of fielding statistics—that I have produced, for the first time, a systematic

fielding analysis that actually rates good fielders as good fielders and poor fielders as poor fielders at least 90% of the time. Nothing like it has ever existed before. It is a radical re-thinking of fielding evaluation—and it works.

Why does it work? Start with the question of why traditional fielding analysis so often fails.

Traditional fielding analysis often fails because *the fielding statistics of a good team are not very much different from the fielding statistics of a poor team.* This is not true of pitching or hitting. The batting stats of good teams are very different from the batting statistics of poor teams; indeed, over time, good teams will outperform poor teams in every batting category, without exception—and the difference between the good teams and the poor teams is fully adequate to explain the successes and failures of the teams. The same is true of pitching: over a period of years, good teams will outperform poor teams in every category of the pitching record except Games Finished (by relievers) and Games in Relief.

But for fielders, the statistics of good teams are, on the whole, no better than the statistics of poor teams. Fielding evaluation is based primarily on three factors: range, double plays, and fielding percentage. The "range" number, on the team level, is constrained by the fact that each team makes only 27 outs per game, regardless of how good their fielders are; you could have an infield of four Omar Vizquels or an infield of four Mo Vaughns, but you're only going to get 27 outs a game either way.

Double plays are not constrained by a boundary, but there is a problem there, too, which is that

1. Bad teams (and bad defensive teams) have more opponents on base than good teams.

2. The more opponents you have on base, the more chances you have to turn a double play.

So bad teams, on the average, don't turn fewer double plays than good teams—in fact, they turn a few more.

So of the three factors which are the basis of fielding evaluation, two are completely unrelated to excellence on the team level, and the third (fielding percentage) favors the better teams by only a small margin. I assembled the fielding records of all major league teams from 1980 to 1990 except 1981—a group of 260 teams, playing 162 games a year with minor exceptions. From this I formed four groups:

1. The fifty best teams.
2. All the teams that had winning records.
3. All the teams that had losing records.
4. The fifty worst teams.

The average fielding records of those four groups of teams are shown in the chart at the bottom of the page.

The best teams have 51 more putouts than the poorest teams (because they more often have to play the bottom of the ninth), but 65 more strikeouts—thus, 14 *fewer* putouts by fielders other than catchers. The worst teams also have 37 more assists, on average, than the best teams. The worst teams have 7 more double plays, on the average, than the best teams.

The best teams do have a small advantage in fielding percentage (.002) and in passed balls (2 per season), but those advantages are more than offset by a series of other quirks in fielding statistics, which favor the players who play on a poor team:

1. The worst teams (in the chart above) make an average of 32.9 plays (putouts plus assists, minus strikeouts) per nine innings. The best teams make an average of only 32.2.

2. All systems of fielding analysis count an assist by a catcher as a positive. But catchers on bad teams record more assists than catchers on good teams, 11% more in the study above. The catchers on the 50 worst teams above recorded an average of 91 assists; the catchers on the best teams averaged only 82.

3. All systems of fielding analysis count assists by outfielders as a positive—but outfielders on bad teams have more assists than outfielders on good teams. In this study, the outfielders on the worst teams averaged 35 assists; those on the best teams, 31.

4. Most systems of fielding analysis totally ignore putouts by first basemen. But first basemen on good teams record more putouts than first basemen on bad teams (because good teams have fewer runners on base against them, hence fewer forceouts at other bases).

	G	PO	As	E	DP	FPct	PB
50 Best Teams	162	4,372	1,749	124	148	.980	12
All Winning Teams	162	4,365	1754	126	150	.980	13
All Losing Teams	162	4,334	1,766	135	151	.978	14
50 Worst Teams	162	4,321	1,786	139	155	.978	14

5. Almost all systems of fielding analysis give credit for putouts by second basemen, shortstops, and third basemen—but bad teams record more putouts by second basemen, shortstops, and third basemen than do good teams (because they have more forceouts).

Traditional fielding analysis thus ignores those putouts which are more common on good teams, but includes the putouts and the assists which are more common on bad teams.

The effect of this is that *traditional fielding analysis, starting with individual fielding statistics, will usually rate a bad team as being better defensively than a good team.* Obviously that's not right; teams that lose 100 games a year are not better defensively than teams that win 100 games in a season. The fielding of poor teams is likely to be weaker by *at least* the same margin as the pitching and the batting. In essence, what happens is that there is a "false normalization" which "corrects" the defensive performance of a bad team so that it appears to be equal—actually slightly better—than the defensive performance of a good team. If a player on a good team makes a spectacular fielding play, that takes one subsequent play away from the team. If a ball whizzes right by a fielder's head, that becomes a bonus play for someone on the team—and also gives the shortstop and second baseman an extra shot at a double play.

The effect of this "false normalization" on fielding statistics can be demonstrated by performing a similar false normalization on pitching stats. Greg Maddux in 1993 was 20-10 with a 2.36 ERA—for a team that won 104 games. If you "normalize" his record to an 80-82 team with an ERA 1% worse-than-league, he's 15-14 with a 3.07 ERA. David Cone in 1998 was 20-7 with a 3.55 ERA—but for a team that won 114 games. If you normalize his record in the same way, he'd be 14-12 with a 4.37 ERA.

On the other hand, Jay Hook with the 1962 Mets was 8-19 with a 4.84 ERA—but if you normalize the team's records to 82-80 with an ERA 1% better than league, he becomes 16-13 with a 3.75 ERA. Bobby Witt in 1993 was 14-13 with a 4.21 ERA—but with a team that was 68-94. If you normalize his record in the same way, he's 17-11 with a 3.68 ERA.

Bobby Witt and Jay Hook are now as good as Greg Maddux and David Cone. Or consider the effect this would have on hitters. Babe Ruth in 1927 hit 60 home runs and drove in 164 runs for a team that hit 158 homers and scored 975 runs. Nate Colbert in 1972 hit 38 homers and drove in 111 runs for a team that hit 102 homers and scored 488 runs. If you normalize the teams, Nate Colbert had a bigger year than Babe Ruth.

This is in no way an exaggeration of the effect of this false normalization on fielding stats; it actually is that dramatic. *Total Baseball* rates Nap Lajoie as a good defensive second baseman in 1914, when he was 39 years old, playing second base for a team that lost 102 games. They rate him as an even better defensive second baseman the following year, when he was 40 years old and playing second base for a team that lost 109 games, and as an absolutely brilliant defensive second baseman in 1916, when he was 41 years old and playing second base for a team that finished 36-117.

These ratings result largely from the false normalization of Lajoie's defensive performance. The proposition that the 1916 Philadelphia A's lost 117 despite the brilliant defensive play of their 41-year-old second baseman is absurd, and is in fact false; Lajoie does *not* deserve to rate as a defensive asset in that season.

Let me say this before we go any further: I am as much responsible for the spread of poor and inaccurate defensive rating schemes as anyone in the world. I have been writing about fielding statistics for twenty-five years. That which I now denounce as "traditional," I am as much as anyone responsible for creating. I am not trying to point fingers at anyone for failed defensive ratings; I am simply trying to explain how to make them better.

Batting statistics of individuals may be successfully related to team wins because there is a natural relationship between individual batting statistics and team success. Pitching statistics of individuals may be successfully related to team wins because there is a natural relationship between individual pitching statistics and team wins. But fielding statistics of individuals are difficult to relate to team wins because *there is no natural relationship between individual fielding statistics and team success.* How do you fix that?

You fix that by starting in a different place. You don't start with the individual fielding statistics. You start with the performance of the team. First, before you do anything else, *establish the overall defensive quality of the team.* Then you can transfer credit (or blame) for that performance to the individuals on the team—but without an implicit assumption that all teams are defensively equal or nearly equal.

How do we establish the overall defensive quality of the team, without relying on their individual fielding statistics? My thinking on this issue is probably not very different than yours, if you have thought about it. There aren't very many options. The characteristics of a good defensive team include:

1. Winning games.
2. Not allowing many runs to score.
3. Not allowing a lot of hits.
4. Avoiding errors.

Win Shares for the team are established on the basis of wins; those that go to defense (pitching and fielding combined) depend on how many runs the team allows, compared to the league average and adjusted for the team's home field. But how do you split the defensive runs between pitchers and fielders?

The pitchers, on an average team, are credited with 67.5% of the team's defensive win shares; the fielders, with 32.5%. But the percentage that go to fielders on any team may be larger or smaller, depending on the team's:

- Strikeouts.
- Walks.
- Home runs allowed.
- Hits allowed.
- Errors and passed balls.
- Double plays compared to expected double plays.

If a team has a poor strikeout/walk ratio and a high number of home runs allowed, but somehow manages to allow a below-average number of runs scored, then obviously, that reflects well on the fielders. If a team has a good strikeout/walk ratio and doesn't allow home runs, but gives up too many runs anyway, obviously the defense has to be held responsible for that.

Each of the six factors above is scored on a scale. The scales are totaled and used to determine the split between the pitchers and the fielders. It's a crude system, and a lot of things could probably be done to refine it. But at its worst, it's a hell of a lot better than allowing fielding analysis to proceed on the assumption that all defenses are created equal.

Other people have attempted to "fix" fielding statistics by starting with the fielding stats, but making sequential adjustments for everything that might bias them. I am not aware that anyone has done this with any great success.

There are two reasons why the Win Shares analysis of fielding works better. One is that outlined above: the elimination of the false normalization of fielding statistics, and the embodiment of the team's defensive success into the individual defensive ratings.

The other reason is this: when you start at a different point and look at something from a different angle, you see different things. Golfers are sometimes advised to walk the course backward. When you walk the course backward, you may see what the course designer has done to you, the tricks he has played on you. Same thing here: starting defensive analysis at a different point has forced me to walk the course backward, and in the process of this, I have discovered a number of amazingly obvious things which I had somehow missed up to that point. Going position by position:

1. *Catcher's fielding percentages look totally different, and are substantially more useful, if you remove the strikeouts.* We can't remove pitcher's strikeouts when evaluating an individual catcher, but we can remove them at the team level. In the Win Shares system we deal with the statistics of *the team's catchers* before we deal with the statistics of the individual catchers.

Let's take the Cincinnati Reds, 1968 through 1980 (the Johnny Bench years). The official fielding percentages of the Cincinnati Reds' catchers in those years don't look notably different from the National League averages:

Fielding Percentages

Year	Cincinnati Reds' Catchers' Averages	National League Catchers' Averages	Difference
1968	.992	.990	+.002
1969	.990	.989	+.001
1970	.984	.987	−.003
1971	.987	.988	−.001
1972	.993	.987	+.006
1973	.995	.987	+.008
1974	.989	.985	+.004
1975	.988	.985	+.003
1976	.992	.986	+.006
1977	.987	.985	+.002
1978	.987	.985	+.002
1979	.987	.985	+.002
1980	.982	.983	−.001

It doesn't show much of anything, right? But strikeouts, as I assume you know, are counted as catcher's putouts, although they virtually never result in catcher's errors. They are, then, "padding" in the catcher's putout record. This works against the Cincinnati catchers, because the Cincinnati pitchers had few strikeouts. Suppose that we take the strikeouts out, and refigure.

If you do that, you discover three things which are quite interesting:

1. Catchers' fielding percentages aren't .990; they're more like .920.
2. The Reds' catchers' fielding percentages are consistently and substantially better than the league averages, and
3. The Reds' catchers have far more "independent putouts"—putouts that AREN'T strikeouts—than the league norms.

| | Fielding Percentages | | | Independent Putouts | |
Year	Cincinnati	National League	Difference	Cincinnati	National League Average
1968	.956	.938	+.018	105	80
1969	.954	.929	+.025	120	84
1970	.914	.916	−.002	87	79
1971	.928	.919	+.009	89	73
1972	.957	.918	+.039	88	68
1973	.970	.917	+.053	93	72
1974	.937	.915	+.022	96	68
1975	.944	.913	+.031	101	76
1976	.959	.923	+.036	103	72
1977	.923	.918	+.005	71	71
1978	.927	.914	+.013	91	72
1979	.928	.917	+.011	67	67
1980	.889	.908	−.019	75	66

Johnny Bench has been a challenge for statisticians to rate defensively. He was a brilliant defensive catcher, winning ten straight Gold Gloves, not to mention two MVP Awards, a Rookie of the Year Award, a World Series MVP, a Major League Player of the Year Award, four National League pennants, and first-ballot selection to the Hall of Fame. If that doesn't convince you, I was actually counting stolen bases allowed by catchers by the mid-1970s, as best I could from box scores, and Bench's totals were sensational; he and Steve Yeager were far better than anybody else in the league. If that doesn't convince you, ask anybody who saw him; the man was a phenomenal defensive catcher.

Total Baseball in one edition had him ranked as the worst defensive catcher of all time, and still has him rated as a negative defensive player. If you base your analysis on individual official fielding statistics, this is what you'll get; there is really nowhere else to go. Bench has pretty good fielding percentages,

but he's just one or two plays a year better than average, so that's nothing. His Passed Ball totals are pretty good, but that's even less significant. That leaves assists—and his assists totals are low, because after he'd been in the league a month, nobody tried to run on him. So what do you do?

I wish I could tell you that we have completely solved this problem, that we have Johnny Bench rated defensively where he deserves to rate. We don't; we still have him rated lower than I think he deserves to rate—but we've made a lot of progress:

1. In the Win Shares system, the catcher on a good defensive team is *presumed* to be better than the catcher on a bad defensive team, unless there is evidence to the contrary.

2. The Claim Percentages of Cincinnati catchers are improved substantially by removing strikeouts before figuring fielding percentage.

3. We have a record of independent putouts by each team's catchers.

These things put us on the way toward having a much more accurate rating for Johnny Bench, and for the great majority of catchers.

2. *Catcher's Assists have to be modified by consideration of the team's won-lost record.* Many more stolen base attempts occur when the team is ahead than when they are behind, which causes bad teams to face many more stolen base attempts, over the course of a season, than good teams. For this reason, bad teams will have more assists by catchers than good teams. You have to adjust for that.

3. *First Basemen's Un-Assisted Putouts can be estimated on the team level.* Putouts by first basemen have always been considered useless, because 90% of them result from plays made by other infielders—4-3, 5-3, or 6-3. But if you study defensive statistics of *teams,* as opposed to individuals, you can remove the assists by other infielders, and estimate with some accuracy the defensive plays actually made by the first baseman—the unassisted putouts. Result: Vic Power, Bill White, Wes Parker, Keith Hernandez, Steve Garvey, and Mark Grace leap forward in the defensive evaluation of first basemen.

4. *A first baseman's throwing arm can be evaluated by studying relationships of fielding stats at other positions.* Again, this comes from studying *team* defensive statistics, as opposed to individual defensive statistics. First basemen's assists are unreliable as an indicator of range or throwing, because

   a. They're almost all 3-1, first baseman flips to the pitcher covering, and

   b. There is a huge discretionary element in throws by first basemen. They represent a *choice,* more than a *skill* or ability.

But if you study teams, you can subtract putouts by pitchers from assists by first basemen, and estimate how many assists the first baseman has that *aren't* just flips to the pitcher. More about this in the first base comments (see Bill Buckner).

5. *The number of ground balls by a team can be simply and accurately estimated.* I am astonished and embarrassed not to have known this before, but this is one of those questions which, when you reach the point of asking, "Is there any way to estimate a team's ground ball/fly ball ratio?" turns out to be dead obvious. Two points:

   a. The great majority of ground ball outs result in assists.

   b. More than 80% of assists result from ground balls.

Thus, a team's assists total is an extremely accurate indicator of the ground ball/fly ball tendencies of their pitching staff.

This simple realization profoundly alters the defensive evaluation of all infielders and all outfielders.

6. *Team double play totals become a heck of a lot more useful once you adjust for the team's ground ball tendency and the opposition runners on base.*

7. *Putouts by third basemen do not indicate defensive range, or anything else useful.* After studying this issue for a week, I concluded that there was no skill factor in putouts by third basemen which is large enough to be identifiable amidst the biases and external factors which create most putouts by third basemen.

8. *Outfield Assists, like catcher's assists, are inversely related to team performance.* A bad team will have more outfield assists than a good team.

There are, of course, other adjustments to be made in the process of evaluating a team's defense, figuring out how much credit belongs to the third baseman, how much to the outfielders, etc. You have to adjust for the left/right balance of the pitching staff; failure to do that can rip your skivvies in this structure, just as it can in a traditional fielding analysis.

A fuller accounting of the Win Shares system can be found in the other book, *Win*

Shares. I am not claiming that we have a perfect system; I am not claiming that this method puts the analysis of Fielding Statistics on the same level as the analysis of Batting Statistics. It doesn't.

If we picked Gold Glove teams for each league every year since 1876, that would be about 2,000 Gold Glove selections. They're not all inevitably right; of those 2,000, there are about 20 that I would like to hide, if I could. Brian Downing gets a Gold Glove one year at catcher. Those things happen. There are statistical flukes in fielding, just as there are in batting and pitching. Norm Cash hit for a higher average in his best year than Roberto Clemente did, Davey Johnson hit more home runs in his best season than Stan Musial did, Ron Bryant won more games in one season than Warren Spahn did. Those things happen.

But for the first time, we have a system by which we can evaluate the defensive performance of the first basemen of 1937, or the second basemen of 1926, or the shortstops of 1907—and feel confident that we've got it right. The Fielding Win Shares contribute heavily to the ratings that follow.

THE 100 GREATEST PLAYERS OF ALL TIME

In the process of drawing up my list of the top 100 players of all time, I studied six other top 100 lists:

1. *The Sporting News* list, from *The Sporting News Selects Baseball's Greatest Players* (*The Sporting News*, 1998).

2. The SABR List, published in 1999 after a poll of SABR members.

3. The *Total Baseball* list, the 100 top players of all time by *Total Baseball*'s "Total Baseball Ranking."

4. The Faber List, a statistical study published by Charles Faber in 1985 (which excludes pitchers).

5. The Maury Allen List, published by Maury Allen in *Baseball's 100* (1981).

6. The Ritter/Honig List, published in *The 100 Greatest Baseball Players of All Time,* also 1981 (which does not have players ranked 1 through 100).

I think there's an updated version of that last one, but I don't have it. I formed a consensus from these lists into a seventh list. I thought about adding my own top 100 from the first version of this book (1984), but decided that was getting a little too cute. Anyway, my purpose in comparing my list to others was not to critique anyone else's list, but to critique my own. There is no point in explaining why I have Frank Robinson ranked as the 24th greatest player of all time, because... well, SABR has him ranked 24th, *The Sporting News* has him ranked 22nd, *Total Baseball* has him 17th, and Faber had him 16th; I have him ranked just like everybody else. If I can see where my ratings are at odds with the experts, then I'll know what to explain. I'll give them to you in groups of ten:

1. Babe Ruth
2. Honus Wagner
3. Willie Mays
4. Oscar Charleston
5. Ty Cobb
6. Mickey Mantle
7. Ted Williams
8. Walter Johnson
9. Josh Gibson
10. Stan Musial

My top ten are consistent with the consensus of the other six lists, with three exceptions: Gibson, Charleston, and Mantle. I have Oscar

Charleston ranked as the fourth greatest player of all time, whereas only one of the other six lists mentions him, and that one (*The Sporting News*) has him 67th.

The rating of the Negro League players is by far the largest discrepancy between my list and the others. Of the other six, five exclude the

There was a stop sign on his chest . . .

Negro League players, for various reasons. The only other list to include Negro League players was *The Sporting News* list, which included five in the top 100—Josh Gibson (18th), Satchel (19th), Buck Leonard (47th), Cool Papa Bell (66th), and Charleston (67th).

I have twelve Negro League players rated in the top 100. What I have to ask myself, but what you have to decide, is whether this discrepancy is caused by my ignorance and my bias, or by the ignorance and blind spots of the people who drew up the other lists. I would hate for anyone to think that I had included twelve Negro League players out of a kind of political correctness. I included them because they belong. Let me point out:

1. I have 34 white players born between 1867 and 1918 in my top 100. I can't see that 12 black players born in the same years is an excessive number; in fact, I think it is low. In terms of getting an accurate list, I am more bothered by the exclusions of Bullet Rogan, Spottswood Poles, and Willard Brown than by dropping Harry Heilman, Ralph Kiner, and Early Wynn.

2. The most inclusive of the other lists included five Negro League players. But the Negro Leagues also produced five of the top 100 in seven years in their death spasms—Jackie Robinson and Roy Campanella (1946), Willie Mays (1949), Hank Aaron (1952), and Ernie Banks (1953). If those leagues could produce five players like that in seven years, what about the previous forty?

3. It's not like one person saw Oscar Charleson play and said that he was the greatest player ever. *Lots* of people said he was the greatest player they ever saw. John McGraw, who knew something about baseball, reportedly said that, at least according to *The Sporting News* book (*Baseball's Greatest Players*).

His statistical record, such as it is, would not discourage you from believing that this was true. I don't think I'm a soft touch or easily persuaded; I believe I'm fairly skeptical. I just don't see any reason not to believe that this man was as good as anybody who ever played the game.

4. I believe that if there were a poll of experts about the Negro Leagues, Oscar Charleston would be selected as the greatest player in the history of the leagues.

5. There are twenty books about Joe DiMaggio, none (that I know of) about Oscar Charleston. DiMaggio appeared on magazine covers hundreds of times, probably thousands; I don't know that Charleston ever appeared on one. It is natural for people to believe that DiMaggio was greater than Charleston. But I believe that if skeptical, intelligent readers would take the time and trouble to learn about Charleston, this is about where he would be commonly rated.

I have Mantle rated higher than anyone else does, but just a little bit higher ... my argument would be that there has been too much talk about Mantle's drinking and too little about the impact of his career on base percentage, .421.

---

11. Tris Speaker
12. Henry Aaron
13. Joe DiMaggio
14. Lou Gehrig
15. Joe Morgan
16. Barry Bonds
17. Satchel Paige
18. Eddie Collins
19. Lefty Grove
20. Pete Alexander

Six of these players (Speaker, DiMaggio, Gehrig, Collins, Grove, and Alexander) are

rated here about the same as everyone else has rated them. Some people have Gehrig in the top ten, and most people have Aaron in the top ten. I wouldn't want to try to justify my rankings by badmouthing Aaron or Gehrig, because ... well, there is nothing bad to say about either one of them, as a man or as a ballplayer. I think that Ted Williams and Mickey Mantle, because they were on base so often, created more runs, at least relative to the game they were playing.

Gehrig also had a .447 career on base percentage. The SABR poll had Babe Ruth ranked as the greatest player of all time, Lou Gehrig second. There is an obvious problem. Gehrig and Ruth were teammates and regulars for ten years, 1925 through 1934. They won four pennants, not that I dismiss winning four pennants, but a lot of teams have won more. If you have the two greatest players in baseball history on one team at one time, shouldn't you at least match the success, let us say, of the St. Louis Cardinals with the young Stan Musial?

Rating Joe Morgan, I have him a little higher than anybody else does, although everybody rates him in the top 60, and most people in the top half of that. Joe Morgan in 1976 hit .320, and led the National League in on-base percentage (.444), slugging percentage (.576), stolen base percentage (60 of 69), sacrifice flies (12), and fewest Grounded Into Double Plays (2). He won the Gold Glove as the league's best defensive second baseman. It seems to me that that season, as a package, is the equal of anything ever done by Lou Gehrig or Jimmie Foxx or Joe DiMaggio or Stan Musial. It wasn't even his best season; his best season was 1975. He had three other seasons as good as 1976.

Morgan had a career batting average of .271—with a secondary average of .431. How can I rate a .271 hitter ahead of Rogers Hornsby? If you count his walks and stolen bases, Morgan accounted for 6,516 career bases, leading to 1,650 runs scored. Hornsby accounted for 5,885 bases, leading to 1,579 runs scored. Hornsby played in a league where team scored 4.43 runs per game; Morgan, an average of 4.11. Hornsby was an average fielder and a jackass; Morgan was a good glove and a team leader. Maybe you know the statistics better than I do, but my reading of the numbers puts Morgan ahead, and I don't see any subjective reason to reject the numbers, and go with Hornsby. I know that a lot of people will never be able to get past the batting average, but I think Joe Morgan was a genuinely great player.

Barry Bonds is still in mid-career, and no one knows where he will eventually rate. This rating is based on the assumption that his career ends with the 1999 season. Bonds' career on-base percentage and slugging percentage are about the same as Musial's. Bonds is as fine a defensive left fielder as anyone; if he was any better he would have been a center fielder.

Barry Bonds will almost certainly claim the position of the game's greatest power/speed combination, and probably will hold that spot for many years. He will probably break the career record for walks drawn, Babe Ruth's record now, Rickey Henderson's perhaps before it becomes Bonds'. He may well break the career record for runs scored, Ty Cobb's record now, with Henderson also in line to intercept that one. Unlike Henderson, he drives in almost as many as he scores. He will break or has already broken the career record for intentional walks. When people begin to take in all of his accomplishments, Bonds may well be rated among the five greatest players in the history of the game.

Satchel Paige is not rated by a lot of people because of the lack of stats for his best years . . . I don't think anyone questions that he was a great player.

21. Mike Schmidt
22. Rogers Hornsby
23. Cy Young
24. Frank Robinson
25. Turkey Stearns
26. Rickey Henderson
27. Pop Lloyd
28. Mel Ott
29. Jimmie Foxx
30. George Brett

My rankings for Schmidt, Cy Young, Frank Robinson, Mel Ott, and George Brett are consistent with everybody else's rankings. Turkey Stearns and Pop Lloyd are exemplars of a group we've already discussed. That leaves Rogers Hornsby, Jackie Robinson, and Rickey Henderson.

Rogers Hornsby is rated in the top ten by most people, who apparently don't feel it is important to have a second baseman who can field. Foxx I have rated a little lower than other people have, I think mostly because I've slipped some new players and some Negro League stars in ahead of him.

Rickey Henderson has a unique ability to alienate fans and sportswriters. I am confident that his greatness as a ballplayer will eventually obscure his obnoxiousness.

31. Mark McGwire
32. Jackie Robinson
33. Pete Rose
34. Eddie Mathews
35. Craig Biggio
36. Warren Spahn
37. Carl Yastrzemski
38. Tom Seaver
39. Arky Vaughan
40. Nap Lajoie

Craig Biggio? OK, Craig Biggio.

Craig Biggio is the best player in major league baseball today. If you compare Craig Biggio very carefully to Ken Griffey Jr. in almost any season, you will find that Biggio has contributed more to his team than Griffey has. Let's do 1998, as a starting point . . . in 1998 Ken Griffey outhomered Biggio, 56 to 20, which is a huge thing, 36 homers. Biggio's advantages were . . . well, everything else; apart from hitting home runs, he did everything better than Griffey.

Biggio's key advantages were 18 doubles (51-33) and 49 singles (137-88). How do you balance those things? Pete Palmer in *The Hidden Game of Baseball* pegged the value of a home run at 1.4 runs, a double at .8 runs, a single at .46, numbers which are probably as good as any other. That appraises Griffey's advantage at 50.4 runs (36 times 1.4), and Biggio's advantages at 37 runs, give or take a tenth (18 times .8, plus 49 times .46, which makes a total of 36.94). Griffey is still 13 and a half runs ahead, but we're just getting started.

Griffey had 76 walks and was hit by seven pitches, total of 83; Biggio drew 64 walks and was hit by 23 pitches, total of 87. Biggio stole 30 more bases (50 to 20) with only three more times caught stealing. Biggio made 436 batting outs (646 at bats, minus 210 hits); Ken Griffey made 453 batting outs (633 minus 180). Griffey hit one more triple but grounded into four more double plays. Biggio hit .360 with runners in scoring position, and homered far more often with men on base than he did with the bases empty. Griffey hit .310 with runners in scoring position, and homered slightly less often with men on base than with the bases empty.

When all of these things are taken into account, I estimate that Craig Biggio created 141 runs for the Houston Astros in 1998, making 459 outs. Griffey created 135 runs, making 476 outs.

But wait a minute; we're not done. Biggio did this in a league in which the average team scored 4.60 runs per game. Griffey was playing in a league where the average was almost 10% higher, 5.01 runs.

We're still not done. Griffey was also playing in a better *park* for a hitter (or should I say, a better dome). According to STATS Inc., the 1996–1998 park run index for the Kingdome was .97; for the Astrodome, .90.

Griffey is a center fielder, and a good one—but Biggio is a second baseman, and a good one. No real advantage there. In the Win Shares system for 1998, I have Biggio evaluated at 35 Win Shares, making him the second-best player in the National League, behind Mark McGwire (who hit 70 home runs), but ahead of Sammy Sosa (who won the MVP Award). I have Griffey at 29 Win Shares, which would still make him the second-best player in the American League.

Well, that's one year. What about 1997, when Griffey was the American League MVP?

Biggio was still better, 38 Win Shares to 36. Biggio scored 146 runs that year, without grounding into a single double play.

How about 1996? Biggio was better, 32 Win Shares to 28. 1995? Griffey broke his wrist that summer; it was Biggio 29, Griffey 9. 1994? Biggio 26, Griffey 20.

Griffey was better in 1993 (30-27), but Biggio was better in 1992 (32-26). In 1999 they were even, at 31 Win Shares apiece.

Look, I'm not knocking Ken Griffey. Ken Griffey Jr. is a great player. Craig Biggio is better. The fact that nobody seems to realize this . . . well, that's not my problem. I'm not going to rate players by how many Nike commercials they do.

I have Napoleon Lajoie rated lower than anyone else except the SABR poll. The other statistical analysts, Charles Faber, and *Total Baseball*, have Lajoie rated as the #1 or #2 player of all time, but they're mis-reading his fielding statistics—a misreading which may also have influenced other people.

Jackie Robinson is more often regarded as a historic figure, rather than a ballplayer. I think that strictly as a player, he's been underrated. I have Robinson evaluated, 100% based on his numbers, as the third-best player in the National League in 1949 (behind Stan Musial and Ralph Kiner), the third-best in 1950 (behind Earl Torgeson and Musial), the best player in the National League in 1951 (tied with Musial), and the second-best in 1952 (behind Stan Musial). In other years, before and after that, he ranks among the top ten.

Jackie hit .311 in his career, and it was far from an empty .311; his secondary average was .357. He is never thought of as a great defensive second baseman, yet his fielding percentage is outstanding, his range numbers are very, very good, and his rate of double plays per game is the third-best in baseball history, behind Bill Mazeroski and Bobby Doerr, and just barely behind them. The double play rate might not be impressive if the Dodgers had a ground ball staff and lots of runners on base, but in fact the Dodgers had *few* runners on base, and a *fly ball* staff; they were always near the bottom of the league in ground ball outs.

Jackie was a great baserunner; his stolen base totals aren't impressive, but if you read accounts of the 1947–1953 World Series, Robinson's baserunning exploits are all over the place. It seems like every time he got on base he made something happen. Several people have Rod Carew ranked ahead of Jackie. Rod Carew could play baseball, too, but I just don't see how you can come up with that answer. Carew has one advantage on Robinson (singles) and one area where he is arguably equal (baserunning). Robinson's got an edge in power, walks, and defense.

Let me write just a few paragraphs here for young readers, who don't remember Pete Rose's career. Pete Rose played the game differently than anyone else. When he drew a walk, he dashed to first base as if he were being chased

by a leopard, as fast as he would run on a ground ball to short. He ran to his defensive position at the start of the inning; he ran full tilt back after the inning was over. He actually *ran* from the on-deck circle to the batter's box; if he struck out he raced back to the dugout. If he had to back up another fielder, he backed him up full speed, as if he fully expected that he would have to make a play. He was not blessed with great speed or strength or quickness or agility, but he was perhaps the most competitive player who ever lived. He hustled, from April first to the end of the season, like nobody else we ever saw; he was called Charlie Hustle. He loved the game of baseball, he loved playing baseball for a living, and he made sure that it showed every day.

Sportswriters worshiped him. This was the guy, the one guy, who played the game the way is was *supposed* to be played, the human training film. More glowing, ecstatic prose was written about Pete Rose than about Michael Jordan, Magic Johnson, John Elway, Mark McGwire, and Twinkie Teletubbie combined. When Pete Rose was discovered to have feet of clay, the sportswriters who had lionized him turned on him like a pack of vultures.

Now, I never particularly *liked* the Pete Rose show, and for a long time about the only thing I ever wrote about him was that he wasn't as good as everybody said he was. But Pete Rose was never my hero, so his personal failings were never a source of pain to me. He is what he is. The man did get 4,256 hits in his career, more than a thousand of them for extra bases. He scored 2,165 runs, a staggering number, led the National League in hits seven times, in doubles five times, in runs scored four times. He drew more than 85 walks six times, won Gold Gloves as an outfielder, made the All-Star team at four positions, led the league in fielding percentage at three positions, led the league in outfield assists twice, won three batting titles, led the league twice in on-base percentage, had a 44-game hitting streak, had two streaks of 500 or more consecutive games played, and took six teams to the World Series.

Pete Rose had more extra base hits in his career than Mike Schmidt, Rogers Hornsby, Ernie Banks, Mickey Mantle, Al Simmons, Eddie Mathews, Willie McCovey, Harmon Killebrew, or Joe DiMaggio. The SABR poll had Pete Rose ranked below Roy Campanella. Pete Rose had almost as many extra base hits in his career as Campanella had hits. Which is better to start a pennant race with, a guy that you *think* might be the MVP, or a guy that you *know* is going to hustle every day and get 200 hits?

The other players I have ranked in a manner that's pretty consistent with how everyone else has ranked them, except for McGwire (who is new to such lists) and Arky Vaughan.

A lot of people seem to forget about Arky Vaughan; I don't know how else to explain him. Almost everybody has him rated below Cronin and Boudreau, who were contemporary shortstops. I don't see that. He was a better hitter than Cronin or Boudreau, he was faster—a lot faster than Boudreau. I'll discuss his ranking more in the ratings section—Shortstop, #2.

---

41. Yogi Berra
42. Christy Mathewson
43. Mule Suttles
44. Johnny Bench
45. Jeff Bagwell
46. Bob Gibson
47. Kid Nichols
48. Cal Ripken
49. Roger Clemens
50. Duke Snider

The most surprising rating in this group of ten, I would suppose, is Kid Nichols. Kid Nichols from 1896 to 1898 led the majors in Wins all three years, finishing 30-14, 31-11,

and 31-12. That three-year span is comparable to the peak years of Christy Mathewson, Walter Johnson, and Pete Alexander, all of whom came along just a few years later.

Nichols won 30 games four other times, 361 total. His career winning percentage was about the same as Greg Maddux's; he ranks ahead of Carl Hubbell, Bob Feller, Cy Young, Tom Seaver, Warren Spahn, Bob Gibson.

I think that Nichols suffers in history from the way that we simplify the data. Analysis is about simplification; what all analysts essentially do is to try to figure out ways to simplify the data with the least possible distortion. For pitchers, we tend to simplify the data by ignoring the records of 19th-century pitchers, which is largely appropriate, since they were playing a different game.

But in the case of Kid Nichols, it probably *isn't* appropriate. Kid Nichols went to the Western Association in mid-career; he went 27-7, then 21-12 for Kansas City (Western), then returned to the National League to go 21-13 for St. Louis. That wasn't in the 19th century; that was 1904. The 34-year-old Nichols was 21-13 with a bad team in the National League. *Total Baseball* has him ranked as the sixth greatest pitcher who ever lived. Maybe they're overrating him; maybe not. They're probably closer than the people who just write him off.

Christy Mathewson was rated 7th by *The Sporting News*, 13th by Maury Allen, 13th by the SABR poll, and 20th by *Total Baseball*, so I have him lower than anyone else does. Since none of us saw him pitch, and since all of us probably have read the same source materials, we are apparently disagreeing on how to interpret his statistics.

Mathewson, as I see it, was the fourth-best pitcher of his generation, behind Cy Young (who was about ten years older than he was), Walter Johnson, and Pete Alexander (who were about five years younger). His won-lost record is great, but then, he pitched for great teams. Mathewson had only one season (1905) when he was the best pitcher in baseball, plus three other years (1908, 1912, and 1913) when he was deserving of the National League Cy Young Award, but not as valuable as the best American League pitcher. I just don't think one year as the best pitcher in baseball is enough to rank him among the twenty greatest players of all time.

---

51. Sandy Koufax
52. Smokey Joe Williams
53. Roy Campanella
54. Tony Gwynn
55. Robin Yount
56. Bob Feller
57. Reggie Jackson
58. Ryne Sandberg
59. Charlie Gehringer
60. Wade Boggs

Second basemen here... the SABR poll ranked Charlie Gehringer 46th, Ryne Sandberg 98th. *The Sporting News* also ranked Gehringer 46th, and didn't include Sandberg at all. I don't see how you get that. To me, these guys are almost the same player, apart from the eras in which they played and the fact that they batted from opposite sides of the plate. Gehringer hit 184 homers, Sandberg 282. Gehringer stole 181 bases, Sandberg 344. Those advantages for Sandberg come from playing in an era when home runs and stolen bases were more common—but why did Gehringer hit .320 to Sandberg's .285? Because he played in an era when batting averages were higher. Other than that, their characteristics as players are about the same. Gehringer led the league in runs scored twice, a few other things; he led the league in batting once and won an MVP Award. Sandberg led the league in runs scored three times, a

few other things; he led the league in home runs once and won one MVP Award.

I don't think that either Sandberg or Gehringer was ever the best *hitter* in his league, even for one season. Gehringer was among the five best hitters in his league four times, Sandberg three times. Sandberg won nine Gold Gloves, and frankly probably didn't deserve quite that many; the Win Shares system shows him as deserving of four Gold Gloves. Gehringer played before Gold Gloves started, but is shown by Win Shares as deserving of six Gold Gloves. I just don't see very much to put any distance between them.

---

61. Eddie Murray
62. Johnny Mize
63. Harmon Killebrew
64. Rod Carew
65. Buck Leonard
66. Joe Jackson
67. Cristobal Torriente
68. Hank Greenberg
69. Willie McCovey
70. Home Run Baker

I have Hank Greenberg rated lower than anybody else except the purely statistical analysts (Faber and *Total Baseball*), both of whom have him rated even lower than I do. He was a big-impact hitter, but his career is short (even if you give him credit for missed seasons), his defensive value is limited, and his stats were inflated by playing in Tiger Stadium, where he hit most of his home runs.

Everybody except me rates Carew ahead of Killebrew. Killebrew played through the sixties; Carew played a little bit later, when there was a little bit more offense in the league. For each 162 games played, Killebrew scored 85 runs and drove in 105. Carew scored 93 runs and drove in 67. Their careers are of roughly the same length. Why is Carew ahead?

Defense? Carew played 1,184 games at first base, 1,130 at second; Killebrew played 969 at first, 791 at third, 470 in the outfield. Killebrew was a first baseman who could be stretched defensively to play third base, but not very well. Carew could play second base, but not very well. I think people rate Carew higher, once again, because they're hung up on batting averages. Carew hit .328, but with a secondary average of .249. Killebrew hit .256, but with a secondary average of .446. I think they're very close, but if push came to shove, I'd take the banger.

---

71. Al Simmons
72. Mickey Cochrane
73. Ken Griffey Jr.
74. Roberto Clemente
75. Frank Thomas
76. Cool Papa Bell
77. Ernie Banks
78. Steve Carlton
79. Mike Piazza
80. Roberto Alomar

Clemente, rated by the consensus of the other sources as the 13th greatest player of all time, has, I think, benefited from a halo effect because of his heroic death. He was a very fine hitter and a great outfielder, but he made a lot of throwing errors, never hit 30 homers in a season, and his strikeout to walk ratio was awful.

The other two players in this group that I have ranked lower than everybody else are Al Simmons and Ernie Banks; actually *Total Baseball* ranks them even lower than I do.

Simmons played in a hitter's park in big hitting era. He hit .334 but didn't walk; he had a lower career on-base percentage than Merv Rettenmund (.271), Earl Torgeson (.265), Bernie Carbo (.264), or Gene Tenace (.241). Simmons was an RBI man, and RBI men are almost always overrated, as opposed to lead-off type hitters, because a lot of people buy into "payoff" statistics without paying attention to the opportunities involved. Simmons piled up RBI, in part, because Maxie Bishop had a .423 on-base percentage.

In the first version of this book I compared Simmons to Al Oliver. I realize now that this was too harsh. Simmons was a better player than Al Oliver, and Al Oliver was a hell of a player. I would still rather have Duke Snider or Reggie Jackson.

Ernie Banks . . . in the first version of this book I had Banks listed as the 40th best player of all time, so what do I know now that I didn't know then?

I was underrating the park effects, and overrating his defense at shortstop. Banks was not regarded as a top-flight defensive shortstop; I argued then that he had been underrated. I was wrong. I'm not saying he was a *bad* shortstop; he was adequate. I pointed out then that he had won the Gold Glove in 1960, which is inconsistent with the idea that he was not a well-respected shortstop. This is true as far as it goes. Banks won the Gold Glove in 1960, as much as anything, by default; there are some leagues where there just isn't a Gold Glove shortstop, but you have to pick somebody.

Banks led National League shortstops in assists in 1959, with 519, and 1960, with 488. This sounds more impressive than it is.

1. The Cubs had a ground ball pitching staff, leading the league in team assists in 1959, finishing second in 1960.

2. Banks played more innings at shortstop than anybody else.

A better indication of the shortstop's range is the percentage of the team's plays made by their shortstops. That figure is just average, for the Cubs. And that has to be looked at in the context of the team's overall defensive performance, which in the Cubs' case was poor.

Banks hit 68 more homers at home (290) than on the road (222); that makes him among the most fortunate home run hitters in history. Banks was a fine player. If I was picking the National League MVPs I would pick Willie Mays in 1958 and Henry Aaron in 1959, but Ernie Banks second both years. I think he was one of the top 100 players of all time, but not one of the top 50.

The other ratings in this group are consistent with the historical consensus, except for the ratings of the 1990s players, who generally haven't been rated before. I doubt that any of them will eventually be rated *lower* than this; some of them will probably be ranked higher.

---

81. Tim Raines
82. Willie Stargell
83. Three Finger Brown
84. Paul Waner
85. Minnie Minoso
86. Willie Wells
87. Ron Santo
88. Frankie Frisch
89. Sam Crawford
90. Al Kaline

Tim Raines has been overlooked by everyone else except *Total Baseball,* which rates him much higher than I do. Raines, in my opinion, is the second-best leadoff man of all time, behind Rickey Henderson, but had the misfortune of being an exact contemporary not only of Henderson, but also of Paul Molitor, the third-greatest leadoff man ever.

No one else has Minnie Minoso in the top 100 except Faber, who excluded pitchers and ranked him 91st. Minoso didn't get to play in the majors until he was 28 years old, but had a better career after age 28 than almost any Hall of Fame left/right fielder. He had a .389 on-base percentage—better than any of the other outfielders in this part of the rankings except

Paul Waner (better than Raines, Clemente, Al Simmons, Stargell, Kaline, Ken Griffey Jr. For that matter, better than Willie Mays or Henry Aaron). Minoso hit for power, drove in 100 runs like clockwork, was a Gold Glove outfielder and one of the best baserunners of his time. Rate that group of outfielders in terms of power, defense, baserunning, batting average, etc., and I think you'll see that Minoso more than holds his own. He led his league at various times in hits, doubles, triples, total bases, hit by pitch (in which he led ten times), sacrifice flies, stolen bases, stolen base percentage, on base percentage, and slugging percentage. He never won a batting title, but was second in hitting twice, in the top five, five times. He was a hustling, aggressive player, immensely popular with fans in both Cleveland and Chicago. Had he gotten the chance to play when he was 21 years old, I think he'd probably be rated among the top thirty players of all time.

Al Kaline is rated 38th by the consensus of the other sources. I love Al Kaline. Dave Winfield has a lot of the same numbers, and he didn't make the top 100.

---

91. Brooks Robinson
92. Greg Maddux
93. Barry Larkin
94. Carl Hubbell
95. Martin Dihigo
96. Robin Roberts
97. Carlton Fisk
98. Kirby Puckett
99. Ed Delahanty
100. Billy Williams

Four of the other six lists have Brooks Robinson in the top 50. I agree that Brooks was the greatest defensive third baseman in baseball history. That's not enough, in my opinion, to make a slow .270 hitter with medium-range power one of the top 50 players in baseball history. I'll say this: if you're going to put Brooks Robinson in your top 50, you had sure better put Ken Boyer in the top 100, because Boyer did everything Robinson did just about as well, out-hit him by twenty points with more power and ran better.

Carlton Fisk has very similar career numbers, as a hitter, to Johnny Bench. Fisk was not rated in the top 100 by any other source except the SABR poll, which rated him about the same as I have. I don't see how you can rate Bench in the top 50, which most people do, and exclude Fisk from the top 100 when

1. They're both catchers.
2. They were born in the same year.
3. Fisk was a good defensive catcher.
4. They have essentially the same batting numbers.

Bench had big years; Fisk did the same things, but took a lot longer to do them, which diluted the impact. Bench deserves to rate ahead for that reason, but Fisk was still one of the best catchers the game has ever produced.

OUT OF THE TOP 100

Comparing my top 100 to other lists, the closest matches are *The Sporting News* list and the SABR poll, each of which has 74 of the same players in the top 100 that I do. I matched *Total Baseball* on 58 players, Maury Allen on 54, Honig and Ritter on 56, and the Faber list on 45.

I made a "consensus list" of the other lists. The number one player on the consensus list who didn't make my list was George Sisler, who was ranked 32nd by the experts.

Sisler hit .340 in his career, but with a secondary average of .231, since he didn't walk or hit for power. Per 162 games, Sisler scored 101 runs and drove in 93. In both categories he ranks below Larry Doby, Dolph Camilli, Heinie Manush, Deacon White, Fred Pfeffer, Ralph

Kiner, Larry Walker, Indian Bob Johnson, Chuck Klein, Dave Foutz, Albert Belle, Billy Nash, Tommy Henrich, Jack Rowe, Oyster Burns, Earl Averill, Henry Larkin, and Pete Browning, among many others who don't make the top 100 list, either. His key seasons were in a hitters era in a hitters park—yet his numbers are thin. He was a good player, but I certainly have no misgivings about leaving him out of the top 100.

The top 20 players who don't make my list, by their consensus rank on the other six lists, are as follows (consensus rank in parenthesis):

1. George Sisler (32)
2. Bill Dickey (44)
3. Bill Terry (53)
4. Whitey Ford (54)
5. Gabby Hartnett (57)
6. Harry Heilmann (58)
7. Jim Palmer (60)
8. Lou Brock (63)
9. Dizzy Dean (66)
10. Juan Marichal (69)
11. Joe Medwick (70)
12. Joe Cronin (71)
13. Luke Appling (72)
14. Steve Garvey (73)
15. Nolan Ryan (74)
16. Pie Traynor (75)
17. Bobby Doerr (77)
18. Ozzie Smith (80)
19. Luis Aparicio (81)
20. George Foster (83)

What do these players have in common? High batting averages, low secondary averages, relatively short careers, playing in big-hitting eras, playing in big-hitting parks, and pitchers whose records were buoyed by pitching for outstanding teams.

The top five hitters above (Sisler, Dickey, Terry, Hartnett, and Heilmann) all played in the big-hitting 1920s and 1930s; so did Medwick, Cronin, Appling, and Traynor. In my list, I ranked in the top 100 as many hitters from that era as from any other . . . here, let me show the time-line breakdown from my study:

19th century	2 players
1900–1924	16 players
1925–1949	27 players
1950–1974	30 players
1975–1999	25 players

Each player placed by the center of his career, as best I could determine that. I don't think I shorted the players from that era in the rankings. As I see it, the fact that a typical outfielder in that era hit .310, whereas in the 1960s the typical outfielder hit .265, doesn't make the hitters of the 1930s better than the hitters of the 1960s. It just means that they played under conditions more favorable to hitters.

The hitters listed above, with three exceptions, had lower secondary averages than batting averages, in all cases at least 11 points lower, and in many cases more than 50 points lower (Sisler, Terry, Traynor, Medwick, Garvey, Aparicio, and Appling all had secondary averages more than 50 points lower than their batting averages. The three exceptions are Cronin, Doerr, and Hartnett, all of whom had secondary averages a few points higher than their batting averages).

Players 101–110 on my list were Bill Dickey, Jim Palmer, Jimmy Wynn, Joe Cronin, Juan Marichal, Dave Winfield, Bobby Grich, Gaylord Perry, Paul Molitor, and Gary Carter.

Ozzie Smith? Yeah, I have misgivings about leaving Ozzie Smith out of my top 100. But if push comes to shove, who do you want: Barry Larkin or Ozzie Smith? I have great respect for Ozzie, but the top 100 spots are crowded with contestants, and I've chosen Barry Larkin.

One more note: I was surprised to see that Ralph Kiner was ranked in the top 100 by the SABR Poll, *The Sporting News, Total Baseball,* and Maury Allen. I don't know if you're old enough to remember this, but when Ralph Kiner was elected to the Hall of Fame in 1975, his selection was widely assailed as a mistake. The Hall of Fame has 200+ members. A consensus seems to have developed placing Kiner in the top 100, meaning the top half of the Hall of Fame.

CATCHER

1 ◆ Yogi Berra

(1946–1965, 2120 G, 358 1430 .285)

Did you ever notice how many great baseball players have what could be loosely described as a Hack Wilson type body? Kirby Puckett once said that his fantasy was to have a body like Glenn Braggs'. Kirby was a short, squat man who didn't look like a baseball player; Braggs was about 6-3, slender, fast, very graceful—and, of course, not one-tenth the player that Kirby Puckett was.

When you look around, there are a lot of good baseball players who have that Kirby Puckett body. Maybe I didn't phrase that right; there aren't very many ballplayers built like Kirby Puckett. But given that premise, they seem to be disproportionately successful—perhaps because scouts don't like them and don't want to sign them unless they're *really* good.

But perhaps, just perhaps, the short, powerful body is actually the best body for a baseball player. Long arms really do not *help* you when you're hitting; short arms work better. Compressed power is more effective than diffuse

power. Yogi Berra had that kind of a body—a short, powerful, funny-looking kind of guy. He wouldn't sign with the Cardinals, his hometown team, because the Cardinals wouldn't give him the same bonus they had given his buddy, Joe Garagiola. He'd been playing ball against Garagiola all his life; he *knew* that he was a better athlete than Joe was. Joe knew it, too. The Cardinals couldn't see it, because Yogi was even shorter and squatter than Joe.

Ducky Medwick was built like that. Matt Stairs has that kind of a body. Wilbert Robinson was built that way. Two or three Negro League stars had that kind of a body—Jud Wilson, Dobie Moore, George Scales. Tim Raines and Rickey Henderson are close to that body style, although not as exaggerated; so was Cupid Childs, and Billy Hamilton. Honus Wagner was 5'11", 200 pounds. Roger Bresnahan was 5'9" and weighed 200 pounds. Smoky Burgess was 5'8" and way over 200 at the end of his career. Roy Campanella was 5'9½" and weighed 205. Kevin Mitchell was short and powerful. That's more than a dozen players I've named so far, most of them great players. Lousy players outnumber great players a hundred to one—but can you name a dozen guys who had bodies like that and were lousy players?

2 ◆ Johnny Bench
(1967–1983, 2158 G, 389 1376 .267)

Of the top ten catchers in major league history, five were what you could call "Born Catchers," three were guys who had caught before they came to the majors, but it was touch-and-go whether they would settle in as catchers or out-fielders, and two were guys who had always been catchers, but didn't really have Grade A catching skills. Yogi, Gary Carter, and Mickey Cochrane were the three who could easily have wound up in the outfield. Torre and Simmons were the two who had always caught, but were born to hit. Bench was the best of the pure catchers.

In the second ten you've got about the same thing—you've got five pure catchers and five guys (Torre, Elston Howard, Bresnahan, Buck Ewing, and Wally Schang) who were "Catchers And."

Bench was a lot more impressive defensively than Berra; Berra was a guy who got the job done. Berra could throw, he could catch the ball, he could call the game, and he knew base-ball like nobody else. Casey Stengel, asked the secret of his success with the Yankees, once said "I never play a game without my man," by which he meant that he never played a big game without Yogi Berra behind the plate. Yogi was very good, but Bench was spectacular, of good size but somehow wiry, quick, active, confident, and blessed with a great arm.

3 ◆ Roy Campanella
(1948–1957, 1215 G, 242 856 .276)

Campanella was taught by Biz Mackey, who was manager of the Baltimore Elite Giants, and took Campanella on when he was fifteen years old. "The sternest, hard-ridingest coach I ever knew," Campanella said years later. "Biz wasn't satisfied for me to do just one or two things good. He wanted me to do *everything* good. And the onli-est way I was going to improve myself was by working at the game, working, working, work-ing, working. There were times when Biz Mackey made me cry with his constant dogging, but nobody ever had a better teacher."

Josh Gibson also went out of his way to help coach Campanella, an opposing catcher, not once but many times spending an hour with him working on his swing, or teaching him, as Campy said (quoting Gibson) that "a catcher has got to have ten eyes."

4 ◆ Mickey Cochrane
(1925–1937, 1482 G, 119 832 .320)

Cochrane, according to his own book, arrived in the majors as a poor defensive catcher. He played so poorly at catcher that Connie Mack tried him at third base, only to discover that he was an even worse third baseman. He could hit and he could throw, and Connie Mack and Cy Perkins taught him to catch; Perkins was the A's number one catcher, but nonetheless worked hard to help Cochrane take his job. On opening day of the 1925 season Perkins, a right-handed hitter, was due up in the eighth inning with the bases loaded, game tied, and a side-arming right-hander, Rudy Kallio, on the mound. Cochrane saw Connie Mack looking for a pinch hitter, and volunteered that he had hit Kallio hard in the Pacific Coast League. Mack let him pinch hit for Perkins. When he delivered a game-winning hit, Perkins, on the bench, said "there goes Cy Perkins job."

See also Muddy Ruel (51).

5 ◆ Mike Piazza
(1992–2000, 1117 G, 278 881 .328)

Too early to rate him with any confidence, but probably the best *hitting* catcher ever to play the game.

6 ◆ Carlton Fisk
(1969–1994, 2499 G, 376 1330 .269)

Trivia Question: Who was the only catcher in history to have 4,000 total bases?
Answer: No one; Fisk retired with 3,999.

The rumor circulated that I had refused to work with Fisk, or that Fisk had refused to catch me. The truth was the Red Sox were just getting Monty some work...Fisk never begged off catching me. Carlton wouldn't ask out of a game if he had both his legs cut off.—Bill Lee, *The Wrong Stuff*

Fisk scored more runs than any other catcher in history, actually a hundred more. He drove in more runs than any catcher except Berra, Bench, and Ted Simmons. He had 200 more total bases than any other catcher, including the guys like Joe Torre who piled careers at other positions onto their seasons as catchers.

If you have a player who

(a) holds major career hitting records for a catcher, and

(b) was an outstanding defensive catcher,

one might think it obvious that he should be rated among the greatest catchers of all time. Apparently it isn't, as nobody else rates him there, but I will point out that there is an argument—an *almost* persuasive argument—that I should have rated Fisk quite a bit higher.

One way to think about the issue is to telescope the player's career into a season, representing the career as if it were a season. Fisk had the longest career of any catcher, but still, he did have some serious injuries early on, so we can't represent him as having played 162 games in his career/season. We might represent him as playing, let's say, 145 games. Per 145 games, Fisk hit 24 doubles, 22 homers, drove in 77 runs, scored 74, stole 7 bases, and hit .269.

Suppose we give proportional representation to Roy Campanella. Campanella played less than one-half as many games as Fisk, 1,215 versus 2,499. If that makes 145 games for Fisk, it makes 70 for Campanella—70 games, 10 doubles, 14 homers, 36 runs scored, 50 RBI, .276 average, 1 stolen base.

Now, if we're picking these catchers on this one season, who are you going to take: the catcher who plays 145 games and hits .269 with 22 homers, or the guy who plays 70 games and hits .276 with 14 homers? It's pretty obvious, isn't it? Nobody's going to take the half-time player.

Well, why isn't this a valid way of thinking about the issue? I can see two opposing arguments:

1. Campanella is missing parts of his career on both ends, at the start because of segregation, at the end because of injuries.

2. Campanella, in part because of his sensational defense, has big-impact seasons.

I don't think you can give Campanella credit for what he might have done without the car wreck, and even if you do, he hadn't played well for two years before the crash. Hand injuries had more or less ended his career before the tragic accident.

We can give him some credit on the other end, but Campanella was in the majors at age 26. Most of his time in the Negro Leagues was more analogous to a training period than to an indefinite extension of his major league career. Let's say we credit him with three additional seasons. That might mean we should telescope Campanella's career to 92 games, rather than 70, but it is hard to see that this brings him up to even with Fisk:

	G	2B	3B	HR	Runs	RBI	Avg
Fisk	145	24	3	22	74	77	.269
Campy	92	13	1	18	47	65	.276

Second argument: Campanella had big seasons.

Well, but if Campanella hits .312 one season but .207 the next, .318 the third season but .219 the fourth—these are his actual averages—why does that make him better than a player who hits .270 every year? Returning to the argument that the career may be represented as a season, would we give favor, in an MVP analysis, to a player who hits .400 one month and .200 the next, as opposed to a player who hits .300 all year?

There is a difference, which is pennants. If Campanella is able to lift the Dodgers to a pennant by driving in 142 runs in one season, they don't take that pennant away because he drives in 50 the next year. A pennant lasts forever, so pennant impact must be considered. Roy Campanella led the Dodgers to the pennant in 1953 and 1955, winning the MVP Award both seasons as well as in 1951.

Yes, but. The fact that Carlton Fisk did not win an MVP Award does not mean that he was not a very good player. Fisk was fourth in the MVP voting in 1972, third in 1983, eighth in 1977 (he was voted first by one writer), and ninth in 1978. And the fact that Campanella won the MVP Award in 1951 and 1955 doesn't necessarily mean that he deserved it. In 1951 Campanella got less than half of the first-place votes, meaning that *most* of the MVP voters *did not* feel that he was the best player in the league. In 1955 he got eight first-place votes out of 24, the same number as Duke Snider, only two more than Ernie Banks. There are three problems with relying too heavily on the MVP vote:

1. It is, after all, merely a record of people's opinions. The same people who gave the National League MVP Award to Roy Campanella in 1951 and 1953 also gave it to Hank Sauer in 1952.

2. The notion that Roy Campanella was the indispensable element of the Dodgers' success in 1955 is somewhat undermined by the fact that the Dodgers had begun winning the National League pennant pretty regularly before they had Campanella, and continued to win it pretty regularly after they lost him. In 1956, when Campanella hit .219, the Dodgers won the pennant anyway.

3. The MVP voters of that era were besotted with the notion of strength up the middle. From 1948 to 1965, the writers gave 14 MVP Awards to catchers or shortstops, several more to second basemen and center fielders. Many of these awards are questionable.

Running at this from a different angle ... Fisk' major league career was more than twice as long as Campanella's. Now, I'm not saying that to get even, Campanella has to be twice as good; he doesn't. But he does have to be, at the very least, 10% better. I can't see that he is. Their batting averages are almost the same. Campanella has a little bit more power, but that's almost entirely due to playing in Ebbets Field; Fisk homered essentially as often in road games as Campanella. Fisk was a better base runner. What else is there?

Defense. Well, OK, but let's break that down to nuts and bolts. What, specifically, did Campanella do better than Fisk? Throwing? Well, OK, but in 1955, Campy's last MVP season, the National League average was 47 stolen bases per team. Let's assume that Campanella eliminated all base stealing against the Dodgers. What is that worth? Something less than ten runs.

Handling the pitching staff? But the Dodger pitching staff in Campanella's era wasn't all that great. They won their pennants with big bats.

Quickness behind the plate? OK. Soft hands? OK. Carlton Fisk was hardly Darrin Fletcher, but what are those worth? Do you see a lot of plays that hinge on the quickness of the catcher?

In any rating scheme, there is an unavoidable need to make arbitrary decisions. One of those choices is whether to rate players strictly on career accomplishments, or to rate them on their best seasons. My ratings attempt to compromise that issue, but give a lot of weight to big seasons. But there is certainly an argument to be made that Carlton Fisk was a better player than I have given him credit for.

7 ◆ Bill Dickey
(1928–1946, 1789 G, 202 1209 .313)
Was more or less a platoon player for much of his career. McCarthy never *said* that he was platooning Dickey, but he did. Dickey joined the Yankees in 1928. For nine years, although he hit .300 almost every year, he was overshadowed by Ruth and Gehrig, teammates, and by Cochrane and Hartnett, who were established as the top catchers in baseball. In 1932 he was suspended for a month after he broke Carl Reynolds' jaw in a fight. He finally broke through in 1936, when he learned to pull the ball down the right field line, and moved into the heart of the Yankee batting order . . .

Joe Gantenbein hit .290 with the Athletics in 1939, then had an off year in 1940 and lost his job. In 1943 he was in uniform, and he happened to run into Bill Dickey outside a hotel, waving for a taxi.

"Don't I know you?" Dickey asked.

"Sure," said Gantenbein.

"I can't remember your name," said Dickey. "But we used to pitch you high and outside."

8 ◆ Gary Carter
(1974–1992, 2296 G, 324 1225 .262)
Essentially interchangeable with Fisk, Bench, Hartnett, or Campanella—a right-handed power hitter and a Gold Glove catcher, ran OK, threw great, and knew what he was doing behind the

mask. He won three Gold Gloves, and in all honesty should have won more than that. Eric Gregg, longtime National League umpire, chose an All-Star team of the best players he had ever worked with in his 1990 book *Working the Plate* (William Morrow). "My catcher," he said, "is not Johnny Bench, but Gary Carter. He's the best I've ever seen, and believe me, we get to work very close to all the catchers."

9 ◆ Gabby Hartnett
(1922–1941, 1990 G, 236 1179 .297)
Al Capone was at Wrigley Field one day, called Gabby over to his box and asked him to sign an autograph for Capone's nephew. Gabby signed, and a photographer took a picture of the two together. When the picture appeared in the paper Judge Landis called Hartnett in and ordered him not to sign anything else for Scarface. "Judge," said Hartnett, "if that's your rule, it's OK by me. But I'm not explaining it to him. Next time you see him, YOU explain it to him."

Hartnett was the oldest of fourteen children. Defying probability, the first seven children were all boys; the last seven were all girls. Several of the children died in infancy, and one of his brothers was shot and killed in a household accident in March 1908.

His father, who was a good amateur catcher, was called "Dowdy," and Hartnett, whose legal name was Charles, became "Young Dowdy"; he was known to his family and close friends as "Dowdy" all his life. He was a marbles champion, like Pee Wee Reese; the book about him, *The Gabby Hartnett Story,* by James Murphy, claims that he had 55,000 marbles as a boy, although it would seem that such a claim should be documented somehow.

Anyway, Hartnett broke an arm when he was about 13, and there were fears that the arm was not set right, and would leave him a cripple. Once the cast came off his mother, Nell Hartnett, made him carry around a bucket of sand for several weeks, to straighten the arm. He had always had a strong throwing arm, and after the accident it was stronger than ever.

John McGraw heard about Hartnett and sent Jesse Burkett to check him out, but Burkett reported that Hartnett would never make it as a catcher because his hands were too small. Hartnett disliked Burkett, and would speak bitterly about him for many years after. He signed with Worcester of the Eastern League. He played fairly well, and Jack Doyle, scouting for the Cubs, took a liking to him, reportedly because he had "a strong puss" (a good face) and didn't back down on contact plays at home plate. Doyle bought him for the Cubs.

He was nicknamed "Gabby" because, as a rookie, he hardly ever said anything; it was an ironic nickname but ironically accurate, for Hartnett, once he got comfortable, was a gregarious, outgoing man. He won the MVP Award in 1935, and, of course, is most famous for the "Homer in the Gloamin'" in 1938, when he was 37 years old. The Win Shares system sees him as being deserving of the National League Gold Glove at catcher in 1927, 1928, 1930, 1932, 1933, 1934, 1935, and 1937—eight altogether, ranking him among the greatest defensive catchers in the history of baseball.

10 ◆ Ted Simmons
(1968–1988, 2456 G, 248 1389 .285)
An exceptional hitter, an underrated defensive catcher. Simmons was an OK catcher his first five years in the league; Bill Deane has studied the records at great length, and demonstrated that Simmons threw out an above-average percentage of opposing base stealers in his prime seasons. But the Cardinals weren't a very good team in those years; they spent most of the time fighting about something and criticizing one another for their failures, and then, too, Johnny Bench set an impossible standard for a young catcher; there was always a feeling that

Simmons' chance to shine would come when the Cardinals developed and Bench faded. But when the time came, Simmons' defense had become problematic and Whitey Herzog traded him, so people remember that Simmons couldn't throw. He handled pitchers well (with some exceptions, like John Denny), was reasonably active behind the plate, but most of his value was as a hitter . . .

Simmons almost wound up occupying Andy Messersmith's seat in baseball history. In 1972, his first All-Star season, Simmons held out, and played most of the season without a contract. The Cardinals finally gave him the money he wanted in August, after he had made the All-Star team.

11 ◆ Joe Torre
(1960–1977, 2209 G, 252 1185 .297)
An even better hitter than Simmons, but even more problematic as a fielder. It was a close call whether to list Torre as a catcher or a third baseman, since he was playing third base in 1971, when he won the MVP Award. He played more games and more innings at catcher. The premise of these ratings is that players are rated by position, but rated as total players; that is, everything Torre did in his career counts toward his rating, even if he did it while playing another position.

Torre's older brother played with the Braves. One of the turning points of his life came in 1955, when he visited the Braves' clubhouse and met one of his idols, Warren Spahn. "Boy, are you fat," said Spahn tactfully. He was fat, but he had been kind of hoping people wouldn't notice. The scouts had been noticing. Torre began to work on his weight, and emerged as a prospect.

When he reached the majors, although he wasn't *exactly* fat, he wasn't exactly thin, either; he always had a kind of a fat kid's body. Torre won a Gold Glove at catcher, in 1965. It was an absurd selection; he won it with his bat. The Gold Glove catcher in the National League in 1965 was John Roseboro or Tom Haller. Whitey Herzog said in *You're Missin' a Great Game* that "Joe Torre was the worst catcher I ever saw. The fans in the centerfield bleachers knew his number better than the ones behind home plate did." That's a little strong; he was a better defensive catcher than Mickey Tettleton or Brian Harper or Russ Nixon or somebody, but he wasn't very good.

12 ◆ Bill Freehan
(1961–1976, 1774 G, 200 758 .262)
Durable power hitter who could throw, very solid in every area of the game. An underrated player historically, in part because he played in an era in which hitters didn't compile big numbers. He was third in the MVP voting in 1967, runner-up to battery mate Denny McLain in 1968. In my opinion he was more valuable than McLain in '68.

13 ◆ Ivan Rodriguez
(1991–2000, 1260 G, 171 704 .304)
Being rated on the first half of his career; will probably be top-ten by the time he is through.

14 ◆ Thurman Munson
(1969–1979, 1423 G, 113 701 .292)
Four of the top 18 catchers of all time were born in 1947—Bench, Fisk, Boone, and Munson. If Fosse hadn't gotten hurt it might have been five . . . I doubt that Munson would rank significantly higher if he hadn't gone to the Ken Hubbs Flight Academy. Most catchers careers are ended by knee and back injuries. Munson already had serious knee and back troubles at the time of his death. His play had declined, and, while he had been an extremely effective player, he did not have the breadth of offensive skills to have stayed in the game as a hitter. He didn't walk, and he didn't have

tremendous power. If you hit .300 and run fairly well, that's one thing, but if you slow down and hit .260, you're out of the game. His career secondary average was .209.

Favorite line about him . . . Sparky Lyle, asked about Thurman being "moody," replied "Nah, Thurman's not moody. When you're moody you're nice sometimes. Thurman's just mean."

15 ◆ Elston Howard
(1955–1968, 1605 G, 167 762 .274)
Howard reached the Yankees in 1955 and, although he played fairly well, was never a star until 1961. Everybody knows that Bill Dickey worked with the young Yogi Berra, teaching Berra to catch. But fewer people know that Dickey stayed with the Yankees for years as a coach, and also worked with Elston Howard when Stengel finally decided that Howard was going to be his next catcher. In 1961, the first year post-Casey, Howard burst into the limelight with a .348 season, 21 homers, and then had four genuinely outstanding seasons, 1961–64, winning an MVP Award with a 1963 season that, in all honesty, was not 1% better than the other three seasons. We have his Win Shares from 1961 through 1964 at 29, 20, 28, and 32. He faded quickly after that, due to injuries.

This is very much the same career pattern that Bill Dickey had. Dickey reached the Yankees in late 1928, but he, too, was never really outstanding until 1936, when he hit .362 with 22 homers. He, also, was then superb for four years, posting Win Share totals of 25, 32, 27, and 27. Then, like Howard, he had injuries and faded away.

Obviously Dickey was better than Howard, although not all that much better, in my opinion, and just a tiny bit better in his four big seasons. And, to the extent that Dickey was better, he was better mostly because the park—Yankee Stadium—favored Dickey, whereas it almost ruined Howard. In his career, Dickey hit more than two-thirds of his home runs in Yankee Stadium—one of the highest home-park home run percentages in history.

Howard, on the other hand, has one of the *lowest* percentages of home runs at home, because Yankee Stadium at that time was a $20 taxi ride to left field. Dickey outhomered Howard 202 to 167, in careers of fairly comparable length, but that's all because of Yankee Stadium. In road games, Howard outhomered Dickey 113 to 67.

16 ◆ Roger Bresnahan
(1897–1915, 1430 G, 26 530 .280)

Roger Bresnahan was elected to the Hall of Fame a few weeks after his death in December 1944. This has been a controversial selection, but then, few men's careers were ever more blessed with controversy. To recount briefly the highlights, Bresnahan first appeared in the major leagues as an eighteen-year-old pitcher on August 28, 1897, pitching for the Washington Senators in the National League. He pitched a six-hit shutout, and showed "a speedy shoot, an outcurve, an inshoot, and a drop ball." Veteran catcher Deacon McGuire was impressed, and said that Bresnahan was made of "the right stuff." He won four games without a loss for Washington that fall, then was released the next spring in a dispute over how much money such a phenom should be paid. That should give you an idea of Roger's temperament, and also a hint as to why the Senators of that era were so terrible.

Bresnahan resurfaced as one of John McGraw's men on the Orioles, and then the Giants, in the first years of the twentieth century. A short 200-pounder who was fast and strong and agile and aggressive, Roger became one of McGraw's best friends, and played every position on the field for him. He caught in 1901, then moved to the outfield, primarily center,

from 1902 to 1904. In 1903 he hit .350. In 1905 he became the Giants' catcher, apparently at the urging of Christy Mathewson.

During 1907 and the fabulous sustained pennant race of 1908, Bresnahan introduced two new pieces of equipment in an effort to stay in the lineup and catch more than the 85-100 games that were normal for a catcher at that time. One was shin guards; the other, equally significant although less famous, was a padded face mask. He caught 139 games in 1908, while George Gibson of Pittsburgh, adopting the equipment, caught 140, and several other catchers also worked very large numbers of games. In 1909, following a beaning, Bresnahan also experimented with a batting helmet, although this would not catch on for almost half a century.

Anyway, in the winter of 1908–1909, Stanley Robison, owner of the St. Louis Cardinals, moaned during a National League meeting that his manager, John McCloskey, had finished last in 1908 with the best pitching staff in the league. He let it be known that he was looking for a new man. Word of this got to John McGraw. McGraw, knowing that Bresnahan wanted to manage (what Bresnahan really wanted, one suspects, was to be John McGraw), and perhaps tired of contending with the explosive catcher's temper, set up a meeting between Bresnahan and Robison. When the two of them reached an agreement, McGraw then extracted three players from St. Louis (Red Murray, Bugs Raymond, and Admiral Schlei) in exchange for Bresnahan, who became player/manager of the Cardinals.

As manager he took over a 49-105 team that had traded its two best players, Murray and Raymond, to acquire him. He brought the team slow progress, to 54-98 in 1909, 63-90 in 1910, and 75-74 in 1911.

Bresnahan was a throwback to the Irish nineties. Almost every paragraph written about him seemed to include the adjective "fiery." He was one of those guys that if you were on his team and played hard he was as nice to you as could be, but if you got on his bad side you'd think he was the Breath of Hell. The 1910 *Reach Guide* reported that "Bresnahan's numerous disputes with, and ejections by, the umpires, in their cumulative effect, caused his team much loss in prestige and possible victories. In all other respects Bresnahan ... scored a decided success, as he infused aggressiveness and ambition and kept the team keyed up to its best efforts nearly all season." In 1911 the same publication reported that the St. Louis catching "was inefficient when Bresnahan was off duty, and he was off a great deal due to frequent suspension for umpire-baiting." A 1910 order from the league office to control vile and unbecoming conduct toward the umpires cited Bresnahan, and only Bresnahan, by name.

At the winter meetings that year Bresnahan became involved in a loud argument with President Murphy, of the Chicago club, in the lobby of the Waldorf Hotel, after which he asserted in the presence of reporters that Murphy had impugned his honor and gone so far as to call him a liar. This incident was argued about in the public presses for a year following, and was of such magnitude that at the league meeting the next year Garry Herrmann, chairman of the National Commission, spoke about it in his address. "I refer to the accusations of Manager Bresnahan, of the St. Louis National League Club, that President Charles W. Murphy, of the Chicago Nationals, openly impugned his motives in the performance of an official act and branded him a liar in a hotel lobby. Such incidents serve to discredit those in control of clubs and to bring the league with which they are associated into disrepute," Herrmann said, and went on to propose a system of reviews and punishments to follow any such future incident. Yet in spite of this record, Bob O'Farrell in *The Glory of Their Times* remembered

Bresnahan kindly, and said that "aside from Bresnahan, nobody helped me any."

In the spring of 1911 Robison died and Lady Bee Britton, remembered as the prettiest young woman ever to own a baseball team, inherited the Cardinals. In the inimical manner of owners of all gender and appearance, Lady Bee began to criticize Bresnahan's managing, in public. When he confronted her about this, relations between the two of them deteriorated quickly. Apparently he used much the same selection of his vocabulary to address the lady that he used on the field. Bresnahan and Britton feuded, the team foundered, and Bresnahan was fired.

This involved him in a monstrous salary hassle, when he insisted, of all things, that the Cardinals honor his contract and pay him both as a player and on the managing contract. He had signed a five-year contract with Robison shortly before Robison's death, and had four years left on it. He refused to report, was traded, couldn't clear waivers, was shipped to Chicago, and continued the battle from there, supported by the infant Player's Union. He eventually won a $20,000 settlement, equivalent to about $300,000 in modern money. He later managed the Cubs for a year, but they had an off season, and he was not destined to be John McGraw, after all.

Was he a great player? He was a very good player. Three things helped to put him in the Hall of Fame—the shin guards, the timing of his death, and a comment that Fred Lieb wrote about him in *The St. Louis Cardinals, the Story of a Great Baseball Club,* published in 1944, which accentuated the normal emotional support that follows the death of a player. Lieb wrote that "Bresnahan was a great catcher, one of the greatest of all time. Roger was really an all-around player, who could have starred at any position." John B. Foster in 1938 also named Bresnahan as the second-greatest catcher of all time, behind Buck Ewing. John

McGraw said of him that "He was the greatest catcher I ever saw. What other catcher was fast enough to lead off? What other catcher could run bases with such speed and cleverness? What other catcher could hit .300, catch as Bresnahan could catch, and play any position where you needed him? What other catcher had his courage?"

And then McGraw added, "If he only didn't have such a temper . . ."

17 ◆ Buck Ewing
(1880–1897, 1315 G, 71 883 .303)
Ewing was an active, athletic catcher like Rick Dempsey or Jim Sundberg, and also a career .300 hitter, led the National League once in homers and once in triples. He was regarded by many people as the best player in nineteenth century baseball. John Foster, a long-time baseball writer, wrote in the 1938 *Spalding/Reach Guide* that "he has been called the greatest all-round player ever connected with the game. I think that he was . . . As a thrower to bases Ewing never had a superior, and there are not to exceed ten men who could come anywhere near being equal to him."

When the Hall of Fame opened there were originally supposed to be ten players selected to open the house—five "modern" players (post-1900) and five "old-timers." The voting system was screwed up, so the five original old-timers were not selected, but Ewing tied with Cap Anson for first place among the pre-1900 players. The Win Shares system also rates him as a superb defensive catcher, with a career rate of 7.29 Win Shares per 1000 defensive innings—fifth all-time among catchers with 5000 or more innings.

For these reasons, I had originally rated Ewing among the top five catchers of all time. I wound up dropping him, for two reasons. One is that in his entire career he caught only about 5,413 innings. Let's assume that he was one

hellacious defensive catcher. So was Gary Carter, and Gary Carter caught 17,373 innings. What could Ewing possibly have done that would make him even?

Ewing caught fewer innings in his major league career than Mike Stanley, Stan Lopata, Joe Ferguson, Ed Herrmann, or Paul Casanova. He caught fewer innings than anyone else rated in the top 100 catchers except Doggie Miller. He caught more than 1,000 innings less than John Romano, who is rated low because his career was short. He caught almost 2,000 innings less than Joe Torre, who moved to third base at age 30.

I know that many catchers in Ewing's era split their time between catching and other positions, but Deacon McGuire, who was a contemporary or Ewing's, caught (about) 13,460 innings in his career—two and a half times as many as Buck. Wilbert Robinson and Chief Zimmer caught twice as many as Ewing. I just don't think you can write that off.

The other reason I dropped him was I realized that I needed to temper the press clippings by remembering that he was a New York player. I've nothing against New York players; five of the top 14 catchers are New York players, six if you count Gary Carter. But sometimes, when you're dealing with a New York player, you do have to let some of the air out of the press notices.

18 ◆ Darrell Porter
(1971–1987, 1782 G, 188 826 .247)
Porter had a career secondary average of .332. Immensely strong, good arm, very disciplined hitter; played almost all of his career in poor home run parks, and lost about 34 homers to the parks he played in. Had a drug problem in mid-career; found Christ, but lost his killer instinct, and started gradually to put on weight. Whitey Herzog said that "the base stealing we were known for wasn't really our foundation.

That came in the form of a guy who couldn't get to first base any faster than I can, wore big glasses, talked softer than a church mouse, missed the highlight reels, and rarely made a dent in those glamour categories you read about in *USA Today*. But if you want to learn about winning, money-making baseball, look no further than the man I brought from Kansas City to squat behind the plate."

19 ◆ Lance Parrish
(1977–1995, 1988 G, 324 1070 .252)

Who would you like to have back, Tiger fans: Freehan or Parrish? Parrish had a stronger arm than Freehan and more power, but had more holes in his game. Freehan's on base percentage (.340) was 27 points higher than Parrish's, more than that if you make era adjustments. Parrish made more errors and was charged with almost twice as many passed balls (192 to 106), mostly because Parrish for much of his career wasn't quick enough to pounce on a ball that bounced a few feet away from him and prevent a runner from advancing.

Don't get me wrong; Parrish was a good player. He was in some ways similar to Ernie Lombardi, who is a Hall of Famer; Lombardi was a .300 hitter and Parrish was a 30-homer guy, but they were both huge catchers with strong arms and very limited mobility. Parrish was charged with more passed balls than any other twentieth-century catcher; Lombardi is third on that list, behind Parrish and Ted Simmons. Nobody ever blocked the plate any better than Parrish.

20 ◆ Wally Schang
(1913–1931, 1840 G, 59 710 .284)

Was the regular catcher for six American League championship teams–the 1913 and 1914 Philadelphia A's, the 1918 Red Sox, and the 1921, 1922, and 1923 Yankees; was also a backup for the Philadelphia A's in 1930. Switch hitter,

walked a lot and ran unusually well for a catcher. Decent defensive catcher, not the equal of Ray Schalk, but good. In the 1921 World Series he gunned down nine runners stealing, effectively stopping the Giants running game; in the next two Series (1922 and 1923) the Giants stole only two bases. Schang threw out 14 of 23 base stealers in those three World Series.

21 ◆ Bob Boone
(1972–1990, 2264 G, 105 826 .254)

A very smart receiver, and worked as hard to stay in shape as anyone who ever played baseball. Not much of a hitter, but one of the five greatest defensive catchers of all time. My favorite Bob Boone story . . . In the 1980 World Series, which Darrell Porter lost for the Royals almost single-handedly, there were two plays on which Porter was out at home plate, and tried to tip-toe in, avoiding a collision. This really wasn't typical of Porter, who was a hard-nosed player, but he chose the wrong time to turn into Darrell Milquetoast. Anyway, after the second play a reporter asked Boone if there was some sort of gentleman's agreement among catchers. "Yeah," said Boone, "the agreement is you get knocked on your ass."

22 ◆ Ernie Lombardi
(1931–1947, 1853 G, 190 990 .306)

Ernie Lombardi was a huge man, with huge, oak-trunk legs and huge feet and huge hands and a promontory with nostrils that protruded from a lumpy face. He had huge arms and wrists like giant power cables that snapped around an unnaturally large bat, the heaviest used by any player of his time, and flicked the ball effortlessly wherever he wanted it to go. As he got older he acquired a huge belly, which he lugged around with a huge effort.

His knees were too low to the ground, and his center of gravity was four feet behind him, so that he was never endowed by nature with adequate speed. As he got older he slowed down, becoming surely the slowest player ever to play major league baseball well. The slowest player today is probably Mo Vaughn. If they raced three times around the bases, Mo would lap him.

Ernie Lombardi was born in Oakland on April 6, 1908. He attended Cole Elementary School through the eighth grade, closing the books on his education at that time, probably 1922. His parents ran a little Italian grocery store, where Ernie helped out for the next several years when not playing baseball on the corner lot or at Bayview Park, where he spent hour after hour working through games with a childhood friend named Abe Rose. In 1926 he played a few games with the Oakland Oaks of the Pacific Coast League, whom he joined for real the next season. Being regarded as raw for this league, Lombardi was dispatched to Ogden in the Utah-Idaho league, where he hit .398 in 50 games, earning a recall to his hometown Oaks. In three seasons in the Pacific Coast League, Ernie hit within a few points of .370 each year, hitting over 20 homers and driving in over 100 runs in 1929 and 1930.

Lombardi was sold that winter to Brooklyn, for $50,000. The Dodgers, who were managed by a huge old catcher (Wilbert Robinson) were apparently of the opinion that you can never get enough catching, but more on that later. Ernie reported to the Dodgers' training camp on March 7, 1931. "Ernest Lombardi travels light," reported Quentin Reynolds the next day in the *World-Telegram*. "He carries nothing but a blue serge suit, a well-worn cap, a small leather bag, the biggest schnozzola ever seen in baseball circles and a .370 batting average."

Introduced to Uncle Robbie (Mgr. Robinson), the big man with the big nose said, "I'm Lombardi, from Oakland." He said this in a tone that, according to Reynolds, seemed to announce as well that he would lick any man in

the house for two dollars. "He weighs 220 pounds right now but he isn't fat. He stands six foot two and his hands are like two enormous hams hanging at the end of his arms. He totes a 42-ounce bat, the heaviest on the club, and as far as any of the players could recall the heaviest in the league . . . (the other players) raised incredulous eyelids at the strange apparition."

Less impressed, Uncle Robbie told him that he would never remember a name like Lombardi and that from now on he was Lumbago, and asked him where his golf clubs were. Lombardi sneered at the idea of a ballplayer playing golf. He and Uncle Robbie became fast friends.

In the minors he had been called Bochy Lombardi, after the kind of lawn bowling popular on the West Coast, but his arrival as a major league player required, in those days, a rechristening with a new name. The fact that Lumbago was a tremendous line drive hitter was immediately apparent, and drew much comment in the papers before he ever played in an intra-squad game. He also "snapped the ball to second base with a whip like motion that brought a look of respect to Al Lopez's eye" (*World-Telegram,* March 8, 1931). Al Lopez was the Dodger's starting catcher. That whip like throw to second was to become one of Ernie's trademarks, along with his nose, his slowness afoot, his heavy bat, his fingers intertwined on the bat.

The fingers—I should explain that. At some point in Lombardi's years with Oakland he had sustained an injury (or, according to one source, had a blister) on one of his fingers. To help protect the sore pinkie, he began interlocking the fingers of his two hands while he gripped the bat. He liked the effect this had on his bat control, and after the injury he continued to do it. The sportswriters sometimes called it a golf grip (or the Gene Sarazen grip) although golf had nothing to do with its origin.

As impressive as Lombardi was as a hitter and thrower, and as much as Uncle Robbie liked him, there just wasn't a place for him. The Dodgers catcher was a defensive wizard and field general named Alfonzo Raymond Lopez, who is also listed here. Lopez was four months younger than Lombardi, who at that time was twenty-two. As a rookie the year before, Lopez had hit .309 in addition to his exceptional defensive skills. Other than Lopez and Lombardi, the Dodgers had a respected veteran in Val Picinich, and another youngster, Paul Richards, who was the same age as Lopez and Lombardi. At first base was Del Bissonette, one of the team's best hitters, and the idea of moving Lombardi to the outfield, given his speed, was out of the question. Playing little, Lombardi "won a big following among many fans" (*World-Telegram*, March 14, 1932).

What, then, to do with him? In September of his rookie year, Robinson hit on the solution: make him a pitcher. Robbie had Lombardi pitch batting practice a few times, and he liked what he saw—a crackling fast ball, an easy motion, excellent control. He didn't have a breaking pitch, but the Dodgers were desperate for pitching, and Robbie figured he could learn that. Some sportswriters were so indiscreet as to compare Lombardi's fastball to that of Walter Johnson.

Robinson's eighteen-year reign at the helm of the Dodgers ended at the close of the season, and the idea of moving Lombardi to the mound died with it. Max Carey was managing the Dodgers in the spring of 1932, and he wanted more of a sleek, aggressive team. During spring training, 1932, Lombardi was thrown in on a three-for-three trade with Cincinnati.

At first the trade didn't seem to work out for Cincinnati. "With his club in the basement," wrote Charles L. Parker that summer, "you might figure that the manager would be ready to admit certain mistakes in assembling such a team, especially when players he yielded in his big trade of the year are making a pennant contender of another outfit. But not so with Dan Howley, of the Cincinnati Reds, who last March gave Joe Stripp, Tony Cuccinello and Clyde Sukeforth to Brooklyn for Babe Herman, Ernie Lombardi and Wally Gilbert."

"It was not the falling down of any of my three men that caused my team to tumble," responded Howley. Lombardi, though charged with a league-leading 17 passed balls, hit .303 and drove in 68 runs in 118 games. He also hit nine triples, evidence that his mobility at that point was not the problem it later became.

In a few years there would be no doubt about who won the trade. The legend of Lombardi was growing in Cincinnati. On May 8, 1935, he hit four doubles and a single in a game. Hitting .300 every year, he landed home runs on the roof of a laundry beyond the left field fence at Crosley Field. It was a tough home run park, and cost him several homers a year. He was such a character, stronger than life. He became, according to many reports, the most beloved player ever to play in Crosley Field. In 1937 he drilled a pitch back to the mound, breaking three fingers on the hand of Cub pitcher Larry French. His strength was legend. His slowness afoot was legend. His disrespect for coaching strategy was legend (he swore that in one game he told the opposing hitters what was coming on every pitch, and the Reds still won). His snoring was legendary. One of his roommates, Chick Hafey, tried everything imaginable to stop him from snoring—tied his big toe to the foot of the bed, tried to get him to sleep with an ice pack on his tummy.

His nose poked out through the slats of his face mask, so that sometimes he would skin his nose on a foul tip. Sportswriters, trying to capture this amazing image in words, gave him nicknames by the bushel—Schnozzola, the

Schnozz, Lumbago, Bocci, Muss, Dogs (after his aching feet), and (my particular favorite) the Cyrano of the Iron Mask. He had the personality of the gentle giant, the man whose sheer physical presence made him feel unthreatened, and magnified any threat he might happen to project. The world calls upon such men to put on a benevolent face, and Lombardi responded. He was quiet, taciturn, yet fully engaged in the clubhouse give and take, handing out vaguely insulting nicknames and accepting them with grace. Dick Bartell reports that he was often the butt of practical jokes, a kind of clubhouse equivalent of school kids teasing the elephant. He hated to be shown up, though.

In *Rowdy Richard*, Dick Bartell recalls that Tony Cuccinello once pulled the hidden ball trick on Ernie, catching him off second base. When he showed him the ball, Lombardi said "You tag me and I'll punch you right in the nose." Cuccinello, naturally, did not tag him, and Ernie walked off the field. He would show this character trait many times over the next forty years. He hated to fall on his face, and he hated to be shown up.

Lombardi was not equally beloved by the Cincinnati management. Beginning in about 1936, Lombardi held out for more money every spring. He just didn't care for spring training, on the one hand, and then on the other hand he never cared for the Cincinnati salary offers. Every spring he held out, and every spring there were rumors that he was as good as traded, usually to the Giants, where Bill Terry was outspoken in his admiration for Lombardi. He held out in 1936, in 1937, in 1938; in the spring of 1938 the rumor had him going to New York with Harry Craft for Gus Mancuso and two other players.

Fortunately for the Reds, they didn't make the trade. Bill McKechnie was hired to manage the Reds in 1938, and Lombardi blossomed under his guidance. He made the All-Star team

for the first time. Johnny Vander Meer pitched his two no-hitters, Lombardi catching both of them; this improved his defensive reputation. Going into the last day of the 1938 season Ernie led Johnny Mize by two points in the race for the batting title. McKechnie offered him the day off, but Lombardi, as Ted Williams would three years later, refused to earn the title sitting on the bench. He played and got two hits to win the title, hitting .342. The Reds moved up to fourth place, and Lombardi was named the Most Valuable Player in the National League. He was given an expensive shotgun as part of the prize for his MVP Award. As a reward for his performance, and to avoid another holdout, Cincinnati General Manager Warren Giles (later NL President) gave him a $3,000 bonus. His salary for the season had been $13,000. He signed in 1939 for $17,000.

It was in this period, according to Lee Allen, that Lombardi emerged as perhaps the most improbable matinee idol in the history of sex. A bashful, retiring man with crooked teeth and a nose like an eggplant, Lombardi, for reasons unclear, began to attract huge crowds of women. According to Allen *(The Cincinnati Reds)* "the ladies shrieked with joy at every move the big catcher made. There was a Sinatra-like adulation of Lom that affected women of all ages, not just bobby-soxers, and after each game they would gather (and wait) to see their hero emerge in street clothes." Lombardi, who lived with his sister in the off season, was petrified of the attention, and would hide out in the training room for hours after the game, drinking beer and waiting for the women to go home.

I believe that it was following the MVP year that the defenses began to get really weird against him. The infielders, realizing that they had extra time against Ernie, had always played him deeper than they played anybody else. Now, however, they recalculated the risks, and backed up even more. Third basemen and shortstops played several feet back on the outfield grass, as deep as their throwing arms would permit them to play. Sometimes they played deeper than their arms would allow; if the ball was hit toward them they would get the ball and run in several steps before throwing. Ernie told Pee Wee Reese that "You had been in the league for five years before I realized you weren't an outfielder." That Ernie could continue to hit .300 by firing bullets between five outfielders nourished his legend. Arthur Daley wrote that "When you look back on . . . his 17 years in the majors, you almost come to the conclusion that he was the greatest hitter of all time." Bill McKechnie said later that he always thought that Lombardi was the only man who could have beat Hugh Duffy's record .438 batting average, if the defenses had had to play honest against him.

The 1939 season was to be, for Lombardi, a painful, glorious, wretched year. On June 11, following a double header in Brooklyn, Lombardi stepped on a broken board in the shower room at Ebbets Field, and ran a splinter into the ball of his left foot. He was out of the lineup for about two weeks. He slumped on his return, but recovered in time to make the All-Star team, again catching the entire game for the National League. The Reds, a last-place team in 1937, were driving toward the pennant. In a crucial game against the Cardinals in September, Ernie's snap throw to second caught Johnny Hopp off second base and stopped a rally. Hitting far below his average following the injury, he hit .343 in September to push him up to .287—50 points below what he usually hit—and reached a career high of 20 home runs. The Reds won the pennant for the first time since 1919.

In the fourth and final game of the 1939 World Series, Lombardi's career was struck by the kind of malevolent media lightning which flashes across the landscape, scarring a random target—a Kato Kaelin here, a Fred Snodgrass there. It was the tenth inning and there were men on first and third when DiMaggio singled to right. Ival Goodman fumbled the ball for a moment before throwing home. The throw arrived just ahead of Charlie Keller, the runner from first base. Keller slammed into Lombardi, knocking the 230-pound receiver flat on his back. While he lay on his back a few feet from home plate, the ball on the ground beside him, DiMaggio raced around the bases to give the Yankees a three-run lead.

Ernie's Snooze. Lombardi's Sit-down Strike. The Schnozz's Swan Dive. The play grew to have as many names as the player. His selection as the series goat was absurd. The Yankees won the series in four straight. Ival Goodman made an error on the same play. Billy Myers had made an error (bobbled a ground ball) to put Keller on first base moments earlier. The run scored by DiMaggio changed the score from 6-4 to 7-4. Bucky Walters, the pitcher, faulted himself for not backing up the play. Anyone could have been the goat; the series was a rout. Nonetheless, the image of the behemoth catcher lying on his back, making no apparent effort to resist the fate that was overpowering his team, became the dominant image of the series, and would haunt Lombardi the rest of his life.

"It was an awful hot day in Cincinnati," Lombardi remembered years later, "and I was feeling dizzy . . . When Keller came in, he spun me around at the plate and I couldn't get up." (*New York Times*, September 28, 1977.) "I was kind of knocked senseless," he told another reporter. "Keller really whacked me."

Keller, oddly enough, insisted that he had run by Lombardi without touching him. Keller was a rookie, perhaps lost in the excitement of the moment. Films are choppy, but suggest that there was a collision. One of the ironies of his career is that Lombardi was famous, among so many other things, for his toughness, and for blocking the plate better than any other catcher.

Lombardi became the Bill Buckner of the 1930s. A sensitive, avuncular man, Lombardi was deeply hurt by the attacks. When Warren Giles used his misfortune against him in contract negotiations in 1940, Lombardi again balked at signing. Giles offered him $14,000, seeing this as a reasonable cut—$3,000—for a player who had dropped 55 points from his MVP season the year before. Lombardi, counting the $3,000 bonus following the 1938 season as part of his 1939 salary, saw this as an attempt to cut him $6,000 for setting a career high in home runs and helping his team to the National League pennant, all based on this stupid World Series fiasco. Rumors were that he would be traded to Brooklyn, for Babe Phelps.

Most of the press supported Lombardi in his battles with Giles. A Cincinnati paper solicited letters on keeping or trading Lombardi. It got 945 answers saying to keep Lombardi, and 23 saying to trade him.

Eventually Lombardi and the Reds worked it out. Lombardi reported determined to redeem himself, and was, according to reports, hustling as never before. The Cincinnati fans forgave him by early May. Once more he made the All Star team. On July 17 he split the middle finger of his right hand, causing him to miss several weeks, but Willard Hershberger filled in for him very well, and once again the Reds were driving to the pennant. In the last days of July, though, the Reds blew a big lead in a game at the Polo Grounds. Some of the Reds players reportedly whispered that the loss would not have happened had Lombardi been available. On August 2, with Hershberger catching again, the Reds lost to a poor Boston team in the twelfth inning. Hershberger killed himself the next day, slitting his wrists and throat with a razor in the bathroom of a Boston hotel.

Lombardi was nearly obsessed by the notion of getting back into the World Series, getting a chance to set things right. On September 15, chasing a foul ball hit by Joe Gallagher of the Cardinals, Ernie twisted an ankle. He went to the hospital for X rays. He would not be able to leave the hospital for at least ten days. The ankle was badly hurt.

The Reds won the pennant with Lombardi in the hospital. Ernie returned for the series, but batted only three times. Jimmy Wilson, a forty-year-old coach, came out of retirement to be the star of the series, won by Cincinnati in seven games. The Reds voted a winner's share of the series, about $6,000, to Hershberger's mother.

Once more, in the spring of 1941, Lombardi held out. They finally settled for a reported $18,000, plus a bonus if he hit .300. When he did report, he showed "a noticeable limp as a hangover of the sprained ankle he suffered near the end of the 1940 season." The sportswriters, less sympathetic this time, alleged that he had not worked out all winter, so that the ankle injury naturally flared up as soon as pressure was put on it.

"Lombardi isn't the best catcher in baseball, but he hits the long ball that breaks up games," wrote Joe Williams that March. "Apparently, he did nothing to condition his ankle during the winter, and as soon as he started to bounce around in the spring his limp came back. Don't ask us why these high-salaried fellows who would be driving trucks if they couldn't hit a baseball are so indifferent as to their physical soundness."

McKechnie insisted that Lombardi would be ready to open the season as his catcher. "Lombardi is probably the greatest magnate [sic] for rumors in the history of the Cincinnati Club," wrote Gabe Paul, then traveling secretary/

publicist for the Reds. "Many times during his Cincinnati career he was rumored to have been killed or seriously injured in auto accidents, while he was snoozing peacefully in his apartment. This past winter the report came in that he weighed 300 pounds. Then he was supposed to have hardening of the arteries, etc.

"Meanwhile, Ernie goes about his business, saying nothing. He knows that time will prove everything, and that as soon as he appears in the lineup, there will have to be a new angle to the rumors about him."

Appear he did, but in 1941, for the first time in his career, Lombardi did not play well. On a road trip in April, $300 was stolen from his hotel room while he was at the game. Overweight, his ankle aching, his feet killing him, Lombardi hit just .264 in 1941. Following the 1938 season there had been a banquet in Cincinnati honoring some of the players. A radio reporter stuck a microphone in front of Lombardi, who had had a few too many, and asked if he had anything to say. Lombardi responded with a few ill-chosen words about the no-good Warren Giles, and—at least as he told the story—passed out on the air. From then on, he felt that Giles was just waiting for a chance to get rid of him. "As soon as I had a bad year," he said, "I was gone."

Lombardi was traded or sold, depending on the source, to the Boston Braves. In March 1942, he was reported to be working at a war-related job, unable to report to the Braves. At 34, coming off a poor season, many assumed that his career was over. In late March, to the astonishment of his critics, he reported to the Boston Braves in shape and ready to go. He had eaten spaghetti only once or twice all winter. "I weigh only 220 pounds," he said. "That's because I stayed away from spaghetti. If you knew how much I love that stuff, you'd realize what a sacrifice I made to get myself in shape."

He returned to the All-Star team. He hit .330, the highest average in the league. He missed several weeks after splitting a finger trying to catch a "flutterball"—a fast knuckleball—thrown by Jim Tobin, with whose family he was boarding, incidentally. This limited him to 105 games, but National League President Ford Frick announced that he was the batting champion anyway, making him, at least if you believe Ford Frick, the only catcher to win two batting championships.

In the spring of 1943 Lombardi again declined to report for spring training. Once more there was talk of his retirement. The health of his father was a concern to him. Lombardi, still a bachelor, now lived with his sister, his sister's family, and his father, who was partially paralyzed. He was exposed to the draft (because he was unmarried), but he was listed as the sole source of support for his father and sister. In March the word appeared that his father's health had improved, but Ernie was unhappy with the Braves' offer. He wanted to be traded. There were allegations of a "sinister influence" on Lombardi's decision—specifically, that another National League team had implied that he could get more money from them than he could get from the Braves.

In any case he finally signed, in April 1943, reportedly for more than the $10,000 he had earned the previous season. Despite these endless salary battles, Dick Bartell says that Lombardi loaned money to players all over the league, and never pressured anyone to get it back. A few days after signing he was traded to the New York Giants, either for $40,000—several times his salary—or for two players, depending on your source.

In May 1943, his father died. Shortly after that he was called in for re-examination by the draft board. A sportswriter wrote that it was "well known that Schnozz has the worst feet in baseball," but he didn't know if that would be enough to keep Lombardi out of the Army. Playing day to day, Lombardi once more made the National League All-Star team. In September it was announced that he had failed his draft physical. He finished his first season with the Giants hitting .305.

In the winter of 1943–44 Lombardi worked as a sheet metal artisan. In the spring of 1944 he held out once more. He finally reported on April 5, weighing about 245 pounds. "Ernie hasn't touched a bat all winter," said Hank De-Berry on April 8. "He is overweight, yet he can rifle pitches to the outfield as if it were mid-July. He laces out those line drives like clay pigeons winging out of a trap . . . He still has one of the best arms in the business."

In mid-April he was hitting .450. Late in the month, though, he hit into three double plays in four games, two of them with the bases loaded. His average dropped to the .220s by early June. The New York fans turned against him. His arrival in New York had been heralded as making the Giants a pennant contender. Instead, they found him a slow, fat old catcher going through the motions with a second-division team.

Cincinnati still loved him. On August 14, 1944, the *World-Telegram* reported that "Ernie Lombardi still is Rhineland's greatest hero. He is cheered here more vociferously than all the Reds put together."

On June 4, 1944, Ernie was cut in the middle of his forehead by the spikes of Pittsburgh outfielder Jim Russell. He had to leave the game. The next day he was married to an Oakland woman named Berice Ayres. He was thirty-six; her age was given as forty-three. His batting rallied. On August 21 he hit two line drive home runs and a game-winning single, driving in all four runs in a Giant win. On September 10, 1944, there was an odd play in which a ball bounced away from Lombardi with a man on base. The umpire, Bill Stewart

(apparently forgetting the base runner) picked up the ball and flipped it to Lombardi. "Maybe that's what Ernie's longed for all along," suggested a writer, "an umpire-retriever."

By the spring of 1945 Ernie was 37 years old. In late April he astonished the crowd by beating out a bunt. He'd do that once in a while; the rule was that if he bunted it was the pitcher's job to field the bunt, no matter where it was. On May 2, 1945, Ernie beat out a bunt again, and once on base moved from second to third on a fly to center, then scored on a foul pop to the second baseman. Two innings later, he scored from second base on a single. Continuing his aggressive play and hitting well, he won over the New York fans. On May 9 Joe King wrote that "the folks for the first time have taken him in lock, stock and proboscis." In early May he was leading the league in home runs.

He became a story. He told sportswriters that he was embarrassed about his performance of the previous season. "Lom is unbelievably sensitive," said Mel Ott. "This year he seems determined to prove that he couldn't possibly have been as bad as he was last year." On May 28 he hit his eleventh home run, one more than he had hit in 1944, and still the most in the league.

In the giddiness over Lombardi's recovery, it seems to have been forgotten that he was 37 years old. It was a forgone conclusion that he would hit 20 home runs. One sportswriter thought he was a candidate to win the triple crown. Mel Ott let him catch 48 of the Giants' first 53 games. By July he had fallen into a slump. On August 20 a foul tip off the bat of Roy Johnson whacked him in the middle finger, driving the nail back into the flesh. He was out about ten days.

The rest did him good. He finished the season at .307 with 19 homers, 70 RBI in 368 at bats. The Giants finished fifth.

On January 5, 1946, the Giants purchased Walker Cooper from the Cardinals. Lombardi was no longer the number one catcher. On May 9 it was reported that he was "doing a grand job while Cooper is shelved." June 18, 1946, was Ernie Lombardi day at the Polo Grounds.

The Giants (and the other New York teams) at this time had a problem with kids stealing their caps as they walked to the clubhouse after games. On September 5, 1946, a twelve-year-old kid swiped Lombardi's hat off his head. Lombardi, who had had enough of this, took off after the kid and, to the astonishment of everybody, caught up with him near the subway entrance. The kid had handed off the cap before the Schnozzola caught him, but Ernie picked him up and hauled him back to face the security force. The Giants did not press charges. "They simply hope that police confrontal will halt the thriving practice of stealing caps and sometimes gloves from the players."

Lombardi finished the 1946 season with a .290 average, 12 homers in 238 at bats. The Giants finished last. In spring, 1947, Lombardi held out again. Walker Cooper had a big year that year, and there were fewer at bats for Ernie, who still hit well (.282 with 21 RBI in 110 at bats). He was released at the end of the season, free to make his own deal with another team.

Lombardi signed to play the 1948 season with Sacramento of the Pacific Coast League. In April, however, his wife became ill, and Lombardi asked for voluntary retirement so that he could stay near her, in Oakland. His request was granted, but then Casey Stengel, who was managing the Oakland Oaks, asked him to come back and play for Oakland, where he had begun his career more than twenty years before. Lombardi agreed, and worked out the details with Sacramento. Oakland won 114 games, helping to propel Casey back to the major leagues. As Stengel went to the Yankees, Lombardi retired from baseball.

As we reach the end of his career, let us pause a moment and evaluate him as a ballplayer. He must have been an amazing hitter.

Harry Craft said "Ernie was the best right-handed hitter I ever saw, and he was an exceptional player in every department except running."

Carl Hubbell said, "I thought he might hurt me, even kill me, with one of those liners." Hubbell many times chose Lombardi as the most difficult player in the league for him to get out, and claimed that when Lombardi was at the plate, Bill Terry would plead with him to pitch Lombardi inside and the third baseman would plead for him to be pitched outside. Neither one wanted to be shot with a line drive.

It was routinely written that he would have hit .400 many times if he could just run.

Arthur Daley wrote that "When Lom would grasp a bat with that interlocking grip of his, his bat looked like a matchstick. And the ball would ricochet off it like a shell leaving a howitzer."

Kirby Higbe said that "He was the best hitter I ever saw, including everybody."

Lombardi almost never struck out. He hit the ball hard, time after time after time. We should not forget, however, that he also grounded into double plays far more often than any other player in history—about once every twenty trips to the plate. The cost to his team was enormous.

Arthur Daley said that "he couldn't outrace a snail, even with a head start."

Lombardi himself, although sensitive about his lack of speed, told a story about once being thrown out at first base after rocketing a ball off the left field wall at the Baker Bowl. He told the story in self defense; he wanted to explain that he just wasn't running, because he was sure it was out of the park. Dick Bartell in *Rowdy Richard* claims that this happened several times, although I doubt that it did.

Lombardi was so slow that his speed was a problem on defense, even at catcher. If a ball bounced away from him, the runner advanced. He could not field a bunt. Foul popups dropped a few feet from home plate, because he could not spring out of a crouch. However, he blocked the plate well, threw exceptionally well, and had good hands.

"Bucky Walters says he was a great catcher," said Waite Hoyt in *Baseball Between the Wars* (Eugene Murdock). "Now among people in baseball the general opinion was that he was a lousy catcher. Any guy who would reach out and catch the ball with his bare hand, and can't shift."

"He was a good hitter," said Bob O'Farrell, who managed him one year, "but he was awfully slow and awkward, as everyone knows. He was a good receiver with a good arm, but I wouldn't call him a great catcher."

For what it may add, the Win Shares system sees Lombardi as a relatively poor defensive catcher, better than many or even most part-time and short-career catchers, but next-to-last (ahead of Blimp Hayes) among the fifty men who have caught 10,000 innings in the major leagues.

In the Hall of Fame dispute that developed later, Lombardi's leading proponents were his former teammates Bucky Walters and Harry Craft, both of whom had stayed in the game after their playing careers. Craft claimed that at times Vander Meer, who was wild, would throw a ball two feet to the right of Ernie, and Ernie would just reach out and catch the ball bare-handed. Dick Bartell says that every player in the league had seen Ernie do this. But Craft also claimed that if Ernie's finger was split or broken by a pitch, he'd just rub some dirt on it, stuff his mitt under his arm, walk back to the dugout, and keep on playing. This is just not true. In fact, Lombardi's career was constantly interrupted by petty injuries such as splinters, foul tips, twisted ankles, and split fingers. Lombardi did take pride in his toughness, his ability to stay in the lineup—but he had many prolonged absences resulting from seemingly small injuries.

Out of baseball, Ernie operated a liquor store in San Leandro, California, for several years. In 1953 he became seriously depressed, seemingly unable to go on. His wife decided to take him to a sanitarium in Livermore, California. Ernie agreed to go. En route to the sanitarium on April 8, 1953, they stopped to stay overnight with Ernie's sister. Ernie went into a bathroom, found a razor, and slit his throat from ear to ear. His wife found him and screamed. He pleaded with her not to save him, to let him die. He fought with the hospital attendants who tried to save him.

Although the newspapers described him as "clinging to life," his injuries were not critical. He was transferred to the sanitarium two days later.

I did not know Lombardi, and I would not speculate too freely on the causes of his pain. Athletes are subject to a uniquely harsh form of mid-life crisis. Losing their skills to time and removed from the athlete's world, they are stripped of a central portion of their identity, forced to fall back on the other elements of their selves, to identify themselves as husbands and fathers and grandfathers, businessmen or sportsmen or whatever. It is difficult for many of them. Lombardi had no children, no father or mother. He had no hobbies to speak of. He wasn't a sportsman or interested in politics. He wasn't a reader, and he didn't play golf. He wasn't cut out to be successful in business, and he was many years too late to be a successful tradesman. He had few friends outside of the National League. Baseball was his world.

Beyond that, one cannot help but notice the similarities between the suicide of Willard Hershberger in 1940 and the attempted suicide thirteen years later of Ernie Lombardi. Did Ernie invent guilt for himself over the tragic death of Hershberger? At the very minimum, he must have said to himself that if he had just been in there playing instead of Hershberger, this would never have happened; for him not to have done that would not be human. Nobody dies without guilt. No one will ever pass from your life without leaving you with the feeling that you should have done something you didn't do and said something you didn't say. Suicides carry more guilt than anything, except maybe the death of a child. Look at the situation: it's a goddamn guilt factory. Lombardi *always* felt that he was supposed to be in the lineup, that he was letting the team down if he had to miss a few days with an injury. He was famous for being tough. He was out of the lineup, and the kid had to play, and the kid couldn't handle it. How much of this did Lombardi bury in the dark corners of his mind, where he would find it fourteen years later in his own black hours?

Following the 1957 season the New York Giants, for whom Lombardi had finished his major league career, moved to San Francisco. Ernie was given a job as a press box attendant. He continued in that job for six years, 1958 to 1963. Though well liked, his personality was not ideal for press relations. He tended to answer questions with a grunt, rarely said very much unless he'd had a couple of beers. When a sportswriter insulted him in 1963, he quit in anger and embarrassment. For several years he dropped out of sight. One day an Oakland sportswriter stopped to fill up his car. A huge man about sixty years of age came to pump his gas. "Look at that nose," the man must have said to himself. He recognized Lombardi.

Interviewed at this point, Lombardi lashed out at the Veterans Committee of the Hall of Fame. "If they elected me now, I wouldn't even show up," he told one reporter. "That sounds terrible, but I'm bitter. All anybody wants to remember about me is that I couldn't run."

"They can take the Hall of Fame and you know what they can do with it," he told another. "Even if they voted me in now, I wouldn't accept. It doesn't mean anything to me anymore."

Berice Lombardi died in Oakland on July 1, 1973. In 1975, in poor health, Lombardi moved to Santa Cruz. A Hall of Fame bandwagon began to get moving for him. On September 26, 1977, Lombardi laid down the mask in a hospital in Santa Cruz, California. Al Lopez, his National League rival, had been inducted into the Hall of Fame just weeks earlier. *The Sporting News* chose to turn Lombardi's obituary into a Hall of Fame plea.

In February 1986, the Veterans' Committee selected Ernie Lombardi for the Hall of Fame.

23 ◆ Gene Tenace
(1969–1983, 1555 G, 201 674 .241)

There are four catchers of the last two generations who all hit around .240, but had very high secondary averages—Gene Tenace (secondary average of .420), Mickey Tettleton (.415), Darren Daulton (.368), and Joe Ferguson (.364). These are the highest secondary averages ever for a catcher; the previous top three were .356 (Roy Campanella and Stan Lopata) and .336 (Mickey Cochrane).

These players rate well because their walks and homers create a lot of runs, despite their .240 batting averages. There is an argument against this position, which goes "I'm not sure that their walks DO create all that many runs. Walks *in general* may result in a lot of runs. Walks to leadoff men, walks to Willie Mays and Mickey Mantle—sure, those result in runs. But these guys hit sixth or seventh most of their careers, and they couldn't run fast enough to stay out of the way of a rabid turtle, so how many runs does that really create?"

But we know that this argument is untrue, for this reason: focus on the runs scored and RBI. See, there are two averages here with pretty much the same norms—batting average, and secondary average. The average batting average for the top 100 catchers in major league history is .261; the secondary average is .228. But there is a third average which can be thrown into the mix: Runs Average. Runs Average is runs scored plus RBI, divided by at bats—dead simple formula, but based on actual runs, rather than run elements. The Runs Average for the top 100 catchers is .242—about the same as the batting average or the secondary average.

Gene Tenace has a Runs Average of .302, Mickey Tettleton .307, Darren Daulton .303, Joe Ferguson .284. Even Ferguson, the weakest of the four, has a higher runs average than Ted Simmons, Gary Carter, Joe Torre, Lance Parrish, Ernie Lombardi, Ivan Rodriguez, Roger Bresnahan, Thurman Munson, Smoky Burgess, or Elston Howard. The only catchers who rank ahead of Tettleton's .307, not in terms of walks and homers but in terms of RUNS per at bat, are the first tier Hall of Famers—Buck Ewing (.375, the highest for a catcher), Mickey Cochrane, Roy Campanella, Yogi Berra, Bill Dickey, Johnny Bench, and Gabby Hartnett.

Of catchers who have higher secondary averages than batting averages, 79% also have higher runs averages than batting averages. Of catchers who have lower secondary averages than batting averages, 89% also have lower runs averages than batting averages. (See also George Brett, #2 at third base.)

24 ◆ Tim McCarver
(1959–1980, 1909 G, 97 645 .271)
Tim McCarver (1966) was the only twentieth-century catcher to lead the league in triples. McCarver hit 13 triples, which ties Johnny Kling (1903) for the modern record.

Buck Ewing hit 13 or more triples nine times, and hit as many as 20. But catchers in Ewing's time didn't squat.

McCarver probably should have won the National League Gold Glove at catcher in 1966 and '67, perhaps '65 as well. He didn't because

his arm wasn't exceptional, and a lot of people focus on the catcher's throwing ability. But while his arm wasn't exceptional, the rest of his defensive skills were. He was very quick behind the plate, he was a good receiver, and he could help a pitcher focus as well as anybody. He was a good baserunner, and a pretty good hitter.

25 ◆ Darren Daulton
(1983–1997, 1161 G, 137 588 .245)
Essentially the same player as Mickey Tettleton, with modest differences. He was a left-handed hitter (Tettleton a switch hitter), didn't hit quite as many home runs as Tettleton or walk quite as much, but had a much better arm and better overall defensive skills. An interesting thing about Daulton is that although he had knee surgery every winter, in his career he was 50-for-60 as a base stealer—the fifth-best stolen base percentage in baseball history—and almost never grounded into a double play. His career high in grounding into double plays was 6, and he did that only once; otherwise his high was 4. In his career he grounded into only one double play for every 104 at bats—the best GIDP rate in history for a catcher (since they began keeping GIDP totals, in the 1930s), and one of the lowest ever. Richie Ashburn grounded into double plays more often, and he was a left-handed leadoff man who could fly. Lou Brock, Maury Wills, and Rickey Henderson grounded into double plays more often than Daulton.

In fact, all of these guys like Daulton had low GIDP rates—Tenace did, Mickey Tettleton did. Tenace grounded into one DP every 58 at bats, Tettleton one every 55 at bats. The norm is about one per 40. Two reasons for it:

1. They hit fly balls, rather than grounders, and

2. They're not afraid to take a walk with a man on base.

A lot of double plays come when a hitter reaches for an outside pitch that he ought to take, and hits a ground ball to shortstop or second base.

26 ◆ Tom Haller
(1961–1972, 1294 G, 134 504 .257)
The next three catchers (and four out of five) were all more or less contemporaries, all National League regulars in 1962. Burgess was the best hitter of the four, Roseboro the best defensive player, Haller the best combination. But they're all really about the same; no one of them is much better than any other.

Haller was one of the biggest catchers of his time—six-foot-four—and a good left-handed hitter, could have been a first baseman and hit 30 homers a year. A college graduate (University of Illinois) and a brother of Bill Haller, longtime American League umpire.

27 ◆ John Roseboro
(1957–1970, 1585 G, 104 548 .249)
Left-handed hitting catcher who is most remembered today as Juan Marichal's assault victim. Roseboro hit .271 with 14 homers as a rookie in 1958, but went backward from there, not because he didn't develop as a hitter—he did—but because baseball moved into the 1960s, when runs scored were at historic lows, and the Dodgers moved into Dodger Stadium, which favored pitchers.

If you compare Roseboro to a 1990s catcher, the adjustment that has to be made for the hitting context is almost mind-bending. Roseboro's best seasons were 1961 (20 Win Shares), 1964 (18 Win Shares), and 1966 (20 Win Shares):

Year	HR	RBI	BAvg	OB + Slg
1961	18	59	.251	.805
1964	3	45	.287	.729
1966	9	53	.276	.741

But what would be comparable seasons for a 1990s catcher? I found four seasons by 1996–97 catchers, all of them pretty good defensive catchers, evaluated at 19 Win Shares apiece. Those four were Benito Santiago (1996) and Dan Wilson, Javy Lopez, and Charles Johnson (all 1997). These are their stats:

Player	HR	RBI	BAvg	OB + Slg
Santiago	30	85	.264	.835
Wilson	15	74	.270	.749
Lopez	23	68	.295	.895
Johnson	19	63	.250	.801

The Win Shares system shows that Roseboro was as valuable as those players, but was he really?

Yes, he was, for two reasons:

1. Value consists in winning games, and
2. Playing in Dodger Stadium in the 1960s, it didn't take very many runs to win a ballgame.

The sixty runs a year that Roseboro created would win as many games, in those conditions, as 80 runs created today.

28 ◆ Smoky Burgess
(1949–1967, 1718 G, 126 673 .295)
One of my favorite paragraphs was written about Smoky Burgess in *The Great American Baseball Card Flipping, Trading, and Bubble Gum Book.* "Smoky Burgess was fat," it begins, "Not baseball fat like Mickey Lolich or Early Wynn. But FAT fat. Like the mailman or your Uncle Dwight. Putsy Fat. Slobby Fat. Just Plain Fat. In fact I would venture to say that Smoky Burgess was probably the fattest man ever to play professional baseball."

Some catchers like to chatter at the hitters to see if they can mess them up while they're trying to hit. Smoky was the world's champion. He used to drive Richie Ashburn nuts. He'd say,

"Get ready, Rich; it's a fastball." Ashburn would pop up or something, so Burgess would say "You didn't do too well on the fastball, Richie; let's try a curve." Of course, Ashburn never could believe him and couldn't ignore him. One time he asked the umpire, "Isn't there some rule that will make that guy shut up?"

Burgess was a church-going man. When he was with the White Sox at the end of his career his teammates made up a song, to the tune of "Get Me to the Church on Time":

> I'm playing baseball in the morning,
> Hey Smoke, Ed Stanky's gonna call,
> The White Sox are in trouble,
> I'll hit a double,
> Just get me out of church on time.

Burgess caught two no-hit games in his career. His team lost both of them. On May 26, 1956, he caught nine no-hit innings by Johnny Klippstein, Herschel Freeman, and Joe Black. The Reds lost the no-hitter in the tenth, and the game in the 11th. With the Pirates exactly three years later—May 26, 1959—Burgess caught Harvey Haddix's 12-inning perfect game, which Harvey, of course, lost in the 13th. Smokey was the guy who noticed that Adcock had passed Aaron on the bases, setting up that game's memorable (if confusing) ending.

Burgess attributed his success as a hitter to two things—one, that he really studied pitchers, which most hitters do not, and two, that he swung as hard at the first pitch as he did at the second or third, rather than "feeling out" the pitcher for a pitch or two and then trying to put the ball in play.

29 ◆ Rick Ferrell
(1929–1947, 1884 G, 28 734 .281)
In his years on the Hall of Fame ballot, Rick Ferrell never received more than one vote—one—from the 300-plus members of the BBWAA. The 1966 book, *Baseball's Greatest Catchers* (Al Hirshberg) has articles on Johnny Kling, Hank Gowdy, Steve O'Neill, Wally Schang, Muddy Ruel, Birdie Tebbets, Mickey Owen, Walker Cooper, Jim Hegan, Del Crandall, and Elston Howard, but no mention of Rick Ferrell.

Of course Ferrell does not belong in the Hall of Fame, but he was a pretty good player. He hit .281 in his career and walked a lot, giving him a .378 career on-base percentage—7th best among the top 100 catchers. You add a long career, a good on-base percentage, and good defense, that doesn't make a Hall of Famer, but it makes a good player.

30 ◆ Del Crandall
(1949–1966, 1573 G, 179 657 .254)
Rushed through the minor leagues in 166 games, because he was born with good defensive skills. Won four Gold Gloves, although Gold Gloves weren't given until his career was more than half over. Hit 20-plus home runs three times. Didn't smoke or drink; was named captain of the Braves by Charlie Grimm. Al Silverman in *Baseball Stars of 1959*: Crandall "is just about the hustlingest operator in baseball, certainly the one Braves' player who displays the animation the old dime baseball novels used to indicate was the prime requirement of a major-leaguer . . . in the World Series just past, Crandall made [Yogi Berra] look like Rip Van Winkle just coming out of his 20-year nap. While Berra trudged after foul pop-ups, chugged wearily to back up the first baseman, caught a conservative, slow-type game behind the plate, Crandall was running here and there and everywhere, as if he were an Olympic sprinter."

> I think the most complete catcher during my time in the league was Del Crandall. He was sound defensively. He could catch the bad pitch and block the plate. He didn't have a strong arm, but he made up for it with a quick release and accuracy.—John Roseboro, *Glory Days with the Dodgers*

31 ◆ Sherm Lollar

(1946–1963, 1752 G, 155 808 .264)

Led his league in fielding percentage five times, in double plays three times, also has the lowest career passed ball rate of any catcher listed here—5.5 passed balls per 162 games played. Actually, Buddy Rosar did better, but he didn't make the top 100.

Lollar came up with Cleveland at the same time they brought along Jim Hegan. Hegan had obvious defensive skills, while Lollar was awkward behind the plate, so the Indians traded Lollar to the Yankees for Gene Bearden, who helped the Indians win the pennant in '48. Lollar battled Yogi Berra for the catcher's job; this was worse than battling Jim Hegan. Berra ran three of the top 60 catchers of all time off the Yankee catching job—Lollar, Gus Triandos, and Elston Howard (for the first half of Howard's career). Lollar was traded to St. Louis, where he played half-time for three years. He hit pretty well, but the Browns at that time couldn't read a Superman comic book and figure out who Clark Kent was, so they included Lollar in a trade to Chicago.

Paul Richards in Chicago made him a regular, and, with Richards' help, Lollar emerged as the American League's second-best catcher, behind Yogi. He won Gold Gloves in 1957, 1958, and 1959; the Win Shares system sees him as deserving of Gold Gloves in 1955, 1959, and 1960. According to *Sport Magazine* (August 1956), Lollar "hunts quail, rabbit and dove during the off-season. Prefers films like *The Desperate Hours* and *The Man in the Gray Flannel Suit*. ('I don't care for musicals.') Called the manager's assistant."

32 ◆ Jim Sundberg

(1974–1989, 1962 G, 95 374 .248)

Below-average hitter, but not an offensive zero, either, and the standard of excellence as a defensive player. Has the best ratio of double plays to errors of any catcher in major league history (1,000 or more games. Actually, Buddy Rosar is better, but he didn't play a thousand games.) A gentleman, and a consummate professional.

33 ◆ Walker Cooper

(1940–1957, 1473 G, 173 812 .285)

Buck Newsom's father died during the 1940 World Series. Newsom pitched twice in the series after his father's death, threw a shutout the first time, then pitched well but lost in the seventh game. This incident became very famous, although that has faded with time; it was prominent in all re-tellings of the 1940 World Series until the mid-1960s.

However, in the 1943 series almost the same thing happened to the Cooper boys, Mort and Walker. Their father died on the morning of October 6, 1943, when Mort was scheduled to pitch against the Yankees. They talked it over and decided that their father would want them to carry on, and they did; Mort pitched a complete game victory over the Yankees, and Walker caught—hours after learning of their father's death. They then rushed home for the funeral (as Newsom had), and returned, Mort making his next start in the fifth and final game of the series, in which he pitched very well, but lost. Walker hit .294 in the series, and Mort had a 2.81 ERA.

This incident, however, received little attention—simply because the story had already been told; that niche had already been filled by the Bobo Newsom story. It's like the 1950 National League pennant race—one of the most exciting and dramatic pennant races in baseball history, but rarely mentioned, because it is buried beneath the story of the 1951 pennant race.

Cooper had one of the greatest games in major league history on July 6, 1949; he went 6-for-6 with 3 homers. He also homered in six consecutive games in 1947, hitting a total of seven homers in the six contests. He made the

All-Star team six times . . . Cooper was identified by Joe Williams as "president of the 'I think Durocher Stinks Club.'"

34 ◆ Tony Pena
(1980–1997, 1988 G, 107 708 .260)
Cheerful, good-natured player, but intense; hit .301 with 15 homers in 1983, also won the Gold Glove. Had his offense stayed at that level he would rank among the top ten catchers of all time, as he was a cat behind the plate—El Gato—and could throw . . . well, maybe not as well as Sundberg, but he could throw. He was also very strong. He was a medium-sized man with a small waist, but extremely strong in the shoulders and forearms. Had a unique way of squatting at the plate, squatting on his left leg with his right leg stretched out in front of him. He could give the pitcher a low target that way, his glove just a foot off the ground sometimes, but his left leg was so powerful that he could explode out of that one-legged squat and throw, or chase down a bunt. Nobody else could do it, because nobody else has knees that good.

35 ◆ Ray Schalk
(1912–1929, 1760 G, 12 594 .253)
Caught four no-hitters . . . One of the "Clean Sox," one of the 1919 White Sox who didn't participate in the fixing of the series; elected to the Hall of Fame on a whim of the Veteran's Committee. Like Muddy Ruel, Johnny Kling and others, Schalk was very small, originally believed to be too small to be a major league catcher. The Win Shares system sees him as deserving of the American League Gold Glove at catcher in 1913, 1914, 1915, 1916, 1917, 1919, 1920, 1921, and 1922. It was taken over at that point by Muddy Ruel . . . participated in more double plays (226) than any other catcher in history. Also had more assists than anyone except Deacon McGuire. The top five in double plays: 1. Schalk, 2. Steve O'Neill (193), 3. Yogi (175), 4. Gabby (163), 5. Bob Boone and Tony Pena (154).

36 ◆ Mike Scioscia
(1980–1991, 1441 G, 68 446 .259)
Scioscia was 6-foot-2 and had arms like a blacksmith, but hit 7 homers a year anyway. He wasn't the quickest guy in the world behind the plate, but he could throw, had good hands, could find a popup and would rank with Parrish and Ed Bailey as the best I ever saw at blocking the plate. Had the reputation of being a very good handler of pitchers, also had the best strikeout/walk ratio of any catcher since World War II, even better than Berra and Smoky Burgess. Very slow, but did not ground into a lot of double plays because of exceptional bat control.

37 ◆ Mickey Tettleton
(1984–1997, 1485 G, 245 732 .241)
Gene Tenace-type player, started with Oakland but never played very much there. He was a .240 hitter, and he wasn't much of a defensive catcher, but his .369 on-base percentage is 11th-best among the top 100 catchers (because he walked a hundred times a year) and his .449 slugging percentage is fifteenth best (because he could hit 30 homers a year). Tettleton was a regular for three teams—Baltimore, 1989–1990, Detroit, 1991–1994, and Texas, 1995–1996. All three teams improved substantially when they put him in the lineup, and declined substantially when they replaced him. The year the Baltimore Orioles made him a regular (1989) they improved their won-lost record by 32 and a half games. After the 1990 season the Orioles traded him to the Tigers. The Orioles declined the next year from 76 wins to 67; the Tigers improved from 79 to 84.

The Tigers, who had lost 103 games in 1989, were around .500 all four years Tettleton was there (1991–1994). After they let him go in

1995 they declined from 53-62 (.461) to 60-84 (.417), then lost 109 games in 1996.

When Texas signed him they improved from 52-62 (.456) to 74-70 (.514), then won 90 games in 1996, their first 90-win season in twenty years. When Tettleton got hurt in '97 they declined by 13 games.

Tettleton was named catcher on *The Sporting News* American League All-Star team in 1989, 1991, and 1992, but he was never really respected even by the organizations that had him. The Oakland A's released him when he was 27 years old, although he had hit 18 homers and driven in 61 runs in 422 at bats over the previous two seasons. He signed with the Orioles as a minor league free agent, won their catching job, made the All-Star team, and led the team to a dramatic 32-game improvement—and was traded even up for a pitcher with a 5.96 ERA.

The Tigers in the four years that Tettleton was a regular there were 14th (last), 11th, 4th, and 10th in the league in batting average—but they were 2nd, 1st, 1st, and 3rd in runs scored.

38 ◆ Terry Steinbach

(1986–1999, 1546 G, 162 745 .271)
Not exceptional in any area of the game, but also has no outstanding weakness, and never really had a bad season.

39 ◆ Ed Bailey

(1953-1966, 1213 G, 155 540 .255)

> Watching this strong, beautifully built man hit, I've often felt that if he didn't try to pull every pitch, but just met the ball, his natural power would carry it out of any ballpark—more often.
> —Stan Musial in *Sport Magazine*, June 1964.

Bailey, whose real first name was "Lonas," was born and raised in Strawberry Plains, Tennessee, a tiny town twelve miles from Knoxville. He made a big reputation as a high school athlete, and wanted to sign a baseball contract, but his parents, who ran a small-town grocery store, insisted he go to college. He went to the University of Tennessee on a football scholarship, where, according to Bob Pille in an article for the *Baseball Digest* in August 1956, Bailey "chafed through five quarters at Tennessee" before his parents relented. He signed with the Cincinnati Reds for $13,000.

The Korean War began. Bailey entered the army in the spring of 1951; by the time he got out he was 22 years old, and had one year of minor league baseball, mixed in with two years of college and two years of military service. In his first appearance against major league pitching (spring training, 1953) Bailey went five for five with two homers. Birdie Tebbetts, who would manage Bailey with the Reds from 1954 through 1958, told Pille it "could have been the worst thing that ever happened to him." Farmed to Tulsa of the Texas League for '53, he swung for the fences and produced 21 homers but an average of only .243.

Nevertheless, in 1954 the Reds kept him as a reserve catcher, behind Andy Seminick and Hobie Landrith. Neither Seminick nor Landrith played well, but Bailey, hitting .197, was unable to fill the void. He was a cocky kid, sometimes irritating the management. One time, before a road trip, he asked Tebbetts sarcastically whether he should bring his glove. Another time, when he put on a couple of pounds, General Manager Warren Giles pulled him aside and told him that a ballplayer couldn't afford to be fat. "You mean like you?" asked Bailey, pinching Giles in his ample mid-section.

"That was a wasted year," Bailey remembered. "After a couple times around the league a guy can tell whether he's ready...and I knew I wasn't." He thought of requesting demotion, but "nobody wants to ask to leave the majors...you may get hurt, get forgotten, and never get back." In early 1955, with his average at .176, the Reds traded for Smoky Burgess, and sent Bailey to the Pacific Coast League.

"They did me a favor," Bailey said later, and although it never showed up in any box score, he did them one during spring training, 1955. According to Jules Tygiel in *Baseball's Great Experiment,* one afternoon in Tampa:

> ...after being removed from a game, [pitcher Brooks Lawrence] and catcher Ed Bailey entered the stands to watch the remainder of the contest. A rope separated the black and white sections and while Bailey sat on the white side, Lawrence sat next to him on the black. "Boy, this is stupid," exclaimed Bailey, a Tennessean. "I'm gonna change this." The catcher removed the rope and, according to Lawrence, no one ever reattached it.

Bailey's batting average rebounded in the PCL, with the aid of some adjustments suggested by Tebbetts, and in the Venezuelan League that winter he was a dominant offensive player. When he reported to the Reds in 1956, Tebbetts noted later in his best Stengelese, "He was more serious, where in the past he had the tendency to be not serious enough when it hurt him."

Smoky Burgess had hit .306 with 20 homers after joining the Reds in 1955, giving him a firm grip on the catching job. Bailey and Burgess were both left-handed hitting catchers, so Bailey was just buried. Bailey had three straight hits as a pinch hitter, however, while the team struggled out of the gate. Bailey had an edge over Burgess, in that he could throw and Burgess couldn't. When Birdie Tebbetts decided to shake up the line-up, Bailey began to play. He finished the 1956 season with what were to be the best offensive numbers of his career, a .300 batting average with 28 homers in 383 at bats.

Bailey made the All-Star team. The Reds hadn't played .500 ball in ten years, but with Bailey and Frank Robinson, who hit 38 homers as a rookie, the 1956 Reds won 91 games, miss-

ing the National League pennant by just two. Tebbetts predicted greatness for him.

It didn't happen. Bailey was never able to match his 1956 offense, and the Reds were not able to contend from 1957 through 1960. Bailey was a solid and consistent player, hitting .250 to .264 every season and keeping his home runs between 11 and 20. He earned a reputation as a sound defensive player, made the All-Star team again in 1957 and 1960.

He'd become serious enough to suit Birdie Tebbetts, but his teammates were in no danger of mistaking him for Mr. Solemnity. Teammate and author Jim Brosnan was only half-kidding when he wrote that Bailey's nickname "Gar" was unquestionably short for "garrulous," and Frank Robinson, after pleading guilty to carrying a concealed weapon, had no doubt who was responsible when he discovered a water pistol in his locker shortly thereafter. In 1959 Ed's brother Jim had a brief pitching trial with the Reds, making the Baileys one of a handful of major league brother batteries.

In early 1961 the Reds traded Bailey to the Giants for Don Blasingame, Sherman Jones, and Bob Schmidt. It was the oddest trade: the Reds, on their way to an unexpected pennant, actually weakened themselves behind the plate (the catcher obtained, Bob Schmidt, was hopeless) while Don Blasingame, expected to fill the second base hole for the Reds, had the worst year of his career. The Giants, expecting to contend, thought they had obtained a cannon arm to be the last piece of the puzzle, but found instead that, in the words of Charles Einstein: "There were times, as the season unfolded, when Bailey could not throw my mother out stealing." The Giants had his arm examined, but X-rays found nothing of interest, and as the season wore on Bailey began to share playing time with Johnny Orsino and Hobie Landrith.

Bailey was never again a regular, but he staged a terrific comeback as a half-time player. In the spring of 1962 the Giants came up with another left-handed hitting catcher, Tom Haller. Haller and Bailey shared the position; between them they hit 35 home runs in 526 at bats (18 for Haller, 17 for Bailey). On the last day of the season Bailey hit a solo home run to help the Giants defeat Houston 2-1, forcing a three-game playoff with the Dodgers.

In the subsequent World Series Bailey managed only one hit in fourteen at-bats, a two-run pinch hit home run with two out in the ninth inning of the third game. Unfortunately the Giants were down three at the time, and the game ended with the next batter.

In 1963 the Bailey/Haller combination again hit 35 home runs, Bailey hitting 21 of those and making the All-Star team for the fourth and final time. Bailey was traded to Milwaukee after the 1963 season. At first glance the trade is puzzling: several players of varying quality were exchanged, but each team included a veteran catcher, Bailey for Del Crandall. Crandall was essentially the same type and quality of catcher as Bailey, about the same age and a player who had made the All-Star team as recently as 1962. Why bother to trade them?

Each team gained a platoon edge. Each team had an outstanding young catcher, Haller in San Francisco and Joe Torre in Milwaukee, but San Francisco had two left-handed hitting catchers and Milwaukee had two right-handed hitting catchers. By exchanging Crandall and Bailey each team created the option of platooning.

Bailey had a respectable 1964 season in Milwaukee, but Joe Torre emerged as a star that year, and Bailey entered the nomadic phase of his career. Lee Allen reported in a 1968 *Sporting News* column that Bailey had found an interesting post-baseball occupation back in Knoxville:

"What are you doing now?" was the obvious question to Bailey.

"I'm a field representative for Congressman John Duncan."

"What does a congressman's field representative do?"

"Just takes care of the district—eight counties—when the Congressman is in Washington, that's all."

"Don't you miss talking to the hitters? Earl Lawson always said you enjoyed talking to the hitters."

"I'm talking to constituents," he replied.

It must be pleasant work. Presumably constituents don't have to be knocked down.

(This entry is based on an article originally written by Mike Kopf. It has been edited down from another book.)

40 ◆ Deacon McGuire
(1884–1912, 1781 G, 45 787 .278)
Started catching when catchers stood upright, stood ten to fifteen feet behind the batter with no one on base, and used gloves with no padding. He stayed in the majors through the introduction of face masks, chest protectors, squatting, catchers mitts, padded face masks, and shin guards.

He played 26 major league seasons, a record he held alone for 80 years, eventually being tied by Nolan Ryan. He was called "Deacon," like Deacon White, because he didn't drink and carouse, and rarely raised his voice. According to James M. Overfield, "It has been said he was never fined and never put out of a game."

Before catchers mitts were developed, McGuire invented the trick of putting a raw steak inside his glove to absorb the beating; this was copied by other catchers. Nonetheless, he had many broken fingers. His hands were so beat up that they were gnarled and twisted every which way, and were often photographed.

41 ◆ Al Lopez
(1928–1947, 1950 G, 52 652 .261)
Rick Dempsey-type player, a light hitter but extremely quick behind the plate, with an

outstanding arm. He never played for a championship team, made the All-Star team only twice (both times as a reserve). His defensive statistics are unremarkable, even making every adjustment that I know how to make, but maybe we're missing something.

Lopez used to hold the record for career games caught, and some related off-beat records (most consecutive years catching 100 games, etc.). He was durable, but he set durability records in large part because of World War II, which kept him in the lineup a couple of years after he was about through.

After the 1935 season Lopez was traded to the Boston Braves for, among others, a journeyman outfielder named Randy Moore. Moore had an uncle in Texas who was trying to finance an oil drilling operation, and persuaded his nephew to see if he could drum up investors among the ballplayers. Lopez, Casey Stengel, Bill McKechnie, and Johnny Cooney were among those who invested in the operation. The uncle found a big oil field, and all of the ballplayers who had invested with him became wealthy men.

42 ◆ Manny Sanguillen
(1967–1980, 1448 G, 65 585 .296)
Manny Sanguillen is the exact opposite of Darren Daulton. Sanguillen was a right-hander; Daulton, a lefty. Daulton hit just .245 but scored 70 runs a year and drove in 80 because he had a high secondary average (.368); Sanguillen hit .296, but drove in and scored fewer runs because he had a secondary average of .153. Daulton was slow but an 80% base stealer who almost never grounded into a double play; Sanguillen was the fastest catcher of his time, but a 48% base stealer who grounded into an above-average number of double plays, 15 to 20 a year.

Sanguillen was overrated, but he was a good player. He never won a Gold Glove, because of

Johnny Bench, but he was a Gold Glove-type catcher and a .300 hitter.

43 ◆ Rick Dempsey
(1969–1992, 1766 G, 96 471 .233)
Light-hitting defensive wizard. Dempsey was signed by the Twins, but hit under .250 in the minors, and the Twins were too busy with guys like George Mitterwald and Glenn Borgmann to take a look at him. They traded him to the Yankees, where he at least had the dignity of backing up a good catcher (Munson) and the opportunity to work with a first-rate coach, (Jim Hegan). He got to play in Baltimore because Earl Weaver was desperate for players after a wave of free agent losses.

When he finally got to play he lasted until he was 40, because people could see that the positives outweighed the negatives. He was small for a catcher and he hit .233 without much power, but had a great arm, was very agile behind the plate, was a good receiver, didn't chase bad pitches, didn't make outs on the bases, and was a surprisingly good hit-and-run man.

Dempsey's parents were actors, and he was a natural entertainer, like Casey Stengel or Nick Altrock. His most famous stunt was dashing out of the dugout during a rain delay, wearing a fat suit and a teammate's jersey, and sliding into every base on the tarp, spraying 50 gallons of water and absorbing another 20. The stunt has been imitated to death, but it was funny as hell at the time.

44 ◆ Jim Hegan
(1941–1960, 1666 G, 92 525 .228)
Hegan grew up a few miles from Fenway Park, but signed with the Indians because a neighbor, Dewey Metivier, had played with the Indians, knew Indians' manager Steve O'Neill, and arranged a tryout with the Indians.

Hegan went to Springfield of the Middle Atlantic League, where he played outfield halftime because the team also had Phil Masi (#94). Masi was four years older and a much better hitter, but Hegan's defensive gifts were apparent from the day he entered baseball. He never did hit much, even in the minors, but progressed rapidly because he was solid gold behind the mask. He had a rifle arm, large, soft hands, and an odd knack for catching pop ups; he always said he could just tell from the sound of the bat where the pop up went. He always anticipated the drift, and caught the ball without staggering or reaching.

He played for Rogers Hornsby in the minors, hit a little bit better under Rajah, so in the winter of 1946–47, when the Indians had decided they wanted him to be their catcher if he could hit his weight, they hired Hornsby to work with him all winter as a personal batting coach. He hit .249 in 1947, which was considered a disappointment. It was to be a career high.

In 1947, unhappy with Hegan's pitch-calling, Lou Boudreau started calling pitches from his shortstop position. This caused tension between Boudreau and Hegan which spread to other members of the organization, and very nearly caused Boudreau to be traded. Bill Veeck, who tended to take Hegan's side in the dispute, tried to trade Boudreau, but couldn't get a satisfactory offer. Hegan held out that winter, and reportedly demanded a trade, although he later denied making such a demand. In any case, Hegan went into the Indians' historic 1948 season with a somewhat awkward relationship to the organization.

In early 1948 Hegan's wife went into premature labor during a road trip. Indians' owner Bill Veeck personally took charge of the situation, arranged day and night nurses for her, arranged child care for their five-year-old son (Mike Hegan), brought flowers to the hospital, and sat up all night at Mrs. Hegan's bedside. They lost the baby, but Hegan was later to say

that "you can tell anyone you please that I think Bill Veeck is the greatest man on earth."

Hegan was retired by the time I became a baseball fan, but all defensive catchers at that time and for many years after that were compared to Hegan. I believe that he was also the first catcher to use multiple catching mitts. He had one mitt that he used to catch Bob Feller, a different mitt that he used to catch Bob Lemon, a third mitt that he used for Early Wynn, and a fourth mitt for some other pitchers.

By the end of Hegan's career Bill Dickey was ready to retire as a Yankee coach, so Hegan was hired to replace Dickey as the tutor of young catchers. He coached for the Yankees for many years, training the young Thurman Munson and Rick Dempsey, among others.

According to the Win Shares system, 63% of Hegan's career value was as a defensive player, the highest percentage of any catcher listed in the top 100. However, among catchers who don't make the top 100 there are many whose value is even more defensive, including Bill Bergen, whose career value is 100% as a defensive catcher . . . the ten catchers with the highest percentage of their value in defense (among the top 100): 1. Hegan, 2. Rollie Hemsley, 3. Luke Sewell, 4. Steve Yeager, 5. Del Rice, 6. Mickey Owen, 7. Jim Sundberg, 8. George Gibson, 9. Jerry Grote, 10. Bob Boone. All had at least 50% of their value in defense.

45 ◆ Duke Farrell
(1888–1905, 1563 G, 51 912 .275)

Grew up in Marlborough, Massachusetts, and was signed by Salem of the New England League. Cap Anson saw him playing for Salem and bought him for Chicago. Harry Stevens, the famous concessionaire who gave baseball hot dogs and peanuts, also gave Farrell his nickname, introducing him before a game one day as "The Duke of Marlborough."

The young Farrell was a tall, thin, elegant-looking man with a handlebar moustache. He jumped from Anson's White Stockings to the Player's League in 1890, played in the American Association (a major league) in 1891, leading the league in Home Runs and RBI. He was a good hitter, an outstanding thrower. Against the Baltimore Orioles on May 11, 1897, he set a record which still stands, throwing out eight would-be base stealers in one game, eight of nine. He played well until 1901, but after that he was bothered by injuries and illnesses, and put on weight whenever he was out of the lineup. He would work hard to get off the weight, play well for a while, then get hurt again. Thirty-six years old, he was hitting around .500 two weeks into the 1903 season when he caught his spikes sliding, was out most of the year, and got out of shape again. According to a fine article by Rich Eldred in *Nineteenth Century Stars* (SABR), *The Sporting Life* suggested that winter that he needed to lose 60 pounds. After his career he worked briefly as a United States Marshall, but came back into baseball as a coach.

46 ◆ Bob O'Farrell
(1915–1935, 1492 G, 58 549 .273)

O'Farrell broke into baseball in the same year as Muddy Ruel (1915) and for the same reason: a newspaper man was trying to drum up a story. Chicago in 1915 had three major league teams—the Cubs, the White Sox, and the Federal League Whales. Somebody at the Chicago Tribune had the idea of having a "tryout contest" among the three teams. The idea was to find three outstanding amateur players, and have each one accompany one of the three Chicago teams on a road trip. The Tribune would interview the kids every day about what it was like to be a member of a major league team, and they'd have an on-going story for a couple of weeks. They invited Cub manager

Roger Bresnahan to come watch the tryouts, but Bresnahan liked O'Farrell so much that he signed him on the spot; O'Farrell never did finish the tryouts.

He had a normal apprenticeship for that era—a few weeks on a major league roster to figure out the drill, three years with a minor league team to learn the basics, three years as a part-time player to finish him off. He took over as the Cubs regular catcher in 1922, and for two years was probably the best catcher in the National League, with Gabby Hartnett backing him up. In early 1924, however, O'Farrell had his skull fractured by a foul tip. He had a new face mask, but the clubhouse boy forgot to bring the new mask up from the clubhouse. O'-Farrell sent him back for it, but he didn't want to hold up the game, so he put on an old mask that didn't really fit him, just to catch the inning. Sure enough, a foul tip hit him right in the forehead, right where the face mask didn't fit, and fractured his skull.

Gabby Hartnett had to fill in when O'Farrell was out. At this point the Cubs realized that Bob O'Farrell was the second-best catcher in the National League. O'Farrell was traded to the Cardinals, the Cardinals won the pennant in 1926, and O'Farrell was named the National League MVP. He threw out Babe Ruth stealing second to end the 1926 World Series, which the Cardinals won.

Rogers Hornsby, player-manager of the Cardinals in 1926, was traded to New York that winter . . . I guess you all know that story. Anyway, O'Farrell managed the Cardinals in 1927; they improved their won-lost record by three and a half games, but fell to second place anyway, and hired Bill McKechnie to manage the team in 1928.

O'Farrell had injuries after that. John McGraw liked to keep a mix of several veteran catchers around; O'Farrell drifted into that role and had two outstanding seasons as a part-time catcher for the Giants. He played a couple of years in the minors, left baseball in 1938, bought a bowling alley in Waukegan, Illinois, and ran that for over thirty years. More information about him can be found by reading *Baseball Players and Their Times: Oral Histories of the Game, 1920–1940,* by Eugene Murdock.

47 ◆ Johnny Bassler

(1913–1927, 811 G, 1 318 .304)

Bassler was an outstanding offensive and defensive player; if his major league career wasn't so short he would rank among the top 20 catchers of all time. He was sixth in the American League MVP voting in 1922, seventh in 1923, fifth in 1924. He was exceptionally slow, even for a catcher, and he had no power, hitting only one home run in 811 major league games. But he was a .300 hitter who walked a lot, giving him the second-best on-base percentage of any catcher (.416), behind Mickey Cochrane (.419); his on-base percentage was over .400 all seven years that he was with the Tigers (1921–1927).

He went back to the Pacific Coast League after that, and starred in the PCL for many years. In 1930 he hit .365 to lead Hollywood to the PCL pennant; in '31 he hit .354 for the same team, in 1933, .336. The PCL didn't record walks, but it would be a safe guess that he wasn't walking any *less* often.

48 ◆ Johnny Kling

(1900–1913, 1260 G, 20 513 .271)

A Kansas City native, the son of a German-born baker. According to Harold U. Ribalow *(The Jew in American Sports),* "Grantland Rice called [Kling] the smartest catcher in baseball." He was a good hitter, the Gold Glove catcher of his time. He became a star as a member of the great Chicago Cubs teams of 1906–1910, and

received a lot of good publicity for holding Ty Cobb without a stolen base in the 1907 series.

In 1909 Kling held out. Kling had a couple of brothers who had made a lot of money in the real estate business. Johnny had also invested in some real estate, and apparently was making pretty good money outside of baseball. Also, according to the *Encyclopedia of Jews in Sports,* Kling had operated a billiard parlor in Kansas City for many years, and, in the year that he held out "he won the world professional billiard championship." The Cubs wouldn't yield, and the holdout went on all season. They called it a draw, and Kling returned in 1910, leading the Cubs to their fourth pennant in five years.

The Cubs lost the World Series, however, and Kling was regarded as the goat of the 1910 series; he hit .077, and there were stories that the A's had picked up a mannerism, and Kling was tipping the pitches. The Cubs traded him, anyway. He managed Boston in 1912 (see Hank Gowdy, #77), played for Joe Tinker at Cincinnati in 1913, then went into real estate full time. In 1933 he purchased the Kansas City Blues of the American Association; he later sold them to the Yankees. At his death in 1947 he was reportedly a millionaire.

"I never thought him as valuable to a ball club as Bresnahan," wrote John McGraw. "Nobody, though, could throw better than Kling."

49 ◆ Charlie Bennett

(1878–1893, 1062 G, 56 420 .256)

Bennett was the subject of the first big court test of baseball's reserve clause. The first reserve clause was instituted in 1879. Bennett signed with Worcester in 1879, and played for them in 1879 and 1880. As the Worcester franchise went out of business they apparently sold Bennett to Pittsburgh of the American Association; anyway, Pittsburgh claimed that they owned him. Bennett claimed they didn't, and signed with Detroit. Pittsburgh sued. Bennett won, the judge ruling that the reserve clause was not a contract in and of itself, but merely an agreement to execute a contract at some later date.

Bennett played for the Detroit Wolverines from 1881 to 1887—the entire period of the Wolverines franchise. He was among the outstanding defensive catchers of that era, perhaps the best. Lee Richmond, interviewed by Elmer Bates in 1910, said that "My partner was a good catcher, but my favorite was Charley Bennett, the best backstop that ever lived in the world. He went after everything, he knew no fear, he kept his pitcher from going into the air." Buck Ewing was supposedly a brilliant catcher, but Bennett caught 50% more innings than Ewing, with a lot fewer mistakes; per 1000 defensive innings, Ewing was charged with 59 errors and 66 passed balls, while Bennett was charged with 46 errors and 43 passed balls. The Wolverines won the National League pennant in 1887, Bennett being one of the most popular members of the team. After the demise of the Detroit franchise, he caught for five years for Boston, helping to win two more National League pennants.

In January 1894, Bennett was on a westward hunting trip. He stopped in Wellsville, Kansas, to visit a friend. When the train started to roll he said goodbye to the friend, and ran to pull himself up on the train. He lost his grip, slipped under the wheels, and his legs were cut off.

Within weeks of the accident, Bennett had written a letter to *The Sporting Life*, expressing thanks for the kindness he had received at the time of the accident, reflecting on all that he still had to be thankful for, and looking "forward to the time when I can stumble around with artificial limbs." He would be in a wheelchair the rest of his life.

He returned to Detroit, and opened a tobacco store/newsstand near the ballpark, by then a minor league park. Fans would go out of their way to go by his store, and he did fairly well. The minor league team, which eventually became the Detroit Tigers, had Charlie Bennett Day, presenting him with a wheelbarrow full of silver dollars donated by the public, among many other gifts. Later, when they built a new park, they had a vote of the fans as to what to call it. The fans selected the name "Bennett Park" in his honor—making him, I believe, the only player to have a major league park named in his honor. He died in Detroit in 1927.

50 ◆ Earl Battey
(1955–1967, 1141 G, 104 449 .270)

Washington Senators catcher at the time they moved to Minnesota. A good hitter, and the best throwing catcher of his time. He won the Gold Glove in 1960, '61, and '62. In '63, when Elston Howard won the American League MVP Award, Battey had almost the same stats as Howard—26 homers, 84 RBI, .285 for Battey, 28, 85, .287 for Howard, plus Battey threw better than Howard, although Howard was more active and athletic behind the plate. He was a very fine player, and would rate in the top twenty if he'd had ten good years, rather than six.

Just something I remember . . . I saw a game in Kansas City, must have been about 1962, with Camilo Pascual on the mound for Minnesota. For some reason, about the fourth inning, Battey started firing his throws back to the mound as hard as he could throw, just ripping the glove off Pascual's hand. Pascual was reluctant to catch the throws, and several of them kicked off his glove toward second base. It created a real buzz in the park; but we didn't know *why* he was doing this. Was he trying to wake Pascual up, trying to say, "Hey, let's see your A material. I've got a fastball; you've got a fastball. Let's see it." Or was he irritated because Pascual had missed a sign and crossed him up or something? It went on for two or three innings, and we never did know what was behind it . . .

The '59 White Sox had Battey, Norm Cash, John Romano, and Johnny Callison all on their bench—but traded all of them away without giving them a chance to play . . . Battey was once asked what it took to be a major league catcher. "You have to be big and you have to be dumb," he responded. "I qualify on both counts." He was big, but he wasn't dumb; he was known as a quick-witted player. He worked with troubled kids in New York City after his playing career, for all I know still does.

51 ◆ Muddy Ruel

(1915–1934, 1461 G, 4 532 .275)

His real name was "Herold." He got the nickname "Muddy" as a kid, playing baseball. When a baseball started to fall apart the kids in his neighborhood would pack it with mud to try to hold it together another hour or so. One time, as Ruel caught the ball, it collapsed and splattered mud all over his face. A man passing by laughed, handed him a quarter, and said, "Hey, muddy kid. Go buy yourself a real baseball." He was "Muddy" the rest of his life.

Muddy grew up in St. Louis. A St. Louis newspaperman formed a baseball club called the Wabadas; he got uniforms for them, and a field. Ruel, a student at Washington University, was the star of the Wabadas, and the news hound arranged for him to have a tryout with the Browns after his college semester was over.

Branch Rickey, running the Browns, liked him and signed him. He wasn't ready to play in the majors, but Branch Rickey encouraged him, told him to stay in college, and sold him to Memphis. Ruel did stay in college, eventually earning a law degree, as Rickey had.

He made it back to the majors, with the Yankees, in 1917. After World War I he seemed to be in control of the Yankee catching job, but Miller Huggins, who weighed 140 pounds himself, thought that the 145-pound Ruel was too small to be a regular catcher, and included him

in a trade. Huggins would later describe this, many times, as the biggest mistake he ever made in baseball. Ruel developed into a tough, durable .300 hitter, and the best defensive catcher in the American League. The Win Shares system sees him as deserving of a Gold Glove in 1923, 1924, and 1925.

He was also, according to Al Hirschberg *(Baseball's Greatest Catchers)* the most respected man on any team he was ever a member of, so much so that teammates who couldn't resolve an issue would turn to him for advice. "He made a pitcher out of me when I was almost through," said Walter Johnson after the 1924 World Series, and Firpo Marberry said that "Without him I'd have been nothing."

Ruel hit .095 in the 1924 World Series, but was a hero of the series anyway (see Hank Gowdy, 77), and stayed in the majors for ten years after that. He hung out a shingle in the winters, and talked often about retiring from baseball to devote full time to the practice of law. He also had some banking interests, but he never did leave the game. He coached for the Cardinals from 1935 to 1945, then spent one year as a special assistant to Commissioner Happy Chandler. It was a brutal year—suspensions, the color line breaking, Chandler constantly under attack—and Ruel didn't enjoy the job. He missed the sidelines, went back to coaching.

Muddy was a devout Catholic, and a good friend of Cardinal Spellman. When Bill Veeck was trying to marry his second wife in 1949 he converted to Catholicism, with Muddy as his baptismal godfather.

In the 1950s Ruel was General Manager of the Tigers. According to Billy Rogell in *Cobb Would Have Caught It,* Mickey Cochrane wanted that job, and tried to get a bunch of old-time Detroit stars to sign a petition calling for Ruel to be fired. Rogell was Cochrane's buddy, but he told him he was nuts. Rogell and Cochrane, by this time men in their fifties, got into a fist fight in a bar in the middle of the night, Rogell knocking out several of Cochrane's teeth and breaking a couple of his own knuckles.

Muddy Ruel is a man who should have a book-length biography, but doesn't because he wasn't a great player. My favorite Muddy Ruel story is actually a Bobby Avila story. Avila got a nice bonus to sign with Cleveland in 1948 and, under the Bonus Baby rule, had to spend two seasons on a major league roster. He was with the Indians in 1949, but he hardly ever played, and sometimes he would fall asleep on the bench, for which Lou Boudreau would give him hell. Avila asked Muddy Ruel for help. "Moddy," he said, "I no want to fall asleep. What can I do? You seet here all day, you no sleep. What you do?" Muddy, who himself had been a gum-chewer until he retired as an active player, told him to chew tobacco. If he started to fall asleep he would swallow the tobacco juice, and that would keep him awake. Advice on how to stay out of trouble—and from a real lawyer.

52 ◆ Terry Kennedy
(1978–1991, 1491 G, 113 628 .264)
Came up with the Cardinals when they already had Ted Simmons. Talk about redundancy . . . Kennedy had the same skills as Simmons, only he didn't have as many good years. He hit close to .300, hit 15-20 homers a year and 42 doubles one year, could drive in runs, but he was slow even for a catcher, and didn't throw well. Simmons was a switch hitter, whereas Kennedy was left-handed, and Simmons had a B− arm as a young player, whereas Kennedy's arm was problematic from the beginning of his career. Kennedy always had a soft body; his face was so pudgy you couldn't tell whether he had a chaw of tobacco in there or not. But he could hit.

"He gave me more gray hairs than any of the guys we sent away," Dick Williams said

later. "Kennedy didn't have a mental or physical problem but an equipment problem. He needed a diaper. He would whine when he didn't feel he was getting enough attention and cry when he felt he got too much."

53 ◆ Johnny Edwards
(1961–1974, 1470 G, 81 524 .242)
Caught for the Reds between Ed Bailey (#35) and Johnny Bench (#2). Edwards had a degree in Ceramic Engineering from Ohio State, signed with the Reds in 1959 and was making orderly progress through their system from '59 through early '61. When the Reds traded Bailey in April, 1961, their intention was to use Bob Schmidt and Darrell Johnson to get them through the year, then bring up Edwards, their catcher of the future, in '62.

Two unexpected things happened, however:

1. The Reds surged into first place.

2. Their other catchers were really, really awful.

Edwards' training wasn't quite done, but he stepped into a major league job, anyway, and caught for the Reds the last two months of their drive to the 1961 pennant. He hit .186, but at least he could catch and throw.

For three years after that he was one of the top two or three catchers in the National League, hitting as high as .281 with as many as 17 homers, in a time when batting numbers were a lot lower than they are now. He won the Gold Glove in '63 and '64, made the All-Star team those two years and in 1965.

He stopped hitting in 1966, probably due to hand injuries. The Reds came up with Johnny Bench in late '67; and quickly forgot that they had ever heard of Johnny Edwards. He backed up Tim McCarver with the '68 Cardinals, getting into his second World Series, then was traded to Houston, where Harry Walker restored him to regular status. He led the National League in fielding percentage for three straight years (1969–71) and in assists twice, but he never did start hitting again, and his career ended after the '74 season.

54 ◆ Steve O'Neill
(1911–1928, 1586 G, 13 537 .263)
O'Neill grew up in Minooka, Pennsylvania, the tenth child of Irish-born parents, the fifth child born in America. He quit school and went to work in the coal mines at the age of ten, playing baseball on weekends.

One of his older brothers, Mike, who had pitched for the Cardinals from 1901 to 1904, was managing Elmira in the New York State League in 1910. Steve was 18 by then; Mike didn't figure his kid brother was much of a ballplayer, but he took him on as a backup catcher, just to get him out of the coal mines.

Steve noticed right away that this beat hell out of working in the coal mines, and he determined to make himself a successful ballplayer. Within weeks, O'Neill's hustle was noticed by a friend of Connie Mack's, and O'Neill was purchased by the A's.

The A's farmed him out in 1911, but late in the season the Cleveland Indians hired Harry Davis, who had played for Connie Mack for years, to manage them in 1912. Davis knew that Connie Mack had another young catcher he liked better, Wally Schang, so he asked Connie if he could take O'Neill with him to Cleveland. Mack agreed, and sold O'Neill to the Indians.

For the better part of a decade—1912 to 1918—O'Neil was regarded as one of the top defensive catchers in the American League, but a light hitter. Lee Fohl, his manager, said that "when you have a catcher like Steve O'Neill you don't care whether he hits or not." (This is what is called baseball logic.) In mid-season, 1919, Tris Speaker replaced Fohl, and, wishing to win more games, decided that he did care whether O'Neill hit or not. "Steve," Speaker told

him, "there is no reason for you to be a .240 hitter. I want you to hit .300."

O'Neill was dumbfounded, but agreeable. He asked Speaker what he needed to do. Speaker told him four things:

1. Go to the plate thinking about getting a hit, rather than thinking about making an out.
2. Guess the pitches sometimes, rather than reading and reacting.
3. Take more batting practice.
4. Stop chasing bad pitches.

It worked. O'Neill's hitting improved dramatically. Of course, hitting stats went way up all over baseball in 1920, but even adjusting for that, O'Neill was a much better hitter after 1919 than he had been before. For a few years O'Neill was the best catcher in baseball. He played until 1928, when he was injured in a car accident, and hospitalized for several weeks, ending his career.

O'Neill was a devout Catholic with black, curly hair. He lost his temper, on the field, about once a season, often with memorable consequences. Mike Sowell described him in *The Pitch That Killed* as "one of the nicest men in baseball. Easygoing and congenial, he was always quick to step into the midst of an argument to try to help the two sides settle their differences peacefully. His good nature and earnestness also made him a popular target for teammates' humor."

55 ◆ Harry Danning
(1933–1942, 890 G, 57 397 .285)
The last product of John McGraw's long quest for a Jewish star. A Los Angeles native, he started in baseball by passing as a Mexican, playing in a semi-pro Mexican League in and south of Los Angeles.

He entered pro ball in 1932, playing for Bridgeport in the Eastern League, where Pancho Snyder learned him all of his experiences, as Yogi said about Bill Dickey. He made the majors quickly, but sat on the Giants bench for almost five years, behind Gus Mancuso. Finally he went to Bill Terry and said it was time for him to play. Terry agreed to give him a shot. Danning responded with a game-winning home run in the second game of a famous double-header at the Polo Grounds (June 9, 1937), in front of 55,577 fans. He took over the catching job after that, and held it until World War II.

He was a good hitter (.306 in 1938, .313 in 1939, .300 in 1940), hit as many as 16 home runs, and he was a good catcher. He was painfully slow and a first-pitch hitter, so he had to hit .300 to play. The war ended his career at age 30.

56 ◆ Gus Triandos
(1953–1965, 1206 G, 167 608 .244)

Triandos was the slowest player of the 1950s, a huge catcher who lost his speed as a result of having two feet that wouldn't move very fast. He trekked slowly through the Yankee system, 1948–1954, pausing two years for the United States Army, but compiling some fun numbers along the way, since he never got promoted until he left black and blue marks all over the league's pitchers. In the Pioneer League in 1948 he hit .323, driving in 85 runs in 92 games. They sent him back to the same team the next year. He hit .435 with 10 homers, 42 RBI in 28 games, at which point they finally said, "OK, OK, you can go to the Piedmont League." He also hit .363 for Amsterdam in the Canadian-American League, and .368 for Birmingham in the Southern League.

Eventually the Yankees decided that he wasn't going to take Yogi Berra's job, and included him in a trade with the Baltimore Orioles, a trade also involving—I am not making this up—Harry Byrd, Jim McDonald, Bill Miller, Hal Smith, Don Leppert, Kal Segrist, Willie Miranda, Gene Woodling, Mike Blyzka, Don Larsen, Bob Turley, Darrell Johnson, Dick Kryhoski, Billy Hunter, Ted del Guercio, and Jim Fridley. Basically, the Orioles traded two pitchers for a dozen or more people the Yankees were never going to use.

Paul Richards, who had successfully molded Sherm Lollar into one of the best catchers in baseball, now undertook the same labor with Triandos. The results were less rewarding, but still worthwhile; Triandos would be a major league regular for eight years. In 1958 he hit 30 home runs, tying the American League record for home runs by a catcher (Yogi's, of course); that year he hit .245 with ten doubles, no triples, but 30 home runs. He also established several records for passed balls, largely because he had the misfortune of catching Hoyt Wilhelm the one season when Wilhelm was a starting pitcher, pitching 200-plus innings. This established the principle that a knuckleball pitcher and a big, slow catcher make an awful combination. "Heaven," Triandos once told a reporter, "is a place where no one throws a knuckleball."

Triandos was a powerful man who, had he not been a catcher and had he reached the majors earlier, could very probably have hit 400 or even 500 major league homers. In December 1961, it was reported that Triandos had been traded to the Dodgers for Charlie Neal and John Roseboro. A reporter called Triandos and asked for his reaction. Triandos let out a loud "Ee-yah," and told the reporter how thrilled he was to be getting out of Baltimore.

Unfortunately, the reporter had been mistaken; there was no trade. Oops.

57 ◆ Andy Seminick
(1943–1957, 1304 G, 164 556 .243)

I'm not sure, but Seminick may be the only player listed in the top 100 at any position who never batted more than 406 times in a season. I always think of him as a long-term regular, because he hit 24 homers twice, 19 another year, hit 11 or more home runs ten times including nine in a row—but he was never a true regular.

58 ◆ Jack Clements

(1884–1900, 1157 G, 77 673 .286)

The only left-handed throwing catcher to have a real career in the major leagues, also the first man to wear a chest protector. Also the only 19th-century player (at any position) who hit more home runs than triples in a career of a thousand or more games. In modern baseball about 80% of players hit more homers than triples—but Clements was the first.

> Where would the Phillies have been this season without Allen and Clements? . . . The latter's clever catching prevented opposing clubs from accomplishing much in the way of run getting. The Phillies' pitchers would not have cut much of a figure, had they had a less competent catcher to back them up, as he made them effective by his superb coaching. He told them by signs where to pitch every ball, and by his fine throwing held runners so closely to their bases, that they could not get around unless by consecutive hitting or through errors by the fielders. The team took a bad tumble when Clements was disabled and unable to play, as during his absence the pitchers did very poorly. But for the accident to Clements and Myer's lay-off the Phillies would probably have captured the League *pennant.—Philadelphia Ledger,* September, 1890, quoted in the 1891 *Spalding Guide.*

> Too indifferent to play for the best that was in him and get into proper shape, Jack Clements, the erstwhile crack backstop of the Phillies, is under contract to do the catching for the Springfield team of the Connecticut State League . . . Clements had all the qualities of a great catcher, but refused to use them.—*Cleveland Plain Dealer,* April 14, 1902.

59 ◆ Luke Sewell

(1921–1942, 1630 G, 20 696 .259)

The Sewell brothers' father was a country doctor in Titus, Alabama, a man who knew the value of an education. There were six children in the Sewell family, all of whom would graduate from college. Luke (and Joe also) fully intended to be a doctor, like their dad. He took pre-med classes at the University of Alabama, but also played baseball, and played summer ball in a real good semi-pro league, which had players like Riggs Stephenson, Hughie Critz, and Bill Terry.

Luke Sewell was connected to the Indians because his brother played for them. They sent a scout, Patsy Flaherty, to watch him play at Alabama. Luke was an infielder at the time, but Flaherty saw immediately that he had the tools to be a catcher. "I'm not a catcher," he told Flaherty. "I'm an infielder."

"No, you're not," Flahery responded. "You're a catcher. You're going to catch for the Cleveland Indians."

"I don't even own a catcher's mitt," replied Sewell.

"You will," said Flaherty.

He spent just a few weeks in the minor leagues, then joined the Indians. In his mind it was still just a detour on the road to being a doctor, but the detour kept getting longer. For a couple of years he backed up Steve O'Neill, then moved into a kind of odd platoon with Glenn Myatt. Myatt, a left-handed hitter, played almost every game at League Park, which was very short to right field, while Sewell played most of the games on the road.

Myatt couldn't throw well, however, and had the bad habit of calling all fastballs when there was a runner on first, to prevent the stolen base. Luke was a better defensive player, and eventually won the job. He was never much of a hitter; he never did hit .300, in an era when anyone who could hit over .300. He was the fourth-best catcher in the American League for most of his career, behind Cochrane, Dickey, and Rick Ferrell. All of them were Gold Glove catchers, but even Ferrell was a lot better hitter than Sewell, and the other guys made Ferrell look like Charlie O'Brien. Sewell helped

Washington win a pennant in 1933, and managed the Browns to their only pennant in 1944.

Sewell, new manager of the Cincinnati Reds, quoted by Joe Williams in the spring of 1950: "It gives me comfort to know there is at least one subject in this country that is creating more anxiety than the H-bomb, the cold war, and the water shortage. In the space of a few weeks I have become the world's leading authority on [Ewell] Blackwell. This, I hasten to add, is a distinction which has been forced upon me. Nobody talks to me about anything else and I do have three or four other players here in camp. But to answer your question: Blackwell has taken on weight, seems to have regained his stamina, his pitching motion is unchanged and I see no reason why he shouldn't work and win regularly for us."

60 ◆ Chief Meyers
(1909–1917, 992 G, 14 363 .291)

His .358 average in 1912 was the highest for a catcher in the dead-ball era. If you don't count the Federal League, his .332 average in 1911 was the second-highest. Like Johnny Bassler and Earl Battey, Meyers was a good hitter and a pretty decent defensive catcher, but had a short career. But a long life; he would live to recite *Casey At the Bat* on the *Today* show when *The Glory of Their Times* came out in 1966. He was in his mid-eighties. There are tapes of that around; he had a marvelous voice and great dignity, great carriage . . .

In 1909 they had "Chief Meyers Day" at the park in Buffalo. Meyers talked back to the umpire, Steamboat Johnson, and Johnson threw him out of the game on his own day, told him to take his loving cup and head home . . .

> Catcher "Jack" Myers, of the New York team, proved one of the real base ball finds of 1909–10. His work in all departments has been first-class, and especially has he excelled as a hard and timely batsman. The big fellow is an Indian, and

Myers is, of course, an assumed name, a college bequest to mark the good-natured aborigine from the sequestered people of his tribe. At the Pala reservation, in California, the notable backstop is known to the mission Indians as "Tortes." Myers is not a reservation Indian, though much of his time has been spent on the California reserves. Reared at Riverside, Cal., where he was born July 29, 1882, Myers had every advantage in securing an education. As a boy he played with his little white brothers of the town. He just naturally took to base ball, and as he was always big and strong, he accepted but one position on the field, that of catcher. From the sand lots he drifted to high-school ball. Then he came East to study at Dartmouth. A year in college, and Harrisburg, of the Tri-State League, persuaded him to seek the diamond as a vocation. He drifted west to Butte, Mont., of the Northwestern League, and made such a reputation there that St. Paul, of the American Association, procured him almost three years ago. From St. Paul he came, in the Fall of 1909, to the Giants. Myers is a bright fellow, despite his native reserve. When warmed to enthusiasm he can discourse on almost any topic intelligently.—1912 *Reach Guide*

61 ◆ Frank Snyder
(1912–1927, 1392 G, 47 525 .265)

Snyder was of Mexican descent, although his name doesn't reflect this (I think his mother was from Mexico); he was called "Pancho," because people at that time didn't have sense enough to be offended by stuff like that. He was originally a *defensive* catcher. When he was 21 years old he took the St. Louis Cardinal catcher's job away from Ivy Wingo, who was a better hitter, because he was quick and could throw. He had 204 assists in 1915, highest season assists total for any of the top 100 catchers, although Bill Rariden had 238 Assists in the Federal League in 1915, and 215 assists in 1914.

As an aside, the top sixteen catchers in assists/season all played between 1903 and 1915, and the top 65 seasons in catchers' assists are all 1920 or before. If you make a list of the top assists totals by catchers since 1920, the top 26 men on that list are all from the 1920s. The highest assist total by a catcher since 1930 was 108, by Gary Carter in 1980.

There are two reasons that the assists totals of catchers in that era were twice or more what they are now. One is that there were a lot of stolen base attempts with very low success rates. Data is spotty, but it is clear that there were a lot of guys in that era who would attempt 50 stolen bases in a season and get thrown out 25 or 30 times. The other reason is that, in addition to the caught stealing, the teams of that era bunted several times a game. A catcher might have registered 80 or more assists per season fielding bunts. Major league catchers in 1914 accounted for 12% of all assists, whereas in 1954 and in 1994 they accounted for less than 5%.

62 ◆ Chief Zimmer

(1884–1903, 1280 G, 26 620 .269)
Pink Hawley was probably the best pitcher in baseball in 1895, but had a very poor self-image, no self-esteem. Zimmer owned a cigar store which he ran in the winter. One day in the middle of January, Hawley burst in and said, "Chief, will you ever forgive me?"

"Certainly," said Chief. The men shook hands, and Hawley left, relieved.

Zimmer had no idea what it was about. He had never had a harsh word with Hawley, and had not the vaguest notion what he was forgiving Hawley for having done . . .

Zimmer grew up in Ironton, Ohio, and played with Ironton town teams until he was in his early twenties; later on he would be called the Ironton Iron Man. He was a carpenter's apprentice, just kind of messing around with baseball, when the Detroit Wolverines, desperate for help during the 1884 player shortages caused by the Union Association, signed him to back up Charlie Bennett. He was 24 years old.

He played badly, and was released after a few games.

In the following years he played in the minors and semi-pro ball. Baseball wasn't very organized in the 1880s; it is difficult to say, sometimes, what is a minor league team, and what is semi-pro ball. The two were really almost the same. Anyway, he played a little bit in the American Association in 1886, just as badly, and in 1887 was playing for a team in the Hudson River League, the Poughkeepsie Indians. That's how he became the "Chief"; he was the best player on the Indians.

Anyway, he played well there, and the Cleveland Spiders bought him. He finally found his major league legs, became the Spiders top catcher in 1888. Zimmer was one of the first catchers to squat behind home plate, rather than standing several feet back. At that time the practice was that teams would carry two or three catchers and rotate them, as they did pitchers; a top pitcher might pitch more innings than a top catcher could catch. Zimmer always insisted that he could catch every day. In 1890 there was a player's strike and another player shortage, as many of the players left to start their own league. The Spiders were one of the hardest hit teams, decimated by defections. The manager decided to let Zimmer catch every day, and he did, 125 of 132 games.

What he hadn't anticipated was Cy Young. In mid-season, 1890, the Spiders signed Cy Young, one of the hardest-throwing pitchers of all time—and remember, in 1890 the pitcher was throwing hard from 50 feet. And the catchers mitt was not padded. Zimmer refused to back off; he put a piece of steak in his glove (a trick he had learned from Deacon McGuire) and continued to catch every day. *The Sporting Life* said that "a game without Zimmer would be a disagreeable novelty," but Zimmer later insisted that he had never in his career had a sore arm, a broken finger, or even a split fingernail. He was Cy Young's catcher for the first half of Young's career, and one of Young's closest friends; the battery of Young and Zimmer probably appeared in the box score as many times as any combination in the history of the game.

The Spiders became a decent team, winning the second half of a split schedule in 1892, and finishing second to Baltimore in 1895 and 1896; at that time the first- and second-place teams played a post-season series, enabling the Spiders to claim the National League championship in 1895, when Zimmer hit a career-high .340. By 1899 the Spiders' best players had been moved to St. Louis by the ownership syndicate, leaving the Spiders as, perhaps, the worst team in history. Zimmer was still there, trying manfully to cope with the frustration of losing almost every game. In April a Cincinnati newspaper criticized his throwing. When the teams met again Zimmer threw out four base stealers in a game; according to *The Sporting Life* he "nipped 'em all a mile or two from the base." Released by Cleveland, he signed with Louisville, and was able to stay in the league in the consolidation year of 1900, when the NL shucked off four teams and a hundred-plus players.

The next spring there was another effort to form a player's union, the "Protective Association of Professional Baseball Players." Zimmer became the first president of this association, and had some success negotiating with the owners. When the American League moved for major league status in 1901, Zimmer played the American League off against the National to win some minor concessions for the players. He hated the job, however, so much that it nearly drove him out of baseball; in March 1901, Zimmer announced that he was going to quit and run his restaurant in Cleveland full time.

That retirement didn't last long; Zimmer was back in the game in a month or two. He played three more seasons, managed the Phillies in 1903, and then umpired for a few years.

There are two things for which Zimmer is most famous, neither of which I have yet mentioned. One is the "200 mile homer," which he supposedly hit over the fence at the old Boston National League Park and onto a passing coal car of the Boston-Albany Railroad. The baseball was recovered when the train stopped in Fall River.

The other thing for which Zimmer is most remembered is "Zimmer's Base Ball Game," described in *The National Pastime* (Spring, 1984) as "the most beautiful baseball table game ever created." Marketed in 1893, it is prized by collectors a hundred years later. According to Mark Cooper (*Baseball's First Stars*, SABR, 1996) it is "played with a pool cue-type spring loaded pitching device and a typical spring-type bat. Metal clasps are located at the nine positions to catch the ball."

Zimmer was quite an entrepreneur, as you can see—the Cigar Store, the restaurant, the game, the Union work. A tee-totaler, he is also sometimes quoted on the subject of temperance. Out of baseball, he took up cabinet making and cigar rolling, among other pursuits, and also owned and managed at least two minor league teams. In his later years he was fond of saying he was "baseball's oldest living ex-catcher," basing his claim on the fact that he was two years older than Connie Mack. He died in Cleveland in 1949, just a couple of months short of his ninetieth birthday.

63 ◆ Jimmie Wilson
(1923–1940, 1525 G, 32 621 .284)

Good defensive catcher in the National League, 1923 to 1940, called "Ace." We have him as deserving of two Gold Gloves, 1929 and 1931. Wilson was traded twice for Spud Davis. Spud was a better hitter than Wilson; Wilson was a better fielder.

Wilson came up with Philadelphia, and played with the rag-tag Phillies for several years; Spud Davis came up with the Cardinals.

When Bill McKechnie was running the Cardinals in the late twenties he traded Davis for Wilson (McKechnie believed that defense was everything), but after McKechnie was gone the Cardinals more or less reversed the trade. It is hard to say who was better, Wilson or Davis, but both times when they were traded for one another Davis's team threw something in WITH Spud Davis to even it up, so that seems to imply that at least the Phillies and Cardinals agreed that Wilson was the better player.

Wilson was the Cardinals catcher when Dizzy Dean came up. He tried to take Dean under his wing, which was kind of like trying to keep a Rhinoceros in your bathroom; Dizzy Dean would make Newk LaLoosh look like a Republican Senator. On their first trip to New York Wilson loaned Dizzy a white silk shirt, saying as tactfully as he could that it wouldn't reflect well on the Cardinals to let their hot rookie pitcher wander around New York City in a plaid cotton shirt with several buttons missing. Diz liked the shirt so much that he cleaned out Wilson's closet, explaining to the enraged Wilson that he jus' *knew* the St. Louis Cardinals would not want to let a great young pitcher like him run around with only one silk shirt. There are a lot of other Jimmie Wilson stories presented peripherally in Dizzy Dean books, and Wilson was also one of Bill Stern's favorite players.

When Frankie Frisch took over the Cardinals (1933) he was apparently jealous of Wilson's status on the team, and/or felt that Wilson was assuming too much authority. At a game in Pittsburgh shortly after Frisch took over the team, an argument developed around home plate. Wilson left the bench, and said something to Pittsburgh manager George Gibson. Frisch snapped at him to get back to the bench, said he didn't need any help running the team. Wilson was benched after that, and traded after the season.

He was player/manager of the Phillies for almost five years, a job that could be compared to being the public relations manager of a toxic waste dump. His main accomplishment as Philadelphia manager was converting Bucky Walters to a pitcher; that, or surviving.

"Wilson had been a great soccer player," wrote Dick Bartell. "He could do tricks with his feet. He came sliding into second base. I was making the tag on him. With a little flip of his foot he knocked the ball right out of my glove."

"Still, that's not the reason I thought he was the worst manager I ever played for. I liked and respected him as a player, but not as manager. He was like a wild man, just couldn't handle the players. He was on my back all the time, no matter what I did."

Wilson is most famous now for the 1940 World Series. Wilson by 1940 was 40 years old, and had basically been retired for three years. He was coaching for Bill McKechnie with the Reds. The Reds' #2 catcher, Willard Hershberger, committed suicide in early August, and their #1 catcher, Ernie Lombardi, got hurt in September. They tried a rookie, Bill Baker, but he didn't hit and didn't field, so Wilson came out of retirement to catch every day for the Reds the last two weeks of the season. The Reds, comfortably ahead anyway, got red-hot the last two weeks of the 1940 season, and won the World Series with Wilson catching six of the seven contests and leading the team in hitting at .353 (6 for 17).

Another story about him . . . the great umpire Bill Klem, who was a funny-looking guy, absolutely hated being called "Catfish." It was understood in the National League for many years that if you were talking to Bill Klem, and the word "Catfish" was mentioned in any context, you were gone.

Well, September 19, 1926; the Cardinals were playing the Phillies in a double-header that was crucial to the Cardinals, but meaningless to the Phillies, who had been virtually eliminated during spring training. The first game of the double-header, Wilson, catching for the Phillies, argued with Klem and got thrown out of the game. At the Baker Bowl there was a window in the Phillies clubhouse that could be seen from the field, so Wilson went back to the clubhouse and wrote out a sign that said "Hi, Catfish," and put the sign in the window.

But before Klem could see the sign, Wilson's manager, Art Fletcher, also got run out of the game. So Klem throws out the manager, turns his attention back to the game, and the next time he looks up he sees this "Hi, Catfish" sign in the window of the clubhouse, where he has just dispatched Art Fletcher. So naturally, Klem thinks Fletcher has put up the sign, and after the game he wires National League president John Heydler to that effect. Heydler suspended Fletcher for the balance of the season, and the Phillies fired him while he was suspended. But both Wilson and Fletcher said that Wilson put up the sign, and Fletcher never even knew it was there until he heard from the league that he had been suspended for putting it there.

Wilson's son, Bob, a promising baseball player himself, was a pilot in World War II, and was killed when his plane was shot down in India. It was said of Wilson that there was never a man who enjoyed life more than Jimmy Wilson, but after his son died all the light went out of his eyes. He died of a heart attack in 1947, aged 46.

64 ◆ Birdie Tebbetts
(1936–1952, 1162 G, 38 469 .270)

Tebbetts was small for a catcher, rather pudgy, one of the slowest runners in the majors, and had no power. He had two assets that kept him in the majors for several years: intelligence, and competitiveness. Birdie was always a very good student, and in fact had turned down a

bonus offer from the Yankees in the late twenties because he wanted to get a college degree before he played baseball. The Tigers agreed to sign him and let him finish his education first, which he did, graduating from Providence College in 1934 with a degree in philosophy.

Mickey Cochrane picked Tebbetts to be his successor as Tiger catcher, and Tebbetts shot quickly through the minors. Unfortunately, Cochrane was seriously hurt before Tebbetts was ready to play, which pushed Tebbetts back into a competition for the job. Rudy York was one of the most talented hitters of his generation, and was a good athlete who could throw. The Tigers tried for a couple of years to make York their catcher. That failing, Tebbetts moved back into the job. York moved to first and drove in 134 runs, Greenberg moved to left field and drove in 150, and Tebbetts hit .296 as the catcher, helping the Tigers to the 1940 American League pennant.

He was a marvel working with pitchers. He knew every hitter's weakness, every hitter's danger zone, what every pitcher liked to throw. He knew how every pitcher *thought;* he made it his responsibility to understand the thinking of every pitcher on his team.

He didn't do anything athletic particularly well, but he always did it the best that he could. He backed up first on every GB6. His particular talent was getting under the skin of opposing players. He worked at it; he knew the magic words that would get anybody in the league thinking about something other than the next pitch—and he chirped those magic words in a high, screechy voice that somehow made it worse. Bill McGowan once threw him out of a game when he was on the bench. "What did I do?" Tebbetts asked.

"Nothing," said McGowan, "but your voice gives me a headache." Many sources say that he was called "Birdie" because of his high, bird-like voice, but actually this is untrue; he was given the nickname the day he was born by an aunt, who said that he had lips like a little birdie.

He was in hundreds of fights. He always said that he didn't *like* to fight, he felt bad about being in so many fights, but he just lost his head in the heat of competition. One of the fights was the big one, World War II; he spent three full seasons in the United States Army.

When he returned to the Tigers in 1946, the Tiger fans for some unknown reason had developed an intense dislike for him, and began to boo him every time he appeared on the field. This eventually forced him to be traded; he became the starting catcher for the Boston Red Sox of the late forties.

Birdie was overjoyed to go to the Red Sox. A bachelor, he lived in the Boston area with his mother in the off-season; now he could live there in-season, too (he was finally married in 1949). He also had an insurance business in the off-season; playing for the Red Sox would be great for that.

The Red Sox of the late forties were virtually an all-star team—Ted Williams, Bobby Doerr, Vern Stephens, Johnny Pesky, Mel Parnell, Dom DiMaggio. They kept finishing second, or sometimes third. After the 1950 season, answering questions after a speech to a booster group, Birdie was asked what the problem was. He expressed the opinion that some of his Boston teammates were "moronic malcontents and juvenile delinquents." This got into the newspapers. Birdie was sold to Cleveland within weeks, and finished his career with the Indians.

One last story. In the early 1940s the Red Sox had a coach named Tom (Four Shows) Daly, who was the Chris Berman of his time, always making puns on the player's names. One time, after the Red Sox had played the Tigers, Daly told a reporter that Birdie Tebbetts had had to pay a $50 fine the previous morning.

"Oh, really," said the reporter. "What did he do?"

"Catching Trout out of season."

65 ◆ Butch Wynegar
(1976–1988, 1301 G, 65 506 .255)

My favorite *Baseball Digest* article title is "How the Tigers Missed Out On Drafting Butch Wynegar." This was about 1977; Wynegar had gone through the minors like a house afire, won the American League Rookie of the Year Award in 1976, and was named to the All-Star team again in 1977. The premise of the article was that the Tigers in 1974 had decided to draft a catcher, and had narrowed the options down to Wynegar and Lance Parrish. They drafted Parrish, hoping that Wynegar would slip to the second round and they could get him, too. He didn't, and after Wynegar's quick start the Tigers were kicking themselves for picking Parrish.

Wynegar more or less cracked up after that; he never made the All-Star team again. He was an OK player, but if he had been able to stay healthy and stay focused, he would have been a great player.

66 ◆ Jerry Grote
(1963–1981, 1421 G, 39 404 .252)

Grote attended Trinity University in San Antonio, signed with the Houston Colts soon after that organization started, and made the majors after less than a year in the bushes. He hit .181 in 100 games for Houston in 1964, and was traded to the Mets for a pitcher who couldn't pitch.

With the Mets he didn't hit .181 any more, but he never hit a whole lot; his skills were similar to Birdie Tebbetts', except that he threw better and didn't hit as many singles. When the Mets developed a fling of outstanding young pitchers (Seaver, Koosman, Gentry, Tug McGraw) Grote got, and probably deserved, some of the credit. He hit .252, his career average, as the 1969 Mets won the pennant. He roomed with Nolan Ryan, a fellow Texan, while Ryan was with the Mets, and was one of the first people remembered by Ryan in his Hall of Fame induction speech.

Grote finished his career with the Kansas City Royals, where he was nicknamed "The Skunk" because of a white streak in his beard. The Royals, who had won the American League in 1980, were going through some difficult straits in 1981, which were symbolized by what happened to Grote. Jim Frey announced on Friday before the game that Grote was now his regular catcher—and on Sunday after the game that Grote had been released.

67 ◆ Don Slaught
(1982–1997, 1327 G, 77 476 .283)
Not much of a defensive catcher, didn't throw particularly well, not the best receiver in the world, and never had the reputation of being particularly good with pitchers. Small for a catcher—they list him at 190 pounds, but I would have guessed 170—and had many injuries. But he was an active, athletic catcher who could really belt out those line drives, hitting .300 six times. I'd compare him to B.J. Surhoff. If somebody had had the sense to tell him to forget about catching and concentrate on what he did well, he'd have rung up some real numbers.

68 ◆ Alan Ashby
(1973–1989, 1370 G, 90 513 .245)
The Indians about 1970 had Ray Fosse, who looked like he was going to be one of the top catchers of his generation. He got hurt after a year or two, but the Indians came up simultaneously with Ashby and Rick Cerone. The Indians couldn't decide between them, so they shipped them both to Toronto and imported a couple of loser has-beens to handle the catching chores. This made Alan Ashby the only man to compete for playing time with Rick Cerone in two different cities.

For several years Ashby didn't hit—he hit .224 in 1975, .210 in 1977, and .202 in 1979. He was a good enough defensive catcher to stay in the league despite these things, and

the longer he stayed around the better he started to hit. By 1987 he hit .288 with 14 homers. He was never great, but he had a seventeen-year career with good defense and some offense.

69 ◆ Rollie Hemsley
(1928–1947, 1593 G, 31 555 .262)
Came up with the Pirates about the same time as Kiki Cuyler and the Waner brothers; the Pirates really had their act together for a few years there. He had exceptional defensive gifts, like Sundberg or Luke Sewell or Al Lopez or Bob Boone, but lacked the seriousness that made those men what they were. Hemsley was called "Rollicking Rollie" because of his great zest for the nation's night life; he seemed to take prohibition as a personal challenge. This caused him to bounce around for most of his career, taking a Cook's tour of the teams that needed a backup catcher, although he was a regular for the Browns in 1934–35. He was enrolled in an Alcoholics Anonymous program by the Indians in 1939 or 1940, and played fairly well for a year or two before he fell off the wagon. Had a post-playing career as a coach and a scout.

70 ◆ Hank Severeid
(1911–1926, 1390 G, 17 539 .289)
St. Louis Browns catcher from 1915 to 1924, hit .324 in 1921, .321 in 1922, over .300 the next three seasons. According to Mike Sowell in *The Pitch That Killed,* Severeid "prided himself on his toughness and durability. Once, a baserunners spikes had caught him above the knee, severing an artery. Severeid was taken to the clubhouse, where he sat and watched as a doctor tied the two ends of the artery together. A week later, he was back behind the plate." Sowell is telling this story because Severeid had a confrontation with Carl Mays, just a few weeks before Mays killed Ray Chapman with a pitch; Severeid had charged

the mound and thrown his bat at Mays after he thought Mays was throwing at him.

Severeid played in the minors for years after his major league career, creating a 29-year career in which he caught 2,357 professional games, which was claimed at the time of his death to be an all-time record. He scouted for the Boston Red Sox from 1944 until his death in 1968.

71 ◆ Spud Davis

(1928–1945, 1458 G, 77 647 .308)
Right-handed hitting catcher, extremely slow and not much of an arm, but a solid line-drive hitter for years and years, lifetime .308 hitter. He was almost exactly the same player as Brian Harper, actually; the only real difference between them is that Harper bounced around for years before he got a chance to play, so Davis' career is a little longer. Don Slaught is similar, too, although Slaught was a little more athletic than the other two.

72 ◆ Ernie Whitt

(1976–1991, 1328 G, 134 534 .249)
The opposite of John Romano (below); Whitt was never a hot prospect, never caught many breaks, didn't get a real look in the majors until he was 28, didn't get 300 at bats in a season until he was past 30. But he worked hard, stayed in shape, just kept doing his best, and wound up having a pretty decent career.

73 ◆ John Romano

(1958–1967, 905 G, 129 417 .255)
The White Sox traded the young John Romano *and* the young Norm Cash to re-acquire the 37-year-old Minnie Minoso.

A handsome Italian who could always hit, Romano became a hot prospect after having a monster season in the Three-I League in 1955. "In those early years," Romano told Stan Isaacs in 1961, "I didn't know I was considered that

bad a catcher. Up until 1958 when I started playing for Walker Cooper . . . I thought I was about as good as the other guys I was playing with." Isaacs' memorable line about Romano: "He is no longer the boy who learned a month after reporting to Dubuque in 1954 that he had started in class D and not double A as he had assumed he would."

Romano was an exceptional player, but only for about two years. He was very strong, had soft hands, and could throw well enough to be a major league catcher, and his .299 average with 21 homers made him one of the best catchers in the majors in 1961. Isaacs reported in the *Sport* magazine article in 1961, however, that Romano "has had to fight a reputation for laziness that traced back to one fateful spring when he reported to camp 30 pounds overweight." The weight began to creep back on after 1961, about five pounds a year, and within a few years that had destroyed his career.

74 ◆ Gus Mancuso

(1928–1945, 1460 G, 53 543 .265)
Played in five World Series. From his rookie year (1930) until 1942 he bounced all over the National League—but played on only one team (the 1932 Cardinals) which had a won-lost record worse than 84-70.

The Cardinals had Mancuso pegged as strictly a backup catcher. Even in the minor leagues, he was never a regular. In 1927 he hit .372 with 54 RBI in 180 at bats at Syracuse (International)—as the backup catcher to a guy named Boyce Morrow, who hit .321, but was supposed to be a better defensive catcher. Mancuso was exceptionally slow, but he kept hitting pretty good, so they put him on the major league roster as a backup catcher/pinch hitter. He hit .366 as a rookie in 1930, driving in 59 runs in 227 at bats. After that, although he never hit .366 again, he hit well enough, but the Cardinals had Jimmie Wilson, and they always had some young catcher like Bill Delancey or Bill Lewis that they liked better. In 1932 Wilson got hurt and Mancuso had to play quite a bit; the Cardinals had a lousy year, which *firmly* convinced them that Mancuso would never be a regular, so they traded him to the Giants.

The Giants made Mancuso their regular catcher, and improved dramatically in 1933, from sixth place (72-82) to the pennant (91-61). All four of the Giants' pitchers were much more effective in 1933 than they had been in 1932. Carl Hubbell, for example, went from 18-11, 2.50 ERA to 23-12, 1.66, and Hal Schumacher went from 5-6, 3.55 to 19-12, 2.16. Mancuso received much credit for this improvement. According to Tom Meany (*Baseball for Everyone*, Joe DiMaggio, ghosted by Meany), the Giants 1932 catcher, Shanty Hogan, was a great big man who always gave a high target, and caught all low pitches by stabbing downward with his glove. The umpires saw the glove bobbing down, and called the low pitches balls—a real problem, since all four New York starters were low-ball pitchers. Mancuso gave a low target and caught the same pitch coming up, making the pitch look like a strike to the men in blue.

An interesting theory—and the team fielding records suggest that at least part of this was true. The Giants in 1933 increased from 1898 assists (fourth in the league) to 2087—highest total in major league baseball in the 1930s. That means they had many, many more ground balls, which probably confirms that they were getting low strikes. And Meany, who wrote about this fifteen years later, certainly never knew about the assists total.

In any case, Mancuso continued as the Giants regular catcher until mid-season, 1937, helping the Giants win three National League pennants . . . He had a brother, Frank, who also

played in the majors, but who achieved more fame as an actor.

75 ◆ Frankie Hayes
(1933–1947, 1364 G, 119 628 .259)

Hayes was not extremely fat; a little pudgy, maybe, but not the blimp suggested by his nickname, which was "Blimp." According to Reverend Jerome C. Romanowski *(The Baseball Padre)*, Hayes "had the tools of a good receiver—strong arm, good hands and an uncanny knack on judging the flight and descent of a foul ball." He was in the majors at age 18, due to his obvious skills, and the A's regular catcher by age 21. He hit between .280 and .308 from 1938 through 1941, and hit as many as 20 homers in a season.

Hayes was traded to the Browns in 1942. According to William B. Mead in *Baseball Goes to War,* "Hayes, a catcher from whom much had been expected, hit .188 and grumped continually about having to play for the Browns." Again quoting the Baseball Padre, Hayes "did not reach his potential. He looked every bit like a major league catcher, but it is sad to report that Hayes left the majors when he was only 32 and died on June 22, 1955, when he was only 40."

76 ◆ Doggie Miller
(1884–1896, 1317 G, 33 518 .267)

Miller was very small, 145 pounds; he was called "Doggie" because he kept dogs, and also "Foghorn" because he had a raspy, booming voice. He was a hard-drinking, fast-living player who played baseball with evident joy, drawing comparisons to King Kelly. He earned good money, as baseball players always have, and spent it as fast as he could get his hands on it.

Miller was in mid-career when the catcher's job changed, baseball moving (1889–1892) from the era of "un-protected" catchers who caught only two-three games a week to modern "protected" full-time catchers. Miller disdained the chest protector and the padded mitt, and thus never caught more than 76 games a season. This forced him out of the majors shortly after his thirtieth birthday, although he played seven more years in the minor leagues. He died of kidney failure in 1909, *The Sporting News* reporting that he was "one of the few players who indulged in intoxicants oftentimes to excess who had an extended career." (See *Baseball's First Stars*, SABR, article by Richard Puff.)

77 ◆ Hank Gowdy
(1910–1930, 1050 G, 21 322 .270)

Gowdy was a tall, skinny guy with bright red hair and freckles. He looked awkward in street clothes and far too tall and skinny to be a catcher, but he was quick and graceful behind the plate, with an excellent arm. He was quiet, very shy, never swore, and never yelled at umpires, but would fight if challenged.

Gowdy had never caught before he came to the majors. John McGraw purchased him for the Giants after he had a big year for Dallas in 1910. McGraw liked him, but he already had a first baseman and Gowdy wasn't really fast enough to play the outfield, so McGraw couldn't find a place for him. The Giants traded him to Boston, where Johnny Kling, managing the Braves, was looking for a young catcher who could hit a little bit. They had Bill Rariden, who was a defensive star but couldn't hit, and Kling himself, who was getting old. Gowdy didn't look anything like a catcher and had never caught, but he was willing to try, so Kling made him a catcher. Kling got fired, and Gowdy went back to the minors to try to get some innings behind the plate.

In 1914 Rariden bolted to the Federal League, leaving George Stallings and the Braves looking for a catcher. They still had an option on Gowdy, so they started the 1914 season with Bert Whaling as their catcher, Gowdy backing him up. Whaling didn't hit or field very well, and Gowdy took over the job, catching almost every game over the last two months as the Miracle Braves made their historic dash from last place to the 1914 pennant.

Gowdy dominated the 1914 World Series as few players ever have. He hit .545 in a pitching-controlled series, swept by the Braves. He was the only player to score three runs in the series, and the only player to drive in three runs in the series. He was the only player to hit a home run in the series, and one of two players to hit triple. He was the only player to hit 3 doubles in the series, thus leading both teams in batting, doubles, triples, and home runs; five of his six hits were for extra bases. One game went 12 innings; Gowdy hit a leadoff double in the bottom of the 12th, all but ending the game. He drew five walks in the series, two more than anyone else. He threw out 3 of 5 opposing base stealers, while he himself stole successfully in his only try. His on-base percentage was .688, his slugging percentage 1.273.

His parents saw the last two games of the series, sneaking into Boston without telling him, because they were concerned that Gowdy, still a young and inexperienced player, would be nervous if he knew they were there. His mother was so religious that this deception bothered her; she told a reporter that telling her son she wouldn't be able to get to Boston was the first time she had lied to him since she told him about Santa Claus.

He was a regular for two years after that, an above-average hitter, and, at least in the opinion of the Win Shares system, deserving of the Gold Glove in 1914 and 1916 (Pancho Snyder deserved it in 1915). Two months into the 1917 season, Gowdy shelved his mask and joined the United States Army. He was the first major league player to go to World War I, leaving a year and a half before most of the others. He saw combat in Europe, in the trenches, and came home a sergeant. His willing patriotism made him a symbol of what was right about the game, and he would forever after remain one of the game's most popular and respected men.

He was, however, unable to get back to regular status. In early 1923 the Braves, now in full retreat as an organization, traded him back to John McGraw, where he split the catching job with Pancho Snyder, and helped the Giants win the 1923 and 1924 pennants. In the seventh game of the 1924 series the game was tied 3-3 in the 12th inning. Muddy Ruel, Washington catcher, was batting with one out. Ruel popped the ball up, a mile high right over the plate. Gowdy failed to throw his mask far enough away, and tripped over the mask as the pop up drifted away from him. It was the first of three misplays that would doom the Giants. Ruel, given a new life, ripped a double past Freddie Lindstrom at third base. Walter Johnson grounded to short, but Travis Jackson fumbled the ball, putting runners on first and second. Earl McNeely hit a ground ball to third base. The ball hit a pebble and hopped over Lindstrom's head, giving Washington the victory, and Gowdy, among others, the goat's horns.

McGraw forgave Gowdy, in part perhaps because McGraw was engaged in a noisy public feud with the man Gowdy had replaced (Oil Smith, #100), who never missed a chance to rip McGraw to the press. Gowdy never forgave himself for his stupid mistake, but returned for the 1925 season, hitting .325, the same as in 1924. He went back to the minors then, played three more years in the minors, eventually getting back to the majors, with Boston, in 1929. Bill McKechnie, Boston manager in 1930, made him a coach; he would coach with McKechnie

for many years. In January 1943, the 53-year-old Gowdy went back into the United States Army, as a captain. He retired from baseball in the late forties.

78 ◆ Steve Yeager
(1972–1986, 1269 G, 102 410 .228)

Most famous among younger fans for inventing the neck guard that hangs down from the catcher's mask. He invented it after a shattered bat stabbed him in the neck, and damn near killed him. He was an extremely good defensive catcher—a lot like Jim Sundberg. He was agile behind the plate, with a terrific arm. He never won a Gold Glove because Johnny Bench had that sewed up before Yeager came along, but Yeager was as good a fielder as Bench was. He wasn't any better, but he was just as good.

One time Yeager posed nude for a women's magazine . . . I think it was *Playgirl*. Later that season he took a foul tip in the mid-section. As he was crumpled over in pain at home plate the pitcher, Jerry Reuss, asked sympathetically, "Where'd it get you Steve? Right in the staples?"

79 ◆ Joe Ferguson
(1970–1983, 1013 G, 122 445 .240)

The Dodgers came up with Ferguson and Yeager at the same time; also Ron Cey, Steve Garvey, Bill Buckner, Dave Lopes, Lee Lacy, Bobby Valentine, Billy Grabarkewitz, and Tom Paciorek, but that's another story. Anyway, the Dodgers decided to make Yeager the catcher and Ferguson a backup catcher/fifth outfielder/pinch hitter. I was never convinced that this was the right play. Yeager was a marvelous defensive player, but Ferguson was an OK catcher and put a lot more runs on that big board in center field. I think it might have been smarter to make Ferguson the catcher and give Yeager one starting pitcher to work with, let him play late-inning defense and backup. But you know how managers are; they always love those Gold Gloves.

80 ◆ Ivy Wingo

(1911–1929, 1327 G, 25 455 .260)

Left-handed hitting catcher, ran exceptionally well for a catcher, and kept his speed through a long career. "Ivey" was his real name, not a nickname, although sportswriters changed him to "Ivy." He was a good-hitting catcher, but his stats are deceptive because he played in the dead ball years, when a lot of catchers hit .220 or less. He led National League catchers in errors eight times.

Did you ever notice how many catchers have brothers who are also major league players? I think the percentage is like three times as high at catcher as at the other positions. Wingo's brother hit .370 for the Tigers in 1924. Luke Sewell's brother was a Hall of Famer; Rick Ferrell's brother wasn't, but could be. Walker Cooper's brother was a bigger star than Walker was, although he had a short career. Joe Torre's brother played in the majors; same for Gus Mancuso, Ed Bailey, Bubbles Hargrave, Harry Danning, Wilbert Robinson, and Wally Schang. Steve O'Neill had three brothers who played in the majors. Gabby Hartnett had several brothers who played in the minors, although they didn't make the majors; Johnny Kling also had at least one brother who played in the minors. Tom Haller's brother was a major league umpire. Several others on the top 100 list had fathers or sons who played in the majors, or in one case, both.

I think this has to do with arm strength and fanaticism, as opposed to athletic ability. Catchers need strong arms. To get an arm, you need to play about ten thousand hours of "catch"— which means you need a brother who also plays. Yogi didn't have a brother in the majors, but he grew up with Garagiola, playing base-

ball sunup to sundown. Jack O'Connor (next) grew up with Patsy and White Wings Tebeau, also in St. Louis.

81 ◆ Jack O'Connor

(1887–1910, 1451 G, 19 738 .263)

Also known as "Pudgy Jack" and "Rowdy Jack." He was a fighter, a tough guy. O'Connor played in the 1890s, baseball's roughest era. The Baltimore Orioles, perhaps the best team of the time, made roughhousing and intimidation a standard part of their game. The Cleveland Spiders, although not as good a team, took the rowdiness a step further; that was pretty much their whole game. The Spiders were managed by Patsy Tebeau, O'Connor's childhood buddy. O'Connor was his right-hand man, his chief minion. He wasn't a great hitter; he wasn't a great fielder. He was a great tough guy. He ran the team when Tebeau was suspended, kicked out of the game, or drunk.

In 1902, during the American League War, O'Connor was hired by American League President Ban Johnson to try to lure some of his Pittsburgh teammates to jump to the American League, where they could play for the New York franchise, the Highlanders. He succeeded at this, persuading Jack Chesbro, Jesse Tannehill, and others to jump, but the National League found out about his efforts, and suspended him.

O'Connor played only 14 games for the St. Louis Browns in 1904. The 1905 *Reach Guide* reported that a "heavy handicap was the season-long lack of condition of Catcher O'Connor." Ban Johnson later would drive O'Connor out of the American League. O'Connor managed the Browns in 1910. On the last day of the Browns season, the St. Louis third baseman played deep, allowing Nap Lajoie to drop bunt hits in front of him, trying to steal the batting title from Ty Cobb; you all know that story. Ban Johnson was embarrassed about this, furious about it, and blamed O'Connor. O'Connor had a contract for the 1911 season, but Johnson eventually persuaded the Browns to fire him anyway. O'Connor sued, and collected most of his 1911 salary. He later worked as a fight promoter.

82 ◆ Heinie Peitz
(1892–1913, 1234 G, 16 560 .271)

Has almost exactly the same career batting stats as Johnny Kling. One time I did a study to find the two players in the Encyclopedia who had the most nearly identical career batting lines (among players playing a thousand or more games). One answer I got was Peitz and Kling. "Similarity" is a somewhat subjective concept, so there are other answers that would be equally accurate . . . Peitz wasn't as good a defensive player as Kling, but had a 16-year major league career, including twelve years as a regular.

Peitz and Ted Breitenstein were known as the "Pretzel Battery"; it sounds obscure now, but apparently this was quite well known at the time. Twin Towers, Heavenly Twins, Bookends, Spahn and Sain; the sports world has had lots of players who were best known as pairs. Line scores, which were sort of short-form box scores, listed the batteries for each game, pitcher and catcher; thus, pitchers and catchers often came to be paired in the public mind.

According to Lee Allen in *The Cincinnati Reds,* there had been an earlier "Pretzel Battery," Charlie Getzein and Charlie Ganzel of Detroit. Peitz and Breitenstein got the name after a game one day, when they were sitting in a back room at the Golden Lion saloon in St. Louis, eating pretzels and drinking beer. A fan came in and shouted to the bartender, "Hey, look who's back there. It's that pretzel battery, Breitentstein and Peitz." The name stuck, and became the lead line of both men's obituaries.

83 ◆ Fred Carroll
(1884–1891, 754 G, 27 366+ .284)

Assuming that his listed birth date is correct (July 2, 1864), Carroll rates as the second-best *young* catcher in baseball history, behind only Johnny Bench. Carroll hit .288 and scored 92 runs in 1886, when he was 21/22 years old, then hit .328 with a .499 slugging percentage in 1887, and hit .330 in 1889. He also walked a lot (85 times in 91 games in 1889) and stole 35 bases in 1890.

It is my belief that Carroll was a fairly decent defensive catcher, although it is hard to say this with confidence. The Win Shares system shows him as an OK defensive catcher. Carroll had a career high of 70 games caught—fairly common at that time . . . When the Chicago White Stockings made their famous around-the-world tour in 1888/1889 they chose an "All-American" team to travel with them, providing their opposition; Carroll was part of the loyal opposition . . .

Carroll was a Californian, one of a handful of Californians in the majors at that time. He always disliked the East, and said so, apparently, pretty often. He played baseball all winter in California, so he was always in shape, but he never wanted to come east for spring training. A hand injury in 1891 forced him to move to the outfield. He had a poor year, hitting just .218, and the Pirates released him.

Baseball was getting more organized on the West Coast, however. Colonel Tom Robinson hired Carroll, at something resembling a major league salary, to be captain of the Oakland team in the California League. He led the California League in batting (.302) and home runs (10) in 1892, but left in a dispute with Robinson; this is according to an article by William E. McMahon in the SABR publication *Baseball's First Stars.* After hitting .338 for San Francisco in 1893 he moved to the Western

League, where he hit .389 in 1894, with 51 doubles, 23 triples, and 22 homers; he had 223 hits and scored 186 runs in 130 games. In 1895 he was perhaps even more dominant, hitting .414 with 58 doubles and 21 homers, collecting 216 hits in 122 games. He left baseball then, for unknown reasons, and died in San Rafael in 1904, a few months after his 40th birthday.

The best *young* catchers in baseball history: 1. Johnny Bench, 2. Fred Carroll, 3. Ted Simmons, 4. Butch Wynegar, 5. Gary Carter. The best catchers in baseball in their prime years (ages 25-29): 1. Yogi Berra, 2. Mike Piazza, 3. Johnny Bench, 4. Mickey Cochrane, and 5. Ted Simmons. The best catchers in baseball in their post-prime years: 1. Roy Campanella, 2. Yogi Berra, 3. Bill Dickey, 4. Gary Carter, and 5. Gabby Hartnett. The best *old* catchers in baseball history: 1. Carlton Fisk (by a huge margin), 2. Gabby Hartnett, 3. Bob Boone, 4. Wally Schang, and 5. Chief Zimmer.

84 ◆ Mike Macfarlane
(1987–1999, 1164 G, 129 514 .252)
Macfarlane actually triggered this project, rating the top 100 players at each position. I was at a game with a friend, Royals game, and I asked my friend whether he thought Mike Macfarlane would be one of the top 100 catchers of all time. He hooted and sneered as if it was ridiculous to suggest such a thing, so my contrarian instincts came out, and I began to argue that he had to be one of the top 50. My friend said he could name 200 better catchers before the game was over. "Go," I said.

He got to about 30, and then he started naming guys who *maybe* were better than Macfarlane, and maybe weren't. It then struck me how few really good players there have been in major league history; there are 20, 30 perennial All-Stars at each position, and then it flattens out so that the difference between #40 and #70, at most positions, is just subtle

things—ten good years against seven, 15 homers a year against 12.

Macfarlane was a trim, powerful athlete who might have been a star outfielder had he been able to run at all. He had Ron Cey's disease (very low knees), as a consequence of which he accelerated quickly but ran real slow. He had power (20 homers in 388 at bats, 1993, 19 homers in 379 at bats, 1996, many other seasons with similar totals) and some small edges. He led the league in hit by pitches twice and always had high HBP totals, which helped his on-base percentage quite a bit, plus he rarely grounded into a double play; indeed, he had the best ratio of HBP to GIDP of any catcher in baseball history. Sure, it's a stupid list, but it helps to explain why he ranks where he ranks; he gains ten bases a year on hit batsmen, another eight on GIDP. Pretty decent defensive player, not a Gold Glove but had years throwing out 40% of opposing base stealers.

85 ◆ Bubbles Hargrave
(1913–1930, 852 G, 29 376 .310)
Cincinnati catcher in the 1920s, a perennial .300 hitter and one of few catchers to win a batting title (under the rules of the time, which required participation in 100 games). He attributed the batting title to an attack of appendicitis which he suffered that spring (1926). The doctors wanted to operate, remove the appendix, but Hargrave refused, and instead went on a liquid diet, apparently consisting mostly of buttermilk. He lost fourteen pounds, which was a good idea, and also claimed that his vision had improved. He hit .400 the first two months, and coasted to the batting title at .353. He liked the diet so much that he would go on "buttermilk binges" for the rest of his life, trying to lose weight and stave off hunger. Just a fair defensive catcher, and never a true regular.

86 ◆ Wilbert Robinson

(1886–1902, 1371 G, 18 622 .273)

Best known, of course, as a manager, described by Fred Lieb as "big, gruff, genial and kindly Wilbert Robinson, heavyweight catcher."

As a youngster Robinson was known as "Billy Fish" because he worked for a fish merchant. One day a housewife yelled at him, as he was leaving, "Come back here, Billy Fish, and take away your fish. They stink!" The nickname stuck with him, among his close friends, for the rest of his life.

He played with the Philadelphia Athletics, 1886–1890, picking up an Irish wife. His wife came to America to visit a friend, met Robby, and never returned to Ireland; she would later be known to tens of thousands of Dodger fans as "Aunt Mary." In 1891 Robinson played for Baltimore in the American Association, which became Baltimore in the National League when the American Association folded. The Old Orioles; the most famous team of their time. Joe Kelley, Willie Keeler, Steve Brodie, Dan Brouthers, Sadie McMahon, Heinie Reitz, John McGraw. McGraw and Robinson were the best of friends, an odd couple; McGraw was tough, pugnacious, sensitive, and widely hated; Robinson was easy-going, gregarious, affectionate, and much beloved—but just as tough as McGraw on the field.

Defying his body type, Robinson was agile and surprisingly fast, but had no power. Even in 1902, when he was 39 years old, playing his last season, he hit 7 triples and stole 11 bases in 91 games. He hit two homers a year, career high of four. He was a fair hitter, hitting .334, .353, and .347, but those figures were in years when several players hit .400. The Orioles jelled as a team in 1894, going 89-39, then went 87-43, 90-39, 90-40, 96-53, and 86-62. Those were fun days; they won almost every day, made good money, drank good whiskey and a lot of it. McGraw and Robinson began bouncing around as a team; they went to St. Louis together in 1900, back to Baltimore with the new American League in 1901, where they were investors in the team.

McGraw and Robinson attracted a couple of the old Orioles, a few other old National Leaguers, and thought that they could dominate the new American League. They couldn't; the franchise didn't have deep pockets, a contract war began, and the Orioles were never able to move into contention. Now the times turned hard. Ban Johnson, when he invited Robinson and McGraw into the new league, had also laid down the law about clean baseball, extracting a promise that the men would not permit or encourage the kind of baseball that the Orioles had made famous. As the Oriole losses mounted, McGraw increasingly chafed at what he felt were restrictions on his team's competitiveness. The team was losing money; McGraw claimed that he had invested in the Orioles, and wound up paying the players' salaries out of his own pocket. When McGraw jumped back to the National League in mid-season, 1902, Robinson took over as manager of the new Orioles, but he, too, was not really happy there. He finished out the season, the franchise half folded and half moved to New York.

Baltimore got a franchise in the Eastern League; Robby managed, still playing a few games.

Wilbert Robinson may have been baseball's first coach. *Total Baseball* says that Arlie Latham was the first "full-time" coach, hired by McGraw to coach with the Giants in 1909. However, if Latham was the first coach, what was Robinson? He had been around the team for a couple of years before then, running errands for McGraw, working with young players, making scouting trips to check out prospects, and coaching from the sidelines. Maybe he wasn't a fulltime coach, but if he wasn't, it was certainly a subtle distinction. In any case, he is listed as a coach with the Giants beginning in 1911, and held that job for three years. The Giants won the pennant all three seasons, 1911–1913. The salad days were back. McGraw and Robinson were better, as a team, than either man by himself.

In 1914 Robinson was hired to manage Brooklyn. At some point McGraw and Robinson had a bitter quarrel, of unknown origin, and stopped speaking to one another. Robby managed the Dodgers/Robins for many years, of course, winning pennants there in 1916 and 1920. The Robins slid out of contention, but Robinson hung around more than ten years.

The real story about Robinson is how much people loved him. Once, meeting Connie Mack unexpectedly at an off-season gathering, he grabbed him and kissed him on both cheeks, embarrassing Connie and astonishing reporters. He let players' children come into the dugout during the game; they would crawl on his lap, during the game, as he signaled his coaches. Once, when Chick Fewster was pounding a bat on the dugout steps during a Dodger rally, Robbie asked him to knock it off because "You might wake up poor old Jesse." Jesse Petty was asleep in a corner.

He wasn't Billy Martin, exactly. He never really adjusted to the lively-ball era, as a manager; his teams got behind the curve, but he was so popular that nobody wanted to fire him. They did, eventually. He managed the Atlanta Crackers in the Southern Association for a couple of years, and died in a bathtub in Atlanta in 1934.

87 ◆ Del Rice
(1944–1961, 1309 G, 79 441 .237)
Light-hitting defensive catcher. A big guy, he played in the NBA in the late forties; he was a teammate of Red Holzman on the Rochester team, just as the league was forming. Scouting report filed by Wid Matthews for the Brooklyn Dodgers, 1947 (this is the only time in 200-plus pages of notes that Matthews breaks into capital letters for emphasis): "HERE IS A FELLOW THAT I WANT YOU TO BE SURE AND REMEMBER THIS ONE THING ABOUT. HE IS THE BEST LOW INSIDE HITTER I EVER SAW. PLEASE, NEVER GIVE HIM ANYTHING LOW INSIDE . . . You can pitch him even low away, but be sure that the pitch is away. Pitch him high away over the plate, from the belt up. You can even come high inside. BUT, AGAIN, NOTHING LOW INSIDE."

Rice was a defensive standout, and hit fairly well his first couple of years in the league. Apparently the word got around the league that he could handle certain pitches in certain zones, after which he had a 15-year career as a defensive player. Rice was Minor League manager of the year in 1971, and managed the Angels in 1972, which was the breakthrough year for Nolan Ryan. He was a nice-guy type of manager, talked a lot about the team having fun, but was let go after one so-so season.

88 ◆ Mickey Owen
(1937–1954, 1209 G, 14 378 .255)
Owen's real name was Arnold Malcolm Owen. When he was in the minor leagues he was known as "Preacher" Owen, but when he came to the majors somebody said he looked like Mickey Cochrane, so he became Mickey Owen . . . anything to avoid being called Arnold Malcolm. He was one of the guys who jumped to the Mexican League in 1946, and was suspended from organized ball for several years. He led the movement to get those guys reinstated a little early.

Owen went into law enforcement after his career, and was Sheriff of Green County, Missouri, from 1964 into the 1970s. It's a large county, the third-largest county in Missouri . . . ran for Lieutenant Governor of Missouri in 1980, but lost in the primary.

89 ◆ Ron Hassey

(1978–1991, 1192 G, 71 438 .266)
Left-handed hitting catcher, painfully slow and never a threat in the Gold Glove voting, but hit .318 in 1980 (130 games), .323 in 1986 (113 games). #1 or #2 catcher for the A's from 1988 through 1990, when they were the best team in baseball.

90 ◆ Jody Davis

(1981–1990, 1082 G, 127 490 .245)
Tall, a little thin for a catcher when he first came up but filled out, hit 17 to 24 homers a year for the Cubs for five years (1983 to 1987), also hit .389 and homered twice in the Championship Series against San Diego (1984). Threw out 45% of base stealers in 1986.

When he first came up he had defensive problems, but was very popular with the Cub fans, probably the most popular player on the team ("Jo-Dee Jo-Dee Jo-Dee Jo-Dee"). Johnny Oates worked with him on his defense, built him into a decent backstop, but the Cubs never had a backup catcher, so Davis played almost every game. This took a toll on his knees. He slowed to a crawl and became prone to slumps, and the fans, predictably, turned on him. His knees went after about five years, and his career was short.

91 ◆ Mike LaValliere

(1984–1995, 879 G, 18 294 .268)
Short, heavy-set player with no power or speed, but excellent defensive skills. Won a Gold Glove in 1987, hit .300 in '87 and '89. Weight shortened his career.

92 ◆ Stan Lopata

(1948–1960, 853 G, 116 397 .254)
Lopata was a big guy, but hit out of an odd, Jeff Bagwell-style crouch, which shrunk his strike zone to the size of a marble. He walked a lot, and pitchers (and managers) used to complain that the stance was, or ought to be, illegal.

Lopata was five years younger than Andy Seminick—five years to the day, oddly enough; they had the same birthday. Anyway, Lopata was a member of the outstanding Utica team in 1947 (see Richie Ashburn—CF, #16), and hit .325 for that team. A bunch of guys on that team went to the majors together, and several of them (including Ashburn and Granny Hamner) stepped right into major league jobs. Andy Seminick, however, had a lock on the Phillies' catching job. Lopata was a better hitter than Seminick, who wasn't a bad hitter either, and incidentally Lopata may have been a better fielder than Seminick; maybe not, but it would be a close call. They were both right-handed, so, after several years of trying to sort this out, the Phillies finally traded Seminick for Smoky Burgess, a left-handed hitter.

The idea was for Burgess to be the catcher and Lopata to back him up, but Lopata's hitting improved substantially after a short conversation with Rogers Hornsby early in the 1953 season. "I notice that you miss the ball quite a lot when you swing," Hornsby told him. "Sometimes you miss the ball by as much as a foot. That simply shouldn't be." Lopata asked Hornsby what he could do to improve. "My guess would be that you are not following the ball properly from the time it leaves the pitcher's hand," Hornsby said. "There must be something you can do about that."

Lopata thought about it, and decided to try to change his angle on the pitcher. Experimenting with the crouch, he got seven hits in three days, and decided to stick with it. He also started wearing tinted glasses on the field; he was the first major league player to do that, and was the first National League catcher to wear glasses behind his mask.

Anyway, he started hitting, and this created one of the most effective catching platoons in baseball history. In 1954 Smoky Burgess hit .368; Lopata, playing 40% of the time, hit .290 with 14 homers, 42 RBI, a .544 slugging percentage. That opened up some playing time for Lopata, but here he was, 30 years old and one of the better catchers in the league, but he has never had a chance to play 100 games a year. He became a regular in 1956, playing 40 games at first base, but then he got hurt after about two years as a regular. A lot of people remember that Lopata had the one great year (1956, when he hit 32 homers and drove in 95 runs), but actually, he had several other years when he was every bit as effective as in 1956, but just batted 250 or 300 times. He was as good a hitter as Gary Carter, Earl Battey, Gus Triandos, Sherm Lollar, or Lance Parrish, but he just didn't get very many at bats to take advantage of it.

93 ◆ Phil Masi
(1939–1952, 1226 G, 47 417 .264)
Hit .326 with 31 homers for Wausau (1937), then hit .308 with 16 homers at Springfield (1938), where he split catching duties with Jim Hegan. He was one of several players set free after the '38 season by Commissioner Landis' ruling that the Indians were controlling the futures of an excessive number of minor leaguers. A free agent, Masi signed with the Braves, where he was a backup catcher for several years.

He was exempt from service for some reason (I'm not sure why), and thus became the Braves number one catcher as soon as the War started. He had some decent years as a hitter, hit over .300 one year, stayed around until the early fifties, and helped the Braves to a National League pennant in 1948.

"Stands up in the batters box. Away from the plate. Runs just average or a shade below. His arm is okay and he is a dandy receiver with good power at the bat."—Wid Matthews, 1947.

According to William Mead *(Baseball Goes to War)* the claim that major league players

were given no special treatment by the Army was refuted by the case of Pfc Phil Masi, stationed at Fort Dix, New Jersey. Masi went three weeks with no kitchen police duty, and wondered why until a sergeant brought him a face mask and shin guards. Masi confessed that he was not *that* Phil Masi, not the catcher—and went on KP the next day.

94 ◆ Shanty Hogan
(1925–1937, 989 G, 61 474 .295)
With the sole exception of Babe Herman, I doubt that any player has been the subject of more anecdotes than Shanty Hogan. All of these anecdotes center on how much he ate, or how much he liked to eat, or how fat he was, or some closely related topic. Pick up any old baseball book at random, and you will probably find an anecdote about Hogan eating something.

He is listed at six-foot-one, 240 pounds, but hit .300 or better six times, anyway. John McGraw, obsessive control freak that he was, reviewed the hotel dinner checks to see what his players were eating. An oft-told story is that Hogan had a deal with a hotel waiter so that he could order pie a la mode, and have it appear on his dinner check as asparagus.

In the spring of 1929 McGraw ordered Hogan to lose weight. Hogan bought a suit three sizes too large for him, rumpled it up, and looked up McGraw. "This old suit is falling off me," he told McGraw.

"You still look like the back end of a truck," said McGraw tactfully.

According to *The Braves: The Pick and the Shovel* (Al Hirshberg, 1948), Hogan "could eat anything, anywhere, under any conditions. He could inhale meals of king size at any hour of the day or night . . . As a result of his ability to pack away enormous amounts of nourishment, Hogan built up both muscles and food bills. He never grew smaller—always bigger."

Frank Graham described him *(McGraw of the Giants)* as "a big, laughing, somewhat boisterous Irish lad . . . one of the best-liked men in the squad," but said that "Hogan had one of the most prodigious appetites ever known in baseball, where big eaters are the rule. Good-natured, never resentful of the occasional ridings he had to take from McGraw, he constantly swore he would stick to a rigid diet. But the sight of a menu never failed to rouse great yearnings within him, and a bottle—or six bottles—of beer had a tremendous lure for him."

The Giants between 1920 and 1940 employed eight of the top 100 catchers of all time—Frank Snyder, Earl Smith, Hank Gowdy, Shanty Hogan, Bob O'Farrell, Ray Schalk, Gus Mancuso, and Harry Danning. They also used Mike Gonzalez, Eddie Ainsmith, Zack Taylor, Paul Richards, Glenn Myatt, Roy Spencer, and Ken O'Dea, none of whom missed the top 100 by a whole lot.

95 ◆ George Gibson
(1905–1918, 1213 G, 15 345 .236)

Outstanding defensive catcher, but had a career secondary average of .163, Runs Average of .170, which is the lowest of any catcher ranked in the top 100.

Gibson was a workhorse; he caught 109 games in 1907, which led the National League, then caught 140 games in 1908, 150 in 1909, and 143 in 1910. The record for games caught before 1907 was 132. Then shin guards were invented, and four major league catchers in one season (1908) caught 132 to 140 games. But actually, some people have over-stated the extent to which Gibson set new standards of durability for a catcher. There were catchers before Gibson who had caught almost all of their teams games, only with a shorter schedule. Chief Zimmer in 1890 had caught 125 of Cleveland's 136 games, and Deacon McGuire in 1895 had caught all 132 of Washington's games.

After shin guards were invented some catchers began catching every day, but after a year or two managers realized that there were

other reasons why this wasn't a good idea, other than just the foul tips which beat up the lower body.

Gibson managed the Pirates in the early twenties (1920–22) and thirties (1932–34). There are many stories about him as a manager, but I'm trying to stick to writing about *players,* for the most part.

96 ◆ Charlie Moore
(1973–1987, 1334 G, 36 408 .261)

Singles hitter, converted to the outfield after the Brewers acquired Ted Simmons, and was a regular outfielder when the Brewers went to the World Series in 1982. Dan Okrent wrote that "he was a solid, unexceptional player whose negotiating leverage derived from his utility as both a catcher and an outfielder."

97 ◆ Bo Diaz
(1977–1989, 993 G, 87 452 .255)

Basically the same player as Jody Davis—a right-handed .250 hitter with mid-range power, OK defense, had a few good years but worked too hard and wore out quickly.

98 ◆ Babe Phelps
(1931–1942, 726 G, 54 345 .310)

A poor man's Smoky Burgess, although he was taller and stronger than Smoky, and World War II deprived him of the opportunity to hang around and hit in his declining years. A left-handed hitter and a really good one; as effective a hitter as Ernie Lombardi, who was ten days older than Phelps. Indifferent catcher who didn't seem to care much about his defense.

In the spring of 1941 the Dodgers trained in Cuba. Phelps, terrified of drowning, reported to Miami for departure, but was unable to get on the boat, and thus missed spring training. Later that season, unhappy with his play and playing time, he jumped the team without warning. He returned to play fairly well in 1942.

99 ◆ Brian Harper
(1979–1995, 1001 G, 63 428 .295)

Harper should have had a much better career than he did. He lost a lot of his career to other people's stupidity. He was drafted by the Angels in 1977, hit .293 with 24 homers, 101 RBI at Quad Cities in 1978, then hit .315 with 37 doubles, 90 RBI at El Paso in 1979. The Angels at that time were building entirely around free agents and veterans, in no mood to give a young player a chance. At Salt Lake City in '81 he hit .350 with 45 doubles, 28 homers, 122 RBI. The Angels traded him to Pittsburgh.

The Pirates already had Tony Pena and Steve Nicosia; they needed another catcher like they needed a fifth baseman. Harper tried to convert to the outfield or first base. He wasn't fast enough to play the outfield; nobody was sure he would hit enough to play first. He bounced over to St. Louis, Detroit, Oakland, Minnesota. He was 30 by the time he got a chance to play.

He caught for Minnesota for five and a half years. He was slow, didn't have real power, didn't walk and didn't throw well, but he could hit .300 in his sleep. Helped the Twins to the World Championship in 1991.

100 ◆ Earl Smith
(1919–1930, 860 G, 46 355 .303)

One of the first really good platoon catchers, caught for the Giants (1919–1923), Braves (1923–24), Pirates (1924–1928), and Cardinals (1928–1930), made the World Series with three different organizations, and hit .335 or better four times. He had a famous feud with John McGraw; I'm not sure how this started, but a lot of people hated McGraw, and he was one guy who wasn't shy about saying so.

McGraw, as an old manager, had many rules. Smith openly ignored them. McGraw fined him; it was reported in 1922 that he had fined him $2,500 during the season, which must have been half his salary. McGraw called

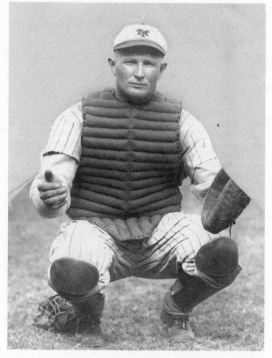

Oil Smith

the pitches from the bench, but Carmen Hill recalled in *Baseball Between the Wars* (Eugene Murdock) that Smith would ignore him. "If I call for something that you don't want, you shake me off," Smith told him. "Don't hesitate. Pitch your own game. As for that little pot-bellied son of a bitch on the bench, you don't look at him and neither will I."

He was a very tough guy, didn't back away from anybody. After the third game of the 1921 World Series, Babe Ruth came into the Giants' clubhouse, looking for Johnny Rawlings. Rawlings had been riding Ruth during the game, and Ruth was planning to beat the hell out of him. Earl Smith walked up to Ruth, face to face, implicitly saying "Pick on somebody your own size—me, for instance." He was small compared to Ruth, but big compared to Rawlings.

"What did he call you?" asked Smith. Ruth told him.

"That's nothing," said Smith, and shot tobacco juice on the floor, near Ruth's feet.

Casey Stengel managed the Giants' B team in spring training, 1923. He recalled in *Casey At the Bat* that "A lot of the men on the B team were put there as a sort of punishment. Earl Smith, a tough young catcher, was one. Evidently they searched our bags when we reported to camp, and they found a pair of handcuffs in Smith's luggage. Why Smith had the handcuffs, nobody knew. I guess some sheriff or somebody gave them to him. But McGraw didn't like it. He said to him, 'Well, any fellow that reports with a pair of handcuffs—you can go with that second team.'"

McGraw had a trainer, a black man named Smoky, who did bed checks for him every night. When he was first traded to Pittsburgh (1924) Smith, having no other residence in the town, was staying in the same hotel where the Giants stayed. Smoky accidentally came into Smith's room during his rounds. Smith grabbed him and locked him in the closet, then went down the hall telling his ex-teammates to go out and have some fun; there would be no bedchecks tonight.

Smith didn't necessarily need a reason to get into a fight. One time, New York was playing Pittsburgh, Dave Bancroft started jawing with the umpire. Smith knocked Bancroft flat, no warning; he just didn't like him. After McGraw traded him, Little Napoleon would order his pitchers to knock him down; Smith, catching for other teams, would call knockdown pitches in retaliation. Smith drank a lot and would fight about anything, and these things shortened his career, but a lot of people liked him, too. He had guts, and there wasn't anything phony about him.

101. Rick Cerone, 102. Bob Brenly, 103. Jocko Milligan, 104. Wes Westrum, 105. Rich Gedman, 106. Ray Fosse, 107. Clay Dalrymple, 108. Mike Heath, 109. Randy Hundley, 110. Ossie Schreckengost, 111. Sammy White, 112. Frankie Pytlak, 113. Cy Perkins, 114. Clyde McCullough, 115. Lou Criger, 116. Art Wilson, 117. Jose Azcue, 118. Bill Rariden, 119. Ron Karkovice, 120. Tom Pagnozzi, 121. Bill Killefer, 122. Mike Gonzalez, 123. Clint Courtney, 124. Matt Nokes, 125. Mike Tresh

CATCHER

Rank	Player Name	Career WS	Top 3	Top 5	Per 162
1.	Yogi Berra	375	34, 32, 31	154	28.66
2.	Johnny Bench	356	37, 34, 34	155	26.72
3.	Roy Campanella	207	33, 33, 28	134	27.60
4.	Mickey Cochrane	275	31, 30, 28	142	30.06
5.	Mike Piazza	234	39, 33, 33	158	33.94
6.	Carlton Fisk	368	33, 31, 30	106	23.86
7.	Bill Dickey	314	33, 27, 27	132	28.43
8.	Gary Carter	337	33, 31, 30	141	23.78
9.	Gabby Hartnett	325	29, 26, 25	114	26.46
10.	Ted Simmons	315	30, 28, 28	127	20.78
11.	Joe Torre	315	41, 29, 28	126	23.10

(continued)

Rank	Player Name	Career WS	Top 3	Top 5	Per 162
12.	Bill Freehan	267	35, 30, 25	126	24.38
13.	Ivan Rodriguez	186	27, 27, 26	121	23.91
14.	Thurman Munson	206	26, 25, 24	111	23.45
15.	Elston Howard	203	32, 29, 28	119	20.49
16.	Roger Bresnahan	231	29, 27, 27	116	25.88
17.	Buck Ewing	241	27, 23, 21	98	29.69
18.	Darrell Porter	222	31, 23, 19	98	20.18
19.	Lance Parrish	248	24, 24, 24	102	20.21
20.	Wally Schang	245	20, 20, 19	77	21.57
21.	Bob Boone	210	20, 18, 17	76	15.03
22.	Ernie Lombardi	218	24, 18, 17	89	19.06
23.	Gene Tenace	231	32, 26, 25	127	24.07
24.	Tim McCarver	204	30, 21, 17	98	17.31
25.	Darren Daulton	159	31, 29, 23	101	22.19
26.	Tom Haller	179	27, 22, 21	106	22.41
27.	John Roseboro	181	21, 20, 19	85	18.50
28.	Smoky Burgess	172	19, 17, 16	71	16.48
29.	Rick Ferrell	206	18, 17, 17	85	17.71
30.	Del Crandall	179	23, 22, 20	93	18.43
31.	Sherm Lollar	209	23, 21, 21	97	19.33
32.	Jim Sundberg	200	23, 22, 18	98	16.51
33.	Walker Cooper	173	23, 19, 18	82	19.03
34.	Tony Pena	175	21, 21, 17	84	14.26
35.	Ray Schalk	191	22, 21, 20	84	17.58
36.	Mike Scioscia	168	26, 20, 16	87	18.89
37.	Mickey Tettleton	184	27, 24, 24	111	20.07
38.	Terry Steinbach	173	20, 18, 16	77	19.40
39.	Ed Bailey	145	23, 17, 17	80	19.38
40.	Deacon McGuire	189	17, 17, 15	65	17.19
41.	Al Lopez	173	16, 14, 13	62	14.37
42.	Manny Sanguillen	157	24, 23, 19	106	17.56
43.	Rick Dempsey	158	17, 15, 14	66	14.49
44.	Jim Hegan	137	17, 15, 15	73	13.32
45.	Duke Farrell	183	24, 17, 16	82	18.97
46.	Bob O'Farrell	161	26, 25, 23	90	17.48
47.	Johnny Bassler	100	21, 19, 15	81	19.83
48.	Johnny Kling	155	22, 22, 21	81	19.93
49.	Charlie Bennett	157	19, 18, 15	78	23.95

Rank	Player Name	Career WS	Top 3	Top 5	Per 162
50.	Earl Battey	142	26, 22, 20	99	20.16
51.	Muddy Ruel	156	23, 20, 18	96	17.19
52.	Terry Kennedy	150	28, 24, 14	92	16.30
53.	Johnny Edwards	149	21, 19, 18	79	16.42
54.	Steve O'Neill	152	25, 18, 16	88	15.53
55.	Harry Danning	111	27, 21, 17	91	20.20
56.	Gus Triandos	127	19, 18, 14	78	17.06
57.	Andy Seminick	142	22, 18, 15	77	17.64
58.	Jack Clements	146	19, 18, 18	73	20.44
59.	Luke Sewell	128	16, 14, 13	58	12.72
60.	Chief Meyers	129	23, 20, 19	94	21.07
61.	Frank Snyder	139	24, 16, 13	66	16.18
62.	Chief Zimmer	153	18, 17, 14	68	19.36
63.	Jimmie Wilson	124	16, 15, 14	66	13.17
64.	Birdie Tebbetts	106	14, 13, 11	51	14.78
65.	Butch Wynegar	136	20, 18, 17	78	16.93
66.	Jerry Grote	127	18, 16, 14	60	14.48
67.	Don Slaught	130	14, 12, 12	59	15.87
68.	Alan Ashby	118	13, 11, 11	47	13.95
69.	Rollie Hemsley	130	15, 15, 14	48	13.22
70.	Hank Severeid	134	18, 18, 16	74	15.62
71.	Spud Davis	149	18, 17, 16	80	16.56
72.	Ernie Whitt	126	16, 16, 16	76	15.37
73.	John Romano	136	26, 25, 20	96	24.34
74.	Gus Mancuso	135	20, 16, 14	71	14.98
75.	Frankie Hayes	130	18, 18, 17	63	15.44
76.	Doggie Miller	135	24, 17, 15	65	16.61
77.	Hank Gowdy	118	17, 16, 15	53	18.21
78.	Steve Yeager	106	16, 15, 13	62	13.53
79.	Joe Ferguson	130	29, 20, 19	84	20.79
80.	Ivy Wingo	115	15, 13, 11	57	14.04
81.	Jack O'Connor	124	21, 12, 12	61	13.84
82.	Heinie Peitz	124	15, 13, 11	59	16.28
83.	Cliff Carroll	109	20, 17, 16	60	23.42
84.	Mike Macfarlane	106	18, 13, 11	60	15.86
85.	Bubbles Hargrave	110	25, 18, 14	79	20.92
86.	Wilbert Robinson	116	15, 12, 9	47	13.71

(continued)

Rank	Player Name	Career WS	Top 3	Top 5	Per 162
87.	Del Rice	110	18, 12, 12	61	13.61
88.	Mickey Owen	88	15, 11, 10	53	11.79
89.	Ron Hassey	115	20, 14, 13	56	15.63
90.	Jody Davis	106	18, 16, 16	78	15.87
91.	Mike LaValliere	95	17, 17, 12	66	17.51
92.	Stan Lopata	104	26, 17, 15	77	19.75
93.	Phil Masi	111	19, 15, 11	65	14.63
94.	Shanty Hogan	111	19, 18, 15	75	18.18
95.	George Gibson	113	24, 18, 12	68	15.09
96.	Charlie Moore	103	15, 14, 9	53	12.51
97.	Bo Diaz	94	21, 15, 15	58	15.34
98.	Babe Phelps	85	16, 15, 14	64	18.97
99.	Brian Harper	83	17, 15, 14	72	13.43
100.	Earl Smith	94	15, 14, 14	55	17.71

Categories of this record are Career Win Shares, Win Shares in the players three best seasons, Win Shares total over the player's five best consecutive seasons, and career Win Shares per 162 games played. For example, Yogi Berra had 375 Career Win Shares, including 34, 32 and 31 in his three best seasons (1950, 1951 and 1954). He had 154 Win Shares in a five-year period, 1950 to 1954, and averaged 28.66 Win Shares per 162 games played over the course of his career.

FIRST BASE

1 ◆ Lou Gehrig
(1923–1939, 2164 G, 493 1990 .340)

Babe Ruth, after he left the Yankees, would regularly deride Gehrig's consecutive game streak. "This Iron Man stuff is just baloney," he said one time. "The guy ought to sit on the bench and rest. They're not going to pay off on how many games he's played in a row. When his legs go, they'll go in a hurry." Well, he was right about that . . .

Gehrig said he reached the decision to end his consecutive-game streak on a road trip early in 1939, when he fielded a routine ground ball and flipped to the pitcher covering. Joe Gordon and Bill Dickey both slapped him on the back, said, "Nice play, big guy." They meant it well, but Gehrig was devastated. He realized he was being congratulated for making a routine play.

2 ◆ Jimmie Foxx
(1925–1945, 2517 G, 534 1921 .325)

Jimmie Foxx was discovered by Home Run Baker, who signed him to play for Easton, Maryland, in the Eastern Shore League, for which Baker also played. Thus, the 1924 Easton Farmers of the Class D Eastern Shore League had two Hall of Famers in their lineup—Baker and

Foxx. Despite this, the Farmers finished last. In fact, the Farmers were so bad (23-57) that they actually pushed the entire rest of the league over .500. It was a six-team league; Easton kept all five of the other teams over .500.

There is a story told about Baker's discovery of Jimmie Foxx that Baker was driving around the Maryland backwoods, got lost, and stopped to ask directions of a boy walking a plow behind a mule. "Where's the nearest town," asked Baker.

"Over that way," said Jimmie Foxx, and pointed—with his plow! Baker said "Hey, you don't happen to play baseball, do you?"

What interests me about this story is that the anecdote is easily recognizable as apocryphal—yet when you walk it through, the story has no improbable elements. I asked several people—my wife, my uncle, Jim Carothers—whether they thought the story might be true. They all scoffed at it. In fact, the story probably is false; Foxx was a well-known amateur player before Baker signed him, and the identical story is also told about Bronco Nagurski, the football star.

But while I do not doubt that the story is false, I can identify no reason that it *could not* be 100% true. Is it unlikely that Baker, driving around scouting ballplayers in the days before the highway system was developed, would get lost? Obviously it is not.

Is it unlikely that he might bump into Jimmie Foxx? Not really. Paul Krichell signed at least a dozen future major league players out of chance encounters.

Would it be impossible for Foxx, a powerful young man, to lift a plow with one arm? I asked my uncle, who was the same age as Foxx, and who spent many hours in his youth walking behind a mule, whether he could have lifted a plow with one hand. He said he could, if he had to.

Would it be out of character for a 16-year-old athlete to show off his great strength by making a gratuitous gesture of this type? Anything but. It is *exactly* the sort of thing that 16-year-old boys do.

If that happened, would Baker respond by asking Foxx if he played baseball? Well, wouldn't you, if you were looking for a ballplayer?

What marks the story as improbable is not its facts, but its form. There is something you can't put your finger on; the story is too pat, too well-formed. And that tells us something about how we distinguish truth from falsehood in our everyday experience.

3 ◆ Mark McGwire
(1986–2000, 1777 G, 554 1350 .267)
My seven-year-old son's favorite player . . . about 55% of McGwire's career value is accounted for by his home runs, a high figure, but not as high as players like Dave Kingman and Steve Balboni. McGwire does do some things well, other than hit home runs.

4 ◆ Jeff Bagwell
(1991–2000, 1476 G, 310 1093 .305)
Pass.

5 ◆ Eddie Murray
(1977–1997, 3026 G, 504 1917 .287)
Here's a challenge for you: Can you identify Eddie Murray's best season?

His best season was probably 1984, when he hit .306 with 29 homers, 110 RBI, and led the league in walks (107) and on-base percentage (.410). But I'm not really sure that's his best season; his best season could be 1980 when he hit .300 with 32 homers, 116 RBI, or 1981, when he led the American League in home runs and RBI (although the strike kept his numbers low), or 1982 (when he hit .316 with 32 homers, 110 RBI), or 1983 (when he hit .306 with 33 homers, 111 RBI), or 1985, when he hit only .297 but drove in a career-high 124 runs, or 1990, when he hit .330, almost leading the National League in batting average, despite playing in Dodger Stadium. His best season could be 1978, or it could be 1995, when he hit .323 and helped Cleveland to their first American League pennant of the modern era. His best year was every year. He never won an MVP Award—but he was an MVP candidate every year.

6 ◆ Johnny Mize
(1936–1953, 1884 G, 359 1337 .312)
Mize was a distant cousin of Babe Ruth's . . . The Giants in 1947 designed a play specifically to take advantage of Jackie Robinson's aggressiveness. When Robinson hit a double to center, the shortstop and second baseman both went into the outfield to cut off the throw, leaving second base (apparently) unguarded. They figured that Robinson would see the base unguarded and run halfway to third, which he did—only to discover that the lead-footed Johnny Mize had trailed him from first base, and had the base covered . . . Mize was probably the best all-around player in the National League in 1940 and 1947, and the second-best in 1937, 1939, and 1948, third-best in 1942. He

missed three prime seasons due to World War II, and became most famous, oddly enough, as a pinch hitter/platoon player with Casey Stengel's early Yankee teams.

7 ◆ Harmon Killebrew
(1954–1975, 2435 G, 573 1584 .256)

A round man with a bull neck, shiny bald head, short arms, couldn't run, didn't have quick feet on defense, but did have good hands and a decent arm. The MLB symbol, the silhouette of a man with a bat, was supposedly based on a picture of Harmon Killebrew . . . Killebrew, who grew up in Idaho, was the son of a college football star. He was recommended to the Senators by an actual Senator, Senator Herman Welker of Idaho, an arch-conservative who used to froth at the mouth about Social Security. Welker was a friend of Clark Griffith, and persuaded Griffith to send a scout to check out Harmon. Killebrew hit five home runs in a three-game weekend, and signed with the Senators for $25,000.

8 ◆ Hank Greenberg
(1930–1947, 1394 G, 331 1276 .313)

Irwin Dickstein, Greenberg's high school basketball coach: "Hank never played games, he worked at them. He wasn't the natural athlete. His reactions were slow and he had trouble coordinating his big body. He couldn't run a lick because of his flat feet. [But] he was a great competitor because he hated to lose."

Greenberg was General Manager of the Indians from 1949 to 1957. Greenberg was a forward-looking man, a very progressive thinker, but there's one thing that always bothers me. My reading of the history of the Cleveland Indians franchise—and I'd be interested to talk to somebody who knows more about this than I do, but I'm just telling you how I see it—my reading is that Hank Greenberg's intransigence and poor decisions probably had as much to do with the collapse of the Indians franchise in the late 1950s as anything else did. But when people write about this collapse, which is variously blamed on Gabe Paul, Frank Lane, Kerby Farrell, and William Daley, Greenberg almost always gets off scot free.

In 1954, when the Indians had a great year, Greenberg authored a famous article in *Life* magazine, "How We Beat the Yankees," in which he claimed that the Indians were getting close to "crush[ing] the head of the Yankee octopus and cut[ting] off all the tentacles." Fine; they did beat the Yankees, he did help design that team. He was entitled to brag about it if he wanted to. But since the franchise crashed and burned three years later, shouldn't we at least take a look at the role he played in that, too?

Who fired Al Lopez? According to his autobiography, Greenberg did. Who tried to chisel a couple of thousand dollars out of Luis Aparicio, and wound up losing the Hall of Famer, who had agreed to sign with Cleveland, to Chicago? Greenberg did.

Greenberg had very clear, strong ideas about how to run a farm system, how to run a franchise. Great. But he drove a lot of good people out of the Indians' system by his stubbornness and his inflexibility. Greenberg remembers, in his autobiography, that in the calendar year he was out of baseball (1958) he received only one phone call from anybody he had known or worked with in his 28 years in the game, a call from Birdie Tebbetts. Greenberg thinks that this is telling about baseball people. I wonder, perhaps, if it isn't more telling about Hank Greenberg.

9 ◆ Willie McCovey
(1959–1980, 2588 G, 521 1555 .270)

McCovey lost three years as a regular at the start of his career because the Giants came up with McCovey and Cepeda at the same time, and couldn't play them both at first base. He lost significant parts of ten other seasons to in-juries. The heart of his career was in the 1960s, the most pitching-dominated decade since Ruth. He overcame all of these things to hit 521 career home runs.

McCovey was 6-foot-4 with shoulders like a condor's wings, but weighed less than 200 pounds. He had long, flat, narrow feet, which always gave him trouble, and a long, sweeping swing, which should have led to 130 strikeouts a year, but never did. He was a hard-working first baseman who could stretch halfway to the pitcher's mound to get a throw, but he did not have good hands, a strong arm, or any innate quickness. But if he played in the 1990s with the DH and the modern parks, he'd hit 800 home runs.

10 ◆ Frank Thomas
(1990–2000, 1530 G, 344 1183 .321)
A couple of years ago, Thomas had a chance to be ranked as one of the three greatest hitters who ever played the game, in a group with Ruth and Williams. That chance has perhaps gotten away from him with a couple of off seasons in the middle of what should be his prime, but he is still young enough to move up among the game's greatest first basemen. Bagwell, born on the same day as Thomas, is a better all-around player.

11 ◆ Cap Anson
(1876–1897, 2276 G, 96 1879 .329)
And, speaking of credit being misplaced . . . as I mentioned in the first section, the notion that Babe Ruth "saved" baseball after the Black Sox scandal is, in my opinion, not well founded. Baseball in 1920 was not threatened by a lack of popularity. Baseball in 1920 was threatened by dishonesty. The man who saved baseball from that threat was not Ruth, but Kenesaw Mountain Landis, who drove the thieves out of the game.

But one man who does deserve the type of credit that Ruth is often given on this account is Cap Anson. The continued existence of pro-fessional baseball, at the end of the 1878 sea-son, was very much in doubt. Five of the original eight franchises had folded or been ex-pelled from the league. Worse, the casualties included teams from the nation's two largest cities, New York and Philadelphia. Baseball failed in New York and Philadelphia, and in 1878 it failed in Milwaukee and Indianapolis, opening the 1879 season with franchises in Troy and Syracuse. Where are we headed here, Youngstown and Hoboken? It was very much unproven, at that time, whether professional baseball would be a viable commercial product. If Chicago and Boston had dropped out of the league in the early 1880s, to be replaced by Des Moines and Springfield, major league baseball as we now know it would never have come into being.

That didn't happen, in large part because of Anson. Cap Anson took over as player/man-ager of the Chicago franchise in 1879, and im-mediately did two things which "saved" or created major league baseball. First, he trolled the other leagues which were operating at the same time, struggling for survival as the Na-tional was, and began stealing their best play-ers. This wasn't totally unprecedented—players had switched teams frequently since before baseball became professional—but teams be-fore Anson tended to focus on stealing the best players from their league competitors. Anson organized the process of identifying and ac-quiring the best players from other leagues. When Anson did this successfully, that forced the other National League teams to do the same, and it was this process—the organized theft of the best players from other leagues—which caused the National League to emerge as the "major" league, the best professional league.

And second, Anson made baseball immensely popular in Chicago, which was the league's largest and most important city. In the National League's first years, the schedule was getting shorter, the league was getting smaller, and the cities in the league were growing more remote. The game was dying. Cap Anson is the man who really changed that—not all by himself, but more than anyone else.

12 ◆ Don Mattingly

(1982–1995, 1785 G, 222 1099 .307)

100% ballplayer, 0% bullshit.

13 ◆ Tony Perez

(1964–1986, 2777 G, 379 1652 .279)

Perez was never called "Tony" until he came to the United States. His name, growing up in Cuba, was "Tany," a shortened form of his given name, Antanasio.

In 1957, as revolution was brewing in Cuba, a man named Tony Pacheco was scouring the island on behalf of the Sugar Kings, the Havana team in the International League. The Sugar Kings were owned by Bobby Madura, a Havana multimillionaire in the sugar industry. Pacheco put together a team of about fifteen young players who traveled Cuba, playing a schedule of exhibition games. On that team were Diego Segui, Tony Gonzalez, Chico Ruiz, Jose Tartabull, and Tony Perez.

Perez was the baby on the team, fourteen years old at the time, just a tall, skinny kid who was unusually strong, but couldn't pull the ball. He was strong because he had already spent a couple of years in the sugar mills, lifting bags of sugar. Most of the other players on that team came to the United States and began their professional careers in 1958. Perez didn't come until a couple of years later, after Castro had nationalized the sugar industry, and relations between the United States and Cuba were beginning to sour. Even then he was only 17,

but precocious, and aware that it was time to get out.

He was given the nickname "The Big Dog" by Dave Bristol, who managed him in the minor leagues and later in the majors. "If the game goes on long enough," Bristol would say, "The Big Dog will bite." This was proven true in the 1967 All-Star game, which was 1-1 in the fifteenth inning, when the Big Dog bit. He was an easy-going, good-natured man who never found any reason to complain about being a major league baseball player.

14 ◆ Will Clark

(1986–2000, 1976 G, 284 1205 .303)

Clark won the Golden Spikes Award as the outstanding college player in the nation in 1985, when he hit .420 with 25 homers in 65 games at Mississippi State, where he was a teammate of Rafael Palmeiro. Clark and Palmeiro have come to be paired in the public's mind since then, as the Texas Rangers in 1993-94 allowed Rafael Palmeiro to walk away as a free agent, then signed Will Clark for more money than would have been required to keep Palmeiro. This didn't work out well, and several years later (1999) the two players swapped teams as free agents, Palmeiro returning to Texas, Clark going to Baltimore.

In general, I don't want to spend a lot of time here justifying the rankings; I've explained the rating system, and explaining exactly how it applies in this case is not going to help all that much. But many of you, I suspect, will think that Rafael Palmeiro has proven to be a better player than Will Clark in the long run, and that I am just wrong in rating Clark higher.

But Will Clark was a truly great player, in my opinion, from 1987 through 1992, when he was with the Giants. The numbers weren't nearly as big then as they are now, and Clark played in Candlestick, where fly balls go to get frostbite. Palmeiro has been a better player since 1993, but if you compare each player in his best seasons—Clark from 1987 to 1992, Palmeiro in the late nineties—I think Clark had more impact on his teams.

Palmeiro's career numbers are better, it is true; he has about a hundred more career homers as of now, and the gap is widening. But the differences in terms of batting average, on base percentage and slugging percentage are not large, and two of the three (batting and on-base percentage) favor Clark. Clark is a better defensive first baseman. When you figure in park effects and league context, I think Clark has had the better of it so far. Palmeiro is gaining on him. (See 19 in this section.)

15 ◆ Dick Allen
(1963–1977, 1749 G, 351 1119 .292)
The second-most controversial player in baseball history, behind Rogers Hornsby. Allen had baseball talent equal to that of Willie Mays, Hank Aaron, or Joe DiMaggio, and did have three or four seasons when he was as good a player as anyone in baseball, but lost half of his career or more to immaturity and emotional instability.

16 ◆ Keith Hernandez
(1974–1990, 2088 G, 162 1071 .296)
Most-comparable players to Keith Hernandez, by decade:

   1880s—Tommy Tucker
   1890s—Fred Tenney
   1900s—Jake Beckley
   1910s—Jake Daubert
   1920s—Joe Judge
   1930s—Bill Terry
   1940s—Joe Kuhel
   1950s—Mickey Vernon
   1960s—Bill White
   1970s—Chris Chambliss

   1980s—Keith Hernandez
   1990s—Mark Grace

Bill White is the poorest match on the list, but there's nobody else in the 1960s who works except Wes Parker, who didn't have enough good years with the bat. Others who could be listed: Will Clark, Phil Cavaretta, Wally Joyner, Cecil Cooper, Ed Konetchy, Charlie Grimm, George Sisler, George Burns, Wally Pipp, Lu Blue.

17 ◆ Orlando Cepeda
(1958–1974, 2124 G, 379 1365 .297)
His career batting stats, through his first six years in the league, closely parallel Henry Aaron's at the same age. A knee injury in 1965 wrecked his chances of hitting 700 homers . . . He was a poor defensive first baseman, and Alvin Dark, who managed him in the early 1960s, thought that his fundamentals were appalling. But he did play with great enthusiasm; he made baseball fun to watch, and he did improve as an all-around player later in his career, although his speed was gone and his batting numbers weren't as big.

18 ◆ Dan Brouthers
(1879–1904, 1673 G, 106 1056 .343)
Name pronounced "Broothers" . . . Brouthers was as big as Cap Anson and, like Anson, had a theatrical bent, used to do things sometimes to amuse the fans, that would be considered out of place in modern baseball. One time he missed a foul ball, which hit him on the head. He dropped like he had been shot, and lay motionless on the ground until he was carried off on a stretcher. As the stretcher reached the exit he hopped up and ran back to the field.

Brouthers had a dog, a beautiful Irish setter named Kelly, probably after King Kelly. He brought the dog with him to every home game, and the dog would watch the game from the "dugout." Parks didn't really have dugouts at that time; some places the players sat on open benches, other places they had above-ground clubhouses which obstructed the fans view of the game. Anyway, Brouthers' dog was very well-behaved, and never ran onto the field or got agitated, no matter how much pandemonium there was in the crowd. On May 6, 1894, Brouthers hit a two-run single to tie the game in the ninth. *The Baltimore Sun* reported the next day that at that point, Brouthers' dog had "turned two back somersaults and gave vent to a series of joyous barks."

> Rusie, by the way, is now assistant watchman at the Polo Grounds. Dan Brouthers is the other watchman. Often we get together and talk over old times. Always I have had a deep sentiment for veteran ball players, and I try to get them a good place any time there is a chance.–John McGraw, *My Thirty Years in Baseball* (1923, Boni and Liveright)

19 ◆ Rafael Palmeiro
(1986–2000, 2088 G, 400 1347 .296)

Now in his late thirties, but playing the best ball of his career. In November 1999, we were in the midst of a mini-controversy, occasioned by the fact that Palmeiro, who played only 28 games at first base, was given the Gold Glove as the best defensive first baseman in the American League.

He wasn't the best defensive first baseman in the league, obviously. He wasn't the best defensive first baseman on his own team. Most of what is being written in this controversy seems to me to miss the central lesson. What people are writing is, in essence, that the voters don't pay attention to the games, the voters are ignorant, the voters don't take the vote seriously, the voters screwed up, etc. The voters who vote for the Gold Gloves are the managers and coaches from the league. I doubt that any of them are ignorant or not paying attention to

the game, but . . . well, they did screw up, so I suppose that's fair.

The larger point, it seems to me, is that *a badly designed voting system will fail sometimes, no matter who votes.* The Gold Glove is decided by what could be called an unconstrained plurality, meaning:

1. A voter can vote for anybody.
2. If the top vote-getter gets 15% of the vote, he wins, the same as if he had received 80%.

A voting structure like this is an open invitation to an eccentric outcome. If the United States were to use a system like this to elect the President, the absolutely certain result would be that, within a few elections, someone like David Duke, Donald Trump, or Warren Beatty would be elected President. If you can win an election with 15% of the vote, sooner or later somebody will. An unconstrained plurality vote gives an opening to someone or something who has a strong appeal to a limited number of people.

If the people who run the Gold Glove vote really want their system to work, there are three things they need to do, none of which is "take the vote away from the coaches and managers." The three things they need to do are:

1. Establish some loose statistical limits on who is eligible for the award. No one should be eligible for the Gold Glove at first base unless he plays at least 500 innings at the position.
2. Have a panel of experts–not a *different* group, but a sub-group of the current voters–review the candidates, and trim it to a list of perhaps five candidates.
3. Get weighted ballots–three points for first, two for second, one for third.

The system as it is now gives the Gold Glove to the most deserving player maybe 50,

60% of the time, and coughs up an embarrassing gaffe like this one every three or four years. If they thought through the voting structure, they could get the honor to the most deserving player perhaps 80% of the time, and eliminate the Palmeiro-type awards.

20 ◆ Norm Cash
(1958–1974, 2089 G, 377 1103 .271)

Cash never played baseball as a youth. "We had 250 acres of good, fertile land and it had to be worked," Cash told *Sport* magazine in 1961. "I can remember driving a tractor some days from sunup to sundown when I was ten. You get strong wrists. Sitting there driving that thing ten or fifteen hours a day takes a tremendous amount of strength." His high school didn't have a baseball team, but he got a scholarship to a junior college as a football player. The Juco didn't have a baseball team either, but some of his teammates organized a town team, and so Cash tried baseball. He was good at it the moment he started . . .

On July 15, 1973, Nolan Ryan was pitching his second no-hitter of the season, against the Tigers at Tiger Stadium. For his third at bat, Norm Cash unscrewed a table leg in the clubhouse, and went to the plate with the table leg instead of a bat. The umpire noticed, unfortunately, and made him switch to a bat. He struck out, and Ryan completed the no-hitter.

21 ◆ Fred McGriff
(1986–2000, 2055 G, 417 1298 .286)

Whitey Herzog in *You're Missin' a Great Game:* "They say McGriff is a fine person, but he's always been an over-rated ballplayer. Here's a guy who hit thirty-plus homers for seven straight years, but in three of those years, he didn't even have 100 RBIs. That's not very good clutch hitting." It's actually four of those years; he drove in 100 runs in only three of the seven seasons. But Mickey Mantle, who hit 30

home runs in a season nine times, drove in 100 runs only three of the nine years—an even worse ratio. Counting their whole careers, McGriff leads Mickey in 100-RBI seasons, six to four. Was Mickey over-rated, too?

22 ◆ Roger Connor
(1880–1897, 1997 G, 138 1322 .317)

Connor hit more career home runs than anyone before Babe Ruth. However, although season records were well circulated, no career records were maintained at that time, and no one knew, until the 1960s, that Connor had held the record, which was variously attributed to Sam Thompson, Dan Brouthers, and Gavy Cravath. Connor died in 1931; he certainly never knew that he had held any career record.

Born in Waterbury, Connecticut, in 1857, Connor was the son of Irish immigrants. His father prohibited him from playing baseball, which he thought was a waste of time. Due to this and other conflicts, Connor ran away from home at the age of fourteen, living on his own in New York City. Unable to catch on as a professional baseball player, he returned home to Waterbury, learning then that his father had died suddenly while he was away.

Connor went to work in a brass factory to support the family; he was the oldest son among eleven children. He continued to play baseball, however, and eventually (six years later) was able to catch on as a professional player. Sold to Troy in 1880, he was sent to a Troy shirt factory to be fitted for a uniform. The blond girl who measured him for the uniform knew a lot about baseball . . . you can see where this is going.

They lost a baby girl, who died just before her first birthday, and adopted a little girl from an orphanage. Eventually the three of them would be the owner/operators of the Waterbury franchise in the Connecticut League as a family business, Roger managing the team, the blond from the shirt factory running the box office, and the little girl who had been abandoned on a doorstep collecting tickets. An excellent article by Bernard J. Crowley, which is the source of much of my information here, can be found in *Baseball's First Stars* (SABR).

A huge, strong man, Connor was one of the original "New York Giants" from whom the Giants franchise got its name.

23 ◆ Mickey Vernon
(1939–1960, 2439 G, 172 1311 .286)

> Mickey Vernon is as silent as a night watchman, as conservative as a banker, and as well behaved as a vicar.—Ira Smith, *Baseball's Famous First Basemen*

Vernon won the 1953 batting title by one point, .337 to .336, over Al Rosen, who would have had the triple crown with one more hit. That battle was marred by machinations almost as bad as those of 1910 (when Lajoie battled Cobb), 1976 (four Twins and Royals), or 1982 (Wilson and Yount). Vernon went into the last game leading by three points, .336 to .333. The pennant race was over; nothing was at stake except the batting crown. The Indians moved Rosen to the leadoff spot, hoping to get him enough at bats to catch Vernon. Rosen had a good day, but Vernon, helped by a bunt single on which the A's third baseman made an indifferent effort, had pushed his average to .338 by the middle of the game. Vernon had stated that he would not come out to protect the title, but after he made an out in his fourth at bat, two of his teammates admitted that they deliberately made outs to prevent him from having to come to bat a fifth time.

24 ◆ George Sisler
(1915–1930, 2055 G, 102 1175 .340)

Perhaps the most over-rated player in baseball history. He hit .340 in his career, hit .400 twice, and at that time there wasn't anyone around to say that batting average is important, but it is less than half of a player's overall offense. Sisler had a lower on-base percentage, in his career, than Fred McGriff (.287), Alvin Davis (.280), Earl Torgeson (.265), Jack Clark (.267), Mike Schmidt (.267), Mark McGwire (.265), or Gene Tenace (.241). Or Ralph Kiner, or Elmer Valo, or a hundred other guys who didn't hit anywhere near .300.

Also, while articles about Sisler invariably claim that he was a fine fielder, the Win Shares system is unable to see that this is true. The Win Shares system does document the defensive excellence of Keith Hernandez, Wes Parker, Bill White, Vic Power, Gil Hodges, Bill Terry, Frank McCormick, Charlie Grimm, and almost all other top defensive first basemen.

25 ◆ Frank Chance
(1898–1914, 1285 G, 20 596 .297)

I know that a lot of people would expect Frank Chance to be in the top ten, and I'm sure I'll get some savage notes from people who think it's an outrage to rate Norm Cash and Fred McGriff ahead of the Peerless Leader. I don't mean to put him down, or Sisler, either; Chance was a great player, at his best. He was an exceptional defensive first baseman, a natural leader, a good hitter, an outstanding baserunner, and a smart percentage player. He was a great player for three or four years. So was Ted Kluszewski. Chance wasn't a great hitter, and he wasn't an impact player like Dick Allen or Willie Stargell. He never played 140 games in a season; only once did he play 130 games. He rates higher than anybody else who played 1,285 career games.

> Chance is the sort of athlete who is likely to get injured . . . If he has to choose between accepting a pair of spikes in a vital part of his anatomy and getting a put-out, or dodging the spikes and losing the put-out, he always takes the put-out. —Christy Mathewson, *Pitching in a Pinch,* Putnam, 1912.

26 ◆ Bill Terry

(1923–1936, 1721 G, 154 1078 .341)

Similar to Sisler, and also one of the more over-rated players in baseball history . . . had more power than Sisler and walked more, better defensive first baseman, but not as fast and his career was not as long.

Terry lost the 1931 batting championship when the last game of the season was rained out after three innings. Terry had gone one-for-one in the game, that one hit being enough to give him the highest batting average in the league. But when the game was rained out, the hit was removed from the records—and Chick Hafey won the batting title . . .

Terry was a cold, sarcastic man. He had a lot of dignity, a very strong presence, and a great deal of self-discipline. He was loyal to his friends; he was intelligent. He was a sharp dresser. He was focused, goal-oriented. When he lost, or when his team lost, he always stepped forward to shoulder the blame. But he was impatient, distrustful, and he didn't project any warmth, except to people that he had known for a long time.

27 ◆ Boog Powell

(1961–1977, 2042 G, 339 1187 .266)

His nickname is short for "Booger," which is what his father would call him when he misbehaved as a very young child (Hey, watch it, you little booger). A lot of the top first basemen had what could be called a "Gentle Giant" personality. That term was certainly applied to Tony Perez, Dan Brouthers, Roger Connor, Dolph Camilli, Frank Howard, maybe Killebrew, certainly Boog. Immensely talented hitter, and actually ran well when he was eighteen, but grew to be the size of an NFL lineman, which forced his move to first base. Won the MVP Award in 1970, and had three other seasons just as good (1964, 1966, 1969).

28 ◆ Cecil Cooper

(1971–1987, 1896 G, 241 1125 .298)

A career .298 hitter, but with a secondary average of only .241. Had medium-range power, led the league in RBI twice and doubles twice, never walked. When he came to the majors he was very quiet, thin as a rail, a little bit awkward, and couldn't hit a left-hander if one laid down in the road in front of him. He couldn't run, and he couldn't throw. The Red Sox left him off their 40-man roster one winter. The Cardinals drafted him, took a look at him in spring training, and sent him back to Boston.

He grew into his body, and began gradually to come out of his shell. In his early years, said Harvey Kuenn, "Coop had as many batting stances as times at bat." In the late 1970s Rod Carew became a big star with a very odd batting stance, pointing his right (front) toe at the pitcher, but his left knee at the catcher, crouched, but with his weight back. Cooper, working with batting coach Harvey Kuenn, adopted Carew's stance and stuck with it. For five years (1979–1983) he was a hell of a player. A good account of his career and personality can be found in Dan Okrent's *Nine Innings* (Ticknor and Fields, 1985).

29 ◆ Dolf Camilli

(1933–1945, 1490 G, 239 950 .277)

Comparing Camilli to Terry, who was a National League first baseman of the same era . . . Terry hit .341 lifetime, but with a secondary average of .257. Camilli hit .277 lifetime, but with a secondary average of .403. Thus, for each 100 hits, Terry had 51 runs scored, 49 RBI—but Camilli, for each 100 hits, had 63 runs scored and 64 RBI.

So if you multiply Terry's batting average by .50, and Camilli's by .63, what do you get? Basically, about the same thing. Camilli's .277 batting average was as productive as Terry's .341.

Defense? Terry Moore, asked by Walter M. Langford to pick an All-Star team of the National Leaguers of his time in *Legends of Baseball,* picked Bill Terry, but added that Camilli was "probably better in the field."

Camilli was the subject of two of the worst trades in major league history. The Cubs brought him to the majors, but after playing him for half a season traded him to the Phillies for Don Hurst. Hurst left the majors after playing 51 games for the Cubs, hitting .199. Camilli led the Phillies in home runs for four seasons, in RBI the last two, completing the run by hitting .339 with 27 homers in 1937.

The Phillies then traded Camilli to the Dodgers for Eddie Morgan and $50,000. Morgan never played in the majors again. Camilli drove in 105 runs a year for five more years, and won the MVP Award in 1941.

Charlie Grimm was managing the Cubs at the time of the first trade. His General Manager was Bill Walker; Warren Brown once wrote that the Cardinal pitcher, Bill Walker, "is not to be confused with the Cubs' General Manager, who is confused enough as it is." Anyway, Walker traded Camilli to the Phillies without asking Grimm or even telling him about it. A newsman called Grimm and asked him if it was true that the Cubs had traded Camilli. Grimm bought some time and called Bill Walker. "I finally got in touch with his chauffeur," wrote Grimm, "who told me that the deal had indeed been made. I was furious that I hadn't been consulted, and every time in the next several years when Camilli smashed a homer for the Phillies or the Dodgers, I muttered to myself that Bill Walker should have stayed in the fish business."

Camilli, although he hardly ever missed a game, couldn't take the ups and downs of baseball in stride. When he went into a slump he would walk the streets for hours on end, trying to get his stomach to stop churning. If he made

a key mistake he would brood about it for days. He wasn't exactly moody; he was just a worrier. A newspaperman wrote that he played baseball as if his life depended on it, rather than just his livelihood.

Camilli hit .212 for the Dodgers in 1945, was a player/manager for a year or two in the minor leagues, then retired. In 1948 the Spokane team in the Western International League, which he had managed, was 57-52 on August 3 when the team's manager, named Buddy Ryan, was ordered to quit by his doctor, who feared that he was near a nervous breakdown. Camilli, who still lived in the area, came out of retirement to manage out the year.

The team got red-hot; they went 45-12 under Camilli, including 27 wins in their last 31 games, and won the league with a record of 102-64.

30 ◆ Gil Hodges
(1943–1963, 2071 G, 370 1274 .273)

A genuinely beloved player. How many players in each generation are genuinely beloved, all around the country? Three or four, I would say; the public always wants to embrace players, but the embrace is stifling and uncomfortable, and most players break free of it as quickly as they can. Only a few players are comfortable accepting the public's adoration, and trying to meet the standard of conduct that goes along, the expectations of being The Nation's Son. Ken Griffey, Cal Ripken, Sammy Sosa in this generation, Kirby Puckett and Don Mattingly in the last. Yogi. Musial.

> Tommy Holmes [said] that with Hodges' hands and his ability as well as his power, he would today be definitely headed for the Hall of Fame had he been able to play at short, his original position . . . like Tommy Holmes, I believe Hodges could have been a great shortstop.—James T. Farrell, *My Baseball Diary*

I remember once seeing a series of photographs showing Dodger first baseman Gil Hodges, at that time in a horrendous batting slump, shopping in a supermarket for his wife. [He was] a patient, devoted man with a fine heart.—Arnold Hano, *A Day in the Bleachers* (Crowell, 1955)

31 ◆ Steve Garvey
(1969–1987, 2332 G, 272 1308 .294)

Here's something to think about: have the changing times made Steve Garvey once more a viable political candidate? I would suspect that he probably is. Not to speak for him, but I think that most people who knew Steve Garvey from 1974 to 1980 assumed that he wanted to be President someday, and that he was going to start running for something as soon as he left baseball. He was thrown off track because he couldn't keep his underpants off the infield, which led to a nasty divorce, a series of public revelations, and a series of paternity suits. At that time—less than twenty years ago—it was assumed that these events would prevent him from entering politics.

Times change, and I suspect that the scandals would no longer be a prohibitive barrier to Garvey's entry into politics. There is, however, a subsidiary problem: Garvey was essentially a Republican. I don't recall that he ever declared his party, but he certainly had a Republican image: a straight-laced, hard-working, goal-oriented image. A lot of people couldn't stand him, for the same reason a lot of people can't stand Ralph Reed or Trent Lott: he seemed smug and self-righteous. I don't think you could sell him as a Democrat, and the loose zipper, which probably wouldn't mean much in a California general election, might be a problem in a Republican primary.

Garvey was a good player. When he was active, I always thought he was a selfish player, and I probably never said a good word about him. After he retired, however, one of his managers (Dick Williams) wrote that he was a selfish player, and his ex-wife wrote a book in which she said he was a selfish everything and gave interviews in which she compared him to Ted Bundy. His image changed so much that a lot of people almost forgot about the things that he could do. He used to get 200 hits a year, regular as clockwork, and they weren't 200 singles. He was an odd player; he had a "program" for getting his 200 hits. He was supposed to bunt for a hit a certain number of times . . . I think it was twice a month. He was supposed to go with the pitch and slap it into right field a certain number of times. He had a certain number of times he was allowed to guess and try to cream the pitch. I never heard of such a thing, but that was Garvey; he was a Clockwork Baseball Player. When he went into a slump, which was basically never, he had a program for getting out of a slump. He was a fine first baseman, although he couldn't throw, and he drove in 110 runs every year in a pitcher's park in an era when you could lead the league in RBI with 120.

32 ◆ Mark Grace
(1988–2000, 1910 G, 148 1004 .308)

People think in terms of images. When the Cubs had Grace at first base and Sandberg at second, they used to bat Sandberg second and Grace third. This makes no sense. Grace, who never had much power, was not a good #3 hitter, but would have been a great #2 hitter. With a .308 career average and a lot of walks, he'd be on base, which is the #1 function of a top-of-the order guy. As a left-handed hitter who could handle the bat, he could hit and run, take advantage of the hole at first if the leadoff man was on, and (as a lefty) be an obstacle to the catcher on stolen base tries.

Sandberg, on the other hand, was a just-fair number two hitter, and much better suited to hitting third—but hit second. Why? Images. We assume, if we don't think about it, that a first baseman hits in the middle of the order, and a second baseman hits at the top of the order if he can hit, the 6-7-8 spots if he doesn't. The Cub managers just never thought about it long enough to get past the images.

33 ◆ Bob Watson
(1966–1984, 1832 G, 184 989 .295)

The absurdity of George Kelly's selection to the Hall of Fame in 1973 can be illustrated by comparing Kelly's career batting stats to those of Bob Watson, who I will assume most of you remember, and don't think of as a Hall of Famer. Watson and Kelly had careers of almost the same length (Watson had 3% more career at bats), had almost the same number of hits (Watson again had 3% more), and scored and drove in almost the same number of runs. Watson hit 36 more homers (184–148), but 30 fewer doubles (307–337):

	AB	Hits	HR	RBI	Avg.
Watson	6,185	1,826	184	989	.295
Kelly	5,993	1,778	148	1,020	.297

Kelly's slugging percentage was five points higher, because he hit some triples, but Watson's on base percentage was 25 points higher, because he would take a walk.

But wait a minute . . . we are missing a key element here. Kelly did this in the 1920s, when teams scored 750 runs a season. Watson played in the 1970s, when teams scored 650–700 runs a season—and played in the worst hitter's park in baseball. In context, Watson was not equal to Kelly, but far better.

34 ◆ Ted Kluszewski
(1947–1961, 1718 G, 279 1028 .298)

Can you name the last three players to hit 40 or more homers in a season with 40 or fewer strikeouts? Ted Kluszewski, 1953, Ted Kluszewski,

1954, and Ted Kluszewski, 1955. Altogether it's been done seven times—Mel Ott, 1929, Gehrig, 1934, DiMaggio, 1937, Johnny Mize, 1948, and the three times by Kluszewski.

Kluzewski's power numbers exploded when the Reds moved in their left field fence from 382 feet to 328. Kluszewski in 1952 hit 16 homers—four at home, 12 on the road. In 1953 his homers on the road increased from 12 to 17, but his home runs in his home park shot from 4 to 23.

Kluszewski, perhaps the strongest player in baseball in the 1950s, was a tight end at the University of Indiana, helping them to a Big Ten championship in 1945. In World War II the major league teams didn't go South for spring training, due to wartime travel restrictions, and the Reds arranged to train in Bloomington. Kluszewski was hired or detailed to help rake the field. The Reds' grounds keeper, Lennie Schwab, saw Kluszewski raking the infield, took a look at his biceps, and went to get Bill McKechnie, the manager. McKechnie worked him out, and the Reds signed him.

Rogers Hornsby, managing the Reds in the early fifties, hated Kluszewski, and kept telling General Manager Gabe Paul that "you oughta trade the big lazy Polack." The feeling was mutual; Kluszewski and his backup, Joe Adcock, used to debate which of them hated Hornsby more. Hornsby wanted to trade Kluszewski for Earl Torgeson . . . .

35 ◆ Jack Fournier
(1912–1927, 1530 G, 136 859 .313)

Asked in 1923 to name the toughest hitter he ever faced, Walter Johnson replied that "I don't believe I ever pitched to a player who took more liberties with my stuff than Jacques Fournier, now a member of the Brooklyn Nationals. When Fournier was with Chicago his specialty was hitting for extra bases when I pitched. No matter how I worked on him he seemed to have no trouble solving my offerings. Fournier was the original tough baby for me."—1924 *Reach Guide*

Jacques Fournier, a picturesque French Canadian ... There was plenty of life in the clubhouse whenever Jack was around; he was never at a loss for words. Frenchy and the fiery Texan, Hornsby, mixed it up in the clubhouse one day ...—Fred Lieb, *The St. Louis Cardinals*

In the 1920s, remembered Roscoe McGowen in *Sport Magazine* years later (June, 1964), the Dodgers spring training home in Clearwater, Florida, was a decrepit old barn known as the Cleveland Hotel. There was one exception, he remembered. "The sophisticated and ruggedly handsome Jack Fournier, along with his beautiful young blond wife Helen, were permitted to put up at the Gray Moss Inn, which normally wouldn't let a ballplayer through the servants' entrance. Jack frequently got into his tux for dinner, which probably over-awed even the stuffy patrons and management of the Inn."

Jacques Fournier will be on first base for the Brooklyn Robins when the National League season of 1926 opens, if we all live and nothing happens. Put a bet on that. Fournier was sincere when he flared up in Pittsburgh and announced that as a result of the profane and obscene abuse to which he had been subjected by the mongrel element in the Brooklyn crowds at Ebbets Field, he would not play base ball next year. When the story had gone abroad, and he had had time to think things over Fournier began to appreciate the advice of friends, who pointed out to him that he was placing himself in a position that would seriously handicap him in business, social and possibly political life for the rest of his days, if he deliberately broke a contract of his own making ...

Fournier's violent protest against profane and obscene language hurled at players from the bleachers and stands has done an enormous service for base ball. The reception of his protest

was amazing. From one end of the country to the other. Some of the largest newspapers and the club owners have suddenly awakened to the fact that they have permitted in base ball parks language and conduct that would have been tolerated in no other sort of gathering of supposedly civilized people.—1926 *Reach Guide*

36 ◆ Jim Bottomley
(1922–1937, 1991 G, 219 1422 .310)

A cheerful, good-natured player, but very competitive, and beloved of the fans in St. Louis. Bottomley wore his hat off to the side of his head and turned up at a slightly comical angle; it was kind of a trade mark. He was one of the great "streak hitters" of all time. He is most famous, of course, for driving in twelve runs in one game in 1924. He also hit seven home runs in a five-game stretch in July, 1929.

Bottomley had grown up on a dairy farm not far from St. Louis. At the end of his career, as he was retiring, the St. Louis fans wanted to give him a day. They asked him what kind of gift he wanted. He asked for a cow. He said he was going to retire to a farm; he wanted a cow. He named the gift bovine Fielder's Choice, and took it to his farm.

37 ◆ Wally Joyner
(1986–2000, 1980 G, 201 1092 .290)

A likeable, innocuous player who vaulted to stardom with a hot streak the first half of his rookie season, and then quietly receded, an inch at a time, for more than a decade. He had no weakness as a player, was an excellent glove, and a decent hitter.

38 ◆ Hal Trosky
(1933–1946, 1347 G, 228 1012 .302)

Trosky drove in 142 runs as a 21-year-old rookie in 1934, then hit 42 homers and drove in 162 runs in 1936. He was a slow runner and an awkward first baseman, but a formidable hitter until stopped by migraine headaches beginning in 1939.

Trosky grew up in Norway, Iowa, a small town which was sort of a baseball hotbed, and produced several quality players. He was born Harold Arthur Troyavesky, and thus goes on an All-Star team with Al Simmons (Aloys Szymanski), Johnny Pesky (John Paveskovich), Eddie Lopat (Edmund Lopatynski), and others. In the last twenty years the story has become common that Trosky's headaches began after he was hit in the head by a line drive during batting practice. This story was rarely if ever printed during Trosky's lifetime, and I am uncertain as to how well documented it is. One source says that Trosky's father had also suffered from headaches. It is very clear, however, that Trosky's demise as a player is solely attributable to migraine headaches that made his life a living hell, and it is also true that Trosky's accomplishments as a hitter, up through age 26, are comparable to those of Gehrig, Foxx, Greenberg, and Mize.

Trosky was a ringleader in the "Cleveland Crybabies" player revolt in 1940, but missed the conference in which the player's petition was discussed with the owner due to the death of his mother, who passed away on the morning of the meeting. His son, Hal Jr., also played briefly in the major leagues.

39 ◆ Bill White
(1956–1969, 1673 G, 202 870 .286)
Very comparable to Bill Terry—a left-handed line drive hitter who hit for a good average, with power, ran well, and carried a Gold Glove. Would have been a Hall of Famer if he'd had a few more good years; may be anyway, because of his service as National League President. White's 199 hits in 1962, 200 in 1963, and 191 in 1964 are almost as impressive, for the 1960s,

as Terry's 225- to 254-hit seasons are in the 1930s . . .

The White All-Star team, if assembled and entered in a tournament, might be able to beat any other surname: C—Sammy White, 1B—Bill White, 2B—Frank White, 3B—Deacon White, SS—Other Bill White (1884–1888), LF—Roy White, CF—Devon White, RF—Rondell White, Pitching Staff—Doc White, Will White, Ernie White, Hal White, others. The Williamses and Robinsons have more stars, but more weaknesses . . .

The great Cardinal team of the mid-1960s was substantially built out of cast-off players. White had a fine rookie season for the New York Giants in 1956, but was drafted into the United States Army after the season. By the time he got out of the Army the Giants had come up with Cepeda and McCovey, and were willing to trade White. Second baseman Julian Javier was similar; the Cardinals got him because the Pirates had Bill Mazeroski at second base, and figured they would never need Javier. Left Fielder Lou Brock was acquired in trade after he didn't hit well his first couple of years in the majors. Shortstop Dick Groat, pitcher Curt Simmons, and (later) right fielder Roger Maris were acquired after they were regarded as washed up. The Cardinals, who had an ability to produce pitchers, traded starting pitchers to pick up almost all of these players, added in three home-grown stars (McCarver, Gibson, and Boyer), and won three pennants in four years.

40 ◆ Kent Hrbek
(1981–1994, 1747 G, 273 1086 .282)
Most-similar players to Kent Hrbek, by decade:

    1880s—Dan Brouthers
    1890s—Harry Davis
    1900s—Tim Jordan
    1910s— Ed Konetchy

1920s—Jacques Fournier
1930s—Dolph Camilli
1940s—Rudy York
1950s—Gil Hodges or Eddie Robinson
1960s—Boog Powell
1970s—John Mayberry
1980s—Kent Hrbek
1990s—Mo Vaughn

41 ◆ Roy Sievers
(1949–1965, 1887 G, 318 1147 .267)

Can you name another player who had the same value pattern as Roy Sievers? I'm not sure there is one. Sievers was a standout rookie in 1949, hitting .306 with 91 RBI, and winning the American League Rookie of the Year Award. After that, however, he drifted into a prolonged slump, lost his regular status, had two serious injuries, drifted completely out of the major leagues, and had to go back to the minors and re-establish himself. He didn't re-emerge as a regular until five years later, 1954, but then became a star, driving in almost 100 runs a year for a decade.

I could name some players who had *somewhat* similar value patterns—Bill White, Matty Alou, Jim Eisenreich, Rico Carty. But Sievers is extreme. I'm not sure there is any player in history who had a value pattern which is truly similar.

A couple of other things about him which are unique: he is one the few players, maybe the only player, I don't know, to lead the league in home runs and RBI while playing for a last-place team (1957). Also, Sievers was one of the few right-handed hitters to have what people call a sweet swing. That peculiar type of "picture swing" that people rave about . . . that's almost always a left-handed hitter, like Paul O'Neill, Ken Griffey Jr., Dave Justice, Billy Williams, etc.

A mild, quiet-mannered person [who] has been slightly embarrassed by the near monopoly he held on the affection of Washington fans . . .

Sievers has developed a picture swing at the plate which [observers] call one of the prettiest in the league. Gripping his bat down at the knob, he takes only a short back swing before whipping the club around gracefully in a flawless arc . . . but the long scar running down Roy's shoulder is a jagged reminder to both him and his wife of the days when baseball as well as medical experts were saying that he probably could never play well again.—Howard Cohn, *Baseball Stars of 1959*

42 ◆ Andres Galarraga
(1985–2000, 1916 G, 360 1272 .291)

Had the best three-year stretch of his career, 1996–1998, beginning when he was 35 years old. Hoping for a comeback at Jack Benny's age after a season battling cancer.

43 ◆ Joe Adcock
(1950–1966, 1959 G, 336 1122 .277)

Lost more home runs to the parks he played in than anyone in history except Joe DiMaggio and Goose Goslin . . . was a teammate of Henry Aaron's for nine seasons, and hit more home runs per at bat in those nine years than Aaron did.

As I suppose you know, Adcock had perhaps the greatest day in the history of major league baseball, hitting four home runs and a shot off the top of the wall for a double at Ebbets Field, July 31, 1954. He was also the first player to hit the ball into the center field bleachers at the Polo Grounds (1953; the bleachers had been there since 1923), and he broke up perhaps the greatest pitching performance in baseball history, Harvey Haddix' 12-inning perfect game, which ended after Adcock hit the ball in the seats.

44 ◆ Joe Judge
(1915–1934, 2170 G, 71 1039 .297)

The day Judge arrived in the majors (September 20, 1915), he delayed the start of the game by 20 minutes. He had led the International League in hitting. His arrival had been trumpeted in the press, and a good crowd was on hand to see him, but his train was late and at game time he wasn't at the park. The umpire held up the start of the game until Judge arrived.

> Joe Judge is another hitter of that type. Goose Goslin will outhit Joe in the averages by 20 to 50 points. But with runners on bases and a hit needed to win the ball game most pitchers would rather pitch to Goose a dozen times over.– *Babe Ruth's Own Book of Baseball* (A. L. Burt and Company, 1928)

> The toughest play for a first baseman to make is to get out of the base path and take a wild throw . . . in the path of a flying runner. Joe Judge and Joe Kuhel were picture performers at this.–Mickey Cochrane, *Baseball: The Fan's Game* (Funk and Wagnalls, 1939)

> Griffith long complained that his veteran, Joe Judge, didn't spur himself to his best job 'unless he has got competition around. I have to keep two first basemen on the payroll to get the best out of Judge.–Shirley Povich, *The Washington Senators* (G.P. Putnam's Sons, 1954)

Judge was Walter Johnson's roommate in Barney's last years in the majors, but basically ended Walter's career by hitting him with a line drive in spring training, 1927. The line drive broke his leg, and Johnson, a 15-game winner in 1926, never really recovered. Later, when Johnson managed the Senators, he had to put Judge on the bench to play Joe Kuhel. Judge resented it, and the two men, who had been the best of friends, wound up in a nasty public feud.

45 ◆ Mike Hargrove
(1974–1985, 1666 G, 80 686 .290)
Hargrove was known as "The Human Rain Delay" because he had a time-consuming routine between pitches, stepping out of the box, re-settling his batting helmet, tugging on his shirt sleeves, loosening his collar, re-fitting his batting gloves, etc. He also took many, many pitches, so that he probably saw more pitches per at bat than any other player of his time, so that a Mike Hargrove at bat could go on for some time.

But my theory is that the game has changed so much in the last twenty years that if Hargrove returned and did all of the same stuff now, nobody would notice. Hargrove in the 1970s was about the only player who stepped out of the batter's box after every pitch. Now everybody does it.

46 ◆ Elbie Fletcher
(1934–1949, 1415 G, 79 616 .271)
Fletcher and Hargrove were both members of a sort of "rump legislature" of first basemen who didn't hit for much power, but made an offensive contribution by hitting for a good average with 10–12 home runs and a hundred walks a year. Ferris Fain, Lu Blue, Joe Cunningham, and Fred Tenney were a few other exemplars of the type, which was never common, and which I believe is now extinct.

47 ◆ Lee May
(1965–1982, 2071 G, 354 1244 .267)
A powerful right-handed hitter, could hit 40–45 homers a year if he played in the 1990s. He was a brutal first baseman, couldn't run and couldn't throw, and, although he later became a batting coach, he wasn't a sophisticated hitter. He couldn't really work a pitcher, and he couldn't go with a pitch and pick up a single to the opposite field; he just basically tried to hit everything into the seats. But he was good at it.

Lee May had a younger brother, Carlos, who also played in the majors. Carlos got 80% of the talent in the family; he was as strong as Lee, which was very strong indeed, but he could also run, and he could throw a little bit. He was a natural hitter, a lefty, and he knew the strike zone. When he was 21 years old he looked like the second coming of Willie Mays.

Carlos blew his thumb off in a military training accident, which cost him a lot, but there was another problem. Whereas Lee May was a hardworking, hustling player within the limits of his ability, a respected clubhouse leader in the early days of the Big Red Machine, Carlos played baseball as if he really didn't give a shit, pardon my French. I have noticed this same syndrome other times, that when you have brothers who are baseball players, very often the youngest brother has or is credited with having the most talent in the family, but turns out to be the one who does the least with it.

The reason I notice this . . . in the town that I grew up in (Mayetta, Kansas), we had a family of brothers who were baseball players. Their father had played in the minors for years, and all the boys were good baseball players with strong arms. But the youngest brother, Danny, was by far the best athlete in the family, the only one who had real *talent*. When I was in the eighth grade I think Danny was in the third grade. We had a "field day" at school once a year, one event of which was the softball throw. Danny won the softball throw—not the third/fourth grade softball throw, the school-wide softball throw. No joke; we were 12 and 13 years old, and this eight-year-old kid could throw a softball further than any of us. We were just astonished; we thought when he got bigger he would really be something.

But whereas all of the older boys in the family were well-liked, responsible, focused kids who did the best they could, Danny just didn't get it. He never did amount to anything, even as an amateur athlete, because he just didn't really care.

So anyway, I've noticed this same thing in baseball families. As the Alou brothers were emerging, Jesus Alou was the one who was always thought to have real, big-time talent, but

he never did very much with it. I think that the reason this happens, perhaps, is that when a boy has several older brothers who play ball, he may play a lot of baseball at a very early age. Because the kid has played way more baseball than the other kids his age, he may be years ahead of them in the development of his skills—and it will look, to those around him, like he has just worlds of talent.

But in reality, the younger sibling is being pulled along by his brothers' interest in the game, while his own interests and his own focus, once it develops, may be somewhere else. Of course, once in awhile you get the younger brother who *does* have the focus and the desire to excel, and then you get Joe DiMaggio or George Brett. But there aren't very many Joe DiMaggios or George Bretts. Most of the time, you get Hector Cruz or Jesus Martinez.

48 ◆ Ed Konetchy
(1907–1921, 2085 G, 74 992 .281)

Konetchy is one of the players most helped by the Win Shares analysis. I had him ranked 69th at the position by subjective impressions, between Earl Torgeson and Moose Skowron, until the Win Shares analysis revealed (a) that his contributions with the bat were worth more than I had thought, and (b) that he was probably the best defensive first baseman of his time.

Ira Smith in *Baseball's Famous First Basemen*, says that Konetchy "was a top-notch fielder, ranging widely. Standing six feet two, he was a fine target for infield throws. His arm was powerful and accurate."

As most of you know, the New York Giants won 26 consecutive games in September, 1916, a major league record. What you probably don't know is that the 25th and 26th games of that streak were both one-hit shutouts, by Ferdie Schupp and Rube Benton. Konetchy got singles to deprive both men of no-hitters, a seventh-inning single against Schupp, an eight-inning single against Benton.

He bounced around a lot, because he was very hard to settle with in salary negotiations. His career ran out just as the lively ball era began, which is ironic, because he was a big, powerful, pull hitter, would have been perfect for the new game. After leaving the majors (1921) he had many outstanding seasons in the minor leagues, including leading the Texas League in Home Runs (41) and RBI (166) in 1925.

49 ◆ John Mayberry
(1968–1982, 1620 G, 255 879 .253)
The same skills and weaknesses as Kent Hrbek. Left-handed hitter, quick bat, hit for power without excessive strikeouts, also had extremely soft hands, fine first baseman. Both players put on weight that they didn't need, and neither could run.

Mayberry in his three best seasons ('72, '73, and '75) was a better player than Hrbek, even in Hrbek's best seasons—in fact, Mayberry was as good as or better than Boog Powell, who was also a similar player. But Mayberry had only those three seasons when he meant anything to his teams; the rest of his career he was just cashing his paychecks.

In 1977 the Royals took a 2-1 lead in the American League playoffs, the fourth game being on a Saturday. They played the fourth game early to accommodate the TV network, which wanted to show a football game at 3:00, so Whitey Herzog told his men that they could skip batting practice and get a good night's sleep before the fourth game. "John Mayberry dragged in real late," wrote Herzog in *White Rat*, "but I put him on first base anyway, which was my big mistake." Mayberry, suffering from an all-night party with his brothers, in from Detroit, played as bad a game as one could possibly play, dropping popups and striking out

twice with men in scoring position. Herzog finally pulled him aside and asked what the hell was wrong. "The man couldn't even talk," wrote Herzog, "and I knew what was wrong ... God only knows the kind of stuff they did. It must have been a hell of a party." Mayberry single-handedly cost the Royals the playoffs, and Herzog insisted that the Royals get rid of him. He was never the same player again.

50 ◆ Andre Thornton
(1973–1987, 1565 G, 253 895 .254)
> Andy was a rock. Andy is a guy that if you had trouble with something, you could go to him for advice. It may not be the advice you want to hear, but it would be good advice because it was what he truly believed.–Mike Hargrove, quoted in *The Curse of Rocky Colavito* (Terry Pluto)

Has almost identical career batting stats to John Mayberry, who was the same age as Thornton. Mayberry rates an edge because of park effects and a better glove. On the other hand, Thornton was a hard-working, respected clubhouse leader; Mayberry was a talented player who floundered and struggled most of his career, and cost the Royals a chance to go to the World Series because he wasn't in condition to play. So if you want to argue it's Thornton over Mayberry, you may well be right.

51 ◆ Mo Vaughn
(1991–2000, 1346 G, 299 977 .298)
Thirty-two years old and carrying a piano, one would suspect that his good years are running out. But he could fool us.

52 ◆ Jake Beckley
(1888–1907, 2386 G, 88 1575 .308)
Casey Stengel, quoted in Arthur Daley's *Sports of the Times* (1959): "Jake Beckley uster turn his bat around and bunt with the handle. I showed our players and they say it's the silliest

thing they ever saw, which it probably is but he done it."

1890s baseball...Beckley attempted to work the hidden ball trick on every rookie in the National League at least once, and often succeeded; he had several variations of the ruse. When he tried it on Honus Wagner, Wagner sniffed it out, so Beckley tried a second version. He snuck an extra baseball on the field and hid it under his armpit, allowing it to stick out far enough that Wagner could spot it. When the umpire turned his back, Wagner grabbed the extra ball and tossed it into the stands, then lit out for second base—only to discover that the pitcher had the legal ball.

53 ◆ John Olerud
(1989–2000, 1555 G, 186 865 .299)
A career .300 hitter who walks 100 times a year and has some power, no speed. His stock will shoot up if and when his career numbers start to pass milestones.

54 ◆ Frank McCormick
(1934–1948, 1534 G, 128 954 .299)
Rates with Keith Hernandez, Wes Parker, Vic Power, and Wally Pipp as a glove man; one of the best defensive first basemen ever to play the game. Won the NL MVP Award in 1940, when he led the NL in hits (191) and doubles (44), also drove in 127 runs. He also led the National League 1939–1941 in fewest strikeouts per at bat.

McCormick was a tall, thin, strikingly handsome man, very graceful in spite of a gangly build. He was slow to get established in the majors because of several injuries in the minor leagues, plus a lack of power. When he did get to the majors he was determined to shake the "brittle" tag, and wouldn't come out of the lineup even when he should have. One time he was beaned in the first inning of a double header, and stumbled around almost in a daze for eighteen innings, but refused to come out.

After Gehrig's streak ended, McCormick had the majors longest consecutive-game streak for some time, eventually reaching 682 games.

55 ◆ Cecil Fielder
(1985–1998, 1470 G, 319 1008 .255)
A big fat guy who hit home runs for a few years.

56 ◆ Rudy York
(1934–1948, 1603 G, 277 1152 .275)
> I roomed with this goddamn Rudy York. He was the silliest bastard I ever met in my life. He was a third-string catcher at the time and I was a regular, and all night long that goddamn phone was ringing. He knew every whore in New York.—Billy Rogell in *Cobb Would Have Caught It* (Richard Bak, Wayne State University Press, 1991)

> Before I knew it, he was drinking again. At least that was the report that I got. He had a tendency to light up a cigarette when he went to bed, then he'd drink and he'd forget about the cigarette and it would burn down to his fingers. Rudy burned up a couple of hotel rooms that way. —Hank Greenberg, *The Story of My Life*

57 ◆ George Scott
(1966–1979, 2034 G, 271 1051 .268)
A power hitter with exceptionally good hands, showy first baseman. A colorful, slightly eccentric player who knew how to play the game. I'll always remember a game that Scott played in Kansas City in August of 1979. He was 35 years old at the time, fat and slow and had warning track power, but he hit a ground ball triple, and then a couple of innings later scored from second base on a fly ball to deep center field. I've seen other ground ball triples, but not very many, and I don't know that I've ever seen any other player score from second on a fly ball, except maybe Alfredo Griffin. But actually, there are a lot of times that a player *could* do that, if he was focused and alert. You get a fly ball to deep center in a big park, it's a tough

play to get the ball home in eight seconds. If the center fielder isn't alert or doesn't make a good throw, the runner from second could tag up and score sometimes.

George Scott, said Dick Williams in *No More Mr. Nice Guy,* "had the striking ability to gain as much as 10 pounds a day." Some days, according to Williams, Scott would "walk into the clubhouse and could barely squeeze into his pants. Once when we were playing the California Angels, he borrowed 20 bucks from Haywood Sullivan to go sight-seeing. I didn't realize that you could sight see in grocery stores, but when Scott returned several hours later, he'd gained seven pounds."

58 ◆ Ron Fairly
(1958–1978, 2442 G, 215 1044 .264)

> Ron Fairly had ordinary ability and became an extraordinary player. As a hitter he knew the strike zone, developed a good swing, and became a difficult out . . . He was willing to do whatever he had to do to become the best player he could.—John Roseboro

His career batting average would be 25 points higher if had played his best years in Cincinnati in the 1970s or St. Louis during the 1980s or Brooklyn during the 1950s, rather than Los Angeles during the 1960s. He hit .322 as a kid in 1961, and he hit .301 as an old man in 1975. But his prime seasons were spent playing in Dodger Stadium when they had their mound built way up in the air for Koufax and Drysdale, and nobody was going to hit .300 in those circumstances. The Dodgers won the pennant in 1963, '65, and '66, and they had more players on those teams who hit under .220 than players who hit over .300.

59 ◆ Phil Cavarretta
(1934–1955, 2030 G, 95 920 .293)

Cavarretta was one of the youngest regular players of this century in 1935, when he played 146 games at first base for the Cubs; he was 18

years old when the season started, turned 19 in July. He won the National League batting championship (.355) and MVP Award ten years later, when he was 28/29. Warren Brown wrote at that time (*The Chicago Cubs,* G.P. Putnam's Sons, 1946) that Cavarretta "broke in as a first baseman of promise. Thereafter he was destined to appear in various outfield positions and at one time was being groomed as a prospective pitcher. Wherever he landed he did more than a fair day's work for a fair day's pay. If the mind-changing Cub management had ever seen fit to station him at one place and keep him there, it is possible that his designation as the league's most valuable player might not have been so long delayed."

Phil Cavarretta claims to be the man who roped off the center field seats in Wrigley Field to protect the batter's hitting background, a policy which was eventually copied by all major league teams. One time on a Sunday there was a big crowd, a lot of white shirts in the center field bleachers. Cavarretta was batting against Curt Simmons, who threw rockets. Cavarretta didn't pick up the ball until the last instant, and it nearly killed him; he just got his arm up at the last second, and the pitch broke his arm. Cavarretta went to the Cubs' General Manager and begged him to rope off the center field bleachers, to prevent somebody from being killed by a pitch.

The Cubs had tried before, in the 1930s, to discourage people with white shirts from sitting in center field. That hadn't worked. They eventually agreed to the more radical solution, and in time the practice spread to all of major league baseball.

> I had two Minor League managers who were not exactly great teachers. One was . . . Phil Cavarretta. He would come out to the mound when you were in a tough spot and say, "Come on, gutless, get the guy out." Another great piece of advice.—Ray Miller in *The Earl of Baltimore* (Terry Pluto)

60 ◆ Harry Davis
(1895–1917, 1755 G, 75 952 .277)

Led the American League in Home Runs in 1904, 1905, 1906, and 1907, but never with more than 12 . . . also led twice in RBI, three times in doubles.

> July 19, 1923, was Harry Davis Day in the camp of the touring Athletics. The man who is known in baseball circles as the smartest and craftiest player in the history of the game is celebrating his fiftieth birthday . . .
>
> "I think we all should look upon Harry Davis as an example for us to follow," was Ralph Perkins' tribute to the man who is so much admired by all the players . . .
>
> [Connie Mack said] "Harry Davis is the squarest man I ever knew. He not only plays the game square himself, but he demands it of all with whom he comes in contact. No man can pull a short trick and expect to escape censure from Davis . . . Davis was a great player—much greater than the public suspected. He was not flashy—more of his work was along scientific lines. This is why he did not stand out like Ruth, Cobb, and some of the latter day stars."
>
> Davis holds some long-distance hitting records that even Babe Ruth has not eclipsed. A home run that he drove over the center-field fence in Detroit is regarded among baseball men as the longest hit ever made in the major leagues. Davis' chief forte, however, was his science . . . Mack said that he (was) the smartest and most scientific of all big league players.— 1924 *Reach Guide*

61 ◆ Jake Daubert
(1910–1924, 2014 G, 56 722 .303)

Casey Stengel, quoted in Arthur Daley's *Sports of the Times*: "Jake Daubert was as good a bunter as I ever saw. He uster put a reverse twist on it like a pool ball. It would hit the ground and—oops—here it is coming back."

Drove in only 31 runs per 100 hits throughout his career, an abysmal ratio . . . died at age 40, still playing in the majors, after an operation to remove his appendix.

62 ◆ Ferris Fain
(1947–1955, 1151 G, 48 570 .290)

Ferris Fain is the only player in major league history who (a) won a batting title, and (b) had a higher ratio of walks to hits than Ted Williams . . . He also had the fourth-best strike-out/walk ratio in major league history, behind Joe Sewell, Mickey Cochrane, and Tommy Holmes.

> Only weeks before, the off-season's biggest trade had sent the 30-year-old controversial firebrand of the Philadelphia Athletics [Fain] to Chicago in exchange for popular Eddie Robinson . . . True, the pennant-hungry Sox had landed the two-time American League batting champion and one of the game's best defensive first basemen. But what about personal relationships? . . . An "angry man" reputation has been pinned on [Fain].—Al Stump, *Sport Magazine,* July, 1953

> Fain supposedly drank a great deal, but I didn't run with him, so I couldn't be sure. He was a loner. On the field he was high-tempered and extremely competitive.—George Kell in *We Played the Game*

Fain's father, Ockie Fain, was a top-notch jockey just before World War I. He (or actually, his horse) finished second in the 1912 Kentucky Derby, riding a 20-1 shot named Duval, and he was the #2 jockey in the nation in 1913. Later, when he grew too big to ride horses, he switched to prize fighting.

Ferris was born in 1921. His parents split up when he was young. Ferris went with his mother, and his father died in 1934, so Ferris never really knew him. At first he also wanted to be a jockey, but as he outgrew that, he also switched to fighting. He liked to fight, and he was good, but the pay was steadier playing baseball, so he drifted into baseball, although he continued to fight regularly in barrooms, bathrooms, bullpens, and dugouts. He burst back into the news in the 1980s, when he was arrested several times for selling marijuana.

63 ◆ Norm Siebern
(1956–1968, 1408 G, 132 636 .272)

Norm Siebern: Hitting consistency, speed and hustle.

Jim Gentile: Defense, power and color.—*The Sporting News* summary of the Gentile/Siebern trade, November, 1963

Working conditions for Norm Siebern are far more pleasant in Kansas City. Ever since he messed up some important fly balls in the 1958 World Series, Norm suffered considerably while playing in Yankee Stadium's difficult left field (and) he was booed regularly.—*Sport Magazine,* September, 1960

Siebern is one of those players that if you could clone him and run his career over again, he might well be a Hall of Famer. His trip through the Yankee farm chain was delayed two full years by Military Service, but in 1957, aged 23, he was the Minor League Player of the year, hitting .349 with great power at Denver. The next year he hit .300 with 14 homers for the Yankees, and also—you can win a bet on this anytime—won a Gold Glove as the top left fielder in the American League.

In the 1958 World Series he was assigned key roles, hitting cleanup in Game 2, hitting fifth in Game 3, then being shifted to the lead-off spot against the lefty (Warren Spahn) in Game Four. He lost a couple of fly balls in the sun that afternoon, got a bad-glove rip, and was shifted to first base, although he had the speed and the arm to play left field, and had always been regarded as a good left fielder. He came back to give Kansas City several outstanding seasons in the early 1960s.

Hits to all fields with power. Great judge of strike zone. Was very poor fielder two years ago, but has made steady improvement. Excellent hitter

with runners in scoring position.—*Sport Magazine,* "American League Managers Secret Player Ratings," August, 1963

(*Sport* rated Siebern the second-best first baseman in the league, behind Gentile but ahead of Norm Cash, who had hit 80 home runs in the previous two seasons.)

64 ◆ Joe Kuhel
(1930–1947, 2105 G, 131 1049 .277)

Kuhel was a skinny guy with huge ears, extremely handsome but slightly clownish, with almost unnaturally bright skin. He was a magician, a student of a famous magician named Candini, and an accredited member of the American Society of Magicians. Occasionally he would do things like pull flowers out of the first base coach's ear, or steal the umpire's cap and make it disappear. This was in Washington, of course, where there was a long tradition of players and coaches clowning around on the sidelines.

Kuhel was an artist with his glove hand. Few balls ever got through him, in a game or in practice. He carried a magic mitt, which probably was one reason why he has been so slick at sleight-of-hand. His nimbleness was just as apparent on the infield as it was in the clubhouse in front of applauding teammates.—Hub Miller, *Baseball Magazine,* March, 1948

65 ◆ George Kelly
(1915–1932, 1622 G, 148 1020 .297)

Asked to name the worst player in the Hall of Fame, I will often cite George Kelly, and point out that Kelly was selected primarily because the Veterans Committee in the early 1970s was strongly biased in his favor. Well, George Kelly's son saw me say this one time on ESPN, and as you can imagine, he was not pleased. He wrote me a letter, laying out his position, and, while he may have forgotten his manners a time or two, obviously one cannot think ill of a man for defending his father's reputation. I wish I could quote the letter, but I wasn't able to get permission, so I'll have to paraphrase.

Essentially, Kelly *fils* made three points in defense of Kelly *pere*. Those three points were:

1. That Kelly was a brilliant defensive first baseman.

2. That Kelly was such an exceptional player that he kept the great Bill Terry on the bench for several years.

3. That Kelly earned his Hall of Fame selection with twenty years of hard work, and it is therefore unfair to suggest that he got in due to favoritism.

As to the first point, that Kelly was a brilliant defensive first baseman, I agree that he was. So was Vic Power, who was nearly as good a hitter as Kelly. So was Wes Parker, whose best season was better than Kelly's. So was Gil Hodges, who was three times the hitter that Kelly was. It's not enough. If Kelly were a marginal case, sure, his glove work at first base might make him a Hall of Famer. Apart from his glove, he's not within ten miles of being a Hall of Famer. His glove work cuts it, let's say, to nine miles. To overstate the case a little, it's like arguing that Greg Minton is a Hall of Famer because he had a great pickoff move to first base. He *did* have a great pickoff move to first base. It's not enough.

The fact that Kelly kept Bill Terry on the bench for a couple of years would be somewhat more impressive if Bill Terry was actually as great a player as people imagine him to have been; Terry was over-rated, too. But what about Walter Holke, who kept Kelly in the minors for a couple of years? Does this make him a Hall of Famer, too? Ed Yost kept Harmon Killebrew out of the Washington lineup for a couple of years. Does this make Ed Yost a Hall of Famer? Carl Furillo blocked Duke Snider's

path for a couple of years; does this make Carl Furillo a Hall of Famer?

It doesn't, because that just isn't how you rationally evaluate a player. You evaluate the player by what he did on the field, not by who he kept on the bench.

As to the "worked hard for everything he got" argument . . . well, I'm sure that he did work hard. I never knew a harder working player than Larry Gura. Bill Pecota worked his ass off to have a major league career. It doesn't make him a Hall of Famer.

One of the things that the general public least understands about major league athletes is how hard they work. The notion that being a professional baseball player is a fun job has strongest appeal to those who know least about it. There are a few players who are born with superb talent and coast through their careers without doing a lot to enhance that talent—Joe Pepitone, Garry Templeton, Bo Belinsky. For most athletes, being a successful player is hard work.

George Kelly was a good ballplayer. So were Chris Chambliss, Bill Buckner, George McQuinn, and Eddie Robinson. He wasn't a Hall of Famer on the best day of his life. What put him in the Hall of Fame was a Veteran's Committee salted with two of his old teammates, one of his old General Managers, and two old reporters who had covered his team in his glory years. And, not wishing to be impolite to Mr. Kelly or his son, or even to the Hall of Fame, I don't think one can denounce that kind of thing in strong enough terms.

66 ◆ Bill Buckner
(1969–1990, 2517 G, 174 1208 .289)

The Dodgers came up with Buckner and Steve Garvey, who are almost the same age, at the same time. The two men reportedly hated each other. Garvey was originally a third baseman, but had to move to first base because he couldn't throw, while Buckner was originally an outfielder, but had to move to first base because of knee and ankle problems. They both had long careers as major league first basemen, Garvey with the Dodgers and Padres, Buckner with the Cubs and Red Sox.

Garvey won the first base job with the Dodgers, in part, because he was a better defensive first baseman than Buckner. Garvey won four Gold Gloves, and would have won more, but Keith Hernandez came into the league at that time. Buckner, although he was a decent defensive first baseman, never won a Gold Glove and never deserved one, and was often replaced for defense after batting in the eighth or ninth inning.

The evaluation of a first baseman's defense by fielding statistics has always been difficult. The essential problem is that there is no "range" number for a first baseman. Putouts by first basemen, in a traditional fielding analysis, are given no weight, since about 80% of first base putouts come from plays originally made by other infielders.

You can't use a first baseman's putouts, but maybe you can use his assists? Trying to find something to stand in for a first baseman's range, traditional fielding analysis has taken up the first baseman's assists total as an indicator of his range. But this, too, has problems, which can be illustrated by contrasting Garvey and Buckner. Buckner, who was not a particularly good first baseman, had more assists per game played than any other first baseman in baseball history. In fact, at one point, Buckner held the league record for assists in both the American League and the National. Garvey, on the other hand, had exceptionally low assists totals.

In the real world, this was a trivial distinction; all it really indicates is the *preference* of each player in making a certain play. Baseball players are taught from a young age that, when a ground ball is hit to the first baseman, it is the pitcher's responsibility to cover first base. Buckner, in part because he had constant pain in his legs, was fanatic about insisting that pitchers do this. I can still see him in my mind's eye, standing five feet from first base, fielding a slow-hit grounder with the glove on his right hand, pointing vigorously to the bag with his left hand, saying "Your play. Get over there. Cover the bag." Yes, he was implicitly saying, I can easily make the play—this time. Yes, it's just two steps away, I've got plenty of time to make the play myself, *but it's your job.* Maybe next time, I won't have time. I'm not going to lose a play later this summer because you got lazy. If a pitcher failed to cover first, Buckner would go immediately to the mound and tell him about it.

Garvey, on the other hand, was paranoid about making unnecessary throws, and strongly preferred to make the play himself if he could. As Garvey saw it, why risk a throw when you can make the play yourself? In part, he saw it this way, no doubt, because he couldn't throw; he was a fine first baseman, but he had no arm.

As a consequence of this essentially trivial distinction, Buckner had many, many more assists per season than did Garvey—60 more per season on average, and twice that in some seasons. Thus, if you use assists by a first baseman to represent "range," you will reach the conclusion that Buckner was a much better defensive first baseman than Garvey. Buckner made more than twice as many errors per season as Garvey (13 to 6), but that's a difference of just a few plays per season. Unless you value one error as ten times more important than one assist, Buckner will rate higher—as, in fact, he does rate much, much higher in *Total Baseball.*

The problem with this is, it's just not true. Buckner was *not* an outstanding defensive first baseman, and Garvey was not a poor defensive first baseman. A hundred and twenty extra assists per season doesn't really have *any* value to the team in this case, because it doesn't reflect anything other than a choice. So how do you make the statistics tell you what you know to be true?

In a traditional fielding model, which uses individual fielding stats as a starting point, I know of no way to do it. But in the Win Shares fielding analysis, which starts with the defensive performance of the team as a whole, I realized that we *could*, in fact, measure a first baseman's range.

How?

Two ways. First, *if you start with the team, rather than the individual, you can estimate fairly accurately how many un-assisted putouts the first baseman has recorded.* First new statistic here: EUPO3. Estimated Un-Assisted Putouts By the First Baseman.

What if we take the putouts of a team's first basemen, and subtract the assists of the other infielders—the assists of the team's second basemen, third basemen, and shortstops?

Once I had reached the point of asking that question and checking the data, it was immediately apparent that it would work. In 1979, for example, Steve Garvey was playing first base for the Los Angeles Dodgers; he recorded 93 assists in 162 games—an above average total for him, but a relatively low total for another first baseman, and is thus rated by traditional fielding statistics as a mediocre defensive first baseman. Bill Buckner played 140 games at first base for the Cubs, recorded 124 assists, and is thus rated as an outstanding first baseman.

But if you look at the TEAM defensive stats, Dodger first basemen had 1,437 putouts, while their second basemen had 422 assists, their third basemen had 311 assists, and their shortstops had 490 assists. That leaves 214 first base putouts unaccounted for. What are those 214 plays?

They're unassisted putouts by the first basemen. The Cubs, on the other hand, had 1,501

putouts by first basemen, but 550 assists by second basemen, 329 assists by third basemen, and 531 assists by shortstops. That leaves only 91 plays un-accounted for. The Cubs' figure is the *lowest* in the National League—as you would expect, since their first baseman hated making plays un-assisted—and the Dodgers figure is the second-highest in the league. If you add together the assists and the estimated assisted putouts, the Dodger first basemen made 309 plays (95 assists, 214 un-assisted), while the Cub first basemen made 236 plays (145 assists, 91 un-assisted).

Nothing in baseball statistics is ever quite that simple; to estimate first base un-assisted putouts accurately, you also need to worry about the assists by the pitcher (most of which go to first base), and you have to adjust for the fact that not ALL assists by second basemen, third basemen, and shortstops are to the first baseman; sometimes a play goes 5-4, rather than 5-3. To use the plays made by the first basemen as an indicator of the first baseman's range, you need to adjust for the number of left-handed pitchers on the staff, because if a team has left-handed pitchers, they will get ground balls to third, rather than ground balls to first. When you get through worrying about all of that, what you have is an estimate, rather than a hard fact, and it is an estimate for the team, rather than for the individual first baseman. Still, you wind up with a much, much better estimate of the first baseman's range than you will have if you don't do the work. Dick Stuart, a comically bad first baseman, had a very high career assists rate, because, like Buckner, he preferred not to go all the way over to first base by himself if he could avoid it. But if you work through this system, you see clearly that Stuart wasn't making any un-assisted putouts. Marv Throneberry, same thing; a high assists rate masks the fact that he was an immobile first baseman. Keith Hernandez, Vic Power, Wes Parker, George Kelly, and Bill

White, to name just a few, all register, if you work through these estimates, as superior defensive first basemen.

That was one of two breakthroughs in the evaluation of first basemen as defensive players; we could call that the Bill Buckner breakthrough. The second revelation, which could be called the Keith Hernandez breakthrough, also has to do with first base assists, and is derived from a similar type of analysis, only simpler. First base assists are not all that meaningful, I realized, because they're almost all just 3-1, first baseman flips to the pitcher covering, and there is a huge element of personal choice in this play. But what about assists by the first basemen which AREN'T to the pitcher?

Studying fielding statistics by *individuals,* again, there is no where to go with this insight. But on the *team* level, we know how many putouts each team's pitchers had. In 1979, when Chicago Cub first basemen had 145 assists (second in the league), Chicago Cub pitchers also had 115 putouts, which led the league. This is just the other side of the same coin.

But if you focus on the assists by first basemen which are not to the pitcher (first base assists, minus pitcher putouts), the Cubs had 30. The Dodgers had only 10, which is not un-expected because, as I mentioned, Steve Garvey couldn't throw. The league average was 22, and the St. Louis Cardinals, with Keith Hernandez at first, had 44, which led the National League.

This yields a second estimate, A3-NP (assists by the first baseman, not to pitcher), which turns out to be even more useful than the first. If you think about it—and please think this through, and tell me if I'm wrong—when the first baseman records an assist which ISN'T to the pitcher, it is almost always a "skill" play, and it is almost always an important play.

If a first baseman has an assist which *isn't* 3-1, what is it? It could 3-2, 3-4, 3-5, or 3-6. If the play goes 3-2, that means the first baseman has thrown out somebody at home plate, which

obviously is an immensely important play. If a play goes 3-4, that usually indicates that the first baseman has fielded a bunt. But that's a key play, too, because bad first basemen don't field bunts. Dick Stuart, Willie Aikens, Dave Kingman—those kind of guys just don't field bunts. They're not quick enough.

If an assist by a first baseman goes 3-5, that means that the first baseman has thrown somebody out at third base—again, an obviously critical play.

If the assist goes 3-6, that would usually mean that the first baseman has fielded a ground ball and thrown to second to get the force out. Probably more assists by first basemen are 3-6 than anything else, other than 3-1. But that's a huge play, over the course of a season, because that means that a runner is on first base, rather than in scoring position.

So while assists by a first basemen which are to the pitcher are common but largely meaningless, assists by first basemen which *aren't* to the pitcher are relatively rare, but extremely significant. This turns out, on examination, to be really interesting data. Keith Hernandez' teams, both in St. Louis and New York, had huge, huge numbers of assists by first basemen other than to the pitcher. Some teams have negative totals, because some few putouts by pitchers are recorded in some other way.

Defensive excellence at first base, as reflected in these two new statistics, does not always go hand in hand with a reputation for defensive excellence. George Scott, to name one, does not show up as a particularly outstanding first baseman, despite winning numerous Gold Gloves. But that doesn't bother me, because I always felt that while Scott was a very good first baseman in his first couple of years in the league, after that he was just living off of his reputation. He had soft hands, but he wasn't mobile. He had a good arm, but I never saw him make a big play by throwing out a runner at another base, the way Hernandez would, or Mark Grace. George Sisler and Hal Chase are a couple of others who have good defensive reputations, but rate, in my analysis, as poor defensive first basemen.

I am not saying that my defensive evaluations of first basemen are absolutely right in all cases—but I do think they are vastly better than any previous statistical evaluations of defensive first basemen.

67 ◆ Chris Chambliss
(1971–1988, 2175 G, 185 972 .279)
Big, strong, left-handed hitter, now the Yankees hitting coach. When he came to the majors Chambliss hit everything to dead center, and people would say that when he learned to pull the ball he would hit 30 homers a year. He didn't have a quick bat, though, and he never really did learn to pull the ball consistently. He was a 90-RBI a year guy.

68 ◆ Stuffy McInnis
(1909–1927, 2128 G, 20 1060 .308)
In the 1924 *Spalding Guide* there is a picture of McInnis reaching out from first base to make a play against the oncoming baserunner, who is Jacques Fournier. Unfortunately I have no way of re-producing the photo, but it shows McInnis stretched almost flat across the infield, in a way that was common 40 years ago, but not anymore. Beneath the photo there is a box with a three-paragraph article entitled "McInnis Famous Knee-Reach."

"For years," reads the note, "John McInnis has been famous as one of the unusually good right-handed first basemen. His height has been against him, because he is not a 'beanpole,' yet he has played first base with a record of chances accepted that compares favorably with that made by players who are left-handed or taller than he is. When at his best his more enthusiastic admirers held that he was the best first baseman among those contemporary with him.

"The success of McInnis is due to his remarkable reach and his success in holding a thrown ball, even if he has to stretch full length to get it. The above photograph, taken in play, shows how McInnis helped to make himself a fine first baseman, and what any first baseman must have if he expects to be of the greatest assistance to his infield.

McInnis has gained practically the length of his body against Fournier, the baserunner, and if the play were at all close Fournier, much to his astonishment, might be out because of the McInnis reach. It would take two steps on the part of Fournier to offset what McInnis has "caught up" on the ball, and as perhaps fifty per cent of the decisions at first base hinge on one step it is apparent what the knee-reach means to a right-handed first baseman. It is this quality of bending and spreading from the knees that has made the "less than six foot first baseman" a success, notwithstanding that old players predicted that short first basemen would always be failures.—1924 *Spalding Guide*

With a few exceptions, first base in the 1990s has become the property of muscle-bound behemoths who would pop a hamstring at the mere thought of stretching themselves almost prone in the infield to gain an extra three feet against the throw. But if you think through the quote above, you'll realize that there are two immense problems with the writer's argument. You spot the problems?

The writer assumes that if the first baseman stretches six feet into the infield so as to gain six feet on the throw, this is equivalent to six feet against the baserunner. But this is only true *if the throw is moving at the same rate of speed as the baserunner.* Of course, the throw is not moving at the same rate of speed as the baserunner. The throw is moving, at a minimum, four times as fast as the baserunner.

Also, the statement that "perhaps fifty per cent of the decisions at first base hinge on one step" is way off. In an average major league game there are about eighteen putouts at first base, about one per half inning (there were more then; about eighteen now). There might be, at the most, one play per game in which a runner beats the throw to first by a step or loses by a step, certainly not nine. The writer, by the combination of these two errors, has overstated the importance of a first baseman's "stretch" probably by a factor of a hundred or more.

69 ◆ Henry Larkin
(1884–1893, 1184 G, 53 836 .303)
Small first baseman, poor fielder, and nothing really recommends him to be listed here except his batting record, which is genuinely impressive. He was a leader in the Player's League effort in 1890, and hit .332 with 112 RBI in that ill-fated season.

70 ◆ Fred Tenney
(1894–1911, 1994 G, 22 688 .294)

> Tenney was not popular at first with the old pros. They called him "The Soiled Collegian."—Harold Kaese, *The Boston Braves*

Singles hitting leadoff man who ran well, had a career on base percentage of .371, scored 125 runs in 1897, and led the National League in runs scored in 1908, when he was 36 years old.

Tenney was a graduate of Brown University, one of the few college men in baseball in the 1890s. He was regarded as a little bit of a gentleman, compared to the ruffians who dominated the era, but he had some coping skills, too. Some of the older players when Tenney came into the league would try to abuse him, because they figured a college boy would be a pushover. Tenney would offer to discuss the matter under the stands after the game.

Tenney had an outstanding arm, and toward the end of his career he and Christy Mathewson developed a trick play to take advantage of it. With a runner on first in a hit and run situation, Mathewson would throw to Tenney, and Tenney would fire it immediately back to Mathewson. Mathewson would then whip it across home plate, before the runner on first base could get off his butt, and often before the batter had any idea the pitch was coming. After a couple of years they changed the rules to make it a balk ...

Stuffy McInnis is generally considered to have been the first first baseman to stretch halfway into the infield for the throw. However, the *Chicago News* in 1897 (twelve years before McInnis) reported that Tenney "reaches his hands far out for the ball, and stretches his legs, so that he is farther out from the bag on every throw than any other first baseman in the league."

71 ◆ Earl Torgeson
(1947–1961, 1668 G, 149 740 .265)
His real first name was "Clifford." Torgeson in 1950 was probably the best player in the National League, hitting .290 with 23 homers, 30 doubles, 15 stolen bases, and 119 walks. It was a fluke year; he was never that good otherwise, but did have a career on-base percentage of .385.

> Faster than most other first basemen in the league. Offensively, seems to be at best with men on base. Good bet to drive in runner from third base but doesn't produce the long ball too often.—*Sport Magazine*, "Secret Ratings of NL Players," February, 1955

72 ◆ John Kruk
(1986–1995, 1200 G, 100 592 .300)
Fun player. Every generation has a few players who are just fun—fun to watch, fun to talk about, fun to make fun of. A lot of these guys are first basemen, like Zeke Bonura, Steve (Bye Bye) Balboni, Marv Throneberry, and Ken Phelps. Kruk was arguably the best of the fun first baseman, except maybe Boog Powell.

73 ◆ Gus Suhr
(1930–1940, 1435 G, 84 818 .279)

His sparkling defensive work in 1936 won for Gus Suhr the rank of leading first-baseman in the National League. This veteran played in all of Pittsburgh's games, 156, and fielded .9934. Gus now has operated in 784 consecutive battles for the Pirates, having launched his league record streak on September 11, 1931. The former mark of 618 was held by Eddie Brown, of Brooklyn and Boston. Suhr was one busy individual for the San Francisco Seals in 1929 when he performed in every inning of 202 contests, batting .381 and handling 2,040 putouts plus 118 assists while making but 24 errors."–*Who's Who in the Major Leagues,* 1937

(The note fails to mention that he also had 299 hits that summer, including 62 doubles and 51 homers, driving in 177 runs and scoring 196.)

Suhr was a tall, thin man with a thin face and an elongated jaw; it must have been four inches from the point of his chin to his perpetual smile. He was a Mark Grace-type player, drove in 100 runs three times and had as many as 95 walks in a season. His consecutive-game streak reached 822 games. The National League record was broken by Stan Musial.

74 ◆ Alvin Davis
(1984–1992, 1206 G, 160 683 .280)

Alvin is younger than Harold Baines, but has been out of baseball for several years. He had a great rookie year in 1984, driving in 116 runs and drawing 97 walks. I wrote a comment about him at that time, speculating that he might have a short career, because, while he was a young player at that time, he had "old players skills"–that is, he had power and strike zone judgment, but no speed, arm, or obvious unexploited athletic ability.

This proved to be true in Alvin's case, but the underlying axiom–that a player with old players skills will have a short career–

remained largely speculation until the development of the Win Shares method, with which it was easy to resolve the issue. See note on Tom Brunansky in the right field section (82).

75 ◆ Moose Skowron
(1954–1967, 1658 G, 211 888 .282)

Hit .300 or better his first four years in the majors (1954–1957)–but didn't really become a full-time player until 1960. Lost a lot of home runs to playing in Yankee Stadium . . . in 1961 he hit 28 homers, only 7 in his home park. In 1956 it was 6 at home, 17 on the road. Good defensive first baseman, .300 hitter, could have hit 35-40 homers a year in a better park for him . . . A gregarious man who loved playing the game.

76 ◆ Hal Chase
(1905–1919, 1917 G, 57 941 .291)

Could he really have existed, or was he perhaps invented by Robert Louis Stevenson, along with the Master of Ballantrae, Long John Silver, and the good Dr. Jekyll? Hal Chase is remembered as a shining, leering, pock-marked face, pasted on a pitch-dark soul. There is some evidence to say that he appeared in the flesh, but I lean more toward the invention theory. What mother, if he was real, what Rosemary could have given birth to such a creature? He was an attractive figure, of this there is no doubt (Susie, knowing nothing of his character, selected him as the ugliest player of the decade, and he was that, too). His parentage is not much discussed in the literature, but he should have been, I would say, the bastard son of a bishop, by way of a woman down on her luck.

Within days of arriving in the majors in 1905, Hal Chase was acclaimed a star. No one ever saw him play without being left gasping for adjectives, and though his statistics may not explain why, he was routinely described as a great player. "His range was incredible," says

Fred Lieb. "No other first baseman played so far off the bag. As a man charging in on a bunt he was fantastic. He was speed and grace personified." According to an article by Robert Hoie in the 1974 *Baseball Research Journal,* a year before he came to the majors the *Los Angeles Examiner* wrote that "If Chase isn't a great natural ballplayer, then Los Angeles never saw one." Within two years of his reaching the major leagues, *The Sporting Life* said that "a more brilliant player does not wear a uniform" and he was "perhaps the biggest drawing card in baseball."

That was in 1907. He was then in the middle of one of his early controversies, seeking to get more money out of the New York Highlanders. In 1908 the first charges appeared that Chase had been "laying down," the terminology of the day for throwing games. Chase, accusing the team of slander, jumped the New Yorkers and went to play in an outlaw league in California. He was suspended for this, but applied for reinstatement, paid a $200 fine and was eligible to begin the 1909 season.

In the spring of 1909 Chase developed small-pox. Some have attributed Chase's later disrepute to this untimely disfigurement, that he felt cheated of his youth and became bitter and greedy thereafter. Chase, in truth, was greedy and disagreeable before this, but never mind . . . reading his life as a work of fiction, we see the pox to have been an external manifestation of the rotten pulp at Chase's center, a clue to the other players and to the readers, if you will, that a wary eye should be kept upon him.

But there was a powerful magnetic force around him. In trying to research something else that happened in the 1909 season, Jim Baker noted that it seemed the only thing the New York papers would report about the Highlanders was the status of Hal Chase. "Chase reported in Albany . . . Chase set to rejoin team next Tuesday . . . Chase reported on train . . .

Hal Chase

Chase in camp." Chase, who had departed the team in a huff the previous September, was presented a loving cup by his teammates when he rejoined them in May, 1909.

George Stallings was now the manager of the Highlanders. He was the second man to have gotten the job after Chase felt that it should have been his. The team did remarkably well; an outfit that had lost 103 games in 1908, the year before Stallings took over, finished near .500 in 1909 and in 1910 improved to 88-63, second in the American League. There were printed charges, however, that Chase was unhappy—indeed, that he was so unhappy that he was laying down, trying to lose games so as to get Stallings fired. In mid-season Stallings accused Chase of trying to throw a game. The two nearly came to blows. Chase began to be mysteriously absent from the team. In late September

Stallings said that he would resign if Chase was not replaced.

A half-century later, interviewed by Lawrence Ritter for *The Glory of Their Times,* Jimmy Austin was still somewhat astonished by what had happened then. Austin, a member of the team, described Stallings as "a fine manager—one of the best," but recalled that Chase "had gone to Mr. Farrell, the president of the club, and complained about Stallings and a lot of other things. Mr. Farrell supported Chase, so Stallings quit, and Chase was made the new manager. God, what a way to run a ball club!"

Gabby Street, a catcher with the club under Chase, told about standing behind Chase once at a poker game. With a big pot on the table, Chase was raising each round. Street, not playing, glanced at Chase's hand and saw three kings. He looked away for a moment and glanced back. Chase had four kings. As he stared at the hand, a low card disappeared as if by magic.

This sort of thing must have been great for morale. Chase was a dismal failure as a player/manager, and resigned after one year.

In 1913 Frank Chance, then managing the team (by now known as the Yankees), approached the sportswriters covering his team and alleged that Chase was throwing games on him. The sportswriters let it pass once, but then printed the charges. Chase was traded to the White Sox shortly after that, and a year later jumped to the Buffalo team of the Federal League, his right to do so becoming the subject of one of the decade's many lawsuits. Rumors were heard surrounding Buffalo's games, which complicated the difficult task of keeping the league alive, but again, nothing was proven. When the Federal League folded their players were auctioned off to other teams, Chase going to Cincinnati.

His first two seasons in Cincinnati were the most productive of his career, but in time there

again began to circulate charges reflecting on the integrity of Chase's efforts. In August of 1918, Reds manager Christy Mathewson suspended Chase for the balance of the season, and charged him with violations of National League Rule 40, which related to "Crookedness and Its Penalties," and specified that "Any person who shall be proven guilty of offering, agreeing, conspiring or attempting to cause any game of ball to result otherwise than on its merits under the playing rules, shall be forever disqualified . . ." Chase immediately filed a civil suit, demanding payment of his salary for the balance of the season, and issued a sweeping denial of the charges against him. National League President John Heydler was assigned by the league to conduct a trial of the issue, and "to render a judgment based on the law and the evidence."

This was the third time that a matter of baseball treason had been heard by the National League, the first relating to the Louisville incident in 1877, and the other to a comparatively trivial clearing up of unsubstantiated charges against Jack Taylor, a Cubs pitcher. The trial of Chase was conducted at Heydler's office in New York on January 30, 1919. Chase was present, and arrived armed with three lawyers, a clerk, and a stenographer. The Cincinnati team sent no one; an attorney from New York represented the National League and cross-examined some witnesses. Christy Mathewson was with the United States Army in France, and was unable to attend. New York pitcher Pol Perritt, who had alleged that Chase had offered to make it worth his while to bear down extra hard in a game against the Reds, was working on his plantation in Louisiana, and was also unable to attend.

This left Greasy Neale, a Cincinnati outfielder most remembered as a football coach, as the leading witness against the infidel. Neale reported several conversations that Chase had

had with other members of the Cincinnati team, each leaving the impression that Chase was betting against his own team. Chase argued that Neale was the head of a clique of Cincinnati players who had it in for him. Pitcher Mike Regan appeared and alleged that Chase had offered him a bribe. Chase denied it and charged that Regan was a part of the clique. He entered into evidence his batting and fielding records for the previous seasons, during one of which he had led the National League in hitting, at .339.

John McGraw appeared, supposedly as a witness to incriminating conversations, but damaged the case by testifying as to Chase's good character, and offering the opinion that the Cincinnati club had no proper basis for their charges. Chase argued that the charges were absurd, that he had been a major league regular at that time longer than any other player, and that he had never before been charged with such dishonesty. When the prior indictments were brought up, Chase "explained previously unknown circumstances in connection with troubles he had had in the American League, particularly while he was with the Yankees" (1919 *Reach Guide*). He had the advantage of being the only person present who was a party to those incidents.

Chase was publicly acquitted. Although John Heydler told friends that he was privately convinced of Chase's guilt, he had in front of him no evidence that would stand up in a court of law, and so he felt that his hands were tied.

Chase was free, then. It had all been brought out into the open, and he had gotten by with it. This seems to have had a liberating effect on Chase's activities, or perhaps it was not that but the fact that as the end of his career grew nearer, he had less to lose and became more reckless. Or perhaps he was just drinking too much. Anyway, John McGraw, to Heydler's irritation, signed Chase to play for the Giants in 1919. Back in New York, where the gamblers were easy to communicate with, Chase enlisted the help of a couple of teammates (Heinie Zimmerman and Jean Dubuc), and between them they seem to have approached almost everyone on the team to see who was interested in making a little money on the side. He was free then, free to bring the gamblers right into the locker room if he chose, free to play his role in arranging the outcome of the World Series.

Heydler, however, had not let the matter drop. He continued to investigate the Chase affair, traveling to Boston to collect information about a gambler there with whom Chase had a connection. Eventually Heydler obtained a signed affidavit from the Boston gambler, as well as a copy of a $500 check given to Chase for throwing a game in 1918. In late 1919, almost a year before the revelation of the Black Sox scandal, Heydler banned Chase from the National League. In 1921 Judge Landis made the ban permanent and universal. Even this did not end Chase's career in dishonesty, but at least it kept it out of organized ball.

Chase's methods in throwing games apparently included bribing teammates, paying bonuses to opponents who played well against his team, and a variety of on-field maneuvers. He collected hits at meaningless times to cover himself, and it has been suggested that opposing pitchers who were co-conspirators may have allowed him to fatten his average. A favorite trick was to break late in covering first, thus failing to make a catch while seeming to make a good effort, often causing the third baseman or shortstop to draw an error on a perfectly good throw.

His methods in arranging a fix are less well documented, and though the destination of his career is well known, much of the scenery has been forgotten. It is my belief, though no one could claim to prove such a thing, that Hal

Chase's personality is one of the keys to the corruption of the era, and that had Chase been a tinker, a tailor, or a cabinet maker, it is quite possible that the whole thing would never have happened—the "whole thing" including the series fix, all of the other scandals, and the arrival of Kenesaw Mountain Landis and the commissioner system to sort it out. Fred Lieb expressed a similar thought in *Baseball As I Have Known It*. "How many good young ballplayers," Lieb asked, "may have said, 'Chase gets by with it, year after year, so why shouldn't we pick up a little extra money when the chance is offered us?'" Visiting a SABR convention in the 1970s, Lieb reportedly said that he thought all of the trouble started with Chase, and he didn't know if any of it would have happened without him.

As ugly as Chase was, something wonderfully masculine and persuasive drew men to him and compelled them to believe not only that he was honest but that he was *right*, that he was something more than ordinary. How else to explain it? The most astonishing thing is that *it all went on so long*. There were printed charges that he was laying down in 1908, *twelve years* before he was expelled from baseball. Fred Lieb said that there was talk among the writers about crookedness when he arrived in New York in 1911. Lee Magee, one of the players that he took with him, charged that the business began in 1906. Three of baseball's most respected managers (Frank Chance, George Stallings, and Christy Mathewson) charged Chase with dishonesty—yet he stayed in the game. Something about him made wrong shine as it were right and evil smell like good. If it seems incredible that one man could so alter the ethics of the sport, consider the rank improbability of what Chase is known to have done. He played in the major leagues for more than a decade during which the cloud of suspicion returned to him again and again and again.

With the greatest of effort, personalities cannot be photographed and preserved. Chase's lost charm is something which can be forever speculated about. When it was alleged that he paid a teammate $25 after the teammate (Jimmy Ring) had lost a game, he said it was just a gift. And he made people believe that. Was that how he did it—did he come bearing gifts? He was known as a generous man. Bob Hoie writes that "He apparently would befriend the young players, was one of the few veterans to invite them home to dinner, etc. Many of them were almost worshipful of him. This appeal carried over to his days of outlaw ball in Douglas, Arizona, where men whose wives and girlfriends had been seduced by Chase were still in awe of him 50 years later." (Quote from private letter.)

There is an evil, a smallness, lust, and greed that lives inside of each of us. The secret of Hal Chase, I believe, was that he was able to reach out and embrace that evil. And he had so much class, don't you see? He was a man of such dignity and bearing, such wit, charm, and grace, that he made you feel that it was alright to have that in you. It's OK; it's just the way we are. We're all professionals, aren't we? We're in this game to make a living, aren't we?

How good a player was Hal Chase? Walter Johnson in 1924 named Chase the greatest first baseman of all time. *Baseball* magazine, choosing an all-time team in July, 1930, did the same. In Babe Ruth's autobiography, *The Babe Ruth Story* with Bob Considine (1948), Ruth chose as the greatest first baseman of all time not Lou Gehrig or Jimmie Foxx or George Sisler or Bill Terry or any of the other great first basemen who were his contemporaries, but Hal Chase, saying that some people "will feel that I should pick Lou Gehrig over Chase, [but Chase] was so much better than anybody else that I ever saw on first base that—to me—it was no contest."

I read old baseball books every day, looking for contemporaneous remarks by which to pin down a player's defensive ability or other features that might have escaped the record books. No other player in baseball history was so richly praised for his defensive skill—no one. His brilliance with the glove is easier to document than Ty Cobb's temper, Hack Wilson's drinking, or Walter Johnson's fastball; it is all over the literature of the sport. John Kieran in the *New York Times* (October 3, 1937) wrote that Hal Chase "was the Fancy Dan of all time around baseball infields. The fellow really was a marvel—all steel springs. And what a man for short-hop throws . . . He would wait until the last part of a split second to sweep his gloved right hand down there and come up with the ball like picking daisies."

There is no doubt that his defensive skills were astonishing, and that you might fully share that conviction, let me give you a few more quotes. One, which I find in Hoie's article, was from a June 1913 issue of *The Sporting News*. "That he can play first base as it never was and perhaps never will be played is a well-known truth," said *TSN*. "That he will is a different matter."

"Gehrig was no Hal Chase," wrote Edward Barrow in 1951. "Indeed no one but Chase ever was. In agility and quickness of movement, Chase was in a class by himself. As a fielding first baseman he was unmatched and without any doubt whatsoever the greatest who ever lived."

"He could be called a dramatic fielder," wrote James T. Farrell. "A left-hander, he could pivot like a ballet dancer; in fact, it is not at all inappropriate to speak of his movements, his footwork and his throwing and fielding as though it were a dance."

The final quote is a poem from the 1915 *Reach Guide,* entitled "You Can't Escape 'Em." It goes:

Sometimes a raw recruit in spring
Is not a pitching find.
He has no Walter Johnson's wing,
Nor Matty's wondrous mind.
He does not act like Harold Chase
Upon the fielding job,
But you will find in such a case,
He hits like Tyrus Cobb.

Lawrence Ritter and Donald Honig chose Chase as one of the top 100 players in baseball history. I would not choose him among a thousand. Okay, so he was the greatest defensive first baseman ever, and he once led the league in homers, and he once led the league in batting. He led the Federal League in home runs with seventeen, but that was playing in a tiny park in a marginal major league. With the exception of that one season, his career high in home runs was five. He was no real power threat. He hit .339 in 1916, and he was a lifetime .291 hitter. But he was an impatient hitter, drawing less than 20 walks a year. That combination—no walks, no power—makes for an empty .291 average. Chase never drove in or scored 100 runs in a season, or even 90. His onfield talents were essentially the same as those of Vic Power. Each player was the best defensive first baseman of his time. Each hit for a pretty good average and had excellent speed for a first baseman. Each had a little power but not much, and each was a contact hitter, but not one to take a walk.

But what greatness as a baseball player comes down to is, "What did he do to help his teams win?" If you were trying to win a pennant, how badly would you want this guy? Hey, this is not Joe Jackson that we are talking about here. This is not the corrupted. This is the corrupt. No matter what his skills, I would not want Hal Chase around, period, and I find it extremely difficult to believe that he ever helped any team, at all, period. He never played for a championship team. Most of the teams that he played for declined precipitously when he joined them and improved dramatically after he was gone. The Highlanders/Yankees declined by twenty games in Chase's rookie year, and improved by eleven the year after he was traded. The White Sox claimed they had the pennant when they acquired Chase. They dropped from fourth to fifth, and improved by twenty-three games in their first full year without Chase. Chase's Federal League teams finished fourth and sixth. Cincinnati declined by ten games the year that Chase joined them and improved by twenty-two the year after he left. That he was a manipulator nonpareil is clear. That he was a great player is not.

77 ◆ Lu Blue
(1921–1933, 1615 G, 44 692 .287)
An athletic first baseman who drew a hundred walks a year and hit .300 four of his first five years in the majors. Blue never hit in the minors, and attributed his good work as a major league hitter to Ty Cobb, who took the time to teach him how to read pitchers. His hitting did decline after Cobb was fired as manager . . . the 1926 Tigers finished in sixth place, but only twelve games out of first. They were in contention until Blue broke his ankle in August, after which the team crumbled.

78 ◆ Dan Driessen
(1973–1987, 1732 G, 152 763 .267)
A reserve on the Big Red Machine, became a regular in 1977, and was a good player for about eight years. Led the National League in walks in 1980, stole 31 bases in 1977, 28 more in 1978, hit 15–18 homers a year and was a quick, agile first baseman who regularly led the league in fielding percentage.

79 ◆ George Burns
(1914–1929, 1866 G, 72 948 .307)
Tris Speaker in 1923 hit 59 doubles, which was a major league record. Speaker at the time was

player/manager of the Cleveland Indians. After the season the Indians traded for Burns—who broke his manager's record, three years later, with 64 doubles. It was broken again five years later (Earl Webb hit 67), but 64 remains the second-highest total of all time.

League Park in Cleveland generated easy doubles for a left-handed hitter; Burns was a right-hander. It was 290 feet to right field, but there was a high fence, so that a fairly-well hit fly ball would bounce off the wall for a double—a left-handed Fenway, essentially. Indian left-handed hitters often led the league in doubles, and one year (1916) two Cleveland lefties tied for the league lead in doubles. I don't know what the data was for Burns, but Tris Speaker in his eleven years in the park hit 306 doubles in Cleveland, only 179 on the road. Burns must have learned to hit the outside pitch in the air and hope for the best, as Yaz did in Fenway.

Burns had an odd batting stance. He stood very straight at the plate with his feet together, his bat resting on his shoulder; it was said that he looked like a soldier standing at attention. The first half of his career was interrupted by constant injuries. In one three-year period (1915–1917) he had malaria, typhoid fever, an operation for appendicitis, a broken ankle suffered on the ball field, and a broken shoulder blade suffered diving into a swimming pool.

In August, 1915, Burns became "the appropriately named George Burns" when he accidentally set a spectator on fire. The man was carrying matches in his pocket. Burns hit him with a foul ball, and the man's coat caught fire. A soda vendor put out the fire by spraying a soft drink in his pocket.

80 ◆ Piano Legs Hickman
(1897–1908, 1081 G, 59 614 .295)
There used to be a man on the Giants, named "Charley" Hickman. He was one of the best natural hitters who ever wormed his way into baseball, but when he got on, the bases were blocked.

He could not run, and it took a hit to advance him a base ... Hickman was not so slow when he first started, but after a while his legs went bad and his weight increased, so that he was built like a box car.—Christy Mathewson, *Pitching in a Pinch* (Putnam, 1912) [slightly edited]

81 ◆ Vic Power
(1954–1965, 1627 G, 126 658 .284)

Power was a spectacular defensive first baseman, an acrobat who would dive for ground balls half way to second base; he had the athletic ability we normally associate with a very good second baseman, but had applied it to playing first base. Power had the same problem as Siebern and McQuinn: he came along in the Yankee farm system at a time when the Yankees were not exactly desperate for help. He had two additional problems: one, that he would be a right-handed hitter in Yankee Stadium, and two, that he was a dark-skinned Latin player before the Yankees had broken the color line. In 1952 he played for Kansas City in the American Association, at that time the Yankees' top farm club. He hit .331 with 40 doubles (leading the league), 17 triples (leading the league), 16 homers and 109 RBI. The Yankees already had Joe Collins and Johnny Mize at first base, plus the Kansas City team also had Moose Skowron, who hit .341 with 31 homers, 134 RBI the same year, playing the outfield. Power returned to Kansas City in 1953, leading the American Association in batting (.349) and hits (217).

One odd thing about Power is that his power zone was right between his eyes; if you threw at his head (which a lot of people did) he was liable to line the knock down pitch into the left field bleachers.

He hit .300 several times in the majors (.288 or better six seasons as a regular), hit 14–19 homers a year, led the league in triples one year, won seven Gold Gloves at first base, and would have won two or three more before that,

but they didn't start giving the award until the middle of his career.

Power was an emotional player, great sense of humor, always laughing, joking, cutting up, playing practical jokes, but he was also a sensitive man with a hair-trigger temper. He would get "hurt angry" rather than "fighting angry," not that he didn't get into his share of fights, but sometimes he would take things the wrong way. Bigots just couldn't stand him. In the vernacular of the 1950s, Power was one of "them" who "didn't know his place." He was a showboat, and he was an uppity n-word who dated white girls.

> Ask any player in the American League who's the biggest showboat and, chances are, you'll get the lightning answer "Vic Power." The rollicking Puerto Rican is upstage most of the time for the Kansas City Athletics, hamming up the most elementary situation at first base. He baits the crowds by making one-hand circus catches of easy bull's-eye pegs, and sometimes succeeds in nauseating his fellow athletes.—James Ellis, *Baseball Digest*, August, 1956

After his playing career, Power was active in youth sports programs in San Pedro de Macoris. He is one of the key reasons—perhaps *the* key reason—why this village became the world's richest source of baseball talent.

My favorite Vic Power story ... Vic Power in a restaurant in Syracuse, 1951. An embarrassed waiter shuffles up to him and explains, "I'm sorry, sir, we don't serve colored people."

"That's OK," says Power. "I don't eat colored people."

82 ◆ George McQuinn
(1936–1948, 1550 G, 135 794 .276)

> The Browns managed to pick up a good first baseman in McQuinn. He could hit well ... and could field with the best.—1939 *Spalding Guide*

McQuinn spent eight full seasons buried in the Yankee system at a time when Lou Gehrig owned first, and a minor league player had no way to seek another path to the majors. He hit .316 with 20 triples, 101 RBI at Scranton in 1931, hit .345 in the Eastern League in 1932, won the NYP League MVP Award in 1933, hitting .357 with 102 RBI for Binghamton, and hit .331 for Toronto, 1934.

After the 1935 season McQuinn was conditionally sold to the Cincinnati Reds. In the Reds camp, according to McQuinn in Ron Mayer's 1937 Newark Bears, "everyone from Larry MacPhail to the bat boy had a suggestion to make to me about my hitting. I changed bats, changed grips, changed stance, but I was so tangled up, I grew worse day by day." McQuinn was rejected by the Reds after a couple of months, and returned to the Yankee farm chain. (The Reds, incidentally, had purchased Johnny Mize from the Cardinals the previous year under a similar arrangement, but had also decided that Mize wasn't worth the money, and had returned him to the Cardinals.)

McQuinn hit .329 for Toronto in 1936, and in 1937 he was the first baseman on the famous Newark Bears team, believed by some to have been the greatest minor league team of all time (McQuinn hit .330 with a .646 slugging percentage).

Believing that Lou Gehrig would go on for several more seasons, the Yankees let McQuinn go in the draft; he was claimed by the St. Louis Browns. As a virtual rookie in 1938 he hit .324, collected 195 hits, had a 34-game hitting streak, hit 42 doubles, and scored 100 runs. He would remain at or near that level for several seasons.

83 ◆ Wally Pipp
(1913–1928, 1872 G, 90 996 .281)
The Yankees got Pipp from a kind of informal expansion draft organized by the stronger teams in the American League. The Highlanders/ Yankees had finished last in the American

League in 1912, seventh in 1913, seventh in 1914, and, with the Federal League launching a threat to the two established major leagues, Ban Johnson felt that the American League would benefit from having a more competitive team in New York. The Yankees were allowed to buy Pipp and a couple of other young players for the waiver price, in part to help the Yankees, and in part to keep the young players from jumping to the Federal League.

Pipp, like the man who replaced him at first base for the Yankees, was a left-handed hitter, a left-handed thrower, and a college man, having studied engineering at Catholic University in Detroit. He was the best defensive first baseman in the American League at that time; Miller Huggins said that he was the best in baseball, by which he meant that Pipp was better than George Kelly, the fancy-fielding first baseman of the New York Giants. Pipp led the American League in home runs in 1916 and 1917, and drove in 97 runs in 1921, 90 in 1922, 108 in 1923, and 113 in 1924, when he hit a league-leading 19 triples.

He lost his job the next summer, of course . . . For two or three weeks after Gehrig started playing, Pipp was pinch hitting, hoping to get back in the lineup. But one day, taking extra batting practice, he was hit in the head by a pitch, suffered a concussion, and wasn't right for the rest of the year.

84 ◆ Fred Merkle
(1907–1926, 1637 G, 61 733 .273)
Merkle was recommended to the Giants by John T. Brush's barber, who raved about the 18-year-old player while giving Brush a shave. The Giants' owner sent Dick Kinsella to check him out, and, a year later, Merkle's mistake was the central focus of the sports world.

Merkle played for five teams which won the National League pennant—the Giants of 1911, 1912, and 1913, the Dodgers of 1916, and the

Cubs of 1918. He also coached and played one game for the 1926 Yankees.

The prototype of the first baseman as a power hitter goes back to the 1880s, when Dan Brouthers, Cap Anson, Roger Connor, and other men of great size took over the position. This model of a first baseman didn't entirely take over until 1925, but there were always some first basemen in that mold. In Merkle's time there were Fred Luderus, Ed Konetchy, Harry Davis, Vic Saier, and others.

John McGraw never had that kind of a first basemen. McGraw had seven first basemen in his years with the Giants—Dan McGann (1902–1907), Fred Tenney (1908–1909), Fred Merkle (1910–1916), Walter Holke (1917–1918), Hal Chase (1919), George Kelly (1920–1926), and Bill Terry (1925 and 1927–1932). All of them were line drive hitters who ran and threw well enough to be outfielders. All except Holke are listed among the top 100 first basemen of all time.

85 ◆ Charlie Grimm
(1916–1936, 2164 G, 79 1078 .290)

Grimm remembered in *Jolly Cholly's Story* that the first man to greet him when he joined Pittsburgh in 1919 was Possum Whitted, who caught the low pitch of his voice and immediately asked "Can you sing bass?" The Bucs had a singing group.

"I'm sure it couldn't happen now," Grimm wrote, "but we gave pre-game concerts . . . Before each game we'd gather behind the batting cage at home plate and serenade the fans. We weren't inflicting our harmony on them, they demanded it. Deep in my memory of those days are the fans who arrived from the coal mines with lamps still attached to their caps."

Grimm had a long career and was as an outstanding defensive first baseman, perhaps the best ever. He was generally a below-average hitter for his era.

86 ◆ Eddie Robinson
(1942–1957, 1315 G, 172 723 .268)

An amiable Texan whose career was delayed several years by World War II. In the 1980s I worked as a consultant to players in salary negotiations, and Eddie worked as a consultant to management, so we used to butt heads in salary arbitration cases about three times a year. At the time, I used to get irritated with him, but as I look back I don't remember why, and have nothing but fond memories of him.

> Eddie Robinson had come out of the service and was having a big year in the minors when I bought the club. Eddie was playing, however, with a dropped foot; the nerves had somehow weakened so that he couldn't control it. We paid for an operation over that winter, and wrote him off for the better part of the next season. By 1948, Robinson was ready to step in and take over at first base, one of our weak spots.—Bill Veeck, *Veeck as in Wreck*

87 ◆ Jack Doyle
(1889–1905, 1564 G, 25 924 .301)

AKA Dirty Jack Doyle and Dashing Jack Doyle. Early in his career, when he was a catcher, he was once reprimanded by the National League for sticking pebbles in the batter's shoes while they were hitting. When the batter leaned forward on his toes Doyle would drop a pebble in the back on his shoe. The batter wouldn't even feel it at the time, but then later, when he was trying to run, he would discover that there was a rock in his shoe.

> [Umpire Bob Emslie] is under cover. It is no secret, or I would not give way on him. But that luxuriant growth of hair, apparent, comes off at night like his collar and necktie . . . I had to laugh to myself . . . when Mr. Lynch appointed "Jack" Doyle, formerly a first baseman and a hot-headed player, an umpire and scheduled him to work with Emslie. I remembered the time several seasons ago when Doyle took offence at one

of "Bob's" decisions and wrestled him all over the infield trying to get his wig off and show him up before the crowd. And then Emslie and he worked together like Damon and Pythias. This business makes strange bed-fellows.—Christy Mathewson, *Pitching in a Pinch,* Putnam, 1912

Doyle scouted for the Cubs for many years after his career . . . there are several stories about him in Peter Golenbock's *Wrigleyville.* "Doyle was a scout of an entirely different tribe," wrote Warren Brown in *The Chicago Cubs* (Putnam, 1946). "Early in his career Doyle had found out that one lasted longer if one kept as far away from the front office as he could. Doyle, the Old Oriole, flew home only when ordered to do so."

88 ◆ Fred Luderus
(1909–1920, 1346 G, 84 647 .277)
A dead ball era power hitter, one of the few. 75% of his career home runs (63 of 84) were hit in his home park, Philadelphia's Baker Bowl . . . career ended just as the lively ball era began.

89 ◆ Bruce Bochte
(1974–1986, 1538 G, 100 658 .282)
> He is still a slashing, yet patient, hitter with no clear weakness . . . Bochte is a fine natural athlete (he played basketball in college), but despite his strong and lean build, he's one of the slowest runners in either league. To compound his problems, his fierce swing finds him lurching toward the catcher on his follow-through.—*The Scouting Report,* 1985

90 ◆ Whitey Lockman
(1945–1960, 1666 G, 114 563 .279)
"Whitey" was a baseball name. To his friends and family, he was called "Pickle" . . .

Lockman played 32 games for the Giants as an 18-year-old early in the 1945 season, and was regarded then as a sensation, hitting .341; at that time he could fly. He went in the Army

for a couple of years, survived that OK, but then had a bad accident in a spring training game in 1947, setting him back a year and costing him some of his speed. He kind of had an "Al Kaline" or "Cesar Cedeno" career after that. He was a terrific player in 1948 and 1949, still very young, but slid slowly away from that standard, rather than building on it.

In 1951 Lockman doubled just ahead of Bobby Thomson's home run. Lockman's double drove in a run, knocked Don Newcombe out of the game, and brought Ralph Branca to the mound.

91 ◆ Jason Thompson
(1976–1986, 1418 G, 208 782 .261)
Left-handed power hitter who started well, had his last good season at age 28.

92 ◆ Dan McGann
(1896–1908, 1436 G, 42 727 .284)
John McGraw's teammate in Baltimore (NL) and St. Louis, his first baseman in Baltimore (AL) and New York. He did a lot of little things well. He led the National League in being hit with the pitch six times, in sacrifice bunts once, in fielding percentage at first base six times. He was a fighter, like all of McGraw's buddies, and most of the references to him in the sport's literature are to fights.

McGann played for McGraw through 1907, but broke an arm that spring, and missed the first half of the season. When he returned in mid-season he was not in shape, and began to quarrel with McGraw. He was included in a big trade that winter. The trade brought in Fred Tenney, who, a reporter pointed out, was the same age as McGann, 36. Yes, explained McGraw, but Tenney has taken better care of himself.

In May, 1908, playing for Boston, McGann grounded into a ninth-inning double play to end a rally. As McGann lumbered toward first, McGraw yelled "ICE WAGON," an ice wagon being notable as something which didn't move very fast. After the game, McGraw explained tactfully to the reporters that "that's how the Giants lost a lot of games last season," and added that there wasn't anyone on his team anymore who wouldn't have been able to beat the throw to first.

McGann took this well; he went to the Copley Square Hotel, where the Giants were staying, and assaulted John McGraw in the middle of a game of billiards. McGraw fled; McGann chased him up the stairs, flailing away behind him until McGraw sprinted for his room and locked the door.

McGann was washed up. He batted 475 times that season, but hit .240 with eight doubles and two homers, and was released after the season. He committed suicide two years later, shooting himself in the temple.

93 ◆ Tommy Tucker
(1887–1899, 1687 G, 42 932 .290)
The first switch hitter to win a batting title (1889). Was hit by pitches 272 times in his career, one of the highest totals in baseball history.

Tucker was a bench jockey, a comedian. In the 1880s and 1890s teams didn't have regular coaches. Managers would assign their loudest mouths and sharpest wits to stand in the first base coach's box, relay signals to the runner, and also do everything possible to annoy the pitcher. Tucker was one of the best; he was called "Foghorn" Tucker, a nickname which has escaped the Encyclopedias, but is mentioned several times in the literature. Apparently he was quite funny, although nothing he said to achieve this reputation survives in a form which is worthy of being quoted. In July, 1894, he succeeded in getting on the nerves of the Philadelphia pitcher sufficiently that the Philadelphia fans rushed the field and broke his cheekbone. The next day the Philadelphia team had extra police on hand to protect the players,

but Tucker was beaten up again on the way back to his hotel.

94 ◆ Jim Gentile
(1957–1966, 936 G, 179 549 .260)
A good defensive first baseman, and a successful power hitter for a few years. Gentile left half of his home runs in the minor league operation of the Brooklyn/LA Dodgers. Gentile hit 34 homers, drove in 102 runs in the minors in 1953, then had 34 and 126, 28 and 109, 40 and 115 . . . he regularly led his league in home runs and RBI. There were three reasons for this:

1. Gil Hodges.
2. A major league team, at that time, could hold a player in the minor leagues for eight years before they let him go.
3. Gentile had a huge, long, violent, sweeping swing, and it was commonly said at the time that he was just a minor league power hitter, that major league pitchers would carve him up, because of his uncontrolled swing.

This is a fallacy. Major league baseball is exactly the same game as minor league baseball, except that it has more good players. If a man hits in the minors, he will hit in the majors. Always. Nonetheless, the fallacy is widely believed now and was universally believed then, and it diminished other team's interest in trying to make a trade for Gentile, who in truth was probably as good a hitter as Hodges was for several years.

He failed brief trials with the Dodgers in 1957 and in 1958. In 1960, when he had a shot to break through with the Orioles, he had an absolutely awful spring training. Paul Richards liked his glove work, however, and was looking for power, so he put him in the lineup as a platoon player. Gentile for two years was the deadliest clutch hitter in baseball.

He was plagued by his own feverish desire and vile temper, at worst cavalier in comparison to the standard of professional deportment.—M.G. Kram, *Baseball Digest*, July 1979

"I guess I was lazy," Gentile told Kram. At this time Gentile was working as a muffler salesman in Tempe, Arizona. "I was a red-ass when I played [but] not everybody is a Brooks Robinson."

95 ◆ Wes Parker
(1964–1972, 1288 G, 64 470 .267)
An elegant first baseman whose best years were played in a park and league where George Sisler would have had a hard time hitting .280. After the league went back to normal (1969) he had one great year, then had some minor injuries, and retired to pursue his acting career. Parker had movie-star looks and played in Los Angeles, for which reason he can still be seen in old episodes of 1960s sitcoms. His acting career floundered after he left baseball.

96 ◆ Pete O'Brien
(1982–1993, 1567 G, 169 736 .261)
Did everything well, but nothing spectacularly well, and was only a real good player for about four–five years.

97 ◆ Don Mincher
(1960–1972, 1400 G, 200 643 .249)
Mincher was a fine platoon player from 1962 through 1965. In those four years he batted only 979 times, but hit 71 homers and drove in 192 runs—44 homers, 118 RBI per 600 at bats. He had a secondary average in those years of .417.

Mincher is a key figure in Bouton's *Ball Four*. Bouton was suspicious of him at first because he had a thick Alabama accent which made him sound stupid to a Yankee. But he turned out, in Bouton's eyes, to be a solid man and a good guy.

Since platooning began there have been more high-level platoon combinations at first base than at any other position. In the 1925 World Series the Washington Senators platooned Joe Judge at first base (.314, 68 RBI) with Joe Harris (.323, 59 more RBI), while the National League champion Pirates platooned George Grantham (.326) with Stuffy McInnis (.368). The 1961–62 Giants platooned Hall of Famers Willie McCovey and Orlando Cepeda, sending Cepeda to the outfield when McCovey played first. The 1987 Toronto Blue Jays platooned Fred McGriff (20 homers) with Cecil Fielder (14 more); Willie Upshaw actually played first base, with Fielder and McGriff working mostly as the Designated Hitters, but that's a lot of talent piled up at first base, anyway. Over a four-year period, I don't know that any platoon player was ever more effective than Mincher was from '62 through '65.

98 ◆ Deron Johnson
(1960–1976, 1765 G, 245 923 .244)
Deron Johnson, wrote Jim Murray in 1965, "had a high school education, but didn't let it interfere seriously with his pass-catching or home run hitting . . . He would split an infinitive if he knew what one was. Up until this year, the only thing he led the league in was silence . . . There was no question of college football for Deron. Fifty colleges wanted him but 1,000 professors didn't."

99 ◆ Joe Pepitone
(1962–1973, 1397 G, 219 721 .258)
> If it weren't for Joe Pepitone, my baseball career probably would have been shorter by many weeks. He kept taking the pressure off me. Every time I got into trouble, there was Peppy, getting into worse trouble.—Jim Bouton, *I'm Glad You Didn't Take it Personally*, Dell, 1971

Joe was mostly bald by the time he was thirty, and, being insecure and blessed with bad judgment, began wearing a wig the size of a grizzly bear. He wrote an autobiography, *Joe, You Coulda Made Us Proud,* with Berry Stainback (Playboy Press, 1975). It's a very 1970s book; it deals at great length with Joe's sex life, and drags the baseball career in now and then to keep the chronology straight.

It's actually a rather good book, and, in all honesty, a much more serious book than the typical baseball biography. Although Pepitone had a decent career, the book is not a record of his successes, but an examination of his failures.

Pepitone was raised by an abusive, half-crazy father. He tells a story about one time, as a kid, when he got a new bike. He took it out around the neighborhood, but his father told him to be home by six o'clock. He got home at 6:03. His father cussed him out, beat him, and, incredibly enough, smashed the new bicycle to pieces.

Pepitone never blames his father for his failures; he's just telling the story of his life. Joe stayed out late too many nights and showed up hung over too many times, mostly because he could not manage his obsession with sex. He wasn't organized enough or mature enough to build a support system—a stable relationship with a woman, friends he could count on, business ventures that made sense, even a career in baseball that didn't depend on his driving in runs. He played his career on a long, slow slide toward prison. But a lot of people have failures; a lot of people are obsessed with meaningless sexual relationships. Not too many people write honestly about it.

100 ◆ Ripper Collins
(1931–1941, 1084 G, 135 659 .296)

The Chicago Cubs were "artists in locating and dealing for major-league players who had established reputations elsewhere. Such a player was Rip Collins . . . while he lasted he was the life of the party at all times."–Warren Brown, *The Chicago Cubs,* Putnam, 1946

G.H. Fleming says in *The Dizziest Season* that Collins "gained his nickname from the way in which he 'ripped' the ball when batting." I doubt it. Collins was probably called "Ripper" after the pitcher of the previous generation, Rip Collins, who was described by Ty Cobb as a "night-walker," meaning that he couldn't keep curfew. The nickname "Ripper" meant that he was a hell-raiser. He had a Jim Gentile-type career—was trapped in the minors for a long time, was one of the best players in baseball in 1934, but had only three-four seasons of any real value.

"Rickey always accused me of being the ringleader," Collins said, "I never could understand why he picked on me—unless it could have been because there was considerable truth in the allegations. Yet I'll wager that no ball club ever got more fun out of playing than we did."–Rob Rains, *The St. Louis Cardinals* (St. Martin's, 1992)

101. Dots Miller, 102. Willie Montanez, 103. Glenn Davis, 104. Dick Hoblitzell, 105. Willie Upshaw, 106. Long John Reilly, 107. Joe Start, 108. Donn Clendennon, 109. John Morrill, 110. Dave Magadan, 111. Eddie Waitkus, 112. Ed Kranepool, 113. Joe Cunningham, 114. Zeke Bonura, 115. Joe Harris, 116. Leon Durham, 117. Dave Orr, 118. Babe Young, 119. Mike Epstein, 120. Earl Sheely, 121. Dick Stuart, 122. John Milner, 123. Jim Spencer, 124. Nate Colbert, 125. Chick Gandil

FIRST BASE

Rank	Player Name	Career WS	Top 3	Top 5	Per 162
1.	Lou Gehrig	489	44, 42, 41	193	36.61
2.	Jimmie Foxx	435	41, 40, 34	173	30.41
3.	Mark McGwire	335	41, 30, 30	148	30.54
4.	Jeff Bagwell	287	41, 37, 32	163	31.50
5.	Eddie Murray	437	33, 31, 31	142	23.40
6.	Johnny Mize	338	34, 33, 33	154	29.06
7.	Harmon Killebrew	371	38, 34, 33	147	24.68
8.	Hank Greenberg	267	34, 33, 31	135	31.03
9.	Willie McCovey	408	39, 34, 34	164	25.54
10.	Frank Thomas	309	39, 36, 33	152	32.72
11.	Cap Anson	381	30, 29, 24	123	27.12
12.	Don Mattingly	263	34, 32, 29	146	23.87
13.	Tony Perez	349	33, 32, 31	144	20.36
14.	Will Clark	330	44, 37, 34	168	27.05
15.	Dick Allen	342	41, 40, 35	170	31.68
16.	Keith Hernandez	311	33, 29, 29	136	24.13
17.	Orlando Cepeda	310	34, 30, 29	130	23.64
18.	Dan Brouthers	355	34, 31, 29	138	34.38
19.	Rafael Palmeiro	308	31, 31, 30	125	23.78
20.	Norm Cash	315	42, 27, 24	130	24.43
21.	Fred McGriff	294	30, 27, 26	132	23.18
22.	Roger Connor	363	36, 32, 30	145	29.45
23.	Mickey Vernon	296	33, 29, 24	112	19.91
24.	George Sisler	292	33, 29, 29	135	23.02
25.	Frank Chance	237	35, 31, 29	143	29.86
26.	Bill Terry	278	32, 32, 29	142	26.17
27.	Boog Powell	282	31, 29, 27	116	22.37
28.	Cecil Cooper	241	29, 27, 25	127	20.59
29.	Dolph Camilli	224	29, 28, 28	135	24.35
30.	Gil Hodges	263	29, 26, 25	129	20.57
31.	Steve Garvey	279	27, 26, 25	124	19.38
32.	Mark Grace	268	27, 25, 25	112	22.73
33.	Bob Watson	236	31, 28, 26	123	20.87
34.	Ted Kluszewski	203	33, 25, 24	125	19.14
35.	Jack Fournier	231	34, 29, 28	127	24.46
36.	Jim Bottomley	258	30, 27, 26	127	20.99
37.	Wally Joyner	253	25, 22, 22	97	20.70

Rank	Player Name	Career WS	Top 3	Top 5	Per 162
38.	Hal Trosky	195	28, 27, 25	120	23.45
39.	Bill White	209	27, 26, 24	121	20.24
40.	Kent Hrbek	230	25, 24, 19	104	21.33
41.	Roy Sievers	231	32, 26, 23	115	19.83
42.	Andres Galarraga	225	27, 25, 25	99	19.03
43.	Joe Adcock	236	25, 22, 22	88	19.52
44.	Joe Judge	278	22, 20, 19	95	20.74
45.	Mike Hargrove	212	25, 25, 24	110	20.61
46.	Elbie Fletcher	185	28, 26, 26	118	21.18
47.	Lee May	215	26, 24, 24	108	16.82
48.	Ed Konetchy	287	27, 27, 26	118	22.30
49.	John Mayberry	199	33, 31, 27	120	19.90
50.	Andre Thornton	186	25, 23, 21	94	19.25
51.	Mo Vaughn	186	29, 25, 24	119	22.39
52.	Jake Beckley	318	23, 21, 21	97	21.59
53.	John Olerud	220	37, 34, 26	118	22.92
54.	Frank McCormick	202	29, 27, 25	112	21.33
55.	Cecil Fielder	160	29, 26, 19	103	17.63
56.	Rudy York	214	27, 26, 26	105	21.63
57.	George Scott	216	24, 23, 23	106	17.20
58.	Ron Fairly	269	26, 21, 21	102	17.85
59.	Phil Cavaretta	237	30, 25, 25	114	18.91
60.	Harry Davis	238	31, 26, 21	117	21.60
61.	Jake Daubert	263	27, 24, 21	101	21.15
62.	Ferris Fain	161	28, 21, 19	104	22.66
63.	Norm Siebern	171	27, 23, 21	109	19.67
64.	Joe Kuhel	243	26, 25, 21	85	18.71
65.	George Kelly	193	26, 24, 22	112	19.28
66.	Bill Buckner	226	21, 21, 20	81	14.55
67.	Chris Chambliss	221	21, 21, 19	94	16.46
68.	Stuffy McInnis	227	26, 24, 21	102	17.28
69.	Henry Larkin	177	29, 23, 19	107	24.22
70.	Fred Tenney	249	25, 25, 22	99	20.23
71.	Earl Torgeson	184	32, 20, 18	87	17.87
72.	John Kruk	156	25, 25, 24	103	21.06
73.	Gus Suhr	170	25, 21, 20	100	19.19
74.	Alvin Davis	153	27, 26, 22	100	20.55

(continued)

Rank	Player Name	Career WS	Top 3	Top 5	Per 162
75.	Bill Skowron	183	24, 21, 17	85	17.88
76.	Hal Chase	231	23, 22, 21	95	19.52
77.	Lu Blue	198	27, 23, 22	89	19.86
78.	Dan Driessen	179	21, 19, 18	91	16.74
79.	George H Burns	200	24, 24, 21	88	17.36
80.	Charlie Hickman	155	23, 21, 21	101	23.23
81.	Vic Power	152	26, 22, 19	89	15.13
82.	George McQuinn	173	24, 20, 18	87	18.08
83.	Wally Pipp	203	22, 20, 18	87	17.57
84.	Fred Merkle	191	22, 22, 20	93	18.89
85.	Charlie Grimm	198	23, 21, 17	77	14.81
86.	Eddie Robinson	127	25, 19, 18	92	15.65
87.	Jack Doyle	176	19, 18, 17	79	18.23
88.	Fred Luderus	160	26, 20, 20	97	19.26
89.	Bruce Bochte	159	19, 19, 17	79	16.75
90.	Whitey Lockman	156	23, 23, 19	96	15.17
91.	Jason Thompson	165	27, 22, 19	92	18.85
92.	Dan McGann	183	24, 22, 21	88	20.64
93.	Tommy Tucker	176	30, 20, 17	96	16.90
94.	Jim Gentile	125	32, 21, 20	108	21.63
95.	Wes Parker	148	29, 20, 18	92	18.61
96.	Pete O'Brien	141	24, 19, 18	91	14.58
97.	Don Mincher	162	28, 19, 18	93	18.75
98.	Deron Johnson	146	23, 21, 19	70	13.40
99.	Joe Pepitone	139	18, 17, 15	75	16.12
100.	Ripper Collins	147	32, 28, 19	109	21.97

Categories of this record are Career Win Shares, Win Shares in the player's three best seasons, Win Shares total over the player's five best consecutive seasons, and career Win shares per 162 games played. For example, Lou Gehrig had 489 Career Win Shares, including 44, 42 and 41 in his three best seasons (1927, 1928, and 1934). He had 193 Win Shares in a five-year period, (1927–1931) and averaged 36.61 Win Shares per 162 games played over the course of his career.

SECOND BASE

1 ◆ Joe Morgan

(1963–1984, 2649 G, 268 1133 .271)

Who is the best percentage player in the history of baseball? Whitey Herzog once said that he liked fast players because speed was the only thing in baseball that could be used both on offense and defense. Mulling this over, I realized that there were "speed indicators" all over a player's batting, baserunning, and fielding records, and that, if one studied the record with that object, one could assess any player's running speed by distilling the pure speed from it's impure measures—triples, stolen bases, GIDP, defensive range, and runs scored as a percentage of times on base.

But re-thinking the issue a year or two later, I realized that Herzog's statement is not literally true; speed is *not* the only thing which is useful both on offense and defense. A player has a second attribute which is useful either on offense or on defense: intelligence. In the same way that we can find a player's speed, I wondered, could we figure his "Baseball IQ" by looking at all of the things in a player's record that might indicate intelligence?

The problem with this theory is that intelligence is so generalized that it might be reflected *everywhere* in the player's record, rather than *anywhere;* anything a player does well might be expanded by intelligence or limited by stupidity. One could be driven toward the conclusion that the most intelligent players are the best players, and the dumbest players the worst players—a conclusion which is only half true, and useless when it happens to be correct.

I decided (a) to call the resulting category "Percentage Player Index," rather than "Baseball IQ," and (b) to use four indicators of how good a percentage player someone is.

The four indicators that make up percentage player index are:

1. The player's fielding percentage, compared to period norms for his era and his position (30%).

2. The player's stolen base percentage (30%).

3. The player's strikeout to walk ratio (30%).

4. The player's walk frequency in absolute terms, rather than compared to strikeouts (10%).

The best percentage player in baseball history, I concluded, was Joe Morgan:

- Joe Morgan had a career fielding percentage of .981, as opposed to a norm for second baseman of his time of .977; I score that at .587 on the 30-percent scale.
- Morgan stole 689 bases in his career, with only 162 times caught stealing, one of the best stolen base percentages in baseball history. I score this at .801 on that 30-percent scale.
- Morgan drew 1,865 walks in his career, with 1,015 strikeouts; I score that at .612 on that 30-percent scale.
- Morgan's rate of walks per plate appearance is the sixteenth-best in baseball history, 1,865 walks with 9,277 at bats. I score that at .768 on the 10-percent scale.

Combining these factors, Morgan's overall rating as a percentage player is .677, the highest in baseball history for any player for whom complete data is available.

One problem here is that the National League didn't record caught stealing until 1951, so a lot of players (most players, in fact) are excluded from consideration. Eddie Collins might well have been as good a percentage player as Morgan, but we can't know because we don't have caught stealing for about half of his career, and we don't even have strikeouts for the first seven years of his career. Anyway, the best percentage players in baseball history, excluding those for whom complete data is not available:

1.	Joe Morgan	.677
2.	Maxie Bishop	.669
3.	Junior Gilliam	.668
4.	Ozzie Smith	.667
5.	Lou Boudreau	.663
6.	Tim Raines	.645
7.	Lu Blue	.643
8.	Willie Kamm	.637
9.	Earle Combs	.634
10.	Barney McCoskey	.630
11.	Tony Gwynn	.629
12.	Joe DiMaggio	.628
13.	Bill Dickey	.627
14.	Buddy Myer	.624
15.	Luke Appling	.622

You can make an All-Star team out of that, by the way; despite the concentration of middle infielders at the top of the list, by the fifteenth spot we've covered all the positions on the all-smart team: C—Bill Dickey, 1B—Lu Blue, 2B—Joe Morgan, 3B—Willie Kamm (or Junior Gilliam), SS—Ozzie Smith, LF—Tim Raines, CF—Earle Combs, RF—Tony Gwynn. One could independently document that almost all of these men were smart players, with no reference to the statistics.

I'll run the antonym list (the poorest percentage players) in an appropriate comment (Dave Kingman). A few other players who were clearly outstanding percentage players, but are excluded from the list because of missing data: Terry Turner, Augie Galan, Eddie Stanky, Hans Lobert, Jackie Robinson, Jack Barry, Frankie Frisch, Home Run Baker, Harry Hooper, Stan Musial, Heinie Groh, Roger Bresnahan, Riggs Stephenson, Richie Ashburn, Johnnie Evers, Honus Wagner, Stuffy McInnis, Muddy Ruel, Ray Schalk, John McGraw, and Johnny Kling . . .

In April 2000, Major League Baseball aired a promotional spot in which Peter Gammons, pitching, struck out Harold Reynolds. Broadcasting on ESPN on April 19, Joe Morgan was frothing at the mouth about this commercial. "Harold Reynolds was a major league baseball player," Morgan said over and over . . . I may be paraphrasing a little, because my VCR wasn't running. "Harold Reynolds was an all-star.

Peter Gammons does not strike him out. It's just wrong, and I'm not going to keep quiet about it. It's wrong. Peter Gammons does not strike out Harold Reynolds."

Dear Joe:

Does the phrase "Get over yourself" mean anything to you? This is not to deny that you were a major league player, and even that you were a better player than Harold Reynolds, who I suppose must have been an All-Star sometime; what the hell, Dave Chalk started two All-Star games. This is not to deny that you were a brilliant player, Joe, but you are becoming a self-important little prig. Grow up, you little weenie. People make fun of one another; this is called friendship. This is life; only self-important twits take offense at that kind of thing. Jeez, man, get a life. Preferably not on television.

Your friend, Bill James

2 ◆ Eddie Collins
(1906–1930, 2826 G, 47 1300 .333)

Under Kid Gleason's distinctive method of managing those oddly assorted personalities, Collins was given more authority than is usually a field captain's portion. This was resented by the anti-Collins faction, which also brooded over the fact that he was the highest paid performer on the club.—Warren Brown, *The Chicago White Sox*

In the rating system that I used here, the top three second basemen (Morgan, Collins, and Hornsby) rank almost even with one another, and far, far ahead of any other second baseman in history. These ratings are based (in this case) 100% on the statistical record, with no adjustment for Hornsby based on his personality or anything of the sort. Eddie Collins rates ahead of Hornsby not because I dislike Hornsby, but because Collins has better numbers. I also dislike Hornsby, but that's incidental; Collins has better numbers. The ranking numbers I have, with the subjective element being even for all

three players, are 243 for Morgan, 241 for Collins, 239 for Hornsby. No other second baseman is higher than 209.

The claim that Eddie Collins has better numbers than Rogers Hornsby is, I would expect, surprising to most people, so let me explain why this is true as best I can, without burying you in decimal points. Rogers Hornsby's best season, 1922, is better than any season of Eddie Collins—not *a lot* better, but a little better. Hornsby in 1922 hit .401 with 250 hits including 42 homers, driving in 152 runs. Collins' best season, taking everything into account, did not have quite the same impact as that monster season, which was the best season ever by a major league second baseman.

However, Collins best season (1909) and his second best (1914) are both better than any other season in Hornsby's career, in my opinion. In addition, Collins had *more* seasons which are at or near the level of his best years.

Why is this true? Hornsby's numbers, without looking at the context, are better. Eddie Collins in 1909 created 118 runs; Hornsby in 1929 hit .380 with 39 homers, creating 178 runs. But the relationship between 1909 baseball and 1929 baseball is like the relationship between 1960s baseball and 1990s baseball. Many, many hitters in the 1990s have better numbers than any hitter posted during the 1960s, not because the players have gotten better, but because the conditions of the game have swung in the hitter's favor. Same thing then: many hitters from 1929 have better numbers than any hitter from 1909. This doesn't prove that they were all better hitters.

In the American League in 1909, when Eddie Collins created 118 runs, the average team scored 3.44 runs per game. Collins, then, created all the runs that would normally be scored by a team in 34 games—actually, 34.3.

In the National League in 1929, when Rogers Hornsby created 178 runs, the average team scored 5.36 runs per game. Hornsby's offense, then, represents all the runs that would normally be scored by a team in 33 games—actually, 33.2.

In context, who is the better hitter? Who had more impact on the games that he was playing? It's close, but Collins did.

Looking at the 1914 season, same thing; Collins created 128 runs (most in the American League) in a league where the average team scored 3.66 runs per game. Collins, then, created all of the offense that would normally be scored by a team in 35 games (actually, 34.97).

Hornsby in 1921 (which matches 1929 as his second-greatest season) created 152 runs, in a league in which the average team scored 4.59 runs per game. Hornsby's 1921 season thus represents all the runs a team would normally be scored in 33 games (actually, 33.1).

The Park Factors for the two players in the seasons I am comparing are almost the same—.96 for Collins in 1909, also .96 for Hornsby in 1929, .91 for Collins in 1914, .88 for Hornsby in 1921. Both of them worked in pitcher's parks in the seasons under scrutiny, so that doesn't do anything to change the comparison between them.

The other factors that I would register on Collins' behalf are things that I would suppose most people would generally accept: defense and consistency. The Win Shares system does show Collins to be a better defensive second baseman than Hornsby. We have Collins with 7.7 Win Shares for his defense in 1909, 5.8 in 1914, and Hornsby with 6.2 Win Shares for defense in 1929, 5.1 in 1921. Thus, we give Collins an edge of about one Win Share per season (about three runs per season) for his defense. Most people who aren't emotional about it would agree, I suspect, that Collins was a better defensive player than Hornsby, and that this is a reasonable and modest advantage for Collins.

The Win Shares system actually does not see Hornsby as a terrible defensive second

baseman. The Win Shares system sees Hornsby as a more or less average defensive second baseman—but also as the worst defensive second baseman who had a long career at the position. There are 71 second basemen in baseball history who played an estimated 10,000 innings or more at second base. Among those 71 players, Hornsby rates dead last in terms of Win Shares per defensive inning.

But actually, Hornsby's defensive performance isn't bad; in fact, we have him as deserving of the National League Gold Glove in 1921 and in 1929, granted that he "deserves" those two Gold Gloves mostly by default, and doesn't rank as the number one second baseman in any other season. It's just that normally, a player never has a long career at second base unless he is a good defensive second baseman. If you compare Hornsby to the men who played 1,000, 2,000, 3,000 innings at the position, there are lots of guys who are far worse than he was. But Hornsby was such a great hitter that he was an exception to the rule—the rule that a player can't have a long career at second base unless he is a good defensive second baseman.

The other statement in Collins' support—that he had more seasons which are near the level of his best seasons—is obvious. Consideration of external factors—leadership, performance of the team, etc.—certainly would not argue that we should re-consider the idea that Collins might have been the better player. Over the course of his career, Collins' teams had far, far better won-lost records than Hornsby's teams. Collins was a regular on six teams that went to the World Series (winning four of them), and played on seven other teams that won 90 or more games. Hornsby went to the World Series twice, and played on three other teams that won 90 or more games, but two of those were years in which Hornsby was injured and missed almost the entire season. Collins played on only three bad teams, and no team that lost more than 92 games; Hornsby played on several teams that were absolutely terrible. See also Tris Speaker (CF, #4).

To this point, I have been writing about Eddie Collins, as contrasted with Rogers Hornsby, rather than about Eddie Collins. Collins joined the Athletics as a result of Andy Coakley's honeymoon. Late in the 1906 season, Andy Coakley asked Connie Mack for a few days off to get married. Mack said OK, the pennant race being about over and Coakley not being a critical player anyway, so Coakley and his bride took off for a few days in Vermont.

Coakley decided to take in a baseball game in Montpelier, where he happened to see the 19-year-old Eddie Collins, playing in a semi-pro game. Collins was a student at Columbia, captain of the Columbia baseball team, and quarterback of the Columbia football team. He was playing under the name of "Eddie Sullivan" in the summer to protect his amateur status, a common practice at the time. (Miller Huggins, for example, played professional baseball under the name "Proctor" while attending college.) Coakley raved about Collins to Connie Mack, and Mack arranged for "Eddie Sullivan" to make a road trip with the A's late in the season.

Mack was impressed. Somebody saw him in a major league uniform, however, and "Eddie Sullivan" was outed as a professional, ending his college athletic career. He finished his education in 1908, and joined the A's full time. He played shortstop for a month, spent a couple of weeks in the outfield, and then settled in as the A's second baseman.

Within two years, he rivaled Nap Lajoie and Johnny Evers as the best second basemen in baseball. A few elements of Collins' career are so well known as to defy us to summarize them quickly enough: Collins became a member of Connie Mack's "$100,000 Infield," a team which dominated baseball from 1910 through 1914 as the Reds did in the mid-seventies, as the

Yankees did in the late 1990s. In 1914 a rival league was launched, the Federal League. Owners in this league targeted the Philadelphia Athletics, driving salaries beyond what Mack could afford to match. Mack sold off the stars of his team, selling Collins and a couple of others to the Chicago White Sox.

The White Sox became one of the better teams in baseball, winning the World Series in 1917 and the American League in 1919. But whereas Connie Mack's A's were a close-knit unit with a family atmosphere, the White Sox were racked with tension. Connie Mack believed strongly in intelligence as a key factor in the success of a team, and preferred to build his team around gentlemen, as much as possible. The White Sox were strictly a bottom-line operation. Making the situation worse, salaries went into a free-fall when the Federal League collapsed, and White Sox owner Charles Comiskey took advantage of the situation, paying no player a dollar more than he absolutely had to.

The White Sox divided into two factions: a gentlemen's faction led by Collins and Ray Schalk, and a bitter, roughneck faction led by Chick Gandil. The two factions hated each other. In 1919 the roughneck faction was paid off by gamblers to lose the World Series, carrying a couple of borderline players with them to their damnation. The fix was discovered in September, 1920, just as the team was on the verge of winning their third American League pennant in four years.

Collins remained with the White Sox for five years thereafter, and managed them the last two of those seasons. He was quite successful as a manager, a point which has been totally overlooked in all accounts that I have found, many of which state inaccurately that he managed the White Sox when they were down and out. The White Sox, who had finished seventh in 1923 and dead last in 1924, rose under Collins to 79-75 in 1925 (their best season since 1920) and to 81-72 in 1926. They would not do as well again for ten years. For some reason, however, the White Sox were not satisfied with the progress, and released Collins—still a fine player—after the 1926 season. He signed with Philadelphia, rejoining Connie Mack as Mack was in the process of sanding and varnishing his second great team.

Collins was small, strong, quick, agile, extremely competitive, and extremely smart. He was a nervous, edgy man, like Johnny Evers, couldn't sit still. On the baseball field, he was aggressive to the point of being arrogant. Off the field, he was modest to the point of being shy.

Collins is described by various sources as the best bunter in the history of baseball, the best hit-and-run man in the history of baseball, the best defensive second baseman in the history of baseball, the best sign-stealer who ever lived, and the greatest World Series star who ever lived. Kid Gleason, who managed Collins on the White Sox, said that Collins was the greatest team player who ever lived. Connie Mack said that Collins was the greatest team player who ever lived. Billy Evans, who was an umpire for many years while Collins was on the field, later a General Manager, said that Collins was the quickest thinker that he ever saw. It seems unlikely that all of these claims could be true.

Collins was, in a less dramatic way, as competitive as Ty Cobb. In 1938 the A's had an old-timers match between their 1910–1914 World Champions and their 1929–1931 team. Lefty Grove, being Lefty Grove, threw a fastball at Collins' chin. Collins by this time was 52, but had been retired only a few years, and was still in shape. He got up, screamed at Grove, and seemed for a moment to be in danger of charging the mound . . .

Connie Mack, picking his all-time all-star team in 1950, wrote that Collins *was* "the greatest second baseman who ever lived. His fighting spirit was contagious . . . Eddie would be my team captain." Eddie, of course, *was* his team captain, not once but twice; perhaps more impartial is the evaluation of John McGraw. McGraw, in *My Thirty Years in Baseball* (Boni and Liveright, 1923) wrote that "I doubt if anybody will dispute my selection of Eddie Collins as the greatest second baseman of all time and, therefore, entitled to a place on the All-American Team of All Time. At any rate, there is no doubt in my mind about it. In picking him I have been fully mindful of the greatness of such men as Napoleon Lajoie. It's pretty hard to select any team and leave Lajoie off. Still, Eddie Collins, in my opinion, is entitled to the honor.

"There is nothing that Collins does not know about playing that important position . . . as a pivot man on a double play, I don't remember ever having seen his equal. As an all around man he is superb. Not only does he play the game, but he thinks it. Rare are the occasions when Collins does not anticipate the play. To cross him is almost impossible. And he is just as forceful on the offensive as on the defensive.

"His mental attitude is an inspiration to his fellow players."

Gordon Mackay, in the 1924 *Reach Guide*, argued that Collins "with seventeen years' experience as a big leaguer, is still the best pivot man in the major leagues on a double play. He can still cover as much ground in as faultless style as anybody whom we have watched . . . Rogers Hornsby may have ousted Eddie from his place as the best second baseman in the business. But had we the say we would not swap Edward for Hornsby or Frankie Frisch."

"I studied Eddie Collins closely from the time I joined Washington," wrote Bucky Harris in *Playing the Game* (Frederick A. Stokes Company, 1925). "He was the greatest second baseman I had ever seen. Plays which were difficult for even a finished infielder, were made to appear easy. I never saw his equal in tagging runners. I tried to copy his style in going after short flies, getting the ball off and in other ways. I never could learn to ride a runner to the bag as he did. A second baseman could watch him every day in the season and learn something.

"Close study of Collins' style helped teach me the value of concentration. I learned that it was necessary to keep mentally as well as physically alert; to figure out the immediate play and what it might develop. Collins knew the batting strength and weakness of the older players in the league. He knew their tricks on the bases. He studied the newcomers until he knew as much about them. I could see that when he was in the game he never thought about anything else. Because he was so intent upon his business he made few mistakes. He was rightly called the king of the second basemen."

One last point ... Eddie Collins has something in common with Hank Aaron. Fresco Thompson had a famous line about Collins. "Eddie Collins was a quick thinker, eh? Well, I'd like to see him outthink the grounders we get these days with the lively ball." But actually, Collins played for eleven years after the lively ball was introduced, 1920 to 1930. He was 33 years old when the lively ball era began—yet he hit .346 in more than 1100 games with the hot baseballs.

What would Eddie Collins career average have been had he started his career ten years later? About the same as Hornsby's—about .358. Collins hit .325 in the dead ball era, .346 with the lively ball. Hornsby, who was nine years younger, hit .310 in the dead ball era, but .374 with the lively ball.

What Collins has in common with Aaron is that both players' records have the illusion of unnatural consistency. Their true consistency is emphasized by the fact that, as they aged,

the circumstances in which they played swung gradually in their favor. Aaron at age 32 moved from a poor home run park to a great home run park, boosting his home run totals just as they were beginning to decline, and then received a second boost three years later, when the mound was lowered and other actions were taken to prevent Bob Gibson from pitching 32 shutouts a year. Neither Collins nor Aaron *actually* became a better player as he aged; Aaron's best five-year period in terms of true value was 1959–1963 (ages 25 to 29), and Collins' was 1911–1915 (ages 24 to 28). But their numbers got better as they aged, because the conditions in which they played became more favorable.

3 ◆ Rogers Hornsby
(1915–1937, 2259 G, 301 1584 .358)
The greatest seasons ever by a second baseman:

1. Rogers Hornsby	1922
2. Nap Lajoie	1910
3. Joe Morgan	1975
4. Eddie Collins	1909
5. Eddie Collins	1914
6. Nap Lajoie	1901
7. Rogers Hornsby	1929
8. Rogers Hornsby	1921
9. Joe Morgan	1973
10. Nap Lajoie	1904

The National League first instituted an official Most Valuable Player Award in 1924. Rogers Hornsby hit .424, but the award went to Dazzy Vance, who, in all fairness, did have an incredible season, going 28-6 and striking out three times as many hitters as any other pitcher in the league, save one. This became a controversial selection, much like the 1947 American League Award, when it was learned that one voter, Jack Ryder of Cincinnati, had left Hornsby off his ten-man ballot. Hornsby, said

Ryder, had hit .424 not for his team but for himself, and his performance had failed to lift the Cardinals above 65 wins.

This logic outraged the St. Louis fans, and a round of name-calling followed, during which, as often happens, a key fact was overlooked. Even if Ryder had voted for Hornsby, even if he had listed him first, Vance would still have won the Award . . .

Rogers Hornsby's mother died October 2, 1926, which was the off day between the end of the 1926 season and the beginning of the 1926 World Series. Hornsby remained with the team, electing not to attend his mother's funeral. "Some thought it was heartless, lacking in the finer sentiments," wrote Fred Lieb. "But it was just like Rogers Hornsby . . ."

"He was a very cold man," said Billy Herman in *Wrigleyville.* "I broke in with the Cubs under Hornsby in 1931. He ignored me completely, and I figured it was because I was a rookie. But then I realized he ignored everybody."

When Bill Veeck fired Rogers Hornsby in 1952, Roy Stockton wrote in defense of Hornsby that Rogers "wanted to win so badly that he was a sourpuss about it." Veeck replied that saying that Hornsby was a sourpuss was like saying that Attila the Hun needed to work on his table manners. Hornsby then moved on to Cincinnati, where, according to Earl Lawson *(Cincinnati Seasons),* the players designated Grady Hatton to go to the front office and complain about the fact that Hornsby insisted on urinating in the showers, even after being asked not to.

If a contest is ever held to determine the biggest horse's ass in baseball history, there are really only seven men, four of them players, who could hope to compete at that level. The four players are Hornsby, Ty Cobb, Dick Allen, and Hal Chase. I think I might choose Hornsby. My favorite Hornsby story: in 1925 Hornsby was on the field, arguing loudly with Art Fletcher, when all of sudden, without warning,

he punched Fletcher in the face. Later, a reporter asked him why he had hit Fletcher.

"Well," replied Hornsby very seriously, "I wasn't making any progress trying to talk to him."

4 ◆ Jackie Robinson
(1947–1956, 1382 G, 137 734 .311)
See comment on Bill Mazeroski (29).

5 ◆ Craig Biggio
(1988–2000, 1800 G, 160 741 .291)
Craig Biggio in 1997 was hit by 34 pitches, while grounding into zero double plays. Both of these figures were historic. He was the fifth player ever to play a full season without grounding into a double play, and missed the major league record for most plate appearances without grounding into a double play by only four. The 34 HBP was the highest total in the National League in 26 years, the second-highest of the twentieth century.

I have always linked these two stats together, long before Biggio, as "little stats." There are a half-dozen batting stats which get left out of *USA Today,* and left off baseball cards, because they're not *generally* significant. The stats include sacrifice hits, sac flies, and intentional walks, but GIDP and hit batsmen are the most important of the group, the two which are most likely to change the way a player should be evaluated.

I have long wanted to make up a stat to summarize the impact of these categories, a "Little Stat Summary," if you will. I have never actually created the formula, because I have already polluted the sport with quite a number of statistical inventions, and I'm afraid of slipping to a lower rung of the inferno if I make up any more. No, seriously, the reason I've never written such a formula is that it's not clear what we would be measuring. For a statistic to have value, it has to be meaningful with reference to something other than its own formula.

Anyway, Biggio has the best "little stats" of any player in baseball history, this being one of the reasons that he has been tremendously underrated. If you compare him to, let's say, Jim Rice in 1984, Biggio has a hidden advantage of 69 extra times on base, since he was hit by pitches 33 more times (34 to 1), and beat the throw to first on a double play attempt 36 more times (0 to 36). Those little stats that get left out of *USA Today*, in this comparison, have an impact roughly equivalent to 100 points of batting average.

6 ◆ Nap Lajoie
(1896–1916, 2480 G, 82 1599 .338)

> Lajoie has no particular style of batting. All curves look alike to him. High or low, in or out, they are all the same to him. This does not mean to imply that big 'Larry' is a chance hitter, and will go after anything. On the contrary, he wants a ball near enough to the plate to allow him to meet it fairly with the bat. He has a good eye for a ball, and seldom is caught 'biting' at wild ones.
>
> Lajoie's success as a batsman lies in the fact that he does not pull his bat back when the ball is delivered, but always swings it in front of him and is ever ready to meet the ball full on the nose. His great strength enables him to drive the leather before him with tremendous force, and many an infielder has been carried off his feet trying to stop the progress of one of "Larry's" line hits.—1905 *Reach Guide*

For sixty years after he retired in 1916, so far as I know, no one ever suggested that Larry Lajoie was a towering defensive figure. Harry Grayson in his 1944 classic *They Played The Game* wrote several paragraphs about Lajoie's batting style (very interesting paragraphs, by the way), but made absolutely no claim for Lajoie's excellence as a fielder. Tom Meany's 1953 standard *Baseball's Greatest Players* gave great weight to Lajoie's "grace," but its only comment about Lajoie in the field was that "he was fluent and unhurried as a second baseman, with an insouciance belying the carefully calculated movements of his big frame." Lajoie was regarded, like Charlie Gehringer, Ryne Sandberg, or Billy Herman, as an exceptional hitter and a capable, efficient second baseman.

In the late 1970s, however, statistical analysis began to force a re-consideration of Lajoie's defensive standing. As I said before and will stress again, I am as much responsible as anyone for the misinterpretation of fielding statistics. I wrote many articles insisting that fielding statistics were meaningful, that defensive range was important, and that the statistical evaluation of any player was incomplete without a consideration of his range factors.

Napoleon Lajoie made a huge number of plays in the field. In the last 20 years several statistical analysts, attempting to give appropriate credit for these defensive plays, have credited Napoleon Lajoie with immense defensive value. This defensive value, combined with Lajoie's unquestioned offensive ability, makes Lajoie appear to be one of the very greatest players in baseball history. Statistical analysts, in essence, are representing Lajoie as if he were a combination of the best features of Rod Carew and Ozzie Smith.

This analysis is incorrect. Lajoie was a competent fielder, even a good fielder. He was *not* a defensive superstar.

The evaluation of Lajoie as a fielder has been led astray by four problems. Those four problems are:

1. The "false normalization" of the defensive statistics of bad teams, which I have already discussed.

2. The unstated assumption that the role of a second baseman in turn-of-the century baseball was the same as it is now.

3. The failure to adjust for some factors which influence the distribution of putouts on a team.

4. A specific problem, peculiar to Lajoie, with placing an appropriate value on his very high putout totals.

The third factor above is not especially prominent in the Lajoie analysis, so I'll save that for some other player . . . let's say Glenn Hubbard.

The role of the second baseman in turn-of-the-century baseball could be called the Gavy Cravath problem, as applied to fielding. In modern baseball, second base is a defense-first position, but second base in 1900 was a *hitter's* position—not exclusively, of course, but certainly to a greater extent than it is now. Until 1930, teams tended to emphasize hitting at second base, and fielding at third base, rather than the other way around.

To document this briefly:

- Between 1900 and 1930, 48 major league second basemen scored 100 runs in a season. Only 23 third basemen scored 100.
- In the same years, 17 major league second basemen hit 15 or more homers. Only four third basemen did.
- From 1900 to 1930, 113 major league second basemen hit .300 in 400 or more plate appearances. Only 89 third basemen hit .300.
- Second basemen won twelve batting titles, third basemen one.
- Twenty-one second basemen had 200 hits in a season. Only ten third basemen had 200 hits.

But on the defensive side, a typical second baseman in the dead ball era might turn 40 or 50 double plays a season. That's very different from modern second basemen, who hit much less than third basemen, but are expected to turn 100 or more double plays in a full season.

There is a relativist logic which assumes that if Lajoie turns 80 double plays in a season

in which the league average is 50 double plays, that's the same as turning 173 double plays in 1950, when the American League average was 143 (by second basemen). It's the "Gavy Cravath" argument. If Gavy Cravath is the best home run hitter of 1915 and Babe Ruth is the best home run hitter of 1925, is Gavy Cravath equal to Babe Ruth? No, he isn't, because 20 homers are not the same as 50, no matter how many home runs anybody else in the league may have hit. The same thing with fielding: if Nap Lajoie leads the league in double plays one year with 78, and Mazeroski leads the league another year with 161, does this make Lajoie equal to Bill Mazeroski with era adjustments? No, it doesn't, because 78 double plays are not the same as 161, no matter how many double plays anybody else in the league may have turned. It is different because *the game has changed*. Defense at second base was simply not as important to the game in 1900 as it was in 1950.

There is, finally, a Lajoie-specific problem with respect to valuing his putouts. All of the elements of Nap Lajoie's fielding record are good—his double plays are good, his assists/game are good, his fielding percentage is good, his putouts/game are good . . . everything's good. He was a good second baseman.

However, among these elements, the one which is most exceptional is his putout total. Lajoie has assists/game numbers above league average for his era, but not all that much above league average. What drives Lajoie's range numbers through the roof is his putout totals, which are phenomenal.

Assists by a second baseman result primarily from ground balls. Probably more than 90% of second base assists result either directly from a ground ball, or from a relay throw to first after a ground ball. But putouts can, in ordinary cases, be any of five things:

1. Line drives caught in the air.

2. Short popups/soft line drives which loop toward the outfield.

3. High popups.

4. Forceouts.

5. Runners caught stealing.

Plays (1) and (2) are Do-or-Die plays, like Ground Balls, which are either going to be made by the second baseman or not made at all. But plays (3), (4), and (5) are "Discretionary" plays, which in most cases can be made by either the second baseman or the shortstop.

Was Lajoie's putout total bolstered by "range" plays, or by plays which were taken away from the Cleveland shortstops? Let's look at the data. Cleveland second basemen in 1908 made 453 putouts, which was far more than any other team in the league.

And their shortstops made 256 putouts, which was far *less* than any other team in the league.

Cleveland second basemen led the league in putouts in 1902, with 364. And their short-stops were last in the league in putouts in 1902, with 244.

Cleveland second basemen led the league in putouts in 1903, with 416. And their shortstops were last in the league in 1903, with 249.

Cleveland second basemen led the league in putouts in 1904, with 385. And their shortstops were last in the league again, with 277.

In the thirteen years that Lajoie was in Cleveland, Cleveland second basemen were above the league average in putouts every year except 1905 and 1907, when they were just a hair under the average. But Cleveland shortstops were below average in putouts every single year.

Nap Lajoie led the league in putouts at sec-ond base five times, not because Lajoie had exceptional range but because *Lajoie took everything at second base.* What the putout totals actually show is that Lajoie was handling all or almost all of the discretionary putouts at second base—the force plays at second, and the runners caught stealing. Remember, teams at this time probably had about 150 to 200 oppo-sition runners a year caught stealing, far more than we have now. That's a lot of putouts for the second baseman, if the second baseman al-ways chooses to make that play.

Nap Lajoie was not only the team's super-star, after 1905 he was also the manager. He was more than that—hell, the team was actually called the "Naps" in his honor, as if Lajoie *was* the team. If Lajoie was in the habit of covering second base every play, the shortstop certainly wasn't going to tell him not to.

Which wouldn't have been unusual, fifteen years earlier. See, Nap Lajoie actually *doesn't* have unusually high putout totals. He has un-usually high putout totals *for his own era*. If you look back to 1880, second basemen made an average of 3.11 putouts per team game, and second basemen made 2.7 times as many putouts as shortstops. How could this be? Easy: second basemen played very near to second base, and second basemen handled all plays at second base.

In the early 1880s Charles Comiskey, or somebody, decided to pull his fielders off the bag. By 1890, putouts by second basemen had declined from 170% more than shortstops to 44% more. By 1900, putouts by second base-men were only 10% more than the putouts of shortstops. In 1909, major league shortstops actually made 2% more putouts than second basemen.

Beginning in 1910, the ratio of second base to shortstop putouts turned around, and headed back up. By 1920, second basemen were again making 14% more putouts than shortstops. By 1950, second basemen were again making 42% more putouts. Lajoie's career, then, spans the trough in this graph. In Lajoie's prime years, the relationship between second base putouts and shortstop putouts was flatter than at any other time in baseball history—for most teams. Not for Cleveland, but for almost everybody else. Lajoie's career average of 2.70 putouts/game is not unusual. Nellie Fox averaged 2.65 putouts/game, Bid McPhee averaged 3.08, Bobby Doerr averaged 2.66, Billy Herman averaged 2.64, Fred Pfeffer averaged 3.07, Bucky Harris averaged 2.71, and Jerry Priddy averaged 2.74.

The question we have to ask, to evaluate the impact of Lajoie's putout numbers on the success of his team, is whether these were plays which otherwise would not have been made, or plays which otherwise would have been made by someone else.

I'm not suggesting that we should throw away the data. I'm not suggesting that we should give him zero credit for making extra plays.

But in the thirteen seasons that Lajoie played in Cleveland, Cleveland second basemen made 537 more putouts than an average American League team. Their shortstops made 460 fewer putouts than an average American League team. I suspect that the net advantage to his team was closer to 77 extra plays than to 537. And, for that reason as well as others, I am convinced that the idea that Nap Lajoie was a defensive player of historic stature is without foundation.

7 ◆ Ryne Sandberg
(1981–1997, 2164 G, 282 1061 .285)

Let's take a look at Ryne Sandberg, not as he will appear on his plaque in Cooperstown, but as he appeared as a rookie in 1982. Sandberg in 1982 was 22 years old, played 156 games for the Cubs, mostly at third base, and hit .271 with 33 doubles, 7 homers, 54 RBI. What is the chance that that player will eventually become a Hall of Famer?

Probably better than you would think—probably at least 20%. I looked at this in two ways, for a reason that I will explain later

(Steve Sax). One way was to generate a list of the most-comparable players in baseball history (to Sandberg in 1982), including age and defensive position. The resulting fifteen-man list included two actual Hall of Famers, George Kell (1945) and Pie Traynor (1922), plus Pete Rose (1963), who could be said to have had a Hall of Fame career or two. The list also included three other players who had outstanding careers, and one player who is still active and still getting better, plus the list contained multiple seasons of Buddy Bell and Milt Stock, which reduced the number of distinct players on the list to 12.

The second way of looking at the issue was to look at the value patterns. Sandberg as a rookie in 1982 earned 16 Win Shares. How often does a 22-year-old rookie who earns 14 to 18 Win Shares go on to a Hall of Fame career?

Through 1998 there have been 58 22-year-old rookies in baseball history who have earned 14 to 18 Win Shares. Of those 58 players, nine are in the Hall of Fame now. Of the other 49, several more will be in the Hall of Fame in twenty years. One more player in the group was Ray Chapman, who was perhaps headed to a Hall of Fame career until killed by a pitch. Most of the others on the list were high quality players such as Roy Sievers, Kent Hrbek, Bill White, Buddy Myer, Bobby Bonds, Rocky Colavito, and Wildfire Schulte. Essentially, I would have to conclude that a 22-year-old rookie non-pitcher who has a season of that quality has a 20 to 35% chance of having a Hall of Fame career.

8 ◆ Charlie Gehringer
(1924–1942, 2323 G, 184 1427 .320)

Gehringer was given the nickname "The Mechanical Man" by members of the Washington Senators. As Doc Cramer explained, "All you do is wind him up on opening day and he runs on and on all season." However, the name came to have a second meaning, that Gehringer was a flat, un-exciting player. He never changed his expression on the field. Edward Barrow wrote of Nap Lajoie that "Lajoie was no Mechanical Man. He was full of spirit and animation, and an alive figure on the ball field."

Gehringer, a bachelor through most of his career, lived with his mother in Detroit, and attended Mass with her every morning . . . I wonder if any player in baseball history had a record of sustained improvement to equal Gehringer? Gehringer was a decent player as a rookie in 1926, hitting .277 with 1 home run but 17 triples, fair defense. He was better his second year in the league (.317 with four homers) and better yet his third (.320 with 6 homers). By his fourth year, he was legitimately outstanding (.339 with 13 homers, leading the league in hits, doubles, triples, runs scored, stolen bases, putouts, and fielding percentage). He was even a little bit better his fifth year. He had an injury his sixth year and took a couple of years to fight his way back, but by 1934 (his ninth year in the league) was better than ever. Two years after that he hit .354 with 60 doubles, 15 homers. The year after that he won his first and only batting title and MVP Award, but the year after that he hit a career-high 20 home runs. I don't know of any other player who took as many steps forward in his career. Frank White, maybe.

Gehringer had a brief, unsuccessful career as the Tigers General Manager in the early 1950s. "'Tis said Charley never wanted the job in the first place, but bowed to the insistence of the elder Briggs," reported John Drebinger in *Baseball Magazine* (November, 1953). "He has revealed no especial talents for front office leadership that would cause him to be regarded as another Ed Barrow or Branch Rickey."

Gehringer was passive to the point of being a victim. He never wanted the GM job in the first place, tried to decline it, but was pressured into accepting it, essentially, because he didn't know how to say "No." "It was a nightmare," he

recalled Gehringer in *Cobb Would Have Caught It.* "We had a lousy ball club, and I'd been away from baseball at that time for ten years. I didn't know who was and who wasn't . . . Brother, what a headache! We couldn't beat anybody, and I made several trades, but it still didn't get us anywhere."

9 ◆ Rod Carew
(1967–1985, 2469 G, 93 1015 .328)
A better hitter than Gehringer (in the context of his own time), but nowhere near the fielder. Carew made some nice plays at second base and didn't make a huge number of errors, plus he was very smart, which counts because the second baseman is in the middle of the diamond, and has to make decisions about which way to go with the play more often than anyone else does. But his arm wasn't good, plus his footwork was never good, and he never could improve it; he couldn't get across the bag and get rid of the ball quickly, which eventually forced his move to first base.

10 ◆ Roberto Alomar
(1988–2000, 1677 G, 170 918 .304)
In mid-career; hasn't won an MVP Award so far, and time may be running out on him if he's going to do that. An overrated fielder, in my opinion; a good fielder, even a very good one, but no better than some guys who don't win Gold Gloves, like Fernando Vina. Offensively, very similar to Frankie Frisch, but better than Frisch, although without Frisch's fire. Frisch and Alomar are both switch-hitting second basemen, very fast, with batting averages over .300 and medium-range power. Alomar is a better hitter; Frisch was a better leader and a better baserunner.

11 ◆ Frankie Frisch
(1919–1937, 2311 G, 105 1244 .316)
Frisch grew up in the Bronx, near Bedford Park. He had a happy childhood. His father was well

off, a linen merchant. His family was intact. He played baseball morning to night and married a girl who lived just down the block from him.

He was a prep school kid, Fordham all the way . . . I'm not exactly sure, but I think that Fordham (and Notre Dame, Holy Cross, and others) at that time had a kind of seamless transition from prep school to college. Anyway, Frisch attended Fordham from a young age, was coached there by Art Devlin, and was named an All-American in 1918. Devlin introduced him to John McGraw, and McGraw signed him for the Giants in 1919, before he had completed his education.

McGraw took personal responsibility for training Frisch. McGraw drove his men hard, as Bobby Knight drives his men today. He was fair to them, even kind to them, but he pushed them to the breaking point. The Giants put the pieces together and won the pennant in 1921, 1922, 1923, and 1924, the World Series the first two of those years. Frisch was the key man on the team, and a hero of the World Series almost every year.

"Frisch is one of the poorest fielders we have ever lamped," wrote Gordon Mackay in the 1924 *Reach Guide,* "but his terrific speed overcomes this in every game. Frisch can knock down more balls with his elbows, knees, chest and head, and by dint of his fleet recovery throw out the runner, than any nine men we know."

By the mid-1920s Frisch began to tire of McGraw's fire-hose pressure. August 20, 1926, was a sweltering day in St. Louis. Frisch was playing on two bad legs, trying to play through a charley horse. McGraw was sick, but forcing himself to go on with his task. The two men had a terrible argument, and Frisch jumped the team.

After a few days they both calmed down, and Frisch re-joined the Giants, but he was there in body only. After that season McGraw

was looking to move Frisch and St. Louis was desperate to get rid of Rogers Hornsby, and so the two were traded, with New York including some little things to balance the trade.

Frisch was thrilled, on joining the Cardinals, to discover a common-sense approach to the game. "What a difference!" he wrote in *Frankie Frisch: The Fordham Flash.* "After those stern years with the regimented Giants, to be in a baseball group where everybody was happy and relaxed, having a good time, enjoying their work. We worked hard, all right, but it was different. There was nobody standing over you with a whip in his hand, telling you to do it his way, or else." Determined to prove himself on his own, Frisch had the greatest year of his career, hitting .337 and setting a major league record, which still stands, with 641 assists at second base.

The Cardinals didn't win that year, but they did win in '28, in '30, in '31, and in '34, making Frisch a regular on eight teams that won the National League pennant—four in New York, and four in St. Louis. Frisch won the MVP Award in 1931, what is now regarded as the first BBWAA Award (although the BBWAA had voted on the same award by the same method for the previous two years). The Cardinals at that time were going through managers like Charlie Sheen working his way down a list of hookers, so by 1933 it was Frisch's turn to handle the Gas House Gang. This was the heyday of the playing manager; in the mid-1930s about half of the major league teams were managed by their stars.

As a manager, to be frank, Frisch was horsebleep. He would manage in the major leagues for sixteen years, with the Cardinals, the Pirates, and the Cubs. He won the World Series his first full year, riding Dizzy Dean's 30 wins, but never won a pennant again; in fact, after 1934 you would be hard pressed to name any Frankie Frisch team that *didn't* have a disappointing season . . . the 1944 Pirates had a pretty decent year, I guess. In the middle of an era when the Cardinal farm system was grinding out Hall of Famers, Frisch managed the Cardinals, after the 1934 championship, to second place, to fourth, to sixth. He had a championship team, added Johnny Mize and Enos Slaughter, and managed them into sixth place. He couldn't run a pitching staff unless he had Dizzy Dean, and he preferred hitters who swung at the first good pitch.

But what he lacked in managerial skill, he made up for in personality. Frisch was a master at charming the press. If you read the books of baseball anecdotes which were popular in the 1940s and 1950s, there are hundreds and hundreds of Frisch anecdotes, almost all of them pointless. Here's a fairly typical one, from *Curve Ball Laughs* (Herman L. Masin, Pyramid Books, 1955):

> Before that hectic 1934 World Series between the Cardinals and the Tigers, Dizzy Dean approached his manager, Frankie Frisch, and informed him that he wanted to pitch every game.
>
> You can't do that, Diz," Frisch told him. "This is the World Series. You can't win four games from the Tigers."
>
> Diz gave this serious consideration, then nodded. "I know," he said, "but I can win four out of five."

Frisch was an effective on-field leader because he had tremendous energy and a forceful personality. But once he could no longer play he began to romanticize the past, to deride his own players, and to launch into long (but apparently entertaining) monologues about all of the great players he used to play with.

12 ◆ Bobby Grich
(1970–1986, 2008 G, 224 864 .266)

The things that a hitter does to help his team can be summarized in two more or less equal groups:

1. Hitting for average.
2. Everything else.

"Secondary average" is a loose and approximate measure of the "everything else" group—walks, power, and stolen bases, per at bat.

Overall secondary averages are almost the same as overall batting averages—but not for middle infielders. Second basemen tend to have secondary averages about 60 points lower than their batting averages, overall. Grich was an exception to that rule: a second baseman who *did* hit for power and did draw walks. The best secondary averages among second basemen:

1.	Joe Morgan	.431
2.	Maxie Bishop	.362
3.	Rogers Hornsby	.362
4.	Jackie Robinson	.355
5.	Joe Gordon	.346
6.	Davey Lopes	.344
7.	Tony Lazzeri	.336
8.	Bobby Grich	.330
9.	George Grantham	.329
10.	Eddie Stanky	.322
11.	Eddie Collins	.322

Focusing on the seven players who rank ahead of Grich, three are ranked higher (Morgan, Hornsby, and Robinson). The other four all had shorter careers than Grich, and only Gordon (among these) was his equal as a defensive player. Grich won four Gold Gloves, and won them over stiff competition—Frank White, Willie Randolph, and Lou Whitaker, among others.

> Bobby Grich "always wore uniforms that looked like 'before' on detergent commercials. Grich looked as if he might have stopped on the way from the clubhouse to the dugout to change the oil in his car. On a bright sunny afternoon in Anaheim, where it might not have rained for three months, Bobby Grich would come out to play the first inning with wet mud drops on his uniform. Where'd he get them? What did he do,

buy them?"—Ron Luciano, *The Fall of the Roman Umpire* (Bantam Books, 1986)

Grich's best friend has long been his minor league and major league roommate, Don Baylor. Baylor in his autobiography remembered one time when they were rookies in 1972, and Earl Weaver pinch hit for Grich with Frank Robinson. Grich, according to Baylor, marched back into the dugout, grabbed Weaver by the throat, and screamed in his face. "How do you expect me to hit in this league when you keep pinch-hitting for me all the time?"

"I couldn't believe my eyes," wrote Baylor, "a rookie, trying to kill baseball's little genius."

13 ◆ Lou Whitaker
(1977–1995, 2390 G, 244 1084 .276)
Whitaker was known as an airhead, the kind of player who in earlier generations, when the distance between the players and the press was less, would have been the butt of countless good-natured stories. One time he showed up in the All Star game wearing an ill-fitting sort-of uniform purchased from a souvenir stand, since he had forgotten to take his uniform to the game. Another time, when an airplane buzzed Tiger Stadium, Whitaker dived to the ground, and was so shaken up that he had to come out of the game. He was a hell of a player, though, and he knew how to play the game. He ranks ninth among all second basemen in runs scored, in RBI, and in total bases, and he was an above-average fielder. He was just excitable, and sometimes needed a little help to focus on the task at hand.

14 ◆ Billy Herman
(1931–1947, 1922 G, 47 839 .304)
In his first major league at bat (August 29, 1931), Herman fouled a pitch off the plate so hard that it bounced up and hit him in the head, knocking him cold. He was carried off the

field on a stretcher, and somebody else had to pinch hit for him.

> Billy was one of the most intelligent infielders as far as positioning himself...He helped me so much learning how to play the game and how to position myself. It made me a better ballplayer. —*Phil Cavarretta in Wrigleyville* (Peter Golenbock, St. Martin's Griffin, 1999)

Herman was widely known as the best hit-and-run man of his time—the best, perhaps, in baseball history.

15 ◆ Nellie Fox
(1947–1965, 2367 G, 35 790 .288)
By the Win Shares method, Nellie Fox is the only man to legitimately take an MVP Award away from Mickey Mantle. The Most Valuable Players in the American League from 1954–1964, by this method, are:

1954 Mickey Mantle
1955 Mickey Mantle
1956 Mickey Mantle
1957 Mickey Mantle
1958 Mickey Mantle
1959 Nellie Fox
1960 Mickey Mantle
1961 Mickey Mantle
1962 Mickey Mantle

Of course, Mantle didn't win all of those awards, as the writers went through an annual process of figuring out, (a) who do we give the MVP Award to this year, other than Mantle, and (b) why is it we're snubbing Mickey this year?

In 1963, when Mantle was injured, there were eleven National League players who rank as better than any American League player, which probably tells us something about why the National League dominated the All-Star game in the 1960s. In 1964, Mantle's last good year, he rates even with Brooks Robinson as the best player in the American League. The award went to Robinson.

1959 actually was not Nellie Fox's best year; Fox was even better in 1957 than he was in 1959.

American League Gold Gloves, 1946–1960, as seen by the Win Shares system: 1946 and 1947—Bobby Doerr, 1948—Pete Suder, 1949—Doerr, 1950—Jerry Priddy, 1951—Bobby Avila, 1952—Nellie Fox, 1953 and 1954—Bobby Avila, 1955—Fox; 1956—Avila; 1957, 1958, and 1959—Fox; 1960—Mark Breeding.

16 ◆ Joe Gordon
(1938–1950, 1566 G, 253 975 .268)

From the odd facts department: Gordon played exactly 1,000 games with the New York Yankees, and had exactly 1,000 hits . . . Gordon would never use the same bat twice in a row. It was an odd superstition—even if he hit a home run in his last at bat, he'd switch to a different bat for the next try.

"Among modern second basemen," wrote Tom Meany in *Baseball for Everyone* (Grosset and Dunlap, 1948), Gehringer, Gordon, and Billy Herman were "the best on the double-play pivot. What made them stand out from other second basemen was that they pivoted and threw *at the same time* that they crossed the bag, not *after* they crossed."

"If I had to put in time on a desert island," wrote Bill Veeck in *Veeck as in Wreck,* "I can think of no one I'd rather have along than Joe, because even on a desert island he would always find ways to keep the hours dancing along." Veeck relates a story about Jackie Price, a shortstop with Cleveland in 1946, who liked to keep snakes. Gordon persuaded Price to turn several of the snakes loose on a train, in the middle of a gathering of women bowlers. This, in turn, led the conductor to seize Gordon by the neck and demand to know his name. "Lou Boudreau," replied Gordon without missing a beat.

(Mike Kopf notes a problem, that being that Gordon and Price were never members of the Indians at the same time. Nonetheless, that's Bill Veeck's story, and I'm sticking to it.)

17 ◆ Willie Randolph
(1975–1989, 2202 G, 54 687 .276)

Of the other people who have rated the top 100 players in baseball history, three put Bill Mazeroski in the top 100, making him a consensus 93rd pick. None even mentioned Willie Randolph. Let's think about this. Their career length is almost the same—2,202 games for Randolph, 2,163 for Mazeroski, a little bigger difference in plate appearances because Randolph hit second most of his career, Mazeroski seventh. Randolph used 6,283 outs in his career, Mazeroski 6,113—no real difference.

The *essential* differences between Randolph and Mazeroski can be reduced to two things: walks, and double plays. There are other differences between them—Mazeroski had a little power, Randolph was faster and his average was 16 points higher, etc. Those things are pretty small; they're essentially comparable players, except that (a) Randolph walked a lot, (b) Mazeroski walked about as often as George Hendrick gave interviews, and (c) Mazeroski was better than anybody who ever lived at turning the double play.

The question, then, is which advantage was larger: Randolph's walks, or Mazeroski's ability to turn the double play?

A lot of people *assume* that the double play advantage must be larger, but was it? The effects of these two things are mirror images. A walk puts a runner on first base; a double play takes a runner off first base.

Randolph drew 1,243 walks in his career, Mazeroski 447. That puts Randolph ahead by 800 times on base, give or take.

Mazeroski, in his career, played about 18,299 innings at second base, and turned 1,706 double plays.

Randolph, in his career, played about 18,717 innings at second, and turned 1,547 double plays.

Adjusting for the innings difference, Mazeroski's advantage is within a hair of 200 double plays.

So Mazeroski's advantage, in truth, is *nowhere near* as significant as Randolph's advantage. In fact, the difference is less than this, because part of Mazeroski's edge is actually explained by external factors—ground ball pitchers, runners on first base, and Gene Alley. But even ignoring those . . . Mazeroski was a heck of a player. The fact that he was the absolute best at turning the double play is attention-getting, and "turning the double play" is, in a sense, the defining characteristic of a second baseman. Randolph's central skill, like his personality, preferred the shadows.

It's easy to see how you could assume that the player who was the absolute best at the specific task which defines his position would have to be among the best ever at the position. I can't see that it holds up if you walk it through.

18 ◆ Bobby Doerr
(1937–1951, 1865 G, 223 1247 .288)
A graceful, quiet player who was never in the newspapers except for his ballplaying. Doerr was a Los Angeles kid who signed with a Pacific Coast League team as a sixteen-year-old high school junior. He hit .342 in the PCL in 1936, when he was eighteen. The Red Sox had an option on him. When Eddie Collins, GM of the Red Sox, flew out to look Doerr over and decide whether to pick up the option, he happened to see a seventeen-year-old the San Diego team had just signed, Ted Williams.

Doerr joined the Red Sox in 1937, struggled for a year, but went on to have a Hall of Fame career. An outstanding hitter and an exceptional second baseman, he was the informal captain of the Red Sox in the late 1940s, the quiet man in the middle of the incendiary Ted Williams, the peppery Johnny Pesky and Birdie Tebbetts, and the odd collection of alcoholics, intellectuals, and country bumpkins who won 473 games between 1946 and 1950.

19 ◆ Tony Lazzeri
(1926–1939, 1740 G, 178 1191 .292)
Lazzeri grew up in the San Francisco Bay area about the same time as several other major league stars; as a kid he played against Joe Cronin, Wally Berger, Ernie Lombardi, and others. Joe Cronin recalled in *The Great Rivalry* (Ed Linn) that Lazzeri, after spending most of his day working at his father's grape press, would arrive at the park at the last minute, and immediately take over the game, as a pitcher and a slugger. "He'd come to the park around the seventh or eighth inning," Cronin recalled, "and always—always—hit a home run, strike everybody out, and beat us."

Lazzeri suffered from epilepsy. The Yankees at that time had their own Pullman railroad car, with assigned seats. One year pitcher Ed Wells was assigned the seat next to Lazzeri. "He told me that if he had [an epileptic] fit, what I should do," recalled Wells in *Baseball Between the Wars* (Eugene Murdock). "He said, 'When I feel it coming on, I'll wake you up and you get a wet towel and put it on my forehead. I'll foam at the mouth, but you take my tongue and hold it so I don't swallow it.' That's what I'd do. The fits lasted about four or five minutes."

Lazzeri "was one of the greatest ballplayers I have ever known," wrote Edward Barrow in *My Fifty Years in Baseball* (Coward-McCann, 1951). "The contrariness of human nature may fix Lazzeri's place as the fellow whom Grover Cleveland Alexander struck out. His rightful place in baseball history should be as one of the greatest Yankees of them all. There was never a time that I didn't watch Lazzeri with the greatest apprehension, fearful that he would have a seizure on the ball field. He never did. Lazzeri was not only a fine mechanical ballplayer and a powerful hitter, getting his great driving force from wrists and forearms developed as a boilermaker in his father's foundry, but had a brilliance on the ball field that was part mental and part instinctive." (Quote has been slightly edited.)

> Tony was the least communicative of all the Cubs. He was not the most colorful character in baseball, either.—Warren Brown, *The Chicago Cubs* (Putnam, 1946)

> Many years ago I made it a point to find out after a huddle between Lefty Gomez [and Lazzeri] what had been said. With the bases loaded and no one out, Lazzeri called for time and walked to the pitcher's box. He looked Gomez squarely in the eye and said "You got yourself into this; get yourself out." And walked back to second base.—*Baseball Wit and Wisdom*, Frank Graham and Dick Hyman (David MacKay and Company, 1962 entry by Jim Farley)

The epilepsy finally killed him, in 1946. He had a seizure at his home, fell down the stairs, and broke his neck. See also entry about Bob Johnson (Left Field, #31).

20 ◆ Larry Doyle
(1907–1920, 1765 G, 74 793 .290)

> At one time in the early part of 1907 four scouts representing four major league clubs were in the stands at Springfield, Ill., at one game, watching Doyle, for whom eight clubs had already made bids. The New York club, fearing some other club would get the player, paid $4,500 for him by telegraph without seeing him play, thus securing

a great second baseman.—*Baseball in the Big Leagues,* Johnny Evers (Reilly and Britton, 1910. Ghosted by Hugh Fullerton)

> Captain and second baseman Lawrence Doyle was purchased by New York from the Springfield Club of the I.I.I. League in July, 1907, for $4500—the highest sum ever payed for a player in that minor league class. In his youth Doyle was a coal minor in Illinois for several years. His work at Springfield was so fine that many offers were made for Doyles release, but the Springfield management refused to sell. Manager McGraw sent Dan Brouthers to watch Doyle at work. Brouthers was so impressed with the youngster's playing that he recommended purchasing his release.—*1912 Reach Guide* (slightly edited)

The Giants played the 1919 season opener in Cincinnati. Before the first game there was a confrontation in the Giants' hotel lobby, which ended with Larry Doyle punching out a fan, and John McGraw demanding police protection for his entire team . . .

21 ◆ Chuck Knoblauch
(1991–2000, 1415 G, 83 549 .297)
A similar player to Larry Doyle, actually. Doyle was a short, stocky player who could drive the ball and hustled. Oddly enough, Doyle also went through several spans in his career when he lost confidence in his ability to throw to first. In 1910 Doyle made 53 errors, many of them Knoblauch-type errors on throws to first.

22 ◆ Dick McAuliffe
(1960–1975, 1763 G, 197 697 .247)
An awkward, odd-looking player who was what you might call functionally effective, but with no style points. He was a left-handed hitter with an odd batting stance . . . it's been 30 years and I can find no photograph, but as best I remember he tucked his right wrist under his chin and held his bat over his head, so it looked

as if he were dodging the sword of Damocles in mid-descent. He pointed his left knee at the catcher and his right knee at the pitcher and spread the two as far apart as humanly possible, his right foot balanced on the toes, so that to have lowered his heel two inches would have pulled his knee inward by a foot. He whipped the bat in a sort of violent pinwheel which produced line drives, strikeouts, and fly balls, few ground balls and not a lot of pop outs.

Coaches were perpetually trying to "correct" him. He was as odd in the field as he was at the plate. "As a second baseman," wrote Chris Stern in *Where Have They Gone*, "he looked like a miner trying to take a shovelful of coal out of the ground."

The press never got what he was about. Searching my library for a photograph of McAuliffe at bat, I found seven photos of Denny McLain playing the organ, but none of McAuliffe's singular batting stance. The book *The Explosive Sixties* makes no mention of McAuliffe, although McAuliffe was as good a player in the 1960s (taking that decade as a whole and no notice of what happened in others) as Lou Brock, Luis Aparicio, or Bill Mazeroski. He was a .250 hitter, but he walked and had more power than any other second baseman of his era, so he led the American League in runs scored in 1968, and created more runs than any other middle infielder of the 1960s except Maury Wills and perhaps Aparicio. Chris Stern, who got the McAuliffe message better than most, said that "his best season was 1964, when he slammed 24 home runs and drove in 77." In fact, that was his fourth best season; his 1966, 1967, and 1968 seasons were not only better, but far better.

"To this day," McAuliffe told Stern, "I can't understand why I never won any Gold Gloves. One year I made only seven errors, but they gave the thing to Bobby Knoop, who, as I recall, had 13." That was probably 1968, when Knoop actually made 15 errors, McAuliffe 9. Knoop was a great defensive second baseman, certainly better than McAuliffe, but I do agree that McAuliffe was worthy of a Gold Glove that one year, 1968.

23 ◆ Davey Lopes
(1972–1987, 1812, 155 614 .263)
As I write this, Davey Lopes is 53 years old, and has just been hired to manage the Milwaukee Brewers. This is late to begin a managerial career; Mike Hargrove, Johnny Oates, Don Baylor, and Dusty Baker, who have all been managing for years, are several years younger than Lopes, and Ray Knight, who was fired as Cincinnati manager some years ago, is younger than they are.

Starting late is not new to Lopes; he was 27 when he played his first major league game, 28 in his rookie season. After the age of 28, he had a better major league career than most of the men listed above him here. From age 34 on, he had a better career than any other second baseman except Joe Morgan, Nap Lajoie, or Eddie Collins. At the age of 40, playing 99 games as a spare outfielder for the Cubs, he stole 47 bases in 51 attempts. If you watched him play in those days he looked like he had arthritis, but he would steal second base standing up. He drew 90+ walks a year in his good years, hit for some power, was a tremendous base stealer, and won and deserved a Gold Glove in 1977, granted that he deserved it mostly on the theory that you have to give the thing to somebody, and there wasn't anybody better in that league that year.

24 ◆ Buddy Myer
(1925–1941, 1923 G, 38 850 .303)
Because he was seldom domineering and tended to the business at hand, "Buddy" Myer never won the plaudits he deserved for his seventeen years ... but the Southern Jewish boy who

played second for the Senators was one of the finest keystoners in the game.—Harold U. Ribalow, *The Jew in American Sports*

Actually, Myer may not have been Jewish. He told a home-town newspaperman shortly before his death in 1974 that he was not Jewish, he was German, but that the writers thought that he was Jewish, and he just didn't think that being German was anything to be proud of at the time, so he never set the record straight.

Myer graduated from Mississippi A&M in 1925, and signed with the Cleveland Indians. The Indians wanted to send him to a low minor league team, however, and Myer refused to report, forcing the Indians to release him, after which he signed with New Orleans, and was sold to Washington.

Myer was the Senators' shortstop in 1926. He was a poor defensive shortstop. In early 1927 the Red Sox offered Topper Rigney, a veteran shortstop who had played well since 1922, in exchange for Myer. Clark Griffith was opposed to making the deal, but the Senators had signed Tris Speaker, who had managed in the league for years, and was known to be one of the smartest players in baseball. Speaker convinced Bucky Harris, the Senators young player/manager, that the deal for Rigney would put the Senators back in the World Series, and Harris pushed Griffith to make the deal.

The Senators regretted the trade immediately, as Rigney didn't play well, and the Senators struggled; the deal led in part to Harris being fired as the Senators' manager, and traded to Detroit. Clark Griffith had to give the Red Sox five players to get Myer back. One of the players the Red Sox insisted on was a young shortstop named Bobby Reeves, who had played well in 1928. The Senators said, "We can't give you Reeves; we'll give you our other young shortstop, Joe Cronin." The Red

Sox, who just three years earlier had refused Lou Gehrig in a trade offer from the Yankees, also refused to accept Joe Cronin, and the Senators eventually agreed to include Bobby Reeves in the deal.

With Harris gone, Myer played second base for the Senators until the early 1940s. He was a .300 hitter, had a great strikeout/walk ratio, and led the league in stolen bases one year. In 1933 he helped the Senators to the American League pennant; in 1935 he won the batting title on the last day of the season, beating out Joe Vosmik with (or without, depending on which story you believe) the cooperation of Jimmie Foxx, who may have allowed Myer to beat out a couple of bunts to boost his average. He was not a great defensive second baseman (I have him as deserving of no Gold Gloves), but was a solid, consistent second baseman, among the best in the league in his better years.

On the first day of the 1933 World Series Myer witnessed a fatal traffic accident on his way to the game. Shaken up, he made three errors in the game, helping the Giants take a one-game lead in the series.

25 ◆ Johnny Evers
(1902–1929, 1782 G, 12 538 .270)

A nervous, high-strung player, Evers had the best strikeout/walk ratio in baseball in his era, and deserved the Gold Glove as the National League's best second baseman in 1904, 1906, and 1907.

Evers, who weighed 125 pounds, was a screamer and fighter; he got on everyone's nerves almost every day, apparently including his own, as he had a nervous breakdown in 1911. He was involved in countless on-field fights, many of them with teammates, most of them just sudden outbursts which ended with someone knocking him silly. He didn't speak to Joe Tinker for several years, and Frank Chance once said that he was a great player but "I wish he had been an outfielder so I wouldn't have to listen to him."

Evers' selection to the Hall of Fame in 1947 has been often ridiculed. While this may not have been the Hall of Fame's finest hour, they have done worse. Evers was essentially the same player as Jim Gilliam: a Gold Glove second baseman, a good baserunner, a guy who drew a lot of walks, and a key part of many championship teams. He was the Most Valuable Player in the National League in 1914, when he led the Braves to a miracle pennant. He played in four World Series, and hit .350 or better in three of them. There are Hall of Famers who don't have as much to sell.

> All there is to Evers is a bundle of nerves, a lot of woven wire muscles, and the quickest brain in baseball. He has invented and thought out more plays than any man of recent years.—Hugh Fullerton, *Touching Second, Fuller and Evers*, (Reilly & Britton, 1910)

Junior Gilliam

26 ◆ Cupid Childs
(1888–1901, 1456 G, 20 743 .306)

A .300 hitter who walked 100-plus times a year and was a good defensive second baseman. His best years are in a hitter's era, so his numbers are a little more impressive than they should be . . . he scored 136 runs in 1892, 145 runs in 1893, 143 in 1894, and had on-base percentages in those years of .443, .463, and .475. There were a lot of runs scored in those years, plus Childs' career is fairly short.

The nickname "Cupid" is of disputed origin, but in my opinion it was a family nickname, not a baseball name. He was also called "The Little Fat Man," as he had a Kirby Puckett-type body.

27 ◆ Jim Gilliam
(1953–1966, 1956 G, 65 558 .265)

Gilliam was a spear carrier, a player whose job was always to help somebody else. He is most remembered as the number two hitter who took pitches to allow Maury Wills to break Ty Cobb's stolen base record. If the Dodgers needed a second baseman, he was their second baseman. If they needed a third baseman, he was their third baseman. If they needed an outfielder, he was an outfielder. If they needed a leadoff man, he was their leadoff man. He was good at all of these things. He was a better leadoff man than Wills, yet he moved happily to the number two spot to make room for Wills. He was a better second baseman than Charlie Neal, yet he moved cheerfully to third base to allow Neal to play second.

Gilliam's nickname on the Dodgers was "The Devil"; he was a good-natured guy with a wicked underside. In 1963 Don Dillard of the Braves slid into second base trying to break up a double play, and Maury Wills hit him right between the eyes with the throw, knocking him out. Everybody gathered around Dillard, afraid he was dead, except Gilliam, who retrieved the ball and tagged Dillard, lying flat on the ground, to make sure he was out. According to John Roseboro in *Glory Days with the Dodgers,* "'That's the first time I tagged out a dead man,' chuckled The Devil."

"I guess my all-time favorite athlete," wrote Jim Murray in 1978, "was Jim Gilliam. He always thought that he was lucky to be a Dodger. I thought it was the other way around."

28 ◆ Red Schoendienst
(1945–1963, 2216 G, 84 773 .289)

Schoendienst grew up in a small town as one of seven brothers, all of whom had brilliant red hair. He had a Mark Twain childhood, fishing in the Kaskaskia river in western Illinois, hunting, playing baseball, and getting into his share of innocuous trouble. When he was a teenager his buddy accidentally hammered a staple that flew into his left eye. His doctor said the eye would have to be removed. Schoendienst, determined to play baseball, refused. The eye never was right. Schoendienst compensated by learning to switch hit, and turning his head toward the pitcher, so that even right-handed he could watch the delivery with his right eye.

He went to a tryout camp the Cardinals ran in his area, got a contract, and made the majors during the War. He was a minor league shortstop. The Cardinals had Marion at shortstop and about two dozen second basemen they liked—Emil Verban in 1945, and a fellow in the service named Lou Klein, who had been tremendous in 1943. They put Schoendienst in the outfield. As a rookie he hit .278, and led the National League in stolen bases.

Something happened to all of the second baseman. Klein got injured and then went to play in the Mexican League, screwing up his career beyond repair. Schoendienst moved back to the infield, to second base.

He was a flawless second baseman, establishing a National League record for consecutive errorless chances in 1949, and then breaking his own record in 1950. On June 5, 1948, he went 4-for-4 with three doubles. June 6 was a double header. In the first game, Schoendienst hit three more doubles and a home run. In the second game he added two more doubles—eight doubles, a single, and a homer in a two-day span.

Schoendienst was a switch hitter with a "mirror" swing; it was said of him that you could take a picture of him batting right-handed, reverse the negative, and he looked exactly the same as he did batting left.

Schoendienst in 1958 was 35 years old, playing the best ball of his life as the captain of the Milwaukee Braves. The Braves had struggled for several years to get the pieces to fit together. When they acquired Schoendienst in early 1957 everything clicked; Schoendienst led them into the World Series in 1957, which they won, and 1958, which they lost although Schoendienst played well. A few weeks after the series, however, Schoendienst was diagnosed with tuberculosis. He missed a season, but fought back again, hitting over .300 as a reserve for the Cardinals in '61 and '62. He remained in the Cardinal organization for many, many years thereafter, as a manager and as a coach.

29 ◆ Bill Mazeroski
(1956–1972, 2163 G, 138 853 .260)

Dave Cash, asked if it was difficult waiting around for Mazeroski to grow old, said, "Not at all. Actually, I learned a lot from Mazeroski. He's a real man, and one of the things he taught me was to keep things in perspective. Maz didn't make many errors, and he hardly ever made any bad plays, but when he did, he didn't let it bother him. He was always the same, whether things were going good, bad or indifferently."

In the Win Shares system I have Mazeroski credited with 113 Win Shares for his defense at second base, which is the highest total of all time. As I mentioned in the Rogers Hornsby comment, there are 71 second basemen in baseball history who have played 10,000 innings or more at the position, as best I can estimate that. Among those 71, the top ten in Win Shares per 1,000 defensive innings are:

1.	Bill Mazeroski	6.18
2.	Glenn Hubbard	6.14
3.	Bobby Grich	5.64
4.	Nellie Fox	5.49
5.	Frank White	5.39
6.	Frankie Frisch	5.39
7.	Manny Trillo	5.38
8.	Red Schoendienst	5.36
9.	Ted Sizemore	5.36
10.	Joe Gordon	5.35

The bottom ten are Rogers Hornsby (3.08), Juan Samuel (3.11), Cub Stricker (3.21), Larry Doyle (3.35), Tony Lazzeri (3.38), Kid Gleason (3.43), Steve Sax (3.53), Ron Hunt (3.66), Joe Quinn (3.68), and Miller Huggins (3.71).

The selection of Mazeroski as the most effective defensive second baseman ever is not a surprise to anyone; *Total Baseball* rates him as the best defensive player at any position, and he won eight Gold Gloves.

Among players who played 3,000 to 9,999 innings, there are twelve with rankings of at least 5.50. Those twelve are:

1.	Hal Lanier	6.38
2.	Jody Reed	6.15
3.	Jackie Robinson	6.00
4.	Fernando Vina	5.70
5.	Mark Lemke	5.69
6.	Bobby Avila	5.61
7.	Eddie Mayo	5.60
8.	Snuffy Stirnweiss	5.55
9.	Morrie Rath	5.54
10.	Jerry Adair	5.50
10.	Marty Barrett	5.50
10.	Burgess Whitehead	5.50

Most of those, again, are not too surprising ...Lanier was the weakest hitter ever to play 1,000 games in the major leagues (except pitchers), but was such a good second baseman that they moved him to shortstop after a couple of years. Avila was a terrific defensive player, Stirnweiss was an MVP, Lemke was a weak hitter who was on TV every October because of his glovework, and Adair was basically Mark Lemke.

The surprises are Jody Reed and Jackie Robinson. Hero worship for Jackie Robinson is virtually an industry, yet even Jackie's devotees rarely claim that he was as good a defensive second baseman as Bill Mazeroski.

What do I make of it? Well, defensive statistics, no matter how carefully interpreted, are still suspect. I have discovered ways to remove many biases from fielding statistics and correct for many illusions, but there may still be wrinkles in there that we don't understand.

I would not rule out the possibility that Jackie may have been a far better defensive second baseman than even the people who watched him regularly realized. Jackie, I would suggest, was such a controversial figure, such a polarizing figure, that it must have been extremely difficult to see him for exactly what he was, even when he was right in front of you.

Also, Jackie was, according to all accounts, unusually intelligent. Is it not possible, I wonder, that Jackie's intelligence created benefits for his team that *only* show up in the statistics? I've made this argument before, and don't want to repeat myself, but if an infielder makes a diving stop of a line drive, he wins recognition as a defensive wizard. But if he anticipates the play, and moves two steps to his left before the ball is hit, it's a routine play, and nobody notices. Invisible range, I call it; anticipating the play creates invisible range. Isn't it possible that Jackie just anticipated the play more often than anybody else did?

Before you answer that, let me point out a couple of other things. Jackie also played about 2,000 innings at third base, at the end of his career. Guess what? As a third baseman, he rates as even more sensational than he was as a second baseman. The average at third base (post-1940) is 3.22 Win Shares per 1,000 innings. The highest figure since 1940, by a player who played 10,000 or more innings, is 4.97, by Clete Boyer.

Jackie is at 5.52.

He's off the charts. Nobody else (post-1940) is even in the same zone.

He also played (about) 1,175 innings in the outfield, mostly in left field. He rates as sensational there, for a left fielder. Figures in the outfield are lower for left/right fielders than they are for center fielders, so Jackie isn't at the top of the list, but he has a per-inning rate which wouldn't be half bad if he was a center fielder. He rates about the same, per inning, as Rick Manning, Earle Combs, Matty Alou, and Roberto Clemente, a little bit ahead of guys like Dwight Evans and Al Kaline and Minnie Minoso, who are the best of the left/right fielders.

Just to complete the record, I don't have him rated as a top-flight defensive first baseman, the position he played when he was breaking into the league. He played about 1,665 innings at first base, rating just a little above average. Still, I think the record would suggest that Robinson may in fact have been a far better defensive player than most people think he was. If it's a statistical illusion of some kind, it's an illusion that chases him all over the diamond. Never underestimate the power of intelligence, particularly when that intelligence is combined with athletic ability, determination, and a formidable competitive instinct.

30 ◆ Bid McPhee
(1882–1899, 2135 G, 53 1057 .271)

> In a rowdy era, Bid was one of the game's gentlemen. He performed spectacularly but was personally sober and sedate, always in prime physical condition and quietly proud of never being ejected from a game.—A. D. Suehsdorf, *Nineteenth Century Stars,* (SABR, 1989)

McPhee was the second baseman of the Cincinnati Reds from 1882, when they played in the American Association, through 1899. (The team switched to the National League in 1890, in the chaos created by the Players' League.) He was the finest defensive second baseman of the 19th century; I have him as deserving of Gold Gloves in the American Association in 1882, 1883, 1887, 1888, 1889, and in the National League in 1890, 1892, 1893, and 1895. He led his league in double plays every year from 1882 through 1890, also in 1892 and 1893, with totals which are genuinely impressive for the era. He also led his league seven times in putouts, six times in assists, five times in fielding percentage—but not even once in errors. Also, in an era of enormous player turmoil which is normally reflected in disjointed careers, McPhee played one position for one team for eighteen years. I doubt that any other 19th century player did that, other than McPhee and Cap Anson.

McPhee never wore a glove until 1896; he was one of the last players to play barehanded. He worked to toughen his hands, and felt that he was more sure-handed without the leather. A broken finger finally forced him to wear a glove in 1896, and that year he fielded .978, a record fielding percentage for a second baseman until well into the twentieth century.

McPhee also recorded 529 putouts in 1886, a major league record which still stands; no one else is within 40 putouts. This record, while it no doubt involved some degree of ability, says as much about the time that McPhee played. McPhee had more putouts than any prior second baseman because the schedule was getting longer almost every year, and new records were set almost every year. He had more putouts than any subsequent second baseman because by the mid-1880s, second basemen were moving off the bag, and sharing forceouts at second with the shortstops. 1886 was about the last year when most second basemen stood right on or very near second base.

31 ◆ Frank White
(1973–1989, 2242 G, 158 865 .256)

The top ten second basemen, ranked by the percentage of their career value which was in fielding, rather than hitting: 1. Frank White, 2. Mazeroski, 3. Julian Javier, 4. Hughie Critz, 5. Ted Sizemore, 6. Tommy Helms, 7. Manny Trillo, 8. Glenn Hubbard, 9. Dick Green, 10. Bobby Richardson.

Frank White was a Kansas City native who grew up in the neighborhood of old Municipal Stadium. The owner of the expansion Royals, Ewing Kauffman, had the idea that he could build up the Royals' talent base by opening a "baseball academy" filled with exceptional athletes who had limited baseball experience. White, who was quick and strong and could run like the wind, was signed for the academy. A couple of notes about the academy, since it came up:

1. John Heydler, the far-sighted President of the National League in the 1920s, had suggested a half-century earlier that major league teams pool their resources and run a "baseball school."

2. The idea of the academy worked great, producing White and two or three other properties of some value in a very short time and at a reasonable cost, but was discontinued after a

few years because professional baseball men didn't want to be associated with any commie pinko radical ideas.

Anyway, White joined the Royals in 1973, also George Brett's rookie season. White became a second baseman simply because the Royals already had a good shortstop, Freddie Patek, while their second baseman, Cookie Rojas, had grown long in the shoelaces. White could have played shortstop, and could have been a good major league shortstop.

Artificial turf had become common in the early 1970s; the Royals moved into Royals Stadium, which had turf, in 1973. White was the first second baseman to fully grasp how the turf had changed the game, and the most successful second baseman at implementing adjustments. With the artificial turf, White realized that the ball would not roll dead in front of him, thus he could set up deeper than second basemen traditionally did. White probably stationed himself further from second base than any other second baseman who ever played the game, playing shallow right field 50, 60, or even 70 feet from second base. He often caught pop ups in foul territory. I saw him many times catch a dying quail over first base, a ball that might have rolled into the corner for a double had White not been playing where he was. More routinely, he would catch the soft single into right field, while with his great quickness and playing deep, he was still able to get to balls hit behind second. Of course he would edge toward second with a right-handed hitter at the plate or a man on first, but even so, for White, cheating toward second base meant setting up 20 or 25 feet behind the bag.

White became an immensely popular player in Kansas City. Being a local boy no doubt helped, but White's class and grace were larger factors. He had a little smile that he would flash many times a game. I always took the smile to be not a sign of enjoyment, but a kind of coping mechanism; when he was dumped at second base, when he got his pitch and fouled it off, when he dived for a ball but was unable to make the play, he would get up and flash the smile. I always took it to be his way of saying to himself "I can deal with this. That was nothing; let's focus on what we need to do."

Over the years, he became a better hitter, eventually hitting cleanup for the Royals in the 1985 World Series. Taking his career as a whole, he was interchangeable with Bill Mazeroski; easily distinguishable, but interchangeable. Both White and Mazeroski were right-handed hitters who hit around .260 with somewhere around 150 home runs. Neither player would take a walk, so both had terrible on-base percentages, below .300. Each player won eight Gold Gloves. Both players had long careers with one team. Both players played on many outstanding teams; each was a regular on one World Championship team. Mazeroski was the best ever at turning the double play; White was faster and probably covered more ground.

32 ◆ Lonny Frey
(1933–1948, 1535 G, 61 549 .269)
The Reds' infield in their 1939–40 championship era dubbed themselves the "Jungle Cats." Frank McCormick was "Wildcat," Frey was "Leopard," shortstop Billy Myers was "Jaguar," and third baseman Billy Werber was "Tiger." They would yell these names to each other during infield practice . . .

Up to a point, Frey could be compared to Jose Offerman. Both players came up as switch-hitting shortstops, in both cases for the Dodgers. Both were very good offensive shortstops, hitting for a good average with a high on-base percentage, and both players could run. Both were outstanding bunters. Both, however, were poor defensive shortstops, which caused their Dodger careers to founder, and forced them to be moved to second base.

Here, however, their career paths separate. Offerman, who was an awful shortstop, became an awful second baseman. Don't get me wrong; I like Jose Offerman. He is one of my favorite players, and I think he's a very underrated player. He makes a lot of mistakes at second base. Frey, on the other hand (a) stopped switch hitting, and (b) became a brilliant defensive second baseman.

Bill McKechnie, the Hall of Fame manager then re-constructing the Cincinnati Reds, realized that Frey just didn't have a shortstop's arm, and that this was putting so much pressure on him that it was causing his whole game to fall apart. McKechnie stationed him at second base, the Reds won two pennants and a World Championship, and Frey for a period of about five years was the best second baseman in the National League.

33 ◆ Gil McDougald
(1951–1960, 1336 G, 112 576 .276)
There are three men who made Casey Stengel a genius—Yogi Berra, Mickey Mantle, and Gil McDougald. Yogi was the only catcher in baseball history who could catch 145 games a year, hit cleanup, and never have an injury or a bad season. Mantle was a devastating offensive player and a solid center fielder; with those two men hitting 3-4, the Yankees were guaranteed to score a lot of runs every year.

And Gil McDougald could do anything. Gil McDougald is the only player in baseball history who rotated between second base, third base, and shortstop and was a Gold Glove fielder at all three positions. I'm sure there are other people who *could* have done this; I'm sure that Marty Marion and Luis Aparicio, had they been asked to play second base or third base, would have been real good at it. They didn't have to. McDougald did.

It was always Casey Stengel's style to re-write his lineup every day. Gil McDougald enabled him to do that successfully. Stengel's Yankees would lead the American League in double plays almost every year, despite massive instability in the middle of their infield. For many years, I could never figure out how they did this—in fact, I have written that several times, that I could never figure out how the Yankees could lead the league in double plays, with Casey Stengel shuffling his second basemen and shortstops in and out of the lineup like a network executive re-programming Tuesday night.

I finally realized, when I did the Win Shares analysis, why this was: Gil McDougald could do anything. There are a lot of books that say this, of course; all the books on the Yankees of the fifties will mention at least in passing that you could put McDougald anywhere and he was as good as anybody in the league. There are books that say anything, and I always thought that was just talk. When I developed the Win Shares system, I realized that this wasn't just talk: Gil McDougald was really outstanding everywhere. As a second baseman, he rates almost even (per inning) with Red Schoendienst, Frank White, and Nellie Fox. As a shortstop, he rates about even with Mark Belanger, Dal Maxvill, and Lou Boudreau. As a third baseman, he rates about even with Ken Boyer, Buddy Bell, and Aurelio Rodriguez.

The way that Stengel used him kept him from becoming a star. The irony is that McDougald would have become a star, in my opinion, had he stayed in baseball just a little longer. The first expansion draft was in December, 1960, stocking the American League's expansion from eight teams to ten. The California Angels acquired the rights to McDougald. McDougald didn't want to have anything to do with the expansion team, and decided to retire instead. The Angels offered him more money than he had ever made in his life. He said no.

Had McDougald agreed to report to the Angels, and had he been healthy, he would have hit at least 30 home runs, maybe 35, possibly 40. Why?

First, playing time. McDougald with the Yankees had averaged 540 plate appearances a year. With an expansion team, a regular position at third base, and eight games added to the schedule, he would probably have had 100 more than that.

Second, park effects. Yankee Stadium at that time was a horrible park for a right-handed hitter. In his ten-year career, McDougald hit 112 home runs—29 in Yankee Stadium, 83 on the road.

Wrigley Field in Los Angeles, on the other hand, was a great home run park, one of the best ever. The old TV show, *Home Run Derby*, was filmed there. In 1961 the Angels hit and allowed 248 home runs at home, as opposed to 121 on the road. Ken Hunt, a right-handed hitter from the Yankee farm system, went to the Angels in 1961 and hit 25 homers—17 at home, 8 on the road. Leon Wagner hit 19 at home, 9 on the road.

Third, of course, the Angels didn't see the same quality of pitching that the Yankees did. People didn't set their rotations to beat the Angels. So McDougald, had he reported, would have gone from *losing* 65% of his home runs in his home park to *gaining* somewhere around 100%. The effect of this, combined with a 20% increase in playing time, would have vaulted his home run total to unimaginable levels. I am confident that McDougald would have at least doubled his previous career high in home runs, which was 14. But then, Gil McDougald wasn't born to be a star. He was born to be a Yankee.

34 ◆ Eddie Stanky
(1943–1953, 1259 G, 29 364 .268)

> Stanky—they called him the Brat—was a clever little guy, but what a nuisance. With some of those guys it was an instinctive reaction. Blame the umpire. That's all they knew.—Tom Gorman, *Three and Two* (Scribner's, 1979)

Stanky's tactics forced major league base-ball into at least two rules changes. In 1945 Stanky developed a trick, when he was on third base with a chance to score on a fly ball, of positioning himself several steps behind third base, on the left field line. Just before the ball was caught he would start running, touch third just as the ball was caught, and break for home on a dead run. No rule prohibited this, and other players realized that it worked, so that by the end of the 1945 season several players were doing it. It was prohibited after the season.

In 1950, when Stanky was playing third for the Giants, he came up with another one. Once in awhile, just as the pitch was being thrown, Stanky would begin jumping up and down and waving his arms, trying to distract the hitter. The maneuver was prohibited by umpires after a few games, and banned by rule after the season ended.

35 ◆ Del Pratt
(1912–1924, 1835 G, 43 968 .292)
Pratt had been an All-American running back at the University of Alabama. He joined the St. Louis Browns in 1912, had an outstanding rookie season, and played every day for several years after that, leading the American League in games played in 1913, 1914, 1915, and 1916. He also led the league in RBI in 1916 (103), and drove in 100 in 1921.

He was a good hitter, and an above-average fielder for the time, which was an era that didn't place as much emphasis on defense at second base as would later be the case. I have him as deserving of the 1919 American League Gold Glove, and as the number two defensive second baseman in the American League in 1914, 1915, 1916, and 1920 (behind Eddie Collins) and in 1918 (behind Joe Gedeon).

Pratt hit .300 as a rookie and as a regular in 1912, and he hit .300 as a regular in 1924, his last year. I can think of only two other major league players (Richie Ashburn and

Tony Cuccinello) who played regularly and hit .300 both in their first major league seasons and their last.

As a college man and a veteran, Pratt emerged as a leader among the players in their battles against management (See article in Part 1, 1917: *Escape from St. Louis*). After becoming *persona non grata* in St. Louis Pratt was sold to the Yankees, where, in 1920, he became one of three designated player spokesmen in an unseemly dispute about the prize money the Yankees won for finishing third in 1919. From the Yankees he moved on to Boston, where he continued to play well, and to play almost every game, and then on to Detroit, where he was more or less a regular for two more years.

Pratt may have been a better player than I have rated him. He played mostly for bad teams, never played in a World Series, and his career is broken into three more or less equal segments—the St. Louis years, the New York phase, and the Boston/Detroit decline phase. Although he played well for all four teams, he failed to become a central figure in the history of any of them, and has largely disappeared from the literature of the sport. It is hard to say with confidence how good a player he was.

36 ◆ Bobby Avila
(1949–1959, 1300 G, 80 467 .281)
> Lockman bunted the ball past the pitcher's mound and toward second base, the kind of bunt that is usually impossible to field, and . . . Lockman is a speedy man. So I yelled, "Attaboy, Whitey," and then I watched in stunned silence as Bobby Avila swooped down, picked up the ball on the dead run, and threw Lockman out at first.—Arnold Hano, *A Day in the Bleachers* (Crowell, 1955)

Avila was born in Vera Cruz, Mexico on April 2, 1924, the ninth and last child of a well-to-do lawyer. A soccer star as a youth, Avila was encouraged to try baseball by an older brother. At Vera Cruz Preparatory High School he pitched and played shortstop, and found an old book on playing baseball by Jack Coombs, which he studied at length. At the age of sixteen he played professional soccer, earning fifty dollars a month, and dreamed of perhaps being a great bullfighter.

His father wanted Roberto to become a professional man. "Some day they will kick your head instead of the ball," he told Roberto, "and I will be hauled into court for having a son with rocks where his brains should be." Over his father's objections Avila signed as a third baseman for Cordoba in the Vera Cruz State League, which operated during the off-season of the dominant Mexican League, and soon moved up to the Mexican major. He batted .250 in his rookie season there, but then improved to .334, .336, .360, and .347.

In 1946 Jorge Pasquel induced a number of quality major-league players to defect to Mexico. When Avila saw the Americans play, he knew that he could make it in North American baseball. "He's a real nice little guy and a helluva hitter," said Sal Maglie in 1950, recalling Avila from the Mexican League. "He's so good I think I will knock him down with my first pitch, just to be on the safe side."

In the winter of 1946–47 Avila played in Cuba, where Leo Durocher was impressed enough to offer Avila $10,000 to sign with the Dodgers. Avila, hardly the stereotype of a hungry Latin player, turned the offer down and also rejected overtures from the Senators' famous man in Havana, Joe Cambria. Another legendary scout, the Indians' Cy Slapnicka, met with him in Mexico City, where Avila demanded $17,500 to sign. Slapnicka reportedly had been prepared to go much higher.

With Baltimore, Cleveland's top farm team in 1947, Avila batted a mere .220. He spoke no English, and his manager recalled that it took him a month to get Avila to understand that he needed to report to the park in time for batting

and fielding drills; in the Mexican League, they just showed up and played the games. In the field he seemed lethargic. The Orioles team doctor examined him and found a severe hernia; going home to Vera Cruz in mid-season, he was operated on by one of his older brothers. Adding to a miserable season, Avila's father died suddenly of a heart attack in the fall of 1948.

The bonus rule in effect at that time allowed a one year minor league option for a player who had received a substantial bonus; after that the bonus baby had to spend two years on the major league roster. Avila roomed with Mike Garcia, whose parents were from Mexico. Garcia was the only person in his world that Avila could talk to, and Bobby nearly drove him nuts asking questions, trying to learn the language. Avila, twenty-five years old and ready to play—Lou Boudreau said that he'd never seen a rookie with as good a grasp of fundamentals—spent a year and a half on the Indians' bench, watching the great Joe Gordon play second, and occasionally falling asleep (see entry on Muddy Ruel, Catcher #51). Joe Gordon ran out of gas in 1950, and Avila replaced him late in the season.

From the day Avila stepped into the lineup, he hit, keeping his average within a few points of .300 for several years. He walked twice as often as he struck out, and had a little line-drive power. On June 20, 1951, he hit three home runs, a single, and a double in one game. Avila hit the ball where it was pitched, pulled the ball when the opportunity arose, and bunted frequently and well. One of the fastest men in the league, Avila was also alert and extremely aggressive on the base paths, this being what he was best known for before 1954. Using his soccer background, he perfected a "scissors-kick" slide. Sliding into the base with his right leg tucked against his body, he would lash out at the last moment, knocking the ball, and sometimes the glove, away from the fielder.

Roberto sent money back home to Mexico to support his mother and a widowed sister, maintaining the family's position by sending a nephew through law school. The father of several children, he spent much of his time writing letters to the people back home. He said he didn't want his son to grow up to be a ballplayer. "Is a fine game for a single man. But for a married man is no good. Too much travel around. Too much away from the family."

Avila played extremely well in the field in 1951, his first season as a regular, but had a defensive slump in 1952. He was criticized for shying away from oncoming baserunners, losing double plays. But that was a one-year thing; from 1951 through 1956 Avila ranks almost dead even with Nellie Fox as the best defensive second baseman in the American League every year except 1952.

In 1954 the Indians, perennial American League runners-up, won 111 games. They did this despite suffering significant injuries to all four regular infielders. Third baseman Al Rosen chipped his right index finger on May 25, and couldn't swing the bat up to his ability the rest of the year. Shortstop George Strickland missed five weeks with a fractured jaw, first baseman Bill Glynn was slowed by hamstrings and replaced in mid-season by Vic Wertz, who missed twenty games with various injuries himself, and Avila, hitting .391 in June, suffered a broken thumb in a collision at second base with Hank Bauer.

Avila reported to spring training in 1954 with ulcers, and was ordered to drink milk. He drank two quarts a day, and it turned out to be power lunch. Avila scored 112 runs that year, went three-for-three in the All-Star game, and hit fifteen home runs, thirteen of which either tied or won the game.

On opening day, 1954, with Ted Williams sidelined by a broken collarbone, Dizzy Dean had wagered a $50 Texas hat that Avila would win the AL batting championship. Despite slumping badly in June with the broken thumb, Avila won Dean his hat with a .341 final mark. The batting title led to a controversy, and thus to a rules change, leaving Avila's imprint on the game. Ted Williams returned to the lineup in mid-May, and finished with a .345 average in 117 games. At the time the rule was that a player had to bat 400 times to be eligible for the batting title, and "The Splinter" just missed that, with 386. Williams, however, had also walked 136 times; altogether he had 526 plate appearances. The rule, said Casey Stengel "was never meant for a guy like Ted Williams, it's for humpty-dumpties trying to steal a batting championship on half a season's work."

Avila offered the opinion that if it hadn't been for his broken thumb there would have been no question as to who deserved the batting championship, leaving open the question of what Ted Williams would have hit had it not been for that painful steel pin in his shoulder. The rule was changed, anyway, so that eligibility for the batting championship was based on plate appearances rather than at bats. Avila could have been the MVP that year, too, but three Cleveland players (Larry Doby, Avila, and Bob Lemon) split the vote, leaving Yogi Berra on top of a rather weird vote.

Avila was the Mike Hargrove of his day, going through a series of motions before he would get into the batter's box—hitching his sleeves, spitting on his hands, getting just the right stance. "He used to drive me nuts when I was umpiring," said Cal Hubbard. "He's the most careful batter in the game." Avila said that until it was pointed out to him, he didn't know that he did all that stuff.

Avila's numbers slipped after 1954, and the Indians slid gradually away from the pennant race. Avila bounced from Cleveland to Baltimore to Boston to Milwaukee, leaving the majors after the 1959 season. He had become a national hero in Mexico—more popular, it was said, than even the greatest bullfighters. During the fifties he became the owner/manager/second baseman of a Mexico City winter league team. "It's terrible," he said. "You playing game and players ask you for money right on the bench." He said that once his major league career was over he would sever his connections with baseball. He didn't, of course; in 1960, his first year out of the majors, he played for the Mexico City Tigers, hitting .333 and leading the league in runs scored and walks. He remained active in baseball as an owner, later as President of the Vera Cruz Eagles, and, for a time in the early 1980s, as President of the Mexican League.

As I said about Del Pratt, Avila could be rated a lot higher than I have him rated here. What we see of Avila in the encyclopedias is only about half of his career, the gringo years. Like Pratt, he was an outstanding hitter, a quality fielder, and a respected team leader.

(Most of the work on this article was done by Mike Kopf. Background articles include *Viva Avila*, by Gordon Cobbledick, in the September, 1953, edition of *Sport Magazine*, an article by Hal Lebovitz in the June, 1955, *Baseball Digest*, a profile of Avila by Harry Jones in *Baseball Stars of 1955*, and another Lebovitz article, *Avila's Flying Feet*, in the 1952 edition of *Best Sports Stories*.)

37 ◆ Miller Huggins
(1904–1916, 1585 G, 9 328 .265)
Most similar players to Miller Huggins, by decade:

> 1890s—Cupid Childs
> 1900s—Johnny Evers
> 1910s—Ralph Young
> 1920s—Sparky Adams
> 1930s—Maxie Bishop
> 1940s—Snuffy Stirnweiss
> 1950s—Johnny Temple or Junior Gilliam

> 1960s—Ron Hunt
> 1970s—Willie Randolph
> 1980s—Wally Backman
> 1990s—Joey Cora or Mark McLemore

Huggins was about halfway between the two New Yorkers that you would remember, Randolph and Backman. He wasn't nearly as good a defensive player as Randolph, nor as bad as Backman . . . As a player he is believed to have invented the delayed steal.

38 ◆ Pete Runnels
(1951–1964, 1799 G, 49 630 .291)
In 1958 Pete Runnels hit .322, losing the American League batting championship on the last day of the season. In 1959 he hit .314, third in the league, and in 1960 he won the title, hitting .320. The next March Runnels arrived at spring training to discover that a rookie, Chuck Schilling, had been handed second base, which was his primary position, and that a polio survivor was playing first base, which was his other position. A reporter asked the manager, Pinky Higgins, where he planned to play Runnels.

"We'll always find a place for him," said Higgins, as if this was the first time he had considered the topic. "He can play any infield position."

In May, 1960, when Runnels was hitting .357, he came up with the bases loaded, facing Dick Stigman, a left-handed pitcher. The manager, Billy Jurges, pinch hit for him with a guy who was hitting under .200 (Ray Boone).

One might think that a perennial .320 hitter who could play any infield position would be considered a valuable man. Runnels opened the 1961 season on the bench. He pinch hit, served as a fifth infielder, and eventually got back into the lineup at first base, hitting .317 for the season. In '62 he came back to win his second American League batting championship, at .326, at which point the Red Sox traded him to Houston.

Pete Runnels could play any infield position, and was a good defensive first baseman. No, actually, Runnels when he came to the majors in 1951 was a decent shortstop. By the early 1960s that was ancient history. He was a first baseman who had the temerity to be a singles hitter, never mind that he was the best singles hitter in baseball. In '63, after they traded Runnels, the Red Sox replaced him with a power-hitting first baseman, Dick Stuart. Stuart hit 42 homers and led the league in RBI—and the Red Sox scored 41 fewer runs than they had with Runnels, and dropped from 76-84 to 76-85 . . .

Runnels attributed his greatly improved batting when he joined the Red Sox to Ted Williams, who, he said, had taught him far more about hitting than everyone else combined. But Runnels had hit .310 at Washington in 1955, before he joined the Sox, and .310 in Washington was at least as impressive as .320 in Fenway.

39 ◆ Hardy Richardson

(1879–1892, 1331 G, 70 822 .299)

Richardson entered professional baseball as the first leagues were just getting organized, and sort of grew up with the game. He played for Buffalo in 1879, with a team that got into the National League because the National League was desperate and on the verge of collapsing. He was pretty decent in his first few years, and as time passed he got better. He played for Buffalo for seven years, the only seven years the Buffalo franchise existed, becoming the first (chronologically) of Buffalo's "Big Four" stars—Richardson, Orator Jim O'Rourke, Dan Brouthers, and Deacon White.

Late in the 1885 season the Detroit Wolverines bought out the Buffalo team for $7,000. Detroit didn't care about the franchise or the rest of the players. What they wanted was to add the Big Four to their roster.

I'm sure you have played this little game, killing time, in which you take two bad teams,

piece them together, and see if you can make one good team. In this case, you could. Detroit in 1885 had gone 41-67; Buffalo was 38-74. But when the Big Four were added to the Detroit lineup, along with one or two other quality players purchased from other sources, the Detroit team vaulted to 87-36 in 1886 (second place), and then to the pennant in 1887.

Richardson in 1886 led the National League in hits (189) and home runs (11). He moved to Boston in 1889, played in the Players League in 1890 (leading the league in RBI, with 146), and left the majors after the 1892 season.

According to Joseph M. Overfield in *Nineteenth Century Stars,* "Richardson was a crackerjack shot, especially in on-the-wing shooting, and left open at all times a $1,000 challenge to anyone who thought he could outshoot him. The challenge was never taken up. When his playing days were over, he operated a hotel in Utica. Later he moved to nearby Ilion, where he was employed in the Remington Typewriter works."

At ballparks in the 1880s the landscaping was often a little shabby. At the Philadelphia park on July 20, 1883, a patch of grass in the left field corner was so high that Richardson and Jack Rowe both got home runs when the ball rolled into the corner and the left fielder, Connie Doyle, couldn't find it.

40 ◆ Tommie Herr

(1979–1991, 1514 G, 28 574 .271)

In the 1982 World Series, Tommie Herr hit a two-run sacrifice fly. He hit a drive to deep center; Gorman Thomas fell down after making the catch, and Willie McGee scored from second. He is the only man in World Series history to drive in two runs with a sacrifice fly.

Fundamentally, he was such a smart player. The whole time I managed him, he never screwed up a ground ball or a play that he should have made. He never made a mental mistake. And he played hurt.—Whitey Herzog, *You're Missin' a Great Game* (Simon & Schuster, 1999)

Ryne Sandberg and Tommie Herr not only have the best fielding percentages of any second baseman listed here (.989), but also the best fielding percentages relative to the league norms for their era. The norm for their era was .981—thus, they committed 42% fewer errors than the league norm. The normal fielding percentage for a second baseman was around .900 in the 1880s. This increased rapidly until 1920, and increased steadily until the early 1950s, but has edged up only four points since 1955. The *worst* fielding percentages by any second baseman listed here were by Juan Samuel (.973 against a league norm of .981) and George Grantham (.949 against .964).

41 ◆ Phil Garner
(1973–1988, 1860 G, 109 738 .260)

Phil Garner's best season was 1979, when he hit .293, 33 points over his career average. The reason? Donnie Moore drilled him in the hand with a fastball. The hand swelled up, Garner was unable to grip the bat properly, and thus was unable to overswing. Playing with the injury, he had the best hot streak of his career, which carried him to the .293 average.

Baseball history is full of stories like this. Ted Williams in 1941 had a broken bone in his right foot. It was painful if he put any weight on it, and consequently it reminded him constantly to keep his weight back. Floyd Robinson attributed his .310 batting average as a rookie in 1961 to an injury. I once heard a player credit a hitting streak to a small hernia, which he said prevented him from overstriding . . .

Garner's father and grandfather were Baptist preachers in small southern towns. "My grandfather was an old fire-and-brimstone-type preacher," Garner said in *The Fall of the Roman Umpire* (Ron Luciano). "He'd stand up

there and he'd tell his parishioners, 'I want to throw all the beer in the river! I want to throw all the wine in the river! I want to throw all the wild women in the river! I want to throw all the cards in the river! Now, let us turn to page two twenty-nine and sing together, Shall We Gather at the River.'"

42 ◆ Robby Thompson
(1986–1996, 1304 G, 119 458 .257)

Good hitter, outstanding fielder, career basically ended at age 31 because of a bad shoulder injury.

43 ◆ Max Bishop
(1924–1935, 1338 G, 41 379 .271)

Maxie had 1,153 walks in his career and 1,216 hits—the highest ratio of walks to hits of any player in baseball history (playing 1,000 or more games). The top ten: Bishop, Gene Tenace, Eddie Yost, Eddie Stanky, Mickey Tettleton, Roy Cullenbine, Ferris Fain, Joe Ferguson, Eddie Joost, and Mark McGwire (through 1999) . . . Also ranks as the second-greatest percentage player in baseball history (see Joe Morgan), has the second-highest secondary average among second basemen (see Bobby Grich), and was a good defensive second basemen, at least according to the Win Shares analysis.

Bishop was a member of the greatest of all minor league teams, the Baltimore Orioles of the early 1920s. He was a Baltimore native (although not born in the city), and was scouted and signed by Jack Dunn, who just three years earlier had scouted and signed Babe Ruth. Bishop was signed off the campus of Baltimore City College; according to Fred Lieb in *The Baltimore Orioles* (G. P. Putnam's Sons, 1955), "the little guy attended there in short pants." When Bishop signed with Dunn, he recommended that Dunn also sign Joe Boley, a Polish kid from Pennsylvania, that Max knew from playing summer ball, and had recruited to play with him at Baltimore City College. Bishop and Boley played second and short together at Baltimore City College, in summer leagues, with the minor league Baltimore Orioles, and eventually with the World Champion Philadelphia Athletics.

44 ◆ Steve Sax
(1981–1994, 1769 G, 54 550 .281)

In the Ryne Sandberg comment I wrote about Sandberg as a rookie. One reason this interests me is that, as a rookie in 1982, Ryne Sandberg (who was playing third at that time) had essentially the same stats as two rookie second basemen, Steve Sax and Johnny Ray. Sandberg hit .271 with 172 hits, 7 homers, 54 RBI, Ray hit .281 with 182 hits, 7 homers, 63 RBI, and Sax hit .282 with 180 hits, 4 homers, 47 RBI. Sax won the Rookie of the Year Award, Ray finished second, and Sandberg was on down the list, behind Willie McGee and Chili Davis. The question of interest is, was there any way to study these players and predict that Sandberg would be the one to emerge as a long-term star?

I suspect that there probably is, if you had enough information. You could certainly eliminate or almost eliminate Ray as a potential star, because he was three years older than Sandberg and Sax, an immense negative factor in assessing his future (See Sam Rice, RF #33). Distinguishing between Sax and Sandberg is harder—in fact, if one were to conclude that Sandberg as a rookie had a 25% chance of becoming a Hall of Famer, one would almost be forced to conclude that the percentage for Sax was somewhat higher than that, since Sax was a few months younger than Sandberg, and outplayed him by a small margin.

Still, I suspect that it might be at least theoretically possible to predict Sandberg's emergence, given the right information. Sax was . . . well, he was a cutup. He had a cheeky, class-clown personality, a smart guy and a smooth

talker, but perhaps with a little more humor than was helpful. Guys like that rarely become superstars . . . Mickey Mantle did; I'm sure others have. Not many. Superstars are fiery talents like Cobb, Hornsby, Ted Williams, and Jackie Robinson, quiet guys like Musial, Brett, Aaron, Ripken, and Wagner (as a player), smoldering personalities like Reggie, Barry Bonds, DiMaggio, Cap Anson, and Al Simmons, and sharp cookies like Eddie Collins, Joe Morgan, and Tris Speaker. What unites these groups is that they all seek attention and "validation" by their success on the baseball field. What separates Sax is that he sometimes sought attention by charm, wit, and personality, as opposed to accomplishments. This would be unusual for a superstar. Personalities are such complex things that it is difficult to generalize, and there are some sports superstars who are narcissists (Reggie, O.J., Steve Garvey, Pete Rose, Jim Brown, Dizzy Dean, Hollywood Henderson), and who seek attention from *everybody* all the time. Sax wasn't like that; he wasn't an obsessed guy who had to be the center of attention all the time.

Ryne Sandberg's personality was in the mold of the Musial/Aaron/Mel Ott/Willie McCovey/Charlie Gehringer type guys. You can never know *everything*, of course; you can never make predictions with 100% accuracy. But if you had known enough about Sax and Sandberg as 22-year-old men, I suspect that you could have made a pretty good guess about where their careers were headed.

45 ◆ Bill Doran
(1982–1993, 1453 G, 84 497 .266)

A low-key member of a team which had most of the elements of a champion, but never got to the top due to injuries to the men who should have been their stars—J.R. Richard, Dickie Thon, Glenn Davis, and Doran. Doran had back trouble . . .

Almost everyone who has held the second base job for the Colts/Astros is one of the top 100 players at the position, mostly in the top 50. Their first second baseman was Joey Amalfitano, a marginal regular, but in '63 they traded for Johnny Temple, then for Nellie Fox. Fox was replaced by Joe Morgan, Morgan was traded for Tommie Helms. Since Helms they've had Phil Garner (1981–82), Bill Doran (1982–1990), and Craig Biggio. Of course, Temple and Fox were washed up before they came to Houston, and the Astros missed Morgan's best years, but only in the late seventies (Art Howe, Rafael Landestoy, Rob Andrews) and for a few odd months here and there have the Astros not put out a second baseman with top-flight credentials.

Bill Doran, a career .277 hitter through 1988, was hitting .280 with 7 homers, 46 RBI on June 25, 1989, then went into the mother of all slumps to finish the season at .219. "I've given the word 'slump' a whole new meaning," Doran said. "Instead of saying, 'I'm in a slump.' they say, 'I'm in a Billy Doran.'"

46 ◆ Davey Johnson
(1965–1978, 1435 G, 136 609 .261)

As most of you know, Davey Johnson had a career high of 18 home runs, other than in 1973, when he hit 43 homers. He had a career high of 77 runs created, other than in 1973, when he created 109.

But here's the question: was Dave Johnson actually a better player in 1973 than he was in any other year? According to the Win Shares system, Johnson was exactly as valuable in 1973 as in his other best seasons. His Win Shares by season, beginning in 1965, read 1, 13, 17, 16, 18, 23, 22, 14, 22, 15, 0, blank (played in Japan), 8, and 3. The 1973 season is the second "22." Johnson did have his best year with the bat in 1973, but much of the apparent increase in his hitting is a park illusion, and the rest of it is offset by his declining defense.

I probably shouldn't mention this, but did you ever notice that Dave Johnson (as a manager) has the world's largest collection of disgusting personal mannerisms? He picks his teeth with his fingers, tucks his hands in his armpits, scratches his head, shakes and pats his unmentionables, spits, drools. Don't get me wrong; he's a terrific manager, one of the very best, but doesn't this man have a wife? Jeez, it's no wonder he gets fired every other year . . .

47 ◆ Tony Taylor
(1958–1976, 2195 G, 75 598 .261)

Between 1900, when the Phillies had Nap Lajoie at second base, and 1960, when they traded for Tony Taylor, the best second baseman the Phillies had was Otto Knabe, who was their second baseman from 1907 to 1913, and who didn't make the top 100. The top five in games played for Philadelphia at second base, 1901–1960, are Knabe (931), Kid Gleason (571), Fresco Thompson (565), Granny Hamner (561), and Bernie Niehoff (401).

This actually happened, July 11, 1963, in Philadelphia, go check the newspapers if you don't believe me. Willie Mays draws a walk leading off the second inning. He has second base stolen standing up, but Orlando Cepeda fouls off the pitch. Second pitch, Mays has second base stolen again, Cepeda fouls off the pitch again, strike two. There's a pitchout and a ball outside; the count reaches two-two, and Mays takes off for second again. Once more, Cepeda fouls the ball off.

Finally, fourth try, Mays goes for second and Cepeda squibs the ball off the end of his bat to the second baseman, Tony Taylor. Mays sees the ball rolling behind him and figures that he can make third on the throw to first, so he heads for third. Tony Taylor, however, has seen Willie Mays play baseball before, so he holds the ball a second before throwing to first. When Mays heads for third, Taylor throws across the infield, Mays is out at third by 40 feet.

Mays, however, decides to stay in a rundown long enough to let Cepeda make second. Catching Willie Mays in a rundown is like trying to assassinate a squirrel with a lawn mower, so this goes on for some time, and Cepeda races down to second base, while Don Hoak (Philadelphia third baseman) chases Mays back to the same base. Mays and Cepeda, both near second base, stare at each other for a moment, while the ball pops loose on the ground before anybody can apply a tag to either one of them.

So Mays heads back to third base.

And Cepeda heads back to first.

Taylor retrieves the ball, and fires to third, and Willie Mays, for the second time on the same play, is caught in a rundown between second and third.

Well, that out is eventually recorded; it's officially scored 4-5-6-1-6-4, but, as the official scorer noted afterward, he couldn't be sure who all had handled the ball, and a player can only get one assist on a play anyway, so he just gave an assist to everybody in the vicinity.

Ed Bailey is up next; he singles, sending Cepeda to third, and then Jim Davenport singles, scoring Cepeda and sending Bailey to third.

The next hitter, Jose Pagan, works the count to 2-2, and Al Dark puts the hit-and-run on again. Pagan strikes out. The catcher fires to Tony Taylor, and Davenport heads back to first base. Taylor throws to first, and the Giants are in the middle of their third rundown of the inning.

At which point Ed Bailey breaks for home plate.

The Giants now have had four baserunners in the inning (Mays, Cepeda, Bailey, and Davenport)—each of whom, at one point or another, has been trapped off base. Roy Sievers ran right at Bailey, freezing him between home and third. Bailey eventually headed back to third, and Sievers threw him out.

They were done for the inning, but not the day; later on, in the sixth, there was another hit-and-run play, as a result of which both Bailey and Cepeda were once more caught off base. In spite of their basepath adventures, Willie McCovey homered in the eighth, and the Giants won, 4-3.

48 ◆ Jeff Kent
(1992–2000, 1191 G, 194 793 .284)
One of the best RBI men to play second base.

49 ◆ Manny Trillo
(1973–1989, 1780 G, 61 571 .263)
Trillo's career tracks that of Frank White. White was born in September, 1950, Trillo on Christmas day of the same year. Both reached the majors in June, 1973. Both became regulars in 1975, Trillo on opening day, White in mid-season. Trillo stayed until 1989; White, until 1990. Both were right-handed hitting second basemen who hit around .260 and didn't walk. Both were outstanding second basemen.

Eventually, due to injuries, White would have a little better career than Trillo; White had more power and more speed and won eight Gold Gloves, while Trillo won three. But in the first ten years of their careers, they were dead even, or Trillo was a little ahead . . .

Of the top 50 second basemen of all time, eight were basically given away by teams which had no idea how good a player they had. Ryne Sandberg was signed and developed by the Phillies, but thrown in on a trade with the Cubs to even up an exchange of shortstops, Ivan DeJesus for Larry Bowa. Nellie Fox was signed by the A's and played a season for the A's, after which they traded him to the White Sox for a backup catcher. Willie Randolph was signed and developed by the Pirates, who gave him 61 at bats and then made him a throw-in on an exchange of pitchers, Dock Ellis for Doc Medich. Buddy Myer was signed by Cleveland, released, signed by Washington, played a year and a half for Washington and was traded for Topper Rigney when he was regarded as a sub-par shortstop. Lonny Frey failed as a short-stop and was dropped by two teams before becoming an outstanding second baseman.

Eddie Stanky spent an eternity in the minor leagues (more than a thousand minor league games), finally reached the majors as a war-time replacement player, was traded even up for a pitcher named Bob Chipman, and actually descended to the level of a 28-year-old war-time utility infielder before Leo Durocher realized that if you let him bat leadoff every-day he would hit .270, draw 140 walks, and lead the league in runs scored. Phil Garner was drafted by Montreal, but demanded a $1,000 bonus to sign, just as a show of respect, and refused to sign when Montreal wouldn't put up even the trivial bonus. He reached the majors with the Oakland A's, played a year with them, hit .246, and was included in a nine-player trade with Pittsburgh. Trillo was a minor league teammate of Phil Garner's at Iowa in 1972, Tucson in 1973 and 1974, in the A's system, but was given away by Oakland even more cheaply than Garner, traded to Chicago with two relief pitchers in exchange for the 37-year-old Billy Williams.

Late in the 1974 season, Dick Williams decided that he had no second baseman but lots of pinch hitters, so he began rotating five second baseman, pinch hitting whenever one of them came to bat. Two of these anonymous second basemen, Garner and Trillo, would go on to be among the best second basemen in the game.

If you checked the top 50 shortstops of all time, I doubt that you would find more than one or two who were given away by organizations that didn't realize they could play . . . I think Joe Cronin may be the only one. Why? Start with a related phenomenon: second basemen are never drafted in the first round of the amateur free agent draft, almost literally never. In the entire history of the amateur draft, which

dates to 1965, only a handful of second basemen have been first-round draft picks.

Why? Teams don't respect an amateur second baseman. They figure if he was any good, he'd be playing shortstop in college. For the same reason, major league teams will often try to develop a young player as a shortstop, decide he's not going to make it as a shortstop, and give him away because he doesn't have a shortstop's arm or a shortstop's quickness. They think of second basemen as guys who aren't good enough to play short.

50 ◆ Dave Cash
(1969–1980, 1422 G, 21 426 .283)
Cash averaged 199 hits a year from 1974 through 1977 (206, 213, 189, 188); he also drew 50 walks a year, giving him a respectable on-base percentage, could run a little, made few errors at second base, had above-average range, and twice hit 40 doubles in a season.

Cash was an intelligent player, consistent and very competitive. He was short, bandy-legged, and didn't look strong, although he was. He was serious about his work. Eventually, like a lot of players, he started to believe that he was a little better player than he actually was. This caused him to bounce from team to team, as a form of reality therapy.

> [Fishing] is what Cash likes to do when he's not playing baseball . . . The 27-year-old Utica, N.Y., product shuns movies and does as little socializing as possible. He prefers to think baseball. Except for rare occasions, he manages to take extra batting practice every day—even when the Phillies are off.—*The Sporting News,* August 21, 1976

51 ◆ Danny Murphy
(1900–1915, 1495 G, 44 702 .290)
Murphy hit .300 several times in an era when runs were scarce, plus he had power, hitting 27 to 34 doubles every year, 11 to 18 triples a year, and finishing among the American League

home run leaders in 1904 (7), 1905 (6), and 1909 (5). He was also a pretty good defensive second baseman, but Eddie Collins' emergence on the team forced him to move to right field to continue his career; as an outfielder he led the American League in fielding percentage (1909) and assists (1911) . . .

There was a building outside the right field fence at Shibe Park in Philadelphia. According to Philip J. Lowrey in *Green Cathedrals* (SABR, 1986), Connie Mack in 1910 sent Murphy to the roof of the building to watch the game with a pair of opera glasses, stealing the catcher's signs and signaling the batters with the weather vane . . .

> Philadelphia is the native burg of Daniel Murphy, the man who guards the right portion of the Athletic outfield. Danny packs away 175 pounds, and has seen 35 years pass over his head without the slightest diminution of playing ability on his part. Seventeen years ago Danny started to draw an envelope by playing base ball. He was originally a second baseman, starting in that capacity with the Worcester (Mass.) team. Three years later Danny found it more profitable to himself to play semi-professional ball. The adjoining towns of Attleboro and North Attleboro, in Massachusetts, are the centers of the cheap jewelry manufacture in the country. Base ball fever hit those burgs, and in the inter-city rivalry the country was scoured for players. Fabulous prices were offered, and inducements of every sort acted as a magnet to draw the stars to the towns. Murphy went with North Attleboro, and as the second baseman in that organization was the idol of the fans. When he tired of the Attleboros Dan went to Norwich, Conn. where he played for a couple of years, to be brought to the New York Giants via the draft. He was turned back to Norwich, and was a member of that club when he was secured by the Athletics. He came as a second baseman, and in his first game with the Connie Clan equaled the world's record established by Clarence Beaumont of making six hits in as many times at bat. Murphy's work at

second was sensational, but when Collins was placed at that position last season Dan was shifted to right field. No outfielder in the country in that position distances Murphy.—1911 *Reach Guide*

52 ◆ Johnny Temple
(1952–1964, 1420 G, 22 395 .284)

> Because Temple and I had once exchanged swings during a clubhouse scuffle, most people figured we had little use for one another. Actually, we were good friends. Temple was a high strung individual . . . with an inferiority complex, which he attempted to conceal beneath a cover of braggadocio.—Earl Lawson, *Cincinnati Seasons*

Temple was an Eddie Stanky, Ron Hunt-type player; a scrappy, annoying leadoff man and a fighter. Joe Garagiola in *Baseball is a Funny Game* (1960, Bantam) picked an all-star team of baseball's best men in an on-field brawl. 1B–Gil Hodges or Ted Kluszewski, 2B–Johnny Temple, 3B–Don Hoak, SS–Johnny Logan, OF–Pete Whisenant, Walt Moryn, and Del Ennis, C–Stan Lopata . . .

Birdie Tebbetts was Temple's manager for several years. Tebbetts gave Temple an automatic "take" sign until the pitcher got two strikes on him; all Temple had was one swing to work with. Temple, naturally enough, hated that. When Jimmy Dykes replaced Tebbetts as manager, he took off the take sign. The next day the Reds were playing the Giants, Johnny Antonelli pitching. Temple drilled the first pitch into the left field seats. Antonelli was furious, and yelled at Temple as he rounded third, "You're not supposed to swing at that pitch." . . .

Temple was a player/coach with the Reds in 1964, but was fired after getting in a fight with another coach (Reggie Ortero). He became a TV newsman in Houston, made good money for a couple of years, and got involved in a business selling RVs and boats. He had a poor choice of partners, however; the business wasn't paying taxes, and after a couple of years it collapsed on Temple's head. He lost everything, including his house, and still couldn't pay the judgments against him.

He got a job with the state of South Carolina, a good job, but was fired after allegations of petty theft, allegations which he always insisted were false. At this point he went into a complete flameout, began to drink heavily, and developed pneumonia. In November, 1977, he was arrested and charged with being involved in a ring of thieves who stole heavy equipment.

Temple's wife, loyal but at the end of her rope, finally wrote a public letter, published in *The Sporting News,* pleading for help. "Johnny was never a favorite player with his fellow players," she wrote. "The fans, though, like Johnny. Would they have compassion for him now?" Hundreds of fans responded, sending $5 to $20 each; the appeal raised several thousand dollars, plus Temple got legal assistance. Eventually, he testified before the South Carolina assembly against his partners in crime.

After that he disappeared for several years, as if he had been wiped off the map. There was speculation that he had been relocated as part of a witness protection program. His troubles finally ended in 1994 ... see also comment on Johnny Logan, (SS #39).

53 ◆ Tony Cuccinello

(1930–1945, 1704 G, 94 884 .280)
Cuccinello grew up in Long Island. He had a neighbor who was a catcher for the Syracuse team in the International League. When he was 17 years old, still in high school, the neighbor saw him playing ball, and asked him to work out for his manager. Cuccinello impressed the manager, and signed with Syracuse.

On his first day with Syracuse they let him pinch hit. He hit a double, but fell down rounding third base on the next hit, and failed to score. At this time good minor league teams ran their own minor league operations, so Cuccinello, after going 3-for-4 for Syracuse, was farmed out to a lower minor league.

Cuccinello sped through the minor leagues in good order, hitting over .300 almost everywhere. Branch Rickey saw him playing, and purchased him for the Cardinals. In 1929 he was assigned to Columbus in the American Association, where he hit .358 in 162 games, leading the league in hits (227) and doubles. At the age of 20, Cuccinello was ready to move on to the major leagues.

The Cardinals, however, had Frankie Frisch at second base. Branch Rickey sold Cuccinello to Cincinnati—one of the first times, incidentally, that Rickey would sell off the surplus of his farm system. His first couple of years in the National League, it looked like Cuccinello was headed for stardom. He hit .312 as a rookie in 1930, and .315 his second season, driving in 93 runs, which would be a record for a Cincinnati second baseman until Joe Morgan, more than 40 years later.

Cuccinello held out that winter, however, which alienated the Reds' owner, who then included him in a trade with Brooklyn. After 1932 he was pestered by an array of minor injuries, and he never got any better. He played for Casey Stengel in Brooklyn, and also formed a life-long friendship with Al Lopez, with whom he would play golf for the next 60 years. In 1935 the Dodgers traded Cuccinello (and Lopez) to the Boston Braves.

In 1931 he had established a National League record for double plays by a second baseman (128). In 1936, proving it wasn't a fluke, he tied his own record. "Lopez and Cuccinello," wrote Al Hirschberg in *The Braves: The Pick and The Shovel,* "were both aggressive ball players, who loved to play the game, knew the league well and cared nothing about what went on in the front office, as long as they could help the team win on the field...Thanks to Cuccinello, the infield became a fairly good unit, which faithfully followed his suggestions." A year later, Casey Stengel was hired as manager, re-uniting the trio. Cuccinello played for the Braves, and well, until 1943.

In 1939 Dick Bartell plowed into him in the middle of a double play, tearing up Cuccinello's knee. He was out for two months, and the knee just got gradually worse for the rest of his life. By the early 1940s he was a bench player, and in July, 1943, he was released.

Cuccinello was 4-F (ineligible for the draft) because he had chronic laryngitis; at one point he was unable to talk above a whisper for three years. He signed with the White Sox the day he was released by the Braves, and by 1945 the War had made him back into a regular. With two days to go in the season, Cuccinello was leading the American League in hitting, at .308; if he had won he would have been, at the time, the oldest man ever to win a batting championship. The White Sox last two games were rained out, however, and Snuffy Stirnweiss edged by him, winning the batting title by .00008—.30854 to .30846. That remains the thinnest margin by which a batting race has ever been decided.

Cuccinello had decided by mid-season, 1945, to retire after the year. His knee was gone; he played in constant pain, and he couldn't run. Cuccinello stayed on the sidelines as a coach for many, many years after his retirement. He coached in the American Association a year, then coached for the Reds for three years, under Bucky Walters and Luke Sewell, and then joined up with Al Lopez, with whom he would work for the rest of his life.

Cuccinello was offered at least four jobs as a manager, but always turned them down, due mostly to his fear of public speaking. Cuccinello had dropped out of high school to play pro baseball, and was always afraid that he would sound ignorant in front of a group of people. That, combined with the chronic laryngitis, left him unable to perform the public relations duties of a manager.

54 ◆ Jimmy Williams
(1899–1909, 1458 G, 49 796 .275)
Williams was called "Button" because he was a small man, no bigger than a button; the Encyclopedias list him at 5-9, 175, but God knows what the source of that is. As a rookie in 1899 he was a great player, hitting .355 with 9 home runs (only two players in baseball hit more), 116 RBI (also third in the league), and 27 triples, which led the league. That remains one of the best rookie seasons in the history of baseball, although it is rarely cited as such because it was before 1900.

A year later, when the American League committed itself to competing with the National, Williams became one of the top prizes of the war between the leagues. He settled with Baltimore, John McGraw's team, further irritating the National League owners by accepting a train ticket to the East Coast from Pittsburgh owner Barney Dreyfuss, but using it to report to Baltimore.

He never matched the brilliance of his rookie season, although he hit over .300 in 1901 and 1902, and led the American League in triples both seasons, with 21. He was an adequate defensive second baseman.

55 ◆ Tom Daly
(1887–1903, 1564 G, 49 811 .278)
A switch hitter, Daly was a regular catcher for four years (1887–1890), switched to third base in 1892, second in 1893. Like Williams, he was a competent but unremarkable second baseman, a pretty decent hitter.

Tom Daly, another irrepressible who never became entirely subdued during all his long career, added gray hairs to the heads of many managers. Nothing stopped Daly and few things ever caused him to hesitate. Mischief bubbled out of him. One hot summer day he was riding westward with the team when the train stopped at a small station. Standing on the platform was a farmer with a benign, fatherly expression and enough whiskers to stuff a chest protector. Daly, leaning from the car window, accosted the farmer most politely, engaged him in conversation regarding crops, the effect of the drought upon the corn, prices and the weather outlook. Just as the train started Daly stretched out his hand. "Well, good-bye," he remarked, and grasping the astonished farmer by the whiskers he dragged him half the length of the platform. —Johnny Evers and Hugh Fullerton, *Baseball in the Big Leagues* (Reilly and Britton, 1910)

56 ◆ Bobby Lowe
(1890–1907, 1820 G, 71 984 .273)

Remembered today as the first player to hit four home runs in a game (May 30, 1894), Lowe in fact was not much of a hitter, but a good second baseman. It was 250 feet to the left field wall at the South End Grounds in Boston, although the *Boston Globe* alleged the next day that all four drives would have been "good for four bases on open prairie." He hit only 15 home runs in his career that did not come in Boston. In 1894, when he hit 17 homers, he hit only one on the road.

I have Lowe as deserving of three Gold Gloves, all of those when he was past his prime (1898, 1899, and 1902). An odd feature of fielding statistics in that era is that as second basemen aged, their plays per game *increased*. In that era, when second basemen got old, they began hanging out near second base, and handling all plays at the bag, resulting in the odd statistical illusion that their range was increasing as they were aging. This happens not only to Lowe, but also to Daly, Cupid Childs, Kid Gleason, Lajoie, and others.

Long after he was retired, Bobby Lowe and his wife once met Larry Lajoie in a hotel lobby. "I'm proud to meet the greatest second baseman the game has ever known," said Mrs. Lowe.

"That's nice of you to say," replied Lajoie, "but it's not true. The greatest second baseman was your husband."

57 ◆ Ron Hunt
(1963–1974, 1483 G, 39 370 .270)

Ron Hunt was about as bad a player as you can be with a .400 on-base percentage. He couldn't run and he had no power, but he learned to crowd the plate and freeze in front of an inside pitch, establishing a "modern" (post-1900) record by being hit with pitches 50 times in 1971. He also held the modern career record for about fifteen years, until Don Baylor took it away from him. He was an arthritic second baseman with a poor arm.

Hunt was not well liked by fans or by other players. An article about him in the April, 1965 issue of *Sport Magazine,* by George Vecsey, is entitled "Ron Hunt, Loner" and describes him as "the latter-day Mean Widdo Kid." Cub pitcher Larry Jackson, later a member of the House of Representatives, tried to counsel Hunt, telling him the story of Darryl Spencer, an infielder of the 1950s, who had become so unpopular around the league that people would go out of their way to plow into him on a double play. This had eventually driven Spencer to Japan. Hunt told Jackson to take his Darryl Spencer stories and shove them.

Hunt, who was smaller than Spencer, was soon spending a couple of months every summer on the disabled list. He rarely struck out, but almost never hit the ball hard. After hitting .303 as a second-year player in 1964, he had fallen by the late 1960s to the .250 range, which, combined with his frequent injuries and substandard defense at second base, had his career in serious jeopardy. He developed then his trick of leaning into the inside pitch, which got him back to regular status, and extended his career by about five years. "Some people give their bodies to science," said Hunt. "I gave mine to baseball."

58 ◆ Marty McManus
(1920–1934, 1831 G, 120 996 .289)
Gil McDougald-type player of the 1920s, played second base and third and was decent at both positions. Hit over .300 several times, led the league in stolen bases once, doubles once, hit some home runs.

59 ◆ Claude Ritchey
(1897–1909, 1671 G, 18 673 .273)
Honus Wagner's roommate and double-play partner. Ritchey was Wagner's teammate at Steubenville (Ohio) of the Inter-State League, later at Warren, Ohio of the Iron-Oil League, then at Louisville, then with the Pirates for many years. He was a tiny, jitterbug-type player, and the best defensive second baseman in baseball between Bid McPhee and Johnny Evers.

Ritchey was a vegetarian; Dennis and Jeanne DeValaria's biography of Honus Wagner notes that "perhaps a difficulty in locating a good salad in a world of steak eaters aggravated [Ritchey's] already surly and unsociable disposition." The story below also comes from the DeValaria book . . .

In 1903 Pittsburgh pitcher Ed Doheny had a breakdown, becoming quite suddenly irrational and violent. Some weeks later Pittsburgh manager Fred Clarke paid a visit to Mrs. Doheny at her home. He returned with an envelope addressed to Ritchey, and, with tears in his eyes, handed it to the second baseman. As he was being led away by police, Clarke explained, Doheny had said to his wife "I owe only two dollars, and that to Claude Ritchey. Won't you pay him?" Inside the envelope were

two dollars, and a note of explanation from Mrs. Doheny.

60 ◆ Felix Millan
(1966–1977, 1480 G, 22 403 .279)
A rail-thin, cat-like second baseman whose .279 average overstates his offensive contribution, but who could play second base with anybody. Millan's major league career ended suddenly on August 12, 1977, when he had the bad judgment to start a fight with Ed Ott, Pittsburgh catcher, who was a high school wrestling champion. Millan, not normally a hot-head, hit Ott in the face with a baseball. Ott body-slammed him, breaking his collarbone. Millan, in his mid-thirties and hitting under .250, had to go to Japan to continue his career.

After a good first season in Japan, according to Robert Whiting in *You Gotta Have Wa* (Macmillan, 1989), the Taiyo Whales offered to allow Millan to train on his own. Millan politely declined the offer, and "instead endured all the rigors of a Japanese preseason camp with his teammates. When he was benched on opening day, he sat quietly in the dugout, a shy smile on his face, intently watching the action. When he got his chance to start a week later, he went 4-for-4, won his spot back, and eventually won the batting title as well, with an average of .324."

61 ◆ Billy Goodman
(1947–1962, 1623 G, 19 591 .300)
Goodman in 1950 came close to being the only utility player to win the MVP Award, when he played 21 games at first base, 2 games at second, 27 games at third, 1 game at short, and 45 games in the outfield. He played 110 games total, won the batting title at .354, and was second (behind Rizzuto) in the MVP voting.

We know the feller at second base (Billy Goodman) gets a pretty good share of hits but he ain't so much with the glove and the arm and can't make double plays.—Casey Stengel, quoted in "Stengel Sizes Up the Red Sox," *Baseball Digest,* September, 1955

62 ◆ George Grantham
(1922–1934, 1444 G, 105 712 .302)

One time, twenty years ago, I did a data base search to see if there was any player in baseball history who:

1. Played 1,200 or more games,
2. Played a key defensive position, and
3. Was above average in every basic offensive category.

Basic offensive categories were batting average, on base percentage, slugging percentage, plus doubles per at bat, triples per at bat, home runs per at bat, runs scored per at bat, RBI per at bat, stolen bases per at bat, walks per at bat, and strikeouts per at bat.

I discovered that there were two such players—Willie Mays, and George Grantham. I just love that kind of crap, so I mentioned that several times in books over the years. While doing this book, I decided to repeat the study, but using a different data file—all players who played 1,000 or more games, as opposed to 1,200. There were about 600 players in the original group; this time, because I'm using a lower standard and twenty years have passed, I had twice as many players. This creates different "norms" in each category, which in this case means different cutoff points. Willie Mays had fallen into the "below average" group in something (I think strikeouts per at bat), but I still found two players who qualified: George Grantham and Jackie Robinson. Their career batting stats actually are very similar. Just to complete the thought, there were three other players who were above average in everything, but didn't play an "up the middle" defensive position: Jacques Fournier, Minnie Minoso, and Kenny Williams.

Grantham was famous as a poor defensive second baseman, which in fact he was; he was nicknamed "Boots" because he booted the ball so often. Statistics aside, he was more similar to Juan Samuel than to Jackie Robinson. As a rookie in 1923 he won the Juan Samuel triple crown, leading the National League in Strike-outs (92), Errors (55), and Caught Stealing (28), in spite of which he was the best rookie in the National League. He played second base that year and in 1927, when the Pirates won the pennant, but otherwise bounced back and forth between first and second.

63 ◆ Jim Gantner
(1976–1992, 1801 G, 47 568 .274)

Gantner, said Dan Okrent, emerged "in the local-boy rounds of the [1974] draft." He was a twelfth-round draft pick, a player of whom nothing was expected, and played third base in the minors because the Brewers had Paul Molitor at second and Robin Yount at short, and didn't expect to need any middle infielders.

Gantner elbowed his way through the minors as an I'll-do-anything, I'll-play-anywhere guy. He kept hitting a little more than was expected, and by 1980 was almost a regular-without-a-position, playing third base in place of the aging Sal Bando and second base in place of the often-injured Molitor. In 1981 he took over second base. "While official Brewer pronouncements said Molitor was being moved to center field because of his vast athletic virtues," wrote Okrent in *Nine Innings,* "everyone connected with the club knew Molitor was being moved because Gantner was, simply, a better second baseman."

64 ◆ Glenn Beckert
(1965–1975, 1320 G, 22 360 .283)

Beckert was so small, coming out of high school, that major league teams were not interested in him, plus he had promised his father that he

would graduate from college. He attended Allegheny College, near Pittsburgh, where he
played for Bob Garbark, a 1930s catcher, and
packed on forty pounds. The Red Sox offered
him an $8,000 bonus, and he took it.

The Red Sox didn't move him along fast
enough, and lost him after a year in the minor
league draft. The Chicago Cubs had been
counting on Ken Hubbs to be their second
baseman. When Hubbs was killed in a private
plane crash on February 15, 1964, they naturally began reviewing their options. Beckert
was playing shortstop, but he was the best
minor league infielder they had at the time,
plus his arm wasn't strong enough to play
shortstop anyway, so . . .

A year later, Leo Durocher brought him to
the majors. "I think maybe I reminded Leo of
some player he admired from the old days,"
Beckert told Rick Talley (*The Cubs of '69*, Contemporary Books, 1989). "All I know is that we
always got along." A hardscrabble player who
sometimes seemed eager to join in collisions at
second base, Beckert was the Billy Herman of
the 1960s, a pretty good second baseman, and
the best hit and run man in baseball. He hit
.280 or better six years in a row beginning in
1966, led the National League in runs scored in
1968, and hit a career-high .342 in 1971.
Arthritis in his knees and ankles forced him out
of the lineup and out of the game soon after
that. He went into business trading farm futures at the Chicago Board of Trade, and has
had a highly successful post-playing career.

65 ◆ Frank Bolling
(1954–1966, 1540 G, 106 556 .254)

Basically the same player as Bill Mazeroski, except that Mazeroski's career was four years
longer and he was just a hair quicker on the
double play. Bolling was damn good, though.

Bolling was always perceived, perhaps unfairly, as a player of unlimited ability. Tom

Meany in the May, 1961, edition of *Sport Magazine* recalled that Harry Craft had once invited
a group of reporters to name the five most talented players in the American League. The reporters suggested Mantle and Kaline. "If you're
all through," Craft said when they were, "I've
got my man. Frank Bolling, the Tigers's sec-
ond-baseman. He's magnificent. He can become one of the big men in the game." Bolling
was quick, strong, and had a good arm.

66 ◆ Fred Pfeffer
(1882–1897, 1670 G, 94 1019 .255)

Of Pfeffer's 94 career home runs, 81 were hit in
his home parks, only 13 on the road. Pfeffer hit
fewer home runs, in road games, than Johnny
Temple (14) or Don Blasingame (16).

The second basemen most helped by their
home parks:

1. Pfeffer	81 home	13 road	+68
2. Doerr	145 home	78 road	+67
3. Whitaker	146 home	98 road	+48
4. Sandberg	164 home	118 road	+46
5. Lowe	57 home	14 road	+43

The five who *lost* the most home runs to
poor home run parks were Gil McDougald (−54),
Bill Mazeroski (−48), George Grantham (−41),
Craig Biggio (−28), and Tony Cuccinello (−28).

67 ◆ Harold Reynolds
(1983–1994, 1374 G, 21 353 .258)

See you at eleven, Harold.

68 ◆ Bobby Richardson
(1955–1966, 1412 G, 34 390 .266)

Religious guy, very handsome; looked like and
talked like Ralph Reed. Jim Bouton suggested
in *Ball Four* that he had difficulty getting along
with black players. Richardson was a small
man with no power, but he used a big, heavy
bat and swung very hard. This wasn't his natural style; he was taught to hit that way by Bill

Dickey in 1959. "Bill felt that I wasn't big enough to hit the ball through the infield holes with a normal swing," Richardson told Dick Kaplan in 1962. "He told me to wind up and cut for all I was worth. It's worked wonderfully for me."

69 ◆ Cookie Rojas
(1962–1977, 1822 G, 54 593 .263)
A scrambling player whose career ran off-track a dozen times, but who always found some way to get it re-started. Rojas was with the Havana team in the International League in 1960, when the owner shifted the team to Miami to avoid having it seized by the government.

He spent six and a half years as a minor leaguer, much of that time as a bench player, because he never hit; he hit less in the minors than he did in the majors. He finally got to the majors by learning to play multiple defensive positions, then hit .291 in 1964, .303 in 1965, taking a regular position away from his fellow Cuban, Tony Taylor. He hit .300 for Kansas City in 1971, reviving his career, then represented the Royals in the All-Star game in 1972, 1973, and 1974.

70 ◆ Bucky Harris
(1919–1931, 1264 G, 9 506 .274)
In 1916 Harris played for Muskegon in the Central League, hitting a robust .166 in 55 games. In 1917 he started the year playing for Norfolk in the Virginia League, hitting .120 in 15 games (6 for 50), after which the league folded. Harris, deciding he wasn't going to make it as a baseball player, went home to Pittston, Pennsylvania, and got a job in the coal mines.

Shortly after that, however, the second baseman of the Reading club in the New York State League got into a fight with an umpire, and was banned from the league. The Reading manager, George Wiltse, needed a second baseman and had seen Harris play—not *Bucky*

Harris, but his older brother, who was also a minor league second baseman. When Bucky got a telegram asking him to report to Reading, he thought it was for him, and reported the next day. Wiltse knew he had the wrong Harris, but needed a second baseman anyway, and decided to give Bucky a chance to impress him.

Three years later, Harris had played 137 games for the Washington Senators, and hit .300.

71 ◆ Don Blasingame
(1955–1966, 1444 G, 21 308 .258)
> Don, who does not have the natural ability of some of the league's other infielders, made himself a good player through sheer determination. He can run, he has a good arm, and he makes all the plays required of a second baseman.—*Sport Magazine,* September, 1957

In 1970, Don Blasingame became the first American to be a head coach on a Japanese team. "There were cries that because Blasingame did not speak the language, he wouldn't be able to function," reported Robert Whiting in *The Chrysanthemum and the Bat* (Dodd, Mead and Company, 1977). "While Blasingame was learning Japanese, he taught the [Nankei] Hawks over 40 defensive plays, ran the team when Nomura was catching, and received a share of credit for the Hawks 1973 Pacific League championship."

72 ◆ Kid Gleason
(1888–1912, 1966 G, 15 823 .261)
A pitcher for seven-plus years, Gleason won 138 major league games, including 38 in 1890. Early in the 1895 season, Baltimore second baseman Heinie Reitz, who had been brilliant in 1894, broke his collarbone. Gleason, bothered by a sore arm, filled in at second base for a few days while Ned Hanlon looked around for a replacement. Gleason played so well that he never went back to the mound, playing twelve

years at second base, 22 years in the majors altogether.

He is most remembered as the manager of the Black Sox. He told his owner after the first game of the series that he was afraid his players had sold out . . . When Ty Cobb was offered the job as manager of the Detroit Tigers, he refused it several times, telling the Tiger owner that he should get Kid Gleason to run the team. From *My Life in Baseball—the True Record,* Ty Cobb with Al Stump (Doubleday, 1961): "The Kid, we all knew, was the real brains of the White Sox. He'd spent twenty-one years as a player, graduating from the Baltimore Oriole and John McGraw school—a brilliant baseball thinker and a grand man."

Warren Brown in *The Chicago White Sox* tells several anecdotes about Gleason, who he describes as "a belligerent little man." One time when Gleason was managing the White Sox and McGraw was managing the Giants both teams conducted spring training in San Antonio, and the players hung out together off hours. McGraw always held a dinner party at the end of spring training, and in this particular year Gleason was seated next to a General, a long-winded, pompous man with a national reputation as a speaker. As the evening wore on, according to Brown, McGraw became aware that Gleason was annoying the officer. He pulled Gleason aside and tried to suggest this.

"Nuts," said Gleason. "Me and the Lieutenant are getting along swell, ain't we, Loot?"

The General nearly exploded. "I, sir, am a full general."

Gleason was unimpressed. "I, sir, am a full manager. How in hell was I to know you're a general? I can't see your leggings."

The ranking of the second basemen past spot 35 is almost impossible. I've done the best job I could, but there are just a lot of players who are the same. What is the difference between Johnny Temple and Don Blasingame? The guys who rate in the seventies were very good players. The guys who rate in the forties weren't great players . . . See also Eddie Collins (2B, #2) and George Davis (SS, #14).

73 ◆ Jerry Priddy
(1941–1953, 1296 G, 61 541 .265)

I wrote a chapter about Priddy in another book *(The Politics of Glory),* and probably shouldn't repeat that. To summarize Jerry Priddy in ten items:

1. California native.
2. Minor-league hot shot, paired with Phil Rizzuto.
3. Dropped out of a regular spot as a rookie, 1941.
4. Quarreled with Joe McCarthy.
5. Bounced around the American League.
6. Played well.
7. Essentially the same skills as Mazeroski and Bolling.
8. Tried his hand as a con man.
9. Went to jail.
10. Died young.

74 ◆ Delino DeShields
(1990–2000, 1422 G, 72 514 .272)

Still building his legend.

75 ◆ Buck Herzog
(1908–1920, 1493 G, 20 445 .259)

Herzog was a fine player, but he was also a tough hombre who would just as soon fight the manager as he would fight umpires and enemy ball players. McGraw wearied of battling with his tough star and, to punish Herzog, traded him to Boston.—Sam Molen, *They Make Me Laugh* (Dorrance and Company, 1947)

A Lutheran whose grandfather was a minister, and a product of the University of Maryland, Herzog is perhaps best remembered for his peculiar relationship with John McGraw . . .

[McGraw] had no use for Herzog personally, a feeling that Buck made mutual. But McGraw had such tremendous admiration for Herzog's talents that he was always selling his contract and then buying it back.–Lee Allen, *The Cincinnati Reds* (G.P. Putnam's Sons, 1948)

In June, 1914, when Herzog was managing the Cincinnati Reds, his friends in New York wanted to give him a "day" at the Polo Grounds. John McGraw refused to allow it. The friends re-scheduled the event as "Buck Herzog Night" at a Manhattan theater. McGraw contacted the theater owner, and persuaded him to also ban the affair.

76 ◆ Jerry Lumpe
(1956–1967, 1371 G, 47 454 .268)

Like 800 other players, Lumpe might have been a Hall of Famer with a few better breaks. His career was derailed for two years by military service when he was half-way through the minor leagues, then he finally reached the majors in 1956 with the Yankees, only to find the team awash in young middle infielders, with a manager who preferred to use each of them two days a week.

Casey Stengel said that the secret of managing is to keep the five guys who hate you away from the ten guys on the fence. Lumpe was too amiable to denounce Stengel, but it would be a safe guess that Lumpe and his buddy Norm Siebern were not among the pro-Casey faction. In May, 1959, Bobby Richardson won the second base job in New York, and Lumpe was traded to Kansas City. He was thrilled. "Now I won't have to look at the lineup card every day to see if I'm playing," he said, and besides "I never liked the city. It's too big. [In KC] I feel like I'm part of something, that I'm wanted. Over there it's just a few guys that are the big men. Everybody else is nothing."

Lumpe was a fine player for about five years, a .290 hitter who had a strong arm and

almost never made a mistake at second base. In the early 1960s he was regarded as the second-best second baseman in the American League, behind Richardson.

77 ◆ Julian Javier
(1960–1972, 1622 G, 78 506 .257)

Trapped in the Pittsburgh farm system behind Bill Mazeroski, Javier was liberated by the Cardinals in exchange for Vinegar Bend Mizell, when the Pirates were cashing in assets to make a run at the pennant in 1960. He was quick as lightning at second base, and deserved a half-dozen Gold Gloves, but never won one because Mazeroski was legitimately better, and owned the award. As a hitter he was up and down, and never all that far up.

> With a strong wind blowing in gusts, Julian hit a high popup to Hoak at third. Don fought the ball and finally lost it in fair ground. But Javier hadn't bothered to run it out, and he wound up on first base.–Ed Richter, *The Man in the Dugout* (Chilton, 1964) . . .

See also comment on Ken Boyer (3B, #12)

78 ◆ Juan Samuel
(1983–1998, 1720 G, 161 703 .259)

A star his first four years as a regular (1984–1987), scoring over 100 runs a season and driving in as many as a hundred. There was a perception, until 1987, that Samuel would develop into a superstar. He was fast, he had some power, and he could play second base; there was a lot of talk about his being the first middle infielder to hit 30 homers and steal 30 bases.

Cracks in his armor soon appeared. He was a second baseman, but a bad one. When you put him anywhere else, he was worse. He had tremendous speed, but a poor on-base percentage, making him less than a desirable leadoff man. He had power, but not enough power to hit in the middle of the order. He was an odd lot, a player who had obvious skills, but didn't fit into any role that you could assign him.

79 ◆ Horace Clarke

(1965–1974, 1272 G, 27 304 .256)

Joe Garagiola, on the Yankees of the mid-1960s. "When I covered the Yankees they had players like Horace Clarke, Ross Moschitto, Jake Gibbs, and Dooley Womack. It was like the first team missed the bus."

Clarke was one of those players, like Brian McRae or Kenny Rogers, who always took a lot of crap for not being better than he was, although he was actually pretty good. Clarke was essentially the same player as Bobby Richardson—a .260 hitting second baseman who didn't walk or have any power, but a quality fielder. But whereas Richardson played with great teams, and thus benefited from a halo effect, Clarke played with teams on which he, unfortunately, was one of the best players, and thus was held responsible for the shortcomings of his teammates.

80 ◆ Johnny Ray

(1981–1990, 1353 G, 53 594 .290)

Good line-drive hitter, a hard-working player in his early years whose career dissolved after his defense deteriorated. *The Scouting Report: 1985* says that "Ray has developed into one of the better second basemen in baseball." The 1990 edition of the same book says that "Ray is a reasonably sure-handed fielder who doesn't have much range [and] has difficulty pivoting on the double play."

81 ◆ Jim Delahanty

(1901–1915, 1186 G, 19 489 .283)

The second-youngest of the five Delahantys who played in the majors, and the second-best. He could hit, and played all over the field because he was a good athlete and managers were always trying to find some place to hide him.

The top ten second basemen, ranked by *the percentage of their total value which was offensive (as a hitter) rather than defensive:* 1. Rogers Hornsby, 2. Rod Carew, 3. Delahanty, 4. Jorge Orta, 5. Nap Lajoie, 6. George Grantham, 7. Joe Morgan, 8. Eddie Collins, 9. Larry Doyle, 10. Jackie Robinson.

82 ◆ Tito Fuentes

(1965–1978, 1499 G, 45 438 .268)

In college I knew a girl named Jane. Jane was a knockout—I mean, absolutely jaw-dropping, drop-dead gorgeous. The odd thing was, however, that few people realized this, because of the way that she dressed. Whereas most coeds in that era dressed in blue jeans with little makeup and long, straight hair, Jane frosted and teased her hair, painted her eyes with blue and green eye shadow, and wore loud dresses with plunging necklines. Only if you caught her off-guard—dressed for a funeral, perhaps—would you realize what a stunning woman she really was. Otherwise, she looked trashy and cheap.

Tito Fuentes was like that. Sparky Lyle in *The Bronx Zoo* described Tito as "one of the most renowned hot dogs in baseball history." But actually, Tito was a very good defensive second baseman, one of the best. He was incapable of making a routine play without trying to make it look like something special, however, and his efforts to look better than he was, like Jane's, backfired on him. Even when he made a legitimately outstanding play, people just wrote it off as part of the show.

83 ◆ Hughie Critz

(1924–1935, 1478 G, 38 531 .268)

Critz, who pronounces his named Crytz (as in cry), was a graduate of Mississippi A&M, where his father was a member of the faculty. Hughie talked with [a] southern drawl . . . and proved to be an exceptional raconteur in addition to a highly skilled infielder.–Lee Allen, *The Cincin-nati Reds*

The Giants in 1927, discovering that Rogers Hornsby was impossible to live with, worked out a deal to trade Hornsby to the Reds for Critz and Bubbles Hargrave. Reds manager Jack Hendricks vetoed the deal. McGraw continued to pursue him, and eventually, after Hendricks was gone, managed to acquire Critz.

The "dimpled end" on the baseball bat is usually credited as a Japanese innovation that Jose Cardenal brought back with him when he returned from the orient. But actually, Hughie Critz carved the end out of his bat in the early 1930s, although it didn't catch on at that time. This fact is documented in Roy Stockton's *The Gashouse Gang,* and is confirmed by a photo in the 1934 *Spalding Guide.*

> Fielding practice "is mostly ignored today. I re-member the Giant infield of Terry, Critz, Jackson and Lindstrom, the 'million-dollar infield' as it was called, and it used to perform up to its name in fielding practice. They were so deft, so quick, so breathtaking that the fans would sit, first in stunned silence, and then in gathering bedlam to roar as each man made his play and the ball sped at dizzying speed about the infield."–Arnold Hano, *A Day In the Bleachers*

On September 14, 1934, in the heat of the pennant race, Dizzy Dean put a black cat on a leash and walked it up and down the New York Giants dugout. "He added insult to in-jury," reported John Lardner in the *New York Post,* "by pointing its nose at second baseman Hughie Critz, an impressionable little fellow from Mississippi, and making all kinds of hex signs and mumbo passes in Hughie's direc-tion . . . Fortunately, the maneuvers of this cloddish person were in vain. Lightning did not strike the Polo Grounds, the Giants won the game, and Mr. Critz performed prodigies at bat and afield."

84 ◆ Jim Lefebvre
(1965–1972, 922 G, 74 404 .251)

Won the National League Rookie of the Year Award in 1965, over Joe Morgan. I have Lefeb-vre that year with 22 Win Shares, which actu-ally is an above-average total for a Rookie of the Year, but Morgan with 31. Morgan may be the only rookie in history to have 31 Win Shares and *not* win the Rookie of the Year Award.

Lefebvre was a good player for two years, 1965–66, more or less in the model of Jeff Kent or Davey Johnson. He was part of the only switch-hitting infield in baseball history–Wes Parker, Lefebvre, Jim Gilliam, and Maury Wills.

He also appeared in episodes of *Gilligan's Island* and *Batman.*

Lefebvre managed the Seattle Mariners for three years, 1989–1991. The Mariners, who had gone 68-93 in 1988, improved under Lefebvre to 73-89, 77-85, and 83-79, at which point they fired him, and dropped back to 64-98.

Lefebvre was hired to manage the Cubs in 1992. They won 78 games his first year (their best season in three years), and 84 in 1993. Then they fired him, and didn't do as well again for five years.

85 ◆ Ted Sizemore
(1969–1980, 1411 G, 23 430 .262)

Replaced Lefebvre when Lefebvre had some in-juries, also won the National League Rookie of the Year Award, and also had some injuries after a couple of good years. Later hit second behind Lou Brock when Brock stole 118 bases, a record at the time.

86 ◆ Yank Robinson
(1882–1892, 978 G, 15 399 .241)

An American Association player who walked a hundred times a year . . . in fact, he established a major league record, at the time, with 116 walks in 1888, then broke the record with 118 the next year. No one knew this, since walks by batters were not calculated until years later.

87 ◆ Jorge Orta
(1972–1987, 1755 G, 130 745 .278)
Excellent left-handed line drive hitter, very poor defensive second baseman—in fact, I have him as the worst-fielding second baseman, per inning played, among the top 250 guys in innings played at second base. He played about 5,796 innings at second base (almost four full seasons), which ranks about 150th all-time, through 1999.

In the 1985 World Series, Orta reached when Don Denkinger blew a call at first base, after which the St. Louis Cardinals self-destructed. Did you ever notice that the ethics chosen by sports writers in reporting blown calls by officials are totally different from the ethics of broadcast journalists? They are. Modern sportswriters dislike second-guessing officials, regard highlighting of officials' mistakes as "homerism" or "boosterism," as bush-league, and generally won't do it unless they have to. I have been to basketball games at which the officiating was just awful, games at which the crowd was focused on the officiating, games in which referees' mistakes were critical elements both to the story of the game and to the outcome. You read about those games the next day in the paper, and the officials have been expunged from the record; their mistakes never happened, the crowd never booed them, the coaches never yelled at them, the game never turned on their blunders.

Broadcasters, on the other hand, absolutely love to catch umpires or referees' mistakes, and to high-light these by showing them again, and again, and again. What they *say* is, "If we see these things, we have an obligation to report them." What they *mean* is "Hoo, boy, I can start a real ruckus out of this." But if you think

about it, the TV guys come a lot closer to having it right. The ethics of modern sports journalism are mostly created by the failure to think through the problem. I know that the sports writers mean well; they don't want to spotlight umpires mistakes because they don't want to embarrass officials, they don't want to focus attention on their mistakes, and they argue, rightly enough, that the story of the game should be what the athletes did or didn't do, not whether some official blew a call. The practical consequence of this is that the TV guys decide when the officiating becomes a story. Sports writers will write about it only if they have to, and they have to only when the TV guys *talk* about it, and show the films over and over, or only when the players bring it up in the post-game interviews. It is frustrating, to me a sports fan, to have an element of a game story covered up or swept under the carpet, even if it's done out of a sense of decency, and I think it's inappropriate for sports writers to do that.

88 ◆ Glenn Hubbard
(1978–1989, 1354 G, 70 448 .244)
Total Baseball has Glenn Hubbard rated as a better player than Pete Rose, Brooks Robinson, Dale Murphy, Ken Boyer, or Sandy Koufax, a conclusion which is every bit as preposterous as it seems to be at first blush.

To a large extent, this rating is caused by the failure to adjust Hubbard's fielding statistics for the ground-ball tendency of his pitching staff. Hubbard played second base for teams which had very high numbers of ground balls, as is reflected in their team assists totals. The Braves led the National League in team assists in 1985, 1986, and 1987, and were near the league lead in the other years that Hubbard was a regular. *Total Baseball* makes no adjustment for this, and thus concludes that Hubbard is reaching scores of baseballs every year that an average second baseman would not reach, hence that he has enormous value.

89 ◆ Fred Dunlap
(1880–1891, 965 G, 41 366+ .292)
Never a legitimate star in a legitimate major league, but a good second baseman and a .275 hitter.

90 ◆ Rennie Stennett
(1971–1981, 1237 G, 41 432 .274)
The Pirates farm system in the years 1969–1976 was churning out players like newspapers, producing at least 15 top-100 players—Manny Sanguillen, Al Oliver, Richie Hebner, Fred Patek, Dave Parker, and Richie Zisk, to name a few. Stennett, a native of Panama, played the outfield in the minors in 1969 and 1970, converted to second base in 1971, and was so impressive that by the end of the season he was the Pirates regular second baseman, blasting aside Dave Cash, who had spent three years being groomed as Mazeroski's successor. Stennett forced the Pirates to trade not only Cash, but also Willie Randolph. In 1974 he had 196 hits, fifth in the National League, plus he probably had as much range as any major league second baseman of that era.

On August 21, 1977, Stennett was hitting .336, looking for his first National League batting title, and had already established a career high with 28 stolen bases. He broke his ankle on that date, never fully recovered, and his career ended within a few years.

91 ◆ Mike Andrews
(1966–1973, 893 G, 66 316 .258)
Like Stennett, Lefebvre, and many others—a good young player who didn't develop because of injuries. He is remembered, of course, for making a couple of errors in the 1973 World Series, neither of them egregious, and in fact

neither of them necessarily his fault; one of them was a bad-hop ground ball, and the other one probably should have been scored as an error on the first baseman. Anyway, Charlie Finley was so mad at Andrews for the misplays that he forced Andrews to sign a false affidavit that he was injured so he could be placed on the disabled list. This led to Dick Williams' resignation as Oakland manager, and also led to the policy still in place which prohibits any roster moves after the World Series has begun.

Andrews played for Dick Williams at Toronto in 1965 and 1966. Williams shifted him from shortstop to second base, moving Reggie Smith from second base to the outfield, then brought both Andrews and Smith to the majors in 1967. Andrews walked a lot and had some power, so he scored quite a few runs, plus he was a decent defensive second baseman until he began having back trouble. His first major league team, the 1967 Red Sox, improved by 20 games. After Williams was fired Andrews was traded to the White Sox. His first team in Chicago, the 1971 Sox, improved by 23 games. The following season they improved by another 12.

92 ◆ Dick Green
(1963–1974, 1288 G, 80 422 .240)
Green had a trick, on a popup, of running to where the ball was going to come down, taking his eye off the ball, looking at the other fielders, looking at the baserunners, waving off the other fielders, motioning with his hands for them to stay back, and then looking back up to find the baseball just as crashed into his glove. It was very odd; I've never seen anybody else do it.

Green never won a Gold Glove, which is unfortunate; he deserved the award in 1971, and was an outstanding fielder all of his career. In 1974 he played so brilliantly in the field that he *almost* won the World Series MVP award although he didn't get a single hit in the series.

93 ◆ Carlos Baerga
(1990–1999, 1280 G, 124 686 .291)
Only 31 right now, but his best years were a long time ago. He could rate higher, I guess.

94 ◆ Ron Oester
(1978–1990, 1276 G, 42 344 .265)
A quiet, efficient player who was always overlooked.

95 ◆ George Cutshaw
(1912–1923, 1516 G, 25 653 .265)

> Cutshaw had the best range of any second baseman in the league and was superb on the double play. Stengel's high regard in later years for second basemen who could make a double play stemmed from his appreciation of what Cutshaw could do.–Robert W. Creamer, *Stengel* (Simon & Schuster, 1984)

> When Cutshaw joined us in 1922, he was a ten-year veteran no longer able to do acrobatics about second base. His arm wasn't much any more. He was nearing the end of the trail. But Cutshaw was a master of the position in many other ways . . . he worked unceasingly with the other infielders, showing them stance on fielding a ball, where to throw on bases-jammed situations and the technique of whipping that arm around the face on a double-play throw to first base. George was simply great, in ways that didn't show to the fans and sportswriters.–Ty Cobb with Al Stump, *My Life in Baseball–The True Record* (Doubleday, 1961)

96 ◆ Cass Michaels
(1943–1954, 1288 G, 53 501 .262)
A war-time teenager who used his early experience as a springboard to a post-war career. In the late 1940s he was one of the best second basemen in baseball, hitting .308, turning 135 double plays, and drawing 101 walks in 1949,

and being named to the All-Star team in 1949 and 1950. He was rotated out of Chicago that fall, when Frank Lane took over the team and traded everybody in sight. Michaels was traded to Washington, which seemed to break his spirit, as he never played as well after the trade. On August 27, 1954, back with the White Sox, he was beaned by Marion Fricano, a hard-throwing pitcher who didn't know the strike zone from a hole in the ground, and suffered a "double fracture of the skull." This ended his career at the age of 28.

Michaels' birth name was Casimir Kwietniewski. This was still his name when he was signed by the White Sox in 1943, and he agonized aloud over what to do with the name. "If I cut it down to Kwiet," he said, "they'll call me quiet or quit and I don't think either of them are very good." He changed his name that winter, without telling the White Sox. According to Richard Goldstein in *Spartan Seasons,* White Sox General Manager Harry Grabiner sent Kwietniewski to Little Rock, and was irritated to find that somebody named "Michaels" was playing shortstop for the team. "An irritated Grabiner finally phoned the farm team to find out why the promising youngster was being benched . . . by the time he retired, there would be twelve years of American League box scores containing Michaels instead of Kw't'ski."

97 ◆ Sparky Adams
(1922–1934, 1424 G, 9 394 .286)
Adams is listed in the Encyclopedias as being 5 feet, 5 inches tall, but according to Lee Allen in *The Hot Stove League* he was actually 5-foot-4, the smallest player ever to play regularly in the National League. According to Allen, Branch Rickey first saw him working out at shortstop, and jumped to his feet shouting, "Get that bat boy out of the shortstop's position!"

"That's not a bat boy, Mr. Rickey," said one of his aides. "That's Earl Adams."

"Judas Priest," Rickey exploded. "Do you mean that is the man we paid seven hundred and fifty dollars for?"

Adams didn't stick with the Cardinals, but did stick with the Cubs two years later. For his first two years he was known as "Rabbit" Adams, but when Rabbit Maranville joined the Cubs in 1925 he said "We can have only one rabbit on this team and it's going to be me. You're a spark plug, so we'll call you Sparky."

Although he had no power and didn't reach the majors until he was nearly thirty, meaning that some of his speed was probably gone, Sparky Adams stayed in the majors by hustle, defense, and contact hitting until he was forty years old. He was the starting third baseman for the 1930 St. Louis Cardinals, the only team of this century for which all eight regulars hit .300.

In retirement, Adams returned to a farm in Schuylkill County, Pennsylvania, where he grew up. Later in life he bought a service station, which he operated until he was past his 90th birthday.

98 ◆ Odell Hale
(1931–1941, 1062 G, 73 573 .289)

A man of many names. He is listed in the encyclopedias as "Odell," although his name actually was "Arvel"—Arvel Odell Hale, a handle which would surely urge anyone to suggest alternatives. The nickname which has stuck in the encyclopedias is "Bad News," which he was given after he hit seven home runs in six games at Alexandria in 1929. In contemporary references, however, he was more often referred to as "Chief" Hale, and he was also frequently called "Sammy" Hale, after an American League third baseman who preceded him.

Hale was a very handsome man. The Alexandria team in 1929 had two stars, Hale and Lon Warneke, who had a near-Hall of Fame career as a pitcher. The Indians had a deal with Alexandria that gave them an option

on either star, and sent Cy Slapnicka to Alexandria to check them out. When he got there, though, it was the middle of a terrible rainstorm, and the only people in the ballpark were one man and two boys. The three of them had a cushion, and they were sitting out at second base in the driving rain, pretending to paddle their "boat" with two barrel staves. It turned out that the comedian was Lon Warneke.

Slapnicka was irritated, and didn't think a guy who did something like that belonged in the major leagues, so he left town without seeing either player. Later, he went back and watched Hale play for a week. He didn't like him, and recommended that the Indians buy another third baseman, but the Alexandria team owed the Indians money, $1,500, and asked whether the Indians would take Hale to cancel the debt. The Indians grumbled, but finally agreed.

His shipmates on the Cleveland Indians call this second-sacker "Chief" because he is part Indian and part Irish. He was born at Hosston, La., Aug. 10, 1909; throws and bats right-handed; is 5 feet 11½ inches tall, weighs 170, and has brown eyes and black hair. Hale is married and his home is at 820 Goodwin Ave., Eldorado, Ark.—Harold (Speed) Johnson, *Who's Who in the American League,* (B. E. Callahan, 1935)

A reformed third-baseman who turned square at second and boosted his season-before swat mark several points. Winter gossip indicates he'll be doing utility infielding and pinch hitting this year, but Bad News had hurled competition for his job before and come up smiling.—John Carmichael, *Who's Who in the Major Leagues,* (B. E. Callahan, 1939)

99 ◆ Tommy Helms
(1964–1977, 1435 G, 34 477 .269)

Harold Reynolds without the speed, Tito Fuentes without the style.

100 ◆ Jerry Remy

(1975–1984, 1154 G, 7 329 .275)

When Remy was playing for El Paso in 1974, he wondered aloud if he would ever make it to the major leagues. His manager, Dave Garcia, overheard him, and said, "Listen, do you know who is playing second base for the Angels?"

"Denny Doyle," said Remy.

"Who runs better, you or Denny?" asked Garcia.

"I do," said Remy.

"Who throws better?"

"I do."

"Who hits better?"

"I do," said Remy.

"Well then," said Garcia, "you're going to the major leagues."

101. Damaso Garcia, 102. Joe Quinn, 103. Marty Barrett, 104. Charlie Neal, 105. Sandy Alomar (Sr.), 106. Wally Backman, 107. John Morrill, 108. Connie Ryan, 109. Frank LaPorte, 110. Billy Wambsganss, 111. Aaron Ward, 112. Bobby Knoop, 113. Lou Bierbauer, 114. Jimmy Brown, 115. Rich Dauer, 116. Julio Cruz, 117. Danny O'Connell, 118. Otto Knabe, 119. Derrel Thomas, 120. Jerry Adair, 121. Danny Richardson, 122. Bill Hallman, 123. Bernie Allen, 124. Don Gutteridge, 125. Hobe Ferris

Before I close the second basemen, I had a few miscellaneous notes that I wanted to include, even though the players involved didn't make the top 100. Let's do these alphabetically: Ross Barnes, Bob Ferguson, Hobe Ferris, Frank LaPorte, Morrie Rath.

You will sometimes see Ross Barnes listed among the best second basemen ever. Barnes was a star in the National Association, forerunner of the National League, from 1871 through 1875, posting reported averages of .401, .422, and .425, and also hit .429 in 1876, the first season of the National League; he was the best player in baseball in that season. After the

1876 season the National League changed the rules so that a ball which landed in fair territory but rolled foul was a foul ball. Prior to that it had been a fair ball. Barnes had mastered the art of bunting so that the ball would bounce once in fair territory and then roll foul wide of third base, making an impossible play for the third baseman. Deprived of this, and fighting some injuries, Barnes was out of the league in a few years.

I know there are some people who want to put Barnes in the Hall of Fame, and maybe they're right, but I just don't see it. It is a reach to describe the National League in 1876 as a "major" league; there is a good argument that the majors became worthy of the distinction about 1885. It seems indefensible, to me, to extend the status backward beyond 1876.

If we disallow the performance in the National Association, Barnes' argument to be considered a top-rank player rests on one season of what might be compared to Double-A baseball. A short season—66 games. His "greatness" as a player is based on his ability to do something which was eliminated from the game 125 years ago because it was perceived as cheap trickery. I don't buy it. I don't think he was one of the top 125 second basemen of all time.

A better argument can perhaps be made for Bob Ferguson, a contemporary of Barnes' who played in the National League until 1883, the American Association in 1884. Ferguson was one of the best players in the nation for many years before the major leagues were organized. *The New York Herald* reported in May, 1871, that "Ferguson, captain of the Atlantic nine, was formerly a quiet hard working member of the nine but since he has been crowned with a little brief authority, he lords it over his men in an insultingly demonstrative way that cannot fail to wound the feelings of the nine, make them sulky and indifferent and act against the interest and success of the club."

Responding to this and other comments, Ferguson threatened to "knock every tooth out of the head of the *Herald* reporter." Forced to choose between the two of them, I guess I'd go with Ferguson, but again, I regard the entire generation as suspect, and I will rate only the legitimate stars among them.

Hobe Ferris was probably the best defensive second baseman in the early days of the American League, a distinction which has unjustifiably settled on Nap Lajoie. He stayed in the game for years afterward as a minor league manager, for which reason he shows up occasionally in the index of old baseball books.

The note about him that I wanted to share was this. On March 10, 1938, Ferris was reading the sports pages in the morning, when he saw a note that Fatty Fothergill, recently of the Tigers, was in very poor health. Ferris was saddened by this, and pointed the item out to his wife. Then he stood up, groaned, keeled over, and died of a heart attack. Fothergill died two days later.

Who was the first player to use a black bat? Any modern fan knows that it was George Foster, mid-1970s, but actually, Frank LaPorte used a black-stained bat almost all of his career, seventy years before Foster "integrated the bat rack." He was a decent player, too; I didn't include him in the top 100, but I could have. I have him at #109.

Finally, there is Morrie Rath, who cannot be listed among the top second basemen because he was a regular in only three seasons—1912, 1919, and 1920. His career average was .254, and he hit only 4 home runs in his career.

If you find a note about Rath in your baseball library, that note will concern the 1919 World Series. When Eddie Cicotte plunked the first batter he faced with a pitch to signal the gamblers that the fix was in, the man that he

hit was Morrie Rath. What interests me about Rath, however, is that while Rath was certainly an *unusual* player for the time, I think he was actually quite a good player, better than some of those listed here, but he spent almost all of his career in the minor leagues, just because his skills were too subtle for the men who managed the major league teams. In 1912, his first real shot at a major league job, he hit .272 with 95 walks, 104 runs scored but only 19 RBI—one of the oddest ratios of runs scored to RBI in major league history. The Win Shares Gold Glove awards at second base in the American League read:

1909—Eddie Collins
1910—Eddie Collins
1911—Eddie Collins
1912—Morrie Rath
1913—Nap Lajoie
1914—Eddie Collins

And he doesn't show as a little bit better than Eddie Collins at second base; he actually shows as quite a lot better—Rath, 9.45, Collins, 6.14, everybody else under four.

So Rath played one season in the majors, played great, but then slumped in the first half the 1913 season, and returned to the minor leagues for the next five seasons.

In 1917, playing for Salt Lake City, Rath won the Pacific Coast League batting title with a .341 average, collecting 246 hits in 197 games—none of them home runs. This event was regarded as so odd that Tex Milliard, in a 1966 book called *Cuttin' the Corners*, recalled Rath as the "batting champion who didn't hit a single home run!" and said that the record was "unique."

He returned to the majors in 1919, when Pat Moran was hired to manage the Cincinnati Reds. The Reds had led the National League in double plays in 1918, but Moran, unhappy with his interior defense, replaced both parts of his double play combination, filling the second base slot by recalling Morrie Rath from the minor leagues.

Did he do the job? The Reds, who hadn't finished within fifteen games of first place since 1898, went 96-44, the best record by a National League team in ten years. Rath led the league in putouts, assists, and double plays, and beat out perennial champion George Cutshaw as the best defensive second baseman in the National League—his second Win Shares Gold Glove in two years as a regular.

There should be a happy ending to this story, but there isn't. Rath led the National League in fielding percentage in 1920, but his playing time decreased, and after the 1920 season he disappeared forever from the major league scene. The Reds returned to the depths of the second division. He was a player, perhaps, who was just too odd to be recognized as valuable.

SECOND BASE

Rank	Player Name	Career WS	Top 3	Top 5	Per 162
1.	Joe Morgan	512	44, 40, 39	197	31.31
2.	Eddie Collins	574	43, 43, 40	193	32.90
3.	Rogers Hornsby	502	47, 42, 41	190	36.00
4.	Jackie Robinson	257	38, 36, 34	162	30.13
5.	Craig Biggio	318	38, 35, 32	165	28.62
6.	Nap Lajoie	496	47, 42, 41	171	32.40
7.	Ryne Sandberg	346	38, 37, 34	154	25.90
8.	Charlie Gehringer	383	37, 34, 31	160	26.71
9.	Rod Carew	384	37, 32, 30	157	25.20
10.	Roberto Alomar	306	35, 34, 31	131	26.41
11.	Frankie Frisch	366	34, 31, 31	135	25.66
12.	Bobby Grich	329	32, 31, 29	143	26.54
13.	Lou Whitaker	351	29, 26, 25	116	23.79
14.	Billy Herman	298	32, 29, 29	135	25.12
15.	Nellie Fox	304	32, 30, 26	128	20.81
16.	Joe Gordon	242	31, 28, 26	134	21.07
17.	Willie Randolph	312	31, 23, 23	114	22.95
18.	Bobby Doerr	281	27, 27, 27	127	22.61
19.	Tony Lazzeri	252	30, 27, 24	115	23.46
20.	Larry Doyle	289	33, 29, 28	130	26.51
21.	Chuck Knoblauch	217	32, 27, 25	129	24.84
22.	Dick McAuliffe	241	28, 27, 26	119	22.15
23.	Dave Lopes	240	27, 26, 25	118	21.46
24.	Buddy Myer	258	33, 24, 23	115	21.73
25.	Johnny Evers	268	28, 27, 27	117	24.34

(continued)

Rank	Player Name	Career WS	Top 3	Top 5	Per 162
26.	Cupid Childs	238	32, 31, 27	127	26.48
27.	Jim Gilliam	247	28, 28, 25	102	20.46
28.	Red Schoendienst	262	27, 26, 25	108	19.15
29.	Bill Mazeroski	219	23, 21, 20	92	16.40
30.	Bid McPhee	305	27, 23, 21	107	23.14
31.	Frank White	211	20, 18, 18	87	14.71
32.	Lonnie Frey	208	25, 25, 24	121	21.95
33.	Gil McDougald	194	27, 24, 24	116	23.52
34.	Eddie Stanky	191	30, 28, 27	113	24.58
35.	Del Pratt	242	26, 25, 24	100	21.36
36.	Bobby Avila	175	34, 24, 24	124	21.81
37.	Miller Huggins	222	27, 23, 22	104	22.68
38.	Pete Runnels	216	26, 24, 24	108	19.45
39.	Hardy Richardson	230	32, 25, 23	111	27.99
40.	Tom Herr	170	30, 20, 18	96	18.19
41.	Phil Garner	195	23, 22, 20	97	16.98
42.	Robby Thompson	155	26, 22, 19	98	19.26
43.	Max Bishop	184	25, 24, 21	100	22.28
44.	Steve Sax	198	31, 24, 24	108	18.13
45.	Bill Doran	193	28, 24, 22	111	21.52
46.	Dave Johnson	171	23, 23, 21	97	19.30
47.	Tony Taylor	198	23, 19, 19	79	14.61
48.	Jeff Kent	170	37, 25, 23	118	23.12
49.	Manny Trillo	146	19, 15, 14	70	13.29
50.	Dave Cash	165	26, 24, 21	99	18.80
51.	Danny Murphy	215	26, 25, 24	104	23.30
52.	Johnny Temple	157	22, 21, 19	94	17.91
53.	Tony Cuccinello	203	23, 23, 23	92	19.30
54.	Jimmy Williams	217	32, 22, 22	110	24.14
55.	Tom Daly	215	28, 25, 20	91	22.27
56.	Bobby Lowe	188	22, 20, 16	87	16.73
57.	Ron Hunt	191	26, 21, 19	94	20.86
58.	Marty McManus	202	21, 20, 20	92	17.87
59.	Claude Ritchey	205	23, 22, 21	100	19.87
60.	Felix Millan	152	20, 19, 18	81	16.64
61.	Billy Goodman	170	20, 20, 17	86	16.97
62.	George Grantham	193	24, 21, 21	101	21.65
63.	Jim Gantner	163	21, 16, 15	76	14.66
64.	Glenn Beckert	125	23, 20, 18	86	15.34
65.	Frank Bolling	141	21, 17, 17	82	14.83

Rank	Player Name	Career WS	Top 3	Top 5	Per 162
66.	Fred Pfeffer	202	21, 20, 20	89	19.60
67.	Harold Reynolds	123	21, 20 19	92	14.50
68.	Bobby Richardson	120	22, 18, 15	81	13.77
69.	Cookie Rojas	144	19, 18, 16	65	12.80
70.	Bucky Harris	133	20, 18, 17	84	17.05
71.	Don Blasingame	140	24, 18, 17	85	15.71
72.	Kid Gleason	294	45, 29, 25	140	24.23
73.	Jerry Priddy	145	24, 20, 20	87	18.13
74.	Delino DeShields	178	24, 21, 21	84	20.28
75.	Buck Herzog	171	21, 20, 20	94	18.55
76.	Jerry Lumpe	127	19, 18, 18	83	15.01
77.	Julian Javier	135	17, 17, 16	68	13.48
78.	Juan Samuel	176	22, 21, 20	98	16.58
79.	Horace Clarke	127	23, 22, 17	86	16.17
80.	Johnny Ray	153	21, 20, 20	88	18.32
81.	Jim Delahanty	149	24, 20, 18	88	20.35
82.	Tito Fuentes	132	19, 17, 16	70	14.27
83.	Hughie Critz	141	20, 19, 16	76	15.45
84.	Jim Lefebvre	106	25, 23, 16	83	18.62
85.	Ted Sizemore	130	22, 17, 15	74	14.93
86.	Yank Robinson	131	24, 21, 20	101	21.70
87.	Jorge Orta	160	22, 21, 18	89	14.77
88.	Glenn Hubbard	140	19, 19, 15	84	16.75
89.	Fred Dunlap	165	38, 17, 17	100	27.70
90.	Rennie Stennett	118	21, 20, 18	84	15.45
91.	Mike Andrews	108	24, 24, 16	93	19.59
92.	Dick Green	117	22, 20, 16	62	14.72
93.	Carlos Baerga	146	28, 28, 23	110	18.48
94.	Ron Oester	112	21, 15, 15	69	14.22
95.	George Cutshaw	140	17, 16, 16	76	14.96
96.	Cass Michaels	121	22, 13, 13	69	15.22
97.	Sparky Adams	144	21, 20, 17	78	16.38
98.	Odell Hale	112	20, 20, 20	88	17.08
99.	Tommy Helms	114	17, 14, 14	63	12.87
100.	Jerry Remy	113	17, 16, 15	69	15.86

Categories of this record are Career Win Shares, Win Shares in the player's three best seasons, Win Shares total over the player's five best consecutive seasons, and career Win Shares per 162 games played. For example, Joe Morgan had 512 Career Win Shares, including 44, 40, and 39 in his three best seasons (1975, 1973, and 1972). He had 197 Win Shares in a five-year period, (1972–1976) and averaged 31.31 Win Shares per 162 games played over the course of his career.

THIRD BASE

1 ◆ Mike Schmidt
(1972–1989, 2404 G, 548 1595 .267)

In the 1971 amateur draft the Kansas City Roy-als had the fifth pick, and the Philadelphia Phillies had the sixth. They chose George Brett and Mike Schmidt with consecutive picks—in the second round. The first ten players taken in that draft were Danny Goodwin, Jay Franklin, Tom Blanco, Condredge Holloway, Roy Branch, Roy Thomas, Roger Quiroga, Ed Kurpiel, David Sloan, and Taylor Duncan . . .

The five worst rookies who went on to Hall of Fame careers:

1. Mike Schmidt, 1973
2. Ty Cobb, 1905
3. Bob Gibson, 1959
4. Red Ruffing, 1925
5. Nellie Fox, 1949

2 ◆ George Brett
(1973–1993, 2707 G, 317 1595 .305)

Brett was the only third baseman in history to have 5,000 Total Bases in his career . . .

The average major league baseball player, now and throughout most of the game's history, will almost match his career hit total in two other columns: Secondary Bases, and (Runs Scored plus RBI). If a player has 2,000 hits in his career, he will also tend to have about 2,000 secondary bases, about 1,000 runs scored, and about 1,000 RBI—on average.

Of the 22 players who have 3,000 career hits (including Cap Anson), 14 also have at least 3,000 secondary bases, and 17 also have at least 3,000 (Runs Plus RBI). Henry Aaron leads the 3,000-hit club in both of these categories—secondary bases, with 4,727, and (Runs Plus RBI), with 4,471. Nap Lajoie is last in secondary bases, with 2,125, and Rod Carew is last is Runs Plus RBI, with 2,439.

Among all the great players in history, George Brett has the most balanced offensive skills—that is, he is the one who most nearly matches his hit total in the other two columns. Brett had 3,154 hits in his career, 3,187 secondary bases, and 3,178 Runs Plus RBI—a 1% spread from the highest figure to the lowest. Thirteen of the 22 players with 3,000 hits have what I would consider to be balanced offensive skills; Brett has the most balanced. Brett is the one player whose career hit total or batting average most accurately reflects his overall offensive contribution. Other players with very balanced offensive skills include:

	Hits	Secondary Bases	R+RBI
Tris Speaker	3,514	3,402	3,419
Cal Ripken	3,070	3,065	3,231
Harold Baines	2,783	2,743	2,853
Rusty Staub	2,716	2,771	2,665
Keith Hernandez	2,182	2,200	2,195
Tim Wallach	2,085	1,984	2,033
Dusty Baker	1,981	1,991	1,977
Bill White	1,706	1,713	1,713
Richie Hebner	1,694	1,721	1,755
Pedro Guerrero	1,618	1,676	1,628
Ben Oglivie	1,615	1,695	1,685
Richie Zisk	1,477	1,459	1,473
Jim Northrup	1,254	1,249	1,213
Bob Skinner	1,198	1,174	1,173
Bill Robinson	1,127	1,119	1,177
Mike Devereaux	949	932	971
Wes Covington	808	785	825
Jerry Martin	666	664	682

Players with *imbalanced* offensive skills can be sorted into two groups: those who are *better* than their batting average reveals, and those who are not as good as their batting average makes them look. The former group is led by Mark McGwire, and includes the other two top third basemen, Schmidt and Mathews. The latter group (players who were not as productive as their batting average would suggest) is led by Jesus Alou, and includes Glenn Beckert, George Sisler, Lloyd Waner, Don Mueller, and Felix Millan, among many others.

3 ◆ Eddie Mathews
(1952–1968, 2388 G, 512 1453 .271)
Eddie Mathews in 1953 had the best season ever by a 21-year-old player, hitting 47 homers and driving in 135 runs. As a 22-year-old and a 23-year-old, he ranks among the top twenty players of all time. An all-star team of the best young players ever:

> C—Johnny Bench
> 1B—Jimmie Foxx
> 2B—Rogers Hornsby
> 3B—Eddie Mathews
> SS—Arky Vaughan
> OF— Mickey Mantle
> OF— Ty Cobb
> OF— Mel Ott
> SP—Babe Ruth
> SP—Amos Rusie
> SP—Christy Mathewson
> SP—Monte Ward

A companion team (the greatest old players in baseball history) can be found under Honus Wagner. The only player who makes both teams is Babe Ruth, who makes this team as a pitcher and that team as an outfielder.

No player holds his franchise record for both stolen bases and home runs. Henry Aaron holds the Milwaukee Braves career record for stolen bases, as well as the records for at bats, hits, doubles, triples, and RBI—but not the record for home runs. Eddie Mathews out-homered him in Milwaukee, 452 to 398.

4 ◆ Wade Boggs
(1982–1999, 2440 G, 118 1014 .328)
Wonder what Margo Adams is doing these days? Her ten minutes ended ten years ago, I guess ... Wade's .328 batting average was the best of any 20th-century third baseman, and is the best of anyone who played 800 or more games at third base. John McGraw hit .334,

but that was in a short nineteenth-century career...No player in baseball history is truly
similar to Wade Boggs. The ten most similar
players are 1. Tony Gwynn, 2. Paul Waner,
3. Rod Carew, 4. Sam Rice, 5. Frankie Frisch,
6. Charlie Gehringer, 7. Tim Raines, 8. Luke Appling, 9. Jimmy Dykes, 10. Heinie Manush. All
except Gwynn, Raines and Dykes are Hall of
Famers.

5 ◆ Home Run Baker
(1908–1922, 1575 G, 93 1012 .307)
You all know that the tradition of the President
throwing out the first ball to open the baseball
season dates to April 14, 1910, when William
Howard Taft threw out the first ball for the
Senators. A little known fact about that game,
however, is that his Vice President and his Secretary of State, Charles Bennett, attended the
game with him. Baker ripped a line drive into
the President's box, hitting Secretary Bennett in
the head. He was not seriously hurt, but everybody was sure shook up for a minute or two.

Frank Baker retired from baseball and sat
out a season twice, the first time (1915) as a
part of a salary dispute with Connie Mack, and
the second time (1921) after his wife died, leaving him with small children to take care of. It is
certainly possible, and I might even argue that
it is likely, that had he not done this, he would
rank still today as the greatest third baseman of
all time. The four years before his first retirement (1911–1914) are by far the best four-year
stretch by a third baseman in baseball history.
He hit .334, .347, .336, and .319, was one of the
best defensive third basemen in the American
League, drove in 113 runs a year, and led the
league in home runs all four seasons. I credit
him with 148 Win Shares in those four years.
The second-best four-year stretch by a third
baseman is 138 Win Shares, by Mike Schmidt,
1980–1983; Schmidt lost 55 games due to the
1981 strike, but gained back eight games every
other year due to a longer schedule.

Ty Cobb, Tris Speaker, Eddie Collins, Walter
Johnson, and Pete Alexander were all basically
the same age as Baker, all born between March,
1886 and April, 1888. In the four years before
his first retirement, the Win Shares for the six
players are:

1.	Johnson	170
2.	Speaker	160
3.	Collins	154
4.	Baker	148
5.	Cobb	145
6.	Alexander	111

But in the four years following his first retirement, Baker had dropped out of the group:

1.	Cobb	149
2.	Speaker	132
3.	Johnson	131
4.	Alexander	112
5.	Collins	102
6.	Baker	81

In the two years after his second retirement,
he was no longer comparable to the other
players:

1.	Speaker	56
2.	Cobb	55
3.	Johnson	45
4.	Collins	44
5.	Alexander	40
6.	Baker	19

Baker, dark-skinned and dour left-handed batter
standing 5 feet 11 and weighing 173 pounds, had
the bowed legs of Hans Wagner and walked like
a soft-shell crab. He appeared so awkward at
third base that such a sharp-eyed baseball man
as Jack Dunn of Baltimore once let him go.

Connie Mack...observed things in the boy
passed up by scouts. Mack grasped the idea that
Baker was a daring fielder who wasn't afraid of
making an error in going far out of his way to

make a play . . . despite his ungainliness and lack of grace, Baker was a superlative baserunner.
—Harry Grayson, *They Played the Game* (A.S. Barnes and Company, 1944)

See also comment on Jimmie Foxx (1B, #2).

6 ◆ Ron Santo
(1960–1974, 2243 G, 342 1331 .277)
Dear Mr. James:

I saw you on ESPN Sunday Night, when you said that Ron Santo should be elected to the Hall of Fame. I just had to write and tell you how wrong you are.

You said that there are fewer third basemen in the Hall of Fame than players at any other position. Well, so what? The Hall of Fame should be only for the very greatest players. If you put in Santo because you need more third basemen, are you going to put in Sal Bando after that and Buddy Bell after that and Gary Gaetti after that? Eventually we'll wind up with Bob Bailey and Pete Ward in the Hall of Fame. The Hall of Fame is supposed to be for players like Willie Mays and Tom Seaver, not for players like Ron Santo and Pete Ward.

—*Cooperstown Defender*

Dear Coop:

Thanks for writing. With regard to there being fewer third basemen in the Hall of Fame than players at any other position, you missed the purpose of the information. My point was not that there are too few third baseman in the Hall of Fame, and therefore we should elect a bunch of third basemen. My point was that Ron Santo was a better player than *most* of the third basemen in the Hall of Fame, and this is true despite the fact that fewer third basemen have been elected to the Hall of Fame than players at any other position.

As to Santo being a better player than most of the Hall of Fame third basemen, I think that if you study this issue carefully, you will be forced to agree that this is true, or was true be-

fore Schmidt and Brett. George Kell is in the Hall of Fame. George Kell in his career drove in 100 runs once, scored 100 runs once; otherwise his career high in RBI was 93. Ron Santo scored 100 runs once, and drove in more than 93 runs every year, eight straight years. Obviously, Santo was doing a lot more to change the scoreboard than Kell was, even though Santo played in the 1960s, when runs were hard to come by.

Santo was not only a better hitter than Kell, he was also a better hitter than Jimmy Collins, Pie Traynor, Fred Lindstrom, and Brooks Robinson. He was a good hitter in a relatively long career, as he ranks eighth all-time in games played at third base. Defense? He won five Gold Gloves. I will agree that Santo was not a brilliant defensive third baseman. Had Brooks Robinson or Clete Boyer been in the National League, Santo's Gold Gloves would have been few and far between. Santo was a sure-handed third baseman with an excellent arm; he was not quick on his feet. I might even agree that Kell was probably a better fielder than Santo was—but Santo was a fine defensive third baseman. Kell, if he was better, could not have been *enough* better to begin to offset the facts that Santo created more runs per year, that he did it for more years, and that he did it in a time when each run was more valuable.

By my reckoning, George Kell was the 30th best third baseman of all time; he is in the Hall of Fame. Fred Lindstrom was the 43rd best third baseman of all time; he is in the Hall of Fame. At several other positions, players have been selected who were not among the top 50. After the Hall of Fame has already honored the 30th-best and 43rd-best players at the position, does it degrade the Hall of Fame to then include the sixth-best? Does it not, in fact, *enhance* the integrity of the honor, to show that the institution is capable of some minimal consistency in its selections?

We could all agree, could we not, that the Hall of Fame is simply *not* going to stop selecting people? It's not going to happen; neither the Veteran's Committee nor the Hall of Fame as a whole is going to stop making selections. What I am saying is, it's not Ron Santo against Willie Mays. It is Ron Santo against Pete Browning, or Babe Herman, or Bob Meusel, or Jake Daubert, or somebody else whose only *real* advantage on Ron Santo is that he played so long ago that his flaws have been forgotten.

The reality is, Willie Mays never was and never can be the standard of the Hall of Fame. In the 1940s, many players were selected to the Hall of Fame who were nowhere near as good as Ron Santo, let alone nowhere near as good as Willie Mays. Players who were nowhere near as good as Ron Santo were elected to the Hall of Fame in the 1950s, players who were nowhere near as good as Ron Santo were elected to the Hall of Fame in the 1960s, players who were nowhere near as good as Ron Santo were elected to the Hall of Fame in the 1970s (lots of them), players who were nowhere near as good as Ron Santo were elected to the Hall of Fame in the 1980s, and players who were nowhere near as good as Ron Santo were elected to the Hall of Fame in the 1990s. It is preposterous to argue that the Hall of Fame standard is Ted Williams, after six decades of honoring players like Tommy McCarthy (1946), Rabbit Maranville (1954), Elmer Flick (1963), Dave Bancroft (1971), George Kell (1983), and Tony Lazzeri (1991). The Ted Williams/Bob Gibson/Honus Wagner standard for Hall of Fame selection has never existed anywhere except in the imaginations of people who don't know anything about the subject.

Look, certain things just do not happen. Rivers do not run uphill, iron does not become gold, time does not go backward, whores do not become virgins, pigs do not give birth to lions, supermodels do not marry auto mechanics, and politicians do not forget about the next election. There is no alchemy by which the Hall of Fame may become what it never has been. Ron Santo towers far above the real standard of the real Hall of Fame.

7 ◆ Brooks Robinson
(1955–1977, 2896 G, 268 1357 .267)

> Paul Richards . . . got me out of bed one morning to look at a young kid to see if he should sign him. He was a nice young man from Little Rock, Arkansas, who hadn't even played high school ball. He couldn't run, he couldn't throw, he couldn't hit. I never would have signed Brooks Robinson.—Gene Woodling in *We Played the Game*

> The amazing thing about *Shoeless Joe* is that I've made an interesting story about a guy who's happily married to a wife he really loves and who loves him. You virtually never see that in fiction because it's hard to write a story about nice people in normal relationships. Stories about nice people who are happy usually are not very interesting.—W.P. Kinsella in *The Writer's Game*

There is an old aphorism that a happy life makes a boring biography. There are three biographies of Brooks Robinson which, meaning them no disrespect, seem to illustrate the point. Brooks' hero, as a child, was Stan Musial, which fits, as Musial was the nicest of superstars. In fact, the third basemen generally, if you'll notice, are the nicest stars in the history of the game. Look at the top ten–twenty players listed at each position. Which is the most likeable group of guys? The third basemen, I think. Four of them are famous for being nice people (Robinson, Mathews, Molitor, and Hack), as were Pie Traynor and Buddy Bell, and the others are all OK, not a real asshole among them. Well, Graig Nettles could be a jerk sometimes. The only position which is comparable is the next position over, shortstop; at shortstop you have Wagner, Ripken, Banks, Ozzie Smith, Pee Wee Reese, Luke Appling, but also guys like Maury Wills, Vern Stephens, and Alvin Dark, who could be nice people if they wanted to.

The catchers are nice people . . . near the top of that group you've got Roy Campanella, who was super nice, and Yogi, who was beloved although he was actually kind of a grouch. There are some egos in there (Ted Simmons) and one really unpleasant person (Munson), but they're a likeable lot.

At first base you've Anson, who was anything but a nice person, and Dick Allen, who was charming but petulant, plus Orlando Cepeda. Eddie Murray was probably not as surly as his reputation, and Johnny Mize did not enjoy a good press. At second, there are some good guys (Gehringer, Sandberg, Lajoie, Collins) but then there was Hornsby, who was just plain nasty, Frisch, who was a hothead, and Jackie Robinson, who was admirable and intelligent, but hardly ingratiating. Johnny Evers, who didn't quite crack the top 20, was never more than about ten minutes away from having a fist fight with somebody.

The left fielders are the worst of the bunch; in the top twenty you've got Ted Williams, Rickey Henderson, Joe Jackson, Goose Goslin, Jim Rice, Jesse Burkett, Joe Medwick, Ralph Kiner, and Al Oliver. Boy, there's a family re-union you can leave me out of . . . the right fielders are almost as bad. You've got Frank Robinson, who has gotten nicer as he has gotten older, plus Reggie, Pete Rose, Clemente. Clemente was a fine person, but hard to get along with. The only really nice guys among the top right fielders were Mel Ott, about whom Durocher said that nice guys finish last, and Al Kaline.

In center field, you've got Ty Cobb, enough said, plus Duke Snider, Willie Davis, Hack Wilson, none of whom was as obnoxious as Cobb, but all of whom had their moments.

Two generalized points:

1. Durocher's law, that nice guys finish last, may well be true of managers, but is almost certainly not true of players. It is kind of striking, in fact, how many unusually nice people you can find among the top ten players at a position. Also, it seems clear that if you took a team of the best player at each position that *everybody* would describe as a nice guy, and a team of the best player at each position that *nobody* would describe as a nice guy, the nice guys would clean their clock.

2. It seems obvious that jerks cluster on the left end of the defensive spectrum, the positions (1B, LF, RF) requiring the least defense, where the big hitters play. The more defense is required of a position, the more nice people seem to congregate there. This seems to extend beyond position, to defensive ability. Rogers Hornsby, although he played a fielder's position, did not play it well; he was basically a hitter. Brooks Robinson, on the other hand, was nowhere near the hitter that some guys are who rank 40th–60th at third base, but he ranks where he does because of his defense.

Of course there are always counter-examples; Leo Durocher was, after all, a weak-hitting shortstop, and Chili Davis, from what I understand, is a prince. There are lots of first basemen who are very nice people. But if you break it down to specialists, think of Dave Kingman on the one hand, Rafael Belliard on the other. Kingman, who couldn't catch the measles in a leper colony, also couldn't get along with people, while Belliard, who lives by his glove, has always been immensely popular with teammates. I could list a dozen other Kingmans—Dick Stuart, Willie Aikens, and Alex Johnson, to name just three—and any number of Rafael Belliard types.

I'm speculating, and argue with me if you disagree, but playing defense is, by it's nature, a selfless, team-oriented skill, while hitting is a glamour job. Thus, it is perhaps natural that defensive positions would attract and develop players whose focus extended beyond their self-interest, while hitting spots would appeal more to people who were looking out for number one. It's not that Alex Johnson or Dave Kingman or Rogers Hornsby *couldn't* play defense. It was just that it was too damn much trouble, and where did it get you? Brooks Robinson represents the other end of that spectrum.

8 ◆ Paul Molitor
(1978–1998, 2683 G, 234 1307 .306)

Only 29% of his career games were at third base, but . . . well, we have to list him somewhere. Treating Molitor as a third basemen, he ranks first among the 100 third basemen listed here in six categories: Career At Bats (10,835), Plate Appearances (12,160), Hits (3,319), Runs Scored (1,782), Caught Stealing (131), and Runs Created (1,876). He also has the most stolen bases of anyone who played with the modern stolen base rule (since 1897), and, despite leading in caught stealing, has the highest stolen base percentage of anyone who has played a full career in the era in which caught stealing have been recorded. Third base leaders in other categories:

Games Played	Brooks Robinson (2,896)
Doubles	George Brett (665)
Triples	Tommy Leach (172)
Home Runs	Mike Schmidt (548)
Total Bases	George Brett (5,044)
RBI	Tie, Brett and Schmidt (1,583)
Runs + RBI	George Brett (3,178)
R + RBI per Game	Bill Joyce (1.47)
Walks	Ed Yost (1,614)
Intentional Walks	George Brett (229)
Strikeouts	Mike Schmidt (1,883)
Hit by Pitch	John McGraw (132)
Sacrifice Hits	Larry Gardner (311)
Sacrifice Flies	George Brett (120)
Stolen Bases	Arlie Latham (739)
SB Percentage	Chipper Jones (81.4%, so far)
Grounded into Double Play	Brooks Robinson (297)
Runs Created/ 27 Outs	John McGraw (9.88)
Batting Average	John McGraw (.334)
On Base Percentage	John McGraw (.465)
Slugging Percentage	Chipper Jones (.529 so far)
Secondary Average	Bill Joyce (.471)

Games at Third	Brooks Robinson (2,870)
Estimated Defensive Innings at Third	Brooks Robinson (25,031)
Defensive Win Shares	Brooks Robinson (106.67)
Defensive Innings per Defensive Game	Pie Traynor (9.02)
Putouts per 9 EDI	Jerry Denny
Assists per 9 EDI	Ned Williamson
Win Shares/1000 Defensive Innings	Lave Cross (6.03)
Putouts at Third	Brooks Robinson (2,697)
Assists at Third	Brooks Robinson (6,205)
Errors at Third	Arlie Latham (822)
Double Plays	Brooks Robinson (618)
Range Factor (Based on Def Games)	Jerry Denny (3.71)
Range Factor (Based on Est Def Innings)	Billy Shindle (3.80)
Fielding Percentage	Brooks Robinson (.971)
Offensive Winning Percentage	John McGraw (.743)
Percentage of Career Games Played at Third Base	Brooks Robinson (99%)

The most remarkable thing about Molitor is that after ten solid years of being regarded as a fragile player (1978–1987), a player who was always hurt, he was so durable over the second half of his career that he was able to go to the plate more times than any other third baseman in history.

9 ◆ Stan Hack
(1932–1947, 1938 G, 57 642 .301)

Everybody always thinks it was the big hitters who gave us pitchers the most trouble. It wasn't them as much as it was those damned 'taperitas' hitters like Stan Hack. They're the ones who really get you in trouble.—Bucky Walters in *Diamond Greats*

I joined the ball club and I'll never forget I walked in the clubhouse and Stan Hack said, "Andy, I heard you were coming. Welcome to Chicago." He made me feel like I was part of the ball club immediately.—Andy Pafko, *Our Chicago Cubs*

Hack used to say that he came from a town so small they didn't have a town drunk; everybody had to take turns . . . Let's compare Stan Hack to Pie Traynor. Stan Hack and Pie Traynor were contemporary third basemen; Traynor actually was ten years older than Hack. They were both National Leaguers, both spending their entire careers with one team (Hack with the Cubs, Traynor with the Pirates). Both men were career .300 hitters, playing almost exactly the same number of games in their careers with almost exactly the same number of home runs. They stole essentially the same number of bases. Both men were known as exceptionally nice people, and both managed their old teams at or after the end of their playing days. Both men broke in playing third base for teams whose regular first baseman was Charlie Grimm.

I am well aware that most historians rank Traynor as a greater player than Hack. Traynor is in the Hall of Fame, Hack is not, and Traynor, before Schmidt and Brett, was often cited as the greatest third baseman of all time. The question is, is this legitimate?

It's an interesting exercise, because the men have so much in common that, when comparing them, you can throw a bunch of things out the window—power, speed, career length, intangible contributions. Traynor ranks higher than Hack in many evaluations, I believe, because:

1. Traynor was a lifetime .320 hitter, whereas Hack hit .301.

2. Traynor drove in more runs. Traynor drove in 100 runs seven times in his career, Hack never did.

3. Traynor was a superior defensive third baseman, whereas Hack was merely a good defensive third baseman.

I don't think that those advantages hold up to a rigorous analysis. Traynor hit .320 to Hack's .301 mostly because National League batting averages in the 1920s were a lot higher than they were in the 1930s. The National League batting averages in Traynor's first nine years as

a regular were .292, .286, .283, .292, .280, .282, .281, .294, and .303. National League batting averages in Hack's years, the first nine years after Traynor was no longer a regular, never reached .280, and dropped as low as .249. Hack's batting averages, compared to the league norms, are as impressive as Traynor's, or more so.

Traynor drove in more runs, but Hack scored more runs; Hack, a leadoff hitter, scored 100 runs seven times. Baseball writers have always overrated RBI, and ignored the fact that runs scored are essentially a function of men on base.

Stan Hack was not only as good a hitter as Traynor, he was better. Traynor created about 1,172 runs in his career, which is 5.61 runs per 27 outs, playing in an era when the league norm was 4.74 runs per game. These are good numbers, but Stan Hack's numbers are pretty much the same, except that he drew 600 more walks. Hack created an estimated 1,240 runs in his career, which is 6.30 runs per 27 outs, playing in an era when the league norm was 4.37 runs per game. Traynor was 182 runs better than an average hitter in his career; Hack was 380 runs better.

As to the third point, that Traynor was a more outstanding fielder than Hack, yes, I agree that he was. I credit Traynor with 77 Win Shares for his defense at third base, Hack with 65—a substantial difference, given that they played almost the same number of innings at third base (16,620 for Traynor, 16,244 for Hack). But Hack was hardly a marginal defensive third baseman; in fact, he was darned good. I see Hack as being deserving of three Gold Gloves as the best third baseman in the National League (1934, 1937, and 1938), the same number as Traynor (1925, 1927, and 1933).

Pie Traynor's career fielding percentage was .947. The league norm for his era was .947. Hack's fielding percentage was .956, against a league norm of .946. Traynor made 78 errors more than Hack—in fact, Traynor led the league in errors five times, whereas Hack never did. Traynor made only 63 more assists than Hack, 3,521 to 3,458. Traynor did make significantly more putouts in his career (2,289 to 1,946), but putouts by third baseman (a) rarely have anything to do with defensive skill, (b) are heavily influenced by other factors, and (c) declined substantially in the ten years that Traynor preceded Hack.

In 1920 National League third basemen recorded 181 putouts per team. In 1930, this figure was 147 per team. (See also entry on Jeremiah Denny, #99.)

Anyway, taking everything into consideration in a systematic way, I do agree that Traynor was a better fielder than Hack—but nowhere near *enough* better to off-set Hack's advantages as a hitter. I will also note that Hack played for four teams that won the National League pennant, whereas Traynor played for only two.

10 ◆ Darrell Evans

(1969–1989, 2687 G, 414 1354 .248)

Darrell Evans is, in my opinion, the most underrated player in baseball history, absolutely number one on the list. There are at least ten characteristics of an underrated player:

1. Specialists and players who do two or three things well are overrated; players who do several things well are underrated.

2. Batting average is overrated; secondary offensive skills, summarized in secondary average, are underrated.

3. Driving in runs is overrated; scoring runs is underrated.

4. Players who play for championship teams are often overrated; players who get stuck with bad teams are often underrated.

5. Players who play in New York and LA are sometimes overrated, while players who play in smaller and less glamorous cities are sometimes underrated, although this factor is not as significant as many people believe it to be.

6. Players who are glib and popular with the press are sometimes overrated, while players who are quiet are sometimes underrated, although, again, this factor is not as significant as many people think it is.

7. Players who play in parks which do not favor their skills are always underrated. Players who play in parks which favor them—hitters in Colorado, lefties in Yankee, pitchers in the Astrodome—are always overrated.

8. Hitters from big-hitting eras (the 1890s, the 1920s and 1930s) are overrated in history, and pitchers from the dead ball era and the 1960s are overrated. Pitchers from the big-hitting era and hitters from the 1960s are underrated.

9. Undocumented skills (leadership, defense, heads-up play) tend to be forgotten over time. Everything else deteriorates faster than the numbers.

10. Anything which "breaks up" a player's career tends to cause him to be underrated. A player who has a good career with one team will be thought of more highly than a player who does the same things, but with three different teams. Switching positions causes a player to be underrated. A player who plays 1,000 games at third base and 1,000 games at second base may be underrated, because it's harder to form a whole image of what he has done.

This is the same principle as camouflage gear—break up the silhouette of a man, break up his colors and his outline, and he's harder to see. This also explains factor (1) above, the overrating of specialists as opposed to players of diverse skills.

Anyway, let's assume that 40% of players are disadvantaged by each of these effects, and that these biases are randomly aligned. If that were the case, then about one player in 10,000 would be disadvantaged in all ten areas.

There aren't 10,000 good players in major league history (there are about 3,000 players who have had real major league careers), so there probably would not be a player who was disadvantaged in *every* area of the evaluation bias. I think that's true, there probably isn't any such player. Darrell Evans is probably the closest.

1. Evans wasn't a specialist; he was a player who did a lot of things pretty well.

2. Evans had a career batting average of .248 (95th among the 100 third basemen listed here), but a secondary average of .373 (9th best among the top 100 third basemen).

3. Evans didn't get to play for a championship team until he was 37 years old, and he had an off year then.

4. Evans never played in New York or LA. He played in Atlanta in the early 1970s, when Atlanta was in its Toledo period, and later played in Detroit, at a time when the only news to escape from Detroit was an occasional gun battle.

5. Evans was not notably glib or quotable.

6. Although Evans did play in good home run parks early in his career and late in his career, the years that should have been his prime seasons were spent in Candlestick Park at a time when Candlestick was one of the worst hitter's parks in baseball.

7. Evans career is broken up into three almost equal phases (Atlanta, San Francisco, and Detroit) and split between two defensive positions.

Hidden behind all of these screens, Evans completely failed to convince the American public that he was anything special as a player—yet he was. Among the 100 third basemen listed here, Evans is eighth in runs scored, sixth in RBI, and he was a very good defensive third baseman.

The player who best makes the Hall of Fame case for Evans (not that I think there is a chance in hell he will ever be elected to the Hall of Fame) is Tony Perez. Perez and Evans are both National League players of the same era (Perez was five years older) who both moved to the American League toward the end of their careers. They were both originally third basemen, and both moved to first base in midcareer. Both were power hitters.

Their careers are of almost the same length—2,687 games for Evans, 2,777 for Perez, 10,737 plate appearances for Evans, 10,861 for Perez. Perez had 500 more hits, including 176 more doubles and more than twice as many triples (79-36), but Evans also has his advantages, including a small advantage in home runs (414-379). More significantly, Evans grounded into less than half as many double plays (133-268), struck out 457 times less, and drew almost 700 more walks (1,605-925). Evans stole twice as many bases (98-49) with essentially the same stolen base percentage. Perez's batting average is 31 points higher than Evans', but his on-base percentage, which is a more important stat than batting average, is 20 points lower (.341 to .361).

Balancing all of the offensive positives and negatives, I have Evans with 1,459 runs created (5.58 per 27 outs) and Perez with 1,475 (5.36 per 27 outs). Basically, they're even.

As defensive players, however, they're not even. Evans is better. Perez played a few years at third base, and he wasn't awful, but it gradually became clear that, as a third baseman, he was a better first baseman. Evans, on the other hand, *could* play third—not at the level of Mike Schmidt, quite, and not at the level of Brooks Robinson, certainly, but he was a good third baseman until he was well into his thirties.

So if Perez wasn't a better hitter, and he wasn't a better fielder, and he wasn't a better baserunner, then why was he a better player? Was he a better player because he played with great teams? Was he a better player because he had a higher batting average and more RBI? Was he a better player because he had a cool nickname and a gregarious personality?

Perez is in the Hall of Fame, and I'm happy that he is, and Evans isn't going to go there, and I'm OK with that, but the fact is that Darrell Evans *was* a better player than Tony Perez.

11 ◆ Sal Bando
(1966–1981, 2019 G, 242 1039 .254)

He's the only player I ever socialized with. I'd invite him to my hotel suite after games or during an off-day, and we'd just talk baseball. The rest of the team saw this and figured I must be all right.–Dick Williams, *No More Mr. Nice Guy* (Harcourt Brace Jovanovich, 1990)

12 ◆ Ken Boyer
(1955–1969, 2034 G, 282 1141 .287)

The best player from one of the great ballplaying families . . . see comment on Felipe Alou.

Boyer was the third baseman on the 1963 Cardinals, all four of whose infielders started the All-Star game–Bill White, Julian Javier, Boyer, and Dick Groat. Two members of that infield had 200 hits (White and Groat), while Boyer had 176 hits and drove in 111 runs. Was that the greatest infield of all time?

The Win Shares system is designed to study a question of this nature. Each player in the Win Shares system has an integer value, and those values bear a constant relationship to team wins. The best infield is the infield which has contributed the most to the wins of their team.

The greatest infield of all time, according to the Win Shares system, is also one of the most famous: Connie Mack's $100,000 infield in 1914:

1914 Philadelphia A's

1B–Stuffy McInnis	22	
2B–Eddie Collins	43	
3B–Home Run Baker	36	
SS–Jack Barry	18	
Total	119	

This infield consisted of two MVP candidates, Collins and Baker, and two other guys who were very good ballplayers. Eddie Collins won the American League MVP Award that year; Home Run Baker was fourth in the voting. According to Win Shares, Collins was actually the second-best player in the league, behind Tris Speaker, while Baker was the fourth-best player in the league, behind Speaker, Collins, and Walter Johnson. Stuffy McInnis hit .314 with 95 RBI. Although nowhere near as valuable as Collins or Baker, he was still the best first baseman in the American League, and by a good margin (22-17). Jack Barry hit just .242, but still ranks as the second-best shortstop in the American League, behind Donie Bush. The A's won 99 games, but made themselves miserable worrying about money, and the infield was broken up that winter.

The second-greatest infield of all time, by this method, is a fluke, the only real fluke team in the top 20. It's the 1908 Pirates:

1908 Pittsburgh Pirates

1B–Alan Storke	5	
2B–Ed Abbaticchio	22	
3B–Tommy Leach	31	
SS–Honus Wagner	59	
Total	117	

Wagner's 1908 season ranks, by the Win Shares system, as the greatest season of the 20th century; even Babe Ruth never matched it. Why?

Well, Wagner hit .354 and drove in 109 runs. This is no big deal; Wagner hit .354 and drove in 109 runs pretty much every year. In baseball history there are lots of guys who hit .370 and drove in 150 runs. What makes Wagner different is (a) defense, and (b) a quite exceptional ratio of wins to runs scored.

The National League ERA in 1908 was 2.35— the lowest ERA of the dead ball era, the lowest ERA for a league in the 20th century.

In modern baseball, the league ERAs are just about twice that, about 4.70. So double the numbers: if you had a Gold Glove shortstop, like Wagner, who drove in 218 runs, what would he be worth?

In addition to that, the Pirates were playing in the poorest hitter's park in the National League, a park which reduced scoring by about 16%. You may remember the Dodgers of the mid-sixties, who won the National League three times in four years without scoring many runs. The 1908 Pirates scored fewer runs, and won more games. Their ratio of wins to runs scored is the highest of all time. On a scale of Wins-to-Runs ratios, the 1930 Phillies are on one end, and the 1908 Pirates are on the other end.

In that context, where runs were extremely scarce, Wagner led the National League in hits (201), in doubles (by 30%), in triples, in total bases (by 40), in stolen bases (53), in runs created (by 28%), in batting average (by 20 points), in RBI (109), in on-base percentage (.415), and in slugging percentage (by almost a hundred points). He was second in home runs and runs scored. At shortstop, he led the league in putouts, by 40. Even Babe Ruth never had as much impact on the game he was playing as Honus Wagner did in that one season.

The contextual oddities which make Wagner's season even greater than it looks, of course, also apply to his teammates. Tommy Leach that year hit .259 with 5 home runs. He's the seventh-best player in the league. Ed Abbaticchio hit .250 with 1 home run. He was the second-best second baseman in the league, behind Johnny Evers.

The Pirate first basemen *weren't* good, even in context; Pirate first baseman Jim Nealon,

who had led the National League in RBI at age 21 in 1906, fell deathly ill, and the Pirates struggled to replace him. But Wagner was *so* great, and Leach and Abbaticchio good enough, that they rank high on the list of greatest infields despite that. No other team in the top ten infields has even one slot filled by a player worth less than 15 Win Shares. Alan Storke, the best of the Pirate first basemen, was worth only one-third of that. But the Pirates overcame that, and won 98 games.

The third-best infield of all-time is the $100,000 infield, again, but in 1912:

1912 Philadelphia A's

1B—Harry Davis	24	
2B—Eddie Collins	37	
3B—Frank Baker	39	
SS—Jack Barry	16	
Total	116	

This is the same as the 1914 team except for Harry Davis, so let's move on. In fourth place is the 1934 Tigers:

1934 Detroit Tigers

1B—Hank Greenberg	31	
2B—Charlie Gehringer	37	
3B—Marv Owen	23	
SS—Billy Rogell	24	
Total	114	

Richard Bak, in *Cobb Would Have Caught It*, says that this team "put together the finest single season of any infield in history." He's wrong, I think, but not by much. The first baseman, Greenberg, hit .339 with 63 doubles, driving in 139 runs. The second baseman, Gehringer, hit .356 with 50 more doubles, 127 RBI, 134 runs scored, and finished second in the MVP voting. The third baseman, Marv Owen, hit .317 with 96 RBI, and was ninth in the MVP vote. The shortstop, Billy Rogell, hit .296, scored 114 runs, and drove in 100. Among the four of them, they played every game except one (Greenberg missed one game), and the Tigers won 101 games and their first American League pennant in a quarter-century.

Gehringer, Owen, and Rogell were all Catholics. Jimmy Dykes, managing the White Sox, used to yell out at Greenberg, "How can you get along with those Catholics and you being a hebe?"

"We didn't like it," said Billy Rogell, "but that's baseball."

Fifth place is a tie between the 1913 version of the $100,000 infield and the 1982 Brewers:

1913 White Elephants

1B—Stuffy McInnis	26
2B—Eddie Collins	39
3B—Home Run Baker	38
SS—Jack Barry	20
Total	113

1982 Milwaukee Brewers

1B—Cecil Cooper	29
2B—Jim Gantner	15
3B—Paul Molitor	30
SS—Robin Yount	39
Total	113

The A's from 1909 through 1914 score at 100, 95, 104, 116, 113, and 119—by far the best run of seasons in baseball history. Dan Okrent wrote a great book about the other team, (Harvey's Wallbangers). Robin Yount hit .331 with 29 homers, 114 RBI, and won the MVP Award. Cecil Cooper hit .313 with 32 homers, 121 RBI, and finished fifth in the MVP voting. Paul Molitor had 201 hits, and led the majors in runs scored, with 136. Jim Gantner, while not a star, was a fine player. They were, at least by this analysis, the greatest infield since the big war.

The 1927 New York Giants had four Hall of Famers in the infield:

1927 New York Giants

1B—Bill Terry	27
2B—Rogers Hornsby	40
3B—Fred Lindstrom	21
SS—Travis Jackson	24
Total	112

None of the four had a career year, but all four were healthy and had solid years, hitting from .306 to .361, with power. Nobody remembers them as an all-time great infield because Hornsby was only there for one year and the Giants didn't win the pennant, although they did win 92 games. As a great infield they are in a 7th/8th place tie with another modern team:

1975 Cincinnati Reds

1B—Tony Perez	19
2B—Joe Morgan	44
3B—Pete Rose	30
SS—Dave Concepcion	19
Total	112

The Big Red Machine. Some of you may wish to argue that this was, in fact, the greatest infield of all time. I might agree with you. The $100,000 infield dominated a game which was not, in all honesty, fully mature. Farm systems hadn't been developed, and scouting was haphazard. The country was small and rural, and blacks weren't allowed to play. The 1975 Reds dominated a modern game. The 1982 Brew Crew scores one point higher, but (a) that one point doesn't mean much, and (b) the Reds were great for six years; the Brewers, for two.

In ninth place is the eastern European infield of the 1946 Cardinals:

1946 St. Louis Cardinals

1B—Stan Musial	44
2B—Red Schoendienst	18
3B—Whitey Kurowski	26
SS—Marty Marion	19
Total	107

Two of the regulars on that unit, Musial and Schoendienst, were converted outfielders who had not played the infield in the major leagues before that season. They seemed to make the transition alright; Musial hit .365 with 50 doubles, 20 triples and 16 homers, Schoendienst hit .281, Kurowski hit over .300 and drove in 89 runs, Marion was a glove wizard, and the Cardinals won the World Championship.

In tenth place is the next installment of the Big Red Machine:

1976 Cincinnati Reds

1B—Tony Perez	16
2B—Joe Morgan	36
3B—Pete Rose	30
SS—Dave Concepcion	23
Total	105

The Reds, from 1972 through 1977, score at 86, 99, 96, 112, 105, and 92—the greatest run of modern times.

The second ten:

11t. 1906 Pirates (Jim Nealon, Claude Ritchey, Tommy Leach, and Honus Wagner), 104 Win Shares.

11t. 1906 Cubs (Frank Chance, Johnny Evers, Joe Tinker, and Harry Steinfeldt), 104 Win Shares.

11t. 1936 Yankees (Lou Gehrig, Tony Lazzeri, Red Rolfe, and Frankie Crosetti), 104 Win Shares.

14t. 1933 Philadelphia Athletics (Jimmie Foxx, Maxie Bishop, Pinkie Higgins, and Dib Williams), 103 Win Shares.

14t. 1983 Brewers (Cooper, Ganter, Molitor, and Yount), 103 Win Shares.

16. 1987 Cardinals (Jack Clark, Tommie Herr, Terry Pendleton, and Ozzie Smith), 102 Win Shares.

17t. 1924 Giants (George Kelly, Frankie Frisch, Heinie Groh, and Travis Jackson), 101 Win Shares.

17t. 1951 Dodgers (Gil Hodges, Jackie Robinson, Billy Cox, and Pee Wee Reese), 101 Win Shares.

17t. 1996 Houston Astros (Jeff Bagwell, Craig Biggio, Sean Berry, and Orlando Miller), 101 Win Shares despite Orlando Miller.

20t. 1909 A's (Harry Davis, Eddie Collins, Frank Baker, and Jack Barry), 100 Win Shares.

20t. 1996 Orioles (Rafael Palmeiro, Roberto Alomar, B.J. Surhoff, and Cal Ripken), 100 Win Shares.

Abbreviating the listings even more:

99 Win Shares

1973	Cincinnati Reds
1990	Detroit Tigers

98 Win Shares

1935	Detroit Tigers
1939	Cincinnati Reds
1963	St. Louis Cardinals
1999	New York Mets

97 Win Shares

1942	Brooklyn Dodgers
1949	Brooklyn Dodgers
1999	New York Yankees

96 Win Shares

1908	Chicago Cubs
1911	Philadelphia A's
1921	St. Louis Cardinals
1953	Brooklyn Dodgers
1954	Brooklyn Dodgers
1998	New York Yankees

95 Win Shares

1910	Philadelphia A's
1932	New York Yankees
1933	Washington Senators
1952	New York Giants
1969	Minnesota Twins
1974	Philadelphia Phillies

So, to answer the question with which we began this exercise, no, the 1963 Cardinals were *not* the greatest infield of all time. They were a terrific infield—in the top 1% of all teams. If Julian Javier had been Joe Morgan, they would have been the greatest infield of all time, by far. And the Cardinals would have won the pennant.

I read an article in September, 1999, suggesting that the 1999 New York Mets may have had the greatest infield of all time (John Olerud, Edgardo Alfonzo, Robin Ventura, and Rey Ordonez). Again, the 1999 New York Mets did have an outstanding infield, in the top 1% of all time. What they lacked was a legitimate MVP candidate, a player with 35 Win Shares. If Rey Ordonez was Derek Jeter, it would be the greatest infield of all time. And the Mets would have won the pennant.

The current New York Yankee infield is as good as the New York Met infield—different, but just as good. Historically, the Yankee infields make surprisingly little impact on the lists above. No Yankee infield is among the ten best of all time, only one is among the top 20 of all time, and only three others have amassed 95 Win Shares among four players. The big Yankee stars have mostly been outfielders—Ruth, DiMaggio, Mantle—and catchers. New York Yankee players have won 20 MVP Awards—9 by outfielders, 5 by catchers, 1 by a pitcher, and 5 by infielders.

Five other notes:

1. Almost all of the greatest infields of all time have at least one superstar. Basically, most of the great infields ever consist of two superstars plus two other good players. The best infield ever that didn't have a real star was the 1939 Cincinnati Reds—25 Win Shares from the first baseman (Frank McCormick), 25 from the second baseman (Lonnie Frey), 25 from the third baseman (Billy Werber), and 23 from the shortstop (Billy Myers).

2. One infield which is conspicuous by its absence is the Orioles of the 1970s, with Boog Powell, Lee May and Eddie Murray at first, Davey Johnson and Bobby Grich at second, Brooks Robinson at third, and Mark Belanger at short.

Those were very good infields, and they are *near* the list almost every year; they just never quite made it somehow. It takes an awful lot to make the list. Brooks Robinson was in his mid-thirties by the time the infield came together, and the infield didn't really have a superstar. Think of all the years the Yankees had Gehrig and Lazzeri and other good players (Rolfe, Crosetti, etc.) but didn't make the list. Think of all the years the Phillies had Mike Schmidt and Larry Bowa, or Schmidt and Bowa and Rose, or Schmidt and Bowa and Rose and Trillo, and still didn't make the list. Think of all the years the Royals had George Brett and Frank White; they never made the list. Think of the years the Red Sox had Doerr and Pesky and Vern Stephens, and they didn't make the list. The 1948 Cleveland Indians, another team often cited as having the best infield ever, didn't make the list. There are lots and lots of teams that had two superstar infielders having good years, but didn't make the list. The 1983 and 1984 Orioles had two of the five best players in the league (Cal Ripken and Eddie Murray), but didn't come close to making the list either year, because the second and third basemen just didn't do enough.

3. Why didn't the 1948 Indians make the list?

The Cleveland shortstop, Boudreau, won the MVP Award. I credit him with 34 Win Shares, which makes him even with DiMaggio and behind Ted Williams, but still, that's an MVP-type season. If you wind up in a tie with Joe DiMaggio, you're doing OK. The third baseman, Ken Keltner, drove in 119 runs and earned 25 Win Shares, and the second baseman, Joe Gordon, drove in 124 runs and earned 24 Win Shares.

But they didn't have a great infield; they had three-fourths of a great infield. If Eddie Robinson had been Lou Gehrig, that would have been the greatest infield of all time. Robinson hit .254 with 16 homers; we credit him with 9 Win Shares. Add it up, and they're one point short.

4. Another team that I expected to make the list was the 1950 Boston Red Sox (Walt Dropo, Bobby Doerr, Johnny Pesky, and Vern Stephens). All four players scored over a hundred runs; all except Pesky drove in over 100, and Dropo and Stephens tied for the league lead, with 144.

But the ratio of runs to wins there is working against them; that was an extremely high-run context. Dropo, despite the 144 RBI, was not really a great player; we credit him with 21 Win Shares, which is a good total, but it's just a regular Gil Hodges-Tino Martinez-type of season, nothing out of the ordinary. We credit Doerr with 23 Win Shares, Pesky with 19, Stephens with 23. Taken together, they are well short of making the list of the greatest infields of all time.

That team would be among the greatest infields ever if we could count their fifth man, Billy Goodman, who played 110 games and won the batting title. The rule of the exercise was, four players is an infield, and there's a good reason for that; Goodman, after all, played almost as much in the outfield as he did in the infield.

5. The 1990 Detroit Tigers had the best infield ever for a sub-.500 team. The first baseman, Cecil Fielder, hit 51 homers, and was second in the MVP voting. Keystone anchors Whitaker and Trammell both had solid seasons, and the third baseman, Tony Phillips, drew 99 walks and scored 97 runs. But their outfield was awful and their pitching was worse, and

they finished 79-83. Almost all of the other teams on the list won 90 or more games.

See also Ron Cey (3B #16) . . .

13 ◆ Graig Nettles
(1967–1988, 2700 G, 390 1314 .248)

In the 1970 World Series, Brooks Robinson became a living legend by making a series of diving stops, several times knocking balls down in foul territory, scrambling after them, and throwing runners out at first. In the 1976–77 Playoffs and the 1977 World Series, Nettles did exactly the same thing, but for some reason, this fact seemed to roll away, leaving the public unimpressed. I never knew quite why that was. It may have been the way the TV network covered the event. It may have been the fact that Brooks was a well-established star before the series, having won the MVP Award six years earlier. It may have been the fact that Nettles was not as likeable as Brooks, that the public sort of refused to put him on the same shelf. It may have been that that slot in the baseball pantheon—defensive wizard at third base—had already been filled in the public's mind. Whatever . . . he was a great defensive player, and he hit almost 400 home runs.

Nettles had a rough, sardonic humor; he could be very funny. He once said that the key to beating Tommy Lasorda's Dodgers was to keep them from hugging each other too much. When Sparky Lyle was traded from the Yankees in 1978, Nettles observed that he had gone from Cy Young to sayonara in one year. He said that to George Steinbrenner, the sweetest words in the world were "Yes, Boss." The Dodgers played on a hard-packed infield. During the 1977 World Series, Nettles said it was like playing on an unnumbered interstate highway.

Nettles "is the best third baseman in baseball and will be for the next five years," wrote Sparky Lyle when Nettles was 34 years old. "Without him at third base, my years on the Yankees would not have been half as productive as they were. He's probably the number one factor in my success here."–Sparky Lyle, *The Bronx Zoo* (Dell, 1979)

14 ◆ Al Rosen

(1947–1956, 1044 G, 192 717 .282)

The best seasons ever by a third baseman:

1. Al Rosen, 1953
2. Home Run Baker, 1912
3. Mike Schmidt, 1974
4. George Brett, 1985
5. Ken Caminiti, 1996

Rosen's career was shortened on both ends, on the front end by three years in the Army and several years trapped in the minor leagues behind Ken Keltner, and on the back end by back trouble, forcing an early retirement. For five years in between, he was every bit as good as Brett and Schmidt. His career average of RBI per game played (111 RBI per 162 games) is the best of any third baseman in history.

15 ◆ Pie Traynor

(1920–1937, 1941 G, 58 1273 .320)

There are four third basemen in history who averaged 200 hits per 162 games in their careers: Deacon White (202), Traynor (202), Paul Molitor (200), and Wade Boggs (200) . . . the idea that Traynor was the greatest third baseman of all time originated in the mid-1950s, about 20 years after Traynor retired. All-time teams chosen prior to 1955 never or almost never list Traynor–for example, Edward Barrow, in *My Fifty Years in Baseball* (1951), took credit for discovering Pie Traynor, and told a long-winded story about how Traynor was stolen from him by a dishonest minor league manager who violated a gentleman's agreement. But when it came time to choose his all-time team, Barrow listed Jimmy Collins as the greatest third baseman ever, although he did pick Traynor second. Babe Ruth with Bob Considine in *The Babe Ruth Story* (1948) also picked Collins as the greatest third baseman of all

time, with no mention of Traynor. Connie Mack in *My 66 Years in the Big Leagues* (1950) also picked Collins as the greatest third baseman of all time, again with no mention of Traynor.

By the time I became a baseball fan ten years later, 1960, it had become common to name Traynor as the greatest third baseman who ever lived. Ty Cobb with Al Stump (1961) chose Traynor as the best ever. Rogers Hornsby in *My War with Baseball* (1962) did the same, as did Casey Stengel in *Casey at the Bat* (1961). There are still people who will insist that he was, but I just don't see why.

> I looked out and watched him. He looked like a real ballplayer, even though he seemed to be all arms and legs and (had) feet like violin cases. He also had big hands and scooped up every ball hit at him and fired it over to first base.–Edward Barrow, *My Fifty Years in Baseball*

> He was an agitator; he started many things that people knew nothing about . . . We were staying at the Almanac Hotel in New York. About two A.M. we heard sirens blasting. Traynor had gotten into some milkman's horse drawn wagon and was driving the thing down Broadway with the police chasing him.–Dick Bartell with Norman L. Macht, *Rowdy Richard* (North Atlantic Books, 1987)

Bartell, Traynor's teammate for several years, disliked him, and thought he was a selfish player. "He had some deficiencies that you weren't aware of unless you played next to him," said Bartell. "When making a throw to second base he would lob the ball like a shot put instead of throwing it."

16 ◆ Ron Cey

(1971–1987, 2073 G, 316 1139 .261)

Cey had a squat, duck-shaped body with very low knees, for which reason he was called "The Penguin."

Cey was a member of the Dodger infield from 1973 through 1982. From '73 through '81 the Dodgers had the same four regular infielders—Garvey, Lopes, Cey, and Russell—the only time in baseball history any team has kept an infield intact for anything remotely resembling that length of time. As a group, they earned 63 Win Shares in 1973, then 88 in 1974, 80 in 1975, 84 in 1976, 81 in 1977, 84 in 1978, 84 in 1979, 73 in 1980, and 39 in the strike-shortened 1981 season.

Those numbers—80 to 88 win shares a season—don't look impressive compared to the historic infields that I identified in the Ken Boyer comment, but they're terrific. Anything above 80 is in the top 10% of all infields. To be there every year is a hell of a foundation for a team.

The infield doesn't rank among the greatest ever in any one season because (a) none of the players was a superstar, and (b) Bill Russell got hurt in '75, which would otherwise have been their best year as a group.

Garvey was the star in the group, but he was overrated, and Cey was actually the best player of the four, although by a thin margin. Cey, Garvey, and Lopes were really almost of the same value, and in any season any one of them might have been the best in the group.

17 ◆ Jimmy Collins
(1895–1908, 1728 G, 65 983 .294)
As I mentioned in the Pie Traynor comment, Collins was almost universally listed, up until the mid-1950s, as the greatest third baseman who ever played. Maybe I should let those who listed him there explain why . . .

> [Collins] completely revolutionized third-base play. Actually, he was the first modern third baseman, developing the technique of coming in for bunts and playing an alert mobile game at third instead of the accustomed style of the third basemen of the nineties of laying back and not "moving off a dime." . . . he had the agility of a cat—he was a sort of third base Hal Chase. Also, he had a keen and astute mind and knew how to match his wits against the crafty players of his day.—Edward Barrow

> Jimmy was another Lajoie, slick and fast. He had a great knack of coming up with the ball between hops. He was also a great base runner and a timely hitter.—Connie Mack.

> I select Jimmy for his general excellence as a fielder, a hitter and a man. He was a great fellow on and off the field and a credit to baseball. Jimmy Collins was particularly adept at going in for bunts. The art of bunting had just come into being when Collins began playing third base and he was one of the first to solve this style of play . . . [he was] the real pioneer of the modern style of playing third base.—John McGraw

18 ◆ Bob Elliott
(1939–1953, 1978 G, 170 1195 .289)
> A solidly built veteran who, besides being one of the most remarkable clutch hitters in the business, was also generally conceded to be the best third baseman in the National League, if not the universe.—Al Hirschberg, *The Braves, the Pick and the Shovel* (Waverly House, 1948)

19 ◆ Buddy Bell
(1972–1989, 2405 G, 201 1106 .279)
The worst percentage base stealer of all time (minimum: 100 attempts)—55 for 134, or 41%. The Indians in the 1970s used to hit and run a lot, so they had a lot of players with atrocious stolen base percentages. Duane Kuiper (52 for 123) is second-worst ever for a player with 100 or more attempts . . . see also comment on Felipe Alou (RF #48), which ranks the best ball-playing families.

20 ◆ Tommy Leach
(1898–1918, 2156 G, 62 810 .269)
A likeable little guy who was a fan favorite at the turn of the century, and was interviewed for *The Glory of Their Times*. Leach, playing for Auburn in the New York State league, was given his choice of going to the major leagues with

Washington or Louisville. He chose Louisville because his minor league manager told him that Wagner, who played third for Washington, was pretty good. It turned out that the manager had confused Honus Wagner with his brother, Butts, and had accidentally pushed Leach into competing with Honus Wagner for playing time. But it worked out alright, as Honus switched to shortstop a year or two later . . . Leach got the first hit in the history of the modern World Series (1903), and scored the first run. The hit was a two-out triple off of Cy Young, which ignited a four-run rally.

21 ◆ Heinie Groh

(1912–1927, 1676 G, 26 566 .292)

Before I did systematic rankings of the top 100 players at each position, I did subjective ratings of the same. In the subjective version, I had Heinie rated 54th at third base, because I didn't make adequate allowances for the fact that his best years were in the dead ball era. In the book, Heinie's 1917 season looks like nothing special—a .304 average, 1 home run, 53 RBI, 71 walks, 94 runs scored. In context, those modest numbers are more than equal to Chipper Jones' MVP season in 1999 (.319 with 45 homers, 119 RBI), and are far better than any season by Edgar Martinez, Ken Boyer, Freddy Lindstrom, Paul Molitor, Graig Nettles, or Pie Traynor. The National League averaged only 551 runs per team in 1917, and Groh played in a pitcher's park. He led the league in hits and doubles, was second in runs scored and runs created, was second in walks, led the league in on base percentage, and was second in total bases, seven behind Rogers Hornsby . . .

Before vanity license plates arrived (about 1980) all license plates had numbers. Some people would line up at the vehicle registration center the first day it was open, to get license plates with special numbers on them. Heinie Groh hit .474 in the 1922 World Series—and for

the rest of his life, always had license plate number 474 . . .

One of the more amazing records in the books is that Heinie Groh still holds to this day the record for the highest fielding percentage by a National League third baseman (.983 in 1924) and fewest errors by a National League third baseman, 140 or more games (7 in 1924). Fielding averages since the 1920s have gone up and up, but no one has broken those two records. Groh led the National League in fielding percentage five times, also a record (since tied by Ken Reitz) and in double plays six times, also a record (since tied by Ron Santo).

22 ◆ Robin Ventura

(1989–2000, 1556 G, 227 945 .273)

Why is it that some organizations get into streaks where they simply cannot find a third baseman? Is this really true, or is it some sort of trick of perception? It certainly *seems* to be more true at third base than at any other position.

The Dodgers, from the time of Billy Cox until the emergence of Ron Cey, chewed through third basemen like Marlon Brando going through a stack of lunch meat. They usually had some young player that they *thought* was going to be good—Don Zimmer, or Dick Gray, or Billy Grabarkewitz, or John Kennedy, or Bill Sudakis, or Johnny Werhas—but who never was. The best young third basemen they came up with in those years were Don Hoak, Ken McMullen, and Bob Aspromonte, all of whom they traded away before allowing them to prove they could play, and none of whom was Chipper Jones, anyway. They tried outfielders at third base—Tommy Davis, Jim Hickman, and Lee Walls. That never works. Well, almost never.

The Dodgers won a lot of pennants in those years anyway, because while Plan A never worked, Plan B was a killer. Plan B was Junior Gilliam. I don't think Gilliam ever started the year as the Dodgers' third baseman, but he finished up the year as the Dodger third baseman more often than not.

After ten years of excellent play, the Dodgers traded Ron Cey for a couple of guys named Dan Cataline and Vance Lovelace, who as I recall were an accountant and a lion tamer. They had two reasons for this:

1. They thought Cey was finished.
2. They thought German Rivera could play.

Cey wasn't, and Rivera couldn't. In no time, the Dodgers were back to the third-baseman-of-the-month plan, trying to make outfielders into third basemen (Pedro Guerrero, Mickey Hatcher, Cory Snyder) and working their way through a seemingly endless series of floundering prospects (Jeff Hamilton, Lenny Harris, Mike Sharperson, Dave Hansen, Dave Anderson, Tracy Woodson). Occasionally they would trade for a "proven" third baseman, like Mike Blowers, Phil Garner, or Bill Madlock, just because, once in awhile, it is fun to watch a veteran crash and burn, rather than a rookie. The best third baseman the Dodgers have had since they dumped Cey, by far, was Tim Wallach, who was 35 years old when he first put on a Dodger uniform, and whose career average with the Dodgers was .251. Finally, in late 1998, the Dodgers came up with Adrian Beltre, who appears to be the genuine article, and you never know; believe it or not, there are two Hall of Famers named "Adrian." If he doesn't work out, maybe they can dig up Junior Gilliam.

The Mets, from their beginnings in 1962 until they came up with Howard Johnson, did the same things, with one difference: the Mets rarely had anybody that they *thought* was going to be good. The Mets mainly were going with desperation options like Roy Staiger, Rod Kanehl, Kevin Collins, and Felix Mantilla, plus help-me-make-it-through-July veterans like Ed Charles, Lenny Randle, Joe Foy, Jim Fregosi, and Joe Torre.

These examples are well known, but there is another case of the same syndrome, which has been even worse: the White Sox. The White Sox traded Willie Kamm in May, 1931. They came up with Robin Ventura in September, 1989. Their third basemen in the period between—58 years—represent a cycle of frustration which even the worst teams in baseball history would be hard pressed to match.

The White Sox, all those 58 years, had exactly two third basemen who were worth a crap: Pete Ward and Bill Melton. Both of them were real good for about two years, and then got hurt. The most amazing sequence is the 1950s. The White Sox in the fifties were a good organization; they had a Hall of Fame double play combination, and they had other good players like Minnie Minoso, Sherm Lollar, Jim Landis, Billy Pierce, and more.

By 1950, however, the White Sox had been struggling for twenty years to replace Willie Kamm. They opened 1950 with a 33-year-old veteran, Hank Majeski, playing third base; as recently as 1948, he had been among the best in baseball, playing for the Athletics. He didn't work out. In 1951, they tried Minnie Minoso at third base. He turned out to be a great player but no third baseman, so they tried Bob Dillinger, a 32-year-old veteran. Dillinger didn't close the hole; in 1952 the regular third baseman was a 32-year-old minor leaguer named Hector Rodriguez.

Hector made the hole, if anything, a little bigger. In 1953 they tried Vern Stephens, a 33-year-old former star who was drinking his way out of the league. He lasted half a season, and was replaced by Bob Elliott, a 36-year-old National League onetime MVP. Elliott gave way to Cass Michaels, yet another player who had been good, and then Grady Hatton, who had been . . . well, not good, but fairly good. Several years ago. Hatton yielded to the 32-year-old George Kell, who lasted one year and was replaced by the 31-year-old Fred Hatfield. Hatfield was replaced by Bubba Phillips, their first third baseman in years who was less than 30. He was 29.

Bubba didn't quite cut it as a third baseman, however, so he became a bench player, and the White Sox traded for 32-year-old Billy Goodman, eight years off his batting crown. He lasted a year, and the White Sox decided maybe they should take a longer look at Bubba Phillips, who by this time was 31, and thus eligible to play third base. Bubba had one more year, and then they traded him to Cleveland, and tried Gene Freese. Freese could hit but not field, so they traded him, and moved an outfielder, Al Smith, into the third base slot.

That's ten years in which the White Sox third baseman was, basically, whoever was available and had once been good. Those ten years are just a slice out of a 58-year period, the other 48 years of which, for the most part, weren't any better. Of those 58 years, there were at least 50 in which the White Sox went into the season hoping that they had finally solved the third base problem. With Robin Ventura, they finally did.

23 ◆ Matt Williams

(1987–2000, 1656 G, 346 1097 .269).
Williams (like Ventura) is in the hunt for a plaque at Cooperstown, but needs to keep hitting. Had the 1994 strike not occurred, there is every likelihood that Williams would have broken Roger Maris' home run record. Had this happened, Williams might have become an idol, as McGwire did, and the public's reaction to the 1998 Sosa/McGwire duel might have been completely different.

Williams had 43 homers in early August, 1994; he was on pace to hit 61, and he was red hot. He did hit 64 home runs in one stretch of 162 games, from early in the 1994 season to early 1995.

24 ◆ Ed Yost

(1944–1962, 2109 G, 139 683 .254)
Yost, who was in the majors when he was 18 years old and never spent a day in the minor leagues, attended NYU in the off season, and earned a master's degree in 1954. In his years in Washington he should have hit 20 homers a year, but lost 90% of his power in his home park, Griffith Stadium. Actually, 90% is conservative . . . through 1953 Yost had 55 career homers: 3 in his home park, 52 on the road. He did hit four at home in 1954, but in 1955 he hit 7 homers on the road, none at home. In a typical year he would hit about 9 homers on the road, but one or none at home. When he finally got to play in a better home run park he was just about finished, but he did hit 20 homers.

Ed Yost in 1952 had only 249 assists in 157 games. In 1954, playing 155 games (he led the league both years in games played) he had 347 assists. Thus, a fielding analysis based on the assumption that Yost's chances in the field fairly reflect his ability will show Yost as a miserable defensive player in 1952, but a brilliant defensive player in 1954. That is in fact what *Total Baseball* shows. The swing in value between those two seasons, based on the assists alone, is about 50 runs—comparable in value to a swing of 40 home runs.

This is incongruous, for a player of Yost's exceptional consistency, to show an immense swing in value like that. What really happened is that the 1952 Senators had almost no left-handed pitching, only 59 innings pitched by left-handers. By 1954 they had added four left-handed starting pitchers, and were one of the most left-handed teams of all time, with 793 innings pitched by left-handed pitchers. The more left-handed pitching you have, the more ground balls will be hit to third base. Yost was the same player in 1954 he was in 1952; he just had a lot more ground balls hit at him.

25 ◆ Ken Caminiti

(1987–2000, 1642 G, 224 942 .275)

Two quick questions:

1. Should Ken Caminiti's MVP year in 1996 be considered a fluke season?

2. If so, is it one of the great fluke seasons of all time?

The answers to those questions appear to be "yes" and "yes"; it was a fluke season, and it was one of the top fluke seasons of all time. I should say . . . Ken Caminiti is a good player. He is not one of the worst players of all time to win an MVP Award (see comment on Zoilo Versalles). He has had many other years when he was among the better players in the National League.

In 1996, however, Caminiti hit .326 with 40 homers, 130 RBI, 109 runs scored. In no other season of his career, which is winding down, has Caminiti hit 30 home runs, driven in 100 runs, or scored 100 runs. He has hit .300 only one other time, that being a .302 average in 1995. His 1996 season was not only better than his other years, but far better, abnormally better.

I set up a simple system to identify fluke seasons by the Win Shares method, by multiplying the player's Win Shares in his best season by the margin between his best season and any other season. In other words, since Caminiti earned 38 Win Shares in 1996 and no more than 26 Win Shares in any other season, his "fluke score" is 456—38 times 12. It's a simple and flawed system, but it generates a list, which gives us a starting point to look at the issue.

Caminiti's 456 Fluke Score in 1996 is among the highest of all time. Among the top 1,000 players in major league history, only about one-third ever had a season which scores at 100 or higher on the fluke scale, and only about one-tenth ever had a season which scores at 200 or higher.

The highest-scoring fluke seasons of all time are all by turn-of-the-last-century pitchers—Amos Rusie in 1894, Jack Chesbro in 1904, Elmer Smith in 1887, Jouett Meekin in 1894, etc. The highest-scoring fluke season by a non-pitcher was by Fred Dunlap in 1884; Dunlap, as I explained in Section I, played the 1884 season in a minor league, which has been included in the encyclopedias as a major league for no good reason. Setting aside pitchers who pitched before 1920 and ignoring a few other seasons for various reasons, this is my list of the top fluke seasons of all time:

1. Kevin Mitchell, 1989. Mitchell won the NL MVP Award, hitting 47 homers and driving in 125 runs. He never drove in 100 runs in any other year, had only one other season when he drove in more than 80. He was a very talented hitter, but most of his career he was more trouble than he was worth.

2. Cy Seymour, 1905. A converted outfielder, Seymour had a Ty Cobb season in 1905, hitting .377 and leading the National League in hits (219), doubles (40), triples (21), and RBI (121). He missed the National League triple crown by one home run. He never led the league in any other hitting category.

3. Norm Cash, 1961. The most famous fluke season in baseball history.

4. Bobby Shantz, 1952. Injuries prevented him from following up on an MVP season.

5. Willie McGee, 1985. Always a good player, but his batting average fell 97 points the next year, and his career average was closer to 1986 than to 1985.

6. Joe Torre, 1971. His average fell 74 points the next year—and just about hit his career mark.

7. Dwight Gooden, 1985.

8. Dolph Luque, 1923.

9. Ken Caminiti, 1996.

10. Steve Carlton, 1972.

Why does Ken Caminiti's season in 1996 rate as a bigger fluke than, let's say, Zoilo Versalles season in 1965? Because it was a better season. Yes, Versalles won the MVP Award, Caminiti won the MVP Award, but Caminiti had a better season. That makes it a bigger fluke, at least in my opinion.

26 ◆ John McGraw
(1891–1906, 1099 G, 13 462 .333)

Do you think it is true that players who walk a lot are more likely to be good managers than free swingers? I think it is probably generally true, but I can't prove it. John McGraw, who had the third-highest on-base percentage of all time, was also one of the greatest managers of all time. Earl Weaver was a minor league player who walked 100 times a year. Miller Huggins walked 100 times a year, even though nobody was counting at the time. Whitey Herzog would have walked 100 times a year (after his rookie year, when he was pressing) if he had played enough.

John McGraw, circa 1898, apparently preparing to take a pot roast out of the oven.

One would assume, intuitively, that (a) anyone who is smart enough to manage should be smart enough not to swing at bad pitches, and (b) any player who doesn't chase bad pitches is going to walk in 12% of his plate appearances or more.

There are some obvious exceptions. Felipe Alou, who I think is a terrific manager, never met a pitch he didn't like.

27 ◆ Tim Wallach
(1980–1996, 2212 G, 260 1125 .257)

A poor man's Brooks Robinson; a rich man's Ken Reitz.

28 ◆ Chipper Jones
(1993–2000, 935 G, 189 635 .303)

Rated here on what he has accomplished through 1999—four straight seasons of 100 runs scored and 100 RBI, capped by an MVP Award. More and better is yet to come, if he can stay away from the Hooter's Girls.

29 ◆ Larry Gardner
(1908–1924, 1922 G, 27 929 .289)

Gardner, like several players of his generation, came to the major leagues as a second baseman, but switched to third because he had the athletic ability to play third, and third base at that time was more of a key defensive position than second.

> Many looked askance when Larry Gardner, supposedly a second baseman, was assigned to third, but the results more than justified the move, and it made room at second for Yerkes, a player who had proved only mediocre on the other side of the diamond.—1913 *Spalding Guide*, reviewing the 1912 season, when the Red Sox won the World Series with Gardner at third base, Yerkes at second

> Larry Gardner, third baseman of the Boston American League club, is a collegian, like Ray Collins, coming from Vermont University. Gardner is of

English parentage, and was born at Enosburg, Vt., on May 13, 1886. From 1905 to 1907 he was a star of the University of Vermont team, and during the vacation played independent ball. A number of clubs were after Gardner, but Boston succeeded in landing him. He was too green and was sent to Lynn, of the New England League, for seasoning in 1908, returning to the Red Sox the following season. At first Gardner was used in utility roles, but the following season he went in at second base when McConnell was taken ill and made good to such an extent that he has since been a regular. In 1912 he was moved over to third base and has filled that position even better than second. He is a splendid fielder and excellent batsman, besides being fast on the bases.—1917 *Reach Guide*

30 ◆ George Kell
(1943–1957, 1795 G, 78 870 .306)

A fine fielder and a fine player, but not an impact hitter. Among the 100 third basemen listed here Kell ranks 10th in batting average (.306) but 84th in secondary average (.208), the combination making him 55th in runs scored per season (80 per 162 games) and 55th in RBI per season (79 per 162 games). Deserved the Gold Glove at third base in 1945, 1946, and 1947.

> "When I got to the majors, I felt like I was in over my head," [Kell] says. "The A's had Al Simmons as a coach, and some of the other greats like Bing Miller and Jimmy Dykes were around. They all tried to change my stance at the plate." [Connie] Mack said, "Leave him alone. He's hit everywhere he's played. He'll hit up here, too."
> —*Diamond Greats* (Rich Westcott)

31 ◆ Edgar Martinez
(1987–2000, 1540 G, 235 925 .320)

Not really a third baseman, but a great hitter, and I have to list him somewhere. There are people who will argue that Martinez is the best hitter of the 1990s . . . I suppose I would go with Frank Thomas, but certainly Martinez is a hitter. His career should have been several years longer, but the Mariners kept sending him to the minors. In 1987 he played 13 games at the end of the year, hitting .372 (16 for 43). Unimpressed, the Mariners returned him to Calgary the next year.

Has there ever been a team which accomplished as little with as much talent as the Mariners of the 1990s? I think not. The standard in this category has long been the Milwaukee Braves of the 1950s, who parlayed the best seasons of Henry Aaron, Eddie Mathews, and Warren Spahn into one World Championship and a long series of excuses. The Mariners appear to have out-done them.

The top ten players of all time in doubles per 162 games:

1.	Ed Delahanty	46.1
2.	Tris Speaker	46
3.	Dan Brouthers	45
4.	Joe Medwick	44
5.	Hank Greenberg	44
6.	Edgar Martinez	44
7.	Chick Hafey	43
8.	Nap Lajoie	43
9.	Bob Meusel	42
10.	Babe Herman	42

32 ◆ Toby Harrah
(1969–1986, 2155 G, 195 918 .264)

Some members of the Washington Senators in 1972 had a club, called the Underminers Club, dedicated to bringing about an end to Ted Williams' career as a manager. According to Shelby Whitfield in *Kiss It Goodbye,* one member of the club was "Toby Harrah, the rookie and baby-faced cynic," who joined the club because "he was the youngest utility player in the major leagues who went away to military summer camp hitting .262 and then couldn't get back in the lineup."

33 ◆ Lave Cross
(1887–1907, 2275 G, 47 1371 .292)

> Lave Cross was captain in more ways than on the ball field. He was always the first one in the old horse-drawn bus, which used to haul the Athletics from their third-rate hotels to the ball parks. The ritual went both for leaving the hotel and after the ball game, and anyone trying to scramble in ahead of Lave had a fight on his hands. Lave was so bowlegged it was a wonder those hot ones down the third-base line didn't roll right through the loop.—Fred Lieb in *Connie Mack* (G.P. Putnam's, 1945)

In baseball history, the era before the Knickerbocker club can be compared to the pre-Assyrian era, about which no specific records remain, and little is actually known. The baseball years between 1858 and 1875 can be likened roughly to the early years of the Old Testament, the era of the Pharaohs and the Trojan Wars, about which there are sketchy records, but debates about which century something occurred in, and disputes among scholars about whether major figures are real or mythical.

The baseball of the 19th century, continuing along this line, can be likened to the classical era, the era of the Greeks and Romans, the time of Christ. Much more is known about this era; there are specific, written records in some detail, but the bones of history have been washed bare by the passage of time, making it impossible to reconstruct certain things. Moving ahead . . . .

Pre-Knickerbocker	Pre-Assyrian
Quasi-Amateur Era	Old Testament Era
19th Century Baseball	Greek and Roman Eras
Dead Ball Era	Dark Ages
Arrival of Babe Ruth	Invention of the Printing Press
Lively Ball Era	1492–1776
Expansion	American Revolution
1981 Strike	Civil War
1994–1995 Strike	World Wars I and II
Bud Selig Era	Television Era

Lave Cross is, I suppose, the Emperor Constantine, a historical figure about whom a great many facts are known, but a man about whom it is difficult to evoke a rich and human image.

34 ◆ Gary Gaetti
(1981–2000, 2507 G, 360 1341 .255)

You know what was odd about Gaetti? His aging pattern. As a player ages there are a few predictable changes that take place in his abilities. His speed declines—I would suppose that 99% of players run better at age 25 than at 35—his defensive range decreases, his batting average normally slips a little, but his fielding percentage should improve some, and his walk rate should improve.

Gaetti is odd in two respects:

1. That his walk rate never improved at all, even an inch.

2. That despite that, he aged at an exceptionally slow rate of speed.

Neither Gaetti's strikeout/walk ratio nor his walk frequency improved at all over the years—in fact, they declined a little. In the 1980s (1981–1989) Gaetti batted 4,412 times, with 322 walks and a 2.41-1 strikeout/walk ratio. In the 1990s he batted 4,529 times with only 312 walks and a 2.64-1 ratio.

His other changes were normal, but exceptionally slow. There is no reason for a player like Gaetti to *last* until he is 40 years old, and not much precedent for it. Gaetti is the same *type* of player as Ken Boyer, Ron Santo, Tim Wallach, Sal Bando, Al Rosen, or Ron Cey, but whereas all of those men were better players than Gaetti at his best, they all aged at a normal rate of speed, losing value at a rate of about 12% per season after age 30, and thus were finished by their mid-thirties.

35 ◆ Ken Keltner
(1937–1950, 1526 G, 163 852 .276)

> Those aren't just ordinary base hits Ken cuts off with those backhand stops, they're sizzlers down

the foul line which would be good for certainly two and maybe three bases if they got by. He had no superior at protecting the foul line.–Joe DiMaggio in *Lucky to Be a Yankee,* explaining why Keltner was the best third baseman he ever saw.

Keltner, a brilliant defensive third baseman with a tremendous arm, was famous for an odd habit of looking carefully at the baseball in his hand before he threw to first. They used to say he counted the stitches before he threw to first. He drove two Hall of Famers off the Indians' third base job–Lou Boudreau and Bob Lemon. Both came to the Indians as third basemen, but switched to shortstop and the mound when they were unable to dislodge Keltner from his job.

There's another thing I'd like to compile, if I had enough lives–a directory of player's mannerisms. They're a large part of the image of a player, but nobody writes them down, so they just get lost when the player retires.

36 ◆ Terry Pendleton
(1984–1998, 1893 G, 140 945 .270)
A line-drive hitter and an excellent defensive third baseman who was a part of championship teams in St. Louis, Atlanta and Florida. In the twelve years of his career for which STATS has records, Pendleton hit .296 with men in scoring position.

37 ◆ Harlond Clift
(1934–1945, 1582 G, 178 829 .272)
Clift has a nickname "Darkie," listed in the encyclopedias. This nickname has a rather unpleasant derivation. His teammate Alan Strange, who broke in with the Browns at the same time as Clift, thought that his first name was "Harlem," and called him "Darkie" because . . .

Clift was a transitional player, really the first modern third baseman. When he hit 29 home runs in 1937 that was a record for a third baseman. He followed that up with 34 the next year, which was the record until Al Rosen hit

37 in 1950. He also walked 110 times every year, and he was a decent defensive third baseman. More clearly than any other player, Clift marks the transition from 1900–1930 style third basemen, who were glove men first and usually singles hitters, to modern third basemen, who are expected to play defense and drive in runs.

At a tryout with the Browns in 1931, Clift reached for a ball, stepped on his glove, did an involuntary somersault, and broke his collarbone. The Browns signed him despite this.

Unfortunately he played for awful teams. The Browns in the early 1930s made two separate efforts to bolster their team, the first under Phil Ball, who died in late 1933, and the second under Bill DeWitt, who put together a coalition of St. Louis businessmen with visions of challenging the Cardinals. After they bought a couple of good young players and didn't improve immediately, however, DeWitt's owners started backing out on him, leaving him to run the operation on a shoestring. Clift was the best of the young players brought in in this era, but within a few years he was playing baseball on an island of despair. This caused sportswriters, as it always does, to blame him for the lack of talent surrounding him.

He avoided getting drafted in World War II, somehow, but his power waned with the balata ball, and he was traded away before the Browns won their only pennant in 1944. He was traded/sold to Washington, but developed testicular mumps, and went home to his farm in the other Washington, Washington state, to recuperate. While he was there he was thrown from a horse, and missed the rest of the year. His career didn't survive the war.

Of the top 100 third baseman, between 35 and 40 are in the same general mold: right-handed power hitters, not fast, hit around .270, good arm and quick enough feet to cope at the position. Harlond Clift was the first player of that type.

38 ◆ Doug DeCinces
(1973–1987, 1649 G, 237 879 .259)

DeCinces is the guy who got to replace Brooks Robinson at third base for the Orioles. That was tough, and after a few years of not being Brooks Robinson, he was happy enough to be traded to California. Gene Mauch said in 1982 that he'd never seen a player have as good a year as DeCinces did that year. DeCinces hit .301 with 42 doubles, 30 homers—numbers that were bigger then than they are now—but also, his defense was good, and he delivered what seemed like a lot of monster, game-breaking hits. DeCinces was a real competitor, but he had broad shoulders and a stiff back, like Al Rosen, Bill Melton, and Jose Canseco, and that always causes back troubles, so he wasn't always able to stay at the top of his game.

39 ◆ Carney Lansford
(1978–1992, 1862 G, 151 874 .290)

I don't think I ever saw a regular third baseman who had less range than Carney Lansford. The reason is, he dived for everything, and I mean *everything*. You could not hit a ball so close to Carney Lansford's left or right that he wouldn't dive for it. You could hit the ball three feet from Lansford on his glove side, and he'd dive for it and come up short half the time. And the cheerleaders in the press box used to rave about his defense because he made all those diving stops. His range was however far he could dive; not a step and a dive, just a dive. He was a good hitter, but he was an awful third baseman.

40 ◆ Buddy Lewis
(1935–1948, 1349 G, 71 607 .297)

The best third basemen in baseball history at age 19: 1. Buddy Lewis, 2. Freddy Lindstrom, 3. John McGraw. The best at age 20: 1. Buddy Lewis, 2. John McGraw, 3. Freddy Lindstrom.

This story probably explains a lot about the collapse of the New York Giants in the 1940s.

The American Legion used to organize Junior Legion ball, including a national championship, the Junior Legion series. Lewis was a sensation in Legion ball, and, for being named the outstanding player in the Legion series, he won a prize, which was a trip to New York City for a three-week stay with the New York Giants, during which he was to wear the uniform of the Giants and work out with the team.

Lewis went to New York dreaming of playing with the Giants, planning to sign with the team if asked. Instead, Bill Terry was rude to him, ignored him, and ordered him off the field every time he went out to take a little infield. Lewis walked off the team, and spent most of his stay in New York hanging out in Central Park. An irony is that Terry and Lewis, both Southerners, both later retired from baseball to return to the South and run auto dealerships.

The Senators signed him a year later for peanuts. For six years, 1936–1941, Lewis created about 100 runs a year, a left-handed line drive hitter who could run and who developed excellent command of the strike zone. He was just reaching maturity when World War II came. He became a pilot, flying a C-47 (which he had named "The Old Fox" after Clark Griffith) on 352 missions over the Himalayas in the China-Burma-India theater. During training in 1943 Lewis buzzed Griffith Stadium during a game, flying the C-47 over the park so low that he almost clipped the flag pole in center field, then wiggling the plane's wings to say hello to his teammates. He was reprimanded by the brass for that stunt, but George Case, who responded to the wiggled wings by throwing his bat in the air, was later to say it was his biggest thrill in baseball, the day Lewis buzzed the stadium. By the war's end he had received the Distinguished Flying Cross and Air Medal.

When the war was over he had trouble getting his heart back into baseball, and left the game in his early thirties... See also Tony Conigliaro (RF, #95).

41 ◆ Bobby Bonilla

(1986–2000, 2020 G, 282 1152 .280)

When I said that Carney Lansford was an awful third baseman, I didn't mean, of course, that he was as bad as Bobby Bonilla. Bonilla, listed at 240 pounds, has played about 8,000 career innings at third base, so I suppose that makes him a third baseman, and if you sent him into space a few times I suppose that would make him an astronaut, but apart from that, he was no more a third baseman than he was an astronaut. But he never gave up; he never let the position beat him, like a lot of people do. He had a good arm and surprisingly quick feet for a big guy, and if you put him at third base he would battle it as hard as he could battle it for nine innings, so managers always felt that they could put him at third base if they needed to, to get his bat in the lineup. He was a terrific hitter, and he helped a lot of teams, at third base and in the outfield.

42 ◆ Denny Lyons

(1885–1897, 1121 G, 62 569 .310)

Five third basemen have career on-base percentages of .400 or better: McGraw (.465), Bill Joyce (.435), Edgar Martinez (.426), Wade Boggs (.415), and Denny Lyons (.407) . . .

43 ◆ Freddie Lindstrom

(1924–1936, 1438 G, 103 779 .311)

Compare Freddy Lindstrom's season in 1928 to Heinie Groh's season eleven years earlier, 1917. Groh hit .304 with 1 home run, 53 RBI, although he did have 39 doubles and 71 walks. Lindstrom has vastly better numbers on a superficial level—.358 with 14 homers, 107 RBI, also 39 doubles although he drew only 25 walks. Both players led the league in hits, but Groh led with 182, whereas Lindstrom had 231.

Obviously, Lindstrom created more runs. Heinie's walks cut into the difference, but we have Groh with 100 runs created, Lindstrom with 116.

But put the runs in a game context. The National League in 1917 averaged 3.53 runs per game. Groh, then, created all the runs a team would normally score in 28 games, plus some. He did this despite playing in a pitcher's park (park factor of .90, based on the 1917 season alone); adjust for that, and Groh moves up to just short of 30 ballgames.

The National League in 1928 averaged 4.70 runs per game. Lindstrom's 116 runs created represent the runs an average team would score in a little less than 25 games. He did that playing in what is essentially a neutral park, favoring neither hitters nor pitchers.

It's not even close. In context, Groh's season is more than 20% better than Lindstrom's.

44 ◆ Red Rolfe

(1931–1942, 1175 G, 69 497 .289)

Same type of player as Pie Traynor, George Kell, Larry Gardner, Stan Hack, John McGraw—that is, a singles hitter, a guy who could get on base, and defensively more or less a second shortstop. Rolfe was, in fact, a minor league shortstop and a good one, could perfectly well have been a major league shortstop had the Yankees not already had Crosetti.

A Dartmouth graduate who played bridge for relaxation, Rolfe was Joe McCarthy's favorite player in the late thirties, and McCarthy apparently intended for Rolfe to succeed him as Yankee manager. He got into a nasty salary dispute in 1941, however, and the front office soured on him. After a poor year in 1942 he took a job as the baseball coach at Yale, coached there a few years between Joe Wood and Ethan Allen. In 1946, his last year at Yale, he had George Bush Sr. on his team, although I don't think Bush played any that year.

He left that for a front office job with the Tigers, and, when the Tigers were looking for a manager, stepped forward to take the job. He was a very peculiar manager; he struck everyone—players, press, and other managers—as having a very strange approach to the job. During the game he carried a little notebook, and after each game he would rush to a typewriter and type out pages and pages of notes about the game. He always said that he did it because he didn't have a good memory; if he didn't get things down quickly he'd lose them. Somewhere, if they haven't been destroyed, there are hundreds of pages of typewritten notes about American League players of that era, notes which I would love to get my hands on.

Anyway, Rolfe was tremendously successful for two years, driving a Detroit team which had guys like Don Kolloway, Aaron Robinson, and Johnny Lipon in the lineup to within three games of the American League pennant—really an astonishing performance. The 1950 Tigers were in first place for four months and played well down the stretch, but the Yankees raced past them in the closing weeks, and after that his team turned on him. He was sort of the opposite of Chuck Tanner; he didn't encourage or support his players very much, offered criticism freely and in the heat of the battle, and he came to be regarded as cold and distant. Hoot Evers, one of his star outfielders, openly hated him, and he began platooning Vic Wertz, his other star outfielder, which Wertz found puzzling, since he had driven in 256 runs over the previous two seasons. Rolfe's managerial career ended quickly after that, and he died young.

45 ◆ Ed Williamson

(1878–1890, 1201 G, 64 667 .255)

> He had lacquered hair, a pug nose, and bright, puckish eyes . . . He had met his wife, Nettie, in New Orleans, where the White Stockings were playing [exhibition] games in the early 1880s . . . She vowed to throw flowers to him if he got a hit and won the game. He did and she did.—*A Clever Base-Ballist,* Bryan Di Salvatore.

> The most remarkable play I ever witnessed on the ball field was made by Ed Williamson, when

he was playing third for Chicago. In an exciting game, when the scoring of a single run meant victory for either side, there was a man on third when a hot one was knocked in Williamson's direction. It struck the ground about midway between home plate and third base, and then bounded high over Williamson's head. Heavy as he was, Ed leaped into the air what seemed to be about four feet, grasped the ball with his right hand, and before again touching the ground snapped the sphere to the catcher, nailing the runner from third several feet from the home plate. How he got the force to make the throw puzzles me to this day.—Fred Pfeffer, quoted in the 1894 *Reach Guide*

The encyclopedias now list Williamson as "Ned"; I don't know why. It's not right, but it's hard to get those things fixed. The same book, the 1894 *Reach Guide,* also had a symposium entitled "Who is the King Player?," seeking to identify the greatest player in professional history up to that point. Eleven old-timers contributed their opinions, three of which I will quote here, followed by a quote from Billy Sunday:

> The ideal player of pre-eminence was Ed Williamson.—Jas. H. O'Rourke

> I consider Ed Williamson the greatest player the National game ever had.—Arthur A. Irwin

> I think Ed Williamson and Hardy Richardson would pretty nearly make a tie as to being the best ball player since professional base ball has existed.—James A. Hart

Ed Williamson, a fellow weighing 225 pounds, was the most active big man you ever saw. He went with them, and while they were on the ship crossing the English channel a storm arose and the captain thought the ship would go down. Williamson tied two life-preservers on himself and one on his wife and dropped on his knees and prayed and promised God to be true. God spoke and the waves were stilled. They came back to the United States and Ed came back to

Chicago and started a saloon on Dearborn Street. I would go through there giving tickets for the YMCA meetings and would talk with them and he would cry like a baby.

I would get down and pray for him, and would talk with him. When he died they put him on the table and cut him open and took out his liver and it was so big it would not go in a candy bucket. Kidneys had shriveled until they were like two stones.

Ed Williamson sat there on the street corner with me, drunk, twenty-seven years ago when I said, "Good-bye, I'm going to Jesus Christ."– Billy Sunday, *The Man and His Message*, L.T. Myers, 1914

46 ◆ Bill Bradley
(1899–1915, 1461 G, 34 552 .271)
One of the best players in the American League from 1903 to 1905 . . . a quiet, well-mannered and popular player who ran a bar near League Park for several years. He was a large, graceful man, the American League's Gold Glove third baseman in 1907 (half a century before the Award was first given), runner-up in other seasons to Jimmy Collins, Lave Cross, and Lee Tannehill. In 1904 a fan asked Jimmy Collins who was the best third baseman in baseball. "If I could field and bat like Bradley," replied Collins, "I should lay claim to that title myself." The next spring a fan shouted at Bradley, between innings, "Who's the greatest third baseman in the country?" Bradley replied quickly that it was Jimmy Collins.

47 ◆ Howard Johnson
(1982–1995, 1531 G, 228 760 .249).
Goes on an All-Star team with Milton Bradley, R.J. Reynolds, Jack Daniels, and John Montgomery Ward. The Phillies in the teens had an outfielder named Bud Weiser; three years later, to get even, the Athletics came up with one named Johnny Walker. Other suggestions from friends: Soup Campbell, Bull Durham, Doc Kerr,

Babe(y) Ruth . . . the top power/speed combinations among third basemen:

	Home Runs	Stolen Bases	Combo
1. Paul Molitor	234	504	319.6
2. Mike Schmidt	548	174	264.1
3. George Brett	317	201	246.0
4. Howard Johnson	228	231	229.5
5. Toby Harrah	195	238	214.4

48 ◆ Bill Madlock
(1973–1987, 1806 G, 163 860 .305)
One thing I was surprised by in researching this book is how many controversies there have been about batting championships . . . somebody does something not entirely fair to help somebody they like win a batting championship. A few of these are famous, of course, like the 1910 American League race (Lajoie and Cobb) and the 1976 race (Brett, McRae, Bostock, and Carew, all playing in the same game). I knew about those and a few others, but there must be 30 batting championships in baseball history about which there have been allegations that an opposing team did somebody a favor to help somebody else win a title.

I never saw any other player who was as focused on batting championships as Bill Madlock. He wasn't a bad third baseman, he was a good baserunner, and obviously he could hit, but sometimes it seemed like all he cared about was winning the batting title. The last month of the season, if he was in the hunt for a title, the guys in the press box used to run a poll to see who could pick the days that Madlock's hamstring would keep him out of the lineup.

49 ◆ Billy Nash
(1884–1898, 1549 G, 60 977 .275)
Nash has the second-highest ratio of RBI to total bases of any player in history, behind Cap Anson . . . One of the few Jewish players of the

19th century, Nash was the captain of the Boston Beaneaters team which won the National League in 1891, 1892, and 1893. Nash was popular with the fans and a fine defensive third baseman, but when Jimmy Collins came along, he was traded to the Phillies for Sliding Billy Hamilton . . . I have him as deserving of the Gold Glove at third base in 1888, 1889, 1890, 1892, 1893, and 1894.

50 ◆ Whitey Kurowski
(1941–1949, 916 G, 106 529 .286)

Kurowski was a tough kid. As a young man he suffered from osteomyelitis, the same condition which destroyed Mickey Mantle's knees, and was missing part of a bone in his right forearm. His right arm was shorter than his left arm, which left him, for reasons that I frankly don't understand, unable to reach out and drive an outside pitch. He compensated by standing right on top of home plate, which supposedly made him vulnerable to pitches high and inside.

In 1937, just before Kurowski left home to begin his baseball career, his brother was killed when a mine caved in on him. In spring training, 1942, when Kurowski was trying to make the Cardinals, his father died of a heart attack. He went home for the funeral, came back, and made the team.

51 ◆ Heinie Zimmerman
(1907–1919, 1456 G, 58 796 .295)

A player about whom one could easily write volumes. In 1912, his second season as a regular, Zimmerman led the National League in batting (.372), and also in hits (207), doubles (41), home runs (14), and total bases (318). He is one of few players to lead the league in home runs and batting average, but *not* win the triple crown.

This was the zenith of the Great Houdini's popularity, and so a Chicago sportswriter began calling Zimmerman "The Great Zim." Zimmerman liked the nickname and, apparently failing to pick up the irony, or perhaps failing to understand the concept of irony, began referring to himself as the Great Zim, even having some of his mail delivered under that name.

The Player's Fraternity, an early union, started that year, and, as Zimmerman was one of the biggest stars of the moment, it was perhaps inevitable that he would become an officer in the Fraternity. Zimmerman, as Warren Brown observed in *The Chicago Cubs* was "no mental giant" and "a man who played baseball by ear mostly," adding that even Franklin P. Adams "would have had trouble reducing him to poetry in motion." As Jim Bouton pointed out, when baseball players are looking for leaders, a player's batting average counts more than his IQ. In the next few years, as the Federal League challenged for status as a third major league, salaries exploded, and the Fraternity thought they were doing great. When the Federal League folded salaries crashed, and the owners told the Fraternity to go to hell, perhaps not quite that politely.

The players, feeling used and betrayed, started selling ballgames. Zimmerman, who had been a solid player although he had never quite matched the standards of his 1912 season, became one of the most prominent crooks. There is an interloping event here: the 1917 World Series. Zimmerman, playing for the New York Giants, had hit .297 that season, his best season in years, leading the National League in RBI with 102. In the World Series he hit .120, with no RBI. In the final game of the series, Zimmerman opened the fourth inning with a wild throw, putting Eddie Collins at second base. Another error, by the right fielder, put runners at second and third.

At this moment, the batter hit a one-hopper back to the mound, fielded by the pitcher, who threw to Zimmerman, trapping Eddie Collins off third base. Zimmerman threw to the catcher, who threw back to Zimmerman. Zimmerman tried to apply the tag, but Collins leaned away from him. Zimmerman chased him. He chased him all the way across the plate, allowing Collins to score and the other runners to reach second and third. They soon scored, putting the Giants in a 3-0 hole, from which they were unable to recover.

Zimmerman blamed his teammates for the blunder, claiming that no one was covering home plate, leaving him with no one to throw to. The public didn't buy that explanation, although it may have been true, and Zimmerman became one of the most famous goats in the history of the World Series. Abused and humiliated, he turned bitter.

In 1919 the Giants acquired Hal Chase. Zimmerman was a moth to the flame. Chase and Zimmerman hung out together constantly, met with gamblers almost every night, and hustled teammates and opponents brazenly to find people who would help them fix games.

The Giants were playing in Chicago on September 11, 1919, Fred Toney on the mound. At the end of the first inning, Zimmerman told Toney that it would be worth his while not to bear down against the Cubs. Toney stewed on that an inning, then reported it to John McGraw, and asked McGraw to remove him from the game so that he could not be suspected of giving less than his best effort. McGraw removed Toney from the game, and immediately, after the game, kicked Zimmerman off the team.

His major league career over, Zimmerman became one the cast of shadowy characters who helped arrange the fix of the World Series. It is not possible to know exactly when Zimmerman began throwing games, and thus we can never be certain that, when he lost the 1917 World Series almost single-handedly, he wasn't doing it on purpose. Reading accounts of the series, Zimmerman must have played as badly in that series as anyone ever.

Zimmerman was not Hal Chase. He was not a heavy drinker, as Chase was, not a charmer, and he had not been throwing games for ten years. He had been, and he should have remained, a lovable eccentric. He wanted more. He got less. His dishonesty and his World Series blunder have long since supplanted any other memory of him.

52 ◆ Jimmy Dykes
(1918–1939, 2282 G, 109 1071 .280)
Frankie-Frisch type player, a sparkplug who played all over the infield, wherever they needed him. Not as fast as Frisch, in part because he was usually a little overweight. Dykes is to Connie Mack as Frisch is to John McGraw—a protégé who was intended to take over the team in time, but then couldn't for some reason.

> Dad had never played baseball . . . but he was nuts about the game. He'd hide quarters under the carpet on the stairs so he could sneak out without my mother knowing he was squandering the family fortune on bleacher tickets.—Jimmie Dykes, *You Can't Steal First Base*

> Dykes was never quite comfortable with black players. . . . He couldn't keep the talented Pinson off the team but he did little to encourage him. —Maury Allen, *Baseball: The Lives Behind the Seams*

53 ◆ Larry Parrish
(1974–1988, 1891 G, 256 992 .263)
Right-handed power hitter with a howitzer for an arm, didn't have quick enough feet or hands to be a good third baseman. Brooks Robinson, Frank Malzone, Clete Boyer, and Tim Wallach establish that players can be slow going to first

base, but have a quick first step going after a line drive. Parrish was like those guys, except he had feet like cement blocks. He played third base because he was too slow to play the outfield, and his arm was so good it seemed like a waste to put him at first base.

54 ◆ Arlie Latham
(1880–1909, 1627 G, 27 562 .269)

Arlie Latham owns as many footnotes in the history of baseball as anyone who has ever played. For starters, he was the first full-time coach, he was the man who brought into existence the third-base coach's box, he was the oldest man ever to steal a base (aged 49), he was a participant in the first sort-of World Series (1885), and he holds the record for errors at third base, 822—more than 200 more than any other player.

A cocky little leadoff man, Latham was one of the biggest stars of Charles Comiskey's St. Louis Browns in the 1880s. In those days teams didn't carry coaches, so players would stand on the sidelines doing coaching duty. Latham, from outside third base, would yell insults at the pitcher, trying to distract him from his pitching. As a bench jockey, actually a sideline jockey, he was clever, funny, rude, and extremely loud. He was a clown, a mimic, and a natural antagonist. One of his techniques was to run up and down the third base line while the pitcher was in mid-delivery, screaming at him all the way. The third base coach's box was created to prevent him from doing this.

While Latham was personally likeable and immensely popular with the St. Louis fans, who considered him a sort of surrogate fan, his private life was a series of disasters. According to Jerry Lansche in *Glory Fades Away* "his first wife attempted suicide and his second wife sued him for divorce on grounds of perversion, desertion, and infidelity." He apparently had

several marriages after this, although no one seems to know the exact number. He drank. In Chicago in May, 1890, he was arrested for beating a small boy. He began to bounce from team to team, somewhere between a journeyman and a pariah.

He stopped drinking. In 1907 Latham was hired by John McGraw as a coach for the Giants, the first full-time official coach. He tried to do the same things in New York that he had done in St. Louis (and later with other teams), but its time had passed. Fred Snodgrass remembered Arlie, in *The Glory of Their Times,* as "probably the worst third-base coach who ever lived." The leagues were trying to make baseball into a family entertainment; they didn't have any place for somebody who was screaming vulgarities and intentionally provoking fights. But Latham, who as a player had stolen over 300 bases in a three-year stretch, worked with the Giant baserunners, and claimed some credit for developing the skills which helped the Giants to steal 347 bases in 1911, a major league record which still stands.

Arlie coached for McGraw for a year or two, then was hired by the league to be an umpire. He didn't like umpiring. It was a lonely profession, and you got booed a lot.

In 1915 he was reported to be working for King George V of England, teaching him about American baseball. According to Lansche, again, he lived in England for seventeen years, and "form[ed] a close friendship with the Prince of Wales." Eventually he returned to the States, and, in his mid-seventies, was hired by the New York Yankees as the press box attendant. He did this job for 17 years, until death took him at the age of 92.

Other notes about Latham:

- In 1885 he had a famous foot race with Billy Sunday, the fastest man on the

Chicago White Stockings. The Browns players bet on Latham; the White Stockings, on Billy Sunday. Sunday beat him easily, ran away from him. Latham was maybe the fastest man in the American Association, but Sunday, as it turned out, was way faster.

- In 1887 a similar stunt backfired on him even worse. Charlie Comiskey put up a $100 prize to see who had the best throwing arm on his team, the top contenders being Latham and Doc Bushong. Latham not only lost the contest but hurt his arm, which was one of his prime assets as a player. His arm never recovered; in fact, he was never able to fully straighten it out again.

- In the 1885 exhibition series which is now somewhat optimistically represented as the first World Series, Latham evaded a tag by Cap Anson by doing a mid-air somersault over Anson's outstretched glove.

- In 1887 Latham set off a firecracker under third base during a game. He had been accused twice by Comiskey of falling asleep at third base. He set off the firecracker, he said, to keep himself awake.

- In 1899 the Philadelphia Phillies had set up an underground wire system to steal the catcher's signs from center field, relaying them to the third base coach by way of a buzzer buried near third base . . . I'm sure most of you know this story. Arlie Latham and Tommy Corcoran are the men who uncovered the ruse. Latham noticed that Cupid Childs, coaching at third, was standing with his foot in a puddle of water. He got curious about why, talked about it with Corcoran, and Corcoran dug up the buzzer.

- When a third baseman stood and watched a hot shot buzz by him without making any effort to stop it, old timers used to say "he Arlie Lathamed it." This expression was used at least into the 1940s, and may have lasted longer.

- Latham once organized a troupe of players who traveled New England in the winter playing a game they called "ice polo."

- Latham was the first man invited by Albert Spalding to go on the famous round-the-world trip in 1889. He had to decline, as he had committed himself to doing a stage show called *Fashions.* According to Robert Smith in *Baseball,* Latham sang a song in the show which went "I'm a daisy on the diamond/I'm a dandy on the stage./I'd ornament a horsecar,/or look pretty in a cage."

- Also according to Smith, Latham "practically invented the characteristic chatter of the ball diamond, the endless lilting encouragement which an infield gives to the pitcher."

- According to Lee Allen in *The Cincinnati Reds,* Latham was also the first player to go on stage.

- Undated anecdote . . . one time Latham, at third base, called time out and began kicking his heels and bouncing on one foot in a bizarre dance, causing spectators to wonder whether Latham had a bumblebee in his pants or had finally lost his marbles. "Sorry," said Latham at length. "My foot was asleep . . ."

- One time late in his career, when he was with Cincinnati, Umpire Tim Hurst made a call against Latham at third base. Latham took off his glove and drop-kicked it. It landed at Hurst' feet, so Hurst kicked the glove back to Latham. Latham kicked it back to Hurst, Hurst to Latham, Latham to Hurst. According to Fred Lieb in *Comedians of Baseball Down the Years,* "taking turns, Arlie and Tim booted the glove all the way to the outfield fence."

55 ◆ Don Money
(1968–1983, 1720 G, 176 729 .261)

Trivia question: What do Don Money, Bill Buckner, Mike Marshall, and Nolan Ryan have in common?

Those are the only men I know of who have held the same record in both leagues, at least post-1970. Money holds the major league record for fewest errors in a season at third base, 150 or more games (5), setting that record in the American League in 1974, and at one time also held the same record in the National League. Bill Buckner holds the major league record for assists by a first baseman (184), and at one time held the same record in the National league. Mike Marshall holds the record for game appearances by a pitcher (106 with the Dodgers in 1974), and also holds the same record in the American League (90, with Minnesota in 1979). Ryan holds or has held several records in both leagues.

56 ◆ Richie Hebner
(1968–1985 1908 G, 203 890 .276)

One of the best platoon players in baseball history, and one of the best grave diggers. For a hundred years baseball players held off-season jobs as truck drivers, school teachers, bartenders, and garbage collectors, and many times a fanatic baseball fan could tell you what any player did for his off-season job. Hebner was one of the last players to be prominently associated with an off-season job, in part because the job (digging graves) was an odd one, and in part because he was in mid-career when the big money rolled into baseball, and he kept doing that job after most of his contemporaries had begun devoting the off-season to staying in shape or getting out of it.

57 ◆ Harry Steinfeldt
(1898–1911, 1648 G, 27 762 .267)

As most of you know, Steinfeldt was the odd man out in the famous infield of Tinker, Evers, and Chance, all of whom got into the Hall of Fame except Harry. In 1906, when the Cubs won an all-time record 116 games, Steinfeldt played as well as anyone on the team, leading the league in hits, tying for the league lead in RBI, and finishing second in total bases. In the rest of his career he was a decent player, but really not the player that the other three guys were. "He was slow," wrote Johnny Evers in *Baseball in the Big Leagues,* "a heavy hitter, a good fielder and a wonderful thrower."

Steinfeldt was an odd and interesting man. In the early 1890s, when he was barely into his early teens, Steinfeldt traveled with a minstrel show, Al Field's minstrels, which toured the nation. I suspect, although I'm not sure, that he had run away from home to join the minstrel show. The minstrels would play baseball against local teams, among other entertainments, and Steinfeldt turned out to be a better baseball player than a minstrel. He entered pro ball, was sold a couple of times, and wound up the property of the Cincinnati Reds, who were owned by Garry Herrmann.

Steinfeldt and Herrmann didn't get along. After Steinfeldt had a good rookie season in 1896 he got into a protracted dispute about his salary, as a result of which he held out for two solid years. He eventually rejoined the Reds, and played for them for seven more years, although he never seemed to be playing up to his ability, and he acquired an awful reputation throughout baseball, so bad that the Cincinnati team couldn't trade him.

Frank Chance, however, had played winter ball with Steinfeldt in California, and thought that most of the stories about him were exaggerated or untrue. The Cubs, close to winning the pennant, needed a third baseman. Chance asked Charles Murphy, owner of the Cubs, to trade for Steinfeldt. Murphy said he would check into it, but when he checked into it he heard so much gossip about Steinfeldt that he didn't want to have anything to do with him, and asked Chance to target somebody else. Chance refused, and insisted that Steinfeldt wasn't the bad actor that a lot of people said he was. The Cubs eventually traded two young players (one of whom was Hans Lobert) to acquire Steinfeldt, and, although no longer young, he had his best years with the Cubs.

Steinfeldt also was involved in a famous freak play in the opening game of the 1907 World Series, a game which ended in a 12-inning tie, and was often described in that era as the greatest game of baseball ever played. With two on and two out in the bottom of the tenth inning, Steinfeldt at bat, a pitch got by the catcher, and the runner from third raced for home. The catcher's throw to the pitcher, covering home, was wide of the plate, apparently allowing the winning run to score. Steinfeldt, however, didn't get out of the way; he leaned into the throw from the catcher, causing the runner to be declared out on interference. This play could easily have cost the Cubs the World Series, although as it turned out it did not.

58 ◆ Art Devlin
(1904–1913, 1313 G, 10 505 .269)
Devlin was a star on the first Giant team to win the World Series, in 1905. Although a college graduate (Georgetown University), Devlin was superstitious to the point of paranoia. If a teammate started to sing or even hum softly on the bench, Devlin would tell him to knock it off, he was killing base hits with that humming. He would enforce this with his fists, which wasn't odd at that time; grown men a hundred years ago would fight over things like that, and nobody thought it strange.

Devlin, one of the few really good fist fighters that baseball ever has known, began swinging at [some fans]. Josh Devore and Larry Doyle, two of Devlin's teammates, knowing he needed no help but wishing to be in on the fun, piled right in with him.—Frank Graham, *The Brooklyn Dodgers*

One of the fans involved in this incident, a man named Bernard J. Roesler, swore out a warrant, and had Devlin arrested. Wee Willie Keeler, retired and well off, went with Devlin to help him make bail, but the judge released Devlin with no bail, and the matter apparently was dropped.

One time a cross-eyed woman sat behind third base, expressing throughout the game a good deal of affection for Devlin. But Devlin, as soon as he noticed her, fell into a terrible slump, and became convinced that the cross-eyed woman was a jinx. Somehow the newspapers got wind of this, and several stories were written about Devlin's cross-eyed jinx. Although none of the stories named her and none of the reporters interviewed her, the woman apparently figured out that she was considered bad luck, and stopped coming to the games. "If she'd stuck much longer," said McGraw *(Pitching in a Pinch),* "I would have had her eyes operated on and straightened. This club couldn't afford to keep on losing ball games because you are such a Romeo, Arthur, that even the cross-eyed ones fall for you."

59 ◆ Frank Malzone
(1955–1966, 1441 G, 133 728 .274)
Malzone scored 107 runs for Milford in the Eastern Shore League in 1948, but didn't make the majors for almost nine years after that because of a serious injury, military service, assorted bad luck, and the fact that the Red Sox were run for much of the 1950s by morons. Playing in the Eastern League in 1950, he shattered his ankle on the second day of the season. He was out for the year, and the doctor who set

the ankle said that his baseball career was over. He came back from that, spent two years in the army, came back from that, and had a good six-game trial late in 1955. The Red Sox handed him the third base job, but that winter his baby daughter died at the age of 15 months. Malzone opened the 1956 season as the Red Sox third baseman, but stumbling around in a daze.

Malzone was a very quiet man. A TV reporter once asked Sammy White to conduct a poll to name the quietest man on the Red Sox. "That's a waste of time," said White. "Malzone would win every vote." He worked for many years after his playing career as a special assignment scout for the Red Sox.

60 ◆ Pinky Higgins
(1930–1946, 1802 G, 141 1075 .292)

Higgins attended the University of Texas, where his older brother had been an All-American football player, and signed with the Philadelphia Athletics in 1930. In 1932 he hit .326 with 33 homers, 126 RBI in the PCL, which brought him to the majors the next year. He was a very good right-handed hitter with some power, but a butcher at third base . . . of course he is famous for getting 12 straight hits.

Higgins was manager and later General Manager of the Red Sox during what might be called the Eddie Bressoud years. He wasn't too bad a manager at first, but he didn't get better. "The first direct indication I had that some Red Sox people were against having a black player," wrote Al Hirshberg in *What's the Matter with the Red Sox?,* was when "Mike Higgins, then the manager, told me 'There'll be no niggers on this ball club as long as I have anything to say about it.'"

He had something to say about it for quite a while, moving into the front office in the 1960s as Boston's general manager. On February 27, 1968, Higgins, driving drunk, plowed into a chain gang near Ruston, Louisiana, killing one man and severely injuring three others. He spent two months in prison, this being an era in which even serious crimes were not taken seriously, but died of a heart attack shortly after his release.

61 ◆ Bill Joyce
(1890–1898, 905 G, 71 607 .294)

The highest secondary averages of any listed third basemen: 1. Bill Joyce, .471, 2. Mike Schmidt, .461, 3. Chipper Jones, .416, 4. Eddie Mathews, .415, 5. John McGraw, .401, 6. Edgar Martinez, .388, 7. Howard Johnson, .384, 8. Al Rosen, .378, 9. Darrell Evans, .373, 10. Harlond Clift, .368 . . . Joyce was a good hitter, and regarded as a very smart player, but he was an immobile third baseman with an erratic arm. The 1890s were an era when a lot of runs were scored, and his career is shorter than that of everybody listed ahead of him, and 90% of those listed below him.

62 ◆ Willie Kamm
(1923–1935, 1692 G, 29 826 .281)

Kamm was purchased by the White Sox from the San Francisco Seals for $100,000, a record price for a minor league player, although the record was broken a year later. He was among the best defensive third basemen in history. Chief Bender, who was in the American League as a player or scout almost continuously from 1903 to 1950, said that Kamm was the best third baseman he ever saw. He led the American League in putouts seven times, in assists four times, in double plays three times, in range factor eight times, and in fielding percentage eight times, which was a record until Brooks Robinson. I have him as deserving of the Gold Glove in 1923, 1924, 1925, 1926, 1928, and 1932.

Kamm was a notorious practical joker. In 1932, when Frankie Pytlak was first called to the majors, Cleveland manager Roger Peckinpaugh assigned him to room with Kamm on the road trip to New York. Pytlak had never been to New York City before, so Kamm took him under his wing, and explained a few things, like the fact that it cost a quarter to ride the elevator in the hotel. Kamm and Pytlak were staying on the 20th floor of the Hotel New Yorker. Pytlak, short on quarters, hauled himself up and down 20 flights of stairs for three days until Peckinpaugh noticed, and asked him what he was doing.

In 1933 the Indians hired Walter Johnson as manager. Walter and Kamm did not get along. The Indians had a divided clubhouse, and Johnson felt, rightly or wrongly, that Kamm was the leader of the anti-Walter faction. He said so, and released Kamm (and Glenn Myatt) with uncharacteristically harsh words. Kamm appealed to the Commissioner to clear his name. The Commissioner announced that Kamm's name was clear, but that he had no authority over Johnson's decision.

Johnson had never been popular with the Cleveland fans, and his blast at Kamm, a popular player, sealed his fate. The front office, trying to quiet the controversy, immediately hired Kamm as a scout. Johnson was fired a few weeks later.

63 ◆ Clete Boyer
(1955–1971, 1725 G, 162 654 .242)

> One day I did the wrong thing with Clete after he'd struck out four times in a game. As he came out of the shower, I squirted him with a Pepsi . . . The next thing I knew he was pulling me up, apologizing. "It's all right, Clete, all right," I said, shaking my head and trying to focus my eyes. I had double vision for three days. I had no idea he was that strong.—Joe Pepitone, *Joe, You Coulda Made Us Proud*

Boyer was a fantastic third baseman. Brooks Robinson got established a year or two before Clete and was a better hitter as well as a fantastic third baseman, so Brooks got the Gold Gloves, but Clete was every bit as good at third. Boyer would dive for a ball, knock it down, then throw the runner out at first from his knees. I've seen other people do it, but Clete did it all the time. He could throw from his knees as well as anybody else could throw standing up.

> Maris' friend Clete Boyer was the kind of guy who would always tell me to be careful who I brought into the clubhouse. Yet he led the league in hosting the obnoxious offspring of clothing manufacturers . . . He and Maris got the sweaters, and we got the kids.—Jim Bouton, *Ball Four*

64 ◆ Doug Rader
(1967–1977, 1465 G, 155 722 .251)

A good player . . . his .251 average wasn't much, but his secondary average was better (.261), he played in a time and place where runs were scarce, and he was a Gold Glove third baseman.

There used to be a lot of wild stories about Rader; he was a character and a half. My favorite story involves the time Rader was doing military training, reserve corps, and his unit was assigned to capture another group's general as a training mission. They never found the general, but at the end of a long, hard day they met the general coming out of the PX. "Where the hell have you been," Rader snapped. "We've been looking for you all day." Royals broadcaster Denny Mathews, who was Rader's teammate in college, can tell you Doug Rader stories by the hour.

In the 1980s, when Rader was trying to make a career as a major league manager, he discouraged the circulation of these wild-and-crazy-Doug-Rader stories, which he thought made him look like a clown (gee, why didn't Casey Stengel ever think of that?). He didn't make it as a manager because, while he is very bright, well organized, and likeable, on a certain level he was insecure, and sometimes under pressure he would turn into a jerk. This isn't unusual; Joe Adcock, Hal McRae, Billy Herman, Bill Joyce, and Walter Johnson were all well-liked, affable men as players, but brusque or hostile as managers. It's a tough job, and there aren't very many people who are good at it.

In 1992, when Mark McGwire's career was in crisis, Rader worked with him on his swing, eliminated mannerisms and motion to make his swing more efficient. McGwire and Rader became close friends, and McGwire credits Rader with making him the hitter he later became.

65 ◆ Willie Jones
(1947–1961, 1691 G, 190 812 .258)

> Willie never seemed in a hurry, but he could fool you. During the period when the scouts were trailing him, one scout brought him to his hotel. The scout excused himself for a moment, went to his room and left Willie alone with the room clerk, a young lady named Carolyn Goodson. "Ah took one look at her," says Willie, "and Ah said, 'Ah'm gonna marry you!' She thought Ah was crazy. But four months later we were married."–Harry Paxton in *Sport Magazine*, June, 1964

The Gary Gaetti of the 1950s . . . most-similar players to Gary Gaetti, by decade:

1880s—Ed Williamson
1890s—Billy Nash
1900s—Harry Steinfeldt (easy one)
1910s— Heinie Zimmerman
1920s—Milt Stock
1930s—Harlond Clift
1940s—Tabor, Keltner, or Kurowski
1950s—Willie Jones
1960s—Ron Santo or Ken McMullen
1970s—Sal Bando
1980s—Gary Gaetti
1990s—Matt Williams or Todd Zeile

The nickname "Puddin' Head" Jones came from a 1933 song, "Wooden Head, Puddin' Head

Jones," popular when Jones was a small boy . . . All Willie team: 1B–Willie McCovey, 2B–Willie Randolph, 3B–Willie Kamm or Willie Jones, SS–Willie Miranda, OF–Willie Stargell, Willie Mays, and Willie Keeler, extra outfielders Willie Davis and Willie McGee, DH–Willie Horton, Pitchers–Willie Sudhoff, Wee Willie Sherdel, Willie Hoffer, Willie McGill, Willie Mitchell, Will White, and Carlton Willey. Relief Ace–Willie Hernandez. Pinch Runner/Sixth Outfielder, Willie Wilson. Pinch Hitters/Defensive Subs at first base, Willie Montanez and Willie Upshaw. (We'll have to trade one of the extra outfielders or first basemen for a catcher.) National Anthem–Willie Nelson, Financial Backer–Willie Sutton, Pharmaceutical Supplies–Willie Aikens.

66 ◆ Ossie Bluege
(1922–1939, 1867 G, 43 848 .272)

"During most of his 18-year career Bluege was regarded as the best in baseball at the position," wrote Henry W. Thomas in *Walter Johnson: Baseball's Big Train*. Since Bluege's career runs parallel to those of Pie Traynor (1920–1937) and Willie Kamm (1923–1935) this statement is open to dispute; however, Bluege was certainly an acknowledged glove wizard, and Calvin Griffith often did say that he was the best he ever saw. He played very shallow, inside the baselines. Thomas credits him with inventing the theory of "cutting down the cone," which is still a popular notion among third basemen, and also says that he was the first third basemen to guard the lines with a one-run lead in the late innings, to prevent the batter getting a double in the corner. I am not personally convinced that either of these theories holds water, but I can't play third base at all, while I have Bluege as deserving of the American League gold glove in 1927 and 1931, and as runner-up in many other seasons. Bluege was a special-assignment coach with the Senators for years after his playing days.

When Bill Dickey was trying to teach Yogi to catch, Bluege was trying to teach Ed Yost to play third base, and when Dickey was working with Elston Howard, Bluege was working with Harmon Killebrew. (Odd fact of the day: Ed Yost was actually only two years older than Elston Howard. This seems completely wrong, because Howard didn't become a regular until 1961, when Yost was finished.) The name, incidentally, was pronounced Blue-Gee, hard G; it rhymes with "Boogie," not "Luge."

67 ◆ Red Smith
(1911–1919, 1117 G, 27 514 .278)
An Atlanta native who played baseball at Auburn. From a chronological standpoint, at least, Smith is one of the keys to the Miracle Braves. Smith hit .296 and led the National League in doubles for Brooklyn in 1913, but in 1914 was not hitting well, and began to feud with Brooklyn manager Wilbert Robinson. The Braves were playing Charlie Deal at third base; he was hitting .210, and the Braves were under .500 in early August. They purchased Smith from Brooklyn for an undisclosed amount of money on August 10. Smith hit .314 with 17 doubles and an on-base percentage over .400 in the closing weeks, and the Braves hardly lost after putting him in the lineup, going 50-14 after August 1.

68 ◆ Hans Lobert
(1903–1917, 1317 G, 32 482 .274)
Lobert was very fast. In 1910 he was clocked circling the bases in 13 $^4/_5$ seconds, which was considered to be the world's record for eleven years. It was finally broken by Maurice Archdeacon. In 1915 he had a famous race against a race horse in Oxnard, California; that story is re-told in *The Glory of Their Times,* and also in Nash and Zullo's *Believe It Or Else.*

The Cubs, who needed a third baseman, traded away Lobert to acquire Harry Steinfeldt. Lobert, by the end of the year, was playing on more or less the same level as Steinfeldt. Within two years, he would be a better player than Steinfeldt, who was several years older than he was. This is one of the commonplace ironies of major league history: very often a team which is anxious to solve a problem will trade away the solution to the problem in the process of solving it. The Mariners, desperate to patch up their bullpen, traded away Derek Lowe to acquire a "proven" reliever.

69 ◆ Ray Boone
(1948–1960, 1373 G, 151 737 .275)
In September, 1957, a woman named Gussie Moran wrote an acutely embarrassing article for *Sport Magazine* entitled "Baseball's Ten Handsomest Men." Both of the men who became patriarchs of three-generation baseball families, Ray Boone and Gus Bell, were included on the list . . . Ray Boone began his career as a catcher, but was switched to the infield in the minor leagues. His son Bob began his career as an infielder, but was switched to catcher . . . Ray, like a lot of guys, could have had a Hall of Fame career with better luck. He came into baseball in 1942, but went to the Army for three years before he could really play. The Indians, with Keltner and Rosen, didn't need him at third base and tried to make him a shortstop, which he wasn't. When he got through all of those things he was 30 years old, but for a period of four years he played like Ken Boyer, hitting 20-26 homers a year, hitting around .300 every year and averaging 99 RBI per season. He was a respected man in baseball, and was hired by the Red Sox as a scout as soon as he retired.

70 ◆ Bill Melton
(1968–1977, 1144 G, 160 591 .253)
In his first few years Melton seemed to be on track for stardom. He hit 33 homers in 1970, a White Sox record at the time, and hit 33 again in 1971, thus becoming the first White Sox

player to lead the league in home runs. His career was de-railed by a back injury in 1972, which may have been worsened by experimental therapy. As a defensive player he struggled to be adequate . . . The 1974 Chicago White Sox had Ron Santo, Dick Allen, and Bill Melton on the team. By the end of the year, they were playing Bill Stein and Lee Richard at third base.

71 ◆ Travis Fryman
(1990–2000, 1482 G, 209 929 .279)
90-RBI a year guy, trying to come back from his first off season.

72 ◆ Ken McMullen
(1962–1977, 1583 G, 156 606 .248)
McMullen's wife died of cancer on the opening day of the 1974 baseball season. McMullen was only 31 at the time, but he was an old 31, balding and slow; he had been a regular for eight years, ending in 1972. He had three small children. "I took off a few weeks to get the kids straightened away," McMullen told Maury Allen later that summer, "Then I went back to work. I had to make a living. There was nothing else I could do."

73 ◆ Don Hoak
(1954–1964, 1263 G, 89 498 .265)
Hoak is probably responsible for Rule 7.09 (g), which reads "If, in the judgment of the umpire, a base runner willfully and deliberately interferes with a batted ball or a fielder in the act of fielding a batted ball with the obvious intent to break up a double play, the ball is dead. The umpire shall call the runner out for interference and also call out the batter-runner because of the action of his teammate. In no event may bases be run or runs scored because of such action by a runner."

This rule was put in the books after a couple of incidents involving the Brooklyn Dodgers in

1955. Jackie Robinson was on first when a double-play ball was hit toward second. Jackie allowed the ball to hit him, perhaps deliberately, which caused Robinson to be called out, but the batter to be awarded first base. A few weeks later a similar play occurred with Hoak on first. Hoak, having seen what Jackie did, grabbed the ball and threw it into the outfield before the fielder could make a play. Hoak was out, of course, but his action averted a double play, as the batter under the old rule was entitled to first base.

> If sheer will were the only criterion, Don Hoak would have hit 1.000 every year. There weren't many men around who fought the world as hard as Hoak did . . . and when he swung you knew a bat had moved. There was nothing half-hearted about the way Don Hoak swung a bat—or did anything else on a ballfield.—Ed Richter, *The Man in the Dugout*

74 ◆ Jim Hart
(1963–1974, 1125 G, 170 578 .278)
A better hitter than 59 of the 73 men listed ahead of him at third base. This should tell you all you need to know about his defense.

75 ◆ Pepper Martin
(1928–1944, 1189 G, 59 501 .298)
"He was a bundle of energy, couldn't sit still for a minute, and was unpredictable," wrote Fred Lieb. When he first reported to a major league team in 1928, he hitchhiked to spring training [Florida]. Riding the railroads (which was technically illegal, although common), Martin was arrested in Thomasville, Georgia, and spent the night in the city jail. He reported to the Cardinals the next day with a scraggly beard, filthy clothes, and his face smeared with grease and oil.

"Later, after he became a star with the Redbirds, he often reported for work looking much the same," said Lieb. "He took up midget auto-racing, and spent the mornings tinkering with his car. He would just have time to reach the park for batting practice, his face, hair and hands still covered with grease."

76 ◆ Deacon White
(1876–1890, 1299 G, 18 602 .303)
See article in Part 1, most-admirable superstar of the 1870s . . . The lowest secondary averages of any listed third basemen:

1. Deacon White   .142
2. Ezra Sutton   .142
3. Joe Dugan   .145
4. Aurelio Rodriguez .168
5. Milt Stock   .170

77 ◆ Kevin Seitzer
(1986–1997, 1439 G, 74 613 .295)
In 1987, when Mark McGwire hit 49 home runs as a rookie, Kevin Seitzer was also a rookie, and also had quite a season, collecting 207 hits (which led the league), scoring 105 runs, drawing 80 walks, and hitting 33 doubles, 8 triples, and 15 homers. I am a Kansas City Royals fan, and, at the time, we all had visions of Seitzer being better than that Brett fellow who used to play third. This didn't work out; Seitzer was a good player, but his rookie season was his best effort.

Seitzer was a rather small man with narrow shoulders, a right-handed hitter, not a fast runner, not a great arm, and giving no obvious evidence of great strength. All of this was apparent even when he was a rookie, but he overcame it by being a disciplined player who hit the ball squarely. He was a born-again Christian who sometimes irritated his teammates and managers, perhaps for good reason or perhaps just because, when things go wrong, it's easy to blame the Christian. He never played badly; he never really had a bad year. He never hit lower than .265, but he never could meet the expectations of his rookie season.

The top ten rookie seasons by third basemen:

1. Dick Allen, 1964
2. Al Rosen, 1950
3. Scott Rolen, 1997
4. Home Run Baker, 1909
5. Pete Ward, 1963
6. Eddie Foster, 1912
7. Max Alvis, 1963
8. Jim Ray Hart, 1964
9. Kevin Seitzer, 1987
10. Pinky Higgins, 1933

78 ◆ Billy Werber
(1930–1942, 1295 G, 78 539 .271)
By all accounts, Billy Werber was a brilliant man. He graduated from Duke University Phi Beta Kappa, which is Greek for "Really Smart Guy." Pinky Higgins and Billy Werber make an interesting contrast. Both were college men, both graduated from college in 1930, and both signed major league contracts at that point with the two American League powerhouses, the A's (Higgins) and the Yankees (Werber). Both men made their major league debuts on June 25, 1930. Both played a few games in the majors, and then returned to the minor leagues for two-plus seasons.

By the spring of 1933, both men were ready to play in the majors. Higgins took over the third base job for the A's, but the Yankees, flush with young infielders, sold Werber to the Red Sox for a reported $100,000. For two years, it appeared that Joe McCarthy might live to regret this. An intense, hustling player, Werber was the best third baseman in the major leagues in 1934, his second season as a regular, when he collected 200 hits, scored 129 runs, hit 41 doubles, and led the major leagues in stolen bases, with 40.

Werber did not play as well in 1935 and 1936, however, and his stock began to slip. In December, 1935, Werber was traded to the

Athletics in exchange for Higgins, in what was reported as a straight-up trade; Higgins also had not been playing as well as he had in 1933–34. Higgins perked up a little bit with the Red Sox, but Werber, with the A's, continued to slide.

After the 1938 season Connie Mack tried to cut Werber's salary. Werber refused to sign but reported to spring training, where he broke his toe kicking a water bucket. (He had seen Lefty Grove kick water buckets for years, he explained. What he didn't realize until he tried it himself was that Lefty always kicked them with the side of his foot.) Anyway, Connie Mack had had it with him. The Cincinnati Reds were trying to build up their team and had asked about Werber, so Connie called Reds manager Bill McKechnie, and sold Werber to the Reds.

Although he always gave his best efforts on the field, Werber had never been well-liked by his teammates, except possibly Moe Berg. A cultured man who read books, worked hard to improve himself, and didn't join his teammates in their nightly carousing, he was sometimes critical of teammates who were less dedicated. He was always a gentleman, but he was regarded, by some, as cold and arrogant. That seemed to change, when he joined the Reds; the Reds accepted him as a part of the team, and included him in their circle of friendship. That was a fun organization to be part of, for a few years; Bill McKechnie, the nicest of Hall of Fame managers, had put together a team of likeable, positive people who played together exceptionally well. The Reds won the pennant in 1939 and 1940, while Werber had probably his best all-around seasons, leading the National League in runs scored in 1939 (115), and scoring 105 more in 1940.

His play slipped in 1941, the war came, and Werber left baseball quickly and without regret. He went into the insurance business, and within a few years was reported to be a wealthy man. "There aren't many players who are wasting their time financially by playing big-league baseball," wrote Lee Allen. "Bill Werber was one of them."

79 ◆ Bob Bailey
(1962–1978, 1931 G, 189 773 .257)
Bailey was paid a big bonus, reportedly the largest ever at the time he signed, and was rushed to the major leagues before he was ready. Like his contemporaries Dick Allen, Jim Ray Hart, and Bill Melton, he was a good right-handed power hitter, but not a very good third baseman. Unable to meet the expectations generated by his bonus, he fell into a frustration cycle, stopped hitting for two years, and lost a good portion of his career.

What do Bob Bailey, Johnny Gochnauer, and Vinny Castilla have in common? Uncannily similar seasons back-to-back. Gochnauer had two consecutive seasons in which he hit .185 with 16 doubles, 4 triples, no homers, the amazing thing being that, having done that once, he survived to do it again. Castilla had two consecutive seasons in which he hit .304 with 40 homers, 113 RBI. Bailey had two consecutive seasons (the frustration years) in which he finished with 73 hits in 322 at bats, a .227 average.

80 ◆ Jeff Cirillo
(1994–2000, 946 G, 77 487 .311)
One of my favorite contemporary players, a .300 hitter with 35–40 doubles every year and great defense. Should move way up the list before he is finished.

81 ◆ Todd Zeile
(1989–2000, 1626 G, 205 884 .268)
A Brooks Robinson clone as a hitter, but more of a Larry Parrish at third base.

82 ◆ Bob Horner

(1978–1988, 1020 G, 218 685 .277)

Perhaps the only player in major league history who was a regular for ten years, and never had a season without an injury. Mantle was famous for constant injuries, but Mickey had nine seasons with more than 600 plate appearances. Horner had none.

"I called him Buddha," remembered Whitey Herzog. "He was a little on the portly side and spent a lot of quality time slouched in his chair in the clubhouse." Herzog had a rule that everybody took infield before the game. During infield drills on Opening Day, 1988, Herzog discovered Horner in the dugout, enjoying a deep trance. Herzog asked him what the hell he was doing. "He looks up a me, blinks like an old frog on a lily pad and says, 'I'm tired.' A hundred and sixty-two games left to play, and the man is gassed!"

83 ◆ Jim Tabor

(1938–1947, 1005 G, 104 598 .270)

> Tall and rangy, he's an ideal hot corner workman with a whipcord arm.—*Who's Who in the Major Leagues*, 1939

Tabor was a rookie with the Red Sox in 1939, the same year that Ted Williams came up (in fact, Williams and Tabor had been teammates the previous season, in the minor leagues). His first three years in the league he was a terrific player, driving in 95 runs as a rookie, 101 runs in 126 games in 1941. He was young (only two years older than Williams), a good third baseman (although he made a lot of errors), and he could run. But he liked the girls, smoked cigars and usually had the stub of a cigar in his mouth off the field, and he drank. In 1941 Joe Cronin suspended him for drinking and missing a game. His career degenerated after 1941. He was back in

the minors by the late 1940s, and died of a heart attack in 1953.

According to Lefty LeFebvre, a teammate of Williams and Tabor at Minneapolis in 1938, one time Ted Williams, then 19 years old, was sulking because the team trainer wouldn't let him have a new baseball for pre-game drills. He was so upset about this that he wouldn't make any effort to play the field; balls landed near him in left-center, and he just stood and looked at them, forcing the center fielder to run over and retrieve the ball. The Millers lost the game. Tabor, in the clubhouse, grabbed Ted Williams and commenced to beat him severely about the head and shoulders. Donie Bush, the manager, rescued Williams, told Tabor to leave him alone, he was just a kid.

"Jim Tabor, he was a twister," said Doc Cramer in *Fenway* (Peter Golenbock, G.P. Putnam's, 1992). "Tabor would drink, get drunk, and be half-drunk when he came to the park." One time the Red Sox hired two private detectives to shadow him, trying to discourage him from drinking. Tabor locked the detectives in the bathroom, and went on to his next bar.

"He had the unfortunate habit of drinking in public," said Tony Lupien (same source). "You can drink in your room, and who the hell knows about it?

"He hustled. He was tough. He'd slide into second base and knock you on your ass."

84 ◆ Pete Ward

(1962–1970, 973 G, 98 427 .254)

Ward attended Lewis and Clark College in Portland, earning a degree in Business Administration. He hit .437 one year in college, but only two teams were interested in him—Baltimore, which offered $6,000, and Kansas City, which didn't.

His rise through the minors was painfully slow, for two reasons. First, Brooks Robinson took control of the third base job in Baltimore just months after Ward signed with the Orioles. Second, Ward in the minor leagues used a split-handed grip, a Ty Cobb grip, his hands separated six to eight inches. Baseball coaches can't stand people who do things *different*, in the first place, and in the second place, it made him a singles hitter. He was a good singles hitter; in the Three-I League in 1960 he hit .345 with 105 RBI, but only 12 homers. The Orioles figured that since Brooks was going to play third, Pete had to play the outfield, and since he had to play the outfield and wasn't fast, he had to hit for power.

Ward finally abandoned the split-handed grip in 1962, hit 22 home runs for Rochester, and was included that winter as a throw-in on an exchange of Hall of Famers, Luis Aparicio and Hoyt Wilhelm. In 1963 he had a Rookie-of-the-year type season (see Kevin Seitzer) although an even better season by a teammate (Gary Peters) deprived him of the award. An odd note: Ward in the majors in 1963 hit exactly the same number of doubles (34), triples (6), and home runs (22) that he had hit the previous year in the minors, and almost matched his hit total (179 in the minors, 177 in the majors).

A series of injuries, the most serious of which was a hernia requiring mid-season surgery in 1966, reduced his effectiveness and shortened his career; he was around baseball for years after that as a coach.

Pete Ward in 1964 hit .282 with 23 homers, 94 RBI—moderately impressive numbers, but remember:

1. The American League batting average in 1963 was .247.

2. The White Sox in 1964 played in the second-worst hitter's park in the league.

Ward was playing in a context of just above 600 runs per team per season.

In a historically normal context of 700 runs per season, equivalent numbers would be .298 with 25 homers, 107 RBI.

In a high-run context of 800 runs per season (still below the norms of the current era), equivalent numbers would be .316 with 27 homers, 122 RBI.

In an extremely high-run context of 900 runs per season (which is still below the levels of Coors Field in the 1990s, although above league norms), equivalent numbers would be .332 with 29 homers, 137 RBI.

See Willie Davis for some explanation of how these numbers are derived.

85 ◆ Jimmy Austin
(1909–1929, 1580 G, 13 390 .246)

> There was peppery Jimmy Austin at third. What an arm! Every fourth heave he made across the diamond went into the right-field bleachers . . . Jimmy shouted a lot. It used to annoy some of the other players.—John Kieran, *New York Times,* October 3, 1937

According to Nash and Zullo's *Believe It Or Else,* Jimmy Austin in 1927 threw out a runner at home plate—as a coach. Austin, coaching for St. Louis, was standing on the steps of the dugout when Bing Miller's throw bounced away from the third baseman, and rolled to a stop at Austin's feet. Sam Rice of the Senators was headed for home. Without thinking, Austin picked up the ball and flipped it to the catcher. The umpire, not having seen the coach interfere with the ball, called Rice out.

Austin was born in Wales, and came to the U.S. at age eight. He grew up in Cleveland, and became a machinist-apprentice at a Westinghouse plant. He was a good amateur baseball player with no notion of turning pro until just after his apprenticeship ended, when the Westinghouse machinists went out on strike. He accepted an offer to play ball (and work) for a factory team in nearby Warren, Ohio.

He was 24 by the time he entered professional baseball, and nearly 30 by the time he reached the majors. In 1913, Browns manager George Stovall was suspended for expectorating tobacco all over an umpire. ("George always did chew an uncommonly large wad, you know," Austin commented.) Austin became interim manager. Branch Rickey arrived to take the helm later that year, and since Rickey never went to the ballpark on the Sabbath, Austin became the Browns' "Sunday Manager" for the next two years.

He had other stints as an interim manager, and a long career as a coach. In 1929, just short of his 50th birthday, he was inserted at third base for the final innings of a meaningless game, and handled two chances flawlessly. Discharged by the Browns after the 1933 season, he coached for the White Sox until his wife's ill health forced him to the sidelines. He was still full of enthusiasm for baseball at age eighty-five when Lawrence Ritter transcribed his reminiscences for *The Glory of Their Times*. He died at his home in Laguna Beach, California, in 1965.

86 ◆ Milt Stock
(1913–1926, 1628 G, 22 696 .289)

Stock, in the majors since 1913, had one of his best seasons in 1925, getting 202 hits including 16 in a four-game span, a record since tied by George Brett. His career basically ended the following spring training, when he sustained serious injuries in a collision with Lou Gehrig during an exhibition game. He remained in baseball for many years after that as a coach and minor league manager. His daughter married Eddie Stanky.

87 ◆ Ray Knight
(1974–1988, 1495 G, 84 595 .271)

How many major league baseball players married women who were perhaps more famous than they were? Knight, Joe DiMaggio, David Justice, Mike Donlin . . . Monte Ward's wife, I guess, was a big deal at the time. Anybody else?

88 ◆ Joe Dugan
(1917–1931, 1446 G, 42 571 .280)

Dugan had a superstitious conviction that it was bad luck to throw the ball back to the pitcher. On most teams, after the players fire the ball around the infield, it is the third baseman who gives the ball to the pitcher. Dugan absolutely wouldn't do it. One time Mark Koenig set up a trick on him; after they flipped him the ball, all three other infielders (Lazzeri, Koenig, and Gehrig) turned their backs on him and walked toward the outfield. Dugan started to throw to Gehrig, realized he couldn't, looked at Lazzeri, double-clutched again, looked at Koenig, wound up, and fired the ball right at Koenig's butt . . .

For many years baseball's trading deadline was June 15. This could be called the "Joe Dugan Rule." On July 23, 1922, with the St. Louis Browns in first place, the Yankees gave $50,000 and a package of players to the also-ran Red Sox for Joe Dugan. This upset the St. Louis sports fans some, and then, on July 30, the exact same thing happened in the National League. With the Cardinals also fighting for the pennant, the New York team (the Giants) gave $100,000 and a couple of pitchers to Boston (the Braves) for veteran pitcher Hugh McQuillen.

Cardinal GM Branch Rickey seized on the bilateral anger of the St. Louis fans, and orchestrated a campaign to get St. Louis city organizations to protest these kind of deals. The City Council, the Rotary Club, and other civic organizations filed protests with Commissioner Landis, complaining that their teams could not hope to compete if the New York teams were allowed to buy off the competition in the heat of the pennant race. Landis agreed, and prohibited any future player deals, except for the waiver price, after June 15.

89 ◆ Hubie Brooks
(1980–1994, 1645 G, 149 824 .269)

A shortstop at Arizona State, Hubie was shifted to third base by the Mets, who then decided he didn't have enough power to play third. He hit 16 homers for the Mets in 1984, and was traded to Montreal, where he became a shortstop again. He wound up playing more games in the outfield (582) than any other position, although this is misleading, because "outfield" is really three positions. That's the kind of player he was, anyway—a third baseman who was a little bit short on power, a shortstop who was a little bit slow, an outfielder who didn't quite produce enough runs, but a valuable player nonetheless because almost every team has a gaping hole somewhere and an extra player they can't use somewhere else. Hubie could change an "F" to a "C" at third base or short-stop or right field or center field, or wherever you put him, and allow somebody else to get into the lineup.

90 ◆ Jim Davenport
(1958–1970, 1501 G, 77 456 .258)

Like Hubie, a player who was just a little bit short of being a shortstop. He was a better third baseman than Hubie—he was outstanding—but not as good a hitter... managed the Giants briefly and unsuccessfully in the 1980s.

91 ◆ Aurelio Rodriguez
(1967–1983, 2017 G, 124 648 .237)

Among the 100 third basemen listed here, Aurelio had the highest percentage of his career value in defensive accomplishments, rather than offensive. The top five third basemen, ranked by the percentage of their total value which was in fielding: 1. Rodriguez, 2. Clete

Boyer, 3. Lave Cross, 4. Billy Shindle, 5. Willie Kamm.

92 ◆ Cookie Lavagetto
(1934–1947, 1043 G, 40 486 .269)

The son of a trash hauler in Oakland, California, Lavagetto broke into baseball in the Pacific Coast League in 1933, playing for Oakland Oaks General Manager "Cookie" Devincenzi. He was called "Cookie's Boy," which became Cookie. He made the majors in one year flat, became a regular in 1937, and was a very solid player with the Dodgers from 1937–1941.

Lavagetto is most famous for a ringing double in the fourth game of the 1947 World Series, which broke up Bill Bevens' no-hitter with two out in the ninth inning, and incidentally won the game for the Dodgers. Neither Lavagetto nor Bevens ever appeared in a major league game after that World Series. Lavagetto's double, one of the most famous hits in major league history, was his last major league hit.

Lavagetto is the missing link between Leo Durocher and Billy Martin. Martin is often described as a latter-day Leo Durocher, but Martin never played for Durocher, and did not know Durocher well. Lavagetto played for Durocher for several years, admired him, and became buddies with Durocher's right-hand man, Charlie Dressen. Out of the major leagues in 1948, Lavagetto returned to Oakland, and played three years for the Oakland Oaks, with whom he had begun his career 15 years earlier. Billy Martin was with that team. Lavagetto took Martin under his wing, roomed with him, and became one of the biggest influences in his life.

Casey Stengel, of course, was the manager of that team. When Casey moved to the Yankees in 1949, the Oaks asked Lavagetto if he was interested in managing the team. Lavagetto said that he wasn't through playing and didn't want to try to do both, but recommended that the

Oaks hire Charlie Dressen, which they did. Lavagetto and Dressen continued to school Martin in the Leo Durocher style of baseball.

Lavagetto became Dressen's Charlie Dressen, so to speak; he coached for Dressen with the Dodgers (1951–53), returned with him to Oakland in 1954, and went with him to Washington in 1955. When that didn't work out for Dressen, Lavagetto replaced him as manager of the Senators on May 7, 1957.

The Senators, a down and out organization for 25 years, were developing the players who would win the American League as the Minnesota Twins in 1965. Although Lavagetto didn't last until the pay day, he helped to develop Killebrew, Pascual, Versalles, Jim Kaat, and others, and produced two consecutive Rookies of the Year, Albie Pearson (1958) and Bob Allison (1959). He also re-acquired Billy Martin when Martin was about through as a player (1961), and made him a Twins' coach, thereby launching Martin's second career. Fired shortly thereafter as Minnesota manager, Lavagetto coached for Casey Stengel with the Mets, and later coached in San Francisco for Alvin Dark, another Durocher protégé.

93 ◆ Pinky Whitney
(1928–1939, 1539 G, 93 927 .293)
Deserved the Gold Glove in 1929 and 1932 (although Pie Traynor would have won the award, based on his reputation). A good defensive third baseman, he also hit .342 with 41 doubles, 8 homers, 117 RBI for the 1930 Phillies, and had several other seasons that look awfully good if you don't realize how many runs it took to win a ballgame in that context. Reversing the question we asked vis-a-vis Pete Ward, what would be equivalent offensive production in a more normal run environment?

Baker Bowl in 1930 was an environment of essentially 1,000 runs per 162 games—compa-rable to Coors Field today. In an environment of 900 runs per season—still an extremely high level of offense—equivalent offensive production would be .326 with 38 doubles, 7 homers, 104 RBI.

In an environment of 800 runs per season (still a high run environment), equivalent production would be .311 with 36 doubles, 7 homers, 93 RBI.

In a "normal" environment of about 700 runs per season, equivalent production would be .294 with 33 doubles, 6 homers, 81 RBI. In other words, it's a decent season, but it's not George Kell, let alone George Brett.

In a low-run environment (600 runs per season), equivalent production would be .276 with 30 doubles, 6 homers, 70 RBI.

94 ◆ George Pinckney
(1884–1893, 1163 G, 21 539, .263)
One of the first good hitters to make a career out of playing third base. His career was basically ended when Ed Delahanty hit a line shot off his ankle in early 1892, breaking the ankle. He was only thirty at the time, and in excellent shape.

95 ◆ Bill Shindle
(1886–1898, 1424 G, 30 758 .269)
There are four contemporary third basemen crowded here at the end of the list—George Pinckney (94), Bill Shindle (95), Ezra Sutton (98), and Jeremiah Denny (99). I don't have a clear image of any of these men, to be honest. Denny is the most "famous" of the four, or the least obscure, I think because he was the most colorful. Shindle, I believe, was the best fielder of the four, but I don't have immense confidence that my defensive evaluation system works well for players of that era; any number of things may have been different enough then that we should be reading the stats in

some other way. There are some good books being written now about baseball in that era, and I suspect that if I live long enough to revise this book in another 15 years, I'll have better source material then than I do now.

96 ◆ Ed Charles
(1962–1969, 1005 G, 86 421 .263)

1. Ed Charles in the 1960s was known as the poet laureate of baseball. You'd see him on television once or twice a year reading or reciting something, but you never see the poetry anywhere; I don't know that any of it was ever published. I think the reason for this is that Charles had a stage presence, a manner and voice, that enabled him to get by with reading his stuff, but when you write it down and somebody else reads it . . . well, there may not be too much left.

2. Charles spent a long, long time trying to get to the major leagues as a shortstop/second baseman. I said that Pete Ward had a slow path to the majors, which he did, but Charles played twice as many minor league games as Ward, plus he missed almost two years with military service; he was in the minors from 1952 through 1961, playing 1,148 minor league games.

3. Like Ward, he finally got to the major leagues when he began to hit for some power. His first season in the majors, 1962, he was outstanding; like Ward, he did not win the Rookie of the Year Award or deserve it given the competition, but he was certainly a lot better than some players who won the same award in other seasons.

4. As pathetic as this may be, Ed Charles was perhaps the best player in the history of the Kansas City Athletics, the team of my childhood; probably not, but you can make an argument for him. Charles played 726 games for the A's, which is (and will always be) the franchise record, and also holds the franchise records for total bases (1,065) and power/speed number (68.8). He is second all-time among KC A's in runs scored (344), hits (703), and RBI (319).

5. However, the 1962 A's, improbably enough, had a legitimately outstanding infield, and could have made the list of the best infields ever (see Ken Boyer, #12) if their shortstop had come through. Norm Siebern at first, Jerry Lumpe at second, and Ed Charles at third all had very strong seasons. And the A's had a good shortstop in 1961 (Dick Howser) and in 1963 (Wayne Causey); either man would have been good enough to put that team on the list of the best infields ever, but Howser didn't play well the first half of the 1962 season and then got hurt, and the A's played Billy Consolo at short for a month before Causey settled in.

97 ◆ Steve Buechele
(1985–1993, 1189 G, 122 486 .248)

Clete Boyer-type player, didn't have as many good years as Clete but could do most of the same things. Slimmer and quicker in the field than many of the third baseman listed here, but deadly slow on the bases and inconsistent at bat.

98 ◆ Ezra Sutton
(1876–1888, 1031 G, 21 518 .288)

Often cited as the best third baseman of his generation, he might deserve to rate higher than I have him. He was a contemporary of Deacon White. White was a better hitter, Sutton a better third baseman. Since hitting ability is captured and recorded in the stats and fielding ability isn't really, White's excellence endures; Sutton's has faded, there existing neither films of him nor even a substantial body of glowing tributes to sustain his image in the absence of concrete records.

How's this for an obscure fact: in 1871 (five years before the founding of the National League) Sutton hit two triples in three consecutive games . . . his closing years were not happy ones. According to an article by Richard Puff in *Nineteenth Century Stars* (SABR), his limbs were paralyzed in 1890, apparently as a result of an accident, a sawmill into which he had sunk his savings failed, and an oil lamp exploded, setting fire to his wife's dress, and eventually killing her. He died in 1907, only 56 years old, but probably more than ready to get it over with.

99 ◆ Jerry Denny

(1881–1894, 1237 G, 74 512+ .260)

Denny was born in New York. His parents moved to California when he was a small boy, however, and then died, leaving Denny to be raised in an orphanage.

I mentioned in passing before that I had reached the conclusion that put outs by a third baseman do not indicate anything of value, and are, as nearly as I can tell, of no value in evaluating a third baseman's defensive play.

As a word of background, the number of putouts by third basemen has dropped constantly throughout baseball history, for reasons which are not entirely clear, but probably related the ever-growing use of the home run, which has gradually replaced sequential offense. The number one player among the 100 listed here, in terms of putouts per inning played at third base, was Jerry Denny, who recorded 244 putouts per 150 full games at third base. Here, I'll chart the top 5 and the bottom 5:

1.	Jerry Denny	244
2.	Denny Lyons	237
3.	Billy Nash	233
4.	Bill Joyce	221
5.	Billy Shindle	220

96.	Travis Fryman	106
97.	Edgar Martinez	104
98.	Todd Zeile	101
99.	Howard Johnson	94
100.	Chipper Jones	87

The top five all played in the 1890s. Denny, Lyons, Nash, and Shindle all started their careers playing bare-handed, and Denny is said to have been the last player to decline to wear a glove in the field.

On the other end are the guys from the 1990s, modern players. There are many other reasons for this change. Increasing strikeouts have caused putouts to drop at every position except catcher—but putouts have dropped more dramatically at third base than at any other position. Decreasing errors have put fewer runners on base, decreasing forceouts at third. As second basemen have gotten more adept at turning the double play, this also has reduced runners on base. Stealing third base has become an unpopular play. All of these things decrease putouts by third basemen. It also seems to me that foul pop ups near third base are nowhere near as common as they were even 25 years ago, although I cannot document that this is true.

Apart from the large number of putouts credited to him there is little or no evidence that Denny was an outstanding defensive player.

100 ◆ Bob Dillinger

(1946–1951, 753 G, 10 213 .306)

Dillinger wore glasses on the field. When he was in the minors in 1939 an umpire called a strike on him, strike two. Dillinger took off his glasses and held them out to the umpire. The umpire calmly took off his mask, put on the glasses, and re-settled the mask. The pitcher threw the next pitch, the umpire yelled "Strike three," and ceremonially handed the glasses back to Dillinger.

101. Eddie Foster, 102. Chris Sabo, 103. Kelly Gruber, 104. Harry Lord, 105. Jimmy Johnston, 106. Vinny Castilla, 107. Max Alvis, 108. Hank Thompson, 109. Jeff King, 110. Andy High, 111. Don Wert, 112. Brook Jacoby, 113. Ken Oberkfell, 114. Sammy Strang, 115. Bobby Byrne, 116. Enos Cabell, 117. Grady Hatton, 118. Wid Conroy, 119. Dave Hollins, 120. Billy Johnson, 121. Vance Law, 122. Wayne Garrett, 123. Joe Foy, 124. Dean Palmer, 125. Mike Mowrey

Two third baseman who didn't make my list, but narrowly missed, were Charlie Dressen

(1925–1933) and Joe Stripp (1928-1938); I didn't list either one, but certainly a good argument could be made on their behalf. They were teammates on the 1931 Cincinnati Reds. Boston coach Tom Daly insisted that the Cincinnati team was going to build a screen around third base. "Why?" asked a reporter.

"Well," replied Daly with a straight face, "I don't think the fans want to see Joe Stripp or Charlie Dressen . . ."

THIRD BASE

Rank	Player Name	Career WS	Top 3	Top 5	Per 162
1.	Mike Schmidt	468	39, 37, 36	171	31.54
2.	George Brett	432	37, 36, 33	154	25.85
3.	Eddie Mathews	447	38, 38, 36	167	30.29
4.	Wade Boggs	394	37, 34, 32	162	26.16
5.	Home Run Baker	301	39, 38, 36	173	30.96
6.	Ron Santo	322	37, 36, 32	162	23.26
7.	Brooks Robinson	355	33, 27, 25	130	19.86
8.	Paul Molitor	412	30, 30, 29	133	24.88
9.	Stan Hack	318	34, 33, 31	140	26.58
10.	Darrell Evans	364	31, 28, 28	117	21.95
11.	Sal Bando	283	36, 31, 29	143	22.71
12.	Ken Boyer	280	31, 28, 27	131	22.30
13.	Graig Nettles	322	28, 27, 26	121	19.32
14.	Al Rosen	185	42, 31, 29	154	28.71
15.	Pie Traynor	271	28, 26, 26	119	22.62
16.	Ron Cey	282	27, 27, 26	126	22.04
17.	Jimmy Collins	273	33, 28, 28	129	25.59
18.	Bob Elliot	287	29, 27, 27	124	23.51
19.	Buddy Bell	299	26, 25, 23	107	20.14
20.	Tommy Leach	329	31, 29, 27	122	24.72
21.	Heine Groh	271	37, 30, 28	147	26.19
22.	Robin Ventura	220	30, 30, 25	109	22.90
23.	Matt Williams	221	28, 28, 27	107	22.95
24.	Eddie Yost	269	27, 27, 24	123	20.66

Rank	Player Name	Career WS	Top 3	Top 5	Per 162
25.	Ken Caminiti	235	38, 26, 25	124	23.19
26.	John McGraw	207	33, 32, 24	122	30.51
27.	Tim Wallach	244	27, 26, 23	102	17.87
28.	Chipper Jones	156	33, 29, 26	136	27.03
29.	Larry Gardner	259	29, 27, 24	106	21.83
30.	George Kell	229	26, 24, 23	106	20.67
31.	Edgar Martinez	239	32, 28, 27	128	25.14
32.	Toby Harrah	284	32, 28, 24	118	21.35
33.	Lave Cross	275	26, 22, 21	97	19.58
34.	Gary Gaetti	251	23, 22, 18	93	16.22
35.	Ken Keltner	199	26, 25, 23	104	21.13
36.	Terry Pendleton	203	35, 27, 21	101	17.37
37.	Harlond Clift	213	25, 24, 23	111	21.81
38.	Doug DeCinces	203	28, 27, 21	99	19.94
39.	Carney Lansford	242	25, 23, 21	96	21.05
40.	Buddy Lewis	179	24, 22, 22	106	21.50
41.	Bobby Bonilla	266	31, 31, 29	132	21.33
42.	Denny Lyons	189	27, 27, 25	122	27.31
43.	Freddy Lindstrom	192	31, 28, 23	116	21.63
44.	Red Rolfe	163	30, 24, 23	118	22.47
45.	Ned Williamson	173	21, 20, 19	87	23.34
46.	Bill Bradley	189	29, 28, 26	124	20.97
47.	Howard Johnson	196	38, 25, 24	133	20.74
48.	Bill Madlock	244	26, 25, 25	112	21.89
49.	Billy Nash	222	25, 23, 22	107	23.22
50.	Whitey Kurowski	138	27, 26, 26	119	24.41
51.	Heinie Zimmerman	215	34, 27, 26	118	23.92
52.	Jimmy Dykes	244	21, 18, 18	81	17.32
53.	Larry Parrish	176	28, 18, 17	75	15.08
54.	Arlie Latham	222	25, 24, 24	102	22.10
55.	Don Money	197	26, 22, 21	95	18.55
56.	Richie Hebner	220	22, 22, 21	97	18.68
57.	Harry Steinfeldt	209	33, 24, 21	109	20.57
58.	Art Devlin	197	36, 25, 24	130	24.31
59.	Frank Malzone	135	19, 18, 18	82	15.18
60.	Mike Higgins	195	23, 22, 20	88	17.53
61.	Bill Joyce	155	28, 25, 18	105	27.78
62.	Willie Kam	201	24, 22, 21	96	19.24
63.	Clete Boyer	161	21, 18, 17	80	15.12

(continued)

Rank	Player Name	Career WS	Top 3	Top 5	Per 162
64.	Doug Rader	166	19, 19, 18	89	18.36
65.	Puddin' Head Jones	188	25, 22, 22	91	18.01
66.	Ossie Bluege	183	18, 18, 17	75	15.88
67.	Red Smith	160	26, 24, 24	116	23.21
68.	Hans Lobert	158	32, 20, 18	92	19.44
69.	Ray Boone	166	28, 22, 22	104	19.59
70.	Bill Melton	124	24, 23, 17	86	17.56
71.	Travis Fryman	188	28, 23, 19	97	20.55
72.	Ken McMullen	175	25, 24, 21	103	17.91
73.	Don Hoak	132	23, 22, 22	96	16.93
74.	Jim Ray Hart	148	29, 27, 25	125	21.31
75.	Pepper Martin	151	29, 24, 19	101	20.57
76.	Deacon White	190	21, 18, 17	82	23.78
77.	Kevin Seitzer	173	23, 22, 21	93	19.48
78.	Bill Werber	162	27, 26, 25	94	20.27
79.	Bob Bailey	190	22, 21, 21	96	15.94
80.	Jeff Cirillo	123	26, 24, 22	111	21.06
81.	Todd Zeile	179	22, 21, 19	90	17.83
82.	Bob Horner	141	21, 19 19	87	22.39
83.	Jim Tabor	97	16, 16, 16	65	15.64
84.	Pete Ward	118	27, 26, 20	95	19.65
85.	Jimmy Austin	144	17, 15, 15	67	14.76
86.	Milt Stock	187	21, 20, 20	93	18.61
87.	Ray Knight	124	20, 20, 18	84	13.44
88.	Joe Dugan	115	17, 17, 14	70	12.87
89.	Hubie Brooks	149	21, 18, 15	80	14.67
90.	Jim Davenport	117	20, 18, 11	67	12.63
91.	Cookie Lavagetto	109	23, 18, 16	85	16.93
92.	Pinky Whitney	149	21, 17, 16	79	15.68
93.	George Pinckney	157	29, 22, 22	110	21.87
94.	Cookie Lavagetto	109	23, 18, 16	85	16.93
95.	Pinky Whitney	149	21, 17, 16	79	15.68
96.	Ed Charles	108	21, 18, 16	81	17.41
97.	Steve Buechele	117	21, 16, 15	71	14.21
98.	Ezra Sutton	159	28, 22, 21	98	24.98
99.	Jerry Denny	140	19, 19, 16	77	18.33
100.	Bob Dillinger	70	17, 16, 14	65	15.06

Categories of this record are Career Win Shares, Win Shares in the player's three best seasons, Win Shares total over the player's five best consecutive seasons, and career Win Shares per 162 games played. For example, Mike Schmidt had 468 Career Win Shares, including 39, 37, and 36 in his three best seasons (1974, 1980, and 1982). He had 171 Win Shares in a five-year period, (1979–1984) and averaged 31.54 Win Shares per 162 games played over the course of his career.

SHORTSTOP

1 ◆ Honus Wagner

(1897–1917, 2792 G, 101 1732 .327)

Aside from Wagner's great artistic achievements he has additional merits that entitle him to special distinction. He has a quiet, unassuming disposition and a remarkable native modesty; is absolutely correct in his living habits; and is a model of deportment on and off the field. Therefore in all ways Wagner represents the greatest development of the model ball player. May his shadow never grow less!—*Reach Guide*, 1905

No one was ever very close to Wagner. His thoughts and feelings, save for a brief, occasional glimpse, are his own. The recollections of twenty years of brilliant deeds on the diamond must be a source of genuine satisfaction to the greathearted but secretive Pirate. But he never allows anyone to share that accumulated treasure save at long intervals and in disconnected fragments.—*Baseball Magazine,* October, 1916

With the exception of a couple of pitchers (Cy Young and Phil Niekro), Honus Wagner was the greatest *old* player in the history of baseball. An all-star team of the best players, based on what the did beginning at age 35:

C– Carlton Fisk
1B–Cap Anson
2B–Nap Lajoie
3B–Pete Rose
SS–Honus Wagner
OF–Ted Williams
OF–Willie Mays
OF–Babe Ruth
SP–Cy Young
SP–Phil Niekro
SP–Jack Quinn
SP–Warren Spahn
RP–Hoyt Wilhelm

Wagner earned 218 Win Shares after age 35—far more than anyone else, other than the pitchers.

Many people who are casual baseball fans will confuse Honus Wagner and Rogers Hornsby, based just on the facts that they were both truly great players, both middle infielders, they both played a long time ago, and their names sound a little bit alike.

A more inappropriate confusion is hard to imagine; it's kind of like confusing Ken Griffey with Bernard Gilkey. Hornsby was a great hitter, but a marginal defensive player. Wagner was among the greatest defensive players in the history of baseball. Hornsby was an arrogant, self-righteous racist who was what might be called creatively rude. He invented ways to offend people, and seemed to take pride in his ability to do so. Wagner as a player was quiet, and thought of as shy; after his career he became gregarious, genial, and widely beloved.

Short biographical sketches of Rogers Hornsby almost always claim that Hornsby was a fanatic about conditioning. The basis of this claim is that Hornsby never smoked or drank (at all), did not go to movies in the baseball season because he was afraid they would affect his eyesight, and, as a manager, tried without much success to impose these rules on his players. But Hornsby also slept 11 or 12 hours a night, ate more than he should have, put on weight in the winters, and was basically finished as a player by the age of 33. Being Hornsby, he instructed his players that they also should sleep 11 or 12 hours a night, and gave occasional impromptu lectures on the health benefits of eating lots of steak. Hornsby's rules, said Billy Herman in *Wrigleyville*, didn't really have anything to do with conditioning, they were just Hornsby's efforts to impose his own habits on everybody else. The success of this effort is reflected, perhaps unfairly, in the fact that Hornsby's wife of 32 years became an alcoholic.

Biographical sketches of Honus Wagner, on the other hand, rarely mention his conditioning, although there is abundant evidence that Wagner was a fitness fanatic. Wagner also never used tobacco, and was strongly against the use of tobacco; this was perhaps the only point on which the two men were alike. Wagner would have a beer or two after the game, but he didn't drink a lot until he was an older man. Wagner played vigorous sports all winter, loved basketball, was careful about what he ate, lifted weights (he may have been the only player of his generation who did, I don't know), and never lectured his teammates about anything.

2 ◆ Arky Vaughan
(1932–1948, 1817 G, 96 926 .318)

Doc Jorgensen, longtime trainer of the Pirates, liked to tell about the first day of spring training with the Pirates, 1933. The Pirates had an infield of Gus Suhr, Tony Piet, Pie Traynor, and Arky Vaughan. In the outfield they had the two Waners and Fred Lindstrom. On the first day of spring training, Jorgensen insisted, George Gibson addressed the troops and insisted that every job on the team was wide open . . .

Vaughan left baseball in 1943 after a clubhouse quarrel with Leo Durocher, returning in 1947 as a bit player. At the time that he left the game he was a viable 3,000-hit candidate . . . he died in a boating accident in 1952.

The selection of Vaughan as the number two shortstop in history was as much a surprise to me as it is to you. Almost any knowledgeable person, asked to name the greatest shortstop in baseball history, would name Honus Wagner. Almost no one, asked to name the second-greatest shortstop of all time, would turn immediately to Arky Vaughan. I believe, nonetheless, that Vaughan is the best answer to the question.

- Arky Vaughan's 1935 season, when he hit .385 with 19 homers and led the National League in walks with 97, was the best season ever by a major league shortstop, other than Honus Wagner.
- Vaughan's three best seasons (1934, 1935, and 1936) are better than the three best seasons of any other shortstop except Wagner. Vaughan hit .351 over the three-year period, led the National League in walks all three years, scored over a hundred runs all three years, and averaged 35

doubles, 11 triples, and 13 homers per season. Defensively, his fielding percentage was above average the first two years, dead on the league average the third season.

- The top five shortstops, rated by their three best seasons: 1. Wagner, 2. Vaughan, 3. Ripken, 4. Yount, 5. Cronin.
- Vaughan's best five-year stretch was far better than the best five consecutive seasons of any other shortstop, other than Wagner. In terms of Win Shares over a five-year period, the top five are:

    | 1. Wagner 1904–08 or 1905–09 | 237 |
    | 2. Vaughan 1933–37 or 1934–38 | 169 |
    | 3. Joe Cronin, 1929–33 | 152 |
    | 4. Hughie Jennings, 1894–1898 | 150 |
    | 5. Cal Ripken, 1982–1986 | 149 |

- Vaughn's career average of Win Shares per game played is also the highest of all time, other than Wagner. The top five in Win Shares per 162 games played:

    | 1. Wagner | 38.0 |
    | 2. Vaughan | 29.4 |
    | 3. Barry Larkin | 28.9 |
    | 4. Alex Rodriguez | 28.0 |
    | 5. Hughie Jennings | 27.1 |

So basically, Vaughan is the number two shortstop in everything I use to rate players, except the raw total; in terms of raw Win Shares, because he left the game during World War II, he ranks behind Yount and Ripken, although still ahead of Banks and Cronin.

A quiet player, Vaughan was not a fan favorite or a flashy defensive player. I do not rate Vaughan as an exceptional *defensive* shortstop, by any means. Among the top 50 shortstops, Vaughan ranks in the bottom half in terms of defensive value per inning. He is nowhere near the guys like Rizzuto, Marion, Tinker, Maranville, Honus, Belanger, and Ozzie, and is substantially below defensive players like Concepcion, Bancroft, and Herman Long. As a defensive shortstop, he ranks a little below Cronin and Ripken.

However, most of the other shortstops who could be ranked second overall weren't brilliant shortstops, either. Ripken and Cronin were good shortstops, but . . . well, they weren't Rizzuto, Marion, or Ozzie. Vaughan was a *better* shortstop than Yount, a far better shortstop than Banks. He was a little better than Appling.

How do you balance the offense against the defense? Of course, many people will think that we should put a greater weight on the defense, particularly at shortstop; I have no doubt that many people will argue that I should have rated Ozzie Smith as the number two shortstop, if not number one.

But logically, it is hard to see how the defensive differences among shortstops could be as large as the offensive differences. Vaughan played about 13,064 innings at shortstop in his career. The best defensive shortstop who played about the same number of innings was Marty Marion, who we rate as the best defensive shortstop in history, per inning played, not counting guys who had short careers. This chart compares their career defensive statistics:

	Vaughan	Marion
Estimated innings:	13,064	13,320
Putouts:	2,995	2.986
Assists:	4,780	4,829
Errors:	397	252
Double plays:	850	978
Fielding percentage (FP):	.951	.969
League norm FP:	.949	.956
Range per nine innings:	5.36	5.28

We credit Marion with an edge of about 80 runs as a defensive player. Looking at their career defensive statistics, it is hard to understand how Marion could have had an advantage much larger than that. Not to minimize 80 runs, but that's nothing compared to the offensive differences between them.

The distance between the number one shortstop (Wagner) and the number two shortstop (whoever it is) is about the same as the distance between the number two shortstop and the number 30 shortstop.

3 ◆ Cal Ripken
(1981–2000, 2873 G, 417 1627 .277)
Underrated as a defensive player, because he doesn't fit the Ozzie Smith/Luis Aparicio image of a shortstop, a little guy with quick feet who can do somersaults. Ripken had the best arm I ever saw on a shortstop. One time about 1988 or 1989 *Baseball America* did a survey of players with the best tools. They listed the Royals shortstop, Kurt Stillwell, as having the "Best Infield Arm" in the American League. I'm a Royals fan; I thought "Wow, I never realized his arm was that good." The Orioles came to town shortly after that, and I went to all three games, and focused on the shortstops' throws. It was preposterous to suggest that Stillwell threw as well as Ripken. Stillwell had a good arm, but Ripken played 5/10 feet deeper than Stillwell, and zinged the ball effortlessly to first base, every throw hitting the first baseman shoulder high. There was no comparison between them.

4 ◆ Robin Yount
(1974–1993, 2856 G, 251 1406 .285)
Robin Yount was a major league regular when he was 18 years old. We always wondered how good he would be, how much he would improve. In 1978, after Yount had been in the major leagues four years, he held out in the spring, mulling over whether he wanted to be a baseball player, or whether he really wanted to be a professional golfer.

When that happened, I wrote him off as a player who would never become a star. If he can't even figure out whether he wants to be a baseball player or a golfer, I reasoned, he's never going to be an outstanding player.

Yount was unhappy about suggestions that the Brewers would move him to the outfield. According to Dan Okrent in *Nine Innings,* "Yount didn't merely reject the suggestion; he brooded about it, resented it, and lost himself in self-doubt. Members of the front office . . . saw Yount's reaction as immature sulking."

But as soon as he returned to baseball, Yount became a better player than he had been before; his career got traction from the moment he returned. What I didn't see at the time was that Yount was in the process of *making* a commitment to baseball. Before he had his golf holiday, he was there every day, he was playing baseball every day, but on a certain level he wasn't participating; he was wondering whether this was really the sport that he *should* be playing. What looked like indecision or sulking was really the process of making a decision.

This is often true. What Watergate was about was not the *corruption* of government, as most people thought, but rather, the establishment of new and higher standards of ethical conduct. Almost all scandals, I think, result not from the invention of new evils, but from the imposition of new ethical standards. Same thing with Yount; he wasn't backing away from baseball; he was just putting the bit in his teeth, accepting new responsibilities. In the biographies of men and nations, success often arrives in a mask of failure.

5 ◆ Ernie Banks
(1953–1971, 2528 G, 512 1636 .274)
Maybe it's sacrilege, but I believe Banks was a con artist . . . No one smiles all the time naturally unless they're putting it on and putting you on.

Every day of our lives isn't a good one.—John Roseboro, *Glory Days with the Dodgers*

As a shortstop, Ernie was sure-handed, but didn't cover enough ground. I was glad to see him make the transfer to first base because he's quite a guy.—Stan Musial in *Sport Magazine,* June, 1964

The governing principle of these ratings is that

1. The player is ranked only at the position where he has the greatest value.

2. Everything the player has done in his career counts to his benefit, whether he was playing that position or another.

Ordinarily, the position where the player has the greatest value is also the position where he plays the most games. Banks is one of the few players for whom this is not true.

Suppose that we separated Ernie Banks into two players—a shortstop (1953–1961) and a first baseman (1962–1971). Where would he rank on each list?

As a first baseman, I think Banks would make the top 100, but it would be close. He would not be in the top 90. In his ten years as a first baseman Banks hit .258 with 214 home runs, 778 RBI. Banks as a first baseman, without his years as a shortstop, would be comparable to Joe Pepitone, Don Mincher, Dick Stuart, Deron Johnson—those kind of guys.

As a shortstop, shorn of his years as a first baseman, where would he rank? About where he does now; maybe a couple of spots lower, but not much. Banks was an OK first baseman, but compared to his good years, his career as a first baseman is just hang around value. My ranking system is designed so that hang around value doesn't really change where a player rates very much. . . .

Who was better: Arky Vaughan in 1935, when Arky hit .385 with 19 homers, 97 walks, or Ernie Banks in 1959, when Banks hit .304 with 45 homers, 143 RBI?

We estimate that Banks created 121 runs. The National League average in 1959 was 4.40 runs per game—thus, Banks created all the runs a team would normally score in 27.5 games.

Vaughan in 1935 created 142 runs, in a league which averaged 4.71 runs per game—thus, Vaughan created all the runs a team would normally score in 30.2 games.

Banks made 443 outs. Vaughan made 319 outs. The park effects are about the same for both players. Thus, unless we have miscalculated by a substantial amount, Vaughan's offensive season is quite a bit better than Banks'.

As a defensive player, Banks had his best season, leading National League shortstops in assists (519) and fielding percentage (.985). Vaughan, who had played brilliantly in the field in 1934, did not have a particularly good defensive season, and I do believe that Banks rates a slim edge as a defensive player, comparing just those two seasons.

However, Banks, as good as his numbers were that year, was not a brilliant shortstop, nor was Vaughan Rafael Ramirez. Banks benefited from a ground ball staff and the false normalization of fielding stats which happens on bad teams. According to *Sport Magazine* in September, 1957, Banks "can fill in at either third or short. Because he has little range at shortstop, third base is his best position . . . His arm is only fair." I rate Banks ahead of Vaughan, comparing these two seasons, by a margin of two Win Shares, 8.7 to 6.7—an advantage of about six runs for Banks.

But adding that together with the offense, Vaughan's 1935 season is significantly better. Yes, batting average is an overrated stat, but still, .385 is .385. Add in the fact that Vaughan led the league in walks, and his on-base percentage is damn near .500. With 19 homers and C+ defense at shortstop, I believe that is the best shortstop's season since Honus retired.

6 ◆ Barry Larkin
(1986–2000, 1809 G, 179 834 .300)

Larkin, now 36 years old but still playing well, is not *likely* to move up further on the short-stop list, but certainly could if he comes through with a big season . . . Larkin is one of the ten most *complete* players in baseball history. He's a .300 hitter, has power, has speed, excellent defense, and is a good percentage player. He ranks with DiMaggio, Mays, and a few others as the most well-rounded stars in baseball history . . .

Larkin is a Cincinnati native. Doesn't it seem like the Reds have had more local players who achieved local stardom than any other city? I don't know if this is true.

7 ◆ Ozzie Smith
(1978–1996, 2573 G, 28 793 .262)

How many ground balls does an outstanding shortstop make a play on, in a season, that an average shortstop would not get?

I don't know the answer to that question, and I don't think anyone does. However, here is one way to approach the problem. A shortstop in modern baseball normally records about 28% of his team's assists—actually 28.3%. This figure has been fairly stable over time; it was 26% from the 1870s through 1900, 25% in the 1900s, 24% in the 1910s, 26% in the 1920s, 27% in the 1930s, 28% in the 1940s, 28% in the 1950s, 28% in the 1960s, 29% in the 1970s, 28% in the 1980s and the 1990s.

You can establish the expected assists for a team's shortstops, then, by multiplying the team's assists total—their ground ball total, essentially—by the league percentage of assists which are recorded by the shortstops, which is a historically stable figure near 28%. The shortstops with the best range, then, should be the shortstops who exceed this figure by the widest margin.

No team in the history of baseball has ever exceeded this figure by 100 plays, and only a limited number of teams—less than 40—have exceeded this figure by even 50. The highest figures of all time were by the 1970 and 1971 St. Louis Cardinals (Dal Maxvill). The Cardinals in 1971 had 614 assists by shortstops—34.6% of the team's total, and 98 more than expected. The 1970 Cardinals had 616 assists by short-stops, 33.6% of the team's total, and 93 more than expected.

Dal Maxvill was certainly an exceptional defensive shortstop, and there may well be an argument that he deserves to be rated among the top 100 shortstops, despite his inability to contribute to the offense. However, the larger points are that:

1. As a rule, the differences between expected and actual assists by the shortstop are not huge.

2. In the cases where they are substantial, it remains unclear to what extent the skill of the shortstop alone is responsible.

It is likely that there are other factors driving up the number of assists by shortstops in the exceptional cases. The 1971 Cardinals, for example, had 563 innings pitched by left-handed pitchers, the second-highest total in the National League. More innings by left-handed pitchers mean more ground balls to shortstop and third base.

There may be other factors involved which are harder to pin down. The '71 Cardinals had an exceptionally hard-throwing staff—a rotation of Bob Gibson, Steve Carlton, plus the 22-year-old Jerry Reuss, and the 23-year-old Reggie Cleveland, all of them healthy all year. It may be that the hard-throwing pitchers were difficult to pull, leading to more ground balls to the middle of the infield, fewer to the corners. Maxvill was playing shortstop next to a converted catcher, Joe Torre, who was just learning how to play third. It may also be that there was something about the park, the pitching patterns, or the positioning favored by the St. Louis manager which tended to cause more ground balls to short.

Ozzie Smith's teams, in his career, had almost exactly 500 more assists by shortstops than expectation:

1978	SD	+46
1979	SD	+30
1980	SD	+67
1981	SD	+42
1982	StL	+82
1983	StL	+26
1984	StL	+23
1985	StL	+33
1986	StL	+ 8
1987	StL	+46
1988	StL	+45
1989	StL	+14
1990	StL	−16
1991	StL	−46
1992	StL	+22
1993	StL	+45
1994	StL	−10
1995	StL	+14
1996	StL	+33
Total		+504

Ozzie wasn't a regular the last two years, and most of the +500 is in the first five years.

I would be surprised if the teams of any other shortstop in history would have a positive assists record as strong as Ozzie's. Many of the individual seasons above are among the best I have figured . . .

The top five shortstops of all time, rated as *offensive* players, are:

1. Honus Wagner.
2. Robin Yount.
3. Arky Vaughan.
4. George Davis.
5. Cal Ripken.

This is rated by career Win Shares, which requires a long career. The top five, rated as defensive players, are:

1. Honus Wagner.
2. Ozzie Smith.
3. Bill Dahlen.
4. Rabbit Maranville.
5. Pee Wee Reese.

This includes defensive Win Shares earned at other positions, as well as shortstop; if you base the rankings only on Defensive Win Shares at shortstop, Ozzie is first.

8 ◆ Joe Cronin
(1926–1945, 2124 G, 170 1424 .301)

> Joseph Edward Cronin was born on October 12, 1906, in San Francisco, only six months after the earthquake had destroyed all the Cronin family's possessions, save for an old rocking chair. His father drove a team of horses, and his two older brothers were "teamos," too.—Ed Linn, *The Great Rivalry*

Joe Cronin was introduced to his future wife, Clark Griffith's daughter Mildred, by Joe Engel, who had purchased Cronin from Kansas City in the American Association. When he introduced the two, Engel reportedly said "Hey, Millie. I brought you a husband from Kansas City." Now *that* is a scout . . .

9 ◆ Alan Trammell
(1977–1996, 2293 G, 185 1003 .285)

Of the top ten shortstops, at least seven are easily associated with a double-play partner—Wagner with Ritchey, Yount with Molitor, Banks with Baker, Smith with Herr, Cronin with Myer, Trammell with Whitaker, and Reese with Robinson. Arky Vaughan and Barry Larkin have no easily identifiable double play partners. The second baseman who played the most games with Cal Ripken at short was actually his brother, Billy . . . Trammell, of course, is permanently linked with Lou Whitaker. I would suppose that the only other double play combination in history which is as closely joined in the public mind as Trammell and Whitaker is Tinker and Evers.

> I remember him in spring training [1978]. He came with a pair of baseball shoes that must have been four sizes too big for him, with yellow shoe-strings. [Jim] Campbell saw that and went out and bought him a new pair of shoes . . .–Ralph Houk, *Talkin' Baseball* (Phil Pepe)

10 ◆ Pee Wee Reese
(1940–1958, 2166 G, 126 885 .269)

In 1939, Tom Yawkey and two "partners," Donie Bush and a man named Frank McKinney, purchased the Louisville Colonels for $100,000. The Colonels had Pee Wee Reese on their roster, a year away from the majors, and Yawkey figured that Reese alone would be worth what he paid for the team. But Bush and McKinney, who were not Red Sox employees, decided they had no reason to let their partner have Reese for free, and voted 2-1 to sell Reese to the highest bidder. Yawkey refused to bid for his own player, and Bush and McKinney sold Reese to the Dodgers for $100,000–the same amount they had paid for the team . . .

National League shortstops deserving of the Gold Glove, 1940-1957: 1940–Marion; 1941–Reese; 1942–Reese; 1943–Eddie Miller; 1944–Marion; 1945–Buddy Kerr; 1946–Marion; 1947–Marion; 1948–Reese; 1949–Granny Hamner; 1950–Hamner; 1951–Hamner; 1952–Roy McMillan; 1953–Johnny Logan; 1954–Al Dark; 1955–McMillan; 1956–McMillan; 1957–McMillan; 1958–Chico Fernandez.

Reese was . . . how do I say this . . . the best career leadoff man among the shortstops. Of the top 100 shortstops, almost exactly one-fourth were essentially leadoff men.

Of the leadoff men, there were three who were probably better leadoff men than Reese, at least in theory. The *most* effective leadoff man in the group, actually, was Solly Hemus. Hemus, however, was not really a shortstop, and thus

was always fighting to stay in the lineup, even after he led the National League in runs scored in 1952.

Johnny Pesky was a highly effective leadoff man, more effective than Reese, but lost his best years to World War II, and had a short career. Lyn Lary was a terrific leadoff man, led the American League in stolen bases in 1936 and was a high percentage base stealer, also drew 117 walks in 1936, but he also was in and out of the lineup due to injuries and marginal defense. Ray Chapman was a quality leadoff man, but . . .

Among the shortstops who were leadoff men and who had long careers–Bartell, Crosetti, Bancroft, Rizzuto, Donie Bush, Maury Wills, Campaneris, Aparicio, Patek–Reese was the most effective leadoff man. Wills was more celebrated in the role, but as a practical matter, Pee Wee's walks led to a lot more runs than Wills' stolen bases.

11 ◆ Luke Appling
(1930–1950, 2422 G, 45 1116 .310)

The best major league shortstops by age

17	Tommy Brown
18 and 19	Robin Yount
20	Alex Rodriguez
21, 22, 23, and 24	Arky Vaughan
25	Lou Boudreau
26	Robin Yount
27	Hughie Jennings
28	Ernie Banks
29 through 35	Honus Wagner every year
36	Luke Appling
37 and 38	Honus Wagner
39 and 40	Luke Appling
41	Honus Wagner
42	Luke Appling

Wagner didn't become a full-time shortstop until he was 29; he was actually more valuable than Jennings at age 27, and more valuable than Banks at age 28, but as a utility man. Once Wagner moved to shortstop, he was better than every other shortstop in history every year, except that Appling was better than Wagner at ages 36, 39, 40, and 42.

Appling is also probably the only man in history moved back to shortstop at the age of 42. When Appling was 41 the White Sox installed Cass Michaels as their shortstop, and moved Appling to third base. Michaels didn't make it at short, however, and Appling moved back to the position in 1949. He played 141 games at short at age 42, and hit .301.

The image of Luke Appling as "Old Aches and Pains," the cheerful baseball-playing hypochondriac...that first arose in June, 1948, when Appling was 41 years old. Before a double header against the Senators on June 20, Appling complained of having a sore arm, being unable to work his arm loose. In the first game, however, Appling collected three hits and also recorded 10 assists at third base, breaking an American League record. Between games of the double header, Appling complained about pain in his legs, but he played the second game anyway, and played well again. A reporter wrote about it, another one picked it up for a magazine article, and this became Appling's dominant image.

The other thing for which Appling was most famous was his ability to hit foul balls at will, wearing down a pitcher and waiting for a walk or a pitch he could slap into the outfield.

12 ◆ Lou Boudreau
(1936–1952, 1646 G, 68 789 .295)

Among the 100 shortstops listed here, Boudreau was probably the slowest runner. In his autobiography he wrote that he was a member of a high school track team, but added that "anybody who has seen me try to beat out an infield grounder will instantly want to know what I

was doing on a track team...people are always reminding me how slow-footed I am on the dead run and they are, of course, as right as rain." *Sport Magazine* in the late 1950s said that Jim Lemon was perhaps the slowest player in the American League since Boudreau retired. Lou had arthritis in his right ankle, severely enough that the draft board rejected him during World War II.

Boudreau graduated from high school in 1935, and won a scholarship to the University of Illinois on a government grant. He was a basketball star at Illinois, a point guard. After two years at Illinois, he signed a deal with the Cleveland Indians, under which he received $1,000 to sign, $100 a month as long as he remained in school, and was to receive an additional $2,200 when he entered the Indians' system. The money, however, was not to go to Boudreau personally, but to his mother and father. Boudreau thought that this would allow him to remain an amateur. The Indians probably knew better, but it wasn't their problem.

That blew up on him, and them, becoming one of a long series of player procurement scandals that the Indians were involved with in the late 1930s.

Apart from the lack of speed, Boudreau was a good athlete; he was strong, exceptionally well coordinated, and a good jumper. His arm was just fair. What made him a star was his intelligence, his competitiveness, and his exceptional self-confidence.

Boudreau in 1948, when he was player/manager of the World Champions, had perhaps the greatest coaching staff in baseball history—Bill McKechnie, Muddy Ruel, Mel Harder, and Burt Shotton.

13 ◆ Luis Aparicio
(1956–1973, 2599 G, 83 792 .262)

Luis Aparicio Jr. was the son of a Venezuelan baseball star, the finest shortstop in Venezuela in the 1930s and 1940s, who turned down a chance to sign with the Washington Senators in 1939. Luis Sr. took his son to the ballpark every day, played catch with him, and let him start taking infield with the grownups as soon as he could throw the ball across the field. At age sixteen (1951) Aparicio began playing professionally in Venezuela, and after three years, on November 18, 1953, the elder Aparicio walked to his shortstop position with his son, handed his son the glove, embraced him, and left the field. Father and son expected that Luis Jr. would play shortstop for Maracaibo for the next twenty years, as Luis Sr. had for the previous twenty.

Red Kress, however, was coaching with the team (Maracaibo), and after watching Luis Jr. for a couple of weeks, he contacted his onetime teammate Hank Greenberg, then general manager of the Cleveland Indians, and urged him to sign Aparicio. Cy Slapnicka went to Venezuela to check him out, and quickly made a handshake agreement to sign Aparicio for $10,500.

Greenberg, however, thought that Slapnicka had gotten carried away in his enthusiasm, and balked at signing the contract. He tried to cut the bonus in half, and also to make it contingent on Aparicio passing a tryout. The Aparicios, offended, backed out of the deal. It is a tale which explains a lot about the collapse of the Cleveland Indians in the late 1950s. The White Sox, alerted to Aparicio Jr. by their incumbent Venezuelan shortstop, Chico Carrasquel, marched into the breach, and signed the Hall of Famer.

Aparicio was a brilliant shortstop, a poor leadoff man. At the time, the perception was that Aparicio was one of the best leadoff men in baseball, because he stole bases; he led the American League in stolen bases his first nine seasons in the league. But each stolen base increases expected runs scored by only .20; a caught stealing decreases expected runs by .35;

thus, Aparicio in his best base-stealing seasons (1959 through 1961) increased his runs scored by only seven. Since he rarely walked and wasn't a .300 hitter, his on-base percentage was poor, and his base stealing didn't begin to offset that. He never scored 100 runs in a season, even once, and was never among the league leaders in runs scored.

In 1966 Mark Belanger was in the Orioles camp behind Luis Aparicio. "He wouldn't talk to me at all," recalled Belanger in *Nine Sides of the Diamond* (David Falkner). "He'd say 'Get away from me, kid, get away from me.' So instead . . . I watched him all the time. I watched every move he made."

14 ◆ George Davis
(1890–1909, 2377 G, 73 1435 .297)

George Davis was born in Cohoes, New York, in 1870. He broke into baseball in Albany in 1889, and a year later was the regular center fielder for the Cleveland Spiders. He hit a respectable .264, drove in 73 runs and led the National League in Baserunner Kills (outfield assists) with 35.

In 1892 he moved to the infield, third base and a little bit of shortstop. He didn't have a particularly good year, hitting .241 (the league average was .245), but the Spiders, previously the doormats of the National League, won 93 games and finished second. At the end of that season Davis was traded to the New York Giants even up for Buck Ewing, one of the biggest stars of nineteenth century baseball.

Davis in New York was a great success. The pitching mound was moved back to 60 feet, 6 inches, and batting totals jumped all around the league. Davis hit .355 in his first season in New York, fifth in the National League, and led the team in RBI (119). The Giants, who had finished eighth in 1892, edged over .500 and into fifth place. Giant manager Monte Ward made a series of other moves, and in 1894 the Giants went 88-44, finishing two and a half games behind one of the great teams of the 19th century. Davis hit .346, second on the team, and played well in the field.

Davis and Monte Ward were close friends, a baseball father and son. In another book, *The Politics of Glory*, I commented that "for one thing, they *looked* a great deal alike. The players at that time did not wear numbers. Fans were told that they could distinguish Davis and Ward on the field because Davis had more curl in his moustache." Emphasizing the point, the book *July 2, 1903* mixed up their photos, identifying Ward as Davis and Davis as Ward.

On January 17, 1895, Andrew Freedman bought the team. Freedman, a millionaire with political connections, was a thug who skated on thin ice above an ocean of lunacy. Monte Ward quit as Giant manager as soon as he heard that Freedman was buying the team, leaving baseball to practice law. The outgoing owner appointed George Davis the new manager. Davis managed the Giants for 33 games (16-17), and then quit in disgust.

Davis asked for his release, which Freedman of course refused to grant. The prime years of George Davis' career were among the strangest seasons that any baseball club has ever endured. Freedman would negotiate salaries with the players, and then reduce the salaries by fining the players hundreds of dollars for petty or unspecified offenses. In one game Freedman, wandering on the field to abuse the umpire, found himself encircled by angry fans. He engaged in a year-and-a-half long salary battle with Hall of Fame pitcher Amos Rusie, a battle which led Rusie to sit out the 1896 season, and to retire at the age of 27.

The Giants had talent, but were never able to overcome the conditions and win the pennant. Davis posted batting averages, beginning in 1895, of .340, .320, .353, .307, .337, .319, and .309. Moving to shortstop in 1897, he led the NL with 134 RBI, and was also among the league leaders in home runs (10), slugging average (.509), and stolen bases (65).

In 1900 the National League contracted from twelve to eight teams. Andrew Freedman and the owner of the Cincinnati Reds, John T. Brush, were friends and business partners. After a winter of confusion and rumors, several Cincinnati stars and the Cincinnati manager, Buck Ewing, were transferred to the New York team. Essentially, the Cincinnati and New York teams were merged into one, as the Louisville and Pittsburgh franchises had earlier been.

Brush and Freedman, trying to stop the blood bath, fired Ewing and appointed Davis to manage the team. Davis attempted for a year and half to patch things up, but the divisions on the team never healed.

On April 26, 1900, Davis was traveling to the ballpark with two teammates. They saw smoke rising from an apartment building, and rushed to the scene. According to the *New York World* on the following day:

> George Davis, Captain of the New York ball team, with "Kid" Gleason and "Mike" Grady, of the same nine, had been among the first on the scene, and had worked like Trojans in carrying down the helpless. They saw Mrs. F. Von Lieben on the top floor of No. 304.
>
> "There's a woman up there!" Capt. Davis exclaimed. He went up the ladder like a squirrel. The heat within blistered his face, but he reached the woman and carried her down. She had nearly fainted from terror. . . .
>
> Firemen Roach, Arene, Browning and Gulick rescued Mrs. Sturges and her three daughters, cut off by flames on the fourth floor of No. 306. Bicycle Policeman Sturden rescued two girls from the third floor of No. 306. Mrs. Tibbetts and a three-year-old child were taken from the fourth floor down the front fire-escape by "Kid" Gleason and Capt. Davis.
>
> Mike Grady and Fireman Frederick Bluemmertt, of Hook and Ladder No. 23, took Mrs.

Pease in safety from the third floor. Bluemmertt's hand was badly cut by crashing glass and he was taken to the J. Hood Wright Memorial Hospital.

Interviewed about it on the scene, Davis told a reporter that "I didn't do much. I just went up the ladder the same as the rest of the boys and helped to carry down women and children. Once I thought I was going to be cut off by the flames and be prevented from reaching a child that was holding out its arms to me. But I got through to the little one and reached the ground without either of us being hurt. I didn't do half as much as Grady and Gleason. We were on our way to the Polo Grounds for preliminary practice before tackling the Bostons when we were attracted by the fire."

The American League opened in 1901, paying better salaries than the NL in an attempt to establish themselves. The Giants, who were miserable to play for, were among the teams hit hardest. Davis was offered $4,000 a year to jump to the White Sox of the new league, and accepted the offer.

Davis played well for the White Sox, hitting .298 with 33 stolen bases in 1902, but John McGraw assumed the management of the New York Giants in mid-summer. McGraw and Brush decided to bring Davis back to New York, and soon reached an agreement with Davis to return to New York in 1903. He was to be paid $6,300 per season on a two-year contract, which would apparently make him the second-highest paid player in the game, behind Lajoie.

A month later, however, the two leagues made peace, agreeing to respect one another's contracts, and to leave the players where they were. George Davis, as a part of the agreement, was ordered to remain in Chicago. Davis had received a $2,700 bonus from the Giants. The peace agreement instructed him to return the bonus, and to play for Chicago for less money than he was expecting to receive in New York.

On January 16, 1903, the New York Giants filed suit to block implementation of the peace agreement between the two leagues. Andrew Freedman, who was connected to Tammany Hall, obtained an injunction from a New York judge, ordering the National League not to implement the peace agreement. Davis was the pretext of the battle; the subtext was that Brush did not want the American League to have a franchise in the city. He hoped to use the George Davis case to get an injunction barring implementation of the peace agreement, and use the injunction (and Freedman's connections) to negotiate a deal under which the American League would stay out of New York.

Injunction was met by injunction, and Brush ultimately failed. Davis, however, still refused to take a 40% pay cut to return to Chicago. On April 4, 1903, the *New York World* reported that "George Davis, on the advice of his counsel John M. Ward, will report to the New York National League Club on April 15 when the league season opens."

National League president Harry Pulliam ordered the Giants not to put Davis in uniform. In June, Davis, Ward, and Brush decided to push the envelope, and Davis actually appeared in four games before Pulliam warned that he would rule any future games in which Davis appeared to be forfeit. Charles Comiskey sought an injunction to stop Davis from playing, and on July 15 Davis was enjoined from playing for the National League team.

Eventually Davis agreed to return to Chicago. Davis had four good years for the White Sox, 1904–1907, slipping some in 1908 and slipping badly in 1909. He was then released from his contract with the White Sox at his own request.

A Chicago paper reported that Davis "had been with Comiskey's team since 1902, and up to the 1909 season always put up a splendid game. He was at all times a clean player and his departure from the big league circles will be regretted."

Another article written at the same time described Davis as "one of the greatest and brainiest players of the present day."

For the next few years Davis moved from job to job, coaching, bowling, scouting, managing in the minors, selling automobiles. He drifted gradually out of the public view, and after 1920 he was lost to history. In the 1960s Lee Allen, creating biographic files about old baseball players for the Hall of Fame library, realized that Davis had disappeared, that no trace of him could be found after 1920. Allen conducted a highly publicized search for Davis, spending hundreds of hours writing letters, making phone calls and conducting interviews to try to find out what had become of him, and reporting periodically in *The Sporting News* about the progress of the search. He eventually learned that Davis had died in a Philadelphia hospital on October 17, 1940.

15 ◆ Jim Fregosi
(1961–1978, 1902 G, 151 706 .265)

A player who did everything well, except that he lacked the quickness of the top-flight shortstops . . . in 1964 Ernie Banks said that Fregosi was "one of the few players who might be able to hit .400 some year." He never hit .300. But he would have, if he had played in any other decade, and if he played in the 1990s, he'd hit 30 homers a year.

16 ◆ Phil Rizzuto
(1941–1956, 1661 G, 38 562 .273)

See also Vern Stephens . . . deserved the American League Gold Glove in 1941, 1942, 1946, and 1950, and did deserve the MVP Award which he won in 1950.

Phil Rizzuto went to Richmond Hill High School in Queens. He was a Dodger fan, and one morning the Dodgers announced that they were holding tryouts for young players. Rizzuto went to the tryout.

"It wasn't much of a tryout," Rizzuto told Arthur Patterson in 1941. "They'd line up about 300 of us on the left-field foul line and run us to the right-field wall. The slowest guys were dropped out. I got there in time, but nobody gave me a second look. I was the smallest man there."

He played well enough in high school to impress a visiting scout, and was asked to work out at Yankee Stadium in front of Paul Krichell, the Yankees' top scout. There were two teams of players, and Krichell organized a series of short games. Rizzuto again was the smallest player there, but Krichell recommended that the Yankees sign him, and they did, assigning him to Bassett, Virginia, to play for the Bassett Furniture Makers.

In his first year in the minors Rizzuto suffered an injury which could have ended his career. A leg injury got infected, and gangrene set in. He was in danger of losing the leg. A local doctor had to cut away a few inches of one muscle, and tied the other end to a big tendon; the surgery left 37 stitches in his leg. After a few weeks' rest the doctor told him to run as hard as he could, saying that "if it doesn't hold now, it never will." He didn't run well, but he didn't crumple in pain. The stitches held.

Rizzuto hit .340 for the Furniture Makers, scoring 53 runs in 67 games. He moved up to the Piedmont League in 1938, then to Kansas City in the American Association in 1939. With the possible exception of the 1937 Newark Bears, the 1939 Kansas City Blues were probably the best minor league team the Yankees ever had. Rizzuto hit .316 and was regarded as one of the three outstanding young shortstops in the league.

The 1939 Yankees were one of the greatest teams ever, finishing 106-45, with Crosetti at short and Joe Gordon at second. Rizzuto returned to Kansas City, where he hit .347, had 201 hits, scored 124 runs, and stole 35 bases. Teaming with Jerry Priddy, also a hot prospect at the time, Rizzuto was named the American Association MVP, and also the Minor League Player of the Year.

While Rizzuto played so brilliantly, the Yankees stumbled to a third-place finish, ending a string of World Championships. Crosetti, only 29 years old, hit .194. The Yankees announced before spring training that Rizzuto would be their shortstop in 1941.

Shortly after the Yankees went to camp, however, Rizzuto received a letter from his draft board. He was later to be given a deferment, which lasted for two years (1941–42). He made the most of them; by the time he was actually drafted, after the 1942 season, Rizzuto was recognized as one of the best shortstops in baseball.

In the years after the war Rizzuto struggled to get back to the level of his pre-war stardom. Having hit .307 in 1941, .284 in 1942, Rizzuto hit .275 or less his first four seasons back in uniform. The Yankees did not win the pennant in 1946, didn't win again in 1948; by 1948 the Yankees had won only one pennant in five years. The Dynasty seemed to be a thing of the past. Rizzuto had injured his shoulder, and was unable to throw well.

In 1949 everything started to come together. While every other Yankee regular battled injuries, Rizzuto played 153 games, glueing the Yankee defense together to take Casey's first pennant. By the end of the year sportswriters were once more arguing that Rizzuto was the best shortstop in baseball. In 1950 he was the best *player* in baseball, at any position.

Rizzuto's playing career came to an end at 4:30 PM on August 25, 1956. Rizzuto, 37 years old, had gradually relinquished the shortstop job, to no one in particular, over a period of two and a half years. In 1954, when the Yankees had

won 103 games and a clear view of Cleveland's rump, Rizzuto had hit only .195. In 1955 Rizzuto batted only 143 times, and the Yankees edged the Indians by three games. In 1956 Billy Hunter suffered an ankle injury, but Gil McDougald became the regular shortstop, sort of; McDougald, or Coleman. Sometimes it could be very hard to tell who Casey's regular was.

Many articles were written then, summarizing Rizzuto's fine career. None of them, that I have seen, suggested that he might be a Hall of Famer. Over the years, however, Rizzuto became the center of the loudest Hall of Fame dispute in the history of Cooperstown. This was finally put to rest when Rizzuto was elected to the Hall of Fame in 1994.

17 ◆ Alex Rodriguez
(1994–2000, 790 G, 189 595 .309)
The best seasons ever by a 20-year-old player:
1. Ty Cobb, 1907
2. Silver King, 1888
3. Alex Rodriguez, 1996
4. Dwight Gooden, 1985
5. Mickey Mantle, 1952
6. Bob Feller, 1939
7. Ted Williams, 1939
8. Mel Ott, 1929
9. Al Kaline, 1955
10. Noodles Hahn, 1899

Of the other nine players on the list, six went on to have Hall of Fame careers. The three who failed to do so were all pitchers—Silver King, Doc Gooden, and Noodles Hahn.

XXX ◆ Nomar Garciaparra and Derek Jeter
It is too early to rate Nomar Garciaparra and Derek Jeter; the same is true of A-Rod, of course. I have nothing to add to the constant hype that accompanies all three men, except that I will observe that it seems likely that all three men will rate among the top 20 at the

position, and that I would regard any stronger statement as speculation. We do not know whether any of these men will eventually have better seasons than they have already had.

18 ◆ Hughie Jennings
(1891–1918, 1285 G, 18 840 .311)

There are four seasons in baseball history in which a player has been hit by pitches 40 or more times in a season–Ron Hunt (1971) and three by Hughie Jennings–51, 46, and 46, from 1896 through 1898 . . . he is also, of course, the only shortstop to hit .400 (1896).

Jennings was known as "Ee-Yah" Jennings, based on something he used to yell on the sidelines, a scream of unrepressed enthusiasm and joy at a teammate's success, which was accompanied by a little jump and a vigorous pumping of both fists. Players of that generation would cheerfully buy into one-note cartoon characterizations of themselves, simplified "images" by which they seemed happy to be known. Willie Keeler, Jennings teammate and friend, signed hundreds of photographs "Hit 'em where they ain't–Wee Willie Keeler." Jennings, for thirty years, posed for hundreds of photos which showed him on the sidelines near a base, one knee in the air and his arms pumping with ever-diminishing enthusiasm for the imaginary exploits of an phantom baserunner.

Jennings made more plays per nine innings in the field than any other shortstop. In about 7,845 innings at short he had 2,390 putouts and 3,147 assists–6.16 plays per nine innings, easily the highest figure of all time. His fielding percentage was also outstanding, and the Win Shares system does rate him as the most effective shortstop of all time, inning for inning, although this could be misleading, as his career is very short.

A skinny, freckle-faced man with brilliant red hair, Jennings was the ninth of twelve children born to a coal miner in Scranton, Pennsylvania.

Most of his brothers worked in the mines, as did Jennings as a young man (like Honus, Napoleon, and countless others). From a young age he was determined that he would not spend his life in the mines; he would go anywhere, he would bear any burden, he would pay any price, but he was not going back to those coal mines. Uncertain how long baseball would sustain him, he took off-season classes at St. Bonaventure. He had two ambitions in life: to become a lawyer, and to meet the pope. He achieved both ambitions, working off-seasons with a law firm in Baltimore, and meeting the pope twice.

Hughey drank a little much, and in 1911 drove a car off a bridge, breaking three of his four limbs and cracking his skull. "Life is full of trials," said Jennings, "which is a good thing for lawyers." Jennings played for the Baltimore Orioles when they won three straight National League championships (1894–1896), managed the Detroit Tigers to three straight American League pennants (1906–1908), and coached for the New York Giants when they won four straight National League pennants (1921–1924). He had a nervous breakdown in 1925, contracted tuberculosis while in the sanitarium, and died of spinal meningitis or TB in 1928. (Burt Solomon's book about Willie Keeler, *Where They Ain't,* was helpful in writing this comment.)

19 ◆ Maury Wills
(1959–1971, 1942 G, 20 458 .281)

1. The stolen base revolution began while Maury Wills was in the minor leagues, and *did not* accelerate after Wills stole 104 bases in 1962. Wills made people aware that stolen bases were coming back into the game, and thus got credit for launching the stolen base revolution. He did not.

2. Wills stole 104 bases in 1962, and was caught stealing only 13 times. You know why?

Catchers couldn't throw. The stolen base had become so uncommon, in the years 1920–1955, that teams had relaxed their standards about catchers throwing arms. If they liked a prospect as a catcher and he didn't throw well, they'd say he threw well enough.

3. After Wills successfully converted in the minor leagues from a right-handed hitter to a switch hitter, it became common to try to convince young players who could run to switch hit. This was the worst idea in the history of coaching. It destroyed dozens of careers. U.L. Washington, as a right-handed hitter, was as good a hitter as Cal Ripken. As a left-hander, he was worse than Dal Maxvill. But they'd made him a switch hitter, and that meant that 70% of the time he was Dal Maxvill. And by the time they figured out that it was a horrible mistake, it was too late to fix it.

4. Let's face facts here: Maury Wills is a creep. He was a lousy father, a lousy teammate, a horrible husband, and probably the worst manager in the history of baseball. He's vulgar and trashy, he doesn't have the sense God give a cockroach, and he blames other people for problems that he has meticulously created for himself. He's a drug addict with an inflated opinion of his own intelligence. He had an affair with Doris Day 35 years ago, and has never stopped bragging about it.

This is all true, but it all sounds worse than it is. He was a hyper-sensitive black kid in a time when the white world thought pissing on black kids was a sport. He's got problems. A lot of us have problems. He's miserable, he's always been miserable, he'll always be miserable. There's nothing unusual about that.

Wills wrote in *On the Run* that "I had married right out of high school because I got my girlfriend pregnant. But I had never been in love with my wife. It was a marriage that produced six children, but for me no deep emotional bonds." How can you *like* somebody who would write something like that? You can't.

But is Maury Wills the only person you know who got his girlfriend pregnant, married her, stayed married for years, but never loved his wife? Of course not; he's just the only one who is tasteless enough to write about it. That's alright. You'll meet worse people than Maury Wills every day of your life. In a perverse way, I admire his honesty. This may be the only thing about him which is admirable.

20 ◆ Johnny Pesky
(1942–1954, 1270 G, 17 404 .307)

Pesky, born John Paveskovitch, loved to play hockey. As a kid in Oregon he was a first-rate hockey player, and he would have loved to play in the NHL. His baseball managers never approved of the hockey playing, for obvious reasons. One time Joe Cronin received a phone call from a friend in Portland who said he had seen a fine looking hockey player in a game in Portland.

"You know, Joe, it's a funny thing," said Cronin's friend, "but he looked a lot like your shortstop. His name wasn't Pesky, though, it was Paveskovitch."

Cronin immediately sent Pesky a telegram, reading "Pesky, Paveskovith or whatever your name is, get off the ice and stay off."

The best seasons ever by a rookie shortstop:

1. Johnny Pesky, 1942
2. Charlie Hollocher, 1918
3. Donie Bush, 1909
4. Nomar Garciaparra, 1997
5. Joe Sewell, 1921
6. Tom Tresh, 1962
7. Ron Hansen, 1960
8. Cal Ripken, 1982
9. Herman Long, 1889
10. Glenn Wright, 1924

Pesky is a gregarious, cheerful man who can tell stories about old-time baseball for hours—not the well-formed, punch line anecdotes retold a hundred times, but random, slice-of-life stories that resist efforts to move them to paper. Are athletes special people? In general, no, but occasionally, yes. Johnny Pesky at 75 was trim, youthful, optimistic, and practically exploding with energy. You rarely meet anybody like that who *isn't* an ex-athlete—and that makes athletes seem special.

21 ◆ Bill Dahlen
(1891–1911, 2443 G, 84 1233 .275)

I traded Charlie Babb and Jack Cronin to Brooklyn for Bill Dahlen. That, by the way, I consider the most successful deal I ever made. It gave me just what I wanted—a great defensive shortstop. There were mighty few better than Dahlen.—John J. McGraw, *My Thirty Years in Baseball*

Shortstop Dahlen ... was a heavy-set, moody, surly man, seemingly lazy and indifferent, who kept mostly to himself, glowering into space like a sick cat. But the seeming indifference, said McGraw years later, "made him an iceberg on the field, keeping the others cool in the tightest situation."—John Devaney, *Sport Magazine,* October, 1963

In the 1890s Dahlen was a high-living, hard-drinking player with a great fondness for horse races. Christy Mathewson in *Pitching in a Pinch* reports that Dahlen discovered that umpire Hank O'Day intensely disliked being called "Henry," and would eject a player from the game for calling him that. Dahlen took advantage of this to get expelled from games, so that he could get to the track.

When his career was threatened by his excesses he stopped drinking; in his years with the Giants, early in the McGraw era, he was a tea drinker. Out of baseball, he began to drink again, and was nearly destitute until rescued by McGraw, who gave him a job at the Polo Grounds. According to the 1924 *Reach Guide:*

Dahlen was the reverse of Brouthers. He was a cat on his feet, a sure fielder and one of the quickest thinking players of his day. He was always a step ahead of the opposition, and usually he thought too quickly even for his partners at second and third base. There never was a ball player with a keener intuition than Dahlen nor one more capable of carrying out his intuitions. But he learned his ethics of baseball and life in the wildest days of baseball. He was a "good fellow" and a spender, and he has come to the same position as those slower-thinking pals who are now with him in uniform.

The "uniform" referred to is a night watchman's. Dahlen, Brouthers, and Amos Rusie were night watchmen at the Polo Grounds.

22 ◆ Vern Stephens
(1941–1955, 1720 G, 247 1174 .286)

Speaking of drinking men ... in *The Politics of Glory* I compared and contrasted Vern Stephens and Phil Rizzuto at perhaps unconscionable length. I know that a lot of people who read the book *thought* that I was saying that Stephens was a better player and a better Hall of Fame candidate than Phil Rizzuto. Obviously I have to take responsibility for the misunderstanding, but it was never my intention to say that. I was trying to present both sides of the argument. Until I developed the Win Shares method (1997–1999), I didn't have any way of determining, to my own satisfaction, whether Rizzuto or Stephens was a better player.

Where I am now ... well, I can still see it either way. I've decided to rate Rizzuto higher. Stephens at his best was not as good as Rizzuto in 1950. Stephens has more good years, but only because Rizzuto missed three prime seasons to World War II.

Stephens and Rizzuto are similar in value, but very different in type—a speedster against a slugger, a defensive player against a hitter, a leadoff man against a cleanup hitter, a player who played in a pitcher's park against a player who plays in a hitter's park, a player who had a good break on playing time against a player who missed three of his best seasons. When you try to balance them against one another, you can't be sure that you have it right unless you can be sure that you're placing exactly the right weight on each element. Baseball stats don't support that degree of confidence.

Stephens, a straight A student in high school, never made his high school baseball team in Long Beach because he was too small. *Famous American Athletes of Today* (11th Series, 1949) says that when he was a senior in high school, he weighed less than a hundred pounds, although frankly I find this difficult to believe. Stephens took to swimming several hours a day, anyway, and had a growth spurt when he was 18, after which, playing for an American Legion post, he began to draw the interest of scouts. As a freshman at Long Beach Junior College he hit .552.

Deferred from military service because of a knee injury, Stevens during the war established himself as perhaps the best wartime position player in the American League, leading the St. Louis Browns to their only American League pennant. In March, 1946, Stephens was holding out for more money and feuding with the Browns at the time that Jorge Pasquel was attempting to raid the major leagues to upgrade the Mexican League. Stephens accepted a bonus, agreed to jump to the Mexican League, signed with Monterrey, and actually played two games in the Mexican League.

Stephens father, however, realized that his son might be making a terrible mistake. Accompanied by Jacques Fournier, a St. Louis scout, Vern Stephens Sr. headed to Monterrey. He quickly persuaded Vern Jr. to return to the states, but the Mexican authorities refused him permission to re-enter the United States, and implicitly threatened to have him arrested for jumping his contract. Stephens had to sneak across the border, wearing borrowed clothes as a makeshift disguise, to get back in the United States.

He returned the bonus he had taken from the Mexican League, made a deal with the Browns, and was allowed to re-join the team, thus avoiding the fate of Max Lanier, Mickey Owen, Sal Maglie, and others.

The Browns traded him to the Red Sox, and he drove in a huge number of runs for the Red Sox; I'm sure you all know that. He had an open stance which pulled the ball naturally to left. Fenway suited him. He faded quickly after 1950, died in 1968, and has not been treated kindly or even fairly by baseball historians; the word "carefree" is one of the more pleasant ones to which his reputation has become accustomed. He was not a superstar, but he was a well-liked player who could play shortstop because he had the best shortstop throwing arm of his generation.

23 ◆ Joe Sewell
(1920–1933, 1902 G, 49 1051 .312)

Sewell is famous, of course, as the player who never struck out, struck out 3 to 5 times a season . . . Described by Franklin Lewis as a "deep-voiced, roundish shortstop."

Sewell, like Freddie Patek and Donie Bush, was only 5-foot-6. When he was called up to Cleveland after the death of Ray Chapman, he not only had never been to a major league baseball game, he had never been to a major league city; although a graduate of the University of Alabama (as a senior he had been president of the student body), he had never been out of the Deep South. He was convinced that he was not ready to play in the major leagues, and tried to talk his way out of the assignment.

He overcame his conviction that he wasn't good enough by pretending to be Ray Chapman. Before each game, he would tell himself that he was Ray Chapman, fighting to bring honor and glory to Cleveland. In the 22 games that he played after being called up in 1920 he made 15 errors at shortstop, yet he refused to yield to self-doubt, batted .329, and launched a Hall of Fame career.

On the day that he stepped into the Cleveland lineup in 1920, Sewell was given a black bat by outfielder George Burns. He hit a triple that day, nicknamed the bat "Black Betsy," and used it (along with other bats) for the rest of his career.

24 ◆ Tony Fernandez
(1983–1999, 2082 G, 92 829 .288)

Hit .300, as a regular, in 1986, 1987, 1998, and 1999—but had an eleven-year stretch in mid-career in which he never hit higher than .287. He is currently (year 2000) playing with the Seibu Lions in Japan. This cuts the number of teams that he has never played for to three.

25 ◆ Bert Campaneris
(1964–1981, 2268 G, 79 635 .258)

The team of my youth was the Kansas City A's. The history of the Kansas City A's can be divided into three parts:

1. The Arnold Johnson years (1955–1960).

2. Charley Finley's false start (1961–1963).

3. The foundation years of the Oakland dynasty (1964–1967).

The third phase began on July 23, 1964, which was Campaneris' first major league game. Campy homered on the first pitch thrown to him, and then, later in the game, hit another home run. He wasn't a home run hitter, but it was apparent from the day he put on

a uniform that Campaneris was a good major league player, which, at the time, gave us a total of one.

I have simplified and distorted, of course . . . there was a transitional stage between parts (2) and (3) above. In the years 1961–1963 the A's were collecting young players, mostly castoffs from other teams, but including some good ones, and they seemed to be making progress. All baseball fans have a fantasy that they could go to the winter meetings, trade this guy for that guy from the other team, exchange this slugger for that pitcher and that pitcher for the other infielder, and convert their team into a champion. At the winter meetings in 1963 Charlie Finley indulged his fan's fantasy, trading his best players for a couple of bigger names, and re-set the team's clock to 100 losses. By July 4 (1964) it was apparent that that hadn't worked, and the A's were back to looking for kids.

By 1964, however, Finley was beginning to develop the system. The A's when they moved to Kansas City did not exactly have a state-of-the-art operation. They had some agreements with minor league teams, and I suppose they must have had some scouts, but 90% of the time, the players the good teams couldn't use were better than the guys coming out of the A's system, so the team was built, for the most part, out of castoffs from other organizations.

Arnold Johnson, the first owner of the Kansas City A's, did not have enough money or foresight to change that; he continued to stumble along with a farm system which, if it ever produced a ball player, did so by accident. Finley inherited that system. It took Finley several years to hire enough scouts, enough minor league coaches and managers, get enough prospects in the system, and so on, to begin producing players.

When Bert Campaneris arrived in 1964, he looked like the future. He wasn't actually the only good player on the team; we had Colavito and Gentile and Ed Charles and Wayne Causey and John Wyatt. Dick Green, who would be a spear carrier for the Oakland dynasty, actually arrived before Campaneris. Even bad teams have four or five players who are as good as some of the players on the good teams. Campy was the only guy who *mattered,* the cornerstone. There was a game in 1966 that symbolized what he meant to the organization. Nobody else in the lineup got a hit; nobody else, as I recall, even reached base, but Campy went 4-for-4, stole several bases, and scored 4 runs. The A's won the game, I think 4-2 or 4-3. There was a feeling of "hang on, Campy, we'll get you some help." Catfish Hunter came along in '65, and by '67 the farm system was growling. But by then, of course, we already knew they were leaving town . . .

The best players on the Kansas City A's, by year: 1955—Vic Power, 1956—Harry Simpson, 1957—Hector Lopez, 1958—Bob Cerv, 1959—Bud Daley, 1960—Norm Siebern, 1961—Norm Siebern, 1962—Siebern, 1963—Wayne Causey, 1964—Rocky Colavito, 1965—Bert Campaneris, 1966—Bert Campaneris, 1967—Catfish Hunter. Campaneris was also the best player on the A's in 1968 and in 1970, when they were in Oakland, and was the team's best position player in 1967. Cerv in 1958 had the best season by a KCA.

26 ◆ Dave Concepcion
(1970–1988, 2488 G, 101 950 .267)

When Concepcion first joined the Reds for spring training (1970) he was 6-foot-2 and weighed 158 pounds. He was out of the lineup with an injury for a couple of days, and Pete Rose asked what was wrong with him. Somebody said he had a pulled muscle. "He may have pulled a bone," said Rose. "But there is no way that man could pull a muscle . . ."

It was Concepcion's fluid motion in the field, his range and his strong throwing arm that first attracted [Sparky] Anderson's attention . . . Not many shortstops in the major leagues have a throwing arm as strong as that of Concepcion, claims Anderson. And none has a stronger arm. —*The Sporting News,* April 26, 1975

27 ◆ Alvin Dark
(1946–1960, 1828 G, 126 757 .289)

"The Lord taught me to love everyone," Alvin Dark once said. "I'm still working on the sportswriters . . ."

> Forty-five minutes of extra batting practice wasn't work to [Ted Williams], it was fun. I know because I was the same.—Alvin Dark, *When In Doubt, Fire the Manager*

Born in 1922 in Comanche, Oklahoma, Dark at the age of six had malaria, pneumonia, and diphtheria. Doctors thought he was a goner, but he pulled through, caught up gradually to normal size, and won an athletic scholarship to LSU in 1940. He was an outstanding football player at LSU, named to some All-American teams, but enlisted in the Marines in April, 1942. He served in China in World War II, mustered out in 1946.

The Braves at this time were negotiating with the St. Louis Cardinals to purchase Marty Marion, who the Cardinals apparently were willing to sell. Ted McGrew, the Braves top scout, talked them out of buying Marion, telling them that for less money they could sign a prospect he had seen, Alvin Dark, and that in two years Dark would be better than Marion. Although Dark was never in Marion's class as a fielder, McGrew was correct: the Braves signed him for a $50,000 bonus, and by 1948 Dark was the National League Rookie of the Year, hitting .322 in 137 games.

The Braves won the National League pennant in 1948, their first in 34 years. Dark roomed with Eddie Stanky, his double-play partner. In 1949, however, the club began to fall apart due to a deep rift between Stanky, the team's veteran leader, and Billy Southworth, the manager. Southworth thought he was being undermined; Stanky thought he was not being supported. Dark and Stanky (and their wives) had become inseparable, best buddies for life, and so that winter Dark and Stanky were traded to the Giants in exchange for Sid Gordon, Willard Marshall, and some other guys.

In Boston Dark had been a singles hitter; in the Polo Grounds he learned to hook the ball into the corner for a short home run, and began to hit about 20 homers a season. In 1951 Dark and Stanky helped the Giants to their first NL title in 13 years, Dark hitting .303 with 41 doubles, 14 homers, 114 runs scored. In 1953 Dark scored 126 runs, and in 1954 the Giants won again; Dark hit .323 in the three World Series.

Dark began to slow down in 1955; he was 33 by then, having started his career late. He bounced around a few years, had a good year with the Cardinals in 1957, and after the 1960 season was hired to manage the San Francisco Giants.

The Giants by this time were struggling. They hadn't really been in the pennant race since 1954. Dark was looked upon as managerial material because he was a college graduate, he was a smart player, he had been an officer in the Marines, he was a Giant, and he had a very good relationship with Willie Mays, the team's star.

Dark was a good, but flawed, manager; he took the Giants to 85 wins in 1961, their best season in years, and to the pennant in 1962. He was not well-liked. A Baptist, he talked a little too much about his religion, and didn't carry through sometimes the way he should have. He was regarded as sour and self-righteous by the press, and, like Eddie Stanky,

was widely suspected of being racist. But he managed in the major leagues for many years, and won a World Championship with the Oakland A's in 1974.

28 ◆ Dave Bancroft
(1915–1930, 1913 G, 32 591 .279)

Frank Graham was one of the most famous baseball writers of his time. The players always called him Frankie. He covered baseball for the *New York Sun* for many years, and wrote several outstanding books about baseball.

Frank and his wife Lillian had a daughter named Mary. When Mary was five years old Lillian needed to go to the hospital to have another baby, and she told Mary that some friends had asked if Mary could stay with them while her mom went away. According to Mary Graham, as an adult, "The friends were Dave Bancroft of the New York Giants and his wife, Edna, a very beautiful woman, and I called them Uncle Dave and Aunt Edna. Living with them was living in a child's paradise. Every evening when Uncle Dave came home (there was no night baseball then) he would have a present for me.

> There was a great day when Aunt Edna took me to the Polo Grounds. Uncle Dave came over to the field box where we were seated to say hello to us. Aunt Edna bought me a hot dog and some chewing gum. They took me up to the press box between games. I was glad to see my father but I also was glad when the second game started so I could go back and watch Uncle Dave play.
> —*Baseball Wit and Wisdom*, Frank Graham Jr. and Dick Hyman (David McKay Company, 1962. Quote has been slightly edited.)

29 ◆ Cecil Travis
(1933–1947, 1328 G, 27 657 .314)

The Washington Senators in 1937 had an infield of Joe Kuhel, Buddy Myer, Buddy Lewis, and Cecil Travis, all good players and all four left-handed hitters. Believe it or not, that is still the only regular infield in major league history in which all four players hit left-handed.

In 1941, when DiMaggio hit in 56 straight, DiMaggio was third in the league in hitting, behind Ted Williams and Cecil Travis. Travis was only 27 then, turned 28 late in the season, but that was his eighth season as a regular, and the seventh time he had hit .317 or better; his .359 season in 1941, leading the American League in hits, was easily his best season. He left for the United States Army before the 1942 season, and was not an effective player after the war. It has been written that he suffered frostbite on his feet in Europe, but Travis has reportedly denied this or denied that the frostbite had anything to do with his inability to play after the war, and said that he simply was unable to get back in playing condition after almost four years away from the game.

30 ◆ Dick Groat
(1952–1967, 1929 G, 39 707 .286)

At the 1959 winter meetings, the Pirates had worked out a deal to trade Groat to the Kansas City A's for Roger Maris. Danny Murtaugh and Pirates' General Manager Joe Brown stepped into the hallway to clear their heads before shaking hands on the deal, and decided to back out of it. Maris was traded to the Yankees the next day, the Pirates kept Groat—and both Groat and Maris won MVP Awards the following season.

> Groat is a prematurely bald man of 30 whose face is chiseled in severe, almost grim lines. He wears blue business suits and enjoys talking politics, which he approaches with strong Republican leanings.—*Sport Magazine*, May 1961.

Groat, a Pittsburgh native and a huge Pirates fan as a kid, went to Duke University on a basketball scholarship, and was one of the best basketball players in the history of that university,

which has a fairly decent basketball history. As a junior he scored 831 points, an NCAA record at the time, and he was an All-American twice in a row.

Like Danny Ainge, Groat was considered fast on a basketball court, but slow on a baseball diamond. He was a determined baseball player with some skills, however, and accepted a $25,000 bonus to sign with the Pirates. The bonus meant he had to go straight to the major leagues, and the Pirates were so terrible that he stepped right into a regular job, hitting .284 in 1952, just off the campus of Duke. He also played briefly in the NBA, and, while he played well (he won a starting job with the Detroit Pistons almost immediately, and averaged in double figures) he was also trying to finish up his degree at Duke. The Pistons, trying to hold on to him, got a plane and a pilot to fly him in to every game, but the juggling act was impossible, and then he got drafted. When he got out of the Army the Pirates insisted he quit the NBA, and he did.

Although Groat hit near .300 from the start of his major league career, he wasn't a star right away; in fact, other than hitting singles, he was pretty awful. He didn't walk, he couldn't run, and all he did was slap soft singles into right field; his only extra base hits in 95 games as a rookie were six doubles, one triple, and one homer. At shortstop he had limited range and made a lot of errors. He may have been the worst .284 hitter in the history of baseball.

Groat was respected by the Pirates—he was named team captain in 1956 by Bobby Bragan, and remained the team's captain when Murtaugh took over the team—but until 1960 he was not well respected around the league. *Sport Magazine* wrote in September, 1957 that Groat "is a step too slow to be a good shortstop. He has even less range than a veteran like Reese," and rated the .300 hitter the sixth-best shortstop in an eight-team league.

That changed in 1960, when Groat won the batting title, and the Pirates won their first pennant since 1927. Groat, who had been mentioned in MVP voting only once previously and had finished 17th then, was voted the MVP.

Groat almost won a second MVP Award, actually; he was second in the MVP voting in 1963. After the 1962 season, for some reason, the Pirates decided to trade Groat to St. Louis. The Cardinals since 1950 had gone through a long series of young shortstops. Trading for veteran leadership is a theory which rarely works, but in this case it did; the Cardinals, perennial under-achievers, were in the pennant race in 1963 for the first time in more than ten years. Groat received much of the credit for the Cardinals coming together.

31 ◆ Jay Bell
(1986–2000, 1830 G, 180 800 .269)

I was never more wrong about a young player than I was about this guy. When he came up with Cleveland in the '80s, I thought his arm would never allow him to play shortstop in the major leagues.

32 ◆ Rico Petrocelli
(1963–1976, 1553 G, 210 773 .251)

Rico made the majors because of his glove, his arm, and his ability to charge a ground ball ... Time spent away from his wife and family has always bothered Rico. He hates long road trips.
—*Baseball Digest*, September, 1969

Billy Herman managed the Red Sox in the mid-1960s, when Rico was just getting established. "The biggest problem," wrote Al Hirshberg in *What's the Matter With the Red Sox,* "was Herman's almost pathological dislike of Rico Petrocelli [who] was a shy, self-effacing kid with almost no self-confidence." Carl Yastrzemski, Petrocelli's locker mate, would tell Rico daily that he was a great shortstop and had a brilliant future ahead of him. "If Yastrzemski

stopped him from quitting baseball once," said Hirshberg, "he stopped him a dozen times."

Rico was a worrier, a worrier's worrier. He fretted constantly over his status on the team, his family, his future ... everything. Once, in the Billy Herman era, he came to the park although his wife was not feeling well. Brooding about her, he left the park in the middle of the game, without telling anyone. Herman insisted that Rico be traded immediately. Rico was eventually located at the hospital, where he had taken his wife. He was allowed to return to the Red Sox but was fined $1,000, reportedly one-ninth of his season's salary.

33 ◆ Joe Tinker
(1902–1915, 1803 G, 31 782 .262)

These are the saddest of possible words:
    Tinker to Evers to Chance.
Trio of bear Cubs and fleeter than birds,
    Tinker to Evers to Chance.
Ruthlessly pricking our gonfalon bubble,
    Making a Giant hit into a double,
Words that are weighty with nothing but trouble,
    Tinker to Evers to Chance.
    —Franklin P. Adams, 1910

Joe Tinker's life reduced to twenty points:

1. July 27, 1880, born in Muscotah, Kansas.

2. 1894, apprenticed to a paper hanger in Kansas City.

3. 1899, signed with Denver in the Western League.

4. 1902, sold to Cubs on trial basis.

5. 1906, Cubs win 116 games.

6. 1907, began feud with Johnny Evers.

7. 1908, starred in game which won the pennant.

8. 1910, Franklin P. Adams wrote famous poem.

9. 1913, managed Cincinnati.

10. 1914, jumped to Federal League.

11. 1916–1920, owner/manager of Columbus, American Association.

12. 1920, moved to Orlando, Florida.

13. 1923, wife committed suicide on Christmas Day.

14. 1923–1929, became wealthy in Florida land dealings.

15. 1929, wiped out when land speculation bubble burst.

16. 1932–1941, instructor at Joe Stripp baseball school.

17. 1937, developed diabetes.

18. 1946, selected to Hall of Fame.

19. 1948, leg amputated due to infection.

20. July 27, 1948, died on his 68th birthday.

34 ◆ Herman Long

(1889–1904, 1874 G, 91 1055 .277)

Long was known as "The Flying Dutchman" before Honus Wagner came to the majors and appropriated the nickname . . . Clark Griffith's all-time All-Star team, chosen in 1914: C–Buck Ewing, 1B–Charlie Comiskey, 2B–Eddie Collins, 3B–Jimmy Collins, SS–Herman Long (over Honus? Really, Clark?), LF–Bill Lange, CF–Tris Speaker, RF–Ty Cobb, Pitchers–Amos Rusie, Cy Young, Christy Mathewson, and Walter Johnson.

The most remarkable play I ever saw was made by Herman Long, of the Boston team, in 1892, on the Boston grounds. With a base runner on first, the batsman hit a hard ground ball to Long's left, directly over second base. He made a great effort, but seeing he could not reach the ball he threw out his left foot and caught the ball on the point of his shoe enough to bring the ball in the air, and by a great left hand catch he was able to get the ball to Joe Quinn in time to catch the base runner at second; all this was done while he was moving at the top of his speed, and the audience went wild over the phenomenal play.–Frank Selee, 1894 *Reach Guide*

35 ◆ Monte Ward

(1878–1894, 1825 G, 26 867 .275)

John Montgomery Ward lived so many lives that even his biography can hardly account for them. Reading about the New York Giants in the first decade of this century, the years of the Andrew Freedman/John T. Brush transition, it is apparent that Ward, while not officially employed by the team, is part of the brain trust running the Giants. He was John McGraw's personal attorney, he represented George Davis in Davis' fight with baseball, and it is apparent that he was meeting regularly with John T. Brush, and acting in concert with him. In every story about the New York Giants from that era, Monte Ward stands quietly in the background. Ward's biography by Bryan DiSalvatore–and I am not faulting the biographer for this, simply commenting on the scope of Ward's life–completely misses this aspect of his life.

36 ◆ Bobby Wallace

(1894–1918, 2383 G, 34 1121 .268)

A pale, angular young man with long arms and legs . . . Bobby was perhaps the best-paid player of his time and before he quit the game was reputed to be the wealthiest.–Robert Smith, *Baseball's Hall of Fame*

Wallace and Honus Wagner were born in the same town, Pittsburgh, in the same year, 1873, and just as Gehrig would play for years in the shadow of Ruth, Bobby would maintain his excellence while all eyes were on the mighty Honus.–Lee Allen and Tom Meany, *Kings of the Diamond*

37 ◆ Dick Bartell

(1927–1946, 2016 G, 79 710 .284)

Bartell was known as a pepperpot, and the fans called him Rowdy Richard. They hated him with a cold fury in Brooklyn. A snarling chatterbox, he had already spiked two of the Dodgers, Joe Judge and Lonnie Frey.–Lee Allen, *The Giants and the Dodgers*

Bartell played with the Cubs in 1939. During spring training two reporters walked by, both of them considerably overweight. "What time does the balloon go up?" Bartell wondered thoughtfully as they walked past.

According to Warren Brown in *The Chicago Cubs,* "No one had ever told Bartell that while a stout man may refer jokingly to his own poundage, nobody else must, least of all a comparative stranger . . . It is doubtful if Bartell ever suspected the coals of critical wrath that he had heaped upon his head with that ill-timed remark."

Bartell didn't drink a lot; he didn't carouse a lot. But he had a big mouth, and he took pride in not backing away from people. Although he was an outstanding player, he bounced from the Pirates to the Phillies to the Giants to the Cubs to the Tigers and back to the Giants. The second half of his career he was a player, like Albert Belle today, who was routinely booed in almost every city.

38 ◆ Rabbit Maranville
(1912–1935, 2670 G, 28 884 .258)

One of baseball's most famous clowns and eccentrics, he lived a kind of Marx Brothers life. He drank frequently, had few inhibitions if any, always had something funny to say whether it was appropriate or not, and was a notorious practical joker. Bill McKechnie, who managed Maranville in Pittsburgh, St. Louis, and Boston, was a quiet, soft-spoken, church-going man known as the Deacon, but Maranville and McKechnie were also the best of friends, and were roommates for over ten years. Many of the best-known Maranville stories concern tricks that Maranville played on the long-suffering McKechnie.

In 1922 McKechnie was sharing a room with Maranville and Chief Yellowhorse, also a drinker. Returning to his room after taking in a movie, McKechnie was surprised to find the room dark, and Maranville and Yellowhorse already in bed. He was even more surprised when he opened a closet, and about 30 pigeons burst out into the room; Maranville and Yellowhorse had spent the evening enticing the pigeons with bread crumbs. As McKechnie started to open the other closet, Maranville said suddenly, "Don't open that one, Bill. Mine are in there . . ."

There are as many Rabbit Maranville stories as Babe Ruth stories. In 1919, on a Saturday night when there was no game on Sunday (as there normally was not at that time), Dick Rudolph's wife gave a team party. Jim Thorpe and Maranville, having had a couple, began climbing through the trees sometime after midnight, swinging off branches, Thorpe yelling "I'm Tarzan" and Maranville yelling "I'm Little Tarzan." According to a witness, they were still in the trees when the Sunday morning sun came up. Years later, in a scene straight out of a hundred movies, Thorpe dangled Maranville by one arm out the 15th story of a Manhattan hotel. "We all knew Jim wasn't going to drop him," said Glenn Wright, "or at least we were pretty sure he wasn't."

Sometimes, while playing shortstop, Maranville would start to mock the basepath umpire. If the umpire swatted a gnat, Maranville would swat away an imaginary gnat. If the umpire brushed back his hair, Maranville would brush back his. He would keep this up until the crowd began to laugh, and then he would drop it for an inning or two, perhaps sneaking in a gesture now and then for the rest of the game, just to keep things lively.

When he tagged out a runner sliding into second base, Maranville would sit triumphantly on top of him for a minute, grinning from ear to ear, and perhaps patting the victim sympathetically on the rump. If he was on base and the pitcher started to let the action drag, he might launch into a pantomime, beginning with an exaggerated yawn and stretch. He

might reach out his arm and check an imaginary watch, or pretend to pull a pocket watch from his jersey. He would pretend to lean against a wall at first base, stretching out gradually until he fell flat on top of the bag.

He once waded into the pool in front of a St. Louis hotel, fully clothed, caught a gold fish with his hands and bit it in half. He once got into a fight with an umpire (which players did in those days), and was ejected. Returning to the field, he apologized profusely, and offered to treat the umpire's cut with iodine. Before the umpire realized what had happened, Maranville had painted iodine streaks all over the poor man's face.

In 1925 Maranville was hired, briefly, to manage the Cubs. He was, remarked a writer, probably the only manager in history who would run up and down the aisles of the train, throwing buckets of ice on complete strangers.

On a trip to Japan in 1931, Maranville decided to see what would happen if you soaped a bat, so he waxed Al Simmons' bat with soap. Simmons hit about 40 foul balls before somebody told what was wrong. Later, invited to watch a Japanese military review, Maranville swiped a uniform and tried to march in the parade. He was arrested, which was not a particularly uncommon event for him, apart from the nationality of the arresting authorities. "I can march in English," Maranville explained, "but I'm damned if I know how to march in Japanese."

Maranville's normal, regular way of catching a popup was the "vest pocket catch." Holding his glove open at his belly button, he would let the ball strike him in the chest and roll down his shirt into the glove. He was, in short, a piece of work. He made a mockery of the game, and he was so good that he got by with it. You and I will never see the like of him.

39 ◆ Johnny Logan
(1951–1963, 1503 G, 93 547 .268)

Like Mickey Rivers, Yogi Berra, Jerry Coleman, and Jim Wohlford, Logan was famous for his malapropisms. He once ordered, for dessert, "Pie la mode with ice cream." Accepting an award, he announced that "I will perish this trophy forever," and he once cited, as the greatest baseball player of all time, "the immoral Babe Ruth."

For several years Logan had a running feud with Johnny Temple of Cincinnati. The feud started, Logan recalled, when he was involved in an altercation at second base with Jim Greengrass, a very large man, and all of a sudden Temple, who had reached first base on the play, jumped him from behind. "I'm not stupid," Logan said, "I was fighting this 210-pounder and I see this 155-pounder wants to take me on. I switched to the little man." Temple and Logan had a terrible fight at second base—not a baseball fight, but an actual street fight, with blood spurting and loose teeth. They were broken up by police and teammates, and Logan was ejected from the game, but as he passed Temple at first he offered a few choice words, and they picked up where they had left off, winding up back near second base.

For years after that, any time Cincinnati and Milwaukee got together the two men could be counted on to have words at the very least. They exchanged blows on many occasions, sometimes in public and sometimes in private. Teammates would get involved, aiming fastballs at their heads and applying tags as enthusiastically as possible. Finally, I think in 1958, Temple pulled into second one day and said, "Johnny, I'm not afraid of you and you're not afraid of me. If this war goes on, somebody is going to get hurt bad. How about we call it off?" They shook hands at second base, and the trouble never flared again.

40 ◆ Travis Jackson
(1922–1936, 1656 G, 135 929 .291)

> Hack Wilson "was as popular in Brooklyn as any visiting ball player could be—always excepting Mel Ott and Travis Jackson, who were unbelievably popular, considering the fact that they were Giants."—*The Brooklyn Dodgers,* Frank Graham

One thing the Win Shares system allows us to do is to take a fresh look at comparable players. We might ask, for example, what postwar players were most comparable to Travis Jackson?

I could identify those using the system of similarity scores, which would look for other players who hit about .291 (Jackson's lifetime average), and who hit about 135 home runs and who had about the same on base percentage and the same slugging percentage and the same doubles total as Jackson. That way of looking at the problem is flawed, however, because the game has changed; a .291 batting average in the 1930s is very different from a .291 batting average in the 1960s. Another way to approach the problem is not to look for similar stats, but to look for players who are similar to Jackson in terms of (a) career value, (b) the percentage of value which is in offense and the percentage which is in defense, and (c) games played.

The most-similar recent players to Jackson, looked at in this way, are Jay Bell, Rico Petrocelli, and Maury Wills.

41 ◆ Art Fletcher
(1909–1922, 1533 G, 32 675 .277)

Fletcher attracted the attention of John McGraw in the spring of 1908, when he was playing for a semi-pro team in Dallas. The bush league outfit played an exhibition game against the Giants, just a training exercise for the big club, but Fletcher, from the start of the game, yelled insults at the Giants and at McGraw. According to McGraw of the Giants

(Frank Graham), when he intervened in a shouting match between Fletcher and Art Devlin, Fletcher called McGraw "The yellow-bellied manager of a yellow-bellied ball club" and told him to "run back to the coaching line, where you won't get hurt."

The Giants spiked him; he spiked them back. They gave him some big-league trash talk, and he demonstrated some refinements on it that they hadn't thought of. They told him they wanted to meet him after the game under the grandstands; he said he'd be there.

John McGraw was impressed with Fletcher's attitude, told his players to call off the battle, and started following Fletcher's career. He purchased him a year later.

42 ◆ Garry Templeton
(1976–1991, 2079 G, 70 728 .271)

His first three and a half years in the majors, Templeton was thought to be a young superstar, almost the way A-Rod and Jeter and Garciaparra are thought of today. He had 200 hits in 1977, his first full season, led the league in triples his first three seasons, and in 1979 became the first major league player to have 100 hits batting left-handed and 100 more batting right-handed; his 211 total led the league. As a shortstop he was erratic but immensely talented, with a great arm and as much range as Ozzie.

I began to get a funny feeling about Templeton when I saw him interviewed before a Game of the Week in 1978. The interviewer asked him what he was doing to improve his game, to bring about the superstar future that was envisioned for him. There was nothing to do, Templeton replied; he just had to wait for it to happen.

That was clearly the wrong answer, but I thought maybe he had flunked Cliches 101, or maybe he knows what he is supposed to say, but just doesn't like to say it. By 1980, however, signs were beginning to appear that there might be a more serious problem. Templeton began to sit out games with minor and unknown injuries. Sometimes he didn't bother to run out ground balls. The St. Louis fans started to boo him. One time, while he was being booed, Templeton made an obscene gesture to the fans, causing Whitey Herzog to grab him by the shirt and pull him forcefully back into the dugout. By the end of the 1981 season, Templeton was finished in St. Louis. That winter, he was traded to San Diego for Ozzie Smith.

To Templeton's credit, he turned himself around in San Diego; he was never a problem child after the trade. He was never a superstar, either. There is an interesting contrast in the books written by Templeton's before-and-after managers, Herzog and Dick Williams. Williams, who liked Templeton, tells a bowdlerized version of Templeton's troubles in St. Louis, in which Herzog pulls Templeton into the dugout to protect him from unruly fans. Herzog, in *You're Missin' a Great Game*, tells the straight story. Templeton helped the Padres get into a World Series in 1984, and was a regular in San Diego for almost ten years. He is one of the fifty finest shortstops ever to play the game, and perhaps does not deserve to be remembered as an unruly kid who blew off superstardom. Unfortunately, he won't get a chance to try it again.

43 ◆ Jack Glasscock
(1879–1895, 1736 G, 27 825 .290)
According to the 1893 *Reach Guide* "a number of ball players lost heavily on the Corbett-Sullivan prize fight, especially Kelly and Glasscock. It was a notable fact that five out of every six ball players were ardent believers in Sullivan's superior powers. . . ."

> Ward hastened to the Middle West to persuade players to stay behind the Brotherhood. He must have done a good job, for a newspaper survey of fifty players showed that with the exception of "Judas" Glasscock, a "spy" and "informer," the men were standing by the Brotherhood "like rocks."–Harold Seymour, *Baseball–The Early Years*

> "Pebbly Jack" Glasscock was the best fielding shortstop of the 1880s and 1890s. The infields of the day contained many pebbles, which often caused the ball to change directions. Glasscock earned his nickname by the tireless way he would pick up small stones from the diamond and toss them away.–James J. Skipper Jr., *Baseball Nicknames*

National League Gold Gloves at shortstop, 1880–1895, as I see them: 1880–Arthur Irwin, 1881–Glasscock, 1882–Glasscock, 1883–Glasscock, 1884–Davy Force, 1885–Monte Ward, 1886–Ward, 1887–Ward, 1888–Arthur Irwin, 1889–Glasscock, 1890–Bob Allen, 1891–Herman Long, 1892–Germany Smith, 1893–Germany Smith, 1894–Hughie Jennings, 1895–Ball Dahlen.

44 ◆ Larry Bowa
(1970–1985, 2247 G, 15 525 .260)
Bowa's father, who looked exactly like Larry, was an infielder in the Cardinal system in the 1940s. His career was ended by a beaning so serious that he was given the last rites.

Like Vern Stephens, Bowa never made his high school baseball team. He went out for the team every year, was cut every year. He went to a Junior College, made the team there, and played well enough that he hoped to be drafted. He wasn't. The scout who covered Northern California for the Phillies had once driven 90 miles to see Bowa play, only to watch Bowa thrown out in the first inning of both games of a double header. The Phillies sponsored a winter league team in the San Francisco area, which the scout, Eddie Bockman, coached. Bockman told Bowa he could play for the team, but if he threw any helmets or abused any umpires, he would be sent home immediately. Bowa went, played well, behaved himself, and got a $2,000 bonus to sign with the Phillies.

45 ◆ Marty Marion
(1940–1953, 1572 G, 36 624 .263)

> He is the best shortstop I've ever seen, and he is the main reason why the Cardinals are as good as they are.—Billy Southworth, *Famous American Athletes of Today* (Ninth Series)

> I never saw Wagner play, so I can truthfully say that Marion is the greatest shortstop that I have ever seen.—Connie Mack (same source)

Many or most major league third basemen are guys who were drafted as shortstops, but moved to third base in the minor leagues. Marion, like Boudreau, was the opposite. He entered pro ball as a third baseman, but the Cardinals at the time had many third base candidates, few shortstops. Burt Shotton, running the Cardinals' minor-league clearinghouse, had to ask himself which of these guys could be a shortstop if he needed to. He decided Marion was the best candidate . . .

Most of the wartime players were 4-F (ineligible to be drafted). Marion actually was never 4-F; he was in a "Limited Service" category, players who could have been drafted, but were deferred for now. He was deferred because of an injury suffered in a childhood accident. He fell off a cliff, seriously fractured his leg, and was unable to walk for several months. He healed up alright, but for some reason it worried the army doctors . . .

46 ◆ Julio Franco
(1982–1999, 1891 G, 141 981 .301)

He's not really a shortstop, but I have to list him somewhere, and he played more games at short than anywhere else. Franco is a better hitter than 24 of the 45 shortstops listed ahead of him, but was always out of position at short.

81% of his value is as a hitter—the highest percentage of any shortstop listed here.

I think Julio is a very bright guy, a fact which has escaped the notice of many people because he seems to have a chip on his shoulder. I worked his arbitration case one year, must have been about 1986. While the lawyers and I were going over his case he slouched in a corner, reading the *Wall Street Journal*. At first I thought he was just hiding behind the newspaper so he wouldn't have to participate in the process of reviewing his strengths and weaknesses, but during a break I asked him about an article I had read in the *Journal* a couple of days earlier. He had seen the article, and had an intelligent reaction to it. This is a guy to whom English is a second language.

47 ◆ Ray Chapman
(1912–1920, 1051 G, 17 364 .278)

> Chappie was a great bunter, one of the best in the business [and] he could really fly . . . I have a hunch that he froze because he had in his mind the idea of starting to bunt.—George Uhle, *Cobb Would Have Caught It*

Ray Chapman and Buck Weaver were the same age. Both came to the majors in 1912, Weaver at the start of the season, Chapman in August. Both were primarily shortstops, although Weaver moved to third in 1917. Both finished their careers in 1920, Chapman because he was killed by a pitch in early August, Weaver because he was expelled from baseball in late September.

In July, 1977, a Yale student named Richard Herrin murdered his girl friend, Bonnie Garland, when she attempted to break up with him. According to Dr. Willard Gaylin, who wrote a book about the crime, "Richard's first encounter after the killing—half naked and smeared with Bonnie's blood—was with a Catholic priest who was a stranger to him. It brought no revulsion, only sympathy and a desire to help. Father

Tartaglia, after twenty-five minutes with Richard, shed tears. Real tears for Richard." Within months the dead girl disappeared into the mists of time, mourned only by her family, while her killer became the focus of a large, well-organized support network. The central question of Dr. Gaylin's book, *The Killing of Bonnie Garland,* is "why is this?" Why do we abandon the dead so quickly, and why are we sometimes so eager to forgive the wrongdoers?

Buck Weaver never killed anything worse than a rally, but I note a related disparity in the historical treatment of Weaver and Chapman. I could show you twenty people writing "Oh, poor Buck Weaver, what a great player he would have been if he had been allowed to finish his career." Although Chapman was clearly a better player than Weaver, I rarely see the same point made about Chapman. Our interest in Ray Chapman ends with his death.

48 ◆ Roger Peckinpaugh
(1910–1927, 2012 G, 48 739 .259)

Peckinpaugh was the same age as Weaver and Chapman. Peckinpaugh grew up in Cleveland, living right across the street from his idol, Nap Lajoie. He signed with the Indians out of high school, made the Indians in 1910, and was their shortstop of the future until they purchased Chapman. As soon as they saw Chapman, they realized they didn't need Peckinpaugh, so they traded him to the Yankees.

Peckinpaugh was the starting shortstop for the American League champions in 1921 (the Yankees), 1924 (the Senators), and 1925 (the Senators). He scored 128 runs in 1921, and was named the league's MVP in 1925, granting that this was probably one of the worst MVP selections of all time. The tradition of not announcing the MVP until the World Series is over dates to Peckinpaugh's selection in 1925. Peckinpaugh, named MVP before the start of the 1925 World Series, then made a record eight errors in the series, prompting a reporter to comment that Peckinpaugh was not only the MVP of the American League, but of the National League as well. There was a feeling that announcing the MVP Award before the series had (a) put pressure on Peckinpaugh, and (b) detracted from the award.

The policy of holding off the MVP announcement until after the series was played began the next season.

Peckinpaugh was a solid player in the dead ball era, but he adapted better to the lively ball than some of his contemporaries, plus his career was extended by an odd thing, which I have never seen any comment upon. In the years 1919–1925 the ranks of the major league shortstops were thinned by an unusual series of events. Between 1919 and 1925:

1. Chapman was killed by a pitch.

2. Charlie Hollocher quit baseball unexpectedly.

3. Two shortstops, Buck Weaver and Swede Risberg, were kicked out of the game for involvement in the 1919 World Series fix.

4. Rogers Hornsby, the best young shortstop in the National League, was switched to second base for defensive reasons.

5. Larry Kopf, shortstop for the Reds in 1919, had a back injury that left him unable to play the position.

6. Chick Galloway, who looked like a brilliant young shortstop in 1922, inexplicably stopped hitting.

These were the best shortstops in baseball, falling like leaves. Combined with the natural aging of guys like Art Fletcher, Donie Bush, Jack Barry, Doc Lavan, and Everett Scott, this created a shortage of short fielders, which made long-term regulars out of some guys like Wally Gerber and Heinie Sand, who probably wouldn't have lasted more than a year or two under more normal circumstances.

Peck, incidentally, was the best shortstop I ever knew, I think. In his prime he could do everything that anyone would ask—and in addition he knew his baseball from front to back. He was smart, and one of the best points he had was an uncanny ability to size up a play.—Babe Ruth, *Babe Ruth's Own Book of Baseball* (ghosted by Ford Frick)

49 ◆ Billy Rogell
(1925–1940, 1481 G, 42 609 .267)

Rogell waited a long time to get his shot as a major league shortstop. Although he was the same age as Mark Koenig, he didn't become a regular until 1932, when Koenig was basically finished. He was one year younger than Travis Jackson, but nine years later getting his shot, and he was two years older than Red Kress, but four years later getting an opportunity to play regularly. He was with the Red Sox in 1925, but the Red Sox wanted him to become a right-handed hitter, thought that would be better in Fenway. He hit .195, and they sent him back to the minors to become a right-handed hitter.

The best account of Rogell's remarkable life and career is in Richard Bok's *Cobb Would Have Caught It.* Rogell was an orphan, raised by a sister. He dropped out of school at the age of 13, went to work trying to help his sister raise a couple of smaller brothers. By his own account, he was a loner, a man who was uncomfortable being the center of attention. He was a functionally effective player, a switch hitter who walked and didn't make mistakes, and he was as tough as a bear. He didn't have tremendous range; he wasn't exciting. He got the job done.

In the 1934 World Series, Rogell hit Dizzy Dean right between the eyes with a relay throw to first. Dean spent the night in the hospital . . . Rogell was a good friend of Eddie Cicotte, who had been a childhood hero (Rogell grew up in Chicago), and who lived in Detroit after he was expelled from the game. Rogell

used to try to get Cicotte to come to the park, said he'd introduce him to his teammates. Cicotte wouldn't go.

One time Gehringer and Rogell messed up covering second base on a hit and run play. Mickey Cochrane, managing the team from behind the plate, rushed out to second base and started to chew them out. Rogell, astonished, looked at Gehringer to see if he was going to say anything. Gehringer, of course, had nothing to say.

"Goddamn you," yelled Rogell. "Don't you come charging out here telling me how to play shortstop. You go back and do the catching, and I'll play shortstop. If I'm not good enough, you can find someone else." Cochrane went back to his own position.

After his playing career Rogell went into Detroit politics, serving on the Detroit City Council for 38 years, 1942 to 1980. He became a resource for old ballplayers in the area. If an old player needed help, Rogell would try to get him a job, or a pension, or something. See comments on Muddy Ruel and Gee Walker.

> You know, every once in a while I give a lot of thought to my oldest boy. He was a good kid. Never hurt anybody, helped everybody he could. They were on maneuvers up in Alpena. He was flying when he blacked out. Everybody's screaming at him and he finally got out of it . . . Doctors told him he had leukemia. I sure miss that boy. —Billy Rogell, *Cobb Would Have Caught It* (Richard Bak)

50 ◆ Leo Cardenas
(1960–1975, 1941 G, 118 689 .257)

Cardenas was almost six foot tall with long, thin arms, and less body fat than a reptile. He looked something like an oversized spider. He was deceptively strong, hit 20 home runs one season, over a hundred in his career, plus he could fire the ball 200 feet on target. I always had the impression that he was skating across the infield, as if he had blades hidden on the bottom of his shoes.

Pete Rose broke in as a second baseman; Cardenas was his double play partner, and his teammate for six years. In most of the books about Rose, Cardenas is literally never mentioned . . . He won only one Gold Glove (1965 NL), but I have him as deserving of four (1964 and 1966 NL, 1969 and 1970 AL).

> Georgia law forbade Cardenas and me to dress with the white players. A separate cubicle was constructed for us. [After our games] Leo would flee to his Spanish sanctuary. He remained fairly happy all summer, drawing comfort from the leisure hours he spent with countrymen. Furthermore, they fed him. I was jealous.—Curt Flood, *The Way It Is*

51 ◆ Donie Bush
(1908–1923, 1946 G, 9 436 .250)

A tiny man who cast a thousand little shadows across the history of the game. He managed four major league teams, and owned and managed other minor league teams, in the process wandering through almost every book ever written about baseball before 1950. He was Ted Williams' manager when Williams had his big season at Mineapolis in 1938.

Bush hit only .250 but led his league in walks five times, thus scoring 90 to 126 runs eight times. The teams for which Bush played had the greatest outfields in baseball history (see Bobby Veach), won the American League in Bush's rookie year (1908—Donie didn't play in the series) and 1909, his first year as a regular, but then never won again, despite 15 years of historic outfields. One key reason they didn't win, as I pointed out in the Decade in a Box, was that Bush was absolutely awful at turning the double play. I'm sure there are teams in history which have won the pennant despite being unable to turn a double play, but frankly, I've

never heard of any. If you make a list of the worst teams ever at turning the double play (see Granny Hamner for some explanation) you'll find two types of teams at the bottom of the list:

1. Donie Bush's Tiger teams, most of which went about 80-74.
2. Teams which lost 100 or more games.

I checked to see whether he had carried this weakness over to his career as a manager. He did, yes. The first team he managed, the 1923 Senators, was +30 in double plays, but they had a double play combination of Peckinpaugh and Harris, had been outstanding at turning the double play before Bush was hired, and were outstanding after he was gone. His second team, the 1927–1929 Pirates, had been +21 turning double plays in 1924, +31 in 1925, and +16 in 1926. Under Bush, although they won the pennant in 1927, they slipped to +3 in 1927 and −17 in 1928. His next team, the 1930–31 White Sox, was −16 in 1930, −21 in 1931.

Bush's career was during an era of rapidly increasing double plays. An average team when Bush broke in would turn about 85 double plays a season. By 1930, the average was over 150 per season. Bush apparently never adjusted; he continued to think about "being sure you get one," which was the prevailing idea at the beginning of his career. It cost him dearly, because in modern baseball you can't win if you can't turn two.

One time in Philadelphia Silk O'Laughlin, a colorful umpire, called Bush out on strikes. At that time the players reached the clubhouse in Philadelphia by a gate in the right field fence, just beyond the first base dugout. When Bush yelled at him O'Laughlin started wandering down the first base line, Bush trailing behind him, paying no attention to where they were headed. When they passed the dugout O'Loughlin opened the gate and said, "Keep on going, son, you're done for today."

52 ◆ Mark Belanger
(1965–1982, 2016 G, 20 389 .228)

The Orioles, to carry through on a theme, had a "positive" double play record every single season between 1957 and 1981, and were +20 in many of those seasons, perhaps most of them . . . Belanger was in the majors for 18 seasons. He played for 13 teams that won 90 or more games. Of the other five teams, two went 88-74, and another was on a 91-71 pace in a strike-shortened season.

Belanger's .228 career average is the second-lowest among shortstops listed in the top 100. But actually, considering all offense (rather than just batting average) and all shortstops who have 1,000-game careers (rather than just the top 100) there have been at least 25 short-stops who had careers of several hundred games although they were worse hitters than Belanger. The ten worst: 1. Hal Lanier, 2. Rafael Belliard, 3. Bobby Wine, 4. Tommy Thevenow, 5. Rabbit Warstler, 6. Dal Maxvill, 7. Joe De-Maestri, 8. Johnnie LeMaster, 9. Skeeter Newsome, 10. Eddie Brinkman. Lanier had the same career batting average as Belanger (.228) but was a far weaker hitter. Per 550 At Bats, Lanier drew only 20 walks, stole 2 bases, and grounded into 20 double plays; Belanger drew 55 walks, stole 16 bases, and grounded into only 8 double plays.

Belanger, a dark, rail-thin man who smoked, was a true believer in the player's union, and worked for the union after he retired. He had three books on his desk: a baseball encyclopedia, Marvin Miller's autobiography, and *Don Baylor,* by Don Baylor. He died in the late 1990s.

53 ◆ Roy McMillan
(1951–1966, 2093 G, 68 594 .243)

> This man has the best hands of anyone I've ever seen.—Stan Musial, *Sport Magazine,* June, 1964

Many people who saw McMillan play suggested that he might be the greatest defensive shortstop ever. Leo Durocher, a defensive stand-out himself, said that McMillan was the best he ever saw. Birdie Tebbetts, asked to compare McMillan to Lou Boudreau, said that "Lou was a wizard at playing the hitters, but it was position play. For sheer range, McMillan has it all over Boudreau." Billy Meyer, who had managed Rizzuto in the minor leagues, said that "I never saw a shortstop who goes into the hole the way McMillan does. Maybe Eddie Miller would do it on occasion . . . but this boy does it all the time."

In 1957 *Sport Magazine* rated McMillan as easily the best shortstop in the National League, ahead of Pee Wee Reese and Al Dark, who were slowing up, but also ahead of Johnny Logan and Dick Groat, who were not. "This great defensive player is all by himself now," said *Sport.* "He has tremendous range; going left, right and everywhere to turn base hits into double plays. He plays each ball well and gets the hop he wants."

54 ◆ Eddie Joost
(1936–1955, 1574 G, 134 601 .239)

In a game at Fenway Park in 1948, Joost lost a ground ball in his shirt. According to Nash and Zullo in *The Baseball Hall of Shame 4,* the ball apparently hit the heel of his glove, rolled up his sleeve, and lodged in the back of his jersey. At first no one could find the ball; it was as if the ball had disappeared into thin air. By the time he finally got the ball out of his shirt, the whole park was roaring with laughter.

But let me tell you what no one has ever pointed out about this play. The disappearing baseball gave Billy Goodman a career batting average of .300. Goodman, who was credited with a hit, retired 14 years later with 1,691 career hits in 5,644 at bats, a .300 average. Had Joost not lost that ball in his shirt when

Goodman was a rookie, Goodman's career average would be .29949.

Joost had a very odd career. He emerged as a purely defensive player in Cincinnati, becoming a regular in mid-season, 1940, when Billy Myers jumped the team due to personal problems. The Reds, of course, won the pennant in 1940, but late in the season Myers was back and second baseman Lonnie Frey was fighting a hamstring, so Joost switched to second, and played there all seven games of the 1940 World Series, which the Reds won. Joost hit only .216 that year, .200 in the series, but Cincinnati manager Bill McKechnie was glove-crazy; he didn't care what a guy hit, if his glove was good enough.

Joost was a regular in Cincinnati the next two seasons, 1941–42; in 1941 he tied a major league record by handling 19 plays in a game. He continued not to hit very much, and the Reds stopped winning, as McKechnie's mania for defense strayed over the line of diminishing returns; the offense was just so weak that they couldn't compete. Joost had a good glove, but after the 1942 season the Reds had a chance to include him in a trade for Eddie Miller, who had a great glove. Joost hit only .185 in Boston, and voluntarily retired after the season, taking a war-time job in a meat-packing plant.

In very early 1945 Joost got a draft notice, and took his physical. According to Joost in *We Played the Game,* "The doctor told me that since the war was about to end and I had two children, he'd give me a six-month deferment. Otherwise I'd have gone to Germany for four years as part of the occupation force." Joost played some with the Braves in 1945, but broke his wrist sliding into third base. He left the Braves and went home after that, and then, as a result of a misunderstanding, found himself suspended from the Braves and banned from baseball for jumping the team. He appealed to the commissioner's office, but the interim commissioner didn't seem to know what to do with the complain. Joost wound up back in the minor leagues in 1946, playing shortstop for Burleigh Grimes at Rochester in the International League.

Joost had gotten a bad reputation. He didn't get along with managers, and he didn't get along with management . . . there had been a steady trickle of little disagreements over the years. Burleigh Grimes, who knew Joost from the Reds system, didn't believe his reputation, and saved his career, and then, too, a funny thing had happened in 1945. Eddie Stanky, a career minor league infielder who was the same age as Joost, suddenly emerged as a star by, among other things, refusing to swing at anything an inch out of the strike zone. Joost, who had always been a disciplined hitter, now recast himself as an Eddie Stanky clone, fouling off close pitches until he forced a walk. The Philadelphia A's at this time had little farm system, and so had to depend on restocking their team out of castoffs and second chance players. Joost got the job as their shortstop in 1947. He hit only .206, with 111 hits in 151 games—but 114 walks. He also led American League shortstops in putouts (370) and in Range Factor, as he would in 1948 and 1949. The A's, who had gone 49-105 in 1946, finished over .500 with Joost and some other veterans added to the lineup.

In 1948 Joost upped his average to .250, hit 16 home runs, and drew 119 more walks, giving him a secondary average of .383, which at the time was the second-highest ever for an American League shortstop. He also established American League records for consecutive errorless games at shortstop (41) and consecutive errorless chances (226). Both records were quickly broken, but the 1948 A's continued to surprise, winning 84 games, their best season in sixteen years, and drawing 945,000 fans, a franchise record.

In 1949 Joost had his best major league season, and quite a season it was; he hit .263 with 23 homers, 81 RBI, drew 149 walks, had an on-base percentage of .429, and scored 128 runs. His secondary average, .478, was a major league record for a shortstop until 1969. The A's turned 217 double plays that season, a major league record which still stands. The A's continued to play well, winning 81 games. To this day, Joost' 1949 season remains one of the ten best seasons ever by a shortstop, not counting Honus Wagner.

The A's bubble burst in 1950, and Joost never played quite as well again, although he remained a regular until 1952, drew over 100 walks a year, and continued to hit about 20 homers and score about 100 runs per season. The A's turned over 200 double plays in 1950 (208) and 1951 (204). Only 11 teams in major league history have turned 200 double plays, and certainly no other team has done it twice in a row. The '49–51 A's did it three times in a row . . . see also Gus Zernial, LF #96.

55 ◆ Roy Smalley Jr.
(1975–1987, 1653 G, 163 694 .257)
Cal Ripken-type shortstop, like Ripken a tall, well-built man who didn't look like a shortstop, like Ripken the son of a player, like Ripken a .270-range hitter who could play short because he had an arm, and he knew how. His best seasons (1978–1979) are simply Cal Ripken seasons, although he was a switch hitter.

Roy Smalley led the American League in putouts, assists, and double plays in both 1978 and 1979, and had 572 assists in 1979, an American League record at the time (since broken by Ripken). For this reason, plus the fact that he was a productive hitter, *Total Baseball* rates Smalley as the best player in the American League in 1978, and again in 1979.

I do not agree with this evaluation; in fact, although he was a good player, I don't think he was one of the ten best players in the league

either year. The Twins at that time had a ground-ball pitching staff—Geoff Zahn, Jerry Koosman, Dave Goltz, Paul Hartzell, all of them ground-ball pitchers. *Total Baseball* seriously overrates Smalley's defense because they fail to adjust for this. The Twins very high double play totals in the late seventies are mostly attributable to runners on base and ground balls; they exceeded their expected double plays, but not by a lot.

The Gold Gloves in Smalley's best years went to Mark Belanger (1977–78) and Rick Burleson (1979). Smalley's reputation as a defensive player, never great, turned sour in the early 1980s when he (a) began having back trouble, and (b) was traded to the Yankees.

Smalley suffered from spondylitis, a congenital back problem. It had troubled him in college, but then hadn't bothered him in Minnesota. Trying to play shortstop for the Yankees, he found himself unable to twist or turn without pain. Smalley became known as an immobile shortstop.

For years, I defended Smalley's defense, trying to say that "the Roy Smalley you saw in New York wasn't the real player. In his prime, Roy Smalley was a great defensive shortstop." But based on recent research, I have to admit that while Smalley was a good shortstop, he was never as good as I used to say that he was. It is clear that the aging Mark Belanger and Rick Burleson were better.

We're going down "injury row" now . . . the next several players were as good as the players ranked 10-50 at shortstop, but had injury-shortened careers.

56 ◆ Rick Burleson
(1974–1987, 1346 G, 50 449 .273)
The five best defensive shortstops of the 1970s, alphabetically: Mark Belanger, Rick Burleson, Dave Concepcion, Dal Maxvill, Ozzie Smith. The five *worst* defensive shortstops of the 1970s, alphabetically: Alan Bannister, Larvell

Blanks, Nelson Norman, Marty Perez, Ron Washington . . .

The Red Sox released Luis Aparicio in the spring of 1974 with the idea that Mario Guerrero, obtained from the Yankees in the Sparky Lyle trade, might be their shortstop, with the rookie Burleson backing him up. Guerrero was a disappointment, and by the end of the 1974 season Burleson was the Red Sox' shortstop.

The 1975 Red Sox, of course, were led to the American League pennant by two rookie outfielders, Lynn and Rice. But the addition of Burleson in the infield, with Lynn in center, made the 1975 Red Sox probably the best defensive team the Red Sox have ever had. "I had never met a red-ass like Rick in my life," wrote Bill Lee in *The Wrong Stuff*. "Some guys didn't like to lose, but Rick got angry if the score was even tied. He was very intense and had the greatest arm of any infielder I had ever seen. The moment he reported to camp, he brought a fire to the club that we had been lacking . . . That was Freddy Lynn's golden year, but Burleson might have been our least expendable player."

"I remember in September against Cleveland," said Jim Willoughby in *Fenway* (Peter Golenbock). In one game "Rick Burleson struck out, and then he went out to his position in the infield and made an error, and he was storming around totally out of control."

Burleson hit around .290 in his best seasons, with 35–40 doubles a year and a few walks. He was one of the best hit and run men of his generation. He left the Red Sox as a free agent as soon as he was eligible to do so, and had one good year for the California Angels before he suffered a torn rotator cuff in April, 1982, essentially ending his career.

"When the Iranians were holding our embassy people captive," said Bill Lee, "instead of the Marines we should have sent Burleson and Petrocelli over there. They would have come back in forty-eight hours with the hostages, the Ayatollah, and a couple of million barrels of oil."

57 ◆ Dickie Thon
(1979–1993, 1387 G, 71 435 .264)

How many beanings are famous enough that the average baseball fan, even years after the fact, would be able to answer the question, "Who was the pitcher who hit . . . ?" Maybe only four—Chapman (by Mays), Cochrane (by Hadley), Conigliaro (by Hamilton), and Thon (by Torrez). Cubs fans all remember Andre Dawson being beaned by Eric Show, and Royals fans remember Ed Farmer breaking Al Cowens' jaw and Frank White's hand in the same game. There must be others . . . a few candidates include Ron Cey, drilled by Goose Gossage in the 1981 World Series, Kirby Puckett's being hit in the face by Dennis Martinez, Mike Schmidt being hit by Bruce Kison, Cass Michaels having his skull fractured by Marion Fricano, and Paul Blair being dropped by Ken Tatum.

Would Dickie Thon be headed for the Hall of Fame, had he not been beaned by Torrez? I think he probably would, yes, at least a 51% shot. Thon, only 25 years old, was one of the five best players in the National League in 1983. He had been real good in 1982. He didn't need to get *better* than he was to make the Hall of Fame; he just needed to stay at a comparable level for six/eight years. In view of the courage and determination that Thon showed in fighting his way back to become a pretty good player years later, it seems likely he would have done so.

58 ◆ Ron Hansen
(1958–1972, 1384 G, 106 501 .234)

Hansen, who had joined the Orioles for the last fourteen games of the 1959 season, was regarded as an acrobatic fielder, but he had yet to make his first major-league hit.—Jack Zanger, *The Brooks Robinson Story*

Ronnie Hansen, the Orioles' dazzling young shortstop, is proof positive that some of baseball's best talent-harvests these days can come from fields far removed from where the heavy bonus oats are being sown.—Jim Ellis, *Baseball Digest*, September 1960

Hansen was an odd player, a low-average power hitter who was also a brilliant defensive shortstop. He was very strong, big but agile. Early in his career, in the minors, he was often compared to Marty Marion as a defensive player, but he got much bigger than Marion, became a different hitter. I'm not sure anyone in history is truly comparable. Darryl Spencer and Woodie Held were similar hitters, but not nearly as good in the field, and Eddie Miller had one year when he hit 19 homers, but he wasn't really a match for Hansen in the power category. Eddie Joost was sort of similar.

Hansen hit .261 with 20 homers, 85 runs scored, 68 RBI in 1964, and hit .235 with 11 homers, 66 RBI in 1965—but those numbers were posted in the 1960s, and in one of the three best pitcher's parks in baseball at that time. Equivalent numbers in a historically normal context (750 runs per team per season) would be .312 with 26 homers, 32 doubles, 83 RBI, 104 runs scored (1964), and .286 with 14 homers, 30 doubles, 85 RBI (1965). He was also the best defensive shortstop in baseball, bar none, in 1963 and 1964.

Hansen's career was shortened by a ruptured disc in his back in 1966.

On the road, I roomed with Ronny, who became my best friend in baseball.—Brooks Robinson

59 ◆ Woody English

(1927–1938, 1261 G, 32 422 .286)
English in 1930 had 214 hits and 100 walks, which enabled him to score 152 runs, and set up Hack Wilson's 191-RBI season. He is one of few players to have had 200 hits and 100 walks

in the same season. He followed that up with another 200-hit season in 1931, and scored 400 runs in a three-year period, 1929–1931. He was not one of the better defensive shortstops of his time, and when he broke his thumb in 1932 he lost his shortstop job to Billy Jurges. He moved to third base, only to be forced out of that job by Stan Hack.

English was a small man but had huge hands. As a child, he was so embarrassed by his large hands that he used to sit on them to hide them. When he became an infielder the big hands were useful, and it was often written that he had the largest hands in the major leagues.

An Ohio farm boy, English broke into pro ball after he played well in a semi-pro league in 1924. He got noticed mostly because he was a fast runner. Playing for Toledo in the American Association in 1925 he didn't hit, but Casey Stengel was hired to manage that team in 1926, the start of Casey's career as a manager. Casey worked with him, and English improved his batting average almost 100 points his second season.

Joe McCarthy had managed in the league the previous season, and had been impressed with English's speed and defense. He made a note to follow English and see if he ever started to hit. When English did start to hit McCarthy went after him, and purchased English, only 19 years old, for $50,000.

The Cubs acquired Rogers Hornsby in 1929. In those days it was traditional to room the shortstop and second baseman together, so English roomed with Hornsby. English liked Hornsby, and enjoyed rooming with him.

If you can get along with Rogers Hornsby you can probably get along with anybody, and that was English. He was a likeable, upbeat person who always had something good to say about everybody. English was the Cubs' team captain in 1932, and conducted the famous clubhouse meeting at which it was decided not to pay a World Series share to Rogers Hornsby, and to pay only a one-half share to Mark Koenig. Hornsby was the Cubs' manager the first four months of the 1932 season, playing a game now and then, concentrating for the most part on alienating as many people as possible. He was fired in early August, with the Cubs in second place, and Mark Koenig was acquired in mid-August. Koenig played brilliantly at shortstop over the last six weeks, and the Cubs won the pennant.

The Cub players, led by English, voted a one-half share to Koenig, and nothing to Hornsby. This became controversial when (a) Hornsby filed a protest with Judge Landis, claiming he was entitled to a share of the money, and (b) a few sportswriters, basically trying to stir up trouble, accused the Cubs of being cheapskates for voting Koenig only a half share.

Judge Landis, forced to rule on Hornsby's claim, called Woody English to his home. English knew the Judge fairly well. Landis attended Cubs games regularly, and sat in a box near third base. English, the Cubs' third baseman, would often go over and exchange a few words with him before the game. Landis (a) ruled that how the Cubs players split up the money was the player's decision, and he had no reason to interfere, and (b) privately expressed the opinion that the Cubs had been generous to Koenig and fair to Hornsby.

A warm account of English's life and career can be found in Eugene Murdock's *Baseball Players and Their Times* (*Oral Histories of the Game, 1920–1940*). The same book is also the best source of information about Glenn Wright (below).

60 ◆ Glenn Wright

(1924–1935, 1119 G, 93 723 .294)

Wright was born and raised in a small town near Kansas City, where his father owned a hardware store. His high school didn't have a baseball team, but he went to the University of Missouri, played baseball there, and caught the attention of the Kansas City Blues, the powerhouse of the American Association. He was a member of the Blues in 1923, when they won the Junior World Series over Jack Dunn's Baltimore Orioles.

That series was the only time Wright ever batted against Lefty Grove, then of the Orioles. Grove's first pitch went behind his head. Years later, Wright asked Grove if he remembered the first pitch he had thrown to him in that series. "Sure," said Grove. "It went behind you, but I didn't mean it to."

"If I had known that," said Wright, "I'd have been even more scared."

Wright was sold that winter to the Pittsburgh Pirates. As Earl Averill would years later with more publicity, Wright demanded—and got—a portion of the sale price. As a rookie in 1924, Wright took a job away from a Hall of Fame shortstop, Rabbit Maranville; Maranville, in mid-career, moved to second to allow Wright to play short, a fact which speaks volumes about Wright's defensive ability. By my analysis, Maranville was the National League's Gold Glove shortstop in 1921, 1922, and 1923; Wright was the Gold Glove shortstop in 1924 and 1925. His arm was powerful but erratic; his range was tremendous. Fred Clarke, interviewed by *Baseball Magazine* after the 1924 World Series, said that "I consider Glenn Wright just as good a defensive player as Wagner. He isn't Wagner on the bases or at bat, but in the field he's the best shortstop in the game today." The 1924–26 Pirates may well have had the greatest defensive infield in baseball history up to that time.

The Pirates won the pennant in 1925. Wright said that his greatest thrill in baseball was standing on the field before the 1925 World Series. The whole team was awed and excited to be there, of course, and an Italian so-prano sang the Star Spangled Banner so beau-tifully it sent chills up and down his spine.

Wright drove in 100 runs four times, and batted cleanup for the Pirates when they won the pennant again in 1927. He was nicknamed "Buckshot" because he sometimes threw wildly, but Al Lopez, his teammate later on, has always insisted that Wright was the best defensive shortstop he ever saw.

In 1926 Wright was beaned by Vic Keen of the Cardinals. A fastball that he never saw hit him in the cheek, making a sound like a rifle shot. He dropped at the plate, unconscious; Keen thought that he had killed him, and it was a couple of days before anyone was sure that he hadn't.

Wright recovered and returned to the lineup in a few weeks—but Vic Keen, a religious, soft-spoken man who would not pitch on Sundays, never recovered his confidence; his career was destroyed by the event.

A series of injuries, the most serious of which was a separated shoulder, diminished Wright's playing time; he was able to work in one more outstanding season, with Brooklyn in 1930, where he was the team captain, and a participant in several of the incidents which defined the Dodgers of the 1930s, including the three-men-on-third incident and the day Boom-Boom Beck fired a baseball against the right-field wall in the Baker Bowl. He was driven out of baseball by injuries before his mid-thirties.

61 ◆ Omar Vizquel
(1989–2000, 1620 G, 41 515 .276)
Although not young, he is still improving, coming off his best major league season as I write this, his best previous season being the one before. Vizquel is a very good defensive shortstop; whether he is actually the glove magician reflected in Gold Glove voting is a

question capable of debate, and I am at best lukewarm about the media practice of anoint-ing one man the king of the shortstops, when there are other guys around (Neifi Perez, Rey Ordonez, Miguel Tejada) who I think may be just as good. Vizquel is still climbing the list; a couple of more good years will put him in the top 50.

62 ◆ Denis Menke
(1962–1974, 1598 G, 101 606 .250)
As a high school player in Bancroft, Iowa, Menke reportedly hit .550 as a shortstop, and went 34-0 as a pitcher. The Braves signed him for $125,000 in 1958, a huge bonus at the time, but couldn't figure out what to do with him . . . let's see, if we make him a pitcher we're wasting his bat; if we play him at first he may not hit enough; if we play him at second we're wasting his arm; if we play him at short he may not have the range. His range wasn't great, but they needed a shortstop, and finally settled on that.

> Menke filled in as the perfect third baseman for the Reds, handling the job through two Western Division titles and one pennant. By 1974, though, he was ready to give up baseball.—Bob Hertzel, *The Big Red Machine*

63 ◆ Freddy Parent
(1899–1911, 1327 G, 20 471 .262)
Parent was one of the best players on the Boston Red Sox from 1901 to 1904, when they won two American League pennants and the first modern World Championship (1903). Par-ent was at bat with an 0-2 count in 1904 when Jack Chesbro threw the most famous wild pitch in major league history, allowing the Red Sox to virtually clinch the pennant.

> Freddy Parent, an agile stubby chap from Bidde-ford, Maine . . . Parent was built close to the ground, [but] he had surprising dexterity in

getting over the ground, took the spikes of the toughest base runners, was a fast runner himself and a dangerous hitter in the clutch.—Fred Lieb, *The Boston Red Sox*

Parent led the American League in errors in 1904 and 1905. However, the 1905 *Reach Guide,* reviewing the fielding records of short-stops, observed that "The shortstops, of whom the American League contained a brilliant array, were headed by Conroy, of New York. But he played only 24 games at the position, and the real leader is Wallace, of St. Louis, who played that field the entire season. A re-markable fact is that Parent, reckoned the greatest of them all, should rank next to last in averages."

> There are rare men, such as Leach of Pittsburgh, Parent of the Chicago White Sox, Hofman of the Cubs, and Wagner, who can play in almost any position . . . Fred Parent, after a brilliant career as a short stop and a fair showing as a second baseman, late in his career discovered that he was a better player in the outfield than in the in-field.—Johnny Evers, *Baseball in the Big Leagues*

He stopped hitting in 1905, for reasons that I do not know—nor, apparently, did the editor of the 1906 *Reach Guide,* who was baffled that "the entire team of veterans had gone back to-gether with such comparatively young players as Parent and Ferris." Leaving the majors in 1911, Parent played for years afterward in the minors. When Babe Ruth made his first appear-ance in pro ball (April 22, 1914), Parent was his third baseman.

64 ◆ Ed McKean
(1887–1899, 1654 G, 66 1124 .302)
McKean broke into pro baseball in 1884, when a rapid expansion of organized leagues created a huge demand for new players. He played well enough to escape the subsequent shakeout, and reached the majors with Cleveland in 1887.

McKean is the weakest defensive player listed among the top 100 shortstops. As a rookie he made 105 errors, 99 at shortstop. Defensive standards were very different at that time, of course, but even so, McKean's error total is among the highest of all time. In the 1890s the Cleveland Spiders became (a) modestly success-ful, and (b) perhaps the most ill-behaved team of baseball's rowdiest decade.

McKean, who hit from .338 to .357 in the years 1894–1896, was field captain of the rowdy lot; according to William Akin in *Nineteenth Century Stars* (SABR), McKean "gained a repu-tation for aggressive base running, hustle, and 'coaching.'" McKean put on weight after the Spiders championship season in 1895, and by 1899 was reduced to a part-time player. He left baseball that season, and made an effort to enter politics. John Phillips in *The Spiders: Who Was Who,* says that McKean "lost an election by 156 votes" running as a Democrat in a Repub-lican district; however, Phillips fails to say what McKean was running for. McKean worked out with the Cleveland team in the American League in 1901, but couldn't latch on. He did play in the minors again in 1902.

65 ◆ Zoilo Versalles
(1959–1971, 1400 G, 95 471 .242)
Who is the worst player to win the MVP Award? I am not debating the merits of the selection. What I'm talking about is players who won MVP Awards and perhaps deserved them, but who did so in the middle of otherwise less than immortal careers.

The weakest players ever to win the MVP Award, it turns out, are all pitchers—pitchers who had half careers for one reason or another. The very weakest was Jim Konstanty, a minor league veteran who was selected by Eddie Sawyer to be the relief ace for the Whiz Kids in 1950, and was voted an MVP Award which he probably did not deserve. Pitchers dominate that list because they have career-ending injuries at many times the frequency of position players, and also because they're inherently unpredictable. The six most-notable pitcher MVPs in otherwise undistinguished careers are Konstanty (83 career Win Shares), Guillermo Hernandez (1984 American League MVP, 110 Win Shares), Denny McLain (114), Spud Chandler (1943 American League MVP, 127 Win Shares), Mort Cooper (1942 National League MVP, 151 Win Shares), and Bobby Shantz (1952 American League, 158 Win Shares).

Other than pitchers, however, the clear winner of this historical booby prize is Zoilo Versalles, 1965 American League MVP, 134 career Win Shares. He actually wasn't a bad MVP pick; I think Tony Oliva probably should have won the Award, but Versalles did have a hell of year. There have certainly been a lot of players who won MVP Awards with seasons nowhere near as good. My list of the ten weakest players to win an MVP Award, not including pitchers, listed by career Win Shares:

1.	Zoilo Versalles, 1965 AL	134
2.	Hank Sauer, 1952 NL	171
3.	George Bell, 1987 AL	172
4t.	Kevin Mitchell, 1989 NL	176
4t.	Marty Marion, 1945 NL	176
6.	Jackie Jensen, 1958 AL	185
7.	Al Rosen, 1953 AL	186
8.	Jeff Burroughs, 1974 AL	193
9t.	Elston Howard, 1963 AL	200
9t.	Frank McCormick, 1940 NL	200

Sauer, Bell, Mitchell, and Burroughs were power hitters and bad defensive outfielders who led their leagues in RBI, and won the award because of sportswriters infantile fascination with Runs Batted In. None of them deserved their awards, in my opinion. Rosen and Jensen were players who retired early; Howard and McCormick were very good players or even great players who didn't get to play regularly until they were almost 30.

In 1959, when he was breaking in with the Washington Senators, Versalles disappeared from training camp for three days. He had no change of clothes, he explained to manager Cookie Lavagetto. He had hocked his clothes. He borrowed the money to go redeem his clothes, and then disappeared.

What Lavagetto had not understood was that the pawn shop was in Havana.

66 ◆ Charlie Hollocher
(1918–1924, 760 G, 14 241 .304)

Hollocher, a St. Louis native, played for the Wabadas, an amateur team, where he was a teammate of Muddy Ruel. John Sheridan, the newsman who had arranged for Ruel to have a tryout with the Browns in 1915, also tried to get a workout for Hollocher, but without success. That failing, Sheridan recommended Hollocher to Keokuk of the Central Association, which signed him on Sheridan's recommendation.

The Cubs purchased Hollocher from the Pacific Coast League in the winter of 1917–18 for $3,500, a pittance. As a rookie in 1918, Hollocher was the best all-around shortstop in baseball, hitting .316, leading the National League in hits (161) and total bases (202) and stealing 26 bases. The Cubs, who hadn't played .500 ball for several seasons, won the National League pennant in a walk.

Hollocher received a draft notice just after the 1918 season, but came down with the Spanish flu before he could report. The Spanish flu was serious stuff; it killed hundreds of thousands of people worldwide. Hollocher survived, and by the time he recovered the war was over.

Back at full strength in 1920, Hollocher played well the first half of the season, hitting .319 in 80 games. On the train from St. Louis to Philadelphia on June 8, 1920, Hollocher fell ill, with what was believed to be ptomaine poisoning. According to an article by Art Ahrens in the 1986 *SABR Research Journal,* Hollocher had three hits in a game two days later, "but was weak from his sickness before the game was over." On July 15, 1920, he was reported suffering from another attack of whatever it was, apparently not ptomaine. He played a couple more games, but then left the lineup again. In August he was reported hospitalized, then he was out of the hospital, but he didn't play again.

In 1921 he played well, and in 1922 he played great, hitting .340 with 37 doubles among his 201 hits, drawing 58 walks while striking out only 5 times all season; this is still the National League record for fewest strikeouts in a season. In January, 1923, however, Hollocher was reported ill, suffering with the stomach flu. He recovered, reported to spring training, and suffered a relapse. The Cubs began to search for what was wrong with him, sending him to high-profile specialists.

He didn't get into a game in 1923 until mid-May, but when he returned he continued to hit, and field, brilliantly; his season's average for 1923 was .342. On July 26, 1923, he was absent from the lineup with an unknown ailment. On August 3 he left the team, leaving a note for the manager (Bill Killefer) reading "Dear Bill— Tried to see you at the clubhouse this afternoon but guess I missed you. Feeling pretty rotten so made up my mind to go home and take a rest and forget baseball for the rest of the year. No hard feelings, just don't feel like playing anymore. Good luck. As Ever, Holly."

The Cubs, understandably, did not pay him his salary for the balance of the season. He thought they should. He held out, missing spring training. On May 20, 1924, again according to Art Ahrens, Irving Vaughan reported in the *Chicago Tribune* that "The X-ray plates of Charlie Hollocher's stomach have definitely determined that there is nothing organically wrong with the star shortstop." Although theoretically healthy, Hollocher did not play well,

hitting .245. In late August, he left the team once more.

Hollocher was only 28. For the better part of ten years, Hollocher talked about returning to the game. He never did. He ran a tavern, worked as a night watchman, and at one time was an investigator for the Prosecuting Attorney's Office in St. Louis. In 1939 he divorced his wife, and married another woman.

On August 14, 1940, Charlie Hollocher was found shot to death on Lindbergh Avenue in a suburb of St. Louis. He had purchased a new shotgun the day before. The shotgun was found cradled in his arm, a note on the dashboard of his nearby car instructing people to notify Mrs. Ruth Hollocher. His death, incidentally, occurred only days after baseball's only in-season suicide by an active player, the death of Willard Hershberger. Hollocher's apparent suicide, reported the *Chicago Herald-American,* was no surprise to those who knew him, since Hollocher from the day the Cubs acquired him was known as "a moody, neurotic boy." We will never know whether his brilliant career was lost to hypochondria, mental illness, or some real but undiagnosable condition of the body.

67 ◆ Frankie Crosetti
(1932–1948, 1682 G, 98 649 .245)

Crosetti is the only shortstop listed here who ever hit under .200 in a season with 502 plate appearances (.190 in 1940). I believe the only players in the top 100 at any position who ever hit under .200 in a full season are Crosetti, Jim Sundberg, and Tom Tresh . . . The ten best seasons by a Yankee shortstop: 1. Derek Jeter, 1999, 2. Phil Rizzuto, 1950, 3. Derek Jeter, 1998, 4. Gil McDougald, 1957, 5. Phil Rizzuto, 1947, 6. Tom Tresh, 1962, 7. Phil Rizzuto, 1942, 8. Frank Crosetti, 1936, 9. Lyn Lary, 1931, 10. Roger Peckinpaugh, 1919. Crosetti's second-best season, 1938, just misses the list.

68 ◆ Chris Speier

(1971–1989, 2260 G, 112 720 .246)

A fine player his first two seasons, he was unable to maintain the same standard because of chronic back problems, but had almost a twenty-year career because he was a sure-handed shortstop with a quality arm.

In 1985 Chris Speier got a big hit to beat the Mets. "We should have won," said Keith Hernandez after the game. "But Gary Carter called for a fastball when everybody in the league knows that Speier can't hit a f—-ing curve ball."

69 ◆ Bill Russell

(1969–1986, 2181 G, 46 627 .263)

Russell was a minor league outfielder who converted to shortstop in 1972, after it became clear that the injuries to the Dodgers' shortstop of the future, Bobby Valentine, were so serious that he would not be able to be a major league star. Among the top 100 shortstops, I think only ten did not reach the majors as shortstops:

Ripken, Boudreau, Al Bridwell, and Kid Elberfeld reached the majors as third basemen, moved to short because of the needs of the team.

Dennis Menke had no obvious position, but was probably more of a natural third baseman, who moved to short because the Braves had Eddie Mathews at third.

Honus Wagner and Bert Campaneris were outstanding athletes who reached the majors as players who could play anywhere, and wound up at shortstop because they helped the team more there than anywhere else.

Monte Ward was a pitcher who moved to short, and George Davis and Bill Russell reached the majors as outfielders.

George Davis "reached the majors" as a 19-year-old in 1890 because a labor war had created a talent shortage.

Bill Russell, then, is really a historical one-of-a-kind, the only major league outfielder to convert to shortstop and have a solid career. His career is not likely to become the template for the next generation. He was an OK player, a fair hitter, and a fair shortstop . . . a poor man's Lou Boudreau, I suppose you could say. He hit .270 and made the plays he was supposed to make.

70 ◆ Jeff Blauser

(1987–1999, 1407 G, 122 513 .262)

Most-similar players to Jeff Blauser, by decade:

    1880s—Sam Wise
    1890s—Tommy Corcoran
    1900s—Danny Murphy
    1910s—Ivy Olson
    1920s—Travis Jackson
    1930s—Eric McNair
    1940s—Granny Hamner
    1950s—Daryl Spencer
    1960s—Dennis Menke
    1970s—Chris Speier
    1980s—Rafael Ramirez
    1990s—Jeff Blauser

71 ◆ Eddie Miller

(1936–1950, 1512 G, 97 604 .238)

> The prize shortstop of the minors last season seems to have the regular short field berth on the Bees nailed down this year. Stengel publicly proclaimed him "the best shortstop Boston has had since Bancroft."—*Who's Who in the Major Leagues,* 1939

"Leo Durocher was a good fielder and we set a double play record together in Cincinnati," Tony Cuccinello recalled in *Diamond Greats* (1988, Meckler). "But the best I ever played with was Eddie Miller. What a shortstop he was. He was one of the best fielders I ever saw in all my years in baseball. On the force at second, he would say to me, 'Where do you want the ball?' I'd tell him, and he put it right where I asked him. He was brilliant."

A shortstop of rare talents . . . Though not a formidable hitter, Miller socked a long ball on occasion. And his work at the short field made the fans gasp in admiration.—Lee Allen, *The Cincinnati Reds*

72 ◆ Don Kessinger
(1964–1979, 2078 G, 14 527 .252)

A lithe, graceful shortstop who will always be remembered for his role in the collapse of the '69 Cubs. Hitting .299 on July 4 and en route to his best major league season—he hit 38 doubles and scored 109 runs—Kessinger played every day through the summer, lost twenty pounds during the season and dropped like a stone in September, finishing the season in a 10-for-65 slump as the Cubs rolled under the wheels of history.

"Sure, it's easy to say now that we should have been rested. But if [Leo Durocher] had come to me in August and asked, 'Do you want a day off?' I would have said no. If he had come in July I would have said no, I was playing great and felt good. I don't think any of us had a clue what might happen."

Kessinger thinks Durocher should not be faulted for playing his regulars until they dropped. I don't buy it. Kessinger was going through his first pennant race; he couldn't be expected to see where they were headed. Durocher was going through maybe his 25th pennant race. Durocher should have had the foresight to see where this was headed.

73 ◆ Freddie Patek
(1968–1981, 1650 G, 41 490 .242)

Freddie Patek was the first major league player I ever interviewed. This must have been 1976. I had written a couple of articles for obscure publications which no longer exist, and I got myself together and asked the Royals' for a press pass.

The guys in the press box did their best to make me feel as if I didn't belong there—and boy, did they succeed at that; to this day, when I go into a press box I always feel like John Rocker at an ACLU convention—and the players, while naturally more polite than writers, were occupied with their assignments. "Mr. Patek," I said. "Do you have a minute?"

He had just grabbed his glove and headed out to do infield, but he grimaced. "OK," he said. "One minute." He sat and talked to me for 45 minutes.

Freddie was very short, but not accurately described as small; he had shoulders and arms. He was very fast, not exceptionally quick but quick, and his arm was no problem at short. He should have been a slap hitter, but he wasn't. In 1971 he was sixth in the American League MVP voting. After that he developed an Albie Pearson syndrome. Albie, who was even shorter than Freddie, was famous for hitting an occasional home run, which would cost him three weeks of singles. "If he could only lick that Ruthian complex," wrote Maury Allen (about Patek), "he would thrill Phil Rizzuto." Sportswriters *thought* that he was trying to hit home runs. I don't know that he was, and I don't believe in evaluating players by what you assume is in their minds, but he did, I am certain, hit more MF8s and MF7s than anybody in the history of baseball. If you threw him a belt-high fastball on the outside half of the plate, he would hit a 370-foot fly ball just to the right of the 385 sign in left center, nine times in ten. But he drew as many as 77 walks in a season, stole 50 bases a year, and was as good as anybody in the league at shortstop, except Belanger and later Burleson.

Late in his career, Patek became the first shortstop ever to hit three home runs in a game. I was so happy for him . . . all those years, all he needed was Fenway Park. Life has not been fair with Freddie since he left baseball; he has had family tragedies, tragedies of a kind which roll unfinished across the years. He is 56 now; his kindness to me was a quarter-century ago, and

I am certain he has long since forgotten it. I have not.

74 ◆ Ozzie Guillen
(1985–2000, 1993 G, 26 619 .264)

A gregarious, friendly player whose abilities escape the statistics, perhaps more so than any other player I ever saw. He lost his speed to an outfield collision with Tim Raines (April 21, 1992), which tore the ligaments in his knee, but if a relay man turned his back on Guillen for a second, Guillen would get a base out of it. I was trying to explain Brent Mayne to a friend of mine, when Mayne first came up. "He's like Ozzie," I said. My friend understood exactly; Mayne looked awful in the stats, but he would make odd plays that nobody else would make. He would figure out a play, cut in behind a runner on the bases, and steal an out. Ozzie once made the hidden-ball trick work twice in two days, against the same team. He would play so well, when the game was on the line, that I could never understand how he could look so mediocre in the end-of-season stats.

75 ◆ Kid Elberfeld
(1898–1914, 1292 G, 10 535 .271)

In 1897 Edward Barrow had Honus Wagner on his team at Paterson, New Jersey, in the Atlantic League. Barrow was trying to get major league managers to come take a look at Wagner, trying to drive up his price. George Stallings, then managing the Phillies, sent Con Lucid to take a look at him. The Phillies were looking for a shortstop, but Lucid was more impressed with Kid Elberfeld, who happened to be playing shortstop for Paterson's opposition. "Wagner big and clumsy; too awkward to play big league ball," cabled Lucid. "Recommend purchase of Elberfeld."

> The way to the clubhouse in those days was through a door in the center-field fence... When the game was over the 25-cent patrons, mostly youngsters, used to leap the fence into

the field and form a human alley at the center-field exit, where they could thump the diamond notables on the back as the heroes ambled to the showers. What a well-meant thumping Big Chief Bender used to take when he went through there! And Jiggs Donahue and Walter Johnson and Charley O'Leary and Ray Caldwell and Wid Conroy. But not Kid Elberfeld. They never touched him. Br-r-r-r! Fielder Jones and Nap Lajoie, Hughey Jennings and Connie Mack, they ran the gantlet (sic) with grins. But Elberfeld stalked through and no boy dared lay a hand on him.—John Kieran, *New York Times*, October 3, 1937.

The term "Kid" was adapted from boxing, and was used to identify a small player with a chip on his shoulder. Boxing used the term "Kid" in promotional nicknames, and in boxing it meant a small, aggressive fighter—The Cleveland Kid or Kid McCauley or whatever. Adapted to baseball it meant small and aggressive but also, since it was a boxing term, implied a willingness to fight.

> Well, this dining room in the hotel had a tile floor, made out of little square tiles. We sat there—way down at the end, as usual—for about 20 minutes and couldn't get any waiters. They wouldn't pay any attention to us at all. Remember Kid Elberfeld? ... Kid Elberfeld says, "I'll get you some waiters, fellows." Darned if he didn't take one of the plates and sail it way up in the air, and when it came down on that tile floor it smashed into a million pieces. In that quiet, refined dining room it sounded like The Charge of the Light Brigade. Sure enough, we had four or five waiters around there in no time.—Sam Crawford in *The Glory of Their Times*, Lawrence S. Ritter (Collier, 1966)

But Elberfeld was not without his softer side. Jimmy Austin in *The Glory of Their Times* says that even though he was a young player backing up Elberfeld with the 1909 Highlanders and obviously after his job, Elberfeld treated him very well. One time Elberfeld got into a serious altercation with an umpire, for which both Elberfeld and the umpire were suspended for a few days. In those days, on the trains, the regulars slept in the lower berths, which were more stable, and the backup players slept in the uppers, which jostled around. While he served his suspension, Elberfeld insisted that Austin take his lower berth.

76 ◆ Granny Hamner
(1944–1962, 1531 G, 104 708 .262)

> When he goes out there in that cocky walk, his chin out, arms swinging, you know what he's thinking—that he can lick anybody and will prove it.—Frank O'Rourke, quoted by Harry Paxton in *Sport Magazine,* June, 1964

Hamner was a fighter; he had the reputation, when a fight broke out on the field, of immediately looking for the biggest guy on the other team. There is an often-told story about him that once, while in the Army, he punched out his Captain—and got by with it.

OK, let's talk a minute about the role of the shortstop in turning a double play. We are in the habit of thinking of the second baseman as the key player in making the double play, and no doubt he is—marginally. The second baseman is marginally more important, in creating double plays, than the shortstop.

Over the course of a season, a team will have 82% as many plays in which the shortstop is the pivot man as plays in which the second baseman is the pivot man. Over the course of a season, the 6-4-3 DP is the most common. However, for each 100 double plays that go 6-4-3 (short to second to first), there will be:

83 which go 4-6-3

53 which go 5-4-3

27 which go 6-3

20 which go 1-6-3

19 which go 4-3

9 which go 3-6-3

5 which go 3-6-1

4 which go 1-4-3

4 which go 3-6

1 which goes 3-6-4

And there are other permutations, but they're rare or involve outfielders or circus elephants. This data was provided, by the way, by Dan Matern of STATS Inc. Anyway, there are 82% as many plays in which the shortstop is the pivot man as plays in which the second baseman is the pivot man. Even when the second baseman is the pivot man, it is most often the shortstop who feeds him the ball—a task which involves, if not as much skill as the pivot itself, certainly almost as much.

The role of the shortstop in making double plays, then, is a substantial part of his defensive responsibility. Who were the best shortstops ever at making this play? Who were the worst?

Raw double play totals can be misleading, for two primary reasons:

1. Some teams have more opposition runners on base than others.

2. Some teams get more ground balls than other teams.

To adjust for these things, we figured the "expected double plays" for every major league team in history . . . I say "we"; it was Jim Henzler who did the work. The expected double plays are defined as:

1. The league average of double plays per inning.

2. Times the team's number of defensive innings.

3. Multiplied by the team's estimated opponents on first base per inning.

4. Divided by the league average of the same.

5. Multiplied by the team's assists (representing ground balls) per inning.

6. Divided by the league assists average.

I would explain how we estimate opponents on first base, except the explanation would go on for several paragraphs, and it's mostly obvious if you take time to think through the problem.

We then compared each team's actual double plays to their expected double plays. Conclusion: the greatest double play combination ever, clearly, was Gordon and Rizzuto. And the best shortstop ever at turning the double play, almost beyond any dispute, was Phil Rizzuto.

This is one reason Rizzuto ranks where he does here, the 16th-best shortstop of all time. In another book I wrote at length about Phil Rizzuto. I did not know this at that time.

Some other guys who were outstanding are cited in the Decade comments, and Donie Bush was the worst ever, as is discussed in his comment.

These evaluations could have been arrived at much more simply, it turns out, by simply comparing the player's double plays to his innings in the field. Phil Rizzuto was credited with 1,217 double plays in his career, playing an estimated 13,614 innings at shortstop. That's 89 double plays per 1,000 innings, which is the highest ratio of all time. Donie Bush participated in only 35 double plays per 1,000 innings, which is the second-lowest ratio among the top 100 shortstops, ahead of a 19th-century guy (Sam Wise).

However, the DPs-to-expected DPs comparison does reveal some things which are not otherwise obvious. In terms of raw DP frequencies, Eddie Joost ranks as the sixth-best in history, turning 82 double plays per 1,000 innings. While Joost's teams were "positive" at turning the double play, his totals were also inflated by playing for teams which had ground-ball pitchers and runners on base. In 1950 the Athletics turned 208 double plays—but had 199 expected double plays. The 1949 A's, who turned an all-time record 217 double plays, were only +26 (217 to 191), and the 1951 A's were only +15 (204 to 189).

The 1973 Kansas City Royals (Patek and Rojas) turned 192 double plays, a huge total—

yet actually missed their expectation, which was 195.

The 1999 Seattle Mariners (Rodriguez and David Bell) turned 182 double plays—but had an expectation of 182.

The 1951 St. Louis Browns turned 179 double plays, which sounds like a lot—but were 23 double plays behind expectation.

The player who is most conspicuously helped by this analysis is probably Granny Hamner. *Total Baseball* rates Hamner as a terrible defensive middle infielder (negative 139 runs). This is a completely inaccurate evaluation.

Hamner played for a team, the Philadelphia Phillies of 1948–1958, whose pitchers got exceptionally few ground balls. The Philadelphia pitchers of 1948–58, led by Robin Roberts, lived on the high fastball. The team had below-average assists totals every season, were last in the league in assists in most seasons, and in fact had the lowest team assists totals of the twentieth century. *Total Baseball* makes no adjustment for this, and thus completely misses the boat on Hamner's defense.

The Phillies of the 1950s also didn't walk people, and thus didn't have a lot of opposition runners on base. Thus, the Phillies of the 1948–58 period, naturally, didn't turn a lot of double plays. Their double plays in that era, and their DP rank in the eight-team league, were:

1948	126	8th
1949	141	7th
1950	155	6th
1951	146	7th
1952	145	5th tie
1953	161	3rd tie
1954	133	8th
1955	117	8th
1956	140	7th tie
1957	117	8th
1958	136	8th

The Phillies were near the bottom of the league in double plays in almost every season. When you figure their expected double plays and compare the actual double plays to the expected, however, you get a very different picture:

Year	Actual	Expected	Difference
1948	126	134	−8
1949	141	138	+3
1950	155	149	+6
1951	146	149	−3
1952	145	138	+7
1953	161	135	+26
1954	133	134	−1
1955	117	127	−10
1956	140	132	+8
1957	117	120	−3
1958	136	141	−5

The Phillies low double play totals, like Hamner's low range factors, are 100% attributable to circumstances of the team. In fact, far from being a *poor* double play infield, it was actually a fairly good infield at turning the double play, when they had the opportunity to do so.

Hamner, who had a good arm, pitched a few innings for the Phillies in 1956–57, as his career was winding down. In 1962 he was managing in the Kansas City A's system, and he was sort of pitching. He started to pitch a little, mostly throwing a knuckle ball, just to soak up some innings and take the pressure off his young pitchers.

Well, a funny thing happened: he started to get people out. Lots of people. He started a game, threw a shutout. He started another game. In the end he pitched in 22 games, started 14 games, completed all of those, finished 10-4, and led the Eastern League in ERA.

Charley Finley was running the A's at that time, and they were desperate for pitchers. So, sure enough, Finley starts pressuring the A's to bring Hamner to the major leagues, and give him a second career as a knuckle ball pitcher.

Hamner's attitude was, "I had my career, thank you. I had a good career; I'd like to go back and manage now, if you don't mind." The A's insisted, brought him back to the majors, and he pitched a little bit, very badly, and then retired in embarrassment, over the objections of the A's management, who thought the 36-year-old Hamner was one of their best pitching prospects. Which, come to think of it, he probably was.

77 ◆ Tony Kubek
(1957–1965, 1092 G, 57 373 .266)

Kubek's father, also named Tony, played shortstop for Milwaukee (American Association) in the 1930s. He was much shorter than Tony (5′9″; Tony-2 was 6′3″), but his career is somewhat similar in shape. He started extremely well, hitting .357 in 101 games in 1931, when he was only 19 years old. He didn't develop from there. I think he had a major injury in the mid-thirties . . . anyway, he started to miss playing time, and didn't make the majors.

This Tony Kubek's career was basically ended by an injury suffered while playing touch football in the Army shortly after the 1961 season. He broke a bone in his neck, didn't get treatment, and it didn't heal right.

Would Kubek have been a Hall of Famer, without the injury? Probably not; he would have had perhaps a 40% shot at it. He would have had to show significant development from the point where he was. Among the 100 shortstops here, he ranks as the 17th best, based on what he accomplished up to age 24 (1961). He was comparable, up to that point, to Boudreau, Sewell, or Pee Wee Reese, who did develop into Hall of Famers, but also to Fregosi, Red Kress, and Mark Koenig, who didn't.

I was raised in Milwaukee, and there were times when I pulled a red wagon through Kosciusko Park to pick up some food because we were on welfare. My father had a fourth-grade education, and he was like a lot of guys in the 1930s, a hard worker who was willing to take about any job so he could support his family. The problem was finding a job—there weren't that many.—Tony Kubek in *Sixty-One,* Tony Kubek and Terry Pluto

78 ◆ Buck Weaver
(1912–1920, 1254 G, 21 421 .272)

Eddie Collins, Weaver's teammate in 1919, never bought the idea that Weaver was an innocent victim of the fix. "I was on first base," Collins told Joe Williams in 1943. "I gave Weaver the hit-and-run sign. He ignored it and I was out a yard at second. Coming back to the bench I said to him, 'You took that sign and did nothing about it. Were you asleep?' Weaver snapped back: 'Quit trying to alibi and play ball.'"

A study of the game accounts shows that this incident occurred in the top of the first inning of the first game—before Eddie Cicotte hit the first Cincinnati batter with the pitch, signaling to them that the fix was in.

Collins also recalled another game, in 1920, in which Dickie Kerr fielded a bunt and threw to third for a force out. Weaver juggled the ball until the runner was safe. Back in the dugout when the inning was over, Kerr screamed at Weaver "If you fellows are throwing this one let me in on it." . . .

79 ◆ Greg Gagne
(1983–1997, 1798 G, 111 604 .254)

I said in the Jay Bell comment that I was never more wrong about a player than I was about Bell. Well, maybe Gagne . . . when the Royals signed Gagne in 1993 I groaned; I thought he was a bad hitter, and nothing special as a shortstop. He was a bad hitter, but not all that bad, and he was by far the best defensive

shortstop the Royals ever had. The Royals, who had finished sixth in a seven-team division in '90, '91, and '92, were well over .500 the next two seasons, and finished second, second, and third in Gagne's three years with the team. I remember saying to a friend early in the '93 season that "watching this guy play shortstop, I understand now how the Twins were able to get into the World Series in '87 and '91." He had wonderful positioning at shortstop, sure hands, excellent arm with a slingshot motion, and the best judgment I ever saw in a shortstop. If he thought he could make a play at second, he'd make the play at second, and he just never seemed to misjudge those kind of things. He was aggressive without making mistakes.

80 ◆ Lyn Lary
(1929–1940, 1302 G, 38 526 .269)

Lyn Lary was purchased by the Yankees along with Jimmy Reese, the guy who coached in the majors until he was 90-something; Reese and Lary had been a double-play combination with the Oakland Oaks for two or three years, and were purchased by the Yankees, as a unit, for a reported $100,000. Lary became the Yankee shortstop in 1929, when Mark Koenig had a sinus infection which interfered with his vision to such an extent that he really couldn't play anymore.

Lary hit .309 as a rookie, scored 93 runs in 117 games in 1930, and in 1931 scored 100 runs and drove in 107, making him one of comparatively few shortstops to drive in and score 100 runs, and probably the only shortstop to drive in and score 100 runs and lose his job. That Yankee team, Joe McCarthy's first Yankee team, could score runs almost at will; they were a better hitting team than either the '27 Yankees or the '36 Yankees, but their pitching and defense were really awful. Lary wasn't a terrible shortstop, but he had a minor injury early in the '32 season, and a rookie, Frankie Crosetti, stepped into the breach. Crosetti was a lot better shortstop, plus the Yankees got red hot while Crosetti was in the lineup; Lary couldn't get his job back.

Lary bounced around the league after that. He played one season for the Red Sox, but didn't play well, and the Red Sox traded him, with a huge stack of cash, for Joe Cronin. He played for the Senators for two months, hitting .194, but got his legs under him when he joined the St. Louis Browns in June, 1935. In 1936 he drew 117 walks, scored 117 runs, and led the American League in stolen bases. The American League at that time had a kind of a caste system; if you failed with one of the good teams, you'd wind up with one of the bad teams; if you played well with a bad team, you'd move up to a better team. In 1937, playing for Cleveland, Lary scored 110 runs, and in 1938, 94 more. He also led the American League in stolen base percentage several times.

81 ◆ Al Bridwell
(1905–1915, 1252 G, 2 348 .255)
Bridwell hit only 95 doubles in his career. All of the other shortstops listed here hit at least 136. He hit only 2 home runs in his career. All of the other listed shortstops hit at least 7.

> Al was not the least disturbed by the importance of the moment. In fact, Bridwell was one of the gamest players I ever knew. We all had a hunch that he was going to nail the ball, and sure enough he did. It was a clean line smack to center.—John McGraw, *My Thirty Years In Baseball*

The hit to which McGraw refers, one of the most famous hits in baseball history, was on September 23, 1908. Fred Merkle was on first base at the time . . . Bridwell had been in a slump. Sid Mercer in the *New York Globe* had reported that morning that "Bridwell has not made a timely hit for a long time."

82 ◆ Shawon Dunston
(1985–2000, 1654 G, 140 634 .270)
A player with speed, some power, a decent batting average, and one of the best arms of his generation, but as bad a percentage player as has ever played the game. He was basically an eternal rookie, a player who continued until the end of his career to make rookie mistakes . . . See also Tony Armas (RF, #89).

83 ◆ Woodie Held
(1954–1969, 1390 G, 179 559 .240)
A quiet, easy-going product of the Yankee farm system, Held hit 35 homers, drove in 125 runs at Denver in 1956. The Yankees at that time had many young infielders—Kubek, Richardson, Lumpe, Clete Boyer, among others. A right-handed power hitter, Held's best shot at stardom would have been as a third baseman or outfielder in Fenway Park or Tiger Stadium or Wrigley, but he didn't have the good fortune to wind up with one of those jobs.

> Woodie Held was a strong kid who could hit the ball a ton and run well. He hit homers and struck out. He also made a lot of errors at short. Woodie wasn't smooth enough to be much of an infielder and was at that position only because Gordon wanted his bat in the lineup. I thought he'd have been better off playing center field like Mantle, who was a converted shortstop.—Billy Moran in *We Played the Game*

84 ◆ Solly Hemus
(1949–1959, 969 G, 51 263 .273)
Hemus followed Marty Marion at shortstop for the Cardinals, which was sort of like following Robin Williams on stage with an accordion solo. Hemus wasn't much of a shortstop, and, following Marion, the Cardinal fans really noticed that he wasn't much of a shortstop. He had surprising power for a little guy, plus he walked a lot and led the league in being hit with the pitch three times, so he scored runs.

He also managed the Cardinals, unsuccessfully, from 1959–1961.

> Solly was easily despised. I thought he could have been a very good manager because of his knowledge, but he simply did not know how to handle different types of people . . . Solly had Harry Walker and Johnny Keane as coaches. I had a feeling that they had sharp knives hidden on their persons.—Jim Brosnan in *The Spirit of St. Louis* (Peter Golenbock)

There is also a letter from Hemus reprinted in Curt Flood's book, *The Way It Is*. Hemus had Flood on that Cardinal team, but didn't play him a lot. Later, after the 1968 World Series, Hemus wrote to Flood, wished him well, and apologized for not recognizing Flood's ability. It's actually a rather remarkable letter; not many people are big enough to face up to their mistakes, apologize, and try to re-build the bridges. But Flood totally misses this, and treats Hemus' letter with contempt.

85 ◆ Scott Fletcher
(1981–1995, 1612 G, 34 510 .262)
A nomadic, modern career, spent a year or two with each team and then moved on. Didn't do anything exceptionally well, but was an adequate shortstop and a pretty good second baseman, punched a few singles, walked some and bunted when asked to do so. He filled a slot.

86 ◆ Ed Bressoud
(1956–1967, 1186 G, 94 365 .252)

> I know what it takes to win. The simple commodity is that a good team makes productive outs, and a bad team does not.—Eddie Bressoud in *Fenway* (Peter Golenbock)

Listen, I don't mean to be rude, but anybody who thinks you can win baseball games by making "productive outs" is delusional. It's a variation of the theory that the big hitters with the big statistics get the glory and the big salaries, but it's the "quiet skills" like hitting the cutoff man and hitting behind the runner that win the games. This is a nice theory, but it has the unfortunate property of being demonstrably false. The difference between winning teams and losing teams isn't the difference between "good outs" and "bad outs"; it's the difference between "outs" and "runners on base." You can take a .500 team, change every one of their outs into "good outs," and they're going to go 83-79. The *only* significant difference among outs, in the long run, is between a double play ball and a regular out.

87 ◆ Red Kress
(1927–1946, 1391 G, 89 799 .286)
An ersatz shortstop for the Browns from 1927 into 1932, he drove in over a hundred runs each season in 1929–1931, also led the American League in fielding percentage and double plays in 1929. He had back and elbow injuries beginning in 1933, later a broken thumb costing him most of a season, and never played consistently well after 1931. He stayed in baseball for many years after his playing career as a coach and scout, coaching with the Giants in the forties, the Indians in the fifties, and the expansion Angels in the early sixties.

> It was in 1948, that [Sid] Gordon really bloomed, and thanks were due to a Giant coach named Red Kress. Kress noticed, in spring training, that Gordon, who was powerfully built, could improve himself by pulling the ball to left field.—Harold U. Ribalow, *The Jew in American Sports*

According to Gordon, Kress:

1. Moved his right-hand grip on the bat.
2. Opened up his stance.
3. Taught him to stride toward third.
4. Taught him to roll his wrists.

Gordon, who had never before hit more than 13 homers in a season, then hit 25 to 30 every year for several years.

Kress, according to Bill Borst in *Still Last in the American League,* "was a classic example of the ninety-pound weakling who made it to the big leagues on guts and sheer determination. He was a sickly youth, plagued by several physical ailments. His complexion was as 'pallid as the dull snow of the Sierra peaks on a drab afternoon.'"

In 1935 Kress was playing for Washington. Before a double header one day in mid-season Kress was informed that he had been released. He left the park, went home, and started to pack, when the phone rang. Buddy Myer, the Senators second baseman, had been thrown out of the first game, and, under an experimental rule then in use, was therefore unable to play in the second game as well. Kress was ordered to hurry back to the stadium. He rushed back to Griffith, started the second game, got four hits—and stayed in the major leagues for five more years . . . See also Luis Aparicio.

88 ◆ Bud Harrelson
(1965–1980, 1533 G, 7 267 .236)
A feisty shortstop most remembered for a fight at second base with Pete Rose in the third game of the 1973 NL Championship Series, a fight which erupted into an on-field brawl. A switch hitter, he wasn't as flashy in the field as Mark Belanger, but he was . . . well, more than "solid." His career high in homers was one, but he was a good bunter and drew as many as 95 walks in a season, so he wasn't a complete zero at home plate, either.

89 ◆ Chico Carrasquel
(1950–1959, 1325 G, 55 474 .258)
The first Venezuelan to play well in the majors. In the late 1950s Vice President Richard Nixon visited Venezuela, where an anti-American demonstration developed into a near-riot. "If those Venezuelans can't hit any better than Chico Carrasquel," said Frank Lane, "Nixon hasn't got a thing to worry about."

90 ◆ Jack Barry
(1908–1919, 1222 G, 10 429 .243)
Marvelous, indeed, was a lad who three years ago was the sensation of the college world—playing in the infield for Holy Cross College. He had played at every corner of the infield, but at shortstop he was a dazzling fielder, and a hitter of fair type. That Fall a tall, slim gentleman walked up to the door of a house in Meriden, Conn., and asked to see "Mr. Barry." John J. Barry, now a familiar figure on the American League circuit, who after a talk with the slender gentleman became a member of the Athletic team. For Connie Mack personally had gone to Meriden, and had secured Jack Barry to play shortstop. Barry, like his running mate, Eddie Collins, is 24 years old, and built on the same plan. To be exact, he entered this world April 26, 1887, and into his comparatively few years has crowded considerable fame. After Barry had been secured by Mack he went back to Holy Cross, playing at shortstop. As a fielder he was a wonderful man on his feet, threw like a rifle shot, and, while not an extensive batsman, was a good man in a pinch. At the close of his college career, in 1908, he came to the Athletics and warmed the bench for a time before he got an opportunity to show the speed that made him famous in the college world. Once Monte Cross, the veteran shortstop, had been allowed to drift to the minors, Connie Mack looked around for a successor. He tried Eddie Collins without success, and then he gave Barry his opportunity. Barry's work from the start was stellar. He was given the berth permanently and his course has been a series of successes. Today he ranks with the best men in the country in the short patch, and vies with the stars in that position in popularity and ability.—1911 *Reach Guide*

91 ◆ Gene Alley

(1963–1973, 1195 G, 55 342 .254)

Alley hit .299 in 1966, .287 in 1967—excellent batting averages for that era—and seemed to be on the verge of emerging as a star until he injured his shoulder in the closing weeks of the '67 season. He expected that a winter of rest would cure whatever was wrong, but it didn't; by June 1, 1968, he was hitting .217, and was unable to throw overhand. He started cortisone treatments at that time, but never got back to where he had been in '66–'67.

The Pirates double plays vs. expected double plays for Alley's years as a regular: 1965, +27; 1966, +49 (215 vs. 166); 1967, +7; 1968 (Alley injured), –1; 1969 (Alley out much of the year), +14; 1970, + 8; 1971, +1; 1972, +31.

92 ◆ Terry Turner

(1901–1919, 1665 G, 8 528 .253)

Turner got his first major league trial with the Pirates in 1901. He went 3 for 7 in two games; a Cincinnati newspaper reported that "The last time the Pirates were in Cincinnati, they had a tow-headed youngster on third base who was 'Johnny Eat-'Em-Up.' The fans called him 'Cotton Top,' and he was the greatest factor both inside and out in downing the Reds." Despite this glowing press report, Turner was returned to the minors after playing in only one more game. According to John Phillips in *Who Was Who in Cleveland Baseball 1901–10*, Turner had played on skinned infields in the minor leagues, hard packed dirt, and did not get enough time to adjust to the grass infields before being rejected by the Pirates.

The only thing that stuck from the Pirate experience was the nickname; he was known as "Cotton" Turner the rest of his career, the nickname becoming so common that he perhaps should be listed in the *Encyclopedias* as Cotton, rather than Terry. He stuck with Cleveland in 1904; boy, did he stick. To this day, Turner holds the Cleveland Indians franchise record for Games Played (1,617), and is among the franchise leaders in hits, stolen bases, and in several other categories; he held the Cleveland stolen base record until Kenny Lofton. He is quite certainly the most obscure player to hold the career games played record for any existing major league franchise.

Turner was actually the Cleveland shortstop 1904–1907; after that he had a long career as a utility infielder. Like Gene Alley, he was brilliant for a few years, and battled injuries for a long time, the differences being that

1. At his best, he wasn't quite as good as Alley.

2. After long battles with injuries and illnesses, he had more good years later in his career (than did Alley).

What his illnesses were I'm uncertain; I know that he suffered a serious beaning, perhaps in 1908, because the Cleveland papers made mention of this at the time of the beaning of Ray Chapman. The 1906 *Reach Guide* reported that "the misfortunes of 1904, which began with the illness of Turner, were repeated in 1905." The 1909 *Reach* reported that Turner had been ill all season, and had been forced to leave the game in mid-season by his condition. Accounts of the great American League pennant race of 1908 also mention his absence and the fact that his inability to play may have cost Cleveland the pennant, but fail to say what had happened to him.

Mike Sowell's amazing book about the death of Ray Chapman, *The Pitch That Killed*, begins with a quote from Terry Turner, describing his own experience. "I can still remember vividly how I was fascinated by seeing that ball coming toward my head," Turner told the *Cleveland Press*. "I was paralyzed. I couldn't make a move to get out of the way, though the ball looked big as a house. I imagine that a person fascinated by a snake feels much the same way, paralyzed and unable to dodge the deadly serpent about to strike. The ball crashed into me. It sounded like a hammer striking a big bell. Then all went dark."

93 ◆ Sam Wise
(1881–1893, 1175 G, 49 672 .272)

In 1882 Wise signed contracts to play with both Cincinnati, of the new American Association, and Boston, of the established National League. When he reported to Boston, Cincinnati filed for an injunction, thus bringing about what is sometimes reported to be "the first court case in professional baseball history." (Of course, it was not.)

He was the Boston shortstop for many years, becoming the first player to strike out 100 times in a season (1884), and the first regular to have more strikeouts in a season than hits (104 to 91). He actually was a pretty good hitter; in his last major league season, 1893, he hit .311 and scored 102 runs. This was one of his better batting lines, not because he was improving with age but because the mound had been moved back before that season. He was an erratic fielder, making many errors; according to an article by Mark Sternman in *Baseball's First Stars* (SABR, 1996) a newspaper reported that "Wise makes hair-raising throws, for which he holds a patent, the ball going among the spectators back of first base."

According to Lee Allen in *Cooperstown Corner,* Wise always carried a potato in his shirt pocket, to guard against rheumatism.

94 ◆ Bucky Dent
(1973–1984, 1392 G, 40 423 .247)

A good fielder and a promising hitter when he first came up, went backward as a hitter . . .

You may have read somewhere that after Bucky's famous playoff game home run in 1978, he played six more years but hit only one more three-run homer. This is true, but another way to look at it is that, of Bucky's 40 career home runs, 8 were hit with two or three men on base. This is a very high percentage, 20%. Among the top 50 home run hitters in baseball history, only Jimmie Foxx, Joe DiMaggio, and George Foster hit 20% of their home runs with two or three men on base.

How many players are known for one hit? It's a short list, I think . . . Dick Nen, Bobby Thomson, and Bill Mazeroski are the only other guys I can think of, although there must be others. Players who had a hit so famous that you can say years afterward "Bucky Dent's home run" and everybody knows which one. Us KC people remember Dane Iorg's hit. Billy Wambsganss used to say about his un-assisted triple play that "you'd think I was born the day before that and died the day after." That must be where Bucky is, now; people think he was born the day before, and died the day after. More people are known, I think, for a single mistake than for a single hit . . . Bill Buckner, Mickey Owen, Fred Merkle, Fred Snodgrass, Gionfriddo's catch, Amoros's too . . . everybody knows what that is.

Another way to think about it: what are the five most famous hits in baseball history, not counting the World Series? I'd have to guess that Bucky is on the list.

95 ◆ Tommy Corcoran
(1890–1907, 2200 G, 34 1135 .256)

From our obscure facts department: Tommy Corcoran is the only major league player to score 1,000 runs and have a career on base percentage below .300 . . .

Corcoran broke into the majors in the Player's League, 1890, when the one-year addition of a third league created a demand for new players. He played well enough to make the American Association in 1891, when the 24 teams folded down to 16, and to stick in the

National League in 1892, when they shrunk down to one league, 12 teams.

He was a bare-handed shortstop when he broke in, a good one, not much of a hitter. He switched to using a glove in 1892, led the National League in fielding four times. His career on-base percentage, .289, is pretty awful, especially when you remember that most of his career was in a hitter's era. The league norm for runs per game through his career was 5.35, a very high figure. But I have him as deserving of the Gold Glove in the American Association in 1891, in the National League in 1898 and 1899.

Corcoran, a quiet, alert player, was noted for his ability to steal signs, and for this reason was the third base coach and team captain of the Cincinnati Reds for the last ten years of his career. It was in this role that he was involved in the most famous incident of his career in 1899, the discovery of the Philadelphia Phillies buried buzzer under the third base coach's box (see Arlie Latham, 3B #54).

In 1901, Corcoran was struck by typhoid fever in mid-season, costing him most of that campaign. Otherwise, he was always healthy, and had a long career and a long life, smoking hand-rolled cigarettes until he was 91 years old.

In St. Louis in 1903 Corcoran was walking around the town sight-seeing with a teammate, Orville Woodruff, when a horse, frightened by an automobile, reared up, creating panic. According Lee Allen in *The Cincinnati Reds,* "pedestrians scattered in all directions. Corcoran was pinned against a building and badly hurt, but Woodruff emerged from the affair a hero, picking up a woman who was lying right in the path of the horse and carrying her away from the danger in the nick of time."

96 ◆ Billy Jurges

(1931–1947, 1816 G, 43 656 .258)

Jurges was shot and seriously wounded by a young woman named Violet Valli in August,

1932, thereby missing much of the 1932 pennant race. He was a young player then; he recovered to play in the World Series, to play 15 more years in the major leagues, and to manage the Red Sox in 1959.

Jurges was offered the Chicago Cubs' player/manager's job in mid-season, 1938, when Charlie Grimm was let go. Jurges turned the job down; it went instead to Gabby Hartnett. In the second inning of the second game of the 1938 World Series, however, Stan Hack and Jurges collided going after a routine ground ball, the blunder creating a costly double. The Cubs crumbled in four straight and Hartnett, perhaps blaming Jurges or perhaps viewing Jurges as a rival, traded him to the Giants after the season.

The greatest day of his life, said Billy Jurges in *Diamond Greats* (Rich Wescott), was the day he got married. "I got married in Birdsboro, Pennsylvania, and then took a train to Philadelphia where we were playing a doubleheader at Baker Bowl. I went 7-for-8, handled about 14 or 15 chances without an error and stole a couple of bases."

He was married for 51 years. When his wife died in 1984, he got a phone call from the President of the United States, Dutch Reagan. Reagan and Jurges had been friends when Reagan broadcast the Cub games, and the two men had stayed in touch ever since.

> When Dick Bartell walked out, Bill Jurges walked in, and a Brooklyn lad crashes Broadway. With the Cubs Bill was one of the ace short-fielders of the league . . . quiet, intense, and a heller in spiked shoes when the going gets tough. His batting average raises no eyebrows, but he's in there to win every minute of every game.—*Who's Who in the Major Leagues,* 1939

Jurges, unfortunately, [was] temperamentally unsuited for the job [as Red Sox manager]. Jurges had been a fine ballplayer, but was high-strung, nervous, and a perfectionist who took every loss personally. By the end of the 1959 season, Jurges was on the verge of a nervous breakdown.—Peter Golenbock, *Fenway*

97 ◆ Everett Scott
(1914–1926, 1654 G, 20 549 .249)

Bob O'Farrell, quoted in *Baseball Players And Their Times* (Eugene Murdock): "I pinch hit three times (in the 1918 World Series) . . . Every time I hit the ball hard through the box and every time shortstop Everett Scott ran over, scooped the ball up and threw me out. I thought I had a hit each time." . . . Scott's career fielding percentage, .965, was 24 points better than the league norm for his era, .941. This is the highest plus factor in fielding percentage of any shortstop in history. He led American League shortstops in fielding percentage eight consecutive years, 1916 to 1923.

Scott, who was known as the Deacon, played in 1,307 consecutive games from 1916 to 1925. This was the record until Lou Gehrig broke it, and is still the third longest consecutive game streak of all time, exceeded only by Ripken and Gehrig. Scott's streak ended just a couple of days before Gehrig's began . . . Babe Ruth reports in *Own Book of Baseball* that Everett Scott and Ernie Johnson were bridge partners, and were the best bridge players on the Yankees.

98 ◆ George McBride
(1901–1920, 1658 G, 7 447 .218)

McBride is on one end of a scale; George Sisler is on the other. The scale is the percentage of a player's total contribution to victory which is represented by his batting average.

Sisler hit .340 in his career; however, Sisler's batting average represents 61% of his total value as a player, which I think the highest figure for any player listed among the top 100 at his position. This estimate is derived by putting two other estimates together. One can estimate what percentage of a player's *offensive* value is

accounted for by his batting average by simply squaring his hits, dividing by his at bats, and dividing the result by his career runs created.

In other words, Sisler had 2,812 hits in 8,267 at bats. How many runs would he have created if he had zero walks in his career, and if all of his hits were singles? Answer: 956. This is a basic application of the runs created formula.

How many runs created did he actually have? 1,404. Thus, 68% of Sisler's runs created (956 of 1404) are attributable to his batting average.

This is a very high figure. There are players who have higher figures, like Jesus Alou, but generally they're not ranked in the top 100 at their position. A normal figure is a little under 50%.

In addition to that, Sisler's offense represents 89% of his value as a player. Thus, multiplying the one by the other, Sisler's batting average alone represents 61% of his total value as a player—89% of 68%. This, I believe, is the highest figure for any player in the top 100 at his position.

McBride, on the other hand, accounts for only 31% of his career value with his offense; most of his value is in his glove work. Of his offensive value, his batting average represents 59%. Thus, McBride's .218 career batting average represents only 18% of his total value as a player—31% of 59%. This, I believe, is the lowest percentage for any player listed in the top 100.

In his second year as the Senator's shortstop (1909) McBride made a bunch of errors early in the season, and the fans began to get on him something awful. McBride was a .220 hitter, so he couldn't afford a bad-glove reputation, and it appeared that he was about to be booed out of the league. Then one day, between innings, a drunk ran onto the field. Players at that time left their gloves on the field while they batted, and this inebriated gentleman picked up

McBride's glove, dashed to the shortstop's position, put on the glove, spit in the pocket, and began to demonstrate for McBride's benefit how shortstop was supposed to be played.

Well, the cops ran out and seized the drunk and, this being 1909, commenced to beat some sense into him, in full view of the public. But the funny thing was, it broke the mood, and ended the fielding slump. McBride retrieved his glove, nodded to the drunk as he was led away, and went about his business. The crowd, which had been riding McBride unmercifully, laughed about the incident, and cheered when McBride fielded cleanly two ground balls in the inning. McBride went on to lead the American League shortstops in fielding that year, and would play shortstop in Washington for the next decade.

99 ◆ Ivan DeJesus
(1974–1988, 1371 G, 21 324 .254)

I had Ivan DeJesus at short and Manny Trillo at second behind me, and they were fantastic. Manny was the best second baseman I ever played with. Of course, later I played with Ozzie Smith, so Ivan is not going to be at the top of the list, but both of those guys were the same way. They came to play every day. We had a lot of good guys on the Cubs teams. We might not have won, but we didn't have guys who complained or sat out. They came to play every day.–Bruce Sutter in *Wrigleyville*, Peter Golenbock

100 ◆ Rafael Ramirez
(1980–1992, 1539 G, 53 484 .261)

A modern Sam Wise–a decent hitter and a fielder with a strong arm, but most remembered for his strikeouts and wild throws.

Marty Marion in his career hit .263, with 1,448 hits in 1,572 games; Ramirez hit .261,

with 1,432 hits in 1,539 games. If you do a computer search for the most similar player to Rafael Ramirez, based on his career batting stats, the computer will tell you that the most similar player is Marty Marion, followed by Scott Fletcher. If you do the same search for Marion, the computer will say that the most similar player is Scott Fletcher, with Ramirez second.

But, of course, neither Rafael Ramirez nor Scott Fletcher is *truly* similar to Marty Marion, because of their defense and for other reasons. If you do a Win Shares analysis, Marion has 178 career Win Shares–80 for offense, 98 for defense. Comparing:

Marion	80 Offense	98 Defense	178 Total
Fletcher	85 Offense	65 Defense	150 Total
Ramirez	64 Offense	50 Defense	114 Total

Looked at in that way, the most-similar players to Marion are Roy McMillan and Larry Bowa. The most-similar players to Scott Fletcher are Monte Cross and Buck Weaver. The most-similar players to Rafael Ramirez are Craig Reynolds and Mark Koenig.

101. Dick Schofield Jr., 102. Mickey Doolan, 103. Jack Rowe, 104. Spike Owen, 105. Mike Bordick, 106. Daryl Spencer, 107. Bill Gleason, 108. Alfredo Griffin, 109. Walt Weiss, 110. Wayne Causey, 111. Heinie Wagner, 112. Craig Reynolds, 113. Germany Smith, 114. Charley Gelbert, 115. Frank Taveras, 116. Topper Rigney, 117. Dick Howser, 118. Billy Myers, 119. Monte Cross, 120. Mark Koenig, 121. Jose Uribe, 122. Kurt Stillwell, 123. U.L. Washington, 124. Ed Brinkman, 125. Tim Foli

SHORTSTOP

Rank	Player Name	Career WS	Top 3	Top 5	Per 162
1.	Honus Wagner	655	59, 46, 45	237	38.01
2.	Arky Vaughan	356	39, 36, 36	169	31.74
3.	Cal Ripken Jr.	419	37, 35, 34	145	23.63
4.	Robin Yount	423	39, 34, 33	144	23.99
5.	Ernie Banks	332	33, 32, 31	143	21.28
6.	Barry Larkin	314	32, 31, 30	130	28.12
7.	Ozzie Smith	326	33, 25, 23	123	20.53
8.	Joe Cronin	333	35, 34, 33	152	25.40
9.	Alan Trammell	318	35, 29, 26	132	22.47
10.	Pee Wee Reese	314	32, 27, 26	134	23.48
11.	Luke Appling	378	40, 29, 29	141	25.28
12.	Lou Boudreau	277	34, 32, 30	135	27.26
13.	Luis Aparicio	293	22, 21, 20	92	18.26
14.	George Davis	398	31, 29, 28	119	27.23
15.	Jim Fregosi	261	33, 28, 28	135	22.23
16.	Phil Rizzuto	231	35, 26, 25	121	22.53
17.	Alex Rodriguez	147	36, 34, 30	145	30.14
xx.	Derek Jeter	123	36, 27, 22	122	25.35
xx.	Nomar Garciaparra	116	32, 29, 27	116	31.58
18.	Hughie Jennings	214	36, 32, 29	150	26.98
19.	Maury Wills	253	32, 28, 27	128	21.11
20.	Johnny Pesky	187	34, 28, 25	130	23.85
21.	Bill Dahlen	393	32, 31, 27	121	26.06
22.	Vern Stephens	265	34, 32, 27	129	24.96
23.	Joe Sewell	277	29, 29, 26	125	23.58
24.	Tony Fernandez	278	25, 25, 24	118	21.63
25.	Bert Campaneris	280	29, 26, 22	109	19.48
26.	Dave Concepcion	269	25, 25, 24	111	17.52
27.	Al Dark	226	28, 27, 23	118	20.03
28.	Dave Bancroft	269	31, 27, 26	115	22.78
29.	Cecil Travis	169	34, 22, 22	111	20.62
30.	Dick Groat	225	31, 25, 21	112	18.90
31.	Jay Bell	232	26, 24, 24	108	20.54
32.	Rico Petrocelli	205	37, 27, 23	125	21.38
33.	Joe Tinker	258	32, 24, 22	118	23.18
34.	Herman Long	265	29, 28, 26	120	22.91

(continued)

Rank	Player Name	Career WS	Top 3	Top 5	Per 162
35.	Monte Ward	409	51, 51, 31	188	36.31
36.	Bobby Wallace	345	26, 25, 25	112	23.45
37.	Dick Bartell	252	28, 24, 21	106	20.25
38.	Rabbit Maranville	302	27, 24, 23	110	18.32
39.	Johnny Logan	181	26, 24, 24	111	19.51
40.	Travis Jackson	211	24, 24, 22	109	20.64
41.	Art Fletcher	218	27, 25, 24	116	23.04
42.	Garry Templeton	209	25, 24, 21	97	16.29
43.	Jack Glasscock	261	27, 25, 22	108	24.36
44.	Larry Bowa	179	22, 16, 15	82	12.91
45.	Marty Marion	177	22, 20, 19	95	18.24
46.	Julio Franco	241	30, 28, 27	121	20.65
47.	Ray Chapman	148	30, 21, 20	99	22.81
48.	Roger Peckinpaugh	239	24, 22, 21	100	19.24
49.	Billy Rogell	161	25, 24, 23	106	17.60
50.	Leo Cardenas	199	23, 22, 22	91	16.61
51.	Donie Bush	232	27, 24, 22	106	19.31
52.	Mark Belanger	162	23, 21, 18	75	13.02
53.	Roy McMillan	172	20, 17, 16	79	13.31
54.	Eddie Joost	209	35, 26, 26	126	21.51
55.	Roy Smalley Jr.	181	24, 22, 20	96	17.74
56.	Rick Burleson	152	21, 21, 19	94	18.29
57.	Dickie Thon	147	30, 22, 20	70	17.17
58.	Ron Hansen	145	30, 24, 19	91	16.97
59.	Woody English	155	28, 24, 17	99	19.91
60.	Glenn Wright	139	24, 22, 21	92	20.12
61.	Omar Vizquel	153	22, 18, 17	87	15.30
62.	Denis Menke	176	29, 24, 21	94	17.84
63.	Freddy Parent	168	29, 26, 23	106	20.51
64.	Ed McKean	221	25, 25, 21	99	21.65
65.	Zoilo Versalles	134	32, 19, 18	98	15.51
66.	Charlie Hollocher	113	28, 24, 16	97	24.09
67.	Frankie Crosetti	189	24, 23, 18	93	18.19
68.	Chris Speier	206	25, 20, 16	93	14.77
69.	Bill Russell	185	18, 17, 16	70	13.74
70.	Jeff Blauser	154	29, 27, 18	85	17.73
71.	Eddie Miller	138	22, 21, 14*	71	14.81
72.	Don Kessinger	159	23, 15, 14	79	12.40
73.	Freddie Patek	150	24, 16, 15	79	14.73

Rank	Player Name	Career WS	Top 3	Top 5	Per 162
74.	Ozzie Guillen	148	18, 17, 15	70	12.03
75.	Kid Elberfeld	184	25, 22, 21	97	23.07
76.	Granny Hamner	144	20, 20, 19	92	15.24
77.	Tony Kubek	120	21, 19, 18	81	17.80
78.	Buck Weaver	152	23, 22, 21	92	19.64
79.	Greg Gagne	157	20, 18, 18	72	14.15
80.	Lyn Lary	145	24, 23, 18	82	18.04
81.	Al Bridwell	138	24, 24, 22	96	17.86
82.	Woodie Held	153	22, 21, 21	102	17.83
83.	Solly Hemus	109	27, 23, 17	84	18.37
84.	Scott Fletcher	148	20, 17, 17	77	14.87
85.	Ed Bressoud	108	25, 21, 17	80	14.75
86.	Red Kress	139	21, 20, 17	90	16.19
87.	Shawon Dunston	148	18, 16, 15	65	14.50
88.	Bud Harrelson	141	19, 17, 14	76	14.90
89.	Chico Carrasquel	132	24, 17, 16	81	16.14
90.	Jack Barry	132	20, 19, 18	89	17.48
91.	Gene Alley	115	22, 19, 15	76	15.59
92.	Terry Turner	171	28, 17, 16	75	16.64
93.	Sam Wise	157	22, 19, 17	84	21.65
94.	Rafael Ramirez	113	21, 18, 18	59	11.89
95.	Bucky Dent	116	19, 16, 16	64	13.50
96.	Tommy Corcoran	214	19, 18, 16	79	15.76
97.	Billy Jurges	170	18, 18, 17	71	15.17
98.	Everett Scott	142	16, 16, 15	70	13.91
99.	George McBride	127	17, 16, 14	68	12.40
100.	Ivan DeJesus	106	19, 16, 15	68	12.53

Categories of this record are Career Win Shares, Win Shares in the player's three best seasons, Win Shares total over the player's five best consecutive seasons, and career Win Shares per 162 games played. For example, Honus Wagner had 655 Career Win Shares, including 59, 46, and 45 in his three best seasons (1908, 1905, and 1906). He had 237 Win Shares in a five-year period, (1904–1908 or 1905–1909) and averaged 38.01 Win Shares per 162 games played over the course of his career.

LEFT FIELD

1 ◆ Ted Williams
(1939–1960, 2292 G, 521 1839 .344)

> The right turn could have made Ted Williams a second Babe Ruth, for he might have become not only the greatest, but the most popular big-league player since the Babe. Instead, Williams's entire career was blighted by intense personality problems, and these problems actually changed the face of baseball.—Al Hirshberg, *What's the Matter with the Red Sox?*

As Hirshberg's quote implies, there is in baseball history a line of "popular" superstars, which includes Honus Wagner, Walter Johnson, Babe Ruth, Stan Musial, Willie Mays, Mickey Mantle, George Brett, and Ken Griffey Jr., and a line of "unpopular" superstars, which includes Ty Cobb, Rogers Hornsby, Barry Bonds, Albert Belle, and Ted Williams. What Hirshberg is suggesting—and I hope I'm not picking on him, because the same suggestion occurs in many other books about the Red Sox—is that Ted Williams fell into the "bad guy" category because the Red Sox didn't handle him well when he came to the majors in 1939, but that if some things had been done differently at that time, he might have—and should have—been pushed over into the popular superstars line.

This may be hard for a younger fan to understand, but Ted Williams was every bit as unpopular, in his time, as Albert Belle is now. In baseball today there are three players who are cheered in every park—Cal Ripken, Tony Gwynn, and Ken Griffey Jr.—and about the same number who are booed in every park, led by Belle and John Rocker. Ted Williams was despised everywhere in the American League, including Boston for at least the first half of his career. He took constant actions to reinforce that relationship. He splattered water coolers, including glass ones. He made obscene gestures at fans, carried on decades-long vendettas against selected reporters, sometimes didn't treat his family well, sometimes didn't hustle or even make any show of hustling in the field or on the bases, was obsessed with his own success, was contemptuous of coaches and some managers, and alternated, in his dealings with the fans, between rugged charm and uncharted rudeness. "When Ted's name is announced," wrote Austin Lake, "the sound is like the autumn wind moaning through an apple orchard."

Could all of this have been avoided, had Williams gotten off on the right track early in his career? I don't see how. There are people who have made similar suggestions about Ty Cobb, that Ty Cobb's angry persona traces back to the mistreatment he received by veteran players when he joined the Tigers in 1905. It doesn't. Ty Cobb's life did not begin in 1905; Ted Williams' life did not begin in 1939. Williams had a miserable childhood. Williams' father abandoned the family. Williams' comment on this was "Well, I wouldn't have wanted to be married to a woman like that, either." By the time he was 20, Williams was insecure, moody, and filled with hate. He was a lot like Rogers Hornsby, whom he knew well and liked, and he is a lot like Bobby Knight, who is a close friend. He had a great deal more in common with Ty Cobb than he did with Babe Ruth.

Cobb has been treated harshly by subsequent generations because he stood on the wrong side of the long arc of history. I'm not making excuses for him, but Ty Cobb didn't invent racism; it was taught to him. It was very common for men of his generation to get into fist fights about nothing; many other players also did this. Gabby Hartnett and Babe Ruth, among countless others, also went into the stands to punch out fans; nobody holds this against their memory. Williams has been treated more kindly by history because he represents the best of what we have taken to calling the Greatest Generation.

One other note about Williams. Hundreds of sources, in discussing Williams' greatness as a hitter, will talk about what amazing eyesight he had, how he could see the seams on the ball, could read the label on a spinning phonograph record, etc. Williams explicitly stated in his autobiography, *My Turn At Bat,* that this was completely false, that his eyesight was good but normal, and that his eyes had little or nothing to do with his hitting ability. And, since he is the only one who would know, I might suggest we should perhaps take his word for this.

2 ◆ Stan Musial
(1941–1963, 3026 G, 475 1951 .331)

> An exact opposite of Williams; the perfect gentleman, the perfect sport. Never angry at draft boards, seldom spits in public, always hits with enthusiasm, smiles often. Successful without arrogance, he represents the milder side of those who admire him.—Roger Kahn, *Sport Magazine,* September 1960

> Like Mays, he saw the world entirely in terms of his own good fortune. He was convinced it was the best of all possible worlds. He not only accepted baseball mythology but propounded it. [Bob] Gibson and I once clocked eight wunnerfuls in a Musial speech that could not have been longer than a hundred words.—Curt Flood, *The Way It Is*

> Stan was just a good ol' country boy. We had a lot of good ol' country boys on our team . . . No, if you don't like Stan, you don't like anybody. —Marty Marion in *The Spirit of St. Louis* (Peter Golenbock)

> See also comment on Willie Mays . . .

3 ◆ Barry Bonds
(1986–2000, 2143 G, 494 1405 .289)

Certainly the most un-appreciated superstar of my lifetime, Bonds, Biggio, and Henderson the three most un-appreciated. Probably the second- or third-best hitter among the 100 listed left fielders (behind Williams and perhaps Musial), probably the third-best baserunner (behind Henderson and Raines), probably the best defensive left fielder. Griffey has always been more popular, but Bonds has been a far, far greater player.

The ten best players of the 1990s:

1. Barry Bonds
2. Craig Biggio
3. Frank Thomas
4. Ken Griffey Jr.
5. Jeff Bagwell
6. Rafael Palmeiro
7. Barry Larkin
8. Roberto Alomar
9. Mark McGwire
10. Greg Maddux

The number two man, Biggio, is closer in value to the number 10 man than he is to Bonds. Biggio passed Bonds as the best player in baseball in 1997.

4 ◆ Rickey Henderson

(1979–2000, 2856 G, 282 1052 .282)

Somebody asked me did I think Rickey Henderson was a Hall of Famer. I told them, "If you could split him in two, you'd have two Hall of Famers." The greatest base stealer of all time, the greatest power/speed combination of all time (except maybe Barry Bonds), the greatest leadoff man of all time, one of the top five players of all time in runs scored . . . yeah, I would think that might make a man a Hall of Famer. Without exaggerating one inch, you could find fifty Hall of Famers who, all taken together, don't own as many records, and as many *important* records, as Rickey Henderson.

The top base stealers of all time, up to age 29:

1. Rickey Henderson, 794
2. Ty Cobb, 649
3. Billy Hamilton, 638
4. Vince Coleman, 586
5. Tim Raines, 585

The greatest base stealers of all time, after age 30:

1. Lou Brock, 604
2. Rickey Henderson, 576 and counting

3. Otis Nixon, 499 and counting
4. Honus Wagner, 464
5. Davey Lopes, 458

Even down through the tenth spot, they're totally separate lists except for Henderson. The top players in career secondary bases:

1. Babe Ruth, 5099
2. Rickey Henderson, 4886
3. Hank Aaron, 4727
4. Willie Mays, 4584
5. Ted Williams, 4273
6. Stan Musial, 4181
7. Carl Yastrzemski, 4133
8. Frank Robinson, 4054
9. Joe Morgan, 3999
10. Mickey Mantle, 3982

5 ◆ Carl Yastrzemski

(1961–1983, 3308 G, 452 1844 .285)

> I always found that in life people respect certain things. One of them is strength, the other is ability, and Yaz had both. He wasn't a Punch-and-Judy hitter, a Pete Rose who hustled, hustled, hustled, and hit singles. Yaz hustled *and* hit the ball out of the park.—Joe Lahoud in *Peter Golenbock's Fenway*

Yastrzemski and Musial are both left-handed hitters, almost the same height, and both listed at 175 pounds. Both played more than 1800 games in the outfield, but also more than 750 at first base. They had about the same number of career hits (3630-3419) and home runs (475-452). Both were of Polish ancestry. Both were likable men who were extremely well respected by teammates.

Both won their first batting titles in their third season in the majors. Both had power surges at age 27. Musial, who had never hit more than 19 home runs in his first six seasons, hit 39 home runs at age 27, which would remain his career high. Yastrzemski, who had never hit more than 20 home runs in his first six seasons, hit 44 home runs at age 27, which would remain his career high.

Yastrzemski, as great as he was, was not Stan Musial. Comparing them at the same ages, Musial was better than Yastrzemski at every age except 24 (when Musial was in the Army in 1945) and several seasons after age 37.

The third member of the group, if there had to be one, would be Al Simmons. Simmons, also of Polish ancestry and about the same size (but of a different build), had never hit more than 24 homers in a season before age 27, and hit 34 homers, driving in 157 runs, at age 27. Simmons was a right-handed hitter, stockier than Yaz and Musial. All three players had very unconventional batting stances. Yastrzemski was a better player than Simmons, not much better, but a little better.

Simmons was 28 years old in 1930, the peak season of the big-hitting era between the wars; Yastrzemski was 28 in 1968, the peak season of the pitching-dominated sixties. There is a book, *Two Spectacular Seasons,* by William B. Mead, which contrasts the two seasons. Simmons at age 28 hit .381 with 36 homers, 165 RBI; Yaz at the same age hit .301 with 23 homers, 74 RBI. Each won the American League batting title. Who had the better season, in context?

Yastrzemski did; it's close, but it's Yastrzemski. Simmons created 156 runs, in a league which averaged 5.41 runs per game, so his offense represents 29 games worth of runs. Yastrzemski in 1968 created 121 runs in a league which averaged 3.41 runs per team per game, so he produced 35 games worth of runs. When you blend in the other factors—park effects, outs used, defense, and the extra eight games on the 1968 schedule—the gap narrows but Yastrzemski is still ahead.

6 ◆ Joe Jackson
(1908–1920, 1330 G, 54 785 .356)

When Jackson played in Cleveland there was a stout woman with a loud voice who sat in a box behind third base, taunting opposing players with personalized insults. After Jackson was traded to Chicago she knew, of course, that he couldn't read or write, and that he was sensitive about this, so the lady started to yell at him, "Hey, Joe! How do you spell Mississippi? How do you spell Mississippi, Joe?" Jackson ripped a triple into the right field corner. As he got to his feet, he looked over at her and said quietly, "How do you spell triple, fat lady?"

> We'd go in for breakfast and the waitress would hand him a menu. Well, he knew they always had ham and eggs and that's what he would order. But we'd go in for dinner and if the waitress went to him first for his order, he'd say, "I haven't made up my mind yet. See what they want." Then he'd listen to what the rest of us were ordering and he'd pick something we said. —Roger Peckinpaugh, *The Man in the Dugout* (Donald Honig)

7 ◆ Al Simmons
(1924–1944, 2215 G, 307 1827 .334)

> "Sign stealing can give you a lot of help," Al Simmons, one of the great modern hitters, once told me, "but only if you can be sure. [With Philadelphia] Eddie Collins was our third base coach, and Eddie was as good as they came. He wouldn't always give the hitter the sign—only when he was sure. I hit many a long ball because he had told me a fast ball was coming down the alley."—Hub Miller, *Baseball Magazine,* December 1950

> One plus for Simmons in 1927 was his association with Ty Cobb who seemed to have a real influence on Al, [and who] seemed to imitate a number of Cobb's mannerisms on the field. They became close friends as Al would spend many of his vacations with Ty in the future.—Dutch Doyle, *Al Simmons: The Best*

One time Al Simmons was in a terrible slump, couldn't buy a hit for a week or more. After going oh-for-four he stumbled out of the shower in a funk and, not really thinking about what he was doing, put on his hat. The sight of a naked man wearing a hat caused somebody to laugh out loud, which caused other people to look and see what was funny, and pretty soon the whole clubhouse was roaring at the sight of Al Simmons, stark naked except for his hat.

The next day, Simmons had four hits. You can imagine what happened then: Simmons began getting dressed after the game every day by putting his hat on first. And, as he got hot and stayed hot, this spread to the rest of the team. After a while, you could go into the A's locker room after a game, and there'd be a dozen men running around naked except for their hats.

8 ◆ Tim Raines

(1979–1999, 2353 G, 168 964 .295)

Eric Gregg, in his 1990 book *Working the Plate,* chose an All-Star team of the best players he had seen in his years as a National League umpire. His outfield was Raines, Tony Gwynn, and Andre Dawson ...

I worked Tim Raines' arbitration case a long time ago, must have been 1984. The arbitrator let Tal Smith drone on at some length, so Raines and I had the same need when we finally took a break. I found the facility a moment before he did. "Ahhh," I said as he pulled up beside me. "Some day I'll be able to tell my grandkids I beat Tim Raines in a foot race." It wasn't that funny, but he laughed so hard he just about peed on my shoe. I rooted for him the rest of his career ...

I always rooted for him to get 3,000 hits. He didn't, mostly because of injuries, but he did get over 3,000 secondary bases.

9 ◆ Willie Stargell

(1962–1982, 2360 G, 475 1540 .282)

> If the Pirates were family, their patriarch was Wilver Dornel "Willie" Stargell. They called him "Pops." He was ... a big teddy bear of a man, and the rest of the Pirates ... brought their problems to him, and he showed them how to win.
> —Phil Pepe, *Talkin' Baseball*

Stargell had the quickest bat I ever saw. Even when he was old, near 40, he could be jammed, spin that big bat like a baton, and drive the ball 370 feet after you were sure he had swung too late. Sometimes it looked like he didn't move anything except his fingers; he'd lock his wrist, rip the bat around with his fingers, and hit the ball hard.

Two questions ...

1. How many home runs would Stargell have hit, had he been healthy throughout his career?

2. What kind of numbers would he have if he played in the 1990s?

First question ... Stargell probably lost less than a hundred career home runs due to injuries. Assuming that he might have played 155 games per season from 1966 through 1979 and that he would have increased his home runs per game slightly with fewer injuries, I can get him up to 568 home runs. That would put him sixth on the all-time home run list at this moment, but still ... it was never in the cards for Stargell to challenge Henry Aaron.

Second question ... Willie Stargell, playing in the 1990s, would probably be pretty comparable to Manny Ramirez or Albert Belle as a hitter. Stargell's 1966, 1969, 1971, and 1973 seasons converted to a standard of 780 runs per team per season:

1966 actual	140	485	84	153	30	0	33	102	.315
Converted	140	501	99	169	33	0	36	120	.337

1969 actual	145	522	89	160	31	6	29	92	.307
Converted	145	540	106	178	34	7	32	109	.330
1971 actual	141	511	104	151	26	0	48	125	.295
Converted	141	532	128	172	30	0	55	154	.323
1973 actual	148	522	106	156	43	3	44	119	.299
Converted	148	537	123	171	47	3	48	138	.318

10 ◆ Minnie Minoso
(1949–1980, 1835 G, 186 1023 .299)

Sooner or later, whenever we talk about hitting, someone will ask me if there will ever be another .400 hitter in the major leagues. Of all the so-called "sluggers" in the big time today, the only one I can think of who really qualifies in all respects is Minnie Minoso.—Ted Williams, "Who Will Hit .400," Ted Williams as told to Paul Gardner, *Baseball Stars of 1955*

The greatest players in history, based on Win Shares between ages 30 and 39, not including pitchers:

1. Honus Wagner   372
2. Babe Ruth   322
3. Willie Mays   294
4. Hank Aaron   270
5. Pete Rose   258
6. Mike Schmidt   257
7. Ty Cobb   255
8. Tris Speaker   255
9. Joe Morgan   255
10. Stan Musial   252
11. Nap Lajoie   242
12. Charlie Gehringer   240
13. Bill Terry   238
14. Frank Robinson   234
15. Eddie Collins   230
16. Minnie Minoso   229
17. Paul Molitor   220
18. Ted Williams   219
19. Willie Stargell   215
20. Jackie Robinson   212

All Hall of Famers except Minoso and Molitor . . .

Minnie Minoso was one of the funniest guys I was ever around. When he thought an umpire made a bad call, he'd argue in half English and half Spanish and you wouldn't know what the heck he was saying.—Les Moss in *We Played the Game,* Danny Peary

What more could I ask of life? I came from nowhere. I worked in the sugar fields as a boy. It was a tough life. I had one pair of shoes and one pair of pants. But I always had a smile on my face. My mother and father . . . taught me to be a good citizen, a good human being, and to love life.—Minnie Minoso in *Diamond Greats* (Rich Wescott)

11 ◆ Billy Williams
(1959–1976, 2488 G, 426 1475 .290)

Billy Williams was Ernie Banks without the PR. Billy took everything as it came to him, soaked everything in, enjoyed it quietly or suffered through it in silence. When a reporter asked him why he didn't get as much publicity as some other players, he said "That's up to you guys. I can't write about myself." When a teammate asked him if he was a hot-weather hitter, he said, "I hope so. That's the only weather I've got right now." When he was asked the secret of his success as a hitter, he said, "When the pitcher hangs a curve ball, hit it. The difference between a good hitter and an average hitter is just 20-30 hits a year. You hit those thirty hangers, you'll be up there in the paper." He enjoyed playing in Wrigley Field, enjoyed playing day baseball, enjoyed hitting, enjoyed playing the field. But unlike Banks, he wouldn't go out of his way to tell you about it.

Williams grew up in a tiny town near Mobile, Alabama; his father played with the Mobile Black Bears, a satellite team in the Negro

Leagues. He had the same kind of youth that I described in the Red Schoendienst comment as a Mark Twain childhood—one of a bunch of kids of a happy family, spent a lot of time swimming in the creeks and fishing, which he still does. A scout for the Cubs, sent to Mobile to check out Henry Aaron's brother Tommie, instead signed Williams for a cigar and a $25 bus ticket.

Williams got discouraged, in the minor leagues, and quit baseball. The Cubs sent Buck O'Neil to Alabama to talk him into returning. "Buck and my dad told me that baseball was good for me," Williams said, "and I listened" . . .

Williams had one of his worst major league seasons in 1966, hitting .276 with 29 homers, 91 RBI. Trying to take advantage of this, Hank Bauer of the Orioles approached Leo Durocher, trying to trade for Williams. The Cubs demanded Mike Epstein, who at the time was the minor league player of the year. The Orioles turned them down . . .

12 ◆ Ed Delahanty
(1888–1903, 1835 G, 101 1464 .346)

When Joe DiMaggio was a rookie in 1936, the old pitcher Bill Dineen was interviewed by Ed Bang of the *Cleveland Plain Dealer*. Dineen said that DiMaggio was the spitting image of Ed Delahanty. "This is the closest replica to Del I have ever seen," said Dineen. "The bat he uses, the way he swings, the manner in which he watches balls he doesn't offer at, are reminiscent of Del. In the outfield, DiMag simply emphasizes the likeness to the old-time star, the way he catches balls, runs and throws. His every move is taken from the same baseball mold that cast Ed Delahanty."

> He stepped to the plate and assumed his majestic pose, his arms raised and his big yellow bat held high over his head.—Mike Sowell, *July 2, 1903*

In a game in 1900 the Phillies led the Pirates 20-4 after five innings. Pittsburgh manager Fred Clarke, out of pitching, sent Honus Wagner to the mound to save some innings. According to Dennis and Jeanne Burke DeValeria in *Honus Wagner*, "When 'Big Ed' Delahanty came to the plate in the eighth, Wagner trembled, knocking his knees together in mock fear." . . .

> Del was a strutter, gathering a coterie of admirers as he moved from one saloon to another. He knew where the best corned beef could be found in every city. A free spender, he was constantly broke.—Norman L. Macht, *Baseball's First Stars*

> A passenger was in altercation with the conductor of the Michigan Central Railroad and at Fort Erie, Ontario, he was forcibly ejected. Later a bridge tender found a man on the International Bridge who had successfully evaded the guard. The bridge tender put a lantern to the man's face, started to ask him questions, and then heard a splash, and the man apparently had plunged into the Niagara River. On the train was found a suitcase and clothes containing complimentary pass No. 26 of your baseball club.—Letter from the Buffalo Pullman Company to Washington manager Tom Loftus, July 7, 1903

13 ◆ Joe Medwick
(1932–1948, 1984 G, 205 1383 .324)

The Albert Belle of the 1930s . . . Medwick was almost universally hated around the National League, as a result of a long string of fights and other incidents. He was nicknamed "Ducky," which was a shortened form of "Ducky Wucky." In 1931, when Medwick was playing for Houston, a female fan gushed, "Oh, isn't he the Ducky Wucky?" This struck a reporter as funny, and the reporters started calling him "Ducky Wucky." He spent almost two years at Houston, and by the time he left the nickname was well established.

He hated the nickname, understandably, even in its shortened form, "Ducky." He childhood nickname had been Mickey, from his middle name Michael, and he preferred that. His teammates also called him Muscles, because he had big ones . . .

In his first at bat after he was traded to the Dodgers in 1940 Medwick was hit in the skull by former teammate Bob Bowman of the Cardinals. Accounts of this event invariably state that Medwick was never the same player after this, or that he was not as aggressive a hitter, and lost his power after this. This is untrue. It's another case of park effects being misinterpreted as actual changes in ability. The National League ERA dropped sharply in 1941 and dropped further in 1942, plus Medwick, in moving from Sportsman's Park to Ebbets Field, was moving to a much tougher home run park. If you adjust for those things, Medwick's value in 1941–42 was almost exactly the same as it had been in 1938–39 . . .

Pepper Martin was very superstitious, and believed that finding hairpins was good luck. This superstition was common inside and outside baseball, and dated back at least fifty years, but Pepper was serious about it, always looking for hairpins. One time in Cincinnati, a couple of writers (Roy Stockton and Ray Gillespie) bought a package of hairpins and scattered them around the hotel lobby, but Joe Medwick got there first and started collecting the pins. "Hey, those are for Pepper Martin," said Stockton.

"Let Pepper find his own hairpins," said Medwick, and walked off with the pins in his pocket . . .

Medwick hit .353 in 1935, .351 in 1936, and .374 in 1937, but fell off to .322 with only 122 RBI in 1938. Cardinal owner Sam Breadon that winter offered him a salary that called for a substantial pay cut, eventually softening his demands to a cut of $2,000. "It's the principle of the thing, Joe," Breadon explained. "I am not giving you the $2,000. I'd rather throw the money out the window."

"Mr. Breadon," Medwick replied. "If you threw two thousand dollars out the window, you would still be holding onto it when it hit the sidewalk."

14 ◆ Jesse Burkett
(1890–1905, 2072 G, 75 952 .341)
Only three men have hit .400 three times: Cobb, Hornsby, and Burkett . . .

> Jesse is one of the most constant and one of the rankest kidders in the business. That would be alright if he could take a kid himself, but the moment that somebody comes back at him with a few facts stated in sarcastic words he goes wild and wants to fight.—*The Sporting News,* 1903

> As a lad of 16, Burkett dove into a flooded river to try to save the lives of two youngsters.—J. Thomas Hetrick, *Misfits!*

> One day, when he was twelve, he saw a little girl fall out of a skiff . . . Jesse plunged into the water, found the girl and dragged her to the shore; but attempts at artificial respiration failed and she died there. It was an incident that haunted him all his life, and on his eighty-third birthday tears welled in his eyes when he told a reporter about it.—Lee Allen and Tom Meany, *Kings of the Diamond*

On August 4, 1897, Cleveland was playing a double-header at Louisville, Jesse Burkett playing for Cleveland. Burkett came to bat in the second inning of the first game, runner on second and two out. The umpire, a man named Jimmy Wolf, called two straight strikes on him, both on pitches which were probably outside.

Burkett went back to the dugout, dropped his bat, picked up a broom, returned to the plate and began sweeping off home plate. Wolf asked him what he was doing, and Burkett called Wolf a thief, packaging the compliment in a string of obscenities. Wolf, naturally, threw him out of the game.

Burkett, however, refused to leave the field. Wolf went over to the Cleveland manager, Patsy Tebeau, and told him that he had three minutes to get Burkett off the field. "You can give us 30 minutes if you want to," Tebeau said. "He won't go out."

"I'll forfeit the game to Louisville, 9 to 0," said Wolf.

"All right," said Tebeau. "Forfeit it. We don't need it."

Wolf wandered out near the pitching mound, pulled out his pocket watch, and made a show of staring at it for three minutes. When three minutes had passed, he declared the game a forfeit; Louisville won.

Burkett, having apparently calmed down, patted Wolf on the back, remarked "Good fellow," and returned to his dugout.

This, however, was only the first game of a double header. What to do about the second game?

They waited 15 minutes, and then they played the second game.

And again, Burkett was thrown out of the game. Again, he refused to go. This time, Wolf called six policemen, and had Burkett forcibly removed from the premises.

Burkett was an interesting personality. He was sharp, never drank, smoked, or chewed tobacco, and had a wicked tongue. At this time the fans were closer to the action, right up on the field, and Burkett would sit with the fans, talk with the fans, and share with the fans his pungent observations on the game. But this wasn't always a friendly relationship because, as noted above, Jesse couldn't take a joke; sometimes the fans would get on him about his

game or about something else, and he would start to mix it up with the spectators. Burkett looked like Jack Glasscock, an older player, and some of the fans used to tease him about being Glasscock's son, just to get under his skin. The nickname "The Crab" was hung on him late in his career, when he took a lot of ribbing about his age, and didn't take it too well.

As an older man, Burkett was hired by John McGraw to be Phil Douglas's "Keeper." Douglas drank a lot and ran wild and liked to fight; Burkett, who was stern and sober and didn't mind if people didn't like him, was hired to baby-sit him full time, walk him out of fights, and keep him from punching out sportswriters.

15 ◆ Lou Brock
(1961–1979, 2616 G, 149 900 .293)

Outfielders and first basemen can be defined in this way:

Those who can throw but can't run are right fielders,

Those who can run but can't throw are left fielders,

Those who can do both are center fielders, and

Those who can't do either are first basemen.

These definitions, of course, are imprecise; if a left fielder can run but not throw, how do you get Willie Stargell in left field? Stargell had a pretty good arm, but played left field because the Pirates had Roberto Clemente for the first half of his career and Dave Parker the second half, plus he was really too slow to be a right fielder.

They put throwing arms in right field, of course, to prevent the runner from going first-to-third on a single, and also to prevent a ball hit into the corner from being a triple. But these plays require a certain degree of speed or at least quickness on the part of the right fielder. A right fielder who was as slow as Stargell (or Frank Howard, or Ted Williams over the second half of his career, or Luzinski, or Kiner, or Zernial, or Sauer, or Horton) would be a disaster, because he could never cut off the ball in the gap quickly enough to keep the runner from first at second, or to keep the ball down the line from becoming a triple.

So there is never, or virtually never, a right fielder who is as slow as the slower left fielders—but also, there is virtually never a right fielder who is as fast as the faster left fielders. Think about it: has there ever, in the history of baseball, been a right fielder who was as fast as Brock, or Henderson, or Raines, or Willie Wilson, or George Burns, or George Case, or Lonnie Smith, or Vince Coleman?

There hasn't, because if a player was that fast and could throw well enough to play right field, he wouldn't be a right fielder, he would be a center fielder. There are fast guys who have played right field for a year or two because of the needs of their team, but there are no true right fielders who steal 50 bases a year. The result is that *there are some left fielders who are too slow to be right fielders, but there are also some left fielders who are too fast to be right fielders*. Odd, isn't it? The fastest players who are left/right fielders are all left fielders—yet on the whole, left fielders are not faster than right fielders, but probably a little slower.

If you graphed the speed of left fielders, you might get a line like the back of a two-humped camel, with slow guys and fast guys. If you graphed the speed of right fielders, you'd get a bell curve but with very steep sides and a high middle.

Brock was ... well, not as bad in left as Lonnie Smith, but never very good. He came up with the Cubs, who tried to make him a center fielder. This led them to conclude that he would never be much of a player. The Cardinals had the great Curt Flood in center, and this enabled Brock to slip into his natural role. Too fast to be a right fielder.

16 ◆ Goose Goslin
(1921–1938, 2287 G, 248 1609 .316)

> He was still using the same exaggerated closed stance with which he had begun at Washington, getting his tremendous power from a swing fuller than any other in the league. Actually, his back was nearly turned to the pitcher, and he stood poised for the pitch while looking over his own left shoulder, with his face in profile.
> —Shirley Povich, *The Washington Senators*

I had always assumed that his nickname was just a pun on his last name, but according to James J. Skipper he was actually given the nickname by a minor league sportswriter "because of his goose-like nose." He did have a huge nose, which he would joke about. In 1924, when he hit .344 and led the American League in RBI, he said "I been hitting .344 as a one-eyed hitter, you know. If I could see around my nose, I'd hit .600."

Goslin lost about as many home runs to playing in poor home run parks as any player in history ... Goose had one of the best arms in the American League the first few years of his career; he is one of few left fielders who had a strong arm. He played left field because

1. like Bob Meusel, he played in a park in which it was so deep to left and left center that the team needed a left fielder who could throw.

2. The Senators had a good right fielder, Sam Rice.

But in 1927 Goslin had a separated shoulder which left him unable to throw. When Goslin fielded a ball the Senators' shortstop had to race 150 feet into the outfield to get the relay throw. His arm came back in a couple of years, but it was never like it had been.

Goslin was well liked by the press and public, but was not well liked by other players. "He was all for Goose," said Chief Hogsett. He was at times accused of not hustling, not hitting in the clutch, being unduly concerned with his own stats, and not being a winning type player. As to not being a winning player, he played in more World Series games than Frankie Crosetti or Tony Perez, being a regular on five championship teams. And as to not hitting in the clutch, one would think that his career RBI record would be a sufficient answer to that. If it isn't, look at the 1935 World Series.

17 ◆ Charlie Keller

(1939–1952, 1170 G, 189 760 .286)

Charlie Keller, had he not been injured, would have been one of the greatest power hitters in the history of baseball; he would rank, if not with Williams and Ruth and Aaron, certainly with Ott and Schmidt and Reggie and Willie McCovey and Al Simmons.

Keller was a 5-foot-11 farm boy with huge muscles and dark black hair growing all over his body like kudzu vines. They called him "King Kong," a nickname which he detested, but it stuck because it worked. "He wasn't scouted," said Lefty Gomez. "He was trapped." When Yogi Berra joined the Yankees in 1946 he was introduced to Spud Chandler, who reportedly remarked afterward, "My God, they found one uglier than Keller."

Keller had milked cows from the age of six, developing wrists like steel, and pitched hay from age seven, developing shoulders like haystacks. He went to the University of Maryland, near his home, and was signed by Gene McCann, a top Yankee scout, who insisted that he be sent directly to Newark, one of the two top spots in the Yankee chain. He hit .353 there as a twenty-year-old, and then, the Yankees not needing outfielders, went back again and hit .365, scoring 149 runs and driving in 129.

Joining the Yankees in 1939, he hit .334 as a rookie, then began concentrating on hitting for power, and did that, too; his career average was .286, but with power and walks giving him a secondary average of .450. Herb Pennock said that of all the left-handed hitters he had ever seen, only Babe Ruth could hit the ball as hard to left field as Keller. He could run—he hit 15 triples in 1940, and 9 or more in every season that he was a regular—he could throw, and he gave A+ effort on the bases and in the field. With Joe DiMaggio, who was even a little bit better, and Tommy Henrich, who was very, very good, he formed one of the greatest outfields in the history of baseball. (See Bobby Veach. In 1942 and in 1946, in my opinion, Keller was actually a better player than DiMaggio.)

Keller was a perfectionist, a man who would go three-for-four and smash his bat if he struck out his fourth time up. He never liked New York City. He played in Newark for two years, but had never been over to New York until he went north with the Yankees in 1939; he said he just wasn't interested in cities. The highlight of every year, to Keller, was getting back to his farm in Maryland when the season was over; he said it was like getting out of the Army every year.

In June, 1947, Keller was trapped in a rundown play in Detroit, when something snapped in his back. He had a ruptured disk. That basically finished him as a player. In 1952 they held a Charlie Keller day at Yankee Stadium. Keller refused all gifts except a plaque, and insisted that all money raised be given to provide scholarships to the University of Maryland.

The highest park-adjusted offensive winning percentages among outfielders:

1.	Babe Ruth	.865
2.	Ted Williams	.851
3.	Mickey Mantle	.833
4.	Ty Cobb	.805

5. Joe Jackson   .802
6. Barry Bonds   .795
7. Charlie Keller   .782
8. Stan Musial   .779
9. Joe DiMaggio   .778
10. Mel Ott   .776

What this means is that it is my best estimate that a team on which Babe Ruth was the typical hitter, given an average pitching staff and an average defense, playing in a leagues in which Ruth played and the parks in which he played, would have a winning percentage of about .865. They would go 140-22 in an average season, whereas a team on which Mel Ott was the typical hitter would go about 126-36.

The second ten are Tris Speaker, Willie Mays, Benny Kauff, Billy Hamilton, Hank Aaron, Frank Robinson, Elmer Flick, Gavy Cravath, Pete Browning, and Ed Delahanty. The opposite list can be found in the Doc Cramer comment (CF #90).

18 ◆ Ralph Kiner
(1946–1955, 1472 G, 369 1015 .279)

He gets an older ballplayer or a former ballplayer on like Willie Mays, and he tries to get Mays to say that the major leagues are bringing ballplayers up too early. [Then when] Mays is gone and Dave Schneck, a rookie, is there in his place, Kiner tells Schneck there's a better crop of young ballplayers in the majors than ever before. He's a two-faced bastard.

"One thing about Kiner," said [Harry] Wendelstedt, "he'll give you a nickel for a dime anytime. That's the kind of guy he is. Only guy worse than Kiner that's been associated with baseball is Leo Durocher."—Lee Gutkind, *The Best Seat in Baseball But You Have to Stand* (First speaker is Art Williams.)

When Ralph Kiner joined the Cubs in 1953, Cub manager Phil Cavarretta shifted Hank Sauer to right field. Sauer told Cavarretta that his arm wasn't good enough to play right. "Yes, it isn't," said Cavarretta. "but it's still better than Kiner's."

Kiner has so many other weaknesses that if you had eight Ralph Kiners on an American Association team, it would finish last.—Branch Rickey

The quotes above are no doubt unfair, but there are others like them . . . a lot of people never liked Kiner. Branch Rickey came to the Pirates as Kiner was at his zenith, and immediately stated his intention to trade Kiner for whatever he could get. The Pirate owner, John Galbreath, said "Wait a minute," and then said "No" and then said "Hell, no."

This provoked Rickey, in one of the oddest moves of his career, to begin systematically destroying Kiner's reputation as a player, so that he could trade him; it's nuts, but that's what he was doing. Kiner was regarded by some Pirate fans as the second coming of Babe Ruth. Rickey went down a check list, comparing Kiner to Babe Ruth. Kiner didn't do well. If he could make his player less popular with the local fans, Rickey reasoned, he would then be free to trade him.

As it turned out, Rickey was right on the narrow point; Kiner had leg, ankle, and back problems which dramatically shortened his career. Had the Pirates traded him in 1950 or 1951 for a package of three young players, they would likely have come out far ahead on the deal, particularly when you consider that Branch Rickey would have been picking the young players.

On another level, Rickey was saying that if Kiner was really as good as the Pirate fans thought he was, the Pirates wouldn't be in last place. This is unfair. Kiner wasn't Babe Ruth, but he was a top flight player, for a few years. No one player is going to keep a team out of last place, year after year, without *some* contributions from the other 24 guys.

During all the time I managed the Pirates there never was a time that Kiner didn't do everything I asked him to do for the general good of the ball club. No matter what I said, it was perfectly okay with him.—Billy Meyer (Kiner's manager, 1947–1952)

XX ◆ Monte Irvin
(1949–1956, 764 G, 99 443 .293)

I'm not going to try to rate Monte Irvin, since his career is half or two-thirds in one world, half or one-third in the other. He hit .394 in ten World Series games.

19 ◆ Frank Howard
(1958–1973, 1895 G, 382 1119 .273)

Howard won the Rookie of the Year of the Award in 1960, then got a reputation for chasing bad balls, and was platooned a good part of the time from 1961 through 1963. He held out in the spring of 1964, threatening to retire rather than continue as a platoon player. It was suggested that the league's pitchers would be happy to take up a retirement fund for him, prompting Jim Murray to write that "You would think that when a man shows such a marked passion for swinging at bouncing curve balls, the pitchers would be more inclined to take up a collection to keep him IN the league. But the catch is that when Frank does get a piece of wood on a breaking pitch, more often than not he hits it straight back at the pitcher. Howard is going to hit a ball back through the box some night and where there once was a 200-lb. pitcher standing, there is only going to be a pair of shoes."

One thing people forget about Frank Howard is that he had an arm. Vic Power managed Howard in Puerto Rico in the winter of 1959–1960, and didn't know where to play him. Howard, who was compulsively polite, told Power that he was happy to play wherever

he was needed, Mr. Power. Power played first himself, and he thought Howard was too slow to be an outfielder (which he was), so he put him on the mound. Howard started two games, and, according to Power, "he pitched against Orlando Cepeda and Roberto Clemente and they were scared of him because he was ten feet tall and threw hard." But as soon as the Dodgers found out about it, they asked Power not to let Howard pitch any more.

20 ◆ Albert Belle
(1989–2000, 1539 G, 381 1239 .295)

Let's try to find ten *good* things to say about Albert Belle:

10. So far as we know, he's never killed any-one.

9. He is handsome, and built like a God.

8. He played every game.

7. He has never appeared on the Jerry Springer Show.

6. He was an underrated base runner who was rarely caught stealing.

5. He hasn't been arrested in several years.

4. He is very bright.

3. He works hard.

2. He has never spoken favorably about Adolf Hitler, Saddam Hussein, or any other foreign madman.

1. The man could hit.

21 ◆ Sherry Magee
(1904–1919, 2087 G, 83 1176 .291)

Philadelphia slugger of a hundred years ago, led the National League in RBI in 1907, 1910, 1914, and 1918, the last time with Cincinnati; also led the league in slugging percentage twice, in batting, on-base percentage, runs scored, and doubles in various seasons.

Magee is indirectly responsible for the sacrifice fly rule. Magee's manager in Philadelphia,

Billy Murray, expressed often the opinion that players should be credited with sacrifices when they hit run-scoring fly balls, as, he argued, Magee very often did. Murray's argument persuaded the league to count sacrifice flies as sacrifices, beginning in 1908. This innovation failed, as it mixed together unlike events to create a kind of "sacrifice mush," but eventually sacrifice flies were split off into their own category.

> The one thing to do, however, is to hold the bat tightly. Players who have loose grips never hit the ball very far. If Sherwood Magee held his bat tighter he would have a couple of dozen home runs each season. But he lets the stick hang loosely in his hands and can't get his full strength into the blow.—Interview with Gavy Cravath, *Philadelphia Public Ledger,* 1919

> In July [1911] outfielder Magee assaulted Umpire Finneran and was suspended by President Lynch for 36 days, thus further weakening the team in batting and fielding.—1912 *Reach Guide*

> Sherwood Nottingham Magee, star outfielder of the crippled Philadelphia Nationals, will again be eligible to return to their home grounds, Wednesday, August 16. Magee was suspended for the remainder of the present season some weeks ago for an inexcusable assault upon umpire Finneran. Through the influence of President Horace Fogel, of the Phillies, Magee was able to secure a rehearing of President Lynch's ruling by appeal to the Board of Directors of the National League. This board upheld the verdict of President Lynch in every particular. But after he was exonerated by the league directors the President's heart began to soften toward the Phillies in their afflictions. Manager Dooin, one of the finest catchers in the circuit, was crippled for the season with a broken leg. Communications to Mr. Lynch, imploring him in the name of sport to make an exception to rigid discipline in the case of a team so badly shattered and reinstate Magee, poured in from every quarter. Finally the executive decided to

reinstate the player on probation. Magee will be permitted to finish the year for his club, provided he keeps the peace.—*The Sporting Life,* August 12, 1911

> Magee came up to bat next, threw his hat on the ground, and started to call me names. He is bad when irritated—and tolerably easy to irritate. —Christy Mathewson, *Pitching in a Pinch*

22 ◆ Fred Clarke
(1894–1915, 2242 G, 67 1015 .312)

> Fred was unanimously selected as the greatest left-fielder of his time. He was a demon base runner, and . . . he was perhaps the best man ever known to baseball coming in to slide for low line drives.—Harold "Speed" *Johnson, Who's Who in the Major Leagues,* 1935

In a game in 1906, Clarke stole home by accident. With the bases loaded and Jim Nealon at bat, Nealon took a 3-1 pitch for what he assumed was ball four. At this time the veteran umpires didn't signal pitches, they called them. Umpire Hank O'Day got a frog in his throat, and couldn't speak for a second, so Cubs catcher Johnny Kling also assumed that the pitch was a ball, and flipped the ball back to the pitcher. By the time O'Day called the pitch a strike the pitcher had the ball, and it was too late to stop Clarke from ambling home. He didn't realize he had stolen home until he was in the dugout.

Clarke was a player who lived by his wits, not that he didn't run well and hit alright. Christy Mathewson in *Pitching in a Pinch* tells many stories about him. In one story, Rube Waddell, the simple-minded pitcher, was warned before the game not to let Clarke distract him from his pitching. Clarke, from the third base box, tried every kind of abuse he could imagine, without effect, until he switched suddenly into Rube's best friend. "Why don't you come out to my ranch in Kansas after the season, George?" Clarke asked. "I've got a pup out there you can train, and you can have him if he takes a fancy to you."

"They all do," replied Waddell. "He's as good as mine."

The next inning, as Christy tells it, Rube was still thinking about the dog—and the Pirates scored five runs.

23 ◆ Zack Wheat
(1909–1927, 2410 G, 132 1248 .317)

> Zack Wheat, half Cherokee, was the most popular ball player Brooklyn ever had. [He was] a typical farmer and old-fashioned ball player with a chaw of tobacco in his face.—Harry Grayson, *They Played the Game*

After the Dodgers won the pennant in 1916 Wheat held out the following spring. Charles Ebbets visited him at his farm in Missouri, but they failed to reach an agreement, and Wheat was still holding out well into spring training, 1917. Finally Wheat received a telegram reading "Report at once. C. H. Ebbets."

Wheat reported to camp, only to discover that the telegram had actually been sent by a sportswriter, Abe Yager. But once he was there, Wheat decided he might as well have dinner with Ebbets and talk turkey, and they reached an agreement that night . . .

> Zack Wheat, a young outfielder with a compact build, muscular shoulders and a keen eye.—Lee Allen, *The Giants and the Dodgers*

> One night Wheat, a somewhat early-to-bed chap, was in his bed with the lights out but still awake when his young roomie came softly into the room about midnight. He stood still for a full minute, then moved closer to Zach and peered down at him. Apparently satisfied that Wheat was asleep, the rookie stealthily lifted Wheat's trousers from the chair they were draped over, took out the wallet and removed a bill from it.—Roscoe McGowen, *Sport Magazine* June 1964

According to McGowen, Wheat simply waited until the unidentified rookie was asleep, retrieved his money, and said nothing about it.

Wheat was one of the first players acquired for the Dodgers by Larry Sutton, the Dodgers' first full-time scout. Sutton saw Wheat playing for Mobile of the Southern Association, and bought him immediately for $1200. When he brought him to Brooklyn, Ebbets asked "What did he hit at Mobile?"

"Two-forty-five," said Sutton.

"Two-forty-five?" said Ebbets. "What are you bringing me a .245 hitter for?"

Wheat in Mobile had had malaria, which cleared up about the time he joined the Dodgers. Sutton didn't know that he had been ill, but knew he wasn't a .245 hitter.

Wheat was named "Zachary" after President Zachary Taylor. His brother Mack, who also played in the majors, was named "McKinley" after President McKinley . . .

Wheat was an easy-going, business-like professional, neither a hothead nor a high liver, extremely well liked by teammates. He was a man who simply took care of business. When Casey Stengel joined the Dodgers in 1912 he knew Wheat a little bit, because Casey was from Kansas City and Wheat was from near Kansas City. Wheat took Casey under his wing, moved Stengel's locker next to his, talked to him constantly on the bench and in the outfield, and worked with him before games.

After his playing career Wheat opened a bowling alley in Kansas City (1928), but lost that to the depression. He worked as a cop for several years, but was involved in a hot-pursuit accident which messed up his neck, so that he carried his head to one side for years afterward (although this apparently cleared up, as photos taken of him at the time of his election to the Hall of Fame in 1959 show him holding his head normally). In 1944 Harry Grayson reported that he was working in a war plant in

Wichita. In 1959 he was running a small vacation resort in the Ozarks, the southern part of Missouri.

Wheat* was a similar player to Sherry Magee, but got into the Hall of Fame in part because he was a few years younger, which made his career last into the lively ball era, and gave him some big-number seasons at the end of his career. See also Rusty Staub (RF #24) . . .

24 ◆ Jimmy Sheckard

(1897–1913, 2122 G, 56 813 .274)

Sheckard drew 147 walks in 1911, which was the National League record until Eddie Stanky, and is still one of the highest figures on record. He also hit as high as .354 (1901), stole as many as 77 bases (1899), and led the National League at various times in triples, home runs, runs scored, walks, sacrifice hits, stolen bases, baserunner kills (outfield assists), on base percentage and slugging percentage.

Sheckard had sort of a Toby Harrah-type career. He did a lot of things well, but not necessarily at the same time. The first half of his career he was a middle-of-the-order hitter, and a good one; the second half of his career he was a leadoff man, and a very good one.

> James Sheckard, a brilliant, clever and much wanted outfielder had disturbed the Brooklyn club by playing hop scotch with the American League during the war. Here the gossip of the club proved valuable. Sheckard was dissatisfied with Brooklyn, and Chance knew it. The Brooklyn management did not think Sheckard was giving his best services, but feared to trade a man who was popular with the spectators.—Johnny Evers, *Baseball in the Big Leagues* (Reilly and Britton, 1910)

25 ◆ Roy White

(1965–1979, 1881 G, 160 758 .271)

Roy White is probably the nicest Goddamn guy on the club. He's quiet. He's well respected by everybody, and he's very classy, he and his wife both.—Sparky Lyle, *The Bronx Zoo* (Dell, 1979)

White never hit .300 but hit .290 four times, never drew 100 walks but drew 95 and 99, never drove in a hundred runs but drove in 94. He did everything well. Still, while acknowledging that he was a good player, I may be the only person who rates Roy White ahead of Jim Rice, George Foster, Joe Carter, and several Hall of Famers, so I suppose I should tackle this rating head on. Let's do Jim Rice . . . let's compare Roy White, 1968–1972, to Jim Rice, 1975–1979; those are each player's five best years.

Over the five seasons, Rice played a few more games than White (778-753) and had a few more plate appearances (3381-3215). Rice had far more hits per season (192-153), and had more hits of each type, more singles (118-107), more doubles (29-26), more triples (10-5), and more home runs (34-15), more than twice as many taters. Rice scored more runs per year (102-83), drove in more (114-74), and hit for a higher average (.311 to .283). Thus, it is easy to see why people would assume that Rice is more valuable; we are comparing a player whose typical triple-crown stats are 34, 114, .311 to one whose trio is 15, 74, .283.

However, White is not without his advantages; he drew almost twice as many walks as Rice (87 per season to 46), struck out less than half as often (58 to 118), and stole more bases (20 to 8) with a better stolen base percentage. White grounded into 10 double plays per season; Rice, into 18. White also had more sacrifice hits and, perhaps surprisingly, more sacrifice flies. These things narrow the gap, but over the five seasons Rice created about 577 runs (115 per season), while White created about 471 (94 per season).

So Rice is well ahead, 106 runs ahead. There are three other offensive factors which have to be considered, to convert "Run Value" into

"Win Value," which is the bottom line. Those three things are:

1. League context.
2. Park context.
3. Outs used.

From 1968 through 1972 the American League average was 3.80 runs per team per game. From 1975 through 1979 the average was 4.34.

White played in a park, Yankee Stadium, which reduced runs scored at that time by about 9%, meaning that there were fewer runs there, which means that each run was more valuable. Rice played in a park which *increased* run scoring by almost twenty percent; the relevant park adjustments are .96 for White, 1.09 for Rice. Making that adjustment, White's 94 runs per season represent about 26 games worth of team offense (94 divided by 3.65), while Rice's 115 runs represent about 24 games worth of offense (115 divided by 4.73).

Roy White, in context, was actually a more productive hitter than Jim Rice. We haven't dealt with outs used. White made 419 outs per season; Rice made 456. We haven't dealt with defense. Jim Rice wasn't a bad outfielder, but Roy White obviously was better.

Roy White has been a tremendously underrated player, for three reasons:

1. His skills were subtle, and not easily summarized into two or three statistics.

2. Like Ralph Kiner, he was blamed for the failures of his teams.

3. He was measured, for much of his career, against a standard of Mickey Mantle and Joe DiMaggio. Bobby Murcer couldn't meet that standard, Tom Tresh couldn't, Roy White couldn't—and Jim Rice couldn't.

There isn't an ocean between them, just a stream. I agree that Jim Rice's best season, 1978, is better than White's best season, 1970—but White's second- and third-best seasons are better than any other Jim Rice campaign. Rice,

in 1977 and again in 1979, hit 39 home runs—12 on the road, 27 in Fenway Park. Roy White in his best years would hit 10 home runs at home, 10 on the road. If Jim Rice had played in Yankee Stadium, how many home runs would he have hit? If Jim Rice had been compared to Mickey Mantle and asked to drag Ron Woods and Jake Gibbs and Jerry Kinney and Gene Michael to the pennant, how would he have fared? I think if you put both players in the same park in the same years, a lot of fans would be able to see that White was a better all-around player.

26 ◆ George Burns
(1911–1925, 1853 G, 41 611 .287, 383 SB)
Jack Coombs was once asked who was the toughest hitter he ever faced. He said George Burns. Another reporter asked George Burns

Ty Cobb and George Burns, about 1921

who the toughest pitcher he ever faced was. He said Jack Coombs . . .

> George was one of the few players for whom [McGraw] had ever indicated a warm personal regard. He had taken him as a raw busher and guided him in his development into what Bill McGeehan had called the almost perfect out-fielder.–Frank Graham, *McGraw of the Giants,* Putnam, 1944

> Burns also was tagged with the moniker of "Silent George" by his teammates and New York sports-writers. Well-behaved and soft-spoken, Burns was never ejected from a game in his career. He was also recognized as one of the best pool players ever to put on a baseball uniform.–Richard Puff, *The Empire State of Base Ball*

Burns, like a lot of other leadoff men, has been largely unappreciated. It would be an interesting study to take a group of leadoff men, form another group of players who played the same positions, played about the same number of games, and earned about the same number of career Win Shares, and then compare the numbers of each group who are in the Hall of Fame, the MVP Awards won, and the number of all-star appearances. I am certain that the leadoff men would be far behind. Burns, for example, played about the same number of career games and was about as good a player as Jim O'Rourke, Joe Kelley, Kiki Cuyler, Heinie Manush, and Earl Averill. I'm not saying he *should* be in the Hall of Fame, because there are better players who aren't, but the only leadoff men to get lucky in the Hall of Fame lottery have been Lloyd Waner, Max Carey, Phil Rizzuto, and Tommy McCarthy.

27 ◆ Jim Rice
(1974–1989, 2089 G, 382 1451 .298)
Probably the most overrated player of the last thirty years. He was a pretty good defensive left fielder, and didn't get credit for that because he wasn't Yastrzemski. But he was a poor runner,

and, as a hitter, he was helped by playing in Fenway. He led the league in grounding into double plays four straight seasons, and has one of the highest GIDP rates in history.

> Jim Rice was one of the best left fielders I ever had out there [but] the fans never liked Jim Rice. No one could like Jim Rice. Jim Rice had one of the biggest egos I've ever seen. He treated people so abruptly, just had no need for anybody, gave no time back to the fans, just was not a nice person.–Bill Lee in *Fenway*

28 ◆ Joe Kelley
(1891–1908, 1842 G, 65 1194 .317)
Kelley's birth name was Joe Kelly. Reporters added the "e" because it was somehow associated with higher status in Ireland; Kelley liked it and adopted it.

> He was powerfully built, and his broad face had a cleft chin and surprisingly delicate features, topped by dirty blond hair that was parted in the

Joe Kelley

middle and plastered to his head. He had a gift for repartee. The ladies loved him, almost as much as he loved himself.—Burt Solomon, *Hit 'em Where They Ain't*

According to Robert I. Tiemann in *Baseball's First Stars,* Kelley carried a mirror in his pocket, which he would use to fix his appearance in mid-game. In 1897, however, he married the daughter of a prominent Baltimore politician, and the marriage lasted. Kelley later managed, not too well, and for many years was a scout for the New York Yankees, noted for his skepticism about young players.

One time the fans in Baltimore got together and presented Kelley a fine watch as a tribute to him. Kelley took the watch to the clubhouse man for safekeeping until after the game, but the clubhouse attendant had to leave, so he turned it over to the umpire. The umpire, George Burnham, said he would keep the watch until after the game.

Well, during the game Burnham called Kelley out on a close play at second base. Kelley argued and argued, and eventually Burnham gave him one minute to get off the field, and pulled a watch to time the minute. Kelley slapped the watch out of Burnham's hand, stomped on it and kicked it across the infield—not realizing that it was his own brand new watch that he was destroying. George Burnham was called "Watch" Burnham as long as he remained in baseball.

29 ◆ Jose Cruz
(1970–1988, 2353 G, 165 1077 .284)
A six-time .300 hitter who stole about 40 bases a season, Cruz's numbers were ruined by playing his best seasons in the Astrodome when it had Park Factors around .80.

Had he played in most other parks, it is clear that Cruz would have won multiple National League batting titles. In 1983 Cruz hit .318, missing the National League batting title

by five points; this was the closest that anyone would ever come to winning a batting title in the Astrodome, and Cruz was one of a handful of Astros ever to finish among the NL leaders in batting. That year he hit .324 with 11 home runs, 48 RBI on the road, making him as good a hitter in "road" games as anyone in the National League.

In 1984 he was better; he hit .349 with 12 home runs in road games—but .274 with no homers in Houston. In his career he lost about 47 home runs to the Astrodome, and probably lost at least ten points off of his career average.

30 ◆ Heinie Manush
(1923–1939, 2009 G, 110 1183 .330)
Cobb made him a hitter. He was from Tuscumbia, Alabama. Ty had a lot of confidence in him . . . I saw Ty try and teach Heinie. He had a lot of patience with Heinie and Heinie did what he was told.—Ed Wells, *Baseball Between the Wars* (Eugene Murdock)

Harry "Heinie" Manush benefited from coaching by Cobb, who urged him to choke up, cut down on his swing, and hit the ball where it was pitched.—Joe Falls, *The Detroit Tigers*

Manush was kind of a pale Ty Cobb. Like Cobb he was:

- A Southerner.
- A high-average hitter who hit doubles and triples.
- A left-handed batter.
- A firebrand, and a bit of a ruffian.

Playing for Cobb in 1926, Manush won the AL batting title at .378. With Cobb gone the next year, he slumped to .298. That finished him in Detroit, as the new Detroit manager, George Moriarty, (a) hated Ty Cobb, and (b) regarded Manush as Cobb's boy.

In dramatic contrast to Bobby Veach, whose role he had inherited, Manush was not a friendly or agreeable man. He would use his spikes, even on ex-teammates. He is one of relatively few men to have been thrown out of a World Series game.

> Never saw Mount Vesuvius in eruption, but saw the next thing to it; that being the spectacle of Heinie Manush fuming and roaring at an umpire.—Ira Smith, *Baseball's Famous Outfielders*

Manush was the youngest of seven brothers, five of whom played professional baseball. You have seen the commercial in which a manager roars out of the dugout and pretends to cuss and yell at an umpire, all the while exchanging pleasantries and inviting the ump to dinner. According to Smith, Manush actually did that at least once, putting on a spectacular display of anger to hide the fact that he was out at second on a stolen base attempt, while actually paying the second base umpire (Bill McGowan) a string of compliments.

31 ◆ Bob Johnson
(1933–1945, 1863 G, 288 1283 .296)
Johnson was a practical joker. One time he was playing left field in a game in which the other left fielder was his brother, Roy Johnson, who incidentally just missed the list of the top 100 left fielders; I have him ranked 125th. Anyway, at that time fielders left their gloves in the field when they went in to bat. Johnson, spotting his brother's glove in the outfield and a bird setting a few feet away, managed to trap the bird, and left it in his brother's glove. Roy went to pick up the glove and jumped about a foot in the air when a bird flew out.

Tony Lazzeri was also a practical joker, and the two of them were always trying to get the best of one another. One time Lazzeri took a used baseball, and doctored it for two weeks. He put it on a bench and pounded on it with his bat, soaked it overnight in soapy water, rubbed dirt into it until it was as dead as Abe Lincoln, then put a little shoe polish on it so it would look white at a glance. When Johnson came up to bat in a nothing game at the end of the season (September 29, 1937), Lazzeri walked to the mound to talk with the pitcher, Kemp Wicker, and switched baseballs.

Wicker threw Johnson a fat pitch, right out in the middle of the plate with nothing on it. Johnson nearly came out of his shoes taking a whack at it. He hit it solid, but the ball went "thud" instead of "crack," and bounced off harmlessly into foul territory. The crowd laughed. "What was that?" Johnson asked. "What'd I hit?"

Bill Summers remembered in a *Look* magazine article 25 years later that he was the home plate umpire, that he called the pitch a strike, and that he stuck with the call over the objections of Johnson and his Philadelphia teammates, apparently to cover Lazzeri's ass. He said that he knew immediately what had happened. "Lazzeri," he said, "turned around." Sure enough, Lazzeri had the other baseball in his back pocket.

The *New York Times* report of the next day, however, says that

1. Summers was the first-base umpire.

2. The home-plate umpire, Johnny Quinn, immediately nullified the pitch.

3. It was the Philadelphia bench that caught on to Lazzeri's deception and told Quinn, who sent Summers to second base to check it out.

4. The incident was immediately reported to the league office, which was expected to fine Lazzeri for tampering with the baseball.

Not that it matters; I would just like to try to straighten these things out. It was, at the time, a game of such importance that neither manager, Connie Mack nor Joe McCarthy, even bothered to attend, Mack because he was nursing a cold, and McCarthy because he just opted to go watch Newark play, the pennant having long since been secured.

32 ◆ Joe Carter

(1983–1998, 2189 G, 396 1445 .259)

Within the world of sabermetrics there is an on-going debate about whether there are actually players who have an *ability* to hit well in the clutch. Joe Carter is, of course, the most famous clutch hitter of the last generation. This is based in part on his ten seasons of 100 or more RBI, in part on his performance in the 1992 World Series, when he homered twice in the series and hit two doubles in the sixth and final game, and in large part on his performance in the 1993 World Series, when he hit a Game-Winning home run in the bottom of the ninth inning of the sixth game. In fairness, however, Carter had a reputation as a clutch hitter dating back to 1986, when he led the American League in RBI with 121.

On the other hand, we have Barry Bonds. Obviously Bonds has much better numbers than Carter overall, but there are people who have been reluctant to accept his greatness as a player, on the theory that he hasn't produced in the clutch.

Since 1987, STATS has scored every major league game, and produced statistical profiles which include things like a player's batting average with runners in scoring position, his batting average in the late innings of close games, etc. Since we have this information for all of Bonds' career and most of Carter's, I thought perhaps it would be instructive to study it and see whether there is any actual evidence therein that Carter was a superior clutch player. OK, let's go:

Batting with runners on base/bases empty: Carter hit .255 overall during the twelve years for which we have data. With no one on base, he hit .252; with men on base, he hit .259.

Bonds hit .280 with the bases empty, .309 with men on base. Advantage: Bonds.

Carter homered 6% more often with the bases empty than he did with men on base.

Bonds homered 11% more often with men on base than with the bases empty; advantage, Bonds, Bonds leads 2-zip.

Batting with runners in scoring position: Most players have a higher average with runners in scoring position than overall, because all sacrifice flies occur with runners in scoring position. If you take those out, most players hit about the same with runners on second or third as they do overall.

Carter hit .271 with runners in scoring position, sixteen points higher than his overall average. Bonds hit .301 with runners in scoring position, thirteen points over his overall average. We'll count that one a draw . . .

Carter batted 2017 times with runners in scoring position, driving in 803 times; that's 40 RBI per 100 at bats. Bonds batted only 1539 times with runners in scoring position, but drove in 774 runs, which is 50 RBI per 100 at bats.

However, Bonds did walk 591 times with runners in scoring position, Carter only 233 times. If you factor those out—that is, if you count a walk as a failure, rather than a non-event—they are almost even in terms of RBI frequency—35.7 for Carter, 36.3 for Bonds. Overall, I think you have to score it as an edge for Bonds; Barry leads, 3-0.

Leading off an inning: Leading off an inning (batting with no one on and no one out) is what might be called a "hidden clutch" situation. A lot of people don't think of it as a clutch situation, but if a batter reaches base leading off an inning, this has a magnified effect on the team's expected runs for the inning, which is essentially how you define a clutch situation—a situation in which there is a magnified impact on runs scored or on game outcome.

Carter, whose overall on-base percentage was .305, dropped to .295 in that situation. Bonds, whose overall on-base percentage is .409, dropped to .369 leading off an inning. I suppose one could, by some theory, count that as an advantage for Carter . . . Bonds 3, Carter 1.

Hitting in the late innings of a close game: Carter, in the late innings of close games, hit .220 and drove in 149 runs in 1004 at bats. Bonds hit .279 and drove in 174 runs in 981 at bats. Clear advantage for Bonds, 4 to 1.

Hitting with the bases loaded: Carter hit .273 with 7 homers with the bases loaded, driving in 124 runs in 143 shots. Bonds has hit .361 with 8 home runs with the bases loaded, driving in 141 runs in 133 opportunities. Bonds leads, 5 to 1.

Batting in September: We'll use On-Base plus slugging here as an easy overall measure . . . Carter, whose overall OB + SLG was .770, dropped to .720 in September, .759 in a few games in early October. Bonds, whose overall OB + SLG is .984, has been at .979 in September, 1.327 in 18 games in October. We'll sit this one aside, as I'm uncertain whether September performance can be equated with clutch performance, and I don't want to bias the outcome in Bonds' favor.

Playoff performance: Bonds has played in four playoffs, 23 games, hitting just .200 with one homer; Carter in 17 games wasn't much better, hitting .236 with 2 homers. Edge to Carter, Bonds still leads, 5 to 2.

World Series performance: Bonds hasn't appeared in a World Series. Carter did play 12 World Series games, hitting 4 homers and driving in 11 runs . . . we'll give him a point for that, making it 5 to 3.

Taking it all in, I think it is hard to say that the record shows that Carter deserves any special credit as a clutch hitter.

33 ◆ Bobby Veach
(1912–1925, 1822 G, 64 1166 .310)

> He was a happy-go-lucky guy, not too brilliant above the ears. His general attitude was that by a stroke of good fortune he was elevated above his

Ty Cobb and Davy Jones

> station and his cue was to mollify his associates rather than compete with them. As a result he was as friendly as a Newfoundland pup with opponents as well as teammates.—Fred Lieb, *The Detroit Tigers*

What is the greatest outfield in the history of baseball? The Win Shares system can address this question by simply adding together the values of the three best outfielders on each team . . . same thing we did with infielders, see Ken Boyer (3B #12).

The greatest outfields of all time, it turns out, all belong to the Tigers and Yankees. We start with the Tigers of 1915—Veach in left, Cobb in center, Crawford in right:

1915 Det   Veach . . 30   Cobb . . 49   Crawford . . 28   107

Even by the standards of the dead ball era, 1915 was a pitcher's year, with an American

League ERA of 2.93, a batting average of .248, and an average of 20 home runs per team. In that run-starved environment (615 runs per team), Ty Cobb hit .369 with 99 RBI, 144 runs scored, Crawford hit .313 and drove in 112 runs, and Veach hit .299 and also drove in 112 runs. Cobb led the league in runs scored and hits, Veach led in doubles, Crawford led in triples. Ty Cobb led the league in total bases, with Crawford second, Veach third, and Veach and Crawford tied for the league lead in RBI, with Cobb third. They were, if not the three best hitters in the league, certainly three of the five best.

This is, of course, a very famous outfield; all of you who read books of baseball stories will remember numerous anecdotes about pitchers in fear of facing this trio. It is something of a surprise that 1915 is the season in which they score best, but they do so by a comfortable margin, six Win Shares.

The 1915 Tigers won 100 games, but did not win the American League pennant, as Boston won 101. This is the only outfield in the top six which did not pull its team to the pennant.

In a second place tie is another Cobb/Crawford outfield, the 1908 Tigers:

1908 Det   McIntyre..33   Crawford..32   Cobb..35   101

Matty McIntyre hit .295 that season with 83 walks, leading the American League in Runs Scored. This is the only outfield in history in which all three outfielders earned 30 Win Shares. Thirty Win Shares is the basic standard of an MVP candidate. Less than half of all teams have one *player* who earns 30 Win Shares; probably less than a fourth of teams have one outfielder at that level.

But superstars crack the 30-level year in and year out. The dead ball Tigers are the only team in history which had two superstars in the outfield for a period of several years—and thus,

they had the greatest outfields of all time. Veach, the usual third, was not a superstar, but he was a very, very good player.

The '08 Tigers are tied with the 1941 Yankees:

1941 NYA   Keller..33   DiMaggio..41   Henrich..27   101

This was the first team in history to have three outfielders hit 30 or more home runs, until the 1980s the *only* team in history to have three outfielders with 30 home runs. All three outfielders scored over a hundred runs. Henrich drove in only 85, but the other two guys were over 120, and the Yankees reduced Ted Williams' bid for .400 into a sideshow.

Then we're back to the Tigers:

1907 Det   D Jones..23   Crawford..36   Cobb..41   100

Who actually are tied with another Yankee team:

1961 NYA   Berra..16   Mantle..48   Maris..36   100

You've probably heard of that team. Left fielder listed first in all cases; the '61 Yankees didn't have a real left fielder, had a catcher platooning out there, but the other two guys were pretty good. And you've probably heard of the next team, too:

1927 NYA   Meusel..21   Combs..32   Ruth..45   98

The '27 Yankees. That's six teams; in a seventh/eighth place tie are the 1902 Pirates:

1902 Pit   Clarke..29   Beaumont..31   Wagner..35   95

Fred Clarke, Ginger Beaumont, and Honus Wagner, in his last year before moving to shortstop. Honus played all over the field, actually, but our rule is, we count the three top players who can reasonably be described as outfielders. The 1902 Pirates, by the way, had a winning percentage almost 30 points higher than the 1927 Yankees. This is the only non-

Yankee, non-Tiger team in the top nine, and then we're back to Bobby Veach:

1917 Det   Veach..31   Cobb..46   Heilmann..18   95

By 1917 the Tigers had replaced Sam Crawford, but fortunately they had replaced him with another Hall of Famer. Ninth place is a three-way tie, led off by (yawn) another Cobb/ Crawford team:

1909 Det   McIntyre..16   Crawford..33   Cobb..44   93

McIntyre dropped off from 1908, but Cobb and Crawford were able to pick up some of the slack. In 1923 Ruth had his greatest all-around season, hitting .393 with 170 walks:

1923 NYA   Meusel..16   Witt..22   Ruth..55   93

The Philadelphia Phillies in the mid-1890s had a Hall of Fame outfield of Ed Delahanty, Sliding Billy Hamilton, and Sam Thompson. That outfield never *quite* cracked the top ten, but by 1899 they had replaced Billy Hamilton with a similar player, Roy Thomas, and Sam Thompson with another Hall of Famer, Elmer Flick:

1899 Phi   Delahanty..41   R Thomas..29   Flick..23   93

Any way you cut it, the Phillies had the greatest outfield of the 19th century. You can argue about which year. Picking it up from there:

92 Win Shares
1928 Yankees (Meusel, Combs, and Ruth)
1968 Red Sox (Yastrzemski, Reggie Smith, and Ken Harrelson)

90 Win Shares
1991 Pirates (Bonds, Van Slyke, and Bonilla)

89 Win Shares
1895 Phillies (Delahanty, Hamilton, and Sam Thompson)

1963 Giants (McCovey, Mays, and Felipe Alou)

88 Win Shares
1905 Phillies (Sherry Magee, Roy Thomas, John Titus)
1911 Tigers (Davy Jones, Cobb, and Crawford)
1912 Red Sox (Duffy Lewis, Tris Speaker, and Harry Hooper)

87 Win Shares
1901 Phillies (Delahanty, Thomas, and Flick)
1934 Giants (Hank Leiber, Jo Jo Moore, Mel Ott)
1972 Astros (Bob Watson, Cesar Cedeno, Jimmie Wynn)

86 Win Shares
1948 Cardinals (Musial, Ron Northey, Slaughter)
1962 Dodgers (Frank Howard, Willie, and Tommy Davis)

85 Win Shares
1914 Red Sox (Lewis, Speaker, and Hooper)
1916 Tigers (Veach, Cobb, and Heilmann)
1921 Yankees (Meusel, Elmer Miller, Ruth)
1942 Red Sox (Ted Williams, Dom DiMaggio, Lou Finney)
1942 Yankees (Keller, Joe DiMaggio, Henrich)
1942 Cardinals (Musial, Terry Moore, Slaughter)
1953 Brooklyn (Jackie Robinson, Snider, Furillo)
1959 Indians (Francona, Minoso, Colavito)
1962 Giants (Harvey Kuenn, Mays, Felipe Alou)

1990 A's (Rickey and Dave Henderson, Canseco)

There appears to be a bias in this method toward older teams, since baseball was less competitive a hundred years ago, and the best players were further from the average than they are now. Still, very few of these all-time great outfields are surprising; it is mostly the teams we would expect to be ranked near the top.

34 ◆ George Foster
(1969–1986 1977 G, 348 1239 .274)

Same type of player as Jim Rice—same strengths, same weaknesses. Like Rice, an underrated outfielder when he wanted to be, but not a player who did a lot of things to help the team.

> Fans cherish a mental kinescope of George streaking across the foul line, snaring a twisting drive, then pivoting those broad shoulders to snap off a throw to the plate, doubling an overconfident runner. There were also times when Foster seemed unconcerned in the field . . .—Hub Walker, *Cincinnati and the Big Red Machine*

> A non-drinking, non-smoking, Bible-reading bachelor, George's idea of a wild evening is taking a long time to decide which flavor he wants at the 31-flavors ice cream store.—Ritter Collett, *Men of the Machine*

> I think one of the reasons Davey wanted McReynolds so much was so he would have a reason to dump George Foster. It would have been easier for Davey to bench Foster if he had another right-handed power hitter available. —Len Dykstra, *Nails*

35 ◆ Greg Luzinski
(1970–1984, 1821 G, 307 1128 .276)

Greg Luzinski was the worst outfielder I ever saw, bar none. The only guy I ever saw that was close to him was that fellow that played with Texas for a couple of years, forget his name . . . Kevin Reimer. Reimer was a good hitter, but not good enough to play. Luzinski was a tremendous hitter, but in addition to being a big, slow guy, he had no arm at all. He couldn't throw the ball across a room. It wasn't just that he couldn't run or throw, though; there are some guys who can't run or throw who are pretty good outfielders anyway (Lou Piniella, Joe Rudi, Bibb Falk, Kevin Bass, Wally Moon, Ron Fairly, Dave Henderson, and Gene Woodling, to name a few), and there are some guys who can run and maybe even throw OK, but are just bad outfielders, like Ralph Garr, Bob Nieman, Leon Wagner, Dave Kingman, Lou Brock, and Billy Ashley. Luzinski, even operating within his limitations, was just a bad outfielder. He had dreadful hands, and he had no confidence in his ability to make a play, so he played everything timidly except the wall, which he seemed to be in denial about. He was always fighting to avoid the sun. He played with his back turned to center field, sort of officially notifying Maddox that he considered anything hit to his left to be Maddox's responsibility. If a ball was hit deep he had no idea whether it was going to hit the wall and come back or not, so he would chase fly balls to the wall, only to see them rocket past him on their way back to the infield. Everything hit out there was a surprise to him; nothing was ever easy. It was like having Herman Munster playing left field. If they didn't have Garry Maddox in center field, there was absolutely no way the Phillies could have gotten by with playing him in left.

Luzinski was a 50s type of player, or a 1990s type of player—a big, slow slugger. In the 50s, and in the 90s, baseball was played in small parks with grass; in the seventies it was played in huge parks with artificial turf, and these parks magnified the defensive weakness of an outfielder. It wasn't like he wasn't *trying;* he wasn't Dave Kingman or Kevin Mitchell or somebody; he always tried. He could hit, though ... he had a very quick stroke which generated tremendous power, seemingly very easily.

36 ◆ Kirk Gibson
(1979–1995, 1635 G, 255 870 .268)

> When he walks through that clubhouse door, everyone knows he's there. There's just something about a player like Gibson ... He's a man. He comes to play and is ready to fight, down and dirty, day after day.—Sparky Anderson, *Bless You Boys*

Kirk Gibson had the lowest rate of Baserunner Kills per 1000 estimated defensive innings of any outfielder listed among the top 100 at his position. He was credited with 41 career assists, playing about 10,554 innings in the outfield:

Player	BK	Inn	BK/1000
1. Kirk Gibson	41	10,554	3.9
2. Don Baylor	27	6,666	4.1
3. Brady Anderson	51	11,915	4.3
4. Willie Wilson	77	16,430	4.7
5. Tito Francona	34	7,095	4.8
6. Bernie Williams	46	9,549	4.8
7. Ron Gant	50	10,223	4.9
8. Eric Davis	54	10,929	4.9
9. Tommy Harper	51	10,138	5.0
10. Dale Mitchell	41	8,101	5.1

37 ◆ Jim O'Rourke
(1876–1904, 1774 G, 51 830 .310)

Jim was a fine-looking lad, somewhat on the order of his teammate George Wright in disposition, always merry, full of life, and of course full of talk. He had an abundant mustache that seemed to make his loud laugh twice as jolly.
—Ira Smith, *Heroes of Baseball*

O'Rourke was called "Orator Jim" because, according to Lee Allen in *The Hot Stove League,* O'Rourke's "command of the English tongue was astonishing and bizarre." In 1890 a lion escaped from the zoo in Bridgeport, Connecticut, O'Rourke's home town. Not knowing there was a lion on the loose, a widow named Mrs. Gilligan went out to her barn and discovered the beast fixing to make a meal of Mrs. Gilligan's calf. Mrs. Gilligan grabbed a pitch fork, and drove the lion from the barn.

The newspapers made a big deal about that, and O'Rourke wrote Mrs. Gilligan a letter in praise of her bravery. The first sentence of his letter reads "The unparalleled bravery shown by you, and the unwavering fidelity extended by you to your calf during your precarious environment in the cowshed, when a ferocious, carnivorous beast threatened your total destruction, has suddenly exalted your fair name to an altitude much higher than the Egyptian pyramids, where hieroglyphics and other undecipherable mementos of the past are now lying in a state of innocuous desuetude, with no enlightened modern scholar able to exemplify their disentangled pronunciation." And he was just warming up ...

Out of superstition or vanity or some mix thereof, O'Rourke recited Hamlet's soliloquy to his teammates before every game.

> He has made a brilliant record for himself as an outfielder, being an excellent judge of a ball, a swift runner, and making the most difficult running-catches with the utmost ease and certainty. His average each season has proved him to be in the front rank in handling the bat, and shows that his usefulness is not merely confined to his fielding abilities. He has always enjoyed the reputation of being a thoroughly reliable and honest player, and one who works hard for the best

interests of the club. His gentlemanly conduct, both on and off the ball field, has won for him a host of friends.—1885 *Spalding Guide*

38 ◆ Brian Downing
(1973–1990, 2344 G, 275 1073 .267)

Downing reached the majors as a bespectacled catcher/third baseman with a soft, slightly pudgy body. He didn't hit much—.225 his first year, .240 his second with 7 homers in 138 games. His defense was OK, nothing special, and it appeared for all the world that he would have a short, unmemorable career perhaps comparable to that of Pat Borders or Joe Oliver.

Over the years he underwent a quite remarkable transformation; in truth, I have never seen anything like it. He started working out, got into strength training. In 1976–77 he had an arm injury or some arm injuries which left him unable to throw well. In 1979 he adopted an odd batting stance, in which he addressed the pitcher with a wide-open stance, almost as if he intended to sell him some life insurance. To the surprise of almost everybody, he hit .326 in 1979 with 12 home runs, making him one of the best-hitting catchers in baseball. Early in the 1980 season he broke his ankle, costing him a season and threatening his career once again, and in 1981 he moved to the outfield, in what appeared to be a desperation effort to keep his career alive.

By this time, however, he had been lifting weights for several years, and had developed into a trim, powerful muscle man. In 1982, his first full year as an outfielder, he hit 28 home runs and 37 doubles, numbers that were more impressive then than they seem now. We assumed that this was a fluke year; in fact, I remember talking to his agent that winter, and even his agent assumed that it was probably a fluke year. This feeling was reinforced in 1983, when he had an injury and an off season; he was, by this time, 33 years old, going through

his fourth career crisis, and apparently near the end of his career.

He was just getting started. He hit 20 homers a year for the next five years, played almost every game, and continued to play well as a part-time player for four years after that, eventually having a 20-year major league career. He was not a great outfielder, but he was a fearless outfielder who almost never made errors—in fact, his career error rate, compared to league norms for his position in his era, is the lowest in major league history, at any position (see Terry Puhl, RF #86)

Along the way he stopped wearing glasses; he didn't start wearing contacts, he just stopped wearing glasses. The shape of his face changed, with the long-term strength training, from a soft, boyish, Terry Kennedy-type face into a man who was almost a dead ringer for the actor Christopher Reeve, Superman. Even his hair seemed to change, to darken gradually over the years.

He was a constant surprise; he wound up his career in a far place from where he started. It was almost as if Mel Rojas or Albie Lopez, struggling as a pitcher, had decided to become a shortstop, and then had decided to become a switch hitter, and then had unexpectedly developed into a power hitter, and then had decided to become a diplomat and was appointed Ambassador to Cameroon.

I always rooted for Brian Downing, and I think a lot of people did, because in some way Brian Downing stood for the proposition that a man can be better than he was supposed to be. He was the incarnation of our universal hopes to escape the ruts of our lazy lives, to metamorphose in mid-life into something finer. The young reporter who interviews me today will not likely become a Nobel-prize winning novelist, my tax lawyer will not likely evolve into even the poorest imitation of Clarence Darrow, my alcoholic neighbor will not likely become

Mother Theresa, and yet we must hope. Brian Downing sustained us in our illusions.

39 ◆ Harry Stovey
(1880–1893, 1486 G, 122 908 .288)

Born Harry Stow, he changed his name to "Stovey" in an effort to prevent his mother from learning that he was playing professional baseball. Breaking into the National League with the Worcester Brown Stockings in 1880, Stovey as a rookie led the NL in triples (14) and home runs (6), although he did not hit for average and his strikeout/walk ratio was poor.

In 1881, in his second season in the National League, Stovey was named captain (manager) of the Brown Stockings. Jumping to Philadelphia of the American Association in 1883, Stovey was the dominant offensive player in the AA for most of its existence, leading the league in doubles, triples, home runs, total bases, runs scored, RBI, stolen bases, and slugging percentage—a total of seventeen titles in those categories. In the Player's League in 1890 he stole 97 bases, leading that league. Moving to the National League in 1891, he led the league in triples, home runs, total bases, and slugging percentage.

Despite his remarkable batting and baserunning stats, and despite often playing for pretty good teams, Stovey was never a big star. Stovey was not a flashy player nor a defensive star. He was not colorful, and he was apparently not quotable, as hardly anything he said is remembered today. The American Association of the 1880s, though now regarded as a major league, was clearly a second class major. The teams Stovey played for were not the glamour teams of 19th century baseball. To the extent that statistics could make a man a star in the 1880s, everything depended on batting average, and Stovey's batting averages were not impressive. I would compare him, perhaps, to Edgar Martinez—a modern player with extremely good numbers, but no star reputation.

Halfway through the 1892 season Stovey was released at the same time as King Kelly, the Boston club proclaiming itself unable to pay the high salaries of veteran stars who were no longer productive. He struggled on for a couple of seasons. After his career he was a policeman in New Bedford, Massachusetts.

40 ◆ Don Baylor
(1970–1988, 2292 G, 338 1276 .260)

> Don is our triple-threat player. He can hit, run and lob.—Merv Rettenmund

Don Baylor is the only outfielder in major league history who never doubled off or doubled up a runner. His career double play total was zero. Everybody else in 500 or more games had at least two . . .

The common statement that Baylor was the first Designated Hitter to win an MVP Award is not exactly true. Baylor actually played 97 games in the outfield in 1979.

That which defines Don Baylor, I think, is the image of strength. He projects an image of great strength, great determination and force of will; as Fred White used to say, "He just *looks* like an RBI standing up there." But personally, I find him almost intolerable, because, to me, he seems to be engaged in a perpetual charade designed to project the image of great strength. As a manager, he seems to be using this image of great strength, great conviction in the rectitude of his actions, as a substitute for having any *reason* for what he is doing. I'm not suggesting that you should react to him that way; that's just me.

41 ◆ Don Buford
(1963–1972, 1286 G, 93 418 .264)

A literate, reserved man who listed his hobbies as chess and reading, Buford attended City College in LA and later USC, not entering baseball until he was 23 years old. In 1963 he led the International League in runs (114), hits (206), and batting average (.336), was named the Minor League Player of the Year, and opened 1964 as the favorite for the American League Rookie of the Year Award. After a so-so rookie year Buford played extremely well in 1965 and 1966, but (a) his accomplishments were largely hidden by a ballpark and an era in which everything favored the pitcher, and (b) his defense was criticized, probably disproportionately to his actual failings.

Buford was playing second and third base then. He wasn't a great infielder, but he was a tremendous leadoff man. After the 1967 season he was traded to Baltimore, where Earl Weaver made him his regular left fielder. He never scored 100 runs in a season, but he scored 99 three straight years, and he only played 144, 144, and 122 games in those three years; that works out to 117 runs scored per 162 games. He was fast, and he was on base.

Buford also had the lowest career GIDP rate of any player for whom full data is available—34 GIDP in 4,583 at bats, or one every 134 at bats. The ten best: 1. Buford, 2. Brett Butler, 3. Mickey Rivers, 4. Don Blasingame, 5. Vince Coleman, 6. Lenny Dykstra, 7. Omar Moreno, 8. Brady Anderson, 9. Darren Daulton, 10. Rob Deer.

42 ◆ Augie Galan
(1934–1949, 1742 G, 100 830 .287)

The Don Buford of the 1930s; I confess to having jiggled the numbers just a little to get Galan right below Buford. Like Buford, Galan was:

    1. A switch hitter.

    2. An outfielder who came up as a second baseman.

    3. A leadoff type hitter.

    4. Fast.

    5. Always on base.

    6. Very underrated.

Tim Raines, incidentally, also meets all six of these criteria.

GREAT SEASONS BY LEFT FIELDERS

I'm going to do a little essay here, Great Seasons by Left Fielders. What left fielder had the most Great Seasons?

In the Win Shares system, a season of 50 Win Shares is extremely rare. Only one left fielder in history ever had a season of 50 Win Shares, that being Ted Williams in 1946, when he won his first MVP Award.

A season of 40 Win Shares is still rare enough to be described as a "Historic" season. With a few exceptions, only Hall of Famers ever have a season of 40 Win Shares, and most Hall of Famers don't approach 40 Win Shares, even in their best seasons. If you get 40, you're usually the MVP, unless you're Ted Williams and the voters hate you or something. In the history of baseball only six left fielders have had seasons of 40 Win Shares—chronologically, Ed Delahanty, Joe Medwick, Ted Williams, Stan Musial, Carl Yastrzemski, and Barry Bonds.

But 30 Win Shares . . . .the truly great players—Williams, Bonds, Musial, Rickey Henderson—those guys earn more than 30 Win Shares as a matter of course. "Good" players rarely have seasons of 30 Win Shares. The really good players, but not great, might get to that level once in their career. Don Baylor never did. Monte Irvin never did, Joe Rudi never did, Kenny Williams never did, Willie Horton never did, Hank Sauer never did, Rico Carty never did. Other guys who never made that level, even once: Del Ennis, Luis Gonzalez, Ben Oglivie, Lonnie Smith, Riggs Stephenson, George Bell, Hal McRae, Wally Moon, Brian Downing, Chick Hafey, Gary Matthews, Gene Woodling, Jim O'Rourke, Dusty Baker, Dave Kingman, Bob Meusel, Leon Wagner; all of those guys, taken together, had zero seasons of 30 Win Shares. You can make the All-Star team, you can win the MVP Award, you can even get into the Hall of Fame without reaching that level, even at your best.

This level, then, is useful for sorting among Hall of Fame candidates: the truly great players do it regularly, but the merely very good players rarely or never get there. Thirty Win Shares is a Great Season—a season typical of a great player. One way of comparing players is to count the number of genuinely Great Seasons that each player has.

Altogether, the 100 left fielders listed here have had a total of 133 Great Seasons—almost one-third of those by five players. The top five:

1. Stan Musial   11
2. Ted Williams   10
3. Barry Bonds   8
4. Joe Jackson   7
5. Ed Delahanty   6

Williams clearly would have the most were it not for his war-time service. Williams was the youngest left fielder to earn 30 Win Shares, when he drove in 145 runs at age 20, and he was the oldest left fielder to earn 30 Win Shares, when he hit .388 at age 38. In between, he missed having Great Seasons only because of injuries or military service; he never fell short on performance until 1958, when he was 39 years old.

Musial was almost as consistent at that level, Bonds is still working on it, Joe Jackson would have been in double figures had he not been banned from the game, and Ed Delahanty might have made it to double figures if he had been a salmon. These men all rank among the greatest left fielders in the history of the game.

Rickey Henderson is the only left fielder in history to have (exactly) five Great Seasons (1980, 1983, 1985, 1989, and 1990). His last Great Season was ten years ago, but he also has a large number of exceptionally good seasons, seasons of 25 or more.

There are three left fielders who had four Great Seasons:

Al Simmons   (1925, 1929, 1930, and 1931)

Tim Raines   (1984, 1985, 1986, and 1987)

Charlie Keller   (1941, 1942, 1943, 1946)

This helps explain, I think, why I have rated Charlie Keller as high as I have. Yes, Keller's career is short; his back injury cut his career in half. But Keller was a genuinely great player for half of a career. Hal McRae and Joe Carter and Don Baylor were very good players and they played until we were tired of them, but Keller was a genuinely great player for a few years.

The players who had three Great Seasons, in general, are Hall of Famers or serious Hall of Fame candidates. There are fourteen left fielders who had (or have had so far) three Great Seasons: Albert Belle, Lou Brock, Jesse Burkett, George Burns, Augie Galan, Frank Howard, Joe Kelley, Ralph Kiner, Sherry Magee, Joe Medwick, Jimmy Sheckard, Bobby Veach, Billy Williams, and Carl Yastrzemski.

At this point we have accounted for 76% of the Great Seasons by left fielders, 101 of 133. Augie Galan is, of course, the wild card here; that's why this is the Augie Galan comment. Few of us, listing the most dominant left fielders of all time, would list Augie Galan with Yastrzemski and Billy Williams.

Galan's numbers for those three seasons are, indeed, quietly impressive—and almost the same for all three seasons. In 1935 Galan had 203 hits, drew 87 walks, led the National League in runs scored with 133, led the National League in stolen bases with 22, and hit .314 with a .399 on base percentage. He hit 41 doubles, 11 triples, and 12 home runs, and grounded into not a single double play in 646 at bats, a major league record which still stands.

His 1944 stats are very much the same—a .318 average with a league-leading 101 walks giving him a .426 on base percentage, 43 doubles, 9 triples, 12 homers, 96 runs scored, 93 RBI.

In 1945 he had a .307 average, 114 walks, 114 runs scored, 92 RBI, 36 doubles, 13 stolen bases, and a .423 on base percentage.

Those are terrific seasons, obviously—Great Seasons. As we all know, there is a problem, which separates Galan from the other guys who had three Great Seasons: the war. Galan was a great player in 1935, but then he wasn't great again until 1944, when he was playing against some good major league players, but also some teenagers, some minor league veterans, and some guys who needed regular surgery.

There's a second problem: Galan, in all three seasons, was hardly mentioned in the MVP voting. One can read that different ways: one can say that the BBWAA voters have always ignored leadoff men, and in particular outfielders who were leadoff men, or one can say that Galan, despite his impressive numbers, was not actually a great player.

But whatever you do, you have to discount Galan's war-time numbers at least a little. Galan was a good player. Fact One: From 1946 through 1948, with the "real" major leaguers back, Galan posted on base percentages of .451, .449, and .471. Other than Ted Williams and Barry Bonds, who can match that? Fact Two: in Galan's first thirteen seasons in the National League, the teams for which he played finished an average of 19 games over .500. But he was good; he wasn't great.

Oddly enough, there are only five Left Fielders who had two Great Seasons: Fred Clarke, Goose Goslin, Lefty O'Doul, Willie Stargell, Zack Wheat. Four of them are Hall of Famers; the other guy (O'Doul) would be a Hall of Famer if his career wasn't so short.

Finally, there are 22 Left Fielders who have had one Great Season. Chronologically, those are: Tip O'Neill (1887), Topsy Hartsel (1905), George Stone (1906), Matty McIntyre (1908), Heinie Manush (1928), Bob Johnson (1944), Jim Russell (1944), Minnie Minoso (1954),

Tommy Davis (1962), Cleon Jones (1969), Tommy Harper (1970), Roy White (1970), George Foster (1977), Greg Luzinski (1977), Jim Rice (1978), Jose Cruz (1983), Kirk Gibson (1988), Kevin McReynolds (1988), Mike Greenwell (1988), Kevin Mitchell (1989), Bernard Gilkey (1996), and Greg Vaughn (1998).

You know what most of those seasons are, don't you? Tip O'Neill's .435 year, Heinie Manush's 241 hits, Tommy Davis' 153-RBI campaign, Cleon Jones' .340 year, Tommy Harper's 30/30 season, Greg Vaughn's 50-homer season, and the MVP seasons from George Foster, Jim Rice, Kirk Gibson, and Kevin Mitchell. And these people, as a rule, are just not Hall of Fame players. They're good players, but they're good players who had one Great Season.

A vaguely related article can be found in the Gus Bell comment (CF, #58).

43 ◆ Del Ennis
(1946–1959, 1903 G, 288 1284 .284)

> Ennis wasn't as pink-cheeked as Ashburn, but he was of the same breed. During one road trip Del's stomach was acting up. It was suggested that his food might settle better if he took a glass of wine. "I can't stand the stuff," said Ennis. "I'd rather have stomach trouble."—Harry Paxton, *Sport Magazine*, June 1964

> Ennis was probably booed more than any player in Phillies' history. It was largely because he was a hometown product, and the fans apparently expected too much of him.—Rich Westcott, *Diamond Greats*

> I remember Del Ennis used to soak his bats in oil. He'd stick a couple of dozen in a barrel of oil at the end of the season and soak them there until the next year. It permeates the structure of the wood.—Richie Ashburn, *It Ain't Cheatin' If You Don't Get Caught* (Dan Gutman)

Ennis was a big, strong, slow player who could drive in 100 runs in his sleep—a Jim Rice,

Greg Luzinski, George Foster-type player. Someday I'll figure out an effective way to measure a player's consistency. Ennis, I'm sure, was as consistent as anybody in history. For many years after his career he ran a bowling alley in Philadelphia.

44 ◆ Jeff Heath
(1936–1949, 1383 G, 194 887 .293)

According to Roger Peckinpaugh, who managed Heath as a young player, Heath "could have been one of the greatest players. He had the ability to do about anything. He could run, he could throw, and he could hit. But he just had no hustle, no nothing. If a ball went by him, he just might walk after it." (Quoted from *Baseball Between the Wars*.)

> There was the inimitable Heath, who . . . should have been one of the greatest players in history. But there were no valves on his temper. He grinned in the manner of a schoolboy or he snarled with the viciousness of a tiger.—*Franklin Lewis*, 1949

Heath was a scary hitter in his best seasons, but he does deserve to be remembered for one other thing, too. In 1947 Willard Brown, a Negro League star, was trying to stick in the American League, which he unquestionably had the ability to do although it didn't work out. The Browns were trying to cash in on the publicity generated by Jackie Robinson's breakthrough in Brooklyn, but neither the front office nor the other St. Louis players actually wanted him to succeed. That was just one of his problems. Another problem was that Brown didn't have any bats that he was comfortable with. He liked to use a heavy bat, but he had left his bats behind when he reported to the team, because he'd been told that the team would furnish bats. When he got to St. Louis everybody was using a lighter bat, and he just couldn't adjust to it.

Jeff Heath used the heaviest bat on the team, and Brown eventually found a bat that had been Heath's, but the knob had broken off on it. Brown taped the knob back on, but the umpire wouldn't let him use a bat with tape over the end, so he had to use the bat with a broken knob. He hit a home run—the first home run by a black player in the American League, and the only home run of Brown's "major league" career. But when he got back to the dugout, Jeff Heath reclaimed the bat, and shattered it against the dugout wall.

45 ◆ Kevin McReynolds
(1983–1994, 1502 G, 211 807 .265)

McReynolds is the same age as Tony Gwynn, and came up with the Padres shortly after Gwynn did. He was a top NL outfielder for a few years, put on weight and disappeared. In his first four years in the league (1985–1988) he had 83% of the value of Tony Gwynn; in his second four (1989–1992) he had 95% of the value of Gwynn, not because he was better but because Gwynn had slipped. From 1993–1996 he had 29% of the value of Tony Gwynn; from 1997–2000, 0%.

46 ◆ Gary Matthews
(1972–1987, 2033 G, 234 978 .281)

For twenty years, the San Francisco Giants used a "Willie Mays" standard to evaluate young outfielders. If a young outfielder came up and he wasn't Willie Mays, they'd get rid of him. Leon Wagner as a rookie in 1958 hit .317 with 13 homers in 221 at bats. That was pretty good, but . . . you know, he wasn't Willie Mays, so they traded him for Don Blasingame. They came up with the Alous, all three of them, and they were pretty good, but . . . well, they weren't Willie Mays, so they traded them. They came up Jose Cardenal and Ollie Brown, neither of whom was Willie Mays. They brought up Bobby Bonds. For a couple of years they thought he was Willie Mays, but then they realized he wasn't, so they got rid of him.

The Giants' system produced Bobby Bonds in 1969, Dave Kingman in 1971, Garry Maddox in 1972, and Gary Matthews, the National League Rookie of the Year in 1973. In 1979 Bonds hit .275 with 25 home runs, 85 RBI, and 34 stolen bases, Kingman hit .288 with 48 homers, 115 RBI, Maddox hit .281 with 13 homers, 61 RBI, and Gold Glove performance in center field, and Gary Matthews hit .304 with 27 homers, 90 RBI. But the Giants, having let them all get away, were playing Bill North, Larry Herndon, and Terry Whitfield in the outfield (although they did have one good outfielder, Jack Clark). North hit .259 with 5 homers, 30 RBI, Herndon hit .257 with 7 homers, 36 RBI, and Whitfield hit .287 with 5 and 44, all of them batting 350 to 460 times.

In the late 1970s Ted Turner and the Atlanta Braves tried to convert a bad team into a good team by throwing lots of money at ballplayers. They were able to sign a number of players, among them Matthews, for more money than they were worth, but the team didn't improve quickly. Mathews was signed for an amount that was, at the time, regarded as outrageous, and there were widespread rumors within baseball that Ted Turner was drunk when he agreed to the deal. I have no idea whether this is true.

When these players failed to move Atlanta out of last place, it was perceived as a failure on the part of the free agents, and the free agents got reputations as overrated bums. Matthews was the only one of these players who was able to overcome that experience, and restore his reputation as a hard-nosed, winning type of player, which in fact he was.

> The secret to hitting, in my mind, is courage. And he has courage to burn. There is no fright in Gary.—Charlie Fox

47 ◆ Topsy Hartsel
(1898–1911, 1356 G, 31 341 .276)

> By a strange kink in the ethics of baseball John Kling, the Chicago catcher, was blamed by the other players on the defeated team for the signs being stolen. They charged that he had been careless in covering his signals and that the enemy's coachers, particularly Topsy Hartsell, a clever man at it, had stolen them from the lines.—Christy Mathewson, *Pitching in a Pinch*

This refers to the 1910 World Series. By another strange kink in ethics, Johnny Kling lost his job after it was charged that he had allowed signs to be stolen during the series, and baseball fans remember this to this day—but how many baseball fans remember who stole the signs? Nobody.

How do you rate the greatest leadoff men of all time? You can do it however you want, but here's one way. First, you can estimate how many runs the player should score by what I call the leadoff man formula, which I have printed many times . . . take the number of times the player has been on first base, multiply by .35, his times on second by .55, his times on third by .8, and his home runs by 1. Many players, and most modern leadoff men, will actually score about the number of runs that the formula says they should score.

One can turn that into a rating of the greatest leadoff men by

1. Converting the Expected Runs Scored into Expected Runs Scored per 27 outs.

2. Contrasting that figure with the league average for runs scored per out during the player's career.

Obviously imperfect, for many reasons, but still . . . sometimes it is helpful to take a fresh look at these kind of issues with new methods, even if the new methods are imperfect.

All of the greatest leadoff men ever, by this method, would be guys who aren't leadoff men, starting with Ted Williams. (Williams, Ruth, Mantle, Barry Bonds, Ty Cobb, Musial, Joe

Jackson, Hornsby, Frank Robinson, and Willie Mays.) Why Robinson ranks ahead of Mays I don't know and don't care, but anyway, this is logical on its own terms: if you had two Ted Williamses, and could afford to use one of them as a leadoff man, he would be the greatest leadoff man who ever lived.

What we want, of course, are the greatest leadoff men who were actually leadoff men. That list is:

1	Rickey Henderson	1.67
2.	Tim Raines	1.64
3.	Topsy Hartsel	1.61
4.	Lenny Dykstra	1.59
5.	Wade Boggs	1.57

The "1.67" for Henderson means that the runs Henderson could be expected to score, as a leadoff man (which is almost the same as the number of runs that he *has* scored) is 67% higher, per 27 outs, than the league runs scored per game for his era.

After that ... 6. Bobby Bonds (1.57), 7. Augie Galan (1.57), 8. Craig Biggio (1.55), 9. Eddie Stanky (1.55), 10. Pete Rose (1.54), 11. Don Buford (1.54), 12. Roy Thomas (1.54), 13. Rod Carew (1.54), 14. Stan Hack (1.53), 15. Elbie Fletcher (1.53), 16. Miller Huggins (1.52), 17. Lonnie Smith (1.51), 18. Bob Bescher (1.52), 19. Billy Hamilton (1.51), 20. John McGraw (1.50).

Hamilton and McGraw are knocked down the list, of course, because they played in a time when so many runs were scored. Of the top 12 leadoff men of all time by this list, not a single one is in the Hall of Fame as of now, emphasizing the historical lack of respect for leadoff men, although this is also because many of them are recent, and one of them is banned. Other notes:

- Roy Cullenbine, who was not actually a leadoff man most of his career, would

rank ahead of Rickey Henderson if he was (1.73), a fact which was utterly lost on managers of the 1940s.
- Eddie Collins, who could have been a leadoff man but never was, also would rank ahead of Henderson (1.68).

Others who wouldn't rank ahead of Henderson, but would rank as top-flight leadoff men had they been leadoff men include Jackie Robinson, Jimmy Wynn, Eric Davis, Joe Cunningham, and Ferris Fain. Rick Monday, who actually did become a leadoff man his last three-four years as a regular, ranks extremely well (higher than Lenny Dykstra). Lou Brock is fairly close to the top 20; he's at 1.44.

Other noted leadoff men: Ed Yost, 1.48; Richie Ashburn, 1.47; Davey Lopes, 1.44; Gary Redus, 1.44; Burt Shotton, 1.44; Ron Hunt, 1.42; Tommy Harper, 1.42; Dom DiMaggio, 1.42; Johnny Pesky, 1.42; George Burns, 1.41; Paul Molitor, 1.40; Maxie Bishop, 1.39; Max Carey, 1.39; Brett Butler, 1.39; Ray Chapman, 1.37; Earle Combs, 1.37; Pee Wee Reese, 1.36; Bill North, 1.35; Brady Anderson, 1.35; Lu Blue, 1.33; Ron LeFlore, 1.33; Junior Gilliam, 1.31; Matty Alou, 1.31; Donie Bush, 1.29; Johnny Temple, 1.28; Vince Coleman, 1.26; Mookie Wilson, 1.25; Billy Werber, 1.24; Mickey Rivers, 1.23; Dave Collins, 1.22; Willie Wilson, 1.21; Bill Bruton, 1.21; Maury Wills, 1.21; Woodie English, 1.21; Lloyd Waner, 1.21; George Case, 1.20; Red Schoendienst, 1.20; Phil Rizzuto, 1.19; Bert Campaneris, 1.18; Luis Aparicio, 1.17; Don Blasingame, 1.16; Gary Pettis, 1.15; Otis Nixon, 1.14; Dummy Hoy, 1.12.

48 ◆ Tip O'Neill
(1883–1892, 1054 G, 52 757 .326)

O'Neill in 1887 led the American Association in doubles, triples, and home runs, making him the only man ever to lead his league in all three species of extra base hits. But he never led the league in any of those categories in any other year . . .

> His gentlemanly bearing made him one of the most popular players of his era . . . A lifelong bachelor, he operated a saloon and restaurant with his brothers.—Robert L. Tiemann and William E. Akin, *Baseball's First Stars*

"O'Neill [had] the reputation of being something of a wit," wrote Lee Allen in *The Cincinnati Reds*. Out for an early stroll on a Sunday in 1892, he met a clergyman.

"Goin' to the game today, Reverend?" asked O'Neill.

"I don't go to baseball games on Sunday," said the minister. "Sunday is my busiest day."

"It's my busiest day, too," said O'Neill.

"Yes," explained the pastor. "But I'm in the right field."

"So am I," countered Tip. "Ain't that sun terrible?"

49 ◆ Sid Gordon
(1941–1955, 1475 G, 202 805 .283)

Gordon, the son of Jewish immigrants, grew up in the streets of Brooklyn. He had a tryout at Ebbets Field in 1936 and impressed Casey Stengel enough to earn promise of a job, but Stengel was fired almost immediately afterward, and the Dodgers didn't follow through. They would regret this for many years, as Gordon tormented his hometown team.

He passed another tryout with the Giants in early 1938; Bill Terry told him he could play for Milford in the Eastern Shore League, but he would have to get there on his own. He did, and hit .352. He reached the majors just as the war was starting, spent two seasons in the Coast Guard, and returned in 1946.

He was slow, had an exceptional arm, usually hit around .290 with 25 homers, 100 RBI. In 1948 they had "Sid Gordon Day" at Ebbets Field, although Sid was still playing for the

Giants; he was given a new car, among other things, and repaid the hospitality by hitting two home runs.

Gordon played for the Giants through 1949, but became expendable when the Giants signed Monte Irvin. He played four years for the Braves, but lost his job after the 1953 season to a kid named Henry Aaron. Traded to Pittsburgh, he was a regular there for a little more than a year, but was pushed aside by a rookie named Roberto Clemente. He retired after the 1955 season . . . see also Red Kress (Shortstop, #87).

50 ◆ Ken Williams
(1915–1929, 1397 G, 196 913 .319)

Ken Williams is the first player I know of to have used a corked bat. Apparently, if I'm reading the source material right, it wasn't strictly illegal when Williams did it, because it was unknown before then. American League President Ban Johnson in 1923 issued a policy prohibiting "trick bats" after Babe Ruth was caught using a bat which consisted of four pieces of wood glued together, and Williams, according to the 1924 *Reach Guide*, "had been knocking 'em out with a bat in which a plug of wood had been inserted."

Even earlier, according to Buck Weaver by way of James T. Farrell's *My Baseball Diary*, George Sisler may have driven nails into his bat. According to Weaver, he once fielded a ground ball from Sisler, and noticed that it had about ten little perforations in it. He asked the umpire to check Sisler's bat, and the umpire found that Sisler "had driven nails in it and filed them down."

51 ◆ Kevin Mitchell
(1984–1998, 1223 G, 234 760 .284)

Talented hitter, had no natural defensive position. Frankie Frisch once said that in baseball you only need to have a good year every five years, because if you have a good year, for several years people will expect you to have another one. Mitchell was a great player in 1989, and was playing outstanding ball at the time of the strike in 1994, but the rest of his career was mostly just waiting for the good years . . .

52 ◆ Lefty O'Doul

(1918–1934, 970 G, 113 542 .349)

Lefty kept a book on all the pitchers in the league, what they threw him, what he did with it, what he hit against them. Any time you asked him, he could pull out his book and tell you what his batting average was against any pitcher in the league. He was the only hitter of that era who did that . . .

> Rabbit Maranville kept the players loose at Pittsburgh and Lefty O'Doul did the same at Brooklyn . . . [O'Doul] was a born politician. He knew what his batting average was all the time, and before we were in some new town half an hour, Lefty knew everybody in the place.–Glenn Wright, *Baseball Players and Their Times* (Eugene Murdock)

> Lefty O'Doul had batted .319 in 1928, but Mc-Graw judged him too old and slow and not serious enough about his work. So off went the colorful San Franciscan, along with a check, to the indigent Phillies for the stolid Fred Leach, who was almost the same age but a better outfielder.–Charles C. Alexander, *John McGraw* (Viking, 1988)

One reason McGraw didn't think Lefty was serious enough about his work is that Lefty, like Ty Cobb, was a fanatic golfer, known on occasion to rush through 36 holes before a 2 o'clock game. The Phillies, for whom Lefty won a batting title in 1929, eventually banned the whole team from playing golf.

Bill Deane, in the 1990 *Baseball Research Journal,* reconstructed O'Doul's career batting records at home and on the road, to see how much O'Doul was aided by his home parks. O'-Doul had a career batting average of .352 in his

home parks–and .347 on the road. He did hit two-thirds of his career home runs at home, but hit more doubles and triples on the road.

53 ◆ Hal McRae

(1968–1987, 2084 G, 191 1097 .290)

While Hal was still playing his son, Brian, was the Royals #1 draft pick. A reporter asked him if that made him feel old. "No," he said. "When they throw fastballs by you consistently, that makes you feel old."

Playing in Puerto Rico in the winter of 1968–69, Hal McRae slid into home plate, and broke his leg in four places. It took him several years to rehab the leg, which was never the same.

The broken leg, beyond any question, cost McRae the Hall of Fame. The accident did three things:

1. It delayed the start of McRae's major league career by several years.

2. It kept him from becoming a part of the Big Red Machine.

3. It cost him his speed.

Before the accident, McRae was a burner, a center fielder who could fly, like his son, Brian. After the accident, his speed was major league average.

Absent the accident, McRae probably would have gotten the job as the Reds' center fielder in 1969, and, if not, would certainly have gotten one of the jobs that went to Bernie Carbo (Reds rookie, 1970), George Foster (whom the Reds acquired in trade in 1971), or Cesar Geronimo (whom the Reds acquired in trade in 1972, after Tolan was injured).

Even starting his career several years late, and even with no speed, McRae was a better player than some of the Hall of Fame left fielders. He hit .300 five times as a regular, plus a couple of times as a part-time player, he hit huge numbers of doubles and 14-27 home runs a season, drove in 133 runs when he was 36 years old, and had over 2,000 major league hits.

McRae was the most aggressive baserunner of the 1970s, a man who left home plate thinking "double" every time he hit the ball. The rule allowing the second base umpire to call a double play if the runner from first leaves the baseline to take out the pivot man is known informally as the McRae Rule. He was probably thrown out on the bases, I would guess, 40 times a season. He took the lessons of the early days of the Big Red Machine, and transmitted them to the Kansas City Royals, becoming the unquestioned clubhouse leader of the team that dominated their division from 1976 through 1985. With a dry wit and a ready needle, he taught the younger players and reminded the veterans to take nothing for granted, and to take no prisoners on the bases.

As a veteran player, McRae was the Royals enlightened man, almost; the players, the management, and the press all had an almost superstitious respect for his character and his intelligence. He just seemed to understand how the world really was, and it was common to hear those guys say that McRae was the smartest man they had ever known.

He was offered the Royal manager's job in 1987, turned it down then, but accepted it the next time it was offered, in 1991. He was actually a successful manager, going 66-58 in 1991, 84-78 in 1993, and 64-51 in 1994, this with an organization that spent the rest of the decade under .500 with several other managers. However, while McRae had been beloved as a player, he was not well liked as a manager. Things he might have said as a player were not always taken the same way as a manager, plus he didn't always seem to have all the answers, as he had as a player, and he didn't always cooperate in the designs of the front office. He hasn't managed since, but Herk Robinson, asked when he left the General Manager's job

in 2000 to name his biggest mistake as the Royals GM, said that it was firing Hal McRae.

54 ◆ Dusty Baker
(1968–1986, 2039 G, 242 1013 .278)
What would you have if you got Dusty Baker together with O. J. Simpson and the architect who designed the old park in San Francisco?

A butcher, a Baker, and a Candlestick maker. Stop groaning; you'll wake the neighbors . . . on June 17, 1984, Dusty Baker stole second, third, and home in the same game. The rest of the season, he stole only one base.

Players who hit exactly as many home runs on the road as they did at home:

	Hm	Rd	Total
1. Carlton Fisk	188	188	376
2. Gary Carter	162	162	324
3. Vic Wertz	133	133	266
4. Dusty Baker	121	121	242
5. Rob Deer	115	115	230
6. Bill Freehan	100	100	200
7. Puddin' Head Jones	95	95	190
8. Charley Gehringer	92	92	184
9. Candy Maldonado	73	73	146
9. Jim Spencer	73	73	146
10. Dave Johnson	68	68	136

55 ◆ Willie Horton
(1963–1980, 2028 G, 325 1163 .273)
Horton drove in 100 runs in his first, second, and last seasons as a regular (1965, 1966, and 1979)—but never drove in 100 runs in the thirteen years in between. This is the longest gap in history between 100-RBI seasons.

Horton was so strong and had such tremendous bat speed that he once snapped a bat in half by stopping his swing . . .

Guys who don't love the game can't play their best.—Willie Horton

He was a ghetto kid, the son of a coal miner and the youngest of nineteen children. He was so poor when he was growing up he almost had to drop out of school because he didn't have shoes. When he signed with the Tigers, the first thing he did was buy a house for his parents. The guy had class.– Rebecca Stowe, *Cult Baseball Players*

A muscular man who reminds baseball people [of] Roy Campanella, Willie Horton takes a belligerent, butcher's slice at the ball . . . It is likely that if he plays long enough (he) may one day top Hank Greenberg's top Tiger total of 58 homers.–Ray Robinson, *Baseball Stars of 1969*

[The Tigers] let Willie go . . . because he couldn't get along with Ralph Houk. But now it turns out they might have done better to let Houk go and make Willie Manager. Last winter, in Venezuela, Willie took over a team that was fifteen games under .500 in mid-season [and managed them to] an incredible sixty wins against only eight losses.–Art Hill, *I Don't Care If I Never Come Back*

56 ◆ Tommy Harper
(1962–1976, 1810 G, 146 678 .257)

Pete Rose and outfielder Tommy Harper broke in together in 1963. Harper had a lot of speed and was talented, but Rose was a great player. He went about his business like nobody I'd ever seen.–Jim O'Toole, *We Played the Game*

Harper was a terrific player in 1970, when he hit .296 with 35 doubles, 31 homers, and 38 stolen bases, and a good player in many other seasons. Like Jimmy Sheckard and Toby Harrah, he did everything well, but not necessarily in the same season. He stole as many as 73 bases, scored as many as 126 runs, hit as high as .296, hit as many as 31 homers, played third base at times, center field at times. He didn't do any of these things with great consistency.

57 ◆ Gene Woodling
(1943–1962, 1796 G, 147 820 .284)

Some of the other guys are harder swingers but Gene manages to ride that ball a long way. He

does it with timing. Beautiful timing. And a smooth swing.–Early Wynn, *Sport Magazine* (My Nine Toughest Batters), March 1961

An Ohio native, Woodling at the age of 17 hit .398 in the Ohio State League, 85 games, winning the batting title in a walk. At 18 he hit .394 in the Mid State League, another batting title, and at 20 hit .344 in the Eastern League, making it to the majors in late September and hitting .320 in 8 games.

Wartime.

Detour.

In 1946, playing 61 games for Cleveland, he hit .188, incidentally the only time in his life Woodling ever failed to hit. He didn't pick the best time.

Back to the minors. He played 22 games for Pittsburgh in '47 and hit OK, but there was a problem there, too: Ralph Kiner. Kiner and Woodling both had to play left. No DH Rule. Kiner hit 40 homers. Figure it out.

1948; by now Woodling is 26, back in the minors. He hit .385 with San Francisco in the Pacific Coast League, 22 homers, 107 RBI. Casey Stengel was managing across the bay; there is no record, but Casey and Woodling both said Woodling hit about .500 against Casey's team. (Tom Ruane, reading this before publication, went to the microfilm to check it out. Woodling in fact hit .493 against Oakland that year, 34-for-39 with 5 home runs.) When Casey returned to the majors in 1949, he took Woodling with him.

Woodling platooned with Hank Bauer for six years, one of the longest platoon combinations in baseball history. The press nicknamed them "The Gold Dust Twins." It wasn't a straight platoon; Bauer would often play right with Woodling in left, and Woodling sometimes played right with another left-handed hitter in left.

Woodling was a better hitter than Bauer, who wasn't a bad hitter either. He hit over .300 five times, walked a lot, had a little power, ran

OK, and was an excellent outfielder other than his just fair arm. He led the league in fielding percentage three times. He was extremely consistent; the 1946 season was literally the only time in his career that he didn't hit. He continued to do these things until he was 40 years old; when he was 40 he hit .276, and it was a productive .276. The platooning kept his numbers smaller; as a regular, he would have driven in and scored over 100 runs in his good years, with home run totals in the 20s. But playing for a team that had talent to burn also put him into five straight World Series.

> We led the league in being "RAs." We had some of the best Red Asses who ever played baseball. If you fooled with Chief Reynolds, Vic Raschi, Hank Bauer, or me, you were in trouble.—Gene Woodling, *We Played the Game*

The only players who scored exactly as many runs as they drove in, playing 1000 or more games:

	Runs	RBI
Gene Woodling	830	830
Howard Johnson	760	760
Bob Kennedy	514	514
Mike Mitchell	514	514
Val Picinich	298	298
Lee Smith	2	2

58 ◆ Rico Carty
(1963–1979, 1651 G, 204 890 .299)

> Joe Tait called Carty a bigger-than-life personality; he was a hulking man, about six feet four, with a baritone voice ... "Rico always played with his wallet in his back pocket," said Kuiper. "He didn't trust the valuables box in the dressing room ... besides, he never slid, so it wasn't like something would happen."—Terry Pluto, *The Curse of Rocky Colavito*

With Alex Johnson and Rico Carty in Texas, I had two good hitters, but I still can't tell you

which in the hell was the worse left fielder. I'd DH one and play the other in left, then switch it around the next day. That way I could hide one of 'em, and they never got tired.—Whitey Herzog, *You're Missin' a Great Game.*

Well, for what it's worth, the Win Shares system places both Rico and Alex in the bottom 10% of defensive outfielders, and ranks them as almost dead even—1.89 Win Shares per 1,000 innings for Johnson, 1.85 for Carty.

The Beeg Boy—later in his career he changed himself to the Beeg Mon—was a friendly, manipulative, emotional Dominican who wore cowboy hats and cowboy boots and smoked big cigars, sort of half Texan and half Dominican. His parents had wanted him to become a doctor, but, or so he would claim, he fainted at the sight of blood. He was much admired by younger Dominican players, many of whom he had gone out of his way to help. He couldn't run at all and he didn't throw particularly well, but he was immensely strong, and the sucker could hit, hitting .330 in 1964 and .366 in 1970, the highest batting average in the National League between 1948 (Stan Musial) and 1987 (Tony Gwynn). He had tuberculosis in mid-career (1968) and missed all of the 1971 season after a serious knee injury, from which it took him several years to recover. He had at least two other major injuries in his career, and these things prevented him from compiling Hall of Fame numbers as a hitter.

59 ◆ Chick Hafey
(1924–1937, 1283 G, 164 833 .317)

The top 20 hitters of Hafey's years (1924 to 1937), minimum 1,000 plate appearances:

1. Rogers Hornsby .366
2. Harry Heilmann .358
3. Lefty O'Doul .353
4. Johnny Mize .349

5. Paul Waner   .348
6. Ty Cobb   .348
7. Lou Gehrig   .344
8. Zack Wheat   .343
9. Eddie Collins   .343
10. Al Simmons   .342
11. Joe Medwick   .342
12. Bill Terry   .341
13. Chuck Klein   .340
14. Babe Ruth   .340
15. Riggs Stephenson   .338
16. Babe Phelps   .336
17. Joe DiMaggio   .335
18. Arky Vaughan   .334
19. Jimmie Foxx   .334
20. Tris Speaker   .332

Hafey, with a .317 average, ranks as the 50th best hitter of those years. He does rank 20th in slugging percentage . . . Hafey was converted from a pitcher to an outfielder after Branch Rickey saw him take batting practice, and immediately ordered him moved to the outfield.

The late Andy High, Hafey's teammate in St. Louis and a great admirer of his, once told me that Hafey's eyesight was so bad that he would see him standing in front of the departure board at the train station, squinting and trying to make out the letters. High said he couldn't imagine what Hafey would have hit if he had been able to see.

> Hafey "was a rangy right-handed hitter whose pull-hitting prowess was almost as awesome as his bazooka-powered throwing arm . . . Hafey threw so powerfully that, as former teammates would concede, if he had played short right field, he would have held virtually all hits in his direction to singles."–Bob Broeg, *Redbirds*

Uh, Bob . . . balls hit AT the right fielder are singles, anyway. Extra base hits are balls hit in the corner, or in the gap, or off the wall. If you moved the right fielder in, that wouldn't make them *singles;* that would make them *triples.*

60 ◆ Hank Sauer
(1941–1959, 1399 G, 288 876 .266)

Putting it as nicely as possible without applying for a British passport, the 1949 edition of *Who's Who in Baseball* reported that "Defensively, Hank still lacks the smoothness and assurance that characterize the top-bracket outer patrols of the majors."

> Don't worry about it. I played center field next to Hank Sauer. You can't be worse than he was.–Willie Mays to Orlando Cepeda, who had expressed concern about his ability to play left
>
> The reason I got the MVP that year over Robin Roberts is because I hurt him. I think I got two home runs off of him that broke up one game he was shutting us out. I hit a home run to beat him 1-0. Then I beat him another game, a couple of games like that I think that's what did it.–Hank Sauer, *Our Chicago Cubs*

Hank Sauer signed with the Yankees in 1938, and spent three years in the Yankee system before being drafted by Cincinnati. He got into a few games late in 1941 with the Reds, hit well, was sent down in 1942, earned another callup, and hit well again in late 1942. The Reds needed outfielders who could hit, but Cincinnati manager Bill McKechnie was convinced that he just couldn't live with Sauer's glove. Sauer went back to the minors for the 1943 season, then spent 1944 and most of 1945 in the Navy. He got out of the service earlier than some of the other guys, which gave him 31 games in the majors in 1945.

Again, he was outstanding. He hit .293 with 5 homers, 20 RBI in the 31 games, including three homers in one game. He had now had three cups of coffee in the major leagues, and had played well all three times.

McKechnie sent him back to Syracuse for 1946. The Reds played Al Libke, Dain Clay, and Bob Usher in the outfield. Libke hit .253 with 5 homers in 431 at bats. Clay hit .228 with 2 homers in 435 at bats. Usher hit .204 with 1 homer in 92 games. The Reds finished 67-87, and were last in the major leagues in runs scored. Sauer drove in 90 runs and scored 99—for Syracuse.

McKechnie got fired, and Johnny Neun got his job.

And sent Hank Sauer back to Syracuse.

Sauer hit 50 home runs for Syracuse in 1947, and was named the minor league player of the year. Johnny Neun announced that winter that Hank Sauer would be his left fielder in 1948.

By the time he got to play in the majors Hank Sauer was 31 years old. He hit 288 major league homers, 281 of them after his 31st birthday. In his first season with the Reds he hit 35 homers, a Cincinnati record at the time. From his 31st birthday on he hit more home runs than Mike Schmidt, Jimmie Foxx, Frank Robinson, Reggie Jackson, Mickey Mantle, Ernie Banks, or Harmon Killebrew. He won an MVP award at age 35, driving in 121 runs for the Cubs. Two years after that he hit 41 homers, and three years after that, at age 40, he hit another 26 homers in 378 at bats.

After he retired Sauer worked for many years as a scout for different organizations.

61 ◆ Riggs Stephenson
(1921–1934, 1310 G, 63 773 .336)

> Speaker tried to make an outfielder out of Stephenson because the muscular Southerner could hit even if he couldn't throw very well. But Stephie rebelled and finally was let go.—Franklin Lewis, *The Cleveland Indians*

Stephenson grew up on a farm near Akron, Alabama; he was a childhood acquaintance and college friend of the Sewell brothers. Two of Stephenson's older brothers (much older) had played pro baseball. Riggs played football, baseball, and basketball at the University of Alabama, and was an outstanding football player, a running back, although he suffered a shoulder

injury playing football which left him unable to throw. He signed with the Cleveland Indians, perhaps on Joe Sewell's recommendation, and went straight to the majors.

In college Sewell had played second base with Stephenson at short; at Cleveland they reversed roles. Stephenson was a poor second baseman to begin with, and in June 1924, battling for the league lead in hitting, he tripped over Earl Sheely's leg on a play at first base, landed on his knee, and pretty much ruined it. He wound up that year hitting .371 in 71 games, but by the spring of 1925 he was back in the minors, trying to learn to play the outfield.

Fortunately, Joe McCarthy was managing in the league, and when McCarthy went to the majors the next year he took Stephenson with him, exactly as Stengel did with Gene Woodling a quarter-century later. He played the outfield for the Cubs for nine years, collecting 199 hits in 1927 and driving in 110 runs in 1929.

Stephenson was a quiet, modest man who retired to Tuscaloosa, Alabama, after his playing career. He was interviewed by Eugene Murdock for the book *Baseball Between the Wars*. Modern players who are comparable to Stephenson in terms of career length and value include Kevin McReynolds, Lenny Dykstra, Don Buford, Danny Tartabull, Mickey Rivers, Richie Zisk, and Kevin Mitchell.

62 ◆ George Bell
(1981–1993, 1587 G, 265 1002 .278)

I helped prepare arbitration cases for George three straight years in the 1980s. I always found him to be an amiable man, which I think most of his teammates also did; he never had a good relationship with the press or with some of his managers, but I don't think he was actually a hard man to get along with.

George had led the American League in errors the first year that we prepared a case for him. We were wondering what to do about that, so I drew up an exhibit entitled "What Was the Cost of George Bell's Errors?" The exhibit showed that while Bell had led the league in errors with 11, none of the errors had actually cost his team anything. Of the 11 errors, only about three led to un-earned runs. Of the three which led to un-earned runs, all had occurred in games which Toronto had won anyway, and in those three games, Bell had driven in something like seven runs.

Well, that case settled at the last minute; George and I had breakfast while the lawyers and the guys from the Blue Jays were upstairs hammering out a settlement. The next year, we were back at it again, and George again had made about ten errors; he hadn't led the league, but he was close. I looked through the errors again, and I found, once again, that he had not made one error which had been costly to the Blue Jays; all of the errors were either innocent (meaning no run had scored as a result) or else had occurred after George had hit two home runs to help the Blue Jays to a 9-2 lead or something.

Once more, the case settled at the last minute. And the next year, the next February, there we were again, drawing up arbitration exhibits for George Bell. And, amazingly enough, once more the exhibit still worked; Bell, despite nearly leading the league in errors, had once again not made an error which led to an un-earned run in a Blue Jay defeat. Over the three years, Bell had made far more errors than any other major league outfielder—but had not been charged with a single error which was costly to his team.

63 ◆ George Stone

(1903–1910, 848 G, 23 268 .301)
Stone played in a pitcher's park in the dead ball era. As it happens, he played in the *most* run-scarce environment, throughout his career, of

any outfielder listed among the top 100. The bottom ten:

1.	George Stone	3.49
2.	Benny Kauff	3.67
3.	Don Buford	3.71
4.	Patsy Dougherty	3.80
5.	Sherry Magee	3.81
6.	Tommie Agee	3.81
7.	Willie Davis	3.82
8.	Terry Puhl	3.84
9.	Tom Tresh	3.84
10.	Paul Blair	3.85

George Stone was 24 when he broke into professional baseball. He was working as a clerk in Coleridge, Nebraska, playing baseball for fun but with no intention of becoming a baseball player. In a game against a team which had several players from the Omaha franchise in the Western League, however, Stone had five hits including three home runs. A year and a half later he was in the major leagues, with the Boston Pilgrims.

Boston manager Jimmy Collins rejected him, however, because his batting style was wildly unorthodox. According to *Baseball Magazine* in 1909 (I am borrowing this quotation from the *Encyclopedia of Jews in Sports*), "Did he not possess arms and hands of wonderful power, Stone could not hit at all. His position at bat would put a weaker man out of the game. He falls back on his left foot, hunches his right shoulder up against himself, so to speak, props against his swing, turns his back on right field, making all ground to the right of second base closed territory to him, and hitting only between second and third bases. Stone is a man of great power. If he stood up . . . and pulled the ball once in a while, I think that he would be the most wonderful batter that baseball ever saw. He hits harder to the 'off-side' between second and third bases than any man who ever stood at bat. Did he but pull them, he would kill first and second basemen."

The book *Nebraska Diamonds* gives a similar account of his batting stance, but also says that Stone would take two quick steps and chop at the ball. In any case, Jimmy Collins didn't want any of it, and he sent Stone to St. Louis, with money, to acquire the aged Jesse Burkett.

Stone in 1905 had a fine rookie season, just missing the league batting title, but leading the league in hits and total bases. In 1906 he was sensational, playing at a Hall of Fame level, hitting .358, and leading the American League in batting, on base percentage, slugging percentage, and total bases. He was, in my opinion, the Most Valuable Player in the American League in that season.

Stone was fast, but couldn't throw. He was a sober man, drinking nothing or almost nothing. He was educated, well spoken, well read, and an eloquent writer. He was very quiet, making noise only with his violin; *The Sporting News* reported that Stone "would rather be a great violinist with a limited income than a great ballplayer with a handsome salary."

His career declined quickly after the brilliant peak of 1906. He held out in 1907, reported to camp sick and underweight, and got off to a slow start. He reported late again in 1908, and played through the season fighting malaria. In 1909 he tore up his ankle, and his career ended in 1911. He returned to his home in Nebraska, went into the banking business, and later served as president of the Nebraska State League.

George Stone and Patsy Dougherty were both left-handed lead-off type hitters in the American League in almost the same seasons. Both reached the majors in 1903, with the Red Sox. Both had brilliant rookie seasons, Dougherty in 1903 and Stone two years later. Both had short careers, after which both went into banking. Both died in the 1940s. But both

rate at the position, despite their short careers, because they were genuinely good players for a few years.

64 ◆ Ben Oglivie
(1971–1986, 1754 G, 235 901 .273)

A skinny left-handed Panamanian with immensely strong wrists and forearms, Oglivie whipped the bat at great speed, pulling almost everything down the first base line.

> His hobbies—martial arts, electronics, reading philosophy—were as consuming as they were varied. One day in 1981, he drove...clear across Phoenix's metropolitan sprawl, while reading—as he drove—a biography of Jean Jacques Rousseau. —Dan Okrent, *Nine Innings*

> i heard you were a quiet man
>   could do a times crossword in 15 minutes
> yet you seemed nervous at the plate
>   waving, wiggling that bat
> a puppy's tail
>   held high by sinew-strong arms
>   —Dan Quisenberry, *Ode to Ben Oglivie*

65 ◆ Lonnie Smith
(1976–1994, 1613 G, 98 533 .288)

> I can still run. I can still hit. I can still make errors.—Lonnie Smith, 1992, denying that he was washed up

Lonnie was a wonderful leadoff man who hit for a good average, would take a walk, led the league in being hit with a pitch three times, and stole more than 50 bases three times. He was a comical outfielder who fell down chasing balls probably once a game on average, or more, for which reason he was nicknamed "Skates." He also had frequent throwing errors. He had very small hands and feet, which were the source of his problems; the small feet caused him to fall down, and his hands were so small and so muscular that it was hard for him to grip the ball properly.

Incidentally, there was a similar player in the 1920s named Red Barnes, whose small feet and frequent falls in the outfield cost him his career. Barnes hit .300 the only year he was a regular (1928), walked some and was fast, but lost his job after one season. Lonnie played in 32 World Series games, getting to the series with Philadelphia (1980), St. Louis (1982), Kansas City (1985), and Atlanta (1991 and 1992). It's not all coincidence; despite the mistakes, he was a hell of a player.

> You have to understand that Lonnie makes defensive mistakes every game; he knows how to handle it. Your average outfielder is inclined to panic when he falls down chasing a ball in the corner; he may just give up and sit there a while, trying to figure it out. Lonnie has a pop-up slide perfected for the occasion. Another outfielder might have no idea where the ball was when it bounded off his glove; Lonnie can calculate with the instinctive astrophysics of a tennis player where a ball will land when it skips off the heel of his glove, what the angle of glide will be when he tips it off the webbing, what the spin will be when the ball skids off the thumb of the mitt. Many players can kick a ball behind them without ever knowing it; Lonnie can judge by the pitch of the thud and the subtle pressure on his shoe in which direction and how far he has projected the sphere. He knows exactly what to do when a ball spins out of his hand and flies crazily into a void on the field, when it is appropriate for him to scramble after the ball and when he needs to back up the man who will have to recover it. He has experience in these matters; when he retires he will be hired to come to spring training and coach defensive recovery and cost containment. This is his specialty, and he is good at it.—1986 *Baseball Abstract*

66 ◆ Tom Tresh

(1961–1969, 1192 G, 153 530 .245)

There are three players who will be rated here higher than almost anyone would expect—Tresh,

Roy White, and Bobby Murcer. All have been historically underrated, for the same reasons:

1. They played in very difficult conditions for a hitter.

2. They played for bad teams.

3. Their offensive ability was more in secondary skills than in batting average.

4. Each, in his turn, was proclaimed the successor to Mickey Mantle (and Joe DiMaggio), and each was proclaimed a failure when he was unable to live up to that standard.

Tresh, White, and Murcer all had secondary averages between .306 and .315. Tresh in 1968 hit just .233—yet he was as valuable in that season as Ed Delahanty was in 1894, when Delahanty hit .407, or as Joe Medwick was in 1938, when Medwick hit .322 with 21 homers, 122 RBI, or as Albert Belle was in 1996, when Belle hit .274 with 45 doubles, 30 homers, and 116 RBI.

> 1—TOM TRESH, New York. Biggest surprise in the balloting. Managers say his versatility and switch-hitting power make him No. 1 over such established stars as Rocky Colavito and Harmon Killebrew. Good fielder. Exceptional baserunner. Accurate arm. Very determined.—*Sport Magazine*, August 1963, "The American League Managers' Secret Player Ratings"

67 ◆ Charley Jones

(1876–1888, 881 G, 56 542 .299)

Born Benjamin Rippy in North Carolina in 1850, Jones was orphaned in the early 1860s, perhaps due to the Civil War, and moved to Indiana where he was raised by a relative named Reuben Jones. The highest level of baseball in the early 1870s was the National Association. A big man and built like a bull, Jones had tryouts with several National Association teams, and finally caught on with Keokuk in 1875.

Once in the league, Jones was a productive hitter and one of the best defensive outfielders of his time, which enabled him to survive the severe shaking-out process of the next several seasons. In 1879, playing for Harry Wright and the Boston Red Stockings, Jones led the National League in home runs, runs scored, RBI, and walks, leading Boston to a second-place finish. He was playing well again in 1880, when he became embroiled in the mother of all salary disputes.

The dispute began, improbably enough, over the timing of his pay envelope. His contract, like that of his teammates, called for the month's salary to be paid at the end of each month. The actual practice, however, was not to pay players when they were on a road trip, but only to advance them what money they needed, since to do otherwise would require the teams to carry large amounts of cash on the road. On September 2, 1880, with the Red Stockings in the midst of a long road trip, Jones demanded that he be paid his full salary for the month of August.

Now, why did Jones need to be paid in the middle of a road trip? Well, he drank, and according to Jim Summer in *Baseball's First Stars* he was nicknamed "The Knight of the Limitless Linen," among other things, because of his huge wardrobe. (Jones was also nicknamed, probably as a result of this conflict, "Baby" and "The Big Baby.") His burn rate, in other words, may have been a little high—but there are other explanations available. Jones and the Red Stockings had been quarrelling all summer, and the August pay envelope may have been a pretext invented by Jones to engineer his release.

In any case, the Red Stockings refused to pay him, since they probably didn't have the money with them, and Jones then refused to play the next day. Harry Wright sent a telegram back to Boston, and the Red Stockings immediately released Jones, and issued a statement saying that his "conduct" had been "aggravat-

ing and beyond the patience of most people." They also expelled him from the league, blacklisted him.

At this point, newspapers began picking sides in the dispute, the *Chicago Tribune* haranguing Jones for staging the conflict, and the *Cincinnati Enquirer,* among others, rallying to Jones' defense, and faulting the Red Stockings. Jones produced a letter from the secretary of the Boston team, a man named Frederick Long, asking Jones to compute how much money the team still owed him. Jones' computations were not to their liking, and the Boston team then refused to pay him anything, even what they clearly owed him.

The newspapers gradually swung around to Jones' side. Jones went to court, and won a judgment in an Ohio court against the Boston team, which they refused to pay. The Red Stockings played in Cleveland, however, so Jones attached Boston's share of the gate receipts for the Cleveland series, which were collected by the sheriff. Jones used the money to purchase a laundry in Cincinnati, and retired from baseball, since he was blacklisted from what was then the only major league.

In late 1881 the American Association announced that they would open 1882 as a new and competing major league. Jones immediately signed to play for the Cincinnati team. The power muggles in the American Association, however, decided to honor the National League's blacklist, and ordered the Cincinnati team not to employ Jones.

Jones, having signed a contract with the Cincinnati team, now sued them for his 1882 salary. There was a trial, a bitter trial at which it was alleged that Jones had been blacklisted not merely for jumping the Boston team, but for alcoholism and insubordination.

Jones lost the lawsuit, but, as other disputes arose between the National League and the

American Association, the AA stopped honoring the blacklist, allowing Jones to return to the game in 1883. He had missed more than two full seasons and endured at least two lawsuits in a dispute that began over when he would be paid a month's salary. He played four more years for Cincinnati, and played extremely well, leading the American Association in runs created in 1884. Retiring from baseball in 1888, Jones moved to New York City, where he was employed as an inspector of elections. The time and place of his death are unknown.

68 ◆ Greg Vaughn
(1989–2000, 1504 G, 320 956 .247)
Have home runs, will travel.

69 ◆ Joe Rudi
(1967–1982, 1547 G, 179 810 .264)

> I just try to keep my mouth shut, do my job, and keep out of people's way.—Joe Rudi

> Oakland's neck was saved by "the greatest catch ever seen" (according to biased observers). Rudi seemed to suspend himself four feet off the ground, one hand against the fence, and the gloved hand, turned backward, placed just right to snare a certain extra-base blow.—Robert Smith, the *Illustrated History of Baseball,* describing a catch in the 1972 World Series (slightly edited)

> "I'll tell you about Joe Rudi," Reggie Jackson said. "Nicest guy in the league—underrated, underpaid, a self-made ballplayer, and the best left fielder in the American League."—Art Berke, *Unsung Heroes of the Major Leagues*

Joe Rudi is the most famous "underrated" player of all time. He wasn't actually underrated, but he came up later than the big stars on the World Championship A's of 1972–74 and wasn't quite as good a player, so he wasn't as well known as Reggie, Rollie, Catfish, and Sal. He played well in the three World Series, however, hitting .300 in 19 games with rather remarkable defense in left field, offering an assortment of sliding, diving, and leaping catches, on all of which he seemed to connect the horsehide to the leather.

The press started saying that Joe was the underrated star of the A's, and continued to say this for years after it was no longer true. Curt Gowdy at that time was the nation's best-known sports broadcaster; he was racing from one assignment to another, broadcasting all of the big events on all three networks. He had lost interest in the sports he was broadcasting, so he would say the same things over and over, every week. If Joe Rudi's name was mentioned he had a Pavlovian response, "Joe Rudi . . . underrated . . . great player . . . never gets any ink." There would be stories about Rudi in *The Sporting News* roughly every third week, all of them claiming that Rudi never got any ink. Rudi himself finally put an end to it when he commented "Well, I don't get a lot of ink about my playing, but I do get a lot of ink about not getting any ink."

70 ◆ Tommy Davis
(1959–1978, 1999 G, 153 1052 .294)

Davis grew up in Brooklyn, as a Dodger fan, and signed with the Dodgers in 1956, hoping to play for the Brooklyn Dodgers. "It broke my heart," he said of his reaction to learning that his employer was moving their home office. "I don't mean I don't like it in Los Angeles. I do. But . . ."

Davis in high school was also an outstanding basketball player, reportedly recruited by more than 40 colleges. The Dodgers closed the deal with him, as an amateur, with a phone call from Jackie Robinson . . .

> He was a big man but could run like hell. In a 60-yard dash, he was just a step behind [Maury] Wills.—Stan Williams, *We Played the Game* (Danny Peary)

Davis broke his ankle, badly, on May 1, 1965, perhaps costing him a Hall of Fame career. Davis, who stole 68 bases in a season in the minor leagues and was clocked going to first base in 3.4 seconds, was never fast again, and never did get back to the level of his 1962–63 performance.

71 ◆ Ron Gant

(1987–2000, 1620 G, 292 910 .256)

Came to the majors as a second baseman, and had a terrific rookie season in 1988. His defense at second was problematic, so they moved him to third base where, in his second season, he hit .177 and fielded .882—among the worst all-around seasons in history for a player playing as many games as he did (88). He went to the outfield the next year, and has been solid ever since, except that he missed the 1994 season due to a motorcycle accident and had a miserable 1997 season.

72 ◆ Patsy Dougherty

(1902–1911, 1233 G, 17 413 .284)

Growing up in Bolivar, New York, Dougherty was a high school teammate of Frank Gannett, founder of the Gannett newspaper chain. He may have come from a family with some money; anyway, Dougherty was a friend of Gannett, and his brother, Frank Dougherty, ran a bank in Bolivar for almost sixty years. A pitcher, Patsy played town baseball against Fielder Jones, who was from a nearby small town, and who was at that time playing in the Eastern League, on his way to the majors. Jones realized that Dougherty could play in the Eastern League, and recommended him to his team.

A good hitter and an exceptional bunter, Dougherty began to play outfield when not pitching. In the winter of 1901–1902 he went to California to play winter ball, a common practice at the time, and wound up on the same team as Jimmy Collins, then managing the team we now call the Red Sox. Collins liked him as an outfielder, and was able to purchase his contract for Boston.

As a rookie in 1902 Dougherty hit .342. In 1903 he hit .331, leading the American League in runs (108) and hits (195), and leading the Red Sox to the pennant.

Early the next season, Dougherty was traded to the New York Highlanders even-up for an infielder named Bob Unglaub, who, at least by comparison, couldn't walk and chew gum at the same time. (Actually, according to an anecdote in Ira Smith's *Low and Outside,* Unglaub was a Salvation Army volunteer who alternated between drunkenness and temperance lectures.) Boston fans were outraged. American League president Ban Johnson had been talking about the need for the American League to have a stronger team in New York, and it was widely suspected that Dougherty's "trade" to New York was some sort of trick to help out the Highlanders.

> Until Frazee ruined the Red Sox in the post-World War I period, it unquestionably was the worst deal made by the Boston club.—Fred Lieb, *The Boston Red Sox*

As far as I know, no one ever admitted that the trade was a set up, but it does seem extremely likely that it was. A footnote is that a Boston newspaper, reporting the trade, ran a headline screaming "DOUGHERTY NOW A YANKEE"—the first known instance of the New York team being referred to in print as the "Yankees." In any case, on the last day of the season the two teams involved, the Red Sox and Highlanders, were to meet in a double header with the pennant on the line; the Red Sox were 94-58, the Highlanders 91-58. The Red Sox needed to win one game; the Highlanders needed to win both. In the first game, after Jack Chesbro's world-famous wild pitch had given the Red Sox the lead in the top of the ninth, Dougherty batted with two out in the bottom of the ninth, with the tying runs on base. He struck out on three pitches, ending the pennant race.

Dougherty never hit .300 again, as the dead ball era deepened and batting averages fell. Unable to reach a contract agreement with New York in 1906, Dougherty jumped the team and went home to Bolivar, quitting baseball. Fielder Jones, now managing the White Sox, rescued him again, working out a deal with the Highlanders and getting Dougherty squared away with Ban Johnson. The White Sox won 19 straight games shortly after Dougherty joined them, still an American League record, and continued their surge until they had claimed the World Championship.

Dougherty was as good a ballplayer in the 1907–1909 era as he had been his first three years in the league, although the dead ball era had queered the numbers. He retired after ten years in the majors, and went home to Bolivar, where he worked at his brother's bank until he died of a heart attack in 1940.

73 ◆ Sam Mertes
(1896–1906, 1190 G, 40 721 .279)
Led National League in RBI in 1903. Mertes, who was enormously strong, was called "Sandow," after a famous circus strongman of that name. Late in September 1903, Roger Bresnahan missed a few games with an injury, forcing Mertes to play center. The *New York Times* described his play in center field as "on the border of the ridiculous." John McGraw, however, recalled Mertes as making categorically the greatest catch that he ever saw, in the heat of the 1905 pennant race.

> The Reds got a man on. A long hit would beat us. And, mind you, the pennant was almost in our grasp. That one game was needed.

The next batter caught one on the nose and it was a wicked line drive to deep center. Mertes, having anticipated the danger of a long hit, played very deep. A short hit—say, a single— would not be so disastrous, but a three-bagger or a home run would be fatal. Mertes realized that and played accordingly.

> Starting with the crack of the bat he looked squarely into the sun and ran with the ball. It seemed certain that it would go over his head. By a sprint, though, he got back and with a jump speared the ball with his bare hand, crashing into the fence as he fell. But he had saved the game and won the pennant.

> That was the greatest catch I ever saw.—John J. McGraw, *My Thirty Years in Baseball* (1923)

Mertes was a quiet man, not popular with the New York fans. In my generation he would probably have been described as "up tight." After being traded to St. Louis he said he had trouble getting along with his teammates in New York because he was a Mason and many of them were Irish Catholics.

74 ◆ Kip Selbach
(1894–1906, 1613 G, 44 779 .293)
Selbach was a small, aggressive player; according to James J. Skipper the nickname "Kip" may have had a meaning similar to "Runt." Skipper also reports that "Selbach was also called 'Baron' and much was made of his German background."

A native of Columbus, Ohio, Selbach's career was a long succession of miserable experiences with his teams, many of which, in all fairness, were not his fault. He played for Washington (NL) from 1894 to 1898, and had his best years there, but that was an awful team, never even close to .500, and hardly anybody came to their games. (In fact, the practice of canceling home games and re-scheduling them as road games to get bigger crowds, which became infamous in 1899 with the Cleveland Spiders, actually began in Washington in 1892.)

Traded to Cincinnati in 1899, Selbach was happy to be on a better team and happy to be near home, but was criticized as a player. Ren Mulford, longtime Cincinnati sportswriter, wrote in 1899 that "Selbach's strongest point is making his toilet while standing at the plate." This wasn't a bathroom joke; "making his toilet" meant dressing himself. Selbach was the Mike Hargrove of his time, the human rain delay, hitching up his trousers, kneeling and fussing with his shoe, and brushing every speck of dust from his uniform before stepping in to hit. A gum chewer, he would, before every at bat, take out his chewing gum and stick it on the bottom of his cap. Perhaps he just wasn't used to playing in front of spectators.

After the 1899 season Selbach and the other better players on the Cincinnati team were transferred to the New York Giants, the two teams being owned by the same men. The idea was to create a super-team, as Brooklyn had done by combining the players from Brooklyn and Baltimore, and as Pittsburgh had done by plucking the best feathers of the Louisville goose. However, as I reported in the comment about George Davis, and wrote about at more length in another book, the two parts of the New York team never merged, but engaged in a long, nasty public feud, accusing one another, in the newspapers, of every offense short of armed robbery. Selbach, who had never wanted to come to New York, was one of the key Cincinnati partisans, and as such was roundly hated by the New York fans, the Giants players, and the New York press. And the feeling was mutual.

Before the 1902 season John McGraw persuaded Selbach to jump to the Baltimore team of the new American League. As soon as Selbach got there, however, McGraw was quarreling with his financial backers and with American League president Ban Johnson, and by mid-season McGraw was gone.

McGraw, of course, took much of the Baltimore team with him when he went to New York, and he tried to persuade Selbach to come back to New York. Selbach, who had endured two years of pure hell playing for the Giants, refused to consider it. After the season, however, the Baltimore team announced that they were moving to New York. Selbach flatly refused to play in New York City, and said that he would jump back to the National League rather than play in New York. Ban Johnson assigned his contract to Washington (AL) rather than lose him to the National League.

But this Washington team was as bad as the other one, and worse yet, they were a bad team with a superstar left fielder, Ed Delahanty. Selbach tried to play right field, and probably could have a few years earlier, but by 1903 his defense in right was unacceptable. According to Mike Sowell in *July 2, 1903,* one time "a fly ball fell between Jimmy Ryan in center field and Kip Selbach in right, and the two players shouted at each other, arguing over who should have made the play. Ryan complained to [manager Tom] Loftus he had no faith in Selbach in right field." Selbach said he wanted to play left field, but Ed Delahanty refused to give it up. The superstar and the minor star had words several times. This problem was solved when Delahanty died, but the team finished last.

Finally, in July 1904, something went right for him. After Patsy Dougherty was "traded" from Boston to New York (see comment on Dougherty), Boston found themselves in the pennant race, and needing a left fielder. They arranged a trade to get Selbach from Washington. In 1904 Selbach helped the Boston Pilgrims hold off a charge from the New York Highlanders, and made a key defensive play in the famous pennant-deciding game which was recounted in the Dougherty comment. That was the highlight of his career, if not the highlight of his life. After years of unhappy experiences, teams that just didn't work out, he had not only helped Boston to win the pennant, but, perhaps more importantly, he had helped them to beat New York.

According to Rich Eldred in *Nineteenth Century Stars* (SABR), Selbach was a world-class bowler, and toured in the off season as "captain of a bowling team." In 1903 Selbach and Herm Collin won the ABC doubles title, with a three-game score of 1,227. "When the old tin can is pulled on him for good," said *The Sporting Life,* "he will give Columbus the best bowling alley they ever had." He left the majors after 1906, played several more seasons in the minor leagues, and returned to Columbus in 1911, where he opened that bowling alley, and lived for the rest of his life.

75 ◆ Elmer E. Smith
(1886–1901, 1239 G, 37 638 .310)

Smith was also a part of that Cincinnati/New York quasi-team of 1901 (see Kip Selbach, if you're not reading this in sequence). Originally a left-handed pitcher, Smith won 34 games for Cincinnati in 1887, when he was 19 years old, and 22 more the next year. He moved to the outfield when his arm gave out, and hit around .350 several times in the 1890s. His pitching accomplishments are counted to his credit in these rankings, which is why he ranks as high as he does.

According to Robert L. Tiemann, Smith "swung one of the heaviest bats in history, up to 54 ounces...He lived his whole life in urban Allegheny City and worked in the iron and steel mills in the winters. But he loved animals, and his home was always surrounded by chickens, ducks and lots and lots of dogs."

76 ◆ Wally Moon
(1954–1965, 1457 G, 142 661 .289)

He was named Wallace Wade Moon, after a famous football coach . . . Wally Moon had a Master's degree from Texas A&M. This probably made him the only player of the 1950s who had more advanced degrees (2) than eyebrows (1).

Moon broke in with the Cardinals in 1954. Eddie Stanky, in his third season as Cardinal manager, was about as popular in St. Louis as Don Denkinger. Moon hit .307 at Rochester in 1953, and, in the spring of 1954, Stanky decided that he was ready to play in the majors. Unfortunately, the Cardinals already had a right fielder, Enos Slaughter. Stanky decided to trade Slaughter to make room in the outfield for Wally Moon—prematurely, as it turned out; Slaughter could still play.

Slaughter was as popular in St. Louis as Stanky was unpopular, and the public was outraged by the trade. Moon, booed daily the first half of the season, had 193 hits as a rookie and won the Rookie of the Year Award, but the Cardinals had an off season, and Stanky was fired early in the 1955 season.

It wasn't Moon's fault that Stanky had decided to trade Slaughter, but, as Morticia said in *The Addams Family* movie, try telling that to an angry mob. Moon was a good outfielder. According to Ray Robinson in *Baseball Stars of 1960,* Moon in 1957 made a catch of a drive by Willie Mays that was the equal of anything Willie himself might have done. A Cardinal fan, applauding half-heartedly, remarked that "Terry Moore would have made it look a lot easier." As soon as he had an off-season Moon was traded out of St. Louis.

He became a part of the Dodgers' world champions of 1959, starting the 1959 All-Star game in the outfield alongside Willie Mays and Henry Aaron. The Dodgers won the pennant that year, with Moon leading the team in batting (.302), and Buzzie Bavasi citing Moon as the team's, if not the league's, MVP, saying that Moon's 19 homers had meant more to the Dodgers than Ernie Banks' 45 had meant to the Cubs.

In the second game of the 1959 World Series, Moon made a defensive play that Casey Stengel, covering the series for *Life* magazine, would cite as the key to the series. The White Sox won the first game 11-0, but trailed in the second game 4-2 entering the bottom of the eighth. They got two men on with none out, when Al Smith blasted a double into deep left-center. Moon, playing left field, realized that he couldn't make the catch, but faked catching the ball for an instant, freezing the runner off first and stopping his momentum. The runner from second scored, making it 4-3, but Moon scrambled after the ball and hit the cutoff man in time to throw out the tying run, the runner from first, at home plate. Moon's bluff and throw saved the game, and prevented the Dodgers from falling into a 2-0 hole in the series.

Moon also ended that series, won by the Dodgers in six, with a fine running catch of a sinking liner by Ted Kluszewski. He hit often around .300 with some power, ran well, won a Gold Glove (1960), and was a part of many fine teams.

77 ◆ Jo-Jo Moore
(1930–1941, 1335 G, 79 513 .298)

> Jo-Jo Moore, whose trademarks were a great throwing arm and extreme competence as a leadoff man despite his habit of swinging at the first pitch.—Fred Stein, *Under Coogan's Bluff*

Born on Christmas Day in 1906, Moore reportedly told everybody that he was going to be a baseball player almost from the time he could walk. He grew up on a spinach farm near Gause, Texas. He briefly attended Texas A&M, left there in 1930, signed with the New York Giants, and was the Giants left fielder in the

Bill Terry years. He had 200 hits in 1935 and 1936, scored 100 runs a year from 1934 through 1936. World War II ended his career a little early, but only a little.

> Some folks call him "The Thin Man" and others refer to him, affectionately, as the "Gause Ghost," for this dynamic Texan is a frail looking hombre.—Speed Johnson, *Who's Who in the Major Leagues,* 1937

> Came up with San Antone in 1930, and mostly since then has held down left field with consummate artistry and a beautiful whip.—Ernest Butt, *Who's Who in the Major Leagues,* 1939

> Gaunt and looking, even as a youngster, as if he were held together with strings and safety pins, he was running out of time now and he had a bad knee, too.—Frank Graham, *The New York Giants*

78 ◆ Leon Wagner
(1958–1969, 1352 G, 211 669 .272)

Leon Wagner in 1963 hit 26 home runs: two in California, and 24 on the road . . .

Wagner was a colorful, quotable player who was always in the news. He liked to refer to himself in the third person, usually as "Daddy Wags" or some variation thereon. He was an odd-looking man, with very high cheekbones, a barrel chest, and long, thin legs. He was not modest about his skills. Asked if he could hit .300 if he concentrated on that, Wagner said "Wags could hit more than .300. Wags could hit .350. But I'm a big guy. When I go in to negotiate my contract, the first thing they ask me is 'How many home runs did you hit?'"

Wagner had an odd batting stance, actually a series of odd batting stances, among which he alternated on the basis of his "hitting mood":

> He come rambling to the plate in a loose-gaited kind of way . . . He takes his left-handed stance, body stooped over the plate, head staring right down the pipe, right leg pointing crazily, and his

hands—look at his hands, will you?—spread apart on the handle.—Jack Zanger, *Baseball Stars of 1963*

One winter Wagner opened a clothing store. Their motto, known coast to coast, was "Get Your Rags From Daddy Wags." By the next winter the clothing store had gone out of business, and Wagner was in the real estate racket. His motto was "Rent Your Pad From Super Dad."

Wagner was a brutal outfielder, cited by a good many fans as the worst they ever saw. After he hit .317 with 13 homers in 74 games as a rookie in 1958, he lost his job because he just couldn't catch the ball. He didn't *know* that he was a bad outfielder, or wouldn't admit that he did; he would insist he was one of the best defensive outfielders in baseball, and would say that "some year Wags is going to go through the season without an error and win me one of them Gold Gloves." He would compare his own fielding, not unfavorably, to that of Willie Mays. He had been Mays' teammate for a couple of years, regarded Willie as one of his closest friends, and would work him into most conversations the way Durocher would drag in Frank Sinatra. "He'd be in a fog out in the field," wrote Zanger, "filling his mind with heroic visions of Wags the hitter, Wags the home run king. Every now and then, balls would whistle by to break the tranquility, and he would generously misplay them into bigger hits." Warming up in the outfield between innings, he would throw the ball underhanded, he explained, to save his arm.

But a left-handed hitter who can hit .280 with 35 homers has his uses, and while Wagner was sometimes irritating, he was harmless. "I don't dig people who put baseball in the same class with goin' to church," said Wagner. "Maybe I don't look it, but I'm givin' it all I got. Only what's wrong with bein' cheerful while I'm at it?"

79 ◆ Bob Meusel
(1920–1930, 1407 G, 156 1067 .309)

Meusel had been one of the greatest—and most misunderstood—players ever to wear a Yankee uniform ... The fans respected him but never could warm up to him. The baseball writers, even those traveling regularly with the team, found him cold, uncommunicative, almost hostile. Recognizing him as a great competitor when the checks were down, they accused him of being lazy.—Frank Graham, *The New York Yankees*

Bob Meusel always looks like the advertisement for what the well-dressed man will wear.—Babe Ruth, *Babe Ruth's Own Book of Baseball*

Meusel was a tall, slender, powerful, elegant man with, by acclamation, the best throwing arm of his generation.

Robert Wm. Meusel, right fielder, the best thrower in the major leagues and one of the best natural hitters, was born in San Jose, Calif., July 19, 1897. He started as a first basemen with the Oakland club in 1917, but had no chance to show. In 1918 he played first baseman for Spokane and batted .311. He jumped into prominence as a third baseman with Vernon in 1919, when his batting earned for him the title of the "Babe Ruth of the Pacific Coast League." He came to the Yanks in 1920, where he alternated as a third baseman and outfielder and batted .328. Only a rather lazy and listless nature prevents Meusel from being one of the greatest stars of the game. He is fast, has a wonderful arm and is a heavy batter. He is erratic in the field, careless on the bases and at times totally indifferent. He stands 6 feet 2$\frac{1}{2}$ inches, weighs 195 pounds and throws and bats right-handed. His home is in Los Angeles.—1922 *Reach Guide*

On February 16, 1924, Boston Braves third baseman Tony Boeckel, a good player, was killed in an automobile accident. Meusel was a passenger in the car at the time of the accident.

80 ◆ Mike Greenwell

(1985–1996, 1269 G, 130 726 .303)

The historical bridge between Ted Williams and Troy O'Leary.

81 ◆ Cleon Jones

(1963–1976, 1213 G, 93 524 .281)

Jones went to high school with Tommie Agee, who was acquired by the Mets in 1968; the two men were teammates on the Mets from 1968 through 1972, and both were among the best players in the National League in 1969; Cleon, in fact, might have been the 1969 MVP were it not for a September injury. They did not handle success well; Agee got fat and paranoid, and Jones was arrested in St. Petersburg sleeping naked in a van with a woman not his wife.

In a 1969 game against Houston, Jones let a fly ball drop in front of him for a hit. Gil Hodges stalked out of the dugout, past the pitcher's mound, out to left field, and told Jones to follow him back to the dugout. Jones, the leading hitter in the National League at that time, was publicly humiliated for not hustling.

After the arrest in St. Pete, Jones was "in a foul mood the next few weeks [and] defied manager Yogi Berra when asked to play defense in one game." According to Maury Allen in *After the Miracle,* "Berra ordered him suspended for insubordination. [The Mets] refused to act, fearing repercussions from the baseball players union, then beginning to feel its power. Berra would not back down and he was soon fired."

In spite of those incidents, I don't think Jones was a bad guy; I think he was well liked by most of his teammates, black and white, and that he was for the most part a positive, upbeat person. There are a lot of very intense pressures to being an athlete in New York City, and Jones just didn't handle them well. After his career he had a fast-food company, which went bankrupt, and worked in community service in Mobile.

82 ◆ Joe Vosmik

(1930–1944, 1414 G, 65 874 .307)

Hit .348 with 47 doubles, 20 triples, 110 RBI in 1935, hit .320 or better five times and usually drove in 90+ runs.

> Broad, blond, and Bohemian, Vosmik had come off the Cleveland sand lots for two years of training in the lower minors. Now the powerful right-handed batter with the strong arm and ready smile was trimmed for his major-league debut.—Franklin Lewis, *The Cleveland Indians*

83 ◆ Ralph Garr

(1968–1980, 1317 G, 75 408 .306)

The top ten rookie seasons by players listed as left fielders:

1. Joe Jackson, 1911
2. Ted Williams, 1939
3. Stan Musial, 1942
4. Rico Carty, 1964
5. George Stone, 1905
6. Del Ennis, 1946
7. Tom Tresh, 1962 (playing shortstop)
8. Kevin McReynolds, 1984
9. Ralph Garr, 1971
10. Joe Medwick, 1933

Not all of these guys were left fielders as rookies. A lot of career left fielders are guys who come up as center fielders and hit pretty well, but can't play center...Ralph Garr in 1971 hit .343 with 219 hits, 30 stolen bases; he was not actually considered a rookie at the time. Garr was fast, but a poor outfielder. He couldn't throw, and he couldn't read the ball well, which made him tentative. Fred White said one time "Ralph Garr played that ball like he thought if he stood real still the ball wouldn't see him." He was a .300 hitter who lived on the Baltimore chop, but his value as a leadoff man was diminished by the fact that he didn't walk.

Garr, I believe, was the first professional athlete to have a registered nickname, "The

Road Runner." My understanding is that the Braves, when Garr was an exciting young player, started calling him "The Road Runner." Warner Brothers or whoever owns the cartoon character objected to the unauthorized use of their character, and the Braves, trying to make a positive out of the challenge, then reached an agreement to license the use of the nickname. After which Garr had an off year and nobody cared anymore.

84 ◆ Tito Francona
(1956–1970, 1719 G, 125 656 .272)

The Cleveland Indians acquired Francona at the end of spring training, 1959, in a trade that was made, Frank Lane stated Frankly, strictly to get rid of Larry Doby; anything he received was an afterthought. Francona had failed trials with the Orioles, White Sox, and Tigers in quick succession.

Playing in Puerto Rico in the winter of 1957–58, Francona had contracted hepatitis; the White Sox, for whom he played in 1958, never knew this, or Al Lopez, who had liked Francona a lot when he traded for him, probably wouldn't have given up on him after half a season. In the spring of 1958 a doctor had told him that there also might be something wrong with his heart. "Go to spring training," said the doctor helpfully, "and if you drop dead, you'll know you have a bad heart." Francona, worrying about his health and kind of moping around, didn't drop dead, but his batting average did. In the winter of 1958–59 he was taking off-season classes at a business school in Aberdeen, South Dakota, expecting to be out of baseball in a year or so.

The hepatitis had forced Francona to go on a strict diet, however, and a year later he was in the best physical condition of his life. Frank Lane didn't know any of this when he traded for him; the only things that Lane knew about Francona were that

1. He had played well enough to draw one vote in the Rookie of the Year voting three years earlier.

2. He had asked in the newspaper to be traded.

3. He wasn't Larry Doby.

It was, oddly enough, the second time that Francona had been traded for Larry Doby. Anyway, Francona pinch hit for the Indians the first two months of the 1959 season, starting only a couple of games. Deciding he was going to live, he worked hard on his swing, Cleveland manager Joe Gordon working with him to reduce his uppercut. In early June the Indians had a seven-game losing streak, the last game of which was a 2-1 loss, Francona's pinch-hit home run in the ninth inning preventing a shutout. The Indians had three pretty good players in the outfield (Colavito, Minoso, and Piersall) and a good first baseman (Vic Power); still, they weren't winning, and Joe Gordon decided it was Francona's turn to play.

> The Francona success story is so unusual that, as fiction, it would be considered unreal. No hero of fiction is allowed to jump from rags to riches so swiftly or so spectacularly as the Indians' left-handed muscle man.—Hal Lebovitz, *Sport Magazine*, January 1960.

Francona stepped into the lineup on Sunday, June 7, 1959, playing a double-header in front of 60,000 Cleveland fans. He hit a single and homer in the first game, driving in three runs to snap the losing streak, and had three more hits in the nightcap. For two months nobody could get Francona out, and the Indians got red-hot the minute Francona went into the lineup, finishing second with an 89-65 record.

Francona, hitting close to .400 in early September, slumped to .363 in 399 at bats at season's end, his late start costing him the

American League batting championship. The Indians presented him with a silver service on the last day of the season, including a silver bowl with 363 silver dollars.

No source says this, but I have always believed that one reason that Rocky Colavito was traded after the 1959 season was because the Indians felt, Frank Lane felt, that Francona could replace him as a matinee idol. As handsome as Colavito was, which is very handsome indeed, Francona was even more so; Francona looked like a movie star. Frank Lane didn't realize that the Cleveland public would turn on him for trading Colavito, in part, because he thought Francona could step in for him with that audience.

That didn't happen, of course. Although he wasn't a .360 hitter, Francona hit .292 in 1960, leading the league in doubles, and .301 with 16 homers, 85 RBI in 1961. He lost his regular job after a sub-par season in '63, but was able to hang around the better part of a decade after that as a pinch hitter.

85 ◆ Duffy Lewis
(1910–1921, 1459 G, 38 793 .284)

> A funny fellow was Duffy Lewis. One of the pleasantest, squarest, friendliest fellows in baseball, he had more friends than any player I ever knew. He had a fad for dress too—and he certainly was the clothes horse of the league. His neckties used to be the envy of everyone on the circuit.—Babe Ruth (Ford Frick) in *Babe Ruth's Own Book of Baseball*

In 1915 Lewis got into a terrible fight with his teammate, Tris Speaker. The trouble started after Lewis, yielding to a heat wave, had his head almost completely shaved—a common thing now, but very unfashionable in 1915. Speaker snuck up behind him during batting practice one day and swiped his hat, letting the fans see his bald head. Lewis threatened to kill him if he did that again, so Speaker came back

the next day and did it again. Lewis threw his bat at Speaker, hitting him across the shins; Speaker had to be carried from the field, and was out of the lineup for a couple of games. It was several weeks before Lewis and Speaker patched up their relationship . . .

The Boston Red Sox 1910–1915 outfield of Duffy Lewis, Tris Speaker, and Harry Hooper is, of course, famous as the greatest defensive outfield of all time. Both Speaker and Hooper were fine defensive center fielders, and the third man, Lewis, was supposed to be a good outfielder, to. Edward Barrow, in *My Fifty Years in Baseball*:

> Bob Meusel, Earle Combs, and Babe Ruth. They were great, to be sure. But defensively, I would rate Speaker, Lewis, and Hooper over them . . . Meusel couldn't range as Duffy Lewis did, or come in for a fly and go back for one with his agility.

A good outfield, sure, but were they actually the best defensive outfield of all time? The Win Shares approach to this issue is to ask a series of questions:

1. How many games did the team win?
2. How much of that success is attributable to their offense, how much to their pitching and defense?
3. Of the success of the pitching and defense, how much do we credit to the fielders?
4. Of that which we credit to the fielders, how much do we credit to the outfielders?

How many games the team won is pretty easy to determine. For each of the other three questions, there is a set of relevant numbers, and there is a set of formulas used to process the data and arrive at the answer.

The answer suggested by this analysis is that that outfield was clearly the best of its own time, but that if they were better than the best of other eras, the system is unable to perceive it. The Red Sox outfield ranks as the best in baseball (defensively) in 1912, 1914, and 1915, and as the best in the American League in 1910. But were they better than, let's say, the Oakland A's outfield of 1980 (Rickey Henderson, Dwayne Murphy, and Tony Armas), or the other best outfields of other eras? The system is unable to see that they were.

86 ◆ John Anderson
(1894–1908, 1635 G, 49 976 .290)

Anderson was a player, like Jackie Brandt or Amos Otis, who never *looked* like he was playing hard. He played well, but he didn't convey intensity ... Anderson, according to *Misfits: The Cleveland Spiders of 1899,* used "a bat heavy enough to be used as a battering ram."

A native of Norway, the switch-hitting Anderson starred in the New England League before making his big league debut with the Brooklyn Dodgers in 1894. He was more or less a regular with Brooklyn from 1895 on, sold to the Washington club on May 19, 1898. The *Washington Post* said that:

> Anderson is one of the most reliable batsmen in the major League, a consistent outfielder, and steady-going, conscientious ball player.
>
> ... Anderson is one of the most stalwart figures in the major League outfield, standing six feet one, and scaling at 190 pounds.

He had a fine season with Washington, leading the league in triples (22) and slugging average (.494).

Despite quality hitting stats he moved from team to team. In 1899 he was with Brooklyn; they won the pennant. In 1900 he jumped to Milwaukee in the American League, at that time a minor league, although gearing up to become a major, which was accomplished in 1901. In 1902 the Milwaukee team moved to St. Louis, becoming the Browns. In 1902 and 1903 Anderson had two amazingly similar seasons, hitting .284 and slugging .385 in both campaigns.

In 1904 he was with the New York Highlanders. They lost the pennant on the final day of the season. The trade register in Macmillan has him being both traded and sold to New York in the space of a few months. After poring over two New York newspapers of the time, we found no evidence of either transaction. He may have been unilaterally assigned to New York by Ban Johnson, as part of Johnson's effort to build up the Highlanders. In May 1905, the Highlanders sold him to Washington. The *Washington Post* noted that "John Anderson is called the 'Human Chattel' because he is shipped from pillar to post."

Anderson—he was also called Big John and Honest John—played well in 1907, but the Senators were a truly bad team, finishing last by a healthy margin. On August 1, while playing first base, he was lustily booed after dropping a throw from an infielder. Two days later, the *Post* reported that "John Anderson has jumped the local ball club." A number of theories were offered, but for whatever reason Anderson had gone home to Worcester, Massachusetts, where he spent the remainder of the season.

There was talk of blacklisting Anderson, but it didn't happen, and he was sold that winter to the Chicago White Sox, for whom he played one season before ending his big league career. Pinch hitting for Ed Walsh, Anderson made the last out of Addie Joss' perfect game in 1908. He hit a hard ground ball over third base, but Bill Bradley made an exceptional play on it, threw to first, and Anderson was called out. Anderson turned to argue, but fans were pouring over the field by the hundreds, and the umpire disappeared into the crowd.

I'm not sure, but this may have been the last at bat of Anderson's career. There were three days left in the season, and he wasn't playing much.

John Anderson was not forgotten after his retirement. On April 29, 1914, the *New York Times* reported that:

Stovall's ball club [the Kansas City Packers] had a chance to score in the second inning, but [Pep] Goodwin pulled a "John Anderson" trying to steal third with the bases loaded ...

A John Kieran article in the March 1932, *New York Times* placed the incident alluded to above specifically in a 1907 Senators-Tigers contest.

The 1939 Pamphlet A Century of Baseball wrote that "Someone other than John Anderson may have been the first to steal an occupied base, but baseball records show that that doubtful distinction is his. Anderson was with the Washingtons when he perpetrated that faux pas, and it happened in the early 1900s.

Baseball by the Rules (1987) also places the origin of the term "John Anderson" as being when Anderson was with the Senators; the authors wrote that "for decades after, a stupid play was described as 'a John Anderson.'"

The Dickson Baseball Dictionary, published in 1990, defines "John Anderson" or "john anderson" as:

Term for the particular boner committed when a runner attempts to steal an occupied base. It has been passed down from John Anderson who, while playing for the New York Highlanders in 1904, pulled a John Anderson with the bases loaded.

Dickson's source appears to be *The New York Yankees: An Informal History,* Frank Graham's 1943 entry in the Putnam team history series, which describes the play.

Facing this mass of contradictory references, Rob Neyer, when he worked with me, decided to do a tracer on the event. He never could find it. It became almost an obsession with him; he spent many hours, many days in the library, trying to find the origin of this story. He never found it. Taking Frank Graham's history of the Yankees to be a reliable source, he went through the accounts of every Highlanders game for the 1904 season. He found no mention of such an incident. That research was done almost ten years ago. To this day, we still have never located the origin of this legend.

87 ◆ Steve Kemp
(1977–1988, 1168 G, 130 634 .278)

There is no such thing as a stop sign on the bases for the hard running Kemp. He gets a good jump out of the batter's box and runs full speed on any ball he hits ... no infielder is safe with Kemp bearing down on him.—*The Scouting Report: 1984*

In his first six years in the majors (1977–1982) Kemp did everything well except run. He hit for average, for power, drew walks, was a decent outfielder. In 1983, playing for the Yankees, he injured his shoulder in an outfield collision early in the season; with a bone chip in his shoulder, he was unable to hit well, but that was the minor injury. In Milwaukee in September he was hit in the face with a line drive during batting practice, scarring the eye. His vision never cleared up, and he was never an effective player after that.

I saw him in the minors several years later, playing baseball for the love of the game, with no hope of being the player he once had been. He reminded me of a ghost ... you know the theory of a ghost is that when a person dies suddenly, without preparation, there is a "life force" left behind, which wanders the earth trying hopelessly to fulfill its destiny. That was Kemp in the late eighties.

88 ◆ Irish Meusel
(1914–1927, 1294 G, 106 819 .310)

Meusel's brother Bob was famous for having, almost by acclamation, the best throwing arm of his generation. What is less known is that Irish's arm was as weak as Bob's was strong. One time, playing right field in an emergency, he picked up the ball and rushed the throw. The ball slipped out of his hand and landed in the bleachers behind him.

Another time, according to Lee Allen's *The Hot Stove League,* Irish was walking down the street with John McGraw when a one-armed man, very drunk, staggered up to them. "Pardon me, sir," the man began. "I had the misfortune to lose my arm . . ."

"Get on your way," McGraw responded. "Irish ain't got it."

The Meusel brothers, similar players except that Irish couldn't throw, were very close; the press used to say that they were "true brothers." In their New York years (1922–1926) they lived together, and often visited one another's clubhouses when the schedule permitted.

89 ◆ Frank Thomas
(1951–1966, 1766 G, 286 962 .266)

> At 6'3" and 200 pounds, Thomas was lumpy and tough, like the Pittsburgh landscape of his birth. In baseball circles, Thomas was known as an agitator. For laughs he would often challenge a pitcher to throw him his hardest pitch. Then he would stand at home plate and catch it barehanded.—Dick Allen and Tim Whitaker, *Crash*

Like Dick Groat, Thomas was a local boy who grew up a Pirate fan. He intended to become a Catholic priest; a note in the old *Baseball Registers* says that he "Studied for priesthood in Roman Catholic Church, 1941–46," although he was only 17 at the end of this period. At 17 he began to attract the attention of baseball scouts, and was close to making a deal with the Cleveland Indians when his parish priest, also a Pirate fan, arranged a meeting with a man from the Pirates front office, who agreed to match the Indians offer.

He served a full minor league apprenticeship and then some, driving in 132 runs at Tallahassee in 1948, and 131 runs for New Orleans in 1952 (35, 131, .303). With the Pirates in 1953 he was hitting .206 in early July. The Pirates hired George Sisler to work with him for a couple of weeks. Sisler got him to move back in the box and stop trying to pull everything. He wound up the year at .255 with 30 homers, 102 RBI.

For the next several seasons he hit 20 to 30 homers a year, usually hit around .280. He couldn't run and he wasn't quick, but he did have a powerful arm. The Pirates, with Bob Skinner and Roberto Clemente as wing outfielders, tried putting him at third to get something out of his arm, and in 1958 he hit .281 with 35 homers, 109 RBI, as the Pirates had their best season in 14 years. Thomas was fourth in the National League MVP voting.

Branch Rickey was running the Pirates then, and Branch Rickey always believed you should trade a player when he was about 30, before his value declined. Thomas, 29 years old and coming off a career year, was traded that winter to the Reds; basically, the Pirates got Don Hoak, Smoky Burgess, and Harvey Haddix for Thomas, which turned out to be a heck of a deal for Pittsburgh. Thomas, the best player on the Pirates in the mid-fifties, thus missed being there for the journey's happy ending in 1960. Instead, playing for the Reds, he wrenched his back, hit .225, and bombed bigtime at third base. He entered the journeyman stage of his career, playing for the Reds in 1959, the Cubs in 1960, the Braves in 1961, the Mets in 1962. He had some good years; he hit .281 with 27 homers in '61, .266 with 34 homers in '62.

In August 1964, the Phillies were looking for first base help to get them through the pennant race. They traded for Thomas . . . . "With Thomas hitting .302, hitting seven homers and driving in 26 runs in 33 games, the Phillies ballooned their lead from 1½ to 6½ games before he fractured his right thumb while sliding, September 8" (1965 *Baseball Guide*). Thomas' injury was one of the key factors which plunged the Phillies into their historic September swoon.

On July 3, 1965, there occurred the most famous and regrettable incident of Thomas' career. The first chapter of Dick Allen's autobiography, *Crash,* is entitled "The Frank Thomas Incident." According to Allen "There was one thing that Frank Thomas used to do that I could never get out of my mind. He would pretend to offer his hand in a soul shake to a young player [but then] grab the player's thumb and bend it back hard. To Thomas, this was a big joke. But I saw too many brothers on the team with swollen thumbs to get any laughs."

Allen doesn't say this in the book, but the player he thought Thomas had been picking on was a quiet youngster named Johnny Briggs, a pretty good player himself, just missed the top 100 at the position. Anyway, according to Allen, most of the team called Thomas "The Big Donkey," but he called him "Lurch," after a member of the Addams Family. Allen and Johnny Callison were around the batting cage, watching Thomas hit and engaging in some rough but good-natured humor, when Allen said something that hit a nerve.

"What are you trying to be," asked Thomas, "another Muhammad Clay?" Allen interpreted this to be a racist remark. Allen punched Thomas, and Thomas hit Allen with a baseball bat. Allen and Thomas were the two strongest men on the Phillies at that time, and it required most of the rest of the roster to separate them.

According to Richie Ashburn, Thomas "didn't get the tag 'The Big Donkey' for his smarts. A lot of guys in baseball could give the needle, but Thomas never knew when to quit. He wasn't an evil guy. His timing was just always off." In any case, Allen hit a triple in the game that day. Frank Thomas pinch-hit and hit a home run—and was released after the game.

This was not Thomas' first well-publicized fight. In 1962, with the Mets, he had taken a swing at Jack Lang, the writer. The Phillies released Thomas, one supposes, because they wanted to heal the rifts on the team, and to put the fight, witnessed by media and a few hundred early-arriving fans, behind them. But the move was a disaster, for the release of Thomas threw a spotlight onto the fight, and became, in itself, a major distraction for the Philadelphia team. Sportswriters from coast to coast editorialized on the appropriateness of releasing a respected veteran ballplayer because he had a fight with a talented kid that a lot of people didn't like anyway. Further, since Thomas had been released, he was free to go to the Philadelphia media and tell them his side of the story—while Allen and the rest of the Phillies were prohibited from talking about it. Thomas denied loudly that he had ever made a racist remark—which, in his own mind, he had not. The Philadelphia fans, suspicious of Allen anyway, turned on him and began to boo loudly at his every appearance. The mishandling of the Frank Thomas incident was one of the three or four critical mistakes which caused Dick Allen's career in Philadelphia, which began so brilliantly, to go so terribly wrong.

Thomas played for three more teams in quick succession, and his career ended in less than a year.

90 ◆ Charlie Jamieson
(1915–1932, 1779 G, 18 550 .303)
Jamieson was a native of Paterson, New Jersey. In the off season Jamieson would return to Paterson, and pass himself off as a fireman to play in a fireman's league. According to Mike Sowell in *The Pitch That Killed* (Macmillan, 1989), "Whenever he was asked his name, he would claim it was O'Reilly.

"'And what precinct are you out of?' they would ask.

"'The second,' Jamieson would tell them.

"'Oh? Do you know Callahan?'

"'Of course I do.'

"'Well, that's funny,' they would say, 'because he died five years ago.'"

Jamieson always donated his cut of the proceeds to the firemen's Widow's Fund, however, so the firemen let him get by with it, and even arranged for a "Charlie Jamieson Day" at the Polo Grounds.

"One of the best laughs I ever had in my life," wrote Babe Ruth in *Babe Ruth's Own Book of Baseball,* "was at the expense of Charley Jamieson." The Cleveland outfield played Ruth swung far around to right field, leaving left field wide open. George Uhle, pitching for Cleveland, tried to jam Ruth, but Ruth hit a rocket right over third base, an apparent triple. But, says Ruth, "the sight of Jamieson tearing across that field on his little short legs as if somebody was chasing him got to me. I was laughing as I left the plate and I was laughing as I turned first base. So were the fans and the rest of the Cleveland Club . . . I got laughing so hard that instead of reaching third base I only got to second." Why this was so funny at the time is not apparent, but, as Ruth says, "It was a lot funnier to see than it was to tell about." An almost identical anecdote is told about Cy Williams.

91 ◆ Bibb Falk

(1920–1931, 1354 G, 59 785 .314)

Bibb Falk was born in Austin, Texas, in 1899; that was his legal name, Bibb. Falk attended his hometown college, the University of Texas, where he played tackle on the football team, well enough to make the All-Southwest Conference team. The Longhorns were organizing a baseball team, and Billy Disch, the baseball coach, talked Falk into coming out for the team.

Falk and Disch were opposite personalities. Disch was a reserved, dignified man who once tried to kick a player off his team for chewing tobacco (Bibb talked him out of it). Falk, although bright and likeable, was intense, vulgar, and sarcastic. Bibb turned out to be a pretty good baseball player, and they got along great.

Falk graduated from the University of Texas at the end of the summer session in 1920. The Black Sox scandal broke in early September 1920, and left the White Sox looking for ballplayers. They signed Falk, and he stepped right into the shoes of Shoeless Joe, never spending a day in the minor leagues. He was not the hitter that Joe Jackson was, but he wasn't bad, either; he was a lifetime .314 hitter, hitting .352 with 99 RBI in 1924, .345 with 108 RBI in 1926. He was a fine outfielder, in the Chad Curtis mold: he was not fast and he did not have a great arm, but he made the plays he was expected to make, and then some. Babe Ruth, in *Babe Ruth's Own Book of Baseball* (1928) recalled a play by Falk as one of the best he had ever seen. With Joe Bush at the plate, Ruth remembered, Falk was playing deep and toward center. Bush lined the ball over third. "Bib came in fast," wrote Ruth's co-author, "made a last dive for the ball and caught it as he was sliding along on his stomach. He took the ball with the gloved hand, not more than two inches off the ground, and then turned a complete flip-flop across the cinder path. His face and both arms were cut with the cinders and when he came to the bench he was covered with blood. But he held the ball." The same book also listed Falk as among the best baserunners in the major leagues.

When his playing career ended he returned to Austin. Billy Disch retired as the Longhorn baseball coach after the 1939 season, and Falk was hired to do that job. He would become one of the most successful college coaches of all time.

He was an unusual man. A lifelong bachelor, he was devoted to baseball, and devoted to his players, and everyone who knew him knew this, but God forbid that he might ever admit it. He was crusty, perhaps a little like Lou Grant on the old Mary Tyler Moore show. He insulted his players freely, often and creatively, but somehow they never took offense; they just got mad as hell and took it out on the other team. "It has been said," wrote Neal Farmer in *Southwest Conference Baseball's Greatest Hits,* "that Falk could curse for an hour and not repeat himself." But somehow, he could do that, too, without offending anybody. "No matter what he said about you," said a former player, "you knew that he just wanted you to do better." He was brusque and rude to the press, and yet the writers doted on him. He was stubborn, yet good-natured. He would leave perfectly good bats and balls in the trash so that the neighborhood kids could have good equipment to play with, but he wouldn't be caught giving them anything.

He coached at the University of Texas for 25 years, winning the Southwestern Conference almost every year—actually, 20 times in 25 years. He coached many future major league players, but (oddly enough) no stars that I am aware of. He squirreled his money away from the day he started earning it, lived quietly, made good investments, and became a wealthy man. Retiring at age 65, he lived in Austin another 24 years before he died, and during that time hardly ever missed a Texas home baseball game. The ballpark where the Longhorns play today, in a program which is still among the best in the nation, is named in his honor.

92 ◆ Gee Walker

(1931–1945, 1784 G, 124 997 .294)

From 1925 to 1950 platooning fell out of favor as a standard strategy. What it was used for in those days was to try out young players; if they came through as platoon players, then they could move up to become regulars.

In 1931, when Gerry Walker was a rookie, the Tigers platooned him with another rookie, a left-handed hitter, with the clear message that one of you is going to make it, and the other one is going home. Gerry won the battle.

The other guy? The other guy was his own brother, Hub Walker . . .

"He used to drive the manager crazy," said Ray Hayworth of Walker in *Baseball Between the Wars,* "but he had so much ability that he offset some of that."

> Still remains the fair-haired boy of the bleacherites because he has the color of a rainbow, the nervous energy of a thoroughbred, and the daring of a trapeze artist. A Detroit alumnus from Ole Mississip.'—*Who's Who in Baseball,* 1939 (Ernest Butt, editor, published by B. E. Callahan, Chicago)

> With the fans, though, he was kind, one of those rare players whose crowd appeal transcends even their unquestioned ability. He was "the people's choice," and if the Tigers had been run by popular vote he would have started every game.—Art Hill, *I Don't Care If I Never Come Back*

Sometime in the 1940s Walker dove into a swimming pool, broke his neck, and was paralyzed from the waist down. Having left baseball just before the player's union was organized, he had no pension. His family wrote to Billy Rogell, who was on the Detroit City Council, and asked for help. Rogell said he would try to do something, so he contacted Joe Cronin, and asked about a pension for Walker. According to Rogell in *Cobb Would Have Caught It,* he told Cronin "Jesus, this All-Star Game was set up for the ball player's pensions. Walker's got a broken neck and he's paralyzed. Can't something be done for him? . . . Him and I almost had a fight at Briggs Stadium. Cronin was president of the American League at that time and he never did anything to help Walker."

93 ◆ Abner Dalrymple

(1878–1891, 951 G, 43 407 .288)

Left fielder and leadoff man for Cap Anson in the first great outfield of major league baseball–Dalrymple, Burns, and Kelly. He was fast, an excellent left-handed line drive hitter with some power, fair arm, and a good fielder. On a team filled with characters and giants, he was a relatively quiet, almost sedate personality. He appears as a background figure in the biographies and stories of Anson, Kelly, Spalding, and many others, but the only anecdote about him which seems to have survived is one about his pulling a baseball out of his shirt and using it to pretend to catch a drive over his head. He worked for the Northern Pacific Railroad for 36 years after his retirement, and is buried in the small town where he was born.

94 ◆ Lou Piniella

(1964–1984, 1747 G, 102 766 .291)

> With Reggie DHing, Piniella is playing right. Everyone always says that Lou is a lousy outfielder because he doesn't run real good or have a great arm, but Goddamn, he catches every ball he can get to. I've always said I'd rather have him out there than most other guys, including Reggie. He's the best slow outfielder in baseball.–Sparky Lyle, *The Bronx Zoo*

For what it is worth, the Win Shares system also rates Piniella as a better defensive outfielder than Reggie. Piniella rates at 2.4 Win Shares per 1,000 defensive innings, which is a mid-range figure for a left/right fielder. Reggie, although he ran much faster than Piniella and had a powerful arm when he was young, rates at 2.2.

95 ◆ Dale Mitchell

(1946–1956, 1127 G, 41 403 .312)

> When I signed Dale Mitchell he could do two things. He could run like hell and he could hit with power. He couldn't throw a lick, and he wasn't a very good fielder, but I thought his speed

and his bat would overcome that, plus the fact that he was a country boy and a gung-ho player, the kind of guy who gets his uniform dirty the first inning.–Hugh Alexander, *Baseball Lives*

Had 200 hits for Cleveland in '48, '49, and hit .300 as long as he was a regular (through 1953). He pinch hit three years after that; his next-to-last major league plate appearance was a strikeout which ended Don Larsen's perfect game. He also pinch hit unsuccessfully in Johnny Kucks' 3-hit shutout two days later, which ended the 1956 World Series.

96 ◆ Gus Zernial

(1949–1959, 1234 G, 237 776 .265)

> Gus Zernial wasn't a leader. He could hit homers but he was a terrible outfielder.–Eddie Joost, *We Played the Game*

Zernial was a comic figure, like John Kruk or Mickey Rivers; a good player, but a player with obvious weaknesses that people made fun of. He had Dave Kingman-type skills, was a better hitter than Kingman in a shorter career, but he was too big and awkward to be a baseball player, compensating for his evident limitations by hitting home runs.

Zernial entered the minors just before World War II, a trim 180-pounder who could run. He spent three years in the Navy, grew an inch and a half, and got into weight lifting; by the time he came out he weighed 230 pounds, solid muscle. He was never fat, he was just huge. He couldn't run anymore but he hit .333 with 41 homers in the Carolina League in 1946, later hit .322 with 40 homers, 156 RBI for Hollywood in the Pacific Coast League, 1948. He appears in the backdrop of the John Gregory Dunne novel *True Confessions*, which is set in Hollywood in 1948; I believe he is also mentioned in the movie version of same, which stars Robert DeNiro and Robert Duvall. At Hollywood he was given his nickname, "Ozark Ike," by Fred

Haney, then broadcasting the Hollywood games, after a comic strip character of prodigious strength.

His first month in the major leagues, May 1949, he broke his collarbone and nearly destroyed his shoulder making a sliding catch, and was out a good part of the season. When he came back he couldn't throw for a year. He was with the White Sox then; in 1950 he hit four home runs in a double-header the last day of the season to establish a White Sox record with 29 home runs in 1950. Frank Lane, the pathological trader, took over the White Sox and traded him to Philadelphia, where he led the American League in home runs and RBI in 1951 (33 and 129), drove in 100 runs in 1952, and hit 42 homers and drove in 108 in 1953.

This wasn't enough for the Philadelphia fans; they boo everybody, and in 1954 Gus Zernial became their favorite target. Eddie Joost was managing the A's then. Joost had been the A's big star before Zernial came along, and Zernial felt that Joost was jealous of him. Joost would do things like hit him seventh in the lineup, just to irritate him. Wally Moses was a former teammate and a friend of Zernial's, now a coach. When Joost prohibited Moses from hanging out with Zernial, told him he couldn't even car pool with him, Gus exploded, and the two men had a loud confrontation in the dugout.

A few days later Zernial tripped over a sprinkler head in the outfield, breaking his other shoulder. He said later he remembered lying there in the outfield, waiting to be carried off on a stretcher, listening to the fans boo him and thinking "Thank God, I don't have to come here anymore."

Eddie Joost, in *We Played the Game*, tells something about the sprinkler incident that Zernial probably didn't know. The A's were losing bad in the first game of a double header. Wally Moses had said to Joost, "Why don't you take him [Zernial] out and save him for the second game?"

"Wally," said Joost, "we're both going to be here for nine innings, so let him stay and suffer with the two of us. If he can't stand it, tough luck." The next inning Zernial did a pratfall in the outfield. Moses looked at Joost and shrugged, as if to say, "I told you so." The incident nearly ended Joost's managerial career.

> It was nothing short of a liberation for Gus Zernial when he came to Kansas City with the A's in 1955. Gone were the unforgiving fans in Philadelphia . . . In Kansas City his strikeouts were pardonable transgressions, a fan's penance until the joy of Zernial's next home run.—Jack Etkin, *Innings Ago*

His first year in Kansas City Zernial hit 30 homers, drove in 84 runs although he batted only 413 times. He was healthy all year, but Lou Boudreau was platooning him. He asked Boudreau what more was expected of him. "You're not very colorful," said Boudreau.

"What do you want me to do," asked Zernial. "Wear a beanie?"

He never got back to regular status, and left baseball four years later, still believing that he could hit (in fact, his batting average, on base, and slugging percentages for the last two years of his career, when he was a part-time player in Detroit, are essentially the same as his career norms). After his career he was a TV sportscaster in Fresno, California, later went into the automobile leasing business.

"I would've liked to have been a better ballplayer," Zernial told Etkin in 1986. "I think I could've hit better, but I wasn't trying to hit better. I was always ready to really jerk one."

97 ◆ B. J. Surhoff
(1987–2000, 1863 G, 160 961 .281)
A catcher the first half of his career, a third baseman for a year or two, now a left fielder.

Like Joe Torre and one or two more, he's hit much better since he stopped catching.

98 ◆ Dave Kingman
(1971–1986, 1941 G, 442 1210 .236)

In 1982 a Mets-Phillies game was delayed briefly when Dave Kingman's glove needed to be fixed. "To fix his glove," Richie Ashburn remarked, "they should have called a welder."

77% of Kingman's career value is his home runs, the highest percentage of any player in history. The top ten: Kingman, Cecil Fielder, Rob Deer, Pete Incaviglia, Tony Armas, Dick Stuart, Gus Zernial, Juan Gonzalez, Sammy Sosa, and Wally Post. This list assumes at least a hundred career win shares. Actually, there are players who had even higher percentages in short careers, led by Steve Balboni, whose home runs were 93% of his value . . .

In the comment on Joe Morgan (2B #1), I outlined a method to figure something I called "Percentage Player Index," looking at several categories of performance to decide whether a man could accurately be described as a percentage player. Dave Kingman, to say the least, was not a percentage player. Actually, he wasn't the worst percentage player in baseball history. The worst percentage player in baseball history, playing 1,000 or more games, was Dick Stuart. This is my list of the ten worst percentage players in baseball history:

1.	Dick Stuart	.136
2.	Jim Lemon	.207
3.	Alex Johnson	.226
4.	Hubie Brooks	.232
5.	Dave Kingman	.242
6.	Brian Harper	.247
7.	Pete Incaviglia	.249
8.	John Bateman	.252
9.	Hector Lopez	.257
10.	Willie Horton	.262

We should point out quickly that (a) there were percentage players worse than Dick Stu-art, but they were so bad they couldn't play in the majors, and (b) Stuart only got to play a few years because he could flat out hit.

Nonetheless, despite driving in 114 to 118 runs three times, Stuart failed to make the list of the 100 top first basemen of all time, depriving me of the opportunity to write a comment about him. Stuart's qualifications as the worst percentage player in baseball history include:

1. 2 career stolen bases in 9 attempts, a 22% stolen base percentage.

2. More than three times as many strikeouts as walks (957 to 301).

3. A .982 career fielding percentage against a norm of .990 for first basemen of his era, which means that he made 80% more errors than an average first baseman.

None of these figures is the worst in major league history. Tony Armas and Mariano Duncan, among others, had much worse strikeout to walk ratios, and two players (Dave Kingman and Alex Johnson) made more than twice as many errors as the league norm. But Stuart is near the bottom of all four lists of the percentage player elements, and thus, on balance, fully merits the title of baseball's worst percentage player.

99 ◆ Charlie Maxwell
(1950–1964, 1133 G, 148 532 .264)

Maxwell was famous for hitting home runs on Sunday. This dates to a 1959 double header in which he hit four home runs against the Yankees. He also hit three home runs against the Yankees in a Sunday double header in 1962. According to *The Sporting News* book *Baseball: A Doubleheader Collection of Facts, Feats & Firsts,* Maxwell hit 148 career home runs, 40 of those on Sundays and 12 of those against the Yankees.

Maxwell played almost 800 games in the minor leagues, despite having several good minor league seasons. Ray Boone says in *We Played the Game* that Maxwell finally got a shot at some playing time after he (Boone) saw Charlie's minor league stats in the Tigers' 1956 media guide, realized he had been waiting a long time for a shot at a job, and convinced Bucky Harris to let Maxwell get some at bats. Maxwell hit .326 that season with 28 homers.

One time Joe Falls (longtime reporter) was having an afternoon snack with Maxwell, and he ordered a coffee milk shake.

"A coffee milk shake?" Maxwell asked.

"I've got to have something to keep me awake while I watch you guys play," said Falls.

"Maybe so," said Maxwell. "But I'll bet more people have fallen asleep reading newspapers than watching ball games."

100 ◆ Hoot Evers

(1941–1956, 1142 G, 98 565 .278)

Evers had two plays in 1946 on which he broke two bones each, perhaps a record of its kind. In spring training, in a game with Cleveland at Lakeland, Florida, he threw up his hand for balance as he was sliding into second in the middle of a double play. The relay throw to first clipped his thumb, and broke the thumb. When that happened he twisted his body in a reflex action, and broke his ankle completing the slide.

Back in the lineup only a few games, Evers collided with Eddie Mayo chasing a pop up, and broke his wrist and his jaw. "That mishap put him on ice again until a few weeks prior to the closing gong," wrote John P. Carmichael in *Who's Who in the Major Leagues*, 1947. "But the skill, stamina, and power he displayed during his limited appearance, his courage in the face of scowling Fate marked him as a star."

Evers later was farm director for the Cleveland Indians. "I had heard about Hoot Evers from some other Cleveland players," wrote Tommy John in *The Sally and Tommy John Story*. "He was, I had been told, a tough, mean, hard-nosed old coot whom nobody could please." But John liked him almost immediately, and found him to be a "a warm-hearted, considerate man" despite the tough façade.

101. Bob Skinner, 102. Bernard Gilkey, 103. Kal Daniels, 104. Greg Jefferies, 105. Ken Henderson, 106. Bip Roberts, 107. Matty McIntyre, 108. Phil Bradley, 109. George Case, 110. Gene Richards, 111. Luis Gonzalez, 112. John Briggs, 113. Tilly Walker, 114. Bob Bescher, 115. Carlos May, 116. Max West, 117. Vince Coleman, 118. Ivan Calderon, 119. Bob Nieman, 120. George Wood, 121. Les Mann, 122. Alex Johnson, 123. Carson Bigbee, 124. Gary Ward, 125. Roy Johnson

LEFT FIELD

Rank	Player Name	Career WS	Top 3	Top 5	Per 162
1.	Ted Williams	555	49, 46, 44	220	39.22
2.	Stan Musial	604	47, 44, 40	193	32.33
3.	Barry Bonds	467	47, 41, 39	187	35.30
4.	Rickey Henderson	519	39, 38, 34	152	29.43
5.	Carl Yasztrzemski	488	42, 39, 36	164	23.89
6.	Joe Jackson	294	39, 37, 37	150	35.81
7.	Al Simmons	375	36, 34, 34	153	27.42

Rank	Player Name	Career WS	Top 3	Top 5	Per 162
8.	Tim Raines	387	36, 34, 32	162	26.64
9.	Willie Stargell	370	36, 35, 29	148	25.39
10.	Minnie Minoso	283	32, 29, 29	133	24.98
11.	Billy Williams	374	33, 32, 31	142	24.35
12.	Ed Delahanty	355	41, 33, 33	159	31.34
13.	Joe Medwick	312	40, 36, 33	157	25.47
14.	Jesse Burkett	389	38, 35, 30	147	30.48
15.	Lou Brock	348	31, 30, 30	134	21.55
16.	Goose Goslin	355	33, 31, 29	147	25.14
17.	Charlie Keller	218	36, 34, 32	148	30.18
18.	Ralph Kiner	242	37, 35, 30	155	26.63
19.	Frank Howard	297	38, 34, 30	153	25.38
20.	Albert Belle	245	37, 31, 30	140	25.78
21.	Sherry Magee	354	38, 36, 31	151	27.47
22.	Fred Clarke	400	31, 30, 29	133	28.90
23.	Zack Wheat	380	35, 32, 28	128	25.54
24.	Jimmy Sheckard	339	33, 33, 30	127	25.88
25.	Roy White	263	34, 29, 29	140	22.65
26.	George Burns	290	34, 32, 31	138	25.35
27.	Jim Rice	282	36, 28, 28	127	21.86
28.	Joe Kelley	305	31, 30, 30	136	26.82
29.	Jose Cruz	313	30, 29, 27	124	21.54
30.	Heinie Manush	285	35, 28, 27	128	22.98
31.	Bob Johnson	287	31, 29, 26	118	24.95
32.	Joe Carter	240	28, 26, 24	109	17.76
33.	Bobby Veach	265	32, 31, 30	137	23.56
34.	George Foster	269	32, 30, 25	132	22.04
35.	Greg Luzinski	247	30, 28, 27	121	21.97
36.	Kirk Gibson	218	31, 26, 24	121	21.60
37.	Jim O'Rourke	305	25, 24, 24	103	27.85
38.	Brian Downing	298	35, 23, 23	102	20.59
39.	Harry Stovey	265	28, 28, 27	121	28.88
40.	Don Baylor	194	29, 24, 23	111	18.51
41.	Don Buford	194	30, 26, 26	118	24.43
42.	Augie Galan	263	32, 32, 30	130	24.45
43.	Del Ennis	233	27, 26, 26	112	19.83
44.	Jeff Heath	217	28, 24, 24	103	25.41
45.	Kevin McReynolds	202	31, 26, 25	118	21.78

(continued)

Rank	Player Name	Career WS	Top 3	Top 5	Per 162
46.	Gary Matthews	257	25, 24, 23	101	20.47
47.	Topsy Harsel	223	30, 29, 27	124	26.68
48.	Tip O'Neill	213	36, 28, 27	137	32.73
49.	Sid gordon	199	29, 25, 25	120	21.85
50.	Ken Williams	202	30, 29, 27	124	23.42
51.	Kevin Mitchell	144	38, 20, 19	109	23.44
52.	Lefty O'Doul	144	33, 30, 22	122	24.04
53.	Hal McRae	230	26, 26, 25	104	17.87
54.	Dusty Baker	245	24, 23, 22	99	19.46
55.	Willie Horton	234	28, 21, 20	105	18.69
56.	Tommy Harper	200	33, 24, 20	113	17.90
57.	Gene Woodling	230	25, 22, 21	97	20.74
58.	Rico Carty	210	27, 27, 24	78	20.60
59.	Chick Hafey	186	25, 25, 23	113	23.48
60.	Hank Sauer	174	28, 22, 19	100	20.14
61.	Riggs Stephenson	190	27, 26, 24	97	23.49
62.	George Bell	172	26, 23, 23	109	17.55
63.	George Stone	146	38, 27, 27	129	28.19
64.	Ben Oglivie	194	27, 21, 20	100	17.91
65.	Lonnie Smith	189	27, 26, 18	89	18.98
66.	Tom Tresh	161	29, 26, 25	122	25.39
67.	Charley Jones	160	27, 24, 20	98	29.42
68.	Greg Vaughn	169	30, 25, 22	85	18.20
69.	Joe Rudi	173	29, 24, 20	103	18.11
70.	Tommy Davis	207	36, 29, 19	102	16.77
71.	Ron Gant	183	26, 25, 21	89	18.30
72.	Patsy Dougherty	188	29, 29, 25	97	24.70
73.	Sam Mertes	181	27, 26, 25	118	24.64
74.	Kip Selbach	213	27, 25, 23	104	21.39
75.	Elmer E Smith	284	54, 31, 29	110	37.25
76.	Wally Moon	176	26, 26, 22	95	19.56
77.	Jo-Jo Moore	169	26, 24, 23	110	20.50
78.	Leon Wagner	156	24, 24, 22	107	18.69
79.	Bob Meusel	183	24, 21, 21	99	21.07
80.	Mike Greenwell	145	30, 19, 17	95	18.51
81.	Cleon Jones	141	30, 24, 20	95	18.83
82.	Joe Vosmik	161	28, 25, 20	98	18.44
83.	Ralph Garr	146	27, 24, 19	100	17.95
84.	Tito Francona	161	27, 23, 21	99	15.17

Rank	Player Name	Career WS	Top 3	Top 5	Per 162
85.	Duffy Lewis	179	24, 24, 21	103	19.87
86.	John Anderson	210	21, 20, 19	91	20.80
87.	Steve Kemp	140	25, 22, 20	83	19.41
88.	Irish Meusel	160	23, 21, 20	101	21.10
89.	Frank Thomas	168	26, 20, 16	93	15.41
90.	Charlie Jamieson	183	25, 19, 19	92	16.66
91.	Bibb Falk	149	24, 21, 21	90	17.84
92.	Gee Walker	177	22, 20, 17	84	16.07
93.	Abner Dalrymple	150	25, 23, 18	86	25.55
94.	Lou Piniella	164	21, 19, 17	70	15.20
95.	Dale Mitchell	140	23, 22, 21	101	21.12
96.	Gus Zernial	123	21, 21, 19	82	16.14
97.	B. J. Surhoff	180	19, 17, 17	82	15.65
98.	Dave Kingman	193	24, 21, 17	82	16.10
99.	Charlie Maxwell	116	25, 21, 18	92	16.58
100.	Hoot Evers	121	25, 20, 18	90	17.16

Categories of this record are Career Win Shares, Win Shares in the player's three best seasons, Win Shares total over the player's five best consecutive seasons, and career Win Shares per 162 games played. For example, Ted Williams had 555 Career Win Shares, including 49, 46, and 44 in his three best seasons (1946, 1942, and 1947). He had 220 Win Shares in a five-year period, (1941–1948 with a 3-year gap for WWII) and averaged 39.22 Win Shares per 162 games played over the course of his career.

1 ◆ Willie Mays

(1951–1973, 2992 G, 660 1903 .302)

According to Sam Levy of the *Milwaukee Journal* (Baseball Digest, June, 1955), the Braves began scouting Willie Mays when he was fifteen years old. The Braves head of scouting, Harry Jenkins, watched Mays play many times, and raved about him often—but lost him in a dispute over $2,500 when two of his assistant scouts, sent to cross-check, doubted that Mays was worth $10,000. If the Braves had signed him they would have had Mays, Aaron, Mathews and Spahn on the team from 1954 through 1965.

In the movie *The Steagle* there is a funny scene in which Richard Benjamin, playing a college professor, goes off the deep end in mid-lecture and starts ranting about the voters shafting Willie Mays in the MVP voting, particularly in 1962. I mentioned in the comment on Nellie Fox that, according to the Win Shares system, Mickey Mantle was really the best player in the American League every year between 1954 and 1964, except for 1959 and 1963. The same is generally true of Mays in the National League, although a little less dramatically. Mays won

only two MVP Awards (1954 and 1965), but is seen by the Win Shares system as the best player in the National League in 1954, 1955, 1958, 1960 (actually tied with Eddie Mathews), 1962 (tied with Frank Robinson), 1965 and 1966. The other years, he's close. In 1957 he's one point behind Henry Aaron (35-34).

This is generally true not only of Mays and Mantle, but of other top-echelon Hall of Famers like Musial, Mike Schmidt and Barry Bonds. Nobody wins more than three MVP Awards because the writers don't want to give the award to the same guy every year, but players of that quality actually have many seasons as the best player in the league, including some surprising seasons, some "off" seasons by their own standards. Willie Mays in 1966 was considered to be slipping; he hit "only" .288 with "only" 37 home runs and "only" 103 RBI. He was still the best player in the league; he just didn't look so good if you compared him to what he had done the previous five years. The same is true of Stan Musial in 1952; he hit "only" .338 with "only" 21 homers and "only" 42 doubles. They gave the MVP Award to Hank Sauer, and I'm glad they did because otherwise nobody would remember Hank Sauer, but realistically, Stan Musial was a lot better player than Hank Sauer, even in 1952. By the Win Shares analysis, Musial was the best player in the National League seven years—1943, 1944, 1946, 1948, 1949, 1951 (tied with Jackie Robinson), and 1952. Musial was the most successful player ever in MVP voting, but really, the vote still under-states his value.

Ted Williams ranks as the best *hitter* in the American League every year from his rookie season (1939) through 1949, except the years he didn't play. I have Mike Schmidt as the clear Most Valuable Player in the National League five times (1977, 1980, 1981, 1982 and 1983), and as the second-best player in the league four other years (1974, 1976, 1979 and 1986).

Comparing Mays to Mantle, I would rate Mays ahead in 1951, Mantle ahead in 1952–53 (when Mays was in the Army), Mays in 1954, Mantle ahead in 1955, '56 and '57, dead even in 1958, Mays in 1959 and 1960, Mantle in 1961, Mays in 1962, 1963, 1964, 1965 and 1966, Mantle in 1967, Mays in 1968, and then Mays in his final years, after Mantle retired. Scoring seasons, that makes it Mays, 15, Mantle, 7, tied, 1, but Mantle's three best seasons (1956, 1957 and 1961) are all better than Mays' best season (1965).

2 ◆ Ty Cobb
(1905–1928, 3034 G, 118 1937 .366)

> A Chinese sage wrote that exaggeration is to paint a snake and add legs. With me, they attached fangs, claws, file-sharpened spikes, and fire snorting out each nostril.—Ty Cobb, *My Life in Baseball: The True Record.*

If one were to take the time to document a thousand instances in which Ty Cobb went out of his way to be kind to other people, including black people, would this change his image? I fear it would not. No one really knows whether

Ty Cobb

or not J. Edgar Hoover was a homosexual, yet stories of his attending parties in a dress, stories which are not only false but preposterous, have stained the culture, and cannot be bleached out. The publication which claimed to have proven that Thomas Jefferson fathered a child by his slave printed a retraction in the next issue, but the bell cannot be unrung. In any case, it isn't that the stories of Ty Cobb as a violent racist are false, but rather, that there is another Ty Cobb as well, undocumented because he is less dramatic.

In the first edition of this book I wrote an essay about a photograph, a photo of Ty Cobb and Christy Mathewson. Here, I'll re-print it . . .

In photographs (make it a point to notice) Ty Cobb is often shown hiding one hand or both, twisting an arm behind his back or burying it in an article of excess clothing. One photograph of him with which I am particularly taken shows

Ty Cobb

him posing with Christy Mathewson in the dugout before the third game of the 1911 World Series. Mathewson, as always, looks poised and confident, staring out toward right field. Cobb is peeking out of the corner of his eye at some unseen distraction—another photographer, probably—but what makes the photograph remarkable is that, to begin with, Cobb is wearing a suit that doesn't look as if it could possibly have fit any of his relatives. Cobb was a big man (he is usually listed at 6'2," 180) yet this suit has got to be four sizes too large for him—it is hard to believe that a reputable haberdasher would have let him leave the store with it. He is holding what looks like an expensive overcoat, and he appears to be dragging it on the ground. His hat is jaunty and his smile is decidedly nervous, and he looks frankly a little bit crazy.

There was such a contradiction in that dugout. Cobb was then a five-time American League batting champion, with more or less seven seasons under his belt—and yet he was also a twenty-four-year-old hick from Nowhere, Georgia, a little in awe of Matty, of the photographers, of the crowd. He had no weapons, at that moment, to defend himself against his inadequacies—no spikes, no bat, no glove. He was so crude that he must have felt that whenever they took those things away from him, his shortcomings glowed like hot iron. And whenever he saw them glowing, he got angry. You can see it in his face, I think, that if he could just put on a uniform and go out on the field it would be such a relief to him, out where manners and taste and style were all defined by bases gained and bases lost. And everyone else, for a change, would have to apologize to him.

Since then I have noticed several other photographs in which Cobb has the same crazy look on his face. It is not an angry look; it is, rather, a look of acute embarrassment, a look of inadequacy. Ty Cobb's racism and his anger, I believe, were fueled not by smugness or even resentment, but by an unusually intense fear of his own limitations. No one is more macho than a man who feels inadequate; no one walks straighter than a man who is half drunk. When Ty Cobb felt threatened he lashed out at the world. He felt threatened a lot—but as long as he wasn't challenged, he was a very nice man.

3 ◆ Mickey Mantle

(1951–1968, 2401 G, 536 1509 .298)

Joe DiMaggio played thirteen seasons in the major leagues. What if you compared Mickey Mantle's first thirteen (full) seasons, 1952–1964, to Joe DiMaggio's career totals. Who would come out ahead?

As a hitter, Mickey Mantle is a long way ahead. First of all, Mantle, despite the publicity given to his bad knee and his aching legs, played more games—1,787 for Mantle, 1,736 for DiMaggio. This is not caused by the expanded schedule, which came in only over the last four years of Mantle's period. DiMaggio had quite a few injuries, and he just missed more time with injuries than Mantle did.

From there on, we should probably compare what they did in seasonal notation (per 162 games) (see the chart at the bottom of the page).

DiMaggio's batting average is a few points higher, but Mantle holds the edge in the more important categories of on base percentage and slugging percentage. Not shown above, Mantle drew almost 40 more walks per season (112-74), and therefore made 40 fewer outs per season (444 to 400). Mantle stole more than four times as many bases (133-30 total, 12-3 per season) and had a better stolen base percentage, although DiMaggio's stolen base percentage is good. Mantle grounded into less than half as many double plays, 72 to about 175.

(There is no GIDP data for the first three seasons of DiMaggio's career.) DiMaggio has his advantages, including RBI, but I don't know of any line of statistical analysis which would *not* show that Mantle was the more productive hitter, even not adjusting for offensive context.

If you adjust for the league run context, it isn't close. The American League in DiMaggio's years averaged 4.83 runs per team per game. DiMaggio created 1,554 runs, meaning that he created all the runs a team would normally score in 322 games. The American League 1952–1964 averaged 4.33 runs per team per game. Mantle created 1,595 runs in those years, so he created all the runs a team would normally score in 368 games. In terms of game impact, Mantle is 46 games better, 14% better.

Of course, DiMaggio was a better center fielder than Mantle, so it remains a legitimate debate as to who was a better all-around player. I think it was Mantle . . .

For this book I have developed a method which translates a player's batting stats into a higher or lower run context; the method is explained in the Willie Davis comment. For the most part, what I have used this method for is to show that certain hitters' numbers are much better than they look; Ron Hansen in 1965, for example, hit .235 with 11 homers, 66 RBI, but in the conditions he was performing in, that was equivalent to about .286 with 14 homers, 85 RBI under normal circumstances.

I have tried to use this method to defend the reputations of hitters whose basic numbers don't look very good—but what if you did the same for Mantle? Mickey Mantle in 1964 *also* played in conditions similar to those of Ron Hansen or Willie Davis, playing in a pitcher's

	Years	AB	R	H	2B	3B	HR	RBI	Avg.	OBA	Slug
DiMaggio	10.72	637	130	207	36	12	34	143	.325	.398	.579
Mantle	11.03	561	128	175	25	6	40	112	.311	.435	.590

park in a pitcher's era. We tend to forget that, because he hit .303 with 35 homers, 111 RBI—but what would those numbers have been like in a historically more normal context?

I'm using 750 runs per team per 162 games as a historically normal context, which is a fairly generous interpretation of "normal." I don't know what the average is, but it's lower than that. 750 runs per 162 games is mid-1980s; the levels of the 1890s, the 1990s and the Babe Ruth era were higher. The chart below compares Mantle's actual triple-crown stats to equivalent numbers in a 750-run context:

	Actual				Adjusted		
Year	HR	RBI	Avg.	HR	RBI	Avg.
1951	13	65	.267	14	70	.275
1952	23	87	.311	25	101	.333
1953	21	92	.295	23	104	.311
1954	27	102	.300	29	117	.319
1955	37	99	.306	40	110	.320
1956	52	130	.353	58	154	.378
1957	34	94	.365	38	109	.389
1958	42	97	.304	46	111	.324
1959	31	75	.285	33	85	.300
1960	40	94	.275	43	105	.289
1961	54	128	.317	57	139	.329
1962	30	89	.321	32	99	.336
1963	15	35	.314	17	41	.335
1964	35	111	.303	38	129	.324
1965	19	46	.255	21	55	.277
1966	23	56	.288	26	69	.317
1967	22	55	.245	26	72	.278
1968	18	54	.237	22	76	.278
Total	536	1,509	.298	588	1,746	.319

Mantle's adjusted 1964 season shows him with a .324 average, 38 homers, 129 RBI, 109 walks, 107 runs scored. Somehow the translation seems less dramatic in Mantle's case than it does for a hitter of less stature.

4 ◆ Tris Speaker
(1907–1928, 2789 G, 117 1529 .345)

> Speaker was a great guy, both on and off the field. I learned a lot just from watching him. He was a good teacher. He'd take you out there and show you how to do it.—Doc Cramer in *Baseball When the Grass Was Real* (Donald Honig)

It is alleged that Speaker was a member of the KKK. This may be true; the KKK in the 1920's had a populist phase in which it toned down its racism, and drew in hundreds of thousands of men who were not racists, including Hugo Black. When Larry Doby broke the color line in the American League, Speaker was strongly on his side, worked with him daily in the outfield, encouraged and supported him, and was remembered by Doby in his Hall of Fame induction speech . . .

Tris Speaker was in the major leagues for 22 years, and played for only four teams which finished under .500. His record is actually better than that, as two of the teams which were under .500 were the 1907–1908 Red Sox, for whom Speaker played a total of 38 games (7 and 31), whereas he played at least 64 games all of the other seasons. So really, 18 of Speaker's 20 teams were .500 or better.

Is this the best record of its kind in baseball history? If not, who had a better one?

I established a method to study this, essentially estimating the won-lost record for each player in the games that he played. Tris Speaker played 2,789 major league games. How many of them did his team win? In 1907 Speaker played 7 games for a team which was 59-90, a .396 percentage. We count that as 2.77 Wins, 4.23 losses. It's an imperfect method, because (a) it assumes that the team's winning percentage is the same whether Speaker is in the game or not, and (b) it makes no allowance for ties, which were pretty common in early baseball.

Also, since we wound up with Babe Ruth in the study, we have to do something else when we have a guy who pitches, since we have a won-lost record to work with or work around . . . still, the method probably isn't off on the player's actual career winning percentage by more than a few points in any case.

I estimate that Speaker's team won 1,572 of his 2,789 career games. I compared this to a list of 25 other players—the top 20 players in games played, plus six other selected players. These are their records:

Player	Won	Lost	Pct
Babe Ruth	1,514	989	.605
Mickey Mantle	1,416	985	.590
Eddie Collins	1,607	1,219	.569
Brooks Robinson	1,637	1,259	.565
Honus Wagner	1,574	1,218	.564
Tris Speaker	1,572	1,217	.564
Reggie Jackson	1,581	1,239	.561
Pete Rose	1,991	1,571	.559
Stan Musial	1,683	1,343	.556
Tony Perez	1,535	1,242	.553
Frank Robinson	1,543	1,265	.550
Willie Mays	1,634	1,358	.546
Ty Cobb	1,641	1,393	.541
Mel Ott	1,473	1,257	.540
Joe Morgan	1,422	1,227	.537
Eddie Murray	1,603	1,423	.530
Henry Aaron	1,742	1,556	.528
George Brett	1,428	1,279	.527
Al Kaline	1,478	1,356	.522
Carl Yastrzemski	1,723	1,585	.521
Rickey Henderson	1,412	1,321	.517
Rogers Hornsby	1,127	1,129	.499
Robin Yount	1,426	1,430	.499
Dave Winfield	1,480	1,493	.498
Rusty Staub	1,388	1,563	.470
Ernie Banks	1,146	1,382	.453

Speaker, it turns out, has almost exactly the same data as Honus Wagner. His record is

good, but there are some better, and we have one more indication of Ruth's excellence. A chart of a few other selected players can be found in the Reggie Smith comment (Right Field #20).

The overall winning percentage of these 26 players, in the games they played, was (about) .536. Does this indicate (a) great players lift their teams about .036 above average over a period of time, or (b) players of this quality tend to wind up on good teams.

It's both, probably a little more (a) than (b). The teams finished about six games a year over .500. A great player can move his team six games over .500 in a season, although it is doubtful that anyone except perhaps Ruth could sustain that over the course of his career.

5 ◆ Joe DiMaggio
(1936–1951, 1736 G, 361 1537 .325)

> Joe was kind of a cold guy; everybody knows that. He never asked me out to dinner alone in all the years I was with the Yankees, but I never asked him either.—Tommy Henrich, *Where Have You Gone, Joe DiMaggio* (Maury Allen).

Vince DiMaggio, in his seventies, was quoted as saying that Joe was a great hitter, but he could play rings around him in center field. Vince was expressing, perhaps, some resentment at the halo effect which has enveloped his little brother's memory, causing aging fans to question whether anyone ever did anything better than Joe DiMaggio. Total Baseball ranks Joe DiMaggio at +51 runs as an outfielder—but rates Dom at +101, Vince at +71. "How can he be the greatest center fielder of all time," asks Bill Deane, "if he's the third best center fielder in his family?"

Literally impossible, of course, but perhaps not quite as far-fetched as one might assume. The Win Shares system gives us a way to pick Gold Glove teams for each league each season. These are the Gold Glove outfielders for the years 1936–1952, when there was a DiMaggio in the major leagues:

1936 AL   Doc Cramer, Ben Chapman, Joe DiMaggio

1936 NL   (No DiMaggio in the league)

1937 AL   Doc Cramer, Joe DiMaggio, Mike Kreevich

1937 NL   Vince DiMaggio, Augie Galan, Lloyd Waner

1938 AL   Doc Cramer, Joe DiMaggio, Mike Kreevich

1938 NL   Harry Craft, Vince DiMaggio, Carl Reynolds

1939 AL   Joe DiMaggio, Mike Kreevich, Barney McCosky

1939 NL   (No DiMaggio in the league)

1940 AL   Mike Kreevich, Barney McCosky, Roy Weatherly (Joe, missing 24 games with a heel injury, ranks 4th)

1940 NL   Harry Craft, Terry Moore, Dixie Walker (Vince played only 109 games)

1941 AL   Joe DiMaggio, Mike Kreevich, Barney McCosky (Dom ranks fifth)

1941 NL   Vince DiMaggio, Terry Moore, Pete Reiser

1942 AL   Doc Cramer, Dom DiMaggio, Barney McCosky (Joe ranks fourth)

1942 NL   Enos Slaughter, Stan Musial, Terry Moore (Vince actually tied for third)

1943 AL   (No DiMaggio in the league)

1943 NL   Vince DiMaggio, Tommy Holmes, Stan Musial

1944 AL   (No DiMaggio in the league)

1944 NL   Buster Adams, Johnny Barrett, Jim Russell (Vince played only 101 games in outfield)

1945 AL   (No DiMaggio in the league)

1945 NL   Cookie Gillenwater, Andy Pafko, Goody Rosen (Vince played only 121 games in outfield)

1946 AL   Dom DiMaggio, Joe DiMaggio, Stan Spence

1946 NL   (No DiMaggio in the league)

1947 AL   Sam Chapman, Dom Dimaggio, Catfish Metkovich

1947 NL   (No DiMaggio in the league)

1948 AL   Dom DiMaggio, Joe DiMaggio, Dale Mitchell

1948 NL   (No DiMaggio in the league)

1949 AL   Sam Chapman, Dom DiMaggio, Hoot Evers

1949 NL   (No DiMaggio in the league)

1950 AL   Dom DiMaggio, Joe DiMaggio, Irv Noren

1950 NL   (No DiMaggio in the league)

1951 AL   Jim Busby, Dom DiMaggio, Irv Noren

1951 NL   (No DiMaggio in the league)

1952 AL   Jim Busby, Dave Philley, Jim Rivera (Dom, playing 123 games, ranks fourth)

1952 NL   (No DiMaggio in the league)

In summary, Joe DiMaggio had eleven seasons in his career in which he played 115 games or more in the outfield. He ranks as deserving of a Gold Glove in eight of those eleven seasons, and ranks as the fourth-best outfielder in the league in two of the other three. Dom DiMaggio had nine seasons in which he played 115 or more games in the outfield. He ranks as deserving of a Gold Glove in six of those nine seasons, and ranks fourth and fifth in two of the other three. Vince had only six seasons playing 115 or more games in the outfield, but he ranks as deserving of a Gold Glove in four of those six seasons, and misses the award on a tie-breaker in one of the other two.

Setting aside hype, resentment and halo effects, the conclusion of this purely mathematical evaluation of outfield play is that all three DiMaggio brothers were quite exceptional defensive outfielders. By the Win Shares method, the top four defensive outfielders whose careers were centered in the 1940s were:

1. Dom DiMaggio
2. Terry Moore
3. Joe DiMaggio
4. Vince DiMaggio

6 ◆ Duke Snider
(1947–1964, 2143 G, 407 1333 .295)

> Back in the 1955 season, Duke Snider blew his top and declared that the Brooklyn fans did not deserve a pennant. This was a brief sensation in the newspapers. Duke explained his hot- headed insult, and all was more or less forgiven.—James T. Farrell, *My Baseball Diary*

Duke always had a somewhat dicey relationship with the press. *Sport* magazine in the 1950s used to alternate between two types of Duke Snider articles, the "Why is Duke Snider Such a Dog?" article and the "Why Doesn't Duke Snider Get the Respect He Deserves?" article. One summer they'd run one article; the next summer they'd run a variation of the other one . . .

7 ◆ Ken Griffey Jr.
(1989–2000, 1680 G, 438 1270 .296)

The second-best left-handed hitting, left-handed throwing outfielder ever born in Donora, Pennsylvania on November 21. My son is a ballplayer; I'm thinking of taking him to be washed in the waters of Donora. In addition to the other things they share, Musial and both Griffeys all seem to be (a) wholly admirable people, and (b) genuinely likeable.

8 ◆ Kirby Puckett
(1984–1995, 1783 G, 207 1085 .318)

Baseball's Buddha. It's been five years and I know better, but I still half expect to pick up the paper and read that there has been a mistake, or a medical breakthrough, and that Kirby will be allowed to come back and finish his career.

Do I think Kirby is a Hall of Famer? Sure. Kirby had 2300 hits at the time of his illness, actually 2304. I estimate that he had a 62% chance to get 3,000 career hits. Missing the decline phase of his career doesn't change where he ranks on this list very much, since the decline phase of a player's career has more to do with padding numbers than with establishing greatness, and I don't see why it should keep him out of the Hall of Fame, either.

9 ◆ Billy Hamilton
(1888–1901, 1591 G, 40 736 .344)

Baseball's first great leadoff man, a Kenny Lofton-type player who established many records which still stand, others which lasted until the 1980s. He scored 196 runs in a season, a record no one has ever approached, and scored more runs per game than anyone else in baseball history.

> Hamilton "had short chunky legs but was fast as a telegraph."—Burt Solomon, *Where They Ain't*

> Hamilton "drove opponents wild with his daring base running. In one game, a Cleveland fielder became so frustrated he picked up the five-foot-six Hamilton, carried him to the edge of the field, and dropped him into the stands."—Mike Sowell, July 2, 1903

> Hamilton was "only five feet, seven in height and very stocky . . . he was one of the few aural outfielders of the early days, racing at the crack of the bat to the spot where the ball would come down."—Lee Allen and Tom Meany, *Kings of the Diamond*

> A ten-second dash man in high school in Newark, and an expert roller skater, Hamilton was "more daring and reckless" than Cobb, according to Sam Thompson who played with both.—Norman L. Macht, *Baseball's First Stars*

Hamilton was completely invisible in the literature of the sport up to 1960, and was not elected to the Hall of Fame until 1961. He left no legend behind him, no stories, no anecdotes. The entry on Hamilton in Alfred Spink's *The National Game* (1910) is shorter than the entry on Ham Hyatt, which appears on the same page. Hamilton was eventually elected to the Hall of Fame purely on the overwhelming quality of his numbers. Even now, in books about nineteenth century baseball, he is often not mentioned at all, and is never presented as a fully-formed character.

The old Boston ballpark, where the Boston Beaneaters played in the 1890s, was built alongside a railroad track, which tended to collect trash. In the space of three years there were two incidents of balls in play lodging in old tin cans. One baseball rolled up to and under the fence by the railroad track. Billy Hamilton, retrieving the ball, discovered it was stuck in a tin can. He tried to shake it lose, but it wouldn't budge, so he threw the can to the shortstop, who threw it to the catcher, who tagged out the runner with a canned baseball.

A year or two later, according to Ira Smith (who is almost always reliable), a similar play occurred when a baseball rolled into and stuck in a tomato can in the outfield. Hugh Duffy immediately tossed the can to the infield, in time to make the play at the plate. The umpire, however, ruled this runner safe, saying that "They's nothin' in the rule book that says you can put out a runner by touchin' him with a tomater can."

10 ◆ Jimmy Wynn
(1963–1977, 1920 G, 291 964 .250)

> Sometimes a team will take a player down with it. Houston is one team that has held back players. I don't know why.—John Roseboro, *Glory Days with the Dodgers*

The Astros came up with both Wynn and Joe Morgan very soon after their creation in 1962. The two men, roommates early in their careers, had most of the same characteristics as players. Both were very small, but strong and also fast. Both had tremendous control of the strike zone, drawing huge numbers of walks. Both played key defensive positions. Both had outstanding years in 1965, their first year as regulars; both were having very good years in 1966, but suffered serious injuries. (Wynn crashed into the center field wall in Philadelphia on August 1, 1966, dislocating his elbow and fracturing his wrist and his hand.) Both continued to fight injuries for some years after that. Wynn was stabbed in the stomach by his wife, Ruth, while celebrating their seventh wedding anniversary, apparently not too happily. After that, he had a shoulder injury which left him unable to throw well.

Overcoming injuries, Morgan hit .271 (career) but with a secondary average of .431. Wynn hit .250 but with a secondary average of .404. Wynn did not reach the heights of stardom attained by Morgan, but he was a very effective player. If the Astros had come up with two more like them and held on to them, they would have been a powerhouse.

11 ◆ Larry Doby
(1947–1959, 1533 G, 253 969 .283)

Ten points about Larry Doby:

1. Doby played for the Newark Eagles under the name "Larry Walker" to protect his status as an amateur athlete.

2. Doby played briefly for legendary college basketball coach and children's author Clair Bee, at Long Island University.

3. In the Negro Leagues, Doby was primarily a middle infielder. He moved to center field because the Indians had one of the best double play combinations of all time (Lou Boudreau and Joe Gordon) already in place.

4. Bill Veeck bought Doby from the Newark Eagles for $15,000. At the same time, the Eagles tried to sell Veeck Monte Irvin for $1,000 for a look, and then Veeck was to pay whatever he thought Irvin was worth. Veeck declined, saying he was buying enough grief with one black player; he didn't think it would be smart to start with two.

5. In 1952, in my opinion, Larry Doby was the most valuable player in the American League. The award went to Bobby Shantz, which is not a bad pick, but if I had a vote, I'd vote for Doby. Doby led the league in home runs (32), runs scored (104) and slugging percentage (.541), also drove in 104 runs, drew 90 walks and played a good center field.

6. Doby was the MVI (Most Valuable Indian) in three seasons—1950, 1951, 1952. He was the team's best position player in 1949, although Bob Lemon was the MVI. Although outplayed by Al Rosen in 1953 and Bobby Avila in 1954, Doby was one of the five best players in the American League, in my opinion, every season between 1950 and 1954.

7. Larry Doby is to Mickey Mantle exactly as Earl Averill is to Joe DiMaggio. All four are Hall of Fame outfielders, all legitimate Hall of Famers in my opinion. Averill came to Cleveland in 1929 and was the best center fielder in the American League until the arrival of DiMaggio. Doby came to Cleveland in 1947 and was the best center fielder in the American League until the arrival of Mantle. Doby was probably a hair better than Averill, but was never able to convince the older Cleveland fans of this, just as Averill had never been able to fully escape the shadow of Tris Speaker. Mantle was probably a hair better than DiMaggio, but was never able to convince the older Yankee fans of this, just as DiMaggio was never able to fully escape the shadow of Babe Ruth. Averill, like DiMaggio, came to the American League from the Pacific

Coast League. Doby, like Mantle, was a converted shortstop.

8. Doby was one of those rare five-tool players: he did everything well. If you scored Doby on hitting for average, hitting for power, speed, defense, throwing, strike zone judgment, probably his lowest score would be hitting for average—yet he hit as high as .326, and his career average of .283 is hardly a gaping wound.

9. The 1949 Indians had a barber shop quartet composed to Doby (lead), Jim Hegan (tenor), Eddie Robinson (baritone) and Satchel Paige (bass).

10. Doby played in Japan in 1962, earning a reported $30,000.

12 ◆ Dale Murphy
(1976–1993, 2180 G, 398 1266 .265)

All-Tall team, composed of the tallest player rated among the top 25 at each position.

C— Lance Parrish
1B—Mark McGwire
2B—Ryne Sandberg
3B—Mike Schmidt
SS—Cal Ripken
LF—Frank Howard
CF—Dale Murphy
RF—Dave Winfield

13 ◆ Wally Berger
(1930–1940, 1350 G, 242 898 .300)

But now, my friends,
The sad part ends,
No more the days are flat;
All Hubits roar
as home runs soar
From Wally Berger's bat.

(Concluding stanza or a poem by Gene Mack, Boston newspaperman, 1930)

Berger was childhood friend of Joe Cronin. The two played together on teams while growing up. Berger dropped out of high school, drove a laundry truck, and worked on the loading docks while trying to break into pro baseball. He was given two short trials by the San Francisco Seals, but was released both times, and went down the ladder to start his career. He made the majors after hitting .335 with 40 home runs for Los Angeles (PCL) in 1929 . . . Berger was the National League's starting center fielder in the first three All Star games (1933, 1934, 1935).

> Berger was a right-handed hitter who swung from his heels . . . during his first season with the Braves (1930), Berger beat the Giants five games by one-run margins with his home runs.—Harold Kaese, *The Boston Braves*

> For four years, Wally Berger had been the Braves' only true claim to fame. Berger could do everything, but his real strength was his big bat . . . no matter how badly the Braves were doing, Berger, single-handed, could keep some customers coming in.—Al Hirshberg, *The Braves, The Pick and the Shovel*

I have pointed out in a couple of other books that Wally Berger has extremely similar career batting stats to those of Hall of Famer Hack Wilson. Berger played 1,350 games, hitting .300 with 242 home runs; Wilson played 1,348 games, batting .307 with 244 home runs. Both were National League center fielders, more or less contemporary. Wilson drew more walks and drove in more runs, Berger hit a few more doubles.

In other books I have stopped short of drawing a conclusion about which was the better player. But having looked at this issue as carefully as I can, I am 100% convinced that Berger was a distinctly better player than Hack Wilson. Berger was better over the course of his career, and he was a better player at his peak.

There are five reasons why this is true:

1. Wilson played in the 1920s, Berger entirely in the 1930s. Wilson created a few more runs, but many more runs were scored in the National League in the 1920s than in the 1930s, and thus each run was less valuable.

2. Wilson played in far better hitter's parks than Berger.

3. Berger was a better defensive player than Wilson.

4. The "high peak" apparent in Wilson's 1929–1930 performance is purely an illusion of context. Had Berger played in the same park in the same years, he would have produced numbers as impressive as Wilson's.

5. There is no evidence that Wilson hit especially well with runners in scoring position. Given Wilson's hitting stats and the hitting stats of the other hitters on the 1930 team, we would expect him to drive in 190-195 runs, even assuming that he has no tendency to hit in the clutch.

There are really three players in this group—Berger, Wilson, and Earl Averill, also a contemporary center fielder, also a Hall of Famer, also has similar batting stats to Berger and Wilson. Averill was the best defensive player of the three, had the longest career of the three. Berger is the only one of the three not in the Hall of Fame—but he was the best player of the group.

14 ◆ Earl Averill
(1929–1941, 1669 G, 238 1165 .318)

For several years as a young man, Earl Averill worked for a living. Among other things, he was a florist. That wasn't a way to survive; that was what he liked, the profession he chose when he was thinking of baseball as a hobby. He was married in 1922, turned twenty a week after his marriage, and didn't play in "organized" baseball until 1926 (although he did play in some very good semi-pro leagues).

Jimmie Foxx and Earl Averill, July 2, 1938

In 1926 he joined the San Francisco Seals, a powerhouse of the Pacific Coast League, and was an immediate star, hitting .348 in 1926, .324 in 1927 and .354 with 36 homers, 173 RBI in 1928.

Late in the 1928 season, with the Pacific Coast League pennant race still several weeks from the finish line, Averill opened the paper on his way to the game, and read that he had been sold to the Cleveland Indians for a reported $50,000. He was to be "delivered" the following season.

"Do I get any of that money?" Averill asked his manager.

"No," replied the manager.

"Well then, I'm going home," replied Averill. And he did.

The Seals immediately went to work on Averill, attempting to convince him that he had no right to the money. Averill said that right or wrong, if he didn't get part of the money, he had no intention of reporting to the Indians.

This got the attention of Judge Landis. Judge Landis—this may be surprising to

younger readers, who have been taught to regard Landis as an ogre–Judge Landis said that
Averill's demand sounded reasonable to him,
and further, that baseball should adopt some
sort of legislation by which, whenever a player
was sold, the player himself would get a cut of
the proceeds.

That went nowhere. Landis in this respect
was forty-five years ahead of his time. His proposal, had it been adopted, would have done
much to alleviate the stresses put on the game
by free agency. Bowie Kuhn, at the outset of
the free agency era, created and unilaterally
imposed a policy by which star players could
not be sold from team to team. This was an ignorant, bone-headed, destructive policy which
had no foundation in anything except that
Kuhn hated Charlie Finley, and saw that he
could drive Finley out of the game by denying
him the right to sell his players. What Kuhn
should have done, if he had been thinking
about the best interests of the game, is adopt
Landis policy: rule that players could be sold
for whatever they would bring, but 30% of the
money had to go to the players. Had he done
that, the effect would have been to allow the
rich teams to acquire more of the best players,
as they do now. But this policy would have allowed the rich teams to strengthen themselves
without inflating the salary structure, and
would have allowed the weaker teams, the Mon-
treal-type teams, to remain financially competitive by profiting from developing young
players.

Averill eventually got a $5000 bonus and a
good salary to report to Cleveland. On the 4th
of July one year (unable to date incident) Averill held a firecracker too long, and burned his
hand. He bandaged it up and went back to
playing baseball, for which he was nicknamed,
like a Cleveland outfielder two decades later,
"The Rock." That incident aside, Averill was a
modest, soft-spoken man who liked flowers

and animals, and didn't like big cities. When he
traveled with the Indians he would visit the
zoos and the gardens; he never cared anything
about the buildings. He was small, not blind-
ingly fast and not blessed with an extraordinary arm, yet he was as productive and capable
in the outfield as he was at the plate.

Averill hit .378 with tremendous power in
1936, his best season, and was hitting .394 on
June 26, 1937, when his back went out during
a game in Philadelphia. The back effected his
swing the rest of his career, and his career went
into a spiral.

Elected to the Hall of Fame in 1975, Averill
paid thousands of dollars out of his own pocket
to bring to Cooperstown the men who had
campaigned for his election, which was laud-
able, and used his inauguration speech to blast
the Hall of Fame for not electing him sooner,
which was regrettable.

15 ◆ Edd Roush
(1913–1931, 1967 G, 68 981 .323)

> Eddie used to take care of the whole outfield, not
> just center field. He was far and away the best
> center fielder I ever saw.–Heinie Groh in *The
> Glory of Their Times*

> Roush "seemed to have the legs of a gazelle and
> the arms of a gibbon."–*Chicago Tribune,* Octo-
> ber, 1919

According to *Baseball's Most Wanted* (Floyd
Conner), on June 8, 1920, Edd Roush was
ejected from the Cincinnati game for falling
asleep in the outfield. The Cincinnati manager
got into an argument with the umpire. Quoting
Conner, "As the debate raged, Roush laid down
in the outfield and took a nap. Roush was so
difficult to wake up that he was ejected for de-
laying the game."

> Edd had a twin brother named Fred, who never
> played baseball . . . "Edd Roush, Cincinnati's star
> center fielder, had declared that unless he was

given five box seats for his family and friends, he would lead the Red Legs in a walkout. Frank Bancroft, the Reds' seventy-one-year-old business manager, steadfastly refused to provide the tickets. During the discussion, Roush began shouting at the older man. Fearing for the old man's safety, Charles Ebbets (and Harry Sparrow) tried to intervene on Bancroft's behalf. When they did, Roush became belligerent. He cursed Ebbets and Sparrow, then pushed Sparrow against a wall."—Mike Sowell, *The Pitch That Killed* (Macmillan, 1989)

16 ◆ Richie Ashburn
(1948–1962, 2189 G, 29 586 .308)

Richie Ashburn was born in Tilden, Nebraska in 1927, the son of a small-town blacksmith. He was such an outstanding athlete that, according to a 1956 article in the *Saturday Evening Post*, it was "taken for granted by the folks in Tilden that Richie Ashburn would be a major-league ballplayer." When he was sixteen the Cleveland Indians mailed him a contract, which he signed and returned. This was prohibited by baseball rules (because of his age), and so Commissioner Landis summoned Ashburn to Chicago to get his testimony, declared him a free agent, and fined the Indians $500.

After graduating from high school Ashburn signed with Nashville, in the Cubs system, signed by the legendary scout Cy Slapnicka. This contract called for him to play for Nashville, but called for a "contingency bonus"; if Ashburn were sold to the majors, he was to receive a portion of the sale price. This contract was also prohibited by baseball rules, and so Ashburn once more had his contract nullified, and was declared a free agent once again.

He signed next with the Philadelphia Phillies for a $3,500 bonus, and began his career, finally, with the 1945 Utica Blue Sox, playing for Eddie Sawyer. As an amateur Ashburn had been a catcher, but after seventeen pro games Sawyer saw the light, and moved him to the outfield. He hit .312 for Utica in 1945, spent a year in the Army, came back to Utica in 1947 and hit .362. Ashburn, Sawyer, Stan Lopata, and Granny Hamner led Utica to a rout of the Eastern League race. Invited to spring training with the Phillies in 1948, Ashburn had no real prospect of making the team, as the Phillies' center fielder was the defending National League batting champion, Harry the Hat Walker, who was actually a very similar player to Ashburn. Walker had hit one point higher at Philadelphia (.363) than Ashburn had hit at Utica.

Walker held out, however, which gave Ashburn a chance to play, and then Harry had a minor injury, which gave Ashburn a chance to play a little more. Harry never got his job back; he went from batting champion to bench warmer in two quick steps. Beginning on May 9, 1948, Ashburn hit safely in 23 consecutive games, then a record for a National League rookie. He finished the season at .333, second to Stan Musial, led the league in stolen bases and walked almost three times as often as he struck out. No rookie since has hit for as high an average as a regular.

Ashburn went top speed all the time. Ted Williams nicknamed him "Put Put" after seeing him tearing down the line in an exhibition game, running as if he had twin motors in his pants. As a young player he threw well; the 1948 edition of *Who's Who In Baseball* said that he had "a throwing arm second to none."

The Phillies, a down and out team for thirty years, won the National League pennant in 1950 with a very young team, the Whiz Kids. It must have been a wonderful team to be a part of. In his first two years in the majors, Richie's parents came to Philadelphia and ran a family-style boarding house for several of the Phillies young stars. Curt Simmons lived with them, and Robin Roberts. The house broke up when the boys started to get married. Ashburn married a Nebraska farm girl. The first time she ever saw a professional baseball game was in 1948, when she traveled to St. Louis to watch Richie play in the All Star game.

On September 29, 1950, the Phillies went to Brooklyn, two games ahead with two to be played. The Dodgers won the first one. Robin Roberts opposed Don Newcombe on October 1, 1950, in one of the greatest baseball games ever played. In the bottom of the ninth, with the score tied 1-1 and Cal Abrams, a fast man, on second base, Duke Snider ripped a single into center field. No one had any doubt that Abrams would score, but Ashburn had been cheating in anticipation of a play at the plate, picked up the single on one hop, and gunned down the startled Abrams by several feet, the most crucial and most famous play of the 1950 season. The Phillies won the game in the tenth inning.

I have always suspected that had it not been for the unbelievable end to the 1951 National League race, this wonderful race, this classic game and this remarkable play might be even more famous than they are. Bobby Thomson, in a sense, blew Richie Ashburn out of the water before the 1950 race had time to settle into myth. The Whiz Kids were annihilated in the 1950 World Series, in any case, and that was the end of that team; they were never serious contenders again.

Ashburn, far from the madding pennant race, was consistently superb. He led the league in hits in 1951, 1953 and 1958, in triples in 1950 and 1958, in walks in 1954, 1957, 1958 and 1960, in stolen bases in 1948, in batting average in 1955 and 1958, and in on-base percentage in 1954, 1955, 1958 and 1960. He is the only leadoff man to lead his league in walks and batting average in the same season, hitting .350 with 97 walks in 1958; other years he walked as many as 125 times. He made far more putouts per season in the outfield than any other player in history, although this is partially due to the fact that the Phillies pitch-

ing staff, led by Robin Roberts, was dominated by fly-ball pitchers. He was durable, playing 731 consecutive games at one point, then missing a week, coming back and playing several hundred more. After a shoulder injury in 1951 his arm was not good, but he compensated with quickness and positioning, and led the league in baserunner kills in 1952, 1953 and 1957. He was, with Phil Rizzuto and Nellie Fox, one of the three best bunters of his era.

Staying in Nebraska in the off seasons, Richie worked as a basketball referee to stay in shape, and invested in real estate. After the 1959 season he was traded to the Cubs. He gave the Cubs a good season in 1960, slipped badly in 1961, and became a member of the infamous 1962 Mets, the lovable losers of Casey Stengel's purgatory. "The 1962 Mets lost one hundred and twenty times," wrote George Vecsey, "and Ashburn went down kicking and screaming one hundred and twenty times."

In the fifth inning of the first game of the Labor Day double header in 1962, Ashburn made a spectacular somersaulting catch of a line drive by Don Hoak. The next hitter, Mazeroski, lifted a fly ball down the right field line. Ashburn crashed into the wall, falling on his face in the Mets bullpen, as the ball bounced over the wall for a ground rule double. Richie staggered to his feet, ran to the infield, and argued that the ball had been foul.

After the game, his teammates began to notice that something was wrong with Richie. Talking to him, they realized that he remembered nothing about the crash, the argument—or the ballgame from that point on. He had played the last five innings on pure reflexes.

He could still play; he hit .306, stole a dozen bases, and had the best on base percentage in the National League, although he was a few plate appearances short of qualifying officially. He had been one of the most popular men ever to play in Philadelphia, however—even the Philadelphia fans hardly ever booed him—and after the 1962 season he was offered a job as a Philadelphia broadcaster. He would hold that job the rest of his life, dying of a heart attack in 1997.

Richie Ashburn combined the Pete Rose virtues and the Pete Rose style of play with the virtues of dignity, intelligence and style. Like Rose, he was a three-hundred-hitting singles hitter who ran out every ground ball of his career, a player who got out of his body every pound of ability that the Lord had put in there. Unlike Rose, Ashburn did not extend his career beyond its natural boundaries to break any records. At the time he retired, he had only 188 hits fewer than Rose had at the same age, and had more than many of the 3,000-hit men had at the same age. He didn't need records to tell him who he was. Ashburn was a reader, a family man, a man of restraint and taste.

My favorite Richie Ashburn story . . . One time Ashburn hit a line drive into the stands, striking a young woman in the side of the face and knocking her unconscious. The stadium gasped, Ashburn stepped out of the box and watched in alarm as medics rushed to her side. In a few minutes the woman revived, the stretcher came, and the ballgame resumed. And Ashburn hit another line drive foul, and struck the poor woman again as she was being carried out of the stadium.

Ashburn visited the woman in the hospital after the game, invited her to come down and meet the players, befriended her and her family, and corresponded with the woman for the rest of his life.

17 ◆ Fred Lynn
(1974–1990, 1969 G, 306 1111 .283)
The only player to win the MVP Award as a rookie, he was even better in 1979, but didn't plaster enough excellent seasons around those two to be a clear-cut Hall of Famer. The ten best seasons by rookie center fielders:

1. Tris Speaker, 1909
2. Fred Lynn, 1975
3. Roy Thomas, 1899
4. Tommie Agee, 1966
5. Dummy Hoy, 1888
6. Vada Pinson, 1959
7. Wally Berger, 1930
8. Earl Averill, 1929
9. Joe DiMaggio, 1936
10. Lloyd Waner, 1927

Actually, Benny Kauff (1914) ranks as even more valuable than Speaker (1909), but I discounted that because Kauff was in the Federal League, which was not *exactly* a major league . . . .The five best rookies (at any position) who did not go on to Hall of Fame careers:

1. Fred Lynn, 1975
2. Hal Trosky, 1934
3. Russ Ford, 1910
4. Walt Dropo, 1950
5. Mark Fidrych, 1976

18 ◆ Vada Pinson
(1958–1975, 2469 G, 256 1170 .286)
Outwardly, he seems totally relaxed, totally carefree, as pleasant and cheerful an athlete as you could ever hope to meet. He is friendly toward teammates and friendly toward newspapermen.
—Dick Schaap, *Sport Magazine*, April, 1962

Vada Pinson moved to Oakland when he was seven years old. His father was a longshoreman, his mother a domestic, and they lived near the bay. Frank Robinson lived nearby, and Vada and Frank where childhood friends. When Frank signed with Cincinnati, it was probably inevitable that Vada would sign with the same organization.

As a young boy Vada was a fanatic trumpet player. He wasn't recognized around the neighborhood as much of an athlete, and he didn't have an athlete's attitude; he was quiet, shy, rather retiring. He could run, however, and his high school baseball coach persuaded him to put baseball on the same level as trumpet practice. When he joined the Reds in 1958 he was so quiet that Jimmy Dykes assumed that he was Cuban, and once, several weeks into spring training, tried communicating with him in pigeon Spanish. Dykes had simply never heard Vada speak.

As a rookie in 1959 Pinson scored 131 runs, and was the fifth-best player in the National League. (He wasn't considered a rookie at the time, but would be by modern standards.) In 1961 he was even better, hitting .343 with 16 homers; the MVP Award went to Frank Robinson, but could easily have gone to Vada.

> I've always wondered whether Pinson's career would have been even more illustrious than it was if he had been voted the National League's Most Valuable Player in 1961 ... I have to think that during the winter of 1961 Pinson came to the conclusion that the top awards and big bucks came with home runs.—Earl Lawson, *Cincinnati Seasons*

Lawson wrote things like that pretty often, and Vada resented it. When Fred Hutchinson chewed him out about regularly missing the cutoff man, Pinson blamed Lawson. On September 4, 1963, before Lawson entered the Reds clubhouse, the other Reds players had been teasing Vada, asking what he was going to do about Lawson. Pinson, riled up, confronted Lawson. The argument escalated, and Vada eventually punched the sportswriter. Lawson went immediately into Fred Hutchinson's office, borrowed his phone, and called the police. The police told Lawson to come down and sign a warrant for Pinson's arrest, and he did.

"It was the only time I had ever done anything like that," Pinson told Maury Allen many years later. "He sued and it was settled out of court. It was very embarrassing ... Except for

the incident with Earl Lawson I can't ever remember losing my head in the all the years I've been in baseball."

Pinson never matched his numbers of 1959 and 1961, and for much of his career was regarded as a disappointment. There were two things which contributed to this. One is, when Pinson had his first great year in 1959, it was believed that he was 21 years old. He wasn't; he was 23. Second, the pitchers took control of the game in 1963, cutting into everybody's numbers, and making "perennial disappointments" of many of the young players of that era, including Willie Davis, Frank Howard, Tom Tresh and Norm Cash. Pinson remained a lifelong friend of Frank Robinson, and remained in the game as a coach until his unexpected death in 1995.

19 ◆ Hack Wilson
(1923-1934, 1348 G, 244 1063 .307)
Could Hack Wilson's 1930 record of 191 RBI be broken?

It could, yes. Wilson in 1930 hit 111 singles, 35 doubles, 6 triples and 56 homers. From the late 1930s until 1993, very few players had numbers in that range, and thus very few players had the opportunity to make a run at the record, even given a good enough string of hitters to set the table for them.

In the last decade, however, combinations of hits comparable to Wilson's have become much more common, thus, in theory, endangering the record. As of yet, no one has made a run at Wilson's record, because modern offenses are different from 1930s style offenses. In 1930, most teams had one or two power hitters, surrounded by players who slapped at the ball and tried to get on base. That meant lots of RBI opportunities for the one or two power hitters.

In modern baseball, *everybody* tries to hit home runs, spreading the offense top to bottom, but creating no "clusters" of RBI opportunities.

The only modern managers who have successfully built a "traditional" style of offense are Johnny Oates and Mike Hargrove—but it will still work. If somebody gets two or three Brett Butler/Kenny Lofton type of hitters and a line drive .340 hitter to bat in front of Vladimir or A-Rod or some other big hitter having a big year, he could drive in 192 runs . . . See also Roger Maris (Right Field, #28).

20 ◆ Hugh Duffy
(1888–1906, 1737 G, 106 1302 .324)
Duffy, who was 5-foot-7 and weighed about 150 pounds, hit .431 in the New England League in 1887, and was purchased by the Chicago Cubs, then known as the White Stockings, the Colts, or the White Colts. He reported to Cap Anson in March, 1888.

"We've got a bat boy," Anson said.

"I'm your new outfielder. I'm on your salary list," said Duffy.

"Where's the rest of you?" Anson demanded.

"I'm all here," Duffy replied, doing the best he could.

Disappointed, Anson parked Duffy on the bench for two months before he played a game. Once he entered the lineup he never came out, leading the National League in games played and at bats in 1889, the Player's League in the same categories in 1890. "Hugh Duffy plays the outfield carrying a crystal ball," Anson said. "He is always there to make the catch." When the Player's League broke up he wound up with Boston, where he paired with Tommy McCarthy in the outfield, the two becoming known as the "Heavenly Twins." They led Boston to several National League championships, but since this was the 1890s you can't really figure out how many.

Leaving the majors after a painful career as a manager, Duffy scouted for the Red Sox from 1924 until he entered his final illness in 1953; he was described by a Boston writer as "Fenway Park's Mr. Chips." It's an old movie about a man who spends a lifetime at an English boarding school . . . Lee Allen wrote that "his record of sixty-eight years in the professional game has been exceeded only by Connie Mack."

Duffy holds one record which you know about, and another which will be even harder to break. Duffy played in four major leagues: the American League, the National League, the Player's League and the American Association—and had a career average over .300 in all four leagues . . . by the Win Shares method I have Duffy as deserving of five Gold Gloves.

21 ◆ Cesar Cedeno
(1970–1986, 2006 G, 199 976 .285)
The best *young* center fielders (career value up to age 25):
1. Ty Cobb
2. Mickey Mantle
3. Tris Speaker
4. Cesar Cedeno
5. Willie Mays
6. Joe DiMaggio
7. Ken Griffey Jr.
8. Richie Ashburn
9. Lloyd Waner
10. Pete Reiser.

In 1985, with Jack Clark hurt, the St. Louis Cardinals picked up the aging Cesar Cedeno for the pennant race. Cedeno played 28 games for the Cards, hitting .434 with 6 homers, 19 RBI. The practice of picking up a veteran for the pennant race goes back at least to the 1920s—but that may well be the greatest late-season pickup of all time.

22 ◆ Amos Otis
(1967–1984, 1996 G, 193 1007 .277)
One time when George Brett had been hitting about .600 for a week he came up with runners

on first and second, two out in the ninth, game tied. Earl Weaver intentionally walked Brett, bringing A.O. to the plate with the bases loaded.

Otis was magnificent. He took two close pitches to make it 2-0, worked the count full, then started fouling off pitches. Knowing that a walk would win the game, he just spoiled pitches until the Oriole pitcher (Tim Stoddard) missed with ball four.

The next morning the Kansas City Star report led off with the statement that "Amos Otis won the game for the Kansas City Royals last night by doing nothing more than the 31,184 paying customers."

I'm a Royals fan, and Amos Otis was my favorite player on the best team the Royals ever had. He was an odd man, sometimes prickly, and he didn't handle either praise or criticism well. He used to put up a sign saying "No Interviews," but he was never actually rude enough not to answer a question, as far as I know; I suppose there must have been somebody he didn't want to talk to. He seemed to resent the fact that Brett and McRae were recognized as the team leaders, but he certainly didn't want the role himself. About once a year or so it would break into the letters to the editor that he had been caught secretly performing some unusual act of good citizenship—stopping on the interstate to pick up a fan having car trouble or something.

Amos was strong, quick, fast, extremely graceful, and smart. He was the best percentage player on that team. He didn't have a quick bat, and the second half of his career he couldn't do much with a good fastball, but he could read a changeup like nobody you ever saw. I'll bet half of his career home runs were hit off of changeups, and he very rarely saw a changeup, because everybody knew he could hit them. He would also steal fifteen bases a year standing up. About once every two weeks he would pick up something in the pitcher's move, and break

for second maybe a full second before the pitcher reached his release point, enabling him to walk into second. He was a magnificent outfielder, hardly ever made an error, and played center in the best defensive outfield of the last forty years—Wilson, Otis, and Cowens, all three of them really center fielders. He won three Gold Gloves and, by my reckoning, deserved five.

23 ◆ Max Carey
(1910–1929, 2476 G, 70 800 .285)

Carey's real name was Maximillian Carnarius. As a young man he was studying at Concordia Seminary in St. Louis, heading for a career as a Lutheran minister, but he spent summers in his home town of Terre Haute, Indiana. The Terre Haute team in the Central League was desperate for a shortstop, and knew that Carnarius was an athlete, so persuaded him to play short. He played under the name of Max Carey so as not to jeopardize his amateur standing (apparently the Lutherans don't believe in rigid fidelity to the concept of amateurism). But he played so well that he never finished studying for the ministry. Other notes:

- In 1925 Carey had three doubles, a single and a stolen base in the seventh game of the World Series. Off of Walter Johnson.
- Carey reportedly lost $100,000 in the stock market crash of 1929.
- Late in life he was a state inspector of the dog racing tracks in Florida.

24 ◆ Dom DiMaggio
(1940–1953, 1399 G, 87 618 .298)

Except for Ted Williams, the greatest student of baseball I ever saw was Dom DiMaggio. Overshadowed by his brother Joe and handicapped by his pedestrian appearance, Dom never got the credit he deserved. With his comparatively short stature and his thick glasses, he hardly looked the part of a ballplayer, but he was a great one.

He could run and throw and field fully as well as Joe.–Curt Gowdy, *Cowboy at the Mike* (Doubleday, 1966)

In 1934 the San Francisco Seals tried to sell Joe DiMaggio to the Cubs. The Cubs made a deal for him, but DiMaggio hurt his leg, and the Cubs backed out. "Take DiMaggio on trial," the Seals' manager said. "Try him for two months. If it doesn't work out, we'll undo the deal." The Cubs still refused.

This part of the story is well known. Less well known is the postscript. In 1938 Cubs sent an unknown scout to the coast to check out Dominic. "We couldn't use him," reported the scout. "He just hits singles . . ."

DiMaggio's career ended early in 1953, when he had an eye operation early in the season. Red Sox manager Lou Boudreau, in the process not only of destroying the Red Sox but of rendering them unable to compete for years afterward, put Tommy Umphlett in center field. Umphlett got hot, and when DiMaggio was ready to play Boudreau wouldn't put him back in center field. DiMaggio wouldn't sit on the bench, so he retired.

As I'm sure most of you know, DiMaggio went into business as a manufacturer, became a multi-millionaire and part owner of the New England Patriots.

He was, in the opinion of many observers, the best center fielder in baseball, even better than Joe.–Al Hirschberg, *What's the Matter with the Red Sox*

25 ◆ Brett Butler
(1981–1997, 2215 G, 54 578 .290)
Another one of my all-time favorite players, a little guy who wasn't even really all that fast, but who hustled and bunted and played smart and kept himself in tremendous shape, and scored 100 runs every year. The best *old* center fielders ever (career value at age 33 or later):

1. Willie Mays
2. Ty Cobb
3. Tris Speaker
4. Brett Butler
5. Cy Williams
6. Dummy Hoy
7. Jimmy Ryan
8. Earl Averill
9. Doc Cramer
10. Billy Bruton

26 ◆ Jimmy Ryan
(1885–1903, 2012 G, 118 1093 .306)
Ryan was left handed, and had the faculty of catching every ball in position and throwing with remarkable quickness, speed and accuracy . . . Ryan and [Tommy] McCarthy after thirty years in baseball still have good arms.–Johnny Evers with Hugh Fullerton, *Touching Second* (1910)

The Chicago team, while en route between Cleveland and Chicago, were caught in a serious "smash up" on the Lake Shore railroad. Several members of the team were badly cut and bruised, but only one, Center-fielder Ryan, was seriously injured. For some time after the wreck occurred Ryan was insensible. He was horribly cut about the face and legs. Though he survived, he remained in the hospital the rest of the season, and it is doubtful his recovery will be entire while he lives. So bad were his injuries, that the railroad company compromised by paying him $10,000.–1894 *Reach Guide*.

Ryan did recover, and played ten years in the major leagues after this was written, but he was never quite the player after the train wreck that he had been before.

Jimmy Ryan, famous as an outfielder 30 years ago, joined the majority of his old teammates on the famous Chicago National League team that Anson managed, when he died October 28, at the age of 60 years. Death came suddenly to the veteran. Ryan and his wife had taken a drive in their motor car during the afternoon; coming home the old player remarked that he didn't feel well and he went out on the sun porch and sat down. There he toppled over and was dead when his wife reached him. Jimmy Ryan was a native of Clinton, Mass., born and schooled in New England. He went to Holy Cross and then to Boston College, but the urge was in him and he took up professional baseball in 1883 . . . Ryan was a wonderful athlete and a great character. At well past 50 he still was rated one of the best players in the Chicago independent ranks. At 60 his heart stopped.—1924 *Reach Guide*

27 ◆ Willie Davis
(1960–1979, 2429 G, 182 1053 .279)

Willie Davis continued to miss signs and cutoff men. It seemed to be his style.—Frank Robinson with Berry Stainback, *Extra Innings*

He was egotistical . . . One time I was asked to help him with his bunting and he told me he didn't need any help. 'How many (bleeping) bunts did you beat out this year?' he asked me. I never tried to help him after that. Willie wasn't willing to work.—John Roseboro, *Glory Days with the Dodgers*

In this book I have occasionally used a new statistical method, designed to express a player's batting abilities in a different run context. In other words, here is a player who hit .238 with 10 home runs and 57 RBI, but in an unusual context, where runs were extremely scarce. What would be equivalent numbers in a more normal run context?

How do we figure this? If you don't remember your high school algebra, I'm going to warn you to skip the next several paragraphs, and just take my word for it. If you want to see the math . . . We want to assume that the player has the same contribution relative to the game, but in a different game.

The Los Angeles Dodgers in 1965 played in a league which averaged 4.03 runs per team

per game—a historically low average. They played in the best pitcher's park in that league, the worst park for a hitter; the fences weren't close, the pitcher's mound was about four feet high, and the foul territory was larger than several national forests. The park factor for Dodger Stadium in 1965 was .76, meaning that it reduced runs scored by about 24%. The Dodgers scored only 608 runs, but they won the pennant.

The .76 Park Factor applies to only half the Dodger games, plus we have to adjust for the fact that the Dodgers' "road" parks were different from any other team's, in that they didn't include Dodger Stadium on their road schedule, and we use multi-year park data. Adjusting for these things, the Dodgers' park adjustment for 1965 is not .76, but .90. Applying that to 162 games and the league average of 4.03 runs per game, the Dodgers were playing in a context of 590 runs per team.

Let's say that a context of 750 runs per team is historically normal. Willie Davis in 1965 hit .238 with 10 homers, 57 RBI; using the basic runs created method, he created about 50 runs. What would be an equivalent number of runs in a 750-run context?

A simple math problem—50, times 750, divided by 590. That's 63 runs created. We then ask the question: in order to create 63 runs, what would Davis' other numbers need to be?

To answer that question, we will make two assumptions:

1. That Davis' games played and batting outs (at bats minus hits) will be the same.

2. That as his hits increase or decrease, everything else will increase or decrease proportionally.

His batting outs are frozen because the number of outs per game is the same regardless of runs scored. A team scoring 900 runs a year makes just as many outs as a team scoring 500 runs. We assume that if Davis' hits increase by ten percent, his doubles will increase by ten percent, his triples, his home runs, his walks, and his stolen bases.

This would be a simple process if, when you increased his run elements by ten percent, his runs created would also increase by ten percent. Unfortunately, that's not the case; if you increased each run element by ten percent and froze the batting outs, a player's runs created would increase by almost twenty percent.

Willie Davis in 1965 had 133 hits, 193 total bases, 558 at bats, drew only 14 walks. His basic runs created, then, are:

$$\frac{(133 + 14) \times 193}{558 + 14}$$

Which is 50—actually, 49.6. We want to make it 63.

We can call his hits H, and express everything else by its relationship to H. In other words:

Hits equal H

Walks equal .105 H.

Total Bases equal 1.451 H.

At Bats equal 425 + H.

$$\frac{(H + .105\,H) \times 1.451\,H}{425 + H + .105\,H} = 63$$

What is H?

Simple seventh-grade algebra. This is the theoretical explanation. You can solve for H above (hits) by making a quadratic equation. As a practical matter, we don't need to wrestle with the damned quadratic equation. I have a spreadsheet which figures the adjusted runs created for the hitter, and which also refigures his runs created for whatever hit number you plug in. I just plug in two or three numbers until I find the one which causes the player to create the appropriate number of runs. In order to create 63 runs, Davis needs to get 153 hits, meaning that he needs to increase his doubles, triples, home runs and walks by 15%.

These are Willie Davis' actual numbers in 1965:

	G	AB	R	H	2B	3B	HR	RBI	BB	SO	SB	Avg
Willie Davis, 1965	142	558	52	133	24	3	10	57	14	81	26	.238

Changing the hits to 153, we then have:

	G	AB	R	H	2B	3B	HR	RBI	BB	SO	SB	Avg
Willie Davis, 1965	142	558	52	133	24	3	10	57	14	81	26	.238
Adjusted to 750 R				153	28	3	12		16		30	

Putting back in the 142 games and the 425 batting outs, we then have:

	G	AB	R	H	2B	3B	HR	RBI	BB	SO	SB	Avg
Willie Davis, 1965	142	558	52	133	24	3	10	57	14	81	26	.238
Adjusted to 750 R	142	578		153	28	3	12		16		30	.265

We will assume that his runs scored and RBI will increase proportionally to his runs created, and we'll leave his strikeouts alone. This creates the adjusted batting record:

	G	AB	R	H	2B	3B	HR	RBI	BB	SO	SB	Avg
Willie Davis, 1965	142	558	52	133	24	3	10	57	14	81	26	.238
Adjusted to 750 R	142	578	66	153	28	3	12	72	16	81	30	.265

Adjusted to a historically normal context, Willie Davis in 1965 would hit .265 with 12 homers, 72 RBI.

OK, guys, we're done with the math. You can come out of the bathroom now.

Willie Davis' 1965 season, even adjusted, is not too good; nobody gets in the Hall of Fame for hitting .265 with 12 homers. But this was his off year; in 1964, in a similar context, he hit .294 with 12 homers, 77 RBI; in 1966 he hit .284 with 11 homers, 66 RBI. What if you adjusted *those* seasons?

His 1964 season adjusts to .323 with 14 homers, 97 RBI, and 206 hits:

	G	AB	R	H	2B	3B	HR	RBI	BB	SO	SB	Avg
Willie Davis, 1964	157	613	91	180	23	7	12	77	22	59	42	.294
Adjusted to 750 R	157	640	115	207	26	8	14	97	25	59	48	.323

His 1966 season adjusts to .306, with 197 hits:

	G	AB	R	H	2B	3B	HR	RBI	BB	SO	SB	Avg
Willie Davis, 1966	153	624	74	177	31	6	11	61	15	68	21	.284
Adjusted to 750 R	153	644	89	197	35	7	12	73	17	68	23	.306

But are these numbers realistic? What I have carefully avoided saying is that these numbers represent what Davis *would have hit* (or even might have hit) in a more normal context. What I have said is that these would be equivalent numbers in a more normal context—not that Davis would have compiled these numbers. But is it realistic to suggest that Davis' 1964 and 1966 seasons should be considered equivalent to .300 seasons with 200 hits?

Well, it is very realistic; we know beyond any question that it is realistic. Look what Davis did, when he played in a more normal context. In 1962, before the pitchers seized control of the league, the 22-year-old Davis hit .285 with 21 home runs. In 1969, when the league returned to a more normal context, Davis hit over .300—in 1969, and again in 1970, and again in 1971.

The essential point I am making is this. Willie Davis, throughout the 1960s, was regarded as a huge disappointment, a player who never played up to his perceived ability. As John Roseboro said, "He has never hit .330 in his career. But he should have." This is completely unfair. Willie Davis was a terrific player. True, he didn't walk, and he was not particularly consistent—but his good years, in context, are quite impressive. The Dodgers won the pennant in 1963, in 1965 and in 1966, and one of the key reasons they did was because they had Willie Davis in center field. He should not be regarded as a failure, merely because he had to play his prime seasons in such difficult hitting conditions.

Willie Davis' entire career, adjusted to a 750-run context:

Year	G	AB	R	H	2B	3B	HR	RBI	BB	SO	SB	Avg.
1960	22	87	12	27	6	1	2	10	4	12	3	.310
1961	128	340	56	87	19	6	12	45	27	46	12	.256
1962	157	612	116	183	19	11	22	95	45	72	34	.299
1963	156	530	73	141	21	9	10	73	28	61	28	.266
1964	157	640	115	207	26	8	14	97	25	59	48	.323
1965	142	578	66	153	28	3	12	72	16	81	30	.265
1966	153	644	89	197	35	7	12	73	17	68	23	.306
1967	143	598	89	175	32	11	7	56	30	65	36	.293
1968	160	687	129	205	31	13	9	47	39	88	46	.298
1969	129	511	75	168	25	9	12	67	36	39	26	.329
1970	146	608	105	196	25	17	9	106	31	54	41	.322
1971	158	665	102	222	37	11	11	90	26	47	22	.334
1972	149	643	103	206	25	8	22	101	31	61	23	.320
1973	152	613	94	185	31	10	17	88	31	62	18	.302
1974	153	619	92	188	28	9	13	95	28	69	26	.304
1975	140	526	61	151	36	8	11	73	19	52	24	.287
1976	141	515	79	154	21	12	6	60	22	34	16	.299
1977	43	57	6	15	2	1	0	2	4	7	1	.263
TOTAL	2,429	9,473	1,462	2,860	447	154	201	1,250	459	977	457	.302

28 ◆ George Van Haltren

(1887–1903, 1984 G, 69 1014 .316)

According to the Baseball Hall of Shame 4, Van Haltren on July 31, 1897, was coaching third base in a game in which his team, the Giants, had just seized a 3-2 lead from Brooklyn. A play occurred on which the catcher turned his back on the action and began to argue with the umpire, but without asking for time. There was a runner on second, no one on third, but Van Haltren, coaching third, began a mad dash for home plate, as if he were trying to steal home. The pitcher, reacting on pure instinct, fired the ball home. The catcher wasn't ready, the ball rolled away, and the runner scored from second base . . .

Van Haltren, who was born in St. Louis but grew up in Oakland, signed with the Pittsburgh Alleghenys (National League) in 1887, as a pitcher, but received permission to report late because his mother was deathly ill in California. Pittsburgh, however, traded him to Chicago, and the White Stockings demanded that he report. Van Haltren refused to leave his dying mother and come east, and Albert Spalding, White Stockings owner, threatened to have him blacklisted. His mother died in late May, and he joined the team in June.

> Amid the glamor of Dedication Day, the clamor had grown for umpires, writers, officials and favorite sons...There was a drive for Johnny Evers, and from the Pacific Coast came a concerted plea for George Van Haltren.—Ken Smith, *Baseball's Hall of Fame* (Grosset and Dunlap, 1952)

The "concerted plea" for Van Haltren to be elected to the Hall of Fame probably occurred in 1945–46, just before and just after Van Haltren's death.

The argument for Van Haltren is simple: read his runs scored. By season beginning in 1889, his runs scored are 126, 84 (in 92 games), 136, 115, 129, 109, 113, 136, 117, 129, 117, 114. He was a left-handed leadoff man, fast, a .316 hitter, and he would take a walk. After his eastern career he played in the Pacific Coast League for six more seasons, and remained in contact with the PCL teams for the rest of his life.

29 ◆ Roy Thomas
(1899–1911, 1471 G, 7 299 .290)

Whenever you draw up a list of the players who have the most or the least of anything, there are certain players who will always be on one end of the spectrum or the other. The two *most* extreme players in history, the far ends of the base spectrum, are Rob Deer and Roy Thomas. I could make a hundred lists of players on which Roy Thomas is either the highest-ranking or the lowest-ranking player in major league history. A few examples:

- Roy Thomas drove in only 299 runs with 1537 major league hits, the lowest ratio ever. The bottom five: Thomas, Frank Taveras, Maury Wills, Miller Huggins and Burt Shotton.

- Roy Thomas was the only player in major league history to score three times as many runs as he drove in (in a real career). The top five:
  1. Roy Thomas
  2. Miller Huggins
  3. Donie Bush
  4. Bill North
  5. Otis Nixon

- Only 7% of Roy Thomas' career hits were doubles, the lowest percentage of all time. The bottom five: Thomas, Willie Keeler, Maury Wills, Al Bridwell, and Patsy Donovan.

- 90% of Roy Thomas' hits were singles, actually 89.6%. This is the highest percentage of all time. The top five:
  1. Roy Thomas (90%)
  2. Mike Tresh (89%)
  3. Al Bridwell (88%)
  4. Maury Wills (87%)
  5. Otis Nixon (87%)

Thomas succeeded Billy Hamilton as Philadelphia leadoff man and center fielder, after a couple of years with a guy named Duff Cooley. He was a little man who probably bunted 200 times a season... Here's one: highest ratios of on base percentage to slugging percentage:

1. Roy Thomas (.413 to .333, 1.24 to 1)
2. Miller Huggins (.382 to .314, 1.22 to 1)
3. Donie Bush (.356 to .300, 1.19 to 1)
4. Mike Tresh (.335 to .283, 1.18 to 1)
5. Eddie Stanky (.410 to .348, 1.18 to 1)

On the other end of that spectrum, if you're wondering, are Juan Gonzalez, Dave Kingman, Tony Armas, Matt Williams and Albert Belle. Highest ratios of walks to extra base hits:

1. Roy Thomas (6.5 to 1)
2. Miller Huggins (4.9 to 1)
3. Mike Tresh (4.5 to 1)
4. Al Bridwell (4.3 to 1)
5. Donie Bush (4.3 to 1)

On the other end are Long John Reilly, Joe Hornung, Charlie Hickman, Dante Bichette and Shawon Dunston. The lowest-ever ratio of RBI to runs created:

1. Roy Thomas
2. Miller Huggins
3. Topsy Hartsel
4. Bill North
5. Billy Hamilton

The players on the other end of that spectrum aren't people you would expect . . . the top five (way more RBI than runs created) are Tommy Thevenow, John Bateman, Hal Lanier, Jimmy Bloodworth and Bobby Wine. The second five are four guys you might expect: Walt Dropo, Dick Stuart, Tony Armas, Dave Kingman, plus Billy Sullivan Sr. One more list: Fewest career RBI, players with 1500 or more hits:

1. Roy Thomas (299)
2. Sparky Adams (394)
3. Felix Millan (403)
4. Ralph Garr (408)
5. Dave Cash (426)

30 ◆ Cy Seymour
(1896–1913, 1528 G, 52 799 .303)

Who lost the game? It was "Cy" Seymour, but perhaps not a dozen of the 30,000 persons who witnessed the struggle know he did. New York had the game won until the third inning in which Tinker was Chicago's first batter. During the entire season Tinker had been hitting Mathewson hard . . . Mathewson feared Tinker, and he signed Seymour to play deep in center field. He was afraid that a long drive by Tinker might turn the tide of battle. Seymour saw the signal, but disregarded it [and] crept a few steps closer to the infield, instead of moving back. Matty dropped his famous "fade away" over the plate, and Tinker drove a long, high, line fly to left center. Seymour made a desperate effort to reach the ball, but fell a few feet short, and the ball rolled into the crowd in the outfield for a

three-base hit, and started a rally that gave Chicago the victory. If Seymour had played a deep field, as he was commanded to do, the probabilities are that New York would have won the pennant.—Johnny Evers, 1910, discussing the decisive game of the 1908 pennant race

Cy Seymour was said to have had the strangest batting stance of the early 1900s—he occupied the rear of the batter's box, with his weight very much forward, and his bat over the shoulder and parallel to the ground.—Lonnie Wheeler and John Baskin, *The Cincinnati Game*

Seymour started with the crack of the bat, hurried over the greensward like a leopard, gave a great leap skyward at the "flycological" moment, and speared the ball with his bare hand. There was a hush for a moment until Seymour lit on the grass with the ball in his possession.

Then . . . [even] the hardened regulars got up in their seats and yelled like Roosevelt rooters. Fair women in the upper tier waved their Merry Widow lids until the hatpins fell into the necks of the fanatics beneath, but the fanatics plucked out the hatpins and kept on shrieking. It was perhaps the greatest ovation ever given a ball player for a fielding performance.—William F. Kirk, *New York American*, June 20, 1908

Latham liked to play practical jokes and otherwise kid around in ways that not everybody appreciated. Cy Seymour had barely got settled at the Hotel Arlington when he took offense at something Latham said or did and proceeded to beat up the little coach in the hallway.—Charles C. Alexander, *John McGraw*

Seymour was a converted pitcher, who had one of the great fluke seasons of all time in 1905, hitting .377 (still the Reds' record) and leading the league in hits (219), doubles (40), triples (21) and RBI (121). With that exception, he never led the league in any batting category, although he had led in strikeouts as a pitcher (1898), and in several "negative" categories as a pitcher.

With the exception of the 1905 season Seymour was a good player, often among the leaders in batting or RBI. He played for John McGraw at Baltimore in 1901–1902; McGraw moved him from the mound to the outfield. He left Baltimore for Cincinnati, where he had his great year, but didn't get along with Ned Hanlon, who was hired to manage that team in 1906, and so was traded back to New York, where he played again for McGraw. In 1908 he was third in the National League in RBI (92), and first in Baserunner Kills (29).

31 ◆ Al Oliver
(1968–1985, 2368 G, 219 1326 .303)
Left-handed line drive hitter. Oliver, very strong, hit the ball right on the nose more often than any other hitter of his generation. While he was active there were always people, including Oliver himself, who would tell you that he was the best hitter in baseball, because he did hit the ball hard almost every time up. He wasn't the best hitter in baseball, by a wide margin, because he didn't walk and he didn't get the ball in the air, which resulted in a lot of hard outs. He grounded into a double play more often than he hit a home run. As an outfielder, he played center because the Pirates had Stargell in left and Clemente and then Zisk in right. He was just an OK outfielder.

32 ◆ Andy Van Slyke
(1983–1995, 1658 G, 164 792 .274)

> [Andy] was able to read the ball on a dead run and make some great plays on shots hit to the alleys. He's always had an outstanding arm."—Syd Thrift, *The Game According to Syd*

A gold glove center fielder. As a hitter he did everything fairly well, drew some walks, stole 30 bases a year with a good stolen base percentage, led the league once in doubles (1992) and once in triples (1988). He was most known for his defense, and his wit. A couple of his more famous lines . . . (see also Lenny Dykstra, #44).

> "I'm not the brightest guy in the world. I wouldn't have graduated from high school, except my dad was the principal."

> "Last year the Pirates had so many people coming and going, they didn't even sew the names on the back of the uniforms. They put them on with Velcro."

33 ◆ Eric Davis
(1984–2000, 1552 G, 278 912 .271)

> Having Eric is like having an atomic bomb sitting next to you in the dugout."—Pete Rose

> When he goes in the game, something is going to happen.—Ray Miller

> Cal Ripken hasn't missed a game in 15 years. Brady Anderson plays [hurt] . .and then there is Eric Davis, who may be a better baseball player than any of them, when he is healthy.—The *Washington Post,* May 14, 1997

Often sick or injured, but has averaged 98 runs scored, 97 RBI per 162 games.

34 ◆ Earle Combs
(1924–1935, 1454 G 58 629 .325)
Combs name, I am fairly sure, was pronounced "Coombs." The reason I assume this is true is that it is often misspelled "Coombs." I would assume that the spelling was following the pronunciation.

> Earl had a bad throwing arm when he came into the league, but gripping exercises have strengthened his wrists and his throwing has improved. —Babe Ruth, *Babe Ruth's Own Book of Baseball*

> What may stop him from ever earning a niche in Cooperstown is his lack of a throwing arm. It was not even fair. It was poor.—Edward Grant Barrow, *My Thirty Years in Baseball*

Combs was the second best batter in the circuit and an outfielder of average ability, but not a player of the fast, hard-throwing type which has made the outfield famous in the major leagues. —1925 *Spalding Guide*

Combs swung late and hit everything to left field. The only time he would pull a ball was when a got a real slow pitch; when that happened he would often line the ball right back through the box. It was reported that, when he first came into the league, he injured three pitchers in a week, all of them by ripping off-speed pitches back through the box.

Combs averaged 8.1 Baserunner Kills per 162 games in the outfield—the worst ratio of any outfielder born 1890 to 1915, playing 1,000 or more games. There are 97 outfielders in the group; he ranks 97th in assists per game.

35 ◆ Clyde Milan
(1907–1922, 1981 G, 17 617 .285)

In 1909 Ty Cobb established an American League record for stolen bases, with 76. In 1910 Eddie Collins broke the record, with 81. In 1911 Cobb reclaimed the record, with 83. In 1912 Milan broke it, with 88. In 1915 Cobb reclaimed it again, with 96—and held the record until Rickey Henderson took it from him after his death.

> Four decades had passed since he broke Ty Cobb's record for stealing bases. And there he was, on that March day, wearing a baseball uniform as he had down through the years since Teddy Roosevelt was President, and displaying his habitual liveliness.
>
> Two hours later, he was the victim of a fatal heart attack.—Ira Smith, *Baseball's Famous Outfielders.*

> Joseph McBride reports, "Chief Bender sarcastically nicknamed Milan 'Deerfoot' because of his lack of speed on the bases."—James J. Skipper, *Baseball Nicknames*

Someone has misunderstood a source. Bender did give Milan the nickname, and it was

sarcastic, but it was a way of suggesting that Milan's whole game was speed, rather than that he didn't have speed. Milan was as fast as anybody in the American League.

Joe Cantillon, making a scouting trip out west, stopped off in Wichita to see Milan, then playing in the Western Association. He purchased Milan, then told him that "I've got to go up to Idaho to inspect a pitcher named Johnson. He's probably some big busher that isn't even worth the car fare to scout."

> Walter Johnson and Clyde Milan were both 19-year-old country boys new to the East and the major leagues. They had personality traits in common also, both being modest, reserved, and quiet . . . [the two men] became best friends, virtually inseparable during the baseball seasons before their marriages. It was a friendship that would last for the rest of their lives.—Henry W. Thomas, *Walter Johnson*

After his career Milan stayed with the Senators as a coach. He was a story teller, well liked by the press, and very good about helping young players with personal problems.

36 ◆ Curt Flood
(1956–1971, 1759 G, 85 636 .293)

By the Win Shares method, Flood rates as the best defensive outfielder in baseball history, per inning played. This claim comes with several caveats. Andruw Jones rates as far better than Flood, but that's just on a few years worth of data, and he'll look different with time. A 19th-century player named Jim Fogarty also rates a little better than Flood, but his career was less than half as long as Flood's, which makes it almost too short to count.

Flood, of course, rates higher than he probably ought to because he skipped the decline phase of his career. There are other guys who rate even with him in his prime years, like Maddox and Blair and the DiMaggios, but as they aged, their per-inning productivity naturally dropped. Flood was a great defensive outfielder; I don't know that I would especially want to argue that he was the best who ever played.

Did Curt Flood sacrifice his career to enable today's baseball players to make millions of dollars a season? Read literally, absolutely not. A lot of people seem to forget: Curt Flood's case ended, for the players, in a solid defeat. Curt Flood carried the banner for baseball players as they marched down the hallway to a doorway that never opened. In a literal sense, all Flood gave to baseball players was the certain knowledge that that door wouldn't open.

Of course, all nations honor patriots whose deaths do not lead directly to victory, and it is traditional for unions to honor the sacrifices of those who fight the good fight, regardless of their won-lost record. I just always notice this, that a lot of people actually seem to think that the Curt Flood case led directly to free agency. It's a confusion of history, vaguely equivalent to thinking that Frederick Douglass wrote the Emancipation Proclamation or that Axis Sally bombed Pearl Harbor.

37 ◆ Bernie Williams
(1991–2000, 1237 G, 181 802 .304)
So far, Bernie Williams has had only two seasons (1992 and 1996) in which he did not establish a new career high in batting average. In those two seasons, he established new career highs in home runs, runs scored and RBI.

38 ◆ Pete Browning
(1882–1894, 1183 G, 46 659 .341)
Pete Browning was, so to speak, a nineteenth century Babe Herman, a great hitter and a great figure of fun. He was a different kind of a hitter—a right-handed slash and run hitter—and a different kind of figure of fun. He drank a lot, and he often said things that didn't quite fit.

When President Garfield was assassinated, Browning asked who he played for. He was once arrested at 3:00 in the morning, fishing in the gutter.

Browning was the original Louisville slugger. He was not much of an outfielder. The story was told that once, when he found a fly in his soup, the waiter told him "Don't worry, Pete. There's no danger of your catching it." In 1886 he led the American Association in batting, .340, but fielded .791 in 112 games in the outfield—the second-lowest single-season fielding percentage in the history of baseball, at any position.

> It was said that Browning could have been replaced in center field by a cigar store Indian to Louisville's advantage. There was always a chance that a drive might bounce off the statue and back to the infield to hold the batter to a double.—William Curran, *Mitts*

> He was a conscientious man and knew that drinking did not help his ballplaying. So he would go dry all winter and show up in spring, lean and fast and sharp. But during the summer [his] moral strength would ebb and he would agree that one, or perhaps two tall ones would hardly harm him at all.—Ira Smith, *Heroes of Baseball*

Browning always touched third base for good luck as he ran in from the outfield at the end of the inning. One time Foghorn Miller stole third base, literally, before Browning could get to third. Browning didn't see Miller swipe that sack, so when he got there he stopped, dumbfounded, and looked around for the bag. Guided perhaps by the laughter from the crowd, he spotted Miller in the opposition dugout with the base, and took off after him. Miller jumped up and ran, carrying the bag. Miller was faster than Browning, so Browning chased him all over the outfield, back to the infield . . . all over the park for several minutes until finally the umpire grabbed him, and told him to go back to the dugout.

In that inning he came up to hit, took two quick strikes, then looked down the line and discovered that third base was back where it belonged. He dropped his bat, raced down to third base and touched the bag, then came back to hit—and ripped the first pitch into right field.

In 1961 a man named Preston D. Orem self-published a book called *Baseball (1845–1881) From the Newspaper Accounts*. It probably sold a couple hundred copies, I don't know . . . the book has its faults, but I'm glad to have read it. After that book came out Mr. Orem continued his work, and prepared a manuscript about baseball in the 1880s, which is the same sort of thing; just snapshots of the game, items taken from newspapers of the 1880s and re-told without much context.

This manuscript contained dozens of marvelous anecdotes about Pete Browning, many of which haven't been published anywhere else. Unfortunately, Mr. Orem died before this manuscript was published. Copies of the manuscript have been passed around for 35 years, but to my great regret I have lost my copy.

39 ◆ Ginger Beaumont
(1899–1910, 1444 G, 38 617 .311)

> [Beaumont] was an extremely fast runner, but his appearance and everyday mannerisms, including dragging his bat to the plate, had him pegged as lazy or even slovenly.—Dennis and Jeanne Burke DeValeria, *Honus Wagner*

Beaumont was the first batter in the first World Series game ever played, the 1903 Boston-Pittsburgh series. He was nicknamed "Ginger" because of his hair; he was a redhead. He was a singles hitter, led the National League in hits four times (1902, 1903, 1904, 1907), once in batting, also led in other things.

Total Baseball ranks Beaumont as a poor defensive player—negative 12 in 1900, +/− zero in 1902, negative 7 in 1903, negative 26 for his career. The Win Shares system ranks him as the 5th-best outfielder in the National League in 1900, the second-best in 1902, and the third-best in 1903, and as a fairly good outfielder for his career, although he declined sharply over the second half of his career.

Why the difference? Three things:

1. Beaumont played on outstanding defensive teams. The Linear Weights system has no correction for the false normalization of defensive statistics, and thus tends to rate the fielders on outstanding defensive teams as being no better than the fielders on poor defensive teams.

2. The Pirates in at least one season (1903) had a ground-ball staff, which resulted in fewer putouts in the outfield.

3. I'm not sure, but I think *Total Baseball* in its current form may evaluate center fielders separately from left/right fielders. If so, this would compare Beaumont to the standard of the league's eight best outfielders, and would tend to rate the league's fifth-best center fielder as below average. In the Win Shares system, the zero point is a player who can't play; in Linear Weights, it's the average.

40 ◆ George Gore
(1879–1892, 1310 G, 46 526 .301)

A "character" who drank heavily. According to Bryan DiSalvatore's biography of Monte Ward, Gore was a clown who would turn his hat backwards and dance on the base paths to entertain the crowd and distract the opposition . . .

According to Ira Smith in *Low And Inside*, the term "Charley Horse" originated in 1882, when members of the Chicago White Sox visited the race track on an off day, and several of them bet on a horse named Charley, who pulled up lame in the stretch.

The next day, playing New York, Gore attempted to steal second, but pulled up lame halfway to the base and was thrown out. Joe Quest, coaching third base, said that Gore was "just an old Charley Horse." The White Sox teased Gore about his "Charley Horse," and the term slipped into the language.

41 ◆ Kenny Lofton

(1991–2000, 1233 G, 78 485 .308)
The Indians fourth great center fielder, but their first since Larry Doby.

One question I was trying to answer, as I was doing these ratings, is "What is the point at which a team composed of players at this level would no longer be a championship team?"

Suppose, for example, that you had a team of the #1 rated player in history at each position—Berra, Gehrig, Morgan, Schmidt, Wagner, Williams, Mays and Ruth. Obviously this team would win the pennant every year—in fact, given average pitching they would win almost every game.

Suppose you had a team composed of the number 10 player at each position—Ted Simmons, Frank Thomas, Roberto Alomar, Darrell Evans, Pee Wee Reese, Minnie Minoso, Jimmie Wynn and Sam Crawford. Again, we would obviously expect this team to win the pennant easily in most seasons. The #1 team, assuming their careers were aligned, would win the pennant every season for a dozen or more years. The #10 team might win 8 pennants in 9 years or something like that.

Suppose, however, that you had a team composed of the 100th-best player of all time at each position? That team would be Oil Smith, Ripper Collins, Jerry Remy, Rafael Ramirez, Bob Dillinger, Hoot Evers, Amos Strunk and Carl Reynolds. Would you win the pennant with that team?

Obviously not; I mean, you *could* win the pennant, if you had enough of them having

their best years (Ripper Collins in 1934, Carl Reynolds in 1930), and if you had enough pitching. But the odds are you'd never win anything, and wouldn't be able to keep the team in contention more than a couple of years.

What, then, is the point at which the team would no longer be a powerhouse, no longer a pennant-winner?

This is about the point at which they start to lose it. A team composed of the 40th best player at each position would be difficult to beat in an ordinary pennant race: C—Deacon McGuire, 1B—Kent Hrbek, 2B—Tommie Herr, 3B—Buddy Lewis, SS—Travis Jackson, LF—Don Baylor, CF—George Gore, RF—Chuck Klein. Pretty salty team; give them a decent manager and a decent pitching staff, they're going to win most pennant races most seasons.

The #70 team, however, is C—Hank Severeid, 1B—Fred Tenney, 2B—Bucky Harris, 3B—Bill Melton, SS—Jeff Blauser, LF—Tommy Davis, CF—Barney McCosky, RF—Ruben Sierra. That's a good team. Those are mostly guys who had two or three good years, but below the standard of the MVP Award. If enough of them got their good years aligned, they could win a pennant, but that's about as far as I could go. It wouldn't be a championship team year-in and year-out. Between the 40th spot and the 70th, the team ceases to be a championship quality team.

42 ◆ Rick Monday

(1966–1984, 1986 G, 241 775 .264)
> My freshman year at [ASU], the big man on campus was Rick Monday . . . he was 6'3" and 190 pounds; he could run the 100 in about 9.7; he had an arm like a cannon; he could hit the ball a cold country mile; he was blond with a deep voice.—Reggie Jackson with Mike Lupica, *Reggie*

When the draft of amateur free agents was first organized in 1965, Rick Monday was the very first player taken, by the Kansas City A's. He made the majors in a year and a half, but wasn't a big star, and was traded away by the A's before they won their three World Championships (1972–1974).

Although he became a good player, until April 25, 1976, Monday seemed likely to be remembered only as the first player drafted. On that date, Monday was playing center field for the Chicago Cubs at Dodger Stadium. Two spectators climbed the wall in center field, and one of them threw down an American flag. As Monday watched, they unfolded the flag and began to pour gasoline on it, intending to set fire to the flag as a protest against something. Monday dashed between them, grabbed the flag, and held it until security arrived.

This event made Monday, for a year or so, a minor national hero. It was the bi-centennial year, and America, its self-image battered by Watergate, Viet Nam, a weak economy and the 1960s, was trying to re-establish patriotism. Monday, for rescuing a flag, came to be seen as a patriot. He was praised by the President of the United States, most of the Senators, the commissioner, the boy scouts of America, all sports television broadcasters, and thousands of other groups and individuals.

43 ◆ Willie McGee
(1982–1999, 2201 G, 73 856 .295)

In the early winter, 1981, the Yankees signed Dave Collins, which forced them to drop a player from their 40-man roster. The player they didn't have room for was Willie McGee, who was then traded to the Cardinals for a pitcher named Bob Sykes.

> The first I heard of the trade was when I read it under the transactions in the newspaper. Nobody called me. I had to call the Yankees two weeks later to find out where I was supposed to go. —Willie McGee, *St. Louis Cardinals* (Rob Rains)

We had Willie McGee in center field, at that time it was 385 to the alleys and 414 to center, and he could cover so much ground I never saw him have to dive."–Joe Magrane in *The Spirit of St. Louis* (Peter Golenbock)

All he has to do today is tap the dirt off his spikes, and the best baseball town in America climbs to its feet and hollers itself silly. It's something to see. They're thanking Willie for years of heads-up, no-bull baseball."–Whitey Herzog and Jonathan Pitts, *You're Missin' a Great Game*

44 ◆ Len Dykstra
(1985–1996, 1278 G, 81 404 .285)

> There's so much tobacco juice out there you can get cancer just by playing center field. It's like a toxic waste dump.–Andy Van Slyke, on playing center field in Philadelphia when Dykstra was the Phillies' center fielder.

> Lenny and I played together on the Mets, who proceeded to trade him...because he's a little on the wild and crazy side. The Phillies acquired him for just this reason. There is nothing corporate about the man.–Keith Hernandez, *Pure Baseball*

45 ◆ Mike Griffin
(1887–1898, 1511 G, 42 719 .296)

Griffin had a career fielding percentage of .956; the norm for outfielders of his era was .916, so Griffin was 40 points better than an average outfielder. This is the largest plus margin of any listed outfielder, although Pop Corkhill, who didn't make the top 100, was +52, and Joe Hornung was also +40. The top ten listed:

1. Mike Griffin	.956 vs. .916	+40
2. Steve Brodie	.959 vs. .925	+34
3. Curt Welch	.933 vs. .899	+34
4. Sam Thompson	.935 vs. .909	+26
5. Ed Delahanty	.951 vs. .927	+24

Only nineteenth century outfielders could make this list, as modern fielding percentages are too high to allow room to exceed them by such margins. Another related list can be found in the Terry Puhl comment (Right Field, #86).

Griffin grew up in Utica, New York, the son of a cigar maker. According to an article by Richard Puff and Mark Rucker in Nineteenth Century Stars, he got a shot at the major leagues as a result of a mistake. Billy Barnie, managing Baltimore in 1887, went to Utica to scout a player he had heard of named Sandy Griffin. Barnie mixed them up, started watching Mike Griffin, and decided to sign him.

He was in the majors for a dozen years, never had an off season, was a good hitter and an excellent center fielder, and managed briefly at the end of his career. He quit baseball in a salary dispute in 1899, returning to Utica, where he worked as a brewer. He died of pneumonia in 1908.

> After thirty-five games [Ebbets] let Barnie go, and named Mike Griffin, the popular center fielder, in his place . . . Griffin was a loose disciplinarian and a popular choice with his teammates.—Burt Solomon, *Where They Ain't*

46 ◆ Pete Reiser
(1940–1952, 861 G, 58 368 .295)

> Of the 100 [players set free by Landis], there was only one Rickey badly wanted to retain, Reiser. Rickey had personally discovered him on the sandlots of St. Louis, and he had used the boy to chauffeur him around before sending him to Class-D ball. Then, to Rickey's dismay, Landis ruled that Reiser was a free agent.—Peter Golenbock, *Bums*

> His name was Harold Reiser and he was from St. Louis, and the boys called him Pistol Pete because of his fondness for Wild West movies. The name stuck; always he would be called Pete. —Frank Graham, *The Brooklyn Dodgers*

> Pete Reiser might have been the best baseball player I ever saw. He was a switch hitter, had power from both sides, could run fast and throw

well . . . He had everything but luck.—Leo Durocher

> There isn't any doubt in my mind that if he would have stayed away from the fences he would have been one of the great players of all time. There was nothing he couldn't do on a ballfield. Run, throw, hit with power. You think Pete Rose hustles? You should have seen Pete Reiser.—Pee Wee Reese

> He's in our memory, cherished, clear and bold on a steamy July day in Brooklyn. The grass gleams, the sun is high. For all the wrong bettors, the disappointed, those who nurture the memory of a loss, dead friends, vanished loves, ambitions unfulfilled, Pistol Pete is always there.—Gerald Green in *Cult Baseball Players*

47 ◆ Dummy Hoy
(1888–1902, 1796 G, 40 726 .287)

> One rainy day in the spring of 1886, the Oshkosh players were assembled in the clubhouse getting ready for opening day. A newspaperman entered to take down the age, height, and weight of each player. When it came my turn to be interviewed, he omitted me because I was a deaf mute. Also, he had not the time to bother with the necessary use of pad and pencil. When I read his writeup the next day, I found he had me down for twenty years of age. He had made what he considered a good guess.

> Now in my school days, I had been taught to refrain from correcting my elders. Then too, he had whiskers! After thinking it over, I decided to let the figures stand . . . What would you have done in my place?—Dummy Hoy, letter to Joseph Overfield, November 15, 1955, explaining the confusion over his age.

> He couldn't talk either, of course, but he'd make a kind of throaty noise, kind of like a little squawk, and when a fly ball came out and I heard this little noise I knew he was going to take it. We never had any trouble about who was

to take the ball.—Sam Crawford, *The Glory of Their Times*

Hoy was born in a small town in Ohio in 1862, lost his voice and his hearing to an attack of meningitis at age three. As a boy he was apprenticed to a shoemaker, and, at about 21, opened up his own cobbler's shop, which was a common profession for a deaf mute in the 19th century.

He was a hell of Sunday baseball player, however, and after a year or two he simply decided to set the shoemaking trade aside, and become a baseball player. He sold his shop, and visited a number of teams in 1885, trying out as a player—actually, as a catcher.

Many managers (or captains, as they were then called) wouldn't even consider a deaf mute ballplayer. Hoy made a trip to Milwaukee to try out for a team there. The manager scoffed at the idea of a deaf mute player, but finally agreed to a tryout, and was impressed enough to offer Hoy a contract. Hoy demanded $75 a month. The manager stuck at $60 a month. Hoy went home.

He later signed with Oshkosh, Northwestern League, as an outfielder. Hoy was very small, but fast, alert, intelligent, and had an outstanding arm. He said that, despite his handicap, he had never had a serious outfield collision in his career.

Playing in the Pacific Coast League in 1903, aged 41, Hoy stole 46 bases. A lifelong baseball fan and a Cincinnati resident, Hoy threw out the first ball at the third game of the 1961 World Series; he was 99 years old. He died about two months later.

> Both Taylor and Hoy, in unfortunate accordance with the high level of insensitivity of the times, were known as 'Dummy.'—Benton Stark, *The Year They Called Off the World Series*

You're walking a fine line there, Mr. Stark, between sensitivity and moral superiority.

Dummy Taylor, I think, should probably be listed in the encyclopedias as Luther. He signed his name Luther, was called Luther by his teammates, and was often referred to as Luther in the press. I think it's a better name for him.

William Hoy, on the other hand, used "Dummy" as his name. We don't do that in the 21st century, but who is to say whether they were insensitive, or we're hyper-sensitive? Is it "unfortunate" that they could call a hammer a hammer and a wrench a wrench, or is it unfortunate that we can't?

I am not debating the merits of the practice; we have the right to make those decisions for our own generation, and we have chosen an antiseptic sensitivity. But the Civil War generation had the right to set the manners for their era, too, and it seems to me to be a dangerous step to begin blandly asserting that ours are better than theirs. If they didn't call him "Dummy," would that mean he could speak? If they called him "Bill," would he have been less aware of his deafness?

Is there not an argument to be made for frankness? Could one not argue that our compulsive sensitivity keeps our nerves raw, and thus makes us *more* aware of our divisions, rather than less? Is it not possible that calling William Hoy "Dummy" was a form of inclusiveness? Is it not possible that this was a recognition of his uniqueness, rather than a denial of his humanity? I take no position on these issues; a historian's role is not to sit in judgment on the dead.

Maybe we could compromise, and list him in future encyclopedias as "Ole' Hearing and Speech Impaired Hoy."

48 ◆ Chet Lemon
(1975–1990, 1988 G, 215 884 .279)

On a good day, Chet Lemon was a great player. Lemon was fast, had a fine arm, was a good outfielder, hit 20 homers a year and hit .300

three times. He walked 60–70 times a year and led his league in being hit with a pitch four times, giving him a good on base percentage. Unfortunately, the following is also true, and a good deal more like it:

> Chet Lemon is an enigma . . . Baserunning is not Lemon's strong suit, despite his above average speed. His instincts are poor . . . He has a bad habit of diving headfirst into first base. That has produced more nagging injuries than base hits. . . . His judgment on throws from the outfield has been questioned and he is prone to missing the cutoff man.—*The Scouting Report: 1987*

49 ◆ Ray Lankford

(1990–2000, 1397 G, 207 768 .276)
What's this? A modern player who is in danger of spending his entire career with one team? Who's in charge here? Pay attention, guys . . .

The top ten players of all time, percentage of balls in play (AB–HR–SO) which resulted in doubles or triples:

1.	Hank Greenberg	.112
2.	Babe Herman	.105
3.	Dan Brouthers	.104
4.	Lou Gehrig	.104
5.	Ray Lankford	.104
6.	Tris Speaker	.103
7.	Chick Hafey	.102
8.	Babe Ruth	.101
9.	Joe Jackson	.100
10.	Larry Walker	.099

50 ◆ Lloyd Waner

(1927–1945, 1993 G, 27 598 .316)
The nicknames "Big Poison" and "Little Poison" came from a New York Giants fan, a big, gregarious guy who would come to the games early and yell at the players. He meant to call them "Big Person" and "Little Person," but he had a Brooklyn accent, and it came out "Big Poison" and "Little Poison." The New York

papers picked it up, and the nicknames stuck. The Waners remained friendly with the fan for years afterward . . .

> I was so small that the other team thought Dad had put me in to try and work out a base on balls. But I hit the first pitch I saw (over third). When I got to third base they were still out in the weeds looking for the ball . . . Gee, I thought, the ball is lost. So I ran out there to help them look for it, and they tagged me out.—Lloyd Waner, *Voices From Cooperstown*

Lowest secondary averages for outfielders listed among the top 100:

1.	Lloyd Waner	.140
2.	Doc Cramer	.149
3.	Matty Alou	.155
4.	Orator Shaffer	.161
5.	Curt Flood	.180
6.	Tommy Davis	.182
7.	Jo Jo Moore	.183
8.	Abner Dalrymple	.185
9.	Lou Piniella	.186
10.	Duffy Lewis	.188

National League Gold Glove outfields, 1927–1937, as I see them (#1 defensive outfielder listed first):

1927 Jigger Statz, Taylor Douthit, Lloyd Waner (1)

1928 Taylor Douthit, Lloyd Waner (2), Paul Waner

1929 Lloyd Waner (3), Paul Waner, Ethan Allen

1930 Johnny Frederick, Jimmy Welsh, Kiki Cuyler

1931 Wally Berger, Lloyd Waner (4), Paul Waner

1932 Lloyd Waner (5), Kiddo Davis, Wally Berger

1933 Wally Berger, Chick Fullis, Freddy Lindstrom

1934 Kiddo Davis, Jack Rothrock, Lloyd Waner (6)

1935 Ethan Allen, Lloyd Waner (7), Terry Moore

1936 Johnny Cooney, Augie Galan, Terry
      Moore
1937 Vince DiMaggio, Lloyd Waner (8), Augie
      Galan

51 ◆ Chick Stahl

(1897–1906, 1304 G, 36 622 .305)
Stahl came to the majors in 1897, hit .354 as a
rookie and .351 in 1899. He was a left-handed
hitter with Sam Crawford type power, hitting
16 to 19 triples a year, as well as a few homers.
He helped the Boston Beaneaters to two National League pennants (1897 and 1898), then
jumped to the American League in 1901, where
he helped the team that was to become the Red
Sox to two more, in 1903 and 1904.

> Taylor was especially enthusiastic about Chick
> Stahl, who had shown signs of putting on weight
> in 1904. "I'm well pleased with 'heavyweight'
> Chick Stahl," laughed the owner. "He looks like a
> new man." Chick explained that through winter
> baths and exercise, he had brought down his
> waistline and generally streamlined himself.
> —Fred Lieb, *The Boston Red Sox*

In 1906 Boston manager Jimmy Collins had
a knee injury which left him unable to play,
and then quarreled with John Taylor, Boston
owner, about the poor performance of his team.
Collins left the team, and handed the managerial reigns to Stahl, by now a respected veteran.

Stahl had never wanted to manage the
team, and did not enjoy the assignment; still,
to all external signs, his life was going well. In
November of that year, 1906, Stahl was married to a woman named Julia Harmon. He was
a Catholic who attended Mass regularly, and
was married in the church. In spring training,
1907, Stahl had a "stone bruise" on his shin,
which was slow to heal. He was given carbolic
acid with which to wash the bruise. Instead, on
March 29, 1907, he drank the acid, killing himself instantly.

According to *Baseball's Most Wanted* (Floyd
Conner), "His wife, Julia, was a drug addict and
committed suicide a year after Stahl's death. In
addition, another woman claimed she was
pregnant with Stahl's child and threatened to
make the news public if he didn't marry her."

> He was the squarest man I ever knew. He had
> only one fault—he was too generous. He was
> often bunkoed because he believed in the good-
> ness of all mankind.—Boston catcher Lou Criger,
> speaking at Stahl's funeral.

52 ◆ Mike Donlin

(1899–1914, 1049 G, 51 543 .333)
One of the most colorful, controversial, and talented players of the 1900–1910 era.

Born in Peoria, Illinois, in 1878, Donlin was
orphaned as a baby when a bridge collapsed
killing a large number of people including his
mother, Donlin being discovered alive in her
arms. Donlin's brothers and sisters went to or-
phanages, but Donlin was raised by a family
named Murphy, who had a boy named Ed
about Donlin's age.

Ed Murphy and Donlin grew up as brothers
in and around Erie, Pennsylvania. When they
were about 18 years old the boys lit out for
California, where they broke into baseball.
Donlin was a left-handed pitcher for Los Angeles in 1897, Santa Cruz in 1898–1899, but
began to have arm troubles, switched to the
outfield, and made the major leagues as an
outfielder in 1899.

In 1900 Donlin was a teammate of John
McGraw and Wilbert Robinson (and Cy Young)
on the St. Louis Perfectos. When the American
League opened in 1901 Donlin and McGraw
jumped to the new league, Donlin thereby
missing the chance to become a teammate of
his "brother," Ed Murphy, who went 10-9 for
St. Louis in 1901. Donlin was one of the better
players in the new league in its first season,
hitting .340 and scoring 107 runs.

Just before the 1902 season, however, Donlin was involved in a couple of nasty incidents on the Baltimore streets. As reported in *The Sporting News,* March 22, 1902:

In Baltimore last Thursday Mike Donlin assaulted an innocent, modest young lady on the street, cutting her face badly. On Saturday night he was arrested in Washington with two other thugs for assaulting a streetcar conductor. He was immediately taken to Baltimore to stand trial for the first offense. When arraigned in court for striking Miss Minnie Fields, an actress, and Ernest Clayton, her escort, Donlin pleaded guilty and said that he was drunk at the time and he didn't know what he was doing. Miss Fields told of the assault, showed her bruised and blackened face, and said the blow felled her to the ground and rendered her unconscious. Clayton's blackened eyes were also in evidence as to the weight of the ruffian's fists. Judge Ritchie sentenced Donlin to six months in jail and a fine of $250.

Minnie Fields and Donlin had been involved in a relationship, which turned into some sort of triangle, rectangle, pentagon or other complicated and unsatisfactory arrangement. Donlin spent the first five months of the 1902 season in jail.

By the time Donlin got out of jail McGraw had split with the Orioles and quarreled with American League President Ban Johnson, who made it clear that Donlin was not welcome to return to his circuit. There were newspaper articles calling for him to be banned from baseball, but he signed with the Cincinnati Reds.

His time with Cincinnati, 1902–1904, was interrupted repeatedly by wayward behavior, but in 1904 John McGraw traded for him, and he rejoined McGraw, this time in New York:

Turkey Mike Donlin, the old Oriole, arrived from the Reds after getting so drunk and rowdy Cincinnati president Garry Herrmann suspended him for a month. He was a notorious drunk and

a carouser, and he had a scar running from his left cheek down to his jaw from a knifing, . . . —Mike Sowell, July 2, 1903.

Mike Donlin, hitter and discipline problem extraordinaire, had been fined and suspended several times in 1904 for breaking team rules and abusing Cincinnati manager Joe Kelley. The Reds made it known that 'Turkey Mike'—called that because of his arrogant, strutting manner—was available.—Benton Stark, *The Year They Called Off the World Series*

Cincinnati asked waivers on Donlin, intending to sell him to St. Louis of the American League. Six NL teams passed on the waivers, but McGraw put in a claim, and arranged a deal for Donlin.

John McGraw was up to the task of managing a difficult player, plus he was Donlin's friend from way back. The two men had a heart-to-heart talk as soon as he joined the Giants, one might surmise, and McGraw probably laid down some ground rules. In 1905 a largely sober Donlin had his greatest season, hitting .356 with 216 hits, leading the National League with 124 runs scored. He was the third-best position player in the National League in 1905, behind Honus Wagner and Cy Seymour, and was almost equal in value to teammate Christy Mathewson, who had one of his best seasons.

On a train in September, 1905, a steward refused to serve him any more drinks, telling him he had had enough. Donlin pulled a gun and mumbled drunkenly that "Mr. Gun barks loud." The steward called the conductor, who telegraphed ahead and had Donlin thrown in jail at the next stop. McGraw had him back in the lineup in a couple of days.

That season he was reportedly involved with a Broadway actress named Trixie Friganza; the New York papers would report on Trixie's visiting the Polo Grounds and flirting with Mike. According to Harry Grayson in *They*

Played the Game (1944), Donlin "hobnobbed with sports and actors, was one of the mob. He hung around the old Metropole, where everybody worth while hung out ... Donlin was the life of the party, held the center of the stage. There was never a dull moment. He told a story better than he knew, struck a neat barber shop chord with a pleasant voice, played practical jokes, was a great kidder."

Early in the 1906 season, Donlin slid into third base, seriously fracturing an ankle. He missed the rest of the 1906 season, and missed all of the 1907 season. There are conflicting reports of what happened here, and I'm unsure who knows what he is talking about; some sources say that Donlin began drinking again and McGraw dismissed him from the team, while others report that he was injured, others that he held out all of the 1907 season in a salary dispute, and yet others that Donlin by this time had fallen in love with another actress, Mabel Hite, whom he married, and left baseball to tour in vaudeville with Mabel. I don't know ... anyway, by the spring of 1908 he was sober and back with the Giants; McGraw, indeed, named him field captain of the team, a position he held throughout the memorable and endlessly re-written 1908 National League pennant race.

He had another outstanding season in 1908, hitting .334 and driving in 106 runs with 198 hits. G. H. Fleming's *The Unforgettable Season* contains frequent stories about him, including periodic rumors that he had, as they said at the time, fallen off the water wagon. Who the hell Mabel Hite was I don't know; however, she was famous enough in her own time that reporters liked to sit beside her at games, and report gushingly on her reactions to her husband's play. She appears to have been at least as famous as Donlin was, and Donlin had become one of the most famous players in the game:

Miss Mabel Hite, Mike Donlin's pretty and talented little wife, who is to star in the 'Merry-Go-Round' opening on Broadway tomorrow, was at the game accompanied by a bevy of enthusiastic stage-beauties.—Sam Crane, New York Evening Journal, April 24, 1908.

Even sober, Donlin was a difficult player. A list of players ejected from 1908 games in David W. Anderson's *More than Merkle* shows that Donlin was ejected from more games than any other player in baseball (6), although he was topped by one manager, McGraw, who had 7. He was also involved in several on-field fights, and at least two fights with spectators. Ed Murphy defended him in a letter to The *Sporting News,* however, saying that "Just because he makes a lot of noise on the field and has a peculiar stride, people look upon him as a rowdy."

"Several of my public appearances I deeply regret," Donlin told a reporter, "and I have tried to atone for my foolishness. My best friends will tell you I could get into trouble easier than the man who invented it."

After the 1908 season Donlin retired from baseball again, this time to pursue a career as an actor. He made periodic efforts to return to the game in later years, not very successfully. He and Mabel moved to Hollywood, where both appeared in films for several years.

Donlin pops up as a footnote to John McGraw again in 1917. McGraw, up to 1916, liked to run a long spring training, getting a large group of young players (this was before strict roster limits) to report early. McGraw would then spend three or four weeks sorting through the prospects, sending home those who didn't have a chance, working with those who did, trying to figure out who might turn out to be really good. The other National League teams didn't want to match his effort and resented McGraw gaining an advantage from it. In December, 1916, they passed a resolution prohibiting teams from starting spring training before March 1.

At this time major league players often played winter ball in California in exhibition games, keeping themselves in shape and picking up a little money. Donlin, by 1916, was promoting games in California. Spring of 1917, then, Donlin turned up in Cuba with a full schedule of promotional games. On one side was a team of veteran major league players. On the other side was a team of McGraw's youngsters. McGraw wasn't officially connected with the team in any way, but, just by coincidence, he was there; he happened to be in the dugout for every game. McGraw, of course, was using Donlin's promotional tour to circumvent the rule preventing the early start of spring training. As the tour broke up, the better youngsters on the tour were sent to the Giants spring training camp in Marlin, Texas.

The details of Donlin's film career are unknown to me, but John McGraw in *My Thirty Years in Baseball* cites three ex-ballplayers who had done well in other fields following baseball—Pennsylvania Governor John K. Tener, Monte Ward, and Mike Donlin. Donlin died in Hollywood in 1933, aged 55.

53 ◆ Paul Hines

(1876–1891, 1481 G, 56 751 .301)
On May 30, 1882, according to Ira Smith, Paul Hines lost a home run when he hit the ball over the fence, but a man walking the sidewalk outside immediately grabbed the ball and flipped it back over the fence. The Detroit left fielder, George Wood, fired the ball back to the infield, and the umpire, thinking the ball had hit the top of the fence, stopped Hines at second base.

Hines was the original center fielder of the team which is now the Chicago Cubs, Cap Anson's team, and was the best player in baseball in 1878 and 1879. He was pushed out of that niche when he slipped a bit and the Cubs

acquired George Gore, who was a very similar player but younger and perhaps a hair better. Hines was a terrific center fielder, a good lead-off man.

He was an affable, well-liked man. Playing for Washington (1886–1887), Hines befriended William McKinley. During the 1886 season, however, he lost his hearing after being beaned by Grasshopper Jim Whitney; he was deaf for the rest of his life. When McKinley became President he appointed Hines, retired from baseball, to be the postmaster of the Department of Agriculture, a job which Hines held for many years.

> Washington—Paul A. Hines, "midfielder" for the Providence baseball club of the old National League in the seventies and for the Washington club in the early eighties, was arrested Tuesday night on a pickpocket charge. He is said to be the first major league player to make a triple play unassisted—on May 8, 1878, when with the Providence club. He was released under bond of $1,000. Hines, who is 69, when confronted with the charge broke down and said, "I have played my last game and *lost*."—*Milwaukee Journal*, November 15, 1921

Hines by 1921 was nearly blind as well as deaf, living a hand-to-mouth existence. I think some provisions were made for him after his arrest, and he died in a nursing home in 1933.

54 ◆ Willie Wilson

(1976–1994, 2154 G, 41 585 .285)
Wilson came to the majors in 1976 as a speed burner whose hitting was suspect. In 1979 Whitey Herzog taught him to swing softly with his wrists, basically just dropping the head of the bat in front of the pitch, and for several years, doing that, he was a highly effective hitter, hitting hundreds of soft popups that settled between the infield and the out. In 1980 he had 230 hits, scored 133 runs, in 1982 he won the

batting title at .332, and he also hit over .300 in 1979, 1981 and 1984.

I suppose it is the Royals fan in me speaking, but I still believe that Wilson may have been the fastest man ever to play major league baseball. He was the only man I ever saw that the shortstop couldn't play at normal depth, because if he did Wilson would be at first base before he picked up the ball. He grounded into only one double play in 1979, 4 in 1980, and those must have been rockets right at somebody, or else Wilson fell down getting out of the box. He led the league in triples regularly, hitting as many as 21, and hit five inside-the-park home runs in 1979, thirteen in his career. The one I remember most clearly was hit August 25, 1979, against Mike Torrez of Boston. It was a PU6, a pop up to the shortstop, only the shortstop couldn't quite get there, and hit the ground at the last minute to avoid being crushed by the charging left fielder, Jim Rice. The ball bounced in front of Rice on the artificial turf, and hopped over his head; Rice had to turn and chase it about 30 feet behind him, and by the time he did Wilson had scored standing up. Dennis Leonard pitched a shutout, and the Royals won the game, 1-0.

It was on defense that his speed was most evident. Everybody (everybody who was around those teams) remembers a sliding catch that Wilson made in Detroit in 1980 or 1981; playing left, he caught a line drive must have been 25 feet in foul territory. What I remember most is the routine plays, for him; the way he would materialize in front of a ball ripped down the left field line, cutting off doubles so quickly that hitters felt lucky to have a single. He ran effortlessly, fluidly, accelerated instantly, and ran without strides, all in one continuous, easy motion. He bounced along the ground as he walked, as if he had springs in his heels; the only other guys I ever saw who did that were Oddibe McDowell and O. J. Simpson.

Of course they moved him to center after a couple of years; George Bamberger remarked that the Royals had the best center fielder in the major leagues playing left field.

Wilson was not an easy man to get along with or to admire; in fact, to be honest, he was often a colossal jerk. He got into cocaine use, and went to jail for that. Cocaine makes you paranoid and hostile, and so this was no big surprise to anybody who ever tried to interview Willie; as Earl Lawson once said about Alex Johnson, what you have to remember is that when Alex says 'Mother', he's just used half of his vocabulary." He got into a fight on a plane once with John Wathan; Wathan used to call him "Herbie," a reference to Herb Washington. Wilson felt that Wathan didn't respect him, so he needed to punch him out. One time there was a nasty incident in Milwaukee when two women showed up at . . . I think it was an airport, and had a bloody fight over which of them was Wilson's legitimate Milwaukee girlfriend. Wilson was married at the time.

Wilson resented being thought of as a speed merchant, and wanted to be respected as a complete player. Well, that's fine, but after 1980 he could have stolen twice as many bases if he had wanted to use his speed a little more. Worse yet, in the mid-1980s the Royals hired Lee May as a hitting coach. Lee May legitimized Wilson's fantasies about being a real hitter, taught him to drive the ball hard to the outfield, so that somebody could run under it and catch it. His batting average dropped 50 points overnight, but Wilson thought it was cool because he was hitting the ball so much harder than he used to. Whitey Herzog says in *You're Missin' a Great Game* that he discovered in the late 1990s that Wilson was still angry at him because Herzog made him slap singles (and hit .320), rather than allowing him to be a real hitter (and hit .265, but with 5 homers a year).

I suppose I am portraying him as worse than he was; he could be as articulate and gracious as the average man in the street, on occasion. He was a hell of a player, though; in 1979–1980 he stole 162 bases in 184 attempts. His last year as a regular, when he was 36 years old, he led the American League in range factor (per nine innings). He could have been better, but ultimately, none of us are judged by what we could have done.

55 ◆ Ben Chapman
(1930–1946, 1717 G, 90 977 .302)

Ben was a very aggressive ballplayer, very aggressive. He was a fighter, and he had a temper. It is unfortunate that he didn't get along with the fans in left field. They used to call him on the carpet all the time.—Ed Wells, interviewed by Eugene Murdock for *Baseball Between The Wars*

He was one of those guys who'd go out of his way to hurt you, but if you ran into him on the bases, he'd scream and holler like hell . . . He hit Gehringer one time in New York. Cut him all the way up to his shinbone. What the hell, Gehringer never said a word. But I told Chapman, "You ever try sliding like that on me, you know what I'll do? I'll hit you right between the eyes."—Billy Rogell, *Cobb Would Have Caught It* (Richard Bak).

Finishing Rogell's story, soon enough Chapman was on first when a double-play ball was hit to Gehringer. As Rogell threw to first Chapman slid into second, and Rogell kicked him in the teeth, sending blood spurting. And you know what? Chapman and Rogell had been teammates in the minor leagues, playing a whole season side by side at third base and short.

"'Hey, nigger, why don't you go back to the cotton field where you belong? Hey, snowflake, which one of those white boys' wives are you shacking up with tonight?'" Alabama-born Philly manager Ben Chapman orchestrated the hate language as the Dodgers tried to concentrate on baseball.—Harvey Frommer, *New York*

City Baseball (Actually Chapman was born in Tennessee.)

Chapman was a lifelong friend of another of Jackie Robinson's most famous antagonists, Dixie Walker. They had become acquainted as teen-agers, when both men worked for the Tennessee Coal and Iron Company. The Tennessee Coal and Iron Company had an internal baseball league—the Sales Force team, the Front Office Team, etc. Both Chapman and Walker played on the Open Hearth team—which, as you might imagine, won the company championship. The two men were similar players, actually—about the same batting stats in their better years and in their careers—but Chapman had his peak very early, and Walker had his very late, so that one doesn't think of them as being of the same generation.

In 1931 Chapman hit .315 with 17 homers, 61 stolen bases, 120 runs scored, 122 RBI—one hell of a year. The New York press compared him to Ty Cobb. He wasn't Ty Cobb, but he was a Ty Cobb type.

I had fun playing ball, but I was a reprobate, a maverick. I haven't changed and I'm not going to change until they put me under. But baseball itself has changed.—Ben Chapman in *For the Love of the Game* (Cynthia J. Wilber)

56 ◆ Garry Maddox
(1972–1986, 1749 G, 117 754 .285)

Vietnam was not as tough on me as it was on some people—a lot of my friends didn't make it back. The guys in the infantry had to go out and beat the bushes for the Viet Cong, not knowing what would happen.—Garry Maddox, quoted by Hal Bodley in *The Team That Would Not Die*

Seventy percent of the earth is covered by water. The other thirty percent is covered by Garry Maddox.—variously attributed

I've seen Garry Maddox do it all. In my estimation, he's the best defensive centerfielder ever to play the game. This may sound like a bold statement, but as his teammate for all these years, I'll stick by it.—Mike Schmidt, *Always on the Offense*

57 ◆ Andy Pafko
(1943–1959, 1852 G, 213 976 .285)

"He was an excellent player and a super guy. The fans loved all the Cubs players, but it was much stronger with Andy."—Rube Walker, We Played the Game

Andy Pafko, the eternal farmboy from Boyceville, Wis., will be remembered for his odd batting stance. He crouched with his bat cocked high at one end and his protruding rump at the other."—Eddie Gold and Art Ahrens, *The New Era Cubs*

He displayed . . . a throwing arm the Cub outfield had not owned since Kiki Cuyler went away, and an ability to travel long stretches in successful pursuit of drives hit in his direction.—Warren Brown, *The Chicago Cubs*

I would rather play baseball than eat.—Andy Pafko

58 ◆ Gus Bell
(1950–1964, 1741 G, 206 942 .281)

At age 22 (1951) Bell led the National League in triples with 12, hit 16 homers and drove in 89 runs for a 7th-place team. After the season, however, Bell asked that in the future his family be allowed to travel with him on the road.

Pirate General Manager Branch Rickey did not react well to this suggestion. A nasty contract dispute ensued, and ended with Bell being a) sent to the minor leagues to start the 1952 season, and b) traded to Cincinnati a year later.

The dispute with Bell, the fact that one of their best players was in the minor leagues, contributed mightily to the 1952 Pirates historically awful season, finishing 42-112. When Bell was sent to the minor leagues for standing up to the front office, the team basically quit. My understanding is that Gus Bell was painfully shy, and not really comfortable except around family and close friends.

Bell, of course, became a star in Cincinnati, which was nearer to his home; in 1953 he hit .300 with 30 homers, 105 RBI. That's what I call a Hall of Fame season—.300 with 30 homers, 100 RBI. There have been 36 Hall of Fame seasons by the center fielders listed here:

Joe DiMaggio	7
Willie Mays	7
Hack Wilson	4
Duke Snider	4
Earl Averill	3
Mickey Mantle	3
Dale Murphy	2
Ken Griffey Jr	2
Wally Berger	1
Gus Bell	1
Fred Lynn	1
Ellis Burks	1

In addition, there was one Hall of Fame season by a center fielder who didn't make the top 100 (Jim Hickman, 1970), and there have been a few Hall of Fame seasons by left/right fielders playing center field, like Al Simmons and Stan Musial. 28 of the 37 Hall of Fame seasons by Center Fielders were by players who are now in the Hall of Fame; the other nine include two by Griffey. Bell met the Hall of Fame standards only once, but was close in two other seasons.

59 ◆ Mickey Rivers
(1970–1984, 1467 G, 61 499 .295)

A reporter once suggested to Whitey Herzog that Willie McGee looked like a young Mickey Rivers. "Yes," said Herzog, "except that Willie doesn't play the horses, shows up on time, and can throw."

Mickey was small and very, very fast. His arm was poor, and he was noted for two other things: an odd throwing motion in which he flapped his arm like a chicken wing, and his malapropisms and wit. About Danny Napoleon, he once said that Napoleon was so ugly when you walked by him your pants would wrinkle, and also that Napoleon was so ugly that when a fly ball was hit to him it would curve away. Cliff Johnson, he said, was so ugly he should be required to wear an oxygen mask. About two of his teammates, he once said they were so old they were eligible for Meals on Wheels. A sampler of the malapropisms:

"My goals this season are to hit .300, score 100 runs and stay injury prone."

"What was the name of that dog on 'Rin Tin Tin'?"

"Me and George and Billy, we're two of a kind."

60 ◆ Terry Moore
(1935–1948, 1298 G, 80 513 .280)
Moore was the field leader of the great Cardinal teams of the 1940s. "We had a good captain in Terry Moore," said Whitey Kurowski. "If we had any troubles or anything, we would go to Terry. He's the one that kept us in good spirits."

"We were a close team," said Harry Walker, "and Terry Moore was a lot of that." These quotes (and there are others) are from Rob Neyer and Eddie Epstein's *Baseball Dynasties*. Moore was also, of course, one of the greatest defensive center fielders of all time.

> As for outfielders one of the best I saw while I was playing was Terry Moore, though not as much in hitting as some others. But he was just like having another infielder out there.—Joe Moore in *Legends of Baseball* (Walter M. Langford).

61 ◆ Marquis Grissom
(1989–2000, 1581 G, 145 663 .273)
Most-similar players to Marquis Grissom:

1900s	Sam Mertes
1910s	Hi Myers
1920s	Taylor Douthit
1930s	Mike Kreevich
1940s	Terry Moore
1950s	Jimmy Piersall

1960s	Jose Cardenal
1970s	Garry Maddox
1980s	Chet Lemon

62 ◆ Dode Paskert
(1907–1921, 1716 G, 42 577 .268)

> "Do you know where I might be able to get a good outfielder?"
>
> "Why sure'" I said. "I can get you the best outfielder in town." So I went to Dode Paskert's house and told him about it, and he went with me to Warren.—Jimmy Austin in *The Glory of Their Times*

Jimmy Austin and Dode Paskert were childhood friends who broke into baseball together in 1903. In 1921 Dode Paskert was the oldest player still playing in the National League—and Austin was the oldest still playing in the American.

When Richie Ashburn first came to the majors, Fred Lieb described him as a new Dode Paskert. This is one of the few recorded instances of the "new" anybody turning out to be better than the original . . .

Of the top 100 center fielders of all time, 35 were essentially leadoff men, 51 were middle-of-the-order hitters, and 14 were players who would normally hit 6, 7 or 8.

63 ◆ Brady Anderson
(1988–2000, 1669 G, 201 771 .261)
Still playing center for Baltimore, which at this writing is trying to win a pennant with an outfield of B.J. Surhoff, who is 35, Brady Anderson, who is 36, and Albert Belle, who is 33. If they were to succeed, which of course they won't, it would be the oldest pennant-winning outfield in baseball history.

64 ◆ Bill Lange
(1890–1899, 811 G, 39 578 .330)
Bill Lange was probably the greatest all-around athlete to play major league baseball in the

nineteenth century. The 1918 *Reach Guide,* writing one of those little asides that made Francis Richter's guide so marvelous, said that "on the ball field speed counts for more than actual physical power in the way of brute strength . . . still there have been a good many Herculean players . . . Such giants of the past were Ed McKean, shortstop of the old Cleveland club [and] Bill Lange, commonly known as 'Little Eva', the old Chicago outfielder, who combined great strength with wonderful speed for so large a man."

Little Eva was 6'2," 200 pounds, with thin legs and a huge upper body. His started playing baseball at the Presidio in San Francisco, where his father was a sergeant, apparently a career soldier. "Despite his size," wrote Ira Smith, "he was very speedy and was forever tearing around the bases." He stole 399 bases in just 811 major league games. Of course, as you know, the definition of a stolen base was a little bit different then, but only a handful of players in that era stole bases with the same frequency.

This combination of size and speed leads to the one thing that Lange is sometimes remembered for, a play that he allegedly made in which he crashed through a wooden fence in a successful effort to make a game-saving catch. Arthur Ahrens in the 1980 *Baseball Research Journal* argues that this play never occurred, but was a confusion of events that took place on August 31, 1896. Kip Selbach (also cited by Richter in the article on the greatest athletes ever to play the game) deliberately smashed through the fence, using a ladder as a battering ram, while helping an injured player to the hospital. Two outs later, Lange fell down making a spectacular catch in the same area, one on which it was reported that ~From the grandstand it looked as if Lange covered almost half the distance spanned by the ball. The crowd rose and cheered him lustily, the players on the [opposing] Washington bench joining in the applause." Several years later the story about Lange's crashing through the fence first surfaced in a filler item in the *Chicago Tribune,* giving specific enough details to convince me that it was, in fact, a confusion of the incidents discussed.

While Ahrens was forced to conclude that Lange's legendary catch never happened, he did find many references to spectacular plays that Lange did make. An article by James D. Smith in *The National Pastime* (Fall, 1982) discusses players who had outstanding seasons in their last major league campaigns. He says that "Bill Lange stands as the finest every day, all-around player to retire from baseball at the peak of his career." Smith writes about Lange's impressive physical tools, and says that he was regarded by some as "the greatest player of the era."

Lange retired early because his prospective father-in-law, a wealthy man, refused to sanction his daughter's marriage to a ballplayer. Lange gave up baseball for love, but the marriage ended in divorce, anyway.

In the 1981 *Baseball Research Journal,* William Akin was trying to identify the greatest defensive outfielders of the 1890s. After twirling through several candidates and selecting a center fielder, he wrote that "in the absence of logically compelling statistical evidence, the impression of contemporary observers must be given greater weight. The evidence points to Bill Lange of Chicago."

Akin credits Little Eva with "unequalled desire." Smith's article, on the other hand, gives the impression that his dedication to his baseball career could have been improved upon in several ways. On the field, there is no doubt that he dashed around like a hurricane. But in 1897, apparently, Lange wanted to stay in his native San Francisco long enough to stop in Nevada on March 5, where he could see Jim

Corbett fight. To delay his reporting, Lange demanded an extra $500, and was surprised when the team met his demand, on condition of secrecy and immediate reporting. So Lange made up a twisted ankle and stalled another week or so, anyway. After finally reporting, he hit .340 and led the National League with 73 stolen bases.

Lange's career average was .330. He hit .389 in 1895, and was fourth in the league in slugging percentage. He was among the top five in the league in stolen bases four times, despite missing some games, and was often in the top twelve in the league in batting. He walked over fifty times a year and rarely struck out. His range and assists totals, while not exceptional, were quite good.

Lange's nephew, George Kelly, is in the Hall of Fame. Lange can't be considered, because he played only seven major-league seasons. Albert Spalding named Lange to his all-time all-star team, over Tris Speaker, saying that "Both men could go back or to either side equally well. Both were lightning fast in handling ground balls. But no man I ever saw could go forward and get a low line drive like Lange." Tim Murnane's all-time all-star outfield was Ty Cobb, Joe Jackson and Bill Lange, but Murnane's picks were mostly from his youth; he also picked Cap Anson, Ned Williamson, Ross Barnes, Bob Caruthers and Charlie Bennett. Francis Richter picked Lange to his all-decade team, but he picked six outfielders. Alfred Spink considered Lange the equal of the young Ty Cobb.

Lange was an exceptionally good-looking man, and the *Chicago Tribune* once said that he was "the most popular man who ever wore a Chicago uniform." In many ways he could be described as a nineteenth-century Mickey Mantle. Another William Akin article, in *Nineteenth Century Stars,* says that Akin was

"fun-loving and carefree [with] a fondness for practical jokes, women and night life." Later in life, after his marriage failed, he coached at Stanford.

This comment, to this point, is essentially a reprint of a comment in the first edition of this book, first published in 1985—edited, and with a little material added, but essentially the same. The original comment, however, makes two statements which I now have analytical tools to better evaluate:

1. That Lange was perhaps the best defensive outfielder of the 1890s, and

2. That Lange was probably the best position player ever to walk away from the game, the best "last year" player.

Akin's 1981 article cites an "absence of statistically compelling evidence," which I think was accurate at that time. My analysis suggests that the best defensive outfielder of the 1890s was Jimmy McAleer, but that the second-best was Bill Lange, the third-best a close call between Steve Brodie and Hugh Duffy. The worst defensive outfielders of the 1890s, if you're curious, were Dan Lally, Tuck Turner, and Bill Hassamer.

With the second statement—that Lange had the best "last season" ever, I disagree. Lange's .325 last-season average looks good, but his all-around 1899 performance was not very impressive. 1899 was a big-hitting year. With adjustments, even among center fielders, I rank Lange's last season as tied for sixth-best. The best last seasons by players who were primarily center fielders, as I would evaluate them:

1. Happy Felsch, 1920	30
2. Mickey Mantle, 1968	25
3. Kirby Puckett, 1995	21
3. Chick Stahl, 1906	21
5. Mike Griffin, 1898	20
6. Bill Lange, 1899	19
6. Jim McTamany, 1891	19

The best "last seasons" by players at any position, including players banned from baseball:

1. Joe Jackson, 1920   36
2. Sandy Koufax, 1966   34
3. Happy Felsch, 1920   30
4. Mickey Mantle, 1968   25
4. Bill Joyce, 1898   25
6. Eddie Cicotte, 1920   24
7. Buck Weaver, 1920   23
8. Jesse Burkett, 1905   22
9. Ted Williams, 1960   21
9. Roy Cullenbine, 1947   21
9. Chick Stahl, 1906   21

65 ◆ Sam Chapman
(1938–1951, 1368 G, 180 773 .266)

> I don't think I ever saw a ball player come on overnight as Chapman did in the 1941 season. —Joe DiMaggio, *Lucky to be a Yankee*

Chapman was an All-American football player at the University of California in the 1930s, playing in the Rose Bowl one year and graduating with a B.A. in 1938. He signed with the Philadelphia Athletics, and went straight to the major leagues with no training (which was common for the A's at that time. They had no real farm system; Mack was trying to survive by signing college players.) Chapman struck out quite a bit at first, but by 1941 was one of the best players in baseball, hitting .322 with 106 RBI.

He went into the Navy after the season, and lost all of his prime seasons except the one to World War II. Returning in 1946, he didn't drive in 100 runs again until 1949 (24, 108, .278), but was a Gold Glove outfielder and a hitter with some power.

Chapman was a great gentleman—reserved, dignified, well spoken, temperate. After leaving baseball he became a successful businessman in the San Francisco/Oakland area.

66 ◆ Paul Blair
(1964–1980, 1947 G, 134 620 .250)

Blair was one of the best players in baseball in 1969, aged 25, but was hit in the face with a fastball from Ken Tatum early in 1970, and never quite got back to the same level as a hitter.

According to one of the Brooks Robinson books, the Oriole players would kid Blair by telling him that he should get hit again; the plastic surgery had made him a lot better looking. When Ed Stroud of the Senators had his jaw broken by a pitch, also requiring surgery, Blair used a variation on the same approach, telling Stroud that "I hope you didn't pay that plastic surgeon for that face of yours. You either got to get your money back, or you got to get another operation."

Blair was called "Motormouth," because he never shut up. He was one of the greatest defensive outfielders of all time. He played shallow, and he could run down everything.

67 ◆ Happy Felsch
(1915–1920, 749 G, 38 446 .293)

Felsch hit .338 with 115 RBI in 1920, making him among the best players in the American League. He was expelled from baseball near the end of that season for participating in the fixing of the 1919 World Series.

> Felsch was a smiling, easygoing, badly educated boy from Milwaukee, constantly seeking raucous pleasure and adventure.—Eliot Asinof, *Eight Men Out*

> His father said he was born laughing.—James J. Skipper, *Baseball Nicknames*

The most-similar center fielders to Felsch in terms of career value and value pattern up to the age at which he was expelled from baseball are (1) George Gore, (2) Andy Pafko,

(3) Hack Wilson, (4) Bernie Williams and (5) Jimmy Barrett.

Felsch played the fewest major league games of any outfielder listed among the top 100 at his position. The bottom ten:

1. Felsch   749
2. Jake Stenzel   766
3. Walt Judnich   790
4. Bill Lange   811
5. Orator Shaffer   842
6. George Stone   848
7. Benny Kauff   859
8. Pete Reiser   861
9. Jimmy Barrett   866
10. Tony Conigliaro   876

The highest-ranking of these players is Pete Reiser, CF #46.

68 ◆ Matty Alou

(1960–1974, 1667 G, 31 427 .307)
The Dom DiMaggio of the Alou brothers, and National League batting champion in 1966.

Alou signed with the San Francisco Giants in 1957 for a $200 bonus, the same amount his older brother had gotten. In '61 and '62 he was the Giants fifth outfielder, hitting a little over .300.

This was followed by three years of frustration. In spring training of 1963, he suffered a knee injury in camp and, hobbled, made a trip back to Tacoma. With the Giants' center field job being guarded by a lion, and their great farm system producing so many hitters that they were always forcing them into the lineup by doing things like putting Orlando Cepeda in the outfield or Jim Ray Hart at third base, Matty couldn't get enough at bats to stay sharp, completely lost his rhythm, and demanded to be traded. On December 1, 1965, Alou was traded to the Pirates.

The Bucs were then managed by Harry "the Hat" Walker, who would today be described as a "hitting guru." Harry worked with Alou, getting him to use a heavy bat and chop down on the ball, rather than using a light bat and uppercutting as do most modern hitters. Alou, who had hit .231 in 1965, won the National League batting title at .342—perhaps the most unexpected NL batting championship since the one claimed by Harry the Hat in 1947. Walker was one of those guys who had a good idea and rode it into the ground, and his idea was to get his players to stop using these damned little bats and trying to pull everything. Matty was his dream come true, his perfect pupil, and he gave interviews about how he had turned Matty's career around until everybody was pretty much sick of hearing about it.

For three years after that Alou was amazingly consistent, hitting .338, .332 and .331. Harry only lasted half a season after Alou's batting title; by the middle of '67 his infield was about ready to arrange a necktie party for him. In 1969 Matty set a major league record, since broken, with 698 at bats, and led the league in hits (231) and doubles (41). At that time the 231 hits were the most by any major league player in 32 years.

Alou had two plusses besides hitting .330: he was fast, and he had a pretty good arm. In 1970, however, his average slipped below three hundred, and after the season he was traded to the Cardinals, thereby missing out on the Pirates' World Championship in '71. Alou edged back over three hundred as he spent the next two years with the Cards and, briefly, the Oakland A's. When Reggie Jackson was injured, Matty played in all seven games of the '72 series, just as his brother would a year later filling the spot left by Bill North. He dropped out of the majors a couple of years later, but played two-plus seasons in Japan before hanging up his spikes.

69 ◆ Dwayne Murphy

(1978–1989, 1360 G, 166 609 .246)

Rates well despite a low average because of four assets:

1. Power
2. Walks
3. Range in center
4. Arm.

Dwayne Murphy, rated between Alou and McCosky, is the meat of a singles sandwich. Alou hit .307, but with a secondary average of .155, and McCosky hit .312, but with a secondary average of .236. Murphy, on the other hand, hit just .246, but with a secondary average of .351, giving him about the same offensive impact as the other two hitters.

70 ◆ Barney McCosky

(1939–1953, 1170 G, 24 397 .312)

A good little left-handed leadoff man who lost his best years to World War II.

McCosky was born in Coal Run, Pennsylvania, the youngest of nine children. His mother died when he was a baby; his father never remarried, leaving McCosky to be raised by older siblings. An older brother got a good job in Detroit, working for Dodge, and the whole family followed him to Detroit. He was an all-city baseball and basketball player at Southwestern High School in Oakwood (Detroit), and signed with the Tigers.

A Tiger fan, McCosky idolized Charlie Gehringer, and copied Gehringer's batting stance. When he got to the Tigers, he had the luxury of getting actual advice from his hero, still starring at second base. McCosky had 190 hits as a rookie in 1939, hitting .311 and also stealing 20 bases in 24 attempts. He had 200 hits his

second season, hitting .340 and leading the league in doubles and hits. Hank Greenberg moved to the outfield that spring to enable Rudy York to play first. Greenberg had never played the outfield before, so he told McCosky, "I need a little help in the outfield . . . I know you're a good center fielder and if I'm going to play alongside of you I'll need your help on where to throw the ball." McCosky worked with Greenberg in the outfield for several days. Greenberg bought McCosky a fancy new suit, drove in 150 runs, won the MVP Award, and the Tigers won the pennant.

My analysis shows McCosky as deserving a Gold Glove in all four of his pre-war seasons (1939–1942). When the war was over he was the same kind of hitter—a consistent .320 hitter with no power—but he had lost his speed, which eliminated most of his value as a center fielder and a leadoff man.

The Barney McCosky Baseball League, a youth baseball league, was formed in Detroit in the late fifties, and as best I know is still going.

71 ◆ Lloyd Moseby

(1980–1991, 1588 G, 169 737 .257)

Brought to the majors before he was ready in 1980, Moseby came into his own in 1983, and was a complete player, above-average in every aspect of the game except perhaps throwing, for five years. He began having trouble with his back and legs in 1988, and was never able to snap out of what seemed at first to be minor, nagging problems.

72 ◆ Jimmy Barrett

(1899–1908, 806 G, 16 255 .291)

Jimmy Barrett was from Athol, Maine, and, as Ty Cobb and Edward Barrow could attest, he could be a real athol thometimeth. You probably know that Ty Cobb and Sam Crawford, Hall of Fame outfielders for the Tigers, had such a bitter feud that at one point Hughie Jennings had to put someone else in center field to keep them apart. Jimmy Barrett is part of the subtext of that feud. Barrett broke in with Sam Crawford at Cincinnati in September, 1899, jumped to the Tigers ahead of Crawford in 1901, and was the Tigers center fielder until he injured his knee just at the time Ty Cobb came along. He was a good player, a left-handed hitting leadoff man, scored 114 runs for Cincinnati in 1900, 110 for Detroit in 1901, hit over .300 in 1900, 1902 and 1903, led the American League in walks in 1903 and 1904, had a .407 on base percentage in 1903, led the American League in putouts in 1902 and 1904 and in Baserunner Kills in 1901, 1903 and 1905. More germane to the story, Crawford and Barrett were tight. When Cobb tried to take his job Barrett became one of Cobb's tormentors, and this aligned Cobb against Crawford.

Edward Barrow had managed the Tigers in 1903, part of 1904. In Barrow's autobiography, *My Fifty Years in Baseball,* he says that he never got along with Barrett, either, and that one of the reasons he quit as the Tigers manager is that he arranged a trade to get rid of Barrett, but Tiger owner Frank Navin blocked the trade because Barrett was popular with the fans. One time, according to Barrow, Barrett said to him, "Mr. Barrow, your methods take all the individuality away from a ballplayer."

"Young man," said Barrow, "if you ever speak to me that way again I will take more than individuality away from you. I will knock your block off."

It's hard to feature a player from a hundred years ago complaining about the manager taking away his "individuality," isn't it? It's an exact quote, though . . .

Two other notes about Barrett.

1. He is the only outfielder listed among the top 100 who did not hit at least 100 career doubles. He hit 83.

2. In 1904, due to tie games, Barrett played 162 games in a 154-game season. He held the record for games played in a season until the schedule was expanded in 1961.

73 ◆ Bill Bruton
(1953–1964, 1610 G, 94 545 .273)

> Bruton is a poor hitter, but once he gets on base, he can upset the opposition with his great speed. Like Ashburn, he can go a long way for a fly ball, and he has a better arm than Richie. He should use his speed by bunting more often.
> —*Sport Magazine,* September, 1957.

Bruton was sometimes described as (or argued to be) the fastest man in baseball in the 1950s. He also has one of the most serious "baseball ages" in history. By the time the color line was firmly broken, Bruton was 24 years old, too old for a lot of teams to be interested in him. John Ogden, scouting for the Braves, told the Braves that Bruton was 20, listing his birth date as 1929 rather than 1925, and got him a chance to play. He blasted through the minors with three outstanding seasons, and played twelve years in the major leagues. After leaving baseball he worked for the Chrysler Corporation for 23 years, starting in sales and becoming a successful executive.

74 ◆ Steve Finley
(1989–2000, 1690 G, 188 745 .275)

Steve Finley and Brady Anderson are very similar players. Anderson originally signed with the Red Sox, but the Red Sox took a quick look at him and decided he couldn't play, so they packaged him *with* Curt Schilling and traded him to Baltimore for a pitcher, Mike Boddicker, who had a couple of good years left. The Orioles should have made out like bandits on the deal, but then they had both Finley and Anderson, so they packaged Finley with Schilling *and* Pete Harnisch, and traded them all to Houston for a washed-up first baseman named Glenn Davis.

75 ◆ Cy Williams
(1912–1930, 2002 G, 251 1005 .292)

The Phillies' long-ball circus of the early 1920s was built around center fielder Fred "Cy" Williams, a gangly left-handed hitter who had been in the league since 1912. Williams, a graduate architect, could not have designed a right-field wall better suited to his talents.—William Curran, *Big Sticks*

Cy Williams, the potent slugger of the Philadelphia National League Club, was discussing this same spirit of aggressiveness, but his philosophic meditations led him to arrive at a different conclusion. "I never have been an aggressive type of player myself," said Williams, "so perhaps I ought not to discuss the subject. But I have, at least, observed, and what I have observed has led me to the conclusion that fighting spirit is often vastly overrated. Much of it is a pure mental delusion.

"I am well aware of Ty Cobb and what he has done. He is a shining exception. John Evers was, in a sense, another. But I think in both these cases aggressiveness was really subordinate to something quite different. Both were great players because they lived and breathed baseball; studied it, analyzed it and themselves. In other words, they were smart, tricky players who were always tough for the opposition to fathom. Aggressiveness was only one of many weapons they employed.

"Most so-called aggressive players that I have known,' continued Williams, 'are aggressive with their mouths rather than their actions. I have in mind one particular veteran who dropped out some time since. He had a loud voice and he was always talking. The crowd rather fell for his line too. He was a peppery ball player, and I suppose, he may have added something to the club spirit. But for all that, he couldn't field the ball four feet on either side. His aggressiveness was mainly noise.

Show me an aggressive player of the Cobb-Evers type who has climbed to the top and I'll show you two or three others who are undoubtedly great stars who have always been quiet, gentlemanly and use none of the bluster and fireworks that you read so much about. That's what it is, fireworks, a lot of noise and brilliant lights, but little *accomplished.*"—*Baseball Magazine,* 1926.

Most of you probably know that several National League teams used the "Williams shift" against Cy Williams twenty years before Lou Boudreau invented it to use against Ted Williams. According to Roscoe McGowen in the third *Fireside Book of Baseball,* one time against the Dodgers Cy Williams decided to slap the ball to left field to cross up the shift, but happened to hit the ball on the nose and lined a shot up the left field line. It should easily have been an inside-the-park home run, McGowen claimed, but Williams started laughing as he ran the bases, apparently at having accidentally hit the ball so hard, and by the time he got to third he was laughing so hard he had to stop running.

76 ◆ Jose Cardenal
(1963–1980, 2017 G, 138 775 .275)

Cardenal is a second cousin of Bert Campaneris. In 1965 and again in 1968, Campaneris led the American League in stolen bases—while Cardenal finished second... When he was 17 years old, playing for El Paso in the Sophomore League, Cardenal hit .355, leading the league in doubles (39), home runs (35), stolen bases (64) and scoring 159 runs in 128 games. Now that is a leadoff man ...

Actually, he might have been better off if they had cut that line out of his record. After his big stats in that dippy little league where everybody hit .300 the Giants sent him straight to triple-A. He wasn't ready. The idea that he was the new Willie Mays lasted about ten minutes, but the idea that he wasn't as good as he was supposed to be lasted ten years . . .

Cardenal played in Japan toward the end of his career, and is credited with bringing the dimpled-end bat back from Japan.

77 ◆ Ellis Burks

(1987–2000, 1672 G, 285 1012 .293)

One of the ten seasons below is Ellis Burks, 1996. Can you spot it?

G	AB	R	H	2B	3B	HR	RBI	BB	SO	SB	Avg.
163	609	113	200	48	3	49	152	81	84	6	.328
139	579	102	197	39	2	40	128	22	96	13	.340
156	613	142	211	45	8	40	126	61	114	32	.344
148	573	129	195	50	8	41	150	93	75	6	.340
154	650	152	226	50	15	38	137	60	49	20	.348
155	576	122	182	34	2	49	122	87	90	8	.316
149	584	120	199	39	10	40	130	84	96	6	.341
161	636	137	205	34	4	42	129	72	65	7	.322
153	585	128	194	34	11	39	155	74	31	37	.332
150	574	135	198	30	5	39	159	78	83	3	.345

Burks' season is the third season down. How many of those seasons can you identify, just based on the numbers?

The ten seasons represent Albert Belle (1998), Dante Bichette (1995), Ellis Burks (1996), Hank Greenberg (1940), Chuck Klein (1932), Frank Robinson (1966), Duke Snider (1954), Billy Williams (1970), Ken Williams (1922), and Hack Wilson (1929).

The most valuable of these ten seasons was Frank Robinson's in 1966, when he was the unanimous MVP. The least valuable of the ten was Dante Bichette, 1995, when he had similar numbers, but barely over one-half the value (41 Win Shares for Robinson, 22 for Bichette).

78 ◆ Tommie Agee

(1962–1973, 1129 G, 130 433 .255)

A short, powerfully built athlete, not quite what you could call a Kirby Puckett type body, but not too far from it.

People in that day still wanted black people to stay "with their own kind." Well, Tommie was my kind—a rugged, good-natured guy [with] as much raw talent as any ballplayer I ever met and he was always good company, ready to go anywhere and not given to quarreling.—Tommy John, *The Sally and Tommy John Story*

We liked Agee, and I knew he was a helluva prospect because he could run. But he also had been up with us a few times and hadn't shown that much. I had to give up something, so I included Agee.—Gabe Paul in *The Curse of Rocky Colavito* (Terry Pluto), explaining why he traded Agee and Tommy John to re-acquire Rocky Colavito in 1965

Agee was a tremendous athlete who didn't compile big numbers in the minor leagues, and went 9-for-53 (.170) in three brief trials with the Cleveland Indians. Traded to the White Sox, he had one of the best rookie seasons ever in 1966, hitting .273 with 22 homers, 86 RBI, and 44 stolen bases, while playing in hitting conditions which were among the very worst in the history of baseball; the White Sox as a team hit .231 with 87 home runs, yet finished over .500.

During that season Agee was frequently compared to a young Willie Mays, and almost universally expected to become a star, if not a superstar. Just one year later, however, Agee was traded to the New York Mets for a package of four players. Agee's manager in Chicago was Eddie Stanky, who was widely suspected of being a racist. Stanky and Agee didn't get along, and Agee didn't seem to be giving the game his best efforts.

The New York press christened him "The Shea Hey Kid," another implied comparison to Willie Mays. In his first year in New York, however, Agee's play continued to degenerate, due to injuries and personal problems:

Said one coach, "Agee doesn't have the salivating greed you need to be a good hitter." Said another, "His knowledge of Greek is greater than his knowledge of the strike zone." That year Agee may have been the least popular athlete in New York.—Chris Stern, *Where Have They Gone*

But Agee bonded with his new manager, Gil Hodges, who became Agee's confidant and supporter. Agee would go into Hodges' office almost every day, close the door, and unload on Gil, sometimes for hours. It was a burden on Hodges, who obviously couldn't do this for everybody on the team, but Hodges and the team seemed to understand that this was something that Agee needed to do.

Agee in 1969 was one of the key players—perhaps *the* key player—in the Mets miracle. He was an adventurous outfielder, not afraid to dive for a sinking line drive that might spell disaster if he didn't connect. In the late stages of 1969, he caught everything that went to center field, an endless string of circus catches wiping out rally after rally. With the bat he was good, not great.

He was never quite as good again; after Hodges died he put on weight, and his career fell apart. Would Agee have been a Hall of Famer, had he played up to the level of his best seasons throughout his career? Probably not. Agee's best seasons were 1966 (29 Win Shares) and 1969 (28 Win Shares). While those were wonderful seasons, they would not ordinarily be enough to put a player in the Hall of Fame, unless he was consistent at that level for twelve years or more. Agee was ninth in the MVP voting in 1966, sixth in 1969; a Hall of Famer should get closer than that to an MVP award. Agee probably did have Hall of Fame ability, but I don't think he ever got to the level of Hall of Fame performance, even in his brief snippets of glory.

By the Win Shares method, the best defensive outfielders whose careers were centered in the 1960s were:

1. Curt Flood
2. Tommie Agee
3. Willie Mays
4. Bill Virdon
5. Ken Berry

79 ◆ Cesar Tovar
(1965–1976, 1488 G, 46 435 .278)

Tovar is most famous for denying Carl Yastrzemski unanimous selection as the MVP in 1967, Yastrzemski's triple-crown season. Tovar in that season played 164 games (the second-highest total ever) despite having no regular position; he played 36 games at second base, 70 at third, 9 at shortstop and 74 in the outfield. He played all four positions fairly well, scored 98 runs, and convinced one Minnesota sportswriter that he was the best player in the league that season. This led to a brief controversy at the BBWAA annual meeting that December, when a resolution was introduced to censure the sportswriter who had voted for Tovar.

Cesar had better years later on, as a regular outfielder; he hit .300 in 1970, leading the league in doubles and triples, and hit .311 in 1971, collecting 204 hits.

80 ◆ Ron LeFlore
(1974–1982, 1099 G, 59 353 .288)

I'm not normally a one-looker, but as far as I was concerned he was the biggest chunk of raw talent I had ever seen.—Ed Katalinas, who signed Al Kaline and Ron LeFlore

I always could run pretty fast. I got a lot of practice running from the police, even when I was young. I liked to throw rocks at police cars, trying to break their windows.—Ron LeFlore, *Breakout*

On January 14, 1970, Ron LeFlore and his two buddies had blown all their money snorting heroin at a dope house. They were hanging around a pool room trying to figure out how to get some money, when LeFlore suggested they should pull a robbery. His friends were agreeable, so the three of them targeted a bar they knew which kept money around to cash payroll checks, got a gun, and held the place up. As they were leaving, however, somebody wrote down their license plate. By the time they had split up the money, they found themselves surrounded by police.

LeFlore was declared a menace to society, and sentenced to Jackson Prison, the toughest prison in Michigan. While incarcerated, he joined the prison baseball team, and became friendly with a veteran con named Jimmy Karalla, doing a long sentence for extortion. Karalla convinced him that he might have the ability to play major league baseball.

LeFlore wrote to Jim Campbell, General Manager of the Tigers, requesting a tryout when he was released. Campbell said no. Later on, however, Billy Martin was hired to manage the Tigers. Jimmy Karalla had a friend who knew Billy Martin (imagine that). Karalla bombarded the friend with rave reviews, and the friend passed some of this along. In May, 1973, the Tigers visited the Jackson prison as a public service activity, and, while there, Martin decided to work out the young man he had been hearing about.

LeFlore was in the major leagues not much more than a year later. Once he got his feet on the ground he was, for four years (1976–1979) a brilliant player. He was incredibly fast, he was strong, alert, and he was a natural hitter. He hadn't played baseball as a kid, and there were certain subtleties of the game that didn't come to him until he had been in the majors for several years. His arm wasn't great, and he would spotlight the weakness of his arm by constantly trying to make long throws.

LeFlore co-authored an autobiography, *Breakout,* and a made-for-TV movie was made about him, starring LeVar Burton. The movie sanitized him, of course. LeFlore did change when he went to prison. He spent three years

locked up, and he grew up some, and he realized that his habits were going to destroy him. He changed; he didn't become a saint. In many ways his roots were always with him. Once he began to slip, he was out of the majors pretty quickly.

81 ◆ Devon White
(1985–2000, 1815 G, 194 799 .263)
Perhaps the best defensive outfielder of the 1990s (until Andruw Jones came up), excellent baserunner, also had one or two years in which he hit enough to be genuinely helpful. Never did gain control of the strike zone.

82 ◆ Tony Gonzalez
(1960–1971, 1559 G, 103 615 .286)
Something I remember a friend of mine saying to me 35 years ago . . . perhaps the best way to describe Tony Gonzalez is that he is the exact opposite of Dick Stuart. Stuart is an infielder; Gonzalez is an outfielder. Stuart is a right-handed hitter; Gonzalez is a left-handed hitter. Stuart is a power hitter; Gonzalez is a singles hitter. Stuart leads the league in errors; Gonzalez hardly ever makes an error. Stuart talks to everything that moves in an endless effort to promote himself; Gonzalez says nothing to nobody. Stuart pulls everything; Gonzalez hits everything to center. Stuart does one thing exceptionally well and a lot of things absolutely as bad as you can do them; Gonzalez does everything fairly well, but doesn't do anything exceptionally well. Stuart is white; Gonzalez is black. Stuart is a middle-of-the order hitter; Gonzalez can hit at the top of the order or the bottom, but rarely in the middle. Stuart is overrated; Gonzalez is underrated.

Who would be more recent players that would fill these roles . . . .Bob Horner and Darryl Hamilton, maybe. Hamilton's a pretty good match for Gonzalez; nobody in modern baseball is really a match for Stuart.

83 ◆ Curt Welch

(1884–1893, 1107 G, 16 503 .263)

Welch broke for the plate—trying to steal home, the ball game, and the series for the Browns. No one will ever know if he would have been safe or out, because Clarkson's pitch sailed high... Whether Welch slid or scored standing up has been lost in the mists of time, but the play has forever been known as Curt Welch's "$15,000 Slide."—Jerry Lansche, *The Forgotten Championships*

Curt Welch's "$15,000 slide" is the most famous play of 19th century baseball. Recent writers have for some reason taken to questioning whether Welch actually slid across the plate. G. W. Axelson in his 1919 biography of Comiskey *(Commy)* quotes Comiskey about the play, and Comiskey clearly states that Welch slid.

> An uncouth and un-educated man, Curt Welch drank himself out of the major leagues at age 31 and into the grave by age 34. In the heyday of his career, however, he was perhaps the finest fielding centerfielder of the 19th century. —Robert L. Tiemann, *Nineteenth Century Stars*

84 ◆ Sammy West

(1927–1942, 1753 G, 75 838 .299)

A quiet, good-natured player, always smiling. Prone to minor injuries but exceptionally graceful, pretty good arm. Missed a lifetime .300 average by only four hits.

The highest range factors in history, compared to league norms:

1.	Richie Ashburn	3.02 vs. 2.31	+ .71
2.	Garry Maddox	2.94 vs. 2.28	+ .66
3.	Sammy West	3.03 vs. 2.40	+ .63
4.	Paul Blair	2.85 vs. 2.23	+ .62
5.	Johnny Mostil	2.99 vs. 2.39	+ .60
6.	Happy Felsch	2.79 vs. 2.19	+ .60
7.	Dwayne Murphy	3.03 vs. 2.45	+ .58
8.	Curt Flood	2.64 vs. 2.06	+ .58
9.	Tris Speaker	2.73 vs. 2.18	+ .55
10.	Sam Chapman	3.00 vs. 2.46	+ .54
11.	Mike Kreevich	2.97 vs. 2.43	+ .54

These are based on plays made (putouts plus assists) per nine estimated defensive innings. The lowest outfielders among the top 100 are listed in the Mike Tiernan comment (RF, #49). See also Dante Bichette (RF, #90).

85 ◆ Baby Doll Jacobson

(1915–1927, 1472 G, 83 819 .311)

According to James J. Skipper's *Baseball Nicknames,* Jacobson became "Baby Doll" Jacobson on April 15, 1912, while playing for Mobile in the Southern Association. It was the home opener, and a band was on hand to celebrate. When Jacobson hit a long home run, the band launched into a crowd-pleasing rendition of "Oh, You Beautiful Doll." The *Mobile Register* reported that the next day, and Bill Jacobson was "Baby Doll" Jacobson for the rest of his life.

The St. Louis outfield of Ken Williams, Jacobson and Jack Tobin is sometimes listed among the best outfields ever—inaccurately, in my opinion. They were all good players, but none of the three was a superstar. When you compare them to outfields led by Babe Ruth or Willie Mays or Ted Williams or Ty Cobb or Joe DiMaggio, they start out way behind because they don't have a player of that caliber.

86 ◆ Gorman Thomas

(1973–1986, 1435 G, 268 782 .225)

"I told him he was lazy," Dave Garcia once said about Gorman Thomas. "It didn't help."

"There was more resentment on the team than Gorman and the general public realized," added Sal Bando. "All the guys were out there doing wind sprints in spring training, and he's in the clubhouse with a sore leg." (*Nine Innings,* Dan Okrent).

Top ten players, career bases per hit:

1. Mark McGwire   2.18
2. Dave Kingman   2.03
3. Babe Ruth   2.02
4. Rob Deer   2.01
5. Gorman Thomas   1.99
6. Harmon Killebrew 1.99
7. Mike Schmidt   1.97
8. Ralph Kiner   1.97
9. Juan Gonzalez   1.96
10. Darryl Strawberry 1.96

Top ten center fielders, ratio of runs scored and RBI to hits:

1. Gorman Thomas	1,463/1,051	1.39–1
2. Hack Wilson	1,946/1,461	1.33–1
3. Eric Davis	1,755/1,321	1.33–1
4. Joe DiMaggio	2,927/2,214	1.32–1
5. Mickey Mantle	3,186/2,415	1.32–1
6. Larry Doby	1,930/1,515	1.27–1
7. Ken Griffey Jr	2,215/1,742	1.27–1
8. Hugh Duffy	2,854/2,282	1.25–1
9. Jimmy Wynn	2,069/1,665	1.24–1
10. Duke Snider	2,592/2,116	1.22–1

The lowest batting averages for outfielders listed among the top 100:

1. Gorman Thomas   .225
2. Dave Kingman   .236
3. Tom Tresh   .245
4. Tom Brunansky   .245
5. Greg Vaughn   .246
6. Dwayne Murphy   .246
7. Jim Landis   .247
8. Jimmy Wynn   .250
9. Paul Blair   .250
10. Tony Armas   .252

The highest-ranking of these players, by far, is Jimmy Wynn, who I regard as the tenth-best center fielder of all time. No one else on this list is ranked higher than 66th at his position. But Reggie Jackson, whose average was only .262, ranks even higher than Wynn.

Thomas also hit the fewest career triples (13) of any outfielder listed among the top 100, including players still active.

87 ◆ Dave Henderson
(1981–1999, 1538 G, 197 708 .258)
A big, friendly, gap-toothed guy, best remembered for his clutch hitting in the 1986, 1988 and 1989 playoffs and World Series.

Henderson played center field most of his career and did a decent job, although he didn't have either the speed or the arm of a top-flight center fielder. I remember in '81, when he first came to the majors, we had heard a lot about him because he had been a first round draft pick and had rung some bells in the minor leagues. The first game I ever saw him play there were three singles to center with a man on second, Henderson had to throw home. All three times his throw tailed up the third base line 15 to 30 feet.

And you know what? He never did fix it. To the end of his career, when Henderson had to throw home he'd put the throw up the third base line two times in three.

88 ◆ Jim Landis
(1957–1967, 1346 G, 93 467 .247)
> Exceptional on defense. Very fast. Has strong arm. No player better going from first to third on hit. Has home-run power, but lacks consistency. Tends to swing at bad *balls.—Sport Magazine*, August, 1963

Landis was rated at that time the second-best center fielder in the American League, behind Mantle.

> I'll tell you something else I've noticed. My men don't even round first when he's out there. —Casey Stengel, quoted in *Baseball Digest*, May, 1962

According to Richard Lindberg in *Who's On 3rd?*, Landis in 1964 had a month-long feud with the White Sox management when the Sox refused to pay him $50 for appearing on a television program. According to Lindberg, "Landis was a quiet family man but had the reputation of being a baseball 'red ass.'"

89 ◆ Jake Stenzel
(1890–1899, 766 G, 32 533 .339)

> The first time his new [Baltimore] teammates got on him for muffing a fly ball, "I got my Dutch up," [Stenzel] said. "But when I cooled down I came to the conclusion that I was not the best outfielder in the world and should not object to taking a lesson occasionally."–Burt Solomon, *Where They Ain't*

> Does anyone ever give ten minutes reflection to the influence this money grubbing fever will have on the future of the youngsters now coming up through the little leagues?–Jake Stenzel in *The Sporting News*, 1915.

The second quote is taken from an article by William E. Akin in the SABR publication *Baseball's First Stars*. By "little leagues" Stenzel probably meant what we now call minor leagues. Little League baseball was not organized at that time.

90 ◆ Tom Brown
(1882–1898, 1786 G, 64 736, .265)

Brown was born in England, but moved to California with his family as a child. In the winter of 1881–1882 John Montgomery Ward played an exhibition tour in California, made the acquaintance of Brown, and brought him east in the spring of 1882 to try out for the Providence team.

Brown failed to stick with Providence, but stayed in the east, and caught on with Baltimore in the American Association, which formed that spring. He was a left-handed leadoff man, very fast and alleged to be an outstanding outfielder, although my statistical analysis does not support this. He had a knockaround career, playing mostly for bad teams and teams on the verge of going out of business, but he did score 177 runs, one of the highest totals on record, in 1891.

91 ◆ Doc Cramer
(1929–1948, 2239 G, 37 842 .296)

The Doc Cramer all-stars:

C– Bob Boone
1B–Charlie Grimm
2B–Tony Taylor
3B–Aurelio Rodriguez
SS–Don Kessinger
LF–Jose Cardenal
CF–Doc Cramer
RF–Wally Moses

These are the weakest players ever to have 2,000-game careers, rated basically by Win Shares per game played, some subjective input. Cramer was the weakest of the outfielders; Aurelio Rodriguez, despite his great defense, was easily the worst major league player to have a 2,000-game career.

Cramer was a consistent .300 hitter, but was about as close to being an offensive zero as you can be if you hit .300; all he did was slap singles. He didn't walk, he was a 46% base stealer, and he once went six-hundred-and-some games without hitting a home run. He was one of the best defensive outfielders of his time.

> Affable and modest, he was popular with fans, players and umpires. Wasn't banished by a major-league umpire until May 1, 1946, that being seventeen years after he played his first game.–Ira Smith, *Baseball's Famous Outfielders*

Playing center field at Comiskey Park on August 3, 1945, Cramer was astonished to see a chicken running loose in center field. Cramer chased the chicken all over center for several minutes, finally caught it, and discovered a note attached saying "This chicken is a present for the pitcher who wins the game." Earl Caldwell pitched a shutout, and Cramer handed him the chicken as he left the mound.

The lowest park-adjusted career winning percentages for outfielders listed among the top 100:

1. Doc Cramer   .465
2. Tony Armas   .474
3. Jimmy Piersall   .476
4. Bill Virdon   .481
5. Paul Blair   .495
6. Tom Brunansky   .507
7. Devon White   .511
8. B. J. Surhoff   .512
9. Mike Kreevich   .514
10. Lloyd Moseby   .523

The highest-ranking of these players is Blair, #66 in center field.

92 ◆ Jimmy Piersall
(1950–1967, 1734 G, 104 591 .272)

When he played in Boston in the 1950s, Jimmy Piersall formed a friendship with John F. Kennedy. In the spring of 1960 Piersall, playing for Cleveland, was in constant hot water with manager Joe Gordon and GM Frank Lane. In the middle of this, he received a wire from JFK. "Dear Jimmy," it read. "Do you have any ideas that might be helpful in the Ohio campaign? Jack Kennedy."

"Dear Jack," responded Piersall in his own wire. "I'm having big troubles with Lane and Gordon. Please don't bother me with your little ones . . ."

His last year in Boston (1958) Piersall hit only .237. One time the Red Sox were playing the Yankees. The Yankee pitcher knocked down Jackie Jensen. Jensen popped up on the next pitch. The pitcher knocked down Frank

Malzone. Malzone grounded out on the next pitch.

"Yogi," said Piersall, "I want you to know something. If you knock me down, I'm going to get up and hit you across the head with this baseball bat. And remember, I'm the guy who can plead temporary insanity, and get by with it."

Yogi pondered this a minute.

"Jim," he said finally. "We haven't knocked down a .230 hitter all year."

93 ◆ Mike Kreevich
(1931–1945, 1241 G, 45 514 .283)

Kreevich was a magnificent outfielder, a kind of a Garry Maddox-type player. He was outstanding for the White Sox from 1936–38, but began to drink. His play slipped, and on December 9, 1941—two days after Pearl Harbor—he was traded to the Philadelphia A's, one of the worst teams in baseball. He tried hard to stop drinking, but he was a likeable, funny guy, and people were always asking him to come along. Al Simmons was a coach with the A's, and Simmons in particular took a liking to him. Not realizing what he was doing, Simmons encouraged Kreevich's drinking, which got so bad that by the end of the 1942 season the A's had to release him.

Kreevich was deferred from the draft because he had small children born before Pearl Harbor. Luke Sewell, managing the Browns, realized that he could pick up a good center fielder for nothing if he could get Kreevich to stop drinking. He got Kreevich to promise to stay sober, which probably wasn't too hard because an alcoholic will promise you that anytime you ask, but also set up a kind of sideline plan to keep Kreevich on track. He took the veterans on his team aside, quietly, and told them not to encourage Kreevich's drinking. He paid him a bonus to stay sober, enlisted the help of a friend who was active in A.A., and, because Kreevich was a good Catholic, scheduled him for regular counseling sessions with a priest. Kreevich had his last good season in 1944, helping the Browns to their only American League pennant.

94 ◆ Benny Kauff
(1912–1920, 859 G, 49 454 .311)

> Benny Kauff is an excellent type of the man who comes into baseball without mental training and who could never grasp the idea of trying to find his faults instead of trying to hide them. Benny had great natural ability. It was almost impossible, though, to get his mind off himself and on the team as a whole. Benny had no early advantages. He wanted to be a star, but he could not realize that a real star must rise with the team to be of value.—John McGraw, *My Thirty Years in Baseball*

> Benny Kauff, a brash young man from the Southeastern Ohio coal fields, was delighted to be a Giant and play for John McGraw. He intended, he said, to become the Ty Cobb of the National League . . . [he] descended on Marlin, Texas, with a trunkload of bats (fifty-two in all), a pocketful of money, and a hearty greeting for everybody.—Charles C. Alexander, *John McGraw*

Kauff was a small man, commonly referred to as "Little Benny." He was known, of course, as the Ty Cobb of the Federal League, a nickname which, by the way, the *real* Ty Cobb genuinely did not appreciate.

Kauff dominated the Federal League in 1914, hitting .370 with 75 stolen bases, 95 RBI for Indianapolis. That winter the Indianapolis franchise broke up, its assets being sold to other Federal League teams. Kauff was sold to Brooklyn, the Brooklyn Tip-Tops of the Federal League.

Kauff, however, signed instead with the New York Giants. McGraw always claimed that the National League had approved of the contract, but league President John K. Tener insisted that he hadn't. The National League, for some reason, decided they did not want their teams "raiding" the Federal League, and prohibited Kauff from playing for the Giants.

On Opening Day, 1915, however, Kauff took the field with the Giants, ready to play against the Boston Braves. The Braves refused to play the game under those circumstances, and pulled their team off the field. Home plate umpire Ernest Quigley then ruled the game forfeited to the Giants.

John McGraw and George Stallings, however, decided that, rather than send the opening-day crowd home angry, they would play an exhibition game. The Braves won the exhibition game, 13–6—and were astonished to discover, the next day, that the league was going to count it as a real game. John Tener ruled that a game was scheduled, a game was played, and there was no basis for a forfeit, so the game counted.

Kauff was ordered to return to the Federal League. He did, and won the batting title again. When the Federal League broke up that fall, McGraw purchased Kauff's contract from the defunct Brooklyn team.

McGraw was initially enthusiastic about Kauff, saying that he was "a player of the old school. He thinks and lives baseball. That's the way I did when I was a youngster . . . there aren't many players like that today."

Kauff's career in the National League was short, and he became a victim of unrealistic expectations. In fact, however, Kauff was a very good player in the National League. His batting average was .287, that in an era with very low averages, very few runs scored. In 1916, his first year with the Giants, he was the best player on the Giants, and the third- or fourth-best position player in the National League. In 1917 he was even better. In 1918 he played just as well, although he left for World War I in mid-season, and in 1919, although he didn't play as well as he had before the war, he was still a very fine player.

Kauff was kicked out of baseball after the 1920 season due to his alleged involvement in his brother's fraud and automobile theft ring. In May, 1921, Kauff was put on trial in the Bronx. John McGraw and other baseball figures appeared to testify to Kauff's good character, and he was acquitted.

Commissioner Landis, however, refused to allow Kauff to return to baseball, saying that "your mere presence in the line-up would inevitably burden patrons of the game with grave apprehension as to its integrity." Kauff sued Landis and baseball, twice, but without success. Kauff's banishment from baseball, wrote Fred Lieb was "one of the worst miscarriages of justice ever to come to my attention." Landis may have had more of a basis for his actions than is known to his critics and detractors. In any case Kauff died in 1961, having outlived the real Ty Cobb by four months.

95 ◆ Billy North
(1971–1981, 1169 G, 20 230 .261)

North was an underrated player. He couldn't throw the ball across a mini-van, and he took a lot of grief for that, plus he played in conditions which depressed batting averages so much that he couldn't hit .300. The A's won the World Series in 1972, 1973 and 1974 with only one regular who hit .300 (Joe Rudi, .305 in 1972). Under normal conditions North would have been a .310-.320 hitter in his good years. He had no power, but he hit singles and walked, stole as many as 75 bases in a season, and was a fine outfielder despite the arm. I have him rated as the sixth-best defensive outfielder of

the 1970s, behind Blair, Maddox, Otis, Geronimo and Tony Scott.

96 ◆ Bill Virdon
(1955–1968, 1583 G, 91 502 .267)

They don't come any better than center fielder Billy Virdon. He'd have guys hit him grounders and flies before every game. You could see the improvement. He made himself into a great outfielder.—Frank Thomas in *We Played the Game*

The big mistake that was made during my year there is that in mid-May we traded Bill Virdon to the Pirates for Bobby Del Greco, another center fielder. What a terrible deal. Virdon would hit over 100 points higher than Del Greco that year—and he was a great fielder, much better than Del Greco.—Hank Sauer, same source

Virdon was a great defensive outfielder; I have him as deserving of Gold Gloves in '56, '57, '58, '59 and '62, and as the fourth- or fifth-most valuable outfielder in the league in '60, '61 and '63. His first two years in the majors it looked like he would be an outstanding hitter as well, but he began having trouble with his vision, and went backward as a hitter.

97 ◆ Walt Judnich
(1940–1949, 790 G, 90 420 .281)

Pitcher Tex Shirley and teammate Walt Judnich got into a fight over a misplayed ball.—William Marshall, *Baseball's Pivotal Era* (1945–1951).

A big man, over 200 pounds, and often called "Wally" at the time he was active. Judnich came out of California (Bay area) about the same time as the DiMaggios, Doerr and Ted Williams. As a young outfielder he was in the Yankee system when the Yankees fourth outfielder was George Selkirk. As a mature player, he lost his prime seasons to World War II. When Joe DiMaggio held out in the spring of '38, the Yankees suggested that Judnich, trapped in the minors, was as good a center fielder as DiMaggio. He wasn't, of course, but he was a legitimate five-tool player, a left-handed hitter who could run, throw, catch, hit and hit for power. His career batting average, on base percentage and slugging percentage are about the same as those of Chili Davis, Wally Moon, Jackie Jensen and Carl Yastrzemski. Had an outstanding arm, led the league three times in fielding percentage, once in putouts.

98 ◆ Steve Brodie
(1890–1902, 1437 G, 25 900 .303)

John McGraw once listed the six most picturesque characters in major league history as Rube Waddell, Bugs Raymond, Ossee Schreckengost, Larry McLean, Babe Ruth and Steve Brodie. "But Brodie was unconsciously funny," McGraw explained. "He actually took baseball very seriously. It was his efforts to be serious and take everything in its full literal sense that made him so amusing to the rest of us on the ball club." Oriole manager Ned Hanlon once bawled out his players before a game for failing to "wait out" the pitchers, make the pitcher throw more pitches. "And that goes especially for you, Steve," he told Brodie. "There is no harm in having a strike called on you once in a while." Brodie went to the plate his first time up, and took three strikes. Returning to the dugout, he yelled at Hanlon, "Now, don't tell me I can't take 'em. And I could have knocked any one of them pitches out of the park." No sense of irony; he was just putting things together in his own way.

Another of McGraw's stories claimed that Brodie was on second base when Roger Bresnahan hit a drive over the center fielder's head. Brodie became so intent on watching Bresnahan try for a game-winning inside-the-park homer that he forgot to run; Bresnahan passed him near home plate, and they were both out. It was a few years before McGraw could laugh about that one.

99 ◆ Johnny Mostil
(1918–1929, 972 G, 23 3767 .301)

Johnny Mostil of the White Sox, and one of the greatest outfielders the game ever has known, managed to steal a lot of bases in the course of a year, and on speed alone. But he's the exception.—Babe Ruth, *Babe Ruth's Own Book of Baseball* (ghosted by Ford Frick).

Johnny Mostil, who was a great center fielder, one of the greatest. It was like turning a rabbit loose when the ball was hit to center field.—Ted Lyons in *Baseball When the Grass Was Real* (Donald Honig)

Speaker was a great outfielder and Johnny Mostil made some sensational catches out there, but Mays does everything better than any outfielder I've ever seen.—Johnny Ogden, quoted by Lee Allen in *The Sporting News*, November 16, 1963

At Fenway Park on August 21, 1926, Ted Lyons reported before the game that he felt nauseous. He walked the leadoff hitter and threw two bad balls to the second man up, prompting action in the White Sox bullpen. At that point, however, the batter drove the 2-0 pitch into center field. Johnny Mostil ran it down, doubled the runner off first—and Lyons recovered to pitch a no-hitter.

Mostil in 1925 and 1926 was a formidable leadoff man, hitting .299 and .328, scoring 135 and 120 runs, leading the league in stolen bases both seasons, leading the league in being hit with a pitch both seasons, also leading in walks and runs scored in 1925.

In Shreveport, Louisiana, in March, 1927, Mostil attempted suicide:

(Mostil) slashed both wrists and wounded himself in the chest, throat and legs with a razor blade and a knife. Early reports, giving him little chance to survive, were wrong . . . The only explanation for his act seems to have been his hypochondriacal nature.—Joseph Overfield, *Total Baseball* (Second Edition)

The popular Johnny Mostil attempted suicide . . . the outfielder was suffering from neuritis, an agonizing nerve condition that affected his jaw. After chatting with Red Faber, Mostil returned to his room and inflicted thirteen cuts to his wrist, neck and chest.—Richard Lindberg, *Who's On 3rd?*

Mostil recovered and played ball again, but never at anything approaching the spectacular level of his 1925–26 performance.

100 ◆ Amos Strunk
(1908–1924, 1509 G, 15 530 .284)

He is one of the fleetest fielders who ever skipped across the green or endeavored to beat the iron arm of an infielder as the latter threw the ball to first. Strunk was born in Philadelphia, and is a chubby-faced chap of 21, who tips the beam at 165 pounds. He is built like a panther, standing six feet in height, and without an ounce of superfluous flesh upon him. Strunk was the schoolboy sensation for several years, and gained the name of "Lightning" [as] he streaked to first and was the pet aversion of catchers when on the paths. In the 1910 season he started with the Athletics, as Connie believed he was ripe. On the Spring training trip Strunk was sent to second to help work out a plan of Connie's. The principal weakness of Harry Krause in the previous season was in keeping runners attached to the sacks. Strunk was sent to the sack and told to steal as often as possible. Krause, on the other hand, was stacked against the fastest man on the team. In skipping back to second to avoid being caught he wrenched his leg, and was out of the game throughout the greater part of the season, and when he seemed destined to create a sensation. —1911 *Reach Guide*

101. Jimmy Slagle, 102. Larry Hisle, 103. Al Bumbry, 104. Burt Shotton, 105. Stan Spence, 106. Solly Hofman, 107. Lance Johnson, 108. Mookie Wilson, 109. Johnny Bates, 110. Johnny Hopp, 111. Bug Holliday, 112. Lee Mazzilli, 113. Jerry Mumphrey, 114. Vince DiMaggio, 115. Fred Snodgrass, 116. Hi Myers, 117. Bobby Tolan, 118. Charlie Hemphill, 119. Ruppert Jones, 120. Brian McRae, 121. Taylor Douthit, 122. Johnny Frederick, 123. Rube Oldring, 124. Roberto Kelly, 125. Jimmy Hall

CENTER FIELD

Rank	Player Name	Career WS	Top 3	Top 5	Per 162
1.	Willie Mays	642	43, 41, 40	197	34.76
2.	Ty Cobb	722	48, 47, 45	213	38.55
3.	Mickey Mantle	565	51, 49, 48	216	38.12
4.	Tris Speaker	630	51, 45, 41	209	36.59
5.	Joe DiMaggio	387	41, 39, 34	175	36.11
6.	Duke Snider	352	39, 37,36,	171	26.60
7.	Ken Griffey Jr.	299	36, 31, 30	148	28.83
8.	Kirby Puckett	281	32, 31, 29	136	25.53
9.	Billy Hamilton	337	36, 33, 30	150	34.31
10.	Jimmy Wynn	305	36, 32, 32	141	25.73
11.	Larry Doby	268	34, 33, 30	152	28.32
12.	Dale Murphy	294	33, 32, 32	150	21.84
13.	Wally Berger	241	36, 33, 31	152	28.92

Rank	Player Name	Career WS	Top 3	Top 5	Per 162
14.	Earl Averill	280	33, 30, 30	143	27.17
15.	Edd Roush	314	33, 33, 30	136	25.86
16.	Richie Ashburn	329	29, 28, 28	137	24.34
17.	Fred Lynn	280	34, 33, 27	131	23.03
18.	Vada Pinson	321	32, 31, 27	137	21.06
19.	Hack Wilson	224	35, 32, 31	152	26.91
20.	Hugh Duffy	295	33, 29, 28	144	27.51
21.	Cesar Cedeno	296	33, 30, 30	140	23.88
22.	Amos Otis	286	29, 29, 27	125	23.18
23.	Max Carey	351	29, 29, 26	133	22.96
24.	Dom DiMaggio	220	28, 26, 26	124	25.47
25.	Brett Butler	295	27, 27, 26	124	21.59
26.	Jimmy Ryan	316	34, 28, 25	129	25.44
27.	Willie Davis	322	26, 26, 25	119	21.47
28.	George Van Haltren	344	30, 29, 26	121	28.08
29.	Roy Thomas	260	31, 30, 28	133	28.63
30.	Cy Seymour	272	42, 26, 25	137	28.83
31.	Al Oliver	305	26, 26, 23	114	20.86
32.	Andy Van Slyke	231	35, 28, 25	122	22.57
33.	Eric Davis	224	30, 27, 26	125	23.38
34.	Earle Combs	227	31, 28, 25	127	25.27
35.	Clyde Milan	266	33, 28, 27	130	21.75
36.	Curt Flood	221	27, 26, 25	120	20.35
37.	Bernie Williams	210	33, 27, 27	137	20.54
38.	Pete Browning	225	30, 28, 23	118	30.81
39.	Ginger Beaumont	229	31, 28, 28	127	25.35
40.	George Gore	250	30, 26, 24	111	30.91
41.	Kenny Lofton	191	25, 24, 23	114	25.09
42.	Rick Monday	258	26, 23, 22	105	21.04
43.	Willie McGee	224	36, 21, 20	102	16.48
44.	Lenny Dykstra	201	35, 32, 23	111	25.47
45.	Mike Griffin	245	30, 23, 23	109	26.26
46.	Pete Reiser	125	34, 28, 19	106	23.51
47.	Dummy Hoy	254	28, 28, 25	106	22.91
48.	Chet Lemon	265	26, 24, 24	109	21.59
49.	Ray Lankford	199	31, 27, 25	114	23.07
50.	Lloyd Waner	245	27, 26, 25	110	19.91
51.	Chick Stahl	211	32, 31, 24	110	26.21

(continued)

Rank	Player Name	Career WS	Top 3	Top 5	Per 162
52.	Mike Donlin	174	36, 31, 24	103	26.87
53.	Paul Hines	249	28, 22, 19	98	27.23
54.	Willie Wilson	237	31, 25, 23	109	17.82
55.	Ben Chapman	233	23, 22, 22	106	21.98
56.	Garry Maddox	203	26, 23, 21	103	18.80
57.	Andy Pafko	220	27, 25, 23	107	19.24
58.	Gus Bell	175	24, 22, 21	100	16.28
59.	Mickey Rivers	185	26, 22, 22	105	20.42
60.	Terry Moore	152	22, 20, 20	89	18.97
61.	Marius Grissom	192	30, 27, 24	116	19.67
62.	Dode Paskert	227	27, 24, 24	98	21.43
63.	Brady Anderson	204	29, 28, 26	109	19.80
64.	Bill Lange	139	29, 24, 21	114	27.76
65.	Sam Chapman	145	25, 24, 17	92	17.17
66.	Paul Blair	183	28, 24, 22	100	15.22
67.	Happy Felsch	123	30, 30, 24	109	26.60
68.	Matty Alou	179	27, 23, 23	112	17.39
69.	Dwayne Murphy	173	27, 24, 22	104	20.60
70.	Barney McCoskey	146	24, 23, 22	99	20.21
71.	Lloyd Moseby	177	26, 25, 22	111	18.05
72.	Jimmy Barrett	135	26, 26, 23	120	25.25
73.	Bill Bruton	190	24, 22, 19	89	19.11
74.	Steve Finley	207	28, 27, 24	106	19.84
75.	Cy Williams	235	24, 21, 19	96	19.01
76.	Jose Cardenal	212	26, 21, 20	95	17.02
77.	Ellis Burks	219	28, 24, 24	101	21.21
78.	Tommie Agee	139	28, 28, 23	104	19.94
79.	Cesar Tovar	178	28, 22, 22	111	19.37
80.	Ron LeFlore	139	26, 24, 23	112	20.48
81.	Devon White	195	24, 20, 19	86	17.40
82.	Tony Gonzalez	183	26, 26 20	92	19.01
83.	Curt Welch	165	26, 24, 22	106	24.14
84.	Sammy West	192	24, 19, 18	93	17.74
85.	Baby Doll Jacobson	178	25, 25, 23	108	19.58
86.	Gorman Thomas	152	26, 25, 21	111	17.15
87.	Dave Henderson	160	26, 25, 20	94	16.85
88.	Jim Landis	151	25, 23, 22	106	18.17
89.	Jake Stenzel	126	28, 24, 24	111	26.64
90.	Tom Brown	218	31, 20, 19	90	19.77

Rank	Player Name	Career WS	Top 3	Top 5	Per 162
91.	Doc Cramer	219	19, 18, 17	79	15.84
92.	Jimmy Piersall	162	21, 20, 19	82	15.13
93.	Mike Kreevich	146	23, 22, 16	92	19.05
94.	Benny Kauff	175	38, 34, 30	144	33.00
95.	Billy North	143	25, 22, 21	92	19.81
96.	Bill Virdon	157	21, 20, 16	82	16.06
97.	Walt Judnich	101	25, 20, 18	93	20.71
98.	Steve Brodie	170	20, 19, 19	86	19.16
99.	Johnny Mostil	128	28, 23, 20	103	21.33
100.	Amos Strunk	174	23, 21, 20	97	18.70

Categories of this record are Career Win Shares, Win Shares in the player's three best seasons, Win Shares total over the player's five best consecutive seasons, and career Win Shares per 162 games played. For example, Willie Mays had 642 Career Win Shares, including 43, 41, and 40 in his three best seasons (1965, 1962, and either 1953 or 1954). He had 197 Win Shares in a five-year period, (1962–1966) and averaged 34.76 Win Shares per 162 games played over the course of his career.

RIGHT FIELD

1 ◆ Babe Ruth

(1914–1935, 2503 G, 714 2213 .342)

In 1983 a traveling Hillerich and Bradsby exhibit featured a Babe Ruth bat. According to Dan Gutman in *It Ain't Cheatin' If You Don't Get Caught,* the Seattle players were admiring the bat "when outfielder Dave Henderson noticed that the round end of the bat didn't exactly match the wood of the barrel. The end was cracked, but the rest of the bat was not.

"'That's a plug!' said Henderson. 'This bat is corked.'"

As I pointed out in the Ken Williams comment, Ruth was caught using an trick bat in a game in August, 1923 (see Ken Williams, LF #50). As I see it, nothing could be more typical of Ruth than to use a corked bat if he could get by with it. Ruth tested the limits of the rules constantly; this was what made him who he was. He refused to be ordinary; he refused to accept that the rules applied to him, until it was clear that they did. Constantly testing the limits of the rules, as I see him, was Babe Ruth's defining characteristic . . .

Is there any such thing as a hitter so good that it would make sense simply to walk him

every time he came to the plate? If there was such a hitter, of course, it would have to be Babe Ruth.

To test this, I established on a computer a lineup with Babe Ruth hitting cleanup in the middle of what is otherwise a worse-than-realistic offense. The team was:

1. Willie Wilson in a bad year, CF
2. Al Weis, 2B
3. Gerald Perry, 1B
4. Babe Ruth, 1921, RF
5. Gino Cimoli, LF
6. Don Wert, 3B
7. Jamie Quirk, C
8. Angel Salazar, SS
9. Sandy Koufax, P (as a hitter only)

To make the distance between Ruth and the other hitters on the team even greater, I modified Ruth's 1921 season slightly, taking away ten outs; instead of going 204 for 540 (.378), I changed him to 204 for 530 (.385), thus increasing his slugging percentage from .846 to .862.

I then ran the team through 1,000 simulated seasons, twice. In one simulation, I instructed the computer to simply walk Ruth every time he came to the plate. In the other run, I allowed the computer to pitch to Ruth (except walking him in those situations in which one normally would).

Conclusion? It's not even close. Walking Ruth every time up does far, far more harm than good, even under these impossibly extreme conditions. The team for which Ruth hit .385 with 61 homers a year scored 601 runs per season, and finished with a winning percentage of .326. The team for which Ruth was walked every time up scored 667 runs per season, and finished with a winning percentage of .380. As great as Ruth was, as terrible as his teammates were, he was still nowhere near the point at which it made sense to simply walk him every time he came to the plate.

Why is this true? Let's assume Ruth come to the plate 726 times per season, which he did in this simulation (when he was being walked). If you pitch to Ruth 726 times, he'll get 210 hits good for 532 Total Bases per season, plus he'll walk 148 times. That's 680 bases, a huge number, and Ruth will account for those bases while making only about 330 outs—a phenomenal bases/outs ratio.

But if you just walk him every time, what do you have then? 726 bases, and zero outs. That's far worse.

If you walk Ruth every time, Gino Cimoli, hitting fifth, drives in 151 runs per year—.267 with 9 homers, 151 RBI. A real hitter would drive in more than 200. It's not worth it; it's not close. There is no such thing as a hitter so good that he should be routinely walked.

2 ◆ Henry Aaron
(1954–1976, 3298 G, 755 2297 .305)
The Boston Braves scouted Willie Mays for years, and at one point thought they had him signed, only to lose him to the Giants. The Giants scouted Aaron for a year, and at one point thought they had acquired him, only to lose him to the Braves.

Throughout his youth, Henry Aaron batted cross-handed, with his left hand on top. He continued to do this while he was in the Negro Leagues, even when he was being scouted by the majors. Dewey Griggs, scouting Aaron for the Braves, told him the major leaguers would look down on the cross-handed grip, and persuaded him to do it "right." Aaron switched, but even when he was in the majors he would occasionally look down at his hands and realize that he had the wrong hand on top.

You know what interests me about that? Aaron was always known for his remarkable wrists. Doesn't it seem at least possible that Aaron developed those amazing wrists *because* he was hitting wrong for all those years? I always notice this: when you have a player who is doing something *different* from everybody else, and that player is exceptionally successful, doesn't it seem like orthodoxy should adapt to that? Ernie Lombardi was the only player in history or one of very few who hit with his fingers interlaced on the bat—and Ernie Lombardi also had phenomenal bat control. Doesn't it seem like other people *should* have tried it, just to see if maybe it would help? If Henry Aaron grew up doing it that way, how wrong can it be?

3 ◆ Frank Robinson
(1956–1976, 2808 G, 586 1812 .294)
> He plays the game the way the great ones played it—out of pure hate.—Jim Murray

> He was a super guy who didn't give anybody any trouble. He got along well with the sportswriters. What could they write bad about him? He was an outstanding player.—Art Fowler

> There were several black players on the Reds [but] only Frank Robinson emerged as a leader. He was a quiet guy, but he was definitely a leader because everyone admired him.—Johnny

Klippstein. (Klippstein and Fowler quotes are from *We Played the Game,* Danny Peary)

I thought that Frank was a terrible example for a young team off the diamond because of his social behavior. He could be very crude. There was a lot of drinking on that team, period, and Frank did nothing to help the situation.—Joe Tait in *The Curse of Rocky Colavito* (Terry Pluto)

[Bill] Russell was a year and a half in front of me at McClymonds but I did play part of one season on the basketball varsity with him. He was a big, awkward six-seven then, but already a very tough defensive player.—Frank Robinson in *My Life is Baseball*

4 ◆ Mel Ott

(1926–1947, 2734 G, 511 1861 .304)

In the first edition of this book, I wrote that "Ott was the one player among the all-time great home run hitters whose totals were seriously inflated by the park that he was playing in, hitting 323 home runs in New York and only 188 in other parks." In the 20th edition of *The Baseball Research Journal* (SABR), Fred Stein responded with an article, "No Cheap Homers for Ott."

The title of Stein's article is of course absurd; Ott hit more cheap home runs than anyone else in the history of baseball, almost beyond any question. Stein broke off part of Ott's career, and then argued that "however, during Ott's prime years, 1928–38, only 58 percent were hit at the Polo Grounds." In response to this: (a) 58% of your home runs in your home park is still one of the highest percentages on record, and (b) Ott's career percentage isn't 58%; it's 63%.

Having said that, Stein does have a good point. According to Stein, "over his career, [Ott] batted fourteen points higher on the road than at home and hit significantly more singles, doubles and triples away from home." I can't confirm that that's true, but I assume it is, and

it makes an important point. The Polo Grounds weren't a great *hitter's* park. The Polo Grounds was (were?) a great *home run* park, but the hitting characteristics of the park in other respects were pitcher-friendly. Ott, had he played in another park, would have 100 fewer home runs, but his overall stats would have been as good or perhaps better than they are. He is not an overrated player . . .

Since the Baseball Writers officially launched their MVP Award in 1931, Mel Ott is the best player who never won the Award. I credit Ott with 525 career Win Shares, making him easily the best player to have struck out in MVP voting:

1.	Mel Ott	525
2.	Eddie Mathews	447
3.	Al Kaline	442
4.	Eddie Murray	433
5.	Dave Winfield	414
6.	Paul Molitor	412
7.	Warren Spahn	411
8.	Wade Boggs	394
9.	Tom Seaver	391
10.	Tony Gwynn	389

Gwynn is still active at this writing, and probably will move up a couple of notches on the list. Mark McGwire is also eligible, and may appear on the list in a year or two.

Not only did Ott not win an Award, he never came really close; his best vote was in 1942, when he finished a distant third. He was fourth in the voting once, fifth once.

Ott's career was underway before the BBWAA Awards begin, and 84 of his career Win Shares were earned in the seasons 1926–1930. If you took those away from him, he would drop to third on the list—and it is quite possible that he might have won the Award in 1929, had the Award been given.

Did Ott actually deserve any MVP Awards? He probably did, yes; I'm a long way from the underlying events, and statistics inevitably leave some things out, but Ott had many years when he *could* have won the Award, and at least one–1938–when he probably should have won it. Ott in 1938 scored 116 runs, drove in 116 runs, and played 118 games at third base, as Bill Terry was unable to find a third baseman he was happy with. Ott, although not a natural third baseman, had an excellent fielding percentage at third, and, according to all accounts, battled the position at least to a draw.

But the Giants, who had won the pennant the previous two years, slipped to third place, and the BBWAA almost never chooses a player from a team which has had a disappointing season. Ott was also equal in value, in my opinion, to Dizzy Dean in 1934 (although nobody was going to take an MVP Award away from Dizzy in that season) and to Carl Hubbell in 1936.

I note that almost all of the best players who never won an MVP Award were well-liked by the press. Ott certainly was, as were Kaline, Molitor, Spahn, Seaver, and Gwynn. Mathews was stern and rather serious, but certainly not disliked.

5 ◆ Pete Rose

(1963–1986, 3562 G, 160 1314 .303)
I don't know if this is helpful to anyone but me, but this is how I have to think about these things to do anything other than just spin my wheels . . .

The crimes of a athlete/gambler can be arranged into a kind of hierarchy of grief, which would go something like this:

Level 1: Associating casually with known (illegal) gamblers.
Level 2: Associating more intimately or having business dealings with known gamblers.
Level 3: Placing small wagers with bookies on other sports, or making casual wagers with friends about baseball.

Level 4: Placing large wagers with bookies on other sports, or allowing oneself to get heavily into debt to a bookie.
Level 5. Making substantial wagers about baseball with acquaintances, or placing small bets on baseball with a bookie.
Level 6: Placing large bets on baseball with a bookie.
Level 7: Being complicit in the fixing of a game or other outcome, or betting against one's own team.
Level 8: Actually assisting in fixing a game or other outcome.
Level 9: Being complicit in the fixing of a championship.
Level 10: Actually participating in the fixing of a championship.

You might look that over and decide if there is some other way you would string things out, but that looks about right to me. Organized baseball discourages steps one and two and punishes everything beyond that.

With respect to Joe Jackson, the issue about which baseball historians argue is whether his culpability reached to Level 10, or whether it is more accurately pegged at Level 9. With respect to Pete Rose, the issue which is endlessly debated is whether his march into degradation had stopped at Level 4, or whether he had gone on to Level 5 or 6.

I might suggest that this may not be the most interesting element of the Pete Rose story. This is where the story has hung up, because there is information missing; in essence, there is a bridge out of the Pete Rose story at that point, and there's a huge traffic jam on both sides of the bridge–not because anybody *wants* to be there, but just because there's no way to move on.

Because of an article I wrote about Pete Rose ten years ago, I am often confronted by people who want to debate me about Pete Rose' guilt or innocence (meaning whether he did or did not bet on baseball). I don't like to be drawn into this debate, for two reasons:

1. I don't know, and
2. You don't know, either.

Major league baseball, through the Dowd report and ever since, has insisted that there is irrefutable evidence that Rose bet on baseball. That issue, I am willing to debate: that there is irrefutable evidence that Pete Rose bet on baseball. I would characterize the evidence that Rose bet on baseball as ... well, not quite nonexistent. It is extremely weak.

In order to understand the evidence against Rose, you first have to understand the nature of the dispute which led to the Rose investigation. Pete Rose, in the mid-1980s, had:

1. Become addicted to gambling, and
2. Largely lost his moral compass.

Rose had entangled his life with a number of shady characters, of whom we will mention only one: Paul Janszen. Janszen and other people squatting near the margins of outright crime were living or virtually living in Rose's house, and were involved with him in a pattern of heavy gambling on football, NCAA basketball, and other sports, involving tens of thousands of dollars per week.

Rose had, for years, used other people to place bets for him. In early 1987 (just a few months after Janszen and Rose had first met), Janszen took over the business of running Rose's bets, due to a dispute between Rose and another lowlife. Janszen placed bets for Rose on other sports, and Janszen also placed bets, by the same manner, on baseball. Janszen told the bookies at that time, as he would tell investigators later on, that he was also placing these bets on behalf of Pete Rose.

Rose insists that the bets Janszen placed on baseball were not his bets, that Janszen placed these bets on his own. Janszen was also a compulsive gambler, and, since Rose's bookies might have been reluctant to accept large bets from Paul Janszen himself, Rose's story—that Janszen used his name to cover Janszen's bets—is reasonable.

That dispute, whether these were Pete Rose's bets or Paul Janszen's, is the crux of the did-Pete-Rose-bet-on-baseball argument. The entire basis of the allegation that Pete Rose bet on baseball is these bets, the Paul Janszen bets, all of which were made in the early part of the 1987 baseball season.

Rose, Janszen, and several other people were living in a cesspool of dirty money. Rose would do card shows for cash, which was not reported or was heroically under-reported to the IRS. Rose and his compatriots made bets in cash (usually), were paid off in cash, and kept everything they could off the books. Janszen, a body builder, was also selling steroids, illegally, and other members of the charmed circle were dealing other drugs. Rose's associates also sold sports memorabilia connected to Rose, including one of his World Series rings. There was a lot of money floating around, all of it beyond the reach of conventional accounting, among a group of people who were not notably honest.

The outcome of that was predictable. Early in 1987 a certain amount of money disappeared from the pool; suddenly there wasn't enough money floating around to keep everybody fat and happy. Some bookies weren't paid, and they got pretty unhappy about it. The bookies began to squeeze Rose and his associates, who then began to bicker among themselves about who owed money to whom, and for what ... I was supposed to get so much money for doing that card show, I only got this much ... I gave you all I got ... I don't owe you, you owe me ... that wasn't your bet, that was my bet ... I gave you 20 autographed bats to sell; that's worth $2,000 ... those bats weren't worth $100 ... I thought you promised to pay for that party...well, I paid for the room, etc. This developed into serious, and ugly, ugly, disputes.

Janszen and Rose became mortal enemies. The two men had known each other less than a year, they had become the best of friends, and now that friendship soured into a furious hatred.

Janszen determined to destroy Pete Rose's life. He would destroy Pete Rose, he decided, by revealing Pete's secret life of gambling and deception. And he did. Rose *did* have a secret life of gambling and deception, Janszen did reveal that, and it did destroy Rose's life, or at least his career.

I hope that no one thinks that I am trying to suggest that Pete Rose was innocent. There wasn't anything very innocent about him. It is fairly evident, I think, that Rose had to be banned from baseball, for some period of time, for the things that he was clearly doing. But it does not follow that everything that Paul Janszen says is true. Janszen said that Rose was betting heavily on other sports; that was true, and Rose admits that it was true. Janszen said that Rose was cheating on his taxes at a massive level; that was true, and Rose was eventually forced to admit that in court.

And Janszen said that the bets he placed on baseball in early 1987 were placed on Pete Rose's behalf. Rose vigorously denies this. Well, then, what evidence is there that these were Rose's bets, rather than Janszen's?

John Dowd, who investigated the case for the commissioner's office, cites a wide range of evidence to support Janszen's claim that these were Pete Rose's bets. The things that he cites include:

1. Supporting statements from a dozen or so other people who were members of the Pete Rose gambling milieu.

2. Tape recordings of conversations between Janszen and other members of the gambling circle.

3. Bank records (cashed checks, etc.) showing that Rose paid money to bookies.

4. Phone records, and

5. The so-called "betting slips," with Pete Rose' fingerprints and perhaps in Pete Rose' handwriting.

But none of these things is very persuasive. Dowd cites a dozen or so people who support Janszen's claim that these are Pete Rose's bets. The problem is that most of these people are not in any position to know. At least two of the people that Dowd lists as confirming Janszen's claim have acknowledged that they never actually *met* Pete Rose. Two of the people that Dowd lists as supporting the claim that Rose bet on baseball acknowledged in secretly taped phone calls that they didn't really know whose bets these were, and another one insists that Rose never bet on baseball.

At least one bookie has come forward, sort of, to support Janszen's story. But what he really says, if you read it carefully, is that *Janszen told him* that these were Pete Rose's bets, and he believed it.

There are only three people cited by Dowd, that I can see, who

1. Claim that these are Pete Rose's bets.

2. Are actually in a position to know.

Those three people are Janszen, his girlfriend, and the guy who was placing Rose's bets before Janszen was honored with that responsibility. The other guy, the Third Man, hasn't given clear, consistent statements; sometimes he suggests that Pete Rose was betting on baseball, sometimes he insists that he wasn't, sometimes he says he doesn't know. Mostly he just says "Leave me alone."

Janszen and his girlfriend both insist that these were Pete Rose's bets, and both took lie detector tests to prove it. And both failed. When Janszen failed his lie detector test John Dowd arranged for him to be re-tested by a more sympathetic polygraph artist, and Janszen got by the second test. When his girlfriend bombed her test, Dowd just wrote her off as a lost cause, and failed to mention in the Dowd Report that she had ever taken the test.

So all of that, to me, is just piles of hot BS; I don't regard *any* of it as meaningful evidence that Rose bet on baseball, other than the claims of Paul Janszen, who has an axe to grind.

The tape recordings have the same problem. Pete Rose's voice never appears on any of the tape recordings which are used to "prove" that he bet on baseball, so obviously he didn't make any incriminating statements. No one else appearing on the tapes, other than Janszen, has any direct knowledge about whether these are Rose's bets or Janszen's. The tape recordings are recordings of conversations between Janszen, who is co-operating with the prosecutors, and other people, bookies and gambling associates. What essentially transpires on these tapes is that Janszen says, "These are Pete Rose's bets. You know that, don't you?" and the other guy says, "Yeah, if you say so." Janszen talks to a bookie, and what the bookie *actually* says, as I read it, is "I don't care if these were Rose's bets or yours. Pete Rose told me that you were placing bets on his behalf. That makes them his bets as far as I'm concerned. Baseball, football, hockey, what do I care . . . you were Pete Rose's guy, and he's responsible for you."

Dowd presents for our inspection bank records, checks that Rose wrote to bookies or to intermediaries. But the great majority of the checks that Dowd shows us were written in *football* season, or in March. There is, for example, one large check ($34,000) that was written the day the NCAA basketball tournament started, which Rose says was written to bring him up to even so that he could bet on the tourney. Janszen insists that the check was in some mysterious way connected to baseball, and Dowd, flying in the face of logic, believes Janszen. The checks connect Rose to betting; the checks connect Pete Rose to book-

ies. The checks do not connect Pete Rose to betting *on baseball*.

There are phone records, phone records which show frequent phone calls between Rose and Janszen. But the phone records, taken as a whole, tend to suggest that these were Paul Janszen's bets, more than they suggest that these were Pete Rose's bets. The phone records show Paul Janszen making incessant phone calls to the sports line, as if he were anxious about the outcome of games. To whatever extent phone calls to the sports line may be considered evidence, they're better evidence against Janszen than Rose.

That leaves, then, the "betting slips," or the alleged betting slips, which are the best evidence against Pete Rose, other than the word of a couple of ne'er-do-wells.

Let me back off from that a moment, and explain what I would see, in a case like this, as being good evidence that Pete Rose placed bets on baseball. What I would like to see, as a starting point, is a specific allegation against him: that is, that on a specific day, Pete Rose bet a specific amount of money on a specific baseball team, with a specific bookie or other person, that this bet was placed in a specific manner (that is, through a named intermediary, by phone, or whatever) and that the result of this bet was win or a loss, and that this money was paid off at some specific time.

This set of specifics should then be pinned down with *some* documentation. The specifics which are missing in the allegations against Pete Rose are . . . well, all of them; the Dowd report contains no allegation of any specific bet, on any specific date, for any specific amount of money. The Dowd report makes damning charges, and drags in eight volumes of supporting information, all of which is supposed to somehow prove that *something* in the charges must be true. The Dowd report doesn't really tie Rose into betting on baseball; it just buries him in rope, and argues that there must be a knot in there somewhere.

On a web site devoted to this issue, I am told, there appears the following note:

> What about what Bill James wrote about the case? He said that the betting slips couldn't be authentic, and that the case was based on rumor, hearsay, and gossip.
>
> In his 1990 book, James assailed the Dowd report. One point of contention was that the gambling slips showed three baseball games that did not take place on the same day. James was mistaken.
>
> In fact, the three games listed on the betting sheet were all played on April 8, 1987.

First, it has never been my position that the betting slips couldn't be authentic. In fact, they *could* be authentic; I just don't think there is sufficient evidence to conclude that they *are*.

As to the dispute about the schedule, my point was 100% correct, and this gentleman is 67% in error. In fact, only one of the three listed games was played on April 8, 1987. One of the games listed was "Philly at Atl." Philadelphia did not play at Atlanta on April 8, 1987. They played on the seventh and on the ninth; they did not play on the eighth. Also, the "betting slips" show a game as "Cin at Mont." Cincinnati did not play at Montreal on April 8, 1987, either. Montreal played at Cincinnati on April 8, 1987. This would be a curious mistake to make if you were the Cincinnati Reds manager. It is a disputed point whether or not Pete Rose actually wrote this note. A fan, a gambler, might easily forget whether a Cincinnati/Montreal game was in Cincinnati or Montreal. As Rose said in *Playboy* (May, 2000), "You think I'd bet on a game and I don't know who the [bleeping] home team is?"

All of that is trivia . . . Cincinnati at Montreal, Montreal at Cincinnati, Philly and Atlanta on the seventh, the eighth, the ninth . . . what difference does it make? Very little.

At the time, Dowd was referring to this as "Pete Rose's betting notebook." At some point,

it occurred to people that calling three sheets of paper a "betting notebook" was kind of grandiose, and the notes became known as "the betting slips." This ominous sounding reference, "the betting slips" has become the chief bulwark of the case against Pete Rose, as it is understood by the average baseball fan. (They found Pete Rose's betting slips . . . they found his betting slips? . . . in his own hand-writing . . . In his own hand-writing? . . . with his fingerprints on them . . . ooh. They found Pete Rose's betting slips in his own handwriting, with his fingerprints all over them. Wow, that's pretty convincing, you can't deny that.")

The "betting slips" *are* the best supporting evidence that Pete Rose was betting on baseball. And there are as many problems with those "betting slips" as you want to take the time to list. To name just a few:

1. The betting slip doesn't match any particular day of the 1987 baseball schedule, or any other season.

2. The notes are, on the surface of them, not even remotely incriminating. If a note said "Philly at Atl., $2000 on Philly," that would be incriminating. All the notes say is "Philly at Atl., L," etc . . . a few lines like that. Why wouldn't we expect a major league manager to have comments about major league baseball games in his possession?

3. The betting slips are not tied to any specific allegation.

4. No one can give any coherent explanation of what exact role these "betting slips" played in any bet.

5. I have never before heard the term "betting slip" used to describe something which would be in the bettor's handwriting, or would normally have his fingerprints on it. The term "betting slip" was a term which was normally used to describe a *bookie's* betting record, in the bookie's handwriting, recovered by police after a raid on the bookie's apartment. With the advent of personal computers, the term is archaic,

but in any case, why would a "betting slip" be in Pete Rose's handwriting, or have his fingerprints on it?

6. Rose's friends have, at times, claimed that the document is a forgery.

7. The entire document is almost too small to determine whether it is a forgery.

I doubt that the document is a forgery, at least in the whole, because I can't imagine that a person forging evidence against Pete Rose would choose to forge something so vague and innocuous. It could be a forgery in part (that is, something could have been added to a document in an attempt to link it to gambling).

But if it is a legitimate document, the question I would ask is, what exact role did it play in Rose's wagering? It wasn't given to a bookie, was it? Obviously it wasn't. Was this a list made *before* bets were made, or after? Is it a note from Rose to himself, or to someone else? Who placed these bets and with what bookie, since the Dowd reports specifically says that Janszen did not begin placing baseball bets until mid-May, and that Rose had broken up with his previous runner/lackey in January or February? If it's a bookkeeping record, why aren't there any dollar amounts? Why does it stop after one or two days of baseball games?

How do we know that this is a "betting slip"? The FBI insists that these are betting slips? The FBI would insist that they were bomb blueprints if Pete Rose were accused of being the Unabomber. At that time the FBI crime lab was a prosecution factory, which would say whatever a prosecutor told them they were supposed to say. If somebody says this is a betting slip, how do they know?

I'm not saying that this is nothing. I'm saying it is almost nothing. It's vague, it's superficially innocuous, and it bears no known relationship to any specific allegation, other than that Pete Rose bet on baseball and that this is evidence of it.

I'm outnumbered on this, a hundred to one. Almost everybody I talk to about this will admit, after a minute or two, that they really have no idea what the evidence is that Pete Rose bet on baseball. But, they will all say quickly, nonetheless I believe he did, because . . . and then will follow their personal interpretation, their personal twist on why they believe that Pete Rose bet on baseball, even though they don't really have the foggiest notion of what the evidence is. The amazing thing about this is that everybody has one, and everybody's is a little bit different . . . he must be guilty, or he wouldn't have signed the agreement; he must be guilty, or he would have sued; or he must be guilty, because he was a compulsive gambler, and a compulsive gambler would bet on anything; or he must be guilty, because major league baseball would re-admit him to get the issue off their agenda if there was any way they could.

There is, I would suggest, a better way to think about it. Pete Rose is innocent unless there is proof that he is guilty. I've looked at the evidence as closely as I can. The closer you look, the less you see.

6 ◆ Tony Gwynn
(1982–2000, 2369 G, 134 1131 .338)
The Tony Gwynn All-Star team:

C–	Ivan Rodriguez
1B–	Frank Thomas
2B–	Craig Biggio
3B–	Edgar Martinez
SS–	Cal Ripken, Jr.
LF–	Ray Lankford
CF–	Bernie Williams
RF–	Tony Gwynn
RHP–	John Smoltz
LHP–	Tom Glavine

The best active players who are still with their first major league team. Also worthy of note: Jeff Bagwell, and Barry Larkin.

Year	G	AB	R	H	2B	3B	HR	RBI	BB	SO	SB	Avg
1973	151	566	127	185	33	2	37	150	89	111	26	.327
1974	148	556	116	175	30	1	35	119	103	105	30	.315
1975	157	615	114	172	45	3	41	130	77	130	19	.280

7 ◆ Reggie Jackson

(1967–1987, 2820 G, 563 1702 .262)

Not really. I had one. I unwrapped it and it told me how good it was.—Catfish Hunter, asked if he had tried a Reggie Bar

I was shocked. I always thought it would be Reggie.—anonymous ex-teammate, asked how he felt on hearing of the charges against O. J. Simpson

The best thing about being a Yankee is getting to see Reggie Jackson play every day.1p4

The worst thing about being a Yankee is having to see Reggie Jackson play every day.—Graig Nettles

Reggie Jackson's 1973–1975 seasons, translated to a 1990s context and to a run-neutral park is shown in the chart at the top of the page.

8 ◆ Roberto Clemente

(1955–1972, 2433 G, 240 1305 .317)

I've been asked if I ever saw anyone better than Willie Mays. The answer is, yes. Roberto Clemente was *much* better than Willie Mays.—Maury Wills, *On the Run*

In the comment on Darrell Evans, I listed the factors which can tend to make a player overrated or underrated. One thing that I didn't discuss there is that defensive excellence, because it has no clear statistical parameters, can at times be exaggerated.

An easy example of this is the impact of a right fielder's throwing arm in preventing runners from going from first to third. Years ago, in rating major league right fielders, I rated Reggie Jackson number one. I received a letter from a reader, who argued that Reggie's home runs were "insignificant compared to his hundreds of strikeouts and the hundreds of times a year that he allows a runner to go from first to third." A *Coors* commercial featuring Willie Mays ran on TV as I was writing this, claiming that Mays "threw out hundreds of runners at home plate."

I am discussing this here, of course, because Clemente had a fantastic throwing arm, and, combining his arm with his quickness, was probably the most successful right fielder ever at preventing runners from going from first to third. But what was that really worth?

Well, it ain't hundreds of bases a year. An average major league team allows about 1000 singles per season; the figure was a little lower in Clemente's time. Of those 1000 singles, about 100 are infield singles. Of the remaining 900, about 270 go to left field, about 360 to center, and about 270 to right field. The right fielder on a typical team fields somewhere around 270 singles per season, if he plays every game. But many of those singles—most of them, in fact—do not occur with runners on first base. Of the 270 singles that a typical full-time right fielder fields in a season, only about 100 will occur with a man on first base.

A hundred bases a year would still be a lot, if the right fielder could stop a hundred men from going from first to third. But, of course, there are four other factors in the play, besides the throwing arm:

1. The speed of the runner.
2. What kind of a break the runner gets.
3. How hard the ball is hit.
4. Where the ball is hit.

Single to right, Charles Johnson on first, he's not going to third no matter who the right fielder is.

Runner on first not moving, line drive single right at the right fielder, he's not going to third no matter who is in right.

Shallow pop up over the second baseman, runner has to hold on to see whether the second baseman can get there, he's not going to third no matter who is in right.

Hit and run play, ball grounded through the hole at second, that runner is going to third no matter who the right fielder is.

Fast runner on first, single driven over the first baseman's head, that man's going to third no matter what the right fielder does.

Sometimes it matters who the right fielder is, but more often it doesn't. STATS has kept track of advances on balls hit to various outfielders for about ten years now. The best right fielders will allow about 35% of opposing runners to go from first to third on a single. Clemente, we might guess, may have been better than that. The worst will allow about 60%, actually not quite 60%. The difference is about 25 bases per season.

Twenty-five bases per season—six/seven runs per season—is not insignificant, and there are other plays on which a right fielder's arm is a factor, although those plays are less common. Still, the right fielder's throwing arm is *not* equal to 20 homers a year, or anything like that. It might be half that, if you're talking about the difference between the very best throwing arm and the very worst, Roberto Clemente and Rudy Law, and if you estimate the difference by how large it might possibly be. Defense is an important part of the game—

but there are also people who will try to stretch it to make it a bigger part of the game than it really is. Willie Mays, in his career, probably threw out no more than 70 runners at home plate, certainly not "hundreds" (he had 195 career Baserunner Kills). The best defense in the world will not turn Shawn Boskie into Pedro Martinez.

9 ◆ Paul Waner
(1926–1945, 2549 G, 113 1309 .333)

John McGraw in 1925 sent a scout out to look at Paul Waner, then playing for the San Francisco Seals. The scout, whose name unfortunately has been lost to history, reported that "That little punk you sent me out to look at, Mr. McGraw—he don't even know how to put on a uniform."

The best rookie seasons ever by right fielders:

1. Paul Waner, 1926
2. Tony Oliva, 1964
3. Frank Robinson, 1956
4. Elmer Flick, 1898
5. Curt Blefary, 1965
6. Reggie Jackson, 1968
7. Buck Freeman, 1899
8. Kiki Cuyler, 1924
9. Tim Salmon, 1993
10. Gene Moore, 1936

Frank Robinson actually played most of the 1956 season in left field, with Wally Post in right. Reggie in 1968 was not considered a rookie by the standards used at the time, but would be now.

The Pirates came up with two of these players, Cuyler and Waner, in three years. Waner forced Cuyler to move to center.

Lloyd didn't drink much when he was playing, but Paul was another story. There were plenty of times he showed up at the ball park and he wasn't sober. In the dugout we had an ice chest. He'd stick a pint of whisky in there and take a swig between innings, before he'd go up to bat. —Dick Bartell, *Rowdy Richard*

In 1940, when Frankie Frisch was managing the Pirates and Waner was near the end of his career, Frisch found a whisky bottle in the Pirate clubhouse. "Waner," yelled Frisch, holding up the bottle, "Is this yours?"

"Does it have anything in it?" Waner asked.

"It's half full," replied Frisch.

"Well, it can't be mine," Waner replied. "If it was mine it would be empty."

10 ◆ Sam Crawford
(1899–1917, 2517 G, 97 1525 .309)

As a young man in Wahoo, Nebraska, Crawford was training to be a barber . . . According to Harry Grayson in *They Played the Game,* "it is too bad that Wahoo Sam Crawford didn't get a shot at the lively ball that came in with Babe Ruth." Indeed it is, but what kind of stats would Crawford have had, had he played his career in the lively ball era?

I converted Crawford's stats to equivalent stats in the lively ball era. Since Crawford's career begins late in 1899, I simply moved it up 20 years, beginning his career in 1919, and converted each season to the league norms of 20 years later—1902 becomes 1922, 1908 becomes 1928, 1910 becomes 1930, etc. Since Crawford played for Cincinnati from 1899–1902, I put him in the National League from 1919 through 1922; then, since he moved to Detroit in 1903, I moved him to the American League in 1923.

Actually, I tried this several different ways before I found something that seemed to work. This transformation assumes:

1. Crawford's games played remain the same.

2. Crawford's batting outs (at bats minus hits) remain the same.

3. The relationship between Crawford's productivity as a hitter and the league average remains exactly the same, however.

4. 2/3 of Crawford's triples would become home runs.

5. 3% of his batting outs would become home runs.

6. 2% of his batting outs would become doubles.

7. Half of his stolen bases would disappear.

8. His hits are pegged at whatever level creates the appropriate level of offense.

9. Everything else rises and falls with the hits or with the total bases.

Points 1–3 above are the same as explained in the Willie Davis comment, but there is an additional wrinkle here, which is that I am also adjusting the ratio of his extra base hits to reflect the changes in the game in the lively ball era.

Crawford in 1903 was 63% more effective than an average American League hitter. When this transformation was finished, he was still 63% more effective than an average hitter, but he was now 63% better than the 1923 American League norm, rather than the 1903 norm, and more of his effectiveness had been wedged into the home run column. But none of this makes Crawford *better* than he actually was; it merely states the same player, playing under different conditions.

Ty Cobb said when Crawford was elected to the Hall of Fame that Crawford would have hit 40 home runs a year with the lively ball. This is a reasonable statement in my opinion, although my translation method does not show him hitting 40 home runs in any season. None of us really knows what Crawford's stats would have been in the lively ball era, but it does seem to me that if Cy Williams could hit 40 home runs

SAM CRAWFORD
Career Beginning 1919

Year	G	AB	R	H	2B	3B	HR	RBI	BB	SO	SB	Avg.
1919	31	116	20	28	4	2	7	20	1	13	2	.228
1920	101	359	52	71	16	4	21	58	20	39	5	.198
1921	131	492	90	147	24	5	33	113	32	52	6	.299
1922	140	552	116	182	25	7	28	100	46	56	8	.330
1923	137	538	104	172	29	8	30	110	23	55	9	.320
1924	150	567	69	148	31	6	26	101	46	56	10	.261
1925	154	591	103	187	50	4	26	100	55	58	12	.316
1926	145	563	84	166	33	5	25	93	38	56	12	.295
1927	144	591	138	197	44	6	28	106	39	58	9	.333
1928	152	602	140	195	43	6	31	106	39	59	8	.324
1929	156	608	119	204	47	5	29	131	52	59	17	.336
1930	154	601	121	183	36	7	32	167	40	59	11	.304
1931	146	556	122	199	40	4	26	127	56	57	17	.358
1932	149	571	95	179	36	7	29	133	40	58	19	.313
1933	153	608	98	191	40	8	37	105	51	28	6	.314
1934	157	587	101	188	31	9	38	140	71	31	13	.320
1935	156	610	102	181	39	6	29	143	65	29	12	.297
1936	100	329	62	99	16	5	16	61	40	10	5	.301
1937	61	105	6	19	6	0	5	16	4	6	0	.181
Total	2,517	9,546	1,743	2,936	590	101	494	1,931	758	839	182	.308

in the Babe Ruth era, Sam Crawford sure as hell could have, under the right conditions.

My translation of Crawford's career stats into lively-ball equivalents appears here in the chart at the top of the page.

11 ◆ Al Kaline
(1953–1974, 2834 G, 399 1583 .297)

Kaline was a great defensive right fielder for the same reason Carl Furillo was—his natural gifts became an extension of his thinking.—David Falkner, *Nine Sides of the Diamond*

I would consider it, yes sir, I would. If the Giants would offer Mays and Marichal and Cepeda for Kaline, I would have to give it some consideration.—Jim Campbell, asked in 1964 if he would consider trading Al Kaline

Still somewhat shy, he has learned to accept the bitter with the sweet, for he gets along well with writers and announcers, the very people he once resented.—Al Hirshberg, *Baseball Stars of 1967*

Kaline was nagged through most of his career by a congenital problem with his left foot, which prevented him from playing as well in some seasons as he did in 1955, '56, '66 and '67.

I quit playing baseball because my son was getting ready to go to college and I had never spent any time with him. I wanted to spend one summer with him before he went to college.—Al Kaline in *For The Love of the Game,* (Cynthia J. Wilber)

12 ◆ Enos Slaughter
(1938–1959, 2380 G, 169 1304 .300)

He's a little old, but he'll pinch-hit any time for you, and even if it weren't for nothing else, he's got the spirit that makes a ballclub go like you'll hardly ever see.—Casey Stengel

His biggest thrill was the 1942 World Series against the Giants. In each of the first two games, Country nailed runners with great throws to choke off Giant rallies. Then, in the fourth game, running like a berserk bull as usual, he scored the winning run all the way from first on Harry Cooper's bloop single.—Chris Stern, *Where Have They Gone?*

Yeah, where have they? Uh, Chris, I don't mean to be rude, but if the Cardinals played the Giants in the World Series, wouldn't that be kind of remarkable? I think that may have been the Yankees. Slaughter threw out one baserunner in that series, not two. And it wasn't Harry Cooper; it was Walker Cooper. And Slaughter wasn't on first; he was on third. He walked, was forced to second on another walk, took third on a wild throw by Bill Dickey, and scored on the bloop single.

And by the way, he didn't score from first on a single in the '46 series, either. That was a double.

13 ◆ Dave Winfield
(1973–1995, 2973 G, 465 1833 .283)

Dave Winfield was the number one draft pick in the country in June, 1973. Asked how he felt about being drafted by the San Diego Padres, Winfield said, "To be honest, I'd never heard of them."

The Padres knew they weren't going to re-sign him, so they started to build a publicity campaign against him. They said he wasn't playing as hard as he had in the past, that he wouldn't run into the wall . . . and once they convinced the public he wasn't playing hard, it was easier to let him get away.—Ozzie Smith, *The Wizard*

14 ◆ Dave Parker
(1973–1991, 2466 G, 339 1493 .290)

One time a reporter told Willie Stargell that Dave Parker had said that he (Stargell) was his idol. "That's pretty good," said Stargell, "considering that his previous idol was himself."

Maybe not quite as tough as it was back in the 60s and 70s, as Pops Parker pointed out to me time and again in that agitated honeybee voice. 'Little 'un, I'm tellin' ya, you used to go in against the Phillies, that Carlton with that slider . . . Pops never missed a beat filling me up with historical details, and he wasn't the kind you interrupt with something as meaningless as your rookie opinion.—Eric Davis, *Born to Play*

15 ◆ Bobby Bonds
(1968–1981, 1849 G, 332 1024 .268)

Did you ever think how improbable it is that Bobby Bonds' record for strikeouts in a season has stood as long as it has? Since Bonds there have been many players, and many good players, who strike out more often, per at bat, than he did, among them Jose Canseco, Reggie Jackson, Cecil Fielder and Sammy Sosa. Rob Deer struck out 46% more often, per at bat, than Bonds. Overall strikeout rates have gone up for most of the last thirty years, and are much higher now than they were at the time Bonds set the record.

Bonds had an "advantage," of course, in that he was a leadoff man, whereas almost all of the other big strikeout guys have been middle-of-the order hitters. Still, Bonds in 1970 went to the plate only 745 times, only about 3% more plate appearances than a middle-of-the-order player might have in a 162-game season, and there *have* been other leadoff men who struck out, more of them every year. It is rare for a record to stand against the current of history. When home run totals go up, home run records are broken, when stolen base totals go up, stolen base records are broken, and when strikeout totals go up, strikeout records are broken. But Bonds and Nolan Ryan have held the single-season strikeout records now for almost thirty years . . .

Bonds was probably a better athlete than his son, although obviously Barry is a greater player. Bobby was muscular; he had long limbs and an almost unnaturally wide frame, giving the impression that he was huge when standing still, but small when in motion. He was 6'1," but he took a long, quick stride, low to the ground, not wasting any time in the air but eating up the ground. Running, he looked so much like Mays in the outfield that occasionally, when they crossed, you could confuse them, and lose track of which was which, although they didn't look anything alike in the face or in the build. He was immensely strong, and a good hitter although he made no compromises; he had one swing, and he used the whole thing every time. Had a much better arm than Barry.

16 ◆ Harry Heilmann
(1914–1932, 2148 G, 183 1539 .342)
Heilmann's parents were immigrants, his father from Germany, his mother from Ireland. The first time he brought home money for playing baseball, his parents were certain he had gotten involved in something underhanded. "Nobody pays such kind of money to a boy for just playing a game," said his father.

Perhaps Cobb's best achievement as a tutor was the job he did on Harry Heilmann . . . "Harry," Ty said, studying Heilmann one morning during batting practice, "I think you'll get a freer swing if you move your hands away from your body." —John McCallum, *The Tiger Wore Spikes*

Heilmann had a career batting average, in even-numbered seasons, of .323. In odd-numbered seasons, his average was .362—a 39-point gap, perhaps the largest in baseball history for a player who had a long career. He hit .400 once and missed it three other times by four hits or less, always in odd-numbered seasons.

Always a "team player" and gave managers no worries. Courageous and a fine competitor. Modest and personable, he was extremely popular. Possessed many virtues, including loyalty, kindness, tolerance and generosity.—Ira Smith, *Baseball's Famous Outfielders*

I never will forget when he came up to me down in St. Petersburg in spring training, and he showed his hands—they were withering all up. He had something. Then he died a few years later.—Ed Wells in *Baseball Between the Wars* (Eugene Murdock)

17 ◆ Bobby Murcer
(1965–1983, 1908 G, 252 1043 .277)
Murcer played center field with the Yankees, right field most of his career after leaving the Yankees. Three of the top seventeen listed right fielders of all time are Tigers (Crawford, Kaline and Heilmann), three are Pirates (Waner, Clemente and Parker), and three are at least partially Yankees (Ruth, Reggie and Murcer). Two played for the Reds (Rose and Robinson), two for the Padres (Gwynn and Winfield), and two for the Giants (Ott and Bonds). Altogether, that's 15 of the 17 right fielders . . .

If you picked an All-Star team by state, the Oklahoma team could compete with anybody, even California and Texas if you let them have Warren Spahn and Carl Hubbell, who weren't born in Oklahoma, but lived there throughout their careers. C–Johnny Bench, 1B–Willie Stargell, 2B–Newt Allen, 3B–Pepper Martin, SS–Alvin Dark, OF–Mickey Mantle, Bobby Murcer and the Waner brothers, LHP–Warren Spahn, RHP–Allie Reynolds . . .

18 ◆ Ken Singleton
(1970–1984, 2082 G, 246 1065 .282)

> He will not swing at a bad pitch and every action he takes on the field has a purpose. Like his speech and dress, Ken Singleton the ballplayer is neat, precise and fluid.—Terry Pluto, *The Earl of Baltimore*

Singleton was the ultimate Earl Weaver player–quiet, functional, and nearly flawless apart from his lack of speed. He drew so many walks and hit so many homers he would produce runs if he hit .220, but he didn't hit .220; he hit .300.

In the first version of this book my wife picked the best-looking players of each decade. She picked Ken Singleton as one of the best-looking players of the 1970s. He sent her a note, thanking her for her comments.

19 ◆ Andre Dawson
(1976–1996, 2627 G, 438 1591 .279)

In *The Scouting Report: 1987*, Jim Rooker commented that "Dawson's peak seasons are behind him." Dawson would win the MVP Award that season, and would almost exactly match his previous career stats after this was written.

In reality, though, Rooker was exactly right: Dawson's peak seasons were 1979–1983. He could still hit and he produced bigger numbers in Wrigley than he did in Montreal, but he was nowhere near the player in 1987 (or later) that he had been earlier.

I'm a great admirer of Andre Dawson; he was a fine gentleman, and a real class act. But his selection as MVP in 1987 is among the worst MVP picks of all time. His defense was good and he hit homers, but his overall game was limited—only 32 walks, only 24 doubles, only 41 runs scored other than home runs. He got a lot of credit for "leadership," but his team finished last. How much leadership can you get credit for on a last-place team? There were more than twenty National League players in 1987 who were more valuable than Andre Dawson.

20 ◆ Reggie Smith
(1966–1982, 1987 G, 314 1092 .287)

All of us are to one degree or another defined by the relationship we bear to others, and all ballplayers are in one sense pegged by the relationship they bear to Babe Ruth. Reggie is defined, for Red Sox fans, by his relationship to Yastrzemski, as Yastrzemski was defined by the comparison to Ted Williams, as Williams was defined by his comparisons to DiMaggio and Babe Ruth.

For non-Red Sox fans, however, Reggie is often defined by an accident of nomenclature: he is the other Reggie. An almost exact contemporary of Reggie Jackson (1967–1987), Reggie Smith was variously distinguished from the loudmouthed superstar as Reggie! and Reggie, or Reggie and reggie, or as the other Reggie. I used to think of him as the anti-Reggie. While Reggie! was a great player and a relentless self-promoter, the anti-Reggie was a quietly efficient player who was almost as good, not quite. There were some seasons (1970, 1977, 1978) in which Reggie was actually a better player than Reggie!, and others (1968, 1972), in which he was just as good.

A third player to whom Reggie is sometimes compared is Fred Lynn. Reggie joined the Red Sox in September, 1966, and helped them to the American League pennant as a 22-year-old rookie in 1967. Fred Lynn joined the Red Sox in late 1974, and led them to the American League pennant as a 23-year-old rookie in 1975. Reggie played in Boston for eight years (seven full years), and then played nine years with three other teams. Lynn played for the Red Sox for seven years (six full years) and then played ten years for four other teams.

Their career stats are almost identical: 1,969 games, 306 homers, 1111 RBI, a .283 average for Lynn, basically the same numbers for Reggie. Lynn was a better hitter with the Red Sox (.308 to .281, comparable power); Reggie was a much better hitter after he left the Red Sox (.294 to .263).

Who was a better player overall? It's close, maybe too close to call. I credit Smith with 324 career Win Shares, Lynn with only 283, a very substantial difference given that their career length is almost the same. However, an important element of my rating system is peak seasons, because much of what we mean by the question "Who was better?" is "Who was better, at his best?" Nobody cares whether Mickey Mantle in 1968 was a better player than Willie Mays in 1971. Lynn's two best seasons, 1975 and 1979, are better than Reggie's best seasons. Reggie has more career Win Shares because he hit just as much, although he played more of his career in low-run parks. Lynn ranks 17th among center fielders, Reggie, who played more games in right field than center, ranks 20th in right field, but that's largely because there have been a few more superstar right fielders than superstar center fielders. Forced to choose, I'd choose Reggie.

Yet another group to which Reggie has some relationship is the Don Buford group—Buford, Galan, and Tim Raines. All of these guys were switch hitters, as Reggie was, all came to the majors as second basemen but switched to the outfield, as Reggie did, all walked a lot and had speed, and all were underrated players. The other three were leadoff men; Reggie was not, but would have been a good one if he had been used that way.

One more note. Reggie played for 18 major league teams—seventeen years, and two teams in 1976. Of those 18 teams, all but three had winning records. The three exceptions were the 1966 Red Sox, for whom Reggie played only six games, the 1976 Cardinals, for whom he played only a third of a season before being traded to the Dodgers, and the 1979 Dodgers, for whom he played only 68 games because of injuries. Every team for which he played 70 or more games in a season had a winning record, thirteen out of thirteen. The won-lost record of teams for which Smith played in games in which he played was about 1081-906, a .544 percentage; see Tris Speaker for details. Smith's .544 percentage ranks him between Willie Mays and Ty Cobb on that chart, but ahead of Joe Morgan, George Brett and Al Kaline. A chart of players related in some way to Reggie or otherwise interesting:

Player	Won	Lost	Pct
Yogi Berra	1,317	803	.621
Don Buford	758	528	.589
Reggie Jackson	1,581	1,239	.561
Ted Williams	1,277	1,015	.557
Augie Galan	952	790	.546
Willie Mays	1,634	1,358	.546
Reggie Smith	1,081	906	.544
Ty Cobb	1,641	1,393	.541
Joe Morgan	1,422	1,227	.537

Player	Won	Lost	Pct
Tim Raines	1,264	1,099	.535
George Brett	1,428	1,279	.527
Al Kaline	1,478	1,356	.522
Carl Yastrzemski	1,723	1,585	.521
Fred Lynn	995	974	.506
George Scott	1,020	1,014	.501
Tony Conigliaro	425	452	.484

I'm surprised Williams' percentage is that high.

21 ◆ Tony Oliva

(1962–1976, 1676 G, 220 947 .304)

Tony Oliva's actual name is Pedro, and he was called Pedro by his family; his older brother was Tony. When Castro was taking over Cuba the Washington Senators gave him a little bit of money and a plane ticket, but he was under-age and had no birth certificate. He borrowed his brother's ID to get out of the country—and became "Tony" for the rest of his life.

> Tony is a man of rather pleasant disposition, al-though still excessively wary and suspicious, as are so many foreign-born when they first emi-grate to a strange land.—Ray Robinson, *Baseball Stars of 1967*

> I roomed with a guy with bad knees for years and used to listen to him cry like a baby at night. I'd be asleep and sometimes I'd hear Tony moan-ing and groaning . . . He'd get up during the night and go down to get ice, wandering all over the hotel trying to find ice to put on his knee. —Rod Carew, *Carew*

22 ◆ Dwight Evans

(1972–1991, 2606 G, 385 1384 .272)

Parker, Winfield, and Evans were all born in 1951. The best player among them, by year:

1972–73	Evans
1974	Winfield
1975	Parker
1976	Winfield
1977–78	Parker
1979–80	Winfield
1981–82	Evans
1983	Winfield
1984	Evans
1985	Parker
1986–87	Evans
1988	Winfield
1989	Evans
1990	Parker
1991–95	Winfield

Winfield "wins" 11 seasons, Evans 9, Parker 5, although Parker has the best seasons. I made up a "best season career" for the three of them, choosing whichever one had the best season that year. It shows a player with 550 home runs, 2074 RBI, 3,531 hits but a career average of just .292 . . .

The Red Sox outfields of Rice, Lynn and Evans and (later) Rice, Armas and Evans were good and were among the best of their era, but were not, in my opinion, truly great. The best outfields of the 1975–1985 era:

1975 Boston—Rice (21), Lynn (33) and Evans (17), total 71, or
Oakland—Washington (22), North (22) and Reggie (27), also total of 71.

1976 Cincinnati—Foster (25), Geronimo (19) and Griffey (25), total 69, or
Philadelphia—Luzinski (23), Maddox (27) and Johnstone (19), also 69, or
Pittsburgh—Zisk (24), Oliver (22) and Parker (23), also 69.

1977 San Diego—Richards (21), Hendrick (29) and Winfield (24), total 74.

1978 Boston—Rice (36), Lynn (27) and Evans (17), total 80.

1979 Boston—Rice (28), Lynn (34) and Evans (15), total 77.

1980 Oakland—Henderson (34), Murphy (27)
and Armas (22), total 83.

1981 Oakland—Henderson (27), Murphy (21)
and Armas (18), total 65.

1982 Los Angeles—Baker (22), Landreaux (17)
and Guerrero (30), total 69.

1983 Montreal—Raines (29), Dawson (27) and
Cromartie (11), total 67.

1984 San Diego—Martinez (21), McReynolds
(25) and Gwynn (35), total 81.

1985 Los Angeles—Marshall (23), Landreaux
(15) and Guerrero (35), total 73, or
St. Louis—Coleman (19), McGee (36) and
Van Slyke (18), also 73.

23 ◆ Elmer Flick

(1898–1910, 1482 G, 46 756 .315)

Flick won the American League batting title in
1906 (.306), and in 1907 led the American
League in triples (22), runs scored (98) and
stolen bases (39). The next year he hit .302, up-
ping his runs scored to 103 (third in the league)
and leading again in triples, with 18, although
Ty Cobb won his first batting title that season.

The next spring, Hughie Jennings contacted
the Indians, trying to trade Cobb for Flick, even
up. "Why are you so anxious to trade Cobb?"
asked Cleveland owner Charley Somers, "Anything wrong with him physically?"

"No, he's fine," said Jennings. "He's healthy.
But he can't get along with our players and we
want to get him away. He's had two fights already this spring. We want harmony on this
team, not scrapping."

"We'll keep Flick," said Somers. "Maybe he
isn't quite as good a batter as Cobb, but he's
much nicer to have on the team."

Lee Allen says that the Cobb-for-Flick offer
was not made in the spring of 1908, but the
spring of 1907. "At the time," wrote Allen, "it
was believed that Cobb would not last long. He
raced his motor so much and his style of play
was so frantic that it was widely believed he

was headed for collapse. But life is ironic, and
it was Flick, not Cobb, whose career was shortened by illness." Flick had stomach trouble in
1908 which kept him out most of the year, and
he was never able to regain his form.

24 ◆ Rusty Staub

(1963–1985, 2951 G, 292 1466 .279)

> He's a great hitter . . . He'd watch for all those lit-
> tle things, little quirks. He was smart. If a guy
> held his glove a certain way, it was going to be a
> fastball. If he took the ball out of glove a certain
> way, it was a breaking ball . . . and he'd always
> be telling something that would help.—Lenny
> Dykstra, *Nails*

Any player's stats reflect two things: his
ability, and the conditions under which he has
played. Once in awhile, due to unusual circumstances or a combination of circumstances, a
player will have a large, sudden change in the
conditions under which he plays, which will
cause us, as baseball fans, to receive entirely
different statistics, emanating from the same
player.

Rusty Staub is one such player—in fact,
Staub is somewhat unique because his career
consists of a series of "condition shocks," in
each of which his run environment changed
rapidly. In 1967–1968, Staub played in a park
(the Astrodome) which reduced home runs by
about 50%. In 1969–1970, he played in a park
(Jarry Park in Montreal) which *increased*
home runs by about 40%. At the same time,
the *league* also moved; the mound was lowered, the strike zone was re-interpreted, and
runs scored increased all around the league.
Combining these effects, Staub moved suddenly from playing in a run environment of
about 600 runs per team per season, to playing in a run environment of about 730 runs
per season.

Without adjusting for this, it would appear
that Staub suddenly "matured" in 1969, became

a much better hitter; after hitting 10 home runs in 1967, only 6 home runs in 161 games in 1968, Staub hit 29 home runs in 1969, 30 in 1970. But how much of the increase is a real increase in Staub's value, and how much is a change in playing conditions?

It's all playing conditions; Staub was exactly the same player in Montreal that he had been in Houston. His Win Shares by season, beginning in 1967, are 28, 28, 26 and 29.

Later on, Staub had two milder "condition shocks," moving from the great hitter's park in Montreal to a tough hitter's park in New York, Shea, and then jumping from that back to a better hitter's park, Tiger Stadium. His true value never really changed; he stayed right around 25 Win Shares per season through all the ups and downs of his other stats. In 1978, when the 34-year-old Staub drove in a career-high 121 runs, his true value was actually only 16 Win Shares, well below the level of his best seasons. He had moved into an RBI slot in a hitter's park, but he *wasn't* a better hitter than he had been five years earlier; he had declined some as a hitter, plus, since he was now a DH, he had lost all defensive value. Staub's best all-around season was actually 1971, his third year in Montreal.

Another example of this is Tilly Walker. Tilly Walker reached the majors in 1911, with the Senators, and became a regular in 1914, with the Browns. He hit 6 home runs in 151 games in 1914, hit 5 home runs in 1915, 3 in 1916 and 2 in 1917. In 1918 he was traded to the Athletics, which put him in a better home run park, and he tied for the American League lead in home runs—with 11. He hit 10 home runs in 1919.

In 1920, however, the lively ball era arrived, and Walker's numbers began to emerge. He hit 17 home runs in 1920, driving in a career-high 82 runs. In 1921 he upped the totals to 23 homers, 101 RBI, and in 1922, at age 34,

he swatted 37 home runs. But how much more valuable was he, in 1922, than he had been before?

It's the same thing as Staub. The lively ball era actually did not increase Walker's *value* at all; he was exactly the same player he had always been. Walker's best season, in fact, was 1914, when he hit .298 with 6 home runs; he was actually quite a bit more valuable that year (28 Win Shares) than he was when he hit 37 homers in 1922 (22 Win Shares). Walker was more valuable in 1916, when he hit .266 with 3 homers, 46 RBI, than he was in 1921, when he hit .304 with 23 homers, 101 RBI. His "improvement" as a hitter is purely an illusion of context.

The same is true of two other players who were almost exact contemporaries of Walker: Harry Hooper and Cy Williams. Hall of Famer Harry Hooper, who hit from .235 to .289 for eight straight seasons in what should have been his prime, was 32 years old when the lively ball era arrived (1920), but established all of his career highs post-1920, hitting for a career-high .328 average in 1924, when he was 36 years old, 37 at the end of the season. In context, his best season was 1918, when he hit .289 with 1 homer, 44 RBI for the Red Sox (who won the World Championship).

Cy Williams, same age as Walker and Hooper, led the National League in home runs four times—in 1916, with 12, in 1920, with 15, in 1923, with 41, and in 1927, when he was 39 years old, with 30 home runs. Williams' best season, all things considered, was actually 1920, when he hit 15 home runs. He was more valuable in 1916, when he led the league in home runs with 12, than he was in 1927, when he led the league in home runs with 30.

But this is not true of *all* players; some players value actually does change when the circumstances in which they play change. Zack Wheat. Wheat, a fine player in the Dead Ball era, had dramatically better stats as an older player, hitting .375 in 1924, when he was 36 years old, and .359 in 1925. It is *not* all an illusion of context; Wheat's best five-year stretch in dead ball era totals up to 114 Win Shares; his five best in the lively ball total 128. Kenny Williams, about the same age, did have his best seasons after 1920, but that was just because he never batted more than 227 times in a season until 1920. Many of the players of that generation had surges in their batting records post-1920—but I do not know of any, other than Wheat, who actually increased in value as they aged.

25 ◆ Pedro Guerrero
(1978–1992, 1536 G, 215 898 .300)

> Former Los Angeles Dodgers baseball player Pedro Guerrero was acquitted on drug conspiracy charges Tuesday in part because jurors believed federal agents took advantage of his low IQ to manipulate and mislead him.—Knight-Ridder Newspapers, June 7, 2000

Pedro was the best hitter in baseball in the early 1980s, bar none, and very probably might have won the triple crown in '82, '83 or '85 had he not been playing in one of the toughest parks for a hitter. He had a Willie Mays-type body, fast and with a strong arm, although he was never a finished defensive player at any position. He never had Mays' mind or spirit, and he lost his speed in an aborted slide into third base during spring training, 1986.

The Dodgers in those days had a fine-tuned public relations operation. Bringing almost all of their players up through the system, they trained them early how to deal with reporters. I remember a reporter who covered the Dodgers telling me that on the one hand it was wonderful, because the players were always available and almost never rude, and everybody in the front office would return your phone calls promptly, but on the other hand it was frustrating because they would never say anything. They were all trained in spin control—accentuate the positive, don't try to explain what's gone wrong, you'll just make it worse, etc.

The one guy who was always off the ranch was Pedro. Pedro would talk to reporters when he felt like it, and if he had something to say, he would say it. Of course, his English wasn't great and his attitude wasn't consistent, but the reporters always hung around him because he was the one guy who *might,* if he felt like it, tell you what was really happening on the team. The fact that he *didn't* buy into the PR program made him, ironically, one of the most popular players with the press.

26 ◆ Rocky Colavito
(1955–1968, 1841 G, 374 1159 .266)

> You want to know why Lane traded Rocky? That's easy. Lane was an idiot.—Mudcat Grant

> Many are aware of Rocky's limitations. They know he is an indifferent outfielder. They know he is a slow and uninspired base runner. They know he is capable of long spells when his bat is a feeble instrument. But they love him because he's Rocky Colavito.—Gordon Cobbledick, *Cleveland Plain Dealer,* April, 1960

> What about age? Lane didn't mention it. Colavito was twenty-six, Kuenn twenty-nine. And Kuenn was an 'old twenty-nine' because he had a distressing injury history.—Terry Pluto, *The Curse of Rocky Colavito*

Age	21	22	23	24	25	26	27	28	29	30	31	32	33	34	35	Total
Colavito	1	16	18	32	29	13	33	25	21	21	28	18	10	7		272
Kuenn	2	19	19	22	26	15	21	25	19	10	18	13	8	3	3	223

Starting his analysis with age, I think Pluto has it almost exactly right. I credit Rocky Colavito with 272 Career Win Shares, Kuenn with 223—a significant but not huge difference. This is how they compare by age:

Comparable careers, Colavito was a little bit better. But what you have to remember is, Kuenn was three years older. So looking backward at the previous four years—ages 22–25 for Colavito, ages 25–28 for Kuenn—they're of about the same value:

Year:	−4	−3	−2	−1	Total
Colavito	16	18	32	29	95
Kuenn	26	15	21	25	87

But looking forward from the point of the trade, they're totally different:

Year	+1	+2	+3	+4	+5	+6	+7	+8	+9	Total
Colavito	13	33	25	21	21	28	18	10	7	176
Kuenn	19	10	18	13	8	3	3			74

They're not only different, they're foreseeably different, because both players have normal career patterns, which peak about age 27, and decline rapidly after 30. Colavito was just heading into his peak seasons; Kuenn was just exiting them.

Bill DeWitt, who made the trade for Detroit, was a Branch Rickey disciple who believed that you should trade a star before his value started to fade. When he did that six years later, trading Frank Robinson from Cincinnati, it was a disaster on a par with Cleveland's fiasco in trading Colavito. But the trade of Harvey Kuenn illustrates why the strategy often worked.

27 ◆ Jack Clark
(1975–1992, 1994 G, 340 1118 .267)
Perhaps the best hitter in baseball in the early eighties, other than Pedro Guerrero, although, as was true with Pedro, *something* was always

standing between Clark and an MVP season. He had a lot of little injuries, and he wasn't a defensive wonder, and his park didn't help him.

> Jack was a wonderful guy [but] he had some quirks. His talent for spending money, for one thing, was top-ten material . . . One day, on his way to the ballpark, he pulled over on a whim, stopped at a car dealer, and bought two $90,000 Porsches.—Whitey Herzog, *You're Missin' a Great Game*

28 ◆ Roger Maris
(1957–1968, 1463 G, 275 851 .260)
> He had a friendly little smile, but he didn't use it much. His face seldom showed much emotion, and he had what many writers called 'cold blue eyes.'"—Robert Creamer in *Musing on Maris*, 17th Baseball Research Journal

> Talking about Yastrzemski not hustling recalled one of the great non-hustlers of all time, Roger Maris. Rodg always went to first base as though he had sore feet . . . [if] he popped up or hit a routine grounder, it would take him a half-hour to get to first base—if he got there at all. He'd often just peel off halfway down and head for the dugout.—Jim Bouton, *Ball Four*

I just quoted Whitey Herzog's *You're Missin' A Great Game,* so I won't again, but Herzog is perhaps the most interesting person on the subject of Roger Maris, who was his best friend. In the winter of 1961–62 Herzog was building a house in Kansas City, building it with his own hands. Maris, coming off two consecutive MVP seasons during one of which he had become the most famous man in the world of sports, reported to work at 7:30 in the morning, one cold morning after the next, packing his own lunch and volunteering to help Whitey build his house. "He loved the game," said Herzog. "It was New York he didn't like."

In the Fall, 1982, issue of *The National Pastime,* a man named Don Nelson cited a long list of profound and superficial similarities between

Maris and Hack Wilson. Skipping the obvious ones:

- Each player reached the majors in his 23rd years, spent twelve seasons in the majors, and retired at age 34.
- Hack Wilson, born in 1900, retired in 1934. Maris, born in 1934, retired 34 years later, in 1968.
- The year before his historic season, Maris lost the American League home run derby to his Hall of Fame teammate, Mickey Mantle, 40-39. The year before his 191-RBI season, Wilson lost the National League home run derby to his Hall of Fame teammate, Rogers Hornsby, 40-39.
- Both players began and ended their careers for teams other than the team with which they achieved stardom.

- Wilson hit only fifteen homers in his last two seasons, 9 and 6; Maris hit only fourteen his last two seasons, 9 and 5.

It's a fascinating exercise . . . I'd recommend you look it up, if you can. At the time Nelson wrote the article Maris was still alive. Since then we can add another: both men died young, Wilson at 48, Maris at 51.

When I figured Win Shares for all players, I was anxious to see how Wilson would compare to Maris, because I had always joined these two men together in my mind, even before Nelson's article. Believe it or not, they wound up in a flat-footed tie: 224 Career Win Shares for Wilson, 224 for Maris. Comparing them by their age at the end of the season:

	23	24	25	26	27	28	29	30	31	32	33	34	Total
Maris	13	17	17	31	36	25	18	25	6	8	17	11	224
Wilson	0	16	4	26	31	28	32	35	13	21	12	6	224

In both cases, 87% of the player's value is as a hitter, 13% as a fielder. This percentage is normally higher for a center fielder than for a right fielder, but Maris was a very good right fielder, while Wilson was not a particularly good center fielder.

29 ◆ Gavy Cravath
(1908–1920, 1221 G, 119 719 .287)
Twenty points about Gavy Cravath:

1. The name was "Gavy," not Gavvy. Gavvy was a reporter's error.

2. "Gavy" was a baseball nickname, but it became the name by which he was known. He signed his name "Gavy," and came to be known as Gavy even to his family.

3. There are at least seven printed accounts as to how he got the nickname. All that can be

said with certainty is that the name was short for "gaviotas"–Spanish for "seagull"–and that the name is a by-product of his baseball career.

4. He was also called "Cactus" because of his prickly personality. He was a practical joker and a warm man with a good sense of humor, but he had a stern, leave-me-alone front which he put on to protect himself from nonsense and BS.

5. From 1899–1902 Cravath worked as a telegraph operator, playing semi-pro ball in his spare time.

6. In 1903 he joined Los Angeles in the Pacific Coast League, where he was a teammate of Hal Chase and Dummy Hoy.

7. In Los Angeles he became a good friend of Charles E. Van Loan, later a famous writer of children's stories, at that time a Los Angeles sportswriter.

8. Van Loan called him "Old Wooden Shoes." Cravath had suffered a knee injury in a high school football game, and was never fast, but he was one of those guys who ran effortlessly, and was faster than he looked. His arm was outstanding. The best one-sentence description of Cravath is from a local obituary: He played ball—and lived his life—with a minimum amount of effort and nervous energy.

9. He was named Most Valuable Player in the Pacific Coast League in 1907, at least according to one source. If true, this would mean that the PCL had an MVP Award before the American League or National League did, which is not improbable.

10. He failed trials with Boston, Washington and Chicago in the American League due to illness, injuries, and competition from other new acquisitions like Tris Speaker and Clyde Milan.

11. Returning to the minors, he had two monster seasons at Minneapolis (American Association) to re-establish his career. Seven teams put in for him in the 1911 winter draft, but Minneapolis had an agreement to sell him to Philadelphia. There was a complicated controversy entangled with the sale, involving a mis-sent telegram, a lot of arcane transaction rules which disappeared during the 1920s, and a disagreement as to whether or not a deal to sell him to Philadelphia had actually been consummated.

12. Cravath was a rare player—an opposite-field power hitter. He was a right-handed hitter, but his power was to right field. Pitchers always tried to work him inside, but he would step back from the plate and slash the ball to right.

13. In 1914 Cravath led the National League with 19 homers—all of them in the Baker Bowl. He did not hit a home run on the road.

14. From 1913 to 1915 Cravath outhomered at least one other National League team every year. In 1915 he hit as many home runs (24) as *any* other National League team.

15. From ages 32-36 (1913–1917) Cravath is the third-greatest right fielder in history (at the same age), behind Ruth and Aaron, just ahead of Clemente, Fielder Jones, Dixie Walker and Mel Ott.

16. In 1915 he invented and applied for a patent on a new kind of catcher's mitt, smaller and lighter than the ones previously in use, and padded with goat hair.

17. Cravath raised as a son a nephew, Jeff Cravath, who became football coach at USC after World War II.

18. Cravath was elected a local judge in Laguna Beach, California in 1927, and was re-elected every two years after that until his death in 1963.

19. He was the last non-lawyer to serve as a judge in California. There are as many stories about him as a judge as there are about him as a player.

20. During World War II he burst briefly into the news when Mrs. James Roosevelt, daughter-in-law of the President, was stopped for speeding in Laguna Beach. The OPA (what was that? Office of Petroleum Allocation? . . . something like that) tried to intervene in the case, asking Cravath to also take away her gasoline ration coupons. Cravath correctly refused to have anything to do with that. "I'm a hard-boiled Republican," he said, "but I'm not going to be a stool pigeon for the OPA. We just enforce the state laws here at Laguna."

30 ◆ Dixie Walker

(1931–1949, 1905 G, 105 1023 .306)

In the spring of 1941 the Dodgers acquired Paul Waner, expecting him to become their regular right fielder. But Dodger fans, who had adopted Walker, sent a telegram, signed by five thousand people, threatening a mass boycott of Ebbets Field if Waner was given Walker's job.

According to Lee Allen, "Larry MacPhail was baffled by the adulation of Walker." It was this incident which gave Walker his nickname, "The People's Cherce."

> Here was a cracker from the South who hated everything black, but he changed when Jackie helped him get into the World Series and make some extra money.–Don Newcombe, *We Played the Game* (Danny Peary)

Walker entered the minor leagues in 1928, and emerged as a prospect by hitting .401 at Greenville (South Atlantic League) in 1930. He hit .350 with 105 RBI for Newark in 1932, and joined the Yankees in 1933. He played well, hitting 15 homers, driving in 51 runs in 98 games; he had a .500 slugging percentage.

Early in the 1934 season, however, Walker dove for a ball in the outfield, separating his shoulder. It would be several years before he could throw well again, and his effort to get back to regular status was complicated by other obstacles:

- The Yankees had many other young out-fielders,
- They didn't win in '33 or '34, and
- Joe McCarthy didn't like Southerners.

I think that Joe McCarthy was the greatest manager who ever lived, but he wasn't perfect, and it is well documented that he just did not like Southerners, who he thought were hot-heads and ignorant. With Chapman and Selkirk in the outfield and DiMaggio on the way, McCarthy sent Walker back to the minors.

He got back to the majors with the White Sox in late 1936, and hit .302 with 95 RBI for the White Sox that season. That winter, however, he was sent to Detroit in a trade involving Gee Walker. There were actually several other players involved in the exchange, but the key players, from the fans standpoint, were the two Walkers, Gee and Dixie, who actually were sim-

ilar players–both line-drive .300 hitters who ran well.

There are two things that the average fan knows about Dixie Walker:

1. That he was a racist, and
2. That he was immensely popular with the Brooklyn fans in the pre-Jackie Robinson era. Whatever he did in Brooklyn, he could do no wrong.

What most people do not know about Walker is that, in Detroit, he was on the other side of this: he could do no right. Gee Walker had been immensely popular in Detroit, exactly as Dixie would be in Brooklyn. Dixie Walker, taking his job, was hated and hooted. Every time Dixie stuck his head out of the dugout, the fans booed him. He hit .300 in Detroit, despite the abuse, but it was an unproductive .300, and, in July, 1939, the Tigers gave up, and put him on waivers.

Dixie, pushing 30, finally landed on his feet in Brooklyn, was adopted by the fans there, and was among the best outfielders in baseball for several years. He put himself on the wrong side of the race question, and this probably cost him a chance to manage in the major leagues, but he hung around the game for many years afterward as a scout and minor league manager.

31 ◆ Ken Griffey Sr.
(1973–1991, 2097 G, 152 859 .296)
Faster than his son and as good an outfielder, probably will wind up with a better career batting average. He had everything Junior has except the power stroke and the endorsement contracts.

32 ◆ King Kelly
(1878–1893, 1455 G, 69 950 .308)
To summarize the obvious for anybody who might have skipped the pre-requisite courses, King Kelly was the first matinee idol of the National League. A handsome man with red

hair and a long moustache, Kelly was regarded as a great defensive outfielder, and as the greatest baserunner of his time. He was, stated Bill Stern with the calm assurance of a man who doesn't give a tinker's damn whether he is right or wrong, "the idol of a nation. He was the first baseball player people followed on the streets. The fans loved him so much they presented him with a glistening white horse and a beautiful carriage so he could ride to the park in style." Kelly was the highest-paid star in baseball for much of his career, but spent every dime on wine, women, song, and fancy clothes. When he died of pneumonia in 1894, aged 36, he was reportedly destitute.

> Kelly reported [to the New York Giants in 1893] with a flourish, in the company of a Japanese valet, one Suzuki, a refugee from a troupe of acrobats that the King encountered during a winter on the boards of vaudeville houses. He could never remember the name of the Japanese and always referred to him as 'Roger Dolan.'"—Lee Allen, *The Giants and the Dodgers*

> Kelly's Greatest Invention, however, was the famous "Chicago slide," now used by every good base runner. The slide, it is conceded by the veterans of Anson's famous White Stocking infield, was the invention of Kelly.—Ira Smith

Whether or not Kelly actually invented sliding is debated; he did, no doubt, contribute many innovations to the game. Kelly was an incessant smoker, smoking on the bench between innings, smoking sometimes in the outfield, and even smoking in the shower after the game. One of the Japanese valet's duties was to light a new cigarette and hand it to him as soon as the last one went out.

Kelly played every position on the field including pitching a few innings in seven different seasons, but he was primarily a catcher and outfielder; we estimate that he caught 4,320 innings in his career, and played the outfield 6,467 innings. To tell the true story of

Mike Kelly is impossible, and even to summarize all of the legends would require at least three books.

It is also almost impossible to explain just how weird are Kelly's defensive statistics. Among all major league outfielders playing 1000 games at the position, the highest rate of baserunner kills (assists) per game is by Hall of Fame outfielder Tommy McCarthy, who had 268 kills in 1,189 games, which is 36.5 kills per 162 games; all of the highest rates are by 19th century players. The highest rate by a 20th-century player is 26.9, by Tris Speaker. Paul Radford, who didn't quite play 1,000 games, has a ratio a little higher than McCarthy, 39.0 kills per 162 games.

And then there is King Kelly, whose kill rate is: 61.6. He must be . . . I don't know, ten standard deviations above the norm or something. OK, I checked . . . taking all outfielders in history playing 500 or more games, he is 7.5 standard deviations above the norm. He has more than 50% more baserunner kills per game than *anybody* else, 55% more than the second-best guy. It's unbelievable. How can you do that?

But wait a minute; I didn't say he was a *great* outfielder; I said he was a *weird* outfielder. *All* of his numbers are that odd. His error rate is every bit as bad as his baserunner kill rate is good. His career fielding percentage, in the outfield, was .820—one error every 5.5 chances. Every other outfielder in history, playing 500 or more games, had a career fielding percentage of at least .844. Kelly's error rate (.180) is 24 points higher than any other outfielder's.

How is this possible? He was playing the position *differently* than anyone else, I think. Kelly, at times when he was listed as an outfielder, may actually have abandoned the outfield to play as a fifth infielder. It is documented that at times, when he was expecting a bunt, he would come in and play within a few feet of the batter.

He may have done this even when he was listed as an outfielder; I don't know.

Kelly's numbers as an outfielder are not a lot stranger than his numbers as a catcher. As a catcher, he was charged with 368 errors and 417 passed balls, in 583 games. His rate of passed balls is astronomical, his error rate easily the worst of all time, for a catcher appearing in 500 or more games. Kelly fielded .892 as a catcher; everybody else, even his contemporaries, is over .900. If statistics can be larger than life, King Kelly's numbers are larger than life.

33 ◆ Sam Rice

(1915–1934, 2404 G, 34 1078 .322)

In the history of baseball through 1999 there have been 161 players who earned 300 or more Win Shares. Of those 161, 35 were primarily pitchers, and of the pitchers, *many* didn't appear in the major leagues or didn't pitch more than a few innings in the major leagues before the age of 25.

But of the 126 non-pitchers, only one—Sam Rice—failed to establish himself as a major league regular before the age of 25. Let me do a count here . . .

2 of the 126 were major league regulars at age 18,

11 were established by age 19,

30 were established by age 20,

68 by age 21,

91 by age 22,

113 by age 23, and

124 by age 24.

The only two players who had careers of that duration and magnitude starting at age 25 or after are Jim O'Rourke (who started in the "majors" at age 25 only because the National League wasn't organized until he was 25; he had been a top player for years before that) and Sam Rice.

This is useful knowledge, because sometimes players aged 25 or 26 have big rookie seasons, and are promoted as potential stars. You can pretty much write them off. A 21-year-old rookie who hits .250 is a better bet for stardom than a 25-year-old rookie who hits .300. A few other points about Rice:

- Rice' entire family, his parents and several siblings, were killed by a tornado when he was a young player, in the minors. Rice never mentioned this to anyone, and this fact was completely unknown to the baseball public to the end of his life.
- The most famous incident of his career was a disputed catch that he made in the third game of the 1925 World Series.
- Rice retired with 2,987 career hits, as the 3,000-hit standard meant little at that time.
- Rice roomed for several years with another Hall of Famer, Goose Goslin.

34 ◆ Tommy Henrich

(1937–1950, 1284 G, 183 795 .282)

On the day that I was born, Tommy Henrich hit one of the most dramatic home runs in baseball history. It was the first World Series game of Casey Stengel's managerial career, Brooklyn at New York. The Yankees at that time had been in the World Series only once in the previous five seasons, and the series was rated a tossup. The game was a scoreless duel into the bottom of the ninth, Allie Reynolds pitching a shutout and Don Newcombe matching him. Tommy Henrich hit the ball into the right field stands, winning the game and launching the Yankees on their way to five consecutive World Series championships.

After that game somebody realized it was the first time a home run had decided a World Series game 1-0 since Casey Stengel did it in 1923. A reporter told Casey after the game that "I really think that Tommy's hit was more dramatic than yours, since he hit it in the ninth inning. You hit yours in the seventh."

"I know," said Casey. "I got nervous and couldn't wait."

His career was short because of World War II, but Henrich's career batting average, on base percentage and slugging percentage were about the same as Dave Justice, Gary Sheffield and Larry Doby.

Tommy Henrich had knee surgery during the 1940 season, as a result of which he spent 28 days in a hospital—and wound up married to one of the nurses.

> Quiet, unassuming, unspectacular, his work is best appreciated by fellow players . . . he is without a peer both as a player and a gentleman. —Frank Waldman, *Famous American Athletes of Today* (Eleventh Series, 1949)

> Joe Gordon and I were talking about the best day we ever had as kid players. I told him I once had fifty hits in a day. It wasn't unusual. When you start playing at eight in the morning and don't stop until eight at night, you get a chance for fifty hits.—Tommy Henrich in *Where Have You Gone, Joe DiMaggio*

> A fellow like Tommy Henrich, whom I'd call an infielder playing the outfield, because he was sure death on ground balls as well as fly balls, is worth a lot to a team.—Joe DiMaggio, *Lucky to be a Yankee*

> Mostly what Henrich was was serious. He was a bad loser, and he worked hard at becoming a success . . . The young players on the team feared Henrich's tongue-lashing even more than they did Stengel's.—Peter Golenbock, *Dynasty*

35 ◆ Willie Keeler
(1891–1910, 2124 G, 34 810 .345)

Keeler was a gregarious player, a chatterbox. In his time most parks had 25-cent bleacher seats, where the kids sat when their parents would give them a quarter and send them to the game. When there was a break Keeler would go lean on the fence and talk to the kids, keep them up on what was happening in the game. He'd explain why a pitching change was being made or why a batter hadn't bunted. He was immensely popular.

Monte Ward traded Keeler away for almost nothing because, Ward explained, he didn't like to use a left-handed third baseman. No one was more brilliant than Ward, but he made the oldest mistake in management: he focused on what the player *couldn't* do, rather than on what he *could*.

> William H. "Wee Willie" Keeler, one of the most famous of old-time baseball players, died January 1 at his home, 1010 Gates Avenue, Brooklyn. He had been a sufferer from heart disease for more than two years. Keeler had expressed a desire to live until the beginning of the new year, and on Sunday, he remarked to his brother, Thomas F. Keeler, that he was fighting a losing fight but would live to see 1923 ushered in. On New Year's eve several members of his family and some friends visited his home. Just before midnight all the members of the party left the room where Keeler was lying and stepped outside to hear the bells. They came back a few minutes later to find a sick man sitting up in bed ringing in the new year with a bell he had for the purpose of calling his attendant. He was playing the game of life as he had played the game of baseball—until the last man was out in the ninth.—1924 *Reach Guide*

36 ◆ Jose Canseco
(1985–2000, 1811 G, 446 1358 .266)

When Mike Boddicker of the Red Sox was with the Orioles, he liked to chide Canseco as "Jose Mistako," meaning the big Cuban-born right-hander could only hit a pitcher's mistakes. —*Baseball Digest,* January, 1989

Twins who have played in the majors:

Ozzie and Jose Canseco

Stan and Stew Cliburn

Marshall and Mike Edwards

Ray and Roy Grimes

Bill and George Hunter

Bubber and Claude Jonnard

Johnny and Eddie O'Brien

Red and Joe Shannon

The best player in the group, other than Jose Canseco, was Ray Grimes. There have been several other stars, among them Edd Rousch and Barry Larkin, who had twin brothers who weren't baseball players.

37 ◆ Sam Thompson
(1885–1906, 1407 G, 127 1299 .331)
Leads all listed outfielders in RBI per game:

1.	Sam Thompson	.923
2.	Joe DiMaggio	.885
3.	Babe Ruth	.884
4.	Juan Gonzalez	.861
5.	Al Simmons	.825
6.	Albert Belle	.813
7.	Ted Williams	.802
8.	Ed Delahanty	.798
9.	Hack Wilson	.788
10.	Jose Canseco	.764

Per plate appearance Thompson ranks fourth, behind Ruth, Gonzalez and DiMaggio. Thompson and Jimmie Foxx are also the only men in major league history to drive in 150 runs with two different teams. Thompson drove in 166 with Detroit in 1887, 165 with Philadelphia in 1895.

Thompson was a tall, powerful, angular man, perhaps built somewhat like Juan Gone, with a bushy handlebar moustache that reached out beyond the edges of his face. As a young man he was a roofer and a carpenter. Organized baseball was expanding rapidly in that era, and eventually drew in Thompson, who had a reputation as a slugger in local

games. He was a sober, cheerful man, popular with the fans and a leader among the players.

> A lifetime tobacco chewer, Thompson regretted it only once. During the flu epidemic of 1918 he wore a surgeon's mask while registering alien women seeking permits to work in war production. One day he forgot he was wearing the mask and expectorated into it.—Norman L. Macht, *Baseball's First Stars*

> Sam was not such a fine outfielder, but a hard and long left-handed hitter, being the Babe Ruth of his day . . . Throughout his career he earned universal respect, as he was . . . a man of exemplary habits and always in perfect playing condition.—1923 *Reach Guide*

38 ◆ Johnny Callison
(1958–1973, 1886 G, 226 840 .264)
Callison was a rather small man, but with powerful forearms; Gene Mauch once said that he was a 200-pounder from his elbows to his fingertips. He ran well and threw extremely well, and was a top flight player for four years (1962–1965).

Until the last two weeks of the 1964 season, when the Phillies collapsed, Callison seemed likely to be the National League MVP. With days left in the season there were five teams in the pennant race. In the closing days of that season—I think it was September 30, 1964—Callison was not in the lineup. He had played every inning all season, but, battling the flu, had been unable to start that game. Called on to pinch hit with the Phillies down two or three runs, Callison lined a single into right field. It was a cool day, and Callison at first base was shaking with the cold and flu. Someone raced out of the dugout and handed him a warmup jacket. This was a technical violation of the rules—only pitchers are allowed to wear warmup jackets on the bases—but the Cardinals, as a sign of respect, did not object, and the umpire did not enforce the rule. Callison, however, was shaking so violently that he was unable to zip up the jacket. Cardinal first baseman Bill White had to assist him in fastening his jacket. A teammate would later say it was the most moving thing he ever saw on a baseball field.

39 ◆ Kiki Cuyler
(1921–1938, 1879 G, 127 1065 .321)

Outfielder Hazen Cuyler is another two year man but already one of the greatest ball players of the day. Cuyler can do everything–hit, throw, cover the ground and run bases. He is the best batter among the Pirates, near the top of the National League hitting list, leads the league in runs scored and is right up among the leaders in stolen bases.–1926 *Reach Guide*

Cuyler is a wonder, one of those all round players that you don't see very often. He can field and hit and run bases. He is fast as a flash and has a great throwing arm . . . Cuyler might well become a second Cobb. Time will tell. In any case, he's the best young outfielder who has broken into baseball for many years.–Fred Clarke in *Baseball Magazine,* 1925

Cuyler his first three years in the National League was a genuine sensation, the best outfielder in the National League. The Pirates, however, came up with the Waner brothers; Paul was as good as Kiki, and Lloyd wasn't far behind. They had other quality outfielders. Cuyler began to quarrel with Donie Bush, then managing the Pirates, and Bush benched him; in 1927 he hardly played the second half of the season. Traded to the Cubs, he had more sensational seasons, and batted third in front of Hack Wilson when Wilson drove in 191 runs . . .

In 1940 Cuyler was managing in the minor leagues. His son Harold had been offered a chance to play for a minor league team. Kiki knew that Harold couldn't play, and wanted to spare him the experience of finding this out the hard way. Harold insisted he could play, so

finally Kiki told him, "Look, son, I had to leave the major leagues because my legs have gone back on me, and that's why I'm through as a player. But I'll race you a hundred yards. If you beat me, I'll say it's all right for you to go ahead. If I beat you, you'll give it up." Harold agreed to the deal, Kiki beat him by fifteen yards, and Harold gave up on the idea of being a baseball player . . .

During World War II Cuyler was Captain of a unit which mostly played ball games to entertain the other troops. Johnny Pesky was, for a time, a member of Cuyler's unit. I once asked Pesky what he remembered about Cuyler. "He had a beautiful voice," said Pesky. "He'd sing all the time, sing in the showers, sing in the locker rooms."

"What would he sing?" I asked.

"He'd sing anything. He'd sing the Lord's Prayer. He'd sing Show Tunes."

Cuyler, of course, was a stutterer; this is where he got the name "Kiki." Many times people who stutter will develop a fondness for singing because they don't stutter in song.

40 ◆ Chuck Klein
(1928–1944, 1753 G, 300 1201 .320)

Kiki Cuyler and Chuck Klein were National League contemporaries. Their initials are reversed–KC and CK. Kiki Cuyler hit .351 through 1925 (283 games), .315 after that (1596 games). Klein hit .359 through 1933 (823 games), but .278 after that (930 games). Both started their careers in Pennsylvania, but were traded to the Cubs after a few years.

According to J. Roy Stockton in *The Gashouse Gang,* the Phillies acquired Klein on the recommendation of Branch Rickey. The Cardinals knew of Klein because they were operating two teams in the Central League, a fact of which Judge Landis did not approve. The Cardinals wanted to acquire Klein, the best player in the league, but were afraid that Landis would

Pos	Player, Year	HR	RBI	Avg	WS	Team Won–Lost
C	Frankie Hayes, 1940	16	70	.308	17	(54–100)
1B	Rusty Staub, 1969	29	79	.302	26	(52–110)
2B	Rogers Hornsby, 1928	21	94	.387	33	(50–103)
3B	Ron Santo, 1966	30	94	.312	30	(59–103)
SS	Cal Ripken, 1988	23	81	.264	25	(54–107)
RF	Chuck Klein, 1930	40	170	.386	28	(52–102)
CF	Roy Thomas, 1904	3	29	.290	28	(52–100)
RF	Charlie Hemphill, 1908	0	44	.297	28	(51–103)

Pos	Player, Year	Won–Lost	ERA	WS	Team Won–Lost
LHS	Irv Young, 1905	20–21	2.90	29	(51–103)
LHS	Dave Roberts, 1971	14–17	2.10	25	(61–100)
LHS	Nap Rucker, 1908	17–19	2.08	23	(53–101)
RHS	Ned Garver, 1951	20–12	3.73	22	(52–102)
RA	John Wyatt, 1964	9–8	3.59	13	(57–105)

pitch a fit if the Cardinals began purchasing the best players from the teams they didn't own outright. Rickey was very fond of Burt Shotton, then managing the Phillies, so instead he called Shotton and strongly urged him to buy Klein before somebody else did.

Just for the hell of it, I drew up an All Star team of the best players ever on teams losing 100 or more games. Chuck Klein, 1930, is the cleanup hitter. The charts are shown at the top of this page.

Special provisions should be made for Steve Carlton, 1972. A pre-season strike shortened the Phillies' schedule by six games, so that they finished with only 97 losses, although they would still have lost 100 games had Carlton finished only 24-13. If the Phillies had lost 100 games, Carlton, with 40 Win Shares, would be by far the best player on the 100-loss team.

This team, if it could be assembled, would win any league easily, and would win well over 100 games.

41 ◆ Fielder Jones
(1896–1915, 1788 G, 21 631 .285)

Only 4% of Fielder Jones career balls in play were doubles or triples—the lowest figure of any right fielder listed here. I know this sounds stupid, but this is an interesting stat. A typical player hits doubles or triples in 6 or 7% of his balls in play (At Bats, minus Home Runs, minus Strikeouts). This figure is almost astonishingly consistent; basically, it's 6 to 8% for almost everybody. Among the 300 out-fielders listed here, 235 got doubles or triples in 6, 7, or 8% of their balls in play. Twenty were below 6%, led by Roy Thomas, at 2.9%. Forty-five were above 8%, led by Babe Herman, at 10.5%. It's been six to eight percent throughout baseball history.

There are two distinct types of players who fall below 6%: slap hitters, and slow runners. There is little overlap between these two groups, and there are few players for whom it is difficult to say whether this guy has a low percentage because he is a slap hitter, or because he is slow.

Why? Because there is nobody who is both a slap hitter and a slow runner. You can be both fast and a power hitter; you cannot be both slow and a slap hitter, and play in the major leagues for any length of time. These are the lowest percentages on record for major league outfielders rated in the top 100, in both groups:

Slap Hitters

1.	Roy Thomas	2.9%
2.	Jimmy Barrett	4.0%
3.	Fielder Jones	4.2%
4.	Willie Keeler	4.5%
5.	Bill North	4.7%

Slow Runners

1.	Leon Wagner	4.6%
2.	Tommy Davis	4.9%
3.	Charlie Maxwell	5.3%
4.	Willie Horton	5.7%
5.	Frank Thomas	5.7%

The lowest figure for a player who was neither slow nor a slap hitter is 4.9%, by Dwayne Murphy.

Jones is a man who shows up frequently in the biographies of players of his era, including Patsy Dougherty and George Davis. A self-starter, he was the manager of the Hitless Wonders, the 1906 White Sox, and was as celebrated in his own time as Frank Chance, manager of the cross-town Cubs.

"Fielder Jones once deliberately tested a rule in Detroit and stirred up one of the biggest discussions baseball has had in many years. With a runner on third Jones ordered him to steal home as the pitcher was in the act of delivering the ball. The pitcher hesitated, changed his pitching motion, and threw the ball to the catcher who ran in front of the batter, caught the ball and touched the runner. The umpire called the runner out. Then Jones raised this point: Was not the runner safe because the catcher interfered with the batter by running in front of him, thereby preventing him from hitting the ball? The umpire ruled that he was not out, as the ball was thrown to the plate and not pitched, therefore the batter had no right to hit it. Jones yielded the point and then argued: Did not the pitcher make a balk, if as the umpire had ruled, he changed his motion and threw to the plate instead of pitching? The umpire was cornered and refused to discuss the case further, beyond ruling the runner out.

> The case stirred up a long discussion. The presidents of the two major leagues ruled in different ways, and the umpires received conflicting orders. Four-fifths of the umpires admit, after studying the play, that Jones was right and that the runner was safe.—Johnny Evers, *Baseball In the Big Leagues* (Reilly and Britton, 1910)

(As an aside, Jones was obviously right on his interpretation of this play. Apparently the practice of the time was for the catcher to break from his position on a steal of home, so as to make the play on the runner. The rules do not permit this.)

> Baseball hasn't meant much to us since the introduction of the TNT ball that robbed the game of the features (which) gave you and Bill Carrigan and Fielder Jones and other really intelligent managers a deserved advantage.—Ring Lardner, to John McGraw upon his retirement in 1932

> Fielder Jones' five-year term as White Sox manager ended on that final day of the 1908 season, amid second guessing, insinuation, and bitter disappointment. The memory of that game tarnished Jones' fine record as manager.—Richard Lindberg, *Who's On 3rd?*

In that hectic game with the Tigers Jones finished his career as manager of the White Sox. As a player he was done with the sport for ever, as he never faced another pitcher. Good-byes were said behind the screen as, true to his scrappy past, the umpires had ordered him off the field. Here he prophesied that the fans would vent their spleen on him for the disaster. It is a fact that they did.—G. W. Axelson, *Commy* (1919)

42 ◆ Harold Baines

(1980–2000, 2798 G, 384 1622 .291)

Harold Baines was the first player taken in the 1977 draft. How much is it actually worth, to have the number one pick? How often does the team which has that pick find a star or a super-star?

The chart below gives the career Win Shares through 1999 of the first 25 men drafted #1, all of those through 1989 (post-1989 most players would still be in mid-career).

1965	Rick Monday (257)
1966	Steve Chilcott (0)
1967	Ron Blomberg (57)
1968	Tim Foli (108)
1969	Jeff Burroughs (193)
1970	Mike Ivie (83)
1971	Danny Goodwin (9)
1972	Dave Roberts (45)
1973	David Clyde (11)
1974	Bill Almon (77)
1975	Danny Goodwin (9)
1976	Floyd Bannister (128)
1977	Harold Baines (305)
1978	Bob Horner (141)
1979	Al Chambers (1)
1980	Darryl Strawberry (254)
1981	Mike Moore (133)
1982	Shawon Dunston (141)
1983	Tim Belcher (131)
1984	Shawn Abner (14)
1985	B. J Surhoff (180)
1986	Jeff King (115)
1987	Ken Griffey Jr. (277)
1988	Andy Benes (122)
1989	Ben McDonald (83)

Baines has been the most valuable player taken #1, although he will be bumped from that slot in 2000 or 2001 by Ken Griffey Jr. The 25 #1 picks can be sorted into four groups:

1. Highly successful players (200 or more Win Shares). There are four of these—Baines, Rick Monday, Darryl Strawberry and Ken Griffey Jr.

2. Good players (100-199 Career Win Shares). There are ten of these—Tim Foli, Jeff Burroughs, Floyd Bannister, Bob Horner, Mike Moore, Shawon Dunston, Tim Belcher, B. J. Surhoff, Jeff King and Andy Benes. More than one-half of the number one draft picks have earned 100 or more career Win Shares.

3. Players who had modest careers (25-99 Career Win Shares). There are five of these—Ron Blomberg, Mike Ivie, Dave Roberts, Bill Almon and Ben McDonald.

4. Washouts (up to 24 Career Win Shares). There are six of these—Steve Chilcott, Danny Goodwin twice, David Clyde, Al Chambers, and Shawn Abner.

Basically, it's a 50-50 shot whether you'll get a good player with the number one draft pick in the country.

Now, let's contrast that with the players picked tenth in the same drafts. Those players and their career Win Shares would be:

1965	Doug Dickerson (0)
1966	Jim Lyttle (16)
1967	Ted Simmons (314)
1968	Junior Kennedy (26)
1969	Bob May (0)
1970	Paul Dade (28)
1971	Taylor Duncan (7)
1972	Dave Chalk (68)
1973	Pat Rockett (4)
1974	Mike Miley (2)
1975	Art Miles (0)
1976	Jamie Allen (3)

1977	Craig Landis (0)
1978	Phil Lansford (0)
1979	Tim Wallach (244)
1980	Kelly Gruber (96)
1981	Mark Grant (26)
1982	John Morris (10)
1983	Ray Hayward (1)
1984	Mark McGwire (316)
1985	Chris Gwynn (19)
1986	Derek Parks (1)
1987	Kevin Garner (0)
1988	Robin Ventura (204)
1989	Charles Johnson (71)

The top four players taken tenth in the draft—Mark McGwire, Ted Simmons, Tim Wallach and Robin Ventura—compare favorably with the top four #1 picks. After that, however, it's a mismatch; the second-line talent taken tenth in the draft does not begin to compare to the second-line talent taken first. Other than the four big stars, the number ten draft picks have yielded *no* good players (100 or more career Win Shares), although Charles Johnson likely will move into that class. But 60% of the players drafted tenth were washouts, having virtually no major league career, whereas only 24% of the #1 picks were washouts. The average value of a number one draft pick over the 25 years was 115 Win Shares. The average value of a number ten pick was one-half that— 58 Win Shares.

43 ◆ Harry Hooper
(1909–1925, 2308 G, 75 817 .281)

> I expected to be an engineer. Went to St. Mary's College and got my degree in Civil Engineering in 1907.—Harry Hooper in *The Glory of Their Times*

Hooper was the king of baseball's right fielders on the defense. Harry had a rare faculty for judging line drives and fly balls, roamed over acres of territory, was fleet as a deer, and had an arm of steel.—Fred Lieb, *The Boston Red Sox*

> There's one man in my experience who was even better than Cobb and Speaker. He comes about as near being the perfect outfielder as any man I ever saw. And that was Harry Hooper.—Babe Ruth (Ford Frick) in *Babe Ruth's Own Book of Baseball* (1928)

> Duffy Lewis in left, Speaker in center and Harry Hooper in right were astonishing fielders.—Bob Creamer, *Babe*

> It was formed in 1910 and played together until Speaker was traded to Cleveland in 1916, and had become in those six years the greatest defensive outfield the game has known.—Edward Barrow, *My Fifty Years in Baseball*

> For years Harry Hooper has been considered one of the greatest outfielders that ever lived. He is also one of the most dangerous hitters in a pinch that the game has ever known.—John McGraw, *My Thirty Years in Baseball*

The Boston team from 1909 to 1915 had two exceptional center fielders, Speaker and Hooper. They couldn't both play center, so Hooper played right. It was as if a team had both Kenny Lofton and Andruw Jones, so Andruw had to play right, or as if a team had had both Paul Blair and Garry Maddox, or Curt Flood and Willie Mays.

Having said that, it may be that too much has been made of this over time. Hooper was a good player, like Blair or Maddox; I do not believe, despite the testimonials of Ruth and Mc-Graw and Barrow, that he was a great player. Tris Speaker and *The Glory of Their Times* put Harry Hooper in the Hall of Fame, much as Johnny Evers and Franklin P. Adams put Joe Tinker in the Hall of Fame, much as Sandy Koufax and Hollywood put Don Drysdale in the Hall of Fame. Hooper, Tinker and Drysdale were good players, but there are a hundred guys who were better who aren't considered Hall of Fame candidates.

44 ◆ Paul O'Neill
(1985–2000, 1916 G, 260 1199 .299)
A .300 hitter, a 100-RBI man and a classic defensive outfielder, he is a worthy inheritor of the position patrolled by Babe Ruth, Tommy Henrich, Hank Bauer, Roger Maris, Reggie Jackson and Dave Winfield.

45 ◆ Sammy Sosa
(1989–2000, 1565 G, 386 1079 .273)
Reggie Jackson-type offensive and defensive player, not on base as much as Reggie was and a ways yet from having as many good years as Reggie did, but a lot easier to root for.

Was it foreseeable that Sammy Sosa would develop into a star? Two teams gave up on him before he broke through in 1993 with the Cubs. They didn't foresee that he would become a star. Should they have?

Absolutely they should have. It was not *inevitable* that he would become a star, but it was always at least a 50/50 shot, and baseball men should have known it. Sosa hit .257 in 58 games when he was 20 years old, hit 15 homers and drove in 70 runs at age 21, before the hitting explosion of the 1990s. There are few examples on record of players who were regulars at age 20 who *didn't* become stars. Sammy had no idea of the strike zone, and he struggled for a couple of years to control the damage that was doing. He could have continued to struggle; he could have devolved into Juan Samuel or Claudell Washington. But his work habits were always good, and his attitude was always good. One should never promote such a player as a star, because that increases the pressure and complicates the player's development, but the Rangers and White Sox were short-sighted not to realize

that he was probably going to be a very good player.

46 ◆ Ross Youngs
(1917–1926, 1211 G, 42 592 .322)
John McGraw had two pictures on the wall of his office: Ross Youngs, and Christy Mathewson. When McGraw retired from the Giants he told Bill Terry that he would never again set foot in the Giants' locker room, unless Terry asked him to. Terry never asked him to, so he never did. But after several years, he sent a friend to the locker room to retrieve the pictures of Matty and Youngs . . .

47 ◆ Darryl Strawberry
(1983–1999, 1583 G, 335 1000 .259)

> Straw lived for it. He lived to make the major leagues. That was life to him. That was reality to him.—Eric Davis, *Born to Run*, on Darryl Strawberry as a child.

> He came from Los Angeles, where all his life he had been ballyhooed. Athletics had always been easy for him. He had never suffered adversity, and adversity is what teaches you and makes you tough.—Davey Johnson, *Bats*

Eric Davis and Darryl Strawberry:

- Were both born in the spring of 1962,
- Were both born and raised in Los Angeles,
- Were childhood friends,
- Were both drafted in 1980,
- Both struck out a great deal. In fact, both struck out more often, per at bat, than Bobby Bonds, who still holds the record for strikeouts in a season.
- Did not hit for a good average, but
- Are 8th and 9th among all listed outfielders in secondary average, because of their walks, stolen bases, and power.
- Have both been injured and out of the lineup for long periods of time in many seasons, but

- Are both are among the 50 best players at their position, despite the career interruptions, and
- Are both cancer survivors.

The top ten secondary averages among listed outfielders:

1.	Babe Ruth	.608
2.	Ted Williams	.555
3.	Barry Bonds	.542
4.	Mickey Mantle	.491
5.	Rickey Henderson	.477
6.	Ralph Kiner	.468
7.	Charlie Keller	.450
8.	Darryl Strawberry	.438
9.	Eric Davis	.431
10.	Ken Griffey, Jr.	.427

48 ◆ Felipe Alou

(1958–1974, 2082 G, 206 852 .286)

What is the greatest baseball-playing family of all time? This is the sort of task for which the Win Shares system is designed—forming estimates of the values of groups of seasons. We might think, then, that we could establish the greatest ball-playing families by simply adding together the career Win Shares of the players from each of the contending families—the Alous, the Boyers, the DiMaggios, etc. Let's compare those:

Felipe Alou	244
Matty Alou	179
Moises Alou	142
Jesus Alou	78
Total	643

Ken Boyer	280
Clete Boyer	161
Cloyd Boyer	16
Total	457

Joe DiMaggio	385
Dom DiMaggio	220
Vince DiMaggio	138
Total	743

Joe DiMaggio is the best individual player from the three families, followed by Ken Boyer, Felipe, Dom DiMaggio, Matty...as a group, the DiMaggios win on this basis.

The problem with this method is that, by a raw count, the greatest ballplaying family of all time was: the Babe Ruth family. There have been some great baseball families—the two Hall of Famers in the Waner family, the Ferrell boys, the Delahantys. Two members of the Perry family won 500 and some games, the Niekros the same. None of these families, all taken together, was worth as much as Babe Ruth by himself.

The answer that the greatest baseball-playing family of all time is Babe Ruth may be technically correct, but it is not what we're looking for. A related problem works through the rankings. The Boyer family, taken as a whole, still doesn't match Lou Gehrig. Technically, this is true: you *wouldn't* trade Lou Gehrig for all of the Boyers taken together, in part because what the hell do you need two third basemen for, but still, it's not the answer we want.

We could eliminate Ruth and Gehrig by requiring all qualifying families to have at least two members who played in the major leagues. But if you do that, the same problem recurs in disguise. Many of the greatest players of all time had brothers or sons who played briefly in the major leagues: Henry Aaron had Tommie, Honus Wagner had Butts, Christy Mathewson had Henry, Eddie Collins had Eddie, Jr., etc. So if you form the list that way, you get a list on which the Aarons, the Wagners and the Younts rank ahead of the Alomars, the Boones, and the Bells.

I designed a method to avoid these problems; we'll call it the Family Score. The way it works is, the number one player in any family (the *best* player in the family) earns the family one point for each Win Share. The second-best player earns the family two points for each Win Share, the third-best player earns three points for each Win Share, the fourth-best player earns the family four points for each Win Share, etc. I'll do the Delahantys:

Ed Delahanty	356
Jim Delahanty	147
Joe Delahanty	21
Frank Delahanty	20
Tom Delahanty	1

This makes a Family Score of 798—356 for Ed, 294 for Jim, 63 for Joe, 80 for Frank, and 5 for Tom. This method places a premium on having multiple members of the same family who can actually play, rather than having a bunch of guys who made the majors but didn't contribute, or rather than having one big star in the family. Contrasting Lee and Carlos May, for example, to Eddie and Rich Murray. Eddie and Rich earned more Win Shares, 435 to 344. But 433 of the Murray's Win Shares were by Eddie, only 2 by Rich, who hit .216 in a third of a season in the major leagues. Lee and Carlos May earned only 344 Win Shares between them, but rank ahead of the Murrays (464 to 437) because both of them could play in the majors.

By the Family Score method, the greatest ball-playing family of all time, through the end of the 1999 season, is the Alous. We have a lot of families active now with star players in mid-career, so these rankings could change rapidly in the next few years, but as of now, the top twenty ball-playing families rank like this:

1. The Alous. (Family Score: 1440)

Felipe Alou	244
Matty Alou	179
Moises Alou	142
Jesus Alou	78

What makes the Alous number one is that they have had four guys who could actually play, at least some. Several families have had four members reach the majors, but none of the others had four guys who actually stuck around and contributed the way the Alous have.

I did not count Mel Rojas (75 Win Shares through 1999) as a member of the Alou family. If I had counted him, that would push their family score to 1815—almost 600 points ahead of any other family.

2. The DiMaggios. (Family Score: 1239)

Joe DiMaggio	385
Dom DiMaggio	220
Vince DiMaggio	138

Without the War, the DiMaggios might rank first, but might not. Joe DiMaggio lost a hundred or more Win Shares to World War II, and Dom lost about 80. That's 260 Win Shares they lost, which would easily put the family in first place.

But Vince DiMaggio, a more marginal player, played through the War, and had some of his best seasons during the War. Without the War, he probably would have lost playing time—and those points count triple, since Vince is the third member of the family.

3. The Bondses (Family Score: 1040)

Barry Bonds	438
Bobby Bonds	301

No other family except possibly the DiMaggios has produced two players as good as Barry and Bobby Bonds. The Waners had two Hall of Famers, yes, but Barry is a greater player than Paul, and Bobby was a better player than Lloyd. But so was Dom DiMaggio.

4. The Waners (Family Score: 913)

Paul Waner	423
Lloyd Waner	245

The only other family to produce two Hall of Famers was the Wright family, Harry and George Wright. But Harry didn't play in the major leagues; he just invented them.

5. The Boones (Family Score: 892)

Bob Boone	209
Ray Boone	166
Bret Boone	89
Aaron Boone	21

This group could move upward very, very rapidly in the next few years. as Bret and Aaron are the third and fourth members of the family to play in the majors. In 1999 the family score moved up by 114 points—and Aaron is just hitting his stride.

6. The Delahantys (Family Score: 798)

Ed Delahanty	356
Jim Delahanty	147
Joe Delahanty	21
Frank Delahanty	20
Tom Delahanty	1

Three of the Delahanty brothers were very marginal players; only one was any kind of a star.

7. The Griffeys (Family Score: 789)

Ken Griffey Jr.	277
Ken Griffey Sr.	256

Junior will move them up at least a couple more spots before he's finished.

8. The Perrys (Family Score: 777)

Gaylord Perry	367
Jim Perry	205

The best of the pitching families. The Niekros have nine more wins—but 39 more losses.

9t. The Alomars (Family Score: 758)

Roberto Alomar	286
Sandy Alomar Sr.	104
Sandy Alomar Jr.	88

They're still moving, but they'll need a third generation to catch the Alous.

9t. Babe Ruth (Family Score: 758)

Babe Ruth	758

Claire never could hit a curve.

11. (751). The Niekros. Phil (375) and Joe (188).

12. (735). The Bells. Buddy (299), Gus (176) and David (28 so far).

13. (726). Ty Cobb.

14. (667). The Aarons. Henry (641) and Tommie (13).

15. (659). The Wagners. Honus (655) and Butts (2).

16. (650). The Boyers. Gave the totals earlier.

17. (649). The Ferrells. Wes (233) and Rick (208).

18. (641). Willie Mays.

19. (635). Cy Young.

20. (633). Tris Speaker.

If we didn't count individuals as families, that would open up five spots, which would allow room for the Bretts (594), Eddie Collins Sr. and Jr. (578), the Sislers (541), the Sewells (540), and the Dixie Walker Clan (also 540). They would be followed by the Clarksons (535), Bob and Roy Johnson (532), the Ripkens (519), Irish and Bob Meusel (503), and the McRaes (490 so far).

49 ◆ Mike Tiernan

(1887–1899, 1476 G, 106 851 .311)

The lowest range factors compared to league norms among listed outfielders:

1.	Greg Luzinski	1.68 vs. 2.28	−.60
2.	Mike Tiernan	1.58 vs. 2.11	−.53
3.	Danny Tartabull	1.87 vs. 2.39	−.52
4.	Jeff Burroughs	1.86 vs. 2.35	−.49
5.	Oyster Burns	1.62 vs. 2.06	−.44
6.	Leon Wagner	1.69 vs. 2.13	−.44
7.	Ken Singleton	1.92 vs. 2.35	−.43
8.	Harry Heilmann	1.94 vs. 2.36	−.42
9.	Bruce Campbell	2.00 vs. 2.41	−.41
10.	Riggs Stephenson	2.09 vs. 2.49	−.40

Tiernan was known as "Silent Mike" because, unlike most of the players of his era, he never argued with umpires. Although he was quiet, he was a very friendly, agreeable man, not at all sour or taciturn. After he retired he ran a saloon near the Polo Grounds until about 1910, when he developed tuberculosis, and went West to try to let the sun burn it out of his system. When that failed he returned to New York to die, signing himself into the hospital under the name of "Joseph Egan, 51, retired, of 2423 Eighth Avenue." No one knew, until he died, that he was the old ballplayer.

"For the information of those who have not been to the New Polo Grounds this season—and there are many, very many such—it should be stated, prior to describing the game played yesterday between the New York and Boston League teams, that it is a long way from the home plate to the center field flag pole.

It was so far last year that none of the Giants was able to hit a ball from point to point; and it is fifty feet further this year, for the grounds have been extended on the north side.

Well, that pole will have a new mission hereafter. That it carries a flag will be a matter not worth noting. It is now a tall monument to Mike Tiernan, for it marks the point at which a ball from his bat—in the thirteenth inning, when the score was a tie at nothing to nothing—cleared the fence and won the game. It was the longest hit ever seen in New York, and the prettiest, for it was a liner; and the most valuable, for it not only won the day, but put a superb climax to a brilliant exhibition of base ball . . ."

One hand was out when Tiernan came to bat. The first ball he tapped foul, and it flew back into the grand stand. A new ball was torn from its case, but before the umpire had tossed it into play the old one was thrown back into the diamond, and it rolled to Pitcher Nichols.

"This ball is all right, isn't it?" he asked of the Umpire, remembering that in the eighth inning Tiernan had hit a new ball safely.

"No; the new ball was on the field first," said Umpire Powers, "and you'll have to use it."

"Oh, all right,:" said Nichols as he exchanged the balls.

"Now, Mike!" cried five hundred folks.

And the first time that sparkling new ball came toward that plate was its last . . . Centerfielder Brodie and Rightfielder Shellhasse both started as if to make a catch, but the ball, though only some thirty or forty feet high, had no time to shake hands with them. On it went beyond the fielders, on beyond the bank, on beyond the fence on top of the bank, on beyond the vision of the happy spectators.

And Mike, he trotted around home amid all the cheering that was possible from the small crowd.

Boston went out in the thirteenth inning in short order, and all who were there rubbed their eyes to make sure the game was not a dream. —O.P. Caylor New York Herald May 13, 1890

50 ◆ Babe Herman
(1926–1945, 1552 G, 181 997 .324)

The Cincy batter smacked a line drive to right field which Herman, displaying his usual aplomb, played into a triple. It wasn't easy. But you could depend on the Babe.—Fresco Thompson, *Every Diamond Doesn't Sparkle*

Floyd Caves Herman, known as Babe, did not always catch fly balls on the top of his head, but he could do it in a pinch. He never tripled into a triple play, but he once doubled into a double play, which is the next best thing.—John Lardner

Never once did I get hit on the head by a fly ball. Once or twice on the shoulder, maybe, but never on the head.—Babe Herman

Any saga of creative fielding must begin with the name of Floyd Caves "Babe" Herman, the only player ever to draw his unconditional release when he was batting .416. It seems that the only day the owner of the Omaha club could get out to the park to check his team, Babe tried to field a pop foul with his head.—William Curran, *Mitts*

Herman slouched to the plate, a gangling blond with an immature look and a chew of tobacco

in his jaw so huge it almost obscured his vision.
—Lee Allen, *The Giants and the Dodgers*

One time on a road trip Babe was assigned to share a locker with Fresco Thompson. He was furious. "It's a hell of a note, having to dress with a .250 hitter," he sulked.

"How do you think I feel," Thompson asked politely, "having to dress with a .250 fielder?"

> The image has cost Babe a spot in the Hall of Fame. He was not a clown, just an affable man who went along with the press when they wrote of his daffy doings. Realistically, he was a very intelligent man, learned about the game, about life, a student of human nature, a deep thinker, a lover of orchids, a dedicated husband and father.—Maury Allen, from the intro to *Brooklyn's Babe*

On the Hall of Fame issue . . . I did a search to try to identify the most profoundly comparable post-war players. Since Herman had 230 Career Win Shares, I started with all outfielders who had about that many, 190 to 270; this gave me a list of about 75 comparable outfielders. From that list, I eliminated all those who played significantly more career games than Herman (more than 1800) or significantly fewer games (less than 1300). Next, I eliminated all whose career rate of Win Shares per game was markedly different from Herman's, and then, since Herman's value was 89% offensive, only 11% defensive, I eliminated those whose value was more than 16% in defense—that is, the center fielders and exceptional defensive players who might have been similar to Herman in overall value, but different in their parts. Finally, I eliminated those who did not have peak seasons comparable to Herman's peak seasons—that is, players who were more consistent but not as brilliant, of whom there were several, and those who were even more brilliant but in just

one or two seasons, of which there were a couple.

This left me with a list of about 20 outfielders. The most comparable post-war outfielders to Babe Herman, I concluded, were Roger Maris, Tony Oliva and Pedro Guerrero, with Guerrero being probably the best match. The fourth-best match would be Danny Tartabull, but Tartabull was really not quite as good a player as Herman; the other three were closer in value.

51 ◆ Carl Furillo
(1946–1960, 1806 G, 192 1058 .299)

> He is one of the toughest hitters in the league when he's hot and he stays hot a good deal of the time. His arm is great and he knows how to play every right-field wall in the league. His lack of speed has always kept him from greatness.
> —*Sport Magazine,* September, 1957

> Furillo has been variously called "The Arm," "The Reading Rifle," "The Rock," and "Peg o' my Heart" [due to] one of the most powerful and accurate arms ever.—Roscoe McGowen, *The Artful Dodgers* (Edited by Tom Meany)

> Even though he was one of my best friends, I was hoping Carl would hurt himself just bad enough so I would get a chance, but unfortunately he was a strong, strong guy, and he continued playing, and I was just sitting.—Cal Abrams in *Bums* (Peter Golenbock)

What are "typical" stats for an outfielder rated here?

The average stats for an outfielder rated 1-10 here are 2,769 career hits, 346 homers, 486 doubles, 1,474 RBI, a .312 batting average and a .511 slugging percentage. I did this in chart form at the tope of page 824.

Furillo has fairly typical stats for a player ranking in the 11 to 40 range, although he ranks 51st. My intention was to find some

Rank	Games	Hits	2B	3B	HR	RBI	SB	Avg	SlPct
1–10	2,431	2,769	486	116	346	1,474	291	.312	.511
11–40	1,921	2,104	354	95	197	1,045	228	.295	.457
41–70	1,572	1,605	274	60	160	783	154	.287	.444
71–100	1,413	1,438	244	63	116	676	145	.283	.425

player who was typical for his range of value, and to introduce this chart for that typical player. However, everybody I could find who had "typical" stats ranked below or at the bottom of his range. Hank Bauer, for example, has fairly typical stats for a player ranking 41-70, but ranks 80th. Al Smith does, too, but he ranks 74th. I have no idea why this happens.

52 ◆ Juan Gonzalez
(1989–2000, 1363 G, 362 1142 .294)

It is my opinion that the Texas Ranger players did not deserve any of the three MVP Awards that they have won in the last four years (1996–1999). In my opinion the best player in the American League in 1996 and 1998 was Alex Rodriguez, in 1999 Derek Jeter. The Rangers have won the MVP Awards, I think, for three reasons:

1.   Despite twenty years of solid research documenting the impact of parks on runs scored, sportswriters still adjust for park effects only in dramatic cases, like Coors Field, and in a haphazard manner. Gonzalez and Ivan Rodriguez, playing in one of the best hitter's parks in the American League, have derived an advantage from this.

2.   Johnny Oates is one of few managers in baseball today who uses a traditional lineup, which creates a large number of RBI opportunities in the middle of the order.

3.   Many sportswriters still tremendously over value RBI in comparison to other offensive contributions.

53 ◆ George Hendrick
(1971–1988, 2048 G, 267 1111 .278)

He did not bust his tail on a ball field at all times, and that annoyed fans . . . At times Hendrick seemed almost to stroll when running to first.
—Frank Robinson with Berry Stainback, *Extra Innings*

He had a lot of problems not running balls out, jogging to fly balls in the outfield, that kind of stuff.—Whitey Herzog, *You're Missin' a Great Game*

Herzog tells about being sent to scout George one year when George was an amateur, and probably the best amateur player in the country. With major league scouts lining up to watch him, George showed up without his uniform, and played the game in blue jeans and a T-Shirt. There was no fence in center, so between innings when he wasn't due up Hendrick would go out beyond the field and stretch out in the grass, rather than coming in to the dugout . . .

After a few conflicts with managers and others George stopped talking to the press. He got a reputation as a bad guy, based on his loafing incidents and the fact that he didn't talk. In reality, he probably wasn't a bad guy; most of his teammates liked him and respected him, and he learned to put himself into the game enough to keep his managers off his back. In the final analysis, he earned his money.

54 ◆ Gary Sheffield

(1988–2000, 1449 G, 279 916 .293)

An urban legend in his own mind. As George Hendrick did, he seems to have matured, and is beginning to put his bad-boy image behind him.

55 ◆ Larry Walker

(1989–2000, 1385 G, 271 906 .311)

Coming off three seasons in which he has hit .366, .363 and .379. In the last seventy years there are seven players who have hit .350 three straight years:

> Al Simmons, 1927–1931 (5 straight)
>
> Joe Medwick, 1935–1937
>
> Joe DiMaggio, 1939–1941
>
> Rod Carew, 1973–1975
>
> Wade Boggs, 1985–1988 (4 straight)
>
> Tony Gwynn, 1993–1997 (5 straight)
>
> Larry Walker, 1997–1999

The last player to hit .363 or better three years in a row was Al Simmons, 1929–1931 (.365, .381, .390). Neither Musial nor Ted Williams hit .350 three straight years as a regular. Neither did Gehrig or Ruth, although their career averages were 30 points higher than Walker's, and they had many seasons when they hit over .350.

It will be interesting to see, as time goes by, how well the Hall of Fame voters can see through the phony batting stats of the 1994–2000 era, and pick out the genuinely great players from those who piled up numbers because of the unusual conditions in which they played.

56 ◆ Bob Allison

(1958–1970, 1541 G, 256 796 .255)

Bob Allison hit .255 in his career, with 256 home runs. No player in major league history has an exact match between these two num-

bers. There are five guys who missed by one: Brooks Robinson (268 homers, .267 average), Allison, Tony Armas (251 homers, .252 average), Andre Thornton (253 homers, .254 average) and Deron Johnson (245 homers, .244 average) . . . .Lenny Dykstra hit .285 and stole 285 bases . . .

> Anyone can be successful at baseball if he follows in the path of Bob Allison. All you have to do is be 6-4, strong as a weightlifter, handsome as a shirt model, have the personality of an honor graduate from Dale Carnegie, and, alas, work your head off.–Leonard Schecter, *Sport Magazine*, September, 1964

> One day Bob Allison said that he had heard I could really go. Allison, the six-foot-four, 225-pound left fielder, had been a star fullback at Kansas State in 1953 and 1954. He said he'd like to race me. I told him, "Bob, forget it. I could beat you backwards."–Rod Carew with Ira Berkow, *Carew*

It was Kansas University, not Kansas State, and he wasn't a star; he just carried the ball a few times. As a high school athlete at Raytown, Missouri, a Kansas City suburb, Allison starred in football, basketball, and track; the high school had no baseball team. He played sandlot ball, however, and was well-known to major league scouts when he enrolled at KU. He played two years of college football and baseball before signing with the Senators.

Allison didn't hit his first three years in the minor leagues, but had such a season at Chattanooga in 1958 that Senator scout Sherry Robertson proclaimed him "another DiMaggio." The Senators' 1958 center fielder was Albie Pearson, the 1958 American League Rookie of the Year. Pearson reported to camp in 1959 with a bad leg, however, while Allison was sensational. Calvin Griffith said that Allison had "the best arm we've had on this club since Jackie Jensen," and trainer Doc Lentz said that

Allison was "the strongest boy I've ever handled." Allison was the Senators' clean-up hitter on opening day.

The American League record for home runs by a rookie at that time was 31, by Ted Williams. Allison, with 29 home runs by September 1, seemed sure to break it. He didn't. He hit just one home run after September first, and wound up with 30. Harmon Killebrew, not a rookie that year but a first-year regular, hit 42 home runs; Killebrew and Allison were dubbed "Mr. Upstairs" and "Mr. Downstairs" for the length of their home runs. Allison and Killebrew had been teammates in the minor leagues, were roommates for years and remained friends the rest of Allison's life. Allison played in the All-Star game, led the league in triples, and was the second consecutive Washington center fielder named the American League Rookie of the Year.

Allison was a fierce competitor and a frightening baserunner. "He looks like a locomotive when he's coming in to break up the double play," said an opposing second baseman. "He's gonna slide into somebody and send him to the moon one of these days."

In *Number 1,* with Peter Golenbock, Billy Martin recalled that Allison "was my leader behind the leader on the bench, a beautiful buffer for me. I'd say to him, 'Bob, tell so-and-so about such-and-such when you get a chance,' and coming from Bob they wouldn't resent it nearly as much as if it came from me. If he wasn't in business now, he'd have made somebody an excellent coach."

Allison had a successful career as a Coca-Cola bottler in the Twin Cities after retiring from baseball, but in the early 1990s was stricken by a painful and debilitating illness, which led to his death in 1995.

57 ◆ Jackie Jensen
(1950–1961, 1438 G, 199 929 .279)

Jensen, a serious athlete and a devoted husband and father . . . had a horror of flying. After trying everything else without success, he got his own personal hypnotist, who managed to help him for a while [but] his fear of flying returned and actually drove him out of baseball.—Al Hirshberg, *What's the Matter with the Red Sox?*

When I was sleeping four in a bed down on the fish docks and my folks were on relief, and I couldn't even make a Peewee League team because I was so little, Jackie was the town hero . . . All-City Jensen, the handsome student body president at Oakland High. All the girls after him. What did he ever suffer? They called me "Banana Nose" and threw me out of the school for fighting.—Billy Martin, explaining why Jackie Jensen threatened to quit baseball in 1953, when his career was slow to gain traction. Martin grew up in Oakland in the shadow of Jackie Jensen, and was Jensen's teammate at Oakland in 1949, and with the Yankees from 1950–1952

58 ◆ Tommy Holmes
(1942–1952, 1320 G, 88 581 .302)

Tommy Holmes was the most popular player in the history of the Boston Braves, or at least in the last 30 years thereof. In 1945 he moved to Right Field (from Center), and had a 37-game hitting streak, which was the National League record until it was broken by Pete Rose in 1978. Holmes was a gregarious, friendly man who would talk to the fans in the right field bleachers, and they just adopted him. According to *The Braves: The Pick and The Shovel* (Al Hirschberg, 1949) "His charm lies in his ball field personality, his ready and constant grin, his friendly blue eyes and the happiness in his somewhat high-pitched voice when he addresses his public."

According to Hirschberg, "out in the jury box, Holmes is always right. When he occasionally throws to the wrong base, or misjudges a fly ball, or kicks a ground ball around, the rest of the fans might bleat, but the boys in the bleachers never raise their voice in anger." He also had some impressive stats. Tommy Holmes was the only outfielder in major league history who had more double plays in his career (37) than errors (33). He is the only player in major league history to lead his league in both home runs and fewest strikeouts per at bats in the same season; this he did in 1945, when he had 28 homers and 9 strikeouts in 636 at bats. His career strikeout/walk ratio was the third-best in major league history, behind Joe Sewell and Mickey Cochrane.

59 ◆ Bobby Thomson
(1946–1960, 1779 G, 264 1026 .270)

It is further curious that Thomson, a mediocre outfielder at best throughout his entire major league career, should emerge the hero of this encounter, and Branca, an excellent pitcher for the Dodgers for many years, the goat.—Brendan C. Boyd and Fred C. Harris, *The Great American Baseball Card Flipping* (Trading and Bubble Gum Book)

Whaddeyer, nuts? Branca couldn't carry Thomson's jock. Branca had two good years, 1947–48, not all that good. Thomson drove in 100 runs four times, 82 or more three other times. Thomson was twice the player Branca was.

60 ◆ Wildfire Schulte
(1904–1918, 1806 G, 92 792 .270)

Schulte was called "Wildfire," according to James J. Skipper, as a consequence of his friendship with the great actress, Lillian Russell. Russell, appearing in Vicksburg, Mississippi in a traveling play called "Wildfire," gave a dinner party for the Cubs, who played an exhibition game in Vicksburg the same day. Schulte, who owned some trotting horses,

named one "Wildfire" in response, and his teammates started kidding him about it, transferring the nickname from horse to owner.

If anyone could have found Schulte up to 1898 a more detailed map would be needed. He was born in Cochocton, New York, and started playing ball with Glen Aubrey. From there he went to Poseyville, from Poseyville to Posytuck, to Hickory Grove, to Glossburg, and finally in 1897 got upon the edge of the map at Waverly, playing there two years. Then he went to Lestershire, and reached Syracuse in 1902.

Schulte proved to be a man needed. In him Chance had found one of the rarest baseball treasures, a "third batter." The third batter in any team is the most important. He must hit long flies, hit hard, bunt and run, because ahead of him in a well constructed team are two batters who are on the team for their ability to "get on," and the third man must be able either to move them up or hit them home.—Johnny Evers with Hugh Fullerton, *Baseball in the Big Leagues* (Reilly and Britton, 1910).

61 ◆ Vic Wertz
(1946–1963, 1862 G, 266 1178 .277)

Wertz was the first player to wear a "shield" on his foot while batting, which is now pretty standard equipment. With a closed stance, he fouled a lot of pitches off his foot . . .

Twelve other players in history have batting averages, slugging percentages and on-base percentages within ten points of Wertz'. Alphabetically, they were Leon Durham, Dwight Evans, Joe Gordon, Jackie Jensen, Ray Lankford, Greg Luzinski, Eddie Murray, Bill Nicholson, Ron Santo, Roy Sievers, Mike Stanley, and Vern Stephens . . .

One time in Cleveland, Vic Wertz caught a line smash at first base. Dizzy Dean, broadcasting the game, observed quickly that "that ball went from bat to Wertz."

Some guys have a career; Vic Wertz had an epic. His career had several movements, and a habit of brushing up against history. Wertz played for five American League teams, plus he played for the Browns/Orioles both in St. Louis and Baltimore, and played for Detroit twice.

- With Detroit, he drove in 256 runs in a two-year period, was a key player in the Tigers' charge at a miracle pennant in 1950, was a cornerstone of the Tigers' "Prague Spring" in 1950–51, and a pivotal figure in Red Rolfe's subsequent self-destruction.
- With Baltimore, he played in the first game for the modern Baltimore Orioles.
- With Cleveland, he filled a key slot on a team that won 111 games, breaking the league record of the 1927 Yankees. The most remembered event in Wertz' career is a drive that he hit in the 1954 World Series, which was caught by Willie Mays, perhaps the most famous defensive play in the history of baseball. What almost no one knows about that fly ball is that Wertz hit .500 in the series (8 for 16), with 2 doubles, a triple, and a homer giving him a .938 slugging percentage. Had Mays not made that remarkable catch, Wertz would have hit .563 in the series with a slugging percentage of 1.129. Except that's not exactly true, because there were two men on at the time of the catch; Wertz' drive would almost certainly have won the game for the Indians, which would have meant a fifth game, thus changing all the stats.
- Wertz drove in 100 runs two more times with Cleveland. When Gil McDougald rifled a line drive off Herb Score's forehead, Vic Wertz recorded the putout.
- With Boston, Wertz came out of retirement to drive in 100 runs again, in 1960.
- In his second trip with Detroit, coming out of his second retirement (during

which he had become a truck driver), Wertz was the best pinch hitter in the American League in 1962.

In between, Wertz had a broken leg costing him half a season, and he had polio. A left-handed slugger, he was born to play in Yankee Stadium. He wound up playing with everybody in the league *except* the Yankees. He wasn't a great player, but then, Dr. Zhivago wasn't a great doctor. He was, like Zhivago, a man to whom everything happened that wasn't supposed to happen, a noble man engaged in a long and arduous battle against vicious and powerful fate.

62 ◆ Harvey Kuenn
(1952–1966, 1833 G, 87 671 .303)

1. Growing up in Milwaukee, Kuenn played for a team called the "Ken Keltners" in the "Stars of Yesterday" League. It works for me.

2. Harvey Kuenn led the Big Ten in hits in 1952—with 28. He hit .444, which means he had 63 at bats. What did they play, an 18-game schedule?

3. Kuenn had suffered two knee injuries in high school, one playing football and one playing basketball, and was rejected by the Army because of his knees. Several scouts backed away from offering him money because of this.

4. He was signed for the Tigers by George Moriarty, who had been with the club since the time of Ty Cobb.

5. When Kuenn reached the majors and played well in late 1952 it was the height of the Korean conflict. Willie Mays and Whitey Ford, among many other players, were in the Army at that time. The Army, careful to avoid favoritism, called him back twice more to examine the knee, but ultimately rejected him.

6. Kuenn led the American League in hits his first two seasons, with 209 and 201. He never had 200 hits again, but led the league twice more.

7. Kuenn led the American League in putouts both as a shortstop and an outfielder. I would guess that Robin Yount, who Kuenn managed, might be the only other player to have done that.

8. On June 4, 1958, he hurt the knee again, running headlong into a fence in Baltimore trying to catch a home run by Gus Triandos. He was out of the lineup about two weeks.

9. Kuenn played center field in the 1959 All-Star game. Willie Mays hit a game-winning triple over his head, and Kuenn moved to right field shortly after that.

10. Harvey Kuenn had a career batting average of .303, a slugging percentage of .408. Pete Rose had a career batting average of .303, with a slugging percentage of .409.

63 ◆ Dave Justice
(1989–2000, 1381 G, 276 917 .283)

> "He's got as sweet a swing as I've ever seen," [Bobby] Cox raved. "I know Billy Williams is in the Hall of Fame, but this is as true a swing as I've seen in baseball."—*Baseball Digest,* December, 1990

Nine rated outfielders reached the majors in 1989–Albert Belle, Steve Finley, Juan Gonzalez, Ken Griffey Jr., Marquis Grissom, Dave Justice, Sammy Sosa, Greg Vaughn and Larry Walker. The best of them, by season (best player listed first):

1989 Ken Griffey, Albert Belle, Greg Vaughn

1990 Ken Griffey, Dave Justice, Sammy Sosa

1991 Ken Griffey, Dave Justice, Greg Vaughn

1992 Marquis Grissom, Steve Finley, Larry Walker

1993 Juan Gonzalez, Ken Griffey, Marquis Grissom

1994 Albert Belle, Larry Walker, Ken Griffey

1995 Albert Belle, Sammy Sosa, David Justice

1996 Albert Belle, Ken Griffey, Steve Finley

1997 Ken Griffey, Larry Walker, David Justice

1998 Albert Belle, Sammy Sosa, Greg Vaughn

1999 Ken Griffey, Sammy Sosa, Greg Vaughn

The overall value of these nine players peaked in 1993, but has declined since then at a miniscule rate, about 2% per season. The rate of decline will explode in the next two-three years, as these players begin to reach the end of the line.

64 ◆ Chili Davis
(1981–1999, 2436 G, 350 1372 .274)

Listing him in right field is a compromise... He was a center fielder when he came up, but ran through the positions quickly due to knee injuries which left him too slow to play the outfield for the last half of his career. But then, how many of the players listed here as right fielders were really career right fielders?

No more than half, probably no more than a third. Few players are career right fielders. Many of the top 100 right fielders—Reggie Smith, Andre Dawson, Bobby Murcer, Carl Furillo, Bob Allison, Jackie Jensen, Chili—played center field for several years early in their careers. A dozen or more of the top 100 (Rose, Kuenn, Tony Phillips) are converted infielders. Some of them are guys like Harold Baines who played right field until they became too slow, then moved to DH. Some of them, like Rusty Staub and Vic Wertz, played about as much in left and at first base as they did in right. Except for a few players who have exceptional arms, Right Field is just a transitional position.

Another note about right fielders—I believe that of the 100 top right fielders, less than 10 ever managed in the major leagues, and that includes some whose managerial careers were brief and unmemorable, like Gavy Cravath.

65 ◆ Bill Nicholson
(1936–1953, 1677 G, 235 948 .268)

He claims that Kiki Cuyler, another great Cubs star fielder, is the man most responsible for the advancement in his career.—Gordon Campbell, *Famous American Athletes of Today,* Ninth Series (1945) (Cuyler had managed Nicholson in the minor leagues)

Nicholson grew up in rural Maryland, in the same little triangle of farm country that produced Home Run Baker, Jimmie Foxx, and Charlie Keller. As a boy he was obsessed with the idea of going to Annapolis and becoming a Naval officer. He read Navy books the way other boys read sports books, studied mathematics diligently, was a straight-A student, and wrangled an appointment to Annapolis on graduation from high school.

When he took his physical, however, the Navy doctors discovered that he was color blind. It is a perfect irony: while dozens of athletes who dreamed of nothing but being baseball players were busy fighting a war, perhaps the best player left in the National League was a man who had grown up dreaming of being a Navy officer.

Nicholson had very broad shoulders, idolized Jimmie Foxx, and returned to Maryland to farm after his playing career. The obvious question about him is to what extent his accomplishments during the war should be discounted because of the quality of competition. Nicholson led the National League in home runs and RBI in 1943 and 1944, also in runs scored in 1944.

Nicholson argued, predictably, that the quality of play during the war was better than it was post-expansion. He made this argument in *Our Chicago Cubs,* by Rick Phalen, among other places; he also whined about how tough it was to hit in Wrigley Field at that time, because of the white shirts in the center field bleachers.

While I don't believe that the quality of baseball in World War II was better than it was post-expansion, I do believe that what could be called the "historic mark down" of the wartime seasons has been disproportionate, and that Nicholson is entitled to more respect than he has received. Nicholson hit .295 in 40% of a season in 1939, and drove in 98 runs in 1940, his first season as a regular, and again in 1941. He was a young man then; in 1943–44 he was 27 and 28. We would expect his numbers to get bigger as he matured.

Yes, a lot of the good pitchers were not there, but on the other hand, the balata ball used during the war was not easy to drive. Many of the players who played through the war failed to match their pre-war power numbers. Whitey Kurowski, a legitimate power hitter, played 139 games in 1943, and hit only 13 home runs, while Frank McCormick hit only 8, Gee Walker only 3, and Bob Elliott only 7.

Also, Nicholson's complaint about Wrigley being a tough place to hit at that time is solid. Nicholson in his career hit 99 home runs at home, 136 on the road. The Park Run Factor for Wrigley Field in that era is very low—as low as .83 in some seasons. Putting these things together, I think Nicholson's war-time numbers are essentially legit.

66 ◆ Tony Phillips
(1982–1999, 2161 G, 160 819 .266)

1. Of the 300 outfielders listed here, almost exactly one-half hit 150 career homers, and almost one-half stole 150 bases. Only 47 players—16%—did both. Phillips is in that 16%.

2. Among the 300 listed outfielders, Phillips ranks 89th in career hits (2023), but 48th in secondary bases (2436).

3. Tony Phillips in a spring training game when he was with the Tigers did something I wonder if anyone else has ever done. He played four positions in that game (Right Field, Center

Field, Third Base and Second) and made brilliant defensive plays at all four positions. I certainly have never seen anybody else do that.

67 ◆ Jesse Barfield

(1981–1992, 1428 G, 241 716 .256)

Chuck Klein has the highest rate of Baserunner Kills per 1000 innings of any outfielder born in the twentieth century, with 195 kills (assists) in about 13,740 innings in the outfield—14.2 per 1000 innings. Barfield was just behind him:

	BK	Innings	Rate
1. Chuck Klein	195	13,740	14.2
2. Jesse Barfield	162	11,547	14.0
3. Roy Cullenbine	100	7,268	13.8
4. Bob Johnson	208	15,302	13.6
5. Mel Ott	257	20,043	12.8
6. Roberto Clemente	266	20,755	12.8
7. Paul Waner	247	19,887	12.4
8. Ben Chapman	159	12,944	12.3
9. Dom DiMaggio	147	12,089	12.2
10. Johnny Callison	175	14,997	11.7

Bob Meusel is just a hair behind Barfield at 13.9, but he was born in 1896. Many outfielders who played before 1920 have higher rates than Klein, with the highest rate being by King Kelly (44.1 per 1000 innings).

Barfield, as I am sure you all remember, had a fantastic arm, and liked to put it on display. Late in his career it became fashionable to say that (a) his habit of trying to make long throws to nail runners was costly to his team, and (b) Mark Whiten actually had the best arm in baseball.

I never did buy that. The cost of Barfield's wasted throws was nowhere near the value of the runners he threw out, and, while Whiten had a hell of an arm, it's my opinion that Barfield's was far better.

The opposite list is given in the comment for Kirk Gibson (LF, #36). The lowest kill rates for players listed as right fielders are:

	BK	Innings	Rate
1. Terry Puhl	57	10,587	5.4
2. Danny Tartabull	46	7,676	6.0
3. Harvey Kuenn	43	6,945	6.2

68 ◆ Roy Cullenbine

(1938–1947, 1181 G, 110 599 .276)

The highest rates of walks per 1000 plate appearances:

1. Ted Williams	206
2. Maxie Bishop	200
3. Babe Ruth	194
4. Ferris Fain	184
5. Eddie Stanky	183
6. Gene Tenace	178
7. Roy Cullenbine	178
8. Frank Thomas	177
9. Eddie Yost	176
10. Mickey Mantle	175

11–20, Charlie Keller, John McGraw, Barry Bonds, Mark McGwire, Mickey Tettleton, Joe Morgan, Rickey Henderson, Earl Torgeson, Bernie Carbo, Ralph Kiner.

> "Cullenbine wouldn't swing the bat," DeWitt recalled. "Sewell would give him the hit sign and he'd take it, trying to get the base on balls. Laziest human being you ever saw."—William B. Mead, *Baseball Goes to War*

In January, 1940, Judge Landis ruled that the Tigers had been guilty of widespread improper manipulation of organized baseball's roster limits, indirectly controlling the baseball fates of 106 players with whom they had no direct contracts. Landis ordered 91 of these 106 players freed from their minor league contracts, and the other 15 to be compensated for their losses. According to Fred Lieb in *The Detroit*

Tigers, "the top players set free were [Benny] McCoy and Outfielder Cullenbine, the latter a former Detroit sand-lotter . . . Cullenbine got a $25,000 check from Larry MacPhail, then head man in Brooklyn."

69 ◆ Richie Zisk
(1971–1983, 1453 G, 207 792 .287)

> Take a drawing out of a book on hitting, put the prescribed stance into real life, and Richie Zisk will come alive. He has a perfect stance, squared at the plate, bat cocked and weight evenly distributed.—*The Scouting Report,* 1983

Zisk was a solid player, but he just couldn't run. He was out of his time, like Greg Luzinski; he would have been more valuable playing in the 1950s or the 1990s, when he could have hit more home runs and his lack of speed in the outfield would have been less noticeable. A poor man's Harry Heilmann or Joe Medwick.

70 ◆ Ruben Sierra
(1986–2000, 1682 G, 240 1054 .269)

> Sierra has lost his plus speed . . . his arm in right field is now no better than average and his range is limited. He also made his share of bonehead plays in Oakland.—*The Scouting Report: 1995* (The Baseball Workshop)

When Sierra came to the majors he was often compared to Roberto Clemente. He had idolized Clemente as a youth, was a good right fielder with a good arm, and, as a right-handed hitter, was very reminiscent of Clemente, bailing out and flinging the head of the bat wildly with strong wrists. Sierra was a switch-hitter, and as a left-handed hitter he was normal, but as a right-hander he was kind of Clemente light, although he insisted that as a kid he had never seen films of Clemente hitting, and that this was just his own natural approach, as it was Clemente's. This may well be true, as Sierra was always a far better hitter with the right-handed Clemente-type approach than he was left-handed, batting "normal."

Clemente was a one-of-a-kind player, and as Sierra matured this became more and more evident. Clemente was able to cover a strike zone from his shoelaces to the bill of his cap. Sierra was not. Sierra, never fat but bigger than Clemente, filled out until he could more easily be mistaken for Dave Parker than Roberto. He had leg injuries. He was a good player, but he never reached the level that I and a lot of other people thought that he would.

71 ◆ Danny Tartabull
(1984–1997, 1406 G, 262 925 .273)

Jose Tartabull played in the majors for nine years, hitting only two home runs. Son Danny had matched that in his first 20 major league at bats, and developed into a consistent 100-RBI man when healthy. Jose, asked where Danny got his power, said "I guess he gets it from his mother."

There has never been a father/son combination in the majors in which the son so little resembled the father as a player except possibly Yogi and Dale Berra. Jose was among the fastest players in baseball in his era, a good outfielder and a decent singles hitter, but not a strong enough hitter to be a regular. Danny was a power hitter but a brutal outfielder and an indifferent baserunner.

Jose was a friendly little guy with a sense of humor, but a man who kind of melted into the woodwork. Danny had a big smile, was articulate and had a sense of style, but he was hypersensitive, moody, and never well liked.

72 ◆ Tim Salmon
(1992–2000, 1113 G, 230 757 .291)

An old-fashioned hard-hat kind of player, good arm, not too much speed, works hard and rarely goes into a slump. Ninety walks a year and a .290 average give him an on-base percentage near .400. Has gone over 200 homers this season (2000) and probably will hit a couple hundred more before the fastballs get too fast for him.

73 ◆ Wally Moses
(1935–1951, 2012 G, 89 679 .291)

Deacon Jones, the umpire, cleaned off the Athletics' bench. Wally Moses was sitting down there in the corner, and Wally, you know, never said an unkind word to anybody in his life. —Spud Chandler, quoted by Donald Honig in *Baseball When the Grass Was Real*

Jones ran Moses off the bench, too. Wally protested that he hadn't said or done anything. "I know," said the umpire. "But when the law raids a house of prostitution, the innocent have to go with the guilty."

Wally Moses hit 25 home runs in 1937, but, despite remaining a regular through the end of the war, never hit more than 9 in any other season—a major league record, most home runs in one season with no other season in double digits. He also set career highs that year in doubles (48), triples (13), hits (208), which of course led to career highs in runs scored and RBI.

When Wally Moses was in the low minors in 1931, a New York Giants scout told him that the Giants were negotiating to buy him. "By the way," said the scout, "you are Jewish, aren't you?" When Moses told the scout that he wasn't Jewish the Giants lost interest in him.

Moses hit .300 or better his first seven seasons in the major leagues—.325, .345, .320, .307, .307, .309 and .301. Time, war, and a trade to Chicago took the threes out of his batting averages, but Moses remained physically fit the rest of his life. He hung around for a long time as a coach, and was famous for being able to step in the batter's box when he was 60 years old and slap line drive after line drive after line drive during batting practice. See also Gus Zernial (LF #96).

74 ◆ Al Smith
(1953–1964, 1517 G, 164 676 .272)

I was traded three times in my career; two of those three times I heard it on the radio while I was sitting in a barber shop.—Al Smith in *When the Cheering Stops* (Heiman, Weiner and Gutman)

When Al Smith came to the Indians in 1953 he took Harry Simpson's job. In 1954 Smith was getting divorced, which at that time required a trial. Simpson showed up to be a character witness. "How can you say nice things about this guy," asked the judge, "after he took your job away?"

Smith was a star high school athlete in Kirkwood, Missouri, a football running back and a Golden Gloves boxing champion. He played with the Cleveland Buckeyes of the Negro American League, and signed with the Indians in 1948, as soon as the color line broke.

Smith thought the world of Bill Veeck, loved being around Veeck and loved playing for him; he says that every major league clubhouse should have a picture of Bill Veeck in it. His first major league manager was Al Lopez, also a good one, and his first major league team (in a full season) won 111 games, an American League record at the time. Ed Lopat used to beat the Indians every time he faced them. About the third time he saw Lopat, Smith told Al Lopez, "This guy's not that quick off the mound. Why don't we see if we can beat him with bunts?" They beat Lopat with bunts, and Lopez decided Smith was his kind of player. When Lopez moved to Chicago he traded Minnie Minoso to get Smith back.

Smith is most famous for a photo taken of him during the 1959 World Series, when a cup of beer was spilled on his head as he faded back to the wall. The Red Sox released him in 1964. Smith took a long, thick nail and drove it into a beam in his house, hung his baseball shoes and his glove on that nail, and told his son that if those things fell off he would go back and play some more baseball, but if they didn't his career was over. They never fell off, and he never went back. He got a job with the Chicago parks department, running baseball programs throughout the city, and worked at that until it was time to retire.

75 ◆ Jeff Burroughs
(1970–1981, 1689 G, 240 882 .261)
When he graduated from high school Burroughs signed an $88,000 bonus contract with the Senators. According to Shelby Whitfield in *Kiss It Goodbye,* he had a clause written into the contract specifying that no matter what happened, his parents were not to get a nickel of the money . . . .

When Burroughs reached the majors in 1970 his first manager was Ted Williams. The two men sincerely hated one another. One incident retold by Whitfield is that Burroughs, who chewed gum constantly, would take out his gum at night and stick it on the bed post. The hotel maids didn't appreciate that, and one of the maids wrote Burroughs a note asking him to throw his gum in the trash. Burroughs (or one of his teammates) wrote back a note telling the hotel maid to go _____ herself. Ted Williams had to talk to the rookie and tell him not to stick gum on the bed post and write nasty notes to the maid.

76 ◆ John Titus
(1903–1913, 1402 G, 38 561 .282)
Titus was a small, quiet man, nicknamed Silent John. Nineteenth century players, as you know, usually wore big handlebar moustaches. Titus was the last player in baseball to have a

moustache like that; they were on the way out before he reached the majors. There were later players who grew a moustache for a year or so, but no player from 1913 to 1965 had a moustache as a regular thing. Titus was the last player before Rollie Fingers to have a big wide moustache.

Titus, like U. L. Washington, Sam Jones and others, played with a toothpick in his mouth. He also chewed tobacco, and he claimed that the toothpick kept the chewing tobacco off his teeth. According to Lee Allen in *The Hot Stove League,* at one point in his career pitchers discovered that he would shift the toothpick to the middle of his teeth and bite down on it when he was determined to swing at the next pitch. Pitchers would exploit this by keeping the ball away from him when he was ready to swing, until Titus discovered the trick and corrected the mannerism.

Titus never cashed his paychecks until the end of the year. He would save them in an envelope in his room, and deposit them in his hometown bank when the season was over. He broke his leg in 1911, and his speed didn't return, forcing him into retirement although he could still hit as well as he ever had.

77 ◆ Von Hayes
(1981–1992, 1495 G, 143 696 .267)
A greyhound who was kind of a career disappointment. Even when he played well, and he had four seasons in which he played very well, he was somehow never as good as he was supposed to be. But he was better than Von Joshua.

78 ◆ Oyster Burns
(1884–1895, 1187 G, 65 832 .300)
Between games of a Fourth of July double header in 1891, Burns was resting on the outfield grass with some of his teammates including Tom Daly, the team's catcher. Just horsing

around, Burns pulled out a pen knife and pushed it against Daly's leg. Daly jerked, rolled over quickly, and snapped a tendon in his leg, putting him out of action the rest of the year.

At Brooklyn on June 27, 1893, Burns was involved in one of the odder plays in baseball history. Burns was on second and Con Daily, the team's catcher, was on third, when a ground ball was hit to shortstop. Dailey broke for home, and Burns, seeing Dailey move, ran to third base.

Half-way home, however, Daily began to retreat. Running full speed back to third base, Dailey discovered that Burns was already occupying the base, so he bolted past him and ran for second. The catcher, chasing Daily, continued the chase toward second. Daily beat him there, and the umpire, temporarily confused, signaled "Safe." The two men had switched bases—Burns to third, Dailey back to second.

On reflection, the umpire reversed himself, and called Dailey out.

The nickname "Oyster" was never commonly applied to Burns during his lifetime. He was called Tom Burns or Tommy; the nickname "Oyster" has been adopted by historians, perhaps to distinguish him from the contemporary third baseman of the same name.

79 ◆ Bing Miller
(1921–1936, 1821 G, 116 990 .312)
Judge Landis' first ruling as Commissioner was that Bing Miller was the property of the Washington Senators. Miller had a big year with Little Rock in 1920. Somehow both Pittsburgh and Washington thought they had purchased him, which was a common thing in those days. Landis first official act, even before banning the Black Sox from returning to baseball, was to sort it out . . . The nickname "Bing" has two published sources. Newspapers from the 1930s

often said that it was a baseball nickname, given to him by sportswriters while he was in the minor leagues. It was supposed to be the sound of the ball coming off his bat. According to James J. Skipper, however, he was nicknamed "Bing" by his brother after a cartoon character. According to Skipper's *Baseball Nicknames*, "It comes from the comic strip character in 'Uncle George Washington Bing, the Village Story Teller', that appeared in the Vinton, Iowa, newspaper, *Eagle*."

According to Ray Hayworth in *Baseball Between the Wars* "Bing Miller was the best curveball hitter of all time. We just couldn't throw him a curveball, he'd wear us out." Miller coached for Connie Mack in the 1940s, one of the group of veterans who ran that team in the years Connie was slipping . . .

80 ◆ Hank Bauer
(1948–1961, 1544 G, 164 703 .277)

> I went into the Marines. Why, I don't know. I saw the poster and saw that blue uniform and all that bullshit. I was 18 going on 19. My dad had to sign the papers, and I told him I could take up a trade in the Marine Corps. Pipefitting or something. Shit, the only thing I traded was a bat for a rifle.—Bauer to Jack Etkin in *Innings Ago*

I realize that nobody cares, but the enduring description of Bauer, that he had a face like a closed fist, has been in recent years credited to *LA Times* columnist Jim Murray. It was in fact offered by a 1960s actor/comedian named Jan Murray.

Hank Bauer and Fuzzy Smith, contemporary right fielders on rival teams, have highly similar career batting stats—the same number of career homers, similar batting averages, slugging percentages and on base percentages in about the same number of games. Both players played for good teams throughout their careers. Bauer's individual won-lost record (see Tris Speaker comment for explanation) was about 927–617, a .601 percentage, among the best ever. Smith's was about 855–662, still an outstanding .564 percentage.

As a Marine in World War II, Bauer was involved in invading four islands—New Georgia, Emirau, Guam, and Okinawa. During one action he caught some shrapnel in the back of his thigh, which he carried with him the rest of his life, it being too dangerous to remove. In the early 1950s a Congressman, trolling for publicity, published a list of athletes who had gotten "soft duty" during World War II, and put Bauer's name on the list. This didn't get the distinguished gentleman the type of publicity he had been hoping for. "Did I say Bauer?" said the Congressman. "I meant *Sauer*, Hank Sauer." Sauer had also seen combat, although not as much as Bauer, so that didn't help much.

Bauer, despite his tough-guy image and willingness to join in on-field and in-the-nightclub brawls, was an easy-going man, popular with the New York press and with other players. He is profiled in countless books about those teams.

81 ◆ Sixto Lezcano
(1974–1985, 1291 G, 148 591 .271)
No relation to Antonio Alfonseca.

82 ◆ Elmer Valo
(1940–1961, 1806 G, 58 601 .282)

> Elmer Valo put out 100 percent every day, running, catching and throwing. He'd run into fences to go after the ball and into the stands. He was a good hitter, a complete player. He was a lot of fun off the field, an easygoing, nice, funny person. Everyone liked Elmer.—Eddie Joost

> Another player I admired was Elmer Valo, a team player who was a lot of fun to be around and

who shared his experiences with younger players.—Joe DeMaestri

Highest on base percentages among outfielders who played 1500 or more games and are not in the All of Fame:

1.	Barry Bonds	.409
2.	Rickey Henderson	.405
3.	Elmer Valo	.398
4.	Bob Johnson	.393
5.	Augie Galan	.390

83 ◆ Jay Buhner
(1987–2000, 1453 G, 308 960 .254)
Having a fine comeback season as I write this . . . Lowest career stolen base percentages for listed outfielders:

1.	Jay Buhner	6 for 30	20%
2.	Vic Wertz	9 for 28	32%
3.	Willie Horton	20 for 58	34%
4.	Richie Zisk	8 for 23	35%
5.	Ken Singleton	21 for 57	37%
6.	Gene Woodling	29 for 74	39%
7.	Frank Thomas	15 for 37	41%
8.	Rocky Colavito	19 for 46	41%
9.	Jim Lemon	13 for 31	42%
10.	Jeff Burroughs	16 for 38	42%

Buhner, who has something close to 0% body fat, is faster than he looks in the stats, although he is not fast. He is a very good outfielder, fine arm and doesn't make mistakes, and a valuable offensive player because he has hit 40 or more homers three times and drawn 100 or more walks twice.

Mariner fans know that the M's acquired Buhner from the Yankees for almost nothing (Ken Phelps), but how many of you know how the Yanks got him? They got him for perhaps even less. The Yankees got Buhner, Dale Berra and a minor leaguer in exchange for Steve Kemp and Tim Foli, both of whom were washed up.

84 ◆ Claudell Washington

(1974–1990, 1912 G, 164 824 .278)

Washington, an undrafted free agent in 1972, was in the majors as a 19-year-old in 1974, and hit .308 as a 20-year-old regular in 1975; he is among the best players ever to slip through the draft. Washington was listed at six foot even but looked taller, with an angular build and a long, loping stride. He was among the best 20-year-old outfielders of all time, and was perceived as a failure most of his career because he did not develop from that platform. The only listed right fielders to have their best seasons at age 20 were Kaline and Claudell.

85 ◆ Tom Brunansky

(1981–1994, 1800 G, 271 919 .245)

In a comment about Tom Brunansky printed many years ago, I described him as a young player with old player's skills, and speculated (there and in other places) that it might be true that such players would tend to peak early and fade away earlier than other players. By "old player's skills," I meant that Brunansky had power and was a disciplined hitter who would take a walk, but that he did not run particularly well or have a high batting average. These are old player's skills because, as a player ages, his batting average declines and his stolen bases decline, but his power increases and his walks increase. Brunansky started out where other players were going.

I decided to check now and see whether this theory was true. Starting with all the outfielders listed 1 to 100, I sorted out 25 players who had:

1. Relatively low batting averages, but
2. Good slugging percentages,
3. Good on-base percentages, and
4. Not too many stolen bases.

I'm not going to list them all, but it's guys you would expect–Brunansky, Jeff Burroughs, Jack Clark, Rocky Colavito, Sid Gordon, Ralph Kiner, Willie Stargell, Greg Luzinski etc. Then I sorted out 25 outfielders who were the exact opposite–Ginger Beaumont, Lou Brock, Ron LeFlore, Willie McGee, Vada Pinson, Mickey Rivers, Edd Roush, Lonnie Smith, etc.

Conclusion? Although the extent to which this is true is not as large as I might have expected, there is no doubt that it is true. The outfielders who had "old players skills" did in fact peak earlier and fade faster than the players who had "young players skills." From ages 21 through 23 the two groups of players were equal in value, 614 Win Shares for the "Young" players, 615 for the "Old" players. But from ages 24-26 the players with "old" skills had 7% less value (1482-1379), and as time passed the gap widened steadily. From ages 28–30 they had 10% less value (1518-1359), from ages 31–33 they had 10% less value (1340-1207), from 34–36 they had 26% less value (916-674), from 37–39 they had 38% less value (346-214), and from 40–42 they had 83% less value (117 to 20).

Brunansky was an outstanding defensive outfielder, had a strong arm, and played everything right. There were others in his group who were good outfielders–Jay Buhner, Dwight Evans, Sid Gordon, Tommy Henrich, Charlie Keller, Sixto Lezcano and Bill Nicholson. Sometimes people assume that a low-average power hitter would be a poor outfielder, but that's not always true.

86 ◆ Terry Puhl

(1977–1991, 1531 G, 62 435 .280)

A fielder's Error Rate is the complement of his fielding percentage. If his fielding percentage is .990, his error rate is .010; if his fielding percentage is .980, his error rate is .020, etc.

Terry Puhl has the second-lowest error rate, compared to league norms for his era, of any outfielder listed here. He fielded .993 against a league norm of .980, thus made only 35% of the normal errors. The ten best:

1. Brian Downing   .995 vs. .982   28%
2. Terry Puhl   .993 vs. .980   35%
3. Pete Rose   .991 vs. .977   39%
4. Brett Butler   .992 vs. .981   42%
5. Amos Otis   .991 vs. .980   45%
6. Joe Rudi   .991 vs. .980   45%
7. Walt Judnich   .988 vs. .974   46%
8. Amos Strunk   .980 vs. .959   48%
9. Tommy Holmes   .989 vs. .978   50%
10. Jimmy Piersall   .990 vs. .980   50%

Darryl Hamilton, not listed, also would rank ahead of Puhl. Puhl was a terrific mechanical player, but just didn't have the power or the arm to be a top-flight right fielder.

87 ◆ Buck Freeman
(1891–1907, 1126 G, 82 713 .293)

> Freeman's hit landed "on a porch on the other side of the street."—*Washington Post,* May 23, 1899

> Freeman, never much of a fielder ... attracted nation-wide attention by hitting twenty-five home runs for the Washington National League club in 1899, a believe-it-or-not feat in that day.—Fred Lieb, *The Boston Red Sox*

There are some players in baseball history about whom nobody really knows much of anything. Freeman appears to be one of them.

88 ◆ Tommy McCarthy
(1884–1896, 1275 G 44 735 .292)

McCarthy played in the 1890s, when many more runs were scored than even in modern baseball (2000), and also played in the best hitter's parks in baseball at that time. Thus, the offensive context in which he performed was the richest for any outfielder listed among the top 100. The top five in Runs Per Game, considering league norms and park effects:

1. Tommy McCarthy   6.30
2. Bill Lange   6.24
3. Tip O'Neill   6.14
4. Hugh Duffy   6.06
5. Billy Hamilton   5.98

The top 25 players on this list are all nineteenth-century players. The top twentieth-century players are listed in the Dante Bichette comment (#90), and the outfielders playing in the most run-scarce environments throughout their career are listed in the George Stone comment (Left Field, #63).

Lowest-rated Hall of Famers:

C– Ray Schalk (35)
1B–George Kelly (65)
2B–Bid McPhee (30)
3B–Freddy Lindstrom (43)
SS–Travis Jackson (40)
LF–Chick Hafey (59)
CF–Lloyd Waner (50)
RF–Tommy McCarthy (88)

Catchers Al Lopez (41) and Wilbert Robinson (86) rate lower than Schalk, but were elected substantially as managers; same thing with Miller Huggins at second (37).

89 ◆ Tony Armas
(1976–1989, 1432 G, 251 815 .252)

Tony Armas went from being underrated to being overrated in about two weeks. Armas had two skills: an outstanding arm, and power. The rest of his game was zeroes; his speed was average, he was a .250 hitter, and his strikeout/walk ratio was the worst in major league history until Shawon Dunston came along. Up to 1979 he was just a platoon player/defensive sub in right field, prone to long slumps. When Billy Martin took over the A's in 1980 he put Armas in the lineup, and got him to cut down on his swing with two strikes on him (and, allegations were, to cork his bat.) He hit 35 homers and drove in 109 runs, anyway, and a lot of people immediately lost sight of his many weaknesses.

Ten worst strikeout/walk ratios in history: 1. Shawon Dunston (888 to 192) 2. Tony Armas (1201 to 260), 3. Mariano Duncan, 4. Cory Snyder 5. Joe Hornung, 6. Cito Gaston, 7. John Shelby, 8. Don Demeter, 9. Luis Salazar, 10. Pete Incaviglia. Dante Bichette (below) was on the list until 1999, when he took 54 walks and pulled himself off the worst-ever list.

90 ◆ Dante Bichette
(1988–2000, 1597 G, 262 1092 .299)

Bichette played in the best-hitting park in the major leagues in the biggest-hitting era of the twentieth century. Thus, he ranks first among all twentieth-century outfielders in "individual offensive context," the number of runs per game scored by a typical team throughout this player's career. The top ten:

1.	Dante Bichette	5.42
2.	Earl Averill	5.37
3.	Joe Vosmik	5.36
4.	Sammy West	5.26
5.	Bruce Campbell	5.21
6.	John Stone	5.21
7.	Al Simmons	5.12
8.	Bing Miller	5.11
9.	Carl Reynolds	5.07
10.	Chuck Klein	5.05

91 ◆ Socks Seybold
(1899–1908, 996 G, 51 556 .294)

The Washington Senators at the turn of the century used to have a flag pole at the wall in dead center field, and a little dog house at the base of the flag pole which was used to store the flag when it was taken down. One time a ball bounced into the dog house, and Seybold reached in to try to retrieve the ball. He couldn't reach it, so he stuck his head in to find the ball—and got stuck. The batter circled the bases while Seybold struggled to free himself from the dog house.

Socks was a roly-poly fellow who played right field with a first-baseman's mitt, by Ban Johnson's special permission. He won as much fame with his omnivorous appetite as with his home-run bat.—Fred Lieb, *Connie Mack*

92 ◆ Jack Tobin
(1914–1927, 1619 G, 64 581 .309)

Tobin was a tiny man, with a listed weight of 142 pounds, plus he was not exceptionally fast. He used a big, heavy bat, and he bunted probably once a game to get on base. As a hitter he could be compared to Nellie Fox, a consistent 200-hit man (he had 236 in 1921), of which about 190 a year were bloops and bunts. Tobin hit 64 homers, but that was just because he played in Sportsmans Park; Nellie actually out-homered him in road games, 30-19.

93 ◆ John Stone
(1928–1938, 1200 G, 77 707 .310)

A college football star (Maryville College) and a college graduate (1928). In 1930 Stone had a 34-game hitting streak, still one of the longest in American League history. In May, 1933, he hit four doubles and two homers in a doubleheader. After the 1933 season he was traded even up for Goose Goslin, although was several years older than Stone. He was a quiet Southerner who hunted and fished with the other Southerners on his teams, but never had much to do with the reporters, and isn't remembered for anything other than the fact that he could hit.

94 ◆ Frank Demaree
(1932–1944, 1155 G, 72 591 .299)

Many of you probably know that Carl Furillo missed a career batting average of .300 by only one at bat; had he made one fewer out in his long career, he would have hit .300. But actually, Demaree missed a .300 career average by even less than Furillo did; Furillo missed his batting average rounding up to .300 by .22 hits, Demaree by .13 hits. The ten players who missed .300 career averages by the thinnest margins (numbers given are hits):

1. Frank Demaree   .13
2. Carl Furillo   .22
3. Bake McBride   .97
4. Hardy Richardson   1.78
5. Rico Carty   2.00
6. Harry Rice   2.13
7. Jack Doyle   2.68
8. Frank McCormick   3.04
9. Sammy West   3.33
10. Pepper Martin   6.04

All except Martin were career .299 hitters; Martin finished at .298 . . .

Demaree was a Carl Furillo-type player, although he didn't have as many good years as Carl, a solid right-handed hitter and a good right fielder. He failed his first shot at a major league job. Playing 134 games for the Cubs in 1933, he hit .272 but with only 6 homers, 22 walks, 51 RBI—numbers not sufficient to keep him in the majors at that time. He returned to Los Angeles of the Pacific Coast League, where he saved his career with one of the best seasons in the history of the PCL, winning the MVP Award and the triple crown (.383, 45, 173), with 41 stolen bases making him one of three players in minor league history to have a 40/40 combination. The Los Angeles Angels of 1934 were one of the best teams in minor league history (see article in Part 1, 1930s).

Returning to the Cubs in 1935, Demaree hit .325 as the Cubs regular center fielder, helping the team to 100 wins and the National League pennant; he hit only two homers in the season, but added two more in the World Series. He started the All-Star game for the National League in 1936 (when he hit .350

with 16 homers, 96 RBI), and in 1937 (when he hit .314 with 17 homers, 115 RBI), and played for four teams which won the NL pennant—the Cubs of '32, '35 and '38, and the Cardinals in '43.

95 ◆ Tony Conigliaro
(1964–1975, 876 G, 166 516 .264)
Nineteen-year-old All-Star team (since 1900):

C— Ivan Rodriguez, 1991
1B— Phil Cavarretta, 1936
2B— Sibby Sisti, 1940
3B— Buddy Lewis, 1936
SS— Robin Yount, 1975
LF— Tony Conigliaro, 1964
CF— Ken Griffey Jr., 1989
RF— Mel Ott, 1928
SP— Wally Bunker, 1964
SP— Dwight Gooden, 1984
SP— Bob Feller, 1938
SP— Gary Nolan, 1967
SP— Chief Bender, 1903
RA—Billy McCool, 1964

Conigliaro is also the only twenty-year-old to lead his league in home runs (32 in 1965), although he is bumped off the 20-year-old all-star team by the emergence of Ted Williams, Ty Cobb, and Al Kaline.

The pitch by Jack Hamilton on August 18, 1967, which hit Conigliaro under the eye, was the third time in his short career that Conigliaro had been hurt by a pitch. On July 26, 1964, Conigliaro's forearm was fractured by a pitch from Pedro Ramos. He was out until September 4, and this prevented Conigliaro from hitting 30+ home runs as a 19-year-old. On July 28, 1965, Conigliaro was hit on the hand by Wes Stock; he suffered a hairline fracture in his left wrist, and was out of action for three and a half weeks, although he returned to lead the league in home runs.

96 ◆ Pete Fox
(1933–1945, 1461 G, 65 695 .298)

"When it came to drinking, you should have seen Pete Fox and that Indian catcher we had, York," Billy Rogell recalled in *Cobb Would Have Caught It* (Richard Bak). Rogell tells about one time when he and a teammate met

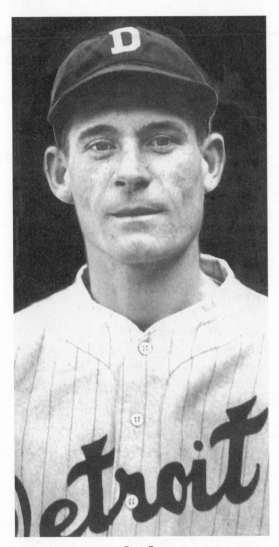

Pete Fox

Fox and Rudy York in a bar. Fox and York had already had ten or twelve beers, but Rogell and his buddy stopped to have one with them, then left. Rogell went to dinner, went out to a movie, and got back to the hotel around eleven. Fox and York were still sitting there drinking, with cases of empty bottles arrayed in front of them.

"Jesus Christ, did you guys eat?" asked Rogell. They said "No," they'd just been sittin' there enjoying the evening.

97 ◆ Jim Lemon
(1950–1963, 1010 G, 164 529 .262)

Lemon thrilled the Washington fans last August when he slammed three consecutive home runs off Whitey Ford, of the Yankees, on a night President Eisenhower attended. No one else in Griffith Stadium history ever slammed out three straight homers.—*Baseball Digest,* April, 1957

The year before, Lemon had become the only man in the history of organized baseball to hit four home runs in an All-Star game. In the Southern Association All-Star Game on July 19, 1955, Lemon homered four times, driving in seven runs in a nine-inning game . . .

According to the Win Shares system, Jim Lemon was the worst defensive outfielder to have a long career in the major leagues . . . we credit him with 1.50 Win Shares per 1,000 innings, meaning that he's about 20% worse than Rico Carty. Actually, there are guys who were worse than Lemon, but those guys, like Kevin Reimer and Danny Walton, were *so* bad that they couldn't stay in the league. Lemon was just good enough, and a big enough power hitter, that he could stay in the league despite his glove. Lemon should have hit 400-500 homers in his career, but didn't get to play more than a few games until he was almost 30 because of military service, bad luck, and the very visible holes in his game.

98 ◆ Bruce Campbell
(1930–1942, 1360 G, 106 766 .290)

> On August 2, 1935, the Indians were "amazed to discover that Campbell was in critical condition at a hospital, victim of cerebral spinal fever, a form of spinal meningitis. The doctors said he had no more than a fifty-fifty chance to recover. All baseball rooted for Bruce Campbell, one of the nicest guys [on the team]."–Franklin Lewis, *The Cleveland Indians*

Campbell recovered from his illness, but had several relapses over the next few years, bouncing him in and out of the hospital, and preventing him from playing up to his ability. Campbell was a left-handed hitter whose ability, had he been healthy, was not quite at a Hall of Fame level, but close.

99 ◆ Orator Shaffer
(1877–1890, 842 G, 10 308 .283)

The Chicago White Stockings traveled to Indianapolis in 1879 to play an exhibition game. Orator Shaffer and Silver Flint, who had played for Indianapolis the year before, had left some heavy debts around town, and, according to Preston Orem (*Baseball: 1845–1881*) Indiana "still had some old fashioned laws, a bit rough on debtors." Before the game, police showed up at the park with warrants for Shaffer and Flint. Cap Anson demanded loudly to see the warrants, studied them ostentatiously, and pronounced them legally insufficient. Of course, Anson was just bluffing, but while he was stalling Flint and Shaffer disappeared into the crowd, and began working their way back to Chicago. After the game police came back and arrested Anson, who posted a $30 bond, and forfeited it. New warrants were sworn for the arrest of Flint and Shaffer, but they were out of state before the warrants could be served.

100 ◆ Carl Reynolds
(1927–1939, 1222 G, 80 695 .302)

> They used to call Carl Reynolds "The One-Man Track Team" when he was burning up college fields during his studious days at Southwestern University, Georgetown, Tex., for he was another Frank Merriwell in all branches of athletic endeavor, also starring at baseball, football and basketball.–*Who's Who In the Major Leagues*, 1935

Many of you probably know that Bill Dickey was suspended for thirty days in 1931 for breaking Carl Reynolds jaw in a fight on July 4, 1931. Dickey had been smarting for a week or so after a Boston baserunner had piled into him at home plate. Reynolds, who weighed 210 pounds and could fly, tagged up on a fly ball, but got to home plate to find the ball waiting for him. He smashed into Dickey full force, knocking the ball loose and scoring the run. As he was returning to the dugout Dickey ran up to him from behind and hit him more or less from the rear, breaking his jaw in two places. Reynolds, hitting .360 and coming off an outstanding 1930 season, had to have his jaw wired shut and was unable to eat solids for six weeks. He lost 25 pounds, and never really got back where he had been.

101. Jim Northrup, 102. Floyd Robinson, 103. Oscar Gamble, 104. Kevin Bass, 105. Jimmy Johnston, 106. Danny Green, 107. Bake McBride, 108. Mike Mitchell, 109. Curt Blefary, 110. Taffy Wright, 111. Ival Goodman, 112. Willard Marshall, 113. George Selkirk, 114. Curt Walker, 115. Casey Stengel, 116. Steve Evans, 117. Mike Marshall, 118. Johnny Wyrostek, 119. Al Cowens, 120. Max Flack, 121. Patsy Donovan, 122. Rob Deer, 123. Willie Crawford, 124. Red Murray, 125. Owen Wilson

RIGHT FIELD

Rank	Player Name	Career WS	Top 3	Top 5	Per 162
1.	Babe Ruth	756	55, 53, 51	233	48.93
2.	Hank Aaron	643	41, 38, 38	183	31.58
3.	Frank Robinson	519	41, 41, 34	164	29.94
4.	Mel Ott	528	38, 36, 36	177	31.33
5.	Pete Rose	547	37, 34, 32	160	24.80
6.	Tony Gwynn	394	39, 35, 30	136	26.94
7.	Reggie Jackson	444	41, 32, 32	148	25.50
8.	Roberto Clemente	377	35, 30, 29	146	25.10
9.	Paul Waner	423	36, 34, 32	154	26.88
10.	Sam Crawford	446	36, 36, 32	159	28.70
11.	Al Kaline	443	31, 31, 30	130	25.32
12.	Enos Slaughter	323	37, 29, 29	141	18.48
13.	Dave Winfield	415	33, 31, 28	132	22.61
14.	Dave Parker	327	37, 33, 31	150	21.48
15.	Bobby Bonds	302	32, 31, 31	149	26.45
16.	Harry Heilmann	356	35, 32, 30	154	26.84
17.	Bobby Murcer	277	38, 36, 27	146	23.51
18.	Ken Singleton	302	36, 33, 32	153	23.49
19.	Andre Dawson	340	29, 28, 26	132	20.96
20.	Reggie Smith	325	29, 29, 26	129	26.49
21.	Tony Oliva	245	33, 30, 28	134	23.68
22.	Dwight Evans	347	31, 29, 26	122	21.57
23.	Elmer Flick	291	37, 32, 31	152	31.80
24.	Rusty Staub	358	32, 30, 28	145	19.65
25.	Pedro Guerrero	246	35, 32, 30	134	25.94
26.	Rocky Colavito	273	33, 32, 29	133	24.02
27.	Jack Clark	316	33, 31, 30	118	25.67
28.	Roger Maris	224	36, 31, 25	135	24.80
29.	Gavy Cravath	202	35, 29, 28	144	21.51
30.	Dixie Walker	278	33, 28, 27	133	23.64
31.	Ken Griffey Sr.	259	25, 25, 23	111	20.00
32.	King Kelly	278	35, 24, 24	130	30.95
33.	Sam Rice	327	24, 24, 24	115	22.03
34.	Tommy Henrich	208	29, 27, 26	122	19.43
35.	Willie Keeler	333	32, 29, 25	131	25.41
36.	Jose Canseco	263	39, 31, 26	126	23.52

(continued)

Rank	Player Name	Career WS	Top 3	Top 5	Per 162
37.	Sam Thompson	236	29, 28, 22	114	27.17
38.	Johnny Callison	241	32, 29, 28	136	20.70
39.	Kiki Cuyler	292	34, 29, 26	116	25.17
40.	Chuck Klein	238	31, 30, 28	140	21.99
41.	Fielder Jones	290	32, 29, 27	135	26.27
42.	Harold Baines	306	25, 24, 23	108	17.71
43.	Harry Hooper	321	29, 26, 24	118	22.53
44.	Paul O'Neill	248	28, 26, 23	117	20.96
45.	Sammy Sosa	203	35, 29, 26	122	21.01
46.	Ross Youngs	206	33, 29, 27	132	27.55
47.	Darryl Strawberry	252	30, 30, 26	133	25.78
48.	Felipe Alou	241	32, 28, 25	108	18.75
49.	Mike Tiernan	251	28, 26, 26	124	27.54
50.	Babe Herman	232	32, 26, 26	131	24.21
51.	Carl Furillo	217	23, 23, 22	91	19.46
52.	Juan Gonzalez	190	31, 25, 24	100	22.58
53.	George Hendrick	237	28, 21, 21	107	18.74
54.	Gary Sheffield	246	34, 32, 31	141	27.50
55.	Larry Walker	216	32, 26, 24	109	25.26
56.	Bob Allison	203	28, 25, 24	115	21.34
57.	Jackie Jensen	187	27, 23, 22	109	21.06
58.	Tommy Holmes	188	29, 27, 25	125	23.07
59.	Bobby Thomson	205	26, 26, 25	112	18.66
60.	Wildfire Schulte	239	31, 26, 24	110	21.43
61.	Vic Wertz	219	26, 24, 23	100	19.05
62.	Harvey Kuenn	223	26, 25, 22	109	19.70
63.	David Justice	214	29, 26, 23	113	25.10
64.	Chili Davis	285	22, 22, 21	91	18.95
65.	Bill Nicholson	223	31, 31, 28	131	21.54
66.	Tony Phillips	268	25, 23, 23	109	20.09
67.	Jesse Barfield	166	28, 26, 22	101	18.83
68.	Roy Cullenbine	182	31, 27, 25	125	24.96
69.	Richie Zisk	178	25, 24, 22	107	19.84
70.	Ruben Sierra	194	34, 28, 21	120	18.68
71.	Danny Tartabull	188	28, 24, 23	99	21.66
72.	Tim Salmon	176	29, 29, 24	117	25.61
73.	Wally Moses	237	28, 21, 21	102	19.08
74.	Al Smith	194	29, 25, 21	105	20.71
75.	Jeff Burroughs	196	33, 27, 23	111	18.79

Rank	Player Name	Career WS	Top 3	Top 5	Per 162
76.	John Titus	201	29, 23, 23	118	23.22
77.	Von Hayes	177	26, 25, 23	107	19.17
78.	Oyster Burns	196	28, 26, 25	113	26.74
79.	Bing Miller	196	23, 22, 20	90	17.43
80.	Hank Bauer	179	21, 21, 20	94	17.11
81.	Sixto Lezcano	159	28, 27, 20	91	19.95
82.	Elmer Valo	187	24, 19, 17	90	14.38
83.	Jay Buhner	176	22, 22, 19	92	19.62
84.	Claudell Washington	194	22, 18, 17	70	16.43
85.	Tom Brunansky	175	20, 18, 17	81	15.75
86.	Terry Puhl	176	23, 23, 19	91	18.62
87.	Buck Freeman	160	25, 25, 24	109	23.01
88.	Tommy McCarthy	170	24, 24, 22	110	21.60
89.	Tony Armas	131	22, 20, 18	80	14.81
90.	Dante Bichette	160	23, 20, 19	90	16.23
91.	Socks Seybold	149	24, 22, 21	109	24.21
92.	Jack Tobin	179	25, 23, 19	98	17.91
93.	John Stone	149	22, 22, 21	88	20.11
94.	Frank Demaree	130	26, 24, 19	96	18.23
95.	Tony Conigliaro	105	20, 18, 17	69	19.41
96.	Pete Fox	149	21, 19, 17	73	16.52
97.	Jim Lemon	103	21, 19, 19	90	16.52
98.	Bruce Campbell	138	16, 16, 15	70	16.43
99.	Orator Shaffer	120	28, 14, 14	68	23.08
100.	Carl Reynolds	139	25, 18, 15	79	18.42

Categories of this record are Career Win Shares, Win Shares in the player's three best seasons, Win Shares total over the player's five best consecutive seasons, and career Win Shares per 162 games played. For example, Babe Ruth had 756 Career Win Shares, including 55, 53, and 51 in his three best seasons (1923, 1921, and 1920). He had 233 Win Shares in a five-year period, (1920–1924) and averaged 48.93 Win Shares per 162 games played over the course of his career.

PITCHERS

1 ◆ Walter Johnson

(1907–1927, 417-279, 2.17 ERA)

Why does Walter rank as the greatest pitcher of all time, you ask?

This is not a revolutionary evaluation. From my standpoint, the argument for Johnson is formed from three tributaries: Johnson against Grove, Johnson against Cy Young, and Johnson against Pete Alexander and everybody else.

If you evaluate all pitchers on the basis of Win Shares per inning (that is, on the basis of contribution to team victories per innings pitched), the highest figures of all time are for modern relievers. Modern relief aces, who pitch only when the game is on the line, have more impact on the won-lost record of the team, per inning pitched, than any other pitcher.

If you adjust for this "timing" factor, however, the highest-impact pitcher of all time was Lefty Grove. Well, Pedro Martinez, but that's a mid-career figure, which is not fixed.

The basic numbers by which pitchers are evaluated are Earned Run Average and Winning Percentage. Walter Johnson, pitching all of his career in pitcher's parks, led his league in ERA six times—but Lefty Grove, pitching all of his career in hitter's parks, led the league in ERA nine times. Grove has the most impressive Earned Run Averages of all time, and, while won-lost records are difficult to disentangle from team performance, he probably also has the most impressive won-lost records of all time, and thus we would expect him to have the highest number of Win Shares per nine innings, as he does.

Walter Johnson was credited with 7.93 Win Shares for each 90 (save-adjusted) innings pitched, which is one of the ten highest ratios of all time. Grove is credited with 8.59 per 90 innings, which is far higher than anyone else, except Pedro Martinez. That puts Grove ahead by eight to nine percent per inning.

Grove, however, pitched 3,941 innings in the major leagues. Johnson pitched 5,914. The difference between them is more innings than the career of Smokey Joe Wood, more than Pedro Martinez (through 2000), more than the career of Dizzy Dean, nearly as many as the career innings of Sandy Koufax. Grove has an 8–9% advantage per inning, but Johnson pitched 50% more innings.

The 8–9% advantage for Grove is a big thing. If it were 8% against 8%, obviously I would rate Grove ahead . . . after all, Johnson, per inning, is only about 10% better than Urban Shocker or Mort Cooper. If it were 8% against 16%, I would rate Grove ahead; if it were 8% against 24%, I would still rate Grove ahead. But 50%?

If we call that even, we then turn our attention to the other question by which I rate players: big impact seasons. Johnson's three best seasons rate at 54, 47, and 42 Win Shares (1913, 1912, and 1915 respectively). Grove's three best score at 42, 37, and 33 Win Shares (1931, 1930, and 1932, respectively). Johnson had more impact because:

   1. He was pitching more innings.

   2. He was also contributing with his bat.

Lefty Grove was a great pitcher for a couple of years before he reached the majors. It is, in my opinion, necessary to make an adjustment for that—but it doesn't change things very much. At 250 innings per year, Johnson had eight more seasons. You can't figure that Grove was a better pitcher in 1923–24 than he was after he reached the majors.

I have a rating system, based on each player's career Win Shares, their three best seasons, their five best consecutive, etc. The system, taking out the subjective element, rates the top two pitchers of all time as 1. Johnson, 2. Grove. If the gap were thin, I would give Grove an edge, and make him the number one man. But it isn't a thin margin . . . the raw numbers are:

   1. Walter Johnson   223.97

   2. Lefty Grove   207.32

   3. Pete Alexander   200.82

   4. Cy Young   191.31

Ultimately, I rate Johnson first because that is what my rating system says, and I don't have a good enough reason to change it.

In comparing Johnson to Cy Young, we have the opposite combination: Johnson is more effective per inning pitched, but Young pitched more innings.

Johnson's three best seasons are scored by the Win Shares system, as I said, at 54, 47, and 42 Win Shares. Young's three best seasons (discounting 1892, when he pitched from 50 feet) are scored at 43, 41, and 38. There are other factors in this case. Again, Johnson was a better hitter than Young. More significantly, three of Young's five best seasons, 1901 through 1903, were posted in what was, in effect, an expansion league.

Young began his career in 1890 under conditions so favorable to pitchers that we simply have to discount them somewhat, unless we want to conclude that all of the greatest pitchers in baseball history pitched before 1893. That effect covers only a corner of Young's career, but still, it's there.

Johnson's value was composed of the facts that (1) he pitched an extraordinary number of innings, and (2) he pitched them at an extraordinary level of effectiveness.

Grove can beat him on the one standard, Young on the other—but nobody can handle the combination. Pete Alexander, born in the same year as Walter, was as effective as Johnson per inning pitched, actually a little bit more effective, 1% more. But Alexander pitched "only" 5200 innings. And from Alexander on, what we have is a long list of pitchers who basically can't match Walter on either standard. Joe Wood, Greg Maddux, Dizzy Dean, Roger Clemens . . . these guys are as effective, per inning, as Walter—but not more so, or not significantly more so. Pud Galvin pitched more innings, but not at anything approaching the same level of effectiveness. After Alexander, Johnson pretty much laps the field.

2 ◆ Lefty Grove
(1925–1941, 300-141, 3.06 ERA)

The best pitching rotation of the 1930s (see Vic Willis, #84), was the rotation of the 1931 Philadelphia A's—Grove, George Earnshaw, Rube Walberg, and Popeye Mahaffey.

Pitcher	W-L	ERA	WS
Grove	31–4	2.06	42
Earnshaw	21–7	3.67	29
Walberg	20–12	3.74	24
Mahaffey	15–4	4.21	13

The Athletics also had Grove, the ultimate stopper. Grove, like Red Ruffing, was a coal miner's son, and he was tough. He made an unusual sociological pairing with the Athletics' other ace, George Earnshaw, who came from a wealthy family and had attended an exclusive prep school—*Two Spectacular Seasons*, William B. Mead

Doc Cramer, describing Grove (same source): "Grove was all man. Ornery. Wanted to win. Didn't care how he won. He just stood out there and threw the ball."

My favorite Lefty Grove story . . . Grove was a loudmouth and a hot-head. His manager, Connie Mack, was a quiet, soft-spoken man who didn't drink, smoke, swear, or raise his voice. In 1932, after a tough defeat, Grove was in the clubhouse raising Cain, throwing chairs, screaming at people and menacing lockers. Finally Connie Mack came out to try to quiet him down. Grove was having none of it. "The hell with you, Mack," he screamed. "To hell with you."

To which Mack responded quietly, as Grove stormed off to the showers, "And to hell with you too, Robert."

3 ◆ Pete Alexander
(1912–1930, 373-208, 2.56 ERA)

The only major league player named after one President of the United States, and portrayed in cinema by another. Also, the only alcoholic among the top twenty pitchers of all time. After you get out of the top twenty, there are a lot of players who have . . . well, *colorful* biographies.

Biographical articles about Alex often suggest that he began drinking after being gassed in a World War I training exercise. While he was gassed in a World War I training exercise, this is clearly false; Alexander's father and grandfather were heavy drinkers, and Alex was well known as a drinking man even before 1918. In fact, the background of his famous strikeout of Lazzeri in the 1926 World Series, the reason that was perceived as such a dramatic event, goes back to rumors about Alexander's drinking during the 1915 World Series. Alexander won 31 games that year with a 1.22 ERA, won the first game of the World Series on October 8, then came back on October 11 to pitch extremely well, although he took a 2-1 loss. The Phillies lost again on October 12, dropping into a 3-1 hole in the series, and Phillies' Manager Pat Moran announced that Alexander would start the next day, October 13.

He didn't, though; Moran switched at the last minute to Erskine Mayer, who lasted only two-plus innings, and Eppa Rixey. It was widely rumored that Alexander had showed up too drunk to take the mound, a charge which Alex loudly denied. He waited eleven years to get another shot at World Series glory, which made Alexander's shot at redemption into one of the natural story lines of the '26 series. When Alex stumbled coming out of the bullpen, the fans thought "Oh, he's drunk again; he's waited all these years to get another shot, and he's drunk again." Which, it is well documented, he was not . . .

4 ◆ Cy Young

(1890–1911, 511–315, 2.63 ERA)

There is a proof offered sometimes that the quality of major league baseball has not improved significantly over time, which goes like this:

Cy Young, one of the best pitchers in baseball in 1893 with a record of 34-16, was still one of the best pitchers in baseball in 1908, going 21-11—therefore, the quality of play in 1908 was not substantially better than in 1893.

Walter Johnson, a .500 pitcher in 1908 (14-14), was 23-7 in 1924—thus, there was no significant improvement in the game in the years 1908–1924.

Ted Lyons, a 12-11 pitcher in 1924, was 14-6 and led the American League in ERA in 1942—therefore, there was no apparent improvement in the years 1924–42.

Early Wynn, 10-16 in the American League in 1942, won 22 games and the Cy Young Award in 1959.

Jim Perry, 12-10 in 1959, won 24 games and the American League Cy Young Award in 1970.

Steve Carlton, 10-19 in 1970, was 23-11 and won the National League Cy Young Award in 1982.

Mike Morgan, 7-11 in 1982, was 16-8 ten years later, was 13-10 in 1999, and is still active in the 21st century—therefore, the quality of play is not dramatically better now than in 1982.

Intuitively, you probably all know that there is something wrong with this analysis, but what is it?

There are two fallacies. First, the argument assumes that distinctions which are small by themselves cannot be large in the aggregate. A parallel argument would be that New York must be at least relatively close to Denver, because Denver is relatively close to Kansas City, Kansas City is close to St. Louis, St. Louis isn't far from 'Cincinnati, Cincinnati is near Pittsburgh, Pittsburgh is just across the state from Philadelphia, and Philadelphia is just an hour from New York.

Second, the argument takes as a constant value a factor—the ability of a single pitcher—which is obviously not a constant. Duke was the NCAA basketball champions in 2001—but by a parallel argument, one could establish that, had they happened to play Kent State, they would have lost by more than 50 points.

Duke played Virginia, and lost by two points.

Virginia played Wake Forest, and lost by 23 points.

Wake Forest played Butler, and lost by 16 points.

Butler played Wisconsin-Green Bay, and lost by 1 point.

Wisconsin-Green Bay played Kent State, and lost by 17 points.

Of course, this argument is unpersuasive, because a team plays better on some nights than it does on others—just as a pitcher pitches better in some years than he does in others. This argument doesn't prove that Kent State would beat Duke, it doesn't prove that they could beat Duke, it doesn't prove that Kent State could stay on the court with Duke without being humiliated—and it doesn't prove that baseball in 2001 is not vastly better than it was in 1893.

5 ◆ Warren Spahn

(1942–1965, 363–245, 3.09 ERA)

Warren Spahn was a cutup. One year Spahn and Lew Burdette tricked the cameraman from Topps, Inc. into posing for one another's pictures—Spahn pretended to be Burdette, pitching right-handed, while Burdette pretended to be Spahn. Had he not been a pre-eminent pitcher, Spahn's image would have rested on his wit.

Books of baseball quotations are full of his one-liners, many of them more insightful than humorous. "Hitting is timing," he said. "Pitching is destroying the hitter's timing."

Willie Mays started his career in an 0-for-21 slump, finally broke out of it with a home run off of Spahn. He was to hit 18 career home runs off Warren, only one off the record for home runs by one hitter off one pitcher (Duke Snider hit 19 against Robin Roberts). "I blame myself for Willie," Spahn said years later. "If I had struck him out in '51, maybe we could have gotten rid of him years ago . . . "

On the other hand, in May 1957, a player named Frank Ernaga hit a home run and a triple against Warren Spahn in his first two major league at bats. He was to collect only ten more hits in the major leagues.

6 ◆ Tom Seaver

(1967–1986, 311-205, 2.86 ERA)

There is actually a good argument that Tom Seaver should be regarded as the greatest pitcher of all time. Of the five pitchers rated ahead of him, four pitched before World War II, the other just after World War II. Three of those four had their best years before World War I, at a time when big pitchers dominated the game much more than they do now. Where Seaver rates relative to those pitchers, then, depends to a large extent on how steep one believes the incline of history to be. Since no one can say with any confidence how much tougher the game has become, it is certainly reasonable to argue that the accomplishments of early pitchers should have been marked off by more than I have discounted them, and thus that Seaver's record, in context, is more impressive than Walter's.

Five of Seaver's contemporaries (Carlton, Sutton, Nolan Ryan, Phil Niekro, and Gaylord Perry) won more games than Seaver did, but none with winning percentages which even

approach Seaver's (.603). Seaver was 106 games over .500. Jim Palmer was 116 games over .500, Juan Marichal 101 games over, and both had better winning percentages than Seaver, but both played for much better teams than Seaver did. If Palmer had had the same number of decisions as he actually did every year and the same won-lost record as the rest of his team, his career record would have been 243-177, 66 (half-) games over .500. He improved that by 25 full games, 50 half-games, up to 116 over.

If Juan Marichal had had his actual decisions every year but the winning percentage of his teammates, his career won-lost mark would have been 206-179, 27 games over. He improved that by 74 half-games, up to +101. But if Tom Seaver had posted the winning percentage of his teammates every year, he would have finished his career 250-266, 16 games under .500. He improved that by 122 half-games, up to +106:

Seaver	250 wins to 311	+122
Marichal	206 wins to 243	+74
Palmer	243 wins to 268	+50

Seaver pitched for eight losing teams, several of them really terrible, and four other teams which had losing records except when Seaver was on the mound. As the Win Shares system sees it, Seaver was dragging his teammates to victory to a larger extent than any of his contemporary stars:

Pitcher	Wins	Win Shares	Diff
Seaver	311	388	+77
Gibson	251	317	+66
Niekro	318	374	+56
Perry	314	369	+55

Pitcher	Wins	Win Shares	Diff
Blyleven	287	339	+52
Palmer	268	312	+44
Jenkins	284	323	+39
Carlton	329	366	+37
Tiant	229	256	+27
Marichal	243	263	+20
Ryan	329	334	+10
John	288	289	+1
Sutton	324	319	−5
Kaat	283	268	−15
Hunter	224	206	−18

The top two pitchers historically are Walter Johnson (560 vs. 417, +143) and Cy Young (634 vs. 511, +123).

7 ◆ Christy Mathewson
(1911–1930, 373-208, 2.56 ERA)
From the "Uh . . . OK" file,

> A statement from Cincinnati has it that Manager Mathewson, like John McGraw of the Giants, has ordered various members of the Reds to have their tonsils removed before they report to camp next spring. Matty is of the opinion that diseased tonsils were the cause of several lame arms on his team last season.—*The Sporting News,* January 10, 1918.

I would have liked Christy Mathewson. When he was in a sanitarium recovering from his injuries in World War I, he spent his time devising an APBA- or Strat-o-matic type game in his head. "When a fellow cannot read, or write, or talk," he told a reporter later, "it requires some resourcefulness to keep his mind off his troubles. I started working out a baseball game, figuring every chance and studying how it should be played mechanically so as to offer the same chances as are offered on a ball field. It interested me and kept my mind engaged."

Larry Doyle, interviewed by Jack Sher years later, said that if you wanted to find Christy Mathewson in spring training, all you had to do was look for a group of rookie pitchers. Christy would be in the middle of them, trying to show them how to pitch successfully in the major leagues.

From 1915 until the Black Sox scandal broke in late summer, 1920, baseball was in denial about its gambling problem. Christy Mathewson was the only man in baseball who wasn't on board with the whitewash. When he had players who sold out on him, he called them on it, and tried to have Hal Chase banned from baseball. During the 1919 World Series, he sat with the reporters and said bluntly that the White Sox were throwing the series. He was the Churchill of this crisis, the only man who would stand up and face what was going on.

8 ◆ Bob Gibson
(1959–1975, 251-174, 2.91 ERA)
You ever see a film of Bob Gibson pitching? Gibson used a pitching motion which sort of looks like he is attempting to fly. If he was drafted now, the first thing the organization would do is start to "correct" his mechanics, get him to maintain his balance during his leg kick, not rock back so far, and stay under control in his follow through. Whether this would actually make him a better pitcher or not I don't know, but I'd say the odds were agin' it. It's like the knuckleball thing (see Hoyt Wilhelm, number 27) . . . pitching coaches come up with ideas which don't seem to be grounded in anything, but which are nonetheless universally adopted within a few years. And maybe they're right, who knows . . .

Most Sacrifice Flies, career, by a pitcher:
1. Bob Gibson   18
2. Warren Spahn   14
3. Steve Carlton   13
4. Phil Niekro   12
5. Johnny Podres   11

The Sacrifice Fly Rule wasn't adopted until 1954, midway through Spahn's career, or he probably would have had more than 18.

9 ◆ Kid Nichols

(1890–1906, 360-205, 2.95 ERA)

Kid Nichols in 1901 hit 7 triples. Actually, at the time, this wasn't that unusual . . . Al Orth hit 7 in 1903, and some guys in the 1890s had hit 8. But since 1955, no pitcher has hit more than three triples in a season . . .

Kid Nichols went 21-13 with a 2.02 ERA for the Cardinals in 1904, and also managed them to a record of 75-79–an exceptional record for that franchise in that era. He was fired early in the 1905 season, however, in a dispute over watching the gate. At that time, as turnstiles did not have counters on them, it was customary for one or two members of the visiting team to position themselves at the gates and count the crowd as it arrived, to prevent the home team from fudging the attendance money. Stanley Robinson, Cardinal co-owner and business manager, instructed Nichols to take his turn at the gate. Nichols said that he had plenty to do managing the team and pitching, and he didn't think he needed to count the gate as well. Robinson and Nichols argued over this, and Robinson fired him . . .

Kid Nichols has been excluded from discussions about the greatest pitchers of all time, as much as anything, because of an accident of the calendar. Baseball exploded in popularity between 1905 and 1910, just as Nichols was leaving the game. Other things happened. Sports coverage by newspapers increased exponentially, and the wire services began to cover and report every game to a national audience. Nichols missed all that; his memory was pushed into baseball's medieval past almost before he got the clay out of his spikes. Although his record is essentially the same as Pete Alexan-

der's or Christy Mathewson's, although he won 30 games seven times, few baseball fans know anything about him.

Nichols was two years younger than Cy Young, but reached the majors in the same season as Cy, 1890. In their first nine seasons in the majors, Nichols out-pitched Young in almost every season. Altogether, he pitched 300 more innings than Young in those years (3642-3352) with a better ERA (2.97 to 3.10), despite pitching in better hitter's parks. He had a better strikeout/walk ratio than Cy Young, fewer baserunners allowed, and a markedly better won-lost record (276-132 for Nichols, 241-135 for Young). He was a better hitter than Cy Young.

Young, of course, pitched equally well over the second half of his career, while Nichols faded at a normal rate . . . Nichols was a tiny man who nonetheless threw very hard. He threw nothing but a fastball, curve, and a change, never fooling with trick pitches . . . see also comment on Vic Willis (number 84).

10 ◆ Sandy Koufax

(1955–1966, 165-87, 2.76 ERA)

1. The Dodgers moved into Dodger Stadium in 1962. In the five years that he pitched there, Koufax had a career record of 57-15 and an ERA of 1.37. On the road his record was just about as good (54-19), but his ERA was 2.57.

2. Koufax and Gibson, two of the greatest pitchers who ever lived, were both born in 1935. Other great years for pitchers: 1876 (Rube Waddell, Vic Willis, and Three Finger Brown), 1887 (Walter Johnson and Pete Alexander), 1944 (Seaver and Carlton), and 1966 (Maddux and Glavine).

3. Koufax, like Gibson, would have an entirely different career if he pitched today. After he missed the end of the 1964 season with a circulatory ailment, he reportedly had a spring training game the next year in which he threw

more than 150 pitches. The Dodgers wanted to see how his arm would hold up to pitching a complete game. Sure enough, his elbow swelled up like a cantaloupe, but the Dodgers didn't back off. Their attitude was "We don't need Sandy to be a spot starter. We don't need Sandy Koufax to be a seven-inning pitcher. We need him to take his turn every fourth day and win, and we need to find out whether he can do that or not."

Now, of course, that approach is unthinkable. In the modern world, the team would think "We've got to protect Sandy at all costs." He'd come out of the game after 6, 7 innings, they'd push his start back if his elbow swelled up, and he'd go on the DL when it really started to hurt. He'd wind up the year 16-5 rather than 26-7, but he'd pitch until he was 40, rather than being forced into retirement at 30.

11 ◆ Roger Clemens
(1984–2000, 260-142, 3.07 ERA)
Like all the modern players, he may deserve to rate higher than I have ranked him. In fact, like Seaver, there is actually a very good argument that he is the greatest pitcher who ever lived.

12 ◆ Bob Feller
(1936–1956, 266-162, 3.25 ERA)
Charlie Gehringer said that Walter Johnson threw "much faster" than Bob Feller. Since Walter was nearing forty by the time Charlie batted against him, while Feller was 17 the first time Gehringer ran into him, this statement seems to be powerful evidence that Johnson threw harder than Feller. But is it really?

When Gehringer saw Johnson for the first time, he was seeing major league fastballs for the first time. He was bowled over. When Gehringer saw Feller, he had been hitting major

league fastballs for more than a decade. He had batted against Grove at Grove's best, against Earnshaw and Wes Ferrell and Dizzy Dean. Is it fair to ask a new pitcher, after that, to duplicate the pyschological impact of seeing a good major league fastball for the first time?

Setting that issue aside, and giving Gehringer all the credit in the world as a credible source, are speed comparisons based on memory really convincing?

If I batted against Bob Feller today and Walter Johnson tomorrow, I could probably tell you which one of them threw harder. But if I batted against Walter Johnson in 1988 and Bob Feller today, how could I really compare the experiences?

After writing the above paragraphs, I later learned that Walter Johnson had been quoted on this exact subject in *Baseball* magazine in 1930, and had said much the same thing, only with more intelligence (although some of his comments no longer apply, with the invention of the radar gun). Asked to compare his own fastball with that of Wes Ferrell and/or George Earnshaw, Walter replied that "It's foolish to compare the speed of one pitcher with another. I might give an opinion and somebody else might give the opposite opinion, and neither of us would know what we were talking about. Pitching speed is impossible to define. It varies with a pitcher. And it varies in the same pitcher from day to day, and often from one pitch to another. In my prime I sometimes had more stuff than I could conveniently use. Other days, when I felt just as well, I wasn't so fast. I never learned why and I don't believe anybody knows.

"The difficulty in deciding between one pitcher and another, however, is the difference in delivery. Some pitchers look faster than they are. Other pitchers don't look so fast. The actual speed of the ball is complicated by wind-up, deceptive delivery and a lot of other things.

People like to talk about pitching speed, but that's as far as they get."

13 ◆ Carl Hubbell
(1928–1943, 253-154, 2.98 ERA)

How many pennants would the Tigers have won, had they given Hubbell a chance to pitch before selling him back to the minor leagues?

Oddly enough, the answer to this historical what-if is extremely clear: they would have won exactly the same number of pennants they won anyway. The Tigers in Hubbell's years never had a season in which they were competitive but did not win . . .

Carl Hubbell, after his pitching career, moved into the Giants' front office, and had a distinguished front office career. Hubbell was director of the New York/San Francisco Giants farm system in the late fifties and the sixties, at a time when that farm system was producing ballplayers like McDonald's produces hamburgers—McCovey, Marichal, Cepeda, the Alou brothers, Leon Wagner, Jim Davenport, Bill White, Mike McCormick, Jose Cardenal, Jim Ray Hart, Gaylord Perry, and many others. It may have been the most productive farm system in the history of baseball.

Hubbell was a man who just loved baseball, loved being around it, even after a twenty-year career as a pitcher and a thirty-year career as a scout and executive. I met him when he was in his eighties, hanging around the batting cage at a spring training game. He lived in Scottsdale at the time, near where the Giants and Cubs trained, and came over often to watch the boys work out.

14 ◆ Greg Maddux
(1986–2000, 240-135, 2.83 ERA)

Maddux and Clemens . . . my friend Dan Okrent, when he was editing *Sports Illustrated*, ran a cover story on Maddux, entitled "The Best Pitcher Since . . . ?" The thesis of the article was

that Maddux was the greatest pitcher, certainly the greatest right-handed pitcher, in many years.

I might have been a part of that article, except that I didn't buy the premise. Greg Maddux, as great a pitcher as he is, has never been the equal of Roger Clemens.

Maddux has had, throughout his career, quite exceptional Earned Run Averages, compared to the league norms. The best of these are:

		Relative
1994	1.56 (Maddux) against 4.21 (League)	.371
1995	1.63 (Maddux) against 4.18 (League)	.390
1997	2.20 (Maddux) against 4.20 (League)	.524
1998	2.22 (Maddux) against 4.23 (League)	.525

You have to go back many years to find ERAs as low as this, relative to league, and this is the basis of the argument for Maddux as the greatest pitcher of his generation. Maddux's best relative ERAs are better than Clemens':

		Relative
1997	2.05 (Clemens) against 4.56 (League)	.450
1990	1.93 (Clemens) against 3.91 (League)	.494
1998	2.65 (Clemens) against 4.65 (League)	.570
1986	2.48 (Clemens) against 4.18 (League)	.593

Maddux is ahead by about .07 times the league norm, which is a difference of seven or eight runs for a pitcher pitching 250 innings.

But while relative ERAs certainly are a valid indicator of pitching excellence, they are not a definitive measure of a pitcher's contribution to his team. There are at least three other things which might be considered, which are:

    1. Park Effects.
    2. Innings Pitched.
    3. The contribution of the defense to the prevention of runs.

Both Maddux and Clemens have pitched most of their careers in hitter's parks, so the adjustment for park effects is minor, but it favors Clemens by 1%.

The larger question is, is pitching at this level for 200 innings the same as pitching at this level for 250 innings?

Of course it is not. Maddux is hardly a wuss; he has led his league in innings pitched five times, and has pitched 250 or more innings in a season four times.

Still, in his busiest seasons Maddux has pitched 268, 267 and 263 innings. Clemens has pitched 281, 271, 264 and 264. In his four best relative-ERA seasons, Maddux pitched a total of 896 innings. (It would have been more except for a strike, but that's spilled milk.) In his four, Clemens pitched a total of 981.

So who do you want: a pitcher with a 1.90 ERA in 224 innings, or a pitcher with a 2.20 ERA in 245 innings?

It's close—maybe too close to call. If the league ERA is 4.20, the former pitcher is saving 57 runs relative to the league average; the latter, 54 runs. But if you compare the pitcher not to the average but to the replacement level, you get a different answer: 102 runs a year for "Maddux," 103 for "Clemens" (assuming a replacement level of 6.00 runs/9 innings).

The other issue, the contribution of the fielders behind a pitcher to his ERA, is a trickier one. To extricate a pitcher's ERA from the fielding behind him is virtually impossible, and I certainly could not claim to have done so in a logically compelling manner. Nonetheless,

(a) my statistical method shows that the defenses behind Maddux have contributed more to his success than the defenses behind Clemens, and

(b) I don't really think there is any doubt that this is true.

The Atlanta Braves' pitching of the last ten years has been great—but their defense has helped. Clemens has not had those kind of defenses behind him.

Maddux has not only exceptional ERAs, but also exceptional won-lost records. However, since Clemens' career winning percentage is better than Maddux's (.647 to .640, through 2000), it is hard to make that into an argument for Maddux. Clemens has a better winning percentage although he has pitched, overall, for teams which were not quite as good.

Clemens' best seasons, as I see them, are 1997 (32 Win Shares), 1986 (29), 1987 (28), and 1990 (also 28). Maddux's best seasons are 1995 (30 Win Shares), 1992 (27), 1994 (26), and 1997 (also 26). I'm not suggesting it is cut and dried or that Maddux is not a worthy candidate. But in my opinion, Roger Clemens is the greatest pitcher of this generation.

15 ◆ Steve Carlton
(1965–1988, 329-244, 3.22 ERA)

Steve Carlton, more than any other player, embodied the cultural rift between sportswriters and players which became manifest in the 1970s.

I don't know when the term "journalism" was thunk up, but I know when it gained currency. Growing up, I never heard of a "journalist." Sportswriters in the early part of the twentieth century, like newspapermen in general, had few pretensions. They had a job to do, and they did it; they had masters to answer to, and they answered.

After World War II newspapermen were caught by the fever of professionalism which was then gripping the nation. Cops became police officers, nurses became health care professionals, garbage men became sanitation workers. Newspapermen were no longer content to be newspapermen; by the late 1960s they had become journalists.

At the same time, baseball players were getting unionized, and emerging as professional athletes. Now, I don't know where you stand on "professionalism," but I think professionalism ranks with socialism, psychology, and twice-baked potatoes as the worst ideas of the twentieth century. Cops became police officers, but the crime rate soared. Professionalism in law has brought us the O. J. Simpson case in lieu of justice. Professionalism in education has given us teachers who know how to administer sophisticated evaluative instruments, but simply don't have the time to deal with the kids who can't read. We would all be far better off if the principle of civilian control of the military was extended to civilian control of the judicial system, civilian control of the schools, civilian control of the police force, and civilian control of the medical profession.

Ah, the doctors. The inevitable defense of professionalism is, "would you rather be operated on by an amateur surgeon, or a professional?" But the costs of professionalism in medicine, as in every field, far outweigh the benefits. Professionalism in medicine has given us medical miracles for the affluent, but hospitals that will charge you $35 for an aspirin, insurance companies that won't pay for an overnight hospital stay after an appendectomy, and no access to health care for 45 million people. My father was a small-town school janitor, but when we got sick a doctor came to the house. Doctors are too professional for that now. We work for them.

Anyway, by the early 1970s sportswriters were no longer just guys who were crazy about sports; they were sports journalists, and they had the college degrees to prove it. And baseball players were no longer just guys who were good at sports; they were professional athletes, and they had the Mercedes to prove it. Professional journalists prize different things than professional athletes, and there was a natural tension between the two groups. An athlete

values loyalty; a journalist wants a source. An athlete wants to keep the focus on the game; a journalist needs something to write about other than what can be seen on television.

Into this mix came Steve Carlton. Steve Carlton in 1972 was the best baseball player in the world. He had a philosophy that guided him . . . I would try to explain it, but I don't understand it. He talked about focus, concentration, far eastern religions, dedication to his work, none of which meant anything to professional sports journalists, but he was winning every start so they wrote it down and passed it along. But the next year, 1973, Carlton had a bad year. Some of the same sportswriters began to make fun of Carlton's metaphysics, suggesting that all of that stuff was deep and profound a year ago, but it didn't work anymore.

An athlete needs to focus on the positive; a journalist needs to write about failure as well as success. By late 1973, Steve Carlton had stopped speaking to reporters.

Carlton was the hardest working, best-conditioned baseball player of his generation, as strong as an NFL linebacker. He used to climb into a vat of dry rice, and exercise by jogging 20 minutes buried in dry rice. Every step was like a marathon. A friend of mine who works in the game used to recommend to baseball players that they adopt Carlton's training regimen, but he learned eventually that the program was so hard that nobody could stay with it. When he was 37 years old, Carlton made 38 starts, pitched 296 innings, struck out 288 batters, and won 23 games.

Carlton was completely committed to his work. He didn't want to deal with the negativity and nuisance that journalists represented. I salute him for that. Not all the consequences of that were necessary, or positive, or appropriate, but Carlton was not wholly responsible for the bad stuff, either; his poor relationship with journalists was in part a consequence of bad journalism.

Is it better now? It's different. I over-simplified, of course; there are legitimate benefits to professionalism, as well as things which are sold as "professionalism" because that sounds better than "organized selfishness." A lot of what was contemplated by professionalism has failed or been discarded; a lot of it has been written into the ground rules. The internet has undermined professionalism in journalism, which is a good thing. Athletes don't come into the game anymore expecting to like sportswriters, sportswriters don't expect to like athletes, and neither side is surprised to discover the enemy camp to be populated by jerks. That was what made Carlton what he was: that as he struggled to make of himself a better man and a better athlete, he was surprised to find himself surrounded by assholes. The modern athlete would never be surprised by this.

16 ◆ Robin Roberts
(1948–1966, 286-245, 3.41 ERA)

> As athletes go, Roberts can safely be called one of the most complex. In conversation, he is at least two IQ notches above most of his compatriots, yet he admits that his intellectual interests are confined mostly to television viewing when he is home and western movies when he is on the road.–Hugh Brown, *Sport Magazine,* August 1956

> Roberts throws the ball to a batter with the idea the bum should hit it some place or miss it, but not stand there and let it slide by. He takes a short, quick windup ... He throws fast balls that dip, fast balls that twist, curves that break rather sharply ... but most of all and best of all he throws.–Franklin Lewis, *Baseball Digest,* June 1956

Robin Roberts threw about as hard as Bob Feller or Walter Johnson or Bob Gibson,

possibly as hard. Because he didn't strike out huge numbers of batters, a lot of people don't realize this.

The Cy Young Award began in 1956. The best pitchers in the National League from 1950–1955, according to the Win Shares system, were:

1950	Robin Roberts
1951	Sal Maglie
1952	Robin Roberts
1953	Robin Roberts
1954	Robin Roberts
1955	Robin Roberts

In 1951, the one year when Roberts does not rank as the best pitcher in the league, he trails Sal Maglie by a margin so thin (27.75 vs. 27.71) that the word "insignificant" hardly does it justice, and actually ranks first in the league, ahead of Maglie 27.96 to 27.75, when his contributions as a hitter are considered. He also ranks ahead of any American League pitcher in every season except 1952, when Roberts went 28-7, but crosstown rival Bobby Shantz was the American League MVP.

The Cy Young Award began, in other words, just as Roberts reign as the best pitcher in baseball was ending. This brings up a question: if the Cy Young Award had started a few years earlier than it did, and if there had been an award for each league, would Roberts now be remembered as a legendary pitcher who dominated his era?

Possibly, but not necessarily. The pitcher perceived by the Win Shares system as the league's best *does* win the Award about half the time, but, in retrospect, we can only be sure that Roberts would have won one award, the 1952 Award (when Roberts was 10 full Win Shares better than any other National League pitcher). Although Roberts *was* the most valuable pitcher in the league every year, the Awards *might* have gone to:

1950   Jim Konstanty
1951   Sal Maglie
1952   Robin Roberts
1953   Warren Spahn
1954   Johnny Antonelli
1955   Don Newcombe

Although '52 would have been Roberts only lock on a Cy Young season, he was actually better in '53 than he was in '52, pitching more innings with a better ERA relative to the league . . .

In 1961 Robin Roberts went 1-10 with an ERA of 5.85. The Phillies sold him to the Yankees that winter, but held a ceremony during spring training, 1962, to retire his number. "It was very touching," said Roberts. "The Yankees were playing the Phillies in spring training, and the Phillies had a ceremony at the Causeway Motel in Tampa. And everybody cried—especially the National League hitters."

Most Grounded Into Double Plays, career, by a pitcher:

Robin Roberts   37
Jim Bunning   36
Phil Niekro   35
Don Drysdale   34
Bucky Walters   34

In a related stupid stat, the only pitchers who were intentionally walked more than once in their careers were Gary Peters, who was intentionally walked three times, and Mickey McDermott, who was intentionally walked twice . . .

17◆   Jim Palmer
(1965–1984, 268-152, 2.86 ERA)
The all-Jim team:

C— Jim Sundberg
1B—Jimmie Foxx

2B—Jim Gilliam
3B—Jimmy Collins
SS—Jim Fregosi
LF—Jimmy Sheckard
CF—Jimmy Wynn
RF—Jimmy Ryan
SP—Jim Palmer, Jim McCormick, Jim Whitney, Jim Kaat, Jim Bunning

I think they would beat any other first name team, except that the Georges would hold their own if they got to use the Bambino . . .

Jim Palmer was the ultimate pretty-boy athlete. Unnaturally handsome, with clear blue eyes and a square, smiling face, he was also highly intelligent and articulate. In his articulate way he whined about the Cy Young voting every time he didn't win it, feuded with his manager, and pulled a face whenever teammates misplayed a ball behind him. He was sort of the exact opposite of Don Zimmer, who is ugly as boiled sin but solid, authentic, tough, and lovable.

18 ◆ Gaylord Perry
(1962–1983, 314-265, 3.11 ERA)
1. For a few days early in 1976, both Gaylord and Jim Perry had career records of 215 wins, 174 losses.

2. Jim Perry *lost* his shot at the Hall of Fame, as much as anything, to the ineptness of his managers. After going 18-10 in 1960 Jim had an off year in 1961, and dropped out of the rotation—for seven years. If you look at Jim Perry's record in 1964, 1965, 1966, 1967, 1968 . . . he pitched well or extremely well every year. But he didn't get back in the rotation until 1969. Even so, his career matches up well against several Hall of Fame pitchers.

3. Gaylord was named "Gaylord," which his family pronounced "Gay-lerd," after a close friend of his father's, who died after having his teeth pulled.

4. Gaylord in 1972 had just a monster season—in my opinion the best season by an American League pitcher since 1931, and better than any season by any major league pitcher since 1972. He was largely obscured, however, because:

    a. he pitched for a bad team, which held his won-lost record to 24-16, and

    b. Steve Carlton had an even better season.

5. Gaylord was also the best pitcher in the American League in 1974, when he pitched 322 innings with a 2.51 ERA, going 21-13 for a team that was well under .500, even with him. The Cy Young vote went 1. Catfish Hunter, 2. Fergie Jenkins, 3. Nolan Ryan, 4. Luis Tiant, 5. Gaylord, but the Win Shares vote would go 1. Gaylord, 2. Tiant, 3. Catfish, 4. Fergie, 5. Bert Blyleven.

6. Gaylord's other Cy Young Award, on the other hand—his 1978 National League Award, won with the Padres—was kind of a fluke, an undeserved award which settled on Gaylord because the Padres scored 162 runs in his 37 starts, which at that time was good offensive support. The five best pitchers in the National League in 1978 were Phil Niekro, Bob Knepper, Vida Blue, Gene Garber, and Ken Tekulve, in that order, but Niekro, Knepper, and Blue all had less than 3.9 runs per start to work with. Gaylord, with a pitcher's park to help his ERA and good offense to boost his won-lost mark, backed into a second Cy Young.

7. From Gaylord's book, *Me and the Spitter:* "Those scouts were a good old bunch, but some of them were really out of place down on the farm. Our mule, Mollie, bit the finger of one scout trying to feed her sugar . . . Another sat down on a pile of mule manure and we never saw him again." The book is very good.

8. When Gaylord's daughter Alison was five years old a reporter asked her if her daddy threw a greaseball. "It's a hard slider," she replied, without missing a beat.

19 ◆ Ed Walsh
(1904–1917, 195-126, 1.82 ERA)

In the last ten days of the 1908 pennant race, Walsh pitched five complete games and relieved twice, pitching a total of $51^2/_3$ innings. He gave up 28 hits and 3 runs, struck out 52 and walked 4. The one game he lost was a 1-0 game in which Walsh struck out 15 batters, but lost when

    (a) Addie Joss pitched a perfect game, and

    (b) His first baseman threw the ball away after he picked a runner off first base . . .

In 1910 the World Series was not scheduled to start until October 17, eight days after the end of the American League schedule. To keep the AL champions from getting out of form during the lull, Ban Johnson and Connie Mack put together an All-Star team from the other seven American League squads to play a series of exhibition games against the American League champs—Ty Cobb, Tris Speaker, and Ed Walsh, among others. Walsh pitched a six-hitter, beating the A's 3 to 1. The A's went on to beat the Cubs in five games . . .

20 ◆ Three Finger Brown
(1903–1916, 239-129, 2.06 ERA)

Because Mordecai worked in the mines as a kid and was called "Miner," many sources say that Brown injured his hand in a mining accident. Actually it was a farm accident. As a young boy, he stuck his hand into a feed chopper on his uncle's farm. His uncle, David Beasley, kept the chopper for many years, and it eventually became a kind of local tourist attraction . . .

On June 13, 1903, Christy Mathewson pitched a no-hitter to beat Brown and the Cubs. Brown himself had a no-hitter heading into the ninth, but lost the no-hitter and the game in the ninth. But he got even: He beat Matty nine straight times from then on. Mathewson didn't beat him again until 1909 . . .

John D. Rockefeller had a grandson, Fowler McCormick, who wanted to be a major league pitcher. Being as rich as Croesus, and able to do whatever the hell he wanted to, McCormick hired Brown in 1912 to work as his personal pitching coach. Brown said the kid had a good arm and good stuff, and he did pitch for Princeton, but he never made it to the encyclopedia . . . After retiring, Brown for many years ran a gas station in a small town in Indiana.

21 ◆ Juan Marichal
(1960–1975, 243-142, 2.89 ERA)

Marichal, says (Ed) Bailey, wants his catchers moving around behind the hitter and never in a predictable position. Further, he wants them moving *after* he has gone into his windup. Says Giant pitching coach Larry Jansen: 'Very few pitchers can adjust to a shifting catcher . . . What he's after is to upset the batter and then keep the ball (away from) the center of the plate.—Al Stump, *Sport Magazine,* September 1964.

Since the Cy Young Award began in 1956, ten National League pitchers have won 25 games in a season:

Don Newcombe won 27 in 1956.

Don Drysdale won 25 in 1962.

Sandy Koufax won 25 in 1963.

Juan Marichal won 25 in 1963.

Sandy Koufax won 26 in 1965.

Sandy Koufax won 27 in 1966.

Juan Marichal won 25 in 1966.

Juan Marichal won 26 in 1968.

Tom Seaver won 25 in 1969.

Steve Carlton won 27 in 1972.

All of these pitchers won the Cy Young Award, except Juan Marichal in 1963, Juan

Marichal in 1966, and Juan Marichal in 1968. Not only did Marichal fail to win any of the three awards, he actually failed to gather a vote in any of the three seasons; Koufax was a unanimous choice in '63 and '66, and Gibson was in '68.

Until I developed the Win Shares system, it was never clear to me whether Koufax and Gibson were actually better than Marichal in those three seasons, or whether Koufax's advantages were just park effects. Had Marichal pitched in Dodgers Stadium and Koufax in Candlestick, it is quite likely that Marichal would have had lower ERAs than Koufax, and Marichal might have won the awards.

However, since I have the Win Shares, I now realize that Koufax was in fact more valuable than Marichal in those key seasons, and Gibson was in fact more valuable in '68. Marichal was great—but he was just in the wrong place to be winning any Cy Young Awards.

22 ◆ Whitey Ford
(1950–1967, 236-106, 2.75 ERA)

The 1961 Yankees, as I mentioned, had only one real quality starting pitcher, Whitey Ford, or two if you count Ralph Terry, who was certainly pretty decent. The 1963 Yankees suffered serious injuries to Maris, Mantle, and Kubek, but won 104 games anyway because they had the strongest starting rotation of the 1960s—Ford, Terry, Jim Bouton, and Al Downing. Bouton was great for two years before his career fell off the edge of the earth, while Downing, in the second half of the '63 season, was on the same level as Sandy Koufax. A 22-year-old kid with a blazing fastball and a huge hook, he struck out 171 men while giving up only 114 hits. He spent the next five years trying to blow people away, before he realized that pitching was a lot easier if you let those seven guys behind you do their jobs.

Let me note again a peculiar phenomenon which I have mentioned before: that historically great pitching staffs have an absolutely terrible record in post-season play:

- The 1922 Yankees, who had the best starting rotation of the 1920s, lost the World Series four-zip (with a tie game).
- The 1931 Philadelphia A's, who had the best starting rotation of the 1930s, lost the World Series to St. Louis.
- The 1954 Cleveland Indians, who had the best starting rotation of the 1950s, lost the World Series in four straight.
- The 1963 Yankees, who had the best starting rotation of the 1960s, lost the World Series in four straight.
- The 1966 Dodgers lost the World Series in four straight.
- The 1971 Orioles, who had four twenty-game winners, the second-best starting rotation of the 1970s, lost the World Series four games to three.
- The 1997 Atlanta Braves, who had the best starting rotation of the last seventy years, if not the best of all time, were eliminated in six games by the Florida Marlins.
- The only team to win the World Series with a decade-best starting rotation was the 1985 Kansas City Royals.

23 ◆ Ferguson Jenkins
(1965–1983, 284–226, 3.34 ERA)

I expected that the strongest starting rotation of the 1970s would be the four twenty-game winners of the 1971 Baltimore Orioles—Jim Palmer, Pat Dobson, Dave McNally and Mike Cuellar. They were great, but they were the second-best rotation of the 1970s, behind the 1970 Chicago Cubs: Jenkins, Ken Holtzman, Bill Hands, and Milt Pappas . . .

All-Canadian team: C—George Gibson, 1B—Bill Phillips, 2B—Pop Smith, 3B—Pete Ward,

SS—Arthur Irwin, OF—Jeff Heath, Tip O'Neill, and Larry Walker, P—Ferguson Jenkins.

Can you name the two Hall of Fame pitchers who played with the Harlem Globetrotters? Bob Gibson and Ferguson Jenkins. Gibson played with them legitimately, when he was a young athlete; Jenkins played with them in the winter a year or two after he was a major league star, more as a promotional stunt . . .

24 ◆ Nolan Ryan
(1966–1993, 324–292, 3.19 ERA)

The mystique of Nolan Ryan was based on two things. First, the other players were somewhat in awe of Ryan. The hitters were in awe of him because they couldn't hit him; the pitchers were in awe of him because they understood how difficult it was to do what he did.

Second, while Ryan was certainly not the greatest pitcher of his time, he was one of the most unusual pitchers of all time. Ryan tried to throw unhittable pitches, one after another, even to weak hitters, even when he was behind in the count. The "ease up and let the fielders do their work" software had never been installed on his machine. From the beginning of his career to the end, a Nolan Ryan game featured strikeouts, walks, and very few hits.

This could be perceived in two ways. On the one hand, it could be perceived as a "no-compromises" position, that Ryan never gave in to the hitter, even in situations when any other pitcher would have. But on the other hand, it could be seen as a sort of permanent compromise. Ryan was saying to the hitters, in essence, "you can have a walk if you want, but I'm not giving you anything to hit." Giving the hitter the walk, in some eyes, was enough.

Sportswriters could have portrayed Ryan either as a heroic pitcher who never compromised, or as a pitcher who was constitutionally compromised. But because Ryan was so respected by the other athletes, the option of portraying him as constitutionally compromised was shut off to sportswriters, who were unwilling to present Ryan in a manner that might not have set well with the other players. Sportswriters—not all of them, but many of them—often seemed to be anxious to send the message back to the athletes that "We get it; we understand. We understand how remarkable Ryan really is, and we would never portray him any other way."

But the other option, the option of portraying Ryan as a very flawed pitcher, was quite obvious, and loomed like an elm tree over all discussions of Nolan Ryan. And this led to a lot of nonsensical information being generated on behalf of Ryan—for example, sportswriters would write that Ryan added 10,000 fans to the gate every time he pitched, when in reality 500 fans was a generous estimate, or point out that between 1972 and 1978 Ryan was 107-1 or something when he entered the eighth inning with a lead (which is a meaningless stat, because managers never allow a starting pitcher to lose the game in the late innings. Everybody wins almost all of his decisions when entering the eighth inning with a lead, because if you're going to lose that game, you'll let the bullpen lose it).

The struggle between these two views of Ryan propelled him out of the class of ordinary players, and lifted his image to a plateau beyond. Ryan has been retired almost ten years; in another ten perhaps we will begin to get a little bit of perspective on him. Ryan's log of spectacular accomplishments is as thick as Bill Clinton's little black book; his list of flaws and failures is lengthy but dry, and will never make for good reading. He rates as well as he does here, in part, because my method compares a pitcher to zero; he ranks not nearly as well if he is compared to the average.

25 ◆ Dizzy Dean
(1930–1947, 150-83, 3.02 ERA)

Dizzy Dean, as most of you know, was a figure of myth and legend, the subject of countless anecdotes still told today. A movie was made about him, books are still written about him regularly although he is now long dead. With just 150 wins, he rushed headlong into the Hall of Fame, and had a lucrative post-playing career as a broadcaster and public speaker.

If you chart his characteristics, however, Dizzy Dean is not exactly a compendium of all that you would want your son to be. He was braggart. He was not entirely honest, he had an ego the size of Pam Anderson's jeeblies, and he was, for many years, the personification of a backward, un-educated, unsophisticated athlete.

To what, then, did Dizzy Dean owe his immense popularity? Two things. First, Dizzy Dean represented good-natured unsophistication. Second, Dizzy represented something which was perceived in his generation to be vanishing.

Dizzy was a hick—but he felt great about himself. He always seemed to be happy. The image of a happy rube has broad appeal. To the extent that each of us feels crude and inadequate to the scrutiny of the sophisticated, the happy rube makes us feel better about ourselves. To the extent that each of us feels clever and "with it," the happy rube makes us feel better about our smugness. The happy rube makes us feel that those who cannot master society's fine details do not or need not suffer from the failing, even though we know this to be generally untrue.

Dizzy Dean, says a friend, was Jethro Bodine of the Beverly Hillbillies, come to life. He was not. Dizzy was clever. Jethroe was dumb as a bag of hammers. "Dizzy loved public speaking more than any man I ever knew," said

Jones Robertson, who had known Dizzy from the time he was a small child. Dizzy could climb up in front of an audience without a moment's preparation and delight them for an hour with stories and quasi-philosophical observations. It is impossible to imagine Jethro Bodine doing this. Dizzy had the appeal of Jethro—combined with the appeal of the raconteur.

Compared to Rube Waddell, Dizzy Dean was a Rhodes scholar. But in Rube's time, rubes were a dime a dozen. We were a rural nation covered by a thin screen of railroads and cities, and many of the major league cities at the time were no bigger than Albany or Wichita is now. Farm boys drifted out of the hills and into the cities like ash seeds floating in limitless number from an ash in summer.

By the time Dizzy appeared, and much more so by the time Dizzy was on NBC every Saturday, America had been knit together by newspapers and magazines, by roads, automobiles, radios, movies, televisions, world wars, airplanes, and big businesses. Isolated pockets of people, authentic, untouched by Paris or by pretension and pretty much unsullied by education, no longer existed in any number. Dizzy was beloved because he represented something which no longer could be seen first-hand on a Sunday drive. People of his ilk dominated television in the 1960s—the Beverly Hillbillies, Green Acres, Gomer Pyle, Petticoat Junction, and Andy Griffith's village of gentle rubes. We watched them because they had been a part of who we were for 150 years, and we missed them.

26 ◆ Phil Niekro
(1964–1987, 318-274, 3.35 ERA)
The best old pitchers ever, based on career Win Shares beginning at age 40:

1.	Jack Quinn	111
2.	Phil Niekro	110
3.	Hoyt Wilhelm	102
4.	Cy Young	88
5.	Nolan Ryan	80
6.	Warren Spahn	78
7.	Charlie Hough	64
8.	Pete Alexander	57
9.	Gaylord Perry	50
10.	Red Faber	49

Honorable mention: Tommy John, Doug Jones, Satchel Paige, Dennis Martinez, Dutch Leonard, Ted Lyons, Early Wynn, Dazzy Vance, Connie Marrero, Don Sutton, Babe Adams, Sad Sam Jones, Don McMahon.

> More than anyone else on the professional level, (Bob Uecker) was responsible for my success. He engrained in my mind that I shouldn't be afraid to throw the knuckler. What happened to it after it left my hand was not my responsibility, but instead his. (He) made it sound as if I alone was responsible for my league-leading ERA. Meanwhile, he took total responsibility for his league-leading twenty-seven passed balls.—*Knuckle Balls,* Phil Niekro with Tom Bird, 1986.

27 ◆ Hoyt Wilhelm
(1952–1972, 143-122, 2.52 ERA, 227 Saves)
One of the interesting things about baseball history—human history, I suppose—is that "beliefs" or "theories" about how the game should be played often sweep the game which have no apparent basis in anything accept consensus. In the period 1958–1963, the notion that a knuckleball was a "specialty" pitch gathered a consensus, and became a part of baseball's accepted dogma. When I became a baseball fan in 1960, pitching coaches would say and announcers would parrot that a knuckleball was a great pitch for a knuckleball pitcher, but a lousy pitch as a part of a repertoire. I have tried

to reconstruct since then what happened to cause this belief to gain credence. One of the things that happened was that Hoyt Wilhelm, who came to the majors throwing a knuckleball and other pitches, went through a career crisis after a brilliant start, and didn't emerge from that crisis until he focused on throwing just the knuckleball. Another thing that happened, I think, is that there were one or two prominent pitchers (Tom Sturdivant) who tried to add the knuckleball to a repertoire of other pitches, and sort of fell out of their saddles in the process. Trying to prevent that from happening, pitching coaches developed the aphorism that a knuckleball was a fine pitch for a knuckleball pitcher, but that for it to be effective you had to throw it almost every pitch.

The only problem with this theory is that for 50 years prior to that, there were countless very successful pitchers who did throw the knuckleball as a part of a standard repertoire. I do not doubt that throwing a knuckleball along with other pitches creates special problems and special challenges, but the indisputable fact is that pitchers had dealt successfully with those challenges for a half-century before that time. Paul Derringer, Wes Ferrell, Freddie Fitzsimmons, Larry French, Warren Hacker, Eddie Lopat, George Pipgras, Nap Rucker, Sherry Smith, and Virgil Trucks, among others, threw the knuckleball mixed into an assortment of pitchers. At that time—about 1960—there were still many of these pitchers active. Early Wynn, Cy Young Award winner in 1959, threw a knuckleball among other pitches, as did Bob Purkey, Bobby Shantz, Ron Kline, Skinny Brown, Bud Daley, Don Elston, Mike Fornieles, Darold Knowles, Frank Lary, Vern Law, Gerry Staley, and others. Purkey went 23-5 in 1962, throwing the knuckleball and other pitches, while pitching coaches in ever-increasing numbers were telling young pitchers that you couldn't do it successfully.

I notice this often about the political process, about television and movies, about culture and art, that ideas seize hold of the public mind like a burr on a pair of fuzzy socks, and will hold on for decades although they contradict history and logic in the most obvious ways. Our government at this moment is forcing universities to spend millions of dollars a year upon the frankly preposterous theory that women care as much about sports as men do, or anyway ought to. It's not mass hysteria, exactly, because who is hysterical about Title IX, who is hysterical about knuckleball pitchers? It is a gentler phenomenon, a massed agreement not to dispute the point.

28 ◆ Amos Rusie

(1889–1901, 248-167, 3.07 ERA)

I am certain that when these rankings are published, I will hear from readers and from friends who feel that I have not given adequate recognition to players from the 19th century.

It is my opinion that the quality of play in major league baseball in the 19th century, and in particular before 1890, was far below the quality of play since 1900, and the ratings do reflect this opinion. There are many reasons to believe that this is true. Of those many arguments for the inferiority of 19th century baseball, perhaps the most compelling is the common success of teenagers, and in particular teenaged pitchers, in the 19th century major leagues:

- In the 1870s, John Montgomery won 69 games as a teen-ager.
- In the 1880s, eight pitchers won 20 or more major league games as teen-agers, led by Jumbo McGinnis with 53 wins.
- In the 1890s, only two teen-agers won 20 or more major league games—Willie McGill (49), and Amos Rusie (42, including 12 in 1889). This decrease in the commonness of

success by teenagers is reflective of an increase in the quality of play in the 1890s as opposed to the 1880s, but still, in all of twentieth century baseball, only one pitcher won 20 or more games as a teenager, that being Bob Feller (31). Altogether there were eleven teenagers who won 20 or more games in 19th century baseball (1876–1899)—as opposed to one in the twentieth century (1900–1999).

How can anyone argue that this does not reflect a lower quality of play in the 19th century? When you have large numbers of teenagers who are successful major league pitchers, isn't that persuasive evidence that the quality of play is not the same? It certainly is to me.

29 ◆ Pedro Martinez
(1992–2000, 125-56, 2.68 ERA)
Seven factorial—that is, seven times six times five, etc.,—is 5,040. Ten is not much larger than seven, but ten factorial is 3.6 million—seven hundred times larger. Stephen Jay Gould once expressed the thought that, when the time comes that we finally understand the difference between the mind of a man and the mind of a monkey, it will turn out to be something simple like this—that a man's mind is not vastly different from a monkey's mind, but rather, the human is capable of vastly more because some small advantages for the human create enormous differences by making combinations with one another, and with the other parts of the mind.

I think of that in connection with Pedro. How can he be *so much* better than the other pitchers? His fastball is good, but there are 20 or 50 people in the league who throw just as hard. His curve isn't better than anyone else's, his control isn't. But he is vastly better *in toto* because he has some additional factors—his

ability to change his arm angle, his ability to change speeds on all of his pitches without losing control—which interact to make geometric combinations.

30 ◆ Jim Bunning
(1955–1971, 224-184, 3.27 ERA)
In his first four years in the minor leagues, Bunning had records of 7-8, 8-10, 5-9, and 5-12, walking more than five batters per nine innings. His career record in the minors was 55-66. Why?

The Tigers tried to make him pitch overhand. Bunning threw with a long, sweeping side-arm/three quarters delivery, culminating with a violent rush or fall toward first base. The Tigers signed him and tried to make him pitch normal—and almost ruined his career.

Although Bunning is now a United States Senator, he was (and is) anything but a glad-hander. Bunning wants you to respect him, but, much like Kevin Brown today, he doesn't seem to care whether you like him or don't. His nickname, as a player, was "lizard." He comes off as very cold, very arrogant.

As I mentioned in another section of the book, Bunning in 1960 was probably the best pitcher in the American League, but finished 11-14. In 1967 he was probably the best pitcher in baseball, but finished 17-15.

Bunning in 1966 allowed 2.61 runs per nine innings. His team scored 4.30 runs per game. We would expect him, then, to have a winning percentage of about .731—the ratio between the squares. Pitching 314 innings, we would expect him to post a record of about 25-9. He was actually 19-14.

I ran these expected won-lost records for Bunning throughout his career. He has an expected career won-lost record of 242-176, thirteen games better than his actual won-lost record. In his four years with the Phillies in the sixties he should have gone 20-11, 21-11, 25-9, and 22-12. He actually went 19-8, 19-9, 19-14, and 17-15.

Why? First, it could be pure luck; the discrepancy certainly does not exceed the bounds of chance. Second, many of Bunning's teammates did not like him. It has been suggested that his lack of offensive support is connected to his lack of warmth, although I pass this along with misgivings, as I think it is unlikely. Players don't play winning baseball because they like the pitcher; they play winning baseball because that's their job.

Third, Gene Mauch once told me that Jim Bunning was the only pitcher he ever had that you couldn't relieve. Bunning's stuff was so good—his fastball so fast, his slider so sharp, his control so precise—that when you brought in a reliever, the hitter's eyes would light up. "We can hit *this* guy," they would say—and they would.

I can't prove it, but I believe that if you studied Bunning's record in his years in Philadelphia, you would find that his bullpen did fail him a lot of times, and that there were times that he stayed in the game when he probably shouldn't have because Mauch didn't want to go to the bullpen.

31 ◆ Don Sutton

(1966–1988, 324-256, 3.26 ERA)

The Dodgers in 1972 became one of the first major league teams to switch from a four-man to a five-man rotation (although they did switch back for one year, in '74). Don Sutton, then:

1. Was probably the first great pitcher to work most of his career on a five-day rotation.

2. Finished his career making more starts than anyone in baseball history except Cy Young (although he was later passed by Nolan Ryan).

These two facts, at a minimum, make an intriguing combination. The biggest reason teams switched from four-man to five-man rotations was to reduce the stress on pitcher's arms. The fact that one of the first pitchers to do that went on to a career of historic length certainly suggests that this effort may have paid off.

At the beginning of major league time, teams used their starting pitchers all game every game, without concern for long-term consequences. Since then, managers have tried to reduce the work loads of their top pitchers, so that they might last longer. This process began in 1876, and continues to this moment.

Contrasting 1970 with 2002, the workload of starting pitchers has been curtailed in two ways. First, teams switched from four-man to five-man rotations. Second, managers go to the bullpen earlier and more often. In 1971, teams averaged 45 complete games per season. Now the average is less than 10 per season.

I would argue that while at least one of these efforts to reduce a pitcher's workload was certainly appropriate, to do both of these things may have been unnecessary, rather like a cat not sitting on a hot stove lid, or a cold one either. My thinking on this is not fixed; I could be persuaded otherwise, but it seems to me, based on what I know, that the strain on a pitcher's arm increases more than proportionally as the number of pitches he throws per start increases. Let us assume that the strain on a pitcher's arm is proportional to the square of the number of pitches thrown—thus, a 120-pitch outing has twice the "strain impact" of an 85-pitch outing, and a 141-pitch outing has twice the strain impact of a 100-pitch outing. (This is probably conservative. In reality, the 141-pitch may be more like ten times as stressful as the 100-pitch outing, rather than twice as stressful.)

Anyway, the point is that there is a counter-vailing interest here: the desire to get as much as you can out of your best pitcher(s). If you assume that both of these things are true—that the strain on the arm increases disproportion-ately in a long outing, and that the team wants to get as many innings as they safely can out of their best pitchers—then the optimal way to use a starting pitcher is to use him *more* fre-quently but not long enough to put undue strain on his arm.

Isn't it possible . . . well, let me be a little more affirmative. I believe that it is possible that a team could get more out of their best pitchers—and thus, could win more games—if they

(a) used a *three*-man starting rotation, and

(b) insisted that their pitchers stay in the game a certain length of time even on off days, but

(c) were more disciplined about not over-running their pitch limits.

Suppose that you put an absolute 100-pitch limit on a pitcher, with other stress indicators pushing that limit even lower. (Other stress in-dicators include long innings, excessive throws to first, clock time, arm stiffness, etc.)

If you did that, you could get about 300 in-nings a year out of a starting pitcher—with, in my opinion, no more stress on the pitcher's arm than pitching 200 innings in the current rou-tine, in which the pitcher makes fewer starts, but sometimes rings up 130 or more pitches in a start.

32 ◆ Dennis Eckersley
(1975–1998, 197-171, 3.50 ERA, 390 Saves)
Only pitcher listed here who had both 100 ca-reer starts and 100 saves. The others who did this (not among the top 100) are Ron Kline, Firpo Marberry, Dave Giusti, Ron Reed, and Ellis Kinder.

The ten most valuable relief seasons ever:
1. John Hiller, 1973
2. Dan Quisenberry, 1983
3. Bruce Sutter, 1977
4. Goose Gossage, 1977
5. Lindy McDaniel, 1960
6. Jim Kern, 1979
7. Dick Radatz, 1964
8. Ted Abernathy, 1967
9. Doug Corbett, 1980
10. Willie Hernandez, 1984

All of the top six except Gossage, in my opinion, were the most valuable pitchers in their leagues, as were Dick Radatz in 1963 and Bruce Sutter again in 1984. Post-1985 relief aces are less valuable, in my opinion, because they don't pitch as many innings, and they often pitch in situations in which the game is not *really* in doubt.

In 1961 a veteran outfielder named Jerry Lynch had a sensational season as a pinch-hitter for the Cincinnati Reds. He hit over .400 as a pinch hitter (19-for-47), with power, and played 44 games in the outfield. Overall he hit .315, but with a slugging percentage of .624 and 50 RBI in 181 at bats—a far better RBI rate than Roger Maris had that same season, hitting 61 homers. More than that, he had big, big hits; game after game, when the Reds were in dan-ger of falling short, Lynch came up with a big hit to put them back in front, and the Reds, picked to finish sixth, won the pennant.

I would liken the Most Valuable Player Award given to Dennis Eckersley in 1992 to giving an MVP Award to Jerry Lynch. Sure, Eckersley was a good pitcher and had a good year, but the MVP? Every argument that was made for Eckersley also works for Lynch. Eck-erlsey faced only 309 batters that season, equivalent to less than half-time play. Cer-tainly, Eckersley pitched at key moments of the game, but the same was true of Lynch. Lynch, as the league's top pinch hitter, was put into the game at critical moments. As Eckersley worked to preserve victories, Lynch was positioned in the contest when he could do the most to stave off defeat.

Lynch was mentioned by only one MVP voter, because he was perceived as a one-way player, contributing only to the offense. But if Lynch was a one-way player, what was Eckersley? What did Eckersley contribute to the Oakland offense that year? He never went to the plate.

Meaning no disrespect to Eckersley, who deserves to be a Hall of Famer, I just think giving a pitcher who faces 309 batters in a season an MVP Award is preposterous. I credit Eckersley with 18 Win Shares in 1992, Roberto Alomar with 34. Kirby Puckett was second in the MVP voting that year; I have him at 31. Kirby went to the plate 696 times that year, hit .329, drove in 110 runs—AND pitched 131 innings, if you want to look at it that way. Kirby was a Gold Glove outfielder, recording 394 putouts. Eckersley retired 240 hitters, which is 80 innings; Kirby retired 394 batters, which would be 131$^1/_3$ innings. I just can't see how anybody can be the MVP, pitching 80 innings with a Designated Hitter Rule.

33 ◆ Don Drysdale
(1956–1969, 209-166, 2.95 ERA)
Per 100 starts, Don Drysdale won 44 games and lost 34. Don Sutton won 42 and lost 33 . . . Drysdale lost 67 games in his career which would now be classed as Quality Starts . . . Drysdale had five games in his career which produce Game Scores over 90:

Date	IP	H	R	ER	BB	SO	Score
May 22, 1959	13	6	1	1	2	10	99
September 9, 1959	9	3	0	0	0	11	92
July 22, 1960	9	4	0	0	1	14	92
September 27, 1964	10	3	0	0	2	6	90
May 25, 1966	9	1	0	0	0	6	91

His average Game Score for his career was 58.3.

In Drysdale's 465 career starts, the Dodgers scored six or more runs 129 times. In those 129 games, Drysdale had a 3.13 ERA, and posted a won-lost record of 85-5.

The Dodgers scored three to five runs 173 times. Drysdale posted a 2.95 ERA in those games, and went 87-46.

The Dodgers scored two or fewer runs 163 times. Drysdale posted a 2.82 ERA in those games, but a won-lost record of 31-109.

Altogether, the Dodgers were 254-211 with Drysdale starting (203-160 for Drysdale, 51-51 for the bullpen).

34 ◆ Eddie Plank
(1901–1917, 326-194, 2.35 ERA)
Plank was a thin, gentlemanly left-hander, a graduate of Gettysburg college in Pennsylvania. He threw with an easy, relaxed, cross-fire delivery . . . after his career he worked as a guide at the battlefield in Gettysburg, where he lived his whole life.

> Thin and just shy of six feet tall, Plank always had a cadaverous look. He was fidgety on the mound and exasperating to the batters as he hitched at his belt, pawed the mound and generally fiddled around.—Ken Smith, Baseball's Hall of Fame

> Level-headed, reliable Plank left no humorous anecdotes. Compared to (Rube) Waddell, he was dull, but Plank's career was ultimately more successful. He played tortoise to Waddell's hare . . . —*The Biographic Encyclopedia: Baseball*

35 ◆ Dazzy Vance
(1915–1935, 197-140, 3.24 ERA)
In baseball history there are only a few outstanding pitchers who have had their best seasons after recovering from arm trouble. Among the top 100 there are perhaps as many as nine

pitchers who had their best years after a serious arm or shoulder injury, although, to get to nine, you have to count all the marginal cases:

- Jim Palmer had a debilitating shoulder problem in 1967–1968, which appeared at the time to have ended his career.
- Dennis Ecklersley was thought to be kind of a rag-arm starter in the early 1980s, before he moved to the bullpen.
- Tommy John, of course, had reconstructive elbow surgery before his best seasons.
- Luis Tiant had arm trouble from 1969 through 1971, recovered to win 20 games three times in the 1970s.
- Ted Lyons had chronic arm trouble in the early 1930s, recovered to pitch effectively for ten years after developing a knuckleball.
- Babe Adams had two years of serious arm trouble and returned to the minor leagues after pitching a 21-inning game in 1914, but came back to win 17 games twice in a row and pitch several more years in the major leagues.
- Eppa Rixey was thought to be washed up in 1919–1920, but had his best seasons after that, and pitched until 1933.
- Sandy Koufax, of course, battled arm injuries through his best seasons.

And Dazzy Vance. Dazzy Vance, blessed with a blazing fast ball, had major league trials beginning in 1915, but did not establish himself as a major league pitcher until 1922, when he was 31 years old. He could not sustain effectiveness for any period of time, up to age 30, because of a chronic sore arm. At New Orleans in 1920, Dazzy banged his arm on the table in the middle of a poker game, and broke something off. What had been a chronic pain became a source of sharp, unbearable pain,

necessitating emergency surgery by a doctor Vance didn't know from Adam. No one knows exactly what the doctor did; my guess is that he took bone chips and debris out of the elbow. In any case, the chronic pain disappeared, and Vance was a hard-throwing, hard-drinking medical miracle for the next fifteen years.

The general point is: don't bet on a sore-arm pitcher to come back. Once a pitcher has arm trouble, it is unlikely he will return to top form. Almost all top-quality starting pitchers come from the thin ranks of those who are able to avoid arm injuries.

When the Dodgers purchased Vance from New Orleans after the 1921 season, they actually didn't want him. The Pelicans had a catcher, Hank DeBerry, that the Dodgers wanted, and they pressured the Dodgers to take Vance in the same deal, two players for $10,000; it was listed as $5,000 each, although Vance always insisted it was really $9,000 for DeBerry, a thousand for Vance. But his arm trouble was behind him, and he was among the best pitchers in the majors from the day he hit the rotation.

36 ◆ Hal Newhouser
(1939–1955, 207-150, 3.06 ERA)

The best starting rotation of the 1940s was the rotation of the 1946 Detroit Tigers—Newhouser, Dizzy Trout, Fred Hutchinson, and Virgil Trucks:

Pitcher	W–L	ERA	WS
Newhouser	26–9	1.94	33
Trout	17–13	2.34	27
Hutchinson	14–11	3.09	19
Trucks	14–9	3.23	16

Newhouser won the American League Most Valuable Player Award in 1944 by a razor-thin margin over his teammate Dizzy Trout, although Trout actually won the plurality of the vote (10 first-place votes for Trout, 7 for New-houser, 7 for other players). The Win Shares system agrees with the plurality, picking Trout as the MVP and Cy Young Award winner for the season—actually, as having the best pitcher's season of the 1940s. However, retroactive Cy Young Awards, American League, 1944–1948:

1944 Dizzy Trout

1945 Hal Newhouser

1946 Hal Newhouser

1947 Hal Newhouser

1948 Hal Newhouser

Newhouser was just 17-17 in 1947, and would have drawn no support in the Cy Young Voting had there been such an award. But he was still the best pitcher in the league; you just can't win if you don't get any runs.

37 ◆ Goose Gossage
(1972–1994, 124-107, 3.01 ERA, 310 Saves)
Many if not most of the great relievers in history spent one or two years as a starter, and were unsuccessful as starters. What is unique about Gossage is that his one year of getting the hell beat out of him as a starting pitcher came not *before* his brilliant career as a reliever, but in the middle of it. In 1975 Gossage pitched 62 games, 142 innings of butt-kicking relief, posting a 1.84 ERA and 26 saves. The next year his manager, Paul Richards, tried to make a starter out of him.

Richards was just an old guy who was be-hind the curve. In Richards' time, the thinking was that your best arms should be in the start-ing rotation. The bullpen was for washed-up veterans and unproven youngsters. When he got a late-in-life shot as a manager in 1976, Richards tried to live by the old wisdom—and got 17 losses from the Goose.

38 ◆ Carl Mays
(1915–1929, 207-126, 2.92 ERA)
Down south in the spring the next year none of the regular players would mix with him. He cor-ralled some of the younger players and told them "If you got to knock somebody down to win a ball game, do it. It's your bread and butter." He says this after killing a man!—Bob Shawkey in *The Man In The Dugout*

Shawkey also claims that, working off-seasons as an insurance agent, he sold Mays a policy on his car. Mays hired somebody to steal the car, and tried to collect on the insurance . . .

The best pitching rotation of the teens (1910–1919; see Vic Willis for explanation) was the rotation of the 1917 Boston Red Sox—Babe Ruth, Carl Mays, Dutch Leonard, and Ernie Shore. This was an expected answer, as that is a famous staff, but less expected was the ranking of the 1922 Yankees as the best staff of the 1920s.

I would have guessed that the best rotation of the 1920s was the 1920 Chicago White Sox, who, of course, had four twenty-game winners. That was a great staff, but they rank fourth in the decade, behind the '22 Yankees, the '23 Yankees, and the 1923 Cincinnati Reds. The odd thing about the '22-'23 Yankees is that they qualify as having the best four-man rota-tion of the decade even though they were using a five-man rotation both years; the front four were that good. The front four of 1922 were Bob Shawkey (27 Win Shares), Joe Bush (26), Waite Hoyt (21), and Sam Jones (20)—with Carl Mays, who had been the Yankee's number one pitcher the previous two seasons, pitching 240 innings and contributing another 17 Win Shares as the fifth man.

39 ◆ Bert Blyleven
(1970–1992, 287-250, 3.31 ERA)
Best known for his monster curve ball . . .

In the early 1970s there were a number of pitchers, particularly American League pitchers, who pitched huge numbers of innings, not only more innings than anyone has pitched since then, but also more than anyone had thrown for fifty years before then. A list of the most innings pitched in a season since 1920 has three types of pitchers:

1. Bob Feller.
2. Robin Roberts.
3. Pitchers from the 1970–1975 era.

Thirty-two pitchers pitched 300 innings in a season between 1970 and 1975, including 15 seasons of 325 innings or more.

Tony Kubek was one of the most visible sports broadcasters at that time. Tony thought, and said, that the Designated Hitter Rule was leading to overuse of American League starters, and thus shortening their careers. I studied the issue at that time and concluded that Kubek was probably right, although frankly after all these years I can't remember what the evidence was or even how I approached the issue.

Looking back at it from this vantage point, there is surprisingly little evidence that pitching 320 to 350 innings did much to shorten any of these pitcher's careers, except maybe Mickey Lolich. Bert Blyleven, a young pitcher at that time, lasted another 20 years after the fact. Gaylord Perry, Steve Carlton, Nolan Ryan, and Fergie Jenkins, who all pitched huge numbers of innings, all were effective pitchers until they were near (and in some cases past) 40. Catfish Hunter lasted long enough to win 224 games, Jim Palmer (323 innings in 1975) lasted. Wilbur Wood lasted long enough to win 164 major league games although he was fat, spent half of his career as a reliever, had a shattered kneecap on a line drive, and pitched 376 innings in a season. Mickey Lolich won 217 major league games,

including 76 after he pitched 376 innings in 1971, although he was even fatter than Wilbur Wood. That generation produced more 300-game winners than the rest of baseball history since 1920, plus several other pitchers who won 260 or more. If pitching 325 innings was destructive to any of these pitchers, the fact is surprisingly subtle in history.

40 ◆ Wes Ferrell
(1927–1941, 193-128, 4.04 ERA)

Wes Ferrell's father was named "Rufus," and he had a brother named "Basil" . . . Wes Ferrell is

(a) the only pitcher listed among the top 100 with a career ERA over 4.00, and

(b) probably the best hitter among the top 100 pitchers—Ferrell or Bob Caruthers.

These two facts are related. Ferrell is listed, despite his high ERA, for three reasons:

1. He pitched in a high-run era.
2. He pitched in hitter's parks.
3. He was an outstanding hitter himself.

What is his value as a hitter, relative to his total contribution? Eleven percent of Ferrell's career value is his value as a hitter, but that is not quite what I am driving at. What I mean to ask is, how much of an off-set should he be given for runs he allowed, since he was such a hitter?

Ferrell as a hitter created about 190 runs in his career. My best estimate is that almost exactly one-sixth of his career plate appearances were as a pinch hitter or an outfielder, so we will remove one-sixth of those 190 runs, leaving him with 159 runs created.

An average hitter for a pitcher, given the same number of plate appearances, would create about 40 runs . . . the number varies over time, being much higher than 40 runs for pitchers in 1876, and much lower in the 21st century. Let's say 40 runs.

This means that Ferrell is as valuable as he would have been had he been an average hitter, but with 119 fewer runs allowed. We are removing 119 runs from each side of the equation—taking 119 runs away from Ferrell's team, and 119 away from the other team. Had Ferrell allowed 119 fewer runs, his career ERA would have been 3.63. In other words, Ferrell's contributions to his team, as a hitter, have a value equal to about 41 points worth of ERA.

Had Ferrell posted a 3.63 career ERA, he would still rank 96th among the top 100 pitchers in career ERA. However, the other two factors listed above would still apply—he would still be pitching in one of the best hitter's eras in baseball history, and he would still be pitching in hitter's parks. All four pitchers who are listed here despite ERAs over 3.63 are American League contemporaries of Ferrell—Ted Lyons (3.67), Mel Harder (3.80), Red Ruffing (3.80), and George Uhle (3.99). The same is true of the next two pitchers on the high-ERA list—Waite Hoyt (3.59) and Tommy Bridges (3.57).

The American League ERA in Ferrell's years was 4.54, which is the highest league-ERA norm for any of the top 100 pitchers. The parks in which Ferrell pitched would push this figure about 3% higher, up to about 4.68. Thus, Ferrell's effective ERA, adjusting for his hitting, is about 1.05 runs better than league, and about 22% better than league.

These figures are comparable to or better than those of other pitchers ranked around here. Ted Lyons career ERA is 51 points, or 12%, better than league, although Lyons' career is longer than Ferrell's, and Lyons also contributed with the bat. Carl Mays' career ERA, with a parallel adjustment for his hitting, was 22% better than the league—the same as Ferrell.

Joe McGinnity (41) was 17% better than league, park adjusted, and was not a good hitter. Hal Newhouser (36) was .92, or 23%, better

than league, park adjusted. Dazzy Vance (35) was .77, or 19%, better than league.

Nolan Ryan (24) was only 10% better than league, and Christy Mathewson, who ranks seventh, was 26% better than league, park-adjusted.

41 ◆ Joe McGinnity
(1899–1908, 246–141, 2.66 ERA)

On August 29, 1902, McGinnity held up the game for ten minutes having a temper tantrum on the mound after the Giants had made several errors behind him . . . In 1906 McGinnity got into a fist fight in Pittsburgh with Pittsburgh catcher Heinie Peitz. This so enraged the mayor of Pittsburgh, who was in attendance at the game, that he demanded that McGinnity be hauled to jail and charged with disorderly conduct. The police lieutenant in charge of game security tried to reason with the mayor, but his honor insisted, and McGinnity was taken downtown and fined $50. The mayor was eventually forced to make a public apology . . . These items taken from Ira Smith, *Baseball's Greatest Pitchers*.

In 1932 Lefty Gomez invited his fiancee, a showgirl named June O'Dea, to Yankee Stadium. She had never seen a game before, and Lefty pitched well in this game, but lost 1-0 in ten innings. "Don't worry, honey," said the future Mrs. Gomez. "You'll go out there and beat them tomorrow."

"Tomorrow!" said Gomez. "Who do you think you're marrying, Iron Man Joe McGinnity?" . . .

McGinnity actually acquired the nickname "Iron Man" from the woman he married, a girl from McAllister, Oklahoma, whose father owned an iron foundry. But he justified the name with his own performance, and thus changed its meaning . . . McGinnity switched between overhand, sidearm, and underhand deliveries. McGinnity believed that this was one of the reasons he was able to pitch a large number of innings and avoid arm trouble—that if his arm got tired throwing overhand, he would simply switch to an underhand delivery, and use different muscles. He was actually not the last pitcher to do this. Remy Kremer, a good pitcher in the 1920s, switched between underhand and overhand pitches, and Clint Brown, Sheriff Blake, George Uhle, and Murry Dickson all threw underhanded at times.

42 ◆ John Clarkson
(1882–1894, 329-177, 2.81 ERA)

Clarkson once bought a huge silver belt buckle, highly polished, which he wore on the mound. He apparently had the idea that the glare from the belt buckle would blind hitters, leaving them unable to pick up the ball. Rival newspapers alleged that Clarkson would wriggle and shake on the mound, trying to get himself into position to shine the reflection into the batter's eyes . . .

> Clarkson was a handsome fellow, of medium size, but he was possessed of great strength in his pitch arm and besides great speed he had as good command of the ball as any man that ever played in the position. When Clarkson passed away in the winter of 1909 Captain Anson said:
>
> John Clarkson was one of the greatest pitchers that ever lived—many regard him as the greatest, but not many know what an amount of encouragement it took to keep him going.
>
> Scold him, find fault with him, and he would not pitch at all.
>
> Say to him after a game: "Grand work, John, I will probably have to use you again to-morrow, for we've got to have that game," and he would go out the next day and stand all the batters on their heads.
>
> In knowing exactly what kind of a ball the batters couldn't hit, and in his ability to serve up just that kind of a ball, John Clarkson probably never had an equal.—Alfred H. Spink, *The National Game*, 1910

43 ◆ Ted Lyons
(1923–1946, 260-230, 3.67 ERA)

Ted Lyons in 1942 was 41 years old. He made 20 starts that year, all of them on Sunday, completed all 20 games, finished 14-6 and led the American League in ERA, at 2.10.

For many years I was puzzled by why the "Sunday Pitcher" trick, which worked so well in the 1940s with Lyons and other pitchers, is never used anymore. There are in baseball many aging pitchers who will pitch well for one or two starts, but can't handle the strain of regular work. If you took one of those old pitchers—David Cone or Bret Saberhagen, let's say—and worked him once a week, doesn't it make sense to think that you could get something out of him that way?

I finally realized why the practice had died out. In 1942, all teams played double-headers on Sundays, almost every Sunday. Thus, to have a Sunday pitcher stabilized the starting rotation, which would otherwise have been under pressure to adjust to the double-headers.

When teams stopped playing Sunday double-headers, to have a Sunday pitcher would have exactly the opposite effect: it would de-stabilize the starting rotation, since the extra pitcher would have to be wedged in where someone else would normally stop. This is not to say that the idea of getting something out of older pitchers by using them on longer rest is not still a good idea; I suspect that it would still work. It's just that different times demand different strategies.

44 ◆ Lon Warneke
(1930–1945, 192-121, 3.18 ERA)

Warneke has the highest career fielding percentage (.988) of any pitcher listed among the top 100. He was charged with only 8 errors in his entire career . . . The top ten in that area: 1. Warneke (.988), 2. Pete Alexander (.985), 3. Ron Guidry (.981), 4. Urban Shocker (.980), 5. Hoyt

Wilhelm (.978), 6. Eppa Rixey (.978), 7. Babe Adams (.976), 8. Tom Glavine (.976), 9. Dazzy Vance (.975), 10. Wes Ferrell (.975) . . .

Usually called "Lonnie" while active . . . National League pitchers deserving the Cy Young Award, 1932–1934:

1932   1. Lon Warneke
         2. Carl Hubbell
         3. Dizzy Dean

1933   1. Carl Hubbell
         2. Lon Warneke
         3. Ed Brandt

1934   1. Dizzy Dean
         2. Carl Hubbell
         3. Lon Warneke

Warneke was by far the best pitcher in the league in 1932 (22-6, 2.37 ERA), and was also among the top five in 1935, which would have been Dizzy's second Cy Young season.

Warneke, although he was not as eccentric or as full of himself as Dizzy Dean, was of the same general mold—an Arkansas hillbilly with a taste for the night life, an over-active sense of humor, and a strong right arm. When he was in the Cotton States League in 1928 he went 6-14, but became locally famous as the pitcher who was always messing around with snakes. Once, when the team bus got a flat tire on the edge of a swamp, Lonnie waded into the swamp, caught a snake, and "cracked the whip" with it. Another time he was thrown out of a game, or actually out of the dugout, for smuggling snakes into the dugout.

His first year in the majors he attracted press attention by buying an unusual number of suits. In 1932 the Cubs wanted him to go to a doctor late in the season, but he refused because he had never been to a doctor in his life, and he wanted to keep it that way. He was droll to the point of being lazy, and was regarded, like Dizzy, as something of a folk-wisdom

philosopher, although unlike Dizzy he was normally quiet.

Warneke carried a ukelele with him throughout his career, and would play it in the clubhouse; later, in the late thirties and early forties, he played with Pepper Martin's "Mudcat Band." His nickname, *The Arkansas Hummingbird*, came from his humming/singing with the band, although some writers have erroneously assumed that the "hum" was his fastball. After his playing career he became an umpire, and was a major league umpire for a few years . . . see also Odell Hale (second base, number 98).

45 ◆ Old Hoss Radbourn
(1881–1891, 309-196, 2.67 ERA)

Old Hoss' 1884 season, when he went 59-12 with 441 strikeouts and a 1.38 ERA, was the biggest-impact season of all time, pitcher or player, according to the Win Shares system. Which makes sense if you think about it . . . Radbourne was pitching with the effectiveness of Pedro Martinez, but pitching three times as many innings. At that time teams used only two or three pitchers. Providence used two pitchers mostly, others occasionally, but their other pitcher, Charlie Sweeney, jumped to the Union Association in mid-season, leaving Providence in a pennant race with only one proven pitcher. Radbourn just pitched every day for a month, 35 of 37 games. When he got up in the morning his arm would be locked up so solid it was all he could do to brush his teeth, but he would stretch and rub the arm until it loosened up, then take the mound.

In 1884, the year overhand pitching became legal, Radbourn pitched 678 2/3 innings. Early in the season he worked in tandem with Charlie Sweeney . . . the two pitchers were rivals more than partners, and both were temperamental. In July, with Radbourn suspended for drunkenness, Sweeney quit the team and jumped to the Union Association. Bargaining to get his suspension lifted and his contract renegotiated, Radbourn declared that he would pitch every remaining Grays' game.–Kevin Kerrane, *The Hurlers*

About the time I came up all the pitchers were trying to beat Charley Radbourne's record for pitching 72 games in a season for Providence during the season of 1884. Nearly all the pitchers that broke in were advertised as another Radbourne the way that the youngsters today are called Alexanders and Johnsons.–Silver King in *The Sporting News,* January 10, 1918.

46 ◆ Don Newcombe
(1949–1960, 149-90, 3.56 ERA)

In 1952, during the Korean War, Willie Mays of the Giants and Don Newcombe of the Dodgers were both drafted. "Losing Newcombe is worse than losing Mays," said Brooklyn manager Charlie Dressen. "Where can you get a pitcher like that? Where can you make up those games? Let the Giants have Mays back. Let 'em have two Mays. It's okay with me, so long as the Army gives me back Newcombe."

Don Newcombe, said Bill Vaughn, was a pretty good pitcher for a hitter. The Cy Young Award began in 1956. Don Newcombe won the first trophy, going 27-7 with 3.06 ERA, but also driving in 16 runs while hitting .234. That was nothing, however, compared to his bat work of the previous season, when he went 20-5, but also hit .359 with 9 doubles, a triple, 7 homers, and 23 RBI. That was, with the exception of one Wes Ferrell season and Babe Ruth, the best-hitting season by a pitcher in the twentieth century.

Newcombe was always a good hitter, but that was easily his best season with the bat, with almost half of his career home runs. Actually, there were four great-hitting seasons in the 1950s by guys who were also great pitchers—Newcombe in 1955, Warren Spahn in 1958, Robin Roberts in 1955, and Bob Lemon in 1950:

Spahn in 1958 hit .333 with 2 homers, 15 RBI. Spahn, like Newcombe and Roberts in '55,

was a good hitter, but way over his head in that particular season.

Robin Roberts in 1955 hit just .252, but did so with 9 doubles, 4 triples, 2 homers, 18 walks and 18 strikeouts. There are lots of pitchers in history who have hit .300 or .350, but for the breadth of accomplishment, that's some season. Normally pitchers who hit, even having good years, have zero triples and absolutely awful strikeout/walk ratios. Earl Wilson in 1968 hit .227 with 7 home runs, but a strikeout/walk ratio of 35 to 2. Catfish Hunter in 1971 hit .350, but with 1 double, 1 triple, 1 homer, and 2 walks. Roberts, projected to full-time play, would have had more than 50 doubles, more than 20 triples, double figures in home runs, and about 100 walks.

Bob Lemon in 1950, on the other hand, was not far over his head; Lemon hit .272 with 9 doubles, a triple, 6 homers, and 26 RBI—the best-hitting season of the 1950s, other than Newcombe in '55. But Lemon could really hit; that season wasn't atypical for him.

47 ◆ Early Wynn
(1939–1963, 300-244, 3.54 ERA)

The best starting rotation of the 1950s, as anyone would have predicted (see Vic Willis, #84) was the rotation of the 1954 Cleveland Indians (Wynn, Garcia, Lemon, and Art Houtteman). The second-best rotation of the 1950s was the 1951 Indians; third-best, the 1956 Indians. Wynn was the number one starter in '51 and '56; Wynn, Garcia, and Lemon were at 24 Win Shares each in 1954.

Early Wynn was famous for throwing inside. Somebody once said that he would knock down his own mother if she crowded the plate on him. "Why shouldn't I?" said Wynn. "My mother was a damned good hitter . . ."

On a sunny day in 1937, a sober-faced boy from Alabama walked into the farm club training camp of the Washington Senators at Sanford, Florida, and announced that he wanted to try out as a pitcher. "What," asked Clyde Milan, then a Senator coach, "makes you think you're a pitcher?"

"Because my daddy says so," said the youth.—Bill Furlong, *Baseball Stars of 1960*

After Early Wynn won his 300th game, somebody asked him if he was upset that Warren Spahn had beaten him to the milestone. Not at all, said Wynn; he was delighted. Because Spahn got there first, he said, he (Wynn) would always be the *last* pitcher to win 300 games. He was a broadcaster for many years after that, always insisting that he would be the last pitcher to ever win 300 games. For many years he was right, but by the time he died in 1999, six other names had been added to the list . . .

48 ◆ Bob Lemon

(1946–1958, 207-128, 3.23 ERA)

Lemon worked as Ronald Reagan's stunt double in the film biography of Pete Alexander . . . Bob Lemon between 1946 and 1950 batted 508 times, hitting .264 with 31 doubles, 24 homers, 75 RBI, and 78 runs scored. No pitcher since has been as effective with the bat, over a period of years.

I have a theory that the quality of play in major league baseball, over time, could be tracked by what we could call "Peripheral Quality Indicia"—PQI, for short. Hitting by pitchers is a peripheral quality indicator; the higher the quality of play, in my opinion, the less the pitchers will hit. I have a list of about a dozen of these:

1. Hitting by pitchers.
2. The average distance of the players, in age, from 27.
3. The percentage of players who are less than six feet tall or more than 6'3".
4. Fielding Percentage and Passed Balls.
5. Double Plays.
6. Usage of pitchers at other positions.

7. The percentage of fielding plays made by pitchers.
8. The percentage of games which are blowouts.
9. The average attendance and seating capacity of the game location.
10. The condition of the field.
11. The use of players in specialized roles.
12. The average distance of teams from .500.
13. The percentage of games which go nine innings.
14. The standard deviation of offensive effectiveness.
15. The standard of record-keeping.
16. The percentage of managers who have 20 years or more experience in the game.

OK, more than a dozen. Anyway, let's array teams in ways which we could all agree represent top to bottom:

1. Major League baseball.
2. Minor League baseball.
3. College baseball.
4. High School baseball.
5. Ten-year-old kids playing baseball.
6. Seven-year-old kids attempting to play baseball.

If you studied that list, you would find that all of these things increased or decreased predictably as the quality of competition improved. The eighth indicator, for example, is the number of blowouts. My seven-year-old son (Reuben) is on a team that lost one game 26-3, and won the next game 31-0. In high school blowouts are still common, but there are more games which *aren't* blowouts. In college ball you get a few 18-0 games—more than you get in the minors or the majors. If you hear that a game has been decided 41-2, don't you tend to assume that that was probably a low-level competition?

Batting stats and pitching stats do not indicate the quality of play, merely which part of that struggle is dominant at the moment. But fielding stats are somewhat inevitably tied to the level of competition, in ways which are reflected in the ratio between double plays and errors. In Reuben's games, most balls in play result in errors, while I have seen only one double play all year. In my thirteen-year-old son's games, there are still about five times as many errors as double plays. In college ball there are still more errors than double plays, but it is closer, while in the majors there are more double plays than errors.

In Reuben's league, the average distance from age 27 is about 20 years; in high school, about ten years, in college, about seven years, in the minor leagues, maybe five years, in the majors, probably three years.

In Reuben's League, the games are attended by a handful of people; in high school, by a few dozen; in college, by hundreds; in the minors, by thousands; in the majors, by tens of thousands.

In Reuben's league, pitchers make far more fielding plays than players at any other position. In high school, they still make as many as at any other position; in college, fewer, but still some, while in the majors the pitchers make only one or two fielding plays per game.

When kids start playing baseball the pitchers are the best hitters. In high school, the pitcher is still very often the cleanup hitter, but as they climb the ladder the pitchers hit less and less.

In Reuben's league there are no statistics at all. In high school baseball there are sketchy statistics kept by some teams. In college ball there are statistics, but not lots of them, while for the major leagues there are nitwits like me who grind them out by the ton.

If you worked at it hard enough, you could make up a set of standards to "score" each of these things, which would track the increases in the quality of competition as Reuben moves to the major leagues, although frankly how you score the quality of the grounds keeping, I don't want to know.

Anyway, my point is that if you track major league baseball from 1876 to the present, all of these indicia, without exception, have advanced steadily. As late as the 1920s, there were still major league managers who had little experience with the game. I know that many people passionately disagree with me when I argue that the quality of play in the majors has continued to increase, but even since 1950, all or virtually all these indicators would suggest that the quality of major league play has improved steadily:

The best-hitting pitchers of the 21st century don't hit anything like what Bob Lemon hit, or Spahn, or Newcombe, or the other good-hitting pitchers of that era.

Success in the majors by very young players has become significantly less common (although success by old players has probably become more common).

In 1950 major league pitchers averaged about 240 assists per team; in 2001, in a longer season, the average will be less than 200.

In 1950 there were about 1.2 double plays for each error. In 2001 the ratio will be at least 1.3 to one.

Player/managers, who were the youngest and least experienced managers, have become extinct.

The stadiums and crowds are bigger, the statistics are better, the grounds keeping standards are far higher. The teams are closer to .500. I haven't studied it, but I would bet there are fewer blowouts, fewer lop-sided games.

During World War II, when we could all agree that the quality of major league play dropped, these indicators reflect the drop.

World War II brought into the game more players who were remote in age from 27—more teenagers, and more old men. The double play to errors ratio, 0.86 to 1 in 1941 and advancing almost every year, dropped slightly during the war years.

When there is an expansion, these indicators reflect the drop in the quality of play. Expansion brings into the league younger players, and keeps in the league older players. Expansion pushes the standard deviation of winning percentage up and the fielding percentage down.

And yet, over time, these effects are not large enough to keep the PQI from moving higher. Is that *proof* that the quality of play is getting better? Perhaps it isn't. But that is what I believe, and this is one of the reasons I believe it.

49 ◆ Randy Johnson
(1988–2000, 179-95, 3.19 ERA)

Early in the 2001 season, Randy had a game in which he struck out 20 batters, walking none. What do you make of the fact that, of the four pitchers who have struck out 20 in nine innings, all had zero walks? I frankly don't know what to make of it . . .

At the time of the 20K game, there was media discussion about whether, if Randy's career ended now, he would go into the Hall of Fame. A consensus was that, with 179 wins, he might not. But Randy opened the 2001 season 84 games over .500 in his career. I think the only pitcher who was 84 games over .500 and has been left out of the Hall of Fame is Bob Caruthers . . .

Randy does not quite have the worst fielding percentage among the top 100 pitchers. His career fielding percentage is .889, while Tim Keefe's was .888. Keefe, however, pitched in an era in which the *average* fielding percentage

for a pitcher was .890, so that's hardly a fair comparison.

The Big Unit has a "relative error rate"—his error percentage, divided by the league norm for his era—of 2.53, meaning he has erred 2.5 times as often as an average pitcher throughout his career. This is easily the worst ratio among the top 100 pitchers, the only other pitcher worse than 1.75 being Nolan Ryan. The top six are 1. Randy, 2. Nolan, 3. Hippo Vaughn, 4. Rube Waddell, 5. Goose Gossage, and 6. Don Drysdale—all power pitchers.

50 ◆ Eddie Cicotte
(1905–1920, 209-149, 2.38 ERA)

Do you remember the mind games that Gaylord Perry used to play with hitters, alternately convincing them that he was throwing a spitball on every pitch and denying that he threw them at all? Cicotte did that with the "shine ball." He would rub the ball on his uniform before every pitch, shining it, which would supposedly make it dive. Then he would confide to the press that "shining" the ball really didn't do anything; it was just to play tricks on the hitters' minds.

> Whether Cicotte does or doesn't use artificial means to get the break on the so-called shine ball, the fact remains he is about the headiest pitcher in the game . . . Perhaps no pitcher in the world has such a varied assortment of wares in his repertory as Cicotte . . . The real inside dope is that Cicotte is the best little mixer on the slab in the world. In pitching for a batter's weakness and cutting the corners when he wants to he has no superior in the game.—*The Sporting News,* May 2, 1918.

51 ◆ Red Ruffing
(1924–1947, 273-225, 3.80 ERA)

Actually called "Chuck" Ruffing by those who knew him, and often called Chuck or Charley by the press while he was active . . .

Ruffing's career won-lost record is actually *worse* than the won-lost record of his teams. Had he matched the won-lost record of his teams every season, his career record would have been 275-223. The odd thing was that when Ruffing was with the Yankees, he was consistently *better* than his teams. When he was with bad teams, the Red Sox (1923–1930) and the White Sox (1947) he was considerably *worse* than his teams. His career record with the Yankees was 231-124 (+7 from his teams); with the Soxes it was 42-101 (–10 from his teams).

On one level this is puzzling. How can a pitcher who drags down the quality of bad teams be good enough to improve a good team? On another level, the reasons for it are fairly obvious: Ruffing was with other teams when he was young and old, with the Yankees in his prime.

But also, when a bad team has one good pitcher, what happens? A, they discourage him, and B, they ride him so hard that they negate his value. Ruffing was 10-25 in 1928, 9-22 in 1929—much worse than his teams' record both years. But was Ruffing actually worse than his teams? Obviously not; he regularly led the team in innings pitched. Perceiving him to be their best pitcher, they let him finish games when he should have come out, they started him when they should have given him a day off, and they communicated to him a daily message that trying to win was a waste of time. The Yankees didn't discourage him, and Joe McCarthy didn't over-use him—and he won 65.1% of his decisions over a period of fifteen years.

> I was 38 years old. I've got four toes missing on my left foot, from a coal mine accident when I was young. I had a wife and kids. I had a mother-in-law; she was my responsibility. But there it was: "Greetings from the President" . . . The regular doctors examined me. They turned me down; 4-F. The last doctor I came to was an Army doctor. He put on his report that what I could do on the outside I could do on the inside. He would have drafted any ballplayer.—Red Ruffing in *Baseball Goes to War,* William B. Mead.

52 ◆ Luis Tiant
(1964–82, 229-172, 3.30 ERA)

Tiant, who ranks near the middle of the top 100, is also closer to the averages for the top 100 pitchers than any other pitcher. Tiant pitched 3,486 innings in his career; the average of the top 100 pitchers was 3,490. Tiant won 229 games and lost 172; the average for the top 100 was 231-162 . . .

Baseball-Reference.com lists the most similar players to Luis Tiant as Catfish Hunter (942) and Jim Bunning (931)—both Hall of Famers. I have noted before that the statistical similarities between Tiant and Hunter, teammates with the 1979 Yankees, are unusually strong. In the past, I have avoided stating a position on whether Tiant or Hunter was actually a better pitcher, in part because I dislike being drawn into Hall of Fame campaigns.

Since we're here, however, Tiant was a better pitcher than Hunter, over the course of his career. Their won-lost records are almost the same—although Hunter pitched for better teams. Their ERAs are almost the same—although Hunter pitched in better parks for pitchers. Adjusting for park effects, Tiant's career ERA was 40 points better than league (3.30 vs. 3.70). Hunter's was 13 points better than league (3.26 vs. 3.39).

It would be easy to over-state the importance of that. *Most* of a player's value, even most of a star player's value, is in being average; only a little bit of the value is in being better than average. The relative era advantage of Tiant to Hunter wasn't 40 to 13, but more like 280 to 253. Most of a player's value is in being average.

53 ◆ Rube Waddell

(1897–1910, 193-143, 2.16 ERA)

In the heat of the 1904 pennant race, according to Bill Dineen (*The Sporting News*, January 3, 1918), Rube Waddell was scheduled to pitch for Philadelphia against Boston. The Boston players decided to try to get Waddell into a wrestling match with Candy LaChance, who was the biggest and strongest player on their team, and thereby perhaps take something away from Rube before the game. In pre-game drills LaChance started bantering with Waddell in a friendly way, slapping his shoulder, punching him in the belly, etc. One thing led to another and, exactly as the Boston players had hoped, a wrestling match began to develop . . .

Without warning, Waddell grabbed LaChance, hoisted him over his head, and slammed him to the ground. LaChance was barely able to play the game and, according to Dineen, Waddell pitched a two-hit shutout . . . .

According to Alan Levy's new biography, this event apparently happened about July 10, 1903, rather than in the heat of the 1904 pennant race. Also, according to the same source, Waddell did pitch a complete game 3-2 victory, but not a shutout . . .

> February 7—At Lynn, Mass., Pitcher Waddell, of the Athletics, prevents a fire by heroically carrying a blazing oil stove out of a building.
>
> February 10—Pitcher Waddell, of the Athletics, flees from Peabody, Mass., under charge of having assaulted and badly injured his wife's parents.—Notes from the Chronology of the 1905 year, 1906 *Reach Guide*

On July 4, 1905, Waddell hooked up with Cy Young in one of the greatest pitching duels of all time. Waddell gave up two in the first; Young surrendered two to tie in the sixth. The game continued in a 2-2 tie until the 21st inning, when the A's finally won it, Waddell finishing the game with 20 consecutive scoreless innings.

An amazing fact is that, through 20 innings, only 18 men had appeared in the game, nine for each side. The first and only substitute of the game was that, in the 21st inning, Connie Mack sent Monte Cross, his 35-year-old backup shortstop, in to pinch-run for Jack Knight, his 19-year-old starting shortstop . . .

> St. Louis, November 18 (1913)—"Rube" Waddell, formerly one of the greatest pitchers in base ball, was picked up wandering about the streets yesterday, exhausted and suffering from consumption. He could not speak above a whisper. Friends took him in charge and provided him with enough money to go to San Antonio, Texas.

You ever read Faulkner? Without actually thinking about it, I had always assumed that Faulkner used Rube Waddell as a model for the character he named Boon Hogganbeck. It occurs to me, when I force this into words, that I have zero evidence for this assumption, other than the facts that Waddell was one of the most celebrated athletes in America in the years 1905 to 1910, when Faulkner would have been an adolescent and teenager, and that Hoggenbeck's description and behavior are indistinguishable from Waddell. My friend Jim Carothers, who knows as much about Faulkner as I know about baseball, assures me that I am probably wrong . . .

54 ◆ Tim Keefe

(1880–1893, 342-226, 2.62 ERA)

1. Keefe was born on New Year's Day, 1857. I will spare you the All-Born-on-Holidays team, Rickey Henderson and all . . .

2. Keefe's father, an engineer, was trapped south of the Mason-Dixon Line when the Civil War broke out. He was taken into custody, and given a choice between fighting for the South and going to a prison camp. He chose the prison

camp, and was held in a southern prison throughout the war.

3. Keefe was nine years old before he saw his father again, early in 1866. By then Keefe had developed a great fondness for baseball, which his father thought was a terrible waste of time, and repeatedly forbade him from playing.

4. Keefe's strikeout total jumped from 116 in 1882 to 359 in 1883 when he learned to throw what has been described as the first modern change-up.

Pitchers had always changed speeds, back into the 1860s, probably the 1850s. Keefe was perhaps the first man to learn to throw a change up with the same arm speed as his fastball, and get the ball over the plate. Although he had an excellent fastball, the change was his best pitch.

5. Keefe was an expert at taking shorthand.

6. Keefe, a native of Cambridge, Massachusetts, was a gentleman, and a close friend of John Montgomery Ward.

7. Keefe and Ward married sisters. Ward, of course, married the famous actress, Helen Dauvray, whose actual name was Helen Gibson. Keefe married her sister, Clara Gibson. Ward and Dauvray broke up after a year or two, as celebrity marriages often do. Keefe and Gibson were together for life.

55 ◆ Wilbur Cooper
(1912–1926, 216-178, 2.89 ERA)

Beyond his wonderful marks he owned a color and a grace that in his period was matchless. He was just fretful enough to be "good copy," and he owned the easiest and most graceful throwing motion of his time. He had wonderful control of his deliveries and he tossed a ball up to the plate with less effort than any hurler in the league . . . His gloved hand moved with the quickness of a cat's paw. He was one of the best fielding pitchers . . . Cooper brooked no sloppy stuff behind him. He was a master at his business and he expected the men behind him to match his ef-

fort.–Harvey J. Boyle, *Pittsburgh Post-Gazette,* February 25, 1933

Cooper, now a successful real estate executive in Mt. Lebanon, conceded that modern pitchers have a tougher job than pitchers in his day—mainly because of the lively ball and so many night games . . . (Cooper would) chew tobacco during a game. Somehow, tobacco juice would get into the pocket of his glove and then on the ball. After an inning or two, the ball would get pretty dark.

"Funny thing, I never did chew the stuff off the field," he joked.–John Carroll, United Press International, September 30, 1959

56 ◆ Red Faber
(1914–1933, 254-213, 3.15 ERA)

As a high school pitcher, Faber struck out 24 batters in a game. Red Faber began pitching professionally in 1909, won 18 games in the Three-I League in 1910, was purchased by the Pirates that fall, and went to spring training with them in 1911.

Faber told James T. Farrell years later *(My Baseball Diary)* that he reported to spring training with no money, and the Pirates didn't pay anything for spring training. He borrowed $5 from Fred Clarke, player/manager of the Pirates, and nursed it along for two weeks, but finally had to go back and ask for another $5. "You must be gambling," Clarke told him.

The Pirates sent him out without putting him in a game, recalled him that fall, sent him out again without pitching him, and recalled him in 1912, once more without pitching him. In spring training games they banned him from throwing the spitball, which was his best pitch. Finally they gave up on him, sold him back to Des Moines, where he won 20 games in 1912 and 1913, and he was purchased by the White Sox, who called him up but didn't pitch him, either.

Faber finally caught his break when Comiskey and John McGraw arranged for the

White Sox and Giants to go on an around-the-world tour in the winter of 1913–1914. Christy Mathewson was scheduled to go on the tour, but backed out at the last moment, leaving Mc-Graw short a pitcher. Comiskey suggested that McGraw could use Faber as a "Giant" on the tour, and McGraw agreed; Faber had still never pitched a major league inning at the time.

After watching Faber pitch a couple of exhibition games on the tour, McGraw asked Comiskey if he could purchase his contract, and keep him with the Giants. Comiskey said no, but McGraw kept asking until, by the time the tour was over, Faber was a solid member of the White Sox staff.

He won 24 games in 1915, and won three games in the 1917 World Series, although he also pulled a famous rock on the bases. Faber, who couldn't hit a lick, ripped a ball into right field with a runner on second, and went to second on the throw home. Assuming that the runner from second had scored, Faber bolted for third when the pitcher went into his full windup, and slid into third base ahead of the tag. When it seemed like the base was more than usually crowded, he looked up and realized that Buck Weaver was still there.

Faber made the list of pitchers allowed to continue throwing the spitball in 1920, and was the Burleigh Grimes of the American League, the last legal spitball pitcher. He was an effective pitcher well into his 40s, but spent his entire career with the White Sox, who (after 1920) were drifting further and further out of contention almost every year . . .

True story . . . Faber was one of Charles Comiskey's favorite players. Comiskey had a hunting lodge in Wisconsin where he kept several moose for atmosphere, and he named one of the moose "Red Faber."

In September, 1916, Red Faber (the moose) escaped from his pen and was shot by a farm boy several miles away when he charged at the boy's brother. One of the Chicago papers ran a headline over the story, "RED FABER KILLED IN SELF-DEFENSE" . . .

> Every time he threw the spitter it seemed like the man would steal. That's about all he had at this stage of his career. He didn't have much of a curve and he threw the spitter about 95 percent of the time. The problem was that the spit is on the bottom. When you grab the ball out of the glove you have your two fingers right on that spit. So when the catcher throws to second base, he's throwing a spitter and it's tough to throw out runners with a spitball.—Bucky Crouse (who caught Faber for eight years), quoted by Eugene Murdock in *Baseball Players and Their Times*.

57 ◆ Bruce Sutter
(1976–1988, 68-71, 2.83 ERA, 300 Saves)

Only pitcher listed among the top 100 who had a losing record in his career . . . also ranks last among the top 100 in career innings pitched . . .

Of the five relief aces who made my list of the top 100 pitchers (Wilhelm, Gossage, Eckersley, Sutter, and Quisenberry), all are right-handed. This brings up a question: who is the best *left-handed* reliever of all time?

The best left-handed reliever specializing in getting out lefties, by far, has been Jesse Orosco. Orosco has been consistently effective for twenty years at a job that most people can't do two years in a row. As to the best left-handed relievers overall, the top candidates are John Franco, Randy Myers, Sparky Lyle, Tug McGraw, Ron Perranoski, and maybe Willie Hernandez and John Hiller. As to where they rate historically . . . well, when I was rating the top 100 pitchers of all time, none of them popped up on the raw-numbers list. If I had to pick one, I'd be inclined to pick Sparky Lyle . . .

58 ◆ Stan Coveleski
(1912–1928, 215-142, 2.89 ERA)

Coveleski's wife died suddenly in May 1920, three months before the death of his teammate and close friend Ray Chapman. Coveleski, who had won 22 games in 1918, 24 in 1919, pushed aside the personal tragedies to win 24 more in 1920, then three more in the World Series, then 23 in 1921.

> A spit baller with legendary control. It was said that Coveleski once pitched seven innings without a single ball being called. Every pitch either was hit or was a strike . . .–Mike Sowell, *The Pitch That Killed*

> The veteran, released to Washington as a back-number, staged quite a comeback with Washington, and ranked as that club's leading pitcher, owing to his own effective work, and the fact that the star pitcher, Walter Johnson, was laid up for a month in mid-season with tonsillitis . . . Coveleskie has depended almost entirely on the spit ball, and is one of the few box men who still use that unsanitary delivery in the major leagues . . . physically he is one of the strongest men on the ball field.–1926 *Reach Guide*

59 ◆ Billy Pierce
(1945–1964, 211-169, 3.27 ERA)

Pierce was a small man (5′10″, 160 pounds), but a power pitcher. *The Sporting News* on August 29, 1956, listed Pierce as having one of the best fastballs in the American League.

Pierce had serious control problems when he came to the majors, and was traded to the White Sox for basically nothing because he was a small pitcher with bad control. His control improved dramatically when, working with Paul Richards, he scrapped his curve ball, and began throwing the slider. From 1952 through 1958 he was one of the best pitchers in the American League every year except 1954, the best pitcher in the league in 1955 and 1958 and a twenty-game winner in '56–'57, but even then, he always had the reputation of being unable to win without his best fastball. Al Lopez, his manager, would tell reporters that his top choice to pitch a big game would be Early Wynn, not Pierce, because Wynn could win even if he didn't have his fastball . . .

Pierce's father ran a drugstore in Detroit, not too far from the ballpark. Paul Richards used to shop there, and sometimes Pierce would wait on him. Pierce, developing a local reputation as an athlete, was working out with the Tigers. "One day he walked up to me on the field," Richards told Donald Honig for *The Man In The Dugout,* "and said, 'You know, you won't even speak to me when you come into our drugstore.'

" 'What are you talking about?' I asked.

" 'That's my father's drugstore,' he said. 'You were in there last night.'

"I took a good hard look at him and, sure enough, he was the clerk."

Pierce was a funny guy, kind of a comic. One time years later . . . this story also courtesy of *The Man In The Dugout* . . . Richards was managing Pierce with the White Sox. The Yankees were hitting line drives and deep flies into center field, but Jim Busby, who was a great defensive player, was running them down. Finally Richards visited the mound. "You feel alright?" he asked Pierce.

"What are you asking me for?" replied Pierce. "Ask Busby how he feels . . ."

60 ◆ Tom Glavine
(1987–2000, 208-125, 3.39 ERA)

The best starting rotations of the 1990s, as you would probably guess, were the Maddux-Smoltz-Glavine rotations of the Atlanta Braves. In their best collective season, 1997, they were joined by Denny Neagle, who went 20-5, to form the only rotation since 1923 in which all four starters earned 20 or more Win Shares—26 for Maddux, 21 for each of the other three. The top starting rotations of the 1990s (see Vic Willis, #84):

1. Atlanta, 1997	215
2. Atlanta, 1993	186
3. Atlanta, 1998	175
4. Atlanta, 1996	167
5. Atlanta, 1999	165

The last team to score over 200, before the Braves of '97, was Cleveland in 1954; the last team to score higher than 215 was the 1931 Philadelphia A's. As a practical matter, the Atlanta rotations of the 1990s are clearly the best in the history of baseball. Some teams in the game's early history score higher than 215, but they didn't perform at the same level year-in and year-out, and the scores were different when starters pitched 350 innings a year.

61 ◆ Virgil Trucks
(1941–1958, 177-135, 3.39 ERA)

Virgil Trucks began his pro career by signing with Andalusia of the Alabama-Florida League, just before that league was entering the 1937 playoffs. He was 18 years old. He didn't get to pitch during the regular season, but pitched twice in the playoffs, and pitched two three-hit shutouts. The next year, pitching for the same team, he was 25-6 with a 1.25 ERA, striking out 418 hitters in 273 innings. I always enjoy looking at those kind of numbers, where a pitcher just has a league overmatched. Bill Kennedy, a so-so major league pitcher, pitched for Rocky Mount in the Coastal Plains League in 1946, going 28-3 with a 1.03 ERA, 456 strikeouts in 280 innings. Kennedy moved up to the Eastern League the next year and went 15-2, but hurt his arm after coming to the majors, then got traded to the Browns, effectively ending his career.

Larry Jackson pitched for Fresno, California League, in 1952, going 28-4 with 351 strikeouts in 300 innings. When I was a kid, collecting baseball cards and studying the old records on the backs, those were the three best pitcher's seasons I could find—Trucks, Kennedy, and Jackson. Trucks and Jackson were top-100 all-time pitchers; Kennedy probably would have been pretty good, too, had he stayed healthy and away from St. Louis.

No pitcher has posted those kind of numbers since then, because, in the modern farm system, a pitcher who has one league overmatched will step up quickly to the next level. A lot of times, I think they do this *too* quickly. If a minor league pitcher now starts out 7-0 with a 1.41 ERA, his organization will think "he's got nothing more to prove at that level; let's move him up a notch." But looked at in a different way, the pitcher *does* have something to prove there, and something important. He has to prove what Jackson and Trucks proved: he has to prove he can keep his focus.

If you think about it, it's not *that* uncommon for a major league pitcher, maybe a .500-type pitcher, to rip off several wins in a row, maybe go 7-0 with a one-something ERA over the space of six weeks, not because he is actually better than everybody else, but just because he hits a stretch where everything is breaking right for him. And the same happens on the other end; a pitcher may lose a bunch of games in a row, just because the breaks aren't going his way.

If that happened to the same pitcher in the minors, a modern organization would drop him down a level, let somebody else have a shot at Double-A. I always wonder if they wouldn't be ahead of the game if they left pitchers alone long enough that they could get a truer read on their ability.

62 ◆ Burleigh Grimes
(1916–1934, 270-212, 3.53 ERA)

> There is a wide difference in the styles of the nine "spitters" who survive. Shocker probably employs the spitball fewer times per game than any of the remaining eight. Mitchell, the south paw, uses it almost exclusively. Grimes, like Shocker, has a curve ball and probably would be a great pitcher without the spitter.—1924 *Reach Guide*

Grimes, like Bob Gibson, had a mean reputation on the mound, but off the mound was an exceptionally nice man. There are many stories in oral histories about Grimes going out of his way to be considerate of rookies or players who had somehow become isolated from the team . . .

Here's a question I get asked 30 times a year on the radio: "It used to be that 300 Wins was the magic number for Hall of Fame selection, but is that still true? With pitchers like Palmer, Jenkins, Jim Bunning, and Catfish Hunter going into the Hall of Fame, is the standard dropping?"

The answer is, 300 Wins was never the standard for the Hall of Fame. The Hall of Fame has *always* selected some pitchers with no more than 150-200 career wins, and that is still true. But as a practical matter, the standard for automatic Hall of Fame selection has always been about 250 wins for post-1900 pitchers, not 300. Yes, there are a few pitchers in the 250-299 Win Range who have not been selected, but only a few, and all of those are either 19th century pitchers or temporary exclusions caused by a backlog of qualified pitching candidates. On the other hand there are a lot of pitchers who *have* been selected with 250-275 wins, winning percentages well short of .600, and not really an awful lot else to sell. Go down the list of pitchers with 250-275 wins, you've got Feller, Gibson, Palmer, Hubbell . . . obvious Hall of Famers. But you've also got Burleigh Grimes, Eppa Rixey, Ted Lyons, Red Ruffing, Red Faber. What put any of those guys in the Hall of Fame, except their career Win totals?

63 ◆ Tommy John

(1963–1989, 288-231, 3.34 ERA)

Tommy John was a college math major . . . Hell of a nice man . . .

On the internet at "Baseballstuff.com" (http://www.baseballstuff.com/fraser/articles/dips.html), a gentleman named Voros McCracken

(which is NekcarcCm Sorov, spelled backwards) has published a very interesting article about pitcher's records. McCracken proposes a way of rating pitchers based on, for example, their strikeouts/inning, their walks/inning, etc., but with a twist. McCracken did not use hits/innings as an element of his system, and this was no mere oversight. McCracken argues that, other than getting strikeouts and allowing home runs, there is little that a pitcher can do to cause his hits allowed to be higher or lower. Therefore, he argues, if the pitcher's hits allowed are higher or lower than we would expect (in view of his strikeouts), this reflects not skill, but pitching in good or bad luck.

This argument has caused some stir in the world of sabermetrics. Without commenting on the nuts and bolts of McCracken's method, my two cents worth:

1. Like most things, McCracken's argument can be taken too literally. A pitcher does have *some* input into the hits/innings ratio behind him, other than that which is reflected in the home run and strikeout columns.

2. With that qualification, I am quite certain that McCracken is correct.

3. This knowledge is significant, very useful.

4. I feel stupid for not having realized this 30 years ago.

I'll address those four points in order in a minute, but let me explain my general approach to testing McCracken's hypothesis. Against each team, one can easily figure

A. The number of balls put into play.

B. The number of hits resulting, and therefore.

C. The percentage of balls in play which become hits.

Against each pitcher, one can easily figure

D. the number of balls in play.

This stuff is so easy to figure that I'm not even going to explain how, assuming that it would be obvious to anyone who cares.

Then, multiplying "C" by "D," we can figure the number of expected hits allowed by each pitcher.

For example, Scott Erickson in 1993 faced 976 batters. Of those 976, 17 hit homers, 116 struck out, 71 walked, 10 were hit by pitches, and 10 laid down sacrifice bunts. Of the 976 batters facing Erickson, then, 752 put the ball in play.

Against the 1993 Minnesota Twins, 31.1% of balls in play became hits. Of the 752 balls in play against Erickson, then, we would expect 234.1 to become hits. Adding in the 17 homers Erickson also allowed, we would expect Erickson in 1993 to have allowed 251 hits, or 251.1 if that were possible. Erickson actually allowed 266 hits. He has a surplus, then, of 15 hits.

One of Erickson's 1993 teammates, Jim Deshaies, allowed 159 hits, but would have been expected to allow 188. Deshaies, then, has a deficit of 29 hits. Since the method is team based, the total of surpluses and deficits for each team is zero.

The key question is whether these "deficits" and "surpluses" are attributable to the pitcher, or whether they have the characteristics of random occurrences. If they're attributable to the pitcher, then we would expect a pitcher who is +15 in one year to be +15 the next—if not +15, then +10 or +20; anyway we would not expect him to be −15. If they're random—if McCracken is correct—then we would expect pitchers who are +15 in one year to be plus or minus zero in the following year.

Addressing the four points above in order:

1. The surpluses and deficits are not totally random. A pitcher does have some impact on the number of hits he allows per nine innings, other than by striking people out.

Tommy John in his career allowed 142 hits more than expected, whereas Nolan Ryan allowed 134 fewer than expected. Bob Gibson allowed 76 fewer than expected. These are not random flukes, over the course of a career.

2. However, while the plusses and minuses are not totally random, they are mostly random. The extent to which any pitcher is reliably over or under his expected hits allowed is just a few hits a year.

3. This knowledge is very useful, because it allows us, in isolated cases, to make observations of value. If a pitcher has allowed 25 or 30 hits fewer than one would expect him to have allowed, then that pitcher has been pitching in extremely good luck, and it is enormously likely—probably almost 100% certain—that his value in the following season will decline. I will document this in a moment. Conversely, if a pitcher has allowed a significant number of hits more than one would expect, we can expect his luck to normalize in the following season, and thus there is some chance that that pitcher's record will improve in the following season, although this is by no means 100% certain.

4. I should have figured this out Christ knows how many years ago. I honestly don't know why I didn't. Wally Bunker in 1964 was 19-5 with a 2.69 ERA as a 19-year-old kid, although his strikeout and walk data was not particularly good. I have always known that there was something funny about that season, that the kid wasn't *really* that good. I should have been able to put my finger on what it was.

Compiling data on about 400 pitcher seasons, I found ten seasons in which pitchers had deficits of 20 or more hits (that is, they allowed 20 or more hits fewer than we would have expected them to allow, given their other data). Those ten seasons are:

Pitcher, Year	W–L	ERA	H	XH	Def
Wally Bunker, 1964	19–5	2.69	161	194	−33
Virgil Trucks, 1949	19–11	2.81	209	240	−31
Jim Deshaies, 1993	11–13	4.41	159	188	−29
Bob Gibson, 1968	22–9	1.12	198	226	−28
Don Sutton, 1980	13–5	2.20	163	191	−28
Nolan Ryan, 1991	12–6	2.91	102	126	−24
Don Wilson, 1967	10–9	2.79	141	162	−21
Tommy John, 1970	12–17	3.27	234	255	−21
Bob Gibson, 1966	21–12	2.44	210	231	−21
Nolan Ryan, 1974	22–16	2.89	221	241	−20

There are some quality pitchers on this list . . . Gibson, Sutton, and Ryan are Hall of Famers, John probably will be eventually, Virgil Trucks is a top-100 pitcher, Don Wilson was a good pitcher. But in the following seasons, all ten of these pitchers suffered significant declines in performance, as their luck returned to normal:

Pitcher, Year	Focus Year		Next Season	
Wally Bunker, 1964	19–5	2.69	10–8	3.38
Virgil Trucks, 1949	19–11	2.81	3–1	3.54
Jim Deshaies, 1993	11–13	4.41	6–12	7.39
Bob Gibson, 1968	22–9	1.12	20–13	2.18
Don Sutton, 1980	13–5	2.20	11–9	2.61
Nolan Ryan, 1991	12–6	2.91	5–9	3.72
Don Wilson, 1967	10–9	2.79	13–16	3.28
Tommy John, 1970	12–17	3.27	13–16	3.61
Bob Gibson, 1966	21–12	2.44	13–7	2.98
Nolan Ryan, 1974	22–16	2.89	14–12	3.45
Averages	16–10	2.75	11–10	3.61

All ten pitchers had higher ERAs in the following season. All except John had poorer won-lost records in the following season. (John was the exception because he pitched for a team which improved from 56-106 in 1970 to 79-83 in 1971, while the league ERA also dropped 25 points. Although John's 1971 record looks similar to his '70 record, his actual value declined by 40%.)

The pitchers who finished 11th, 12th, 13th, 14th, and 15th on my list of "hit lucky" pitchers also suffered significant declines in performance in the following seasons. The first pitcher on the list who did not suffer a significant performance decline was Bob Gibson, 1962—a young Bob Gibson. Gibby's improvement as a pitcher was more than equal to his decline in "hit luck."

That can happen, of course; if you studied enough pitchers, you would probably find somebody who was −30 in one season, but nonetheless was able to improve his performance the following season. But it would be extremely uncommon. Among pitchers who are −20 or more, I suspect that 99% would suffer performance declines in the following season.

It would be nice to report that there were also pitchers who were 99% certain to improve in the following year. There aren't. It's not a parallel universe. Pitchers who are +20 are much fewer in number, for one thing, because pitchers who pitch in tough luck are very prone to losing their jobs in mid-season. Pitchers who do finish +20 in hits allowed don't have the same tendency to improve in the following season because, among other things, they often don't have starting jobs in the following season. Still, about 65% of pitchers who are +15 or more in "hit luck" will improve their ERAs in the following season (although often in fewer innings pitched).

A pitcher's luck can be analyzed in several different ways, which we have known for years. A pitcher can be "run support lucky," and finish 20-8 with a 4.70 ERA, and there's a pitcher you don't want on your team the following year. A pitcher can be "run element lucky" and post a 4.00 ERA when, given the number of hits and walks and homers he has allowed, his ERA should be 4.86, and there, again, is a pitcher you don't want on your team in the following season.

And here is another one—a pitcher can be "hit lucky," and there's a man you don't want to bet on. Voros McCracken, I thank you for the edge.

64 ◆ Catfish Hunter
(1965–1979, 224-166, 3.26 ERA)

> I used to wonder how in the hell he ever won a game. His fast ball is ordinary and his breaking stuff isn't all that good. But he knows what he's doing out there, and he has excellent control. Good guy, too.—Denny McLain in *Nobody's Perfect*.

I have a son, Isaac, who never makes anything harder than it is. We don't know where he gets this, but it's an interesting thing to watch. Homework isn't hard for him, because he simply sits down when he gets home from school and does it. Keeping his room clean isn't hard, because he throws dirty clothes in the laundry to begin with. Good things come to him, because unlike the rest of us, he doesn't fight the world; he simply does what needs to be done.

Catfish was like that; he caught some good breaks in life because people simply liked him, and he caught some more because he never made pitching harder than it was. He never worried about making perfect pitches; he just tried to stay away from the hitter's strengths. He didn't get behind the hitters; he didn't start to fight himself or the umpire or the press or his manager or the fielders behind him. He just threw strikes. Because of the way he pitched, he could pitch more than his share of innings, and because he was a country boy with good manners and not much of an ego, there was a tendency sometimes to let him have more than his share of the credit.

His name wasn't "Catfish," of course; it was "Jim," but if Charley Finley wanted him to be "Catfish"... well, why fight it? When he was a high school pitching phenom his brother's shotgun went off, and filled Jim's foot with buckshot. The scouts could have backed off from him, but... well, he was Jim Hunter, and they liked him. He probably wasn't the best pitcher in the American League in 1974, but he was one of the best, and... well, he was Catfish, and the Cy Young voters liked him. Maybe his career numbers didn't scream "Hall of Fame" at you, but... well, he was Catfish.

George Steinbrenner paid him a record salary to get one good year out of him, and was asked later whether he felt it was a bad investment. "Absolutely not," said Steinbrenner, "Catfish brought respectability back to this organization." The record book shows that the Yankees won six fewer games the year Catfish joined them then they had the year before, but... well, he was Catfish. The Yankees were glad to have him anyway.

I was Catfish's biggest fan his first few years in the league. I was a Kansas City A's fan; Catfish was special from the moment he stepped on the field. When he was 19 years old, he was just on the roster because he had to be, but he turned out to be one of our best pitchers, pitched a two-hit shutout in which he himself got three hits. Three years later, determined to keep rooting for the Athletics even though they had abandoned us, I listened to every pitch of a faint, scratchy broadcast from Minnesota, as Catfish pitched a perfect game against the Twins. I haven't worshiped athletes in that way since I grew up, but I certainly wouldn't want anyone to think I was being critical of Catfish, rating him where I have. Catfish was special. But in rating the pitchers, I have to face the facts, too.

65 ◆ Jim Kaat

(1959–1983, 283-237, 3.45 ERA)

Jim Kaat was usually taken for granted. First he was taken for granted because consistent players are always taken for granted, and Kaat was unnaturally consistent. Between 1962 and 1975 Kaat had a winning record every year except 1963, when he was 10-10, and 1971, when he was 13-14. But while he was always over .500, he was never *way* over .500; he was never over .658 in his career, except in 1972, when he was injured and missed most of the season, but did go 10-2. As Billy Loes said, if you win 20 games once, people will expect you to do it every year. Jim Kaat won 18 games every year, but well . . . he was *expected* to.

Late in his career he won 20 games twice in a row, with the White Sox in 1974 and 1975. These twenty-win seasons were almost entirely overlooked, however, because it was an unusual time, and the league was knee deep in twenty-game winners. Between 1970 and 1975 there were 49 twenty-game winners in the American League . . . here, let me chart how unusual that is:

AL 20-game winners, 1950–1955	20
AL 20-game winners, 1960–1965	15
AL 20-game winners, 1970–1975	49
AL 20-game winners, 1980–1985	12
AL 20-game winners, 1990–1995	9

Kaat won 20 twice in a row, but nobody noticed, because there were so many 20-game winners in the league that you couldn't keep track of them.

Kaat at that time was working extremely quickly; this was what he was known for—he was the old pitcher who worked real fast. He would just get the ball back from the catcher and immediately fire it back to the plate. Somebody asked him why he worked so quickly, and he said "Because if the game goes over two hours, my fastball turns into a pumpkin." I quote that line often, because it makes a point: that it is not merely the number of pitches which cause fatigue in a pitcher, but also the length of the game. One of the primary reasons we have almost no complete games now is that the games take so long to play.

Kaat reached the major leagues in the Eisenhower administration, played through the Kennedy administration, the Johnson administration, the Nixon administration, the Ford administration, the Carter administration, and three years into the Reagan administration. He had a losing record in the Carter administration, but then, everybody did.

Jim Kaat's won-lost records between 1962 and 1969 were:

1962	18-14
1963	10-10
1964	17-11
1965	18-11
1966	25-13
1967	16-13
1968	14-12
1969	14-13
1970	14-10

You can make Kaat's into a first-ballot Hall of Fame career, not by *improving* his luck, but merely by re-arranging it a little bit. Suppose that Kaat had won a couple games more in 1962 and '65, but given them back in other years:

1962	20-12
1963	10-10
1964	16-12
1965	20-9
1966	24-14
1967	15-14
1968	14-12
1969	14-13
1970	13-11

His overall record would be exactly the same, but he would be in the Hall of Fame because that would give him five 20-win seasons. Five 20-win seasons do not guarantee the Hall of Fame—but they come pretty close. 283 career wins probably do guarantee eventual selection to the Hall of Fame, but only in the long run. And Kaat *did* pitch better than his record in 1962 and in 1965, and probably deserved to win 20 both years.

Are there other players like this, who could be converted into first-ballot Hall of Fame selections just by modestly re-arranging their luck? Maybe, but I don't know of any. It works for Kaat because

(a) Kaat is on the edge of the Hall of Fame anyway, and

(b) Kaat was exceptionally consistent, and thus lacks Big Years.

66 ◆ Ron Guidry
(1975–1988, 170-91, 3.29 ERA)
You know how you can spot those left-handers who are going to have super control? They're exceptionally graceful. Remember Guidry on the mound, how graceful he was? He was like a dancer. He would balance on the mound, his feet so close together they almost formed a point, and he hovered above the point like an exclamation mark.

Jim Kaat was like that; although he was much bigger than Guidry, he had exceptional grace for a large man. Larry Gura was the most graceful player I ever saw with the Royals, except maybe Charlie Leibrandt or Bud Black. Warren Spahn was like that, even at 40. Joe Sambito . . . remember him? He was Fred Astaire. Bobby Shantz was famous for his grace.

You see a young left-hander, trying to establish himself in the major leagues, you look for two things. First of all, you look for the great fastball. If he has that, he has a chance. Second, you look for awkwardness. If he is

even the tiniest bit awkward, and he *doesn't* have a Grade A fastball, write him off. He'll never make it.

67 ◆ Lefty Gomez
(1930–1943, 189-102, 3.34 ERA)
Before television, and before Satan invented the business of selling autographs, retired ballplayers would sometimes sustain themselves by speaking to rooms full of people. There used to be thousands of Lions clubs, and Moose, and Elk, and Oddfellows, and Knights of Columbus, and all of these groups met once or twice a month, and sometimes brought in speakers. In the winter, or after retirement, a ballplayer could speak three or four times a week if he wanted to, and earn a good income, and also that was how young athletes proved that they had something upstairs, that they could handle responsibilities that didn't involve hitting a curve ball. Joe Garagiola was a great after-dinner speaker (while he was a player), and Billy Martin was, and Tommy Lasorda, and Whitey Herzog, and Dizzy Dean, and Fresco Thompson.

The best, however, was supposed to be Lefty Gomez. Baseball books are rife with Lefty Gomez anecdotes, retold from his years of public speaking. I almost never use his anecdotes . . . as I think about it, what made a story good for Gomez was often the opposite of what makes a story useful for me. Gomez wanted a story that was clean and quick, nothing to distract from the punch line. I want a story that tells us something about the time and the place—and thus, a story that looks around as it progresses. Lefty didn't care whether a story was true as long as it would get a laugh; I can't use a story unless I believe it to be true.

I want a story that tells us something about the character or the style of the player. Lefty made caricatures of his friends and teammates, so that he could pull them onstage quickly with just a line or two.

Don't get me wrong; he *was* funny. Phil Rizzuto, said Lefty, was so short that he had to stand on a stool to take a shower, otherwise the water would be cold before it got to him. Jimmie Foxx, said Gomez, "Has muscles in his hair."

"I was the worst hitter I ever saw," Gomez used to say. "I never even broke a bat until last year. I backed over it as I was pulling out of the garage." When he had triple-bypass surgery in 1979, Lefty said that it was the first triple he had ever had.

Lefty claimed that one time he hit a double, but was picked off second base. "What the hell happened out there," Joe McCarthy demanded. "How should I know?" replied Lefty. "I've never been there before."

He said that one time Willie Mays hit a home run in the Polo Grounds that didn't come down until Utica. "I know," he explained, "because I was managing there at the time." When he was managing in the minors he lost 14 straight games, then had a game rained out. "It felt so good," said Gomez, "we had a victory dinner."

One time Johnny Broaca, a Yale man, addressed Gomez as "Goofy." Gomez yelled at Broaca never to call him that again. Bill Dickey, puzzled, asked Gomez why he had gotten mad. "You don't get mad when Pat Malone calls you goofy," Dickey said.

"Malone didn't go to Yale," explained Gomez.

"Lefty, to what do you attribute your success?" he was asked when he was elected to the Hall of Fame. "Clean living and a fast outfield," he replied.

Here's a Lefty Gomez story I *don't* like. One time, when Joe DiMaggio was a rookie, Hank Greenberg hit a ball over his head. Lefty asked Joe why he was playing so shallow. "I'm going to make them forget Tris Speaker," replied DiMaggio.

"Roomie," said Gomez, "you keep playing Greenberg shallow, and you're going to make them forget Lefty Gomez."

I don't like the story because I can't feature Joe DiMaggio claiming he is going to make people forget Tris Speaker, I don't believe he ever said it, and without that, there's no story.

But here's one I do . . . one time, with runners on first and third, the batter hit a sharp one-hopper back to the mound. Lefty bobbled the ball a moment, too late to make the play at home, then spun and threw to Tony Lazzeri at second, way too late to make the play at second. "What did you do that for?" asked Lazzeri.

"I've been reading in the papers about what a smart player you are," said Gomez. I figured you'd think of something."

68 ◆ Dan Quisenberry
(1979–1990, 56-46, 2.76 ERA, 244 Saves)
Most and fewest career wild pitches among the top 100 pitchers:

1. Nolan Ryan	277
2. Tim Keefe	233
3. Phil Niekro	226
4. Old Hoss Radbourn	217
5. Tommy John	187

1. Dan Quisenberry	4
2. Dizzy Dean	12
3. Urban Shocker	20
4. Don Newcombe	22
5. Babe Adams	26

Most and fewest walks per nine innings, among the top 100:

1. Nolan Ryan	4.67
2. Bob Feller	4.15
3. Amos Rusie	4.07
4. Bob Lemon	3.95
5. Lefty Gomez	3.94

1. Tommy Bond	0.58
2. Babe Adams	1.29

3. Dan Quisenberry   1.40
4. Addie Joss   1.41
5. Cy Young   1.49

Quisenberry is the only one of the top eight control pitchers to have reached the majors later than 1911. And of the 162 walks that he issued in his career, almost half (70) were intentional . . .

Dan Quisenberry had neither the body nor the ego of a major league athlete, and yet he was one of the best. He was a skinny man with a long nose and small teeth and a pencil moustache, and he was a beautiful man.

I couldn't say that we were close, but Quiz and I did a radio show together one summer . . . some of you may remember it. He was funny and quirky, and he was brilliant. Quiz used to play a game with Denny Matthews, Royals broadcaster, which tells you something about him. "Your word for today is 'homily,' he would tell Matthews, or 'xenophobic,' or 'divaricate.'"

"Your word is 'penumbra,'" Matthews would respond, or "triumvirate," or something. Denny would have to figure out some way to work the word "homily" into his broadcast without the listeners realizing that anything was going on, and Quiz would have to figure out some way to work the word "penumbra" into his post-game interview.

One time a guy called up the show, told us about a time when he was ten years old and met Quisenberry in a grocery store. He asked for his autograph, which Quiz gave, but then the Quiz started talking to him, just like (he said years later) a real person. "You playin' baseball?" Dan asked him.

"Yes," the kid said, he was playing baseball.

"You got your glove with you?"

Quiz wound up playing catch with the kid for twenty minutes in the supermarket parking lot.

Unusually approachable, very comfortable, more human than athlete. He loved words, loved to play with oddball ideas, and wrote poetry. He was, in fact, a gentle man, but he had an edge to him, too. Like a lot of bright people, he was very aware that he was living in a world inhabited by more than a few morons. A lot of times, when he said the funny things that are collected in all of the quote books, he was actually directing attention away from something that he didn't want to talk about. Privately, he regarded a fairly good percentage of his ex-managers and a comfortable majority of his ex-coaches as dullards and frauds, and he could take offense at things you might say, not offense like he was going to punch you, but offense like "don't you realize what you are saying?" He hated being patronized, and didn't particularly like being analyzed or evaluated.

I never knew anyone who would give an unexpected answer to a question more often than Quiz, unexpectedly honest, unexpectedly profound, or just off-the-wall. "I never asked 'Why me?'" he said about the brain tumor. "Why not me?"

Now, it is a fair question how I can evaluate a player like Quisenberry, who I knew and liked, along a list of players most of whom I didn't personally know, and some of whom I didn't particularly like. But there's a simple answer: I just go by the numbers. I've got a rating system; I don't move a player up or down from where the numbers rate him unless I have a specific reason to move him.

One element of the rating system is a subjective factor, a number between 0 and 50. But the subjective factor is 25 for everybody unless there is a reason to make it higher or lower. For Quisenberry, I made it 16. Two reasons:

1. The system is kind—perhaps too kind—to relievers of that era, as opposed to the earlier and later relievers.

2. I don't want people to think I'm over-rating the players I knew and liked.

Quiz ranks 68th when he probably deserves to rank 60th ... what's that? That matter to somebody? I've worked as hard as I possibly can to rate the players accurately, but at a certain point rating systems just become opinions, stated as numbers. It isn't the subjective factor which makes them subjective; it is the subjective decisions which go into the construction of the formulas. The difference between the 100th and 200th best pitchers of all time is thin enough that good arguments exist for players who didn't make the top 200, let alone the top 100. I rated Quisenberry here not because I liked him, but because this is where he rates. There has never been a pitcher who made fewer mistakes than Dan Quisenberry.

69 ◆ Bucky Walters
(1934–1950, 198-160, 3.30 ERA)

I have had this idea for twenty years, and it hasn't gone anywhere yet, but you never know ...

Did you ever try to sort pitchers into "families." The only family of pitchers that I have written much about is the Tommy John family. The Tommy John family of pitchers has five defining characteristics:

1. Left-handers.
2. With good control.
3. With outstanding moves to first.
4. Who get *lots* of ground balls.
5. Relatively few strikeouts.

This combination enabled John to win for many years in the major leagues despite high opposition batting averages. The career average against John was .265, but he had years late in his career when it was close to .300, but he was still able to win because, when you take away the walk, the stolen base, and the home run, it takes a lot of singles to beat you.

Tommy John, however, is the only member of the Tommy John family who made the list of the top 100 pitchers. Well, I *think* he was ... there's Eddie Plank and Eppa Rixey, but I am getting ahead of myself.

Why do you want to sort out families of pitchers, James? It's a way of organizing our thinking. I'll give you an example. A major league team once asked me to evaluate the outlook for one of their pitchers, who they were thinking about signing to a five-year contract. I looked at him for two days, and reported that, in my opinion, the pitcher would go through a career crisis in the middle of the five-year period, but would emerge from that, and would still be a solid pitcher. The prediction turned out to be exactly accurate; he is still a good major league pitcher today.

I based that prediction on the experience of comparable pitchers—good right-handed power pitchers. You look at those guys, a lot of them go through a career crisis at age 31, 32, where they have to learn how to pitch without their Grade A fastball.

Another example: members of the Tommy John family of pitchers can't pitch effectively with a bad team. Why? Too much pressure on the defense. Without strikeouts, there are a lot of hard-hit balls in play. A bad team can't get enough outs from those to save the pitcher's ass—but a good team can. Thus, members of this family tend to be valuable to good teams, but useless to bad teams. If you know that, then maybe once in awhile you can make a judgment that you can't otherwise make.

Players who share four, five, or six characteristics may—or may not, you never know—be expected to have similar career progressions, or to have other characteristics in common. The problem is knowing who to put in what family. Among the top 100 pitchers, there is probably only one absolutely clean match: Bucky Walters and Bob Lemon. Bucky Walters and Bob

Lemon have *everything* in common, as pitchers, and no significant differences that I am aware of. Both were right-handers, about the same size. Both were originally third basemen, and both were good enough to reach the majors as third basemen. Both were outstanding hitters.

Both were power pitchers in the sense that they threw hard, rather than throwing to spots, but neither had a real strikeout pitch. Most batters who strike out do so on a curve or a change; both Lemon and Walters became major league pitchers after learning to throw the pitch which is now called the slider. Walters was taught to throw the slider by Chief Bender in 1935, although Bender didn't have a name for the pitch. Lemon learned to throw the pitch, which he called a curve, during World War II, but both of them lived and died on the pitch now known as the slider. Both had poor strikeout/walk ratios (about 1-1. Among the top 100 pitchers of all time, they rank 95th and 96th in strikeout/walk ratio.) Both got tremendous ground-ball support. Their career ERAs are about the same, and most of their other stats are, as well; even their fielding stats are almost the same. Lemon was a little better, but they're an essentially perfect match.

My point here is: That's the exception. If that's a perfect match, it's probably the only one. Most of the time, the problem with discussing "families" of pitchers is figuring out who is in which family. I'll list families by the best pitcher who is a member of the family, which makes this the Bob Lemon family. Here are a few others:

The Lefty Grove Family—Blow 'em Away Lefties—includes Randy Johnson, Steve Carlton, Sandy Koufax, Hal Newhouser, Rube Waddell, Vida Blue, and Hippo Vaughn. With eight members, this is probably the most-represented family within the top 100. Secondary characteristics include a relatively slow maturation process (several of these guys lost big for years

before figuring it out) and really, really bad offense. None of these guys could hit a lick except Newhouser and Carlton, who could hit a little, and most of them also had some difficulty fielding the ball.

The Bob Feller Family—Right-handed Power Pitchers Who Will Give You the Walk—includes Nolan Ryan, Goose Gossage, Dazzy Vance, Amos Rusie, and probably Virgil Trucks.

The Tom Seaver Family—Right-handed Power Pitchers Who Won't Give You Anything They Don't Have To—is perhaps the most plentiful group among what could be called "Ordinary High Quality Pitchers"—Curt Schilling, Alex Fernandez, Brad Radke, etc. Among the top 100, however, we have only four clear-cut members of this family—Seaver, Clemens, Bob Gibson, and Doc Gooden.

The Jim Bunning Family—The Picture-Perfect Pitchers—These are the guys who maybe don't have Bob Gibson fastballs, but who just have the whole package—a good fastball backed up with a curve, a slider, a change, and pinpoint control. These are the guys, you see them on a good day and you think "I don't understand how this bastard ever loses," but they do lose sometimes because they throw strikes, and if you put the ball over the plate sometimes the batter is going to hit it. Jim Bunning, Don Sutton, Lon Warneke, Dave Stieb, Bret Saberhagen, possibly Jim Palmer.

The Juan Marichal Family—The What-The-Hell-Was-THAT Family—includes Pedro Martinez, David Cone, Old Hoss Radbourn, Luis Tiant, and Joe McGinnity, also includes assorted other pitchers like Orlando Hernandez, Livan Hernandez, Ron Kline, Remy Kremer, and all of the Cubans. These are the guys who have good fastballs and good control, but who bamboozle hitters by changing speeds and arm angles, leaving hitters—even *good* hitters sometimes—completely over-matched. An interesting note about these pitchers is that all of them except Marichal have high Indexes of Self-Destruction (see Orel Hershiser, number 83), probably because they experiment on the mound constantly, and sometimes things will get away from them.

The Robin Roberts Family is the "tightest" family of the group, containing Roberts, Catfish Hunter, and Fergie Jenkins. Roberts, Hunter, and Jenkins have all but indistinguishable records; they would all go 23-14, 22-15, 21-13 year after year, pitching lots of innings with exceptional strikeout to walk ratios, but tons of home runs allowed. These are the right-handed pitchers who have good fastballs and a strong commitment to strike one. These guys are going to throw their fastball down the middle of the plate on the first pitch, batter after batter. If you can hit it, power to you, buddy, and they're going to give up some home runs because of that. But they're also going to get a huge number of first-pitch outs, and they're going to be working ahead of 65 or 70% of the hitters. These things enable them to work 300 innings a year, and win a lot more often than they lose. These guys were also good hitters, and they also—all three of them—had high ratios of fly balls to ground balls.

Another characteristic of this family of pitchers is that they have exceptionally "regular" careers. Their careers, if you graph them, rise to a peak and then settle gradually down, in a way that pitchers' careers almost never do. They don't really have off seasons, the way that a lot of pitchers do.

And they are also useful for explaining the basic problem with the concept of pitching families. Look, Roberts, Jenkins, and Hunter are almost a perfect group, the *most* perfect group except for Walters and Lemon. There is no doubt that they belong in a family. The problem is knowing who *doesn't* belong in the family. Jim Bunning, example one. I have chosen Jim Bunning to be the eponym of a different group, the

picture-perfect pitchers, but the reality is that he can almost equally well be placed in the Robin Roberts group. Like the Robin Roberts group, Bunning had a strong faith in strike one. Like the Roberts group, he gave up a lot of home runs because he would rather risk a home run than work behind a hitter.

Why isn't he in the Roberts family, then? It's just a judgment call. His stuff was a little different; he relied on the slider more than Roberts or Hunter did. But as a practical matter, he *could* be in the Robin Roberts family, and he could also be in the Tom Seaver family, and he could *almost* be in the Juan Marichal family, maybe not quite. Don Newcombe could be in the Robin Roberts family. The only real reason he is not is that Newcombe's career was torn up by the color line, military service, and his battles with the bottle, so that he doesn't have the regular career shape that the other three pitchers do.

Bert Blyleven had seasons which look, statistically, exactly like they belong in the Robin Roberts family, although he was a different kind of a pitcher, relying heavily on that huge hook, while the other three used mostly the fastball and the slider.

Which leads us to the second big problem with this line of analysis: what, exactly, is a defining characteristic for a pitcher? Is the fact that Blyleven relied on his curve a sufficient reason to distinguish him from this family? Or is Blyeleven really a completely different type of pitcher, who merely happens to have records which *look* a lot the same? Is the fact that Don Newcombe lacks a complete career a sufficient reason to distinguish him from pitchers whose stuff and style and results were very much the same? Is that a defining characteristic, or just misfortune?

What about Babe Adams? Adams, like this family of pitchers, had a good fastball, a strong belief in strike one, and a level-headed, no-nonsense approach to pitching. He didn't give up a lot of home runs, however, simply because he played in an era when there *weren't* many home runs.

A secondary characteristic of the Robin Roberts family of pitchers is that they tend to have lower component ERAs than actual ERAs. The component ERA is a formula which looks at a pitcher's hits allowed, walks allowed, and home runs allowed, and says "this is the ERA that these should add up to." It's a good formula, but it's not a *perfect* formula, and pitchers like Roberts, Newcombe, Jenkins, and Hunter tend to have higher actual ERAs than component ERAs. Robin Roberts never led his league in ERA, but led his league in component ERA twice.

But Babe Adams never led his league in ERA, either, but led his league in component ERA an astonishing six times. This certainly suggests that Adams might be a member of this family. On the other hand, maybe not. Roberts had a great fastball and a strong belief that you should throw it. Adams had a good fastball and a strong belief that you should save it until you really needed it. He didn't walk people, but he threw curves and change ups like pennies. If he had come along later, would Adams have given up 30 homers a year? He didn't throw a slider because he pitched before the slider became popular, but does that mean that nobody from 1910 could be considered a Robin Roberts-type pitcher?

Does Walter Johnson belong with the Tom Seaver family, or not? I think somehow that he doesn't, but I'm really not sure. Walter didn't throw a curve much, and his mechanics were a lot different, with that sidearm delivery and odd follow-through. His records are unique; nobody else really has records that look like that. Can a great pitcher be put into the same family with a mediocrity, or is quality, at some level, a defining characteristic? If Walter doesn't belong with Seaver, where does he belong?

Is John Smoltz in the Jim Bunning family, or does his fondness for throwing eleven pitches put him into the Juan Marichal class? We just don't know. The "families" approach to evaluating pitchers is fun and useful, but a lot of times it is limited because you just don't know what family a pitcher belongs to. Carrying on:

The Don Drysdale Family—Big, Scary Right-Handed Power Pitchers Who Can Really Hit—includes Wes Ferrell, Don Drysdale, and, I suppose, Don Newcombe. Frightening pitchers, and good athletes as well as good pitchers.

The Warren Spahn Group—the "Easy Motion" Left-Handers. Here again the exact limits of the family are crucial, and impossible to pin down. I have placed five of the top 100 pitchers in this group—Spahn, Tom Glavine, Eddie Plank, Jesse Tannehill, and Wilbur Cooper, but I am only certain that the grouping is appropriate for three of them (Spahn, Glavine, and Cooper), and it is also arguable that Jim Kaat, Eppa Rixey, Mickey Lolich, and even Tommy John should be placed in the same family.

This is one of the most common groups of "good" pitchers historically. The Royals used to pile them up in layers—Bud Black, Charlie Leibrandt, Larry Gura, Paul Splittorff. The Orioles used to have them, too—Dave McNally certainly, maybe Cuellar as well. Jamie Moyer is in this group.

In 2001, every third pitcher who comes along is described as a Tom Glavine clone. When I was a kid, they were described as Eddie Lopat-types, although Lopat had been retired for ten years by then.

Do Plank and Tannehill actually belong in this group, or were they more like Tommy John? What about Eppa Rixey, or Mel Parnell? Maybe with more research, we could be sure, but I'm really just sorting people based on a best guess. Here, quickly, are a few remaining groups:

The Christy Mathewson Family, Mathewson and Greg Maddux. If you don't consider throwing left- or right-handed to be a defining characteristic, Carl Hubbell is also in this family.

The Kevin Brown Family contains only three representatives among the top 100 pitchers, those being Kevin Brown, Rick Reuschel, and Larry Jackson. Ground Ball pitchers who also had a strikeout pitch. Historically, there aren't many of these. I think Scott Erickson is the only other guy in this group right now. Burleigh Grimes *might* belong in this group, although I chose to put him in . . .

The Gaylord Perry Family, spitball pitchers who pitched a ton of innings. Gaylord, Ed Walsh, Red Faber, Urban Shocker, and Burleigh Grimes.

The Dizzy Dean Family—a Great Half of A Career—contains Dizzy Dean, Smokey Joe Wood, Bob Caruthers, and Addie Joss, although Joss might more properly be included with the Kevin Brown family. This group has countless members who did not make the top 100, and also has filed a claim to count Don Newcombe.

The Phil Niekro Family—Pure Knuckle Ball Pitchers—has two top-100 representatives, Phil and Hoyt Wilhelm, although I have some misgivings about classifying starters and relievers together.

The Ted Lyons Family is right-handers who throw everything up there but the kitchen sink. We have four of those among the top 100—Lyons, Early Wynn, Eddie Rommel, and Eddie Cicotte.

The Bert Blyleven 125 Curve Balls A Game Family has two top-100 pitchers, Blyleven and Tommy Bridges. Camilo Pascual was also in this family.

I'm drifting down to "sets" or "pairs" here, rather than full families.

Ron Guidry and Lefty Gomez seem like they should be paired. These two have similar career records as well, which many times similar pitchers really do not. Guidry and Gomez were thin guys, very graceful, and both had a couple of years early in their careers when they could blow people away. Neither really fits with the Lefty Grove group, however, because they weren't true power pitchers throughout their careers, relying for much of their careers on breaking stuff and control.

Red Ruffing and George Uhle can be put together—guys who weren't big and didn't throw 95, but were extremely good athletes, good hitters who knew how to pitch.

Jim Kaat can be linked with Eppa Rixey as BIG lefties who were graceful and threw strikes, although, as I mentioned, there are other claimants for Rixey. Frank Viola, who could have made the top 100, could also be in this class, although Viola on the mound really looked more like Mickey Lolich than he did like Kaat.

Altogether I have classified 72 of the top 100 pitchers so far; the other 28, I don't know what to do with. Mel Harder, I think, may be the third member of the Bob Lemon family, unless you regard "starting your career as a third baseman" to be an essential characteristic of the group. Of the other 28 many are not put with any group because they're unique—Carl Hubbell, Whitey Ford, Bruce Sutter, Carl Mays, Three Finger Brown, Pete Alexander, etc.—and many are not put into any group because I don't know enough about them to know where to put them. Some, like Mickey Lolich and Dan Quisenberry, have clear counterparts, but no clear counterparts within the top 100 pitchers.

Every pitcher is an individual, of course. John Heydler was President of the National League in 1909. He was a brilliant man, a real student of the game. Before the 1909 World Series Heydler was in Washington on business, and he happened to see a game at which Dolly Gray, a mediocre Washington pitcher, beat the American League champion Detroit Tigers, with Cobb and Crawford.

Heydler thought that Dolly Gray reminded him of Babe Adams, a rookie sixth starter with the National League champion Pittsburgh Pirates. Heydler recommended to Pirates manager

Fred Clarke that he pitch Adams against the Tigers. When his top starters developed some minor injuries, Clarke did choose Adams to start the series. Adams started three games, and beat the Tigers three times.

That is the essence of the "Families" approach to pitching: looking for useful similarities between pitchers.

70 ◆ Clark Griffith
(1891–1914, 236-143, 3.31 ERA)

> In a honky-tonk music hall, Griffith and Cantillon finally found work. The wild Indian yells he had learned in his native Missouri served Griffith in good stead. He gained a job as a "bad Indian" in a Barbary Coat "mellerdrammer," and Cantillon, as an Indian in the same skit, emptied a six-shooter at Griffith twice a night.—Shirley Povich in *The Washington Senators*

Ira Smith and H. Allen Smith, in *Three Men on Third,* allege that Clark Griffith was superstitious about shutouts, that he thought that throwing a shutout was bad luck. "When he appeared to be headed for such an achievement," report the Smiths, "he'd beg his teammates to ease up and let the opposition score a run, lest the special curse descend upon him." Griffith led the National League in shutouts in 1900 and 1901, but his career shutout total (22 in 372 starts) *does* appear to be lower than we would expect.

A short, square man who changed speeds and had outstanding control . . . who would be in a "family" with him? Nobody I ever saw, except maybe some minor guys like Scott Bankhead. Mario Soto, maybe . . . Griffith was much admired in the Washington area, thought of as a clever man who cared about his players and cared about the team. Douglass Wallop portrayed him sympathetically in *The Year the Yankees Lost the Pennant* as Adam Welch, a kindly old pater familias whose first priority was the welfare of his players. In the modern world we don't much admire businessmen or team owners, even when they are genuinely worthy of admiration.

Griffith's cleverness had short borders. He resisted changes, ridiculed night baseball, refused to build a farm system, and hired clowns as coaches. He did have a decent record on civil rights, employing Cubans who were almost black before the color line broke, and hiring out his stadium to black baseball. He was sharp enough to survive, sharp enough to make himself wealthy, and sharp enough to win into the 1930s. Like Connie Mack, his only real fellow traveller, he fell behind the game when he refused to build a farm system.

71 ◆ Urban Shocker
(1916–1928, 187-117, 3.17 ERA)

> Shocker is reading the newspapers, and his berth is messed up with a dozen sports pages, torn from as many different papers. Now and then he makes some discovery and pauses to discuss baseball with Pennock.—Ford Frick in *Babe Ruth's Own Book of Baseball*

Two of the top-100 pitchers were named "Urban." Red Faber was the other . . . Shocker was a career .209 hitter, but with almost as many walks (139) as hits (167), making him one of very few pitchers to have a higher secondary average than batting average. These are the top ten secondary averages for pitchers with higher secondary than batting averages:

		BAvg	SecAvg
1.	Jack Harshman	.179	.337
2.	Willie McGill	.202	.277
3.	Earl Wilson	.195	.265
4.	Pat Luby	.235	.240
5.	Bob Lemon	.232	.235
6.	Matt Kilroy	.222	.232
7.	Mickey Harris	.188	.229
8.	Urban Shocker	.209	.216
9.	Frank Allen	.135	.215
10.	Silver King	.199	.215

Most outfielders and first basemen have higher secondary than batting averages, and some middle infielders do, as well. But very few pitchers . . .

Shocker was an obsessive newspaper reader, particularly the sports pages. He bought every newspaper he could find, and studied them at length, in consequence of which he knew more than anybody else about what was going on around the league—who was hot, who was cold, who was playing, who was not, and who was hitting what. If a player went 0-for-4 against Tom Zachary, Shocker would reason that the player was having trouble reading change ups, and would throw him slow stuff.

Shocker was an outstanding bunter, one of the best fielding pitchers of his time, and a crossword puzzle wizard. Ford Frick claimed that in 1927 he drove in 11 runs, six of them on squeeze bunts, although I wouldn't want to bet on this claim checking out. He was not an easy man to get along with. While with the Browns he was once suspended in a dispute over bringing his wife along on a road trip, and he reportedly did not get along with either Lee Fohl or George Sisler, his manager and superstar teammate in St. Louis.

Shocker won 27 games in 1921 for a team that was under .500 with other pitchers, won 20 four times in a row for a team that was under .500 otherwise in three of the four years. He never had a losing record in his career. In a thirteen-year career he went 12-12 in '25, 0-0 in 1928, otherwise had a winning record every year. He died of pneumonia in 1928, less than a year after winning 18 games for the '27 Yankees.

72 ◆ Mickey Lolich
(1963–1979, 217-191, 3.44 ERA)

> Lolich was blessed with one of the finest arms I've ever seen . . . Too bad the good Lord didn't give him more of an ability to think on the mound. Had Mickey Lolich concentrated more

on opposing batters, and less on his personal battle with Denny McLain, he'd have been a bigger and more consistent winner over the years.–Denny McLain in *Nobody's Perfect*

> Mickey and I have had some curious conversations on the mound during games. In the sixth inning of the seventh game of the 1968 World Series . . . I asked Mickey "Anything I can do for you?"
> "Yeah," he said. "Can you get me a couple of hamburgers between innings?"–Bill Freehan, *Behind the Mask*

Lolich was the David Wells of the 1970s, a fat, motorcycle-riding lefty who was, with due respect to Denny McLain, very heady on the mound. He was friendlier than Wells, I think . . . he seemed like a friendly fat uncle, rather than kind of a fat sour neighbor with big dogs. He was of the same pitching family as Sid Fernandez and John Candelaria: lefties with good stuff who were never thought of as rocket scientists off the baseball diamond, but who simply "got it" when they took the mound.

73 ◆ Kevin Brown
(1986–2000, 170-114, 3.21 ERA)

I don't root for him, either, but he is a great pitcher.

74 ◆ Dave Stieb
(1979–1998, 176-137, 3.44 ERA)

Oooh . . . should have realized this before. Stieb is probably a member of the Bob Lemon family of pitchers. Like Lemon and Walters, Stieb began his career as a position player (an outfielder), converted to the mound, and relied very heavily on the slider. Like the other two (Lemon and Walters) he did not have a good strikeout/walk ratio, but was an outstanding fielder.

Despite being a converted outfielder, Stieb never had a hit in the major leagues, because of the Designated Hitter Rule. The only pitchers listed among the top 100 who never had a hit in the majors are Stieb and Ron Guidry, who had only one major league at bat between them, not counting the World Series. The lowest batting averages among those who *did* get a hit were:

1. Hoyt Wilhelm .088
2. Bruce Sutter .088
3. Sandy Koufax .097
4. Pedro Martinez .098
5. Vida Blue .104

Stieb, like Kevin Brown, Bunning, Palmer, Shocker, Steve Rogers, Lefty Grove, and many others, was difficult to get along with because he was a perfectionist. It's a common disease among pitchers, but actually it is *more* common for outstanding pitchers to be players who *don't* put a lot of pressure on themselves, like Babe Adams, Juan Marichal, Luis Tiant, Pete Alexander, Cy Young, and Catfish Hunter.

75 ◆ Eppa Rixey
(1912–1933, 266–251, 3.15 ERA)

When the Phillies sold Pete Alexander to the Cubs in late 1917, Eppa Rixey was so disgusted that he joined the Army. With World War I underway everybody had conflicts about whether to stay or go. Rixey said that he had hoped to pitch one more year in the majors and had planned to take his chances on the draft, but the sale of Alexander (and Bill Killefer) had wrecked the team, and he decided the heck with it. He fought a year in Europe, returned to the Phillies—and pitched fifteen more seasons in the National League . . .

Eppa was a southern gentleman, a basketball and baseball star at the University of Virginia who came straight to the major leagues after earning his degree. He would throw temper tantrums and break furniture after a loss, but was regarded as a cultured and sophisticated player. Because he was a southerner, opposition players and teammates would whistle "Marching Through Georgia" or make cracks about the Civil War to get under his skin . . .

Eppa was the Babe Ruth of sacrifice hits allowed, allowing more than anyone else in history. This was not just a function of time and place; Eppa led his league in Sac Hits allowed pretty regularly, with large numbers. I do not know why this is. I first thought it was because of his size (6'5"), perhaps he wasn't quick enough to field a bunt. But researching it further, I don't think that was it . . .

76 ◆ Dwight Gooden
(1984–2000, 194–112, 3.51 ERA)

When a young player comes to the major leagues and has success right away, writers will almost always write about what a fine young man he is as well as a supreme talent. Never pay any attention to those articles or those descriptions. Albert Pujols is going through this now . . . people who didn't know Albert Pujols from Jack the Ripper six months ago and have never talked to him more than six feet from his locker are writing very sincerely about what an exceptional young man he is. Doc Gooden, his first three years in baseball, was supposed to be mature beyond his years, polite to everybody, and kind to stray kittens. Rickey Henderson was routinely described, from 1980 through 1982, as "a Jack Armstrong type kid."

Sportswriters, despite their cynicism or because of it, desperately want to believe in athletes as heroes, and will project their hopes onto anyone who offers a blank slate. The problem with this is that, when the player turns out to be human and fallible, people feel betrayed. It is a disservice to athletes to try to make them more than they really are.

77 ◆ Tommy Bridges
(1930–1946, 194–138, 3.57 ERA)

A short, skinny, funny-looking man with huge ears and the best curve ball of his generation.

He was quiet, professional, the son of a small-town Tennessee doctor, the grandson of another. Bridges also attended the University of Tennessee, although he didn't graduate. He had long, strong fingers, despite his short stature, which enabled him to grip the ball in an unusual way, applying pressure with the second finger.

In 2001 there was a controversy in the major leagues when a rookie beat out a bunt to prevent an opposition pitcher from throwing a no-hitter, and some blockhead manager, inventing old-school ethics as he went along, decided that this was a bush-league play and that nobody in his generation would have done anything like that. Actually, a similar thing happened to Tommy Bridges on August 5, 1932. Bridges retired the first 26 Washington hitters that day, and was leading the game 13-0. Walter Johnson sent up a pinch hitter, Dave Harris, who broke up the no-hitter. Reporters criticized Johnson for sending up a pinch hitter in that situation, but Bridges would have none of it. "I didn't want the perfect game to be given me on a platter," Tommy said. "I wanted it with the opposition doing its best to keep me from winning."

Bridges, during his career, was a sober, sensible man, intelligent, friendly, and almost universally liked. "Every time I see one of those T-shirts you see nowadays, the ones that say, 'Baseball is Life,' I think of Tommy Bridges," said Elden Auker. "Baseball was everything to him." He was a family man who called his wife every night, and fretted about his children.

At some point during the war Bridges began to drink. After World War II he went to the Pacific Coast League, where he pitched for several years, and began to drink in earnest, finally passing out drunk on the mound during a game. Out of baseball, he burst into the headlines when he was caught in bed with a woman by the woman's husband, who fired a couple of shots at him. He divorced his wife, married the woman he had been caught with, who was a waitress at a bar he frequented. They went back to the Detroit area and met up with some of his old teammates, including Elden Auker and Billy Rogell, who reported in later books that they were shocked to see him in such dissolute condition. Rogell, a Detroit city councilman, arranged for a sales job for him, a good job, but Bridges never showed up to work. "It was terrible to see that," said Rogell in *Cobb Would Have Caught It*, "But nice guys go, too, you know."

78 ◆ Waite Hoyt
(1920–1938, 237-182, 3.59 ERA)

Waite Hoyt signed a contract with the New York Giants when he was 15 years old, although he didn't actually play pro ball until he was 17, or play for the Giants until he was 18. After an inning with the Giants (and a whole lot of batting practice) he went back to the minors, but was purchased by the Red Sox in 1919, sold to the Yankees after the 1920 season. With the Yankees he was a rotation anchor for eight years, and went 22-7 for the '27 Yankees.

> Waite always said that the secret of success in pitching lay in getting a job with the Yankees, and that a Yankee pitcher never should hold out or rile the manager because if he did he might be traded and then he would have to pitch against those murderous hitters. He was to prove the soundness of these observations. The first time he pitched against the Yankees they knocked him out in the second inning.—Frank Graham, *The New York Yankees*

Waite Hoyt would sing while Mark Koenig played the piano . . . not an odd thing in those days. That kind of thing will come back someday. Electronics have brought the world's best singers and performers into our living rooms, which unfortunately has intimidated us into thinking that we can't sing to one another any more, as people did for thousands of years, because we don't meet the standard. But it will come back, because sooner or later people will rediscover that half the joy of music is in making it. Or more than half . . .

> A lot of theatrical folks who know, tell me that Waite could make a success on the stage as well as in baseball. But he isn't interested. During the off-season, instead, he spends his time at his profession. He's a mortician, and has an office with his father-in-law in Brooklyn.—Ford Frick, *Babe Ruth's Own Book of Baseball*

After his pitching career he decided to leave the stiffs, and stayed in baseball for 30 years as a Cincinnati broadcaster, giving countless interviews about Babe Ruth and baseball in the 1920s, becoming grouchier and grouchier as he did so, until, at the end, he appeared to deeply resent anybody else pretending to have any knowledge or understanding of anything connected with baseball before 1930. Mel Allen said that Hoyt was the best "of all the former athletes who went to the microphone—highly intelligent, industrious, great story teller."

Hoyt and Urban Shocker . . . Hoyt's career won-lost record, 237-182, is two games worse than his team's winning percentage with other pitchers. Shocker's career record, 187-117, is 31 games *better* than his team's record without him. Shocker had a worse winning percentage than his teammates only once, in 1922, when he was 24-17 for a good team; otherwise he was better than his team every year. Hoyt had a worse winning percentage than his team fifteen times in his career, double-counting 1931 and 1932, when he pitched for two teams each year and had lower winning percentages than both teams. In the three years that they were teammates, 1925-1927, Hoyt was 25 to 27 years old; Shocker was 34 to 36 years old. Shocker went 49-29; Hoyt went 49-33.

79 ◆ Bret Saberhagen
(1984–1999, 166-115, 3.33 ERA)
The best starting rotation of the 1980s belonged to the 1985 Kansas City Royals: Saberhagen, Charlie Leibrandt, Mark Gubicza, and Danny Jackson. The second-best rotation of the 1980s belonged to the 1987 Royals, and consisted of the same four pitchers . . .

Of the ten teams which rank as having the best rotations of their decades, all ten are anchored by at least one pitcher among the 100 best in the history of the game. In fact, among the forty pitchers who comprise these ten rotations, almost all 40 are legitimately good major league pitchers, as opposed to pitchers who happened to have a good year.

80 ◆ Addie Joss
(1902–1910, 160-97, 1.89 ERA)
If you rank the 100 pitchers here by their ERAs, Addie ranks second:

1.	Ed Walsh	1.82
2.	Addie Joss	1.89
3.	Joe Wood	2.03
4.	Three Finger Brown	2.06
5.	Christy Mathewson	2.13
6.	Rube Waddell	2.16
7.	Walter Johnson	2.17
8.	Tommy Bond	2.25
9.	Eddie Plank	2.35
10.	Eddie Cicotte	2.38

While Wes Ferrell ranks last:

1.	Wes Ferell	4.04
2.	George Uhle	3.99
3.	Red Ruffing	3.80
4.	Mel Harder	3.80
5.	Ted Lyons	3.67

However, all of the top ten pitched at the same time—the Dead Ball Era, when ERAs were very low, and all of the bottom five pitched in the same league at the same time—the American League in the 1930s, when ERAs were very high.

I adjusted the ERAs of the top 100 pitchers for the league ERAs at the time, and also for the parks in which the pitcher played. I adjusted everyone to a normal ERA of 3.75 in a neutral park . . . for example, since Addie Joss pitched in an era in which the league ERA was 2.72, I adjusted his ERA by multiplying it by 3.75 over 2.72, which is 1.38. Also, since Joss pitched in parks which favored the pitchers by 1%, I adjusted this upward by another 1%, which makes Joss's ERA equivalent to 2.63 in a normal league in an neutral park. The top ten now become:

1. Pedro Martinez   2.24
2. Lefty Grove   2.52
3. Joe Wood   2.56
4. Roger Clemens   2.56
5. Dan Quisenberry   2.58
6. Walter Johnson   2.58
7. Hoyt Wilhelm   2.58
8. Greg Maddux   2.60
9. Ed Walsh   2.61
10. Addie Joss   2.63

While the bottom five (of the 100 greatest pitchers) become:

1. Mickey Lolich   3.61
2. Catfish Hunter   3.59
3. Early Wynn   3.52
4. George Uhle   3.52
5. Vida Blue   3.50

In context, Wes Ferrell's 4.04 ERA is actually more impressive than Tommy Bond's 2.25 mark. The pitchers most effected by this adjustment are:

1. Tommy Bond   up 1.07, from 2.25 to 3.31
2. Wes Ferrell   down .80, from 4.04 to 3.24
3. Ed Walsh   up .79, from 1.82 to 2.61
4. Addie Joss   up .74, from 1.89 to 2.63
5. Eddie Cicotte up .69, from 2.38 to 3.07

81 ◆ Rick Reuschel
(1972–1991, 214-191, 3.37 ERA)

In 1987 Rick Reuschel reported to camp with Pittsburgh four pounds heavier than he had been the year before. A reporter asked Kent Biggerstaff, Pirates trainer, for a comment. "Four pounds on him?" asked Biggerstaff. "That's like adding one more suitcase to the *Queen Mary.*"

Reuschel was a big guy who looked fat even when he wasn't. He could run, and he could hit a little.

82 ◆ Tony Mullane
(1881–1894, 287-214, 3.05 ERA)

Tony Mullane of Cincinnati received a pay cut from forty-two hundred dollars to thirty-five hundred in mid-season. When he objected, owner John T. Brush informed him his contract was not "worth the paper it was written on" Mullane walked out, refusing to play the second half of the season, but few others followed his lead.—Mike Sowell, *July 2, 1903*

Five pitchers who won 250 or more games are not listed here among the top 100 pitchers of all time. Those five are Pud Galvin (360-308), Mickey Welch (309-211), Jim McCormick (265-214), Gus Weyhing (264-232), and Jack Morris.

Contrasting Mullane with . . . say, Mickey Welch. Welch had a better won-lost record, but pitched for far better teams. Mullane in his career was a robust 48 games better than his teams, which had a .477 winning percentage when he was not on the mound. I doubt that there is any pitcher who was 48 games better than his teams, and *isn't* listed among the top 100 . . .

The fact which every baseball fan knows about Tony Mullane is that he was ambidextrous, pitched with both hands. Thirty years ago, when historical research about baseball was in a sorry state, there were widely differing accounts about how much Mullane pitched left-handed, with some sources saying that he did so regularly, and others questioning whether he ever did so at all. There is now a consensus that Mullane did pitch to a few batters left-handed on July 18, 1882, and did so in some exhibition games, and may have done so on other occasions, but never did so more than a few times.

The second fact that baseball fans may know about Tony Mullane is that he was the father of a now-extinct custom called Ladies Day. Mullane, a handsome man, was known as "The Apollo of the Box," and was a big favorite with female fans. The Cincinnati Reds in the late 1880s, trying to take advantage of this, would schedule "Ladies Day" when Mullane was on the mound.

Mullane was the star pitcher for Toledo in 1884, when they employed a black catcher named Fleet Walker. According to *Baseball's Most Wanted* (Floyd Conner) "Mullane threw the ball in the dirt, hoping to injure him. Mullane refused to take Walker's signals, but grudgingly admitted, 'He was the best catcher I ever worked with.'" How Mullane hoped to injure his catcher by throwing the ball in the dirt is unclear to the author, but apparently I'm missing something . . .

Career walks drawn by pitchers listed here:

1.	Tony Mullane	221
2.	Tim Keefe	175
3.	Red Faber	169
4.	Clark Griffith	166
5.	Old Hoss Radbourn	158

83 ◆ Orel Hershiser

(1983–2000, 204-150, 3.48 ERA)

I have a stat that I've figured once in awhile for 25 years called the "Index of Self-Destructive

Acts." The Index of Self-Destructive Acts is the total number of hit batsmen, wild pitches, balks, and errors by a pitcher, per nine innings.

The Index of Self-Destructive Acts is kind of a garbage stat, because it puts together separate and unrelated acts into a single category. I like it, nonetheless, because it makes useful information out of four statistical categories which are, by themselves, too small to sustain any conclusions.

The highest and lowest Indexes of Self-Destruction, among the top 100 pitchers:

1.	Robin Roberts	0.23
2.	Pete Alexander	0.23
3.	Dan Quisenberry	0.25
4.	Urban Shocker	0.25
5.	Dizzy Dean	0.27
6.	Babe Adams	0.28

1.	David Cone	0.96
2.	Nolan Ryan	0.93
3.	Randy Johnson	0.92
4.	Orel Hershiser	0.90
5.	Tim Keefe	0.88
6.	Rube Waddell	0.88

The Index of Self-Destructive acts tracks control, as you can see; control pitchers do well, power pitchers don't. This chart breaks out more data for the top two:

	IP	HB	WP	Bk	Err
Robin Roberts	4,689	54	33	3	31
Pete Alexander	5,190	70	39	1	25
David Cone	2,745	96	140	32	26
Nolan Ryan	5,386	158	277	33	90

The surprise of the chart is that Orel Hershiser has one of the higher self-destructive rates among the top 100 pitchers. First of all, Hershiser is surrounded on the chart by power pitchers, so that doesn't seem quite right, but we all think of Hershiser as a pitcher who never beat himself. I don't mean to challenge that assumption, but Hershiser ranks 16th among the top 100 pitchers in career hit batsmen, 18th in Wild Pitches, 7th in balks, and 25th in errors, so all four elements of his Self-Destructive Index are high. Of course, he is being compared here to the best pitchers who ever lived . . .

84 ◆ Vic Willis

(1898–1910, 248-208, 2.63 ERA)

One of the fun things about doing research is that occasionally you find things which you not only had never known, but which you had never suspected—conclusions which, in some cases, nobody had ever suspected, but which nonetheless seem to withstand scrutiny. When I set out to identify objectively the greatest starting rotations in the history of baseball, I had one of those experiences.

The method, first. I decided to rate starting rotations by Win Shares, of course, but counting one point for each Win Share by the team's number one starter, two points for the number two starter, three points for the number three starter, and four points for the number four starter. This is an arbitrary choice and you're free to reject the conclusion, but I think that what most people mean by a great starting rotation is not one superstar and three other guys, but a rotation which is solid top to bottom. To identify those teams, the teams which are solid top to bottom, we put extra weight on the ass end of the rotation.

For example, in 1985 the New York Mets and the Los Angeles Dodgers each had 72 Win Shares from four starting pitchers (which is a lot). The Dodgers had Orel Hershiser (19-3, 2.03 ERA), Fernando Valenzuela (17-10, 2.45), Bob Welch (14-4, 2.31), and Jerry Reuss (14-10, 2.92). The Mets had Doc Gooden, who was by far the best pitcher in baseball that season (24-4, 1.53 ERA), backed by Ron Darling (16-6, 2.90), Sid Fernandez (9-9, 2.90), and Ed Lynch (10-8, 3.44). The Dodgers 2-3-4 starters

were obviously better than the Mets, but because Gooden was so good, he evens out the totals:

Gooden	33
Darling	17
Fernandez	12
Lynch	10
Total	72
Hershiser	23
Valenzuela	21
Welch	15
Reuss	13
Total	72

When I scored the rotations, I scored the Dodgers at 162 (making them the third-best rotation of the 1980s), and the Mets at 143.

This "weighting system" also plays a key role in determining the best starting rotation of the 1960s. The team that I thought had the best starting rotation of the 1960s, the team I assumed would come out on top, was the 1966 Dodgers, whose starting rotation consisted of three Hall of Fame pitchers, all among the top 33 (Sandy Koufax, Don Drysdale, Don Sutton), plus Claude Osteen, who was a hell of a pitcher for somebody with a wimpy French name.

In total Win Shares, this foursome earned 79, which is more than the '63 Yankees, but less than the '69 Cubs. But when I converted the individual Win Shares into a rotation score, the '63 Yankees took the lead:

'63 YANKEES

Pitcher	W–L	ERA	WS
Ford	24–7	2.74	23
Bouton	21–7	2.53	22
Terry	17–15	3.22	17
Downing	13–5	2.56	16
Totals	75–34	2.79	78
SCORE			182

'66 DODGERS

Pitcher	W–L	ERA	WS
Koufax	27–9	1.73	35
Osteen	17–14	2.85	17
Sutton	12–12	2.99	14
Drysdale	13–16	3.42	12
Totals	69–41	2.68	79
SCORE			163

'69 CUBS

Pitcher	W–L	ERA	WS
Hands	20–14	2.49	28
Jenkins	21–15	3.21	25
Holtzman	17–13	3.58	17
Selma	10–8	3.63	11
Totals	68–50	3.16	81
SCORE			173

The Cubs replaced Selma in mid-1970 with Milt Pappas, which gave the 1970 Cubs the strongest starting rotation of the 1970s, which was also a surprise. Anyway, comparing the '66 Dodgers to the '63 Yankees, we have the same thing: Koufax is far better than anyone else, but otherwise, the Yankee staff is stronger. I set up the system so that depth and balance counts more than having a superstar.

I also decided not to simply rate the best rotations of all time, but to choose the best of each decade. Pitching patterns have changed so much, over the last hundred years, that the numbers are just different over time, and a rotation from 1935, when starting pitchers are pitching 15 times a year in relief, is not directly comparable to a starting rotation from 1998.

When I did this, the rotation which scored as the best of the decade for the years 1900–1909—and, incidentally, the highest-scoring of the entire twentieth century—was the rotation of the 1901 Boston Beaneaters.

Who?

The team which I had expected to represent that decade was the 1906 or 1907 Cubs (Three Finger Brown, Carl Lundgren, Ed Reulbach, and Orval Overall). That was a great rotation, too; they score at 249 in 1907, the second-highest total of the last hundred years. The highest total, however, belongs to the 1901 Beaners—Vic Willis, Kid Nichols, Bill Dineen, and Togie Pittinger.

Now, those are all good pitchers. Willis and Nichols are Hall of Famers, Dineen won 170 games, and Pittinger added 115. They were managed by a Hall of Fame manager, Frank Selee, who incidentally also put together that Cubs rotation, although his health failed before the Cubs reached their crest.

Still, if you glance at the 1901 Boston records, you don't see much. Willis was 20-17, 2.36 ERA, while Kid Nichols was 19-16, 3.22, Dineen was 15-18, 2.94, and Pittinger was 13-16, 3.01. The ERAs of the 1907 Cubs range from 1.17 to 1.69, and they all had winning percentages over .700.

The Cubs won 107 games and lost 45; the Beaneaters played .500 ball (69-69). How in the world, then, can the Boston rotation be rated as better?

First, 1901 is a lot different from 1907. In 1901 the National League average was more than four and a half runs per game; in 1907 it was less than three and a half. ERAs from 1907 are not on the same scale as ERAs from 1901.

Second, the won-lost records of the Boston pitchers were nailed to the .500 mark because the team's offense was genuinely pathetic—probably among the worst offenses of all time. The Beaneaters played in the best hitter's park in the National League, increasing runs scored by 17%—yet they were dead last in the league in runs scored.

But if you focus on what the pitchers themselves did, the big four pitched an average of

304 innings apiece, in the best hitter's park in the league—and all four of them had better-than-league ERAs. I don't think you can find any other four-man rotation in the history of baseball which matches those numbers. Baseball is half offense, half defense. This was a team that had zero offense—but a pitching staff good enough to carry them to a .500 record.

85 ◆ Eddie Rommel
(1920–1932, 171-119, 3.54 ERA)

> Working as a steam fitter's helper on a ship in World War I, Rommel scalded his hand severely. While recovering, he began experimenting with the knuckle ball, a pitch he learned from Cutter Drury, a veteran minor league first baseman. Rommel knew he was not too fast and needed something extra ...—Lee Allen, *The Hot Stove League*

Rommel gave an interview in 1945 in which he suggested that, within a few years, *everybody* would be throwing the knuckleball. He threw a "modern" knuckleball—that is, he held the ball with finger tips and threw it very softly. There were "knuckleball" pitchers in that era who actually held the ball with their knuckles, and there were also pitchers who threw a pitch which they called a knuckleball, but threw hard. Rommel clearly did not throw the knuckleball every pitch, however, because he said in the interview that he found the knuckleball to be a great change-up ...

Highest and lowest strikeouts per nine innings, among the top 100 pitchers:

1.	Randy Johnson	10.95
2.	Pedro Martinez	10.38
3.	Nolan Ryan	9.55
4.	Sandy Koufax	9.28
5.	Roger Clemens	8.60
1.	Eddie Rommel	2.11
2.	Ted Lyons	2.32

3.	Clark Griffith	2.54
4.	Carl Mays	2.57
5.	Eppa Rixey	2.70

86 ◆ Vida Blue
(1969–1986, 209-161, 3.26 ERA)

Vida, his first full year in the majors, was 17-2 at the All-Star break, wound up winning the Cy Young Award and the MVP Award, striking out 301 batters and leading the league in shutouts (8), lowest opposition batting average (.189), opposition on-base percentage (.251), component ERA (1.81), and actual ERA (1.82). The rest of his career, he never struck out 200 men in a season, and the only categories in which he led the league were hits allowed, earned runs allowed, losses, and sacrifice flies allowed ...

He wasn't a one-year wonder, though; he won twenty games two other seasons, and won as many games in his career as Drysdale, with fewer losses. He had three 20-win seasons, which is more than many of the pitchers listed here.

He pitched for Kansas City during their cocaine seasons. One year he was in the starting rotation until the All-Star break, and never won a game. Even then, though, you could see that he was just a few steps away from being a dominant pitcher. He was throwing about five pitches an inning in the dirt. He'd break off that big curve ball and have no idea where it was going, but neither did the hitter. Unfortunately, he was behind 99.7% of the hitters, so he'd have to come in with a fastball, and get nailed.

87 ◆ John Smoltz
(1988–1999, 157-113, 3.35 ERA)

Still attempting to make a comeback with the Braves ... Smoltz in 1996 won 29 major league games: 24 during the regular season, one against the Dodgers in the Division Series, two against the Cardinals in the league championship series, one against the Yankees in the World Series, and the All-Star game . . .

88 ◆ Bob Caruthers
(1884–1892, 217-98, 2.83 ERA)

Caruthers was 119 games over .500 in his career, which is the tenth best figure of all time, not counting active pitchers. All of the other top pitchers on this list—all of the other pitchers who are +100—are in the Hall of Fame. Caruthers is not. All of the other pitchers who are +100 (20 of them) are rated by me among the top 54 pitchers of all time, eight of them ranked among the top 10 pitchers of all time.

Caruthers' career winning percentage is the third-best among the top 100 pitchers, behind Pedro Martinez and Whitey Ford, just ahead of Lefty Grove. Caruthers was also an outstanding hitter—in fact, on the basis of runs created per out or runs created relative to his league, he was the *best* hitting pitcher among the top 100 guys.

There is an argument, then, that Caruthers has been short-sheeted by history, and shafted again by me. That argument *could* be correct, but here's why I didn't buy it:

1. Caruthers career is very short. He won over 200 games because pitchers in his time routinely won 40 games a season, but he was only a good pitcher for five years.

2. The quality of competition that Caruthers dominated was probably the weakest of any pitcher listed among the top 100. Nineteenth century baseball wasn't very good to begin with, and Caruthers was pitching in the American Association, which was the weaker of the two leagues.

3. Caruthers was carried to his outstanding winning percentages in part by playing for teams which were far better than their competition. The winning percentage of his teams, when he *wasn't* on the mound, was .613. Yes, he was 24 games better than his teams, which

is good, but it's not great; there are guys who are +24 and *don't* make the top 100 pitchers list.

I don't deny that he was a good pitcher, but the pitcher to whom he is most comparable is Smokey Joe Wood, who ranks 94th. I can't tell you that I have it exactly right, but this is my best estimate of where he deserves to rank.

89 ◆ Larry Jackson
(1955–1968, 194-183, 3.40 ERA)

Larry Jackson retired to go into politics after a 1968 season in which he pitched 244 innings with a 2.77 . . . his career record, while not all that good, was nine games better than his teams, and he had an ERA better-than-league every year of his career except the first two seasons and 1965 . . . In his entire career, as best I can determine, Larry Jackson was never in the vicinity of a humorous anecdote.

90 ◆ Dolf Luque
(1914–1935, 193-179, 3.24 ERA)

One year Dolf Luque held out, and got into a nasty salary battle with Cincinnati Reds owner Garry Herrmann. Herrmann wrote Luque, back in Cuba, that if he did not sign, he would be placed on a blacklist. This was not an idle threat; Judge Landis, battling Ban Johnson, needed the support of Herrmann, and would do almost anything to retain it. Another Cincinnati pitcher, Ray Fisher, had in fact been blacklisted for doing not much more than holding out.

Enraged, but having limited command of the English language, Luque asked Pepe Conte to compose a letter back to Herrmann. Herrmann saved the letter resulting, which begins:

> I read your letter to him (Luque), and as he is the most illiterate man on captivity he raised cain and started to say at the top of his voice that you

and Landis could go plump to _____. Of course, this is mere empty words pronounced by a man that has no education and that outside of his ability to pitch is a most perfect jack-ass.

Looking for the greatest pitching season of the 1920s, I was sure the answer would be "Dazzy Vance, 1924." Dazzy in 1924 went 28-6, 2.16 ERA—but actually Dolf Luque the year before was even better. Dolf was 27-8, 1.93 ERA . . .

Following up on the idea developed in the comment about Tommy John (#63), I thought I would take a look at the role that "hit luck" may have played in giving pitchers historically great seasons. I began by making a list of 12 pitchers who had tremendous seasons and less impressive seasons in consecutive years, although they were healthy both years and pitching for the same team both years:

Pitcher, Season	Won–Lost	ERA
Dolf Luque, 1922	13–23	3.31
Dolf Luque, 1923	27–8	1.93
Eddie Rommel, 1922	27–13	3.28
Eddie Rommel, 1923	18–19	3.27
George Uhle, 1925	13–11	4.10
George Uhle, 1926	27–11	2.63
Lefty Gomez, 1934	26–5	2.33
Lefty Gomez, 1935	12–15	3.18
Early Wynn, 1943	18–12	2.91
Early Wynn, 1944	8–17	3.38
Jim Kaat, 1965	18–11	2.83
Jim Kaat, 1966	25–13	2.75
Luis Tiant, 1967	12–9	2.74
Luis Tiant, 1968	21–9	1.60
Vida Blue, 1971	24–8	1.82
Vida Blue, 1972	6–10	2.80
Steve Carlton, 1972	27–10	1.97
Steve Carlton, 1973	13–20	3.90
Rick Reuschel, 1976	14–12	3.46
Rick Reuschel, 1977	20–10	2.79
Dwight Gooden, 1985	24–4	1.53
Dwight Gooden, 1986	17–6	2.84
Orel Hershiser, 1987	16–16	3.06
Orel Hershiser, 1988	23–8	2.36

Having compiled this list, I then figured the "expected hits allowed" for each pitcher each season, and compared the actual to the expected hits allowed.

In the process of doing this, I discovered a pitcher who had the At 'Em ball working even more consistently than Wally Bunker in 1964. Eddie Rommell in 1922 had 1027 balls in play, for a team which allowed 30.4% of balls in play to become hits. We would thus expect him to have allowed 334 hits that season—22 home runs, plus 312 hits on balls in play.

He actually allowed only 294 hits—39 fewer than expected. This is the most fortunate season, in this respect, that I have yet discovered.

Actually, apart from the bad fortune of pitching for a lousy team, Eddie Rommel in 1922 must have been just about the luckiest pitcher of all time. Rommel had an absolutely amazing season, finishing 27-13 for a team that narrowly escaped finishing last, at 65-89. Other than Rommel's games, they won exactly one-third of their decisions—38 of 114.

However, even having balls hit at fielders all year, Rommel allowed 3.92 runs per nine innings, for a team which scored only 4.55 runs per game. Given 40 decisions, you would expect him to go 23-17. He beat that by four full games.

Anyway, the conclusion of the study was that having the At 'Em ball working one year and not working the other year was a significant factor in eight of these twelve cases where pitchers had strong turnarounds, although, of course, there were always other factors as well. In addition to Rommel:

- Dolf Luque in 1923 allowed 20 hits fewer than expected, whereas his hit luck was neutral in 1922.

- Lefty Gomez allowed 25 hits fewer than expected in 1934, whereas he allowed ten *more* than expected in 1935.

- Early Wynn was −11 in 1943, +10 in 1944.

- Luis Tiant was neutral in 1967, −16 in 1968.

- Steve Carlton was −22 in 1972, +6 in 1973.

- Orel Hershiser was −5 in 1987, −27 in 1988.

The odd one of these eight cases where the hit luck was a factor was Jim Kaat, 1966. Jim Kaat in 1966, when he went 25-13, was not lucky in allowing hits; he actually allowed one more than expected. This was a tremendous improvement, however, over 1965, where he was extremely *un*-lucky, allowing 25 hits more than expected. Actually, Kaat pitched at the same level in 1965 that he did in 1966—he just didn't get the results he deserved until the second year.

Rick Reuschel in '77 improved from −2 to −9 . . . I wouldn't say that was a "significant" change in his luck. In the other three cases—George Uhle in 1926, Vida Blue in 1971, and Dwight Gooden in 1985—hit luck was not a factor in the pitcher having a better year in one season than the other.

91 ◆ George Uhle

(1919–1936, 200-166, 3.99 ERA)

In the "pitching families" discussion—ostensibly a comment about Bucky Walters—I classified George Uhle with Red Ruffing. Later I ran across an interview with Red Ruffing (Leonard Schecter, 1962) in which Ruffing confessed that he had a sore arm most of his career, and was constantly visiting doctors to have his arm stretched or treated. I thought that was interesting, and added it to the comment about Ruffing.

But then, researching Uhle (*Cobb Would Have Caught It*), I found exactly the same thing about Uhle—he also had a sore arm throughout his career, and was constantly visiting doctors to have the arm stretched. Both claimed to have "adhesions" on the shoulder, which could be removed by systematic (but painful) stretching—a theory which also had a brief vogue in the 1970s. My point, anyway: players who have several characteristics in common will often also share additional characteristics of which we otherwise have little knowledge . . .

George Uhle probably was the first quality pitcher to rely heavily on the pitch now known as the slider. George Blaeholder, who came after Uhle, is often credited with inventing the pitch, but he may have simply invented the terminology. Uhle taught Waite Hoyt to throw the pitch in 1930. "It was a wonderful pitch," said Hoyt. "Uhle threw overhanded with his fastball motion. It didn't curve, but actually skidded, almost at right angles, like an auto on ice. He practiced it hour after hour. Sometimes the umpire would be about to call it a ball when it would hop over into the strike zone at the last fraction of a second."

> George was one of three pitchers I ever saw that I thought could pitch a ball game by themselves—in other words make their own selection at any stage of the game and go ahead and pitch without any trouble. The other two were Wes Ferrell and Alvin Crowder. Never bothered those fellows how many men might be on base.—Luke Sewell in *The Man In The Dugout* (Donald Honig)

Career leaders in batting average by a pitcher, minimum 300 plate appearances:

1.	Erv Brame	.306
2.	Jack Stivetts	.297
3.	Jim Devlin	.293
4.	Jack Bentley	.291
5.	George Uhle	.289

Stivetts and Devlin were nineteenth century pitcher/position players; Brame and Bentley had short careers. Thus, Uhle is sometimes, and not unreasonably, listed as having the highest career batting average of any pitcher. Some people will proceed from that, and argue that he was the best-hitting pitcher of all time. He wasn't. He was a very good hitter, but, hitting only nine home runs in his career, nowhere near the all-around hitter that Wes Ferrell was.

92 ◆ Mel Harder
(1928–1947, 223-186, 3.80 ERA)
In the second All-Star game, July 10, 1934, Mel Harder pitched five innings, allowing only one hit, no runs, and was the winning pitcher. That was the game in which Carl Hubbell struck out six straight hitters—but at the time, Mel Harder was almost universally reported as the star of the game. Only a couple of newspapers, at the time, focused their reports on Hubbell's strike-out skein . . . Harder pitched three more shutout innings in the All-Star game the next year (1935), two more the year after that, and three more in 1937—13 shutout innings in four consecutive All-Star games.

93 ◆ Babe Adams
(1906–1926, 194-140, 2.76 ERA)
Thirty facts about Babe Adams:

1. Born on a farm in Indiana in 1882.

2. Family very poor; spent adolescent years with a farmer named Lee Sarver in north-central Missouri.

3. Shown how to hold a curve by a shortstop on a team which had beaten him badly. Practiced throwing the curve against a barn for a year.

4. Pitched one-hit shutout in first game as a professional player, May 11, 1905, in Missouri Valley League.

5. Purchased by Cardinals in 1905, but sold back to minor leagues. Purchased by Pirates in 1907.

6. Was nicknamed "Babe" by female fans at Louisville in 1908 because . . . well, he was a Babe. He was an exceptionally handsome man.

7. He was the only significant "Babe" in baseball before Ruth.

8. Was married in March 1909.

9. Member of one of greatest teams of all time as a rookie in 1909.

10. Posted 1.11 ERA as a rookie—a record for a rookie.

11. Started the first game of the 1909 World Series on the recommendation of National League President John Heydler.

12. Became the hero of the World Series, winning three complete games, and throwing a shutout in the seventh game. Got Ty Cobb out consistently by never throwing him a fastball.

13. Had several outstanding seasons following that.

14. Issued the fewest walks per nine innings of any pitcher since 1900 except teammate Deacon Phillippe, any pitcher among the top 100 except Tommy Bond.

15. Pitched 21-inning complete game against Rube Marquard and the Giants on May 17, 1914, walking no one.

16. Had arm trouble for three years (as did Marquard), and dropped out of the major leagues in 1916.

17. Arm came back, winter of 1916–1917.

18. Pitched brilliantly in the minors, 1917–1918.

19. Got back to the majors during war-time player shortages, late 1918.

20. Won 17 games in 1919, again in 1920.

21. Walked 18 men in 263 innings in 1920.

22. By 1923 was the oldest player in baseball (41).

23. June 30, 1923, was Babe Adams Day at Forbes Field. Adams told a reporter after the game, "I cannot explain my lasting much longer than many other pitchers on any other theory than this: I always take things easy, and I never worry. I discovered many years ago that when I exerted myself I was not so effective, for the mere effort of trying to be uncommonly good distracted my mind from the simple task of pitching."

24. Pitched one inning in World Series of 1925—his first World Series since 1909.

25. Inadvertently became central figure in Pirates famous clubhouse revolt in 1926. He backed into this controversy by uttering the phrase, "The manager is the manager. Nobody else should interfere."

26. Was released at that time. He was well fixed financially.

27. Worked as a sportswriter in the 1930s.

28. Went to the Pacific during World War II as a foreign correspondent.

29. In Korean War, past 70, returned to Korea as a war correspondent.

30. Died in 1968.

94 ◆ Smokey Joe Wood
(1908–1920, 116-57, 2.03 ERA)

Here's a stat for you: Smokey Joe Wood allowed only ten home runs in his entire career. Modern baseball, that's just a month . . . Everybody else listed here allowed at least 19 career home run . . . Also ranks last among the top 100 pitchers in games pitched (225) . . .

Joe Wood's career, like Dizzy Dean's, was cut in half by a broken bone in another part of his body, which spread to his arm. Dizzy, of course, tried to pitch with a broken toe, and ruined his arm . . . I assume you all know that story. After his 34-5 season in 1912, Wood broke his thumb in spring training, 1912. His hand was in a cast for two months. When the cast came off he tried to come back too quickly,

without rebuilding his arm, and his arm was never the same.

95 ◆ Bob Shawkey
(1913–1927, 196-150, 3.09 ERA)

> Born in Brookville, Pa., and, after a brief minor league experience, purchased by the Athletics from Baltimore in 1913, he had been obtained by the Yankees on waivers in 1916 and had been with them continuously . . . He was a sound student of baseball from the time he began to play professionally.—Frank Graham, *The New York Yankees*

> Bob is one of the best hunters in the business, and knows the moose trails of Canada as well as most of the professional guides.—Ford Frick, *Babe Ruth's Own Book of Baseball*

Shawkey was known as "Sailor Bob" or "Bob the Gob," "Gob" being a slang term for a sailor. At the outbreak of World War I, Shawkey joined the Navy—but not to fight. He joined to play baseball. He apparently knew a naval commander or had an "in" of some sort, so he joined the navy to pitch for a service team, and the navy used him to promote enlistment in the New York City area. Since a lot of people didn't know the Navy had baseball players until Shawkey made them aware of it, that became a central part of his identity for the rest of his career. As a pitcher he mostly threw curves—a hard curve, a slow curve, a fastball, and a change.

According to Mike Sowell in *The Pitch That Killed*, Shawkey had a terrible run-in with home plate umpire George Hildebrand on May 27, 1920. After the initial argument calmed down and Hildebrand signalled for play to resume, Shawkey knelt down and began to tie his shoelaces. He kneeled on the mound and continued to tie his shoelaces for about five minutes, infuriating Hildebrand further, and finally, after Hildebrand called a batter out on strikes, bowed low in an exaggerated gesture of appreciation. When he was thrown out the game he took a swing at Hildebrand, who retaliated by taking off his mask and whacking Shawkey with it, hard enough to draw quite a bit of blood. Shawkey had to have stitches behind his ear . . .

96 ◆ Hippo Vaughn
(1908–1921, 178-137, 2.49 ERA)

Vaughn's career won-lost record is weak for a top-100 pitcher, but he pitched most of his career with bad teams. After pitching for a couple of 100-loss teams in the American League he joined the Cubs in 1913, just as the team was degenerating, and was the ace of their staff through a series of awful seasons. In 1917 he was 23-13, 2.01 ERA for a team that was sixteen games under .500 when he wasn't pitching.

In 1918, given an infusion of cash and optimism, the Cubs geared up for a run at the pennant, starting with the purchase of Grover Cleveland Alexander from the Philadelphia Phillies. Alexander was at his peak, coming off three straight 30-win seasons, and was regarded as the only pitcher in the league better than Vaughn.

"It has always been Vaughn's ambition to be on a winner," reported *The Sporting News* (January 3, 1918). "That he is a remarkable twirler goes without saying, and he can be greater when he makes up his mind. He has determined to equal or better the record of Alexander next season. Many believe that Vaughn is the best left-handed pitcher in baseball, and that when he extends himself seriously he can achieve anything Alexander has ever done."

At this time *The Sporting News* would interview players, in the winter, by mail; they would send the player a postcard with a few questions, and the players would actually write back. "I am not going to predict how many games I will win," Vaughn wrote, "but will

venture to say that Alexander will have to step some to beat me. He has been winning 30 games a year for three years, and it is now my determination to pass that mark."

It was funny how this worked out . . . Alexander, shortly after being sold to the Cubs, was drafted into the United States Army, but the Cubs, with Charlie Hollocher having a great year as a rookie shortstop, won the pennant anyway. Vaughn had 22 wins when the war stopped the season in August . . .

He also threw a 17-inning no-hitter in the minor leagues, as I mentioned earlier, and matched up with Fred Toney in a double no-hitter on May 2, 1917. (Vaughn lost the game when his defense betrayed him in the tenth inning.) When I was a kid the double no-hitter was one of the most famous games in baseball history, but you rarely hear about it anymore because baseball history has become the purview of the television people, who aren't interested in anything for which there is no tape.

It's kind of off the subject, but . . . the top three winners of the 1917 season had been Alexander (30 Wins), Toney (24 Wins), and Vaughn (23 Wins). While Alexander went into the Army, Toney had an adventurous and perilous 1918 season of his own. The Army draft began in late 1917. In early January 1918, Toney was arrested and charged with attempting to evade the draft by providing false information on his draft form.

Toney volunteered to join the Army to square the matter, but the draft board refused to accept this, and insisted on putting Toney on trial. The trial began in early April. The allegation was that "Toney had misrepresented the status of his family as dependents."

That trial ended in a hung jury, but Toney was immediately re-arrested, and indicted on new charges. The testimony at the first trial had revealed that Toney "had been living with a woman and passing her off as his wife for three years, while his real wife worked as a telephone operator in Nashville for $20 a month." He was indicted under the Mann Act, and faced the possibility of a substantial stretch in the state pen.

Exactly how this all got settled I'm not sure; my impression is that Toney agreed to make back payments to his lawfully wedded, and they dropped the Mann Act. He returned to baseball, in any case, and had several more good seasons.

But not as many as Hippo Vaughn. Hippo left the majors in 1922, but continued to pitch 200–300 innings a year in the minors, the low minors and then semi-pro baseball until he was past 50 years old. The 178 games he won in the majors are less than half of his career total.

97 ◆ Tommy Bond
(1876–1884, 193-115, 2.25 ERA)
The best pitcher's seasons of all time, by decade:

> 1870s—Tommy Bond, 1878
>
> 1880s—Old Hoss Radbourn, 1884
>
> 1890s—Amos Rusie, 1894
>
> 1900s—Jack Chesbro, 1904
>
> 1910s—Walter Johnson, 1913
>
> 1920s—Dolf Luque, 1923
>
> 1930s—Lefty Grove, 1931
>
> 1940s—Dizzy Trout, 1944
>
> 1950s—Robin Roberts, 1953
>
> 1960s—Bob Gibson, 1968
>
> 1970s—Steve Carlton, 1972
>
> 1980s—Dwight Gooden, 1985
>
> 1990s—Roger Clemens, 1997

98 ◆ David Cone
(1986–2000, 184-116, 3.40 ERA)
> Pitching Here,
> Pitching There,
> David Cone,
> Staff Ace on Loan.

99 ◆ Jesse Tannehill
(1894–1911, 195-117, 2.79 ERA)
A tiny man, perhaps comparable to Bobby Shantz, Harvey Haddix, or . . . I guess we're out of those, aren't we? Jimmy Key, although Jimmy wasn't that small.

In 1902, after a series of exceptional seasons with the Pirates, Tannehill and several of his teammates were secretly negotiating with Ban Johnson about jumping to the American League. According to Dennis and Jeanne Burke DeValeria's *Honus Wagner,* Tannehill got into a fight with a teammate, Jimmy Burke, which dislocated his shoulder. Tannehill was rushed to a hospital and given ether (an anesthetic) while doctors popped the arm back into its socket. Under the influence of the ether, Tannehill blabbed to his team owner, Barney Dreyfuss, about his conversations with Ban Johnson, and also gave the names of his teammates who were involved in the negotiations . . .

The last two pitchers here, Tannehill and Parnell, were lefties. Among the top 100 pitchers of all time, 77 were right-handed, 23 lefties. I thought I would study the data a little bit, just to see what differences there might be between the right-handers and the lefties.

In the aggregate, the differences are not large. The right-handed pitchers among the top 100 have an average won-lost record of 232-164 with an ERA of 3.06; the lefties, of 231-158, with an ERA of 3.05. All of the left-handers were starters, whereas five of the right-handers were relievers, so that queers the numbers a little bit, plus there are a few more left-handers later in history, so that skews the numbers a little bit, not too seriously in either case. Other differences:

The right-handers gave up more *un*-earned runs—0.73 for right-handers, 0.56 for left-handers. I don't know why that is; I would have guessed that the lefties would give up more unearned runs, since left-handers have more balls hit to third base and short, which require longer throws, hence more errors.

The left-handers give up a few more sacrifice bunts (202 average vs. 177), because a manager is more likely to order a bunt to stay out of a double play when there is a lefty on the mound.

The left-handers in this group had more strikeouts (2038 to 1911 on average) and more walks (1034 to 986), about 10% more per inning, since the right-handers had a few more innings. The two groups gave up identical batting averages of .245, but the on-base percentage was a fraction higher against the lefties (.305 to .301) because of the walks.

The left-handers in this group were significantly worse hitters than the right-handers. Only five of the 23 lefties had career batting averages over .200, led by Tannehill at .256, whereas seven of the right-handed pitchers hit .268 or higher, and 33 of the 77 hit .200 or better.

The right-handers in this group recorded a lot more putouts than the lefties, 212 to 134 on average. This was un-expected . . . I would guess it might be because a right-hander comes off the mound with his motion carrying him toward first base, whereas a lefty comes off going toward third, which probably makes it harder for him to recover and get to first, unless he is Jim Kaat or Bobby Shantz or somebody.

The differences are small, but I just thought I should check . . .

100 ◆ Mel Parnell

(1947–1956, 123-75, 3.50 ERA)

By decade, the number of pitchers among the top 100 is as follows:

1870s	1
1880s	6
1890s	13
1900s	19
1910s	27
1920s	26
1930s	23
1940s	21
1950s	19
1960s	26
1970s	24
1980s	28
1990s	17
2000s	9

Pitchers are counted in every decade in which they pitched, even if, like Joe Wood in 1920, they pitched only two innings in the decade.

The low number in the 1990s is caused by the fact that we have, as yet, only a partial view of the accomplishments of the pitchers of the 1990s. There are many more 1990s pitchers—Mike Mussina, Kevin Appier, Chuck Finley, Brad Radke, etc.—who *might*, when their careers are complete, rank among the top 100.

The low numbers of the 1870s/1880s are caused by the same effect on the other end. There are (almost) no pitchers from the 1870s because no one who had been great in the 1860s or even the 1850s was hanging around into the 1870s. Same with the 1880s . . . the game was too new to have "hanger-on" stars.

The blip in the teens is just caused by an unusual number of pitchers whose careers straggled into the beginning of the decade— Rube Waddell, Vic Willis, Jesse Tannehill, Cy Young, Clark Griffith, Addie Joss. The numbers increase very slightly after the expansion in 1960s, although the increase is less than proportional to the increase in the number of teams, and much less than proportional to the increase in the population.

This leaves the tic downward in the 1950s to be explained. It is difficult to attribute this to anything other than a simple, very slight shortage of great pitchers during the decade. On a list of the top winners of the 1950s, seven of the top ten are among the top 100 pitchers of all time. Those seven are Warren Spahn (202 Wins during the 1950s), Robin Roberts, Early Wynn, Billy Pierce, Bob Lemon, Don Newcombe, and Whitey Ford. The top winners of the 1950s who did not make the list were Mike Garcia (128-91 during the decade), Lew Burdette (126-82), and Johnny Antonelli (116-92).

Antonelli did little outside the 1950s, and I don't think one can argue that he was one of the top 100 pitchers of all time, although he was a fine pitcher. Garcia and Burdette, on the other hand, can be argued to be among the top 100. I have rated Garcia 126th, Burdette 177th, but their records are comparable to those of some pitchers among the top 100, including Mel Parnell. Emphasizing different factors in different ways, one could make an argument that these two belong.

But if there are pitchers with records similar to Garcia and Burdette who are in the top 100, there are many more who are not. Of the ten pitchers with career records most similar to Garcia (Rip Sewell, Sonny Siebert, Joe Dobson, Jack Sanford, Pat Malone, Dutch Ruether, Jack Billingham, Larry Dierker, Dock Ellis, and Johnny Sain), none made the list of the top 100. Of the ten most similar to Lew Burdette, three made the list (George Uhle, Stan Coveleski, and Carl Mays) but seven did not (Charlie Root, Jesse Haines, Freddie Fitzsimmons, Larry French, Guy Bush, Dutch Leonard, and Art Nehf).

Garcia and Parnell . . . Garcia and Parnell were contemporary American League pitchers, Garcia's career running 1948–1960, and Parnell's 1947–1956. Parnell had a breakout season in 1948 (15-8, 3.14 ERA), then had four outstanding seasons (25-7, 18-10, 18-11 and 21-8), with a .500 season thrown in (12-12). Garcia had a breakout season in 1949 (14-5,

2.36 ERA), then had four outstanding seasons (20-13, 22-11, 18-9, 19-8) with four .500-type seasons thrown in (11-11, 11-13, 11-12, 12-8). Parnell led the league in ERA in 1950; Garcia led the league in ERA in 1954. Parnell and Garcia pitched for Boston and Cleveland, who were the 2-3 teams in the American League in that era, and very competitive.

Garcia had a longer career (2175 innings to 1752), more wins (142 to 123), and a lower ERA (3.27 to 3.50)—thus, I suspect, most people would rate Garcia ahead of Parnell. They're close, and I certainly wouldn't try to tell you that that was the wrong answer.

But the ERA advantage for Garcia is a park illusion, since Parnell pitched in Fenway Park, while Garcia pitched in cold, cavernous Cleveland Memorial Stadium, which at that time had a pitcher's mound higher than the white cliffs of Dover. Adjusting for park effects, Garcia's ERA was 56 points, or 15%, better than league, while Parnell's was 90 points, or 20%, better than league. Garcia had more wins because he hung around a little longer, but hang around value has little impact on the ratings, as I see them. Parnell was 48 games over .500 in his career; Garcia, 45 games. I give Parnell a slight edge.

Completing the top 100 pitchers of all time, I would ordinarily now list the next 25. Actually, I planned to list the next 100, but the computer which had that list crashed yesterday, and the list is, perhaps permanently, beyond my reach.

Working from memory, there are about a dozen Hall of Fame pitchers who didn't make my list of the top 100 pitchers of all time, and there were at least two who didn't make my list of the second 100, either. Those two were Pop Haines and Rube Marquard. Meaning neither man any disrespect . . . they were fine pitchers, after all . . . but Haines had a career record of 210-158, Marquard of 201-177. Yes, it is true that I have picked some pitchers among the top 100 who have won-lost records worse than that, but it is also true that in the history of baseball there are just dozens of pitchers who have won-lost records like that ... Lew Burdette, and Chuck Finley, and Jerry Koosman, and Jack Morris, and Frank Tanana, and Allie Reynolds, and Jerry Reuss, and Ed Reulbach, and Bob Welch, and Charlie Buffinton, and Milt Pappas, and Dave McNally, and Mike Cuellar, and Sad Sam Jones, and Dutch Leonard, and Curt Simmons, and Dennis Martinez, and Paul Derringer, and Jim Perry. You may choose to believe that the Hall of Fame plucked Haines and Marquard from this long list of pitchers by their special wisdom and deep insight. I am more inclined to believe that it was a product of bias, impulse, and superficial research, but in any case the reality is that there isn't much difference between the 100th best pitcher in baseball history, and the 200th. I set up a process to rank them; these are the results, this is my list. I can't really tell you that Babe Adams is necessarily a better choice for the top 100 than George Mullin or Fat Freddie Fitzsimmons or Hooks Dauss or Charlie Root.

One player that I will be criticized for omitting is the Hall of Fame's second reliever, Rollie Fingers. But again, meaning no disrespect to Fingers, or anyone else who has a moustache you could weave into a carpet, I don't really see what is uniquely wonderful about Rollie Fingers' career. Yes, Fingers won an MVP Award in 1981, but ... why? He faced 297 batters that year. Yes, he posted a 1.04 ERA, but Goose Gossage posted an ERA of 0.77 that same season, Rob Murphy posted an ERA of 0.77 in 1986, Dale Murray had a 1.03 ERA in 1974, Tim Burke had a 1.19 ERA in 1987, Frank Williams a 1.20 ERA in 1986. Jim Brewer and Ted Abernathy had ERAs of 1.27. Bob Veale in 1963 pitched the same number of innings (78) and allowed the same number of earned runs

(9) as Fingers in 1981. It's just not a remarkable accomplishment.

Veale, for pitching 78 innings and allowing 9 earned runs, was credited with 10 Win Shares. Fingers, for doing the same, was credited with 17 Win Shares. That is a reasonable recognition of the importance of Fingers' role on the team. The BBWAA, however, gave Fingers an MVP Award. This is excessive. In my opinion, the BBWAA did something dumb when they gave Fingers an MVP award, and compounded the dumbitude by using that as a reason to put him in the Hall of Fame.

Rollie Fingers' proponents used the argument that Fingers was remarkably consistent for a relief ace. But for a relief ace, an ERA a full run better than the league is a basic standard of competence. Fingers met that standard only six times in his career, and pitched all of his career in pitcher's parks. Gossage met that standard 11 seasons, seven straight seasons, and pitched as many innings per year in tougher parks while doing it. Quisenberry met that standard his first nine seasons in the league, ten overall, also pitching more innings in tougher parks.

Fingers' ERA, adjusted for the parks he played in, was 16% better than league (2.90 vs. 3.45). Quisenberry's ERA was 31% better than league, Gossage's was 20% better than league, Sutter's 26% better, Wilhelm's 31% better. Kent Tekulve and Lee Smith were 24% better than league, Sparky Lyle 21% better than league. Fingers is more in a class with Jeff Reardon (17% better than league), Ron Perranoski (18% better), Gene Garber (15% better), and Don McMahon (16% better).

What lifted Fingers out of that class, I believe, was simply that he had exceptionally good taste in teammates—and the same is true of Jesse Haines and Rube Marquard. Haines in his career was ten games better than his teams; Marquard was two better than his.

But again, if I tried to tell you I was completely confident who should be rated where, I'd be lying to you. Why Virgil Trucks rather than Ed Lopat? Why Hippo Vaughn, rather than Harry Brecheen? Why Don Newcombe, rather than Johnny Allen?

Rating pitchers is a 40-way balancing act. A good ERA for one pitcher must be balanced against a better won-lost record for another. A .625 winning percentage on a great team must be balanced against a .550 percentage for bad teams. Two Cy Young seasons must be balanced against five twenty-win seasons. Twenty-win seasons in 1995 must be balanced against 30-win and 40-win seasons in 1895. One pitcher's contribution with his bat must be balanced against another pitcher's 7-1 record in World Series play. One pitcher's star power must be balanced against another's quiet consistency. One pitcher posts a 3.30 ERA in a pitcher's park in an era when a lot of runs are scored; another posts a 2.90 ERA, but in a deadball era, but in

hitter's parks. And all of these complicating factors occur in every case, and from the very top of the spectrum (500 wins, a 1.80 ERA, a .700 winning percentage) in a continuous line to the bottom.

Walter Johnson is not too hard to rate, because there is only one Walter Johnson. But when you have many pitchers who have about the same records, who comes out on top depends to a large extent on which features you decide to put weight on. Don Drysdale does well on this list because I focused on big seasons and consistent performance over a five-year period. This is a system in which a pitcher who starts 40 times a year for four years does much better than a pitcher who starts 32 times a year for five years. I'm not saying that is inevitably right, but I did the best I could. There are a hundred other pitchers who have a legitimate argument that they should have made the list.

Rank	Player Name	Career WS	Top 3	Top 5	Per Season
1.	Walter Johnson	564	54, 47, 42	217	34.09
2.	Lefty Grove	391	42, 37, 29	167	36.94
3.	Pete Alexander	477	44, 43, 40	180	34.31
4.	Cy Young	635	44, 42, 41	200	32.63
5.	Warren Spahn	411	32, 31, 28	120	29.23
6.	Tom Seaver	391	33, 29, 26	142	31.49
7.	Christy Mathewson	426	39, 39, 37	161	32.85
8.	Bob Gibson	320	36, 33, 29	143	31.07
9.	Kid Nichols	479	48, 44, 43	208	35.42
10.	Sandy Koufax	194	35, 33, 32	139	31.85
11.	Roger Clemens	314	32, 29, 28	125	34.88
12.	Bob Feller	292	34, 32, 32	151	29.02
13.	Carl Hubbell	305	37, 33, 32	153	31.82
14.	Greg Maddux	272	30, 27, 26	130	34.52
15.	Steve Carlton	367	40, 29, 26	111	27.19
16.	Robin Roberts	339	35, 32, 31	153	27.04

Rank	Player Name	Career WS	Top 3	Top 5	Per Season
17.	Jim Palmer	313	31, 29, 28	126	30.34
18.	Gaylord Perry	367	39, 30, 26	134	26.49
19.	Ed Walsh	265	47, 40, 37	177	32.73
20.	Three Finger Brown	296	36, 35, 34	163	34.13
21.	Juan Marichal	263	33, 30, 29	134	28.69
22.	Whitey Ford	261	24, 23, 22	105	30.90
23.	Ferguson Jenkins	323	37, 26, 26	135	27.32
24.	Nolan Ryan	334	28, 24, 22	102	23.84
25.	Dizzy Dean	181	37, 31, 31	145	34.08
26.	Phil Niekro	375	30, 28, 28	118	26.45
27.	Hoyt Wilhelm	256	23, 21, 19	85	33.69
28.	Amos Rusie	293	56, 41, 40	205	29.11
29.	Pedro Martinez	155	29, 27, 26	117	37.59
30.	Jim Bunning	257	30, 27, 26	100	26.06
31.	Don Sutton	318	24, 22, 21	99	23.30
32.	Dennis Eckersley	300	24, 23, 19	95	25.90
33.	Don Drysdale	258	27, 26, 25	117	28.14
34.	Eddie Plank	360	31, 29, 29	133	30.08
35.	Dazzy Vance	241	36, 32, 26	124	31.03
36.	Hal Newhouser	264	38, 35, 33	157	32.86
37.	Goose Gossage	223	26, 23, 20	90	31.42
38.	Carl Mays	256	35, 30, 27	140	29.46
39.	Bert Blyleven	339	29, 23, 23	114	26.36
40.	Wes Ferrell	233	35, 32, 28	129	30.25
41.	Joe McGinnity	269	42, 40, 35	162	29.52
42.	John Clarkson	398	62, 61, 51	249	32.69
43.	Ted Lyons	311	30, 26, 23	110	27.93
44.	Lon Warneke	220	31, 29, 26	125	29.44
45.	Old Hoss Radbourn	346	89, 59, 49	249	30.19
46.	Don Newcombe	176	27, 25, 22	103	28.25
47.	Early Wynn	308	28, 25, 24	110	24.64
48.	Bob Lemon	232	31, 26, 25	126	28.11
49.	Randy Johnson	200	26, 26, 23	99	30.98
50.	Eddie Cicotte	247	35, 32, 27	124	28.76
51.	Red Ruffing	322	27, 25, 24	116	25.53
52.	Luis Tiant	256	29, 28, 22	108	27.43
53.	Rube Waddell	240	35, 33, 32	145	30.59

(continued)

Rank	Player Name	Career WS	Top 3	Top 5	Per Season
54.	Tim Keefe	413	70, 47, 42	236	30.06
55.	Wilbur Cooper	266	31, 27, 27	133	28.26
56.	Red Faber	292	37, 31, 25	118	26.81
57.	Bruce Sutter	168	27, 23, 22	94	33.41
58.	Stan Coveleski	245	32, 29, 29	142	29.85
59.	Billy Pierce	248	24, 23, 23	101	27.73
60.	Tom Glavine	220	23, 23, 22	101	29.33
61.	Virgil Trucks	198	27, 25, 22	82	27.45
62.	Burleigh Grimes	286	32, 30, 29	122	25.19
63.	Tommy John	289	23, 19, 19	86	23.73
64.	Catfish Hunter	206	29, 27, 24	117	22.49
65.	Jim Kaat	268	26, 22, 22	88	22.64
66.	Ron Guidry	174	31, 22, 19	96	28.14
67.	Lefty Gomez	185	31, 29, 20	106	28.35
68.	Dan Quisenberry	157	28, 24, 23	107	34.12
69.	Bucky Walters	258	38, 32, 32	132	29.10
70.	Clark Griffith	273	34, 32, 30	143	29.25
71.	Urban Shocker	225	30, 29, 25	128	30.87
72.	Mickey Lolich	224	29, 26, 20	111	23.63
73.	Kevin Brown	200	26, 26, 23	114	29.25
74.	Dave Stieb	210	25, 24, 24	113	28.13
75.	Eppa Rixey	315	26, 26, 24	118	26.49
76.	Dwight Gooden	187	33, 18, 17	95	25.30
77.	Tommy Bridges	225	26, 22, 20	106	30.46
78.	Waite Hoyt	262	24, 23, 22	100	25.98
79.	Bret Saberhagen	193	28, 24, 23	98	29.37
80.	Addie Joss	191	35, 28, 25	131	31.51
81.	Rick Reuschel	240	26, 20, 20	95	26.05
82.	Tony Mullane	401	58, 55, 46	183	29.45
83.	Orel Hershiser	210	25, 23, 21	102	25.49
84.	Vic Willis	293	39, 33, 29	138	28.10
85.	Eddie Rommel	209	27, 25, 21	113	30.11
86.	Vida Blue	202	30, 25, 22	96	23.33
87.	John Smoltz	181	27, 21, 18	99	28.46
88.	Bob Caruthers	338	57, 54, 51	255	32.72
89.	Larry Jackson	225	25, 22, 21	99	26.09
90.	Dolf Luque	241	39, 27, 23	121	27.24
91.	George Uhle	231	32, 29, 23	106	25.34

Rank	Player Name	Career WS	Top 3	Top 5	Per Season
92.	Mel Harder	234	27, 27, 24	111	25.91
93.	Babe Adams	243	29, 27, 25	107	29.80
94.	Smokey Joe Wood	193	44, 26, 20	111	34.59
95.	Bob Shawkey	223	27, 27, 27	114	27.76
96.	Hippo Vaughn	205	30, 28, 24	128	28.43
97.	Tommy Bond	243	60, 50, 47	225	31.50
98.	David Cone	197	21, 20, 19	93	27.90
99.	Jesse Tannehill	233	34, 27, 26	130	28.82
100.	Mel Parnell	141	31, 23, 22	111	30.48

Categories of this record are Career Win Shares, Win Shares in the pitcher's three best seasons, Win Shares total over the pitcher's five best consecutive seasons, and career Win Shares per season. For example, Walter Johnson had 564 Career Win Shares, including 54, 47, and 42 in his three best seasons (1913, 1912, and 1915). He had 217 Win Shares in a five-year period, (1912–1916) and averaged 34.09 Win Shares per 43 starts over the course of his career.

LAST MINUTE NOTES

It has been almost a year since I finished most of these ratings, the year between mid-summer, 2000 and early season, 2001. The ratings presented here were based on performance through the 1999 season. Since then the following things have changed.

At Catcher, it has by now become apparent that Mike Piazza *is* the best-hitting catcher in the history of baseball; not maybe, not "so far." He simply is. Yes, he has played through a hitting explosion which queers the numbers, but we know how to adjust for that, don't we? There is no longer any doubt: even if you adjust for everything, he is the best hitter to play that position.

Other than Piazza, there are hardly any active catchers among the top 100; there's Ivan, but he had an injury year. But in the 2000 season four young catchers vaulted onto the list of the top 100 catchers of all time: Javy Lopez, Jason Kendall, Charles Johnson, and Todd Hundley. All of these players now have between 91 and 108 career Win Shares, a raw number which would suggest a rating between 81 and 100, but all four have had big enough seasons that they clearly will rate higher than that. If a catcher gets to 200 career Win Shares—any of

them might except Hundley—that would place them somewhere around the 30th spot.

At First Base there were eleven active players on the top-100 list a year ago, so every year stirs that list quite a bit. Mark McGwire, injured, did not move. Frank Thomas, with another MVP-type season, has probably vaulted ahead of McCovey, Greenberg, Killebrew, and Mize, and is again fighting a more or less even fight with Jeff Bagwell for a spot among the four best ever to play that position. Will Clark closed out his career without advancing further. Palmeiro had another fine season but didn't really move his historical rank. Wally Joyner, while still active, is inert so far as the list is concerned.

John Olerud, ranked 53rd a year ago, had a good enough year to edge into the forties. The other active first basemen—Mark Grace, Fred McGriff, Mo Vaughan, and Andres Galarraga—had solid but not exceptional seasons, and each edged forward one to three notches.

Other first basemen fighting for a spot . . . J. T. Snow, Tino Martinez, Jim Thome, and Eric Karros are all probably top-100 players by now. Four young players—Mike Sweeney, Carlos Delgado, Todd Helton, and Jason Giambi—are certainly *going to be* top-100 players, top 50, top 10 maybe, but I don't see what would be gained by trying to rank them now. There sure are a bunch of first basemen right now of historic stature. Greg Jefferies probably deserves to rank somewhere on pure merit, but screw 'im. Ryan Klesko is fairly close. Tony Clark and David Segui are not on the list as yet.

At **Second Base**, the big news in 2000 was the MVP season of Jeff Kent, and the MVP-type season of Edgardo Alfonzo. Kent, rated 48th a year ago, has moved up in history 15 to 20 spots, ranking now probably even with the Hall of Fame trio ranked 28th to 30th (Rod Schoendienst, Bill Mazeroski, Bid McPhee). He's not a Hall of Famer, but at the rate the Hall of Fame is electing second basemen . . . .

Edgardo would now rank somewhere on the top 80, but is probably passing two or three players a month, so we'll wait until he slows down a little to worry about him. Roberto Alomar, rated tenth a year ago, has not moved.

Of all the rankings I did a year ago, there is only one that I now regret enough to mention the fact. A year ago, I rated Craig Biggio fifth at second base, ahead of Nap Lajoie. This may have been a mistake. While I yield to no one in my admiration for Biggio—the greatest unappreciated player of my lifetime—it has been my policy, in doing these ratings, to avoid getting ahead of events. In this case, I did. Biggio had a poor and injury-plagued season in 2000, and it is no longer apparent that he deserves to rate ahead of Lajoie.

Chuck Knoblauch is no longer a second baseman, and will need to turn things around if he is going to move up *any* list . . . come to think of it, I may have done that rating the same day I did Biggio's, so to speak. Delino DeShields had a solid 2000; his 74th rank at the position might now be regarded as conservative.

Two second basemen, other than Edgardo, probably climbed into the top 100 in 2000,

those being Bret Boone and Ray Durham, who would be top-100 performers if we rated them now, but not top-80. Fernando Vina, Damion Easley, Quilvio Veras, Jose Vidro . . . not yet. Jose Offerman . . . I'm still rooting for you, son, but I'll have to wait 20 years to let people forget about your defense. Mickey Morandini has an argument, but no advocate.

At **Third Base** Chipper Jones, ranked 28th a year ago, would probably rank 19th now. Nobody active was in the top 20 a year ago. Robin Ventura (22nd), Matt Williams (23rd), Ken Caminiti (25th), and Bobby Bonilla (41st) all looked old and about gone, and none of them moved the list. Edgar Martinez (31 a year ago) had another great year as a DH . . . in all candor, I didn't know where to rank him a year ago, and I don't know now.

Travis Fryman had a pretty decent year; he would move from 71st up perhaps eight to ten spots. Jeff Cirillo, 80th a year ago, hit .326 again and would now rank about even with Fryman. Todd Zeile, now a first baseman, ranked 81st a year ago and is just treading water.

Gary Gaetti has passed into legend. Dean Palmer, as awful as his defense has become, probably now has to rate in the top 100 at third base. Vinny Castilla has credentials as good the guys rated 90-100—Steve Buechele, Ed Charles, etc. It seems clearly premature to rank Scott Rolen, and I'm not even going to talk about Troy Glaus or Adrian Beltre.

The Great Young **Shortstops** are still hard to rate. A year ago I said that they were all probably top 20. That is still about as much as I could say, without getting the argument out in front of the facts. Barry Larkin (sixth) didn't move. Jay Bell (31) is now a second baseman, but still a good player, and he probably has moved into the top 30. Tony Fernandez (24) has bowed out gracefully, and Jeff Blauser (70) is gone.

Omar Vizquel (61) moved up in 2000 to about 54th. Ozzie Guillen (74) and Shawon Dunston (87) are playing out the string; Walt Weiss also, although Walt didn't quite make the 100. Jose Valentin and Miguel Tejada are stalking the list, but not exactly storming it...the same for Royce Clayton and Rich Aurilia. No young shortstop jumped onto the list in 2000.

In Left Field, Barry Bonds and Rickey Henderson ranked third and fourth a year ago, and would rank the same today. Albert Belle retired, apparently, without moving from his perch at number 20.

Ron Gant (71 a year ago) didn't change the shape of his career any; neither did B. J. Surhoff (97), although he had a better year than Gant, or Greg Vaughn (68), although he had a better year than Surhoff. Brian Giles and Bobby Abreu are not yet top-100 players, although they likely will be. Bobby Higginson probably is in the top 100 now...if he isn't, he's certainly close.

A year ago I rated Gary Sheffield 54th in right field. This clearly is no longer an accurate raking, since he is now no longer a right fielder, and he has added another season of big numbers to his puzzling curriculum vitae. Ranked as a left fielder, he would be within the top 40, and in his case, I have real enthusiasm for the principle of giving conservative ratings to active players. We need perspective here.

Other than Sheffield, I'm not sure any left fielder made the list in 2000. Rusty Greer is a good top-100 candidate, and Darrin Erstad will make the list in a couple of years.

In Center, Ken Griffey (7) had a relatively poor year, and did not enhance his position. Eric Davis (33) is still active but has not moved up the list, and probably will not.

Bernie Williams (37) might have moved up the list, but I probably was a year ahead of myself in rating him anyway. He's a hell of a player. Kenny Lofton (41) had a decent year, but still has fewer career Win Shares than any

center fielder ranked ahead of him. Ray Lankford (49), is now a left fielder...I may have been a year early on *all* of these guys, come to think of it. Marquis Grissom (61) is still playing regularly, but I'm not sure why.

Brady Anderson (63) and Steve Finley (74) both advanced modestly in the rankings, Anderson perhaps to 60th, Finley perhaps to 65th. Ellis Burks (77) hit .344, and moved up at least a half-dozen spots. Devon White (81) did not move.

Four young center fielders—Carl Everett, Johnny Damon, Jim Edmonds, and Andruw Jones—seem likely to be comfortably within the top 100, but probably shouldn't be rated until they hit their peak. Andruw, I am guessing, will be in the top fifteen, but let's wait and see.

In Right Field, Sammy Sosa was ranked 45th a year ago. With another 50-homer campaign, he would now rank 30th or better. Vladimir is climbing the charts...no idea what his destination might be. He wouldn't be in the top 50 yet, and it would be an insult to a man of his talents to rate him lower than 50th. Manny Ramirez may ultimately rank as a right fielder, a left fielder, a DH, or something else...as a right fielder, he ranks now about where Sammy Sosa ranked a year ago, about 45th.

The old guys on the right field list—Gwynn, Canseco, Baines, and O'Neill—none of them have moved in the last year except possibly O'Neill, who hasn't moved much. Juan Gone (52nd a year ago) and Larry Walker (55) both had sub-par years.

David Justice (63) had a good year, and would move up perhaps five spots. Tim Salmon (72) hit 34 homers, and would move up about ten spots. No one else did enough to move the list or make the list, although Shawn Green and Raul Mondesi remain candidates.

The ratings for pitchers were done after the 2000 season, and wouldn't benefit from review here.

PART III

REFERENCE

WIN SHARES

Throughout this book I have used and referred to Win Shares as a way of evaluating players. While it would (will) require a book to give the Win Shares for every player every season for all players who:

1. Earned at least 300 career Win Shares.

2. Have completed their careers with a career Win Share total which is evenly divisible by 50.

3. A few still active-players who obviously will exceed 300 career Win Shares.

The players with 300 or more career Win Shares are listed in chronological order by date of birth.

DECADE OF THE 1870s

Player	70	71	72	73	74	75	76	77	78	79	Decade	B	F	P	Career
O'Rourke, Jim							17	14	12	17	60	85	15	0	304
Anson, Cap							14	11	9	9	43	89	11	0	377
Galvin, Pud										61	61	3	0	97	402
McCormick, Jim									6	33	39	6	0	94	335
Brouthers, Dan										5	5	93	7	0	356
Ward, Monte									24	51	75	39	19	42	410
Gore, George										8	8	80	20	0	250
Dalrymple, Abner								8	9	17	79	21	0		150
Brown, Lew							5	9	12	9	35	69	31	0	50
Force, Davy							3	8		5	16	27	73	0	50

DECADE OF THE 1880s

Player	80	81	82	83	84	85	86	87	88	89	Decade	B	F	P	Career
Born 1850s															
O'Rourke, Jim	17	14	11	17	25	24	24	13	17	19	181	85	15	0	304
Anson, Cap	20	21	18	15	19	23	30	18	29	21	214	89	11	0	377
Radbourn, Old Hoss	0	24	49	59	89	39	32	22	11	21	346	8	1	91	389
Galvin, Pud	14	36	29	47	56	12	32	33	30	16	305	3	0	97	402
McCormick, Jim	54	34	42	40	54	21	33	18			296	6	0	94	335
Keefe, Tim	11	23	24	70	47	42	38	39	35	27	356	5	0	95	413
Connor, Roger	17	11	19	19	23	30	36	21	31	26	233	89	11	0	362
Brouthers, Dan	0	15	21	24	22	26	31	26	27	28	220	93	7	0	356
Mullane, Tony		0	36	55	58		34	46	34	24	287	12	1	87	401
Welch, Mickey	42	25	12	31	47	57	29	27	31	31	332	6	0	93	354
McPhee, Bid			8	11	19	13	23	19	17	20	130	68	32	0	306
Born 1860s															
Ward, Monte	51	28	31	28	16	12	21	25	15	17	244	39	19	42	410
Clarkson, John			1		11	62	43	51	32	61	261	3	0	97	398
Ryan, Jimmy					1	14	18	34	25		92	80	18	2	315
Caruthers, Bob					10	51	57	54	46	47	265	27	2	71	338
Hamilton, Billy								3	23		26	86	14	0	336
Van Haltren, George							14	24	21		59	74	14	12	346
Beckley, Jake								14	18		32	88	12	0	318
Delahanty, Ed								7	6		13	88	12	0	356
Gore, George	24	15	17	22	16	30	26	14	7	23	194	80	20	0	250
Dalrymple, Abner	23	15	16	12	18	25	10	6	3		128	79	21	0	150
Henderson, Hardie				12	32	36	14	6	0		100	7	0	93	100
Kuehne, Bill				6	15	9	10	13	18	8	79	55	45	0	100
Brown, Lew		4	1		10						15	69	31	0	50
Force, Davy	3	5	7	5	8	3	3				34	27	73	0	50

DECADE OF THE 1890s

Player	90	91	92	93	94	95	96	97	98	99	Decade	B	F	P	Career
Born 1850s															
O'Rourke, Jim	21	16	15	11							63	85	15	0	304
Anson, Cap	24	20	18	11	11	14	12	10			120	89	11	0	377
Radbourn, Old Hoss	34	9									43	8	1	91	389
Galvin, Pud	10	15	11								36	3	0	97	402
Connor, Roger	25	23	24	16	14	12	14	1			129	89	11	0	362
Brouthers, Dan	19	29	33	16	21	3	10				131	93	7	0	356
Mullane, Tony	28	25	26	27	8						114	12	1	87	401
Welch, Mickey	19	3	0								22	6	0	93	354
McPhee, Bid	21	19	27	21	17	15	17	11	15	13	176	68	32	0	306
Born 1860s															
Ward, Monte	27	15	23	17	9						91	39	19	42	410
Clarkson, John	33	42	33	16	13						137	3	0	97	398
Ryan, Jimmy	23	22	24	12	13	14	14	16	28	17	183	80	18	2	315
Caruthers, Bob	30	22	19	2							73	27	2	71	338
Hamilton, Billy	25	36	25	20	29	30	30	28	33	15	271	86	14	0	336
Van Haltren, George	30	26	21	21	21	22	23	23	29	18	234	74	14	12	346
Young, Cy	8	28	44	36	39	37	42	28	34	35	331	1	0	99	635
Beckley, Jake	21	16	19	17	17	18	10	16	14	20	168	88	12	0	318
Delahanty, Ed	13	12	20	28	22	31	31	23	33	41	254	88	12	0	356
Burkett, Jesse	14	4	23	24	21	35	29	23	29	30	232	86	14	0	389
Nichols, Kid	43	39	48	41	37	34	33	41	44	31	391	2	0	98	479
Born 1870s															
Dahlen, Bill		21	32	17	21	20	31	14	27	23	206	64	36	0	392
Davis, George	14	21	19	22	25	21	20	31	20	20	213	75	25	0	396
Kelley, Joe		1	6	20	30	27	31	26	22	30	193	83	17	0	304
Keeler, Willie			2	3	22	23	25	32	23	29	159	85	15	0	331
Clarke, Fred					5	16	17	30	25	25	118	84	16	0	399
Wallace, Bobby					2	15	15	21	25	25	103	58	33	9	348
Wagner, Honus								9	22	26	57	78	22	0	655
Lajoie, Nap							5	21	26	19	71	81	19	0	496
Leach, Tommy									0	13	13	71	29	0	329
Sheckard, Jimmy								2	13	20	35	80	20	0	339
Born 1880s															
Crawford, Sam										4	4	89	11	0	448
Gore, George	18	18	12								48	80	20	0	250
Donovan, Patsy	4	14	19	14	10	15	17	12	19	9	133	84	16	0	200
Seybold, Socks										1	1	84	16	0	150
Carsey, Kid		9	21	17	15	21	8	3	1	5	100	4	0	95	100
Kuehne, Bill	10	8	3								21	55	45	0	100
Daub, Dan			2	7	8	12	16	5			50	3	0	97	50
Hill, Bill							14	11	16	9	50	2	0	98	50
Klobedanz, Fred							8	25	15	1	49	10	0	90	50
McFarland, Herman							0		3		3	80	20	0	50
Taylor, Harry	19	12	13	6							50	82	18	0	50

DECADE OF THE 1900s

Player	0	1	2	3	4	5	6	7	8	9	Decade	B	F	P	Career
Born 1860s															
Ryan, Jimmy	12		19	9							40	80	18	2	315
Hamilton, Billy	23	16									39	86	14	0	336
Van Haltren, George	21	23	3	6							53	74	14	12	346
Young, Cy	22	41	39	38	35	28	13	27	27	20	290	1	0	99	635
Beckley, Jake	21	18	18	17	23	16	5	0			118	88	12	0	318
Delahanty, Ed	19	33	31	6							89	88	12	0	356
Burkett, Jesse	25	38	25	22	25	22					157	86	14	0	389
Nichols, Kid	18	32			27	11	0				88	2	0	98	479
Born 1870s															
Dahlen, Bill	21	18	23	23	25	24	19	12	16	5	186	64	36	0	392
Davis, George	18	24	26	0	28	28	29	16	14	0	183	75	25	0	396
Kelley, Joe	22	18	15	15	16	9	8		8		111	83	17	0	304
Keeler, Willie	22	20	23	20	26	19	19	2	10	11	172	85	15	0	331
Clarke, Fred	17	28	29	25	14	24	21	29	28	31	246	84	16	0	399
Wallace, Bobby	13	26	22	20	23	21	23	20	22	13	203	58	33	9	348
Wagner, Honus	34	37	35	35	43	46	45	44	59	43	421	78	22	0	655
Lajoie, Nap	22	42	21	31	41	13	33	32	33	28	296	81	19	0	496
Plank, Eddie		19	25	28	29	31	16	29	19	22	218	2	0	98	360
Leach, Tommy	3	17	27	21	25	17	19	29	31	26	215	71	29	0	329
Mathewson, Christy	0	21	22	37	34	39	20	29	39	34	275	3	0	97	426
Sheckard, Jimmy	14	33	25	33	11	21	25	24	15	23	224	80	20	0	339
Born 1880s															
Crawford, Sam	13	24	23	25	21	36	23	36	32	33	266	89	11	0	448
Magee, Sherry			12	28	31	37	26	20			154	87	13	0	354
Baker, Home Run									1	27	28	78	22	0	301
Cobb, Ty						4	16	41	36	44	141	89	11	0	726
Collins, Eddie							0	0	12	43	55	81	19	0	572
Hooper, Harry										9	9	83	17	0	321
Johnson, Walter								4	20	13	37	5	0	94	564
Speaker, Tris								0	3	34	37	81	19	0	633
Wheat, Zack										4	4	85	15	0	380
Titus, John				7	21	29	23	22	23	20	145	87	13	0	200
Donovan, Patsy	12	17	22	13	3		0	0			67	84	16	0	200
Bates, Johnny							12	15	13	19	59	86	14	0	150
Seybold, Socks		21	24	21	21	21	20	19	2		149	84	16	0	150
Smith, Frank					17	22	6	24	21	30	120	6	0	94	150
Coughlin, Bill		15	17	9	11	17	12	13	6		100	64	36	0	100
Harmon, Bob										4	4	2	0	98	100
Tannehill, Lee			8	17	13	10	4	14	14		80	37	63	0	100
Burch, Al							8	8	11	17	44	75	25	0	50
Clarke, Nig					3	11	17	10	5		46	74	26	0	50
Dygert, Jimmy					0	10	20	11	6		47	0	0	100	50
Klobedanz, Fred		1									1	10	0	90	50
McConnell, Amby									20	13	33	76	24	0	50
McFarland, Herm		21	10	16							47	80	20	0	50

DECADE OF THE 1910s

Player	10	11	12	13	14	15	16	17	18	19	Decade	B	F	P	Career
Born 1870s															
Young, Cy	10	4									14	1	0	99	635
Clarke, Fred	15	20		0	0	0					35	84	16	0	399
Wallace, Bobby	20	7	9	2	1	1	1	0	1		42	58	33	9	348
Wagner, Honus	30	30	35	18	19	23	17	5			177	78	22	0	655
Lajoie, Nap	47	14	22	23	7	12	4				129	81	19	0	496
Plank, Eddie	16	22	25	16	11	29	16	7			142	2	0	98	360
Leach, Tommy	16	10	14	24	27	8			2		101	71	29	0	329
Mathewson, Christy	31	32	31	30	19	4	4				151	3	0	97	426
Sheckard, Jimmy	23	31	21	5							80	80	20	0	339
Born 1880s															
Crawford, Sam	23	32	24	27	31	28	13	0			178	89	11	0	448
Magee, Sherry	36	19	17	19	29	26	17	14	18	5	200	87	13	0	354
Baker, Home Run	25	35	39	38	36		17	21	23	20	254	78	22	0	301
Cobb, Ty	46	48	40	31	26	49	40	46	31	32	389	89	11	0	726
Alexander, Pete		34	24	27	26	43	44	40	2	26	266	2	0	98	477
Collins, Eddie	38	35	37	39	43	40	30	31	15	26	334	81	19	0	572
Hooper, Harry	19	20	15	21	20	20	25	22	29	17	208	83	17	0	321
Johnson, Walter	36	31	47	54	38	42	36	29	39	27	379	5	0	94	564
Speaker, Tris	34	27	52	36	45	37	41	37	27	27	363	81	19	0	633
Wheat, Zack	21	16	15	16	26	24	32	16	16	21	203	85	15	0	380
Born 1890s															
Carey, Max	1	14	22	20	17	16	24	23	22	11	170	73	27	0	348
Rice, Sam						2	8	24	1	18	53	83	17	1	326
Rixey, Eppa			14	12	0	12	24	20		4	86	0	0	100	315
Maranville, Rabbit			1	17	24	20	27	22	2	18	131	53	47	0	300
Roush, Edd				0	6	22	10	30	22	33	123	81	19	0	315
Heilmann, Harry					3		17	18	12	23	73	91	9	0	355
Ruth, Babe					1	23	37	37	40	43	181	81	6	13	758
Hornsby, Rogers						0	28	37	18	26	109	88	12	0	502
Frisch, Frankie										3	3	71	29	0	365
Titus, John	17	9	16	13							55	87	13	0	200
Bates, Johnny	25	23	12	15	16						91	86	14	0	150
Ruether, Dutch							6	0	25		31	10	0	90	150
Smith, Frank	8	5	0		11	6					30	6	0	94	150
Weaver, Buck			7	23	8	20	14	21	15	20	128	58	42	0	150
Bassler, Johnny				0	1						1	66	34	0	100
Harmon, Bob	6	23	12	13	16	15	7		4		96	2	0	98	100
Tannehill, Lee	5	15	0								20	37	63	0	100
Burch, Al		4	2								6	75	25	0	50
Clarke, Nig	1	2								1	4	74	26	0	50
Coumbe, Fritz					7	5	9	11	10	1	43	3	0	97	50
Dygert, Jimmy	3										3	0	0	100	50
James, Bill		1	0		15	11	4	13	2	4	50	2	0	98	50
McConnell, Amby	6	11									17	76	24	0	50

DECADE OF THE 1920s

Player	20	21	22	23	24	25	26	27	28	29	Decade	B	F	P	Career
Born 1880s															
Baker, Home Run		12	7								19	78	22	0	301
Cobb, Ty	20	26	29	24	27	25	10	22	13		196	89	11	0	726
Alexander, Pete	36	22	18	27	14	20	16	29	19	10	211	2	0	98	477
Collins, Eddie	38	21	23	24	25	22	18	11	1	0	183	.81	19	0	572
Hooper, Harry	24	15	21	15	19	10					104	83	17	0	321
Johnson, Walter	10	24	21	17	30	26	15	5			148	5	0	94	564
Speaker, Tris	39	27	29	36	21	25	29	21	6		233	81	19	0	633
Wheat, Zack	28	23	27	15	35	27	11	7			173	85	15	0	380
Born 1890s															
Carey, Max	20	24	29	29	25	26	5	13	7	0	178	73	27	0	348
Rice, Sam	23	23	20	25	24	24	23	16	19	20	217	83	17	1	326
Rixey, Eppa	18	22	23	26	21	26	14	15	22	14	201	0	0	100	315
Maranville, Rabbit	14	23	22	17	15	3	5	1	11	16	127	53	47	0	300
Roush, Edd	33	18	9	28	20	23	21	16	3	15	186	81	19	0	315
Heilmann, Harry	16	28	24	35	29	30	27	32	22	19	262	91	9	0	355
Ruth, Babe	51	53	29	55	45	13	45	45	45	32	413	81	6	13	758
Hornsby, Rogers	38	41	47	26	39	35	21	40	33	42	362	88	12	0	502
Frisch, Frankie	15	31	20	31	30	20	20	34	22	20	243	71	29	0	365
Born 1900s															
Grove, Lefty						9	25	24	27	28	113	0	0	100	391
Goslin, Goose		1	12	21	29	31	33	28	26	19	200	86	14	0	355
Hartnett, Gabby			2	9	19	19	13	21	26	1	110	66	34	0	326
Lyons, Ted				0	8	23	23	30	15	16	115	2	0	98	311
Simmons, Al					17	34	27	26	23	34	161	82	18	0	375
Waner, Paul							29	36	35	30	130	86	14	0	423
Gehringer, Charlie					1	0	11	20	23	27	82	77	23	0	385
Gehrig, Lou			2	1	15	30	44	42	32		166	93	7	0	489
Hubbell, Carl								11	19		30	0	0	100	305
Ruffing, Red				0	9	8	8	21	11		57	10	0	90	322
Cronin, Joe					2	0	4	19			25	70	30	0	333
Dickey, Bill							0	18			18	70	30	0	315
Foxx, Jimmie				1	1	6	22	34			64	89	11	0	435
Ott, Mel					2	4	19	31			56	90	10	0	525
Brandt, Ed							6	7			13	3	0	97	150
Davis, Spud							3	9			12	67	33	0	150
Ruether, Dutch	18	15	20	15	9	20	9	13			119	10	0	90	150
Weaver, Buck	22										22	58	42	0	150
Bassler, Johnny		13	15	19	21	13	10	8			99	66	34	0	100
Coumbe, Fritz	1	6									7	3	0	97	50
Swanson, Evar										14	14	82	18	0	50

DECADE OF THE 1930s

Player	30	31	32	33	34	35	36	37	38	39	Decade	B	F	P	Career
Born 1890s															
Rice, Sam	23	13	11	2	7						56	83	17	1	326
Rixey, Eppa	8	5	9	6							28	0	0	100	315
Maranville, Rabbit	17	9	11	5		0					42	53	47	0	300
Roush, Edd		6									6	81	19	0	315
Heilmann, Harry	20		0								20	91	9	0	355
Ruth, Babe	39	38	36	29	20	2					164	81	6	13	758
Hornsby, Rogers	3	20	1	5	1	0	0	1			31	88	12	0	502
Frisch, Frankie	25	22	14	21	18	12	7	0			119	71	29	0	365
Born 1900s															
Grove, Lefty	37	42	33	23	2	29	29	27	17	23	262	0	0	100	391
Goslin, Goose	26	25	19	20	22	17	22	4	0		155	86	14	0	355
Hartnett, Gabby	29	16	19	21	24	26	18	25	16	15	209	66	34	0	326
Lyons, Ted	26	6	14	12	10	20	9	13	14	20	144	2	0	98	311
Simmons, Al	36	34	25	24	23	13	20	11	16	9	211	82	18	0	375
Waner, Paul	25	25	31	28	30	22	32	28	15	15	251	86	14	0	423
Gehringer, Charley	29	10	25	28	37	31	34	30	28	20	272	77	23	0	385
Gehrig, Lou	39	36	38	36	41	34	38	36	25	0	323	93	7	0	489
Hubbell, Carl	18	20	25	33	32	26	37	23	15	14	243	0	0	100	305
Ruffing, Red	16	15	27	14	17	22	23	24	25	22	205	10	0	90	322
Cronin, Joe	33	35	31	34	17	16	7	24	29	22	248	70	30	0	333
Appling, Luke	0	5	11	24	14	24	29	28	9	24	168	71	29	0	376
Dickey, Bill	15	20	19	25	19	20	25	33	27	28	231	70	30	0	315
Foxx, Jimmie	34	24	41	41	31	30	26	23	34	30	314	89	11	0	435
Ott, Mel	28	26	33	31	38	35	36	31	35	28	321	90	10	0	525
Hack, Stan			4	5	13	21	19	23	33	23	141	79	21	0	318
Born 1910s															
Medwick, Joe			4	24	24	33	36	40	22	24	207	86	14	0	312
Vaughan, Arky			21	34	36	39	36	24	34	25	249	78	22	0	356
Mize, Johnny							26	34	28	33	121	92	8	0	337
DiMaggio, Joe							25	38	30	34	127	84	16	0	385
Slaughter, Enos									10	23	33	85	15	0	325
Williams, Ted										32	32	92	8	0	558
McCormick, Frank						0		2	19	25	46	86	14	0	200
Brandt, Ed	8	27	13	29	19	3	17	14	7		137	3	0	97	150
Cooper, Mort									2	16	18	1	0	99	150
Davis, Spud	8	16	18	18	15	14	13	5	2	6	115	67	33	0	150
Fox, Pete				14	13	21	7	19	13	11	98	79	21	0	150
Mueller, Ray						2	1	7	9	3	22	53	47	0	100
Almada, Mel				2	1	14	3	15	12	3	50	60	40	0	50
Cain, Sugar			2	11	12	9	14	2	0		50	0	0	100	50
Davis, Kiddo			17	12	12	3	1	5	0		50	65	35	0	50
Desautels, Gene	2	0	2	1				8	13	8	34	30	70	0	50
Hayworth, Ray	4	4	12	8	6	7	6	3	0	0	50	44	56	0	50
Powell, Jake	0				1	17	14	6	3	1	42	74	26	0	50
Ripple, Jimmy							12	15	10	4	41	82	18	0	50
Ryba, Mike					1	1	8	0			10	4	1	96	50
Swanson, Evar	5		2	19	10						36	82	18	0	50

DECADE OF THE 1940s

Player	40	41	42	43	44	45	46	47	48	49	Decade	B	F	P	Career
Born 1900s															
Grove, Lefty	11	5									16	0	0	100	391
Hartnett, Gabby	1	6									7	66	34	0	326
Lyons, Ted	15	13	21			3					52	2	0	98	311
Simmons, Al	2	0		1	0						3	82	18	0	375
Waner, Paul	7	9	11	10	5	0					42	86	14	0	423
Gehringer, Charley	20	10	1								31	77	23	0	385
Hubbell, Carl	12	11	7	2							32	0	0	100	305
Ruffing, Red	16	15	15			7	7	0			60	10	0	90	322
Cronin, Joe	23	23	4	4	5	1					60	70	30	0	333
Appling, Luke	28	29	20	40		6	26	22	17	19	207	71	29	0	376
Dickey, Bill	13	17	11	20			5				66	70	30	0	315
Foxx, Jimmie	24	20	5		0	8					57	89	11	0	435
Ott, Mel	24	26	35	16	25	22	0	0			148	90	10	0	525
Born 1910s															
Hack, Stan	26	31	27	21	13	34	17	8			177	79	21	0	318
Medwick, Joe	19	23	21	10	19	5	3	5	0		105	86	14	0	312
Vaughan, Arky	31	19	19	28				7	3		107	78	22	0	356
Mize, Johnny	33	26	32				22	32	30	12	187	92	8	0	337
DiMaggio, Joe	31	41	32				24	29	34	21	212	84	16	0	385
Slaughter, Enos	21	20	37				30	20	26	30	184	85	15	0	325
Reese, Pee Wee	13	14	28				27	26	23	32	163	65	35	0	315
Williams, Ted	30	42	46				50	44	39	40	291	92	8	0	558
Born 1920s															
Wynn, Early		4	3	19	8		9	20	2	8	73	5	0	95	308
Musial, Stan		3	28	39	38		44	25	47	40	264	89	11	0	604
Spahn, Warren			0				9	32	14	24	79	2	0	98	411
Berra, Yogi							2	11	18	21	52	72	28	0	375
Snider, Duke							1	5	24		30	84	16	0	354
Roberts, Robin								12	17		29	2	0	98	339
Ashburn, Richie								21	19		40	78	22	0	328
Fox, Nellie							0	0	6		6	63	37	0	301
McCormick, Frank	26	20	17	19	29	16	16	8	3		154	86	14	0	200
Cooper, Mort	15	11	29	28	24	9	13	3		0	132	1	0	99	150
Davis, Spud	14	3			5	1					23	67	33	0	150
Fox, Pete	7	7	5	13	17	3					52	79	21	0	150
Mueller, Ray	0		24	26			12	6	0	6	74	53	47	0	100
Desautels, Gene	4	4	3	3		0	2				16	30	70	0	50
Powell, Jake	0		3	3	2						8	74	26	0	50
Ripple, Jimmy	6	2		1							9	82	18	0	50
Ryba, Mike		7	3	9	9	11	1				40	4	1	96	50

DECADE OF THE 1950s

Player	50	51	52	53	54	55	56	57	58	59	Decade	B	F	P	Career
Born 1900s															
Appling, Luke	1										1	71	29	0	376
Born 1910s															
Mize, Johnny	12	11	3	3							29	92	8	0	337
DiMaggio, Joe	29	17									46	84	16	0	385
Slaughter, Enos	16	14	23	17	5	12	7	7	6	1	108	85	15	0	325
Reese, Pee Wee	20	22	23	21	26	18	14	4	4		152	65	35	0	315
Williams, Ted	20	34	1	9	29	24	25	38	25	9	214	92	8	0	558
Born 1920s															
Wynn, Early	21	24	21	16	24	21	28	10	11	23	199	5	0	95	308
Musial, Stan	32	38	37	33	31	29	26	30	21	8	285	89	11	0	604
Spahn, Warren	21	25	22	31	23	19	24	22	28	23	238	2	0	98	411
Berra, Yogi	32	31	29	28	34	24	31	23	21	23	276	72	28	0	375
Snider, Duke	29	22	25	37	39	36	34	25	13	17	277	84	16	0	354
Roberts, Robin	26	28	32	35	31	27	12	11	20	13	235	2	0	98	339
Ashburn, Richie	23	28	21	26	26	29	28	26	28	14	249	78	22	0	328
Fox, Nellie	5	22	22	21	25	25	19	31	22	30	222	63	37	0	301
Born 1930s															
Banks, Ernie			2	16	32	22	28	31	33		164	80	20	0	333
Mays, Willie		19	5		40	40	27	34	39	32	236	84	16	0	641
Mathews, Eddie			19	38	33	34	29	33	24	36	246	87	13	0	447
Mantle, Mickey		13	33	26	36	41	49	51	39	30	318	90	10	0	565
Aaron, Hank				13	29	30	35	31	38		176	89	11	0	641
Clemente, Roberto					7	14	5	16	10		52	84	16	0	375
Cash, Norm								0	4		4	89	11	0	311
Kaline, Al			0	7	31	26	20	23	27		134	87	13	0	442
Robinson, Frank					26	27	20	25			98	90	10	0	520
Gibson, Bob								5			5	2	0	98	320
Killebrew, Harmon			0	1	1	2	0	23			27	91	9	0	371
Pinson, Vada						3	27				30	78	22	0	321
Robinson, Brooks			0	1	2	7	9				19	70	30	0	355
Cepeda, Orlando					20	24					44	91	9	0	312
McCovey, Willie					12						12	93	7	0	408
Gordon, Sid	29	22	25	19	16	6					117	87	13	0	200
Mueller, Ray	3	1									4	53	47	0	100
O'Toole, Jim							1	3			4	0	0	100	100

DECADE OF THE 1960s

Player	60	61	62	63	64	65	66	67	68	69	Decade	B	F	P	Career
Born 1910s															
Williams, Ted	21										21	92	8	0	558
Born 1920s															
Wynn, Early	16	9	5	6							36	5	0	95	308
Musial, Stan	13	14	19	9							55	89	11	0	604
Spahn, Warren	16	25	23	22	1	7					94	2	0	98	411
Berra, Yogi	16	16	6	9		0					47	72	28	0	375
Snider, Duke	10	11	9	14	3						47	84	16	0	354
Roberts, Robin	13	0	16	15	15	13	3				75	2	0	98	339
Ashburn, Richie	22	6	11								39	78	22	0	328
Fox, Nellie	20	11	16	12	13	1					73	63	37	0	301
Born 1930s															
Banks, Ernie	29	19	14	10	15	18	11	17	18	14	165	80	20	0	333
Mays, Willie	38	34	41	38	38	43	37	21	30	17	337	84	16	0	641
Mathews, Eddie	38	32	26	31	20	22	15	15	2		201	87	13	0	447
Mantle, Mickey	36	48	32	14	33	16	18	25	25		247	90	10	0	565
Aaron, Hank	35	35	34	41	33	31	27	34	32	38	340	89	11	0	641
Clemente, Roberto	20	26	20	21	29	27	29	35	25	28	260	84	16	0	375
Cash, Norm	16	42	22	23	18	23	27	20	18	20	229	89	11	0	311
Kaline, Al	17	29	19	25	24	19	31	30	18	17	229	87	13	0	442
Robinson, Frank	23	34	41	23	33	26	41	30	24	32	307	90	10	0	520
Gibson, Bob	0	18	21	17	24	26	26	13	36	33	214	2	0	98	320
Killebrew, Harmon	20	27	25	23	24	22	32	38	12	34	257	91	9	0	371
Pinson, Vada	20	32	26	31	22	24	19	24	15	11	224	78	22	0	321
Robinson, Brooks	22	18	27	19	33	25	24	24	24	17	233	70	30	0	355
Cepeda, Orlando	26	29	26	30	22	0	19	35	17	20	224	91	9	0	312
McCovey, Willie	11	13	12	29	11	29	34	24	34	40	237	93	7	0	408
Williams, Billy	2	15	18	27	28	33	20	28	31	24	226	88	12	0	373
Perry, Gaylord			1	1	18	5	21	20	19	26	111	0	0	100	367
Niekro, Phil					0	6	2	21	18	28	75	0	0	100	375
Brock, Lou		0	9	15	26	22	21	30	31	23	177	86	14	0	349
Yastrzemski, Carl		12	21	28	20	21	21	42	39	26	230	87	13	0	486

DECADE OF THE 1960s

Player	60	61	62	63	64	65	66	67	68	69	Decade	B	F	P	Career
Born 1940s															
Santo, Ron	6	18	9	26	36	32	30	37	27	26	247	79	21	0	322
Stargell, Willie			1	7	13	21	25	20	15	27	129	91	9	0	369
Davis, Willie	3	10	26	16	26	15	21	15	18	22	172	75	25	0	321
Torre, Joe	0	13	9	20	28	22	29	17	15	23	176	82	18	0	312
Rose, Pete				19	12	27	25	24	32	38	177	84	16	0	546
Allen, Dick				0	41	33	35	29	32	22	192	91	9	0	340
Wynn, Jimmy				9	4	31	14	28	32	37	155	86	14	0	307
Perez, Tony				0	7	4	23	24	31		89	86	14	0	347
Morgan, Joe				1	1	31	19	26	2	24	104	82	18	0	518
Jenkins, Fergie					2	12	21	25	25		85	1	0	99	323
Staub, Rusty				12	5	13	18	28	28	26	130	90	10	0	357
Nettles, Graig							0	3	5		8	71	29	0	322
Seaver, Tom							21	24	33		78	0	0	100	391
Carlton, Steve						2	3	13	11	24	53	1	0	99	367
Sutton, Don							14	7	13	14	48	0	0	100	318
Smith, Reggie							0	19	25	24	68	84	16	0	324
Carew, Rod								19	12	21	52	86	14	0	386
Palmer, Jim						4	11	3		18	36	0	0	100	313
Bonds, Bobby									15	31	46	86	14	0	301
Jackson, Reggie								2	25	40	67	91	9	0	444
Oliver, Al									0	13	13	85	15	0	304
Ryan, Nolan							0		6	6	12	0	0	100	334
Bench, Johnny								2	23	28	53	72	28	0	355
Harper, Tommy			0	13	8	17	15	10	7	17	87	82	18	0	200
Millan, Felix							1	3	17	19	40	61	39	0	150
Hall, Jimmie				21	19	26	10	15	3	5	99	78	22	0	100
Knowles, Darold						0	10	12	3	11	36	1	0	99	100
O'Toole, Jim	10	22	16	18	19	0	8	3			96	0	0	100	100
Bruce, Bob	6	1	9	8	18	8	0	0			50	1	0	99	50

DECADE OF THE 1970s

Player	70	71	72	73	74	75	76	77	78	79	Decade	B	F	P	Career
Born 1930s															
Banks, Ernie	4	0									4	80	20	0	333
Mays, Willie	24	27	12	5							68	84	16	0	641
Aaron, Hank	24	33	21	20	13	9	5				125	89	11	0	641
Cash, Norm	16	24	18	15	5						78	89	11	0	311
Clemente, Roberto	23	24	16								63	84	16	0	375
Kaline, Al	19	22	14	8	16						79	87	13	0	442
Robinson, Frank	26	23	14	26	19	6	1				115	90	10	0	520
Gibson, Bob	28	17	29	12	13	2					101	2	0	98	320
Killebrew, Harmon	30	23	19	5	5	5					87	91	9	0	371
Pinson, Vada	15	11	20	9	10	2					67	78	22	0	321
Robinson, Brooks	21	23	16	12	23	6	2	0			103	70	30	0	355
Cepeda, Orlando	21	7	3	13	0						44	91	9	0	312
McCovey, Willie	33	16	7	22	25	16	4	16	7	11	157	93	7	0	408
Williams, Billy	29	26	32	20	16	17	7				147	88	12	0	373
Perry, Gaylord	24	17	39	24	30	21	17	16	18	16	222	0	0	100	367
Niekro, Phil	11	22	22	17	28	19	21	20	30	24	214	0	0	100	375
Brock, Lou	20	31	21	26	22	18	13	10	1	10	172	86	14	0	349
Yastrzemski, Carl	36	21	19	24	24	20	18	24	19	13	218	87	13	0	486
Born 1940s															
Santo, Ron	19	19	21	13	3						75	79	21	0	322
Stargell, Willie	17	35	26	36	29	22	17	8	22	18	230	91	9	0	369
Davis, Willie	24	25	26	23	20	15	16			0	149	75	25	0	321
Torre, Joe	25	40	18	19	16	8	10	0			136	82	18	0	312
Rose, Pete	29	28	32	34	27	30	30	23	27	27	287	84	16	0	546
Allen, Dick	19	29	40	15	23	8	11	3			148	91	9	0	340
Wynn, Jimmy	28	7	28	17	32	21	18	1			152	86	14	0	307
Perez, Tony	33	23	25	31	20	19	16	17	18	13	215	86	14	0	347
Morgan, Joe	24	30	39	40	37	44	36	31	18	18	317	82	18	0	518
Jenkins, Fergie	26	37	22	15	26	15	14	14	21	14	204	1	0	99	323
Staub, Rusty	29	32	12	24	17	25	26	12	16	8	201	90	10	0	357
Nettles, Graig	18	27	21	19	21	21	28	25	26	15	221	71	29	0	322
Seaver, Tom	25	33	22	29	16	26	20	25	19	16	231	0	0	100	391
Carlton, Steve	14	16	40	14	22	14	18	26	20	18	202	1	0	99	367
Sutton, Don	11	21	24	22	15	17	20	17	11	10	168	0	0	100	318
Smith, Reggie	25	29	26	23	25	20	13	29	24	9	223	84	16	0	324
Carew, Rod	11	17	23	29	32	30	30	37	22	16	247	86	14	0	386
Palmer, Jim	25	23	25	28	9	31	27	29	27	12	236	0	0	100	313
Bonds, Bobby	31	32	24	31	23	24	16	24	22	21	248	86	14	0	301
Jackson, Reggie	17	32	26	32	30	27	26	28	23	23	264	91	9	0	444
Oliver, Al	15	18	23	22	26	21	22	21	21	18	207	85	15	0	304
Ryan, Nolan	8	4	24	28	21	12	17	22	12	13	161	0	0	100	334
Evans, Darrell	2	10	20	31	28	28	9	13	26	23	190	81	19	0	364
Singleton, Ken	5	11	18	28	16	33	24	36	28	32	231	90	10	0	302
Cruz, Jose	1	13	8	12	5	11	21	24	26	26	147	84	16	0	309
Bench, Johnny	34	19	37	26	34	30	19	22	20	22	263	72	28	0	355
Fisk, Carlton		2	33	17	11	15	19	29	30	6	162	69	31	0	367
Grich, Bobby	2	2	23	28	31	29	30	7	20	29	201	72	28	0	329
Simmons, Ted	6	20	23	28	21	28	20	28	30	20	224	77	23	0	314
Schmidt, Mike			1	10	39	28	36	33	23	33	203	81	19	0	468

DECADE OF THE 1970s

Player	70	71	72	73	74	75	76	77	78	79	Decade	B	F	P	Career
Born 1950s															
Blyleven, Bert	10	20	19	29	23	21	20	21	16	13	192	0	0	100	339
Parker, Dave				4	6	25	23	33	37	31	159	87	13	0	326
Winfield, Dave				3	17	20	24	24	28	33	149	90	10	0	414
Evans, Dwight			2	7	15	17	15	9	17	15	97	85	15	0	346
Brett, George				0	9	25	33	29	23	33	152	86	14	0	432
Hernandez, Keith					1	3	13	24	19	29	89	89	11	0	312
Carter, Gary					2	18	6	25	22	28	101	64	36	0	338
Randolph, Willie						1	17	20	24	23	85	69	31	0	307
Dawson, Andre							1	18	21	24	64	82	18	0	341
Eckersley, Dennis						17	11	18	24	23	93	0	0	100	300
Smith, Ozzie									20	7	27	57	43	0	329
Yount, Robin					8	14	14	16	19	14	85	76	24	0	423
Clark, Jack						0	3	11	30	23	67	92	8	0	314
Murray, Eddie								21	28	24	73	91	9	0	433
Molitor, Paul									12	26	38	89	11	0	412
Whitaker, Lou								0	18	20	38	75	25	0	357
Trammell, Alan								0	14	13	27	71	29	0	316
Henderson, Rickey										10	10	89	11	0	519
Harper, Tommy	33	19	24	20	6	9	2				113	82	18	0	200
Millan, Felix	15	18	9	19	12	17	16	4			110	61	39	0	150
Stanley, Bob								11	17	15	43	0	0	100	150
Hall, Jimmie	1										1	78	22	0	100
Heath, Mike									1	4	5	56	44	0	100
Jones, Randy				9	6	28	20	3	14	13	93	0	0	100	100
Knowles, Darold	15	6	9	6	1	3	9	5	7	3	64	1	0	99	100
Ruthven, Dick				5	10	1	14	9	16	6	61	1	0	99	100
Bradley, Tom	1	20	16	11	2	0					50	0	0	100	50
Cubbage, Mike					0	3	12	11	12	5	43	72	28	0	50
Littell, Mark				1		1	14	10	9	14	49	0	0	100	50

DECADE OF THE 1980s

Player	80	81	82	83	84	85	86	87	88	89	Decade	B	F	P	Career
Born 1930s															
McCovey, Willie	2										2	93	7	0	408
Perry, Gaylord	11	7	10	6							34	0	0	100	367
Niekro, Phil	17	8	14	9	15	10	9	4			86	0	0	100	375
Yastrzemski, Carl	10	7	12	9							38	87	13	0	486
Born 1940s															
Stargell, Willie	7	1	2								10	91	9	0	369
Rose, Pete	17	17	17	7	8	13	3				82	84	16	0	546
Perez, Tony	13	6	4	6	1	9	4				43	86	14	0	347
Morgan, Joe	22	14	29	19	13						97	82	18	0	518
Jenkins, Fergie	12	2	14	6							34	1	0	99	323
Staub, Rusty	10	6	3	4	1	2					26	90	10	0	357
Nettles, Graig	10	12	10	17	16	17	9	2	0		93	71	29	0	322
Seaver, Tom	9	17	0	12	16	18	10				82	0	0	100	391
Carlton, Steve	29	16	25	19	12	4	4	3	0		112	1	0	99	367
Sutton, Don	20	10	17	9	11	11	13	9	2		102	0	0	100	318
Smith, Reggie	17	0	16								33	84	16	0	324
Carew, Rod	20	12	17	16	9	13					87	86	14	0	386
Palmer, Jim	12	6	20	3	0						41	0	0	100	313
Bonds, Bobby	4	3									7	86	14	0	301
Jackson, Reggie	31	9	22	4	10	18	13	6			113	91	9	0	444
Oliver, Al	21	13	26	14	8	2					84	85	15	0	304
Ryan, Nolan	11	15	16	12	9	8	11	15	8	18	123	0	0	100	334
Evans, Darrell	27	14	20	28	12	18	17	22	11	5	174	81	19	0	364
Singleton, Ken	27	15	12	17	0						71	90	10	0	302
Cruz, Jose	25	14	18	30	29	21	17	8	0		162	84	16	0	309
Bench, Johnny	15	9	7	8							39	72	28	0	355
Fisk, Carlton	18	13	19	27	10	24	6	16	15	18	166	69	31	0	367
Schmidt, Mike	37	29	37	35	26	27	31	26	14	3	265	81	19	0	468
Simmons, Ted	22	8	19	19	1	13	3	4	1		90	77	23	0	314
Grich, Bobby	20	21	21	20	16	19	11				128	72	28	0	329

DECADE OF THE 1980s

Player	80	81	82	83	84	85	86	87	88	89	Decade	B	F	P	Career
Born 1950s															
Blyleven, Bert	9	14	1	10	20	23	18	18	4	22	139	0	0	100	339
Parker, Dave	17	6	7	12	17	29	20	13	10	15	146	87	13	0	326
Winfield, Dave	22	16	20	22	26	21	17	18	31		193	90	10	0	414
Evans, Dwight	18	26	31	13	29	21	23	25	23	21	230	85	15	0	346
Brett, George	36	14	27	24	14	37	19	15	27	17	230	86	14	0	432
Hernandez, Keith	28	20	24	23	33	27	29	21	13	4	222	89	11	0	312
Carter, Gary	30	17	31	24	30	33	23	13	12	2	215	64	36	0	338
Randolph, Willie	30	9	18	15	21	19	17	21	13	20	183	69	31	0	307
Dawson, Andre	29	25	26	27	12	16	16	20	20	13	204	82	18	0	341
Eckersley, Dennis	10	6	17	3	16	15	8	13	15	14	117	0	0	100	300
Smith, Ozzie	18	8	19	18	19	25	23	33	22	21	206	57	43	0	329
Yount, Robin	25	20	39	33	27	16	23	26	32	34	275	76	24	0	423
Clark, Jack	24	15	25	20	12	22	9	32	21	31	211	92	8	0	314
Murray, Eddie	26	21	29	31	33	28	20	20	20	21	249	91	9	0	433
Molitor, Paul	18	8	30	23	0	20	14	29	27	27	196	89	11	0	412
Whitaker, Lou	11	14	22	30	23	24	19	20	20	25	208	75	25	0	357
Trammell, Alan	20	14	16	26	29	16	26	35	22	13	217	71	29	0	316
Boggs, Wade			15	34	28	31	37	32	31	29	237	81	19	0	394
Henderson, Rickey	34	27	28	31	28	38	27	20	28	30	291	89	11	0	519
Baines, Harold	8	10	19	20	24	25	19	13	18	18	174	92	8	0	306
Raines, Tim	0	18	21	29	31	36	32	34	19	25	245	86	14	0	386
Sandberg, Ryne		0	17	18	39	28	20	20	22	28	192	72	28	0	346
Born 1960s															
Gwynn, Tony			7	10	35	20	29	29	23	29	182	88	12	0	394
Ripken, Cal		0	23	36	37	25	28	20	25	26	220	68	32	0	419
Clemens, Roger				8	7	29	28	22	18		112	0	0	100	333
McGwire, Mark						1	30	28	20		79	94	6	0	335
Clark, Will						14	24	37	44		119	92	8	0	330
Larkin, Barry						6	11	28	15		60	71	29	0	314
Bonds, Barry						14	22	26	24		86	91	9	0	467
Palmeiro, Rafael						1	7	17	16		41	89	11	0	308
Biggio, Craig							1	18			19	78	22	0	318
Maddux, Greg						1	2	20	20		43	0	0	100	297
Alomar, Roberto							22	22			44	74	26	0	306
Griffey, Ken, Jr.								15			15	84	16	0	299

DECADE OF THE 1980s

Player	80	81	82	83	84	85	86	87	88	89	Decade	B	F	P	Career
Dykstra, Lenny						8	23	17	15	13	76	81	19	0	200
Fletcher, Scott		1	0	9	13	7	20	17	17	11	95	57	43	0	150
Stanley, Bob	15	6	20	21	13	10	6	5	9	2	107	0	0	100	150
Heath, Mike	4	8	9	9	12	14	6	10	6	11	89	56	44	0	100
Higuera, Teddy						14	25	20	22	9	90	0	0	100	100
Jones, Randy	5	0	2								7	0	0	100	100
McDowell, Roger						13	16	9	10	11	59	1	0	99	100
Ruthven, Dick	14	2	10	7	3	3	0				39	1	0	99	100
Salazar, Luis	7	11	12	15	4	7	0	3	15	11	85	70	30	0	100
Swift, Bill						4	2	6		6	18	0	0	100	100
Berryhill, Damon							0	7	12		19	50	50	0	50
Candaele, Casey							1	12	3		16	54	46	0	50
Crim, Chuck								12	11	11	34	0	0	100	50
Cubbage, Mike	6	1									7	72	28	0	50
Fermin, Felix							1	2	9		12	35	65	0	50
Heep, Danny	3	1	4	7	4	9	8	0	3	9	48	82	18	0	50
Hill, Donnie				4	2	9	10	6	2		33	61	39	0	50
Hulett, Tim				0	0	11	8	2		5	26	59	41	0	50
King, Eric							11	6	5	9	31	0	0	100	50
Lea, Charlie	4	2	11	14	15			0	4		50	0	0	100	50
Leach, Terry		3	3			4	0	10	7	2	29	1	0	99	50
Littell, Mark	0	1	0								1	0	0	100	50
Williamson, Mark								10	4	12	26	0	0	100	50

DECADE OF THE 1990s

Player	90	91	92	93	94	95	96	97	98	99	Decade	B	F	P	Career
Born 1940s															
Ryan, Nolan	15	13	8	2							38	0	0	100	334
Fisk, Carlton	22	13	4	0							39	69	31	0	367
Born 1950s															
Blyleven, Bert	3		5								8	0	0	100	339
Parker, Dave	15	6									21	87	13	0	326
Winfield, Dave	13	18	26	10	5	0					72	90	10	0	414
Evans, Dwight	9	10									19	85	15	0	346
Brett, George	26	8	11	5							50	86	14	0	432
Hernandez, Keith	1										1	89	11	0	312
Carter, Gary	8	7	7								22	64	36	0	338
Randolph, Willie	11	22	6								39	69	31	0	307
Dawson, Andre	22	20	16	7	2	4	2				73	82	18	0	341
Eckersley, Dennis	19	14	18	9	5	6	8	8	3		90	0	0	100	300
Smith, Ozzie	11	25	21	20	9	2	8				96	57	43	0	329
Yount, Robin	18	16	20	9							63	76	24	0	423
Clark, Jack	17	15	4								36	92	8	0	314
Murray, Eddie	31	16	19	15	8	16	6	0			111	91	9	0	433
Molitor, Paul	19	30	28	29	19	12	18	13	10		178	89	11	0	412
Whitaker, Lou	19	26	24	20	11	11					111	75	25	0	357
Trammell, Alan	29	12	4	17	3	6	1				72	71	29	0	316
Boggs, Wade	24	25	14	20	18	19	15	10	6	6	157	81	19	0	394
Henderson, Rickey	39	25	25	25	11	19	16	14	20	16	210	89	11	0	519
Baines, Harold	11	22	15	15	6	11	13	14	8	16	131	92	8	0	306
Raines, Tim	19	19	28	19	14	14	7	9	11	1	141	86	14	0	386
Sandberg, Ryne	34	37	33	13	7		19	11			154	72	28	0	346
Born 1960s															
Gwynn, Tony	17	21	18	18	17	24	17	38	19	18	207	88	12	0	394
Ripken, Cal	20	34	21	17	18	16	22	18	13	12	191	68	32	0	419
Clemens, Roger	28	25	26	11	16	10	20	32	25	9	202	0	0	100	333
McGwire, Mark	28	18	29	6	6	24	29	26	41	30	237	94	6	0	335
Clark, Will	25	34	28	15	19	18	11	14	19	7	190	92	8	0	330
Larkin, Barry	25	26	33	19	19	30	31	12	25	24	244	71	29	0	314
Bonds, Barry	37	37	41	47	25	36	39	36	34	20	352	91	9	0	467
Palmeiro, Rafael	23	26	24	31	17	21	30	18	25	31	246	89	11	0	308
Biggio, Craig	18	19	32	27	26	29	32	38	35	31	287	78	22	0	318
Maddux, Greg	15	17	27	25	26	30	22	26	25	16	229	0	0	100	297
Alomar, Roberto	18	24	34	31	13	16	31	21	19	35	242	74	26	0	306
Thomas, Frank	14	33	33	32	25	28	27	39	25	16	272	98	2	0	309
Bagwell, Jeff		23	29	22	30	20	41	31	28	37	261	92	8	0	287
Griffey Jr., Ken	24	29	26	30	20	9	28	36	29	31	262	84	16	0	299

DECADE OF THE 1990s

Player	90	91	92	93	94	95	96	97	98	99	Decade	B	F	P	Career
Dykstra, Lenny	35	13	17	33	13	8	5				124	81	19	0	200
Fletcher, Scott	13	3	18	14	3	4					55	57	43	0	150
Heath, Mike	5	1									6	56	44	0	100
Higuera, Teddy	8	2		0	0						10	0	0	100	100
McDowell, Roger	9	10	3	6	0	9	4				41	1	0	99	100
Salazar, Luis	7	6	2								15	70	30	0	100
Swift, Bill	12	14	16	19	7	7	2	1	4		82	0	0	100	100
Berryhill, Damon	1	1	10	8	5	1		5			31	50	50	0	50
Candaele, Casey	11	15	4	2			1	1			34	54	46	0	50
Crim, Chuck	7	4	2	0	3						16	0	0	100	50
Fermin, Felix	9	8	5	8	6	2	0				38	35	65	0	50
Heep, Danny	1	1									2	82	18	0	50
Hill, Donnie	8	8	1								17	61	39	0	50
Hulett, Tim	6	1	6	8	3	0					24	59	41	0	50
King, Eric	12	5	2								19	0	0	100	50
Leach, Terry	7	4	8	2							21	1	0	99	50
Williamson, Mark	9	4	2	4	5						24	0	0	100	50

WIN SHARE BY TEAMS

Our next chart takes a cross-section of 24 teams, some of them very good and some of them awful, and looks at the Win Shares assigned to each member of those teams. The 24 teams are:

Year	Team	Won–Lost
1998	New York Yankees	114– 48
1954	Cleveland Indians	111–143
1975	Cincinnati Reds	108– 54
1953	Brooklyn Dodgers	105– 49
1977	Kansas City Royals	102– 60
1989	Oakland As	99– 63
1986	Houston Astros	96– 66
1964	St. Louis Cardinals	93– 69
1971	San Francisco Giants	90– 72
1978	California Angels	87– 75
1983	Pittsburgh Pirates	84– 78
1988	Montreal Expos	81– 81
1989	Milwaukee Brewers	81– 81
1996	Minnesota Twins	78– 84
1967	Cleveland Indians	75– 87
1986	Chicago White Sox	72– 90
1999	Tampa Bay Devil Rays	69– 93
1963	Houston Astros	66– 96
1969	Philadelphia Phillies	63– 99
1983	Seattle Mariners	60–102
1973	Texas Rangers	57–105
1979	Oakland Athletics	54–108
1969	San Diego Padres	52–110
1962	New York Mets	40–120

Each team has three Win Shares for each win. The following charts give the batting and pitching stats of all members of these teams who had value, with the Win Shares resulting from these stats and from the fielding performance, for which stats are not included.

1998 New York Yankees (114-48)

Pos	Player	WS	G	AB	R	H	2B	3B	HR	RBI	BB	SB	Avg
C	Jorge Posada	15	111	358	56	96	23	0	17	63	47	0	.268
1B	Tino Martinez	21	142	531	92	149	33	1	28	123	61	2	.281
2B	Chuck Knoblauch	22	150	603	117	160	25	4	17	64	76	31	.265
3B	Scott Brosius	26	152	530	86	159	34	0	19	98	52	11	.300
SS	Derek Jeter	27	149	626	127	203	25	8	19	84	57	30	.324
LF	Curtis	14	151	456	79	111	21	1	10	56	75	21	.243
CF	Bernie Williams	28	128	499	101	169	30	5	26	97	74	15	.339
RF	Paul O'Neill	26	152	602	95	191	40	2	24	116	57	15	.317
DH	Darryl Strawberry	11	101	295	44	73	11	2	24	57	46	8	.247
C2	Joe Girardi	7	78	254	31	70	11	4	3	31	14	2	.276
I5	Homer Bush	3	45	71	17	27	3	0	1	5	5	6	.380
I6	Luis Sojo	1	54	147	16	34	3	1	0	14	4	1	.231
O4	Tim Raines	11	109	321	53	93	13	1	5	47	55	8	.290
O5	Shane Spencer	6	27	67	18	25	6	0	10	27	5	0	.373
X1	Ricky Ledee	2	42	79	13	19	5	2	1	12	7	3	.241
X2	Chili Davis	2	35	103	11	30	7	0	3	9	14	0	.291

Pos	Player	WS	G	IP	Won-Lost	Pct	H	SO	BB	ERA	CG	Sv
S1	David Wells	18	30	214	18-4	.818	195	163	29	3.49	8	0
S2	David Cone	17	31	208	20-7	.741	186	209	59	3.55	3	0
S3	Andy Pettitte	13	33	216	16-11	.593	226	146	87	4.24	5	0
S4	Orlando Hernandez	13	21	141	12-4	.750	113	131	52	3.13	3	0
S5	Hideki Irabu	12	29	173	13-9	.591	148	126	76	4.06	2	0
RA	Mariano Rivera	14	54	61	3-0	1.000	48	36	17	1.91	0	36
SW	Ramiro Mendoza	12	41	130	10-2	.833	131	56	30	3.25	1	1
M1	Graeme Lloyd	5	50	38	3-0	1.000	26	20	6	1.67	0	0
M2	Mike Stanton	4	67	79	4-1	.800	71	69	26	5.47	0	6
M3	Darren Holmes	4	34	51	0-3	.000	53	31	14	3.33	0	2
P1	Jeff Nelson	4	45	40	5-3	.625	44	35	22	3.79	0	3
P2	Mike Buddie	1	24	42	4-1	.800	46	20	13	5.62	0	0
P3	Jim Bruske	1	3	9	1-0	1.000	9	3	1	3.00	0	0
P4	Jay Tessmer	1	7	9	1-0	1.000	4	6	4	3.12	0	0
P5	Ryan Bradley	1	5	13	2-1	.667	12	13	9	5.68	0	0

1954 Cleveland Indians (111–43)

Pos	Player	WS	G	AB	R	H	2B	3B	HR	RBI	BB	SB	Avg
C	Jim Hegan	15	139	423	56	99	12	7	11	40	34	0	.234
1B	Vic Wertz	12	94	295	33	81	14	2	14	48	34	0	.275
2B	Bobby Avila	35	143	555	112	189	27	2	15	67	59	9	.341
3B	Al Rosen	27	137	466	76	140	20	2	24	102	85	6	.300
SS	George Strickland	10	112	361	42	77	12	3	6	37	55	2	.213
LF	Dave Philley	9	133	452	48	102	13	3	12	60	57	2	.226
CF	Larry Doby	33	153	577	94	157	18	4	32	126	85	3	.272
RF	Al Smith	25	131	481	101	135	29	6	11	50	88	2	.281
C2	Hal Naragon	3	46	101	10	24	2	2	0	12	9	0	.238
I5	Sam Dente	5	68	169	18	45	7	1	1	19	14	0	.266
I6	Rudy Regalado	4	65	180	21	45	5	0	2	24	19	0	.250
O4	Wally Westlake	9	85	240	36	63	9	2	11	42	26	0	.263
O5	Dave Pope	5	60	102	21	30	2	1	4	13	10	2	.294
X1	Bill Glynn	4	111	171	19	43	3	2	5	18	12	3	.251
X2	Hank Majeski	3	57	121	10	34	4	0	3	17	7	0	.281
X3	Dale Mitchell	2	53	60	6	17	1	0	1	6	9	0	.283
X4	Mickey Grasso	1	4	6	1	2	0	0	1	1	1	0	.333

Pos	Player	WS	G	IP	Won–Lost	Pct	H	SO	BB	ERA	CG	Sv
S1	Early Wynn	24	40	271	23–11	.676	225	155	83	2.73	20	2
S2	Mike Garcia	24	45	259	19–8	.704	220	129	71	2.64	13	5
S3	Bob Lemon	23	36	258	23–7	.767	228	110	92	2.72	21	0
S4	Art Houtteman	14	32	188	15–7	.682	198	68	59	3.35	11	0
S5	Bob Feller	11	19	140	13–3	.813	127	59	39	3.09	9	0
RA	Ray Narleski	12	42	89	3–3	.500	59	52	44	2.22	1	13
M1	Don Mossi	13	40	93	6–1	.857	56	55	39	1.94	2	7
M2	Hal Newhouser	7	26	47	7–2	.778	34	25	18	2.51	0	7
P1	Bob Chakales	2	3	10	2–0	1.000	4	3	12	0.87	0	0
P2	Dave Hoskins	1	14	27	0–1	.000	29	9	10	3.04	0	0

1975 Cincinnati Reds (108-54)

Pos	Player	WS	G	AB	R	H	2B	3B	HR	RBI	BB	SB	Avg
C	Johnny Bench	30	142	530	83	150	39	1	28	110	65	11	.283
1B	Tony Perez	19	137	511	74	144	28	3	20	109	54	1	.282
2B	Joe Morgan	44	146	498	107	163	27	6	17	94	132	67	.327
3B	Pete Rose	30	162	662	112	210	47	4	7	74	89	0	.317
SS	Dave Concepcion	19	140	507	62	139	23	1	5	49	39	33	.274
LF	George Foster	21	134	463	71	139	24	4	23	78	40	2	.300
CF	Cesar Geronimo	16	148	501	69	129	25	5	6	53	48	13	.257
RF	Ken Griffey Sr.	18	132	463	95	141	15	9	4	46	67	16	.305
C2	Bill Plummer	4	65	159	17	29	7	0	1	19	24	1	.182
I5	Doug Flynn	4	89	127	17	34	7	0	1	20	11	3	.268
I6	Darrel Chaney	4	71	160	18	35	6	0	2	26	14	3	.219
O4	Merv Rettenmund	5	93	188	24	45	6	1	2	19	35	5	.239
O5	John Vuckovich	1	31	38	4	8	3	0	0	2	4	0	.211
X1	Dan Driessen	8	88	210	38	59	8	1	7	38	35	10	.281
X2	Terry Crowley	1	66	71	8	19	6	0	1	11	7	0	.268

Pos	Player	WS	G	IP	Won–Lost	Pct	H	SO	BB	ERA	CG	Sv
S1	Don Gullett	15	22	160	15–4	.789	127	98	56	2.42	8	0
S2	Gary Nolan	15	32	211	15–9	.625	202	74	29	3.16	5	0
S3	Fred Norman	9	26	188	12–4	.750	163	119	84	3.73	2	0
S4	Jack Billingham	8	33	208	15–10	.600	222	79	76	4.11	5	0
S5	Pat Darcy	7	27	131	11–5	.688	134	46	59	3.58	1	1
RA	Rawly Eastwick	13	58	90	5–3	.625	77	61	25	2.60	0	22
M1	Will McEnaney	10	70	91	5–2	.714	92	48	23	2.47	0	15
M2	Pedro Borbon	10	67	125	9–5	.643	145	29	21	2.95	0	5
M3	Clay Carroll	9	56	96	7–5	.583	93	44	32	2.62	0	7
P1	Clay Kirby	3	26	111	10–6	.625	113	48	54	4.72	1	0
P2	Tom Carroll	1	12	47	4–1	.800	52	14	26	4.98	0	0

1953 Brooklyn Dodgers (105–49)

Pos	Player	WS	G	AB	R	H	2B	3B	HR	RBI	BB	SB	Avg
C	Roy Campanella	33	144	519	103	162	26	3	41	142	67	4	.312
1B	Gil Hodges	25	141	520	101	157	22	7	31	122	75	1	.302
2B	Junior Gilliam	25	151	605	125	168	31	17	6	63	100	21	.278
3B	Billy Cox	12	100	327	44	95	18	1	10	44	37	2	.291
SS	Pee Wee Reese	21	140	524	108	142	25	7	13	61	82	22	.271
LF	Jackie Robinson	25	136	484	109	159	34	7	12	95	74	17	.329
CF	Duke Snider	37	153	590	132	198	38	4	42	126	82	16	.336
RF	Carl Furillo	25	132	479	82	165	38	6	21	92	34	1	.344
C2	Rube Walker	3	43	95	5	23	6	0	3	9	7	0	.242
I5	Bobby Morgan	7	69	196	35	51	6	2	7	33	33	2	.260
O4	Gene Shuba	4	74	169	19	43	12	1	5	23	17	1	.254
O5	Don Thompson	1	96	153	25	37	5	0	1	12	14	2	.242
X1	Wayne Belardi	4	69	163	19	39	3	2	11	34	16	0	.239

Pos	Player	WS	G	IP	Won–Lost	Pct	H	SO	BB	ERA	CG	Sv
S1	Carl Erskine	20	39	247	20–6	.769	213	187	95	3.54	16	3
S2	Russ Meyer	9	34	191	15–5	.750	201	106	63	4.56	10	0
S3	Preacher Roe	9	25	157	11–3	.786	171	85	40	4.36	9	0
S4	Billy Loes	8	32	163	14–8	.636	165	75	53	4.54	9	0
S5	Johnny Podres	7	33	115	9–4	.692	126	82	64	4.23	3	0
RA	Clem Labine	13	37	110	11–6	.647	92	44	30	2.77	0	7
SW	Bob MIlliken	9	37	118	8–4	.667	94	65	42	3.37	3	2
M1	Jim Hughes	9	48	86	4–3	.571	80	49	41	3.47	0	9
M2	Ben Wade	7	32	90	7–5	.583	79	65	33	3.79	0	3
P1	Joe Black	4	34	73	6–3	.667	74	42	27	5.33	0	5

1977 Kansas City Royals (102-60)

Pos	Player	WS	G	AB	R	H	2B	3B	HR	RBI	BB	SB	Avg
C	Darrell Porter	18	130	425	61	117	21	3	16	60	53	1	.275
1B	John Mayberry	14	153	543	73	125	22	1	23	82	83	1	.230
2B	Frank White	12	152	474	59	116	21	5	5	50	25	23	.245
3B	George Brett	29	139	564	105	176	32	13	22	88	55	14	.312
SS	Freddie Patek	15	154	497	72	130	26	6	5	60	41	53	.262
LF	Tom Poquette	11	106	342	43	100	23	6	2	33	19	1	.292
CF	Amos Otis	18	142	478	85	120	20	8	17	78	71	23	.251
RF	Al Cowens	27	162	606	98	189	32	14	23	112	41	16	.312
DH	Hal McRae	25	162	641	104	191	54	11	21	92	59	18	.298
C2	John Wathan	5	55	119	18	39	5	3	2	21	5	2	.328
C3	Buck Martinez	1	29	80	3	18	4	0	1	9	3	0	.225
I5	Cookie Rojas	2	64	156	8	39	9	1	0	10	8	1	.250
I6	Bob Heise	2	54	62	11	16	2	1	0	5	2	0	.258
O4	Joe Zdeb	5	105	195	26	58	5	2	2	23	16	6	.297
O5	Joe Lahoud	3	34	65	8	17	5	0	2	8	11	1	.262
X1	Pete LaCock	6	88	218	25	66	12	1	3	29	15	2	.303
X2	Clint Hurdle	1	9	26	5	8	0	0	2	7	2	0	.308
X3	Willie Wilson	1	13	34	10	11	2	0	0	1	1	6	.324
X4	U L Washington	1	10	20	0	4	1	1	0	1	5	1	.200

Pos	Player	WS	G	IP	Won-Lost	Pct	H	SO	BB	ERA	CG	Sv
S1	Dennis Leonard	24	38	293	20-12	.625	246	244	79	3.04	21	1
S2	Jim Colborn	16	36	239	18-14	.563	233	103	81	3.62	6	0
S3	Paul Splittorff	15	37	229	16-6	.727	243	99	83	3.69	6	0
S4	Andy Hassler	7	29	156	9-6	.600	166	83	75	4.20	3	0
RA	Doug Bird	11	53	118	11-4	.733	120	83	29	3.88	0	14
SW	Marty Pattin	9	31	128	10-3	.769	115	55	37	3.58	4	0
M1	Larry Gura	11	52	106	8-5	.615	108	46	28	3.13	1	10
M2	Mark Littell	10	48	105	8-4	.667	73	106	55	3.61	0	12
P1	Steve Mingori	5	43	64	2-4	.333	59	19	19	3.09	0	4
P2	George Throop	1	4	5	0-0	.000	1	1	4	0.00	0	1
P3	Tom Hall	1	6	8	0-0	.000	4	10	6	3.52	0	0

1989 Oakland Athletics (99-63)

Pos	Player	WS	G	AB	R	H	2B	3B	HR	RBI	BB	SB	Avg
C	Terry Steinbach	14	130	454	37	124	13	1	7	42	30	1	.273
1B	Mark McGwire	20	143	490	74	113	17	0	33	95	83	1	.231
2B	Tony Phillips	14	143	451	48	118	15	6	4	47	58	3	.262
3B	Carney Lansford	21	148	551	81	185	28	2	2	52	51	37	.336
SS	Mike Gallego	12	133	357	45	90	14	2	3	30	35	7	.252
LF	Rickey Henderson	20	88	306	72	90	13	2	9	35	70	52	.294
CF	Dave Henderson	19	152	579	77	145	24	3	15	80	54	8	.250
RF	Jose Canseco	14	65	227	40	61	9	1	17	57	23	6	.269
DH	Dave Parker	15	144	553	56	146	27	0	22	97	38	0	.264
C2	Ron Hassey	6	97	268	29	61	12	0	5	23	24	1	.228
I5	Walt Weiss	7	84	236	30	55	11	0	3	21	21	6	.233
I6	Glenn Hubbard	5	53	131	12	26	6	0	3	12	19	2	.198
O4	Stan Javier	9	112	310	42	77	12	3	1	28	31	12	.248
O5	Luis Polonia	6	59	206	31	59	6	4	1	17	9	13	.286
X1	Lance Blankenship	2	53	131	12	26	6	0	3	12	19	2	.198
X2	Billy Beane	2	37	79	8	19	5	0	0	11	0	3	.241
X3	Felix Jose	1	20	57	3	11	2	0	0	5	4	0	.193

Pos	Player	WS	G	IP	Won-Lost	Pct	H	SO	BB	ERA	CG	Sv
S1	Mike Moore	19	35	242	19–11	.633	193	172	83	2.61	6	0
S2	Dave Stewart	16	36	258	21–9	.700	260	155	69	3.32	8	0
S3	Bob Welch	14	33	210	17–8	.680	191	137	78	3.00	1	0
S4	Storm Davis	7	31	169	19–7	.731	187	91	68	4.36	1	0
S5	Curt Young	4	25	111	5–9	.357	117	55	47	3.73	1	0
RA	Dennis Eckersley	14	51	58	4–0	1.000	32	55	3	1.56	0	33
M1	Todd Burns	11	50	96	8–5	.615	68	49	28	2.24	0	8
M2	Rick Honeycutt	10	64	79	2–2	.500	58	52	26	2.35	0	12
P1	Gene Nelson	6	50	80	3–5	.375	60	70	30	3.26	0	3
P2	Jim Corsi	4	22	38	1–2	.333	26	21	10	1.88	0	0
P3	Eric Plunk	3	23	29	1–1	.500	17	24	12	2.20	0	1
P4	Greg Cadaret	2	26	28	0–0	.000	21	14	19	2.28	0	0

1986 Houston Astros (96–66)

Pos	Player	WS	G	AB	R	H	2B	3B	HR	RBI	BB	SB	Avg
C	Alan Ashby	11	120	315	24	81	15	0	7	38	38	1	.257
1B	Glenn Davis	24	158	574	91	152	32	3	31	101	64	3	.265
2B	Bill Doran	19	145	550	92	152	29	3	6	37	81	42	.276
3B	Denny Walling	19	130	382	54	119	23	1	13	58	36	1	.312
SS	Dickie Thon	8	106	278	24	69	13	1	3	21	29	6	.248
LF	Jose Cruz	17	141	479	48	133	22	4	10	72	55	3	.278
CF	Billy Hatcher	12	127	419	55	108	15	4	6	36	22	38	.258
RF	Kevin Bass	26	157	591	83	184	33	5	20	79	38	22	.311
C2	John Mizerock	3	44	81	9	15	1	1	1	6	24	0	.185
C3	Mark Bailey	3	57	153	9	27	5	0	4	15	28	1	.176
I5	Phil Garner	9	107	313	43	83	14	3	9	41	30	12	.265
I6	Craig Reynolds	7	114	313	32	78	7	3	6	41	12	3	.249
O4	Terry Puhl	3	81	172	17	42	10	0	3	14	15	3	.244
O5	Tony Walker	3	84	90	19	20	7	0	2	10	11	11	.222
X1	Dave Lopes	3	37	98	11	23	2	1	1	13	12	9	.235
X2	Jim Pankovits	3	70	113	12	32	6	1	1	7	11	1	.263
X3	Ty Gainey	3	26	50	6	15	3	1	1	6	6	3	.300
X4	Dan Driessen	1	17	24	5	7	1	0	1	3	5	0	.292

Pos	Player	WS	G	IP	Won–Lost	Pct	H	SO	BB	ERA	CG	Sv
S1	Mike Scott	27	37	275	18–10	.643	182	308	72	2.22	7	0
S2	Bob Knepper	17	40	258	17–12	.586	232	143	62	3.14	8	0
S3	Nolan Ryan	11	30	178	12–8	.600	119	194	82	3.34	1	0
S4	Jim Deshaies	10	26	144	12–5	.706	124	128	59	3.25	1	0
S5	Danny Darwin	5	12	54	5–2	.714	50	40	9	2.32	1	0
RA	Dave Smith	11	54	56	4–7	.364	39	46	22	2.73	0	33
M1	Charlie Kerfeld	12	61	94	11–2	.846	71	77	42	2.59	0	7
M2	Aurelio Lopez	6	45	78	3–3	.500	64	44	25	3.46	0	7
P1	Larry Andersen	5	38	65	2–1	.667	64	33	23	2.78	0	1
P2	Matt Keough	3	10	35	3–2	.600	22	25	18	3.09	0	0
P3	Frank DiPino	3	31	40	1–3	.250	27	27	16	3.57	0	3
P4	Mike Madden	1	13	40	1–2	.333	47	30	22	4.08	0	0
P5	Manny Hernandez	1	9	28	2–3	.400	33	9	12	3.90	0	0
P6	Jeff Calhoun	1	20	27	1–0	1.000	28	14	12	3.71	0	0
P7	Mark Knudson	1	9	43	1–5	.167	48	20	15	4.22	0	0

1964 St. Louis Cardinals (93–69)

Pos	Player	WS	G	AB	R	H	2B	3B	HR	RBI	BB	SB	Avg
C	Tim McCarver	16	143	465	53	134	19	3	9	52	40	2	.288
1B	Bill White	26	160	631	92	191	37	4	21	102	52	7	.303
2B	Julian Javier	11	155	535	66	129	19	5	12	65	30	9	.241
3B	Ken Boyer	28	162	628	100	185	30	10	24	119	70	3	.295
SS	Dick Groat	20	161	636	70	186	35	6	1	70	44	2	.292
LF	Lou Brock	22	103	419	81	146	21	9	12	44	27	33	.348
CF	Curt Flood	25	162	679	97	211	25	3	5	46	43	8	.311
RF	Mike Shannon	7	88	253	30	66	8	2	9	43	19	4	.261
C2	Bob Uecker	2	40	106	8	21	1	0	1	6	17	0	.198
I5	Phil Gagliano	1	40	58	5	15	4	0	1	9	3	0	.259
I6	Jerry Bucheck	1	35	30	7	6	0	2	0	1	3	0	.200
O4	Carl Warwick	4	88	158	14	41	7	1	3	15	11	2	.259
O5	Bob Skinner	3	55	118	10	32	5	0	1	16	11	0	.271
X1	Johnny Lewis	2	40	94	10	22	2	2	2	7	13	2	.234
X2	Charlie James	2	88	233	24	52	9	1	5	17	11	0	.223
X3	Doug Clemens	1	33	78	8	16	4	3	1	9	6	0	.205
X4	Jeoff Long	1	28	43	5	10	1	0	1	4	6	0	.233

Pos	Player	WS	G	IP	Won–Lost	Pct	H	SO	BB	ERA	CG	Sv
S1	Bob Gibson	24	40	287	19-12	.613	250	245	86	3.01	17	1
S2	Curt Simmons	16	34	244	18-9	.667	233	104	49	3.43	12	0
S3	Ray Sadecki	15	37	220	20-11	.645	232	119	60	3.68	9	1
S4	Roger Craig	12	39	166	7-9	.438	180	84	35	3.25	3	5
S5	Ray Washburn	3	15	60	3-4	.429	60	28	17	4.05	0	2
RA	Barney Schultz	10	30	49	1-3	.250	35	29	11	1.64	0	14
SW	Gordie Richardson	5	19	47	4-2	.667	40	28	15	2.30	1	1
M1	Ron Taylor	6	63	101	8-4	.667	109	69	33	4.62	0	7
M2	Bob Humphreys	5	28	43	2-0	1.000	32	36	15	2.53	0	2
P1	Ernie Broglio	4	11	69	3-5	.375	65	36	26	3.50	3	0
P2	Mike Cuellar	3	32	72	5-5	.500	80	56	33	4.50	1	4
P3	Glen Hobbie	2	13	44	1-2	.333	41	18	15	4.28	1	1
P4	Bobby Shantz	1	16	17	1-3	.250	14	12	7	3.12	0	0
P5	Lew Burdette	1	8	10	1-0	1.000	10	3	3	1.80	0	0

1971 San Francisco Giants (90–72)

Pos	Player	WS	G	AB	R	H	2B	3B	HR	RBI	BB	SB	Avg
C	Dick Dietz	19	142	453	58	114	19	0	19	72	97	1	.252
1B	Willie McCovey	16	105	329	45	91	13	0	18	70	64	0	.277
2B	Tito Fuentes	17	152	630	63	172	28	6	4	52	18	12	.273
3B	Alan Gallagher	13	136	429	47	119	18	5	5	57	40	2	.277
SS	Chris Speier	16	157	601	74	141	17	6	8	46	56	4	.235
LF	Ken Henderson	23	141	504	80	133	26	6	15	65	84	18	.264
CF	Willie Mays	27	136	417	82	113	24	5	18	61	112	23	.271
RF	Bobby Bonds	32	155	619	110	178	32	4	33	102	62	26	.288
C2	Fran Healy	3	47	93	10	26	3	0	2	11	15	1	.280
I5	Hal Lanier	3	109	206	21	48	8	0	1	13	15	0	.233
I6	Chris Arnold	1	6	13	2	3	1	0	0	2	3	0	.231
O4	Jimmy Rosario	5	92	192	26	43	6	1	0	13	33	7	.224
O5	George Foster	2	36	105	11	28	5	0	3	8	6	0	.267
X1	Dave Kingman	6	41	115	17	32	10	2	6	24	9	5	.278
X2	Jim Ray Hart	1	31	39	5	10	0	0	2	5	6	0	.256
X3	Jimmy Howarth	1	7	13	3	3	1	0	0	2	3	0	.231

Pos	Player	WS	G	IP	Won–Lost	Pct	H	SO	BB	ERA	CG	Sv
S1	Juan Marichal	18	37	279	18–11	.621	244	159	56	2.94	18	0
S2	Gaylord Perry	17	37	280	16–12	.571	255	158	67	2.76	14	0
S3	John Cumberland	13	45	185	9–6	.600	153	65	55	2.92	5	2
S4	Ron Bryant	5	27	140	7–10	.412	146	79	49	3.79	3	0
S5	Steve Stone	3	24	111	5–9	.357	110	63	55	4.15	2	0
RA	Jerry Johnson	12	67	109	12–9	.571	93	85	48	2.97	0	18
SW	Don Carrithers	3	22	80	5–3	.625	77	41	37	4.03	2	1
M1	Don McMahon	5	61	82	10–6	.625	73	71	37	4.06	0	4
M2	Steve Hamilton	5	39	45	2–2	.500	29	38	11	3.02	0	4
P1	Frank Reberger	2	13	44	3–0	1.000	37	21	19	3.92	0	0
P1	Jim Barr	2	17	35	1–1	.500	33	16	5	3.57	0	0

1978 California Angels (87-75)

Pos	Player	WS	G	AB	R	H	2B	3B	HR	RBI	BB	SB	Avg
C	Brian Downing	18	133	412	42	105	15	0	7	48	52	3	.255
1B	Ron Jackson	14	105	387	49	115	18	6	6	57	16	2	.297
2B	Bobby Grich	20	144	497	68	122	16	2	6	42	75	4	.251
3B	Carney Lansford	17	121	453	63	133	23	2	8	52	31	20	.294
SS	Dave Chalk	10	135	470	42	119	12	0	1	34	38	5	.253
LF	Joe Rudi	14	133	497	58	127	27	1	17	79	28	2	.256
CF	Rick Miller	13	132	475	66	125	25	4	1	37	54	3	.263
RF	Lyman Bostock	19	147	568	74	168	24	4	5	71	59	15	.296
DH	Don Baylor	23	158	591	103	151	28	0	34	99	56	22	.255
C2	Terry Humphrey	3	53	114	11	25	4	1	1	9	6	0	.219
C3	Ike Hampton	1	19	14	2	3	0	1	1	4	2	1	.214
I5	Jim Anderson	2	48	108	6	21	7	0	0	7	11	0	.194
I6	Rance Mulliniks	1	50	119	6	22	3	1	1	6	8	2	.185
O4	Merv Rettenmund	5	50	108	16	29	5	1	1	14	30	0	.269
O5	Ken Landreaux	5	93	260	37	58	7	5	5	23	20	7	.223
X1	Ron Fairly	4	91	235	23	51	5	0	10	40	25	0	.217
X2	Danny Goodwin	3	24	58	9	16	5	0	2	10	10	0	.276
X3	Tony Solaita	2	60	94	10	21	3	0	1	14	16	0	.223
X4	Dave Machemer	1	10	22	6	6	1	0	1	2	2	0	.273

Pos	Player	WS	G	IP	Won–Lost	Pct	H	SO	BB	ERA	CG	Sv
S1	Frank Tanana	14	33	239	18–12	.600	239	137	60	3.65	10	0
S2	Nolan Ryan	12	31	235	10–13	.435	183	260	148	3.72	14	0
S3	Chris Knapp	9	30	188	14–8	.636	178	126	67	4.21	6	0
S4	Don Aase	8	29	179	11–8	.579	185	93	80	4.03	6	0
S5	Dave Frost	7	11	80	5–4	.556	71	30	24	2.58	2	0
RA	Dave LaRoche	14	59	96	10–9	.526	73	70	48	2.82	0	25
SW	Paul Hartzell	10	54	157	6–10	.375	168	55	41	3.44	5	6
M1	Dyar Miller	7	41	85	6–2	.750	85	34	41	2.66	0	1
M2	Tom Griffin	1	24	56	3–4	.429	63	35	31	4.02	0	0
P1	Al Fitzmorris	3	9	32	1–0	1.000	26	8	14	1.71	0	0
P2	Ken Brett	1	31	100	3–5	.375	100	43	42	4.95	1	1

1983 Pittsburgh Pirates (84–78)

Pos	Player	WS	G	AB	R	H	2B	3B	HR	RBI	BB	SB	Avg
C	Tony Pena	21	151	542	51	163	22	3	15	70	31	6	.301
1B	Jason Thompson	17	152	517	70	134	20	1	18	76	99	1	.259
2B	Johnny Ray	20	151	576	68	163	38	7	5	53	35	18	.283
3B	Bill Madlock	17	130	473	68	153	21	0	12	68	49	3	.323
SS	Dale Berra	19	161	537	51	135	25	1	10	52	61	8	.251
LF	Mike Easler	11	115	381	44	117	17	2	10	54	22	4	.307
CF	Marvell Wynne	8	103	366	66	89	16	2	7	26	38	12	.243
RF	Dave Parker	12	144	552	68	154	20	4	12	69	28	12	.279
C2	Steve Nicosia	1	21	46	4	6	2	0	1	1	1	0	.130
I5	Jim Morrison	6	66	158	16	48	7	2	6	25	9	2	.304
O4	Lee Lacy	9	108	288	40	87	12	3	4	13	22	31	.302
O5	Lee Mazzilli	7	109	246	37	59	9	0	5	24	49	15	.240
X1	Richie Hebner	4	78	162	23	43	4	1	5	26	17	8	.265
X2	Doug Frobel	2	32	60	10	17	4	1	3	11	4	1	.283
X3	Brian Harper	1	61	131	16	29	4	1	7	20	2	0	.221
X4	Gene Tenace	1	53	62	7	11	5	0	0	6	12	0	.177

Pos	Player	WS	G	IP	Won–Lost	Pct	H	SO	BB	ERA	CG	Sv
S1	Rick Rhoden	16	36	244	13–13	.500	256	153	68	3.09	7	1
S2	Larry McWilliams	15	35	238	15–8	.652	205	199	87	3.25	8	0
S3	John Candelaria	15	33	198	15–8	.652	191	157	45	3.23	2	0
S4	Lee Tunnell	10	35	178	11–6	.647	167	95	58	3.65	5	0
S5	Jose DeLeon	9	15	108	7–3	.700	75	118	47	2.83	3	0
RA	Kent Tekulve	17	76	99	7–5	.583	78	52	36	1.64	0	18
M1	Cecilio Guante	7	49	100	2–6	.250	90	82	46	3.32	0	9
M2	Manny Sarmiento	6	52	84	3–5	.375	74	49	36	2.99	0	4
P1	Don Robinson	1	6	36	2–2	.500	43	28	21	4.46	0	0

1988 Montreal Expos (81-81)

Pos	Player	WS	G	AB	R	H	2B	3B	HR	RBI	BB	SB	Avg
C	Nelson Santovenia	8	92	309	26	73	20	2	8	41	24	2	.236
1B	Andres Galarraga	25	157	609	99	184	42	8	29	92	39	13	.302
2B	Tom Foley	12	127	377	33	100	21	3	5	43	30	2	.265
3B	Tim Wallach	16	159	592	52	152	32	5	12	69	38	2	.257
SS	Luis Rivera	5	123	371	35	83	17	3	4	30	24	3	.224
LF	Tim Raines	19	109	429	66	116	19	7	12	48	53	33	.270
CF	Otis Nixon	7	90	271	47	66	8	2	0	15	28	46	.244
RF	Hubie Brooks	18	151	588	61	164	35	2	20	90	35	7	.279
C2	Mike Fitzgerald	5	63	155	17	42	6	1	5	23	19	2	.271
C3	Jeff Reed	2	43	123	10	27	3	2	0	9	13	1	.220
I5	Rex Hudler	6	77	216	38	59	14	2	4	14	10	29	.273
I6	Johnny Parades	2	35	91	6	17	2	0	1	10	9	5	.187
O4	Mitch Webster	7	81	259	33	66	5	2	2	13	36	12	.255
O5	Tracy Jones	6	53	141	20	47	5	1	2	15	12	9	.333
X1	Dave Martinez	5	63	191	24	49	3	5	2	12	17	16	.257
X2	Herm Winningham	2	47	90	10	21	2	1	0	6	12	4	.233
X3	Casey Candaele	2	36	116	9	20	5	1	0	4	10	1	.172
X4	Wallace Johnson	1	86	94	7	29	5	1	0	3	12	0	.309
X5	Jeff Huson	1	20	42	7	13	2	0	0	3	4	2	.310
X6	Tom O'Malley	1	34	37	4	8	3	0	0	1	5	0	.216
X7	Wilfredo Tejada	1	8	15	1	4	2	0	0	2	0	0	.267

Pos	Player	WS	G	IP	Won–Lost	Pct	H	SO	BB	ERA	CG	Sv
S1	Dennis Martinez	15	34	235	15–13	.536	215	120	55	2.72	9	0
S2	Pascual Perez	14	27	188	12–8	.600	133	131	44	2.44	4	0
S3	Bryn Smith	11	32	198	12–10	.545	179	122	32	3.00	1	0
S4	John Dopson	7	26	169	3–11	.214	150	101	58	3.04	1	0
S5	Brian Holman	5	18	100	4–8	.333	101	58	34	3.23	1	0
RA	Tim Burke	7	61	82	3–5	.375	84	42	25	3.40	0	18
M1	Jeff Parrett	10	61	92	12–4	.750	66	62	45	2.65	0	6
M2	Andy McGaffigan	9	63	91	6–0	1.000	81	71	37	2.76	0	4
P1	Joe Hesketh	7	60	73	4–3	.571	63	64	35	2.85	0	9
P2	Floyd Youmans	4	14	84	3–6	.333	64	54	41	3.21	1	0
P3	Randy Johnson	2	4	26	3–0	1.000	23	25	7	2.42	1	0
P4	Mike Smith	1	5	9	0–0	.000	6	4	5	3.12	0	1

1989 Milwaukee Brewers (81-81)

Pos	Player	WS	G	AB	R	H	2B	3B	HR	RBI	BB	SB	Avg
C	B. J. Surhoff	8	126	436	42	108	17	4	5	55	25	14	.248
1B	Greg Brock	10	107	373	40	99	16	0	12	52	43	6	.265
2B	Jim Gantner	13	116	409	51	112	18	3	0	34	21	20	.274
3B	Paul Molitor	27	155	615	84	194	35	4	11	56	64	27	.315
SS	Bill Spiers	8	114	345	44	88	9	3	4	33	21	10	.255
LF	Glenn Braggs	10	144	514	77	127	12	3	15	66	42	17	.247
CF	Robin Yount	34	160	614	101	195	38	9	21	103	63	19	.318
RF	Rob Deer	12	130	466	72	98	18	2	26	65	60	4	.210
DH	Joey Meyer	3	53	147	13	33	6	0	7	29	12	1	.224
C2	Charlie O'Brien	9	62	188	22	44	10	0	6	35	21	0	.234
I5	Gary Sheffield	6	95	368	34	91	18	0	5	32	27	10	.247
I6	Gus Polidor	2	79	175	15	34	7	0	0	14	6	3	.194
O4	Greg Vaughn	6	38	113	18	30	3	0	5	23	13	4	.265
O5	Mike Felder	6	117	315	50	76	11	3	3	23	23	26	.241
X1	Terry Francona	3	90	233	26	54	10	1	3	23	8	2	.232
X2	Dave Engle	1	27	65	5	14	3	0	2	8	4	0	.215
X3	George Canale	1	13	26	5	5	1	0	1	3	2	0	.192

Pos	Player	WS	G	IP	Won-Lost	Pct	H	SO	BB	ERA	CG	Sv
S1	Chris Bosio	17	33	235	15-10	.600	225	173	48	2.95	8	0
S2	Teddy Higuera	9	22	135	9-6	.600	125	91	48	3.46	2	0
S3	Jamie Navarro	7	19	110	7-8	.467	119	56	32	3.12	1	0
S4	Tom Filer	5	13	72	7-3	.700	74	20	23	3.61	0	0
S5	Don August	2	31	142	12-12	.500	175	51	58	5.31	2	0
RA	Dan Plesac	11	52	61	3-4	.429	47	52	17	2.35	0	33
SW	Mark Knudson	8	40	124	8-5	.615	110	47	29	3.35	1	0
M1	Chuck Crim	11	76	118	9-7	.563	114	59	36	2.83	0	7
M2	Tony Fossas	4	51	61	2-2	.500	57	42	22	3.54	0	1
P1	Bill Krueger	5	34	94	3-2	.600	96	72	33	3.84	5	3
P2	Bryan Clutterbuck	2	14	67	2-5	.286	73	29	16	4.14	1	0
P3	Jay Aldrich	2	16	26	1-0	1.000	24	12	13	3.81	0	1
P4	Jeff Peterek	1	7	31	0-2	.000	31	16	14	4.02	0	0

1996 Minnesota Twins (78-84)

Pos	Player	WS	G	AB	R	H	2B	3B	HR	RBI	BB	SB	Avg
C	Greg Myers	6	97	329	37	94	22	3	6	47	19	0	.286
1B	Scott Stahoviak	12	130	405	72	115	30	3	13	61	59	3	.284
2B	Chuck Knoblauch	32	153	578	140	197	35	14	13	72	98	45	.341
3B	Dave Hollins	11	121	422	71	102	26	0	13	53	71	6	.242
SS	Pat Meares	8	152	517	66	138	26	7	8	67	17	9	.267
LF	Marty Cordova	18	145	569	97	176	46	1	16	111	53	11	.309
CF	Rich Becker	20	148	525	92	153	31	4	12	71	68	19	.291
RF	Roberto Kelly	9	98	322	41	104	17	4	6	47	23	10	.323
DH	Paul Molitor	18	161	660	99	225	41	8	9	113	56	18	.341
C2	Matt Walbeck	3	63	215	25	48	10	0	2	24	9	3	.223
C3	Mike Durant	1	40	81	15	17	3	0	0	5	10	3	.210
I5	Jeff Reboulet	2	107	234	20	52	9	0	0	23	25	4	.222
I6	Chip Hale	2	85	87	8	24	5	0	1	16	10	0	.276
O4	Matt Lawton	7	79	252	34	65	7	1	6	42	28	4	.258
X1	Ron Coomer	5	95	233	34	69	12	1	12	41	17	3	.296
X2	Denny Hocking	1	49	127	16	25	6	0	1	10	8	3	.197
X3	Todd Walker	1	25	82	8	21	6	0	0	6	4	2	.256

Pos	Player	WS	G	IP	Won–Lost	Pct	H	SO	BB	ERA	CG	Sv
S1	Brad Radke	14	35	232	11–16	.407	231	148	57	4.46	3	0
S2	Frank Rodriguez	11	38	207	13–14	.481	218	110	78	5.05	3	2
S3	Rich Robertson	8	36	186	7–17	.292	197	114	116	5.12	5	0
S4	Scott Aldred	6	25	122	6–5	.545	134	75	42	5.09	0	0
S5	Rick Aguilera	6	19	111	8–6	.571	124	83	27	5.42	2	0
RA	Dave Stevens	6	49	58	3–3	.500	58	29	25	4.66	0	11
M1	Mike Trombley	9	43	69	5–1	.833	61	57	25	3.01	0	6
M2	Eddie Guardado	6	83	74	6–5	.545	61	74	33	5.25	0	4
P1	Dan Naulty	6	49	57	3–2	.600	43	56	35	3.79	0	4
P2	Greg Hansell	4	50	74	3–0	1.000	83	46	31	5.69	0	3
P3	Jose Parra	2	27	70	5–5	.500	88	50	27	6.04	0	0

1967 Cleveland Indians (75-87)

Pos	Player	WS	G	AB	R	H	2B	3B	HR	RBI	BB	SB	Avg
C	Jose Azcue	13	86	295	33	74	12	5	11	34	22	0	.251
1B	Tony Horton	12	106	363	35	102	13	4	10	44	18	3	.281
2B	Vern Fuller	7	73	206	18	46	10	0	7	21	19	2	.223
3B	Max Alvis	17	161	637	66	163	23	4	21	70	38	3	.256
SS	Larry Brown	14	152	485	38	110	16	2	7	37	53	4	.227
LF	Leon Wagner	12	135	453	56	105	15	1	15	54	37	3	.242
CF	Vic Davalillo	9	139	359	47	103	17	5	2	22	10	6	.287
RF	Chuck Hinton	11	147	498	55	122	19	3	10	37	43	6	.245
C2	Duke Sims	10	88	272	25	55	8	2	12	37	30	3	.202
I5	Chico Salmon	5	90	203	19	46	13	1	2	19	17	10	.227
I6	Pedro Gonzalez	2	80	189	19	43	6	0	1	8	12	4	.228
O4	Lee Maye	11	115	297	43	77	20	4	9	27	26	3	.259
O5	Rocky Colavito	5	63	191	10	46	9	0	5	21	24	2	.241
X1	Fred Whitfield	5	100	257	24	58	10	0	9	31	25	3	.218
X2	Richie Scheinblum	3	18	66	8	21	4	2	0	6	5	0	.318
X3	Don Demeter	2	51	121	15	25	4	0	5	12	6	0	.207
X4	Gus Gil	1	51	96	11	11	4	0	0	5	9	0	.115

Pos	Player	WS	G	IP	Won-Lost	Pct	H	SO	BB	ERA	CG	Sv
S1	Luis Tiant	17	33	214	12-9	.571	177	219	67	2.74	9	2
S2	Steve Hargan	16	30	223	14-13	.519	180	141	72	2.62	15	0
S3	Sonny Siebert	15	34	185	10-12	.455	136	136	54	2.38	7	4
S4	Sam McDowell	8	37	236	13-15	.464	201	236	123	3.85	10	0
S5	John O'Donoghue	7	33	131	8-9	.471	120	81	33	3.24	5	2
RA	Orlando Pena	6	48	88	0-3	.000	67	72	22	3.36	0	8
SW	Stan Williams	6	16	79	6-4	.600	64	75	24	2.62	2	1
M1	George Culver	4	53	75	7-3	.700	71	41	31	3.96	0	3
M2	Bob Allen	3	47	54	0-5	.000	49	50	25	2.98	0	5
P1	Steve Bailey	2	32	65	2-5	.286	62	46	42	3.90	0	2
P2	Gary Bell	1	9	61	1-5	.167	50	39	24	3.71	1	0
P3	Bobby Tiefenauer	1	5	11	0-1	.000	9	6	3	0.79	0	0

1986 Chicago White Sox (72-90)

Pos	Player	WS	G	AB	R	H	2B	3B	HR	RBI	BB	SB	Avg
C	Carlton Fisk	6	125	457	42	101	11	0	14	63	22	2	.221
1B	Greg Walker	10	78	282	37	78	10	6	13	51	29	1	.277
2B	Julio Cruz	4	81	209	38	45	2	0	0	19	42	7	.215
3B	Tim Hulett	8	150	520	53	120	16	5	17	44	21	4	.231
SS	Ozzie Guillen	9	159	547	58	137	19	4	2	47	12	8	.250
LF	Darryl Boston	7	56	199	29	53	11	3	5	22	21	9	.266
CF	John Cangelosi	11	137	438	65	103	16	3	2	32	71	50	.235
RF	Harold Baines	19	145	570	72	169	29	2	21	88	38	2	.296
DH	Ron Kittle	5	86	296	34	63	11	0	17	48	28	2	.213
C2	Ron Hassey	7	49	150	22	53	11	1	3	20	22	0	.353
C3	Ron Karkovice	4	37	97	13	24	7	0	4	13	9	1	.247
I5	Wayne Tolleson	7	81	260	39	65	7	3	3	29	38	13	.250
I6	Jack Perconte	1	24	73	6	16	1	0	0	4	11	2	.219
O4	Bobby Bonilla	7	75	234	27	63	10	2	2	26	33	4	.269
O5	Reid Nichols	2	74	136	9	31	4	0	2	18	11	5	.228
X1	Jerry Hairston	5	101	225	32	61	15	0	5	26	26	0	.271
X2	Russ Morman	3	49	159	18	40	5	0	4	17	16	1	.252
X3	Joel Skinner	3	60	149	17	30	5	1	4	20	9	1	.201
X4	Steve Lyons	1	42	123	10	25	2	1	0	6	7	2	.203
X5	Ivan Calderon	1	13	33	3	10	2	1	0	2	3	0	.303
X6	Marc Hill	1	22	19	2	3	0	0	0	1	3	0	.158
X7	Bryan Little	1	20	35	3	6	1	0	0	2	4	0	.171

Pos	Player	WS	G	IP	Won–Lost	Pct	H	SO	BB	ERA	CG	Sv
S1	Floyd Bannister	11	28	165	10–14	.417	162	92	48	3.54	6	0
S2	Joe Cowley	10	27	162	11–11	.500	133	132	83	3.88	4	0
S3	Neil Allen	8	22	113	7–2	.778	101	57	38	3.82	2	0
S4	Jose DeLeon	7	13	79	4–5	.444	49	68	42	2.96	1	0
S5	Richard Dotson	4	34	197	10–17	.370	226	110	69	5.48	3	0
RA	Bob James	4	49	58	5–4	.556	61	32	23	5.25	0	14
M1	Gene Nelson	9	54	115	6–6	.500	118	70	41	3.85	0	6
M2	Dave Schmidt	8	49	92	3–6	.333	94	67	27	3.31	0	8
P1	Bill Dawley	7	46	98	0–7	.000	91	66	28	3.32	0	2
P2	Bobby Thigpen	7	20	36	2–0	1.000	26	20	12	1.77	0	7
P3	Steve Carlton	4	10	63	4–3	.571	58	40	25	3.69	0	0
P4	Ray Searage	4	29	29	1–0	1.000	15	26	19	0.62	0	0
P5	Joel McKeon	4	30	33	3–1	.750	18	18	17	2.45	0	1
P6	Joel Davis	4	19	105	4–5	.444	115	54	51	4.70	1	0
P7	Tom Seaver	3	12	72	2–6	.250	66	31	27	4.38	1	0

1999 Tampa Bay Devil Rays (69–93)

Pos	Player	WS	G	AB	R	H	2B	3B	HR	RBI	BB	SB	Avg
C	John Flaherty	12	117	446	53	124	19	0	14	71	19	0	.278
1B	Fred McGriff	24	144	529	75	164	30	1	32	104	86	1	.310
2B	Miguel Cairo	10	120	465	61	137	15	5	3	36	24	22	.295
3B	Wade Boggs	6	90	292	40	88	14	1	2	29	38	1	.301
SS	Kevin Stocker	7	79	254	39	76	11	2	1	27	24	9	.299
LF	Bubba Trammell	9	82	283	49	82	19	0	14	39	43	0	.290
CF	Randy Winn	3	79	303	44	81	16	4	2	24	17	9	.267
RF	Dave Martinez	13	143	514	79	146	25	5	6	66	60	13	.284
DH	Jose Canseco	12	113	430	75	120	18	1	34	95	58	3	.279
C2	Mike DiFelice	8	51	179	21	55	11	0	6	27	8	0	.307
I5	Tony Graffanino	7	39	130	20	41	9	4	2	19	9	3	.315
I6	Aaron Ledesma	3	93	294	32	78	15	0	0	30	14	1	.265
O4	Paul Sorrento	7	99	294	40	69	14	1	11	42	49	1	.235
O5	Terrell Lowery	3	66	185	25	48	15	1	2	17	19	0	.259
X1	Herb Perry	4	66	209	29	53	10	1	6	32	16	0	.254
X2	Quinton McCracken	2	40	148	20	37	6	1	1	18	14	6	.250
X3	Bobby Smith	2	68	199	18	36	4	1	3	19	16	4	.181
X4	David Lamb	1	55	124	18	28	5	1	1	13	10	0	.226
X5	Jose Guillen	1	47	168	24	41	10	0	2	13	10	0	.244

Pos	Player	WS	G	IP	Won–Lost	Pct	H	SO	BB	ERA	CG	Sv
S1	Wilson Alvarez	10	28	160	9–9	.500	159	128	79	4.22	1	0
S2	Ryan Rupe	8	24	142	8–9	.471	136	97	57	4.55	0	0
S3	Rolando Arrojo	6	24	141	7–12	.368	162	107	60	5.18	2	0
S4	Bobby Witt	5	32	180	7–15	.318	213	123	96	5.84	3	0
S5	Dave Eiland	2	21	80	4–8	.333	98	53	27	5.60	0	0
RA	Roberto Hernandez	14	72	73	2–3	.400	68	69	33	3.07	0	43
SW	Bryan Rekar	3	27	95	6–6	.500	121	55	41	5.80	0	0
M1	Rick White	7	63	108	5–3	.625	132	81	38	4.08	0	0
M2	Albie Lopez	4	51	64	3–2	.600	66	37	24	4.64	0	1
P1	Norm Charlton	3	42	51	2–3	.400	49	45	36	4.44	0	0
P2	Mike Duvall	3	40	40	1–1	.500	46	18	27	4.05	0	0
P3	Jim Mecir	2	20	23	1–1	.500	20	16	20	5.79	0	0
P4	Esteban Yan	2	50	61	3–4	.429	77	46	32	5.90	0	0
P5	Scott Aldred	2	37	24	3–2	.600	26	22	14	5.18	0	0
P6	Dan Wheeler	1	6	31	0–4	.000	35	32	13	5.87	0	0
P7	Jeff Sparks	1	8	10	0–0	.000	6	17	12	5.40	0	1

1963 Houston Astros (66-96)

Pos	Player	WS	G	AB	R	H	2B	3B	HR	RBI	BB	SB	Avg
C	John Bateman	6	128	404	23	85	8	6	10	59	13	0	.210
1B	Rusty Staub	12	150	513	43	115	17	4	6	45	59	0	.224
2B	Johnny Temple	12	100	322	22	85	12	1	1	17	41	7	.264
3B	Bob Aspromonte	7	136	468	42	100	9	5	8	49	40	3	.214
SS	Bob Lillis	6	147	469	31	93	13	1	1	19	15	3	.198
LF	Al Spangler	18	120	430	52	121	25	4	4	27	50	5	.281
CF	Jimmy Wynn	9	70	250	31	61	10	5	4	27	30	4	.244
RF	Carl Warwick	15	150	528	49	134	19	5	7	47	49	3	.254
C2	Jim Campbell	2	55	158	9	35	3	0	4	19	10	0	.222
I5	Ernie Fazio	3	102	228	31	42	10	3	2	5	27	4	.184
I6	J C Hartman	1	39	90	2	11	1	0	0	3	2	1	.122
O4	Howie Goss	8	133	411	37	86	18	2	9	44	31	4	.209
O5	Johnny Weekly	2	34	80	4	18	3	0	3	14	7	0	.225
X1	Pete Runnels	9	124	388	35	98	9	1	2	23	45	2	.253
X2	John Paciorek	1	1	3	4	3	0	0	0	3	2	0	1.000
X3	Joe Morgan	1	8	25	5	6	0	1	0	3	5	1	.240
X4	Carroll Hardy	1	15	44	5	10	3	0	0	3	3	1	.227

Pos	Player	WS	G	IP	Won-Lost	Pct	H	SO	BB	ERA	CG	Sv
S1	Turk Farrell	15	34	202	14–13	.519	161	141	35	3.02	12	1
S2	Ken Johnson	15	37	224	11–17	.393	204	148	50	2.65	6	1
S3	Don Nottebart	12	31	193	11–8	.579	170	118	39	3.17	9	0
S4	Bob Bruce	8	30	170	5–9	.357	162	123	60	3.59	1	0
S5	Hal Brown	7	26	141	5–11	.313	137	68	8	3.31	6	0
RA	Hal Woodeshick	17	55	114	11–9	.550	75	94	42	1.97	0	10
M1	Jim Umbricht	7	35	76	4–3	.571	52	48	21	2.61	0	0
M2	Don McMahon	3	49	80	1–5	.167	83	51	26	4.07	0	5
P1	Joe Hoerner	1	1	3	0–0	.000	2	2	0	0.00	0	0

1969 Philadelphia Phillies (63-99)

Pos	Player	WS	G	AB	R	H	2B	3B	HR	RBI	BB	SB	Avg
C	Mike Ryan	7	133	446	41	91	17	2	12	44	30	1	.204
1B	Dick Allen	22	118	438	75	126	23	3	32	89	64	9	.288
2B	Cookie Rojas	3	110	391	35	89	11	1	4	30	23	1	.228
3B	Tony Taylor	12	138	557	68	146	24	5	3	30	42	19	.262
SS	Don Money	10	127	450	41	103	22	2	6	42	43	1	.229
LF	Deron Johnson	14	138	475	51	121	19	4	17	80	60	4	.255
CF	Larry Hisle	18	145	482	75	128	23	5	20	56	48	18	.266
RF	Johnny Callison	17	134	495	66	131	29	5	16	64	49	2	.265
C2	Dave Watkins	2	69	148	17	26	2	1	4	12	22	2	.176
I5	Terry Harmon	5	87	201	25	48	8	1	0	16	22	1	.239
O4	Johnny Briggs	12	124	361	51	86	20	3	12	46	64	9	.238
O5	Ron Stone	3	103	222	22	53	7	1	1	24	29	3	.239
X1	Rick Joseph	7	99	264	35	72	15	0	6	37	22	2	.273

Pos	Player	WS	G	IP	Won-Lost	Pct	H	SO	BB	ERA	CG	Sv
S1	Rick Wise	15	33	220	15-13	.536	215	144	61	3.23	14	0
S2	Grant Jackson	14	38	253	14-18	.438	237	180	92	3.34	13	1
S3	Woodie Fryman	6	36	228	12-15	.444	243	150	89	4.41	10	0
S4	Jerry Johnson	5	33	147	6-13	.316	151	82	57	4.28	4	1
S5	Billy Champion	2	23	117	5-10	.333	130	70	63	5.01	4	1
RA	Billy Wilson	4	37	62	2-5	.286	53	48	36	3.32	0	6
SW	Lowell Palmer	1	26	90	2-8	.200	91	68	47	5.20	1	0
M1	Turk Farrell	4	46	74	3-4	.429	92	40	27	4.00	0	3
M2	John Boozer	3	46	82	1-2	.333	91	47	36	4.28	0	6
P1	Al Raffo	3	45	72	1-3	.250	81	38	25	4.11	0	1

1983 Seattle Mariners (60-102)

Pos	Player	WS	G	AB	R	H	2B	3B	HR	RBI	BB	SB	Avg
C	Rick Sweet	3	93	249	18	55	9	0	1	22	13	2	.221
1B	Pat Putnam	12	144	469	58	126	23	2	19	67	39	2	.269
2B	Tony Bernazard	9	80	300	35	80	18	1	6	30	38	21	.267
3B	Todd Cruz	3	65	216	21	41	4	2	7	21	7	1	.190
SS	Spike Owen	3	80	306	36	60	11	3	2	21	24	10	.196
LF	Ron Roenecke	7	59	198	23	50	12	0	4	23	33	6	.253
CF	Dave Henderson	13	137	484	50	130	24	5	17	55	28	9	.269
RF	Steve Henderson	12	121	436	50	128	32	3	10	54	44	10	.294
DH	Richie Zisk	5	90	285	30	69	12	0	12	36	30	0	.242
C2	Orlando Mercado	3	66	178	10	35	11	2	1	16	14	2	.197
C3	Jamie Nelson	2	40	96	9	21	3	0	1	5	13	4	.219
I5	Julio Cruz	6	61	181	24	46	10	1	2	12	20	33	.254
I6	Domingo Ramos	3	53	127	14	36	4	0	2	10	7	3	.283
O4	Rickey Nelson	4	98	291	32	74	13	3	5	36	17	7	.254
O5	Al Cowens	1	110	356	39	73	19	2	7	35	23	10	.205
X1	Ken Phelps	3	50	127	10	30	4	1	7	16	13	0	.236
X2	Jamie Allen	3	86	273	23	61	10	0	4	21	33	6	.223
X3	Phil Bradley	1	23	67	8	18	2	0	0	5	8	3	.269
X4	Al Chambers	1	31	67	11	14	3	0	1	7	18	0	.209
X5	Manny Castillo	1	91	203	13	42	6	3	0	24	7	1	.207
X6	John Moses	1	93	130	19	27	4	1	0	6	12	11	.208
X7	Darnell Coles	1	27	92	9	26	7	0	1	6	7	0	.283
X8	Harold Reynolds	1	20	59	8	12	4	1	0	1	2	0	.203

Pos	Player	WS	G	IP	Won–Lost	Pct	H	SO	BB	ERA	CG	Sv
S1	Matt Young	16	33	204	11–15	.423	178	130	79	3.27	5	0
S2	Jim Beattie	13	30	197	10–15	.400	197	132	66	3.84	8	0
S3	Bob Stoddard	8	35	176	9–17	.346	182	87	58	4.41	2	0
S4	Mike Moore	5	22	128	6–8	.429	130	108	60	4.71	3	0
S5	Glenn Abbott	4	14	82	5–3	.625	116	42	23	4.94	2	0
RA	Bill Caudill	6	63	73	2–8	.200	70	73	38	4.71	0	26
SW	Bryan Clark	9	41	162	7–10	.412	160	76	72	3.91	2	0
M1	Mike Stanton	6	50	65	2–3	.400	65	47	28	3.32	0	7
M2	Roy Thomas	6	43	89	3–1	.750	95	77	32	3.45	0	1
P1	Ed VandeBerg	5	68	64	2–4	.333	59	49	22	3.36	0	5
P2	Gaylord Perry	3	16	102	3–10	.231	116	42	23	4.94	2	0
P3	Edwin Nunuez	1	14	37	0–4	.000	40	35	22	4.38	0	0

1973 Texas Rangers (57–105)

Pos	Player	WS	G	AB	R	H	2B	3B	HR	RBI	BB	SB	Avg
C	Ken Suarez	6	93	278	25	69	11	0	1	27	33	1	.248
1B	Jim Spencer	8	102	352	35	94	12	3	4	43	34	0	.267
2B	Dave Nelson	15	142	576	71	165	24	4	7	48	34	43	.286
3B	Bill Sudakis	8	82	235	32	60	11	0	15	43	23	0	.255
SS	Toby Harrah	13	118	461	64	120	16	1	10	50	46	10	.260
LF	Elliott Maddox	3	100	172	24	41	1	0	1	17	29	5	.238
CF	Vic Harris	10	152	555	71	138	14	7	8	44	55	13	.249
RF	Jeff Burroughs	22	151	526	71	147	17	1	30	85	67	0	.279
DH	Alex Johnson	12	158	624	62	179	26	3	8	68	32	10	.287
C2	Dick Billings	2	81	280	17	50	11	0	3	32	20	1	.179
I5	Jim Fregosi	5	45	157	25	42	6	2	6	16	12	0	.268
I6	Jim Mason	4	92	238	23	49	7	2	3	19	23	0	.206
O4	Tom Grieve	5	66	123	22	38	6	0	7	21	7	1	.309
O5	Rico Carty	3	86	308	24	71	12	0	3	33	36	2	.232
X1	Bill Madlock	4	21	77	16	27	5	3	1	5	7	3	.351
X2	Larry Biitner	4	83	258	19	65	8	2	1	12	20	1	.252
X3	Mike Epstein	1	27	85	9	16	3	0	1	6	14	0	.188
X4	Pete Mackanin	1	44	90	3	9	2	0	0	2	4	0	.100

Pos	Player	WS	G	IP	Won–Lost	Pct	H	SO	BB	ERA	CG	Sv
S1	Jim Bibby	10	26	180	9–10	.474	121	155	106	3.24	11	1
S2	Jim Merritt	6	35	160	5–13	.278	191	65	34	4.05	8	1
S3	Sonny Siebert	5	25	120	7–11	.389	120	76	37	3.99	1	2
S4	Mike Paul	2	36	87	5–4	.556	104	49	36	4.95	1	2
S5	Pete Broberg	2	22	119	5–9	.357	130	57	66	5.61	1	0
RA	Steve Foucault	3	32	56	2–4	.333	54	28	31	3.88	0	8
SW	Bill Gogolewski	5	49	124	3–6	.333	139	77	48	4.22	0	6
M1	Jackie Brown	3	25	67	5–5	.500	82	45	25	3.92	2	2
M2	Charlie Hudson	2	25	62	4–2	.667	59	34	31	4.62	1	1
P1	Rick Henninger	2	6	23	1–0	1.000	23	6	11	2.74	0	0
P2	Don Stanhouse	1	21	70	1–7	.125	70	42	44	4.76	1	1
P3	David Clyde	1	18	93	4–8	.333	106	74	54	5.01	0	0
P4	Dick Bosman	1	7	40	2–5	.286	42	14	17	4.24	1	0
P5	Steve Dunning	1	23	94	2–6	.250	101	38	52	5.34	2	0
P6	Rich Hand	1	8	42	2–3	.400	49	14	19	5.40	1	0

1979 Oakland A's (54-108)

Pos	Player	WS	G	AB	R	H	2B	3B	HR	RBI	BB	SB	Avg
C	Jeff Newman	12	143	516	53	119	17	2	22	71	27	2	.231
1B	Dave Revering	18	125	472	63	136	25	5	19	77	34	1	.288
2B	Mike Edwards	2	122	400	35	93	12	2	1	23	15	10	.233
3B	Wayne Gross	13	138	442	54	99	19	1	14	50	72	4	.224
SS	Rob Picciolo	4	115	348	37	88	16	2	2	27	3	2	.253
LF	Rickey Henderson	10	89	351	49	96	13	3	1	26	34	33	.274
CF	Dwayne Murphy	16	121	388	57	98	10	4	11	40	84	15	.255
RF	Tony Armas	7	80	278	29	69	9	3	11	34	16	1	.248
DH	Mitchell Page	8	133	478	51	118	11	2	9	42	52	17	.247
C2	Jim Essian	9	98	313	34	76	16	0	8	40	25	0	.243
I5	Dave Chalk	3	66	212	15	47	8	0	2	13	29	2	.222
I6	Mike Guerrero	1	46	166	12	38	5	0	0	18	6	0	.229
O4	Mike Heath	4	74	258	19	66	8	0	3	27	17	1	.256
O5	Larry Murray	1	105	226	25	42	11	2	2	20	28	6	.186

Pos	Player	WS	G	IP	Won–Lost	Pct	H	SO	BB	ERA	CG	Sv
S1	Rick Langford	12	34	219	12–16	.429	233	101	57	4.28	14	0
S2	Steve McCatty	10	31	186	11–12	.478	207	87	80	4.22	8	0
S3	Brian Kingman	7	18	113	8–7	.533	113	58	33	4.31	5	0
S4	Mike Norris	5	29	146	5–8	.385	146	96	94	4.80	3	0
S5	J. H. Johnson	4	14	85	2–8	.250	97	40	42	4.36	1	0
RA	Dave Heaverlo	6	62	86	4–11	.267	97	40	42	4.20	0	9
SW	Dave Hamilton	6	40	83	3–4	.429	80	52	43	3.70	1	5
P1	Matt Keough	3	30	177	2–17	.105	220	95	78	5.04	7	0
P2	Craig Minetto	1	36	118	1–5	.167	131	64	58	5.55	0	0

1969 San Diego Padres (52–110)

Pos	Player	WS	G	AB	R	H	2B	3B	HR	RBI	BB	SB	Avg
C	Chris Cannizzaro	5	134	418	23	92	14	3	4	33	42	0	.220
1B	Nate Colbert	16	139	483	64	123	20	9	24	66	45	6	.255
2B	Jose Arcia	2	120	302	35	65	11	3	0	10	14	14	.215
3B	Ed Spiezio	9	121	355	29	83	9	0	13	43	38	1	.234
SS	Roberto Pena	7	139	472	44	118	16	3	4	30	21	0	.250
LF	Al Ferrara	12	138	366	39	95	22	1	14	56	45	0	.260
CF	Cito Gaston	4	129	391	20	90	11	7	2	28	24	4	.230
RF	Ollie Brown	15	151	568	76	150	18	3	20	61	44	10	.264
C2	Walt Hriniak	1	31	66	4	15	0	0	0	1	8	0	.227
I5	Van Kelly	3	73	209	18	51	7	1	3	15	12	0	.244
I6	Tommy Dean	2	101	273	14	48	9	2	2	9	27	0	.176
O4	Ivan Murrell	5	111	247	19	63	10	6	3	25	11	3	.255
O5	Tony Gonzalez	3	53	182	17	41	4	0	2	8	19	1	.225
X1	John Sipin	2	68	229	22	51	7	1	3	15	12	0	.244
X2	Larry Stahl	2	95	162	10	32	6	2	3	10	17	3	.198
X3	Ron Slocum	1	13	24	6	7	1	0	1	5	0	0	.292
X4	Jim Williams	1	13	25	4	7	1	0	0	2	3	0	.280

Pos	Player	WS	G	IP	Won–Lost	Pct	H	SO	BB	ERA	CG	Sv
S1	Joe Niekro	12	37	202	8–17	.320	213	55	45	3.70	8	0
S2	Clay Kirby	10	35	216	7–20	.259	204	113	100	3.80	2	0
S3	Al Santorini	8	32	185	8–14	.364	194	111	73	3.95	2	0
S4	Dick Kelley	8	27	136	4–8	.333	113	96	61	3.57	1	0
S5	Johnny Podres	3	17	65	5–6	.455	66	17	28	4.31	0	0
RA	Frank Reberger	7	67	88	1–2	.333	83	65	41	3.59	0	6
M1	Jack Baldschun	4	61	77	7–2	.778	90	67	29	4.79	0	1
M2	Billy McCool	3	54	59	3–5	.375	59	35	42	4.30	0	7
SW	Gary Ross	4	48	110	3–12	.200	104	58	58	4.19	0	3
P1	Tommie Sisk	4	53	143	2–13	.154	160	59	48	4.78	1	6
P2	Dick Selma	2	4	22	2–2	.500	19	20	9	4.09	1	0
P3	Dave Roberts	1	22	49	0–3	.000	65	19	19	4.81	0	1

1962 New York Mets (40-120)

Pos	Player	WS	G	AB	R	H	2B	3B	HR	RBI	BB	SB	Avg
C	Choo Choo Coleman	3	55	152	24	38	7	2	6	17	11	2	.250
1B	Marv Throneberry	5	116	357	29	87	11	3	16	49	34	1	.244
2B	Charlie Neal	7	136	508	59	132	14	9	11	58	56	2	.260
3B	Felix Mantilla	8	141	466	54	128	17	4	11	59	37	3	.275
SS	Elio Chacon	5	118	368	49	87	10	3	2	27	76	12	.236
LF	Frank Thomas	12	156	571	69	152	23	3	34	94	48	2	.266
CF	Richie Ashburn	11	135	389	60	119	7	3	7	28	81	12	.306
RF	Jim Hickman	7	140	392	54	96	18	2	13	46	47	4	.245
C2	Sammy Taylor	2	68	158	12	35	4	2	3	20	23	0	.222
C3	Chris Cannizzaro	2	58	133	9	32	2	1	0	9	19	1	.241
I5	Rod Kanehl	3	133	351	52	87	10	2	4	27	23	8	.248
I6	Cliff Cook	1	40	112	12	26	6	1	2	9	4	1	.232
O4	Joe Christopher	5	119	271	36	66	10	2	6	32	35	11	.244
O5	Gene Woodling	4	81	190	18	52	8	1	5	24	24	0	.274
X1	Gil Hodges	2	54	127	15	32	1	0	9	17	15	0	.252
X2	Jim Marshall	1	17	32	6	11	1	0	3	4	3	0	.344
X3	Hobie Landrith	1	23	45	6	13	3	0	1	7	8	0	.289
X4	Joe Pignatano	1	27	56	2	13	2	0	0	2	2	0	.232
X5	Don Zimmer	1	14	52	3	4	1	0	0	1	3	0	.077
X6	Gus Bell	1	30	101	8	15	2	0	1	6	10	0	.149
X7	Rick Herrscher	1	35	50	6	11	3	0	1	6	5	0	.220

Pos	Player	WS	G	IP	Won–Lost	Pct	H	SO	BB	ERA	CG	Sv
S1	Roger Craig	9	42	233	10–24	.294	261	118	70	4.51	13	3
S2	Al Jackson	8	36	231	8–20	.286	244	118	78	4.40	12	0
S3	Jay Hook	7	37	214	8–19	.296	230	113	71	4.84	13	0
S4	Bob Miller	3	33	144	1–12	.077	146	91	62	4.89	1	0
S5	Craig Anderson	1	50	131	3–17	.150	150	62	63	5.35	2	4
RA	Ken MacKenzie	3	42	80	5–4	.556	87	51	34	4.95	0	1
M1	Willard Hunter	1	27	63	1–6	.143	67	40	34	5.57	1	0
SW	Bob Moorhead	3	38	105	0–2	.000	118	63	42	4.53	0	0
P1	Galen Cisco	1	4	19	1–1	.500	15	13	11	3.26	1	0
P2	Larry Foss	1	5	12	0–1	.000	17	3	7	4.63	0	0

WIN SHARE TEAM COMPARISON

Our final chart summarizes these 24 teams into one chart, making position-by-position comparisons, in a way which I hope helps us to see the strengths and weaknesses of each team. This is useful for, for example:

1. Picking All-Star teams,
2. Comparing groups of players (comparing infields, comparing starting staffs, etc.),
3. Evaluating generalizations about strong teams as opposed to weak teams, or
4. Studying how pennants are won in one era as opposed to another.

Yr Team	C	1B	2B	3B	SS	LF	CF	RF	DH	S1	S2	S3	S4	S5	RA	Bench	Stf	Total
'98 Yanks	15	21	22	26	27	14	28	26	11	18	17	13	13	12	14	32	33	342
'54 Cle	15	12	35	27	10	9	33	25		24	24	23	14	11	12	36	23	333
'75 Reds	30	19	44	30	19	21	16	18		15	15	9	8	7	13	27	33	324
'53 Bums	33	25	25	12	21	25	37	23		20	9	9	8	7	13	19	29	315
'77 KC	18	14	12	29	15	11	18	27	25	24	16	15	7		11	27	37	306
'89 Oak	14	20	14	21	12	20	19	14	15	19	16	14	7	4	14	38	36	297
'86 Hou	11	24	19	19	8	17	12	26		27	17	11	10	5	11	38	33	288
'64 Cards	16	26	11	28	20	22	25	7		24	16	15	12	3	10	17	27	279
'71 SF	19	16	17	13	16	23	27	32		18	17	13	5	3	12	22	17	270
'78 Cal	18	14	20	17	10	14	13	19	23	14	12	9	8	7	14	27	22	261
'83 Pit	21	17	20	17	19	11	8	12		16	15	15	10	9	17	31	14	252
'88 Mon	8	25	12	16	5	19	7	18		15	14	11	7	5	7	41	33	243
'89 Mil	8	10	13	27	8	10	34	12	3	17	9	7	5	2	11	34	33	243
'96 Twins	6	12	32	11	8	18	20	9	18	14	11	8	6	6	6	22	27	234
'67 Cle	13	12	7	17	14	12	9	11		17	16	15	8	7	6	44	17	225
'86 ChA	6	10	4	8	9	7	11	19	5	11	10	8	7	4	4	43	50	216
'99 TB	12	24	10	6	7	9	3	13	12	10	8	6	5	2	14	38	28	207
'63 Hous	6	12	12	7	6	18	9	15		15	15	12	8	7	17	28	11	198
'69 Phil	7	22	3	12	10	14	18	17		15	14	6	5	2	4	29	11	189
'83 Sea	3	12	9	3	3	7	13	12	5	16	13	8	5	4	6	31	30	180
'73 Tex	6	8	15	8	13	3	10	22	12	10	6	5	2	2	3	29	17	171
'79 A's	12	18	2	13	4	10	16	7	8	12	10	7	5	4	6	18	10	162
'69 Padres	5	16	2	9	7	12	4	15		12	10	8	8	3	7	20	18	156
'62 Mets	3	5	7	8	5	12	11	7		9	8	7	3	1	3	25	5	120

INDEX